VIVEKANANDA
The Yogas and Other Works

VIVEKANANDA
The Yogas and Other Works

*Including the Chicago Addresses, Jnāna-Yoga,
Bhakti-Yoga, Karma-Yoga, Rāja-Yoga, Inspired
Talks, and Lectures, Poems, and Letters*

Chosen and with a Biography by
SWAMI NIKHILANANDA

Revised Edition

Ramakrishna Vedanta Centre,
Bourne End, Bucks, SL8 5LG.
Telephone: 01628 526464

NEW YORK
Ramakrishna-Vivekananda Center

VIVEKANANDA: The Yogas and Other Works

Fourth Printing 1996

ISBN 0-911206-04-3

Library of Congress Catalog Card Number: 53-7534

PREFACE

THE CONTENTS of the present volume, carefully selected from the *Complete Works of Swami Vivekananda*, published in eight volumes in India, will present to Western readers the essentials of the religion and philosophy of the Hindus as interpreted by an outstanding thinker and saint of modern India. It contains such well-known books by the Swami as *Jnāna-Yoga*, *Karma-Yoga*, *Bhakti-Yoga*, *Rāja-Yoga*, and *Inspired Talks*, and in addition some of his lectures, poems, and letters. A perusal of this book, it is hoped, will acquaint the Western reader with the general thought-current of Swami Vivekananda, who was the first Indian to come to America as India's unofficial cultural ambassador and to build a bridge between East and West for the exchange of spiritual ideas and ideals.

The reader of this volume will be struck by the wide sweep of Swami Vivekananda's mind. All facets of man's spiritual life, in both its theoretical and its practical aspects, are discussed.

According to the Swami, yoga is the science of religion. *Jnāna-Yoga*, based upon the teachings of the Upanishads, which form the philosophical section of the Hindu scriptures, the Vedas, shows the way to realize the oneness of the individual soul and the Supreme Soul, through the discipline of discrimination between the real and the unreal. The contents of this book, originally delivered as lectures in America and England, are based upon the Swami's direct experience of Truth. Therein lie their vividness and irresistible appeal. Free from dogmas demanding unquestioning belief for acceptance, *Jnāna-Yoga* teaches the divinity of the soul, the non-duality of the Godhead, the harmony of religions, and the unity of all existence.

Karma-Yoga, perhaps the outstanding book among the works of Swami Vivekananda, shows the way to perfection for the active man of the world, who may be sceptical about the God of the theologians or the various untested dogmas of religion. The Swami contends that a man may, through the right performance of work, reach the same exalted state of consciousness that a genuine Buddhist obtains largely through meditation, and a Christian devotee through prayer. But the performance of work is often irksome. It seldom leaves time for the other pursuits of life. One activity leads to another. Furthermore, success in work is often accompanied by a desire for power and name; and failure, by frustration and gloom. Yet the life of an inactive recluse is neither possible nor desirable for all. The Swami asks the active man, conscious of his social duties and responsibilities, to plunge into the world and learn the secret of work; and that is the way of karma-yoga. Man need not fly from the wheels of the world-machine, but may stand inside it and learn work's secret. Work properly performed within the machine opens the way out. The secret is non-attachment. Even when the body and sense-organs are intensely active, one can enjoy serenity of soul through non-attachment and realize "non-activity in activity."

Bhakti-Yoga teaches man how to train emotion in order to attain his spiritual end; untrained emotion creates a terrible bondage and brings endless miseries. The first part of *Bhakti-Yoga* deals with the preliminaries, such as the definition of God, the qualifications of teacher and disciple, the meaning of symbols, the characteristics of Divine Incarnations and the Chosen Ideal, and the details of concrete worship. Next the aspirant is asked to practise the higher discipline described in the second part, which is pure love of God, free from dogmas, rituals, and symbols. This is love for love's sake, devoid of fear of punishment or expectation of reward. Through such love the devotee attains the highest intuitive knowledge and realizes the oneness of the lover, love, and the beloved God.

Rāja-Yoga, consisting of the Yoga aphorisms of Patanjali with Swami Vivekananda's masterly introduction and penetrating commentary, is perhaps the most widely read of his books in Europe and America. A standard treatise on Hindu psychology, *Rāja-Yoga* deals with various disciplines for the practice of self-control, concentration, and meditation, by means of which the truths of religion are directly experienced. It was written during the last decade of the nineteenth century, when the physical sciences emphasized the mechanistic interpretation of life and the universe, defining truth as a logical proposition supported by reason based upon sense-experience, and condemning religion as mere speculation incapable of verification by the well-established scientific method of experimentation. The Swami accepted the challenge of science and demonstrated, through *Rāja-Yoga*, that religion could stand the test of reason and was valid, besides, on the higher basis of man's inner experience, a support that the physical sciences lacked. He showed, further, that the mind possesses unlimited powers, which, when properly exercised, enable a man to realize in the end the isolation of the Spirit from the body, this constituting his Highest Good.

Thus the four yogas explained by Swami Vivekananda serve a very useful purpose for the spiritual development of the four types of men: the intellectual, the active, the emotional, and the psychic or introspective. They also help the individual to integrate his diverse faculties and thus endow his action with grace and meaning.

Inspired Talks, containing the Swami's instruction to a select group of disciples at Thousand Island Park, records some of his most profound religious experiences.

The letters, selected from hundreds written by him in longhand, show his intimate relationship with his disciples as well as the great heights and depths of his unique mind.

The notes on pronunciation, the glossary, and the index will, it is hoped, add to the usefulness of the volume. The appendices contain the testimonial given by the Swami's students in London on the eve of his departure for India in 1896, and also a schedule of his activities in America during the winter of 1895-96, showing the strenuousness of his public work.

The reader will be disappointed if he tries to find in Vivekananda's statements a systematic, academic philosophy. His words will appear now rigorously logical and now wildly inconsistent, like those of the Prophets of the Old Testament or of many of the Christian mystics. Yet from them philosophical systems are being formulated. These utterances of his reveal Vivekananda not only as a Godlike person but also as a warm-blooded, passionate, sensitive, and breathing human being. The infinite variety of his thought will remain for ever vivid and fresh despite the passage of time and the changing tastes of society.

Swami Vivekananda's public life covered a period of ten years—from 1893, when he appeared at the Parliament of Religions in Chicago, to 1902, when he gave up his mortal body. These were years of great physical and mental strain as a result of extensive travels, adaptation to new environments, opposition from detractors both in his native land and abroad, incessant public lectures and private instruction, a heavy correspondence, and the organizing of the Ramakrishna Order in India. Hard work and ascetic practices undermined his health. The Swami thus had no time to revise his books, which either were dictated by him or consisted of lectures delivered without notes and taken down in shorthand or longhand. A number of the lectures included under "Miscellaneous Lectures" were delivered when he no longer had Mr. J. J. Goodwin as his stenographer, and were taken down by unskilled persons. I have therefore felt the need of editing the present collection, making changes wherever they were absolutely necessary, but being always mindful to keep intact the Swami's basic thought.

I have deemed it necessary to add to the book a rather lengthy biography of Swami Vivekananda; for in religious matters the teacher is intimately related to what he teaches. His teaching is the outpouring of his life and experiences. The Swami, during his lifetime, left an indelible impression upon all with whom he came in contact, whether in India or in the course of his travels in America and Europe. Anyone who saw him even once could never forget him. But the generation that knew him is passing away. The biography is included in this book to keep his memory alive for coming generations. The materials of the biography have been gathered from *The Life of Swami Vivekananda*, by his Eastern and Western disciples, published by the Advaita Āśrama, Mayavati, India; *The Life of Vivekananda and the Universal Gospel*, by Romain Rolland, published by the Advaita Āśrama; the letters of the Swami; and unpublished but authenticated reports from persons who knew him. I am immensely grateful to the Advaita Āśrama for materials obtained from its publications.

My friends Joseph Campbell, Nelson S. Bushnell, and Howard Van Smith have revised this introductory chapter, written by myself, on the life of Swami Vivekananda, and thus contributed greatly to whatever literary merit it possesses. I am deeply indebted to them.

No one but Elizabeth Davidson and Brahmachari Yogatmachaitanya will, perhaps, ever know how much hard work has gone into the preparation of the manuscript for the press and the correction of the proofs. Patiently and cheerfully they rendered their assistance in both these matters. It is a real joy to acknowledge my gratitude to them.

The expenses for the publication of this book have been met partly from the Estate of Swami Vivekananda in America, a trust fund created by the Swami for the propagation of his writings, and partly from a contribution made by the Government of India. A generous donation from Doris Kellogg Neale provided the additional funds needed for this undertaking. To her, also, I express my sincere gratitude.

Sixty years ago, this day, Swami Vivekananda was introduced to America and the Western world through the historic Parliament of Religions in Chicago. It appears as if the stage was set by a divine power in order to give him an opportunity to present to the West the message of Vedānta, the religious philosophy of India. Though everything else that was said in the Parliament has been forgotten, Vivekananda's message of the divinity of the soul, the unity of existence, and the harmony of religions has found an abiding place in the thought of America.

Swami Vivekananda is an unusual phenomenon in our time—a philosopher, a man of action, a devotee of God, and an introspective yogi, all in one. A writer, a poet, a dreamer, and a dynamic speaker, he was also the founder of the Rama-krishna Order of monks, which is dedicated to religious, educational, and philanthropic activities. But in his inmost heart he was a passionate lover of God. His message is not merely for the hour, but for the modern age; not for a particular nation, but for humanity. Even his message for India does not aim at partial social or religious reform, but at complete rejuvenation of her national life. The reader will be stirred, whether or not he agrees with the Swami; for every word he spoke is charged with power. And what he accomplished in the short span of his thirty-nine years will nourish humanity for centuries.

Contemplating the malady of our times one wistfully asks, in the words of the bard of Avon, "When comes such another?"

NIKHILANANDA

Vivekananda Cottage
Thousand Island Park, New York
September 11, 1953

CONTENTS

x　　　　　　　　　　　　　　　Contents

Contents

POEMS

LETTERS

ILLUSTRATIONS

NOTE ON THE PRONUNCIATION OF
SANSKRIT AND VERNACULAR WORDS

a	has the sound of				o in *come*.
ā	"	"	"	"	a in *far*.
e	"	"	"	"	e in *bed*.
i	"	"	"	"	ee in *feel*.
o	"	"	"	"	o in *note*.
u	"	"	"	"	u in *full*.
ai, ay	"	"	"	"	oy in *boy*.
au	"	"	"	"	o pronounced deep in the throat.
ch	"	"	"	"	ch in *church*.
ḍ	"	"	"	"	hard d (in English).
g	"	"	"	"	g in *god*.
jn	"	"	"	"	hard gy (in English).
ś	"	"	"	"	sh in *shut*.
th	"	"	"	"	*t-h* in *boat-house*.

sh may be pronounced as in English.

t and d are soft as in French.

Other consonants appearing in the transliterations may be pronounced as in English.

Diacritical marks have generally not been used in proper names belonging to recent times or in modern and well-known geographical names.

VIVEKANANDA

Vivekananda in Meditation

VIVEKANANDA

S WAMI VIVEKANANDA, the great soul loved and revered in East and West alike
as the rejuvenator of Hinduism in India and the preacher of its eternal
truths abroad, was born at 6:49, a few minutes after sunrise, on Monday,
January 12, 1863. It was the day of the great Hindu festival Makarasamkrānti,
when special worship is offered to the Ganges by millions of devotees. Thus
the future Vivekananda first drew breath when the air above the sacred river
not far from the house was reverberating with the prayers, worship, and religious
music of thousands of Hindu men and women.

While Vivekananda was still in his mother's womb, she, like many other
pious Hindu mothers, had observed religious vows, fasted, and prayed so that
she might be blessed with a son who would do honour to the family. She
requested a relative who was living in Benares to offer special worship to the
Vireśwara Śiva of that holy place and seek His blessings; for Śiva, the great god
of renunciation, dominated her thought. One night she dreamt that this
supreme Deity aroused Himself from His meditation and agreed to be born as
her son. When she woke she was filled with joy.

The mother, Bhuvaneswari Devi, accepted the child as a boon from Vireśwara
Śiva and named him Vireśwara. The family, however, gave him the name of
Narendranath Datta, calling him, for short, Narendra, or more endearingly,
Naren.

The Datta family of Calcutta, into which Narendranath had been born, was
well known for its affluence, philanthropy, scholarship, and independent spirit.
The grandfather, Durgacharan, after the birth of his first son, had renounced
the world in search of God. The father, Viswanath, an attorney-at-law of the
High Court of Calcutta, was versed in English and Persian literature and often
entertained himself and his friends by reciting from the Bible and the poetry
of Hafiz, both of which, he believed, contained truths unmatched by human
thinking elsewhere. He was particularly attracted to the Islāmic culture, with
which he was familiar because of his close contact with the educated Moslems
of Northwestern India. Moreover, he derived a large income from his law
practice and, unlike his father, thoroughly enjoyed the worldly life. An expert
in cookery, he prepared rare dishes and liked to share them with his friends.
Travel was another of his hobbies. Though agnostic in religion and a mocker
of social conventions, he possessed a large heart and often went out of his way
to support idle relatives, some of whom were given to drunkenness. Once, when
Narendra protested against this lack of judgement, his father said: "How can

1

you understand the great misery of human life? When you realize the depths
of men's suffering, you will sympathize with these unfortunate creatures who
try to forget their sorrows, even though only for a short while, in the oblivion
created by intoxicating drink." Naren's father, however, kept a sharp eye on
his children and would not tolerate the slightest deviation from good manners.

Bhuvaneswari Devi, the mother, was cast in a different mould. Regal in
appearance and gracious in conduct, she belonged to the old tradition of Hindu
womanhood. As mistress of a large household, she devoted her spare time to
sewing and singing, being particularly fond of the great Indian epics, the
Rāmāyana and the Mahābhārata, large portions of which she had memorized.
She became the special refuge of the poor, and commanded universal respect
because of her calm resignation to God, her inner tranquillity, and her dignified
detachment in the midst of her many arduous duties. Two sons were born to
her besides Narendranath, and four daughters, two of whom died at an early age.

Narendra grew up to be a sweet, sunny-tempered, but very restless boy. Two
nurses were necessary to keep his exuberant energy under control, and he was
a great tease to his sisters. In order to quiet him, the mother often put his head
under the cold-water tap, repeating Śiva's name, which always produced the
desired effect. Naren felt a child's love of birds and animals, and this characteristic reappeared during the last days of his life. Among his boyhood pets
were a family cow, a monkey, a goat, a peacock, and several pigeons and
guinea-pigs. The coachman of the family, with his turban, whip, and bright-
coloured livery, was his boyhood ideal of a magnificent person, and he often
expressed the ambition to be like him when he grew up.

Narendra bore a striking resemblance to the grandfather who had renounced
the world to lead a monastic life, and many thought that the latter had been
reborn in him. The youngster developed a special fancy for wandering monks,
whose very sight would greatly excite him. One day when such a monk appeared
at the door and asked for alms, Narendra gave him his only possession, the
tiny piece of new cloth that was wrapped round his waist. Thereafter, whenever a monk was seen in the neighbourhood, Narendra would be locked in a
room. But even then he would throw out of the window whatever he found
near at hand as an offering to the holy man. In the meantime, he was receiving
his early education from his mother, who taught him the Bengali alphabet
and his first English words, as well as stories from the Rāmāyana and the
Mahābhārata.

During his childhood Narendra, like many other Hindu children of his age,
developed a love for the Hindu deities, of whom he had learnt from his mother.
Particularly attracted by the heroic story of Rāma and his faithful consort Sitā,
he procured their images, bedecked them with flowers, and worshipped them in
his boyish fashion. But disillusionment came when he heard someone denounce
marriage vehemently as a terrible bondage. When he had thought this over
he discarded Rāma and Sitā as unworthy of worship. In their place he installed
the image of Śiva, the god of renunciation, who was the ideal of the yogis.
Nevertheless he retained a fondness for the Rāmāyana.

At this time he daily experienced a strange vision when he was about to fall
asleep. Closing his eyes, he would see between his eyebrows a ball of light of

changing colours, which would slowly expand and at last burst, bathing his whole body in a white radiance. Watching this light he would gradually fall asleep. Since it was a daily occurrence, he regarded the phenomenon as common to all people, and was surprised when a friend denied ever having seen such a thing. Years later, however, Narendra's spiritual teacher, Śri Ramakrishna, said to him, "Naren, my boy, do you see a light when you go to sleep?" Ramakrishna knew that such a vision indicated a great spiritual past and an inborn habit of meditation. The vision of light remained with Narendra until the end of his life, though later it lost its regularity and intensity.

While still a child Narendra practised meditation with a friend before the image of Śiva. He had heard that the holy men of ancient India would become so absorbed in contemplation of God that their hair would grow and gradually enter into the earth, like the roots of the banyan tree. While meditating, therefore, he would open his eyes, now and then, to see if his own hair had entered into the earth. Even so, during meditation, he often became unconscious of the world. On one occasion he saw in a vision a luminous person of serene countenance who was carrying the staff and water-bowl of a monk. The apparition was about to say something when Naren became frightened and left the room. He thought later that perhaps this had been a vision of Buddha.

At the age of six he was sent to a primary school. One day, however, he repeated at home some of the vulgar words that he had learnt from his classmates, whereupon his disgusted parents took him out of the school and appointed a private tutor, who conducted classes for him and some other children of the neighbourhood in the worship hall of the house. Naren soon showed a precocious mind and developed a keen memory. Very easily he learnt by heart the whole of a Sanskrit grammar and long passages from the Rāmāyana and the Mahābhārata. Some of the friendships he made at this age lasted his whole lifetime. At school he was the undisputed leader. When playing his favourite game of "King and the Court," he would assume the rôle of the monarch and assign to his friends the parts of the ministers, commander-in-chief, and other state officials.

He was marked from birth to be a leader of men, as his name Narendra (lord of men) signified, yet even at that early age he could not tolerate caste arrogance. In his father's office separate tobacco pipes were provided for clients belonging to the different castes, as orthodox Hindu custom required, and the pipe from which the Moslems smoked was set quite apart. Narendra once smoked tobacco from all the pipes, including the one marked for the Moslems, and when reprimanded, remarked, "I cannot see what difference it makes."

During these early years, Narendra's future personality was influenced by his gifted father and his saintly mother, both of whom kept a chastening eye upon him. The father had his own manner of discipline. For example, when, in the course of an argument with his mother, the impetuous boy once uttered a few rude words and the report came to the father, Viswanath did not directly scold his son, but wrote with charcoal on the door of his room: "Narendra today said to his mother—" and added the words that had been used. He wanted Narendra's friends to know how rudely he had treated his mother.

Another time Narendra bluntly asked his father, "What have you done for me?"

Instead of being annoyed, Viswanath said, "Go and look at yourself in the mirror, and then you will know."

Still another day, Narendra said to his father, "How shall I conduct myself in the world?"

"Never show surprise at anything," his father replied.

This priceless advice enabled Narendranath, in his future chequered life, to preserve his serenity of mind whether dwelling with princes in their palaces or sharing the straw huts of beggars.

The mother, Bhuvaneswari, played her part in bringing out Narendranath's innate virtues. When he told her, one day, of having been unjustly treated in school, she said to him, in consolation: "My child, what does it matter, if you are in the right? Always follow the truth without caring about the result. Very often you may have to suffer injustice or unpleasant consequences for holding to the truth; but you must not, under any circumstances, abandon it." Many years later Narendranath proudly said to an audience, "I am indebted to my mother for whatever knowledge I have acquired."

One day, when he was fighting with his play-fellows, Narendra accidentally fell from the porch and struck his forehead against a stone. The wound bled profusely and left a permanent scar over his right eye. Years later, when Ramakrishna heard of this accident, he remarked: "In a way it was a good thing. If he had not thus lost some of his blood, he would have created havoc in the world with his excessive energy."

In 1870, at the age of seven, Narendra entered high school. His exceptional intelligence was soon recognized by his teachers and classmates. Though at first reluctant to study English because of its foreign origin, he soon took it up with avidity. But the curriculum consumed very little of his time. He used most of his inexhaustible energy in outside activities. Games of various kinds, many of which he invented or improvised, kept him occupied. He made an imitation gas-works and a factory for aerating water, these two novelties having just been introduced in Calcutta. He organized an amateur theatrical company and a gymnasium, and took lessons in fencing, wrestling, rowing, and other manly sports. He also tried his hand at the art of cooking. Intensely restless, he would soon tire of one pastime and seek a new one. With his friends he visited the museums and the zoological garden. He arbitrated the disputes of his play-fellows and was a favourite with the people of the neighbourhood. Everybody admired his courage, straightforwardness, and simplicity.

From an early age this remarkable youth had no patience with fear or superstition. One of his boyish pranks had been to climb a flowering tree belonging to a neighbour, pluck the flowers, and do other mischief. The owner of the tree, finding his remonstrances unheeded, once solemnly told Naren's friends that the tree was guarded by a white-robed ghost who would certainly wring their necks if they disturbed his peace. The boys were frightened and kept away. But Narendra persuaded them to follow him back, and he climbed the tree, enjoying his usual measure of fun, and broke some branches by way of further mischief. Turning to his friends, he then said: "What asses you all are! See, my neck is still there. The old man's story is simply not true. Don't believe what others say unless you yourselves know it to be true."

These simple but bold words were an indication of his future message to the world. Addressing large audiences in later years, he would often say: "Do not believe in a thing because you have read about it in a book. Do not believe in a thing because another man has said it was true. Do not believe in words because they are hallowed by tradition. Find out the truth for yourself. Reason it out. That is realization."

The following incident illustrates his courage and presence of mind. He one day wished to set up a heavy trapeze in the gymnasium, and so asked the help of some people who were there. Among them was an English sailor. The trapeze fell and knocked the sailor unconscious, and the crowd, thinking him dead, ran away for fear of the police. But Naren tore a piece from his cloth, bandaged the sailor's wound, washed his face with water, and gradually revived him. Then he moved the wounded man to a neighbouring schoolhouse where he nursed him for a week. When the sailor had recovered, Naren sent him away with a little purse collected from his friends.

All through this period of boyish play Narendra retained his admiration for the life of the wandering monk. Pointing to a certain line on the palm of his hand, he would say to his friends: "I shall certainly become a sannyāsin. A palmist has predicted it."

ON THE THRESHOLD OF YOUTH

As Narendra grew into adolescence, his temperament showed a marked change. He became keen about intellectual matters, read serious books on history and literature, devoured newspapers, and attended public meetings. Music was his favourite pastime. He insisted that it should express a lofty idea and arouse the feelings of the musician.

At the age of fifteen he experienced his first spiritual ecstasy. The family was journeying to Raipur in the Central Provinces, and part of the trip had to be made in a bullock cart. On that particular day the air was crisp and clear; the trees and creepers were covered with green leaves and many-coloured blossoms; birds of brilliant plumage warbled in the woods. The cart was moving along a narrow pass where the lofty peaks rising on the two sides almost touched each other. Narendra's eyes spied a large bee-hive in the cleft of a giant cliff, and suddenly his mind was filled with awe and reverence for the Divine Providence. He lost outer consciousness and lay thus in the cart for a long time. Even after returning to the sense-perceived world he radiated joy.

Another interesting mental phenomenon may be mentioned here; for it was one often experienced by Narendranath. From boyhood, on first beholding certain people or places, he would feel that he had known them before; but how long before he could never remember. One day he and some of his companions were in a room in a friend's house, where they were discussing various topics. Something was mentioned, and Narendra felt at once that he had on a previous occasion talked about the same subject with the selfsame friends in that very house. He even correctly described every nook and corner of the building, which he had not seen before. He tried at first to explain this singular phenomenon by the doctrine of reincarnation, thinking that perhaps he had lived in that house in a previous life. But he dismissed the idea as improbable. Later he concluded that before his birth he must have had previsions of the people, places, and events that he was to experience in his present incarnation; that was why, he thought, he could recognize them as soon as they presented themselves to him.

At Raipur Narendra was encouraged by his father to meet notable scholars and discuss with them various intellectual topics usually considered too abstruse for boys of his age. On such occasions he exhibited great mental power. From his father, Narendra had learnt the art of grasping the essentials of things, seeing truth from the widest and most comprehensive standpoints, and holding to the real issue under discussion.

In 1879 the family returned to Calcutta, and Narendra within a short time graduated from high school in the first division. In the meantime he had read a great many standard books of English and Bengali literature. History was his favourite subject. He also acquired at this time an unusual method of reading a book and acquiring the knowledge of its subject matter. To quote his own words: "I could understand an author without reading every line of his book. I would read the first and last lines of a paragraph and grasp its meaning. Later I found that I could understand the subject matter by reading only the first and last lines of a page. Afterwards I could follow the whole trend of a writer's argument by merely reading a few lines, though the author himself tried to explain the subject in five or more pages."

COLLEGE DAYS

Soon the excitement of his boyhood days was over, and in 1879 Narendranath entered the Presidency College of Calcutta for higher studies. After a year he joined the General Assembly's Institution, founded by the Scottish General Missionary Board and later known as the Scottish Church College. It was from Hastie, the principal of the college and the professor of English literature, that he first heard the name Śri Ramakrishna.

In college Narendra, now a handsome youth, muscular and agile, though slightly inclined to stoutness, enjoyed serious studies. During the first two years he studied Western logic. Thereafter he specialized in Western philosophy and the ancient and modern history of the different European nations. His memory was prodigious. It took him only three days to assimilate Green's *History of the English People*. Often, on the eve of an examination, he would read the whole night, keeping awake by drinking strong tea or coffee.

About this time he came in contact with Śri Ramakrishna; this event, as we shall presently see, was to become the major turning-point of his life. As a result of his association with Śri Ramakrishna, his innate spiritual yearning was stirred up, and he began to feel the transitoriness of the world and the futility of academic education. The day before his B.A. examination, he suddenly felt an all-consuming love for God and, standing before the room of a college-mate, was heard to sing with great feeling:

> Sing ye, O mountains, O clouds, O great winds!
> Sing ye, sing ye, sing His glory!
> Sing with joy, all ye suns and moons and stars!
> Sing ye, sing ye, His glory!

The friend, surprised, reminded him of the next day's examination, but Narendra was unconcerned; the shadow of the approaching monastic life was fast falling on him. He appeared for the examination, however, and easily passed.

About Narendra's scholarship, Professor Hastie once remarked: "Narendra is a real genius. I have travelled far and wide, but have not yet come across a lad of his talents and possibilities even among the philosophical students in the German universities. He is bound to make his mark in life."

Narendra's many-sided genius found its expression in music, as well. He studied both instrumental and vocal music under expert teachers. He could play on many instruments, but excelled in singing. From a Moslem teacher he learnt Hindi, Urdu, and Persian songs, most of them of devotional nature.

He also became associated with the Brāhmo Samāj, an important religious movement of the time, which influenced him during this formative period of his life.

THE BRĀHMO SAMĀJ

The introduction of English education in India following the British conquest of the country brought Hindu society in contact with the intellectual and aggressive European culture. The Hindu youths who came under the spell of the new, dynamic way of life realized the many shortcomings of their own society. Under the Moslem rule, even before the coming of the British, the dynamic aspect of the Hindu culture had been suppressed and the caste-system stratified. The priests controlled the religious life of the people for their own selfish interest. Meaningless dogmas and lifeless ceremonies supplanted the invigorating philosophical teachings of the Upanishads and the Bhagavad Gītā. The masses were exploited, moreover, by the landlords, and the lot of women was especially pitiable. Following the breakdown of the Moslem rule, chaos reigned in every field of Indian life, social, political, religious, and economic. The newly introduced English education brought into sharp focus the many drawbacks of society, and various reform movements, both liberal and orthodox, were initiated to make the national life flow once more through healthy channels.

The Brāhmo Samāj, one of these liberal movements, captured the imagination of the educated youths of Bengal. Rājā Rammohan Roy (1774-1833), the founder of this religious organization, broke away from the rituals, image worship, and priestcraft of orthodox Hinduism and exhorted his followers to dedicate themselves to the "worship and adoration of the Eternal, the Unsearchable, the Immutable Being, who is the Author and the Preserver of the universe." The Rājā, endowed with a gigantic intellect, studied the Hindu, Moslem, Christian, and Buddhist scriptures and was the first Indian to realize the importance of the Western rational method for solving the diverse problems of Hindu society. He took a prominent part in the introduction of English education in India, which, though it at first produced a deleterious effect on the newly awakened Hindu consciousness, ultimately revealed to a few Indians the glorious heritage of their own indigenous civilization.

Among the prominent leaders of the Brāhmo Samāj who succeeded Rammohan Roy were Devendranath Tagore (1817-1905), a great devotee of the Upanishads, and Keshab Chandra Sen (1838-1884), who was inclined to the rituals and doctrines of Christianity. The Brāhmo Samāj, under their leadership, discarded many of the conventions of Hinduism, such as rituals and the worship of God through images. Primarily a reformist movement, it directed its main energy to the emancipation of women, the remarriage of Hindu widows, the abolition of early marriage, and the spread of mass education. Influenced by Western culture, the Brāhmo Samāj upheld the supremacy of reason, preached against the uncritical acceptance of scriptural authority, and strongly supported the slogans of the French Revolution. The whole movement was intellectual and eclectic in character, born of the necessity of the times; unlike traditional Hinduism, it had no root in the spiritual experiences of saints and seers. Narendra, like many other contemporary young men, felt the appeal of its progressive ideas and became one of its members. But, as will be presently seen, the Brāhmo Samāj could not satisfy the deep spiritual yearning of his soul.

About this time Narendra was urged by his father to marry, and an opportunity soon presented itself. A wealthy man, whose daughter Narendra was asked to accept as his bride, offered to defray his expenses for higher studies in England so that he might qualify himself for the much coveted Indian Civil Service. Narendra refused. Other proposals of similar nature produced no different result. Apparently it was not his destiny to lead a householder's life.

From boyhood Narendra had shown a passion for purity. Whenever his warm and youthful nature tempted him to walk into a questionable adventure, he was held back by an unseen hand. His mother had taught him the value of chastity and had made him observe it as a matter of honour, in loyalty to herself and the family tradition. But purity to Narendra was not a negative virtue, a mere abstention from carnal pleasures. To be pure, he felt, was to conserve an intense spiritual force that would later manifest itself in all the noble aspirations of life. He regarded himself as a brahmachārin, a celibate student of the Hindu tradition, who worked hard, prized ascetic disciplines, held holy things in reverence, and enjoyed clean words, thoughts, and acts. For according to the Hindu scriptures, a man, by means of purity, which is the greatest of all virtues, can experience the subtlest spiritual perceptions. In Naren it accounts for the great power of concentration, memory, and insight, and for his indomitable mental energy and physical stamina.

In his youth Narendra used to see every night two visions, utterly dissimilar in nature, before falling asleep. One was that of a worldly man with an accomplished wife and children, enjoying wealth, luxuries, fame, and social position; the other, that of a sannyāsin, a wandering monk, bereft of earthly security and devoted to the contemplation of God. Narendra felt that he had the power to realize either of these ideals; but when his mind reflected on their respective virtues, he was inevitably drawn to the life of renunciation. The glamour of the world would fade and disappear. His deeper self instinctively chose the austere path.

For a time the congregational prayers and the devotional songs of the Brāhmo Samāj exhilarated Narendra's mind, but soon he found that they did not give him any real spiritual experience. He wanted to realize God, the goal of religion, and so felt the imperative need of being instructed by a man who had seen God.

In his eagerness he went to Devendranath, the venerable leader of the Brāhmo Samāj, and bluntly asked him, "Sir, have you seen God?"

Devendranath was embarrassed and replied: "My boy, you have the eyes of a yogi. You should practise meditation."

The youth was disappointed and felt that this teacher was not the man to help him in his spiritual struggle. But he received no better answer from the leaders of other religious sects. Then he remembered having heard the name of Ramakrishna Paramahamsa from Professor Hastie, who, while lecturing his class on Wordsworth's poem *The Excursion*, had spoken of trances, remarking that such religious ecstasies were the result of purity and concentration. He had said, further, that an exalted experience of this kind was a rare phenomenon, especially in modern times. "I have known," he had said, "only one person who has realized that blessed state, and he is Ramakrishna of Dakshineswar. You will understand trances if you visit the saint."

Narendra had also heard about Śri Ramakrishna from a relative, Ramchandra Datta, who was one of the foremost householder disciples of the Master. Learning of Narendra's unwillingness to marry and ascribing it to his desire to lead a spiritual life, Ramchandra had said to him, "If you really want to cultivate spirituality, then visit Ramakrishna at Dakshineswar."

Narendra met Ramakrishna for the first time in November 1881 at the house of the Master's devotee Surendranath Mitra, the young man having been invited there to entertain the visitors with his melodious music. The Paramahamsa was much impressed by his sincerity and devotion, and after a few inquiries asked him to visit him at Dakshineswar. Narendra accepted. He wished to learn if Ramakrishna was the man to help him in his spiritual quest.

RAMAKRISHNA

Ramakrishna, the God-man of modern times, was born on February 18, 1836, in the little village of Kamarpukur, in the district of Hooghly in Bengal. How different were his upbringing and the environment of his boyhood from those of Narendranath, who was to become, later, the bearer and interpreter of his message! Ramakrishna's parents, belonging to the brāhmin caste, were poor, pious, and devoted to the traditions of their ancient religion. Full of fun and innocent joys, the fair child, with flowing hair and a sweet, musical voice, grew up in a simple countryside of rice-fields, cows, and banyan and mango trees. He was apathetic about his studies and remained practically illiterate all his life, but his innate spiritual tendencies found expression through devotional songs and the company of wandering monks, who fired his boyish imagination by the stories of their spiritual adventures. At the age of six he experienced a spiritual ecstasy while watching a flight of snow-white cranes against a black sky overcast with rain-clouds. He began to go into trances as he meditated on gods and goddesses. His father's death, which left the family in straitened circumstances, deepened his spiritual mood. And so, though at the age of sixteen he joined his brother in Calcutta, he refused to go on there with his studies; for, as he remarked, he was simply not interested in an education whose sole purpose was to earn mere bread and butter. He felt a deep longing for the realization of God.

The floodgate of Ramakrishna's emotion burst all bounds when he took up the duties of a priest in the Kāli temple of Dakshineswar, where the Deity was worshipped as the Divine Mother. Ignorant of the scriptures and of the intricacies of ritual, Ramakrishna poured his whole soul into prayer, which often took the form of devotional songs. Food, sleep, and other physical needs were completely forgotten in an all-consuming passion for the vision of God. His nights were spent in contemplation in the neighbouring woods. Doubt sometimes alternated with hope; but an inner certainty and the testimony of the illumined saints sustained him in his darkest hours of despair. Formal worship or the mere sight of the image did not satisfy his inquiring mind; for he felt that a figure of stone could not be the bestower of peace and immortality. Behind the image there must be the real Spirit, which he was determined to behold. This was not an easy task. For a long time the Spirit played with him a teasing game of hide-and-seek, but at last It yielded to the demand of love on the part of the young devotee. When he felt the direct presence of the Divine Mother, Ramakrishna dropped unconscious to the floor, experiencing within himself a constant flow of bliss.

This foretaste of what was to follow made him God-intoxicated, and whetted his appetite for further experience. He wished to see God uninterruptedly, with eyes open as well as closed. He therefore abandoned himself recklessly to the practice of various extreme spiritual disciplines. To remove from his mind the least trace of the arrogance of his high brāhmin caste, he used to clean the dirty places at a pariah's house. Through a stern process of discrimination he effaced all sense of distinction between gold and clay. Purity became the very breath of his nostrils, and he could not regard a woman, even in a dream, in any other way except as his own mother or the Mother of the universe. For several years his eyelids did not touch each other in sleep. And he was finally thought to be insane.

Indeed, the stress of his spiritual practice soon told upon Ramakrishna's delicate body and he returned to Kamarpukur to recover his health. His relatives and old friends saw a marked change in his nature; for the gay boy had been transformed into a contemplative young man whose vision was directed to something on a distant horizon. His mother proposed marriage, and finding in this the will of the Divine Mother, Ramakrishna consented. He even indicated where the girl was to be found, namely, in the village of Jayrambati, only three miles away. Here lived the little Saradamani, a girl of five, who was in many respects very different from the other girls of her age. The child would pray to God to make her character as fragrant as the tuberose and purer than the full moon, which, pure as it was, showed a few dark spots. The marriage was celebrated and Ramakrishna, participating, regarded the whole affair as fun or a new excitement.

In a short while he came back to Dakshineswar and plunged again into the stormy life of religious experimentation. His mother, his newly married wife, and his relatives were forgotten. Now, however, his spiritual disciplines took a new course. He wanted to follow the time-honoured paths of the Hindu religion under the guidance of competent teachers, and they came to him one by one, nobody knew from where. One was a woman, under whom he practised the disciplines of Tantra and of the Vaishnava faith and achieved the highest result in an incredibly short time. It was she who diagnosed his physical malady as the manifestation of deep spiritual emotions and described his apparent insanity as the result of an agonizing love for God; he was immediately relieved. It was she, moreover, who first declared him to be an Incarnation of God, and she proved her statement before an assembly of theologians by scriptural evidence. Under another teacher, the monk Jatadhari, Ramakrishna delved into the mysteries of Rāma worship and experienced Rāma's visible presence. Further, he communed with God through the divine relationships of Father, Mother, Friend, and Beloved. By an austere sannyāsin named Totapuri, he was initiated into the monastic life, and in three days he realized his complete oneness with Brahman, the undifferentiated Absolute, which is the culmination of man's spiritual endeavour. Totapuri himself had had to struggle for forty years to realize this identity.

Ramakrishna turned next to Christianity and Islām, to practise their respective disciplines, and he attained the same result that he had attained through Hinduism. He was thereby convinced that these, too, were ways to the realization of God-consciousness. Finally, he worshipped his own wife—who in the meantime had grown into a young woman of seventeen—as the manifestation of the Divine Mother of the universe and surrendered at her feet the fruit of his past spiritual practices. After this he left behind all his disciplines and struggles. For according to Hindu tradition, when the normal relationship between husband and wife, which is the strongest foundation of the worldly life, has been transcended and a man sees in his wife the divine presence, he then sees God everywhere in the universe. This is the culmination of the spiritual life.

Ramakrishna himself was now convinced of his divine mission on earth and came to know that through him the Divine Mother would found a new religious order comprising those who would accept the doctrine of the Universal Religion which he had experienced. It was further revealed to him that anyone who had prayed to God sincerely, even once, as well as those who were passing through their final birth on earth, would accept him as their spiritual ideal and mould their lives according to his universal teaching.

The people around him were bewildered to see this transformation of a man whom they had ridiculed only a short while ago as insane. The young priest had become God's devotee; the devotee, an ascetic; the ascetic, a saint; the saint, a man of realization; and the man of realization, a new Prophet. Like the full-blown blossom attracting bees, Ramakrishna drew to him men and women of differing faith, intelligence, and social position. He gave generously to all from the inexhaustible storehouse of divine wisdom, and everyone felt uplifted in his presence. But the Master himself was not completely satisfied. He longed for young souls yet untouched by the world, who would renounce everything for the realization of God and the service of humanity. He was literally consumed with this longing. The talk of worldly people was tasteless to him. He often compared such people to a mixture of milk and water with the latter preponderating, and said that he had become weary of trying to prepare thick milk from that mixture. Evenings, when his anguish reached its limit, he would climb the roof of a building near the temple and cry at the top of his voice: "Come, my boys! Oh, where are you all? I cannot bear to live without you!" A mother could not feel more intensely for her beloved children, a friend for his dearest friend, or a lover for her sweetheart.

Shortly thereafter the young men destined to be his monastic disciples began to arrive. And foremost among them was Narendranath.

RAMAKRISHNA AND NARENDRANATH

The first meeting at Dakshineswar between the Master and Narendra was momentous. Śri Ramakrishna recognized instantaneously his future messenger. Narendra, careless about his clothes and general appearance, was so unlike the other young men who had accompanied him to the temple. His eyes were impressive, partly indrawn, indicating a meditative mood. He sang a few songs, and as usual poured into them his whole soul.

His first song was this:

> Let us go back once more, O mind, to our proper home!
> Here in this foreign land of earth
> Why should we wander aimlessly in stranger's guise?
> These living beings round about,
> And the five elements,
> Are strangers to you, all of them; none are your own.
> Why do you so forget yourself,
> In love with strangers, foolish mind?
> Why do you so forget your own?
>
> Mount the path of truth, O mind! Unflaggingly climb,
> With love as the lamp to light your way.
> As your provision on the journey, take with you
> The virtues, hidden carefully;
> For, like two highwaymen,
> Greed and delusion wait to rob you of your wealth.
> And keep beside you constantly,
> As guards to shelter you from harm,
> Calmness of mind and self-control.
>
> Companionship with holy men will be for you
> A welcome rest-house by the road;
> There rest your weary limbs awhile, asking your way,
> If ever you should be in doubt,
> Of him who watches there.
> If anything along the path should cause you fear,
> Then loudly shout the name of God;
> For He is ruler of that road,
> And even Death must bow to Him.

When the singing was over, Śri Ramakrishna suddenly grasped Narendra's hand and took him into the northern porch. To Narendra's utter amazement, the Master said with tears streaming down his cheeks: "Ah! You have come so late. How unkind of you to keep me waiting so long! My ears are almost seared listening to the cheap talk of worldly people. Oh, how I have been yearning to unburden my mind to one who will understand my thought!" Then with folded hands he said: "Lord! I know you are the ancient sage Nara—the Incarnation of Nārāyaṇa—born on earth to remove the miseries of mankind." The rationalist Naren regarded these words as the meaningless jargon of an insane person. He was further dismayed when Śri Ramakrishna presently brought from his room some sweets and fed him with his own hands. But the Master nevertheless extracted from him a promise to visit Dakshineswar again.

They returned to the room and Naren asked the Master, "Sir, have you seen God?" Without a moment's hesitation the reply was given: "Yes, I have seen God. I see Him as I see you here, only more clearly. God can be seen. One can talk to Him. But who cares for God? People shed torrents of tears for their wives, children, wealth, and property, but who weeps for the vision of God? If one cries sincerely for God, one can surely see Him."

Narendra was astounded. For the first time, he was face to face with a man who asserted that he had seen God. For the first time, in fact, he was hearing that God could be seen. He could feel that Ramakrishna's words were uttered from the depths of an inner experience. They could not be doubted. Still he could not reconcile these words with Ramakrishna's strange conduct, which he had witnessed only a few minutes before. What puzzled Narendra further was Ramakrishna's normal behaviour in the presence of others. The young man returned to Calcutta bewildered, but yet with a feeling of inner peace.

During his second visit to the Master, Narendra had an even stranger experience. After a minute or two Śri Ramakrishna drew near him in an ecstatic mood, muttered some words, fixed his eyes on him, and placed his right foot on Naren's body. At this touch Naren saw, with eyes open, the walls, the room, the temple garden—nay, the whole world—vanishing, and even himself disappearing into a void. He felt sure that he was facing death. He cried in consternation: "What are you doing to me? I have my parents, brothers, and sisters at home."

The Master laughed and stroked Naren's chest, restoring him to his normal mood. He said, "All right, everything will happen in due time."

Narendra, completely puzzled, felt that Ramakrishna had cast a hypnotic spell upon him. But how could that have been? Did he not pride himself in the possession of an iron will? He felt disgusted that he should have been unable to resist the influence of a madman. Nonetheless he felt a great inner attraction for Śri Ramakrishna.

On his third visit Naren fared no better, though he tried his utmost to be on guard. Śri Ramakrishna took him to a neighbouring garden and, in a state of trance, touched him. Completely overwhelmed, Naren lost consciousness.

Śri Ramakrishna, referring later to this incident, said that after putting Naren into a state of unconsciousness, he had asked him many questions about his past, his mission in the world, and the duration of his present life. The answers had only confirmed what he himself had thought about these matters. Ramakrishna told his other disciples that Naren had attained perfection even before this birth; that he was an adept in meditation; and that the day Naren recognized his true self, he would give up the body by an act of will, through yoga. Often he was heard to say that Naren was a Saptarshi, one of the Seven Sages, who live in the realm of the Absolute. He narrated to them a vision he had had regarding the disciple's spiritual heritage.

Absorbed, one day, in samādhi, Ramakrishna had found that his mind was soaring high, going beyond the physical universe of the sun, moon, and stars, and passing into the subtle region of ideas. As it continued to ascend, the forms of gods and goddesses were left behind, and it crossed the luminous barrier separating the phenomenal universe from the Absolute, entering finally the transcendental realm. There Ramakrishna saw seven venerable sages absorbed in meditation. These, he thought, must have surpassed even the gods and goddesses in wisdom and holiness, and as he was admiring their unique spirituality he saw a portion of the undifferentiated Absolute become congealed, as it were, and take the form of a Divine Child. Clambering upon the lap of one of the sages and gently clasping his neck with His soft arms, the Child whispered something in his ear, and at this magic touch the sage awoke from meditation. He fixed his half-open eyes upon the wondrous Child, who said in great joy: "I am going down to earth. Won't you come with me?" With a benign look the sage expressed assent and returned into deep spiritual ecstasy. Ramakrishna was amazed to observe that a tiny portion of the sage, however, descended to earth, taking the form of light, which struck the house in Calcutta where Narendra's family lived, and when he saw Narendra for the first time, he at once recognized him as the incarnation of the sage. He also admitted that the Divine Child who brought about the descent of the rishi was none other than himself.

THE MASTER AND THE DISCIPLE

The meeting of Narendranath and Śri Ramakrishna was an important event in the lives of both. A storm had been raging in Narendra's soul when he came to Śri Ramakrishna, who himself had passed through a similar struggle but was now firmly anchored in peace as a result of his intimate communion with the Godhead and his realization of Brahman as the immutable essence of all things.

A genuine product of the Indian soil and thoroughly acquainted with the spiritual traditions of India, Śri Ramakrishna was ignorant of the modern way of thinking. But Narendra was the symbol of the modern spirit. Inquisitive, alert, and intellectually honest, he possessed an open mind and demanded rational proof before accepting any conclusion as valid. As a loyal member of the Brāhmo Samāj he was critical of image worship and the rituals of the Hindu religion. He did not feel the need of a guru, a human intermediary between God and man. He was even sceptical about the existence of such a person, who was said to be free from human limitations and to whom an aspirant was expected to surrender himself completely and offer worship as to God. Ramakrishna's visions of gods and goddesses he openly ridiculed, and called them hallucinations.

For five years Narendra closely watched the Master, never allowing himself to be influenced by blind faith, always testing the words and actions of Śri Ramakrishna in the crucible of reason. It cost him many sorrows and much anguish before he accepted Śri Ramakrishna as the guru and the ideal of his spiritual life. But when the acceptance came, it was wholehearted, final, and irrevocable. The Master, too, was overjoyed to find a disciple who doubted, and he knew that Naren was the one to carry his message to the world.

The inner process that gradually transformed the chrysalis of Narendra into a beautiful butterfly will for ever remain, like all deep spiritual mysteries, unknown to the outer world. People, however, noticed the growth of an intimate relationship between the loving, patient, and forgiving teacher and his imperious and stubborn disciple. The Master never once asked Naren to abandon reason. He met the challenge of Naren's intellect with his superior understanding, acquired through first-hand knowledge of the essence of things. When Naren's reasoning failed to solve the ultimate mystery, the teacher gave him the necessary insight. Thus, with infinite patience, love, and vigilance, he tamed the rebellious spirit, demanding complete obedience to moral and spiritual disciplines, without which the religious life cannot be built on a firm foundation.

The very presence of Narendranath would fill the Master's mind with indescribable joy and create ecstatic moods. He had already known, by many indications, of the disciple's future greatness, the manifestation of which awaited only the fullness of time. What others regarded in Naren as stubbornness or haughtiness appeared to Śri Ramakrishna as the expression of his manliness and self-reliance, born of his self-control and innate purity. He could not bear the slightest criticism of Naren and often said: "Let no one judge him hastily. People will never understand him fully."

Ramakrishna loved Narendranath because he saw him as the embodiment of Nārāyana, the Divine Spirit, undefiled by the foul breath of the world. But he was criticized for his attachment. Once a trouble-maker of twisted mind named Hazra, who lived with the Master at Dakshineswar, said to him, "If you long for Naren and the other youngsters all the time, when will you think of God?" The Master was distressed by this thought. But it was at once revealed to him that though God dwelt in all beings, He was especially manifest in a pure soul like Naren. Relieved of his worries, he then said: "Oh, what a fool Hazra is! How he unsettled my mind! But why blame the poor fellow? How could he know?"

Śri Ramakrishna was outspoken in Narendra's praise. This often embarrassed the young disciple, who would criticize the Master for what he termed a sort of infatuation. One day Ramakrishna said in the presence of Keshab Sen and the saintly Vijay Goswami, the two outstanding leaders of the Brāhmo Samāj: "If Keshab possesses one virtue which has made him world-famous, Naren is endowed with eighteen such virtues. I have seen in Keshab and Vijay the divine light burning like a candle flame, but in Naren it shines with the radiance of the sun."

Narendra, instead of feeling flattered by these compliments, became annoyed and sharply rebuked the Master for what he regarded as his foolhardiness. "I cannot help it," the Master protested. "Do you think these are my words? The Divine Mother showed me certain things about you, which I repeated. And She reveals to me nothing but the truth."

But Naren was hardly convinced. He was sure that these so-called revelations were pure illusions. He carefully explained to Śri Ramakrishna that, from the viewpoint of Western science and philosophy, very often a man is deceived by his mind, and that the chances of deception are greater when a personal attachment is involved. He said to the Master, "Since you love me and wish to see me great, these fancies naturally come to your mind."

The Master was perplexed. He prayed to the Divine Mother for light and was told: "Why do you care about what he says? In a short time he will accept your every word as true."

On another occasion, when the Master was similarly reprimanded by the disciple, he was reassured by the Divine Mother. Thereupon he said to Naren with a smile: "You are a rogue. I won't listen to you any more. Mother says that I love you because I see the Lord in you. The day I shall not see Him in you, I shall not be able to bear even the sight of you."

On account of his preoccupation with his studies, or for other reasons, Narendra could not come to Dakshineswar as often as Śri Ramakrishna wished. But the Master could hardly endure his prolonged absence. If the disciple had not visited him for a number of days, he would send someone to Calcutta to fetch him. Sometimes he went to Calcutta himself. One time, for example, Narendra remained away from Dakshineswar for several weeks; even the Master's eager importunities had failed to bring him. Śri Ramakrishna knew that he sang regularly at the prayer meetings of the Brāhmo Samāj, and so one day he made his way to the Brāhmo temple that the disciple attended. Narendra was singing as the Master entered the hall, and when he heard Narendra's voice, Śri Ramakrishna fell into a deep ecstasy. The eyes of the congregation turned to him, and soon a commotion followed. Narendra hurried to his side. One of the Brāhmo leaders, in order to stop the excitement, put out the lights. The young disciple, realizing that the Master's sudden appearance was the cause of the disturbance, sharply took him to task. The latter answered, with tears in his eyes, that he had simply not been able to keep himself away from Narendra.

On another occasion a comical incident occurred that reveals a different side of Narendra's character. That day, too, Śri Ramakrishna had been unable to bear Narendra's absence, and he had gone to Calcutta to visit the disciple at his own home. He was told that Naren was studying in an attic that could be reached only by a steep ladder. A disciple named Latu, who was a sort of caretaker of the Master, had accompanied him, and with Latu's help Śri Ramakrishna climbed a few steps of the ladder. Narendra opened the door, and at the very sight of him Śri Ramakrishna exclaimed, "Naren, my beloved!" and went into ecstasy. With considerable difficulty the two disciples helped him to finish climbing the ladder, and as he entered the room the Master fell into deep samādhi. A fellow student who was with Naren at the time and did not know anything of religious trances, asked Naren in bewilderment, "Who is this man?"

"Never mind," replied Naren. "He is an *idiot*. You had better go home now."

After a while Śri Ramakrishna regained ordinary consciousness. Latu, who was illiterate, had heard the English word *idiot* and remembered it. He now asked Naren its meaning. When the word was explained to him, he flew into a rage, asking Naren how he dared apply such an insulting word to Śri Ramakrishna. Naren tried to pacify him and declared that since his friend did not have the slightest idea about ecstasy, and since he could not possibly have explained to him the meaning of samādhi, he had thought that the easiest way of avoiding an endless discussion with his friend was simply to describe Śri Ramakrishna as an idiot.

Naren often said that the "Old Man," meaning Ramakrishna, bound the disciple for ever to him by his love. "What do worldly men," he remarked, "know about love? They only make a show of it. The Master alone loves us genuinely." Naren, in return, bore a deep love for Śri Ramakrishna, though he seldom expressed it in words. He took delight in criticizing the Master's spiritual experiences as evidences of a lack of self-control. He made fun of his worship of Kāli.

"Why do you come here," Śri Ramakrishna once asked him, "if you do not accept Kāli, my Mother?"

"Bah! Must I accept Her," Naren retorted, "simply because I come to see you? I come to you because I love you."

"All right," said the Master, "ere long you will not only accept my blessed Mother, but weep in Her name."

Turning to his other disciples, he said: "This boy has no faith in the forms of God and tells me that my visions are pure imagination. But he is a fine lad of pure mind. He does not accept anything without direct evidence. He has studied much and cultivated great discrimination. He has fine judgement."

TRAINING OF THE DISCIPLE

It is hard to say when Naren actually accepted Śri Ramakrishna as his guru. As far as the Master was concerned, the spiritual relationship was established at the first meeting at Dakshineswar, when he had touched Naren, stirring him to his inner depths. From that moment he had implicit faith in the disciple and bore him a great love. But he encouraged Naren in the independence of his thinking. The love and faith of the Master acted as a restraint upon the impetuous youth and became his strong shield against the temptations of the world. By gradual steps the disciple was then led from doubt to certainty, and from anguish of mind to the bliss of the Spirit. This, however, was not an easy attainment.

Śri Ramakrishna, perfect teacher that he was, never laid down identical disciplines for disciples of diverse temperaments. He did not insist that Narendra should follow strict rules about food, nor did he ask him to believe in the reality of the gods and goddesses of Hindu mythology. It was not necessary for Narendra's philosophic mind to pursue the disciplines of concrete worship. But a strict eye was kept on Naren's practice of discrimination, detachment, self-control, and regular meditation. Śri Ramakrishna enjoyed Naren's vehement arguments with the other devotees regarding the dogmas and creeds of religion and was delighted to hear him tear to shreds their unquestioning beliefs. But

when, as often happened, Naren teased the gentle Rakhal for showing reverence
to the Divine Mother Kāli, the Master would not tolerate these attempts to
unsettle the brother disciple's faith in the forms of God.

As a member of the Brāhmo Samāj, Narendra accepted its doctrine of monotheism and the Personal God. He also believed in the natural depravity of man.
Such doctrines of non-dualistic Vedānta as the divinity of the soul and the
oneness of existence he regarded as blasphemy; the view that man is one with
God appeared to him pure nonsense. When the Master warned him against
thus limiting God's infinitude and asked him to pray to God to reveal to him
His true nature, Narendra smiled. One day he was making fun of Śri Ramakrishna's non-dualism before a friend and said, "What can be more absurd
than to say that this jug is God, this cup is God, and that we too are God?"
Both roared with laughter.

Just then the Master appeared. Coming to learn the cause of their fun, he
gently touched Naren and plunged into deep samādhi. The touch produced
a magic effect, and Narendra entered a new realm of consciousness. He saw
the whole universe permeated by the Divine Spirit and returned home in a
daze. While eating his meal, he felt the presence of Brahman in everything—
in the food, and in himself too. While walking in the street, he saw the carriages, the horses, the crowd, and himself as if made of the same substance.
After a few days the intensity of the vision lessened to some extent, but still
he could see the world only as a dream. While strolling in the public park of
Calcutta, he struck his head against the iron railings, several times, to see if
they were real or a mere illusion of the mind. Thus he got a glimpse of non-
dualism, the fullest realization of which was to come only later, at the Cossipore garden.

Śri Ramakrishna was always pleased when his disciples put to the test his
statements or behaviour before accepting his teachings. He would say: "Test
me as the money-changers test their coins. You must not believe me without
testing me thoroughly." The disciples often heard him say that his nervous
system had undergone a complete change as a result of his spiritual experiences,
and that he could not bear the touch of any metal, such as gold or silver. One
day, during his absence in Calcutta, Narendra hid a coin under Ramakrishna's
bed. After his return, when the Master sat on the bed, he started up in pain as if
stung by an insect. The mattress was examined and the hidden coin was found.

Naren, on the other hand, was often tested by the Master. One day, when he
entered the Master's room, he was completely ignored. Not a word of greet-
ing was uttered. A week later he came back and met with the same indifference,
and during the third and fourth visits saw no evidence of any thawing of the
Master's frigid attitude.

At the end of a month Śri Ramakrishna said to Naren, "I have not exchanged
a single word with you all this time, and still you come."

The disciple replied: "I come to Dakshineswar because I love you and want
to see you. I do not come here to hear your words."

The Master was overjoyed. Embracing the disciple, he said: "I was only
testing you. I wanted to see if you would stay away on account of my outward

indifference. Only a man of your inner strength could put up with such indifference on my part. Anyone else would have left me long ago."

On one occasion Śri Ramakrishna proposed to transfer to Narendranath many of the spiritual powers that he had acquired as a result of his ascetic disciplines and visions of God. Naren had no doubt concerning the Master's possessing such powers. He asked if they would help him to realize God. Śri Ramakrishna replied in the negative but added that they might assist him in his future work as a spiritual teacher. "Let me realize God first," said Naren, "and then I shall perhaps know whether or not I want supernatural powers. If I accept them now, I may forget God, make selfish use of them, and thus come to grief." Śri Ramakrishna was highly pleased to see his chief disciple's single-minded devotion.

NARENDRA'S STRUGGLE

Several factors were at work to mould the personality of young Narendranath. Foremost of these were his inborn spiritual tendencies, which were beginning to show themselves under the influence of Śri Ramakrishna, but against which his rational mind put up a strenuous fight. Second was his habit of thinking highly and acting nobly, disciplines acquired from a mother steeped in the spiritual heritage of India. Third were his broadmindedness and regard for truth wherever found, and his sceptical attitude towards the religious beliefs and social conventions of the Hindu society of his time. These he had learnt from his English-educated father, and he was strengthened in them through his own contact with Western culture.

With the introduction in India of English education during the middle of the nineteenth century, as we have seen, Western science, history, and philosophy were studied in the Indian colleges and universities. The educated Hindu youths, allured by the glamour, began to mould their thought according to this new light, and Narendra could not escape the influence. He developed a great respect for the analytical scientific method and subjected many of the Master's spiritual visions to such scrutiny. The English poets stirred his feelings, especially Wordsworth and Shelley, and he took a course in Western medical science to understand the functioning of the nervous system, particularly the brain and spinal cord, in order to find out the secrets of Śri Ramakrishna's trances. But all this only deepened his inner turmoil.

John Stuart Mill's *Three Essays on Religion* upset his boyish theism and the easy optimism imbibed from the Brāhmo Samāj. The presence of evil in nature and man haunted him and he could not reconcile it at all with the goodness of an omnipotent Creator. Hume's scepticism and Herbert Spencer's doctrine of the Unknowable filled his mind with a settled philosophical agnosticism. After the wearing out of his first emotional freshness and naïveté, he was beset with a certain dryness and incapacity for the old prayers and devotions. He was filled with an ennui which he concealed, however, under his jovial nature. Music, at this difficult stage of his life, rendered him great help; for it moved him as nothing else and gave him a glimpse of unseen realities that often brought tears to his eyes.

Narendra did not have much patience with humdrum reading, nor did he care to absorb knowledge from books as much as from living communion and personal experience. He wanted life to be kindled by life, and thought kindled by thought. He studied Shelley under a college friend, Brajendranath Seal, who later became the leading Indian philosopher of his time, and deeply felt with the poet his pantheism, impersonal love, and vision of a glorified millennial humanity. The universe, no longer a mere lifeless, loveless mechanism, was seen to contain a spiritual principle of unity. Brajendranath, moreover, tried to present him with a synthesis of the Supreme Brahman of Vedānta, the Universal Reason of Hegel, and the gospel of Liberty, Equality, and Fraternity of the French Revolution. By accepting as the principle of morals the sovereignty of Universal Reason and the negation of the individual, Narendra achieved an intellectual victory over scepticism and materialism, but no peace of mind.

Narendra now had to face a new difficulty. The "ballet of bloodless categories" of Hegel and his creed of Universal Reason required of Naren a suppression of the yearning and susceptibility of his artistic nature and joyous temperament, the destruction of the cravings of his keen and acute senses, and the smothering of his free and merry conviviality. This amounted almost to killing his own true self. Further, he could not find in such a philosophy any help in the struggle of a hot-blooded youth against the cravings of the passions, which appeared to him as impure, gross, and carnal. Some of his musical associates were men of loose morals for whom he felt a bitter and undisguised contempt.

Narendra therefore asked his friend Brajendra if the latter knew the way of deliverance from the bondage of the senses, but he was told only to rely upon Pure Reason and to identify the self with it, and was promised that through this he would experience an ineffable peace. The friend was a Platonic transcendentalist and did not have faith in what he called the artificial prop of grace, or the mediation of a guru. But the problems and difficulties of Narendra were very different from those of his intellectual friend. He found that mere philosophy was impotent in the hour of temptation and in the struggle for his soul's deliverance. He felt the need of a hand to save, to uplift, to protect—a śakti or power outside his rational mind that would transform his impotence into strength and glory. He wanted a flesh-and-blood reality established in peace and certainty, in short, a living guru, who, by embodying perfection in the flesh, would compose the commotion of his soul.

The leaders of the Brāhmo Samāj, as well as those of the other religious sects, had failed. It was only Ramakrishna who spoke to him with authority, as none had spoken before, and by his power brought peace into the troubled soul and healed the wounds of the spirit. At first Naren feared that the serenity that possessed him in the presence of the Master was illusory, but his misgivings were gradually vanquished by the calm assurance transmitted to him by Ramakrishna out of his own experience of Satchidānanda Brahman—Existence, Knowledge, and Bliss Absolute.[1]

Narendra could not but recognize the contrast of the *Sturm und Drang* of

[1] This account of the struggle of Naren's collegiate days summarizes an article on Swami Vivekananda by Brajendranath Seal, published in the *Life of Swami Vivekananda* by the Advaita Āśrama, Mayavati, India.

his soul with the serene bliss in which Śri Ramakrishna was always bathed. He begged the Master to teach him meditation, and Śri Ramakrishna's reply was to him a source of comfort and strength. The Master said: "God listens to our sincere prayer. I can swear that you can see God and talk with Him as intensely as you see me and talk with me. You can hear His words and feel His touch." Further the Master declared: "You may not believe in divine forms, but if you believe in an Ultimate Reality who is the Regulator of the universe, you can pray to Him thus: 'O God, I do not know Thee. Be gracious to reveal to me Thy real nature.' He will certainly listen to you if your prayer is sincere."

Narendra, intensifying his meditation under the Master's guidance, began to lose consciousness of the body and to feel an inner peace, and this peace would linger even after the meditation was over. Frequently he felt the separation of the body from the soul. Strange perceptions came to him in dreams, producing a sense of exaltation that persisted after he awoke. The guru was performing his task in an inscrutable manner. Narendra's friends observed only his outer struggle; but the real transformation was known to the teacher alone—or perhaps to the disciple too.

BEREAVEMENT

In 1884, when Narendranath was preparing for the B.A. examination, his family was struck by a calamity. His father suddenly died, and the mother and children were plunged into great grief. For Viswanath, a man of generous nature, had lived beyond his means, and his death burdened the family with a heavy debt. Creditors, like hungry wolves, began to prowl about the door, and to make matters worse, certain relatives brought a lawsuit for the partition of the ancestral home. Though they lost it, Narendra was faced, thereafter, with poverty. As the eldest male member of the family, he had to find the wherewithal for the feeding of seven or eight mouths. He attended the law classes clad in coarse clothes, barefoot, and hungry, and often refused invitations for dinner from friends, remembering his starving mother, brothers, and sisters at home. He would skip family meals on the fictitious plea that he had already eaten at a friend's house, so that the people at home might receive a larger share of the scanty food. The Datta family was proud and would not dream of soliciting help from outsiders. With his companions Narendra was his usual gay self. His rich friends no doubt noticed his pale face, but they did nothing to help. Only one friend sent occasional anonymous aid, and Narendra remained grateful to him for life. Meanwhile, all his efforts to find employment failed. Some friends who earned money in a dishonest way asked him to join them, and a rich woman sent him an immoral proposal, promising to put an end to his financial distress. But Narendra gave to these a blunt rebuff. Sometimes he would wonder if the world were not the handiwork of the Devil—for how could one account for so much suffering in God's creation?

One day, after a futile search for a job, he sat down, weary and footsore, in the big park of Calcutta. There some friends joined him and one of them sang a song, perhaps to console him, describing God's abundant grace.

Furiously Naren said: "Will you please stop that song? Such fancies are, no doubt, pleasing to those who are born with silver spoons in their mouths.

Yes, there was a time when I, too, thought like that. But today these ideas appear to me a mockery."

The friends were bewildered.

One morning, as usual, Naren left his bed repeating God's name, and was about to go out in search of work after seeking divine blessings. His mother heard the prayer and said bitterly: "Hush, you fool! You have been crying yourself hoarse for God since your childhood. Tell me what has God done for you?" Evidently the crushing poverty at home was too much for the pious mother.

These words stung Naren to the quick. A doubt crept into his mind about God's existence and His Providence.

It was not in Naren's nature to hide his feelings. He argued before his friends and the devotees of Śrī Ramakrishna about God's non-existence and the futility of prayer even if God existed. His over-zealous friends thought he had become an atheist and ascribed to him many unmentionable crimes, which he had supposedly committed to forget his misery. Some of the devotees of the Master shared these views. Narendra cried in anguish and roared with anger, mortified to think that they could believe him to have sunk so low. He became hardened and justified drinking and the other dubious pleasures resorted to by miserable people for a respite from their suffering. He said, further, that he himself would not hesitate to follow such a course if he were assured of its efficacy. Openly asserting that only cowards believed in God for fear of hell-fire, he argued the possibility of God's non-existence and quoted Western philosophers in support of his position. And when the devotees of the Master became convinced that he was hopelessly lost, he felt a sort of inner satisfaction.

A garbled report of the matter reached Śrī Ramakrishna, and Narendra thought that perhaps the Master, too, doubted his moral integrity. The very idea revived his anger. "Never mind," he said to himself. "If good or bad opinion of a man rests on such flimsy grounds, I don't care."

But Narendra was mistaken. For one day Bhavanath, a devotee of the Master and an intimate friend of Narendra, cast aspersions on the latter's character, and the Master said angrily: "Stop, you fool! The Mother has told me that it is simply not true. I shan't look at your face if you speak to me again that way."

The fact was that Narendra could not, in his heart of hearts, disbelieve in God. He remembered the spiritual visions of his own boyhood and many others that he had experienced in the company of the Master. Inwardly he longed to understand God and His ways. And one day he gained this understanding. It happened in the following way:

He had been out since morning in a soaking rain in search of employment, having had neither food nor rest for the whole day. That evening he sat down on the porch of a house by the roadside, exhausted. He was in a daze. Thoughts began to flit before his mind, which he could not control. Suddenly he had a strange vision, which lasted almost the whole night. He felt that veil after veil was removed from before his soul, and he understood the reconciliation of God's justice with His mercy. He came to know—but he never told how—that misery could exist in the creation of a compassionate God without impairing His sovereign power or touching man's real self. He understood the meaning of it all and was at peace. Just before daybreak, refreshed both in body and in mind, he returned home.

This revelation profoundly impressed Narendranath. He became indifferent to people's opinion and was convinced that he was not born to lead an ordinary worldly life, enjoying the love of a wife and children and physical luxuries. He recalled how the several proposals of marriage made by his relatives had come to nothing, and he ascribed all this to God's will. The peace and freedom of the monastic life cast a spell upon him. He determined to renounce the world, and set a date for this act. Then, coming to learn that Śrī Ramakrishna would visit Calcutta that very day, he was happy to think that he could embrace the life of a wandering monk with his guru's blessings.

When they met, the Master persuaded his disciple to accompany him to Dakshineswar. As they arrived in his room, Śrī Ramakrishna went into an ecstatic mood and sang a song, while tears bathed his eyes. The words of the song clearly indicated that the Master knew of the disciple's secret wish. When other devotees asked him about the cause of his grief, Śrī Ramakrishna said, "Oh, never mind, it is something between me and Naren, and nobody else's business." At night he called Naren to his side and said with great feeling: "I know you are born for Mother's work. I also know that you will be a monk. But stay in the world as long as I live, for my sake at least." He wept again.

Next day Naren procured a temporary job, which was sufficient to provide a hand-to-mouth living for the family.

One day Narendra asked himself why, since Kālī, the Divine Mother, listened to Śrī Ramakrishna's prayers, should not the Master pray to Her to relieve his poverty. When he spoke to Śrī Ramakrishna about this idea, the latter inquired why he did not pray himself to Kālī, adding that Narendranath suffered because he did not acknowledge Kālī as the Sovereign Mistress of the universe.

"Today," the Master continued, "is a Tuesday, an auspicious day for the Mother's worship. Go to Her shrine in the evening, prostrate yourself before the image, and pray to Her for any boon; it will be granted. Mother Kālī is the embodiment of Love and Compassion. She is the Power of Brahman. She gives birth to the world by Her mere wish. She fulfils every sincere prayer of Her devotees."

At nine o'clock in the evening, Narendranath went to the Kālī temple. Passing through the courtyard, he felt within himself a surge of emotion, and his heart leapt with joy in anticipation of the vision of the Divine Mother. Entering the temple, he cast his eyes upon the image and found the stone figure to be nothing else but the living Goddess, the Divine Mother Herself, ready to give him any boon he wanted—either a happy worldly life or the joy of spiritual freedom. He was in ecstasy. He prayed for the boon of wisdom, discrimination, renunciation, and Her uninterrupted vision, but forgot to ask the Deity for money. He felt great peace within as he returned to the Master's room, and when asked if he had prayed for money, was startled. He said that he had forgotten all about it. The Master told him to go to the temple again and pray to the Divine Mother to satisfy his immediate needs. Naren did as he was bidden, but again forgot his mission. The same thing happened a third time.

Then Naren suddenly realized that Śri Ramakrishna himself had made him forget to ask the Divine Mother for worldly things; perhaps he wanted Naren to lead a life of renunciation. So he now asked Śri Ramakrishna to do something for the family. The Master told the disciple that it was not Naren's destiny to enjoy a worldly life, but assured him that the family would be able to eke out a simple existence.

The above incident left a deep impression upon Naren's mind; it enriched his spiritual life, for he gained a new understanding of the Godhead and Its ways in the phenomenal universe. Naren's idea of God had hitherto been confined either to that of a vague Impersonal Reality or to that of an extra-cosmic Creator removed from the world. He now realized that the Godhead is immanent in the creation, that after projecting the universe from within Itself, It has entered into all created entities as life and consciousness, whether manifest or latent. This same immanent Spirit, or the World Soul, when regarded as a person creating, preserving, and destroying the universe, is called the Personal God, and is worshipped by different religions through such a relationship as that of father, mother, king, or beloved. These relationships, he came to understand, have their appropriate symbols, and Kāli is one of them.

Embodying in Herself creation and destruction, love and terror, life and death, Kāli is the symbol of the total universe. The eternal cycle of the manifestation and non-manifestation of the universe is the breathing-out and breathing-in of this Divine Mother. In one aspect She is death, without which there cannot be life. One of Her hands is smeared with blood, since without blood the picture of the phenomenal universe is not complete. To the wicked who have transgressed Her laws, She is the embodiment of terror, and to the virtuous, the benign Mother. Before creation She contains within Her womb the seed of the universe, which is left from the previous cycle. After the manifestation of the universe She becomes its preserver and nourisher, and at the end of the cycle She draws it back within Herself and remains as the undifferentiated Śakti, the creative power of Brahman. She is non-different from Brahman. When free from the acts of creation, preservation, and destruction, the Spirit, in Its acosmic aspect, is called Brahman; otherwise It is known as the World Soul or the Divine Mother of the universe. She is therefore the doorway to the realization of the Absolute; She is the Absolute. To the daring devotee who wants to see the transcendental Absolute, She reveals that form by withdrawing Her garment of the phenomenal universe. Brahman is Her transcendental aspect. She is the Great Fact of the universe, the totality of created beings. She is the Ruler and the Controller.

All this had previously been beyond Narendra's comprehension. He had accepted the reality of the phenomenal world and yet denied the reality of Kāli. He had been conscious of hunger and thirst, pain and pleasure, and the other characteristics of the world, and yet he had not accepted Kāli, who controlled them all. That was why he had suffered. But on that auspicious Tuesday evening the scales dropped from his eyes. He accepted Kāli as the Divine Mother of the universe. He became Her devotee.

Many years later he wrote to an American lady: "Kāli worship is my especial fad." But he did not preach Her in public, because he thought that all that

modern man required was to be found in the Upanishads. Further, he realized
that the Kāli symbol would not be understood by universal humanity.

Narendra enjoyed the company of the Master for six years, during which
time his spiritual life was moulded. Śri Ramakrishna was a wonderful teacher
in every sense of the word. Without imposing his ideas upon anyone, he taught
more by the silent influence of his inner life than by words or even by personal
example. To live near him demanded of the disciple purity of thought and
concentration of mind. He often appeared to his future monastic followers as
their friend and playmate. Through fun and merriment he always kept before
them the shining ideal of God-realization. He would not allow any deviation
from bodily and mental chastity, nor any compromise with truth and renunciation. Everything else he left to the will of the Divine Mother.

Narendra was his "marked" disciple, chosen by the Lord for a special mission.
Śri Ramakrishna kept a sharp eye on him, though he appeared to give the disciple every opportunity to release his pent-up physical and mental energy.
Before him, Naren often romped about like a young lion cub in the presence
of a firm but indulgent parent. His spiritual radiance often startled the Master,
who saw that māyā, the Great Enchantress, could not approach within "ten
feet" of that blazing fire.

Narendra always came to the Master in the hours of his spiritual difficulties.
One time he complained that he could not meditate in the morning on account
of the shrill note of a whistle from a neighbouring mill, and was advised by
the Master to concentrate on the very sound of the whistle. In a short time he
overcame the distraction. Another time he found it difficult to forget the body
at the time of meditation. Śri Ramakrishna sharply pressed the space between
Naren's eyebrows and asked him to concentrate on that sensation. The disciple
found this method effective.

Witnessing the religious ecstasy of several devotees, Narendra one day said
to the Master that he too wanted to experience it. "My child," he was told,
"when a huge elephant enters a small pond, a great commotion is set up, but
when it plunges into the Ganges, the river shows very little agitation. These
devotees are like small ponds; a little experience makes their feelings flow over
the brim. But you are a huge river."

Another day the thought of excessive spiritual fervour frightened Naren. The
Master reassured him by saying: "God is like an ocean of sweetness; wouldn't
you dive into it? Suppose there is a bottle, with a wide mouth, filled with
syrup, and that you are a fly, hungry for the sweet liquid. How would you like
to drink it?" Narendra said that he would sit on the edge of the bottle, otherwise he might be drowned in the syrup and lose his life. "But," the Master said,
"you must not forget that I am talking of the Ocean of Satchidānanda, the
Ocean of Immortality. Here one need not be afraid of death. Only fools say
that one should not have too much of divine ecstasy. Can anybody carry to excess
the love of God? You must dive deep in the Ocean of God."

On one occasion Narendra and some of his brother disciples were vehemently
arguing about God's nature—whether He was personal or impersonal, whether

Divine Incarnation was fact or myth, and so forth and so on. Narendra silenced his opponents by his sharp power of reasoning and felt jubilant at his triumph. Śri Ramakrishna enjoyed the discussion and after it was over sang in an ecstatic mood:

> How are you trying, O my mind, to know the nature of God?
> You are groping like a madman locked in a dark room.
> He is grasped through ecstatic love; how can you fathom Him without it?
> Only through affirmation, never negation, can you know Him;
> Neither through Veda nor through Tantra nor the six darśanas.

All fell silent, and Narendra realized the inability of the intellect to fathom God's mystery.

In his heart of hearts Naren was a lover of God. Pointing to his eyes, Ramakrishna said that only a bhakta possessed such a tender look; the eyes of the jnāni were generally dry. Many a time, in his later years, Narendra said, comparing his own spiritual attitude with that of the Master: "He was a jnāni within, but a bhakta without; but I am a bhakta within, and a jnāni without." He meant that Ramakrishna's gigantic intellect was hidden under a thin layer of devotion, and Narendra's devotional nature was covered by a cloak of knowledge.

We have already referred to the great depth of Śri Ramakrishna's love for his beloved disciple. He was worried about the distress of Naren's family and one day asked a wealthy devotee if he could not help Naren financially. Naren's pride was wounded and he mildly scolded the Master. The latter said with tears in his eyes: "O my Naren! I can do anything for you, even beg from door to door." Narendra was deeply moved but said nothing. Many days after, he remarked, "The Master made me his slave by his love for me."

This great love of Śri Ramakrishna enabled Naren to face calmly the hardships of life. Instead of hardening into a cynic, he developed a mellowness of heart. But, as will be seen later, Naren to the end of his life was often misunderstood by his friends. A bold thinker, he was far ahead of his time. Once he said: "Why should I expect to be understood? It is enough that they love me. After all, who am I? The Mother knows best. She can do Her own work. Why should I think myself to be indispensable?"

The poverty at home was not an altogether unmitigated evil. It drew out another side of Naren's character. He began to feel intensely for the needy and afflicted. Had he been nurtured in luxury, the Master used to say, he would perhaps have become a different person—a statesman, a lawyer, an orator, or a social reformer. But instead, he dedicated his life to the service of humanity.

Śri Ramakrishna had had the prevision of Naren's future life of renunciation. Therefore he was quite alarmed when he came to know of the various plans made by Naren's relatives for his marriage. Prostrating himself in the shrine of Kāli, he prayed repeatedly: "O Mother! Do break up these plans. Do not let him sink in the quagmire of the world." He closely watched Naren and warned him whenever he discovered the trace of an impure thought in his mind.

Naren's keen mind understood the subtle implications of Śri Ramakrishna's teachings. One day the Master said that the three salient disciplines of Vaishnavism were love of God's name, service to the devotees, and compassion for all living beings. But he did not like the word *compassion* and said to the devotees: "How foolish to speak of compassion! Man is an insignificant worm crawling on the earth—and he to show compassion to others! This is absurd. It must not be compassion, but service to all. Recognize them as God's manifestations and serve them."

The other devotees heard the words of the Master but could hardly understand their significance. Naren, however, fathomed the meaning. Taking his young friends aside, he said that Śri Ramakrishna's remarks had thrown wonderful light on the philosophy of non-dualism with its discipline of non-attachment, and on that of dualism with its discipline of love. The two were not really in conflict. A non-dualist did not have to make his heart dry as sand, nor did he have to run away from the world. As Brahman alone existed in all men, a non-dualist must love all and serve all. Love, in the true sense of the word, is not possible unless one sees God in others. Naren said that the Master's words also reconciled the paths of knowledge and action. An illumined person did not have to remain inactive; he could commune with Brahman through service to other embodied beings, who also are embodiments of Brahman.

"If it be the will of God," Naren concluded, "I shall one day proclaim this noble truth before the world at large. I shall make it the common property of all—the wise and the fool, the rich and the poor, the brāhmin and the pariah."

Years later he expressed these sentiments in a noble poem which concluded with the following words:

> Thy God is here before thee now,
> Revealed in all these myriad forms:
> Rejecting them, where seekest thou
> His presence? He who freely shares
> His love with every living thing
> Proffers true service unto God.

It was Śri Ramakrishna who re-educated Narendranath in the essentials of Hinduism. He, the fulfilment of the spiritual aspirations of the three hundred millions of Hindus for the past three thousand years, was the embodiment of the Hindu faith. The beliefs Narendra had learnt on his mother's lap had been shattered by a collegiate education, but the young man now came to know that Hinduism does not consist of dogmas or creeds; it is an inner experience, deep and inclusive, which respects all faiths, all thoughts, all efforts, and all realizations. Unity in diversity is its ideal.

Narendra further learnt that religion is a vision which, at the end, transcends all barriers of caste and race and breaks down the limitations of time and space. He learnt from the Master that the Personal God and worship through symbols ultimately lead the devotee to the realization of complete oneness with the Deity. The Master taught him the divinity of the soul, the non-duality of the Godhead, the unity of existence, and the harmony of religions. He showed Naren by his own example how a man in this very life could reach perfection, and the disciple found that the Master had realized the same God-consciousness by following the diverse disciplines of Hinduism, Christianity, and Islām.

One day the Master, in an ecstatic mood, said to the devotees: "There are many opinions and many ways. I have seen them all and do not like them any more. The devotees of different faiths quarrel among themselves. Let me tell you something. You are my own people. There are no strangers around. I clearly see that God is the whole and I am a part of Him. He is the Lord and I am His servant. And sometimes I think He is I and I am He."

Narendra regarded Śri Ramakrishna as the embodiment of the spirit of religion and did not bother to know whether or not he was an Incarnation of God. He was reluctant to cast the Master in any theological mould. It was enough for Naren if he could see through the vista of Ramakrishna's spiritual experiences all the aspects of the Godhead.

How did Narendra impress the other devotees of the Master, especially the youngsters? He was their idol. They were awed by his intellect and fascinated by his personality. In appearance he was a dynamic youth, overflowing with vigour and vitality, having a physical frame slightly over middle height and somewhat thickset in the shoulders. He was graceful without being feminine. He had a strong jaw, suggesting his staunch will and fixed determination. The chest was expansive, and the breadth of the head towards the front signified high mental power and development. But the most remarkable thing about him was his eyes, which Śri Ramakrishna compared to lotus petals. They were prominent but not protruding, and part of the time their gaze was indrawn, suggesting the habit of deep meditation; their colour varied according to the feeling of the moment. Sometimes they would be luminous in profundity, and sometimes they sparkled in merriment. Endowed with the native grace of an animal, he was free in his movements. He walked sometimes with a slow gait and sometimes with rapidity, always a part of his mind absorbed in deep thought. And it was a delight to hear his resonant voice, either in conversation or in music.

But when Naren was serious his face often frightened his friends. In a heated discussion his eyes glowed. If immersed in his own thoughts, he created such an air of aloofness that no one dared to approach him. Subject to various moods, sometimes he showed utter impatience with his environment, and sometimes a tenderness that melted everybody's heart. His smile was bright and infectious. To some he was a happy dreamer, to some he lived in a real world rich with love and beauty, but to all he unfailingly appeared a scion of an aristocratic home.

And how did the Master regard his beloved disciple? To quote his own words:

"Narendra belongs to a very high plane—the realm of the Absolute. He has a manly nature. So many devotees come here, but there is no one like him.

"Every now and then I take stock of the devotees. I find that some are like lotuses with ten petals, some like lotuses with a hundred petals. But among lotuses Narendra is a thousand-petalled one.

"Other devotees may be like pots or pitchers; but Narendra is a huge water-barrel.

"Others may be like pools or tanks; but Narendra is a huge reservoir like the Hāldārpukur.

"Among fish, Narendra is a huge red-eyed carp; others are like minnows or smelts or sardines.

THE TEMPLE OF KĀLI AT DAKSHINESWAR

Śri Ramakrishna

The Holy Mother

The Cossipore Garden House

"Narendra is a 'very big receptacle,' one that can hold many things. He is like a bamboo with a big hollow space inside.

"Narendra is not under the control of anything. He is not under the control of attachment or sense pleasures. He is like a male pigeon. If you hold a male pigeon by its beak, it breaks away from you; but the female pigeon keeps still. I feel great strength when Narendra is with me in a gathering."

RAMAKRISHNA'S ILLNESS AND DEATH

Sometime about the middle of 1885 Sri Ramakrishna showed the first symptoms of a throat ailment that later was diagnosed as cancer. Against the advice of the physicians, he continued to give instruction to spiritual seekers, and to fall into frequent trances. Both of these practices aggravated the illness. For the convenience of the physicians and the devotees, he was at first removed to a house in the northern section of Calcutta and then to a garden house at Cossipore, a suburb of the city. Narendra and the other young disciples took charge of nursing him. Disregarding the wishes of their guardians, the boys gave up their studies or neglected their duties at home, at least temporarily, in order to devote themselves heart and soul to the service of the Master. His wife, known among the devotees as the Holy Mother, looked after the cooking; the older devotees met the expenses. All regarded this service to the guru as a blessing and privilege.

Narendra time and again showed his keen insight and mature judgement during Sri Ramakrishna's illness. Many of the devotees, who looked upon the Master as God's Incarnation and therefore refused to see in him any human frailty, began to give a supernatural interpretation of his illness. They believed that it had been brought about by the will of the Divine Mother or the Master himself to fulfil an inscrutable purpose, and that it would be cured without any human effort after the purpose was fulfilled. Narendra said, however, that since Sri Ramakrishna was a combination of God and man the physical element in him was subject to such laws of nature as birth, growth, decay, and destruction. He refused to give the Master's disease, a natural phenomenon, any supernatural explanation. Nonetheless, he was willing to shed his last drop of blood in the service of Sri Ramakrishna.

Emotion plays an important part in the development of the spiritual life. While intellect removes the obstacles, it is emotion that gives the urge to the seeker to move forward. But mere emotionalism without the disciplines of discrimination and renunciation often leads him astray. He often uses it as a short-cut to trance or ecstasy. Sri Ramakrishna, no doubt, danced and wept while singing God's name and experienced frequent trances; but behind his emotion there was the long practice of austerities and renunciation. His devotees had not witnessed the practice of his spiritual disciplines. Some of them, especially the elderly householders, began to display ecstasies accompanied by tears and physical contortions, which in many cases, as later appeared, were the result of careful rehearsal at home or mere imitation of Sri Ramakrishna's genuine trances. Some of the devotees, who looked upon the Master as a Divine Incarnation, thought that he had assumed their responsibilities, and therefore they relaxed their own efforts. Others began to speculate about the part each of them was destined to play in the new dispensation of Śri Ramakrishna. In short, those who showed the highest emotionalism posed as the most spiritually advanced.

Narendra's alert mind soon saw this dangerous trend in their lives. He began to make fun of the elders and warned his young brother disciples about the harmful effect of indulging in such outbursts. Real spirituality, he told them over and over again, was the eradication of worldly tendencies and the development of man's higher nature. He derided their tears and trances as symptoms of nervous disorder, which should be corrected by the power of the will, and, if necessary, by nourishing food and proper medical treatment. Very often, he said, unwary devotees of God fall victims to mental and physical breakdown. "Of one hundred persons who take up the spiritual life," he grimly warned, "eighty turn out to be charlatans, fifteen insane, and only five, maybe, get a glimpse of the real truth. Therefore, beware." He appealed to their inner strength and admonished them to keep away from all sentimental nonsense. He described to the young disciples Śri Ramakrishna's uncompromising self-control, passionate yearning for God, and utter renunciation of attachment to the world, and he insisted that those who loved the Master should apply his teachings in their lives. Śri Ramakrishna, too, coming to realize the approaching end of his mortal existence, impressed it upon the devotees that the realization of God depended upon the giving up of lust and greed. The young disciples became grateful to Narendranath for thus guiding them during the formative period of their spiritual career. They spent their leisure hours together in meditation, study, devotional music, and healthy spiritual discussions.

The illness of Śri Ramakrishna showed no sign of abatement; the boys redoubled their efforts to nurse him, and Narendra was constantly by their side, cheering them whenever they felt depressed. One day he found them hesitant about approaching the Master. They had been told that the illness was infectious. Narendra dragged them to the Master's room. Lying in a corner was a cup containing part of the gruel which Śri Ramakrishna could not swallow. It was mixed with his saliva. Narendra seized the cup and swallowed its contents. This set at rest the boys' misgivings.

Narendra, understanding the fatal nature of Śri Ramakrishna's illness and realizing that the beloved teacher would not live long, intensified his own spiritual practices. His longing for the vision of God knew no limit. One day he asked the Master for the boon of remaining merged in samādhi three or four days at a stretch, interrupting his meditation now and then for a bite of food. "You are a fool," said the Master. "There is a state higher than that. It is you who sing: 'O Lord! Thou art all that exists.'" Śri Ramakrishna wanted the disciple to see God in all beings and to serve them in a spirit of worship. He often said that to see the world alone, without God, is ignorance, ajnāna; to see God alone, without the world, is a kind of philosophical knowledge, jnāna; but to see all beings permeated by the spirit of God is supreme wisdom, vijnāna. Only a few blessed souls could see God dwelling in all. He wanted Naren to attain this supreme wisdom. So the Master said to him, "Settle your family affairs first, then you shall know a state even higher than samādhi."

On another occasion, in response to a similar request, Śri Ramakrishna said to

Naren: "Shame on you! You are asking for such an insignificant thing. I thought that you would be like a big banyan tree, and that thousands of people would rest in your shade. But now I see that you are seeking your own liberation." Thus scolded, Narendra shed profuse tears. He realized the greatness of Śri Ramakrishna's heart.

An intense fire was raging within Narendra's soul. He could hardly touch his college books; he felt it was a dreadful thing to waste time in that way. One morning he went home but suddenly experienced an inner fear. He wept for not having made much spiritual progress, and hurried to Cossipore almost unconscious of the outside world. His shoes slipped off somewhere, and as he ran past a rick of straw some of it stuck to his clothes. Only after entering the Master's room did he feel some inner peace.

Śri Ramakrishna said to the other disciples present: "Look at Naren's state of mind. Previously he did not believe in the Personal God or divine forms. Now he is dying for God's vision." The Master then gave Naren certain spiritual instructions about meditation.

Naren was being literally consumed by a passion for God. The world appeared to him to be utterly distasteful. When the Master reminded him of his college studies, the disciple said, "I would feel relieved if I could swallow a drug and forget all I have learnt." He spent night after night in meditation under the trees in the Panchavati at Dakshineswar, where Śri Ramakrishna, during the days of his spiritual discipline, had contemplated God. He felt the awakening of the Kundalini[2] and had other spiritual visions.

One day at Cossipore Narendra was meditating under a tree with Girish, another disciple. The place was infested with mosquitoes. Girish tried in vain to concentrate his mind. Casting his eyes on Naren, he saw him absorbed in meditation, though his body appeared to be covered by a blanket of the insects.

A few days later Narendra's longing seemed to have reached the breaking-point. He spent an entire night walking around the garden house at Cossipore and repeating Rāma's name in a heart-rending manner. In the early hours of the morning Śri Ramakrishna heard his voice, called him to his side, and said affectionately: "Listen, my child, why are you acting that way? What will you achieve by such impatience?" He stopped for a minute and then continued: "See, Naren. What you have been doing now, I did for twelve long years. A storm raged in my head during that period. What will you realize in one night?"

But the master was pleased with Naren's spiritual struggle and made no secret of his wish to make him his spiritual heir. He wanted Naren to look after the young disciples. "I leave them in your care," he said to him. "Love them intensely and see that they practise spiritual disciplines even after my death, and that they do not return home." He asked the young disciples to regard Naren as their leader. It was an easy task for them. Then, one day, Śri Ramakrishna initiated several of the young disciples into the monastic life, and thus himself laid the foundation of the future Ramakrishna Order of monks.

Attendance on the Master during his sickness revealed to Narendra the true import of Śri Ramakrishna's spiritual experiences. He was amazed to find that

[2] The spiritual energy, usually dormant in man, but aroused by the practice of spiritual disciplines. See glossary.

the Master could dissociate himself from all consciousness of the body by a mere wish, at which time he was not aware of the least pain from his ailment. Constantly he enjoyed an inner bliss, in spite of the suffering of the body, and he could transmit that bliss to the disciples by a mere touch or look. To Narendra, Śri Ramakrishna was the vivid demonstration of the reality of the Spirit and the unsubstantiality of matter.

One day the Master was told by a scholar that he could instantly cure himself of his illness by concentrating his mind on his throat. This Śri Ramakrishna refused to do since he could never withdraw his mind from God. But at Naren's repeated request, the Master agreed to speak to the Divine Mother about his illness. A little later he said to the disciple in a sad voice: "Yes, I told Her that I could not swallow any food on account of the sore in my throat, and asked Her to do something about it. But the Mother said, pointing to you all, 'Why, are you not eating enough through all these mouths?' I felt so humiliated that I could not utter another word." Narendra realized how Śri Ramakrishna applied in life the Vedāntic idea of the oneness of existence and also came to know that only through such realization could one rise above the pain and suffering of the individual life.

To live with Śri Ramakrishna during his illness was in itself a spiritual experience. It was wonderful to witness how he bore with his pain. In one mood he would see that the Divine Mother alone was the dispenser of pleasure and pain and that his own will was one with the Mother's will, and in another mood he would clearly behold the utter absence of diversity, God alone becoming men, animals, gardens, houses, roads, "the executioner, the victim, and the slaughter-post," to use the Master's own words.

Narendra saw in the Master the living explanation of the scriptures regarding the divine nature of the soul and the illusoriness of the body. Further, he came to know that Śri Ramakrishna had attained to that state by the total renunciation of "woman" and "gold," which, indeed, was the gist of his teaching. Another idea was creeping into Naren's mind. He began to see how the transcendental Reality, the Godhead, could embody Itself as the Personal God, and the Absolute become a Divine Incarnation. He was having a glimpse of the greatest of all divine mysteries: the incarnation of the Father as the Son for the redemption of the world. He began to believe that God becomes man so that man may become God. Śri Ramakrishna thus appeared to him in a new light.

Under the intellectual leadership of Narendranath, the Cossipore garden house became a miniature university. During the few moments' leisure snatched from nursing and meditation, Narendra would discuss with his brother disciples religions and philosophies, both Eastern and Western. Along with the teachings of Śankara, Krishna, and Chaitanya, those of Buddha and Christ were searchingly examined.

Narendra had a special affection for Buddha, and one day suddenly felt a strong desire to visit Bodh-Gayā, where the great Prophet had attained enlightenment. With Kali and Tarak, two of the brother disciples, he left, unbeknown to the others, for that sacred place and meditated for long hours under the sacred Bo-tree. Once while thus absorbed he was overwhelmed with emotion and, weeping profusely, embraced Tarak. Explaining the incident, he said afterwards that during the meditation he keenly felt the presence of Buddha and saw vividly how the history of India had been changed by his noble teachings; pondering all this he could not control his emotion.

Back in Cossipore, Narendra described enthusiastically to the Master and the brother disciples Buddha's life, experiences, and teachings. Śri Ramakrishna in turn related some of his own experiences. Narendra had to admit that the Master, after the attainment of the highest spiritual realization, had of his own will kept his mind on the plane of simplicity.

He further understood that a coin, however valuable, which belonged to an older period of history, could not be used as currency at a later date. God assumes different forms in different ages to serve the special needs of the time.

Narendra practised spiritual disciplines with unabating intensity. Sometimes he felt an awakening of a spiritual power that he could transmit to others. One night in March 1886, he asked his brother disciple Kali to touch his right knee, and then entered into deep meditation. Kali's hand began to tremble; he felt a kind of electric shock. Afterwards Narendra was rebuked by the Master for frittering away spiritual powers before accumulating them in sufficient measure. He was further told that he had injured Kali's spiritual growth, which had been following the path of dualistic devotion, by forcing upon the latter some of his own non-dualistic ideas. The Master added, however, that the damage was not serious.

Narendra had had enough of visions and manifestations of spiritual powers, and he now wearied of them. His mind longed for the highest experience of non-dualistic Vedānta, the nirvikalpa samādhi, in which the names and forms of the phenomenal world disappear and the aspirant realizes total non-difference between the individual soul, the universe, and Brahman, or the Absolute. He told Śri Ramakrishna about it, but the master remained silent. And yet one evening the experience came to him quite unexpectedly.

He was absorbed in his usual meditation when he suddenly felt as if a lamp were burning at the back of his head. The light glowed more and more intensely and finally burst. Narendra was overwhelmed by that light and fell unconscious. After some time, as he began to regain his normal mood, he could feel only his head and not the rest of his body.

In an agitated voice he said to Gopal, a brother disciple who was meditating in the same room, "Where is my body?"

Gopal answered: "Why, Naren, it is there. Don't you feel it?"

Gopal was afraid that Narendra was dying, and ran to Śri Ramakrishna's room. He found the Master in a calm but serious mood, evidently aware of what had happened in the room downstairs. After listening to Gopal the Master said, "Let him stay in that state for a while; he has teased me long enough for it."

For a long time Narendra remained unconscious, and when he regained his normal state of mind he was bathed in an ineffable peace. As he entered Śri Ramakrishna's room the latter said: "Now the Mother has shown you everything. But this realization, like the jewel locked in a box, will be hidden away from you and kept in my custody. I will keep the key with me. Only after you

have fulfilled your mission on this earth will the box be unlocked, and you
will know everything as you have known now."

The experience of this kind of samādhi usually has a most devastating effect
upon the body; Incarnations and special messengers of God alone can survive
its impact. By way of advice, Śri Ramakrishna asked Naren to use great discrimination about his food and companions, only accepting the purest.

Later the Master said to the other disciples: "Narendra will give up his body
of his own will. When he realizes his true nature, he will refuse to stay on this
earth. Very soon he will shake the world by his intellectual and spiritual powers.
I have prayed to the Divine Mother to keep away from him the Knowledge of
the Absolute and cover his eyes with a veil of māyā. There is much work to be
done by him. But the veil, I see, is so thin that it may be rent at any time."

Śri Ramakrishna, the Avatār of the modern age, was too gentle and tender
to labour, himself, for humanity's welfare. He needed some sturdy souls to carry
on his work. Narendra was foremost among those around him; therefore Śri
Ramakrishna did not want him to remain immersed in nirvikalpa samādhi
before his task in this world was finished.

The disciples sadly watched the gradual wasting away of Śri Ramakrishna's
physical frame. His body became a mere skeleton covered with skin; the suffering was intense. But he devoted his remaining energies to the training of
the disciples, especially Narendra. He had been relieved of his worries about
Narendra; for the disciple now admitted the divinity of Kāli, whose will controls all things in the universe. Naren said later on: "From the time he gave
me over to the Divine Mother, he retained the vigour of his body only for six
months. The rest of the time—and that was two long years—he suffered."

One day the Master, unable to speak even in a whisper, wrote on a piece of
paper: "Narendra will teach others." The disciple demurred. Śri Ramakrishna
replied: "But you must. Your very bones will do it." He further said that all the
supernatural powers he had acquired would work through his beloved disciple.

A short while before the curtain finally fell on Śri Ramakrishna's earthly life,
the Master one day called Naren to his bedside. Gazing intently upon him,
he passed into deep meditation. Naren felt that a subtle force, resembling an
electric current, was entering his body. He gradually lost outer consciousness.
After some time he regained knowledge of the physical world and found the
Master weeping. Śri Ramakrishna said to him: "O Naren, today I have given
you everything I possess—now I am no more than a fakir, a penniless beggar.
By the powers I have transmitted to you, you will accomplish great things in
the world, and not until then will you return to the source whence you have
come."

Narendra from that day became the channel of Śri Ramakrishna's powers and
the spokesman of his message.

Two days before the dissolution of the Master's body, Narendra was standing
by the latter's bedside when a strange thought flashed into his mind: Was the
Master truly an Incarnation of God? He said to himself that he would accept
Śri Ramakrishna's divinity if the Master, on the threshold of death, declared
himself to be an Incarnation. But this was only a passing thought. He stood

looking intently at the Master's face. Slowly Śri Ramakrishna's lips parted and he said in a clear voice: "O my Naren, are you still not convinced? He who in the past was born as Rāma and Krishna is now living in this very body as Ramakrishna—but not from the standpoint of your Vedānta." Thus Śri Rama-krishna, in answer to Narendra's mental query, put himself in the category of Rāma and Krishna, who are recognized by orthodox Hindus as two of the Avatārs, or Incarnations of God.

A few words may be said here about the meaning of the Incarnation in the Hindu religious tradition. One of the main doctrines of Vedānta is the divinity of the soul: every soul, in reality, is Brahman. Thus it may be presumed that there is no difference between an Incarnation and an ordinary man. To be sure, from the standpoint of the Absolute, or Brahman, no such difference exists. But from the relative standpoint, where multiplicity is perceived, a difference must be admitted. Embodied human beings reflect godliness in varying measure. In an Incarnation this godliness is fully manifest. Therefore an Incarnation is unlike an ordinary mortal or even an illumined saint. To give an illustration: There is no difference between a clay lion and a clay mouse, from the stand-point of the clay. Both become the same substance when dissolved into clay. But the difference between the lion and the mouse, from the standpoint of form, is clearly seen. Likewise, as Brahman, an ordinary man is identical with an Incarnation. Both become the same Brahman when they attain final illu-mination. But in the relative state of name and form, which is admitted by Vedānta, the difference between them is accepted. According to the Bhagavad Gitā (IV. 6-8), Brahman in times of spiritual crisis assumes a human body through Its own inscrutable power, called māyā. Though birthless, immutable, and the Lord of all beings, yet in every age Brahman appears to be incarnated in a human body for the protection of the good and the destruction of the wicked.

As noted above, the Incarnation is quite different from an ordinary man, even from a saint. Among the many vital differences may be mentioned the fact that the birth of an ordinary mortal is governed by the law of karma, whereas that of an Incarnation is a voluntary act undertaken for the spiritual redemption of the world. Further, though māyā is the cause of the embodiment of both an ordinary mortal and an Incarnation, yet the former is fully under māyā's control, whereas the latter always remains its master. A man, though potentially Brahman, is not conscious of his divinity; but an Incarnation is fully aware of the true nature of His birth and mission. The spiritual disciplines practised by an Incarnation are not for His own liberation, but for the welfare of humanity; as far as He is concerned, such terms as bondage and liberation have no meaning, He being ever free, ever pure, and ever illumined. Lastly, an Incarnation can bestow upon others the boon of liberation, whereas even an illumined saint is devoid of such power.

Thus the Master, on his death-bed, proclaimed himself through his own words as the Incarnation or God-man of modern times.

On August 15, 1886, the Master's suffering became almost unbearable. At midnight he summoned Naren to his bedside and gave him the last instructions, almost in a whisper. The disciples stood around him. At two minutes past one

in the early morning, Śrī Ramakrishna uttered three times in a ringing voice
the name of his beloved Kāli and entered into the final samādhi, from which
his mind never again returned to the physical world.

The body was given to the fire in the neighbouring cremation ground on the
bank of the Ganges. But to the Holy Mother, as she was putting on the signs
of a Hindu widow, there came these words of faith and reassurance: "I am not
dead. I have just moved from one room to another."

As the disciples returned from the cremation ground to the garden house,
they felt great desolation. Śrī Ramakrishna had been more than their earthly
father. His teachings and companionship still inspired them. They felt his
presence in his room. His words rang in their ears. But they could no longer
see his physical body or enjoy his seraphic smile. They all yearned to commune
with him.

Within a week of the Master's passing away, Narendra one night was strolling
in the garden with a brother disciple, when he saw in front of him a luminous
figure. There was no mistaking: it was Śrī Ramakrishna himself. Narendra
remained silent, regarding the phenomenon as an illusion. But his brother
disciple exclaimed in wonder, "See, Naren! See!" There was no room for further
doubt. Narendra was convinced that it was Śrī Ramakrishna who had appeared
in a luminous body. As he called to the other brother disciples to behold the
Master, the figure disappeared.

THE BARANAGORE MONASTERY

Among the Master's disciples, Tarak, Latu, and the elder Gopal had already
cut off their relationship with their families. The young disciples whom Śrī
Ramakrishna had destined for the monastic life were in need of a shelter. The
Master had asked Naren to see to it that they should not become householders.
Naren vividly remembered the Master's dying words: "Naren, take care of the
boys." The householder devotees, moreover, wanted to meet, from time to time,
at a place where they could talk about the Master. They longed for the company of the young disciples who had renounced the world and totally dedicated
their lives to the realization of God. But who would bear the expenses of a
house where the young disciples could live? How would they be provided with
food and the basic necessaries of life?

All these problems were solved by the generosity of Surendranath Mitra, the
beloved householder disciple of Śrī Ramakrishna. He came forward to pay the
expenses of new quarters for the Master's homeless disciples. A house was
rented at Baranagore, midway between Calcutta and Dakshineswar. Dreary and
dilapidated, it was a building that had the reputation of being haunted by evil
spirits. The young disciples were happy to take refuge in it from the turmoil
of Calcutta. This Baranagore Math, as the new monastery was called, became
the first headquarters of the monks of the Ramakrishna Order.[3] Its centre was

[3] The monastery remained at Baranagore from 1886 to 1892; then it was shifted to
Alambazar, in the neighbourhood of Dakshineswar, where it functioned till 1897. Next
it was removed to the garden house of Nilambar Mukherjee, on the bank of the Ganges
across from Baranagore. Finally, the permanent monastery was dedicated in 1898 at the
Belur Math, adjacent to Nilambar Mukherjee's garden house.

NARENDRANATH AT THE COSSIPORE GARDEN (1886)

VIVEKANANDA AS A WANDERING MONK

the shrine room, where the copper vessel containing the sacred ashes of the Master was daily worshipped as his visible presence.[4]

Narendranath devoted himself heart and soul to the training of the young brother disciples. He spent the daytime at home, supervising a lawsuit that was pending in the court and looking after certain other family affairs; but during the evenings and nights he was always with his brothers at the monastery, exhorting them to practise spiritual disciplines. His presence was a source of unfailing delight and inspiration to all.

The future career of the youths began to take shape during these early days at Baranagore. The following incident hastened the process. At the invitation of the mother of Baburam, one of the disciples, they all went to the village of Antpur to spend a few days away from the austerities of Baranagore. Here they realized, more intensely than ever before, a common goal of life, a sense of brotherhood and unity integrating their minds and hearts. Their consecrated souls were like pearls in a necklace held together by the thread of Ramakrishna's teachings. They saw in one another a reservoir of spiritual power, and the vision intensified their mutual love and respect. Narendra, describing to them the glories of the monastic life, asked them to give up the glamour of academic studies and the physical world, and all felt in their hearts the ground-swell of the spirit of renunciation. This reached its height one night when they were sitting for meditation around a fire, in the fashion of Hindu monks. The stars sparkled overhead and the stillness was unbroken except for the crackling of the firewood. Suddenly Naren opened his eyes and began, with an apostolic fervour, to narrate to the brother disciples the life of Christ. He exhorted them to live like Christ, who had had no place "to lay his head." Inflamed by a new passion, the youths, making God and the sacred fire their witness, vowed to become monks.[5] When they had returned to their rooms in a happy mood,

[4] Some of the ashes were later buried at Kankurgachi, a suburb of Calcutta, where a temple was built by the Master's disciple Ramchandra Datta. The place had been hallowed by Śri Ramakrishna's visit during his lifetime. But most of the ashes are now preserved in the shrine at the Belur Math.

[5] Some time after, these chosen disciples of the Master performed the formal sacrifice called virajā and took the monastic vows of celibacy and poverty. Further, they dedicated their lives to the realization of God and the service of men. They assumed new names to signify their utter severance from the world. Narendra, who later became world-famous as Swami Vivekananda, did not take that name till his departure for America in 1893. Prior to that he assumed the names of Vividishananda and Satchidananda in order to conceal his identity from the public. The monastic names of the Master's disciples who renounced the world soon after his death were as follows:

Narendra . . . . Swami Vivekananda	Hari . . . . Swami Turiyananda
Rakhal . . . . Swami Brahmananda	Sarat . . . . Swami Saradananda
Jogin . . . . Swami Jogananda	Sashi . . . . Swami Ramakrishnananda
Niranjan . . . . Swami Niranjanananda	Kali . . . . Swami Abhedananda
Latu . . . . Swami Adbhutananda	Gangadhar . . . . Swami Akhandananda
Baburam . . . . Swami Premananda	Gopal (elder) . . . . . . Swami Advaitananda
Tarak . . . . Swami Shivananda	Sarada Prasanna . . Swami Trigunatitananda
	Subodh . . . . Swami Subodhananda

someone found out that it was Christmas Eve, and all felt doubly blest. It is no wonder that the monks of the Ramakrishna Order have always cherished a high veneration for Jesus of Nazareth.

The young disciples, after their return to Baranagore, finally renounced home and became permanent inmates of the monastery. And what a life of austerity they lived there! They forgot their food when absorbed in meditation, worship, study, or devotional music. At such times Sashi, who had constituted himself their caretaker, literally dragged them to the dining-room. The privations they suffered during this period form a wonderful saga of spiritual discipline. Often there would be no food at all, and on such occasions they spent day and night in prayer and meditation. Sometimes there would be only rice, with no salt for flavouring; but nobody cared. They lived for months on boiled rice, salt, and bitter herbs. Not even demons could have stood such hardship. Each had two pieces of loin-cloth, and there were some regular clothes that were worn, by turns, when anyone had to go out. They slept on straw mats spread on the hard floor. A few pictures of saints, gods, and goddesses hung on the walls, and some musical instruments lay here and there. The library contained about a hundred books.

But Narendra did not want the brother disciples to be pain-hugging, cross-grained ascetics. They should broaden their outlook by assimilating the thought-currents of the world. He examined with them the histories of different countries and various philosophical systems. Aristotle and Plato, Kant and Hegel, together with Śankarāchārya and Buddha, Rāmānuja and Madhva, Chaitanya and Nimbārka, were thoroughly discussed. The Hindu philosophical systems of Jnāna, Bhakti, Yoga, and Karma, each received a due share of attention, and their apparent contradictions were reconciled in the light of Śri Ramakrishna's teachings and experiences. The dryness of discussion was relieved by devotional music. There were many moments, too, when the inmates indulged in light-hearted and witty talk, and Narendra's bons mots on such occasions always convulsed them with laughter. But he would never let them forget the goal of the monastic life: the complete control of the lower nature, and the realization of God. "During those days," one of the inmates of the monastery said, "he worked like a madman. Early in the morning, while it was still dark, he would rise from bed and wake up the others, singing, 'Awake, arise, all who would drink of the Divine Nectar!' And long after midnight he and his brother disciples would still be sitting on the roof of the monastery building, absorbed in religious songs. The neighbours protested, but to no avail. Pandits came and argued. He was never for one moment idle, never dull." Yet the brothers complained that they could not realize even a fraction of what Ramakrishna had taught.

Some of the householder devotees of the Master, however, did not approve of the austerities of the young men, and one of them teasingly inquired if they had realized God by giving up the world. "What do you mean?" Narendra said furiously. "Suppose we have not realized God; must we then return to the life of the senses and deprave our higher nature?"

Soon the youths of the Baranagore monastery became restless for the life of the wandering monk with no other possessions except staff and begging-bowl. Thus they would learn self-surrender to God, detachment, and inner serenity.

They remembered the Hindu proverb that the monk who constantly moves on remains pure, like water that flows. They wanted to visit the holy places and thus give an impetus to their spiritual life.

Narendra, too, wished to enjoy the peace of solitude. He wanted to test his own inner strength as well as teach the others not to depend upon him always. Some of the brother disciples had already gone away from the monastery when he began his wanderings. The first were in the nature of temporary excursions; he had to return to Baranagore in response to the appeal of the inmates of the monastery. But finally in 1891, when he struck out again—without a companion, without a name, with only a staff and begging-bowl—he was swallowed in the immensity of India and the dust of the vast sub-continent completely engulfed him. When rediscovered he was no longer the unknown Naren, but the Swami Vivekananda who had made history in Chicago in 1893.

IN NORTHERN INDIA

In order to satisfy his wanderlust, Narendra went to Benares, considered the holiest place in India—a city sanctified from time out of mind by the association of monks and devotees. Here have come prophets like Buddha, Śankarāchārya, and Chaitanya, to receive, as it were, the commandment of God to preach their messages. The Ganges charges the atmosphere with a rare holiness. Narendra felt uplifted by the spirit of renunciation and devotion that pervades this sacred place. He visited the temples and paid his respects to such holy men as Trailanga Swami, who lived on the bank of the Ganges constantly absorbed in meditation, and Swami Bhaskarananda, who annoyed Naren by expressing doubt as to the possibility of a man's total conquest of the temptation of "woman" and "gold."[6] With his own eyes Naren had seen the life of Śri Ramakrishna, who had completely subdued his lower nature.

In Benares, one day, hotly pursued by a troop of monkeys, he was running away when a monk called to him: "Face the brutes." He stopped and looked defiantly at the ugly beasts. They quickly disappeared. Later, as a preacher, he sometimes used this experience to exhort people to face the dangers and vicissitudes of life and not run away from them.

After a few days Naren returned to Baranagore and plunged into meditation, study, and religious discourses. From this time he began to feel a vague premonition of his future mission. He often asked himself if such truths of the Vedānta philosophy as the divinity of the soul and the unity of existence should remain imprisoned in the worm-eaten pages of the scriptures to furnish a pastime for erudite scholars or to be enjoyed only by solitary monks in caves and the depths of the wilderness; did they not have any significance for the average

[6] The words woman and gold occur again and again in the teachings of Śri Ramakrishna to designate the two chief impediments to spiritual progress. By these words he really meant lust and greed, the baneful influence of which retards the aspirant's spiritual growth. He used the word woman as a concrete term for the sex instinct when addressing his men devotees; while speaking to women, however, he warned them against man. The word gold symbolizes greed, which is the other obstacle. Śri Ramakrishna never taught his disciples to hate any woman, or womankind in general. He regarded women as so many images of the Divine Mother of the universe.

man struggling with life's problems? Must the common man, because of his
ignorance of the scriptures, be shut out from the light of Vedānta?

Narendra spoke to his brother disciples about the necessity of preaching the
strength-giving message of the Vedānta philosophy to one and all, and especially to the down-trodden masses. But these monks were eager for their own
salvation, and protested. Naren said to them angrily: "All are preaching. What
they do unconsciously, I will do consciously. Ay, even if you, my brother monks,
stand in my way, I will go to the pariahs and preach in the lowest slums."

After remaining at Baranagore a short while, Naren set out again for Benares,
where he met the Sanskrit scholar Pramadadas Mitra. These two felt for each
other a mutual respect and affection, and they discussed, both orally and
through letters, the social customs of the Hindus and abstruse passages of the
scriptures. Next he visited Ayodhyā, the ancient capital of Rāma, the hero of
the Rāmāyana. Lucknow, a city of gardens and palaces created by the Moslem
Nawabs, filled his mind with the glorious memories of Islāmic rule, and the
sight of the Tāj Mahal in Agra brought tears to his eyes. In Vrindāvan he
recalled the many incidents of Krishna's life and was deeply moved.

While on his way to Vrindāvan, trudging barefoot and penniless, Naren saw
a man seated by the roadside enjoying a smoke. He asked the stranger to give
him a puff from his tobacco bowl, but the man was an untouchable and shrank
from such an act; for it was considered sacrilegious by Hindu society. Naren
continued on his way, but said to himself suddenly: "What a shame! The
whole of my life I have contemplated the non-duality of the soul, and now I
am thrown into the whirlpool of the caste-system. How difficult it is to get
over innate tendencies!" He returned to the untouchable, begged him to lend
him his smoking-pipe, and in spite of the remonstrances of the low-caste man,
enjoyed a hearty smoke and went on to Vrindāvan.

Next we find Naren at the railroad station of Hathras, on his way to the
sacred pilgrimage centre of Hardwar in the foothills of the Himālayas. The
stationmaster, Sarat Chandra Gupta, was fascinated at the very first sight of
him. "I followed the two diabolical eyes," he said later. Narendra accepted Sarat
as a disciple and called him "the child of my spirit." At Hathras he discussed
with visitors the doctrines of Hinduism and entertained them with music, and
then one day confided to Sarat that he must move on.

"My son," he said, "I have a great mission to fulfil and I am in despair at
the smallness of my power. My guru asked me to dedicate my life to the regeneration of my motherland. Spirituality has fallen to a low ebb and starvation
stalks the land. India must become dynamic again and earn the respect of the
world through her spiritual power."

Sarat immediately renounced the world and accompanied Narendra from
Hathras to Hardwar. The two then went on to Hrishikesh, on the bank of the
Ganges several miles north of Hardwar, where they found themselves among
monks of various sects, who were practising meditation and austerities. Presently Sarat fell ill and his companion took him back to Hathras for treatment.
But Naren, too, had been attacked with malarial fever at Hrishikesh. He now
made his way to the Baranagore monastery.

Naren had now seen northern India, the Āryāvarta, the sacred land of the

Āryans, where the spiritual culture of India had originated and developed. The main stream of this ancient Indian culture, issuing from the Vedas and the Upanishads and branching off into the Purānas and the Tantras, was subsequently enriched by contributions from the Śaks, the Huns, the Greeks, the Pathans, the Moghuls, and numerous other foreign peoples. Thus India developed a unique civilization based upon the ideal of unity in diversity. Some of the foreign elements were entirely absorbed into the traditional Hindu consciousness; others, though flavoured by the ancient thought of the land, retained their individuality. Realizing the spiritual unity of India and Asia, Narendra discovered the distinctive characteristics of Oriental civilization: renunciation of the finite and communion with the Infinite.

But the stagnant life of the Indian masses, for which he chiefly blamed the priests and the landlords, saddened his heart. Naren found that his country's downfall had not been caused by religion. On the contrary, as long as India had clung to her religious ideals, the country had overflowed with material prosperity. But the enjoyment of power for a long time had corrupted the priests. The people at large were debarred from true knowledge of religion, and the Vedas, the source of the Hindu culture, were completely forgotten, especially in Bengal. Moreover, the caste-system, which had originally been devised to emphasize the organic unity of Hindu society, was now petrified. Its real purpose had been to protect the weak from the ruthless competition of the strong and to vindicate the supremacy of spiritual knowledge over the power of military weapons, wealth, and organized labour; but now it was sapping the vitality of the masses. Narendra wanted to throw open the man-making wisdom of the Vedas to all, and thus bring about the regeneration of his motherland. He therefore encouraged his brothers at the Baranagore monastery to study the grammar of Pānini, without which one could not acquire first-hand knowledge of the Vedas.

The spirit of democracy and equality in Islām appealed to Naren's mind and he wanted to create a new India with Vedāntic brain and Moslem body. Further, the idea began to dawn in his mind that the material conditions of the masses could not be improved without the knowledge of science and technology as developed in the West. He was already dreaming of building a bridge to join the East and the West. But the true leadership of India would have to spring from the soil of the country. Again and again he recalled that Śri Ramakrishna had been a genuine product of the Indian soil, and he realized that India would regain her unity and solidarity through the understanding of the Master's spiritual experiences.

Naren again became restless to "do something," but what, he did not know. He wanted to run away from his relatives since he could not bear the sight of their poverty. He was eager to forget the world through meditation. During the last part of December 1889, therefore, he again struck out from the Baranagore monastery and turned his face towards Benares. "My idea," he wrote to a friend, "is to live in Benares for some time and to watch how Viśwanāth and Annapurnā deal out my lot. I have resolved either to realize my ideal or to lay down my life in the effort—so help me Lord of Benares!"

On his way to Benares he heard that Swami Jogananda, one of his brother disciples, was lying ill in Allahabad and decided to proceed there immediately. In Allahabad he met a Moslem saint, "every line and curve of whose face showed that he was a paramahamsa." Next he went to Ghazipur and there he came to know the saint Pavhari Baba, the "air-eating holy man."

Pavhari Baba was born near Benares of brāhmin parents. In his youth he had mastered many branches of Hindu philosophy. Later he renounced the world, led an austere life, practised the disciplines of Yoga and Vedānta, and travelled over the whole of India. At last he settled in Ghazipur, where he built an underground hermitage on the bank of the Ganges and spent most of his time in meditation. He lived on practically nothing and so was given by the people the sobriquet of the "air-eating holy man"; all were impressed by his humility and spirit of service. Once he was bitten by a cobra and said while suffering terrible pain, "Oh, he was a messenger from my Beloved!" Another day, a dog ran off with his bread and he followed, praying humbly, "Please wait, my Lord; let me butter the bread for you." Often he would give away his meagre food to beggars or wandering monks, and starve. Pavhari Baba had heard of Śri Ramakrishna, held him in high respect as a Divine Incarnation, and kept in his room a photograph of the Master. People from far and near visited the Baba, and when not engaged in meditation he would talk to them from behind a wall. For several days before his death he remained indoors. Then, one day, people noticed smoke issuing from his underground cell with the smell of burning flesh. It was discovered that the saint, having come to realize the approaching end of his earthly life, had offered his body as the last oblation to the Lord, in an act of supreme sacrifice.

Narendra, at the time of his meeting Pavhari Baba, was suffering from the severe pain of lumbago, and this had made it almost impossible for him either to move about or to sit in meditation. Further, he was mentally distressed, for he had heard of the illness of Abhedananda, another of his brother disciples, who was living at Hrishikesh. "You know not, sir," he wrote to a friend, "that I am a very soft-natured man in spite of the stern Vedāntic views I hold. And this proves to be my undoing. For however I may try to think only of my own good, I begin, in spite of myself, to think of other people's interests." Narendra wished to forget the world and his own body through the practice of Yoga, and went for instruction to Pavhari Baba, intending to make the saint his guru. But the Baba, with characteristic humility, put him off from day to day.

One night when Naren was lying in bed thinking of Pavhari Baba, Śri Ramakrishna appeared to him and stood silently near the door, looking intently into his eyes. The vision was repeated for twenty-one days. Narendra understood. He reproached himself bitterly for his lack of complete faith in Śri Ramakrishna. Now, at last, he was convinced. He wrote to a friend: "Ramakrishna has no peer. Nowhere else in the world exists such unprecedented perfection, such wonderful kindness to all, such intense sympathy for men in bondage." Tearfully he recalled how Śri Ramakrishna had never left unfulfilled a single prayer of his, how he had forgiven his offenses by the million and removed his afflictions.

But as long as Naren lived he cherished sincere affection and reverence for Pavhari Baba, and he remembered particularly two of his instructions. One of these was: "Live in the house of your teacher like a cow," which emphasizes the spirit of service and humility in the relationship between the teacher and the disciple. The second instruction of the Baba was: "Regard spiritual discipline in the same way as you regard the goal," which means that an aspirant should not differentiate between cause and effect.

Narendranath again breathed peace and plunged into meditation. After a few days he went to Benares, where he learnt of the serious illness of Balaram Bose, one of the foremost lay disciples of Śri Ramakrishna. At Ghazipur he had heard that Surendranath Mitra, another lay disciple of the Master, was dying. He was overwhelmed with grief, and to Pramadadas, who expressed his surprise at the sight of a sannyāsin indulging in a human emotion, he said: "Please do not talk that way. We are not dry monks. Do you think that because a man has renounced the world he is devoid of all feeling?"

He came to Calcutta to be at the bedside of Balaram, who passed away on May 13. Surendra Mitra died on May 25. But Naren steadied his nerves, and in addition to the practice of his own prayer and meditation, devoted himself again to the guidance of his brother disciples. Sometime during this period he conceived the idea of building a permanent temple to preserve the relics of Śri Ramakrishna.

From his letters and conversations one can gain some idea of the great storm that was raging in Naren's soul during this period. He clearly saw to what an extent the educated Hindus had come under the spell of the materialistic ideas of the West. He despised sterile imitation. But he was also aware of the great ideals that formed the basis of European civilization. He told his friends that in India the salvation of the individual was the accepted goal, whereas in the West it was the uplift of the people, without distinction of caste or creed. Whatever was achieved there was shared by the common man; freedom of spirit manifested itself in the common good and in the advancement of all men by the united efforts of all. He wanted to introduce this healthy factor into the Indian consciousness.

Yet he was consumed by his own soul's hunger to remain absorbed in samādhi. He felt at this time a spiritual unrest like that which he had experienced at the Cossipore garden house during the last days of Śri Ramakrishna's earthly existence. The outside world had no attraction for him. But another factor, perhaps unknown to him, was working within him. Perfect from his birth, he did not need spiritual disciplines for his own liberation. Whatever disciplines he practised were for the purpose of removing the veil that concealed, for the time being, his true divine nature and mission in the world. Even before his birth, the Lord had chosen him as His instrument to help Him in the spiritual redemption of humanity.

Now Naren began to be aware that his life was to be quite different from that of a religious recluse: he was to work for the good of the people. Every time he wanted to taste for himself the bliss of samādhi, he would hear the piteous moans of the teeming millions of India, victims of poverty and ignorance. Must they, Naren asked himself, for ever grovel in the dust and live like brutes? Who would be their saviour?

He began, also, to feel the inner agony of the outwardly happy people of

the West, whose spiritual vitality was being undermined by the mechanistic
and materialistic conception of life encouraged by the sudden development of
the physical sciences. Europe, he saw, was sitting on the crater of a smouldering
volcano, and any moment Western culture might be shattered by its fiery eruption. The suffering of man, whether in the East or in the West, hurt his tender
soul. The message of Vedānta, which proclaimed the divinity of the soul and the
oneness of existence, he began to realize, could alone bind up and heal the
wounds of India and the world. But what could he, a lad of twenty-five, do?
The task was gigantic. He talked about it with his brother disciples, but received
scant encouragement. He was determined to work alone if no other help was
forthcoming.

Narendra felt cramped in the monastery at Baranagore and lost interest in
its petty responsibilities. The whole world now beckoned him to work. Hence,
one day in 1890, he left the monastery again with the same old determination
never to return. He would go to the Himālayas and bury himself in the depths
of his own thought. To a brother disciple he declared, "I shall not return until
I gain such realization that my very touch will transform a man." He prayed
to the Holy Mother that he might not return before attaining the highest
Knowledge, and she blessed him in the name of Śri Ramakrishna. Then she
asked whether he would not like to take leave of his earthly mother. "Mother,"
Naren replied, "you are my only mother."

WANDERINGS IN THE HIMĀLAYAS

Accompanied by Swami Akhandananda, Naren left Calcutta and set out for
Northern India. The two followed the course of the Ganges, their first halting-
place being Bhagalpur. To one of the people who came to visit him there
Naren said that whatever of the ancient Āryan knowledge, intellect, and genius
remained could be found mostly in those parts of the country that lay near the
banks of the Ganges. The farther one departed from the river, the less one
saw of that culture. This fact, he believed, explained the greatness of the Ganges
as sung in the Hindu scriptures. He further observed: "The epithet 'mild
Hindu,' instead of being a word of reproach, ought really to point to our glory,
as expressing greatness of character. For see how much moral and spiritual
advancement and how much development of the qualities of love and compassion have to be acquired before one can get rid of the brutish force of one's
nature, which impels a man to slaughter his brother men for self-aggrandize-
ment."

He spent a few days in Benares and left the city with the prophetic words:
"When I return here the next time, I shall burst upon society like a bomb-
shell, and it will follow me like a dog."

After visiting one or two places, Naren and Akhandananda arrived at Nainital,
their destination being the sacred Badarikāśrama, in the heart of the Himālayas.
They decided to travel the whole way on foot, and also not to touch money.
Under an old peepul tree by the side of a stream they spent many hours in
meditation. Naren had a deep spiritual experience, which he thus jotted down
in his note-book:

In the beginning was the Word, etc.

The microcosm and the macrocosm are built on the same plan. Just as the individual soul is encased in a living body, so is the Universal Soul, in the living prakriti (nature), the objective universe. Kāli is embracing Śiva. This is not a fancy. This covering of the one (Soul) by the other (nature) is analogous to the relation between an idea and the word expressing it. They are one and the same, and it is only by a mental abstraction that one can distinguish them. Thought is impossible without words. Therefore in the beginning was the Word, etc.

This dual aspect of the Universal Soul is eternal. So what we perceive or feel is the combination of the eternally formed and the eternally formless.

Thus Naren realized, in the depths of meditation, the oneness of the universe and man, who is a universe in miniature. He realized that all that exists in the universe also exists in the body, and further, that the whole universe exists in the atom.

Several other brother disciples joined Naren. But they could not go to Badarikāśrama since the road was closed by Government order on account of famine. They visited different holy places, lived on alms, studied the scriptures, and meditated. At this time, the sad news arrived of the suicide of one of Naren's sisters under tragic conditions, and reflecting on the plight of Hindu women in the cruel present-day society, he thought that he would be a criminal if he remained an indifferent spectator of such social injustice.

Naren proceeded to Hrishikesh, a beautiful valley at the foot of the Himālayas, which is surrounded by hills and almost encircled by the Ganges. From an immemorial past this sacred spot has been frequented by monks and ascetics. After a few days, however, Naren fell seriously ill and his friends despaired of his life. When he was convalescent he was removed to Meerut. There he met a number of his brother disciples and together they pursued the study of the scriptures, practised prayer and meditation, and sang devotional songs, creating in Meerut a miniature Baranagore monastery.

After a stay of five months Naren became restless, hankering again for his wandering life; but he desired to be alone this time and break the chain of attachment to his brother disciples. He wanted to reflect deeply about his future course of action, of which now and then he was getting glimpses. From his wanderings in the Himālayas he had become convinced that the Divine Spirit would not allow him to seal himself within the four walls of a cave. Every time he had thought to do so, he had been thrown out, as it were, by a powerful force. The degradation of the Indian masses and the spiritual sickness of people everywhere were summoning him to a new line of action, whose outer shape was not yet quite clear to him.

In the later part of January 1891, Naren bade farewell to his brother disciples and set out for Delhi, assuming the name of Swami Vividishananda. He wished to travel without being recognized. He wanted the dust of India to cover up his footprints. It was his desire to remain an unknown sannyāsin, among the thousands of others seen in the country's thoroughfares, market-places, deserts, forests, and caves. But the fires of the Spirit that burnt in his eyes, and his aristocratic bearing, marked him as a prince among men despite all his disguises.

In Delhi, Naren visited the palaces, mosques, and tombs. All around the modern city he saw a vast ruin of extinct empires dating from the prehistoric days of the *Mahābhārata*, revealing the transitoriness of material achievements. But gay and lively Delhi also revealed to him the deathless nature of the Hindu spirit.

Some of his brother disciples from Meerut came to the city and accidentally discovered their beloved leader. Naren was angry. He said to them: "Brethren! I told you that I desired to be left alone. I asked you not to follow me. This I repeat once more. I must not be followed. I shall presently leave Delhi. No one must try to know my whereabouts. I shall sever all old associations. Wherever the Spirit leads, there I shall wander. It matters not whether I wander about in a forest or in a desert, on a lonely mountain or in a populous city. I am off. Let everyone strive to realize his goal according to his lights."

Narendra proceeded towards historic Rajputana, repeating the words of the Dhammapāda:

> Go forward without a path,
> Fearing nothing, caring for nothing,
> Wandering alone, like the rhinoceros!
> Even as a lion, not trembling at noises,
> Even as the wind, not caught in a net,
> Even as the lotus leaf, untainted by water,
> Do thou wander alone, like the rhinoceros!

Several factors have been pointed out as influencing Naren's life and giving shape to his future message: the holy association of Śri Ramakrishna, his own knowledge of Eastern and Western cultures, and his spiritual experiences. To these another must be added: the understanding of India gained through his wanderings. This new understanding constituted a unique education for Naren. Here, the great book of life taught him more than the printed words of the libraries.

He mixed with all—today sleeping with pariahs in their huts and tomorrow conversing on equal terms with Mahārājās, Prime Ministers, orthodox pandits, and liberal college professors. Thus he was brought into contact with their joys and sorrows, hopes and frustrations. He witnessed the tragedy of present-day India and also reflected on its remedy. The cry of the people of India, the God struggling in humanity, and the anxiety of men everywhere to grasp a hand for aid, moved him deeply. In the course of his travels Naren came to know how he could make himself a channel of the Divine Spirit in the service of mankind.

During these wandering days he both learnt and taught. The Hindus he asked to go back to the eternal truths of their religion, hearken to the message of the Upanishads, respect temples and religious symbols, and take pride in their birth in the holy land of India. He wanted them to avoid both the outmoded orthodoxy still advocated by fanatical leaders, and the misguided rationalism of the Westernized reformers. He was struck by the essential cultural unity of India in spite of the endless diversity of form. And the people who came to know him saw in him the conscience of India, her unity, and her destiny.

TRAVELS IN RAJPUTANA

As already noted, Narendranath while travelling in India often changed his name to avoid recognition. It will not be improper to call him, from this point of his life, by the monastic title of "Swami," or the more affectionate and respectful appellation of "Swamiji."

In Alwar, where Swamiji arrived one morning in the beginning of February 1891, he was cordially received by Hindus and Moslems alike. To a Moslem scholar he said: "There is one thing very remarkable about the Koran. Even to this day it exists as it was recorded eleven hundred years ago. The book has retained its original purity and is free from interpolation."

He had a sharp exchange of words with the Mahārājā, who was Westernized in his outlook. To the latter's question as to why the Swami, an able-bodied young man and evidently a scholar, was leading a vagabond's life, the Swami retorted, "Tell me why you constantly spend your time in the company of Westerners and go out on shooting excursions, neglecting your royal duties." The Mahārājā said, "I cannot say why, but, no doubt, because I like to." "Well," the Swami exclaimed, "for that very reason I wander about as a monk."

Next, the Mahārājā ridiculed the worship of images, which to him were nothing but figures of stone, clay, or metal. The Swami tried in vain to explain to him that Hindus worshipped God alone, using the images as symbols. The Prince was not convinced. Thereupon the Swami asked the Prime Minister to take down a picture of the Mahārājā, hanging on the wall, and spit on it. Everyone present was horror-struck at this effrontery. The Swami turned to the Prince and said that though the picture was not the Mahārājā himself, in flesh and blood, yet it reminded everyone of his person and thus was held in high respect; likewise the image brought to the devotee's mind the presence of the Deity and was therefore helpful for concentration, especially at the beginning of his spiritual life. The Mahārājā apologized to Swamiji for his rudeness.

The Swami exhorted the people of Alwar to study the eternal truths of Hinduism, especially to cultivate the knowledge of Sanskrit, side by side with Western science. He also encouraged them to read Indian history, which he remarked should be written by Indians following the scientific method of the West. European historians dwelt mainly on the decadent period of Indian culture.

In Jeypore the Swami devoted himself to the study of Sanskrit grammar, and in Ajmere he recalled the magnificence of the Hindu and Moslem rules. At Mount Abu he gazed in wonder at the Jain temples of Dilwara, which, it has been said, were begun by titans and finished by jewellers. There he accepted the hospitality of a Moslem official. To his scandalized Hindu friends the Swami said that he was, as a sannyāsin belonging to the highest order of paramahamsas, above all rules of caste. His conduct in dining with Moslems, he further said, was not in conflict with the teachings of the scriptures, though it might be frowned upon by the narrow-minded leaders of Hindu society.

At Mount Abu the Swami met the Mahārājā of Khetri, who later became one of his devoted disciples. The latter asked the Swami for the boon of a male heir and obtained his blessing.

Next we see the Swami travelling in Gujrat and Kathiawar in Western India.

In Ahmedabad he refreshed his knowledge of Jainism. Kathiawar, containing
a large number of places sacred both to the Hindus and to the Jains, was mostly
ruled by Hindu Mahārājās, who received the Swami with respect. To Babu
Haridas Beharidas, the Prime Minister of the Moslem state of Junagad, he
emphasized the need of preaching the message of Hinduism throughout the
world. He spent eleven months in Porebandar and especially enjoyed the company of the Prime Minister, Pandit Sankar Pandurang, a great Sanskrit scholar
who was engaged in the translation of the Vedas. Impressed by the Swami's
intellectuality and originality, the pandit said: "Swamiji, I am afraid you cannot
do much in this country. Few will appreciate you here. You ought to go the
West, where people will understand you and your work. Surely you can give to
the Western people your enlightening interpretation of Hinduism."

The Swami was pleased to hear these words, which coincided with something
he had been feeling within. The Prime Minister encouraged the Swami to
continue his study of the French language since it might be useful to him in
his future work.

During this period the Swami was extremely restless. He felt within him a
boundless energy seeking channels for expression. The regeneration of India
was uppermost in his mind. A reawakened India could, in her turn, help the
world at large. The sight of the pettiness, jealousy, disunion, ignorance, and
poverty among the Hindus filled his mind with great anguish. But he had no
patience with the Westernized reformers, who had lost their contact with the
soul of the country. He thoroughly disapproved of their method of social,
religious, and political reform through imitation of the West. He wanted the
Hindus to cultivate self-confidence. Appreciation of India's spiritual culture
by the prosperous and powerful West, he thought, might give the Hindus
confidence in their own heritage. He prayed to the Lord for guidance. He became
friendly with the Hindu Mahārājās who ruled over one-fifth of the country and
whose influence was great over millions of people. Through them he wanted
to introduce social reforms, improved methods of education, and other measures
for the physical and cultural benefit of the people. The Swami felt that in this
way his dream of India's regeneration would be realized with comparative ease.

After spending a few days in Baroda, the Swami came to Khandwa in Central
India. Here he dropped the first hint of his willingness to participate in the
Parliament of Religions to be held shortly in Chicago. He had heard of this
Parliament either in Junagad or Porebandar.

After visiting Bombay, Poona, and Kolhapur, the Swami arrived at Belgaum.
In Bombay he had accidentally met Swami Abhedananda and in the course of
a talk had said to him, "Brother, such a great power has grown within me that
sometimes I feel that my whole body will burst."

All through this wandering life he exchanged ideas with people in all stations
and stages of life and impressed everyone with his earnestness, eloquence,
gentleness, and vast knowledge of Indian and Western culture. Many of the
ideas he expressed at this time were later repeated in his public lectures in
America and India. But the thought nearest to his heart concerned the poor
and ignorant villagers, victims of social injustice: how to improve the sanitary

condition of the villages, introduce scientific methods of agriculture, and procure pure water for daily drinking; how to free the peasants from their illiteracy
and ignorance, how to give back to them their lost confidence. Problems like
these tormented him day and night. He remembered vividly the words of Śri
Ramakrishna that religion was not meant for "empty bellies."

To his hypochondriac disciple Haripada he gave the following sound advice:
"What is the use of thinking always of disease? Keep cheerful, lead a religious
life, cherish elevating thoughts, be merry, but never indulge in pleasures which
tax the body or for which you will feel remorse afterwards; then all will be well.
And as regards death, what does it matter if people like you and me die? That
will not make the earth deviate from its axis! We should not consider ourselves
so important as to think that the world cannot move on without us."

When he mentioned to Haripada his desire to proceed to America, the
disciple was delighted and wanted to raise money for the purpose, but the
Swami said to him that he would not think about it until after making his
pilgrimage to Rameswaram and worshipping the Deity there.

SOUTH INDIA

From Belgaum the Swami went to Bangalore in the State of Mysore, which
was ruled by a Hindu Mahārājā. The Mahārājā's Prime Minister described the
young monk as "a majestic personality and a divine force destined to leave his
mark on the history of his country." The Mahārājā, too, was impressed by his
"brilliancy of thought, charm of character, wide learning, and penetrating
religious insight." He kept the Swami as his guest in the palace.

One day, in front of his high officials, the Mahārājā asked the Swami,
"Swamiji, what do you think of my courtiers?"

"Well," came the bold reply, "I think Your Highness has a very good heart,
but you are unfortunately surrounded by courtiers who are generally flatterers.
Courtiers are the same everywhere."

"But," the Mahārājā protested, "my Prime Minister is not such. He is
intelligent and trustworthy."

"But, Your Highness, a Prime Minister is 'one who robs the Mahārājā and
pays the Political Agent.' "

The Prince changed the subject and afterwards warned the Swami to be
more discreet in expressing his opinion of the officials in a Native State; otherwise those unscrupulous people might even poison him. But the Swami burst
out: "What! Do you think an honest sannyāsin is afraid of speaking the truth,
even though it may cost him his very life? Suppose your own son asks me about
my opinion of yourself; do you think I shall attribute to you all sorts of virtues
which I am quite sure you do not possess? I can never tell a lie."

The Swami addressed a meeting of Sanskrit scholars and gained their applause
for his knowledge of Vedānta. He surprised an Austrian musician at the Prince's
court with his knowledge of Western music. He discussed with the Mahārājā
his plan of going to America, but when the latter came forward with an offer
to pay his expenses for the trip, he declined to make a final decision before
visiting Rameswaram. Perhaps he was not yet quite sure of God's will in the

matter. When pressed by the Mahārājā and the Prime Minister to accept some gifts, the costlier the better, the Swami took a tobacco pipe from the one and a cigar from the other.

Now the Swami turned his steps towards picturesque Malabar. At Trivandrum, the capital of Travancore, he moved in the company of college professors, state officials, and in general among the educated people of the city. They found him equally at ease whether discussing Spencer or Śankarāchārya, Shakespeare or Kālidāsa, Darwin or Patanjali, Jewish history or Āryan civilization. He pointed out to them the limitations of the physical sciences and the failure of Western psychology to understand the superconscious aspect of human nature.

Orthodox brāhmins regarded with abhorrence his habit of eating animal food. The Swami courageously told them about the eating of beef by the brāhmins in Vedic times. One day, asked about what he considered the most glorious period of Indian history, the Swami mentioned the Vedic period, when "five brāhmins used to polish off one cow." He advocated animal food for the Hindus if they were to cope at all with the rest of the world in the present reign of power and find a place among the other great nations, whether within or outside the British Empire.

An educated person of Travancore said about him: "Sublimity and simplicity were written boldly on his features. A clean heart, a pure and austere life, an open mind, a liberal spirit, wide outlook, and broad sympathy were the outstanding characteristics of the Swami."

At Rameswaram the Swami met Bhaskara Setupati, the Rājā of Ramnad, who later became one of his ardent disciples. He discussed with the Prince many of his ideas regarding the education of the Indian masses and the improvement of their agricultural conditions. The Rājā urged the Swami to represent India at the Parliament of Religions in Chicago and promised to help him in his venture. From Rameswaram the Swami went to Kanyākumāri (Cape Comorin), which is the southernmost tip of India.

THE GREAT VISION

At Cape Comorin the Swami became as excited as a child. He rushed to the temple to worship the Divine Mother. He prostrated himself before the Virgin Goddess.[7] As he came out and looked at the sea his eyes fell on a rock. Swimming to the islet through shark-infested waters, he sat on a stone. His heart thumped with emotion. His great journey from the snow-capped Himālayas to the "Land's End" was completed. He had travelled the whole length of the Indian subcontinent, his beloved motherland, which, together with his earthly mother, was "superior to heaven itself."

Sitting on the stone, he recalled what he had seen with his own eyes: the pitiable condition of the Indian masses, victims of the unscrupulous whims of their rulers, landlords, and priests. The tyranny of caste had sapped their last drop of blood. In most of the so-called leaders who shouted from the housetops for the liberation of the people, he had seen selfishness personified. And now

[7] The Deity worshipped in the temple is known as Kanyākumāri, the Virgin Goddess, the Jungfrau.

he asked himself what his duty was in this situation. Should he regard the world as a dream and go into solitude to commune with God? He had tried this several times, but without success. He remembered that, as a sannyāsin, he had taken the vow to dedicate himself to the service of God; but this God, he was convinced, was revealed through humanity. And his own service to this God must begin, therefore, with the humanity of India. "May I be born and reborn," he exclaimed, "and suffer a thousand miseries, if only I may worship the only God in whom I believe, the sum total of all souls, and above all, my God the wicked, my God the afflicted, my God the poor of all races!"

Through austerity and self-control the Swami had conserved great spiritual power. His mind had been filled with the wisdom of the East and the West. He had received in abundance Śri Ramakrishna's blessings. He also had had many spiritual experiences of his own. He must use all of these assets, he concluded, for the service of God in man.

But what was to be the way?

The clear-eyed prophet saw that religion was the backbone of the Indian nation. India would rise through a renewal and restoration of that highest spiritual consciousness which had made her, at all times, the cradle of nations and the cradle of faith. He totally disagreed with foreign critics and their Indian disciples who held that religion was the cause of India's downfall. The Swami blamed, rather, the falsehood, superstition, and hypocrisy that were practised in the name of religion. He himself had discovered that the knowledge of God's presence in man was the source of man's strength and wisdom. He was determined to awaken this sleeping divinity. He knew that the Indian culture had been created and sustained by the twin ideals of renunciation and service, which formed the core of Hinduism. And he believed that if the national life could be intensified through these channels, everything else would take care of itself. The workers for India's regeneration must renounce selfishness, jealousy, greed, and lust for power; and they must dedicate themselves to the service of the poor, the illiterate, the hungry, and the sick, seeing in them the tangible manifestations of the Godhead. People required education, food, health, and the knowledge of science and technology to raise their standard of living. The attempt to teach metaphysics to empty stomachs was sheer madness. The masses everywhere were leading the life of animals on account of ignorance and poverty; therefore these conditions should be removed.

But where would the Swami find the fellow workers to help him in this gigantic task?

He wanted whole-time servants of God, workers without worldly ties or vested interests. And he wanted them by thousands. His eyes fell upon the numerous monks who had renounced the world in search of God. But alas, in present-day India most of these led unproductive lives. He would have to infuse a new spirit into them, and they in their turn would have to dedicate themselves to the service of the people. He hit upon a plan, which he revealed later in a letter to a friend. "Suppose," the Swami wrote, "some disinterested sannyāsins, bent on doing good to others, went from village to village, disseminating education and seeking in various ways to better the condition of all down to the untouchable, through oral teaching and by means of maps, magic lanterns, globes, and other accessories—would that not bring forth good in time? All these plans I cannot write out in this brief letter. The long and short of it is that if the mountain does not come to Mahomet, Mahomet must go to the mountain. The poor are too poor to go to schools; they will gain nothing by reading poetry and all that sort of thing. We, as a nation, have lost our individuality. We have to give back to the nation its lost individuality and raise the masses."

Verily, the Swami, at Kanyākumāri, was the patriot and prophet in one. There he became, as he declared later to a Western disciple, "a condensed India."

But where were the resources to come from, to help him realize his great vision?

He himself was a sannyāsin, a penniless beggar. The rich of the country talked big and did nothing. His admirers were poor. Suddenly a heroic thought entered his mind: he must approach the outside world and appeal to its conscience. But he was too proud to act like a beggar. He wanted to tell the West that the health of India and the sickness of India were the concern of the whole world. If India sank, the whole world would sink with her. For the outside world, in turn, needed India, her knowledge of the Soul and of God, her spiritual heritage, her ideal of genuine freedom through detachment and renunciation; it needed these in order to extricate itself from the sharp claws of the monster of material-ism.

Then to the Swami, brooding alone and in silence on that point of rock off the tip of India, the vision came; there flashed before his mind the new con-tinent of America, a land of optimism, great wealth, and unstinted generosity. He saw America as a country of unlimited opportunities, where people's minds were free from the encumbrance of castes or classes. He would give the receptive Americans the ancient wisdom of India and bring back to his motherland, in exchange, the knowledge of science and technology. If he succeeded in his mission to America, he would not only enhance India's prestige in the Occident, but create a new confidence among his own people. He recalled the earnest requests of his friends to represent India in the forthcoming Parliament of Religions in Chicago. And in particular, he remembered the words of the friend in Kathiawar who had been the first to encourage him to go to the West: "Go and take it by storm, and then return!"

He swam back to the continent of India and started northwards again, by the eastern coast.

It may be mentioned here that during the Swami's trip across the country, just described, there had taken place many incidents that strengthened his faith in God, intensified his sympathy for the so-called lower classes, and broadened his general outlook on life and social conventions.

Several times, when he had had nothing to eat, food had come to him unsought, from unexpected quarters. The benefactors had told him that they were directed by God. Then, one day, it had occurred to the Swami that he had no right to lead the life of a wandering monk, begging his food from door to door, and thus depriving the poor of a few morsels which they could otherwise share with their families. Forthwith he entered a deep forest and walked the whole day without eating a grain of food. At nightfall he sat down under a tree, footsore and hungry, and waited to see what would happen next.

Presently he saw a tiger approaching. "Oh," he said, "this is right; both of us are hungry. As this body of mine could not be of any service to my fellow men, let it at least give some satisfaction to this hungry animal." He sat there calmly, but the tiger for some reason or other changed its mind and went off in another direction. The Swami spent the whole night in the forest, meditating on God's inscrutable ways. In the morning he felt a new surge of power.

During his wanderings in the Himālayas, he was once the guest of a Tibetan family and was scandalized to see that polyandry was practised by its members, six brothers sharing a common wife. To the Swami's protest, the eldest brother replied that a Tibetan would consider it selfishness to enjoy a good thing all by himself and not share it with his brothers. After deep thought the Swami realized the relativity of virtue. He saw that many so-called good and evil practices had their roots in the traditions of society. One might argue for or against almost anything. The conventions of a particular society should be judged by its own standards. After that experience, the Swami was reluctant to condemn hastily the traditions of any social group.

One day Swamiji was sharing a railway compartment with two Englishmen, who took him for an illiterate beggar and began to crack jokes in English at his expense. At the next station they were astonished to hear him talking with the station master in perfect English. Embarrassed, they asked him why he had not protested against their rude words. With a smile, the Swami replied, "Friends, this is not the first time that I have seen fools." The Englishmen became angry and wanted a fight. But looking at the Swami's strong body, they thought that discretion was the better part of valour, and apologized.

In a certain place in Rajputana, the Swami was kept busy for three days and nights by people seeking religious instruction. Nobody cared about his food or rest. After they left, a poor man belonging to a low caste offered him, with great hesitation, some uncooked food, since he, being an untouchable, was afraid to give him a prepared meal. The Swami, however, persuaded the kind-hearted man to prepare the meal for him and ate it with relish. Shedding tears of gratitude, the Swami said to himself, "Thousands of such good people live in huts, and we despise them as untouchables!"

In Central India he had to pass many hard days without food or shelter, and it was during this time that he lived with a family of outcaste sweepers and discovered the many priceless spiritual virtues of those people, who cowered at the feet of society. Their misery choked him and he sobbed: "Oh, my country! Oh, my country!"

To resume the story of Swamiji's wandering life: From Cape Comorin he walked most of the way to Madras, stopping at Ramnad and Pondicherry. His fame had already spread to the premier city of South India, and he was greeted by a group of enthusiastic young men. In Madras he publicly announced his intention of going to America. His devotees here collected funds for the trip, and it was through them that he later started his Indian work in an organized form.

Here, in Madras, he poured his whole soul into the discussion of religion, philosophy, science, literature, and history. He would blaze up at people who, for lack of time or zeal, did not practise meditation. "What!" he thundered at a listener. "Those giants of old, the ancient rishis, who never walked but strode, standing by whose side you would shrivel into a moth—they, sir, had time for meditation and devotions, and you have none!"

To a scoffer he said: "How dare you criticize your venerable forefathers in such a fashion? A little learning has muddled your brain. Have you tested the wisdom of the rishis? Have you even as much as read the Vedas? There is a challenge thrown by the rishis. If you dare oppose them, take it up."

At Hyderabad, the capital of the Nizam's State, he gave his first public lecture, the subject being "My Mission to the West." The audience was impressed and the Swami was pleased to see that he could hold his own in this new field of activity.

When the devotees in Madras brought him the money for his voyage to America, he refused to accept it and asked them to distribute it among the poor. How was he to know that the Lord wanted him to go to America? Perhaps he was being carried away by his own ambition. He began to pray intensely for divine guidance. Again money was offered to him by some of his wealthy friends, and again he refused. He said to his disciples: "If it is the Mother's wish that I should go to the West, then let us collect money from the people. It is for them that I am going to the West—for the people and the poor!"

The Swami one day had a symbolic dream, in which he saw Śrī Ramakrishna walking into the water of the ocean and beckoning him to follow. He also heard the authoritative word "Go!" In response to a letter that he had written to Sarada Devi, the Holy Mother, she gave him her blessings for the fulfilment of his desire, knowing that it was Ramakrishna's wish that he should undertake the journey to America. And now, at last, he felt sure of his call.

When everything was arranged for the departure, there suddenly arrived in Madras the private secretary of Swamiji's disciple the Mahārājā of Khetri, bearing the happy news of the birth of a royal son. The Swami was earnestly desired to bless the heir apparent. He consented, and the Mahārājā was overjoyed to see him.

The Swami assumed at the Mahārājā's request the name of Vivekananda, and the Mahārājā accompanied him as far as Jeypore when he departed for Bombay.

Here in Jeypore an incident occurred that the Swami remembered all his life. He was invited by the Mahārājā to a musical entertainment in which a nautch-girl was to sing, and he refused to come, since he was a monk and not permitted to enjoy secular pleasures. The singer was hurt and sang in a strain of lamentation. Her words reached the Swami's ears:

> Look not, O Lord, upon my sins!
> Is not Same-sightedness Thy name?
> One piece of iron is used
> Inside the holy shrine,
> Another for the knife
> Held in the butcher's hand;
> Yet both of these are turned to gold
> When touched by the philosophers' stone.

Sacred the Jumnā's water,
Foul the water in the ditch;
Yet both alike are sanctified
Once they have joined the Ganges' stream.
So, Lord, look not upon my sins!
Is not Same-sightedness Thy name?

The Swami was deeply moved. This girl, whom society condemned as impure, had taught him a great lesson: Brahman, the Ever Pure, Ever Free, and Ever Illumined, is the essence of all beings. Before God there is no distinction of good and evil, pure and impure. Such pairs of opposites become manifest only when the light of Brahman is obscured by māyā. A sannyāsin ought to look at all things from the standpoint of Brahman. He should not condemn anything, even a so-called impure person.

The Swami then joined the party and with tears in his eyes said to the girl: "Mother, I am guilty. I was about to show you disrespect by refusing to come to this room. But your song awakened my consciousness."

On his way to Bombay the Swami stopped at the Abu Road station and met Brahmananda and Turiyananda. He told them about his going to America. The two brother disciples were greatly excited. He explained to them the reason for his going: it was India's suffering. "I travelled," he said, "all over India. But alas, it was agony to me, my brothers, to see with my own eyes the terrible poverty of the masses, and I could not restrain my tears! It is now my firm conviction that to preach religion amongst them, without first trying to remove their poverty and suffering, is futile. It is for this reason—to find means for the salvation of the poor of India—that I am going to America."

Addressing Turiyananda, he said, "Brother, I cannot understand your so-called religion." His face was red with his rising blood. Shaking with emotion, he placed his hand on his heart, and said: "But my heart has grown much, much larger, and I have learnt to feel. Believe me, I feel it very sadly." He was choked, and then fell silent. Tears rolled down his cheeks.

Many years later Turiyananda said, while describing the incident: "You can imagine what went through my mind when I heard these pathetic words and saw the majestic sadness of Swamiji. 'Were not these,' I thought, 'the very words and feelings of Buddha?'" And he remembered that long ago Naren had visited Bodh-Gayā and in deep meditation had felt the presence of Buddha.

Another scene of the same nature, though it occurred much later, may be recounted here. Swami Turiyananda called on his illustrious brother disciple, after the latter's triumphant return from America, at the Calcutta home of Balaram Bose, and found him pacing the veranda alone. Deep in thought, he did not notice Turiyananda's presence. He began to hum under his breath a celebrated song of Mirābāi, and tears welled up in his eyes. He stopped and leaned against the balustrade, and hid his face in his palms. He sang in an anguished voice, repeating several times: "Oh, nobody understands my sorrow!" And again: "Only he who suffers knows the depth of my sorrow!" The whole atmosphere became heavy with sadness. The voice pierced Swami Turiyananda's heart like an arrow; but he could not understand the cause of Vivekananda's suffering. Then he suddenly realized that it was a tremendous universal sympathy with the suffering and oppressed everywhere that often made him shed tears of burning blood; and of these the world would never know.

The Swami arrived in Bombay accompanied by the private secretary to the Mahārājā of Khetri, the Prince having provided him with a robe of orange silk, an ochre turban, a handsome purse, and a first-class ticket on the S.S. "Peninsular" of the Peninsular and Orient Company, which would be sailing on May 31, 1893. The Mahārājā had also bestowed on him the name by which he was to become famous and which was destined to raise India in the estimation of the world.

The ship steamed out of the harbour on the appointed day, and one can visualize the Swami standing on its deck, leaning against the rail and gazing at the fast fading landscape of his beloved motherland. What a multitude of pictures must have raced, at that time, through his mind: the image of Śrī Ramakrishna, the Holy Mother, and the brother disciples, either living at the Baranagore monastery or wandering through the plains and hills of India! What a burden of memories this lad of twenty-nine was carrying! The legacy of his noble parents, the blessings of his Master, the wisdom learnt from the Hindu scriptures, the knowledge of the West, his own spiritual experiences, India's past greatness, her present sorrow, and the dream of her future glory, the hopes and aspirations of the millions of India's brown men toiling in their brown fields under the scorching tropical sun, the devotional stories of the Purānas, the dizzy heights of Buddhist philosophy, the transcendental truths of Vedānta, the subtleties of the Indian philosophical systems, the soul-stirring songs of the Indian poets and mystics, the stone-carvings and the frescoes of the Ellora and Ajanta caves, the heroic tales of the Rajput and Marhatta fighters, the hymns of the South Indian Alwars, the snow peaks of the towering Himālayas, the murmuring music of the Ganges—all these and many such thoughts fused together to create in the Swami's mind the image of Mother India, a universe in miniature, whose history and society were the vivid demonstration of her philosophical doctrine of unity in diversity. And could India have sent a son worthier than Vivekananda to represent her in the Parliament of Religions—a son who had learnt his spiritual lessons at the feet of a man whose very life was a Parliament of Religions—a son whose heart was big enough to embrace the whole of humanity and to feel for all in its universal compassion?

Soon the Swami adjusted himself to the new life on board the ship—a life completely different from that of a wandering monk. He found it a great nuisance to look after his suitcases, trunk, valise, and wardrobe. His orange robe aroused the curiosity of many fellow passengers, who, however, were soon impressed by his serious nature and deep scholarship. The vessel ploughed through the blue sea, pausing at various ports on the way, and the Swami enjoyed the voyage with the happy excitement of a child, devouring eagerly all he saw.

In Colombo he visited the monasteries of the Hinayāna Buddhists. On the way to Singapore he was shown the favourite haunts of the Malay pirates, whose descendants now, as the Swami wrote to an Indian friend, under the "leviathan guns of modern turreted battleships, have been forced to look about for more peaceful pursuits." He had his first glimpse of China in the busy port of Hongkong, where hundreds of junks and dinghies moved about, each with the wife of its boatman at the helm, for a whole family lived in each floating craft. The traveller was amused to notice the Chinese babies, most of whom were tied to the backs of their mothers, while the latter were busy either pushing heavy loads or jumping with agility from one craft to another. And there was a rush of boats and steam launches coming in and going out.

"Baby John," the Swami wrote humorously to the same friend, "is every moment in danger of having his little head pulverized, pigtail and all, but he does not care a fig. The busy life seems to have no charm for him, and he is quite content to learn the anatomy of a bit of rice-cake given to him by the madly busy mother. The Chinese child is quite a little philosopher and calmly goes to work at the age when your Indian boy can hardly crawl on all fours. He has learnt the philosophy of necessity too well, from his extreme poverty."

At Canton, in a Buddhist monastery, the Swami was received with respect as a great yogi from India. He saw in China, and later in Japan, many temples with manuscripts written in the ancient Bengali script. This made him realize the extent of the influence of India outside her own borders and strengthened his conviction about the spiritual unity of Asia.

Next the boat reached Japan, and the Swami visited Yokohama, Osaka, Kyoto, and Tokyo. The broad streets, the cage-like little houses, the pine-covered hills, and the gardens with shrubs, grass-plots, artificial pools, and small bridges impressed him with the innate artistic nature of the Japanese people. On the other hand, the thoroughly organized Japanese army equipped with guns made in Japan, the expanding navy, the merchant marine, and the industrial factories revealed to him the scientific skill of a newly awakened Asiatic nation. But he was told that the Japanese regarded India as the "dreamland of everything noble and great."

His thoughts always returned to India and her people. He wrote to a disciple in Madras: "Come out and be men! India wants the sacrifice of at least a thousand of her young men—men, mind you, and not brutes. How many men, unselfish and thoroughgoing men, is Madras ready to supply, who will struggle unto death to bring about a new state of things—sympathy for the poor, bread for hungry mouths, enlightenment for the people at large, who have been brought to the level of beasts by the tyranny of your forefathers?"

From Yokohama he crossed the Pacific Ocean and arrived in Vancouver, British Columbia. Next he travelled by train to Chicago, the destination of his journey and the meeting-place of the Parliament of Religions.

THE NEW WORLD

The first sight of Chicago, the third largest city of the New Continent, the great civic queen of the Middle West, enthroned on the shore of Lake Michigan, with its teeming population and strange way of life—a mixture of the refinement of the Eastern coast and the crudities of the backwoods—must have bewildered, excited, and terrified the young visitor from India. Swami Vivekananda walked through the spacious grounds of the World's Fair and was speechless with amazement. He marvelled at what the Americans had achieved through hard work, friendly co-operation with one another, and the application of scientific knowledge. Not too many years before, Chicago had consisted of only a few fishermen's huts, and now at the magic touch of human ingenuity, it was turned into a fairyland. Never before had the Swami seen such an accumulation of wealth, power, and inventive genius in a nation. In the fair-grounds he attracted people's notice. Lads ran after him, fascinated by his orange robe and turban. Shopkeepers and porters regarded him as a Mahārājā from India and tried to impose upon him. On the Swami's part, his first feeling was one of unbounded admiration. But a bitter disillusionment was to come.

Soon after his arrival in Chicago, he went one day to the information bureau of the Exposition to ask about the forthcoming Parliament of Religions. He was told that it had been put off until the first week of September (it was then only the middle of July) and that no one without credentials from a bona fide organization would be accepted as a delegate. He was told also that it was then too late for him to be registered as a delegate. All this had been unexpected by the Swami; for not one of his friends in India—the enthusiastic devotees of Madras, the Mahārājās of Khetri, Ramnad, and Mysore, the Ministers of the native states, and the disciples who had arranged his trip to America —had taken the trouble to make any inquiries concerning the details of the Parliament. No one had known what were to be the dates of the meetings or the conditions of admission. Nor had the Swami brought with him any letter of authority from a religious organization. All had felt that the young monk would need no letter of authorization, his personality being testimonial enough.

"The Swami himself," as his Irish disciple, Sister Nivedita, wrote some years later, "was as simple in the ways of the world as these his disciples, and when he was once sure that he was divinely called to make this attempt, he could see no difficulties in the way. Nothing could have been more typical of the lack of organizedness of Hinduism itself than this going forth of its representative unannounced, and without formal credentials, to enter the strongly guarded door of the world's wealth and power."

In the meantime, the purse that the Swami had carried from India was dwindling; for things were much more expensive in America than he or his friends had thought. He did not have enough to maintain him in Chicago until September. In a frantic mood he asked help from the Theosophical Society, which professed warm friendship for India. He was told that he would have to subscribe to the creed of the Society; but this he refused to do because he did not believe in most of the Theosophical doctrines. Thereupon the leader declined to give him any help. The Swami became desperate and cabled to his friends in Madras for money.

Finally, however, someone advised him to go to Boston, where the cost of living was cheaper, and in the train his picturesque dress, no less than his regal appearance, attracted a wealthy lady who resided in the suburbs of the city. She cordially invited him to be her guest, and he accepted, to save his dwindling purse. He was lodged at "Breezy Meadows," in Metcalf, Massachusetts, and the lady was delighted to display to her inquisitive friends this strange curiosity from the Far East. The Swami met a number of people, most of whom annoyed him by asking queer questions regarding Hinduism and the social customs of India, about which they had read in the tracts of Christian missionaries and sensational writers. However, there came to him a few serious-minded people, and among these were Mrs. Johnson, the lady superintendent of a women's prison, and J. H. Wright, a professor of Greek at Harvard University. On the invitation of the superintendent, he visited the prison and was impressed by the humanitarian attitude of its workers towards the inmates. At once there came to his mind the sad plight of the masses of India and he wrote to a friend on August 20, 1893:

How benevolently the inmates are treated, how they are reformed and sent back as useful members of society—how grand, how beautiful, you must see to believe! And oh, how my heart ached to think of what we think of the poor, the low, in India. They have no chance, no escape, no way to climb up. They sink lower and lower every day, they feel the blows showered upon them by a cruel society, and they do not know whence the blows come. They have forgotten that they too are men. And the result is slavery. . . . Ah, tyrants! You do not know that the obverse is tyranny and the reverse, slavery.

Swami Vivekananda had no friends in this foreign land, yet he did not lose faith. For had not a kind Providence looked after him during the uncertain days of his wandering life? He wrote in the same letter: "I am here amongst the children of the Son of Mary, and the Lord Jesus will help me."

The Swami was encouraged by Professor Wright to represent Hinduism in the Parliament of Religions, since that was the only way he could be introduced to the nation at large. When he announced, however, that he had no credentials, the professor replied, "To ask you, Swami, for your credentials is like asking the sun about its right to shine." He wrote about the Swami to a number of important people connected with the Parliament, especially to the chairman of the committee on selection of delegates, who was one of his friends, and said, "Here is a man more learned than all our learned professors put together." Professor Wright bought the Swami's railroad ticket for Chicago.

The train bearing Vivekananda to Chicago arrived late in the evening, and he had mislaid, unfortunately, the address of the committee in charge of the delegates. He did not know where to turn for help, and no one bothered to give information to this foreigner of strange appearance. Moreover the station was located in a part of the city inhabited mostly by Germans, who could hardly understand his language. He knew he was stranded there, and looking around saw a huge empty wagon in the railroad freight-yard. In this he spent the night, without food or a bed.

In the morning he woke up "smelling fresh water," to quote his own words, and he walked along the fashionable Lake Shore Drive, which was lined with the mansions of the wealthy, asking people the way to the Parliament grounds. But he was met with indifference. Hungry and weary, he knocked at several doors for food and was rudely treated by the servants. His soiled clothes and unshaven face gave him the appearance of a tramp. Besides, he had forgotten that he was in a land that knew thousands of ways of earning the "almighty dollar," but was unfamiliar with Franciscan poverty or the ways of religious vagabonds. He sat down exhausted on the sidewalk and was noticed from an opposite window. The mistress of the house sent for him and asked the Swami if he was a delegate to the Parliament of Religions. He told her of his difficulties. The lady, Mrs. George W. Hale, a society woman of Chicago, gave him breakfast and looked after his needs. When he had rested, she accompanied him to the offices of the Parliament and presented him to Dr. J. H. Barrows, the President of the Parliament, who was one of her personal friends. The Swami was thereupon cordially accepted as a representative of Hinduism and lodged with the other Oriental delegates. Mr. and Mrs. Hale and their children became his life-long friends. Once again the Swami had been strengthened in his conviction that the Lord was guiding his footsteps, and he prayed incessantly to be a worthy instrument of His will.

THE PARLIAMENT OF RELIGIONS

On Monday, September 11, 1893, the Parliament of Religions opened its deliberations with due solemnity. This great meeting was an adjunct of the World's Columbian Exposition, which had been organized to celebrate the four hundredth anniversary of the discovery of America by Christopher Columbus. One of the main goals of the Exposition was to disseminate knowledge of the progress and enlightenment brought about in the world by Western savants and especially through physical science and technology; but as religion forms a vital factor in human culture, it had been decided to organize a Parliament of Religions in conjunction with the Exposition.

Dr. Barrows, in his history of the Parliament of Religions, writes:

> Since faith in a Divine Power to whom men believe they owe service and worship has been, like the sun, a life-giving and fructifying potency in man's intellectual and moral development; since Religion lies back of Hindu literature with its marvellous and mystic developments; of the European Art, whether in the form of Grecian statues or Gothic cathedrals; and of American liberty and the recent uprisings of men in behalf of a juster social condition; and since it is as clear as the light that the Religion of Christ has led to many of the chief and noblest developments of our modern civilization, it did not appear that Religion, any more than Education, Art, or Electricity, should be excluded from the Columbian Exposition.

It is not altogether improbable that some of the more enthusiastic Christian theologians, among the promoters of the Parliament, thought that the Parliament would give them an opportunity to prove the superiority of Christianity, professed by the vast majority of the people of the progressive West, over the other faiths of the world. Much later Swami Vivekananda said, in one of his jocular moods, that the Divine Mother Herself willed the Parliament in order to give him an opportunity to present the Eternal Religion of the Hindus before the world at large, and that the stage was set for him to play his important rôle, everything else being incidental. The appropriateness of this remark can be appreciated now, half a century after the great event, from the fact that whereas all else that was said and discussed at the Parliament has been forgotten, what Vivekananda preached is still cherished in America, and the movement inaugurated by him has endeared itself to American hearts.

"One of the chief advantages," to quote the words of the Hon. Mr. Merwin-Marie Snell, president of the Scientific Section of the Parliament, "has been in the great lessons which it has taught the Christian world, especially the people of the United States, namely, that there are other religions more venerable than Christianity, which surpass it in philosophical depth, in spiritual intensity, in independent vigour of thought, and in breadth and sincerity of human sympathy, while not yielding to it a single hair's breadth in ethical beauty and efficiency."

At 10 a.m. the Parliament opened. In it every form of organized religious belief, as professed among twelve hundred millions of people, was represented. Among the non-Christian groups could be counted Hinduism, Jainism, Buddhism, Confucianism, Shintoism, Mohammedanism, and Mazdaism.

The spacious hall and the huge gallery of the Art Palace were packed with seven thousand people—men and women representing the culture of the United States. The official delegates marched in a grand procession to the platform, and in the centre, in his scarlet robe, sat Cardinal Gibbons, the highest prelate of the Roman Catholic Church in the Western hemisphere. He occupied a chair of state and opened the meeting with a prayer. On his left and right were grouped the Oriental delegates: Pratap Chandra Mazoomdar of the Calcutta Brāhmo Samāj, and Nagarkar of Bombay; Dharmapala, representing the Ceylon Buddhists; Gandhi, representing the Jains; Chakravarti and Annie Besant of the Theosophical Society. With them sat Swami Vivekananda, who represented no particular sect, but the Universal Religion of the Vedas, and who spoke, as will presently be seen, for the religious aspiration of all humanity. His gorgeous robe, large yellow turban, bronze complexion, and fine features stood out prominently on the platform and drew everybody's notice. In numerical order the Swami's position was number thirty-one.

The delegates arose, one by one, and read prepared speeches, but the Hindu sannyāsin was totally unprepared. He had never before addressed such an assembly. When he was asked to give his message he was seized with stage-fright, and requested the chairman to call on him a little later. Several times he postponed the summons. As he admitted later: "Of course my heart was fluttering and my tongue nearly dried up. I was so nervous that I could not venture to speak in the morning session."

At last he came to the rostrum and Dr. Barrows introduced him. Bowing to Sarasvati, the Goddess of Wisdom, he addressed the audience as "Sisters and Brothers of America." Instantly, thousands arose in their seats and gave him loud applause. They were deeply moved to see, at last, a man who discarded formal words and spoke to them with the natural and candid warmth of a brother.

It took a full two minutes before the tumult subsided, and the Swami began his speech by thanking the youngest of the nations in the name of the most ancient monastic order in the world, the Vedic order of sannyāsins. The keynote of his address was universal toleration and acceptance. He told the audience how India, even in olden times, had given shelter to the religious refugees of other lands—for instance, the Israelites and the Zoroastrians—and he quoted from the scriptures the following two passages revealing the Hindu spirit of toleration:

"As different streams, having their sources in different places, all mingle their water in the sea, so, O Lord, the different paths which men take through different tendencies, various though they appear, crooked or straight, all lead to Thee."

"Whosoever comes to Me, through whatsoever form, I reach him. All men are struggling through paths which in the end lead to Me."

In conclusion he pleaded for the quick termination of sectarianism, bigotry, and fanaticism.

The response was deafening applause. It appeared that the whole audience had been patiently awaiting this message of religious harmony. A Jewish intellectual remarked to the present writer, years later, that after hearing Vivekananda he realized for the first time that his own religion, Judaism, was true, and that the Swami had addressed his words on behalf of not only his religion, but all religions of the world. Whereas every one of the other delegates had spoken for his own ideal or his own sect, the Swami had spoken about God, who, as the ultimate goal of all faiths, is their inmost essence. And he had learnt that truth at the feet of Śri Ramakrishna, who had taught incessantly, from his direct experience, that all religions are but so many paths to reach the same goal. The Swami gave utterance to the yearning of the modern world to break down the barriers of caste, colour, and creed and to fuse all people into one humanity.

Not a word of condemnation for any faith, however crude or irrational, fell from his lips. He did not believe that this religion or that religion was true in this or that respect; to him all religions were equally effective paths to lead their respective devotees, with diverse tastes and temperaments, to the same goal of perfection. Years before, young Narendra had condemned before his Master, in his neophyte zeal, a questionable sect that indulged in immoral practices in the name of religion, and Ramakrishna had mildly rebuked him, saying: "Why should you criticize those people? Their way, too, ultimately leads to God. There are many doors to enter a mansion. The scavenger comes in by the back door. You need not use it."

How prophetic were the Master's words that his Naren would one day shake the world! Mrs. S. K. Blodgett, who later became the Swami's hostess in Los Angeles, said about her impressions of the Parliament: "I was at the Parliament of Religions in Chicago in 1893. When that young man got up and said, 'Sisters and Brothers of America,' seven thousand people rose to their feet as a tribute to something they knew not what. When it was over I saw scores of women walking over the benches to get near him, and I said to myself, 'Well, my lad, if you can resist that onslaught you are indeed a God!' "

Swami Vivekananda addressed the Parliament about a dozen times. His outstanding address was a paper on Hinduism in which he discussed Hindu metaphysics, psychology, and theology. The divinity of the soul, the oneness of existence, the non-duality of the Godhead, and the harmony of religions were the recurring themes of his message. He taught that the final goal of man is to become divine by realizing the Divine and that human beings are the children of "Immortal Bliss."

In the final session of the Parliament, Swami Vivekananda said in the conclusion of his speech: "The Christian is not to become a Hindu or a Buddhist, nor is a Hindu or a Buddhist to become a Christian. But each must assimilate the spirit of the others and yet preserve his individuality and grow according to his own law of growth. If the Parliament of Religions has shown anything to the world, it is this: It has proved to the world that holiness, purity, and charity are not the exclusive possessions of any church in the world, and that every system has produced men and women of the most exalted character. In the face of this evidence, if anybody dreams of the exclusive survival of his own religion and the destruction of the others, I pity him from the bottom of my heart and point out to him that upon the banner of every religion will soon be written, in spite of resistance: 'Help and not Fight,' 'Assimilation and not Destruction,' 'Harmony and Peace and not Dissension.' "

The Parliament of Religions offered Swami Vivekananda the long desired opportunity to present before the Western world the eternal and universal truths of his Āryan ancestors. And he rose to the occasion. As he stood on the platform to give his message, he formed, as it were, the confluence of two great streams of thought, the two ideals that had moulded human culture. The vast audience before him represented exclusively the Occidental mind—young, alert, restless, inquisitive, tremendously honest, well disciplined, and at ease with the physical universe, but sceptical about the profundities of the supersensuous world and unwilling to accept spiritual truths without rational proof. And behind him lay the ancient world of India, with its diverse religious and philosophical discoveries, with its saints and prophets who investigated Reality through self-control and contemplation, unruffled by the passing events of the transitory life and absorbed in contemplation of the Eternal Verities. Vivekananda's education, upbringing, personal experiences, and contact with the God-man of modern India had pre-eminently fitted him to represent both ideals and to remove their apparent conflict.

To Vivekananda the religion of the Hindus, based upon the teachings of the Vedas, appeared adequate to create the necessary synthesis. By the Vedas he did not mean any particular book containing the words of a prophet or deriving sanction from a supernatural authority, but the accumulated treasure of spiritual laws discovered by various Indian seers in different times. Just as the law of gravitation existed before its discovery, and would continue to exist even if all humanity forgot it, so do the laws that govern the spiritual world exist independently of our knowledge of them. The moral, ethical, and spiritual relations between soul and soul, and between individual spirits and the Father of all spirits, were in existence before their discovery, and will remain even if we forget them. Regarding the universal character of the Hindu faith the Swami said: "From the high spiritual flights of the Vedānta philosophy, of which the latest discoveries of science seem like echoes, to the low ideas of idolatry with its multifarious mythology, the agnosticism of the Buddhists, and the atheism of the Jains, each and all have a place in Hindu religion."

The young, unknown monk of India was transformed overnight into an outstanding figure of the religious world. From obscurity he leapt to fame. His life-size portraits were posted in the streets of Chicago, with the words "The Monk Vivekananda" written beneath them, and many passers-by would stop to do reverence with bowed heads.

Dr. J. H. Barrows, the President of the Parliament of Religions, said: "Swami Vivekananda exercised a wonderful influence over his auditors," and Mr. Merwin-Marie Snell stated, more enthusiastically: "By far the most important and typical representative of Hinduism was Swami Vivekananda, who, in fact, was beyond question the most popular and influential man in the Parliament. . . . He was received with greater enthusiasm than any other speaker, Christian or pagan. The people thronged about him wherever he went and hung with eagerness on his every word. The most rigid of orthodox Christians say of him, 'He is indeed a prince among men!' "

Newspapers published his speeches and they were read with warm interest all over the country. The *New York Herald* said: "He is undoubtedly the greatest figure in the Parliament of Religions. After hearing him we feel how foolish it is to send missionaries to this learned nation." The *Boston Evening Post* said: "He is a great favourite at the Parliament from the grandeur of his sentiments and his appearance as well. If he merely crosses the platform he is applauded; and this marked approval of thousands he accepts in a childlike spirit of gratification without a trace of conceit. . . . At the Parliament of Religions they used to keep Vivekananda until the end of the programme to make people stay till the end of the session. . . . The four thousand fanning people in the Hall of Columbus would sit smiling and expectant, waiting for an hour or two to listen to Vivekananda for fifteen minutes. The chairman knew the old rule of keeping the best until the last."

It is one of the outstanding traits of Americans to draw out the latent greatness of other people. America discovered Vivekananda and made a gift of him to India and the world.

The reports of the Parliament of Religions were published in the Indian magazines and newspapers. The Swami's vindication of the Hindu faith filled with pride the hearts of his countrymen from Colombo to Almora, from Calcutta to Bombay. Naturally Calcutta, his birthplace, and Madras, which had taken the initiative for his adventurous trip to Chicago, felt the greatest jubilation. Meetings were held in the principal cities to congratulate him on his triumph. The brother monks at the Baranagore monastery were not, at first, clear about the identity of Vivekananda. A letter from the Swami, six months after the Parliament, removed all doubts, however, and how proud they felt at the achievement of their beloved Naren!

But how did Vivekananda himself react to this triumph, which had been the fulfilment of his long cherished desire? He knew that his solitary life as a monk in constant communion with God was at an end; he could no longer live in obscurity with his dreams and visions. Instead of dwelling in peace and serenity, he was thrown into the vortex of a public career with its ceaseless turmoil and demands. When he returned to his hotel the night after the first meeting of the Parliament, he wept like a child.

AFTER THE PARLIAMENT

After he had delivered his message in the Parliament, the Swami suffered no longer from material wants. The doors of the wealthy were thrown open. Their lavish hospitality made him sick at heart when he remembered the crushing poverty of his own people. His anguish became so intense one night that he rolled on the floor, groaning: "O Mother, what do I care for name and fame when my motherland remains sunk in utmost poverty? To what a sad pass have we poor Indians come when millions of us die for want of a handful of rice, and here they spend millions of rupees upon their personal comfort! Who will raise the masses of India? Who will give them bread? Show me, O Mother, how I can help them." While addressing one session of the Parliament, the Swami had said that what India needed was not religion, but bread. Now he began to study American life in its various aspects, especially the secret of the country's high standard of living, and he communicated to his disciples in India his views on the promotion of her material welfare.

Swami Vivekananda was invited by a lecture bureau to tour the United States, and he accepted the offer. He wanted money in order to free himself from obligation to his wealthy friends and also to help his various philanthropic and religious projects in India. Further, he thought that through a lecture bureau he could effectively broadcast his ideas all over the American continent and thus remove from people's minds erroneous notions regarding Hindu religion and society. Soon he was engaged in a whirlwind tour covering the larger cities of the East and the Middle West. People called him the "cyclonic Hindu." He visited, among other places, Iowa City, Des Moines, St. Louis, Indianapolis, Minneapolis, Detroit, Buffalo, Hartford, Boston, Cambridge, New York, Baltimore, and Washington. Cherishing a deep affection for the members of the Hale family, he made his headquarters with George W. Hale in Chicago.

But his path was not always strewn with rose petals. Vivekananda was an outspoken man. Whenever he found in American society signs of brutality, inhumanity, pettiness, arrogance, and ignorance concerning cultures other than its own, he mercilessly criticized them. Often small-minded people asked him irritating questions about India, based upon malicious and erroneous reports, and the Swami fell upon them like a thunderbolt. "But woe to the man," wrote the *Iowa State Register*, "who undertook to combat the monk on his own ground, and that was where they all tried it who tried it at all. His replies came like flashes of lightning and the venturesome questioner was sure to be impaled on the Indian's shining intellectual lance. . . . Vivekananda and his cause found a place in the hearts of all true Christians."

Many Christian ministers became his warm friends and invited him to speak in their churches.

Swami Vivekananda was especially bitter about false Christianity and the religious hypocrisy of many Christian leaders. In a lecture given in Detroit he came out in one of his angriest moods, and declared in the course of his speech:

You train and educate and clothe and pay men to do what?—to come over to my country and curse and abuse all my forefathers, my religion, my everything. They walk near a temple and say, "You idolaters, you will go to hell." But the Hindu is mild; he smiles and passes on, saying, "Let the fools talk." And then you who train men to abuse and criticize, if I just touch you with the least bit of criticism, but with the kindest purpose, you shrink and cry: "Do not touch us! We are Americans; we criticize, curse, and abuse all the heathens of the world, but do not touch us, we are sensitive plants." And whenever your missionaries criticize us, let them remember this: If all India stands up and takes all the mud that lies at the bottom of the Indian Ocean and throws it up against the Western countries, it will not be doing an infinitesimal part of what you are doing to us.

Continuing, the Swami said that the military conquests of the Western nations and the activities of the Christian missionaries, strangely enough, often proceeded side by side. Most people were converted for worldly reasons. But the Swami warned:

Such things tumble down; they are built upon sand; they cannot remain long. Every-thing that has selfishness for its basis, competition for its right hand, and enjoyment as its goal, must die sooner or later.

If you want to live, go back to Christ. You are not Christians. No, as a nation you are not. Go back to Christ. Go back to him who had nowhere to lay his head. Yours is a religion preached in the name of luxury. What an irony of fate! Reverse this if you want to live; reverse this. You cannot serve God and Mammon at the same time. All this prosperity—all this from Christ? Christ would have denied all such heresies. If you can join these two, this wonderful prosperity with the ideal of Christ, it is well; but if you cannot, better go back to him and give up these vain pursuits. Better be ready to live in rags with Christ than to live in palaces without him.

On one occasion the Swami was asked to speak in Boston on Ramakrishna, a subject dear to his heart. When he looked at the audience—the artificial and worldly crowd of people—and contrasted it with his Master's purity and renun-ciation, he practically dropped the subject and mercilessly inveighed against the materialistic culture of the West. The audience was resentful and many left the meeting in an angry mood. But Vivekananda, too, had his lesson. On returning home he recalled what he had said, and wept. His Master had never uttered a word of condemnation against anybody, even the most wicked person; yet he, while talking about Ramakrishna, had criticized these good-hearted people who were eager to learn about the Master. He felt that he was unworthy of Sri Ramakrishna and resolved not to discuss him in public or even to write about him again.

Swami Vivekananda's outspoken words aroused the bitter enmity of a large section of the Christian missionaries and their American patrons, and also of Christian fanatics. Filled with rancour and hatred, these began to vilify him both openly and in private. They tried to injure his reputation by writing false stories traducing his character. Some of the Indian delegates to the Parliament, jealous of the Swami's popularity and fame, joined in the vilification. Mission-aries working in India and some of the Hindu organizations started an infamous campaign against the Swami's work. The Theosophists were particularly vin-dictive. They declared that the Swami was violating the laws of monastic life in America by eating forbidden food and breaking caste laws.

His friends and disciples in India were frightened and sent him cuttings from Indian papers containing these malicious reports. One article stated that one of the Swami's American hostesses had had to dismiss a servant girl on account of the Swami's presence in the house. But the lady published a vehement denial and said that the Swami was an honoured guest in her home and would always be treated with affection and respect. The Swami wrote to his timorous devotees in India concerning a particular American paper that had criticized him, telling them that it was generally known in America as the "blue-nosed Presbyterian paper," that no educated American took it seriously, and that, following the well-known Yankee trick, it had tried to gain notoriety by attacking a man lionized by society. He assured them that the American people as a whole, and many enlightened Christian clergymen, were among his admiring friends, and he asked them not to send him any more of such newspaper trash with articles from his vilifiers. He told them, furthermore, that he had never deviated from the two basic vows of the monastic life, namely, chastity and poverty, and that as regards other things, he was trying to adjust himself to the customs of the people among whom he lived.

To the accusation from some orthodox Hindus that the Swami was eating beef and other forbidden food at the table of infidels, he retorted:

Do you mean to say I am born to live and die as one of those caste-ridden, super-stitious, merciless, hypocritical, atheistic cowards that you only find among the educated Hindus? I hate cowardice. I will have nothing to do with cowards. I belong to the world as much as to India, no humbug about that. What country has a special claim on me? Am I a nation's slave? . . . I see a greater power than man or God or Devil at my back. I require nobody's help. I have been all my life helping others.

To another Indian devotee he wrote in similar vein:

I am surprised that you take the missionaries' nonsense so seriously. . . . If the people of India want me to keep strictly to my Hindu diet, please tell them to send me a cook and money enough to keep him. . . . On the other hand, if the missionaries tell you that I have ever broken the two great vows of the sannyāsin—chastity and poverty—tell them that they are big liars. As for me, mind you, I stand at nobody's dictation, and no chauvinism about me. . . . I hate cowardice; I will have nothing to do with cowards or political nonsense. I do not believe in any politics. God and truth are the only politics in the world; everything else is trash.

Swami Vivekananda remained unperturbed by opposition. His lectures, intensely religious and philosophical, were attended everywhere by eminent people. Many came to him for private instruction. His aim was to preach the eternal truths of religion and to help sincere people in moulding their spiritual life. Very soon his dauntless spirit, innate purity, lofty idealism, spiritual personality, and spotless character attracted to him a band of sincere and loyal American disciples, whom he began to train as future Vedānta workers in America.

AMERICA AT THE TIME OF VIVEKANANDA

It must be said to the credit of America that she was not altogether unprepared to receive the message of Vivekananda. Certain spiritual ideas, which were congenial for the reception of the Vedāntic ideals presented by the Swami, had already begun to ferment underneath the robust, picturesque, gay, and dynamic surface of American life. Freedom, equality, and justice had always been the cherished treasures of American hearts. To these principles, which the Americans applied in politics and society for the material and ethical welfare of men, Swami Vivekananda gave a spiritual basis and interpretation.

Religion had played an important part from the very beginning of American

Colonial history. The pilgrims who crossed the Atlantic in the "Mayflower" and landed on the barren coast of Cape Cod in November 1620, were English people who had first left England and gone to Holland for freedom of worship. Later they were joined by other dissenters who could not submit to the restrictions placed upon their religious beliefs by the English rulers of the time. These were the forbears of the sturdy, religious-minded New Englanders who, two centuries later, became the leaders of the intellectual and spiritual culture of America. Swami Vivekananda found among their descendants many of his loyal and enthusiastic followers.

Both the Holy Bible and the philosophy of Locke influenced the Bill of Rights and the American Constitution. Leaders imbued with the Christian ideal of the Fatherhood of God and the brotherhood of men penned the second paragraph of the Declaration of Independence, which clearly set forth its political philosophy, namely, the equality of men before God, the state, and society. Thomas Paine, one of the high priests of the American Revolution, was an uncompromising foe of tyranny, and an upholder of human freedom. The same passion for equality, freedom, justice, enduring peace, and righteousness was later to permeate the utterances of the great Lincoln.

The political structure of America shows the sagacity and lofty idealism of her statesmen, who built up the country after the War of Independence. The original thirteen colonies, which had wrested freedom from England, gradually became the United States of America. The architects of the American Government might have created, following the imperialistic pattern of England, an American Empire, with the original thirteen states as a sort of mother country and the rest as her colonies. But instead, the newly acquired territories received complete equality of status. It may also be mentioned that, with the exception of the Mexican War of 1845, America has never started a war.

Within a hundred years of her gaining independence, America showed unprecedented material prosperity. The country's vast hidden wealth was tapped by European immigrants, who brought with them not only the flavour of an older civilization, but technical skill, indomitable courage, and the spirit of adventure. Scientists and technologists flooded the country with new inventions. Steamboats, a network of railroads, and various mechanical appliances aided in the creation of new wealth. Towns grew into cities. As big business concerns expanded, workmen and mechanics formed protective organizations. Ambition stirred everywhere, and men's very manners changed with the new haste and energy that swept them on.

Material prosperity was accompanied by a new awakening of men's minds and consciousness. Jails were converted into penitentiary systems, based upon humanitarian principles, and anti-slavery societies were inaugurated. During the five years between 1850 and 1855 were published some of the greatest books in American literature, hardly surpassed in imaginative vitality. Democracy was in full swing and it was the people's day everywhere. The crude frontier days were fast disappearing.

The Transcendentalist Movement, of which Emerson was the leader, with Thoreau and Alcott as his associates, brought spiritual India into the swift current of American life. The old and new continents had not been altogether strangers. Columbus had set out to find the short route to India, known far and wide for her fabulous wealth, and had stumbled upon America instead. The chests of tea of the Boston Tea Party, which set off the War of Independence, had come from India. Moreover, the victory of the English over the French in the eighteenth-century colonial wars in India contributed to the success of the American colonists in their struggle for freedom begun in 1775. And finally, Commodore Perry in 1853 made it possible for American merchant ships to trade with the Far East and thus visit Indian coastal towns on their long journeys.

The development of Emerson's innate idealism had been aided by the philosophy of Greece, the ethics of China, the poetry of the Sufis, and the mysticism of India. Emerson, a keen student of the Bhagavad Gītā, was familiar with the Upanishadic doctrines and published translations of religious and philosophical tracts from the Oriental languages. His beautiful poem "Brahma" and his essay "The Over-Soul" show clearly his indebtedness to Hindu spiritual thought. But Emerson's spirit, pre-eminently ethical and intellectual, could not grasp the highest flights of Hindu mysticism; it accepted only what was in harmony with a somewhat shallow optimism. Emerson's writings later influenced the New Thought movement and Mary Baker Eddy's Christian Science.

Thoreau, Emerson's neighbour for twenty-five years, read and discussed with him in great detail the Hindu religious classics. Thoreau wrote: "I bathe my intellect in the stupendous and cosmogonal philosophy of the Upanishads and the Bhagavad Gītā, in comparison with which our modern world and literature seem puny and trivial." He wanted to write a joint Bible, gathering material from the Asiatic scriptures, and took for his motto *Ex Oriente Lux*.

Alcott was a genuine friend of Indian culture. He was instrumental in bringing out the American edition of Sir Edwin Arnold's *The Light of Asia*, and this made the life and teachings of Buddha accessible, for the first time, to American readers.

The Transcendental Club, founded in Concord, near Boston, reached its height by 1840. The American Oriental Society was formed in 1842, with aims similar to those of the European Oriental societies.

Walt Whitman (1819-1892), a contemporary of the Concord philosophers, seems to have come very near to Vedāntic idealism. There is no reliable evidence to show that Whitman was directly influenced by Hindu thought. He is reputed to have denied it himself. A great religious individualist, he was free from all church conventions and creeds. To him, religion consisted entirely of inner illumination, "the secret silent ecstasy." It is not known if he practised any definite religious disciplines; most probably he did not. Yet Swami Vivekananda once called Whitman "the sannyāsin of America." *Leaves of Grass*, which Swami Vivekananda read, breathes the spirit of identity with all forms of life, and Whitman's "Song of the Open Road" is full of the sentiments that were nearest to the heart of Vivekananda. Here, for example, are three stanzas:

I inhale great draughts of space;
The east and the west are mine, and the north and the south are mine.

I am larger, better than I thought;
I did not know I held so much goodness.

*   *   *

Allons! We must not stop here!
However sweet these laid-up stores—however convenient this dwelling, we cannot remain
    here;
However shelter'd this port, and however calm these waters, we must not anchor here;
However welcome the hospitality that surrounds us, we are permitted to receive it but a
    little while.

*   *   *

Allons! Be not detain'd!
Let the paper remain on the desk unwritten, and the book on the shelf unopen'd!
Let the tools remain in the workshop! let the money remain unearn'd!
Let the school stand! mind not the cry of the teacher!
Let the preacher preach in the pulpit! let the lawyer plead in the court, and the judge
    expound the law.

The marriage of East and West dreamt of by Emerson and Thoreau was not consummated for several reasons. The Gold Rush of 1849, to California, had turned people's attention in other directions. Then had come the Civil War, in which brother had fought brother and men's worst passions had been let loose. Lastly, the development of science and technology had brought about a great change in people's outlook, intensifying their desire for material prosperity.

The publication of Darwin's *Origin of Species* in 1859 changed the *Weltanschauung* of the Western world, and its repercussions were felt more in the New World than in Europe. Within a decade, intellectual people gave up their belief in the Biblical story of creation and did not hesitate to trace man's origin back to an apelike ancestor, and beyond that to a primordial protoplasmic atomic globule. The implications of evolution were incorporated into every field of thought—law, history, economics, sociology, philosophy, religion, and art; transcendentalism was replaced by empiricism, instrumentalism, and pragmatism. The American life-current thus was turned into a new channel. When America had been comparatively poor she had cherished her spiritual heritage. In the midst of her struggle for existence she had preserved her spiritual sensitivity. But in the wake of the Civil War the desire to possess "bigger and better things" cast its spell everywhere. Big utilities and corporations came into existence; the spiritual and romantic glow of the frontier days degenerated into the sordidness of competitive materialistic life, while the unceasing flow of crude immigrants from Europe made difficult the stabilization of American culture.

Emerson was disillusioned by the aftermath of the Civil War. He had hoped "that in the peace after such a war, a great expansion would follow in the mind of the country, grand views in every direction—true freedom in politics, in religion, in social science, in thought. But the energy of the nation seems to have expended itself in the war."

Walt Whitman was even more caustic. He wrote bitterly:

Society in the States is cramped, crude, superstitious, and rotten. . . . Never was there, perhaps, more hollowness of heart than at present, and here in the United States. Genuine belief seems to have left us. . . . The great cities reek with respectable, as much as non-respectable, robbery and scoundrelism. In fashionable life, flippancy, tepid amours, weak infidelism, small aims, or no aims at all, only to kill time. . . . I say that our New World Democracy, however great a success in uplifting the masses out of their sloughs in materialistic development, and in a certain highly deceptive superficial popular intellectuality, is so far an almost complete failure in its social aspects. In vain do we march with unprecedented strides to empire so colossal, outvying the antique, beyond Alexander's, beyond the proudest sway of Rome. In vain we annexed Texas, California, Alaska, and reach north for Canada or south for Cuba. It is as if we were somehow being endowed with a vast and thoroughly appointed body, and left with little or no soul.

But the material prosperity or the triumph of science could not destroy the innate idealism of the American mind. It remained hidden like embers under ashes. Thoughtful Americans longed for a philosophy which, without going counter to the scientific method, would show the way to a larger vision of life, harmonizing the diverse claims of science, the humanities, and mystical experience. Now the time was ripe for the fulfilment of Thoreau's dream of the marriage of East and West, a real synthesis of science and religion. And to bring this about, no worthier person could have been found than Swami Vivekananda of India. This accounts for the spontaneous welcome received by this representative of Hinduism, who brought to America an ancient and yet dynamic philosophy of life.

VEDĀNTA IN AMERICA

After the meetings of the Parliament of Religions were concluded, Swami Vivekananda, as already noted, undertook a series of apostolic campaigns in order to sow the seed of the Vedāntic truths in the ready soil of America. Soon he discovered that the lecture bureau was exploiting him. Further, he did not like its method of advertisement. He was treated as if he were the chief attraction of a circus. The prospectus included his portrait, with the inscription, proclaiming his cardinal virtues: "An Orator by Divine Right; a Model Representative of his Race; a Perfect Master of the English Language; the Sensation of the World's Fair Parliament." It also described his physical bearing, his height, the colour of his skin, and his clothing. The Swami felt disgusted at being treated like a patent medicine or an elephant in a show. So he severed his relationship with the bureau and arranged his own lectures himself. He accepted invitations from churches, clubs, and private gatherings, and travelled extensively through the Eastern and Midwestern states of America, delivering twelve to fourteen or more lectures a week.

People came in hundreds and in thousands. And what an assorted audience he had to face! There came to his meetings professors from universities, ladies of fine breeding, seekers of truth, and devotees of God with childlike faith. But mixed with these were charlatans, curiosity-seekers, idlers, and vagabonds. It is not true that he met everywhere with favourable conditions. Leon Landsberg, one of the Swami's American disciples, thus described Vivekananda's tribulations of those days:

The Americans are a receptive nation. That is why the country is a hotbed of all kinds of religious and irreligious monstrosities. There is no theory so absurd, no doctrine so

irrational, no claim so extravagant, no fraud so transparent, but can find their numerous
believers and a ready market. To satisfy this craving, to feed the credulity of the people,
hundreds of societies and sects are born for the salvation of the world, and to enable the
prophets to pocket $25 to $100 initiation fees. Hobgoblins, spooks, mahātmās, and new
prophets were rising every day. In this bedlam of religious cranks, the Swami appeared
to teach the lofty religion of the Vedas, the profound philosophy of Vedānta, the sublime wisdom of the ancient rishis. The most unfavourable environment for such a task!

The Swami met with all kinds of obstacles. The opposition of fanatical
Christian missionaries was, of course, one of these. They promised him help if
he only would preach their brand of Christianity. When the Swami refused,
they circulated all sorts of filthy stories about him, and even succeeded in persuading some of the Americans who had previously invited him to be their
guest, to cancel the invitations. But Vivekananda continued to preach the
religion of love, renunciation, and truth as taught by Christ, and to show him
the highest veneration as a Saviour of mankind. How significant were his words:
"It is well to be born in a church, but it is terrible to die there!" Needless to
say, he meant by the word church all organized religious institutions. How like
a thunderbolt the words fell upon the ears of his audience when one day he
exclaimed: "Christ, Buddha, and Krishna are but waves in the Ocean of Infinite
Consciousness that I am!"

Then there were the leaders of the cranky, selfish, and fraudulent organizations, who tried to induce the Swami to embrace their cause, first by promises
of support, and then by threats of injuring him if he refused to ally himself
with them. But he could be neither bought nor frightened—"the sickle
had hit on a stone," as the Polish proverb says. To all these propositions his
only answer was: "I stand for Truth. Truth will never ally itself with falsehood.
Even if all the world should be against me, Truth must prevail in the end."

But the more powerful enemies he had to face were among the so-called
free-thinkers, embracing the atheists, materialists, agnostics, rationalists, and
others of similar breed who opposed anything associated with God or religion.
Thinking that they would easily crush his ancient faith by arguments drawn
from Western philosophy and science, they organized a meeting in New York
and invited the Swami to present his views.

"I shall never forget that memorable evening," wrote an American disciple,
"when the Swami appeared single-handed to face the forces of materialism,
arrayed in the heaviest armour of law, and reason, and logic, and common
sense, of matter, and force, and heredity, and all the stock phrases calculated
to awe and terrify the ignorant. Imagine their surprise when they found that,
far from being intimidated by these big words, he proved himself a master in
wielding their own weapons, and as familiar with the arguments of materialism
as with those of Advaita philosophy. He showed them that their much vaunted
Western science could not answer the most vital questions of life and being,
that their immutable laws, so much talked of, had no outside existence apart
from the human mind, that the very idea of matter was a metaphysical conception, and that it was much despised metaphysics upon which ultimately
rested the very basis of their materialism. With an irresistible logic he demonstrated that their knowledge proved itself incorrect, not by comparison with

that which was true, but by the very laws upon which it depended for its basis; that pure reason could not help admitting its own limitations and pointed to something beyond reason; and that rationalism, when carried to its last consequences, must ultimately land us at something which is above matter, above force, above sense, above thought, and even consciousness, and of which all these are but manifestations."

As a result of his explaining the limitations of science, a number of people from the group of free-thinkers attended the Swami's meeting the next day and listened to his uplifting utterances on God and religion.

What an uphill work it was for Swami Vivekananda to remove the ignorance, superstition, and perverted ideas about religion in general and Hinduism in particular! No wonder he sometimes felt depressed. In one of these moods he wrote from Detroit, on March 15, 1894, to the Hale sisters in Chicago:

> But I do not know—I have become very sad in my heart since I am here. I do not know why. I am wearied of lecturing and all that nonsense. This mixing with hundreds of human animals, male and female, has disturbed me. I will tell you what is to my taste. I cannot write—cannot speak—but I can think deep, and when I am heated can speak fire. But it should be to a select few—a very select few. And let them carry and sow my ideas broadcast if they will—not I. It is only a just division of labour. The same man never succeeded in thinking and in casting his thoughts all around. Such thoughts are not worth a penny. . . . I am really not "cyclonic" at all—far from it. What I want is not here—nor can I longer bear this cyclonic atmosphere. Calm, cool, nice, deep, penetrating, independent, searching thought—a few noble, pure mirrors which will reflect it back, catch it until all of them sound in unison. Let others throw it to the outside world if they will. This is the way to perfection—to be perfect, to make perfect a few men and women. My idea of doing good is this—to evolve a few giants, and not to strew pearls to the swine and lose time, breath, and energy. . . . Well, I do not care for lecturing any more. It is too disgusting to bring me to suit anybody's or any audience's fad.

Swami Vivekananda became sick of what he termed "the nonsense of public life and newspaper blazoning."

The Swami had sincere admirers and devotees among the Americans, who looked after his comforts, gave him money when he lacked it, and followed his instruction. He was particularly grateful to American women, and wrote many letters to his friends in India paying high praise to their virtues.

In one letter he wrote: "Nowhere in the world are women like those of this country. How pure, independent, self-relying, and kind-hearted! It is the women who are the life and soul of this country. All learning and culture are centred in them."

In another letter: "[Americans] look with veneration upon women, who play a most prominent part in their lives. Here this form of worship has attained its perfection—this is the long and short of it. I am almost at my wit's end to see the women of this country. They are Lakshmi, the Goddess of Fortune, in beauty, and Sarasvati, the Goddess of Learning, in virtues—they are the Divine Mother incarnate. If I can raise a thousand such Madonnas—incarnations of the Divine Mother—in our country before I die, I shall die in peace. Then only will our countrymen become worthy of their name."

Perhaps his admiration reached its highest pitch in a letter to the Mahārājā of Khetri, which he wrote in 1894:

American women! A hundred lives would not be sufficient to pay my deep debt of gratitude to you! Last year I came to this country in summer, a wandering preacher of a far distant country, without name, fame, wealth, or learning to recommend me— friendless, helpless, almost in a state of destitution; and American women befriended me, gave me shelter and food, took me to their homes, and treated me as their own son, their own brother. They stood as my friends even when their own priests were trying to persuade them to give up the "dangerous heathen"—even when, day after day, their best friends had told them not to stand by this "unknown foreigner, maybe of dangerous character." But they are better judges of character and soul—for it is the pure mirror that catches the reflection.

And how many beautiful homes I have seen, how many mothers whose purity of character, whose unselfish love for their children, are beyond expression, how many daughters and pure maidens, "pure as the icicle on Diana's temple"—and withal much culture, education, and spirituality in the highest sense! Is America, then, only full of wingless angels in the shape of women? There are good and bad everywhere, true—but a nation is not to be judged by its weaklings, called the wicked, for they are only the weeds which lag behind, but by the good, the noble, and the pure, who indicate the national life-current to be flowing clear and vigorous.

And how bitter the Swami felt when he remembered the sad plight of the women of India! He particularly recalled the tragic circumstances under which one of his own sisters had committed suicide. He often thought that the misery of India was largely due to the ill-treatment the Hindus meted out to their womenfolk. Part of the money earned by his lectures was sent to a foundation for Hindu widows at Baranagore. He also conceived the idea of sending to India women teachers from the West for the intellectual regeneration of Hindu women.

Swami Vivekananda showed great respect for the fundamentals of American culture. He studied the country's economic policy, industrial organizations, public instruction, and its museums and art galleries, and wrote to India enthusiastically about them. He praised highly the progress of science, hygiene, institutions, and social welfare work. He realized that such noble concepts as the divinity of the soul and the brotherhood of men were mere academic theories in present-day India, whereas America showed how to apply them in life. He felt indignant when he compared the generosity and liberality of the wealthy men of America in the cause of social service, with the apathy of the Indians as far as their own people were concerned.

"No religion on earth," he wrote angrily, "preaches the dignity of humanity in such a lofty strain as Hinduism, and no religion on earth treads upon the necks of the poor and the low in such a fashion as Hinduism. Religion is not at fault, but it is the Pharisees and Sadducees."

How poignant must have been his feelings when he remembered the iniquities of the caste-system! "India's doom was sealed," he wrote, "the very day they invented the word mlechcha[8] and stopped from communion with others." When he saw in New York a millionaire woman sitting side by side in a tram-

[8] The non-Hindu, with whom all social intercourse is forbidden.

car with a negress with a wash-basket on her lap, he was impressed with the democratic spirit of the Americans. He wanted in India "an organization that will teach the Hindus mutual help and appreciation" after the pattern of Western democracies.

Incessantly he wrote to his Indian devotees about the regeneration of the masses. In a letter dated 1894 he said:

Let each one of us pray, day and night, for the downtrodden millions in India, who are held fast by poverty, priestcraft, and tyranny—pray day and night for them. I care more to preach religion to them than to the high and the rich. I am no metaphysician, no philosopher, nay, no saint. But I am poor, I love the poor. . . . Who feels in India for the three hundred millions of men and women sunken for ever in poverty and ignorance? Where is the way out? Who feels for them? Let these people be your God— think of them, work for them, pray for them incessantly—the Lord will show you the way. Him I call a mahātmā, a noble soul, whose heart bleeds for the poor; otherwise he is a durātmā, a wicked soul. . . . So long as the millions live in hunger and ignorance, I hold every man a traitor who, having been educated at their expense, pays not the least heed to them. . . . We are poor, my brothers, we are nobodies, but such have always been the instruments of the Most High.

Never did he forget, in the midst of the comforts and luxuries of America, even when he was borne on the wings of triumph from one city to another, the cause of the Indian masses, whose miseries he had witnessed while wandering as an unknown monk from the Himālayas to Cape Comorin. The prosperity of the new continent only stirred up in his soul deeper commiseration for his own people. He saw with his own eyes what human efforts, intelligence, and earnestness could accomplish to banish from society poverty, superstition, squalor, disease, and other handicaps of human well-being. On August 20, 1893, he wrote to instil courage into the depressed hearts of his devotees in India:

Gird up your loins, my boys! I am called by the Lord for this. . . . The hope lies in you—in the meek, the lowly, but the faithful. Feel for the miserable and look up for help—it shall come. I have travelled twelve years with this load in my heart and this idea in my head. I have gone from door to door of the so-called "rich and great." With a bleeding heart I have crossed half the world to this strange land, seeking help. The Lord is great. I know He will help me. I may perish of cold and hunger in this land, but I bequeath to you young men this sympathy, this struggle for the poor, the ignorant, the oppressed. . . . Go down on your faces before Him and make a great sacrifice, the sacrifice of a whole life for them, for whom He comes from time to time, whom He loves above all—the poor, the lowly, the oppressed. Vow, then, to devote your whole lives to the cause of these three hundred millions, going down and down every day. Glory unto the Lord! We will succeed. Hundreds will fall in the struggle—hundreds will be ready to take it up. Faith—sympathy, fiery faith and fiery sympathy! Life is nothing, death is nothing—hunger nothing, cold nothing. Glory unto the Lord! March on, the Lord is our General. Do not look back to see who falls—forward—onward!

Swami Vivekananda was thoroughly convinced by his intimate knowledge of the Indian people that the life-current of the nation, far from being extinct, was only submerged under the dead weight of ignorance and poverty. India still produced great saints whose message of the Spirit was sorely needed by the Western world. But the precious jewels of spirituality discovered by them were hidden, in the absence of a jewel-box, in a heap of filth. The West had created the jewel-box, in the form of a healthy society, but it did not have the jewels. Further, it took him no long time to understand that a materialistic culture contained within it the seeds of its own destruction. Again and again he warned the West of its impending danger. The bright glow on the Western horizon might not be the harbinger of a new dawn; it might very well be the red flames of a huge funeral pyre. The Western world was caught in the maze of its incessant activity—interminable movement without any goal. The hankering for material comforts, without a higher spiritual goal and a feeling of universal sympathy, might flare up among the nations of the West into jealousy and hatred, which in the end would bring about their own destruction.

Swami Vivekananda was a lover of humanity. Man is the highest manifestation of God, and this God was being crucified in different ways in the East and the West. Thus he had a double mission to perform in America. He wanted to obtain from the Americans money, scientific knowledge, and technical help for the regeneration of the Indian masses, and, in turn, to give to the Americans the knowledge of the Eternal Spirit to endow their material progress with significance. No false pride could prevent him from learning from America the many features of her social superiority; he also exhorted the Americans not to allow racial arrogance to prevent them from accepting the gift of spirituality from India. Through this policy of acceptance and mutual respect he dreamt of creating a healthy human society for the ultimate welfare of man's body and soul.

VARIOUS EXPERIENCES AS A TEACHER

The year following the Parliament of Religions the Swami devoted to addressing meetings in the vast area spreading from the Mississippi to the Atlantic. In Detroit he spent six weeks, first as a guest of Mrs. John Bagley, widow of the former Governor of Michigan, and then of Thomas W. Palmer, President of the World's Fair Commission, formerly a United States Senator and American Minister to Spain. Mrs. Bagley spoke of the Swami's presence at her house as a "continual benediction." It was in Detroit that Miss Greenstidel first heard him speak. She later became, under the name of Sister Christine, one of the most devoted disciples of the Swami and a collaborator of Sister Nivedita in her work in Calcutta for the educational advancement of Indian women.

After Detroit, he divided his time between Chicago, New York, and Boston, and during the summer of 1894 addressed, by invitation, several meetings of the "Humane Conference" held at Greenacre, Massachusetts. Christian Scientists, spiritualists, faith-healers, and groups representing similar views participated in the Conference.

The Swami, in the course of a letter to the Hale sisters of Chicago, wrote on July 31, 1894, with his usual humour about the people who attended the meetings:

They have a lively time and sometimes all of them wear what you call your scientific dress the whole day. They have lectures almost every day. One Mr. Colville from Boston is here. He speaks every day, it is said, under spirit control. The editor of the *Universal Truth* from the top floor of Jimmy Mills has settled herself down here. She is conducting religious services and holding classes to heal all manner of diseases, and very soon I expect them to be giving eyes to the blind, etc., etc. After all, it is a queer gathering. They do not care much about social laws and are quite free and happy. . . .

There is a Mr. Wood of Boston here, who is one of the great lights of your sect. But he objects to belonging to the sect of Mrs. Whirlpool.[9] So he calls himself a mental healer of metaphysical, chemico, physical-religioso, what-not, etc.

Yesterday there was a tremendous cyclone which gave a good "treatment" to the tents. The big tent under which they held the lectures developed so much spirituality under the treatment that it entirely disappeared from mortal gaze, and about two hundred chairs were dancing about the grounds under spiritual ecstasy. Mrs. Figs of Mills Company gives a class every morning, and Mrs. Mills is jumping all about the place. They are all in high spirits. I am especially glad for Cora, for she suffered a good deal last winter and a little hilarity would do her good. You would be astounded with the liberty they enjoy in the camps, but they are very good and pure people—a little erratic, that is all.

Regarding his own work at Greenacre, the Swami wrote in the same letter:

The other night the camp people all went to sleep under a pine tree under which I sit every morning à la India and talk to them. Of course I went with them and we had a nice night under the stars, sleeping on the lap of Mother Earth, and I enjoyed every bit of it. I cannot describe to you that night's glories—after the year of brutal life that I have led, to sleep on the ground, to meditate under the tree in the forest! The inn people are more or less well-to-do, and the camp people are healthy, young, sincere, and holy men and women. I teach them all Śivoham, Śivoham—"I am Śiva, I am Śiva"—and they all repeat it, innocent and pure as they are, and brave beyond all bounds, and I am so happy and glorified.

Thank God for making me poor! Thank God for making these children in the tents poor! The dudes and dudines are in the hotel, but iron-bound nerves, souls of triple steel, and spirits of fire are in the camp. If you had seen them yesterday, when the rain was falling in torrents and the cyclone was overturning everything—hanging on to their tent-strings to keep them from being blown off, and standing on the majesty of their souls, these brave ones—it would have done your hearts good. I would go a hundred miles to see the like of them. Lord bless them! . . .

Never be anxious for me for a moment. I will be taken care of, and if not, I shall know my time has come—and pass out. . . . Now good dreams, good thoughts for you. You are good and noble. Instead of materializing the spirit, i.e. dragging the spiritual to the material plane as these fellers do, convert matter into spirit—catch a glimpse at least, every day, of that world of infinite beauty and peace and purity, the spiritual, and try to live in it day and night. Seek not, touch not with your toes, anything which is uncanny. Let your souls ascend day and night like an unbroken string unto the feet of the Beloved, whose throne is in your own heart, and let the rest take care of themselves, i.e. the body and everything else. Life is an evanescent, floating dream; youth and beauty fade. Say day and night: "Thou art my father, my mother, my husband, my love, my Lord, my God—I want nothing but Thee, nothing but Thee, nothing but Thee. Thou in me, I in Thee—I am Thee, Thou art me." Wealth goes, beauty vanishes, life flies, powers fly—but the Lord abideth for ever, love abideth for ever. If there is glory in keeping the machine in good trim, it is more glorious to withhold the soul from suffering with the body. That is the only demonstration of your being "not matter"—by letting matter alone.

Stick to God. Who cares what comes, in the body or anywhere? Through the terrors

[9] A reference to Mrs. Mary Baker Eddy, the founder of Christian Science.

of evil, say, "My God, my Love!" Through the pangs of death, say, "My God, my Love!" Through all the evils under the sun, say: "My God, my Love! Thou art here, I see Thee. Thou art with me, I feel Thee. I am Thine, take me. I am not the world's, but Thine—leave Thou not me." Do not go for glass beads, leaving the mine of diamonds. This life is a great chance. What! Seekest thou the pleasures of this world? He is the fountain of all bliss. Seek the highest, aim for the highest, and you *shall* reach the highest.

At Greenacre the Swami became a friend of Dr. Lewis G. Janes, Director of the School of Comparative Religions organized by the Greenacre Conference, and President of the Brooklyn Ethical Association. The following autumn he lectured in Baltimore and Washington.

During the Swami's visit in New York he was the guest of friends, mostly rich ladies of the metropolitan city. He had not yet started any serious work there. Soon he began to feel a sort of restraint put upon his movements. Very few of his wealthy friends understood the true import of his message; they were interested in him as a novelty from India. Also to them he was the man of the hour. They wanted him to mix with only the exclusive society of "the right people." He chafed under their domination and one day cried: "Śiva! Śiva! Has it ever come to pass that a great work has been grown by the rich? It is brain and heart that create, and not purse." He wanted to break away from their power and devote himself to the training of some serious students in the spiritual life. He was fed up with public lectures; now he became eager to mould silently the characters of individuals. He could no longer bear the yoke of money and all the botheration that came in its train. He would live simply and give freely, like the holy men of India. Soon an opportunity presented itself.

Dr. Lewis Janes invited the Swami to give a series of lectures on the Hindu religion before the Brooklyn Ethical Association. On the evening of December 31, 1894, he gave his first lecture, and according to the report of the *Brooklyn Standard*, the enthusiastic audience, consisting of doctors and lawyers and judges and teachers, remained spellbound by his eloquent defence of the religion of India. They all acknowledged that Vivekananda was even greater than his fame. At the end of the meeting they made an insistent demand for regular classes in Brooklyn, to which the Swami agreed. A series of class meetings was held and several public lectures were given at the Pouch Mansion, where the Ethical Association held its meetings. These lectures constituted the beginning of the permanent work in America which the Swami secretly desired.

Soon after, several poor but earnest students rented for the Swami some unfurnished rooms in a poor section of New York City. He lived in one of them. An ordinary room on the second floor of the lodging-house was used for the lectures and classes. The Swami when conducting the meetings sat on the floor, while the ever more numerous auditors seated themselves as best they could, utilizing the marble-topped dresser, the arms of the sofa, and even the corner wash-stand. The door was left open and the overflow filled the hall and sat on the stairs. The Swami, like a typical religious teacher in India, felt himself in his own element. The students, forgetting all the inconveniences, hung upon every word uttered from the teacher's deep personal experiences or his wide range of knowledge.

The lectures, given every morning and several evenings a week, were free. The rent was paid by the voluntary subscriptions of the students, and the deficit was met by the Swami himself, through the money he earned by giving secular lectures on India. Soon the meeting-place had to be removed downstairs to occupy an entire parlour floor.

He began to instruct several chosen disciples in jnāna-yoga in order to clarify their intellects regarding the subtle truths of Vedānta, and also in rāja-yoga to teach them the science of self-control, concentration, and meditation. He was immensely happy with the result of his concentrated work. He enjoined upon these students to follow strict disciplines regarding food, choosing only the simplest. The necessity of chastity was emphasized, and they were warned against psychic and occult powers. At the same time he broadened their intellectual horizon through the teachings of Vedāntic universality. Daily he meditated with the serious students. Often he would lose all bodily consciousness and, like Śri Ramakrishna, have to be brought back to the knowledge of the world through the repetition of certain holy words that he had taught his disciples.

It was sometime about June 1895 when Swami Vivekananda finished writing his famous book Rāja-Yoga, which attracted the attention of the Harvard philosopher William James and was later to rouse the enthusiasm of Tolstoy. The book is a translation of Patanjali's Yoga aphorisms, the Swami adding his own explanations; the introductory chapters written by him are especially illuminating. Patanjali expounded, through these aphorisms, the philosophy of Yoga, the main purpose of which is to show the way of the soul's attaining freedom from the bondage of matter. Various methods of concentration are discussed. The book well served two purposes. First, the Swami demonstrated that religious experiences could stand on the same footing as scientific truths, being based on experimentation, observation, and verification. Therefore genuine spiritual experiences must not be dogmatically discarded as lacking rational evidence. Secondly, the Swami explained lucidly various disciplines of concentration, with the warning, however, that they should not be pursued without the help of a qualified teacher.

Miss S. Ellen Waldo of Brooklyn, a disciple of the Swami, was his amanuensis. She thus described the manner in which he dictated the book:

"In delivering his commentaries on the aphorisms, he would leave me waiting while he entered into deep states of meditation or self-contemplation, to emerge therefrom with some luminous interpretation. I had always to keep the pen dipped in the ink. He might be absorbed for long periods of time, and then suddenly his silence would be broken by some eager expression or some long, deliberate teaching."

SWAMI VIVEKANANDA AT THOUSAND ISLAND PARK

By the middle of the year 1895 the Swami was completely exhausted. The numerous classes and lectures, the private instruction, the increasing correspondence, and the writing of Rāja-Yoga had tired him both physically and mentally. It was a herculean task to spread the message of Hinduism in an alien land

and at the same time to mould the lives of individuals according to the highest ideal of renunciation. Besides there were annoyances from zealous but well-meaning friends, especially women. Some suggested that he should take elocution lessons, some urged him to dress fashionably in order to influence society people, others admonished him against mixing with all sorts of people. At times he would be indignant and say: "Why should I be bound down with all this nonsense? I am a monk who has realized the vanity of all earthly nonsense! I have no time to give my manners a finish. I cannot find time enough to give my message. I will give it after my own fashion. Shall I be dragged down into the narrow limits of your conventional life? Never!" Again, he wrote to a devotee: "I long, oh, I long for my rags, my shaven head, my sleep under the trees, and my food from begging."

The Swami needed rest from his strenuous work, and accepted the invitation of his devoted friend Francis H. Leggett to come to his summer camp at Percy, New Hampshire, and rest in the silence of the pine woods. In the meantime Miss Elizabeth Dutcher, one of his students in New York, cordially asked the Swami to take a vacation in her summer cottage at Thousand Island Park on the St. Lawrence River. The Swami gratefully accepted both invitations.

About his life at the camp, he wrote to a friend on June 7, 1895: "It gives me a new lease of life to be here. I go into the forest alone and read my Gītā and am quite happy." After a short visit at Percy, he arrived in June at Thousand Island Park, where he spent seven weeks. This proved to be a momentous period in his life in the Western world.

When the students who had been attending Swami Vivekananda's classes in New York heard of Miss Dutcher's proposal, they were immensely pleased, because they did not want any interruption of their lessons. The Swami, too, after two years' extensive work in America, had become eager to mould the spiritual life of individual students and to train a group that would carry on his work in America in the future. He wrote to one of his friends that he intended to manufacture "a few yogis" from the materials of the classes. He wanted only those to follow him to Thousand Island Park who were completely earnest in their practice of spiritual disciplines, and he said that he would gladly recognize these as his disciples.

By a singular coincidence just twelve disciples were taught by him at the summer retreat, though all were not there the full seven weeks; ten was the largest number present at any one time. Two, Mme. Marie Louise and Mr. Leon Landsberg, were initiated at Thousand Island Park into the monastic life. The former, French by birth but a naturalized American, a materialist and socialist, a fearless, progressive woman worker known to the press and platform, was given the name Abhayananda. The latter, a Russian Jew and member of the staff of a prominent New York newspaper, became known as Kripananda. Both took the vows of poverty and chastity.

In many respects the sojourn in Miss Dutcher's cottage was ideal for the Swami's purpose. Here, to this intimate group, he revealed brilliant flashes of illumination, lofty flights of eloquence, and outpourings of the most profound wisdom. The whole experience was reminiscent of the Dakshineswar days when the Swami, as the young Narendra, had been initiated into the mysteries of the spiritual life at the feet of his Master, Ramakrishna.

Thousand Island Park, near the western tip of Wellesley Island, the second largest of the seventeen hundred islands in the St. Lawrence River, has for its setting one of the scenic show-places of America. A prosperous village during the last part of the nineteenth century, it was, at the time of the Swami's visit, a stronghold of orthodox Methodist Christianity. The local tabernacle, where celebrated preachers were invited to conduct the divine service on Sunday mornings, attracted people from the neighbouring islands. Since secular activities were not allowed on the Sabbath, the visitors would arrive at Thousand Island Park the previous day and spend the night camping out. No such profanities as public drinking, gambling, or dancing were allowed in the summer resort—a rule that is still enforced half a century later. Only people of serious mind went there for their vacation.

Miss Dutcher's cottage[10] was ideally located on a hill, which on the north and west sloped down towards the river. It commanded a grand view of many distant islands, the town of Clayton on the American mainland, and the Canadian shores to the north. At night the houses and hotels were brightly illuminated by Chinese lanterns.

Miss Dutcher, an artist, had built her cottage literally "on a rock," with huge boulders lying all around. It was surrounded by rock-gardens with bright-coloured flowers. At that time the trees at the base of the hill had not grown high; people from the village often visited the upstairs porch to survey the magnificent sweep of the river.

After inviting the Swami, Miss Dutcher added a new wing to the cottage for his accommodation. This wing, three storeys high, stood on a steep slope of rock, like a great lantern-tower with windows on three sides. The room at the top was set apart exclusively for the Swami's use; the lowest room was occupied by a student; the room between, with large windows, and several doors opening on the main part of the house, was used as the Swami's classroom. Miss Dutcher thoughtfully added an outside stairway to the Swami's room so that he might go in and out without being noticed by the others.

On the roofed-in porch upstairs, extending along the west side of the cottage, the students met the Swami for his evening talks. There, at one end, close to the door of his room, he would take his seat and commune with his pupils both in silence and through the spoken word. In the evening the cottage was bathed in perfect stillness except for the murmur of insects and the whisper of the wind through the leaves. The house being situated, as it were, among the tree-tops, a breeze always relieved the summer heat. The centre of the village was only a five minutes' walk from the cottage, and yet, on account of the woods around it, not a single house could be seen. Many of the islands that dotted the river were visible in the distance and, especially in the evening,

[10] The cottage, which was acquired by the Ramakrishna-Vivekananda Center of New York in December 1947 and extensively restored without interfering with the original design, is now used as a summer retreat for Swamis of the Ramakrishna Order. It has been dedicated as "Vivekananda Cottage" and Swami Vivekananda's room has been set apart as a shrine for the devotions of the inmates.

appeared like a picture. The glow of the sunset on the St. Lawrence was breath-taking in its beauty, and the moon at night was mirrored in the shining waters beneath.

In this ideal retreat, "the world forgetting, by the world forgot," the devoted students spent seven weeks with their beloved teacher, listening to his words of wisdom and receiving his silent benediction. Immediately after the evening meal they would assemble on the upstairs porch. Soon the Swami would come from his room and take his seat. Two hours and often much longer would be spent together. One night, when the moon was almost full, he talked to them until it set below the western horizon, both the teacher and the students being unaware of the passage of time. During these seven weeks the Swami's whole heart was in his work and he taught like one inspired.

Miss Dutcher, his hostess, was a conscientious little woman and a staunch Methodist. When the Swami arrived at the house, he saw on the walls of his living quarters scrolls bearing the words "Welcome to Vivekananda" painted in bold letters. But as the teaching began, Miss Dutcher often felt distressed by the Swami's revolutionary ideas. All her ideals, her values of life, her concepts of religion, were, it seemed to her, being destroyed. Sometimes she did not appear for two or three days. "Don't you see?" the Swami said. "This is not an ordinary illness. It is the reaction of the body against the chaos that is going on in her mind. She cannot bear it."

The most violent attack came one day after a timid protest on her part against something he had told them in the class. "The idea of duty is the midday sun of misery, scorching the very soul," he had said. "Is it not our duty—" she had begun, but got no farther. For once the great free soul broke all bounds in his rebellion against the idea that anyone should dare bind with fetters the soul of man. Miss Dutcher was not seen for some days.

Referring to the students who had gathered around the Swami, a village shopkeeper said to a new arrival who inquired for the cottage, "Yes, there are some queer people living up on the hill; among them there is a foreign-looking gentleman." A young girl of sixteen, living with her family at the foot of the hill, one day expressed the desire to talk to the Swami. "Don't go near him," her mother said sternly. "He is a heathen." Mr. Tom Mitchell, a carpenter who helped to restore the cottage for the Ramakrishna-Vivekananda Center in 1948, and had originally built the Swami's quarters in 1895, told the present writer that he had read the Swami's lectures in Chicago from the newspapers long before his arrival at the island.

The students wanted, at first, to live as a community without servants, each doing a share of the work. Nearly all of them, however, were unaccustomed to housework and found it uncongenial. The result was amusing; as time went on it threatened to become disastrous. When the tension became too great, the Swami would say with utmost sweetness, "Today, I shall cook for you." At this Landsberg would ejaculate, in an aside, "Heaven save us!" By way of explanation he declared that in New York, whenever the Swami cooked, he, Landsberg, would tear his hair, because it meant that afterwards every dish in the house required washing. After a few days an outsider was engaged to help with the housework.

Swami Vivekananda started his class at Thousand Island Park on Wednesday, June 19. Not all the students had arrived. But his heart was set on his work; so he commenced at once with the three or four who were with him. After a short meditation, he opened with the Gospel according to Saint John, from the Bible, saying that since the students were all Christians, it was proper that he should begin with the Christian scriptures. As the classes went on, he taught from the Bhagavad Gītā, the Upanishads, the Vedānta Sutras, the Bhakti Sutras of Nārada, and other Hindu scriptures. He discussed Vedānta in its three aspects: the non-dualism of Śankara, the qualified non-dualism of Rāmānuja, and the dualism of Madhva. Since the subtleties of Śankara appeared difficult to the students, Rāmānuja remained the favourite among them. The Swami also spoke at length about Śri Ramakrishna, of his own daily life with the Master, and of his struggles with the tendency to unbelief and agnosticism. He told stories from the inexhaustible storehouse of Hindu mythology to illustrate his abstruse thoughts.

The ever recurring theme of his teaching was God-realization. He would always come back to the one, fundamental, vital point: "Find God. Nothing else matters." He emphasized morality as the basis of the spiritual life. Without truth, non-injury, continence, non-stealing, cleanliness, and austerity, he repeated, there could be no spirituality. The subject of continence always stirred him deeply. Walking up and down the room, getting more and more excited, he would stop before someone as if there were no one else present. "Don't you see," he would say eagerly, "there is a reason why chastity is insisted on in all monastic orders? Spiritual giants are produced only where the vow of chastity is observed. Don't you see there must be a reason? There is a connexion between chastity and spirituality. The explanation is that through prayer and meditation the saints have transmuted the most vital force in the body into spiritual energy. In India this is well understood and yogis do it consciously. The force so transmuted is called ojas, and it is stored up in the brain. It has been lifted from the lowest centre to the highest. 'And I, if I be lifted up, will draw all men unto me.'" He would plead with the students as if to beg them to act upon this teaching as something most precious. Further, they could not be the disciples he required if they were not established in chastity. He demanded a conscious transmutation. "The man who has no temper has nothing to control," he said. "I want a few, five or six, who are in the flower of their youth."

He would frequently exhort the students to attain freedom. As the words came in torrents from the depths of his soul, the atmosphere would be charged with the yearning to break free from the bondage of the body, a degrading humiliation. As he touched upon "this indecent clinging to life," the students would feel as if the curtain that hid the region beyond life and death were lifted for them, and they would long for that glorious freedom. "Āzād! Āzād! the Free! the Free!" he would cry, pacing back and forth like a caged lion; but for him the bars of the cage were not of iron, but of bamboo. "Let us not be caught this time," would be his refrain on other occasions.

Some of these precious talks were noted down by his disciple Miss S. Ellen Waldo and later published as Inspired Talks. Students of Swami Vivekananda will for ever remain indebted to her for faithfully preserving his immortal words, and the title of this book was well chosen, for they were indeed inspired. One day Miss Waldo was reading her notes to some tardy arrivals in the cottage while the Swami strode up and down the floor, apparently unconscious of what was going on. After the travellers had left the room, the Swami turned to Miss Waldo and said: "How could you have caught my thought and words so perfectly? It was as if I heard myself speaking."

During these seven weeks of teaching the Swami was most gentle and lovable. He taught his disciples as Śri Ramakrishna had taught him at Dakshineswar: the teaching was the outpouring of his own spirit in communion with himself. The Swami said later that he was at his best at Thousand Island Park. The ideas he cherished and expressed there grew, during the years that followed, into institutions, both in India and abroad.

The Swami's one consuming passion, during this time, was to show his students the way to freedom. "Ah," he said one day, with touching pathos, "if I could only set you free with a touch!" Two students arrived at the Park one dark and rainy night. One of them said, "We have come to you as we would go to Jesus if he were still on the earth and ask him to teach us." The Swami looked at them kindly and gently said, "If I only possessed the power of the Christ to set you free!" No wonder that Miss Waldo one day exclaimed, "What have we ever done to deserve all this?" And so felt the others also.

One cannot but be amazed at the manifestation of Swami Vivekananda's spiritual power at Thousand Island Park. Outwardly he was a young man of thirty-two. All his disciples at the cottage, except one, were older than himself. Yet everyone looked upon him as a father or mother. He had attained an unbelievable maturity. Some marvelled at his purity, some at his power, some at his intellectuality, some at his serenity, which was like the depths of the ocean, unperturbed by the waves of applause or contumely. When had he acquired all these virtues which had made him, at thirty, a teacher of men? From the foregoing pages the reader will have formed an idea of him as a stormy person, struggling, in early youth, against poverty and spiritual unbelief. Afterwards he is seen wandering from the Himālayas to Cape Comorin, raging against the grievances and sufferings of the Indian masses. During his first two years in America he had had to fight tooth and nail against malicious critics in order to establish his reputation as a religious teacher. When had he, then, tapped the secret spring of inner calmness and assurance without which a teacher cannot transmit spirituality to his disciples?

One must not forget that Vivekananda, as Ramakrishna had said, was not an ordinary man, but a nityasiddha, perfect even before birth, an Iśvarakoti, or special messenger of God born on earth to fulfil a divine mission. The silent but powerful influence of the guru always guided his feet. The outer world saw only the struggles and restlessness of his wandering days, but not the inner transformation brought about through the practice of purity, detachment, self-control, and meditation. The veil of māyā, without which no physical embodiment is possible, and which in him was very thin, was rent through the spiritual struggle of a few years. People were astonished to see his blossoming forth at Thousand Island Park.

At Dakshineswar, though Śri Ramakrishna had offered young Naren various supernatural powers of Yoga as a help for his future work, the disciple had refused to accept them, as being possible impediments to spiritual progress. But later these powers began to manifest themselves as the natural fruit of his spiritual realizations. Thus one sees him at Thousand Island Park reading the inmost soul of his followers before giving them initiation, and foretelling their future careers. He prophesied for Sister Christine extensive travels in Oriental countries and work in India. He explained that his method of foresight was simple, at least in the telling. He first thought of space—vast, blue, and extending everywhere. As he meditated on that space intently, pictures appeared, and he then gave interpretations of them which would indicate the future life of the person concerned.

Even before his arrival at Thousand Island Park the Swami had had other manifestations of such Yoga powers. For instance, while busy with his lecture tour, sometimes giving twelve or fourteen speeches a week, he would feel great physical and mental strain and often wonder what he would speak of the next day. Then he would hear, at dead of night, a voice shouting at him the very thoughts he was to present. Sometimes it would come from a long distance and then draw nearer and nearer, or again, it would be like someone delivering a lecture beside him as he lay listening in bed. At other times two voices would argue before him, discussing at great length ideas, some of which he had never before consciously heard or thought of, which he would find himself repeating the following day from the pulpit or the platform.

Sometimes people sleeping in the adjoining rooms would ask him in the morning: "Swami, with whom were you talking last night? We heard you talking loudly and enthusiastically and we were wondering." The Swami often explained these manifestations as the powers and potentialities of the soul generally called inspiration. He denied that they were miracles.

At that time he experienced the power of changing a person's life by a touch, or clearly seeing things happening at a great distance. But he seldom used these and the other powers he had acquired through Yoga. One day, much later, Swami Turiyananda entered the room while the Swami was lying on his bed, and beheld, in place of Vivekananda's physical body, a mass of radiance. It is no wonder that today in America, half a century later, one meets men and women who saw or heard Swami Vivekananda perhaps once, and still remember him vividly.

But it must not be thought that the Swami did not show his lighter mood at Thousand Island Park. He unfailingly discovered the little idiosyncrasies of the students and raised gales of laughter at the dinner-table, with some quip or jest—but never in sarcasm or malice. One of the inmates of the Dutcher Cottage was Dr. Wight, a very cultured man of well over seventy who had attended the Swami's classes and lectures in New York. He became so absorbed in the class talks that at the end of every discourse he would invariably ask the teacher: "Well, Swami, it all amounts to this in the end, doesn't it?—I *am* Brahman, I *am* the Absolute." The Swami would smile indulgently and answer gently, "Yes, Dockie, you are Brahman, you are the Absolute, in the real essence of your being." Later, when the learned doctor came to the table a trifle late, the Swami, with the utmost gravity but with a merry twinkle in his eyes, would say, "Here comes Brahman" or "Here is the Absolute."

Sometimes he would say, "Now I am going to cook for you, 'brethren.'" The food he cooked would be delicious, but too hot for Western tastes. The students, however, made up their minds to eat it even if it strangled them. After the meal was cooked, the Swami would stand in the door with a white napkin draped over his arm, in the fashion of the negro waiters in a dining-car, and intone in perfect imitation their call for dinner: "Last call fo' the dining cah. Dinner served." And the students would rock with laughter.

One day he was telling the disciples the story of Sitā and of the pure woman-hood of India. The question flashed in the mind of one of the women as to how some of the beautiful society queens would appear to him, especially those versed in the art of allurement. Even before the thought was expressed, the Swami said gravely, "If the most beautiful woman in the world were to look at me in an immodest or unwomanly way, she would immediately turn into a hideous green frog, and one does not, of course, admire frogs."

At last the day of the Swami's departure from Thousand Island Park arrived. It was Wednesday, August 7, 1895. In the morning he, Mrs. Funke, and Sister Christine went for a walk. They strolled about half a mile up the hill, where all was forest and solitude, and sat under a low-branched tree. The Swami suddenly said to them: "Now we shall meditate. We shall be like Buddha under the Bo-tree." He became still as a bronze statue. A thunderstorm came up and it poured; but the Swami did not notice anything. Mrs. Funke raised her umbrella and protected him as much as possible. When it was time to return, the Swami opened his eyes and said, "I feel once more I am in Calcutta in the rains." It is reported that one day at Thousand Island Park he experienced nirvikalpa samādhi.

At nine o'clock in the evening the Swami boarded the steamer for Clayton, where he was to catch the train for New York. While taking leave of the Islands he said, "I bless these Thousand Islands." As the steamer moved away, he boyishly and joyously waved his hat to the disciples still standing at the pier.

Some of his devotees thought that the Swami had planned at Thousand Island Park to start an organization. But they were mistaken. He wrote to a disciple:

We have no organization, nor want to build any. Each one is quite independent to teach, quite free to teach, whatever he or she likes. If you have the spirit within, you will never fail to attract others. . . . Individuality is my motto. I have no ambition beyond training individuals. I know very little; that little I teach without reserve; where I am ignorant I confess it. . . . I am a sannyāsin. As such I hold myself as a servant, not as a master, in this world.

Vivekananda, the awakener of souls, was indeed too great to be crammed within the confines of a narrow organization. He had had a unique experience of inner freedom at Thousand Island Park, which he expressed eloquently in his poem "The Song of the Sannyāsin." He wrote from there to a friend: "I am free, my bonds are cut, what do I care whether this body goes or does not go?

I have a truth to teach—I, the child of God. And He that gave me the truth will send me fellow workers from earth's bravest and best."

IN THE COMPANY OF SOME NOTABLES

A month after his return from Thousand Island Park, Swami Vivekananda sailed for Europe. Before we take up that important chapter of his life, however, it will be well to describe some of his interesting experiences in America, especially his meeting with noted personalities.

Robert Ingersoll, the famous orator and agnostic, and Swami Vivekananda had several conversations on religion and philosophy. Ingersoll, with a fatherly solicitude, asked the young enthusiast not to be too bold in the expression of his views, on account of people's intolerance of all alien religious ideas. "Forty years ago," he said, "you would have been hanged if you had come to preach in this country, or you would have been burnt alive. You would have been stoned out of the villages if you had come even much later." The Swami was surprised. But Ingersoll did not realize that the Indian monk, unlike him, respected all religions and prophets, and that he wanted to broaden the views of the Christians about Christ's teachings.

One day, in the course of a discussion, Ingersoll said to the Swami, "I believe in making the most of this world, in squeezing the orange dry, because this world is all we are sure of." He would have nothing to do with God, soul, or hereafter, which he considered as meaningless jargon. "I know a better way to squeeze the orange of this world than you do," the Swami replied, "and I get more out of it. I know I cannot die, so I am not in a hurry. I know that there is no fear, so I enjoy the squeezing. I have no duty, no bondage of wife and children and property, so I can love all men and women. Everyone is God to me. Think of the joy of loving man as God! Squeeze your orange my way, and you will get every single drop!" Ingersoll, it is reported, asked the Swami not to be impatient with his views, adding that his own unrelenting fight against traditional religions had shaken men's faith in theological dogmas and creeds, and thus helped to pave the way for the Swami's success in America.

Nikola Tesla, the great scientist who specialized in the field of electricity, was much impressed to hear from the Swami his explanation of the Sāmkhya cosmogony and the theory of cycles given by the Hindus. He was particularly struck by the resemblance between the Sāmkhya theory of matter and energy and that of modern physics. The Swami also met in New York Sir William Thomson (afterwards Lord Kelvin) and Professor Helmholtz, two leading representatives of Western science. Sarah Bernhardt, the famous French actress, had an interview with the Swami and greatly admired his teachings.

Madame Emma Calvé, the well-known prima donna, described the Swami as one who "truly walked with God." She came to see him in a state of physical and mental depression. The Swami, who did not at that time know even her name, talked to her about her worries and various personal problems. It was clear that he was familiar with them, even though she had never revealed them to him or to anyone else. When Madame Calvé expressed surprise, the Swami assured her that no one had talked to him about her. "Do you think that is necessary?" he asked. "I read you as I would an open book." He gave her this parting advice: "You must forget. Be gay and happy again. Do not dwell in silence upon your sorrows. Transmute your emotions into some form of external expression. Your spiritual health requires it. Your art demands it."

Madame Calvé later said: "I left him, deeply impressed by his words and his personality. He seemed to have emptied my brain of all its feverish complexities and placed there instead his clean and calming thoughts. I became once again vivacious and cheerful, thanks to the effect of his powerful will. He used no hypnosis, no mesmerism—nothing of that sort at all. It was the strength of his character, the purity and intensity of his purpose, that carried conviction. It seemed to me, when I came to know him better, that he lulled one's chaotic thoughts into a state of peaceful acquiescence, so that one could give complete and undivided attention to his words."

Like many people, Madame Calvé could not accept the Vedāntic doctrine of the individual soul's total absorption in the Godhead at the time of final liberation. "I cannot bear the idea," she said. "I cling to my individuality—unimportant though it may be. I don't want to be absorbed into an eternal unity." To this the Swami answered: "One day a drop of water fell into the vast ocean. Finding itself there, it began to weep and complain, just as you are doing. The giant ocean laughed at the drop of water. 'Why do you weep?' it asked. 'I do not understand. When you join me, you join all your brothers and sisters, the other drops of water of which I am made. You become the ocean itself. If you wish to leave me you have only to rise up on a sunbeam into the clouds. From there you can descend again, little drop of water, a blessing and a benediction to the thirsty earth.'"

Did not the Swami thus explain his own individuality? Before his present embodiment, he had remained absorbed in communion with the Absolute. Then he accepted the form of an individual to help humanity in its spiritual struggle. A giant soul like his is not content to remain eternally absorbed in the Absolute. Such also was the thought of Buddha.

In the company of great men and women, the Swami revealed his intellectual and spiritual power. But one sees his human side especially in his contact with humble people. In America he was often taken to be a negro. One day, as he alighted from a train in a town where he was to deliver a lecture, he was given a welcome by the reception committee. The most prominent townspeople were all there. A negro porter came up to him and said that he had heard how one of his own people had become great and asked the privilege of shaking hands with him. Warmly the Swami shook his hand, saying, "Thank you! Thank you, brother!" He never resented being mistaken for a negro. It happened many times, especially in the South, that he was refused admittance to a hotel, a barber shop, or a restaurant, because of his dark skin. When the Swami related these incidents to a Western disciple, he was promptly asked why he did not tell people that he was not a negro but a Hindu. "What!" the Swami replied indignantly. "Rise at the expense of another? I did not come to earth for that."

Swami Vivekananda was proud of his race and his dark complexion. "He was scornful," wrote Sister Nivedita, "in his repudiation of the pseudo-ethnology of privileged races. 'If I am grateful to my white-skinned Āryan ancestors,' he said, 'I am far more so to my yellow-skinned Mongolian ancestors, and most of all to the black-skinned negroids.' He was immensely proud of his physiognomy, especially of what he called his 'Mongolian jaw,' regarding it as a sign of 'bulldog tenacity of purpose.' Referring to this particular racial characteristic, which is believed to be behind every Āryan people, he one day exclaimed: 'Don't you see? The Tartar is the wine of the race! He gives energy and power to every blood.' "

The Swami had a strange experience in a small American town, where he was confronted by a number of college boys who had been living there on a ranch as cowboys. They heard him describe the power of concentration, through which a man could become completely oblivious of the outside world. So they decided to put him to test and invited him to lecture to them. A wooden tub was placed, with bottom up, to serve as a platform. The Swami commenced his address and soon appeared to be lost in his subject. Suddenly shots were fired in his direction, and bullets went whizzing past his ears. But the Swami continued his lecture as though nothing was happening. When he had finished, the young men flocked about him and congratulated him as a good fellow.

In his lectures and conversations the Swami showed a wonderful sense of humour. It was a saving feature in his strenuous life, and without it he might have broken down under the pressure of his intense thinking. Once, in one of his classes in Minneapolis, the Swami was asked by a student if Hindu mothers threw their children to the crocodiles in the river. Immediately came the reply: "Yes, Madam! They threw me in, but like your fabled Jonah, I got out again!" Another time, a lady became rather romantic about the Swami and said to him, "Swami! You are my Romeo and I am your Desdemona!" The Swami said quickly, "Madam, you'd better brush up your Shakespeare."

As already stated, Swami Vivekananda was particularly friendly with Mr. and Mrs. Hale, of Chicago, and their young daughters and two nieces, named Mary, Isabel, Harriet, and Jean. He affectionately called Mr. Hale "Father Pope" and Mrs. Hale "Mother Church." The girls he addressed as "sisters" or "babies." A very sweet and warm relationship grew up between them and the Swami. His relationship with the eldest girl, Mary, was especially close. He wrote to her many light-hearted letters. In a letter to the sisters, dated July 26, 1894, the Swami said:

Now, don't let my letters stray beyond the circle, please—I had a beautiful letter from Sister Mary—See how I am getting the dash—Sister Jeany teaches me all that—She can jump and run and play and swear like a devil and talk slang at the rate of five hundred a minute—only she does not much care for religion—only a little. . . . Darn it, I forget everything—I had duckings in the sea like a fish—I am enjoying every bit of it—What nonsense was the song Harriet taught me, "Dans la Plaine"—the deuce take it!—I told it to a French scholar and he laughed and laughed till the fellow was wellnigh burst at my wonderful translation—That is the way you would have taught me French—You are a pack of fools and heathens, I tell you—How you are gasping for breath like huge fish stranded—I am glad that you are sizzling[11]—Oh! how nice and cool it is here—and it is increased a hundredfold when I think about the gasping, sizzling, boiling, frying four old maids—and how cool and nice I am here—Whoooooo! ! ! . . .

Well—dear old maids—you sometimes have a glimpse of the lake and on very hot

[11] Referring to the summer heat of Chicago.

noons think of going down to the bottom of the lake—down—down—down—until it
is cool and nice, and then to lie down on the bottom, with just that coolness above and
around—and lie there still—silent—and just doze—not sleep, but a dreamy, dozing,
half unconscious sort of bliss—very much like that which opium brings—That is delicious—and drinking lots of iced water—Lord bless my soul!—I had such cramps several
times as would have killed an elephant—So I hope to keep myself away from the cold
water—

May you all be happy, dear fin de siècle young ladies, is the constant prayer of
VIVEKANANDA.

One realizes how deeply Swami Vivekananda had entered into the American
spirit, when one sees how facile he was in his use of American slang. Surely this
letter is an example. As we have stated before, the Swami also needed diversions
of this kind in order to obtain relief from his intensely serious life and thinking
in America. One recalls that Śri Ramakrishna, too, would often indulge in light
talk in order to keep his mind on the level of ordinary consciousness.

Shortly after his success at the Parliament of Religions, the Swami began,
as we have seen, to write to his devotees in India, giving them his plans for
India's regeneration. He urged them to take up work that would lead to better
systems of education and hygiene throughout India. He wanted a magazine to
be started for disseminating among his fellow countrymen the broad truths of
Vedānta, which would create confidence in their minds regarding their power
and potentialities, and give them back their lost individuality. He exhorted his
devotees to work especially for the uplift of women and the masses, without
whose help India would never be able to raise herself from her present state
of stagnation. He sent them money, earned through his lectures, for religious,
educational, and other philanthropic activities. His enthusiastic letters inspired
them. But they wanted him to return and take up the leadership. They were
also distressed to see the malicious propaganda against him by the Christian
missionaries in India. The Swami, however, repeatedly urged them to depend
upon themselves. "Stand on your own feet!" he wrote to them. "If you are
really my children, you will fear nothing, stop at nothing. You will be like lions.
You must rouse India and the whole world."

About the criticism from the Christian missionaries, he wrote: "The Christianity that is preached in India is quite different from what one sees here.
You will be astonished to hear that I have friends in this country amongst the
clergy of the Episcopal and Presbyterian Churches, who are as broad-minded,
as liberal, and as sincere as you are in your own religion. The real spiritual man—
everywhere—is broad-minded. His love forces him to be so. They to whom
religion is a trade are forced to become narrow-minded and mischievous by their
very introduction into religion of the competitive, fighting, selfish methods of
the world." He requested the Indian devotees not to pay any heed to what the
missionaries were saying either for or against him. "I shall work incessantly,"
he wrote, "until I die, and even after death I shall work for the good of the
world. Truth is infinitely more weighty than untruth. . . . It is the force of character, of purity, and of truth—of personality. So long as I have these things,

you can feel easy; no one will be able to injure a hair of my head. If they try, they will fail, saith the Lord."

FIRST VISIT TO EUROPE

For some time Swami Vivekananda had been planning a visit to London. He wished to sow the seed of Vedānta in the capital of the mighty British Empire. Miss Henrietta Muller had extended to him a cordial invitation to come to London, and Mr. E. T. Sturdy had requested him to stay at his home there. Mr. Leggett, too, had invited the Swami to come to Paris as his guest.

Mr. Francis H. Leggett, whose hospitality the Swami had already enjoyed at Percy, was a wealthy business man of New York. He and two ladies of his acquaintance, Mrs. William Sturges and Miss Josephine MacLeod (who were sisters), had attended the Swami's lectures in New York during the previous winter. They were all impressed by the Swami's personality and his message, and Mr. Leggett remarked, one day, that the teacher was a man of "great common sense." An intimate relationship gradually developed between the Swami, the two sisters, and Mr. Leggett. Mrs. Sturges, who was a widow, and Mr. Leggett became engaged and announced their engagement at the summer camp at Percy. They decided to be married in Paris, and Mr. Leggett invited the Swami to be a witness at the ceremony.

This invitation, coming at the same time as Miss Muller's and Mr. Sturdy's, seemed to the Swami, as he described it in a letter, a "divine call." The Swami's New York friends thought that a sea voyage would be most beneficial for his weary body and mind. At this time the Swami began to feel a premonition of his approaching end. One day he even said, "My day is done." But the awareness of his unfulfilled mission made him forget his body.

The Swami and Mr. Leggett sailed from New York about the middle of August 1895, reaching Paris by the end of the month. The French metropolis with its museums, churches, cathedrals, palaces, and art galleries impressed him as the centre of European culture, and he was introduced to a number of enlightened French people.

When Swami Vivekananda arrived in London he was enthusiastically greeted by Miss Muller, who had already met him in America, and Mr. Sturdy, who had studied Sanskrit and had to a certain degree practised asceticism in the Himā-layas. The Swami's mind, one can imagine, was filled with tumultuous thoughts as he arrived in the great city. He was eager to test his ability as an interpreter of the spiritual culture of India in the very citadel of the English-speaking nations. He also knew that he belonged to a subject race, which had been under the imperialistic domination of England for the past one hundred and fifty years. He attributed India's suffering, at least in part, to this alien rule. He was not unaware of the arrogance of the British ruling class in India, to whom India was a benighted country steeped in superstition. Would the Britishers give a patient hearing to the religion and philosophy of his ancestors, of which he was so proud? Would they not rather think that nothing good could ever come "out of Nazareth"? He did not, as we learn from his own confession, set foot on English soil with the friendliest of feelings. But how he felt when he left England after his short visit will be presently described.

After a few days' rest the Swami quietly began his work. Through friends he was gradually introduced to people who were likely to be interested in his thoughts; he also devoted part of his time to visiting places of historical interest. Within three weeks of his arrival he was already engaged in strenuous activity. A class was started and soon the hall was found inadequate to accommodate the students. Newspapers interviewed him and called him the "Hindu yogi." Lady Isabel Margesson and several other members of the nobility became attracted to the Swami's teachings. His first public lecture was attended by many educated and thoughtful people; some of the leading newspapers were enthusiastic about it. The *Standard* compared his moral stature with that of Rammohan Roy and Keshab Chandra Sen. The *London Daily Chronicle* wrote that he reminded people of Buddha. Even the heads of churches showed their warm appreciation.

But the Swami's greatest acquisition in London was Miss Margaret E. Noble, who later became his disciple, consecrating her life to women's education in India. She also espoused the cause of India's political freedom and inspired many of its leaders with her written and spoken words.

Miss Noble, the fourth child of Samuel Noble, was born in Northern Ireland in 1867. Both her grandfather and her father were Protestant ministers in the Wesleyan church and took active part in the political agitation for the freedom of Ireland. Her grandmother and her father gave her instruction in the Bible.

Her father, who died at the age of thirty-four, had a premonition of his daughter's future calling. One of the last things he whispered to his wife was about Margaret. "When God calls her," he said, "let her go. She will spread her wings. She will do great things."

After finishing her college education, Margaret took the position of a teacher at Keswick, in the English Lake District, where contact with the High Church stirred her religious emotions. Next she taught in an orphanage in Rugby, where she shared the manual labour of the pupils. At twenty-one, Miss Noble was appointed as mistress at the secondary school in Wrexham, a large mining centre, and participated in the welfare activities of the town, visiting slum households and looking for waifs and strays. Next she went to Chester and taught a class of eighteen-year-old girls. Here she delved into the educational systems of Pestalozzi and Froebel. And finally she came to London, where, in the autumn of 1895, she opened her own school, the Ruskin School, in Wimbledon.

The metropolis of the British Empire offered Miss Noble unlimited opportunities for the realization of her many latent desires—political, literary, and educational. Here she joined the "Free Ireland" group, working for Ireland's home rule. She was also cordially received at Lady Ripon's exclusive salon, where art and literature were regularly discussed. This salon later developed into the Sesame Club, with rooms in Dover Street, where Bernard Shaw, T. H. Huxley, and other men of literature and science discussed highly intellectual subjects. Margaret Noble became the secretary of the club, and lectured on "The Psychology of the Child" and "The Rights of Women." Thus even before she met Swami Vivekananda she was unconsciously preparing the ground for her future activities in India.

At this time Margaret suffered a cruel blow. She was deeply in love with a man and had even set the wedding date. But another woman suddenly snatched him away. A few years before, another young man, to whom she was about to be engaged, had died of tuberculosis. These experiences shocked her profoundly, and she began to take a more serious interest in religion. She was very fond of a simple prayer by Thomas à Kempis: "Be what thou prayest to be made."

One day her art teacher, Ebenezer Cook, said to Margaret: "Lady Isabel Margesson is inviting a few friends to her house to hear a Hindu Swami speak. Will you come?" Swami Vivekananda had already been a topic of discussion among certain members of the Sesame Club. Mr. E. T. Sturdy and Miss Henrietta Muller had told of his extraordinary success in America as a preacher and orator.

Miss Noble first met Swami Vivekananda on a Sunday evening in the drawing-room of Lady Isabel Margesson, situated in the fashionable West End of London. He was to address a group of people on Hindu thought. Miss Noble was one of the last to arrive. Fifteen people sat in the room in absolute silence. She nervously felt as if all eyes were turned on her, and as she took the first vacant chair, she gathered her skirt to sit down without making any noise. The Swami sat facing her. A coal fire burnt on the hearth behind him. She noticed that he was tall and well built and possessed an air of deep serenity. The effect of his long practice of meditation was visible in the gentleness and loftiness of his look, which, as she was to write later, "Raphael has perhaps painted for us on the brow of the Sistine Child."

The Swami looked at Lady Isabel with a sweet smile, as she said: "Swamiji, all our friends are here." He chanted some Sanskrit verses. Miss Noble was impressed by his melodious voice. She heard the Swami say, among other things: "All our struggle is for freedom. We seek neither misery nor happiness, but freedom, freedom alone."

It was at first difficult for Miss Noble to accept Swami Vivekananda's views. But before he left London she had begun to address him as "Master."

Recalling those first meetings in London, and their decisive influence on her life, Nivedita wrote in 1904 to a friend: "Suppose he had not come to London that time! Life would have been like a headless dream, for I always knew that I was waiting for something. I always said that a call would come. And it did. But if I had known more of life, I doubt whether, when the time came, I should certainly have recognized it. Fortunately, I knew little and was spared that torture. . . . Always I had this burning voice within, but nothing to utter. How often and often I sat down, pen in hand, to speak, and there was no speech! And now there is no end to it! As surely I am fitted to my world, so surely is my world in need of me, waiting—ready. The arrow has found its place in the bow. But if he had not come! If he had meditated, on the Himalayan peaks! . . . I, for one, had never been here."

Swami Vivekananda and Mr. Sturdy soon began an English translation of the Bhakti aphorisms of Nārada. At this time the idea came to the Swami's mind that a religion could not have a permanent hold upon people without organization and rituals. A mere loose system of philosophy, he realized, soon lost its appeal. He saw the need, therefore, of formulating rituals, on the basis of the

Upanishadic truths, which would serve a person from birth to death—rituals that would prepare for the ultimate realization of the supra-mental Absolute.

His stay in England was very short, but his insight enabled him to appraise the English character with considerable accuracy. He wrote to a devotee on November 18, 1895: "In England my work is really splendid. I am astonished myself at it. The English do not talk much in the newspapers, but they work silently. I am sure of having done more work in England than in America." And in another letter, written on November 13, to a brother disciple in India: "Every enterprise in this country takes some time to get started. But once John Bull sets his hand to a thing, he will never let it go. The Americans are quick, but they are somewhat like straw on fire, ready to be extinguished."

The Swami had been receiving letters from American devotees asking him to come back; a rich lady from Boston promised to support his work in New York throughout the winter. Before leaving England, however, he arranged that Mr. Sturdy should conduct the classes in London till the arrival of a new Swami from India, about the need of whom he was writing constantly to his brother disciples at the Baranagore monastery.

ESTABLISHING THE WORK IN AMERICA

On December 6, 1895, Swami Vivekananda returned to New York, after his two months' stay in England, in excellent health and spirits. During his absence abroad, regular classes had been carried on by his American disciples Kripananda, Abhayananda, and Miss Waldo, who taught rāja-yoga in both its practical and its theoretical aspects.

Together with Kripananda he took up new quarters, consisting of two spacious rooms, which could accommodate one hundred and fifty persons. The Swami at once plunged into activity and gave a series of talks on work as a spiritual discipline. These talks were subsequently published as *Karma-Yoga*, which is considered one of his best books. In the meantime the devotees of the Swami had been feeling the need of a stenographer to take down his talks in the classes and on public platforms. Many of his precious speeches had already been lost because there had been no reporter to record them. Fortunately there appeared on the scene an Englishman, J. J. Goodwin, who was at first employed as a professional stenographer; in a few days, however, he was so impressed by the Swami's life and message that he became his disciple and offered his services free, with the remark that if the teacher could give his whole life to help mankind, he, the disciple, could at least give his services as an offering of love. Goodwin followed the Swami like a shadow in America, Europe, and India; he recorded many of the public utterances of Vivekananda, now preserved in published books, and thereby earned the everlasting gratitude of countless men and women.

The Swami spent Christmas of 1895 with Mr. and Mrs. Leggett at their country home, Ridgely Manor, which he frequently visited in order to enjoy a respite from his hard work in New York. But even there he would give exalted spiritual discourses, as will be evident from the following excerpt from a letter written by Mr. Leggett on January 10, 1896, to Miss MacLeod:

One night at Ridgely we were all spellbound by his eloquence. Such thought I have never heard expressed by mortal man—such as he uttered for two and a half hours. We were all deeply affected. And I would give a hundred dollars for a typewritten verbatim report of it. Swami was inspired to a degree that I have never seen before or since. He leaves us soon and perhaps we shall never see him again, but he will leave an ineffaceable impress on our hearts that will comfort us to the end of our earthly careers.

After a short visit to Boston as the guest of Mrs. Ole Bull, the Swami commenced a series of public lectures in New York at Hardeman Hall, the People's Church, and later at Madison Square Garden, which had a seating capacity of fifteen hundred people. In the last mentioned place he gave his famous lectures on love as a spiritual discipline, which were subsequently published as *Bhakti-Yoga*. Both the lectures of the Swami and his personality received favourable comment from the newspapers. He initiated into monastic life Dr. Street, who assumed the name of Yogananda.

Mrs. Ella Wheeler Wilcox, one of the founders of the New Thought movement in America, spoke highly of the Swami's teachings. She and her husband first went to hear him out of curiosity, and what happened afterwards may be told in her own words:

Before we had been ten minutes in the audience, we felt ourselves lifted up into an atmosphere so rarefied, so vital, so wonderful, that we sat spellbound and almost breathless to the end of the lecture. When it was over we went out with new courage, new hope, new strength, new faith, to meet life's daily vicissitudes. . . . It was that terrible winter of financial disasters, when banks failed and stocks went down like broken balloons, and business men walked through the dark valleys of despair, and the whole world seemed topsy-turvy. Sometimes after sleepless nights of worry and anxiety, my husband would go with me to hear the Swami lecture, and then he would come out into the winter gloom and walk down the street smiling and say: "It is all right. There is nothing to worry over." And I would go back to my own duties and pleasures with the same uplifted sense of soul and enlarged vision. . . . "I do not come to convert you to a new belief," he said. "I want you to keep your own belief; I want to make the Methodist a better Methodist, the Presbyterian a better Presbyterian, the Unitarian a better Unitarian. I want to teach you to live the truth, to reveal the light within your own soul." He gave the message that strengthened the man of business, that caused the frivolous society woman to pause and think; that gave the artist new aspirations; that imbued the wife and mother, the husband and father, with a larger and a holier comprehension of duty.

Having finished his work in New York, the Swami, accompanied by Goodwin, left for Detroit. The main theme of his lectures and class talks there was bhakti, or love of God. At that time he was all love. A kind of divine madness seemed to have taken possession of him, as if his heart would burst with longing for the beloved Mother. He gave his last public lecture at Temple Beth-El, of which Rabbi Louis Grossman, an ardent admirer of the Swami, was the leader. The Swami cast a spell, as it were, over the whole audience. "Never," wrote Mrs. Funke, "had I seen the Master look as he looked that night. There was something in his beauty not of earth. It was as if the spirit had almost burst the bonds of flesh, and it was then that I saw a foreshadowing of the end. He was much exhausted from the years of overwork, and it was even then to be seen that he was not long for this world. I tried to close my eyes to it, but in my heart I knew the truth. He had needed rest but felt that he must go on."

The idea that his years were numbered came to Swami Vivekananda again and again. He would often say at this time, "Oh, the body is a terrible bondage!" or "How I wish that I could hide myself for ever!" The note-book that he had carried during his wanderings in India contained these significant words: "Now to seek a corner and lay myself down to die!" In a letter to a friend, he quoted these words and said: "Yet all this karma remained. I hope I have now worked it out. It appears like a hallucination that I was in these childish dreams of doing this and doing that. I am getting out of them. . . . Perhaps these mad desires were necessary to bring me over to this country. And I thank the Lord for the experience."

On March 25, 1896, he delivered his famous lecture on "The Philosophy of Vedānta" before the graduate students of the philosophy department of Harvard University. It produced such an impression that he was offered the Chair of Eastern Philosophy in the university. Later a similar offer came from Columbia University. But he declined both on the ground that he was a sannyāsin.

In February 1896, Swami Vivekananda established the Vedānta Society of New York as a non-sectarian organization with the aim of preaching the universal principles of Vedānta. Tolerance and religious universalism formed its motto, and its members generally came to be known as "Vedāntins."

In the meantime the Swami's great works Rāja-Yoga, Bhakti-Yoga, and Karma-Yoga were receiving marked attention from many thoughtful people of the country. The Swami was serious about organizing Hinduism on a sound, universal, ethical, and rational basis so that it would appeal to earnest thinkers in all parts of the world. He wanted to reinterpret, in keeping with the methods of modern science, the Hindu view of the soul, the Godhead, the relationship between matter and energy, and cosmology. Further, he wanted to classify the apparently contradictory passages of the Upanishads bearing on the doctrines of dualism, qualified non-dualism, and absolute non-dualism, and show their ultimate reconciliation. In order to achieve this end, he asked his devotees in India to send him the Upanishads and the Vedānta Sutras with their commentaries by the leading āchāryas, and also the Brāhmana portions of the Vedas, and the Purānas. He himself wanted to write this Maximum Testamentum, this Universal Gospel, in order to translate Hindu thought into Western language. He expressed his objective in a letter written to one of his disciples on February 17, 1896:

To put the Hindu ideas into English and then make out of dry philosophy and intricate mythology and queer, startling psychology, a religion which shall be easy, simple, popular, and at the same time meet the requirements of the highest minds, is a task which only those can understand who have attempted it. The abstract Advaita must become living—poetic—in everyday life; and out of bewildering yogism must come the most scientific and practical psychology—and all this must be put into such a form that a child may grasp it. That is my life's work. The Lord only knows how far I shall succeed. To work we have the right, not to the fruits thereof.

The Swami always wanted a healthy interchange of ideas between East and West; this was one of the aims of the Vedānta Society of New York. He felt the need of centres of vital and continual communication between the two worlds to make "open doors, as it were, through which the East and the West could pass freely back and forth, without a feeling of strangeness, as from one home to another." Already he had thought of bringing to America some of his brother disciples as preachers of Vedānta. He also wanted to send some of his American and English disciples to India to teach science, industry, technology, economics, applied sociology, and other practical things which the Indians needed in order to improve their social conditions and raise their standard of living. He often told his American disciples of his vision that the time would come when the lines of demarcation between East and West would be obliterated. From England he had already written to Swami Saradananda to prepare to come to the West.

In the spring of 1896 letters began to pour in from England beseeching Swami Vivekananda to return there and continue his activities. The Swami felt the need of concentrating on the work in both London and New York, the two great metropolises of the Western world. Therefore he made arrangements with Miss Waldo and other qualified disciples to continue his program in America during his absence. Mr. Francis Leggett was made the president of the Vedānta Society.

The Swami had also been receiving letters from his friends in India begging for his return. He said he would come as soon as possible, but he encouraged them to organize the work, warning them against the formation of any new cult around the person of Śri Ramakrishna, who, to the Swami, was the demonstration of the eternal principles of Hinduism. On April 14, 1896, he wrote to India: "That Ramakrishna Paramahamsa was God—and all that sort of thing—has no go in countries like this. M——— has a tendency to put that stuff down everybody's throat; but that will make our movement a little sect. You keep separate from such attempts; at the same time, if people worship him as God, no harm. Neither encourage nor discourage. The masses will always have the person; the higher ones, the principle. We want both. But principles are universal, not persons. Therefore stick to the principles he taught, and let people think whatever they like of his person."

The Swami now made definite arrangements to leave for London on April 15, and, after carrying out his plans there, to sail for his motherland.

It should be apparent to readers of Swami Vivekananda's life that he worked under great pressure, from a fraction of which a lesser person would have collapsed in no time. Naturally he spent his few spare moments in fun and joking. He would read a copy of *Punch* or some other comic paper, and laugh till tears rolled down his cheeks. He loved to tell the story of a Christian missionary who was sent to preach to the cannibals. The new arrival proceeded to the chief of the tribe and asked him, "Well, how did you like my predecessor?" The cannibal replied, smacking his lips, "Simply de-li-cious!"

Another was the story of a "darky" clergyman who, while explaining the creation, shouted to his congregation: "You see, God was a-makin' Adam, and He was a-makin' him out o' mud. And when He got him made, He stuck him up agin a fence to dry. And den—" "Hold on, dar, preacher!" suddenly cried out a learned listener. "What's dat about dis 'ere fence? Who's made dis fence?" The preacher replied sharply: "Now you listen 'ere, Sam Jones. Don't you be askin' sich questions. You'll be a-smashin' up all theology!"

By way of relaxation he would often cook an Indian meal at a friend's house. On such occasions he brought out from his pockets tiny packets of finely ground spices. He would make hot dishes which his Western disciples could hardly eat without burning their tongues. They were, no doubt, soothing to his high-strung temperament.

But the Swami's brain was seething with new ideas all the time. He very much wanted to build a "Temple Universal" where people of all faiths would gather to worship the Godhead through the symbol Om, representing the un-differentiated Absolute. At another time, in the beginning of the year 1895, he wrote to Mrs. Bull about buying one hundred and eight acres of land in the Catskill Mountains where his students would build camps and practice medi-tation and other disciplines during the summer holidays.

A touching incident, which occurred in 1894, may be told here; it shows the high respect in which some of the ladies of Cambridge, Massachusetts, held the Swami and his mother. The Swami one day spoke to them about "The Ideals of Indian Women," particularly stressing the ideal of Indian motherhood. They were greatly moved. The following Christmas they sent the Swami's mother in India a letter together with a beautiful picture of the Child Jesus on the lap of the Virgin Mary. They wrote in the letter: "At this Christmastide, when the gift of Mary's son to the world is celebrated and rejoiced over with us, it would seem the time of remembrance. We, who have your son in our midst, send you greetings. His generous service to men, women, and children in our midst was laid at your feet by him, in an address he gave us the other day on the Ideals of Motherhood in India. The worship of his mother will be to all who heard him an inspiration and an uplift."

The Swami often spoke to his disciples about his mother's wonderful self-control, and how on one occasion she had gone without food for fourteen days. He acknowledged that her character was a constant inspiration to his life and work.

The love and adoration in which the Swami was held by his Western disciples can hardly be over-emphasized. Some described him as the "lordly monk," and some as a "grand seigneur." Mrs. Leggett said that in all her experience she had met only two celebrated personages who could make one feel perfectly at ease without for an instant losing their own dignity, and one of them was Swami Vivekananda. Sister Nivedita described him aptly as a Plato in thought and a modern Savonarola in his fearless outspokenness. William James of Harvard addressed him as "Master" and referred to him in Varieties of Religious Experi-ence as the "paragon of Vedāntists."

MEETING WITH MAX MÜLLER

A pleasant surprise awaited Swami Vivekananda on his arrival in London. Swami Saradananda had already come and was staying as the guest of Mr. Sturdy. The two Swamis had not seen each other in a very long time. Swami

Vivekananda was told all the news of his spiritual brothers at the Alambazar monastery and their activities in India. It was a most happy occasion.

Swami Vivekananda soon plunged into a whirlwind of activity. From the beginning of May he conducted five classes a week and a Friday session for open discussion. He gave a series of three Sunday lectures in one of the galleries of the Royal Institute of Painters in Water-Colours, in Piccadilly, and also lectured at Princes' Hall and the Lodge of Annie Besant, in addition to speaking at many clubs, and in educational institutions and drawing-rooms. His audiences consisted mostly of intellectual and serious-minded people. His speeches on jnāna-yoga, containing the essence of the Vedānta philosophy, were mostly given in England. Canon Wilberforce held a reception in the Swami's honour, to which he invited many distinguished people.

At one of the meetings, at the close of his address, a white-haired and well-known philosopher said to the Swami: "You have spoken splendidly, sir, but you have told us nothing new." Quick came the Swami's reply: "Sir, I have told you the Truth. That, the Truth, is as old as the immemorial hills, as old as humanity, as old as creation, as old as the Great God. If I have told you in such words as will make you think, make you live up to your thinking, do I not do well in telling it?" Loud applause greeted him at the end of these remarks.

The Swami was quick in repartee. During the question period a man, who happened to be a native of Scotland, asked, "What is the difference between a baboo and a baboon?"[12] "Oh, not much," was the instantaneous reply of the Swami. "It is like the difference between a sot and a Scot—just the difference of a letter."

In one of his public lectures in England he paid the most touching tribute to his Master, Śri Ramakrishna. He said that he had not one little word of his own to utter, not one infinitesimal thought of his own to unfold; everything, every single thing, all that he was himself, all that he could be to others, all that he might do for the world, came from that single source, from that pure soul, from that illimitable inspiration, from him who, seated "there in my beloved India, had solved the tremendous secret, and bestowed the solution on all, ungrudgingly and with divine prodigality." The Swami's own self was utterly forgotten, altogether ignored. "I am what I am, and what I am is always due to him; whatever in me or in my words is good and true and eternal came to me from his mouth, his heart, his soul. Śri Ramakrishna is the spring of this phase of the earth's religious life, of its impulses and activities. If I can show the world one glimpse of my Master, I shall not have lived in vain."

It was Ramakrishna who brought him in contact with Max Müller, the great German Sanskritist and Indologist, who had been impressed by the eloquence of Keshab Chandra Sen and his religious fervour, and had also come to know of the influence that Śri Ramakrishna had exerted in the development of Keshab's life. From the information that he had been able to gather from India, Max Müller had already published an article on Ramakrishna in the

[12] In Northern India the word baboo is used at the end of a man's first name as a sign of respect, somewhat as the English word Mr. before the name of a gentleman. The questioner was evidently making fun of the Swami.

Nineteenth Century, entitled "A Real Mahātman." Now he was eager to meet a direct disciple of the Master, and invited Swami Vivekananda to lunch with him in Oxford on May 28, 1896.

The Swami was delighted to meet the savant. When the name of Rama-krishna was mentioned, the Swami said, "He is worshipped by thousands today, Professor."

"To whom else shall worship be accorded, if not to such?" was Max Müller's reply.

Regarding Max Müller and his wife, the Swami later wrote:

The visit was really a revelation to me. That little white house, its setting in a beauti-ful garden, the silver-haired sage, with a face calm and benign, and forehead smooth as a child's in spite of seventy winters, and every line in that face speaking of a deep-seated mine of spirituality somewhere behind; that noble wife, the helpmate of his life through his long and arduous task of exciting interest, overriding opposition and contempt, and at last creating a respect for the thoughts of the sages of ancient India—the trees, the flowers, the calmness, and the clear sky—all these sent me back in imagination to the glorious days of ancient India, the days of our brahmarshis[13] and rājarshis,[14] the days of the great vānaprasthins,[15] the days of Arundhatis and Vaśishthas.[16] It was neither the philologist nor the scholar that I saw, but a soul that is every day realizing its oneness with the universe.

The Swami was deeply affected to see Max Müller's love for India. "I wish," he wrote enthusiastically, "I had a hundredth part of that love for my mother-land. Endowed with an extraordinary, and at the same time an intensely active, mind, he has lived and moved in the world of Indian thought for fifty years or more, and watched the sharp interchange of light and shade in the interminable forest of Sanskrit literature with deep interest and heartfelt love, till they have sunk into his very soul and coloured his whole being."

The Swami asked Max Müller: "When are you coming to India? All men there would welcome one who has done so much to place the thoughts of their ancestors in a true light."

The face of the aged sage brightened up; there was almost a tear in his eye, a gentle nodding of the head, and slowly the words came out: "I would not return then; you would have to cremate me there."

Further questions on the Swami's part seemed an unwarranted intrusion into realms wherein were stored the holy secrets of a man's heart.

Max Müller asked the Swami, "What are you doing to make Śrī Rama-krishna known to the world?" He himself was eager to write a fuller biography of the Master if he could only procure the necessary materials. At the Swami's request, Swami Saradananda wrote down the sayings of Śrī Ramakrishna and the facts of his life. Later Max Müller embodied these in his book *The Life and Sayings of Śrī Ramakrishna.*

One day Saradananda asked the Swami why he himself had not written about the Master's life for Max Müller. He answered: "I have such deep feeling for

---

[13] Sages illumined by the Knowledge of Brahman.

[14] Kings illumined by the Knowledge of Brahman.

[15] A vānaprasthin is a man who, during the third stage of life, lives with his wife in solitude, both devoting themselves to the contemplation of the Godhead.

[16] Arundhati was the wife of the great Hindu sage Vaśishtha.

the Master that it is impossible for me to write about him for the public. If I had written the article Max Müller wanted, then I would have proved, quoting from philosophies, the scriptures, and even the holy books of the Christians, that Ramakrishna was the greatest of all prophets born in this world. That would have been too much for the old man. You have not thought so deeply about the Master as I have; hence you could write in a way that would satisfy Max Müller. Therefore I asked you to write."

Max Müller showed the Swami several colleges in Oxford and the Bodleian Library, and at last accompanied him to the railroad station. To the Swami's protest that the professor should not take such trouble, the latter said, "It is not every day that one meets with a disciple of Ramakrishna Paramahamsa."

Besides doing intensive public work in England, the Swami made there some important personal contacts. The names of Goodwin, Henrietta Muller, Margaret Noble, and Sturdy have already been mentioned. These knew him intimately during his second visit and had become his disciples. Now came the turn of Captain and Mrs. Sevier. The captain was a retired officer of the English army, forty-nine years old, and had served for many years in India. Both were earnest students of religion and had sought the highest truth in various sects and creeds, but had not found it anywhere. When they heard Swami Vivekananda, they intuitively realized that his teachings were what they had so long sought. They were deeply impressed by the non-dualistic philosophy of India and the Swami's personality.

Coming out of one of the Swami's lectures, Captain Sevier asked Miss MacLeod, who had already known the Swami in America: "You know this young man? Is he what he seems?"

"Yes."

"In that case one must follow him and with him find God."

The Captain went to his wife and said, "Will you let me become the Swami's disciple?"

"Yes," she replied.

She asked him, "Will you let me become the Swami's disciple?"

He replied with affectionate humour, "I am not so sure!"

The very first time the Swami met Mrs. Sevier in private he addressed her as "Mother" and asked her if she would not like to come to India, adding, "I will give you my best realizations."

A very affectionate relationship sprang up between the Swami and the Seviers, and the latter regarded him as their son. They became his intimate companions and offered him all their savings. But the Swami, anxious about their future worldly security, persuaded them to keep the greater portion of their fortune. Captain and Mrs. Sevier, together with Miss Noble and Goodwin, were the choicest among the followers that Swami Vivekananda gathered in England, and all of them remained faithful to him and his work till the last days of their lives.

Through the generosity of the Seviers, the Swami, as will be seen, established the Advaita Āśrama at Mayavati in the Himālayas for the training of his disciples, both Eastern and Western, in the contemplation of the Impersonal Godhead. After Captain Sevier's death in the monastery, Mrs. Sevier lived there for fifteen years—the only Western woman in that remote region of the mountains, which is inaccessible for long months of the year—busying herself with the education of the children of the neighbouring hills. Once Miss MacLeod asked her, "Do you not get bored?" "I think of him," she replied, referring to Swami Vivekananda.

Though preoccupied with various activities in England, the Swami never for one moment forgot his work in India. After all, it had been his intense desire to find means to ameliorate the condition of his countrymen that had brought him to the West. That hope he always cherished in a corner of his mind, both in Europe and in America. He had to train his brother disciples as future workers in India. And so he is seen writing to them in detail regarding the organization of the monastery at Alambazar, where they had been living for some time.

On April 27, 1896, he sent instructions about the daily life of the monks, their food and clothing, their intercourse with the public, and about the provision of a spacious library at the monastery, a smaller room for interviews, a big hall for religious discussions with the devotees, a small room for an office, another for smoking, and so forth and so on. He advised them to furnish the rooms in the simplest manner and to keep an eye on the water for drinking and cooking. The monastery, he suggested, should be under the management of a President and a Secretary to be elected by vote. Study, preaching, and religious practices should be important items among the duties of the inmates. He also desired to establish a math for women, directly under the control of the Holy Mother. The monks were not to visit the women's quarters. In conclusion, he recommended Swami Brahmananda as the President of the math, and said: "He who is the servant of all is their true master. He never becomes a leader in whose love there is a consideration of high or low. He whose love knows no end and never stops to consider high or low has the whole world lying at his feet." For his workers the Swami wanted men with "muscles of iron and nerves of steel, inside which dwells a mind of the same material as that of which the thunderbolt is made."

To quote the Swami's words again: "I want strength, manhood, kshatra-virya, or the virility of a warrior, and brahma-teja, or the radiance of a brāhmin. . . . These men will stand aside from the world, give their lives, and be ready to fight the battle of Truth, marching on from country to country. One blow struck outside of India is equal to a hundred thousand struck within. Well, all will come if the Lord wills it."

TOUR IN EUROPE

The Swami was exhausted by his strenuous work in England. Three of his intimate disciples, the Seviers and Henrietta Muller, proposed a holiday tour on the continent. He was "as delighted as a child" at the prospect. "Oh! I long to see the snows and wander on the mountain paths," he said. He recalled his travels in the Himālayas. On July 31, 1896, the Swami, in the company of his three friends, left for Switzerland. They visited Geneva, Mer-de-Glace, Montreux, Chillon, Chamounix, the St. Bernard, Lucerne, the Rigi, Zermatt, and Schaffhausen. The Swami felt exhilarated by his walks in the Alps. He wanted to climb Mont Blanc, but gave up the idea when told of the difficulty of the ascent. He found that Swiss peasant life and its manners and customs resembled those of the people who dwelt in the Himālayas.

In a little village at the foot of the Alps between Mont Blanc and the Little St. Bernard, he conceived the idea of founding a monastery in the Himālayas. He said to his companions: "Oh, I long for a monastery in the Himālayas, where I can retire from the labours of my life and spend the rest of my days in meditation. It will be a centre for work and meditation, where my Indian and Western disciples can live together, and I shall train them as workers. The former will go out as preachers of Vedānta to the West, and the latter will devote their lives to the good of India."

Mr. Sevier, speaking for himself and his wife, said: "How nice it would be, Swami, if this could be done. We must have such a monastery."

The dream was fulfilled through the Advaita Āśrama at Mayavati, which commands a magnificent view of the eternal snows of the Himālayas.

In the Alps the Swami enjoyed some of the most lucid and radiant moments of his spiritual life. Sometimes he would walk alone, absorbed in thought, the disciples keeping themselves at a discreet distance. One of the disciples said: "There seemed to be a great light about him, and a great stillness and peace. Never have I seen the Swami to such advantage. He seemed to communicate spirituality by a look or with a touch. One could almost read his thoughts, which were of the highest, so transfigured had his personality become."

While still wandering in the Alps, the Swami received a letter from the famous orientalist, Paul Deussen, Professor of Philosophy at the University of Kiel. The professor urgently invited the Swami to visit him. The Swami accepted the invitation and changed his itinerary. He arrived at Kiel after visiting Heidelberg, Coblenz, Cologne, and Berlin. He was impressed by the material power and the great culture of Germany.

Professor Deussen was well versed in Sanskrit, and was perhaps the only scholar in Europe who could speak that language fluently. A disciple of Schopenhauer and follower of Kant, Deussen could easily appreciate the high flights of Śankarāchārya's philosophy. He believed that the system of Vedānta, as founded on the Upanishads and the Vedānta Sutras, is one of the "most majestic structures and valuable products of the genius of man in his search for Truth, and that the highest and purest morality is the immediate consequence of Vedānta."

The Swami and the Seviers were cordially received by the German scholar. In the course of the conversation Deussen said that a movement was being made back towards the fountainhead of spirituality, a movement that would in the future probably make India the spiritual leader of the nations, the highest and the greatest spiritual influence on earth. He also found in the Swami a vivid demonstration of concentration and control of the mind. On one occasion he saw his guest turning over the pages of a poetical work and did not receive any response to a query. Afterwards the Swami apologized, saying that he had been so absorbed in the book that he did not hear the professor. Then he repeated the verses from the book. The conversation soon turned to the power of concentration as developed in the Yoga philosophy. One of the purposes of Deussen's meeting the Swami, it is said, was his desire to learn from the latter the secrets of the Yoga powers.

Deussen showed the Swami the city of Kiel. Thereafter the Swami wished to leave immediately for England, though the professor insisted that he should stay at Kiel a few days more. As that was not possible, Deussen joined the party in Hamburg and they travelled together in Holland. After spending three days in Amsterdam all arrived in London, and for two weeks Deussen met with the Swami daily. The Swami also visited Max Müller again at Oxford.

Swami Vivekananda spent another two months in England, giving lectures and seeing important men of their day, such as Edward Carpenter, Frederick Myers, Canon Wilberforce, and Moncure D. Conway. The most notable lectures he gave at this time were those on māyā, about which he spoke on three occasions, dealing with its various aspects. It is said that some members of the British royal family attended these lectures incognito. He created such an intense atmosphere during these talks that the whole audience was transported into a realm of ecstatic consciousness, and some burst into tears. The lectures were the most learned and eloquent among his speeches on non-dualistic Vedānta.

Swami Abhedananda arrived from India, and Vivekananda was immensely pleased to have his brother disciple assist him in his foreign work. The maiden speech of Abhedananda at a club in Bloomsbury Square, on October 27, was highly appreciated by all, and the Swami said about his spiritual brother, "Even if I perish on this plane, my message will be sounded through these dear lips, and the world will hear it." The report of the continued popularity of Swami Saradananda, who had in the meantime gone to New York, likewise gratified him.

Despite the rush of his European work Swami Vivekananda maintained his contact with America. He took a personal interest in the spiritual development of his students. The affectionate relationship of the Swami with the Hale family of Chicago has been mentioned before, especially with the four unmarried girls. Hearing of the proposed marriage of Harriet, he wrote to her on September 17, 1896, "Marriage is the truest goal for ninety-nine per cent of the human race, and they will live the happiest life as soon as they have learnt and are ready to abide by the eternal lesson—that we are bound to bear and forbear and that to everyone life must be a compromise." He sent the young lady his blessings in these terms: "May you always enjoy the undivided love of your husband, helping him in attaining all that is desirable in this life, and when you have seen your children's children, and the drama of life is nearing its end, may you help each other in reaching that infinite ocean of Existence, Knowledge, and Bliss, at the touch of whose waters all distinctions melt away and we all become One."

But Mary Hale could not make a decision between marriage and lifelong celibacy. She was full of idealism and the spirit of independence; but she was warm in her affection. Swami Vivekananda was particularly fond of Mary. On the day he wrote to Harriet he also wrote to Mary, congratulating Harriet for her discrimination, and prophesying for her a life of joy and sweetness, since she was "not so imaginative and sentimental as to make a fool of herself and has enough of common sense and gentleness to soften the hard points of life which must come to everyone." But he wanted to tell Mary "the truth, and my language is plain." He wrote:

My dear Mary, I will tell you a great lesson I have learnt in this life. It is this: "The higher your ideal is, the more miserable you are," for such a thing as an ideal cannot be attained in the world—or in this life, even. He who wants perfection in the world is a madman—for it cannot be. How can you find the infinite in the finite?

You, Mary, are like a mettlesome Arab—grand, splendid. You would make a splendid queen—physically, mentally—you would shine alongside of a dashing, bold, adventurous, heroic husband. But, my dear sister, you will make one of the worst wives. You will take the life out of our easy-going, practical, plodding husbands of the everyday world. Mind, my sister, although it is true that there is much more romance in actual life than in any novel, yet it is few and far between. Therefore my advice to you is that until you bring down your ideals to a more practical level, you ought not to marry. If you do, the result will be misery for both of you. In a few months you will lose all regard for a commonplace, good, nice young man, and then life will become insipid. . . .

There are two sorts of persons in the world—the one strong-nerved, quiet, yielding to nature, not given to much imagination, yet good, kind, sweet, etc. For such is this world—they alone are born to be happy. There are others, again, with high-strung nerves, tremendously imaginative, with intense feeling—always going high, and coming down the next moment. For them there is no happiness. The first class will have almost an even tenor of happiness. The second will have to run between ecstasy and misery. But of these alone what we call geniuses are made. There is some truth in a recent theory that genius is "a sort of madness."

Now persons of this class, if they want to be great, must fight to be so—clear the deck for battle. No encumbrance—no marriage—no children, no undue attachment to anything except the one idea, and live and die for that. I am a person of this sort. I have taken up the one idea of "Vedānta," and I have "cleared the deck for action." You and Isabel are made of this metal—but let me tell you, though it is hard, you are spoiling your lives in vain. Either take up one idea, clear the deck, and to it dedicate the life, or be contented and practical, lower the ideal, marry, and have a happy life. Either "bhoga" or "yoga"—either enjoy this life or give up and be a yogi. None can have both in one. Now or never—select quick. "He who is very particular gets nothing," says the proverb. Now sincerely and really and for ever determine to "clear the deck for the fight," take up anything—philosophy or science or religion or literature—and let that be your God for the rest of your life. Achieve happiness or achieve greatness. I have no sympathy with you and Isabel—you are neither for this nor for that. I wish to see you happy, as Harriet is, or great. Eating, drinking, dressing, and society nonsense are not things to throw away a life upon—especially for you, Mary. You are rusting away a splendid brain and abilities, for which there is not the least excuse. You must have ambition to be great. I know you will take these rather harsh remarks from me in the right spirit, knowing I like you really as much as or more than what I call you, my sister. I had long had a mind to tell you this and as experience is gathering I feel like telling you. The joyful news from Harriet urged me to tell you this. I will be overjoyed to hear that you are married also, and happy so far as happiness can be had here, or would like to hear of your doing great deeds.

Mary Hale later married a gentleman from Florence, and became known as Mme. Matteini.

For some time the Swami had been feeling an inner urge to return to India. From Switzerland he wrote to friends in India: "Do not be afraid. Great things are going to be done, my children. Take heart. . . . In the winter I am going back to India and will try to set things on their feet there. Work on, brave hearts, fail not—no saying nay; work on—the Lord is behind the work. Mahāśakti, the Great Power, is with you."

On November 29, 1896, he wrote to a disciple in India about his proposed Himālayan monastery. He further said that his present plan was to start two centres, one in Madras and the other in Calcutta, and later others in Bombay and Allahabad. He was pleased to see that the magazine *Brahmavādin*, published in English in Madras, was disseminating his ideas; he was planning to start similar magazines in the vernaculars also. He also intended to start a paper, under the management of writers from all nations, in order to spread his ideas to every corner of the globe. "You must not forget," he wrote, "that my interests are international and not Indian alone."

Swami Vivekananda could no longer resist the voice of India calling him back. Sometime during the middle of November, after a class lecture, he called Mrs. Sevier aside and quietly asked her to purchase four tickets for India. He planned to take with him the Seviers and Mr. Goodwin. Reservations were accordingly made on the "Prinz Regent Luitpold," of the North German Lloyd Steamship Line, sailing from Naples for Ceylon on December 20, 1896. The Seviers wanted to lead a retired life in India, practising spiritual disciplines and helping the Swami in carrying out the idea of building a monastery in the Himālayas. Faithful Goodwin, who had already taken the vows of a brahmachārin, would work as the Swami's stenographer. It was also planned that Miss Muller and Miss Noble would follow the party some time after, the latter to devote her life to the cause of women's education in India.

The Swami was given a magnificent farewell by his English friends, devotees, and admirers on December 13 at the Royal Society of Painters in Water-Colours, in Piccadilly. There were about five hundred people present. Many were silent, tongue-tied and sad at heart. Tears were very near in some eyes. But the Swami, after his farewell address, walked among the assembled friends and repeated over and over again, "Yes, yes, we shall meet again, we shall." It was decided that Swami Abhedananda would continue the work after the Swami's departure.

Of the impressions left by the Swami's teachings in England, Margaret Noble writes:

To not a few of us the words of Swami Vivekananda came as living water to men perishing of thirst. Many of us have been conscious for years past of that growing uncertainty and despair, with regard to religion, which has beset the intellectual life of Europe for half a century. Belief in the dogmas of Christianity has become impossible for us, and we had no tool, such as now we hold, by which to cut away the doctrinal shell from the kernel of Reality, in our faith. To these, the Vedānta has given intellectual confirmation and philosophical expression of their own mistrusted intuitions. "The people that walked in darkness have seen a great light." . . .

It was the Swami's *I am God* that came as something always known, only never said before. . . . Yet again, it was the Unity of Man that was the touch needed to rationalize all previous experiences and give logical sanction to the thirst for absolute service, never boldly avowed in the past. Some by one gate, and some by another, we have all entered into a great heritage, and we know it.

The practical Englishman saw in the Swami's life the demonstration of fearlessness which was the necessary corollary of his teaching regarding the divinity of the soul. It was revealed in many incidents.

One in particular illustrates this. He was one day walking with Miss Muller and an English friend across some fields when a mad bull came tearing towards them. The Englishman frankly ran, and reached the other side of the hill in safety. Miss Muller ran as far as she could, and then sank to the ground, incapable of further effort. Seeing this, and unable to aid her, the Swami—thinking, "So this is the end, after all"—took up his stand in front of her, with folded arms.

He told afterwards how his mind was occupied with a mathematical calculation as to how far the bull would be able to throw him. But the animal suddenly stopped a few paces off, and then, raising its head, retreated sullenly. The Englishman felt ashamed of his cowardly retreat and of having left the Swami alone to face the bull. Miss Muller asked the Swami how he could muster courage in such a dangerous situation. He said that in the face of danger and death he felt—and he took two pebbles in his hands and struck the one against the other—as strong as flint, for "I have touched the feet of God." He had shown a like courage in his early youth, when he quickly stepped up to a runaway horse and caught it, in a street of Calcutta, thus saving the life of a woman who occupied the carriage behind.

Regarding his experience and work in England, he told the Hale sisters, in a letter, that it was a roaring success. To another American friend he wrote that he believed in the power of the English to assimilate great ideas, and that though the process of assimilation might be slow, it would be all the more sure and abiding. He believed that the time would come when distinguished ecclesiastics of the Church of England, imbued with the idealism of Vedānta, would form a liberal community within the Anglican Church itself, supporting the universality of religion both in vision and in practice.

But what he admired most in England was the character of the English people—their steadiness, thoroughness, loyalty, devotion to the ideal, and perseverance to finish any work that they undertook. His preconceived idea about the English was thoroughly changed when he came to know them intimately. "No one," he said later, addressing the Hindus of Calcutta, "ever landed on English soil feeling more hatred in his heart for a race than I did for the English. [The iniquities of the colonial rule in India were deeply impressed in his mind.] . . . There is none among you who loves the English people more than I do."

He wrote to the Hale sisters on November 28, 1896: "The English are not so bright as the Americans, but once you touch their heart it is yours for ever. . . . I now understand why the Lord has blessed them above all other races—steady, sincere to the backbone, with great depths of feeling, only with a crust of stoicism on the surface. If that is broken you have your man." In another letter: "You know, of course, the steadiness of the English; they are, of all nations, least jealous of each other and that is why they dominate the world. They have solved the secret of obedience without slavish cringing—great freedom with law-abidingness." On still another occasion he called the English "a nation of heroes, the true kshattriyas. . . . Their education is to hide their feelings and never to show them. If you know how to reach the English heart, he is your friend for ever. If he has once an idea put into his brain, it never comes out; and the immense practicality and energy of the race makes it sprout up and immediately bear fruit."

The Swami felt that the finger of God had brought about the contact between India and England. The impact created by the aggressive British rule, on the one hand, awakened the Hindu race from its slumber of ages, and on the other hand, offered India opportunities to spread her spiritual message throughout the Western world.

He wrote to Mr. Leggett on July 6, 1896:

The British Empire with all its evils is the greatest machine that ever existed for the dissemination of ideas. I mean to put my ideas in the centre of this machine, and it will spread them all over the world. Of course, all great work is slow and the difficulties are too many, especially as we Hindus are a conquered race. Yet that is the very reason why it is bound to work, for spiritual ideals have always come from the downtrodden. The downtrodden Jews overwhelmed the Roman Empire with their spiritual ideals. You will be pleased to learn that I am also learning my lesson every day in patience and above all in sympathy. I think I am beginning to see the Divine even inside the bullying Anglo-Indians. I think I am slowly approaching to that state when I would be able to love the very "Devil" himself, if there were any.

Though Swami Vivekananda himself spoke highly of the effect of his teachings in England, he did not start any organized work there as he did in the United States of America. From his letters and conversations one learns that he was growing weary of the world. Though he was at the peak of his success, as far as public activity was concerned, he began to feel a longing for the peace that comes from total absorption in the Supreme Spirit. He sensed that his earthly mission was over. On August 23, 1896, he wrote to a friend, from Lucerne:

"I have begun the work, let others work it out. So you see, to set the work going I had to defile myself by touching money and property for a time.[17] Now I am sure my part of the work has been done, and I have no more interest in Vedānta or any philosophy in the world, or in the work itself. I am getting ready to depart, to return no more to this hell, this world. . . . Even its religious utility is beginning to pall on me. . . . These works and doing good, and so forth, are just a little exercise to cleanse the mind. I have had enough of it."[18] He was losing interest even in the American programme, which he himself had organized.

In the letter quoted above, the Swami wrote: "If New York or Boston or any other place in the U. S. needs Vedānta teachers, they must receive them, keep them, and provide for them. As for me, I am as good as retired. I have played my part in the world." To Swami Abhedananda he confided one day, about this time, that he was going to live for five or six years at the most. The brother disciple said in protest that he was a young man and that he should not think of death. "But," Vivekananda said, "you are a fool; you do not understand.

[17] Where money was concerned, he shared the physical repulsion towards it of Śri Ramakrishna.

[18] That work serves as a discipline for the realization of freedom, and is not freedom itself, has been fully discussed by Swami Vivekananda in his *Karma-Yoga*.

My soul is getting bigger and bigger every day; the body can hardly contain it. Any day it may burst this cage of flesh and bone!"

The world was leaving him. The string of the kite by which it was fastened to earth was breaking.

The reader may recall that Śri Ramakrishna spoke of Vivekananda as a free soul whom he had dragged down from the realm of the Absolute to help him in his mission on earth. A temporary veil, necessary for physical embodiment and work, was put on this soul so that it might dwell in the world to help men in their search for spiritual freedom. But now, as the veil was becoming thinner, the Swami began to get a glimpse of the real freedom. He realized that the world was the lilā, the play, of the Divine Mother, and it would continue as long as She wanted it. On August 8, 1896, he wrote from Switzerland to Goodwin:

I am much refreshed now. I look out of the window and see the huge glaciers just before me—and feel that I am in the Himālayas. I am quite calm. My nerves have regained their accustomed strength, and little vexations like those you write of do not touch me at all. How shall I be disturbed by this child's play? The whole world is mere child's play—preaching, teaching, and all included. "Know him to be a sannyāsin who neither hates nor desires." What is to be desired in this little mud-puddle of a world, with its ever recurring misery, disease, and death? "He who has given up all desires, he alone is happy." This rest—eternal, peaceful rest—I am catching a glimpse of it now in this beautiful spot. "If a man knows the Ātman as 'I am this,' then desiring what and for whose sake will he suffer in the wake of the body?"

I feel as if I have had my share of experience in what they call "work." I am finished. I am longing to get out now.

With this growing detachment from the world, the idea of good and evil, without the consciousness of which no work is possible, began to drop away. The Swami was realizing an intense love for God. In that mood a great exaltation would come over him, and the whole universe would seem to him an Eternal Garden where an Eternal Child plays an Eternal Game. In that mood of delirious joy he had written on July 6, 1896, to Francis Leggett, his friend and disciple:

At twenty I was a most unsympathetic, uncompromising fanatic. I would not walk on the foot-path on the theatre side of the street in Calcutta. At thirty-three I can live in the same house with prostitutes and never would think of saying a word of reproach to them. Is it degeneration? Or is it that I am broadening out into that universal love which is the Lord Himself? . . . Some days I get into a sort of ecstasy. I feel that I must bless everyone, every being, love and embrace every being, and I literally see that evil is a delusion. . . . I bless the day I was born. I have had so much of kindness and love here, and that Love Infinite who brought me into being has guided every one of my actions, good or bad (don't be frightened); for what am I, what was I ever, but a tool in His hands—for whose service I have given up everything—my Beloved, my Joy, my Life, my Soul? He is my playful darling, I am His playfellow. There is neither rhyme nor reason in the universe. What reason binds Him? He, the Playful One, is playing—these tears and laughter are all parts of the play. Great fun, great fun! as Joe[19] says.

It is a funny world, and the funniest chap you ever saw is He, the Beloved. Infinite

[19] Referring to Miss MacLeod.

fun, is it not? Brotherhood or playmatehood? A shoal of romping children let out to play in this playground of the world, isn't it? Whom to praise, whom to blame? It is all His play. They want an explanation, but how can you explain Him? He is brain-less, nor has He any reason. He is fooling us with little brains and reasons, but this time He won't find me napping—"you bet." I have learnt a thing or two. Beyond, beyond reason and learning and talking is the feeling, the "Love," the "Beloved." Ay, "Sakē,"[20] fill the cup and we will be mad.—Yours ever in madness, VIVEKANANDA.

In a philosophical mood he spoke about the illusion of progress. He did not believe in the possibility of transforming this earth into a heaven where misery would be totally eliminated and happiness alone would reign in its place. True freedom and bliss could be attained only by the individual and not by the masses as a whole. He wrote to Goodwin on August 8, 1896: " 'A good world,' 'a happy world,' 'social progress' are equally intelligible as 'hot ice,' 'dark light,' etc. If it were good it would not be the world. The soul foolishly thinks of manifesting the Infinite in finite matter—the intelligence through gross particles—and at last finds out its error and tries to escape. This going back is the beginning of religion, and its method, destruction of self, that is, love. Not love for wife or child or anybody else, but love for everything else except this little self. Never be deluded by the tall talk, of which you will hear a lot in America, about 'human progress' and such stuff. There is no progress without regression."

On November 1, 1896, in the course of a letter to Mary Hale, Swami Vivekananda wrote from London:

"An objective heaven or millennium therefore has existence only in the fancy, but a subjective one is already in existence. The musk-deer, after vain search for the cause of the scent of the musk, at last will have to find it in himself."

But Swami Vivekananda's mission to the world was not yet finished. An arduous task was awaiting him in his beloved motherland. The Indian work had to be organized before he could bid farewell to this earth. He left England on December 16, 1896, and travelled overland for the port of departure at Naples.

The party headed directly for Milan, passing through Dover, Calais, and Mont Cenis. The Swami enjoyed the railroad journey and entertained his companions, the Seviers, with his stimulating conversation. But a part of his mind was drawn to India. He said to the Seviers: "Now I have but one thought, and that is India. I am looking forward to India." On the eve of his departure from London, an English friend had asked him, "Swami, how will you like your motherland after three years' experience in the luxurious and powerful West?" His significant reply was: "India I loved before I came away. Now the very dust of India has become holy to me, the very air is now holy to me; it is the holy land, the place of pilgrimage." Often the Swami said that the West was the karma-bhumi, the land of action, where through selfless work a man purified his heart; and India was the punya-bhumi, the land of holiness, where the pure in heart communed with God.

In Milan the Swami was much impressed by the great cathedral and by

[20] Friend.

Leonardo's "Last Supper." Pisa, with the leaning tower, and Florence, with its magnificent achievements in art, immensely delighted him. But the peak of his happiness was reserved for Rome, where he spent Christmas week. Many things there reminded him of India: the tonsure of the priests, the incense, the music, the various ceremonies of the Catholic Church, and the Holy Sacrament—the last of these recalling to his mind the prasādam of the Hindu temples, the food partaken of by devotees after it has been offered to God.

When asked by a lady companion about the church ritual, the Swami said, "If you love the Personal God, then give Him your best—incense, flowers, fruit, and silk." But he was a little bewildered by the imposing High Mass at St. Peter's on Christmas Day, and whispered to the Seviers: "Why all this pageantry and ostentatious show? Can it be possible that the Church which loves such a display of pomp and ceremonies is the true follower of the humble Jesus, who had nowhere to lay his head?" He could never forget that Christ was a sannyāsin, a world-renouncing monk, and that the essence of his teachings was renunciation and detachment.

He enjoyed his visit to the catacombs, associated with the memories of early Christian martyrs and saints. The Christmas festival at Santa-Maria d'Ara Coeli, with the stalls where sweets, toys, and cheap pictures of the Bambino were sold, reminded him of similar religious fairs in India. Christmas in Rome filled his heart with a warm devotion for Jesus Christ, who was an Asiatic and whom Asia had offered to the West as a gift to awaken its spiritual consciousness.

The Swami spent a few days in Naples, visiting Vesuvius, Pompeii, and other places of interest. Then the ship at last arrived from Southampton with Mr. Goodwin as one of her passengers. The Swami and his friends sailed from Naples on December 30, 1896, expecting to arrive in Colombo on January 15, 1897.

On board the ship the Swami had a significant vision. One night, somewhere between Naples and Port Said, he saw in a vivid dream a venerable, bearded old man, like a rishi of India, who said: "Observe carefully this place. You are now in the Island of Crete. This is the land where Christianity began. I am one of the Therapeutae who used to live here." The apparition uttered another word, which the Swami could not remember. It might have been "Essene," a sect to which John the Baptist belonged.

Both the Therapeutae and the Essenes had practised renunciation and cherished a liberal religious outlook. According to some scholars, the word Therapeutae may be derived from the Buddhist word sthaviraputta, meaning the sons or disciples of the Theras, or Elders, the superiors among the Buddhist monks. The word Essene may have some relation with Iśiyāna, meaning the Path of the Lord, a well-known sect of Buddhist monks. It is now admitted that the Buddhists at an early time had monasteries in Asia Minor, Egypt, and generally along the eastern part of the Mediterranean.

The old man in the dream concluded his statement by saying: "The truths and ideas preached by us were presented as the teachings of Jesus. But Jesus the person was never born. Various proofs attesting this fact will be brought to light when this place is dug up." At that moment—it was midnight—the

Swami awoke and asked a sailor where the ship was; he was told that it was fifty miles off Crete.

The Swami was startled at this singular coincidence. The idea flashed in his mind that the Acts of the Apostles might have been an older record than the Gospels, and that Buddhist thought, coming through the Therapeutae and the Essenes, might have helped in the formulation of Christianity. The person of Christ might be a later addition. He knew that Alexandria had been a meeting-place of Indian and Egyptian thought. Later, when the old sites in Crete were excavated, evidence was found connecting early Christianity with foreign sources.

But Swami Vivekananda never refused to accept the historical Christ. Like Krishna, Christ, too, has been revealed in the spiritual experiences of many saints. That, for Vivekananda, conferred upon him a reality which was more real than historical realities. While travelling in Switzerland, the Swami one day plucked some wild flowers and asked Mrs. Sevier to offer them at the feet of the Virgin in a little chapel in the mountains, with the remark, "She too is the Mother." One of his disciples, another day, gave him a picture of the Sistine Madonna to bless. But he refused in all humility, and piously touching the feet of the child said, "I would have washed his feet, not with my tears, but with my heart's blood." It may be remembered that the monastic Order of Ramakrishna was started on Christmas Eve.

During the two weeks' voyage, Swami Vivekananda had ample time to reflect on the experiences of his three years in the Western world. His mind was filled with memories of sweet friendship, unflinching devotion, and warm appreciation from both sides of the Atlantic. Three years before, he had come to America, unknown and penniless, and was regarded somewhat as a curiosity from the glamorous and inscrutable East. Now he was returning to his native land, a hero and prophet worshipped by hundreds and admired by thousands. Guided by the finger of God he had gone to Chicago. In the New World he had seen life at its best and its worst. He found there a society based on the ideals of equality, justice, and freedom, where a man—in sad contrast with India—was given every opportunity to develop his potentialities. There the common people had reached a high standard of living and enjoyed their well-earned prosperity in a way unimaginable in any other part of the world. The American mind was alert, inquisitive, daring, receptive, and endowed with a rare ethical sensitivity. He saw in America, in her men and women of letters, wealth, and position, sparks of spirituality which kindled at the touch of his magic words. He was impressed to see the generous confidence and richness of heart manifested through the pure and candid souls who gave themselves to him once they had recognized him as a trustworthy spiritual guide. They became his noble friends and slaves of love, and did not shrink from the highest sacrifice to help in the fulfilment of his mission.

But withal, the Swami saw the vulgarity, garishness, greed, lust for power, and sensuality among this vast country's heterogeneous elements. People had been swept off their feet by the newly acquired prosperity created with the aid of science, technology, and human ingenuity. They often appeared to him naïve and noisy, and he may have wondered if this new nation, l'enfant terrible, the last hope of Western culture and also the source of potential fear for the rest of the world, would measure up to the expectations of its Founding Fathers and act as the big brother of the world, sharing with all the material amenities of life.

America had given him the first recognition and he was aware of it. In America he had started the work of Vedānta in an organized form, and he hoped America would be the spiritual bridge between the East and the West. Though his scholarly and conservative mind often felt at home among the intellectuals of England and Germany, yet to America his heart was devoted. The monuments of Western culture no doubt fascinated him, but, as he wrote to Mary Hale from London, in May 1896: "I love the Yankee land—I like to see new things. I do not care a fig to loaf about old ruins and mope a life out about old histories and keep sighing about the ancients. I have too much vigour in my blood for that. In America is the place, the people, the opportunity for everything new. I have become horribly radical."

In that same letter he wrote, too, that he wished he could infuse some of the American spirit into India, into "that awful mass of conservative jelly-fish, and then throw overboard all old associations and start a new thing, entirely new—simple, strong, new and fresh as the first-born baby—throw all of the past overboard and begin anew."

Swami Vivekananda bestowed equally high praise upon the Englishman. He felt that in a sense his work in England was more satisfactory than his work in America. There he transformed the life of individuals. Goodwin and Margaret Noble embraced his cause as their own, and the Seviers accompanied him to India, deserting Europe and all their past to follow him.

But what of Swami Vivekananda's early dream of gathering from America the material treasures to remedy the sufferings of the Indian masses and raise their standard of living? He had come to America to obtain, in exchange for India's spiritual wealth, the needed monetary help and scientific and technological knowledge to rebuild the physical health of his own people. Though on his return he did not take with him American scientists and technologists, or carry in his pocket gold and silver from the New World, yet he had left behind a vast storehouse of goodwill and respect for India. He had been India's first spiritual ambassador to America, India's herald, who, remembering the dignity of the royal land whence he had come, had spoken in her name and delivered her message with appropriate dignity.

The full effect of this contact will be known only in years to come; but a beginning can be seen even now. Half a century after Swami Vivekananda's visit to America, India gained her freedom from British rule. When she thus obtained facilities to arrange her national affairs in her own way, India sent thousands of students to the New World to acquire advanced knowledge in the physical sciences and technology. Further, American money is now being spent to improve the material condition of the Indian masses. Thus it appears that, after all, Swami Vivekananda was not a mere visionary, but had insight into the shape of things to come.

The immediate task before him, the Swami felt, was to work for India's regeneration from within the country itself. India could be liberated by her own efforts alone. But he was carrying from the West a priceless asset to help him in his herculean task: The West had given him an authority which, it appears, he did not have before in the land of his birth. He had been successful in planting the seeds of India's spiritual ideas in the very heart of the English-speaking world—in New York and London. Did he know then that within a half century these ideas would be broadcast over the Western world, and earn its respect for his motherland? Though he had come to America as a giver, he was now, in a sense, going back to India as a gift from the New World.

THE RETURN TO INDIA

Swami Vivekananda enjoyed the sea voyage back to India, relaxing from his strenuous activities in the West. But his mind was full of ideas regarding his future plan of work in his motherland.

There were on the boat, among other passengers, two Christian missionaries who, in the course of a heated discussion with the Swami, lost their tempers and savagely criticized the Hindu religion. The Swami walked to one of them, seized him by the collar, and said menacingly, "If you abuse my religion again, I will throw you overboard."

"Let me go, sir," the frightened missionary apologized; "I'll never do it again."

Later, in the course of a conversation with a disciple in Calcutta, he asked, "What would you do if someone insulted your mother?" The disciple answered, "I would fall upon him, sir, and teach him a good lesson."

"Bravo!" said the Swami. "Now, if you had the same positive feeling for your religion, your true mother, you could never see any Hindu brother converted to Christianity. Yet you see this occurring every day, and you are quite indifferent. Where is your faith? Where is your patriotism? Every day Christian missionaries abuse Hinduism to your face, and yet how many are there amongst you whose blood boils with righteous indignation and who will stand up in its defense?"

When the boat stopped at Aden, the party went ashore and visited the places of interest. The Swami saw from a distance a Hindusthāni betel-leaf seller smoking his hookah, or hubble-bubble. He had not enjoyed this Indian way of smoking for the past three years. Going up to him, the Swami said, "Brother, do give me your pipe." Soon he was puffing at it with great joy and talking to him as to an intimate friend.

Mr. Sevier later on said to Swamiji teasingly: "Now we see! It was this pipe that made you run away from us so abruptly!" Speaking of this incident, the Swami's companions said later: "The shopkeeper could not have resisted him; for he had such an endearing way about him, when asking for anything, that he was simply irresistible. We shall never forget that ingenuous look on his face when he said to the shopkeeper, with childlike sweetness, 'Brother, do give me your pipe.' "

In the early morning of January 15, 1897, the coast of Ceylon with its majestic coco palms and gold-coloured beach was seen at a distance. The Swami's heart leapt with joy; and his disciples caught his excitement as the boat approached the beautiful harbour of Colombo. But no one in the party had the slightest idea of what they were to witness while disembarking.

Since the day of his success at the Parliament of Religions in Chicago, which had filled with joy and pride the hearts of his countrymen, especially of his disciples and brother monks at the Baranagore Math, Swami Vivekananda had been inspiring his faithful followers to lay down their lives for the uplift of the masses of India, and in particular to help the hungry and illiterate. In his heart of hearts he felt that India would not be able to resist his appeal. Many months before, while discussing with some of his disciples in Detroit the great difficulties that he had encountered in presenting Hinduism to bigoted Christians in America, he had said: "But India shall listen to me. I will shake India to her foundations. I will send an electric thrill through her veins. Wait! You will see how India receives me. It is India, my own India, that knows truly how to appreciate what I have given so freely here, and with my life's blood. India will receive me in triumph."

When the news of Swami Vivekananda's departure from Europe reached India, the hearts of the people were stirred. The spiritual ambassador of their ancient land was coming back after fulfilling his mission. They must give a regal welcome to this great crusader. In big towns committees were formed for his reception. His brother disciples and friends were impatient. Swami Shivananda came ahead of time to Madras and Swami Niranjanananda to Colombo; so also many of his disciples from Bengal and the Northern Provinces came to Madras to await his arrival. The newspapers published articles eulogizing his personality and work.

A gaily decorated steam launch carried the Swami and his party from the ship to the harbour. When the monk with his yellow robe and luminous eyes touched the dust of his motherland, a mighty shout arose from the human throng crowding the quays. Thousands flung themselves on the ground to touch his feet. A deputation of the notables of Ceylon welcomed him, and he was taken in a huge procession through many triumphal arches. Flags were unfurled, religious hymns chanted; an Indian band played. Rose-water and the sacred water of the Ganges were sprinkled before him, and flowers were strewn in his path. Incense was burnt before the houses as he passed. Fruit and other offerings were brought by hundreds of visitors.

Swami Vivekananda accepted all these honours without losing his poise. He was not the man to flee from triumph any more than from battle. He regarded the tributes paid to him, a penniless beggar, as tributes paid to the spiritual ideal of India. In the course of his reply to the address of welcome given in Colombo, he said: "The spirituality of the Hindus is revealed by the princely reception which they have given to a beggar sannyāsin." He pointed out that though he was not a military general, not a prince nor a wealthy man, yet men great in the transitory possessions of the world and much respected by society had nevertheless come to honour him, a homeless monk. "This," he exclaimed, "is one of the highest expressions of spirituality." He disclaimed any personal glory in the welcome he received, insisting that it was but the recognition of a principle.

Swami Vivekananda's progress from Colombo to Madras and the welcomes he received at Kandy, Anuruddhapura, Jaffna, Pamban, Rameswaram, Ramnad, Paramakudi, Madura, Trichinopoly, and Kumbhakonum demonstrated how deeply he had endeared himself to the men and women of India. At Anuruddhapura a band of fanatical Buddhists tried to break up the meeting, but did not succeed. At Rameswaram the Swami exhorted the people to "worship Śiva in the poor, the diseased, and the weak."

He received a touching welcome there from the Rājā of Ramnad, his disciple, who had encouraged him to go to America and had helped him materially for that purpose. At Ramnad the horses were unhitched from the carriage bearing the Swami, and the people themselves, the Rājā among them, drew it. At Rameswaram the Rājā erected, in the Swami's honour, a victory column forty feet high with a suitable inscription. He also gave a liberal donation to the Madras famine-relief fund to commemorate the home-coming of the Swami.

At a small railroad station near Madras, hundreds of people gathered for a glimpse of Vivekananda. The stationmaster did not want to delay the train since no stop was scheduled. But the crowd of admirers flung themselves on the track, and the train had to be halted. The Swami was visibly moved and blessed the multitude.

The enthusiasm of the people reached its peak in Madras, where extensive preparations had been made for the Swami's reception. It was Madras that had first recognized the greatness of Vivekananda and equipped him for the journey to Chicago. At that time, when he had first come there, he had been, in effect, only an obscure individual. He had spent some two months in an unknown bungalow at St. Thome, holding conversations on Hinduism. Yet even then a few educated young men of keen foresight had predicted that there was something in the man, a "power" that would lift him above all others and enable him to be a leader of men. These youths, who had been ridiculed as "misguided enthusiasts" and "dreamy revivalists," now, four years later, had the supreme satisfaction of seeing "our Swami," as they loved to call him, return to them a famous personage in both Europe and America.

The streets and thoroughfares of Madras were profusely decorated; seventeen triumphal arches were erected. The Swami's name was on everybody's lips. Thousands jammed the railway station, and as the train steamed in he was received with thundering shouts of applause. An elaborate procession was formed, and he was taken to "Castle Kernan," the palatial home of Billigiri Iyengar, where arrangements had been made for his stay in the city.

On the third day after his arrival Swami Vivekananda was honoured in a public meeting on behalf of the people of Madras. As Victoria Hall, chosen for the purpose, was too small to hold the large crowd, the people cried for an open-air gathering. The Swami came out and addressed them from the top of a coach; it was, as it were, Śri Krishna, standing in the chariot, exhorting Arjuna to give up his unmanliness and measure up to his Āryan heritage. In a brief speech he told the people how India, through her love of God, had expanded the limited love of the family into love of country and of humanity. He urged them to maintain their enthusiasm and to give him all the help he required to do great things for India.

During his short stay in Madras, Swami Vivekananda gave four public lectures, his subjects being, "My Plan of Campaign," "The Sages of India," "Vedānta in its Relation to Practical Life," and "The Future of India." In these lectures he reminded the Indians of both their greatness and their weakness, and urged them to be proud of their past and hopeful for their future.

While speaking on "My Plan of Campaign," the Swami exposed the meanness of some of the Theosophists, who had tried their utmost to injure his work in America but later claimed that they had paved the way for his success in the New World. He told the audience that when, in desperation, he had cabled to India for money, the Theosophists had come to know about it and one of them had written to a member of the Society in India: "Now the devil is going to die. God bless us all!" But it must be said that there were many among the Theosophists, especially in India, who were his genuine well-wishers.

Swami Vivekananda had hardly a moment's respite during his nine days in Madras. When asked by a disciple how he found the strength for such incessant activity, he answered, "Spiritual work never tires one in India." But he would lose patience if asked about matters that had no bearing on practical life. One day a pandit asked him to state clearly whether he was a dualist or a non-dualist. The Swami said: "As long as I have this body I am a dualist, but not otherwise. This incarnation of mine is to help put an end to useless and mischievous quarrels, which only distract the mind and make men weary of life, and even turn them into sceptics and atheists."

Meanwhile heart-warming letters had been arriving from America informing the Swami of the progress of the Vedānta work in the New World under the leadership of Swami Saradananda, and also in appreciation of his own achievements. One letter was signed by Lewis G. Janes, President of the Brooklyn Ethical Association; C. C. Everett, Dean of the Harvard Divinity School; William James and Josiah Royce, both professors of philosophy at Harvard University; Mrs. Sara C. Bull of Boston, and others. It said: "We believe that such expositions as have been given by yourself and your co-labourer, the Swami Saradananda, have more than mere speculative interest and utility—that they are of great ethical value in cementing the ties of friendship and brotherhood between distant peoples, and in helping us to realize that solidarity of human relationship and interests which has been affirmed by all the great religions of the world. We earnestly hope that your work in India may be blessed in further promoting this noble end, and that you may return to us again with assurances of fraternal regard from our distant brothers of the great Āryan family, and the ripe wisdom that comes from reflection and added experience and further contact with the life and thought of your people."

Another letter from Detroit, signed by forty-two of his friends, said in part: "We Western Āryans have been so long separated from our Eastern brothers that we had almost forgotten our identity of origin, until you came and with your beautiful presence and matchless eloquence rekindled within our hearts the knowledge that we of America and you of India are one."

Swami Vivekananda, after his strenuous work in South India, needed rest. On the advice of friends, he decided to travel to Calcutta by steamer. Monday, February 15, was the date of his sailing. Several devotees boarded the steamer

to see him off, and one of them, Professor Sundarama Iyer, asked the Swami
if his mission had achieved lasting good in America and Europe. The Swami
said: "Not much. I hope that here and there I have sown a seed which in time
may grow and benefit some at least."

Swami Vivekananda's lectures delivered during his progress from Colombo to
Madras were inspiring and enthusiastic. He yearned to awaken the masses of
India from the slumber of ages. He had seen the dynamic life of the West;
he now felt more deeply the personality of India, which only needed his fiery
exhortation to assert itself once more among the nations of the world. Again one
is reminded of Krishna's admonition to Arjuna on the battlefield of Kurukshetra:
"In this crisis, O Arjuna, whence comes such lowness of spirit, unbecoming to
an Āryan, dishonourable, and an obstacle to the attaining of heaven? Do not
yield to unmanliness, O Arjuna. It does not become you. Shake off this base
faint-heartedness and arise, O scorcher of enemies!"

In his famous lecture "My Plan of Campaign," delivered in Madras, he called
upon the people to assert their soul-force:

> My India, arise! Where is your vital force? In your Immortal Soul. Each nation, like
> each individual, has one theme in this life, which is its centre, the principal note round
> which every other note comes to form the harmony. If any one nation attempts to
> throw off its national vitality, the direction which has become its own through the
> transmission of centuries, that nation dies. . . . In one nation political power is its
> vitality, as in England. Artistic life, in another, and so on. In India religious life forms
> the centre, the keynote of the whole music of the national life. And therefore, if you
> succeed in the attempt to throw off your religion and take up either politics or society,
> the result will be that you will become extinct. Social reform and politics have to be
> preached through the vitality of your religion. . . . Every man has to make his own
> choice; so has every nation. We made our choice ages ago. And it is the faith in an
> Immortal Soul. I challenge anyone to give it up. How can you change your nature?

He asked the Indians to stop complaining. Let them make use of the power
that lay in their hands. That power was so great that if they only realized it
and were worthy of it, they could revolutionize the world. India was the Ganges
of spirituality. The material conquests of the Anglo-Saxon races, far from being
able to dam its current, had helped it. England's power had united the nations
of the world; she had opened paths across the seas so that the waves of the spirit
of India might spread until they had bathed the ends of the earth.

What was this new faith, this word that the world was awaiting?

> The other great idea that the world wants from us today—more perhaps the lower
> classes than the higher, more the uneducated than the educated, more the weak than
> the strong—is that eternal, grand idea of the spiritual oneness of the whole universe, the
> only Infinite Reality, that exists in you and in me and in all, in the self, in the soul. The
> infinite oneness of the soul—that you and I are not only brothers, but are really one—is
> the eternal sanction of all morality. Europe wants it today just as much as our down-
> trodden races do, and this great principle is even now unconsciously forming the basis
> of all the latest social and political aspirations that are coming up in England, in Ger-
> many, in France, and in America.[21]

[21] Extracts from the lecture "The Mission of the Vedānta."

What Swami Vivekananda preached was the essence of the non-dualistic
Vedānta, the deepest and the unique expression of India's spirit.

I heard once the complaint made that I was preaching too much of Advaita, absolute
non-dualism, and too little of dualism. Ay, I know what grandeur, what oceans of love,
what infinite, ecstatic blessings and joy there are in dualistic religion. I know it all. But
this is not the time for us to weep, even in joy; we have had weeping enough; no more
is this the time for us to become soft. This softness has been with us till we have
become like masses of cotton. What our country now wants is muscles of iron and nerves
of steel, gigantic will, which nothing can resist, which will accomplish their purpose in
any fashion, even if it means going down to the bottom of the ocean and meeting death
face to face. That is what we want, and that can only be created, established, and
strengthened by understanding and realizing the ideal of Advaita, that ideal of the oneness of all. Faith, faith, faith in ourselves! . . . If you have faith in the three hundred
and thirty millions of your mythological gods, and in all the gods which foreigners have
introduced into your midst, and still have no faith in yourselves, there is no salvation
for you. Have faith in yourselves and stand upon that faith. Why is it that we three
hundred and thirty millions of people have been ruled for the last thousand years by
any and every handful of foreigners? Because they had faith in themselves and we had
not. I read in the newspapers how, when one of our poor fellows is murdered or ill-
treated by an Englishman, howls go up all over the country; I read and I weep, and the
next moment comes to my mind the question of who is responsible for it all. Not the
English; it is we who are responsible for all our degradation. Our aristocratic ancestors
went on treading the common masses of our country underfoot till they became helpless,
till under this torment the poor, poor people nearly forgot that they were human beings.
They have been compelled to be merely hewers of wood and drawers of water for centuries, so that they are made to believe that they are born as slaves, born as hewers of
wood and drawers of water.[22]

He exhorted the leaders to cultivate the indispensable virtue of feeling for
the people: "Feel, therefore, my would-be reformers, my would-be patriots! Do
you feel? Do you feel that millions and millions of the descendants of gods
and of sages have become next-door neighbours to brutes? Do you feel that
millions are starving today and millions have been starving for ages? Do you
feel that ignorance has come over the land as a dark cloud? Does it make you
restless? Does it make you sleepless? Has it made you almost mad? Are you
seized with that one idea of the misery of ruin, and have you forgotten all about
your name, your fame, your wives, your children, your property, even your own
bodies? If so, that is the first step to becoming a patriot. For centuries people
have been taught theories of degradation. They have been told that they are
nothing. The masses have been told all over the world that they are not human
beings. They have been so frightened for centuries that they have nearly become
animals. Never were they allowed to hear of the Ātman. Let them hear of the
Ātman—that even the lowest of the low have the Ātman within, who never
dies and never is born—Him whom the sword cannot pierce, nor the fire burn,
nor the air dry, immortal, without beginning or end, the all-pure, omnipotent,
and omnipresent Ātman."[23]

[22] Extracts from "The Mission of the Vedānta."
[23] Extracts from "My Plan of Campaign."

"Ay, let every man and woman and child, without respect of caste or birth, weakness or strength, hear and learn that behind the strong and the weak, behind the high and the low, behind everyone, there is that Infinite Soul, assuring all the infinite possibility and the infinite capacity to become great and good. Let us proclaim to every soul: Arise, arise, awake! Awake from this hypnotism of weakness. None is really weak; the soul is infinite, omnipotent, and omniscient. Stand up, assert yourself, proclaim the God within you, do not deny Him!"[24]

"It is a man-making religion that we want. It is a man-making education all round that we want. It is man-making theories that we want. And here is the test of truth: Anything that makes you weak physically, intellectually, and spiritually, reject as poison; there is no life in it, it cannot be true. Truth is strengthening. Truth is purity, truth is all knowledge. Truth must be strengthening, must be enlightening, must be invigorating. Give up these weakening mysticisms and be strong. The greatest truths are the simplest things in the world, simple as your own existence.

"Therefore my plan is to start institutions in India to train our young men as preachers of the truths of our scriptures in India and outside India. Men, men—these are wanted: everything else will be ready; but strong, vigorous, believing young men, sincere to the backbone, are wanted. A hundred such and the world becomes revolutionized. The will is stronger than anything else. Everything must go down before the will, for that comes from God: a pure and strong will is omnipotent."[25]

"If the brāhmin has more aptitude for learning on the grounds of heredity than the pariah, spend no more money on the brāhmin's education, but spend all on the pariah. Give to the weak, for there all the gift is needed. If the brāhmin is born clever, he can educate himself without help. This is justice and reason as I understand it."[26]

"For the next fifty years let all other vain Gods disappear from our minds. This is the only God that is awake: our own race—everywhere His hands, everywhere His feet, everywhere His ears, He covers everything. All other Gods are sleeping. Why should we vainly go after them, when we can worship the God that we see all around us, the Virāt? The first of all worships is the worship of the Virāt, of those all around us. These are all our Gods—men and animals; and the first Gods we have to worship are our own countrymen."[27]

These stirring words did not fall on deaf ears. The spirit of India vibrated to the Swami's call. India became aware of the power of the soul—of God sleeping in man and of His illimitable possibilities. Ramakrishna and Vivekananda were the first awakeners of India's national consciousness; they were India's first nationalist leaders in the true sense of the term. Ramakrishna was the power and Vivekananda the voice. The movement for India's liberation started from Dakshineswar. The subsequent political leaders of the country, consciously or unconsciously, received their inspiration from Vivekananda's

[24] Extracts from "The Mission of the Vedānta."
[25] Extracts from "My Plan of Campaign."
[26] From "The Mission of the Vedānta."
[27] From "The Future of India."

message, and some of them openly acknowledged it. The Bengal revolutionaries were ardent readers of Vivekananda's books, some of which were frowned upon by the British Government. The uplift of the masses, the chief plank in Gandhi's platform, was Vivekananda's legacy.

Yet the militant Vivekananda was not a politician. "Let no political significance ever be attached falsely to my writings or sayings. What nonsense!"— he had said as early as September 1894. A year later he wrote: "I will have nothing to do with political nonsense. I do not believe in politics. God and Truth are the only policy in the world. Everything else is trash."

Swami Vivekananda longed for India's political freedom; but he thought of a free India in relation to her service to humanity. A free India would take her rightful place in the assembly of nations and make a vital contribution towards bringing peace and goodwill to mankind. His message was both national and international.

BACK TO BENGAL

While Swami Vivekananda was enjoying the restful boat trip from Madras to Calcutta, a reception committee was busy preparing for him a fitting welcome in the metropolis of India, the city of his birth. The steamer docked at Kidderpore, and the Swami and his party arrived by train in Calcutta. The reception was magnificent, with an enthusiastic crowd at the railroad station, triumphal arches, the unharnessed carriage drawn by students, and a huge procession with music and religious songs. A princely residence on the bank of the Ganges was placed at the Swami's disposal.

On February 28, 1897, he was given a public reception. Rājā Benoy Krishna Deb presided, and five thousand people jammed the meeting. As usual, the Swami asked the people to go back to the perennial philosophy of the Upanishads. He also paid a touching tribute to Ramakrishna, "my teacher, my master, my hero, my ideal, my God in life." "If there has been anything achieved by me," he said with deep feeling, "by thoughts or words or deeds, if from my lips has ever fallen one word that has ever helped anyone in the world, I lay no claim to it; it was his. But if there have been curses falling from my lips, if there has been hatred coming out of me, it is all mine, and not his. All that has been weak has been mine; all that has been life-giving, strengthening, pure, and holy has been his inspiration, his words, and he himself. Yes, my friends, the world has yet to know that man." A few days after, he gave another public lecture, on "Vedānta in All its Phases."

Shortly after the Swami's arrival in Calcutta the anniversary of Sri Ramakrishna's birth was celebrated at Dakshineswar. Accompanied by his brother disciples, the Swami joined the festival. He walked barefoot in the holy grounds. Deep emotions were stirred up as he visited the temples, the Master's room, the Panchavati, and other spots associated with the memory of Sri Ramakrishna. The place was a sea of human heads.

The Swami said to Girish, a beloved disciple of the Master, "Well, what a difference between those days and these!"

"I know," replied Girish, "but I have the desire to see more."

For a little while the Swami spent his days at the palatial house on the river;

nights, however, he spent with his spiritual brothers at the Alambazar monastery. He had hardly any rest. People streamed in at all times to pay him their respects or to hear his exposition of Vedānta, or just to see him. There were also people who came to argue with him on scriptural matters and to test his knowledge.

But the Swami's heart was with the educated, unmarried youths whom he could train for his future work. He longed to infuse into their hearts some of his own burning enthusiasm. He wanted them to become the preachers of his "man-making religion." The Swami deplored the physical weakness of Indian youths, denounced their early marriage, and reproached them for their lack of faith in themselves and in their national ideals.

One day a young man complained to the Swami that he could not make progress in spiritual life. He had worshipped images, following the advice of one teacher, and had tried to make his mind void according to the instruction of another, but all had been fruitless.

"Sir," the young man said, "I sit still in meditation, shutting the door of my room, and keep my eyes closed as long as I can, but I do not find peace of mind. Can you show me the way?"

"My boy," replied the Swami in a voice full of loving sympathy, "if you take my word, you will have first of all to open the door of your room and look around, instead of closing your eyes. There are hundreds of poor and helpless people in your neighbourhood; you have to serve them to the best of your ability. You will have to nurse and procure food and medicine for the sick. You will have to feed those who have nothing to eat. You will have to teach the ignorant. My advice to you is that if you want peace of mind, you shall have to serve others to the best of your ability."

Another day a well-known college professor, who was a disciple of Śri Ramakrishna, said to the Swami: "You are talking of service, charity, and doing good to the world; these, after all, belong to the domain of māyā. Vedānta says that the goal of man is the attainment of mukti, liberation, through breaking the chain of māyā. What is the use of preaching about things which keep one's mind on mundane matters?"

The Swami replied: "Is not the idea of mukti in the domain of māyā? Does not Vedānta teach that the Ātman is ever free? Why should It, then, strive for mukti?"

He said on another occasion: "When I used to roam about all over India, practising spiritual disciplines, I passed day after day in caves absorbed in meditation. Many a time I decided to starve myself to death because I could not attain mukti. Now I have no desire for mukti. I do not care for it as long as a single individual in the universe remains in bondage."

Swami Vivekananda often used to say that different forms of spiritual discipline were especially efficacious for different ages. At one period it was the practice of austerities; at another period, the cultivation of divine love; and at a third period, it was philosophical discrimination accompanied by renunciation. But in modern times, he emphasized, unselfish service of others, karma-yoga, would quickly bring spiritual results. Therefore he advocated the discipline of selfless action. He particularly advocated this discipline for the

Indians because they were under the spell of tamas, inertia. The Swami realized that only after cultivating rajas would they be able to acquire sattva and attain liberation. As regards himself, the Swami had already known mukti through the realization of oneness with Brahman in nirvikalpa samādhi. But by the will of God he had brought himself down to consciousness of the phenomenal world, and lived like a bodhisattva, devoting himself to the welfare of humanity.

Swami Vivekananda found it most difficult to convert some of his own brother disciples to his new conception of religion and its discipline and method. These brother disciples were individualists, eager for their personal salvation. They wanted to practise austerities and penances, enjoy peaceful meditation, and lead a quiet life of detachment from the world. To them God was first, and next the world. At least that was the way they understood Śri Ramakrishna's teachings. These young monks thought that for one who had taken the monastic vows the world was māyā; therefore all activities, including the charitable and philanthropic, ultimately entangled one in worldly life.

But Vivekananda's thought flowed through a different channel. Śri Ramakrishna had once admonished him to commune with God with eyes open, that is to say, through the service of the poor, the sick, the hungry, and the ignorant. During his days of wandering the Swami had seen with his own eyes the suffering of the people and had felt the voiceless appeal of India for his help. In America and Europe he had witnessed the material prosperity of the people, the dynamic social life, and the general progress made through science, technology, and organized action. Time and again he remembered the words of Ramakrishna: "Religion is not for empty stomachs."

To his brother disciples, therefore, he pointed out that the idea of personal liberation was unworthy of those who called themselves disciples of Ramakrishna, an Incarnation of God. The very fact that they had received the grace of a Saviour should have convinced them of their sure salvation. Their duty, he emphasized, was to serve others as the visible manifestations of God. He said that he wanted to create a new band of monks, who would take not only the traditional vow of personal salvation, but also a new vow of service to humanity.

The brother disciples, who respected the superior spirituality of Vivekananda and bore him great love as the one especially chosen by the Master to carry on his work, obeyed him without always agreeing with him wholeheartedly. Thus at his behest Swami Ramakrishnananda—who had been the keeper of Śri Ramakrishna's shrine for twelve long years after the passing away of the Master, regarding his worship as the supreme spiritual discipline, and had not been absent even for a single day from the monasteries at Baranagore and Alambazar—left for Madras to found a centre for the propagation of Vedānta in South India. Swami Akhandananda went to Murshidabad to carry on relief work among the famine-stricken people there. Swamis Abhedananda and Saradananda had already gone to America.

As for himself, Swami Vivekananda was constantly talking to people, instructing them in the Upanishads, and enjoining them to cultivate the inner strength that comes from the knowledge of God residing in all human hearts. The strain of work and the heat of the plains soon told upon his health. At the advice of physicians he went for a short change to Darjeeling, in the Himālayas, and felt somewhat refreshed. Returning to Calcutta he again devoted himself to the work of teaching.

Several young men, inspired by the Swami's fiery words, joined the Order. Four others, who had been practising disciplines in the monastery under the guidance of the older Swamis while Vivekananda was abroad, were now eager to receive the monastic initiation formally from their great leader. His brother disciples expressed hesitation about one of them, because of some incidents of his past life.

This aroused Swami Vivekananda's emotion. "What is this?" he said. "If we shrink from sinners, who else will save them? Besides, the very fact that someone has taken refuge at the monastery, in his desire to lead a better life, shows that his intentions are good, and we must help him. Suppose a man is bad and perverted; if you cannot change his character, why then have you put on the ochre robe of a monk? Why have you assumed the rôle of teachers?" All four received their monastic initiation.

On the day previous to this sacred ceremony the Swami spoke to them only about the glories of renunciation and service. He said: "Remember, for the salvation of his soul and for the good and happiness of many, a sannyāsin is born in the world. To sacrifice his own life for others, to alleviate the misery of millions rending the air with their cries, to wipe away tears from the eyes of widows, to console the hearts of bereaved mothers, to provide the ignorant and depressed masses with ways and means for the struggle for existence and make them stand on their own feet, to broadcast the teachings of the scriptures to one and all, without distinction, for their spiritual and material welfare, to rouse the sleeping lion of Brahman in the hearts of all beings by the knowledge of Vedānta—a sannyāsin is born in the world." Turning to his brother disciples the Swami said: "Remember, it is for the consummation of this purpose in life that we have taken birth, and we shall lay down our lives for it. Arise and awake, arouse and awaken others, fulfil your mission in life, and you will reach the highest goal." Then addressing the aspirants for the monastic life he said: "You must renounce everything. You must not seek comfort or pleasure for yourself. You must look upon gold and objects of lust as poison, name and fame as the vilest filth, worldly glory as a terrible hell, pride of birth or of social position as 'sinful as drinking spirituous liquor.' In order to be teachers of your fellow men, and for the good of the world, you will have to attain freedom through the knowledge of the Self."

From the following incident one can learn the depths of the Swami's compassion. Many inmates of the math thought that he was not very discriminating in the choice of his disciples. Almost anyone could obtain spiritual initiation from him after a little supplication, and some of them were found later to indulge in wicked actions. One of his own monastic disciples, Swami Nirmalananda, spoke to him about his lack of proper judgement and his inability to understand human nature. The Swami's face became red with emotion. He exclaimed: "What did you say? You think that I do not understand human nature? About these unfortunate people I know not only all they have done in their present lives, but also what they did in their previous ones. I am fully aware of what they will do in the future. Then why do I show kindness to them? These hapless people have knocked at many doors for peace of mind and a word of encouragement, but everywhere have been repulsed. If I turn them down they will have no place to go."

Another incident indicating the tender and compassionate heart of Swami Vivekananda may be mentioned here. One day he was engaged in teaching a disciple the Vedas, with the abstruse commentary of Sāyanāchārya, when Girish Chandra Ghosh, the great playwright of Bengal and an intimate disciple of Śri Ramakrishna, arrived. By way of teasing him, the Swami said, addressing him by his familiar name: "Well, G. C., you have spent your whole life with Krishna and Vishnu.[28] You are quite innocent of the Vedas and other scriptures."

Girish Chandra admitted his ignorance of the scriptures and said, "Hail Śri Ramakrishna, the very embodiment of the Vedas!"

An adept in the knowledge of human nature, Girish was well aware that Swami Vivekananda, in spite of his preaching the austere philosophy of Vedānta, had a heart that was tender in the extreme. He wanted to reveal that side of the Swami's nature before the disciple, and began to paint, in his usual poetic language, a heart-rending picture of the afflictions of the Indian people—the starvation of the masses, the humiliation of Hindu women, the ill health and general suffering of the people everywhere. Suddenly, addressing the Swami, he said, "Now please tell me, do your Vedas teach us how to remedy this state of affairs?"

As the Swami listened to his friend's words, he could hardly suppress his emotion. At last it broke all bounds and he burst into tears.

Drawing the attention of the Swami's disciple to the great leader, Girish Chandra said: "Perhaps you have always admired your teacher's intellect. Now you see his great heart."

On May 1, 1897, Swami Vivekananda called a meeting of the monastic and lay devotees of Śri Ramakrishna at the house of the Master's intimate disciple Balaram Bose, for the purpose of establishing his work on an organized basis. He told them that by contrasting Hindu society with American society, he was convinced that lack of an organizing spirit was one of the great shortcomings of the Hindu character. Much of the intelligence and energy of the Hindus was being expended without producing any fruitful result. He also recalled how Buddhism had spread both in India and abroad through Buddhist organizations. Therefore he asked the co-operation of the monastic and householder disciples of Śri Ramakrishna in order to organize the educational, philanthropic, and religious activities which he had already inaugurated, but which had hitherto been carried out in an unsystematic way. Further, the Swami declared that in a country like India, in its then current state of development, it would not be wise to form an organization on a democratic basis, where each member had an equal voice and decisions were made according to the vote of the majority. Democratic principles could be followed later, when, with the spread of education, people would learn to sacrifice individual interests and

[28] An allusion to the dramas written by Girish Chandra Ghosh, in which Krishna, Vishnu, and other characters of Hindu mythology play prominent parts.

personal prejudices for the public weal. Therefore, said the Swami, the organization for the time being should be under the leadership of a "dictator," whose
authority everybody must obey. In the fullness of time, it would come to be
guided by the opinion and consent of others. Moreover, he himself was only
acting in the capacity of a servant of the common Master, as were they all.[29]

Swami Vivekananda proposed to the members present that the Association
should "bear the name of him in whose name we have become sannyāsins,
taking whom as your ideal you are leading the life of householders, and whose
holy name, influence, and teachings have, within twelve years of his passing
away, spread in such an unthought-of way both in the East and in the West."
All the members enthusiastically approved of the Swami's proposal, and the
Ramakrishna Mission Association came into existence.

The aim of the Association was to spread the truths that Ramakrishna, for
the good of humanity, had preached and taught through the example of his
own life, and to help others to put them into practice for their physical, mental,
and spiritual advancement.

The duty of the Association was to direct, in the right spirit, the activities
of the movement inaugurated by Śri Ramakrishna for the establishment of fel-
lowship among the followers of different religions, knowing them all to be so
many forms of one undying Eternal Religion.

Its methods of action were to be: (a) to train men so as to make them
competent to teach such knowledge and sciences as are conducive to the material
and spiritual welfare of the masses; (b) to promote and encourage arts and
industries; (c) to introduce and spread among the people in general Vedāntic
and other ideas as elucidated in the life of Śri Ramakrishna.

The Ramakrishna Mission Association was to have two departments of
action: Indian and foreign. The former, through retreats and monasteries established in different parts of India, would train such monks and householders as
might be willing to devote their lives to the teaching of others. The latter would
send trained members of the Order to countries outside India to start centres
there for the preaching of Vedānta in order to bring about a closer relationship
and better understanding between India and foreign countries.

The aims and ideals of the Ramakrishna Mission Association, being purely
spiritual and humanitarian, were to have no connexion with politics.

Swami Vivekananda must have felt a great inner satisfaction after the estab-

[29] A touching incident that happened shortly afterwards and expresses the complete
self-effacement of the Swami, may be narrated here. He handed over to Swami Brahmananda, the newly appointed President of the Ramakrishna Mission Association, all the
money he had brought from America for the purpose of carrying on his Indian activities,
with the request that "only the kids should be eaten and the mother goat be spared,"
meaning that the Association should spend only the interest and not touch the capital.
Thus he himself was left without any personal income. A few minutes later he said that
he would like to go to Calcutta and requested one of his disciples to ask Swami
Brahmananda for a few pennies for the ferry-boat across the Ganges. Swami Brahmananda
felt embarrassed and told him that the whole money belonged to him and that he must
not ask for it in that way. But Swami Vivekananda insisted on being counted as any
other member of the monastery.

lishment of the Association. His vision of employing religion, through head, heart, and hands, for the welfare of man was realized. He found no essential conflict among science, religion, art, and industry. All could be used for the worship of God. God could be served as well through His diverse manifestations as through the contemplation of His non-dual aspect. Further, as the great heart of Ramakrishna had embraced all of mankind with its love, so also the Ramakrishna Mission was pledged to promote brotherhood among different faiths, since their harmony constituted the Eternal Religion.

Swami Vivekananda, the General President, made Brahmananda and Yogananda the President and the Vice-president of the Calcutta centre. Weekly meetings were organized at Balaram's house to discuss the Upanishads, the Bhagavad Gītā, the Vedānta scriptures, and religious subjects in general.[30]

Even now Swami Vivekananda could not completely convince some of his brother disciples about his new conception of religion, namely, the worship of God through the service of man. They had heard Śri Ramakrishna speak time and again against preaching, excessive study of the scriptures, and charitable activities, and exhort aspirants to intensify their love of God through prayer and meditation in solitude. Therefore they regarded Vivekananda's activities in the West as out of harmony with the Master's teachings. One of them said bluntly to the Swami, "You did not preach our Master in America; you only preached yourself." The Swami retorted with equal bluntness, "Let people understand me first; then they will understand Śri Ramakrishna."

On one occasion Swami Vivekananda felt that some of these brother disciples wanted to create a narrow sect in the name of Ramakrishna and turn the Ramakrishna Math into a cult of the Temple, where the religious activities would centre around devotional music, worship, and prayer alone. His words burst upon them like a bomb-shell. He asked them how they knew that his ideas were not in keeping with those of Śri Ramakrishna. "Do you want," he said, "to shut Śri Ramakrishna, the embodiment of infinite ideas, within your own limits? I shall break these limits and scatter his ideas broadcast all over the world. He never enjoined me to introduce his worship and the like."

[30] In 1899 Swami Vivekananda established the Belur Math, the present Headquarters of the Ramakrishna Order, and turned it over to a Board of Trustees drawn from the monastic members of the Ramakrishna Order; the main purpose of the Math was to train monks in spiritual practice and to serve humanity in all possible ways. It was, however, restricted in its public activities. With the establishment of the Belur Math, the Ramakrishna Mission Association ceased to function as an independent organization. Soon the need was felt to conduct extensive philanthropic, charitable, educational, and missionary work. Therefore a separate organization, called the Ramakrishna Mission, was set up to carry on these activities, and a legal status was given to it in 1909. Its membership was open to monks and laymen. But the management of the Ramakrishna Mission was vested in a Governing Body, which, for the time being, consisted of the Trustees of the Belur Math. Both the Ramakrishna Math at Belur, also called the Belur Math, and the Ramakrishna Mission now have branches all over India. The members of the Math devote themselves mainly to the spiritual practices of study, prayer, worship, and meditation, whereas the members of the Mission carry on public activities in various fields.

Had it not been demonstrated to Vivekananda time and again that Śri Ramakrishna was behind him in all his actions? He knew that through the Master's grace alone he had come out triumphant from all ordeals, whether in the wilderness of India or in the busy streets of Chicago.

"Śri Ramakrishna," the Swami continued, "is far greater than the disciples understand him to be. He is the embodiment of infinite spiritual ideas capable of development in infinite ways. . . . One glance of his gracious eyes can create a hundred thousand Vivekanandas at this instant. If he chooses now, instead, to work through me, making me his instrument, I can only bow to his will."

Vivekananda took great care lest sentimentalism and narrowness in one form or another should creep in, for he detested these from the bottom of his heart.

But things came to a climax one day at Balaram's house in Calcutta, when Swami Jogananda, a brother disciple whom Śri Ramakrishna had pointed out as belonging to his "inner circle" of devotees, said that the Master had emphasized bhakti alone for spiritual seekers and that philanthropic activities, organizations, homes of service for the public good, and patriotic work were the Swami's own peculiar ideas, the result of his Western education and travel in Europe and America.

The Swami at first retorted to his brother with a sort of rough humour. He said: "What do you know? You are an ignorant man. . . . What do you understand of religion? You are only good at praying with folded hands: 'O Lord! how beautiful is Your nose! How sweet are Your eyes!' and all such nonsense. . . . And you think your salvation is secured and Śri Ramakrishna will come at the final hour and take you by the hand to the highest heaven! Study, public preaching, and doing humanitarian works are, according to you, māyā, because he said to someone, 'Seek and find God first; doing good to the world is a presumption!' As if God is such an easy thing to be achieved! As if He is such a fool as to make Himself a plaything in the hands of an imbecile!

"You think you have understood Śri Ramakrishna better than myself! You think jnāna is dry knowledge to be attained by a desert path, killing out the tenderest faculties of the heart! Your bhakti is sentimental nonsense which makes one impotent. You want to preach Śri Ramakrishna as you have understood him, which is mighty little! Hands off! Who cares for your Ramakrishna? Who cares for your bhakti and mukti? Who cares what your scriptures say? I will go into a thousand hells cheerfully if I can rouse my countrymen, immersed in tamas, to stand on their own feet and be men inspired with the spirit of karma-yoga. I am not a follower of Ramakrishna or anyone, but of him only who serves and helps others without caring for his own bhakti and mukti!"

The Swami's voice was choked with emotion, his body shook, and his eyes flashed fire. Quickly he went to the next room. A few moments later some of his brother disciples entered the room and found him absorbed in meditation, tears flowing from his half-closed eyes. After nearly an hour the Swami got up, washed his face, and joined his spiritual brothers in the drawing-room. His features still showed traces of the violent storm through which he had just passed; but he had recovered his calmness. He said to them softly:

"When a man attains bhakti, his heart and nerves become so soft and delicate

VIVEKANANDA AS HINDU TEACHER

BRAHMANANDA

PREMANANDA

SARADANANDA

JOGANANDA

NIRANJANANANDA

ADVAITANANDA

ADBHUTANANDA

SHIVANANDA

RAMAKRISHNANANDA

TURIYANANDA

TRIGUNATITANANDA

AKHANDANANDA

SUBODHANANDA

VIJNANANANDA

ABHEDANANDA

Śri Ramakrishna Monastery at Belur

(Vivekananda's room is at left front of second storey.)

that he cannot bear even the touch of a flower! . . . I cannot think or talk of Śri Ramakrishna long without being overwhelmed. So I am always trying to bind myself with the iron chains of jnāna, for still my work for my mother-land is unfinished and my message to the world not fully delivered. So as soon as I find that those feelings of bhakti are trying to come up and sweep me off my feet, I give a hard knock to them and make myself firm and adamant by bringing up austere jnāna. Oh, I have work to do! I am a slave of Ramakrishna, who left his work to be done by me and will not give me rest till I have finished it. And oh, how shall I speak of him? Oh, his love for me!"

He was again about to enter into an ecstatic mood, when Swami Jogananda and the others changed the conversation, took him on the roof for a stroll, and tried to divert his mind by small talk. They felt that Vivekananda's inmost soul had been aroused, and they remembered the Master's saying that the day Naren knew who he was, he would not live in this body. So from that day the brother disciples did not again criticize the Swami's method, knowing fully well that the Master alone was working through him.

From this incident one sees how Vivekananda, in his inmost heart, relished bhakti, the love of God. But in his public utterances he urged the Indians to keep their emotionalism under control; he emphasized the study of Vedānta, because he saw in it a sovereign tonic to revivify them. He further prescribed for his countrymen both manual and spiritual work, scientific research, and service to men. Vivekananda's mission was to infuse energy and faith into a nation of "dyspeptics" held under the spell of their own sentimentality. He wished in all fields of activity to awaken that austere elevation of spirit which arouses heroism.

As with his Master, the natural tendency of Vivekananda's mind was to be absorbed in contemplation of the Absolute. Again, like Śri Ramakrishna, he had to bring down his mind forcibly to the consciousness of the world in order to render service to men. Thus he kept a balance between the burning love of the Absolute and the irresistible appeal of suffering humanity. And what makes Swami Vivekananda the patriot saint of modern India and at the same time endears him so much to the West is that at the times when he had to make a choice between the two, it was always the appeal of suffering humanity that won the day. He cheerfully sacrificed the bliss of samādhi to the amelioration of the suffering of men. The Swami's spirit acted like a contagion upon his brother disciples. One of them, Akhandananda, as stated before, fed and nursed the sufferers from famine at Murshidabad, in Bengal; another, Trigunatita, in 1897 opened a famine-relief centre at Dinajpur. Other centres were established at Deoghar, Dakshineswar, and Calcutta.

Swami Vivekananda was overjoyed to see the happy beginning of his work in India. To Mary Hale he wrote on July 9, 1897:

Only one idea was burning in my brain—to start the machine for elevating the Indian masses, and that I have succeeded in doing to a certain extent.

It would have made your heart glad to see how my boys are working in the midst of famine and disease and misery—nursing by the mat-bed of the cholera-stricken pariah and feeding the starving chandāla, and the Lord sends help to me, to them, to all. . . . He is with me, the Beloved, and He was when I was in America, in England, when I was roaming about unknown from place to place in India. What do I care about what they say?[31] The babies—they do not know any better. What? I, who have realized the Spirit, and the vanity of all earthly nonsense, to be swerved from my path by babies' prattle? Do I look like that? . . . I feel my task is done—at most three or four years more of life are left. I have lost all wish for my salvation. I never wanted earthly enjoyments. I must see my machine in strong working order, and then, knowing for sure that I have put in a lever for the good of humanity, in India at least, which no power can drive back, I will sleep without caring what will be next.

And may I be born again and again, and suffer thousands of miseries, so that I may worship the only God that exists, the only God I believe in, the sum total of all souls. And above all, my God the wicked, my God the miserable, my God the poor of all races, of all species, is the especial object of my worship.

IN NORTHERN INDIA

From May 1897 to the end of that year, the Swami travelled and lectured extensively in Northern India. The physicians had advised him to go as soon as possible to Almora, where the air was dry and cool, and he had been invited by prominent people in Northern India to give discourses on Hinduism. Accompanied by some of his brother disciples and his own disciples, he left Calcutta, and he was joined later by the Seviers, Miss Muller, and Goodwin.

In Lucknow he was given a cordial welcome. The sight of the Himālayas in Almora brought him inner peace and filled his mind with the spirit of detachment and exaltation of which these great mountains are the symbol. But his peace was disturbed for a moment when he received letters from American disciples about the malicious reports against his character spread by Christian missionaries, including Dr. Barrows, who had been the President of the Parliament of Religions in Chicago. Evidently they had become jealous of the Swami's popularity in India. Dr. Barrows told the Americans that the report of the Swami's reception in India was greatly exaggerated. He accused the Swami of being a liar and remarked: "I could never tell whether to take him seriously or not. He struck me as being a Hindu Mark Twain. He is a man of genius and has some following, though only temporary."

The Swami was grieved. At his request the people of Madras had given Dr. Barrows a big reception, but the missionary, lacking religious universalism, had not made much of an impression.

In a mood of weariness the Swami wrote to a friend on June 3, 1897:

As for myself, I am quite content. I have roused a good many of our people, and that was all I wanted. Let things have their course and karma its sway. I have no bonds here below. I have seen life, and it is all self—life is for self, love is for self, honour for self, everything for self. I look back and scarcely find any action I have done for self—even my wicked deeds were not for self. So I am content—not that I feel I have done anything especially good or great, but the world is so little, life so mean a thing, existence so, so servile, that I wonder and smile that human beings, rational souls, should be running after this self—so mean and detestable a prize.

This is the truth. We are caught in a trap, and the sooner one gets out the better for one. I have seen the truth—let the body float up or down, who cares? . . .

[31] Referring to some scurrilous remarks about Swami Vivekananda by certain American missionaries.

I was born for the life of a scholar—retired, quiet, poring over my books. But the Mother dispensed otherwise. Yet the tendency is there.

In Almora the Swami's health improved greatly. On May 29 he wrote to a friend: "I began to take a lot of exercise on horseback, both morning and evening. Since then I have been very much better indeed. . . . I really began to feel that it was a pleasure to have a body. Every movement made me conscious of strength—every movement of the muscles was pleasurable. . . . You ought to see me, Doctor, when I sit meditating in front of the beautiful snow-peaks and repeat from the Upanishads: 'He has neither disease, nor decay, nor death; for verily, he has obtained a body full of the fire of yoga.' "

He was delighted to get the report that his disciples and spiritual brothers were plunging heart and soul into various philanthropic and missionary activities.

From Almora he went on a whirlwind tour of the Punjab and Kashmir, sowing everywhere the seeds of rejuvenated Hinduism. In Bareilly he encouraged the students to organize themselves to carry on the work of practical Vedānta. In Ambala he was happy to see his beloved disciples Mr. and Mrs. Sevier. After spending a few days in Amritsar, Dharamsala, and Murree, he went to Kashmir.

In Jammu the Swami had a long interview with the Mahārājā and discussed with him the possibility of founding in Kashmir a monastery for giving young people training in non-dualism. In the course of the conversation he sadly remarked how the present-day Hindus had deviated from the ideals of their forefathers, and how people were clinging to various superstitions in the name of religion. He said that in olden days people were not outcasted even when they committed such real sins as adultery, and the like; whereas nowadays one became untouchable simply by violating the rules about food.

On the same topic he said a few months later, at Khetri: "The people are neither Hindus nor Vedāntins—they are merely 'don't touchists'; the kitchen is their temple and cooking-pots are their objects of worship. This state of things must go. The sooner it is given up, the better for our religion. Let the Upanishads shine in their glory, and at the same time let not quarrels exist among different sects."

In Lahore the Swami gave a number of lectures, among which was his famous speech on the Vedānta philosophy, lasting over two hours. He urged the students of Lahore to cultivate faith in man as a preparation for faith in God. He asked them to form an organization, purely non-sectarian in character, to teach hygiene to the poor, spread education among them, and nurse the sick. One of his missions in the Punjab was to establish harmony among people belonging to different sects, such as the Ārya Samājists and the orthodox Hindus. It was in Lahore that the Swami met Mr. Tirtha Ram Goswami, then a professor of mathematics, who eventually gained wide recognition as Swami Ram Tirtha. The professor became an ardent admirer of Swami Vivekananda.

Next the Swami travelled to Dehra-Dun, where, for the first ten days, he lived a rather quiet life. But soon he organized a daily class on the Hindu scriptures for his disciples and companions, which he continued to conduct during the whole trip. At the earnest invitation of his beloved disciple the Rājā of Khetri, he visited his capital, stopping on the way at Delhi and Alwar, which were familiar to him from his days of wandering prior to his going to America. Everywhere he met old friends and disciples and treated them with marked affection. The Rājā of Khetri lavished great honours upon him and also gave him a handsome donation for the Belur Math, which was being built at that time.

Before returning to Calcutta, he visited Kishengarh, Ajmere, Jodhpur, Indore, and Khandwa and thus finished his lecture tour in North India. During this tour he explained to his fellow countrymen the salient features of Hinduism and told them that they would have a glorious future if they followed the heritage of their past. He emphasized that the resurgent nationalism of India must be based on her spiritual ideals, but that healthy scientific and techno-logical knowledge from the West, also, had to be assimilated in the process of growth. The fundamental problem of India, he pointed out, was to organize the whole country around religious ideals. By religion the Swami meant not local customs which served only a contemporary purpose, but the eternal prin-ciples taught in the Vedas.

Wherever the Swami went he never wearied of trying to rebuild individual character in India, pointing out that the strength of the whole nation depended upon the strength of the individual. Therefore each individual, he urged, what-ever might be his occupation, should try, if he desired the good of the nation as a whole, to build up his character and acquire such virtues as courage, strength, self-respect, love, and service of others. To the young men, especially, he held out renunciation and service as the highest ideal. He preached the necessity of spreading a real knowledge of Sanskrit, without which a Hindu would remain an alien to his own rich culture. To promote unity among the Hindus, he encouraged intermarriage between castes and sub-castes, and wanted to revive the Indian universities so that they might produce real patriots, rather than clerks, lawyers, diplomats, and Government officials.

Swami Vivekananda's keen intellect saw the need of uniting the Hindus and Moslems on the basis of the Advaita philosophy, which teaches the oneness of all. On June 10, 1898, he wrote to a Moslem gentleman at Nainital:

The Hindus may get the credit for arriving at Advaitism earlier than other races, they being an older race than either the Hebrew or the Arab; yet practical Advaitism, which looks upon and behaves towards all mankind as one's own soul, is yet to be developed among the Hindus universally. On the other hand, our experience is that if ever the followers of any religion approach to this equality in an appreciable degree on the plane of practical work-a-day life—it may be quite unconscious generally of the deeper mean-ing and the underlying principle of such conduct, which the Hindus as a rule so clearly perceive—it is those of Islām and Islām alone.

Therefore we are firmly persuaded that without the help of practical Islām, the theories of Vedāntism, however fine and wonderful they may be, are entirely valueless to the vast mass of mankind. We want to lead mankind to the place where there is neither the Vedas nor the Bible nor the Koran; yet this has to be done by harmonizing the Vedas, the Bible, and the Koran. Mankind ought to be taught that religions are but the varied expressions of the Religion which is Oneness, so that each may choose the path that suits him best.

For our own motherland a junction of the two great systems, Hinduism and Islām— Vedāntic brain and Islāmic body—is the only hope.

I see in my mind's eye the future perfect India rising out of this chaos and strife, glorious and invincible, with Vedāntic brain and Islāmic body.

For the regeneration of India, in the Swami's view, the help of the West was indispensable. The thought of India had been uppermost in his mind when he had journeyed to America. On April 6, 1897, the Swami, in the course of a letter to the lady editor of an Indian magazine, had written: "It has been for the good of India that religious preaching in the West has been done and will be done. It has ever been my conviction that we shall not be able to rise unless the Western countries come to our help. In India no appreciation of merit can be found, no financial support, and what is most lamentable of all, there is not a bit of practicality."

TRAINING OF THE DISCIPLES

The year 1898 was chiefly devoted to the training of Vivekananda's disciples, both Indian and Western, and to the consolidation of the work already started. During this period he also made trips to Darjeeling, Almora, and Kashmir.

In February 1898, the monastery was removed from Alambazar to Nilambar Mukherjee's garden house in the village of Belur, on the west bank of the Ganges. The Swami, while in Calcutta, lived at Balaram Bose's house, which had been a favourite haunt of Śri Ramakrishna's during his lifetime. But he had no rest either in the monastery or in Calcutta, where streams of visitors came to him daily. Moreover, conducting a heavy correspondence consumed much of his time and energy; one cannot but be amazed at the hundreds of letters the Swami wrote with his own hand to friends and disciples. Most of these reveal his intense thinking, and some his superb wit.

While at the monastery, he paid especial attention to the training of the sannyāsins and the brahmachārins, who, inspired by his message, had renounced home and dedicated themselves to the realization of God and the service of humanity. Besides conducting regular classes on the Upanishads, the Bhagavad Gitā, the physical sciences, and the history of the nations, he would spend hours with the students in meditation and devotional singing. Spiritual practices were intensified on holy days.

In the early part of 1898, the site of the Belur Math, the present Head-quarters of the Ramakrishna Math and Mission, was purchased with the help of a generous donation from Miss Muller, the devoted admirer of the Swami. Mrs. Ole Bull gave another handsome gift to complete the construction, and the shrine at the Belur Math was consecrated, as we shall see, on December 9, 1898. Sometime during this period the Swami initiated into the monastic life Swami Swarupananda, whom he considered to be a real "acquisition." This qualified aspirant was given initiation after only a few days' stay at the monastery, contrary to the general rule of the Ramakrishna Order. Later he became editor of the monthly magazine *Prabuddha Bhārata*, and president of the Advaita Āsrama at Mayavati, in the Himālayas.

Among the Western devotees who lived with Swami Vivekananda at this time were Mr. and Mrs. Sevier, Mrs. Ole Bull, Miss Henrietta F. Muller, Miss Josephine MacLeod, and Miss Margaret E. Noble, all of whom travelled with him at various times in Northern India. The Seviers identified themselves completely with the work at the Mayavati Advaita Āśrama. Mrs. Ole Bull, the wife of the famous Norwegian violinist, and a lady of social position, great culture, and large heart, had been an ardent admirer of the Swami during his American trip. Miss Muller, who knew the Swami in both England and America and had helped defray, together with the Seviers and Mr. Sturdy, the expenses of his work in England, had come to India to organize an educational institution for Indian women.

Miss MacLeod had attended Swami Vivekananda's classes in New York, and for months at a time he had been the guest of her relatives at their country home, Ridgely Manor. She became his life-long friend and admirer and cherished his memory till the last day of her life, but though she was devoted to him, she never renounced her independence, nor did he demand that she should. By way of spiritual instruction, the Swami had once asked Miss MacLeod to meditate on Om for a week and report to him afterwards. When the teacher inquired how she felt, she said that "it was like a glow in the heart." He encouraged her and said: "Good, keep on." Many years later she told her friends that the Swami made her realize that she was in eternity. "Always remember," the Swami had admonished her, "you are incidentally an American and a woman, but always a child of God. Tell yourself day and night who you are. Never forget it." To her brother-in-law, Francis H. Leggett, the Swami had written, on July 6, 1896, in appreciation of Miss MacLeod: "I simply admire Joe Joe for her tact and quiet ways. She is a feminine statesman. She could wield a kingdom. I have seldom seen such strong yet good common sense in a human being."

When Miss MacLeod asked the Swami's permission to come to India, he wrote on a postcard: "Do come by all means, only you must remember this: The Europeans and Indians live as oil and water. Even to speak of living with the natives is damning, even at the capitals. You will have to bear with people who wear only a loin-cloth; you will see me with only a loin-cloth about me. Dirt and filth everywhere, and brown people. But you will have plenty of men to talk philosophy to you." He also wrote to her that she must not come to India if she expected anything else, for the Indians could not "bear one more word of criticism."

On one occasion, while travelling in Kashmir with the Swami and his party, she happened to make a laughing remark about one of his South Indian disciples with the caste-mark of the brāhmins of his sect on his forehead. This appeared grotesque to her. The Swami turned upon her "like a lion, withered her with a glance, and cried: 'Hands off! Who are you? What have you ever done?' "

Miss MacLeod was crestfallen. But later she learnt that the same poor brāhmin had been one of those who, by begging, had collected the money that had made it possible for the Swami to undertake his trip to America.

"How can I best help you," she asked the Swami when she arrived in India. "Love India," was his reply.

One day Swami Vivekananda told Miss MacLeod that since his return to India he had had no personal money. She at once promised to pay him fifty dollars a month as long as he lived and immediately gave him three hundred dollars for six months in advance. The Swami asked jokingly if it would be enough for him.

"Not if you take heavy cream every day!" she said.

The Swami gave the money to Swami Trigunatita to defray the initial expenses of the newly started Bengali magazine, the *Udbodhan*.

But of all Swami Vivekananda's Western disciples, the most remarkable was Margaret E. Noble, who was truly his spiritual daughter. She had attended the Swami's classes and lectures in London and resolved to dedicate her life to his work in India. When she expressed to him her desire to come to India, the Swami wrote to her, on July 29, 1897: "Let me tell you frankly that I am now convinced that you have a great future in the work for India. What was wanted was not a man but a woman, a real lioness, to work for the Indians—women especially. India cannot yet produce great women; she must borrow them from other nations. Your education, sincerity, purity, immense love, determination, and above all, your Celtic blood, make you just the woman wanted.

"Yet the difficulties are many. You cannot form any idea of the misery, the superstition, and the slavery that are here. You will be in the midst of a mass of half-naked men and women with quaint ideas of caste and isolation, shunning the white-skins through fear or hatred, and hated by them intensely. On the other hand, you will be looked upon by the white as a crank, and every one of your movements will be watched with suspicion.

"Then the climate is fearfully hot, our winter in most places being like your summer, and in the south it is always blazing. Not one European comfort is to be had in places out of the cities. If in spite of all this you dare venture into the work, you are welcome, a hundred times welcome. As for me, I am nobody here as elsewhere, but what little influence I have shall be devoted to your service.

"You must think well before you plunge in, and afterwards if you fail in this or get disgusted, on my part I promise you *I will stand by you unto death*, whether you work for India or not, whether you give up Vedānta or remain in it. 'The tusks of the elephant come out but never go back'—so are the words of a man never retracted. I promise you that." He further asked her to stand on her own feet and never seek help from his other Western women devotees.

Miss Noble came to India on January 28, 1898, to work with Miss Muller for the education of Indian women. The Swami warmly introduced her to the public of Calcutta as a "gift of England to India," and in March made her take the vow of brahmacharya, that is to say, the life of a religious celibate devoted to the realization of God. He also gave her the name of Nivedita, the "Dedicated," by which she has ever since been cherished by the Indians with deep respect and affection. The ceremony was performed in the chapel of the monastery. He first taught her how to worship Śiva and then made the whole ceremony culminate in an offering at the feet of Buddha.

"Go thou," he said, "and follow him who was born and gave his life for others five hundred times before he attained the vision of the Buddha."

The Swami now engaged himself in the training of Sister Nivedita along with the other Western disciples. And certainly it was a most arduous task. They were asked to associate intimately with the Holy Mother, the widow of Śri

Ramakrishna, who at once adopted them as her "children." Then the Swami would visit them almost daily to reveal to them the deep secrets of the Indian world—its history, folklore, customs, and traditions. Mercilessly he tried to uproot from their minds all preconceived notions and wrong ideas about India. He wanted them to love India as she was at the present time, with her poverty, ignorance, and backwardness, and not the India of yore, when she had produced great philosophies, epics, dramas, and religious systems.

It was not always easy for the Western disciples to understand the religious ideals and forms of worship of the Hindus. For instance, one day in the great Kāli temple of Calcutta, one Western lady shuddered at the sight of the blood of the goats sacrificed before the Deity, and exclaimed, "Why is there blood before the Goddess?" Quickly the Swami retorted, "Why not a little blood to complete the picture?"

The disciples had been brought up in the tradition of Protestant Christianity, in which the Godhead was associated only with what was benign and beautiful, and Satan with the opposite.

With a view to Hinduizing their minds, the Swami asked his Western disciples to visit Hindu ladies at their homes and to observe their dress, food, and customs, which were radically different from their own. Thus he put to a severe test their love for Vedānta and India. In the West they had regarded the Swami as a prophet showing them the path of liberation, and as a teacher of the universal religion. But in India he appeared before them, in addition, in the rôle of a patriot, an indefatigable worker for the regeneration of his motherland.

The Swami began to teach Nivedita to lose herself completely in the Indian consciousness. She gradually adopted the food, clothes, language, and general habits of the Hindus.

"You have to set yourself," he said to her, "to Hinduize your thoughts, your needs, your conceptions, your habits. Your life, internal and external, has to become all that an orthodox brāhmin brahmachārini's ought to be. The method will come to you if you only desire it sufficiently. But you have to forget your past and cause it to be forgotten." He wanted her to address the Hindus "in terms of their own orthodoxy."

Swami Vivekananda would not tolerate in his Western disciples any trace of chauvinism, any patronizing attitude or stupid criticism of the Indian way of life. They could serve India only if they loved India, and they could love India only if they knew India, her past glories and her present problems. Thus later he took them on his trip to Northern India, including Almora and Kashmir, and told them of the sanctity of Benares and the magnificence of Agra and Delhi; he related to them the history of the Moghul Emperors and the Rajput heroes, and also described the peasant's life, the duties of a farm housewife, and the hospitality of poor villagers to wandering monks. The teacher and his disciples saw together the sacred rivers, the dense forests, the lofty mountains, the sun-baked plains, the hot sands of the desert, and the gravel beds of the rivers, all of which had played their parts in the creation of Indian culture. And the Swami told them that in India custom and culture were one. The visible manifestations of the culture were the system of caste, the duties determined by the different stages of life, the respect of parents as incarnate gods, the appointed hours of religious service, the shrine used for daily worship, the chanting of the Vedas by the brāhmin children, the eating of food with the right hand and its use in worship and japa, the austerities of Hindu widows, the kneeling in prayer of the Moslems wherever the time of prayer might find them, and the ideal of equality practised by the followers of Mohammed.

Nivedita possessed an aggressively Occidental and intensely English outlook. It was not easy for her to eradicate instinctive national loyalties and strong personal likes and dislikes. A clash between the teacher and the disciple was inevitable. Ruthlessly the Swami crushed her pride in her English upbringing. Perhaps, at the same time, he wanted to protect her against the passionate adoration she had for him. Nivedita suffered bitter anguish.

The whole thing reached its climax while they were travelling together, some time after, in the Himālayas. One day Miss MacLeod thought that Nivedita could no longer bear the strain, and interceded kindly and gravely with the Swami. "He listened," Sister Nivedita wrote later, "and went away. At evening, however, he returned, and finding us together on the veranda, he turned to her (Miss MacLeod) and said with the simplicity of a child: 'You were right. There must be a change. I am going away to the forests to be alone, and when I come back I shall bring peace.' Then he turned away and saw that above us the moon was new, and a sudden exaltation came into his voice as he said: 'See, the Mohammedans think much of the new moon. Let us also, with the new moon, begin a new life.' " As he said these words, he lifted his hand and blessed his rebellious disciple, who by this time was kneeling before him. It was assuredly a moment of wonderful sweetness of reconciliation.

That evening in meditation Nivedita found herself gazing deep into an Infinite Good, to the recognition of which no egotistic reasoning had led her. "And," she wrote, "I understood for the first time that the greatest teachers may destroy in us a personal relation only in order to bestow the Impersonal Vision in its place."

To resume our story, on March 30, 1898, the Swami left for Darjeeling, for he badly needed a change to the cool air of the Himālayas. Hardly had he begun to feel the improvement in his health, when he had to come down to Calcutta, where an outbreak of plague was striking terror.

Immediately he made plans for relief work with the help of the members of the monastery and volunteers from Calcutta.

When a brother disciple asked him where he would get funds, the Swami replied: "Why, we shall sell if necessary the land which has just been purchased for the monastery. We are sannyāsins; we must be ready to sleep under the trees and live on alms as we did before. Must we care for the monastery and possessions when by disposing of them we could relieve thousands of helpless people suffering before our own eyes?" Fortunately this extreme step was not necessary; the public gave him money for the relief work.

The Swami worked hard to assuage the suffering of the afflicted people. Their love and admiration for him knew no bounds as they saw this practical application of Vedānta at a time of human need.

The plague having been brought under control, the Swami left Calcutta for

Nainital on May 11, accompanied by, among others, his Western disciples. From there the party went to Almora where they met the Seviers. During this tour the Swami never ceased instructing his disciples. For his Western companions it was a rare opportunity to learn Indian history, religion, and philosophy direct from one who was an incarnation of the spirit of India. Some of the talks the Swami gave were recorded by Sister Nivedita in her charming book *Notes of Some Wanderings with the Swami Vivekananda.*

In Almora the Swami received news of the deaths of Pavhari Baba and Mr. Goodwin. He had been closely drawn to the former during his days of wandering. Goodwin died on June 2. Hearing of this irreparable loss, the Swami exclaimed in bitter grief, "My right hand is gone!" To Goodwin's mother he wrote a letter of condolence in which he said: "The debt of gratitude I owe him can never be repaid, and those who think they have been helped by any thought of mine ought to know that almost every word of it was published through the untiring and most unselfish exertions of Mr. Goodwin. In him I have lost a friend true as steel, a disciple of never-failing devotion, a worker who knew not what tiring was, and the world is less rich by the passing away of one of those few who are born, as it were, to live only for others."

The Swami also sent her the following poem, which he had written in memory of Goodwin, bearing witness to the affection of the teacher for the disciple:

REQUIESCAT IN PACE

Speed forth, O soul! upon thy star-strewn path;
Speed, blissful one! where thought is ever free,
Where time and space no longer mist the view;
Eternal peace and blessings be with thee!

Thy service true, complete thy sacrifice;
Thy home the heart of love transcendent find!
Remembrance sweet, that kills all space and time,
Like altar roses, fill thy place behind!

Thy bonds are broke, thy quest in bliss is found,
And one with That which comes as death and life,
Thou helpful one! unselfish e'er on earth,
Ahead, still help with love this world of strife!

Before the Swami left Almora, he arranged to start again the monthly magazine *Prabuddha Bhārata,* which had ceased publication with the death of its gifted editor, B. R. Rajam Iyer. Swami Swarupananda became its new editor, and Captain Sevier, the manager. The magazine began its new career at Almora. Then, on June 11, the Swami, in the company of his Western disciples, left for Kashmir as the guest of Mrs. Ole Bull.

The trip to Kashmir was an unforgettable experience for the Westerners. The natural beauty of the country, with its snow-capped mountains reflected in the water of the lakes, its verdant forests, multi-coloured flowers, and stately poplar and chennar trees, make the valley of Kashmir a paradise on earth. Throughout the journey the Swami poured out his heart and soul to his disciples. At first he was almost obsessed with the ideal of Śiva, whom he had worshipped since boyhood, and for days he told the disciples legends relating to the great God of renunciation. The party spent a few days in house-boats, and in the afternoons the Swami would take his companions for long walks across the fields. The conversations were always stimulating. One day he spoke of Genghis Khan and declared that he was not a vulgar aggressor; he compared the Mongol Emperor to Napoleon and Alexander, saying that they all wanted to unify the world and that it was perhaps the same soul that had incarnated itself three times in the hope of bringing about human unity through political conquest. In the same way, he said, one Soul might have come again and again as Krishna, Buddha, and Christ, to bring about the unity of mankind through religion.

In Kashmir the Swami pined for solitude. The desire for the solitary life of a monk became irresistible; and he would often break away from the little party to roam alone. After his return he would make some such remark as: "It is a sin to think of the body," "It is wrong to manifest power," or "Things do not grow better; they remain as they are. It is we who grow better, by the changes we make in ourselves." Often he seemed to be drifting without any plan, and the disciples noticed his strange detachment. "At no time," Sister Nivedita wrote, "would it have surprised us had someone told us that today or tomorrow he would be gone for ever, that we were listening to his voice for the last time."

This planlessness was observed in him more and more as his earthly existence drew towards its end. Two years later, when Sister Nivedita gave him a bit of worldly advice, the Swami exclaimed in indignation: "Plans! Plans! That is why you Western people can never create a religion! If any of you ever did, it was only a few Catholic saints who had no plans. Religion was never, never preached by planners!"

About solitude as a spiritual discipline, the Swami said one day that an Indian could not expect to know himself till he had been alone for twenty years, whereas from the Western standpoint a man could not live alone for twenty years and remain quite sane. On the Fourth of July the Swami gave a surprise to his American disciples by arranging for its celebration in an appropriate manner. An American flag was made with the help of a brāhmin tailor, and the Swami composed the following poem:

TO THE FOURTH OF JULY

Behold, the dark clouds melt away
That gathered thick at night and hung
So like a gloomy pall above the earth!
Before thy magic touch the world
Awakes. The birds in chorus sing.
The flowers raise their star-like crowns,
Dew-set, and wave thee welcome fair.
The lakes are opening wide, in love,
Their hundred thousand lotus-eyes
To welcome thee with all their depth.
All hail to thee, thou lord of light!
A welcome new to thee today,
O sun! Today thou sheddest liberty!

Bethink thee how the world did wait
And search for thee, through time and clime!
Some gave up home and love of friends
And went in quest of thee, self-banishèd,
Through dreary oceans, through primeval forests,
Each step a struggle for their life or death;
Then came the day when work bore fruit,
And worship, love, and sacrifice,
Fulfilled, accepted, and complete.
Then thou, propitious, rose to shed
The light of freedom on mankind.

Move on, O lord, in thy resistless path,
Till thy high noon o'erspreads the world,
Till every land reflects thy light,
Till men and women, with uplifted head,
Behold their shackles broken and know
In springing joy their life renewed!

As the Swami's mood changed he spoke of renunciation. He showed scorn for the worldly life and said: "As is the difference between a fire-fly and the blazing sun, between a little pond and the infinite ocean, a mustard seed and the mountain of Meru, such is the difference between the householder and the sannyāsin." Had it not been for the ochre robe, the emblem of monasticism, he pointed out, luxury and worldliness would have robbed man of his manliness.

Thus the party spent their time on the river, the teacher providing a veritable university for the education of his disciples. The conversation touched upon all subjects—Vedic rituals, Roman Catholic doctrine, Christ, St. Paul, the growth of Christianity, Buddha.

Of Buddha, the Swami said that he was the greatest man that ever lived. "Above all, he never claimed worship. Buddha said: 'Buddha is not a man, but a state. I have found the way. Enter all of you!' "

Then the talk would drift to the conception of sin among the Egyptian, Semitic, and Āryan races. According to the Vedic conception, the Swami said, the Devil is the Lord of Anger, and with Buddhists he is Māra, the Lord of Lust. Whereas in the Bible the creation was under the dual control of God and Satan, in Hinduism Satan represented defilement, never duality.

Next the Swami would speak about the chief characteristics of the different nations. "You are so morbid, you Westerners," he said one day. "You worship sorrow! All through your country I found that. Social life in the West is like a peal of laughter, but underneath it is a wail. The whole things ends in a sob. The fun and frivolity are all on the surface; really, it is full of tragic intensity. Here it is sad and gloomy on the outside, but underneath are detachment and merriment."

Once, at Islamabad, as the group sat round him on the grass in an apple orchard, the Swami repeated what he had said in England after facing a mad bull. Picking up two pebbles in his hand, he said: "Whenever death approaches me all weakness vanishes. I have neither fear nor doubt nor thought of the external. I simply busy myself making ready to die. I am as hard as that"

—and the stones struck each other in his hand—"for I have touched the feet of God!"

At Islamabad the Swami announced his desire to make a pilgrimage to the great image of Śiva in the cave of Amarnāth in the glacial valley of the Western Himālayas. He asked Nivedita to accompany him so that she, a future worker, might have direct knowledge of the Hindu pilgrim's life. They became a part of a crowd of thousands of pilgrims, who formed at each halting-place a whole town of tents.

A sudden change came over the Swami. He became one of the pilgrims, scrupulously observing the most humble practices demanded by custom. He ate one meal a day, cooked in the orthodox fashion, and sought solitude as far as possible to tell his beads and practise meditation. In order to reach the destination, he had to climb up rocky slopes along dangerous paths, cross several miles of glacier, and bathe in the icy water of sacred streams.

On August 2 the party arrived at the enormous cavern, large enough to contain a vast cathedral. At the back of the cave, in a niche of deepest shadow, stood the image of Śiva, all ice. The Swami, who had fallen behind, entered the cave, his whole frame shaking with emotion. His naked body was smeared with ashes, and his face radiant with devotion. Then he prostrated himself in the darkness of the cave before that glittering whiteness.

A song of praise from hundreds of throats echoed in the cavern. The Swami almost fainted. He had a vision of Śiva Himself. The details of the experience he never told anyone, except that he had been granted the grace of Amarnāth, the Lord of Immortality, not to die until he himself willed it.

The effect of the experience shattered his nerves. When he emerged from the grotto, there was a clot of blood in his left eye; his heart was dilated and never regained its normal condition. For days he spoke of nothing but Śiva. He said: "The image was the Lord Himself. It was all worship there. I have never seen anything so beautiful, so inspiring."

On August 8 the party arrived at Srinagar, where they remained until September 30. During this period the Swami felt an intense desire for meditation and solitude. The Mahārājā of Kashmir treated him with the utmost respect and wanted him to choose a tract of land for the establishment of a monastery and a Sanskrit college. The land was selected and the proposal sent to the British Resident for approval. But the British Agent refused to grant the land. The Swami accepted the whole thing philosophically.

A month later his devotion was directed to Kālī, the Divine Mother, whom Ramakrishna had called affectionately "my Mother."

A unique symbol of the Godhead, Kālī represents the totality of the universe: creation and destruction, life and death, good and evil, pain and pleasure, and all the pairs of opposites. She seems to be black when viewed from a distance, like the water of the ocean; but to the intimate observer She is without colour, being one with Brahman, whose creative energy She represents.

In one aspect She appears terrible, with a garland of human skulls, a girdle of human fingers, her tongue dripping blood, a decapitated human head in one hand and a shining sword in the other, surrounded by jackals that haunt the cremation ground—a veritable picture of terror. The other side is benign and gracious, ready to confer upon Her devotees the boon of immortality. She reels as if drunk: who could have created this mad world except in a fit of drunkenness? Kāli stands on the bosom of Her Divine Consort, Śiva, the symbol of Brahman; for Kāli, or Nature, cannot work unless energized by the touch of the Absolute. And in reality Brahman and Kāli, the Absolute and Its Creative Energy, are identical, like fire and its power to burn.

The Hindu mind does not make a sweepingly moralistic distinction between good and evil. Both are facts of the phenomenal world and are perceived to exist when māyā hides the Absolute, which is beyond good and evil. Ramakrishna emphasized the benign aspect of the Divine Mother Kāli and propitiated Her to obtain the vision of the Absolute. Swami Vivekananda suddenly felt the appeal of Her destructive side. But is there really any difference between the process of creation and destruction? Is not the one without the other an illusion of the mind?

Vivekananda realized that the Divine Mother is omnipresent. Wherever he turned, he was conscious of the presence of the Mother, "as if She were a person in the room." He felt that it was She "whose hands are clasped with my own and who leads me as though I were a child." It was touching to see him worship the four-year-old daughter of his Mohammedan boatman as the symbol of the Divine Mother.

His meditation on Kāli became intense, and one day he had a most vivid experience. He centred "his whole attention on the dark, the painful, and the inscrutable" aspect of Reality, with a determination to reach by this particular path the Non-duality behind phenomena. His whole frame trembled, as if from an electric shock. He had a vision of Kāli, the mighty Destructress lurking behind the veil of life, the Terrible One, hidden by the dust of the living who pass by, and all the appearances raised by their feet. In a fever, he groped in the dark for pencil and paper and wrote his famous poem "Kāli the Mother"; then he fell exhausted:

The stars are blotted out,
The clouds are covering clouds,
It is darkness, vibrant, sonant;
In the roaring, whirling wind
Are the souls of a million lunatics,
Loosed from the prison-house,
Wrenching trees by the roots,
Sweeping all from the path.
The sea has joined the fray
And swirls up mountain-waves
To reach the pitchy sky.
The flash of lurid light
Reveals on every side
A thousand thousand shades
Of death, begrimed and black.

Scattering plagues and sorrows,
Dancing mad with joy,
Come, Mother, come!

> For terror is Thy name,
> Death is in Thy breath,
> And every shaking step
> Destroys a world for e'er.
> Thou Time, the All-destroyer,
> Come, O Mother, come!
>
> Who dares misery love,
> And hug the form of death,
> Enjoy destruction's dance—
> To him the Mother comes.

The Swami now talked to his disciples only about Kāli, the Mother, describing Her as "time, change, and ceaseless energy." He would say with the great Psalmist: "Though Thou slay me, yet I will trust in Thee."

"It is a mistake," the Swami said, "to hold that with all men pleasure is the motive. Quite as many are born to seek pain. There can be bliss in torture, too. Let us worship terror for its own sake.

"Learn to recognize the Mother as instinctively in evil, terror, sorrow, and annihilation as in that which makes for sweetness and joy!

"Only by the worship of the Terrible can the Terrible itself be overcome, and immortality gained. Meditate on death! Meditate on death! Worship the Terrible, the Terrible, the Terrible! And the Mother Herself is Brahman! Even Her curse is a blessing. The heart must become a cremation ground—pride, selfishness, and desire all burnt to ashes. Then, and then alone, will the Mother come."

The Western disciples, brought up in a Western faith which taught them to see good, order, comfort, and beauty alone in the creation of a wise Providence, were shaken by the typhoon of a Cosmic Reality invoked by the Hindu visionary. Sister Nivedita writes:

And as he spoke, the underlying egoism of worship that is devoted to the kind God, to Providence, the consoling Deity, without a heart for God in the earthquake or God in the volcano, overwhelmed the listener. One saw that such worship was at bottom, as the Hindu calls it, merely "shopkeeping," and one realized the infinitely greater boldness and truth of teaching that God manifests through evil as well as through good. One saw that the true attitude for the mind and will that are not to be baffled by the personal self, was in fact that determination, in the stern words of Swami Vivekananda, "to seek death, not life, to hurl oneself upon the sword's point, to become one with the Terrible for evermore."

Heroism, to Vivekananda, was the soul of action. He wanted to see Ultimate Truth in all its terrible nakedness, and refused to soften it in any shape or manner. His love of Truth expected nothing in return; he scorned the bargain of "giving to get in return" and all its promise of paradise.

But the gentle Ramakrishna, though aware of the Godhead in all its aspects, had emphasized Its benign side. One day several men had been arguing before him about the attributes of God, attempting to find out, by reason, their meaning. Śri Ramakrishna stopped them, saying: "Enough, enough! What is the use of disputing whether the divine attributes are reasonable or not? . . . You say that God is good: can you convince me of His goodness by this reasoning? Look at the flood that has just caused the death of thousands. How can you prove that a benevolent God ordered it? You will perhaps reply that the same flood swept away uncleanliness and watered the earth, and so on. But could not a good God do that without drowning thousands of innocent men, women, and children?"

Thereupon one of the disputants said, "Then ought we to believe that God is cruel?"

"O idiot," cried Ramakrishna, "who said that? Fold your hands and say humbly, 'O God, we are too feeble and too weak to understand Thy nature and Thy deeds. Deign to enlighten us!' Do not argue. Love!"

God is no doubt Good, True, and Beautiful; but these attributes are utterly different from their counterparts in the relative world.

The Swami, during these days, taught his disciples to worship God like heroes. He would say: "There must be no fear, no begging, but demanding—demanding the Highest. The true devotees of the Mother are as hard as adamant and as fearless as lions. They are not in the least upset if the whole universe suddenly crumbles into dust at their feet. Make Her listen to you. None of that cringing to Mother! Remember, She is all-powerful; She can make heroes out of stones."

On September 30 Swami Vivekananda retired to a temple of the Divine Mother, where he stayed alone for a week. There he worshipped the Deity, known as Kshirbhavāni, following the time-honoured ritual, praying and meditating like a humble pilgrim. Every morning he also worshipped a brāhmin's little daughter as the symbol of the Divine Virgin. And he was blessed with deep experiences, some of which were most remarkable and indicated to him that his mission on earth was finished.

He had a vision of the Goddess and found Her a living Deity. But the temple had been destroyed by the Moslem invaders, and the image placed in a niche surrounded by ruins. Surveying this desecration, the Swami felt distressed at heart and said to himself: "How could the people have permitted such sacrilege without offering strenuous resistance? If I had been here then, I would never have allowed such a thing. I would have laid down my life to protect the Mother." Thereupon he heard the voice of the Goddess saying: "What if unbelievers should enter My temple and defile My image? What is that to you? Do you protect Me, or do I protect you?" Referring to this experience after his return, he said to his disciples: "All my patriotism is gone. Everything is gone. Now it is only 'Mother! Mother!' I have been very wrong. . . . I am only a little child." He wanted to say more, but could not; he declared that it was not fitting that he should go on. Significantly, he added that *spiritually* he was no longer bound to the world.

Another day, in the course of his worship, the thought flashed through the Swami's mind that he should try to build a new temple in the place of the present dilapidated one, just as he had built a monastery and temple at Belur to Śri Ramakrishna. He even thought of trying to raise funds from his wealthy American disciples and friends. At once the Mother said to him: "My child!

If I so wish I can have innumerable temples and monastic centres. I can even this moment raise a seven-storied golden temple on this very spot."

"Since I heard that divine voice," the Swami said to a disciple in Calcutta much later, "I have ceased making any more plans. Let these things be as Mother wills."

Śri Ramakrishna had said long ago that Narendranath would live in the physical body to do the Mother's work and that as soon as this work was finished, he would cast off his body by his own will. Were the visions at the temple of Kshirbhavāni a premonition of the approaching dissolution?

When the Swami rejoined his disciples at Srinagar, he was an altogether different person. He raised his hand in benediction and then placed some marigolds, which he had offered to the Deity, on the head of every one of his disciples. "No more 'Hari Om!' " he said. "It is all 'Mother' now!" Though he lived with them, the disciples saw very little of him. For hours he would stroll in the woods beside the river, absorbed within himself. One day he appeared before them with shaven head, dressed as the simplest sannyāsin and with a look of unapproachable austerity on his face. He repeated his own poem "Kāli the Mother" and said, "It all came true, every word of it; and I have proved it, for I have hugged the form of death."

Sister Nivedita writes: "The physical ebb of the great experience through which he had just passed—for even suffering becomes impossible when a given point of weariness is reached; and similarly, the body refuses to harbour a certain intensity of the spiritual life for an indefinite period—was leaving him, doubtless, more exhausted than he himself suspected. All this contributed, one imagines, to a feeling that none of us knew for how long a time we might now be parting."

The party left Kashmir on October 11 and came down to Lahore. The Western disciples went to Agra, Delhi, and the other principal cities of Northern India for sight-seeing, and the Swami, accompanied by his disciple Sadananda, arrived at Belur on October 18. His brother disciples saw that he was very pallid and ill. He suffered from suffocating attacks of asthma; when he emerged from its painful fits, his face looked blue, like that of a drowning man. But in spite of all, he plunged headlong into numerous activities.

On November 12, 1898, the day of the worship of Kāli, the Nivedita Girls' School was opened in Calcutta. At the end of the inaugural ceremony the Holy Mother, Śri Ramakrishna's consort, "prayed that the blessing of the Great Mother of the universe might be upon the school and that the girls it should train might be ideal girls." Nivedita, who witnessed the ceremony with the Swamis of the Order, said: "I cannot imagine a grander omen than her blessing spoken over the educated Hindu womanhood of the future."

The dedication of the school was the beginning of Nivedita's work in India. The Swami gave her complete freedom about the way to run it. He told her that she was free from her collaborators if she so chose; and that she might, if she wished, give the work a "definite religious colour" or even make it sectarian. Then he added, "You may wish through a sect to rise beyond all sects."

On December 9, 1898, the Ramakrishna Monastery at Belur was formally consecrated by the Swami with the installation of the Master's image in the chapel. The plot of land, as already stated, had been purchased the previous year and had been consecrated with proper religious ceremony in March that year. The Swami himself had performed the worship on that occasion and afterwards had carried on his shoulder the copper vessel containing the Master's sacred relics. While bearing it he said to a disciple: "The Master once told me, 'I will go and live wherever you take me, carrying me on your shoulder, be it under a tree or in the humblest cottage.' With faith in that gracious promise I myself am now carrying him to the site of our future Math. Know for certain, my boy, that so long as his name inspires his followers with the ideal of purity, holiness, and charity for all men, even so long shall he, the Master, sanctify this place with his presence."

Of the glorious future he saw for the monastery the Swami said: "It will be a centre in which will be recognized and practised a grand harmony of all creeds and faiths as exemplified in the life of Śri Ramakrishna, and religion in its universal aspect, alone, will be preached. And from this centre of universal toleration will go forth the shining message of goodwill, peace, and harmony to deluge the whole world." He warned all of the danger of sectarianism's creeping in if they became careless.

After the ceremony, he addressed the assembled monks, brahmachārins, and lay devotees as follows: "Do you all, my brothers, pray to the Lord with all your heart and soul that He, the Divine Incarnation of the age, may bless this place with his hallowed presence for ever and ever, and make it a unique centre, a holy land, of harmony of different religions and sects, for the good of the many, for the happiness of the many."

Swami Vivekananda was in an ecstatic mood. He had accomplished the great task of finding a permanent place on which to build a temple for the Master, with a monastery for his brother disciples and the monks of the future that should serve as the headquarters of the Ramakrishna Order for the propagation of Śri Ramakrishna's teachings. He felt as if the heavy responsibility that he had carried on his shoulders for the past twelve years had been lifted. He wanted the monastery at Belur to be a finished university where Indian mystical wisdom and Western practical science would be taught side by side. And he spoke of the threefold activities of the monastery: annadāna, the gift of food; vidyādāna, the gift of intellectual knowledge; and jnānadāna, the gift of spiritual wisdom. These three, properly balanced, would, in the Swami's opinion, make a complete man. The brahmachārins of the monastery, through unselfish service of men, would purify their minds and thus qualify themselves for the supreme knowledge of Brahman.

Swami Vivekananda in his vivid imagination saw the different sections of the monastery allotted to different functions—the free kitchen for the distribution of food to the hungry, the university for the imparting of knowledge, the quarters for devotees from Europe and America, and so forth and so on. The spiritual ideals emanating from the Belur Math, he said, would influence the thought-currents of the world for eleven hundred years.

"All these visions are rising before me"—these were his very words.

It was a few months before the buildings of the new monastery were com-

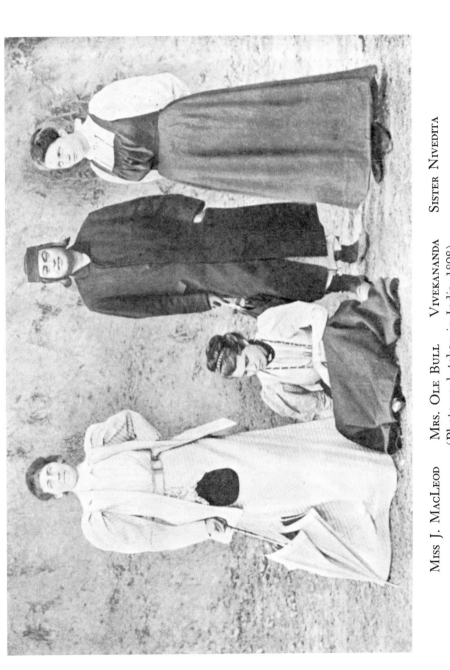

Miss J. MacLeod   Mrs. Ole Bull   Vivekananda   Sister Nivedita
(Photograph taken in India, 1898)

TRIGUNATITANANDA   SHIVANANDA   TURIYANANDA
                                    VIVEKANANDA   BRAHMANANDA
                          SADANANDA

pleted and the monastery was finally removed to its present site. The date of
the momentous occasion was January 2, 1899. The Bengali monthly magazine,
the Udbodhan, was first published on January 4 of the same year, and regarding
its policy, the Swami declared that nothing but positive ideas for the physical,
mental, and spiritual improvement of the race should find a place in it; that
instead of criticizing the thoughts and aspirations of ancient and modern man,
as embodied in literature, philosophy, poetry, and the arts, the magazine should
indicate the way in which those thoughts and aspirations might be made conducive to progress; and finally that the magazine should stand for universal
harmony as preached by Śri Ramakrishna, and disseminate his ideals of love,
purity, and renunciation.

The Swami was happy to watch the steady expansion of the varied activities
of the Order. At his request Swami Saradananda had returned from America to
assist in the organization of the Belur Math. Together with Swami Turiyananda,
he conducted regular classes at the Math for the study of Sanskrit and of Eastern
and Western philosophy. Somewhat later the two Swamis were sent on a preaching mission to Gujrat, in Western India, and for the same purpose two of the
Swami's own disciples were sent to East Bengal. Swami Shivananda was deputed
to Ceylon to preach Vedānta. Reports of the excellent work done by Swamis
Ramakrishnananda and Abhedananda in Madras and America were received
at the Math. Swami Akhandananda's work for the educational uplift of the
villages and also in establishing homes for the orphans elicited praise from
the Government.

One of the most remarkable institutions founded by Swami Vivekananda was
the Advaita Āśrama at Mayavati in the Himālayas. Ever since his visit to the
Alps in Switzerland, the Swami had been cherishing the desire to establish
a monastery in the solitude of the Himālayas where non-dualism would be
taught and practised in its purest form. Captain and Mrs. Sevier took up the
idea, and the Āśrama was established at Mayavati, at an altitude of 6800 feet.
Before it there shone, day and night, the eternal snow-range of the Himālayas
for an extent of over six hundred miles, with Nandā Devi rising to a height
of 25,500 feet.

Spiritual seekers, irrespective of creed and race, were welcome at the monastery
at Mayavati. No external worship of any kind was permitted within its bound-
aries. Even the formal worship of Śri Ramakrishna was excluded. It was required
of the inmates and guests always to keep before their minds the vision of the
nameless and formless Spirit.

Swami Vivekananda in the following lines laid down the ideals and principles
of this Himālayan āśrama:

"In Whom is the Universe, Who is in the Universe, Who is the Universe;
in Whom is the Soul, Who is in the Soul, Who is the Soul of man; to know
Him, and therefore the Universe, as our Self, alone extinguishes all fear, brings
an end to misery, and leads to infinite freedom. Wherever there has been
expansion in love or progress in well-being of individuals or numbers, it has been
through the perception, realization, and the practicalization of the Eternal
Truth—the Oneness of All Beings. 'Dependence is misery. Independence is
happiness.' The Advaita is the only system which gives unto man complete

possession of himself and takes off all dependence and its associated superstitions, thus making us brave to suffer, brave to do, and in the long run to attain to Absolute Freedom.

"Hitherto it has not been possible to preach this Noble Truth entirely free from the settings of dualistic weakness; this alone, we are convinced, explains why it has not been more operative and useful to mankind at large.

"To give this ONE TRUTH a freer and fuller scope in elevating the lives of individuals and leavening the mass of mankind, we start this Advaita Āśrama on the Himālayan heights, the land of its first formulation.

"Here it is hoped to keep Advaita free from all superstitions and weakening contaminations. Here will be taught and practised nothing but the Doctrine of Unity, pure and simple; and though in entire sympathy with all other systems, this Āśrama is dedicated to Advaita and Advaita alone."

After the Swami's return from Kashmir his health had begun to deteriorate visibly. His asthma caused him great suffering. But his zeal for work increased many times.

"Ever since I went to Amarnāth," he said one day, "Śiva Himself has entered into my brain. He will not go."

At the earnest request of the brother monks, he visited Calcutta frequently for treatment; yet even there he had no respite from work. Visitors thronged about him for religious instruction from morning till night, and his large heart could not say no to them. When the brother monks pressed him to receive people only at appointed hours, he replied: "They take so much trouble to come, walking all the way from their homes, and can I, sitting here, not speak a few words to them, merely because I risk my health a little?"

His words sounded so much like those of Śri Ramakrishna during the latter's critical illness, no wonder that Swami Premananda said to him one day, "We do not see any difference between Śri Ramakrishna and you."

But the Swami's greatest concern was the training of the sannyāsins and brahmachārins—the future bearers of his message—and to this task he addressed himself with all his soul. He encouraged them in their meditation and manual work, himself setting the example. Sometimes he would cook for them, sometimes knead bread, till the garden, or dig a well. Again, he would train them to be preachers by asking them to speak before a gathering without preparation. Constantly he reminded the monks of their monastic vows, especially chastity and renunciation, without which deep spiritual perception was impossible. He attached great importance to physical exercise and said: "I want sappers and miners in the army of religion! So, boys, set yourselves to the task of training your muscles! For ascetics, mortification is all right. For workers, well developed bodies, muscles of iron and nerves of steel!" He urged them to practise austerities and meditation in solitude. For the beginners he laid down strict rules about food. They were to rise early, meditate, and perform their religious duties scrupulously. Health must not be neglected and the company of worldly people should be avoided. But above all, he constantly admonished them to give up idleness in any shape or form.

Of himself he said: "No rest for me! I shall die in harness! I love action! Life is a battle, and one must always be in action, to use a military phrase. Let me live and die in action!" He was a living hymn of work.

To a disciple who wanted to remain absorbed in the Brahman of Vedānta, the Swami thundered: "Why? What is the use of remaining always stupefied in samādhi? Under the inspiration of non-dualism why not sometimes dance like Śiva, and sometimes remain immersed in superconsciousness? Who enjoys a delicacy more—he who eats it all by himself, or he who shares it with others? Granted, by realizing Ātman in meditation you attain mukti; but of what use is that to the world? We have to take the whole world with us to mukti. We shall set a conflagration in the domain of great Māyā. Then only will you be established in the Eternal Truth. Oh, what can compare with that Bliss immeasurable, 'infinite as the skies'! In that state you will be speechless, carried beyond yourself, by seeing your own Self in every being that breathes, and in every atom of the universe. When you realize this, you cannot live in this world without treating everyone with exceeding love and compassion. This is indeed practical Vedānta."

He wanted his disciples to perform with accuracy and diligence the every-day tasks of life. "He who knows even how to prepare a smoke properly, knows also how to meditate. And he who cannot cook well cannot be a perfect sannyāsin. Unless cooking is performed with a pure mind and concentration, the food is not palatable."

Work cannot produce real fruit without detachment on the part of the worker. "Only a great monk," the Swami said one day, "can be a great worker; for he is without attachment. . . . There are no greater workers than Buddha and Christ. No work is secular. All work is adoration and worship."

The first duty of the inmates of the monastery was renunciation. How the Swami idolized the monastic life! "Never forget, service to the world and the realization of God are the ideals of the monk! Stick to them! The monastic is the most immediate of the paths. Between the monk and his God there are no idols! 'The sannyāsin stands on the head of the Vedas!' declare the Vedas, for he is free from churches and sects and religions and prophets and scriptures. He is the visible God on earth. Remember this, and go thou thy way, sannyāsin bold, carrying the banner of renunciation—the banner of peace, of freedom, of blessedness!"

To a disciple who wanted to practise spiritual discipline to attain his own salvation, the Swami said: "You will go to hell if you seek your own salvation! Seek the salvation of others if you want to reach the Highest. Kill out the desire for personal mukti. This is the greatest spiritual discipline. Work, my children, work with your whole heart and soul! That is the thing. Mind not the fruit of work. What if you go to hell working for others? That is worth more than to gain heaven by seeking your own salvation. . . . Śri Ramakrishna came and gave his life for the world. I will also sacrifice my life. You also, every one of you, should do the same. All these works and so forth are only a beginning. Believe me, from the shedding of our lifeblood will arise gigantic, heroic workers and warriors of God who will revolutionize the whole world."

He wanted his disciples to be all-round men. "You must try to combine in your life immense idealism with immense practicality. You must be prepared to go into deep meditation now, and the next moment you must be ready to go and cultivate the fields. You must be prepared to explain the intricacies of the scriptures now, and the next moment to go and sell the produce of the fields in the market. . . . The true man is he who is strong as strength itself and yet possesses a woman's heart."

He spoke of the power of faith: "The history of the world is the history of a few men who had faith in themselves. That faith calls out the inner divinity. You can do anything. You fail only when you do not strive sufficiently to manifest infinite power. As soon as a man loses faith in himself, death comes. Believe first in yourself and then in God. A handful of strong men will move the world. We need a heart to feel, a brain to conceive, and a strong arm to do the work. . . . One man contains within him the whole universe. One particle of matter has all the energy of the universe at its back. In a conflict between the heart and the brain, follow your heart."

"His words," writes Romain Rolland, "are great music, phrases in the style of Beethoven, stirring rhythms like the march of Handel choruses. I cannot touch these sayings of his, scattered as they are through the pages of books at thirty years' distance, without receiving a thrill through my body like an electric shock. And what shocks, what transports must have been produced when in burning words they issued from the lips of the hero!"

The Swami felt he was dying. But he said: "Let me die fighting. Two years of physical suffering have taken from me twenty years of life. But the soul changes not, does it? It is there, the same madcap—Ātman—mad upon one idea, intent and intense."

SECOND VISIT TO AMERICA

On December 16, 1898, Swami Vivekananda announced his plan to go to the West to inspect the work he had founded and to fan the flame. The devotees and friends welcomed the idea since they thought the sea voyage would restore his failing health. He planned to take with him Sister Nivedita and Swami Turiyananda.

Versed in the scriptures, Turiyananda had spent most of his life in meditation and was averse to public work. Failing to persuade him by words to accompany him to America, Vivekananda put his arms round his brother disciple's neck and wept like a child, saying: "Dear brother, don't you see how I am laying down my life inch by inch in fulfilling the mission of my Master? Now I have come to the verge of death! Can you look on without trying to relieve part of my great burden?"

Swami Turiyananda was deeply moved and offered to follow the Swami wherever he wanted to go. When he asked if he should take with him some Vedānta scriptures, Vivekananda said: "Oh, they have had enough of learning and books! The last time they saw a warrior;[32] now I want to show them a brāhmin."

June 20, 1899, was fixed as their date of sailing from Calcutta. On the night of the 19th a meeting was held at the Belur Math at which the junior members

[32] Referring to himself, who had delivered his message in a combative spirit.

of the monastery presented addresses to the two Swamis. The next day the
Holy Mother entertained them and other monks with a sumptuous feast.

The steamship "Golconda," carrying the Swami and his two companions,
touched Madras, but the passengers were not allowed to land on account of the
plague in Calcutta. This was a great disappointment to Swami Vivekananda's
South Indian friends. The ship continued to Colombo, Aden, Naples, and
Marseilles, finally arriving in London on July 31.

The voyage in the company of the Swami was an education for Turiyananda
and Nivedita. From beginning to end a vivid flow of thought and stories went
on. One never knew what moment would bring the flash of intuition and the
ringing utterance of some fresh truth. That encyclopaedic mind touched all
subjects: Christ, Buddha, Krishna, Ramakrishna, folklore, the history of India
and Europe, the degradation of Hindu society and the assurance of its coming
greatness, different philosophical and religious systems, and many themes more.
All was later admirably recorded by Sister Nivedita in *The Master as I Saw Him*,
from which the following fragments may be cited.

"Yes," the Swami said one day, "the older I grow, the more everything seems
to me to lie in manliness. This is my new gospel. Do even evil like a man! Be
wicked, if you must, on a grand scale!" Some time before, Nivedita had com-
plimented India on the infrequency of crime; on that occasion the Swami said
in sorrowful protest: "Would to God it were otherwise in my land! For this is
verily the virtuousness of death." Evidently, according to him, the vilest crime
was not to act, to do nothing at all.

Regarding conservative and liberal ideas he said: "The conservative's whole
ideal is submission. Your ideal is struggle. Consequently it is we who enjoy life,
and never you! You are always striving to change yours to something better,
and before a millionth part of the change is carried out, you die. The Western
ideal is to be doing; the Eastern, to be suffering. The perfect life would be a
wonderful harmony between doing and suffering. But that can never be."

To him selfishness was the greatest barrier to spiritual progress:

"It is selfishness that we must seek to eliminate. I find that whenever I have
made a mistake in my life, it has always been because *self* entered into the
calculation. Where self has not been involved, my judgement has gone straight
to the mark."

"You are quite wrong," he said again, "when you think that fighting is the
sign of growth. It is not so at all. Absorption is the sign. Hinduism is the very
genius of absorption. We have never cared for fighting. Of course, we struck
a blow now and then in defense of our homes. That was right. But we never
cared for fighting for its own sake. Everyone had to learn that. So let these races
of new-comers whirl on! They all will be taken into Hinduism in the end."

In another mood, the theme of his conversation would be Kāli, and the worship of the Terrible. Then he would say: "I love terror for its own sake, despair
for its own sake, misery for its own sake. Fight always. Fight and fight on, though
always in defeat. That's the ideal! That's the ideal!" Again: "Worship the
Terrible! Worship Death! All else is vain. All struggle is vain. This is the last
lesson. Yet this is not the coward's love of death, not the love of the weak or
the suicide. It is the welcome of the strong man, who has sounded everything

to the depths and knows that there is no alternative." And who is Kāli, whose will is irresistible? "The totality of all souls, not the human alone, is the Personal God. The will of the totality nothing can resist. It is what we know as Law. And this is what we mean by Śiva and Kāli and so on."

Concerning true greatness: "As I grow older I find that I look more and more for greatness in little things. I want to know what a great man eats and wears, and how he speaks to his servants. I want to find a Sir Philip Sidney greatness. Few men would remember to think of others in the moment of death.

"But anyone will be great in a great position! Even the coward will grow brave in the glow of the footlights. The world looks on. Whose heart will not throb? Whose pulse will not quicken, till he can do his best? More and more the true greatness seems to me that of the worm, doing its duty silently, steadily, from moment to moment and hour to hour."

Regarding the points of difference between his own schemes for the regeneration of India and those preached by others: "I disagree with those who are for giving their superstitions back to my people. Like the Egyptologist's interest in Egypt, it is easy to feel an interest in India that is purely selfish. One may desire to see again the India of one's books, one's studies, one's dreams. My hope is to see the strong points of that India, reinforced by the strong points of this age, only in a natural way. The new state of things must be a growth from within. So I preach only the Upanishads. If you look you will find that I have never quoted anything but the Upanishads. And of the Upanishads, it is only that one idea—strength. The quintessence of the Vedas and Vedānta and all, lies in that one word. Buddha's teaching was of non-resistance or non-injury. But I think ours is a better way of teaching the same thing. For behind that non-injury lay a dreadful weakness—the weakness that conceives the idea of resistance. But I do not think of punishing or escaping from a drop of sea-spray. It is nothing to me. Yet to the mosquito it would be serious. Now, I will make all injury like that. Strength and fearlessness. My own ideal is that giant of a saint whom they killed in the Sepoy Mutiny, and who broke his silence, when stabbed to the heart, to say—'And thou also art He.'"

About India and Europe the Swami said: "I see that India is a young and living organism. Europe is also young and living. Neither has arrived at such a stage of development that we can safely criticize its institutions. They are two great experiments, neither of which is yet complete." They ought to be mutually helpful, he went on, but at the same time each should respect the free development of the other. They ought to grow hand in hand.

Thus time passed till the boat arrived at Tilbury Dock, where the party was met by the Swami's disciples and friends, among whom were two American ladies who had come all the way to London to meet their teacher. It was the off-season for London, and so the two Swamis sailed for New York on August 16.

The trip was beneficial to the Swami's health; the sea was smooth and at night the moonlight was enchanting. One evening as the Swami paced up and down the deck enjoying the beauty of nature, he suddenly exclaimed, "And if all this māyā is so beautiful, think of the wondrous beauty of the Reality behind it!" Another evening, when the moon was full, he pointed to the sea and sky, and said, "Why recite poetry when there is the very essence of poetry?"

The afternoon that Swami Vivekananda arrived in New York, he and his brother disciple went with Mr. and Mrs. Leggett to the latter's country home, Ridgely Manor, at Stone Ridge in the Catskill Mountains, Swami Abhedananda being at that time absent from New York on a lecture tour. A month later Nivedita came to Ridgely, and on September 21, when she decided to assume the nun's garb, the Swami wrote for her his beautiful poem "Peace." The rest and good climate were improving his health, and he was entertaining all with his usual fun and merriment.

One day Miss MacLeod asked him how he liked their home-grown strawberries, and he answered that he had not tasted any. Miss MacLeod was surprised and said, "Why Swami, we have been serving you strawberries with cream and sugar every day for the past week." "Ah," the Swami replied, with a mischievous twinkle in his eyes, "I am tasting only cream and sugar. Even tacks taste sweet that way."

In November the Swami returned to New York and was greeted by his old friends and disciples. He was pleased to see how the work had expanded under the able guidance of Swami Abhedananda. Swami Vivekananda gave some talks and conducted classes.

At one of the public meetings in New York, after addressing a tense audience for about fifteen minutes, the Swami suddenly made a formal bow and retired. The meeting broke up and the people went away greatly disappointed. A friend asked him, when he was returning home, why he had cut short the lecture in that manner, just when both he and the audience were warming up. Had he forgotten his points? Had he become nervous? The Swami answered that at the meeting he had felt that he had too much power. He had noticed that the members of the audience were becoming so absorbed in his ideas that they were losing their own individualities. He had felt that they had become like soft clay and that he could give them any shape he wanted. That, however, was contrary to his philosophy. He wished every man and woman to grow according to his or her own inner law. He did not wish to change or destroy anyone's individuality. That was why he had had to stop.

Swami Turiyananda took up his work at Montclair, New Jersey, a short distance from New York, and began to teach children the stories and folklore of India. He also lectured regularly at the Vedānta Society of New York. His paper on Śankarāchārya, read before the Cambridge Conference, was highly praised by the Harvard professors.

One day, while the Swami was staying at Ridgely Manor, Miss MacLeod had received a telegram informing her that her only brother was dangerously ill in Los Angeles. As she was leaving for the West coast, the Swami uttered a Sanskrit benediction and told her that he would soon meet her there. She proceeded straight to the home of Mrs. S. K. Blodgett, where her brother was staying, and after spending a few minutes with the patient, asked Mrs. Blodgett whether her brother might be permitted to die in the room in which he was then lying; for she had found a large picture of Vivekananda, hanging on the wall at the foot of the patient's bed. Miss MacLeod told her hostess of her surprise on seeing the picture, and Mrs. Blodgett replied that she had heard Vivekananda at the Parliament of Religions in Chicago and thought that if ever there was a

God on earth, it was that man.[33] Miss MacLeod told her that she had just left the Swami at Ridgely Manor, and further, that he had expressed the desire to come to Los Angeles. The brother died within a few days, and the Swami started for the West Coast on November 22. He broke his trip in Chicago to visit his old friends, and upon his arrival in Los Angeles became the guest of Mrs. Blodgett, whom he described in a letter to Mary Hale as "fat, old, extremely witty, and very motherly."

The impression the Swami left in the mind of this good woman can be gathered from the following lines of a letter written by her to Miss MacLeod after Swamiji's passing away:

I am ever recalling those swift, bright days in that never-to-be-forgotten winter, lived in simple freedom and kindliness. We could not choose but to be happy and good. . . . I knew him personally but a short time, yet in that time I could see in a hundred ways the child side of Swamiji's character, which was a constant appeal to the mother quality in all good women. . . . He would come home from a lecture, where he had been compelled to break away from his audience—so eagerly would they gather around him—and rush into the kitchen like a boy released from school, with "Now we will cook!" Presently Joe would appear and discover the culprit among the pots and pans, and in his fine dress, who was by thrifty, watchful Joe admonished to change to his home garments. . . . In the homely, old-fashioned kitchen, you and I have seen Swamiji at his best.

Swami Vivekananda gave many lectures before large audiences in Los Angeles and Pasadena; but alas! there was no Goodwin to record them, and most of what he said was consequently lost. Only a little has been preserved in the fragmentary notes of his disciples.

At the Universalist Church of Pasadena he gave his famous lecture "Christ, the Messenger"; and this was the only time, Miss MacLeod said later, that she saw him enveloped in a halo. The Swami, after the lecture, was returning home wrapped in thought, and Miss MacLeod was following at a little distance, when suddenly she heard him say, "I know it, I know it!"

"What do you know?" asked Miss MacLeod.

"How they make it."

"How they make what?"

"Mulligatawny soup. They put in a dash of bay leaf for flavour." And then he burst into a laugh.

The Swami spent about a month at the headquarters of the "Home of Truth" in Los Angeles, conducted regular classes, and gave several public lectures, each of which was attended by over a thousand people. He spoke many times on the different aspects of rāja-yoga, a subject in which Californians seemed to be especially interested.

The Swami endeared himself to the members of the Home of Truth by his simple manner, his great intellect, and his spiritual wisdom. *Unity*, the magazine of the organization, said of him: "There is a combination in the Swami Vivekananda of the learning of a university president, the dignity of an archbishop, with the grace and winsomeness of a free and natural child. Getting

[33] See p. 62.

upon the platform, without a moment's preparation, he would soon be in the midst of his subject, sometimes becoming almost tragic as his mind would wander from deep metaphysics to the prevailing conditions in Christian countries of today, whose people go and seek to reform the Filipinos with the sword in one hand and the Bible in the other, or in South Africa allow children of the same Father to cut each other to pieces. In contrast to this condition of things, he described what took place during the last great famine in India, where men would die of starvation beside their cows rather than stretch forth a hand to kill."

The members of the Home of Truth were not permitted to smoke. One evening the Swami was invited for dinner by a member of the organization along with several other friends who were all opposed to the use of tobacco. After dinner the hostess was absent from the room for a few minutes, when the Swami, perhaps due to his ignorance of the rule about tobacco, took out his pipe, filled it up, and began to puff. The guests were aghast, but kept quiet. When the hostess returned, she flew into a rage and asked the Swami if God intended men to smoke, adding that in that case He would have furnished the human head with a chimney for the smoke to go out.

"But He has given us the brain to invent a pipe," the Swami said with a smile.

Everybody laughed, and the Swami was given freedom to smoke while living as a guest in the Home of Truth.

Swami Vivekananda journeyed to Oakland as the guest of Dr. Benjamin Fay Mills, the minister of the First Unitarian Church, and there gave eight lectures to crowded audiences which often numbered as high as two thousand. He also gave many public lectures in San Francisco and Alameda. People had already read his *Rāja-Yoga*. Impressed by his lectures, they wanted a centre in San Francisco. The Swami was offered a gift of land, measuring a hundred and sixty acres, in the southern part of the San Antone valley; surrounded by forest and hills, and situated at an altitude of 2500 feet, the property was only twelve miles from the Lick Observatory on Mt. Hamilton. He at once thought of Swami Turiyananda, who could be given charge of the place to train earnest students in meditation.

During his trip back to New York, across the American continent, the Swami was very much fatigued. He stopped in Chicago and Detroit on the way. In Chicago he was the guest of the Hale family, and many old reminiscences were exchanged. On the morning of his departure, Mary came to the Swami's room and found him sad. His bed appeared to have been untouched, and on being asked the reason, he confessed that he had spent the whole night without sleep. "Oh," he said, almost in a whisper, "it is so difficult to break human bonds!" He knew that this was the last time he was to visit these devoted friends.

In New York the Swami gave a few lectures at the Vedānta Society, which by this time had enlisted the active co-operation of several professors of Harvard and Columbia University. At the earliest opportunity he spoke to Turiyananda about the proposed gift of land in northern California, but the latter hesitated to accept any responsibility. The Swami said, "It is the will of the Mother that you should take charge of the work there."

Swami Turiyananda was amused and said with good humour: "Rather say it is your will. Certainly you have not heard the Mother communicate Her will to you in that way. How can you hear the words of the Mother?"

"Yes, brother," the Swami said with great emotion. "Yes, the words of the Mother can be heard as clearly as we hear one another. But one requires a fine nerve to hear Mother's words."

Swami Vivekananda made this statement with such fervour that his brother disciple felt convinced that the Divine Mother was speaking through him. He cheerfully agreed, therefore, to take charge of Śanti Āśrama, the Peace Retreat, as the new place was called.

In parting, the Swami said to Turiyananda: "Go and establish the Āśrama in California. Hoist the flag of Vedānta there; from this moment destroy even the memory of India! Above all, lead the life and Mother will see to the rest."

The Swami visited Detroit again for a week and on July 20 sailed for Paris.

GLIMPSES OF THE SWAMI'S MIND

Before continuing the thread of Swami Vivekananda's life, it will be interesting for the reader to get a glimpse of his state of mind. During the past two years, the Swami wrote to his friends, he had gone through great mental anguish. His message, to be sure, had begun to reach an ever increasing number of people both in India and in America, and naturally he had been made happy by this fact; yet he had suffered intensely on account of "poverty, treachery, and my own foolishness," as he wrote to Mary Hale on February 20, 1900. Though his outward appearance was that of a stern non-dualist, he possessed a tender heart that was often bruised by the blows of the world. To Margaret Noble he wrote on December 6, 1899: "Some people are made that way—to love being miserable. If I did not break my heart over the people I was born amongst, I would do it for somebody else. I am sure of that. This is the way of some—I am coming to see it. We are all after happiness, true, but some are only happy in being unhappy—queer, is it not?"

How sensitive he was to the sufferings of men! "I went years ago to the Himālayas," he wrote to an American friend on December 12, 1899, "never to come back—and my sister committed suicide, the news reached me there, and that weak heart flung me off from the prospect of peace! It is the weak heart that has driven me out of India to seek some help for those I love, and here I am! Peace have I sought, but the heart, that seat of bhakti, would not allow me to find it. Struggle and torture, torture and struggle! Well, so be it then, since it is my fate; and the quicker it is over, the better."

His health had been indifferent even before he had left for the West. "This sort of nervous body," he wrote on November 15, 1899, "is just an instrument to play great music at times, and at times to moan in darkness." While in America, he was under the treatment of an osteopath and a "magnetic healer," but received no lasting benefit. At Los Angeles he got the news of the serious illness of his brother disciple Niranjan. Mr. Sturdy, his beloved English disciple, had given up the Swami because he felt that the teacher was not living in the West the life of an ascetic. Miss Henrietta Muller, who had helped him financially to buy the Belur Math, left him on account of his illness; she could not associate sickness with holiness. One of the objects of the Swami's visit to California was to raise money to promote his various activities in India: people came to his meetings in large numbers, but of money he received very little. He suffered a bereavement in the passing away of his devoted friend Mr. George Hale of Chicago. Reports about the work in New York caused him much anxiety. Swami Abhedananda was not getting on well with some of Vivekananda's disciples, and Mr. Leggett severed his relationship with the Society. All these things, like so many claws, pierced Vivekananda's heart. Further, perhaps he now felt that his mission on earth was over. He began to lose interest in work. The arrow, however, was still flying, carried by its original impetus; but it was approaching the end, when it would fall to the ground.

The Swami longed to return to India. On January 17, 1900, he wrote to Mrs. Ole Bull that he wanted to build a hut on the bank of the Ganges and spend the rest of his life there with his mother: "She has suffered much through me. I must try to smooth her last days. Do you know, this was just exactly what the great Śankarāchārya himself had to do. He had to go back to his mother in the last few days of her life. I accept it. I am resigned."

In the same letter to Mrs. Ole Bull he wrote: "I am but a child; what work have I to do? My powers I passed over to you. I see it. I cannot any more *tell* from the platform. Don't tell it to anyone—not even to Joe. I am glad. I want rest; not that I am tired, but the next phase will be the *miraculous touch and not the tongue*—like Ramakrishna's. The word has gone to you, the boys, and to Margot."[34]

He was fast losing interest in active work. On April 7, 1900, he wrote to a friend:

"My boat is nearing the calm harbour from which it is never more to be driven out. Glory, glory unto Mother![35] I have no wish, no ambition now. Blessed be Mother! I am the servant of Ramakrishna. I am merely a machine. I know nothing else. Nor do I want to know."

To another friend he wrote, on April 12, in similar vein:

Work always brings dirt with it. I paid for the accumulated dirt with bad health. I am glad my mind is all the better for it. There is a mellowness and a calmness in life now, which never was before. I am learning now how to be attached as well as detached —and mentally becoming my own master. . . . Mother is doing Her own work. I do not worry much now. Moths like me die by the thousands every minute. Her work goes on all the same. Glory unto Mother! . . . For me—alone and drifting about in the will-current of the Mother has been my life. The moment I have tried to break it, that moment I was hurt. Her will be done. . . . I am happy, at peace with myself, and more of the sannyāsin than I ever was. The love for my own kith and kin is growing less every day—for Mother, increasing. Memories of long nights of vigil with Śri Ramakrishna, under the Dakshineswar banyan tree, are waking up once more. And work? What is work? Whose work? Whom to work for? I am free. I am Mother's child. She works, She plays. Why should I plan? What shall I plan? Things came and went, just

[34] Referring to Sister Nivedita.
[35] Referring to the Divine Mother of the Universe.

as She liked, without my planning, in spite of my planning. We are Her automata. She is the wire-puller.

With the approaching end of his mission and earthly life, he realized ever more clearly how like a stage this world is. In August 1899 he wrote to Miss Marie Halboister: "This toy world would not be here, this play could not go on, if we were knowing players. We must play blindfolded. Some of us have taken the part of the rogue of the play; some, of the hero—never mind, it is all play. This is the only consolation. There are demons and lions and tigers and what not on the stage, but they are all muzzled. They snap but cannot bite. The world cannot touch our souls. If you want, even if the body be torn and bleeding, you may enjoy the greatest peace in your mind. And the way to that is to attain hopelessness. Do you know that? Not the imbecile attitude of despair, but the contempt of the conqueror for the things he has attained, for the things he has struggled for and then thrown aside as beneath his worth."

To Mary Hale, who "has been always the sweetest note in my jarring and clashing life," he wrote on March 26, 1900:

This is to let you know "I am very happy." Not that I am getting into a shadowy optimism, but my power of suffering is increasing. I am being lifted up above the pestilential miasma of this world's joys and sorrows. They are losing their meaning. It is a land of dreams. It does not matter whether one enjoys or weeps—they are but dreams, and as such must break sooner or later. . . . I am attaining peace that passeth understanding—which is neither joy nor sorrow, but something above them both. Tell Mother[36] that. My passing through the valley of death—physical, mental—these last two years, has helped me in this. Now I am nearing that *Peace*, the eternal *Silence*. Now I mean to see things as they are—everything in that Peace—perfect in its way. "He whose joy is only in himself, whose desires are only in himself," he has *learnt* his lessons. This is the great lesson that we are here to learn through myriads of births and heavens and hells: There is nothing to be sought for, asked for, desired, beyond one's self. The greatest thing I can obtain is myself. I am free—therefore I require none else for my happiness. Alone through eternity—because I was free, am free, and will remain free for ever. This is Vedāntism. I preached the theory so long, but oh, joy! Mary, my dear sister, I am realizing it now every day. Yes, I am. I am free—Alone—Alone. I am the One without a second.

Vivekananda's eyes were looking at the light of another world, his real abode. And how vividly and touchingly he expressed his nostalgic yearning to return to it, in his letter of April 18, 1900, written from Alameda, California, to Miss MacLeod, his ever loyal Joe:

Just now I received your and Mrs. Bull's welcome letter. I direct this to London. I am so glad Mrs. Leggett is on the sure way to recovery.

I am so sorry Mr. Leggett resigned the presidentship.

Well, I keep quiet for fear of making further trouble. You know my methods are extremely harsh, and once roused I may rattle Abhedananda too much for his peace of mind.

I wrote to him only to tell him his notions about Mrs. Bull are entirely wrong.

Work is always difficult. Pray for me, Joe, that my work may stop for ever and my whole soul be absorbed in Mother. Her work She knows.

[36] Referring to Mrs. Hale.

You must be glad to be in London once more—the old friends—give them all my love and gratitude.

I am well, very well mentally. I feel the rest of the soul more than that of the body. The battles are lost and won. I have bundled my things and am waiting for the Great Deliverer.

Śiva, O Śiva, carry my boat to the other shore!

After all, Joe, I am only the boy who used to listen with rapt wonderment to the wonderful words of Ramakrishna under the banyan at Dakshineswar. That is my true nature—works and activities, doing good and so forth, are all superimpositions. Now I again hear his voice, the same old voice thrilling my soul. Bonds are breaking—love dying, work becoming tasteless—the glamour is off life. Now only the voice of the Master calling.—"I come, Lord, I come."—"Let the dead bury the dead. Follow thou Me."—"I come, my beloved Lord, I come."

Yes, I come. Nirvāna is before me. I feel it at times, the same infinite ocean of peace, without a ripple, a breath.

I am glad I was born, glad I suffered so, glad I did make big blunders, glad to enter peace. I leave none bound, I take no bonds. Whether this body will fall and release me or I enter into freedom in the body, the old man is gone, gone for ever, never to come back again!

The guide, the guru, the leader, the teacher, has passed away; the boy, the student, the servant, is left behind.

You understand why I do not want to meddle with Abhedananda. Who am I to meddle with any, Joe? I have long given up my place as a leader—I have no right to raise my voice. Since the beginning of this year I have not dictated anything in India. You know that. Many thanks for what you and Mrs. Bull have been to me in the past. All blessings follow you ever! The sweetest moments of my life have been when I was drifting. I am drifting again—with the bright warm sun ahead and masses of vegetation around—and in the heat everything is so still, so calm—and I am drifting, languidly— in the warm heart of the river. I dare not make a splash with my hands or feet—for fear of breaking the wonderful stillness, stillness that makes you feel sure it is an illusion!

Behind my work was ambition, behind my love was personality, behind my purity was fear, behind my guidance the thirst for power. Now they are vanishing and I drift. I come, Mother, I come, in Thy warm bosom, floating wheresoever Thou takest me, in the voiceless, in the strange, in the wonderland, I come—a spectator, no more an actor.

Oh, it is so calm! My thoughts seem to come from a great, great distance in the interior of my own heart. They seem like faint, distant whispers, and peace is upon everything, sweet, sweet peace—like that one feels for a few moments just before falling into sleep, when things are seen and felt like shadows—without fear, without love, without emotion—peace that one feels alone, surrounded with statues and pictures.— I come, Lord, I come.

The world is, but not beautiful nor ugly, but as sensations without exciting any emotion. Oh, Joe, the blessedness of it! Everything is good and beautiful; for things are all losing their relative proportions to me—my body among the first. Om That Existence!

I hope great things come to you all in London and Paris. Fresh joy—fresh benefits to mind and body.

THE PARIS CONGRESS

But the arrow of Swami Vivekananda's life had not yet finished its flight. Next he was to be seen in Paris participating in the Congress of the History of Religions, held on the occasion of the Universal Exposition. This Congress, compared with the Parliament of Religions of Chicago, was a rather tame affair.

The discussion was limited to technical theories regarding the origin of the rituals of religion; for the Catholic hierarchy, evidently not wanting a repetition of the triumph of Oriental ideas in the American Parliament, did not allow any discussion of religious doctrines. Swami Vivekananda, on account of his failing health, took part in only two sessions. He repudiated the theory of the German orientalist Gustav Oppert that the Śiva lingam was a mere phallic symbol. He described the Vedas as the common basis of both Hinduism and Buddhism, and held that both Krishna and the Bhagavad Gītā were prior to Buddhism. Further, he rejected the theory of the Hellenic influence on the drama, art, literature, astrology, and other sciences developed in India.

In Paris he came to know his distinguished countryman J. C. Bose, the discoverer of the life and nervous system in plants, who had been invited to join the scientific section of the Congress. The Swami referred to the Indian scientist as "the pride and glory of Bengal."

In Paris Swami Vivekananda was the guest of Mr. and Mrs. Leggett, at whose house he met many distinguished people. Among these was the young Duke of Richelieu, a scion of an old and aristocratic family of France. The title had been created by Louis XIII, and one of the ancestors of the Duke had been Premier under Louis XVIII. Born in Paris, educated at a Jesuit school in France, and later graduated from the University of Aix-en-Provence, the Duke of Richelieu became greatly attached to the Swami and visited him frequently. On the eve of Vivekananda's departure from Paris, the Swami asked the Duke if he would renounce the world and become his disciple. The Duke wanted to know what he would gain in return for such renunciation, and the Swami said, "I shall give you the desire for death." When asked to explain, the Swami declared that he would give the Duke such a state of mind that when confronted by death he would laugh at it. But the Duke preferred to pursue a worldly career, though he cherished a life-long devotion to Swami Vivekananda.

During his stay in Paris the Swami met such prominent people as Professor Patrick Geddes of Edinburgh University, Père Hyacinthe, Hiram Maxim, Sarah Bernhardt, Jules Bois, and Madame Emma Calvé. Père Hyacinthe, a Carmelite monk who had renounced his vows, had married an American lady and assumed the name of Charles Loyson. The Swami, however, always addressed him by his old monastic name and described him as endowed with "a very sweet nature" and the temperament of a lover of God. Maxim, the inventor of the gun associated with his name, was a great connoisseur and lover of India and China. Sarah Bernhardt also bore a great love for India, which she often described as "very ancient, very civilized." To visit India was the dream of her life.

Madame Calvé the Swami had met in America, and now he came to know her more intimately. She became one of his devoted followers. "She was born poor," he once wrote of her, "but by her innate talents, prodigious labour and diligence, and after wrestling against much hardship, she is now enormously rich and commands respect from kings and emperors. . . . The rare combination of beauty, youth, talents, and 'divine' voice has assigned Calvé the highest place among the singers of the West. There is, indeed, no better teacher than misery and poverty. That constant fight against the dire poverty, misery, and hardship of the days of her girlhood, which has led to her present triumph over them, has brought into her life a unique sympathy and a depth of thought with a wide outlook."

After the Swami's passing away, Madame Calvé visited the Belur Math, the headquarters of the Ramakrishna Mission. In old age she embraced the Catholic faith and had to give up, officially, her allegiance to Swami Vivekananda. But one wonders whether she was able to efface him from her heart.

Jules Bois, with whom the Swami stayed for a few days in Paris, was a distinguished writer. "We have," the Swami wrote to a disciple, "many great ideas in common and feel happy together."

Most of the Swami's time in Paris was devoted to the study of French culture and especially the language. He wrote a few letters in French. About the culture, his appreciation was tempered with criticism. He spoke of Paris as the "home of liberty"; there the ethics and society of the West had been formed, and its university had been the model of all others. But in a letter to Swami Turiyananda, dated September 1, 1900, he also wrote: "The people of France are mere intellectualists. They run after worldly things and firmly believe God and souls to be mere superstitions; they are extremely loath to talk on such subjects. This is truly a materialistic country."

After the Congress of the History of Religions was concluded, the Swami spent a few days at Lannion in Brittany, as the guest of Mrs. Ole Bull. Sister Nivedita, who had just returned from America, was also in the party. There, in his conversations, the Swami dwelt mostly on Buddha and his teachings. Contrasting Buddhism with Hinduism, he one day said that the former exhorted men to "realize all this as illusion," while Hinduism asked them to "realize that within the illusion is the Real." Of how this was to be done, Hinduism never presumed to enunciate any rigid law. The Buddhist command could only be carried out through monasticism; the Hindu might be fulfilled through any state of life. All alike were roads to the One Real. One of the highest and the greatest expressions of the Faith is put into the mouth of a butcher, preaching, by the orders of a married woman, to a sannyāsin.[37] Thus Buddhism became the religion of a monastic order, but Hinduism, in spite of its exaltation of monasticism, remains ever the religion of faithfulness to daily duty, whatever it may be, as the path by which man may attain to God.

From Lannion, on St. Michael's Day, he visited Mont St. Michel. He was struck by the similarity between the rituals of Hinduism and Roman Catholicism. He said, "Christianity is not alien to Hinduism."

Nivedita took leave of the Swami in Brittany and departed for England in order to raise funds for her work on behalf of Indian women. While giving her his blessings, the Swami said: "There is a peculiar sect of Mohammedans who are reported to be so fanatical that they take each new-born babe and expose it, saying, 'If God made thee, perish! If Ali made thee, live!' Now this which they say to the child, I say, but in the opposite sense, to you, tonight—'Go forth into the world, and there, if I made you, be destroyed! If Mother made you, live!' " Perhaps the Swami remembered how some of his beloved Western dis-

[37] The butcher and the woman, in the story referred to, which is found in one of the Purānas, were householders who had received spiritual illumination through the performance of their respective duties.

ciples, unable to understand the profundity of his life and teachings, had
deserted him. He also realized the difficulties Westerners experienced in identifying themselves completely with the customs of India. He had told Nivedita,
before they left India, that she must resume, as if she had never broken them
off, all her old habits and social customs of the West.

On October 24, 1900, Swami Vivekananda left Paris for the East, by way of
Vienna and Constantinople. Besides the Swami, the party consisted of Monsieur
and Madame Loyson, Jules Bois, Madame Calvé, and Miss MacLeod. The
Swami was Calvé's guest.

In Vienna the Swami remarked, "If Turkey is called 'the sick man of Europe,'
Austria ought to be called 'the sick woman of Europe'!"

The party arrived in Constantinople after passing through Hungary, Serbia,
Romania, and Bulgaria. Next the Swami and his friends came to Athens. They
visited several islands and a Greek monastery. From Athens they sailed to Egypt
and the Swami was delighted to visit the museum in Cairo. While in Cairo,
he and his women devotees, one day, in the course of sightseeing, unknowingly
entered the part of the city in which the girls of ill fame lived, and when the
inmates hurled coarse jokes at the Swami from their porches, the ladies wanted
to take him away; but he refused to go. Some of the prostitutes came into the
street, and the ladies saw from a distance that they knelt before him and kissed
the hem of his garment. Presently the Swami joined his friends and drove away.

In Cairo the Swami had a presentiment that something had happened to
Mr. Sevier. He became restless to return to India, took the first available boat,
and sailed for Bombay alone.

Throughout his European tour the Swami's friends had noticed that he was
becoming more and more detached from the spectacle of external things, and
buried in meditation. A sort of indifference to the world was gradually over-
powering him. On August 14 he had written to a friend that he did not expect
to live long. From Paris he wrote to Turiyananda: "My body and mind are
broken down; I need rest badly. In addition there is not a single person on
whom I can depend; on the other hand, as long as I live, all will be very selfish,
depending upon me for everything." In Egypt the Swami had seemed to be
turning the last pages of his life-experience. One of the party later remarked,
"How tired and world-weary he seemed!" Nivedita, who had had the opportunity of observing him closely during his second trip to the West, writes:

The outstanding impression made by the Swami's bearing during all these months of
European and American life, was one of almost complete indifference to his surroundings.
Current estimates of value left him entirely unaffected. He was never in any way startled
or incredulous under success, being too deeply convinced of the greatness of the Power
that worked through him, to be surprised by it. But neither was he unnerved by external
failure. Both victory and defeat would come and go. He was their witness. . . . He moved
fearless and unhesitant through the luxury of the West. As determinedly as I had seen
him in India, dressed in the two garments of simple folk, sitting on the floor and eating
with his fingers, so, equally without doubt or shrinking, was his acceptance of the com-
plexity of the means of living in America or France. Monk and king, he said, were the
obverse and reverse of a single medal. From the use of the best to the renunciation of
all was but one step. India had thrown all her prestige in the past round poverty. Some
prestige was in the future to be cast round wealth.

For some time the Swami had been trying to disentangle himself from the responsibilities of work. He had already transferred the property of the Belur Math from his own name to the Trustees of the organization. On August 25, 1900, he had written to Nivedita from Paris:

Now I am free, as I have kept no power or authority or position for me in the work. I also have resigned the Presidentship of the Ramakrishna Mission. The Math etc. belong now to the immediate disciples of Ramakrishna except myself. The Presidentship is now Brahmananda's—next it will fall on Premananda etc., in turn. I am so glad a whole load is off me. Now I am happy. . . .

I no longer represent anybody, nor am I responsible to anybody. As to my friends, I had a morbid sense of obligation. I have thought well and find I owe nothing to anybody —if anything. I have given my best energies, unto death almost, and received only hectoring and mischief-making and botheration. . . .

Your letter indicates that I am jealous of your new friends. You must know once for all I am born without jealousy, without avarice, without the desire to rule—whatever other vices I may be born with.

I never directed you before; now, after I am nobody in the work, I have no direction whatever. I only know this much: So long as you serve "Mother" with a whole heart, She will be your guide.

I never had any jealousy about what friends you made. I never criticized my brethren for mixing up in anything. Only I do believe the Western people have the peculiarity of trying to force upon others whatever seems good to them, forgetting that what is good for you may not be good for others. As such I am afraid you would try to force upon others whatever turn your mind might take in contact with new friends. That was the only reason I sometimes tried to stop any particular influence, and nothing else.

You are free. Have your own choice, your own work. . . .

Friends or foes, they are all instruments in Her hands to help us work out our own karma, through pleasure or pain. As such, "Mother" bless them all.

How did America impress Swami Vivekananda during his second visit to the West? What impressions did he carry to India of the state of things in the New World? During his first visit he had been enthusiastic about almost everything he saw—the power, the organization, the material prosperity, the democracy, and the spirit of freedom and justice. But now he was greatly disillusioned. In America's enormous combinations and ferocious struggle for supremacy he discovered the power of Mammon. He saw that the commercial spirit was composed, for the most part, of greed, selfishness, and a struggle for privilege and power. He was disgusted with the ruthlessness of wealthy business men, swallowing up the small tradespeople by means of large combinations. That was indeed tyranny. He could admire an organization; "but what beauty is there among a pack of wolves?" he said to a disciple. He also noticed, in all their nakedness, the social vices and the arrogance of race, religion, and colour. America, he confided to Miss MacLeod, would not be the instrument to harmonize East and West.

During his trip through Eastern Europe, from Paris to Constantinople, he smelt war. He felt the stench of it rising on all sides. "Europe," he remarked, "is a vast military camp."

But the tragedy of the West had not been altogether unperceived by him even during his first visit. As early as 1895 he said to Sister Christine: "Europe

is on the edge of a volcano. If the fire is not extinguished by a flood of spirituality, it will erupt."

One cannot but be amazed at the Swami's prophetic intuition as expressed
through the following remarks made to Christine in 1896: "The next upheaval
will come from Russia or China. I cannot see clearly which, but it will be either
the one or the other." He further said: "The world is in the third epoch, under
the domination of the vaiśya. The fourth epoch will be under that of the
śudra."[38]

TOWARDS THE END

Swami Vivekananda disembarked in Bombay and immediately entrained for
Calcutta, arriving at the Belur Math late in the evening of December 9, 1900.
The Swami had not informed anybody of his return. The gate of the monastery
was locked for the night. He heard the dinner bell, and in his eagerness to join
the monks at their meal, scaled the gate. There was great rejoicing over his
home-coming.

At the Math Swami Vivekananda was told about the passing away of his
beloved disciple Mr. Sevier at Mayavati in the Himālayas. This was the sad
news of which he had had a presentiment in Egypt. He was greatly distressed,
and on December 11 wrote to Miss MacLeod: "Thus two great Englishmen[39]
gave up their lives for us—us, the Hindus. This is martyrdom, if anything is."
Again he wrote to her on December 26: "He was cremated on the bank of the
river that flows by his āśrama, à la Hindu, covered with garlands, the brāhmins
carrying the body and the boys chanting the Vedas. The cause has already two
martyrs. It makes me love dear England and its heroic breed. The Mother is
watering the plant of future India with the best blood of England. Glory unto
Her!"

The Swami stayed at the Math for eighteen days and left for Mayavati to see
Mrs. Sevier. The distance from the railroad station to the monastery at Mayavati was sixty-five miles. The Swami did not give the inmates sufficient time to
arrange for his comfortable transportation. He left the railroad station in a
hurry in the company of Shivananda and Sadananda. The winter of that year
was particularly severe in the Himālayas; there was a heavy snowfall on the way,
and in his present state of health he could hardly walk. He reached the monastery, however, on January 3, 1901.

The meeting with Mrs. Sevier stirred his emotions. He was delighted, how-

---

[38] The vaiśya, or the merchant, and the śudra, or the worker, represent the third and
fourth castes in Hindu society. Swami Vivekananda said that the four castes, by turn,
governed human society. The brāhmin dominated the thought-current of the world
during the glorious days of the ancient Hindu civilization. Then came the rule of the
kshattriya, the military, as manifested through the supremacy of Europe from the time
of the Roman Empire to the middle of the seventeenth century. Next followed the rule
of the vaiśya, marked by the rise of America. The Swami prophesied the coming supremacy of the śudra class. After the completion of the cycle, he said, the spiritual culture
would again assert itself and influence human civilization through the power of the
brāhmin. Swami Vivekananda often spoke of the future greatness of India as surpassing
all her glories of the past.

[39] The other was Mr. Goodwin.

ever, to see the magnificent view of the eternal snow and also the progress of
the work. Because of the heavy winter, he was forced to stay indoors most
of the time. It was a glorious occasion for the members of the āśrama. The
Swami's conversation was inspiring. He spoke of the devotion of his Western
disciples to his cause, and in this connexion particularly mentioned the name
of Mr. Sevier. He also emphasized the necessity of loyalty to the work undertaken, loyalty to the leader, and loyalty to the organization. But the leader,
the Swami said, must command respect and obedience by his character. While
at Mayavati, in spite of a suffocating attack of asthma, he was busy with his
huge correspondence and wrote three articles for the magazine Prabuddha
Bhārata. The least physical effort exhausted him. One day he exclaimed, "My
body is done for!"

The Advaita Āśrama at Mayavati had been founded, as may be remembered,
with a view to enabling its members to develop their spiritual life through the
practice of the non-dualistic discipline. All forms of ritual and worship were
strictly excluded. But some of the members, accustomed to rituals, had set apart
a room as the shrine, where a picture of Śri Ramakrishna was installed and
worshipped daily. One morning the Swami chanced to enter this room while
the worship was going on. He said nothing at that time, but in the evening
severely reprimanded the inmates for violating the rules of the monastery. As
he did not want to hurt their feelings too much, he did not ask them to discon-
tinue the worship, but it was stopped by the members themselves.

One of them, however, whose heart was set on dualistic worship, asked the
advice of the Holy Mother. She wrote: "Śri Ramakrishna was all Advaita and
preached Advaita. Why should you not follow Advaita? All his disciples are
Advaitins."

After his return to the Belur Math, the Swami said in the course of a conversation: "I thought of having one centre at least from which the external
worship of Śri Ramakrishna would be excluded. But I found that the Old Man
had already established himself even there. Well! Well!"

The above incident should not indicate any lack of respect in Swami Vivekananda for Śri Ramakrishna or dualistic worship. During the last few years of
his life he showed a passionate love for the Master. Following his return to
the Belur Math he arranged, as will be seen presently, the birthday festival
of Śri Ramakrishna and the worship of the Divine Mother, according to traditional rituals.

The Swami's real nature was that of a lover of God, though he appeared
outwardly as a philosopher. But in all his teachings, both in India and abroad,
he had emphasized the non-dualistic philosophy. For Ultimate Reality, in the
Hindu spiritual tradition, is non-dual. Dualism is a stage on the way to non-
dualism. Through non-dualism alone, in the opinion of the Swami, can the
different dualistic concepts of the Personal God be harmonized. Without the
foundation of the non-dualistic Absolute, dualism breeds fanaticism, exclusiveness, and dangerous emotionalism. He saw both in India and abroad a caricature
of dualism in the worship conducted in the temples, churches, and other places
of worship.

In India the Swami found that non-dualism had degenerated into mere dry intellectual speculation. And so he wanted to restore non-dualism to its pristine purity. With that end in view he had established the Advaita Āśrama at Mayavati, overlooking the gorgeous eternal snow of the Himālayas, where the mind naturally soars to the contemplation of the Infinite, and there he had banned all vestiges of dualistic worship. In the future, the Swami believed, all religions would receive a new orientation from the non-dualistic doctrine and spread goodwill among men.

On his way to Mayavati Swami Vivekananda had heard the melancholy news of the passing away of the Mahārājā of Khetri, his faithful disciple, who had borne the financial burden of his first trip to America. The Mahārājā had undertaken the repairing of a high tower of the Emperor Akbar's tomb near Agra, and one day, while inspecting the work, had missed his footing, fallen several hundred feet, and died. "Thus," wrote the Swami to Mary Hale, "we sometimes come to grief on account of our zeal for antiquity. Take care, Mary, don't be too zealous about your piece of Indian antiquity."[40] "So you see," the Swami wrote to Mary again, "things are gloomy with me just now and my own health is wretched. Yet I am sure to bob up soon and am waiting for the next turn."

The Swami left Mayavati on January 18, and travelled four days on slippery slopes, partly through snow, before reaching the railroad station. He arrived at the Belur Math on January 24.

Swami Vivekananda had been in this monastery for seven weeks when pressing invitations for a lecture trip began to pour in from East Bengal. His mother, furthermore, had expressed an earnest desire to visit the holy places situated in that part of India. On January 26 he wrote to Mrs. Ole Bull: "I am going to take my mother on pilgrimage. . . . This is the one great wish of a Hindu widow. I have brought only misery to my people all my life. I am trying to fulfil this one wish of hers."

On March 18, in the company of a large party of his sannyāsin disciples, the Swami left for Dacca, the chief city of East Bengal, and arrived the next day. He was in poor health, suffering from both asthma and diabetes. During an asthmatic attack, when the pain was acute, he said half dreamily: "What does it matter! I have given them enough for fifteen hundred years." But he had hardly any rest. People besieged him day and night for instruction. In Dacca he delivered two public lectures and also visited the house of Nag Mahashay, where he was entertained by the saint's wife.

Next he proceeded to Chandranāth, a holy place near Chittagong, and to sacred Kāmākhyā in Assam. While in Assam he spent several days at Shillong in order to recover his health, and there met Sir Henry Cotton, the chief Government official and a friend of the Indians in their national aspiration. The two exchanged many ideas, and at Sir Henry's request the Government physician looked after the Swami's health.

Vivekananda returned to the Belur Monastery in the second week of May. Concerning the impressions of his trip, he said that a certain part of Assam was endowed with incomparable natural beauty. The people were more sturdy,

[40] Referring to himself.

active, and resolute than those of West Bengal. But in religious views they were rather conservative and even fanatical. He had found that some of the gullible people believed in pseudo-Incarnations, several of whom were living at that time in Dacca itself. The Swami had exhorted the people to cultivate manliness and the faculty of reasoning. To a sentimental young man of Dacca he had said: "My boy, take my advice; develop your muscles and brain by eating good food and by healthy exercise, and then you will be able to think for yourself. Without nourishing food your brain seems to have weakened a little." On another occasion, in a public meeting, he had declared, addressing the youths of Bengal, who had very little physical stamina, "You will be nearer to God through football than through the Bhagavad Gitā."

The brother disciples and his own disciples were much concerned about the Swami's health, which was going from bad to worse. The damp climate of Bengal did not suit him at all; it aggravated his asthma, and further, he was very, very tired. He was earnestly requested to lead a quiet life, and to satisfy his friends the Swami lived in the monastery for about seven months in comparative retirement. They tried to entertain him with light talk. But he could not be dissuaded from giving instruction to his disciples whenever the occasion arose.

He loved his room on the second storey, in the southeast corner of the monastery building, to which he joyfully returned from his trips to the West or other parts of India. This large room with four windows and three doors served as both study and bedroom. In the corner to the right of the entrance door stood a mirror about five feet high, and near this, a rack with his ochre clothes. In the middle of the room was an iron bedstead with a spring mattress, which had been given to him by one of his Western disciples. But he seldom used it; for he preferred to sleep on a small couch placed by its side. A writing-table with letters, manuscripts, pen, ink, paper, and blotting-pad, a call-bell, some flowers in a metal vase, a photograph of the Master, a deer-skin which he used at the time of meditation, and a small table with a tea-set completed the furnishings.

Here he wrote, gave instruction to his disciples and brother monks, received friends, communed with God in meditation, and sometimes ate his meals. And it was in this room that he ultimately entered into the final ecstasy from which he never returned to ordinary consciousness. The room has been preserved as it was while the Swami was in his physical body, everything in it being kept as on the last day of his life, the calendar on the wall reading July 4, 1902.

On December 19, 1900, he wrote to an American disciple: "Verily I am a bird of passage. Gay and busy Paris, grim old Constantinople, sparkling little Athens, and pyramidal Cairo are left behind, and here I am writing in my room on the Ganges, in the Math. It is so quiet and still! The broad river is dancing in the bright sunshine, only now and then an occasional cargo boat breaking the silence with the splashing of the waves. It is the cold season here, but the middle of the day is warm and bright every day. It is like the winter of southern California. Everything is green and gold, and the grass is like velvet, yet the air is cold and crisp and delightful."

After the Swami's return from East Bengal he lived a relaxed life in the monastery, surrounded by his pet animals: the dog Bāghā, the she-goat Hansi, an antelope, a stork, several cows and sheep and ducks and geese, and a kid called Mātru who was adorned with a collar of little bells, and with whom the Swami ran and played like a child. The animals adored him; Mātru, the little kid, who had been—so he pretended—a relation of his in a previous existence, slept in his room. When it died he grieved like a child and said to a disciple: "How strange! Whomsoever I love dies early." Before milking Hansi for his tea, he always asked her permission. Bāghā, who took part in the Hindu ceremonies, went to bathe in the Ganges with the devotees on sacred occasions, as for instance when the gongs and conchs announced the end of an eclipse. He was, in a sense, the leader of the group of animals at the Math. After his death he was given a burial in the grounds of the monastery.

Referring to his pet animals he wrote to an American disciple on September 7, 1901: "The rains have come down in right earnest, and it is a deluge—pouring, pouring, pouring, night and day. The river is rising, flooding the banks; the ponds and tanks have overflowed. I have just now returned from lending a hand in cutting a deep drain to take off the water from the Math grounds. The rain-water stands at places some feet deep. My huge stork is full of glee and so are the ducks and geese. My tame antelope fled from the Math and gave us some days of anxiety in finding him out. One of my ducks unfortunately died yesterday. She had been gasping for breath more than a week. One of my waggish old monks says, 'Sir, it is no use living in the Kaliyuga, when ducks catch cold from damp and rain, and frogs sneeze!' One of the geese had her plumes falling off. Knowing no other method of treatment, I left her some minutes in a tub of water mixed with mild carbolic, so that it might either kill or heal—and she is all right now."

Thus Swami Vivekananda tried to lead a carefree life at the monastery, sometimes going about the grounds clad in his loin-cloth, sometimes supervising the cooking arrangements and himself preparing some delicacies for the inmates, and sometimes joining his disciples and brother monks in the singing of devotional music. At other times he imparted spiritual instruction to the visitors, or engaged in deep thought whenever his inner spirit was stirred up, occupied himself with serious study in his room, or explained to the members of the Math the intricate passages of the scriptures and unfolded to them his scheme of future work.

Though his body was wearing away day by day, his mind was luminous. At times his eyes assumed a far-away look, showing how tired he was of the world. One day he said, "For one thing we may be grateful: this life is not eternal."

The illness did not show any sign of abatement, but that did not dampen his spirit to work. When urged to rest, he said to a disciple: "My son, there is no rest for me. That which Śri Ramakrishna called 'Kāli' took possession of my body and soul three or four days before his passing away. That makes me work and work and never lets me keep still or look to my personal comfort." Then he told the disciple how the Master, before his passing away, had transmitted his spiritual power to him.[41]

During the later part of 1901 the Swami observed all the religious festivals

[41] See p. 34.

at the Math. The Divine Mother was worshipped in strict orthodox fashion during the Durgā-pujā, Lakshmi-pujā, and Kāli-pujā. On the occasion of the Durgā-pujā the poor were given a sumptuous feast. Thus the Swami demonstrated the efficacy of religious rituals in the development of the spiritual life. In February 1902 the birth anniversary of Śri Ramakrishna was celebrated at the Belur Math, and over thirty thousand devotees gathered for the occasion. But the Swami was feverish. He was confined to his room by the swelling of his legs. From the windows he watched the dancing and the music of the devotees.

To the disciple who was attending him the Swami said: "He who has realized the Ātman becomes a storehouse of great power. From him as the centre a spiritual force emanates, working within a certain radius; people who come within this circle become inspired with his ideas and are overwhelmed by them. Thus without much religious striving they derive benefit from the spiritual experience of an illumined person. This is called grace."

"Blessed are those," the Swami continued, "who have seen Śri Ramakrishna. All of you, too, will get his vision. When you have come here, you are very near to him. Nobody has been able to understand him who came on earth as Śri Ramakrishna. Even his own nearest devotees have no real clue to it. Only some have a little inkling of it. All will understand in time."

It is said that the spot immediately beneath a lamp is dark. And so it was that the orthodox people of the neighbouring villages hardly understood the ideas and ideals of the Belur Math. The monks there did not in all respects lead the life of orthodox sannyāsins. Devotees from abroad frequented the monastery. In matters of food and dress the inmates were liberal. Thus they became the butt of criticism. The villagers invented scandals about them and the passengers on the boats passing along the Ganges would point out the monastery with an accusing finger.

When the Swami heard all this he said: "That is good. It is a law of nature. That is the way with all founders of religion. Without persecution superior ideas cannot penetrate into the heart of society."

But the criticism of the neighbours in time gave place to pride in having in their midst so many saintly souls.

Many distinguished Indians used to visit the Swami at this time. With some of them he discussed the idea of founding a Vedic Institution for the promotion of the ancient Āryan culture and the knowledge of Sanskrit. This was one of the Swami's favourite thoughts, on which he dwelt even on the last day of his life on earth.

Towards the end of 1901 two learned Buddhists from Japan came to the Belur Math to induce the Swami to attend a Congress of Religions that was being contemplated in Japan at that time. One of them was the famous artist and art critic Okakura, and the other Oda, the abbot of a Buddhist monastery. The Swami became particularly fond of Okakura and said, "We are two brothers who meet again, having come from the ends of the earth." Though pressed by the visitors, he could not accept the invitation to go to Japan, partly because of his failing health and partly because he was sceptical that the Japanese would appreciate the monastic ideal of the Non-dualistic Vedānta. In a letter to a Western lady written in June 1902, the Swami made the following interesting observation about the connexion between the monastic ideal and fidelity in married life:

> In my opinion, a race must first cultivate a great respect for motherhood, through the sanctification and inviolability of marriage, before it can attain to the ideal of perfect chastity. The Roman Catholics and the Hindus, holding marriage sacred and inviolate, have produced great chaste men and women of immense power. To the Arab, marriage is a contract or a forceful possession, to be dissolved at will, and we do not find there the development of the idea of the virgin or the brahmachārin. Modern Buddhism—having fallen among races who had not yet come up to the evolution of marriage—has made a travesty of monasticism. So until there is developed in Japan a great and sacred ideal about marriage (apart from mutual attraction and love), I do not see how there can be great monks and nuns. As you have come to see that the glory of life is chastity, so my eyes also have been opened to the necessity of this great sanctification for the vast majority, in order that a few lifelong chaste powers may be produced.

The Swami used to say that absolute loyalty and devotion between husbands and wives for three successive generations find their expression in the birth of an ideal monk.

Okakura earnestly requested the Swami to accompany him on a visit to Bodh-Gayā, where Buddha had attained illumination. Taking advantage of several weeks' respite from his ailment, the Swami accepted the invitation. He also desired to see Benares. The trip lasted through January and February 1902, and was a fitting end to all his wanderings. He arrived at Bodh-Gayā on the morning of his last birthday and was received with genuine courtesy and hospitality by the orthodox Hindu monk in charge of the temple. This and the similar respect and affection shown by the priests in Benares proved the extent of his influence over men's hearts. It may be remembered that Bodh-Gayā had been the first of the holy places he had visited during Śri Ramakrishna's lifetime. And some years later, when he was still an unknown monk, he had said farewell to Benares with the words: "Till that day when I fall on society like a thunderbolt I shall visit this place no more."

In Benares the Swami was offered a sum of money by a Mahārājā to establish a monastery there. He accepted the offer and, on his return to Calcutta, sent Swami Shivananda to organize the work. Even before Swami Vivekananda's visit to Benares, several young men, under the Swami's inspiration, had started a small organization for the purpose of providing destitute pilgrims with food, shelter, and medical aid. Delighted with their unselfish spirit, the Swami said to them: "You have the true spirit, my boys, and you will always have my love and blessings! Go on bravely; never mind your poverty. Money will come. A great thing will grow out of it, surpassing your fondest hopes." The Swami wrote the appeal which was published with the first report of the "Ramakrishna Home of Service," as the institution came to be called. In later years it became the premier institution of its kind started by the Ramakrishna Mission.

The Swami returned from Benares. But hardly had he arrived at Belur when his illness showed signs of aggravation in the damp air of Bengal. During the last year and a half of his life he was, off and on, under the strict supervision of his physicians. Diabetes took the form of dropsy. His feet swelled and certain parts of his body became hypersensitive. He could hardly close his eyes in sleep.

A native physician made him follow a very strict regime: he had to avoid water and salt. For twenty-one days he did not allow a drop of water to pass through his throat. To a disciple he said: "The body is only a tool of the mind. What the mind dictates the body will have to obey. Now I do not even think of water. I do not miss it at all. . . . I see I can do anything."

Though his body was subjected to a devitalizing illness, his mind retained its usual vigour. During this period he was seen reading the newly published *Encyclopaedia Britannica*. One of his householder disciples remarked that it was difficult to master these twenty-five volumes in one life. But the Swami had already finished ten volumes and was busy reading the eleventh. He told the disciple to ask him any question from the ten volumes he had read, and to the latter's utter amazement the Swami not only displayed his knowledge of many technical subjects but even quoted the language of the book here and there. He explained to the disciple that there was nothing miraculous about it. A man who observed strict chastity in thought and action, he declared, could develop the retentive power of the mind and reproduce exactly what he had heard or read but once, even years before.

The regeneration of India was the ever recurring theme of the Swami's thought. Two of the projects dear to his heart were the establishment of a Vedic College and a convent for women. The latter was to be started on the bank of the Ganges under the direction of the Holy Mother and was to be completely separated from the Belur Monastery. The teachers trained in the convent were to take charge of the education of Indian women along national lines.

But the Swami's heart always went out in sympathy for the poor and neglected masses. During the later part of 1901 a number of Sonthāl labourers were engaged in digging the grounds about the monastery. They were poor and outside the pale of society. The Swami felt an especial joy in talking to them, and listened to the accounts of their misery with great compassion. One day he arranged a feast for them and served them with delicacies that they had never before tasted. Then, when the meal was finished, the Swami said to them: "You are Nārāyanas. Today I have entertained the Lord Himself by feeding you."

He said to a disciple: "I actually saw God in them. How guileless they are!"

Afterwards he said, addressing the inmates of the Belur Math:

"See how simple-hearted these poor, illiterate people are! Will you be able to relieve their miseries to some extent at least? Otherwise of what use is our wearing the ochre robe of the sannyāsin? To be able to sacrifice everything for the good of others is real monasticism. Sometimes I think within myself: 'What is the good of building monasteries and so forth? Why not sell them and distribute the money among the poor, indigent Nārāyanas? What homes should we care for, we who have made the tree our shelter? Alas! How can we have the heart to put a morsel into our mouths, when our countrymen have not enough wherewith to feed or clothe themselves? . . . Mother, shall there be no redress for them?' One of the purposes of my going out to preach religion to the West, as you know, was to see if I could find any means of providing for the people of my country. Seeing their poverty and distress, I think sometimes: 'Let us throw away all the paraphernalia of worship—blowing the conch and ringing the bell and waving the lights before the image. . . . Let us throw away all pride of learning and study of the scriptures and all spiritual disciplines for the attainment of personal liberation. Let us go from village to village, devoting ourselves to the service of the poor. Let us, through the force of our character and spirituality and our austere living, convince the rich about their duties to the masses, and get money and the means wherewith to serve the poor and the distressed. . . . Alas! Nobody in our country thinks for the low, the poor, the miserable! Those who are the backbone of the nation, whose labour produces food, those whose one day's absence from work raises a cry of general distress in the city—where is the man in our country who sympathizes with them, who shares in their joys and sorrows? Look how, for want of sympathy on the part of the Hindus, thousands of pariahs are becoming Christians in the Madras Presidency! Don't think that it is merely the pinch of hunger that drives them to embrace Christianity. It is simply because they do not get your sympathy. You are continually telling them: 'Don't touch me,' 'Don't touch this or that!' Is there any fellow-feeling or sense of dharma left in the country? There is only 'Don't-touchism' now! Kick out all such degrading usages! How I wish to abolish the barriers of 'Don't-touchism' and go out and bring together one and all, crying: 'Come, all ye that are poor and destitute, fallen and downtrodden! We are one in the name of Ramakrishna!' Unless they are elevated, the Great Mother India will never awake! What are we good for if we cannot provide facilities for their food and clothing? Alas, they are ignorant of the ways of the world and hence fail to eke out a living though labouring hard day and night for it. Gather all your forces together to remove the veil from their eyes. What I see clear as daylight is that the same Brahman, the same Śakti, is in them as in me! Only there is a difference in the degree of manifestation—that is all. Have you ever seen a country in the whole history of the world rise unless there was a uniform circulation of the national blood all over the body? Know for certain that not much can be done with that body one limb of which is paralysed, even though the other limbs are healthy."

One of the lay disciples pointed out the difficulty of establishing unity and harmony among the diverse sects in India. Vivekananda replied with irritation:

"Don't come here any more if you think any task too difficult. Through the grace of the Lord, everything becomes easy of achievement. Your duty is to serve the poor and the distressed without distinction of caste and creed. What business have you to consider the fruits of your action? Your duty is to go on working, and everything will set itself right in time, and work by itself. My method of work is to construct, and not to destroy that which is already existing. . . . You are all intelligent boys and profess to be my disciples—tell me *what* you have done. Couldn't you give away one life for the sake of others? Let the reading of Vedānta and the practice of meditation and the like be left for the next life! Let this body go in the service of others—and then I shall know you have not come to me in vain!"

A little later he said: "After so much tapasyā, austerity, I have known that the highest truth is this: 'He is present in all beings. These are all the manifested forms of Him. There is no other God to seek for! He alone is worshipping God, who serves all beings.' "

In this exhortation is found Vivekananda's message in all its vividness. These words are addressed to India and the Western world alike. The West, too, has its pariahs. He who exploits another man, near or distant, offends God and will pay for it sooner or later. All men are sons of the same God, all bear within them the same God. He who wishes to serve God must serve man—and in the first instance, man in the humblest, poorest, most degraded form. Only by breaking down the barriers between man and man can one usher in the kingdom of heaven on earth.

There were moments when Vivekananda felt gloomy. His body was wasting away, and only a few young men came forward to help him in his work. He wanted more of them who, fired with indomitable faith in God and in themselves, would renounce everything for the welfare of others. He used to say that with a dozen such people he could divert into a new channel the whole thought-current of the country. Disregarding his physical suffering, he constantly inspired his disciples to cultivate this new faith.

Thus we see him, one day, seated on a canvas cot under the mango tree in the courtyard of the monastery. Sannyāsins and brahmachārins about him were busy doing their daily duties. One was sweeping the courtyard with a big broom. Swami Premananda, after his bath, was climbing the steps to the shrine. Suddenly Swami Vivekananda's eyes became radiant. Shaking with emotion, he said to a disciple:

"Where will you go to seek Brahman? He is immanent in all beings. Here, here is the visible Brahman! Shame on those who, neglecting the visible Brahman, set their minds on other things! Here is the visible Brahman before you as tangible as a fruit in one's hand! Can't you see? Here—here—here is Brahman!"

These words struck those around him with a kind of electric shock. For a quarter of an hour they remained glued to the spot, as if petrified. The broom in the hand of the sweeper stopped. Premananda fell into a trance. Everyone experienced an indescribable peace. At last the Swami said to Premananda, "Now go to worship."

The brother disciples tried to restrain the Swami's activities, especially instruction to visitors and seekers. But he was unyielding. "Look here!" he said to them one day. "What good is this body? Let it go in helping others. Did not the Master preach until the very end? And shall I not do the same? I do not care a straw if the body goes. You cannot imagine how happy I am when I find earnest seekers after truth to talk to. In the work of waking up Ātman in my fellow men I shall gladly die again and again!"

Till the very end the Swami remained the great leader of the monastery, guiding with a firm hand the details of its daily life, in spite of his own suffering. He insisted upon thorough cleanliness and examined the beds to see that they were aired and properly taken care of. He drew up a weekly time-table and saw that it was scrupulously observed. The classes on the Vedas and the Purānas were held daily, he himself conducting them when his health permitted. He dis-

couraged too much ritualism in the chapel. He warned the monks against
exaggerated sentimentalism and narrow sectarianism.

But the leader kept a stern watch on the practice of daily meditation on the
part of the inmates of the monastery. The bell sounded at fixed hours for meals,
study, discussion, and meditation. About three months before his death he
made it a rule that at four o'clock in the morning a hand-bell should be rung
from room to room to awaken the monks. Within half an hour all should be
gathered in the chapel to meditate. But he was always before them. He got up
at three and went to the chapel, where he sat facing the north, meditating
motionless for more than two hours. No one was allowed to leave his seat before
the Swami set the example. As he got up, he chanted softly, "Śiva! Śiva!"
Bowing to the image of Śri Ramakrishna, he would go downstairs and pace the
courtyard, singing a song about the Divine Mother or Śiva. Naturally his presence
in the chapel created an intense spiritual atmosphere. Swami Brahmananda
said: "Ah! One at once becomes absorbed if one sits for meditation in company
with Naren! I do not feel this when I sit alone."

Once, after an absence of several days on account of illness, he entered the
chapel and found only two monks there. He became annoyed; in order to discipline the absentees he forbade them to eat their meals at the monastery. They
had to go out and beg their food. He did not spare anyone, even a beloved
brother disciple for whom he cherished the highest respect and who happened
to be absent from the chapel that morning.

Another day, he found a brother disciple, Swami Shivananda, in bed at the
hour of meditation. He said to the latter: "Brother! I know you do not need
meditation. You have already realized the highest goal through the grace of
Śri Ramakrishna. But you should daily meditate with the youngsters in order
to set an example to them."

From that day on, Shivananda, whether ill or well, always communed with
God during the early hours of the morning. In his old age, when it became
physically impossible for him to go to the chapel, he used to sit on his bed for
meditation.

But the Swami, preoccupied as he was with the training of his Indian disciples, never forgot his Western ones. Their welfare, too, was always in his
thought and prayer.

To Miss MacLeod he wrote on June 14, 1901:

Well, Joe, keep health and spirits up. . . . *Gloire et honneur* await you—and mukti.
The natural ambition of woman is, through marriage, to climb up leaning upon a man;
but those days are gone. You shall be great without the help of any man, just as you are,
plain, dear Joe—our Joe, everlasting Joe. . . .

We have seen enough of this life not to care for any of its bubbles, have we not, Joe?
For months I have been practising to drive away all sentiments; therefore I stop here,
and good-bye just now. It was ordained by Mother that we should work together; it has
been already for the good of many; it shall be for the good of many more. So let it be. It
is useless planning useless high flights; Mother will find her own way . . . rest assured.

To Mary Hale, on August 27, 1901, he wrote with his usual wit:

I would that my health were what you expected—at least to be able to write you a long letter. It is getting worse, in fact, every day—and so many complications and botherations without that, I have ceased to notice it at all.

I wish you all joy in your lovely *Suisse* chalet—splendid health, good appetite, and a light study of Swiss or other antiquities just to liven things up a bit. I am so glad that you are breathing the free air of the mountains, but sorry that Sam is not in the best of health. Well, there is no anxiety about it; he has naturally such a fine physique.

"Woman's moods and man's luck—the gods themselves do not know, not to speak of men." My instincts may be very feminine—but what I am exercised with just this moment is that you get a little bit of manliness about you. Oh! Mary, your brain, health, beauty, everything, is going to waste just for the lack of that one essential—assertion of individuality. Your haughtiness, spirit, etc. are all nonsense—only mockery. You are at best a boarding-school girl—no backbone! no backbone!

Alas! this life-long leading-string business! This is very harsh, very brutal—but I can't help it. I love you, Mary—sincerely, genuinely. I can't cheat you with namby-pamby sugar candies. Nor do they ever come to me.

Then again, I am a dying man; I have no time to fool in. Wake up, girl! I expect now from you letters of the right slashing order. Give it right straight—I need a good deal of rousing. . . .

I am in a sense a retired man. I don't keep much note of what is going on about the Movement. Then the Movement is getting bigger and it is impossible for one man to know all about it minutely. I now do nothing—except try to eat and sleep and nurse my body the rest of the time.

Good-bye, dear Mary. Hope we shall meet again somewhere in this life—but meeting or no meeting, I remain ever your loving brother, VIVEKANANDA.

To his beloved disciple Nivedita he wrote on February 12, 1902: "May all powers come unto you! May Mother Herself be your hands and mind! It is immense power—irresistible—that I pray for you, and, if possible, along with it infinite peace. . . .

"If there was any truth in Śri Ramakrishna, may He take you into His leading, even as He did me, nay, a thousand times more!"

And again, to Miss MacLeod: "I can't, even in imagination, pay the immense debt of gratitude I owe you. Wherever you are you never forget my welfare; and there, you are the only one that bears all my burdens, all my brutal outbursts. . . ."

MAHĀSAMĀDHI

The sun, enveloped in a golden radiance, was fast descending to the horizon. The last two months of the Swami's life on earth had been full of events foreshadowing the approaching end. Yet few had thought the end so near.

Soon after his return from Benares the Swami greatly desired to see his sannyāsin disciples and he wrote to them to come to the Belur Math, even if only for a short time. "Many of his disciples from distant parts of the world," writes Sister Nivedita, "gathered round the Swami. Ill as he looked, there was none probably who suspected how near the end had come. Yet visits were paid and farewells exchanged that it had needed voyages half round the world to make."

More and more the Swami was seen to free himself from all responsibilities, leaving the work to other hands. "How often," he said, "does a man ruin his disciples by remaining always with them! When men are once trained, it is essential that their leader leave them, for without his absence they cannot develop themselves." "Plants," he had said some time before, "always remain small under a big tree." Yet the near and dear ones thought that he would certainly live three or four years more.

He refused to express any opinion on the questions of the day. "I can no more enter into outside affairs," he said; "I am already on the way." On another occasion he said: "You may be right; but I cannot enter any more into these matters. I am going down into death." News of the world met with but a far-away rejoinder from him.

On May 15, 1902, he wrote to Miss MacLeod, perhaps for the last time: "I am somewhat better, but of course far from what I expected. A great idea of quiet has come upon me. I am going to retire for good—no more work for me. If possible, I will revert to my old days of begging. All blessings attend you, Joe; you have been a good angel to me."

But it was difficult for him to give up what had been dearer to him than his life: the work. On the last Sunday before the end he said to one of his disciples: "You know the work is always my weak point. When I think *that* might come to an end, I am all undone." He could easily withdraw from weakness and attachment, but the work still retained its power to move him.

Śri Ramakrishna and the Divine Mother preoccupied his mind. He acted as if he were the child of the Mother or the boy playing at the feet of Śri Ramakrishna at Dakshineswar. He said, "A great tapasyā and meditation has come upon me, and I am making ready for death."

His disciples and spiritual brothers were worried to see his contemplative mood. They remembered the words of Śri Ramakrishna that Naren, after his mission was completed, would merge for ever into samādhi, and that he would refuse to live in his physical body if he realized who he was. A brother monk asked him one day, quite casually, "Do you know yet who you are?" The unexpected reply, "Yes, I now know!" awed into silence everyone present. No further question was asked. All remembered the story of the great nirvikalpa samādhi of Naren's youth, and how, when it was over, Śri Ramakrishna had said: "Now the Mother has shown you everything. But this realization, like the jewel locked in a box, will be hidden away from you and kept in my custody. I will keep the key with me. Only after you have fulfilled your mission on this earth will the box be unlocked, and you will know everything as you have known now."

They also remembered that in the cave of Amarnāth, in the summer of 1898, he had received the grace of Śiva—not to die till he himself should will to do so. He was looking death in the face unafraid as it drew near.

Everything about the Swami in these days was deliberate and significant, yet none could apprehend its true import. People were deceived by his outer cheerfulness. From the beginning of June he appeared to be regaining his health.

One day, about a week before the end, he bade a disciple bring him the Bengali almanac. He was seen several times on subsequent days studying the book intently, as if he was undecided about something he wanted to know. After the passing away, the brother monks and disciples realized that he had been debating about the day when he should throw away the mortal body. Ramakrishna, too, had consulted the almanac before his death.

Three days before the mahāsamādhi, Vivekananda pointed out to Swami Premananda a particular spot on the monastery grounds where he wished his body to be cremated.

On Wednesday the Swami fasted, following the orthodox rule: it was the eleventh day of the moon. Sister Nivedita came to the monastery to ask him some questions about her school; but he was not interested and referred her to some other Swamis. He insisted, however, on serving Nivedita the morning meal. To quote the Sister's words:

Each dish, as it was offered—boiled seeds of the jack-fruit, boiled potatoes, plain rice, and ice-cold milk—formed the subject of playful chat; and finally, to end the meal, he himself poured the water over her hands, and dried them with a towel.

"It is I who should do these things for you, Swamiji! Not you for me!" was the protest naturally offered. But his answer was startling in its solemnity—"Jesus washed the feet of his disciples!"

Something checked the answer, "But that was the last time!" as it rose to the lips, and the words remained unuttered. This was well. For here also, the last time had come.

There was nothing sad or grave about the Swami during these days. Efforts were made not to tire him. Conversations were kept as light as possible, touching only upon the pet animals that surrounded him, his garden experiments, books, and absent friends. But all the while one was conscious of a luminous presence of which the Swami's bodily form seemed only a shadow or symbol. The members of the monastery had never felt so strongly as now, before him, that they stood in the presence of an infinite light; yet none was prepared to see the end so soon, least of all on that Friday, July the Fourth, on which he appeared so much stronger and healthier than he had been for years.

On the supreme day, Friday, he rose very early. Going to the chapel, alone, he shut the windows and bolted the doors, contrary to his habit, and meditated for three hours. Descending the stairs of the shrine, he sang a beautiful song about Kāli:

> Is Kāli, my Mother, really black?
> The Naked One, though black She seems,
> Lights the Lotus of the heart.
> Men call Her black, but yet my mind
> Does not believe that She is so:
> Now She is white, now red, now blue;
> Now She appears as yellow, too.
>
> I hardly know who Mother is,
> Though I have pondered all my life:
> Now Purusha, now Prakriti,
> And now the Void, She seems to be.
> To meditate on all these things
> Confounds poor Kamalākānta's wits.

Then he said, almost in a whisper: "If there were another Vivekananda, then he would have understood what this Vivekananda has done! And yet—how many Vivekanandas shall be born in time!"

He expressed the desire to worship Mother Kāli at the Math the following day, and asked two of his disciples to procure all the necessary articles for the ceremony. Next he asked the disciple Suddhananda to read a passage from the Yajur-Veda with the commentary of a well-known expositor. The Swami said that he did not agree with the commentator and exhorted the disciple to give a new interpretation of the Vedic texts.

He partook of the noon meal with great relish, in company with the members of the Math, though usually, at that time, he ate alone in his room because of his illness. Immediately afterwards, full of life and humour, he gave lessons to the brahmachārins for three hours on Sanskrit grammar. In the afternoon he took a walk for about two miles with Swami Premananda and discussed his plan to start a Vedic College in the monastery.

"What will be the good of studying the Vedas?" Premananda asked.

"It will kill superstition," Swami Vivekananda said.

On his return the Swami inquired very tenderly concerning every member of the monastery. Then he conversed for a long time with his companions on the rise and fall of nations. "India is immortal," he said, "if she persists in her search for God. But if she goes in for politics and social conflict, she will die."

At seven o'clock in the evening the bell rang for worship in the chapel. The Swami went to his room and told the disciple who attended him that none was to come to him until called for. He spent an hour in meditation and telling his beads, then called the disciple and asked him to open all the windows and fan his head. He lay down quietly on his bed and the attendant thought that he was either sleeping or meditating.

At the end of an hour his hands trembled a little and he breathed once very deeply. There was a silence for a minute or two, and again he breathed in the same manner. His eyes became fixed in the centre of his eyebrows, his face assumed a divine expression, and eternal silence fell.

"There was," said a brother disciple of the Swami, "a little blood in his nostrils, about his mouth, and in his eyes." According to the Yoga scriptures, the life-breath of an illumined yogi passes out through the opening on the top of the head, causing the blood to flow in the nostrils and the mouth.

The great ecstasy took place at ten minutes past nine. Swami Vivekananda passed away at the age of thirty-nine years, five months, and twenty-four days, thus fulfilling his own prophecy: "I shall not live to be forty years old."

The brother disciples thought that he might have fallen into samādhi, and chanted the Master's name to bring back his consciousness. But he remained on his back motionless.

Physicians were sent for and the body was thoroughly examined. In the doctor's opinion life was only suspended; artificial respiration was tried. At midnight, however, Swami Vivekananda was pronounced dead, the cause, according to medical science, having been apoplexy or sudden failure of the heart. But the monks were convinced that their leader had voluntarily cast off his body in samādhi, as predicted by Śri Ramakrishna.

In the morning people poured in from all quarters. Nivedita sat by the body and fanned it till it was brought down at 2 p.m. to the porch leading to the courtyard. It was covered with ochre robes and decorated with flowers. Incense was burnt and a religious service was performed with lights, conch-shells, and bells. The brother monks and disciples took their final leave and the procession started, moving slowly through the courtyard and across the lawn, till it reached the vilva tree near the spot where the Swami himself had desired his body to be cremated.

The funeral pyre was built and the body was consigned to the flames kindled with sandalwood. Across the Ganges, on the other bank, Ramakrishna had been cremated sixteen years before.

Nivedita began to weep like a child, rolling on the ground. Suddenly the wind blew into her lap a piece of the ochre robe from the pyre, and she received it as a blessing. It was dusk when the flames subsided. The sacred relics were gathered and the pyre was washed with the water of the Ganges. The place is now marked by a temple, the table of the altar standing on the very spot where the Swami's body rested in the flames.

Gloom and desolation fell upon the monastery. The monks prayed in the depths of their hearts: "O Lord! Thy will be done!" But deep beneath their grief all felt that this was not the end. The words of the leader, uttered long before his death, rang in their ears:

"It may be that I shall find it good to get outside my body—to cast it off like a worn-out garment. But I shall not cease to work. I shall inspire men everywhere, until the world shall know that it is one with God."

And: "May I be born again and again, and suffer thousands of miseries, so that I may worship the only God that exists, the only God I believe in, the sum total of all souls."

For centuries to come people everywhere will be inspired by Swami Vivekananda's message: O Man! first realize that you are one with Brahman—*aham Brahmāsmi*—and then realize that the whole universe is verily the same Brahman—*sarvam khalvidam Brahma.*

CHICAGO ADDRESSES

VIVEKANANDA ENTERING THE PARLIAMENT OF RELIGIONS (1893)

VIVEKANANDA AT THE PARLIAMENT OF RELIGIONS

RESPONSE TO WELCOME

At the World's Parliament of Religions

(Chicago, September 11, 1893)

SISTERS AND BROTHERS OF AMERICA:
It fills my heart with joy unspeakable to rise in response to the warm and cordial welcome which you have given us. I thank you in the name of the most ancient order of monks in the world. I thank you in the name of the mother of religions. And I thank you in the name of the millions and millions of Hindu people of all classes and sects.

My thanks, also, to some of the speakers on this platform, who, referring to the delegates from the Orient, have told you that these men from far-off nations may well claim the honour of bearing to different lands the idea of toleration.

I am proud to belong to a religion which has taught the world both tolerance and universal acceptance. We not only believe in universal toleration, but we accept all religions as true. I am proud to belong to a nation which has sheltered the persecuted and the refugees of all religions and all nations of the earth. I am proud to tell you that we have gathered in our bosom the purest remnant of the Israelites, who came to Southern India and took refuge with us in the very year in which their holy temple was shattered by Roman tyranny. I am proud to belong to the religion which has sheltered and is still fostering the remnant of the grand Zoroastrian nation.

I will quote to you, brethren, a few lines from a hymn that I remember to have repeated from my earliest boyhood, which is every day repeated by millions of human beings: "As the different streams, having their sources in different places, all mingle their water in the sea, so, O Lord, the different paths which men take through different tendencies, various though they appear, crooked or straight, all lead to Thee." The present convention, which is one of the most august assemblies ever held, is in itself a vindication, a declaration to the world, of the wonderful doctrine preached in the Gītā: "Whosoever comes to Me, through whatsoever form, I reach him. All men are struggling through paths which in the end lead to Me."

Sectarianism, bigotry, and its horrible descendant, fanaticism, have long possessed this beautiful earth. They have filled the earth with violence, drenched it often and often with human blood, destroyed civilization, and sent whole nations to despair. Had it not been for these horrible demons, human society would be far more advanced than it is now. But their time is come; and I fervently hope that the bell that tolled this morning in honour of this convention may be the death-knell of all fanaticism, of all persecutions with the sword or with the pen, and of all uncharitable feelings between persons wending their way to the same goal.

WHY WE DISAGREE

(September 15, 1893)

I WILL TELL YOU a little story. You have heard the eloquent speaker who has just finished say, "Let us cease from abusing each other," and he was very sorry that there should always be so much variance. But I think I should tell you a story which will illustrate the cause of this variance.

A frog lived in a well. It had lived there for a long time. It was born there and brought up there, and yet it was a little, small frog. Of course, the evolutionists were not there then to tell us whether the frog lost its eyes or not, but for our story's sake we must take it for granted that it had eyes and that every day it cleansed the water of all the worms and bacilli that lived there, with an energy that would do credit to our modern bacteriologists. In this way it went on and became a little sleek and fat. Well, one day another frog, which lived in the sea, came and fell into the well.

"Where are you from?"

"I am from the sea."

"The sea! How big is that? Is it as big as my well?" And it took a leap from one side of the well to the other.

"My friend," said the frog of the sea, "how can you compare the sea with your little well?"

Then the frog took another leap and asked, "Is your sea so big?"

"What nonsense you speak, to compare the sea with your well!"

"But," said the frog of the well, "nothing can be bigger than my well; there can be nothing bigger than this. This fellow is a liar, so turn him out."

That has been the difficulty all the while.

I am a Hindu. I am sitting in my own little well and thinking the whole world is my little well. The Christian sits in his little well and thinks the whole world is his well. The Mohammedan sits in his little well and thinks that is the whole world. I have to thank you of America for the great attempt you are making to break down the barriers of this little world of ours, and I hope that in the future the Lord will help you to accomplish your purpose.

HINDUISM

(Paper read at the Parliament, September 19, 1893)

THREE RELIGIONS NOW STAND in the world which have come down to us from times prehistoric: Hinduism, Zoroastrianism, and Judaism. They have all received tremendous shocks, and all of them have proved, by their survival, their internal strength. But while Judaism failed to absorb Christianity and was driven out of its place of birth by its all-conquering daughter, and a handful of Parsees is all that remains to tell the tale of their grand religion, sect after sect arose in India and seemed to shake the religion of the Vedas to its very foundations; but like the waters of the seashore in a tremendous earthquake, it receded only for a while, to return in an all-absorbing flood, a thousand times more vigorous; and when the tumult of the rush was over, these sects were all sucked in, absorbed, and assimilated into the immense body of the mother faith.

From the high spiritual flights of the Vedānta philosophy, of which the latest discoveries of science seem like echoes, to the low ideas of idolatry with its multifarious mythology, the agnosticism of the Buddhists, and the atheism of the Jains, each and all have a place in the Hindu religion.

Where, then, the question arises, where is the common centre upon which all these widely diverging radii converge? Where is the common basis upon which all these seemingly hopeless contradictions rest? This is the question I shall attempt to answer.

The Hindus have received their religion through revelation: the Vedas. They hold that the Vedas are without beginning and without end. It may sound ludicrous to this audience that a book can be without beginning or end. But by the Vedas no books are meant. They mean the accumulated treasure of spiritual laws discovered by different persons in different times. Just as the law of gravitation existed before its discovery and would exist if all humanity forgot it, so is it with the laws that govern the spiritual world. The moral, ethical, and spiritual relations between soul and soul and between individual spirits and the Father of all spirits were there before their discovery and would remain even if we forgot them.

The discoverers of these laws are called rishis, and we honour them as perfected beings. I am glad to tell this audience that some of the very greatest of them were women.

Here it may be contended that these laws, as laws, may be without end, but they must have had a beginning. The Vedas teach us that creation is without beginning or end. Science is said to have proved that the sum total of cosmic energy is always the same. Then, if there was a time when nothing existed, where was all this manifested energy? Some say it was in a potential form in

185

God. In that case God is sometimes potential and sometimes kinetic, which would make Him mutable. Everything mutable is a compound, and every compound must undergo that change which is called destruction. So God would die—which is absurd. Therefore there never was a time when there was no creation.

If I may be allowed to use a simile, creation and Creator are two lines, without beginning and without end, running parallel to each other. God is the ever active Providence, by whose power systems after systems are being evolved out of chaos, made to run for a time, and again destroyed. This is what the brāhmin boy repeats every day: "The sun and the moon, the Lord created like the suns and moons of previous cycles."

Here I stand, and if I shut my eyes and try to conceive my existence—"I," "I," "I"—what is the idea before me? The idea of a body. Am I, then, nothing but a combination of material substances? No, the Vedas declare, I am a spirit living in a body. I am not the body. The body will die, but I shall not die. Here I am in this body; it will fall, but I shall go on living. I had also a past. The soul was not created; for creation means a combination, which means a certain future dissolution. If the soul was created, it must die.

Some are born happy, enjoy perfect health, have beautiful bodies, mental vigour, and all wants supplied. Others are born miserable: some are without hands or feet; others, again, are idiots and only drag on a wretched existence. Why, if they are all created, why does a just and merciful God create one happy and another unhappy? Why is He so partial? Nor would it mend matters in the least to hold that those who are miserable in this life will be happy in a future one. Why should a man be miserable, even here, in the reign of a just and merciful God?

In the second place, the idea of a Creator God does not explain the anomaly, but simply asserts the cruel fiat of an all-powerful Being. There must have been causes, then, before a man's birth, to make him miserable or happy; and those were his past actions.

Are not all the tendencies of the mind and the body accounted for by inherited aptitude? Here are two parallel lines of existence—one of the mind, the other of matter. If matter and its transformations answer for all that we have, there is no necessity for supposing the existence of a soul. But it cannot be proved that thought has been evolved out of matter; and if a philosophical monism is inevitable, spiritual monism is certainly logical and more desirable than a materialistic monism. But it is not necessary to discuss either of these here.

We cannot deny that bodies acquire certain tendencies from heredity; but those tendencies only mean the physical configuration through which a peculiar mind alone can act in a peculiar way. There are other tendencies peculiar to a soul, caused by its past actions. And a soul with a certain tendency will by the law of affinity take birth in that body which is the fittest instrument for the display of that tendency. This is in accord with science; for science wants to explain everything by habit, and habit is acquired through repetition. So repetition is necessary to explain the natural habits of a new-born soul. And since they were not obtained in this present life, they must have come down from past lives.

There is another suggestion. Taking all this for granted, how is it that I do not remember anything of my past life? This can be easily explained. I am now speaking English. It is not my mother tongue; in fact no words of my mother tongue are now present in my consciousness; but let me try to bring them up, and they rush in. That shows that consciousness is only the surface of the mental ocean, and within its depths are stored up all our experiences. Try and struggle —and they will come up and you will be conscious even of your past life.

This is direct and demonstrative evidence. Verification is the perfect proof of a theory, and here is the challenge thrown to the world by the rishis. We have discovered the secret by which the very depths of the ocean of memory can be stirred up. Try it—and you will get a complete reminiscence of your past life.

So, then, the Hindu believes that he is Spirit. Him the sword cannot pierce, him fire cannot burn, him water cannot melt, him the air cannot dry. The Hindu believes that every soul is a circle whose circumference is nowhere, but whose centre is located in the body, and that death means the change of this centre from body to body. The soul is not bound by the conditions of matter. In its very essence it is free, unbounded, holy, pure, and perfect. But somehow or other it finds itself tied down to matter and thinks of itself as matter.

Why the free, perfect, and pure Being should be thus under the thraldom of matter is the next question. How can the perfect soul be deluded into the belief that it is imperfect? We have been told that the Hindus shirk the question and say that there can be no such question. Some thinkers want to answer it by positing one or more quasi-perfect beings, and use big scientific names to fill up the gap. But naming is not explaining. The question remains the same. How can the perfect become the quasi-perfect; how can the pure, the absolute, change even a microscopic particle of its nature? But the Hindu is sincere. He does not want to take shelter under sophistry. He is brave enough to face the question in a manly fashion, and his answer is: "I do not know. I do not know how the perfect Being, the soul, came to think of itself as imperfect, as joined to and conditioned by matter." But the fact is a fact for all that. It is a fact in everybody's consciousness that one thinks of oneself as the body. The Hindu does not attempt to explain why one thinks one is the body. The answer that it is the will of God is no explanation. This is nothing more than what the Hindu says: "I do not know."

Well, then, the human soul is eternal and immortal, perfect and infinite, and death means only a change of centre from one body to another. The present is determined by our past actions, and the future by the present. The soul will go on evolving up or reverting back, from birth to birth and death to death.

But here is another question: Is man a tiny boat in a tempest, raised one moment on the foamy crest of a billow, and dashed down into a yawning chasm the next, rolling to and fro at the mercy of good and bad actions—a powerless, helpless wreck in an ever raging, ever rushing, uncompromising current of cause and effect; a little moth placed under the wheel of causation, which rolls on crushing everything in its way and waits not for the widow's tears or the orphan's cry? The heart sinks at the idea. Yet this is the law of nature.

Is there no hope? Is there no escape?—was the cry that went up from the bottom of the heart of despair. It reached the Throne of Mercy, and words of hope and consolation came down and inspired a Vedic sage; and he stood up before the world and in trumpet voice proclaimed the glad tidings: "Hear, ye children of immortal bliss, even ye that reside in higher spheres! I have found the Ancient One, who is beyond all darkness, all delusion. By knowing Him alone will you be saved from death over again." "Children of immortal bliss"—what a sweet, what a hopeful name! Allow me to call you, brethren, by that sweet name—heirs of immortal bliss. Yea, the Hindu refuses to call you sinners. We are the children of God, the sharers of immortal bliss, holy and perfect beings. Ye divinities on earth—sinners! It is a sin to call a man so; it is a standing libel on human nature. Come up, O lions, and shake off the delusion that you are sheep. You are souls immortal, spirits free, blest, and eternal. You are not matter, you are not bodies; matter is your servant, not you the servants of matter.

Thus it is that the Vedas proclaim, not a dreadful combination of unforgiving laws, not an endless prison of cause and effect, but that at the head of all these laws, in and through every particle of matter and force, stands One "by whose command the wind blows, fire burns, the clouds rain, and death stalks upon the earth."

And what is His nature?

He is everywhere, the pure and formless One, the Almighty and All-merciful. "Thou art our Father, Thou art our Mother, Thou art our beloved Friend, Thou art the Source of all strength: give us strength. Thou art He that beareth the burdens of the universe: help me bear the little burden of this life." Thus sang the rishis of the Vedas.

And how are we to worship Him? Through love. "He is to be worshipped as the one Beloved, dearer than everything in this and the next life."

This is the doctrine of love declared in the Vedas. Let us see how it is fully developed and taught by Krishna, whom the Hindus believe to have been God incarnate on earth.

Krishna taught that a man ought to live in this world like a lotus leaf, which grows in water but is never moistened by the water: so a man ought to live in the world—his heart to God and his hands to work.

It is good to love God in the hope of reward in this or the next world, but it is better to love God for love's sake; and the prayer goes: "Lord, I do not want wealth or children or learning. If it is Thy will, I shall go from birth to birth; but grant me this—that I may love Thee without hope of reward, love unselfishly for love's sake."

One of Krishna's disciples, the emperor of India, was driven from his kingdom by his enemies and had to take shelter, with his queen, in a forest in the Himālayas. And there one day the queen asked him how it was that he, the most virtuous of men, should suffer so much misery. Yudhishthira answered: "Behold, my queen, the Himālayas—how grand and beautiful they are. I love them. They do not give me anything; but it is my nature to love the grand, the beautiful; therefore I love them. Similarly, I love the Lord. He is the source of all beauty, of all sublimity. He is the only object to be loved. My nature is to love Him, and therefore I love. I do not pray for anything; I do not ask for anything. Let Him place me wherever He likes. I must love Him for love's sake. I cannot trade in love."

The Vedas teach that the soul is divine, only held in the bondage of matter, and that perfection will be reached when this bond bursts. And the word they use for it is therefore mukti, freedom—freedom from the bonds of imperfection, freedom from death and misery. This bondage can only fall off through the mercy of God; and this mercy comes to the pure. So purity is the condition of His mercy. How does that mercy act? He reveals Himself to the pure heart; the pure and the stainless see God, yea, even in this life. Then and then only is all the crookedness of the heart made straight. Then all doubt ceases. Man is no more the victim of a terrible law of causation.

This is the very centre, the most vital conception of Hinduism. The Hindu does not want to live upon words and theories. If there are existences beyond the ordinary sensuous existence, he wants to come face to face with them. If there is a soul in him which is not matter, if there is an all-merciful Universal Soul,[1] he will go to Him direct. He must see Him; that alone can destroy all doubts. So the best proof a Hindu sage gives about the Soul, about God, is: "I have seen the Soul; I have seen God." And that is the only condition of perfection. The religion of the Hindus does not consist in struggles and attempts to believe a certain doctrine or dogma, but in realization—not in believing, but in being and becoming. Thus the whole object of their system is by constant struggle to become perfect, to become divine, to reach God and see God; and this reaching God, seeing God, becoming perfect even as the Father in heaven is perfect, constitutes the religion of the Hindus.

And what becomes of a man when he attains perfection? He lives a life of bliss infinite. He enjoys infinite and perfect bliss, having obtained the only thing in which man ought to have pleasure, namely, God, and enjoys the bliss with God.

So far all the Hindus are agreed. This is the common religion of all the sects of India. But then perfection is absolute, and the absolute cannot be two or three. It cannot have any qualities. It cannot be an individual. And so, when a

---

[1] Non-dualistic Vedānta speaks of two souls, as it were: the Real Soul and the apparent soul, the Universal and the individual, the Absolute and the phenomenal. The Real Soul, which is the same as Brahman, is Pure Consciousness, birthless, deathless, and beyond time, space, and the law of causation. The apparent soul is the one with which we deal in our daily practical life, which identifies itself with the body, senses, and mind, and is subject to birth, death, and other phenomenal changes. In reality there is only one Existence, designated as Brahman. Through māyā, or metaphysical ignorance, the apparent multiplicity is created and Brahman appears as the individul soul and the universe. By means of spiritual discipline the individual soul ultimately recognizes its oneness with the Universal Soul. Throughout this book the word soul, when it denotes Brahman, or Pure Consciousness, has been spelt with a capital s; when it denotes the individual soul it has been spelt with a small s, except in a few instances, where, in order to emphasize the soul's potential divine nature, it has been spelt with a capital. The same applies to the word self.

soul becomes perfect and absolute, it must become one with Brahman, and it will then realize itself as Existence Absolute, Knowledge Absolute, and Bliss Absolute.

We have often and often heard this called losing one's individuality and becoming a stock or a stone. "He jests at scars that never felt a wound." I tell you it is nothing of the kind. If it is happiness to enjoy the consciousness of this small body, it must be greater happiness to enjoy the consciousness of two bodies, the measure of happiness increasing with the consciousness of an increasing number of bodies, the aim, the peak of happiness being reached when it has become a universal consciousness.

Therefore to gain this infinite universal individuality, this miserable little prisoner individuality must go. Then alone can death cease when I am one with Life; then alone can misery cease when I am one with Happiness; then alone can all errors cease when I am one with Knowledge. This is the necessary scientific conclusion. Science has proved to me that physical individuality is a delusion, that really my body is one little continuously changing body in an unbroken ocean of matter; and Advaita, non-duality, is the necessary conclusion with regard to my other part, the Soul.

Science is nothing but the finding of unity. As soon as science reaches perfect unity, it will stop from further progress, because it will have reached the goal. Thus chemistry cannot progress farther when it discovers one element out of which all others are made. Physics will stop when it is able to fulfil its services in discovering one energy of which all the others are but manifestations. And the science of religion will become perfect when it discovers Him who is the one Life in a universe of death, who is the constant basis of an ever changing world, One who is the only Soul, of whom all souls are but delusive manifestations. Thus it is, through multiplicity and duality, that the ultimate unity is reached. Religion can go no farther. This, too, is the goal of all science.

All science is bound to come to this conclusion in the long run. Manifestation, and not creation, is the word of science today; and the Hindu is only glad that what he has been cherishing in his bosom for ages is going to be taught in more forcible language, and with further light, from the latest conclusions of science.

Descend we now from the aspirations of philosophy to the religion of the ignorant. At the very outset, I may tell you that there is no polytheism in India. In every temple, if one stands by and listens, one will find the worshippers applying all the attributes of God, including omnipresence, to the images. It is not polytheism, nor would the name *henotheism* explain the situation. "A rose by any other name would smell as sweet." Names are not explanations.

I remember, as a boy, hearing a Christian missionary preach to a crowd in India. Among other sweet things, he said to them, "If I give your idol a blow with my stick, what can it do?" One of his hearers sharply answered, "If I abuse your God, what can He do?" "You will be punished," said the preacher, "when you die." "So my idol will punish you when you die," retorted the Hindu.

A tree is known by its fruits. When I have seen, amongst those that are called idolaters, men the likes of whom in morality and spirituality and love I have never seen anywhere, I stop and ask myself, "Can sin beget holiness?"

Superstition is a great enemy of man, but bigotry is worse. Why does a Christian go to church? Why is the Cross holy? Why is the face turned towards the sky in prayer? Why are there so many images in a Catholic church? Why are there so many images in the minds of Protestants when they pray?

My brethren, we can no more think about anything without a mental image than we can live without breathing. By the law of association the material image calls up the mental idea and vice versa. This is why the Hindu uses an external symbol when he worships. He will tell you that it helps to keep his mind fixed on the Being to whom he prays. He knows as well as you do that the image is not God, is not omnipresent. After all, how much does omnipresence mean to most of the world? It stands merely as a word, a symbol. Has God superficial area? Even if we do not admit that, still, when we repeat that word *omnipresent*, we think of the extended sky or of space—that is all.

As we find that somehow or other, by the laws of our mental constitution, we have to associate our ideas of infinity with the image of the blue sky or of the sea, so we naturally connect our idea of holiness with the image of a church, a mosque, or a cross. The Hindus have associated the ideas of holiness, purity, truth, omnipresence, and other such ideas with different images and forms— but with this difference, that while some people devote their whole lives to their idol of a church and never rise higher, because with them religion means an intellectual assent to certain doctrines and doing good to their fellows, the whole religion of the Hindus is centred in realization.

Man is to become divine by realizing the divine. Idols or temples or churches or books are only the supports, the helps, of his spiritual childhood; but on and on he must progress. He must not stop anywhere. "External worship, material worship," say the Hindu scriptures, "is the lowest stage; struggling to rise higher, through mental prayer, is the next stage; but the highest stage is when the Lord has been realized."

Mark that the same earnest man who is kneeling before the idol tells you: "Him the sun cannot express, nor the moon, nor the stars; the lightning cannot express Him, not to speak of fire. Through Him they shine." But he does not abuse anyone's idol or call its worship sin. He recognizes in it a necessary stage of life. "The child is father of the man." Would it be right for an old man to say that childhood is a sin or youth a sin?

If a man can realize his divine nature with the help of an image, would it be right to call that a sin? Or, even when he has passed that stage, should he call it an error? To the Hindu, man is not travelling from error to truth, but from truth to truth—from lower to higher truth. To him all religions, from the lowest fetishism to the highest absolutism, mean so many attempts of the human soul to grasp and realize the Infinite, each determined by the conditions of its birth and association; and each of these marks a stage of progress; and every soul is a young eagle soaring higher and higher, gathering more and more strength till it reaches the glorious Sun.

Unity in variety is the plan of nature, and the Hindu has recognized it. Every other religion lays down certain fixed dogmas and tries to force society to adopt them. It places before society only one coat, which must fit Jack and John and Henry all alike. If it does not fit John or Henry, he must go without a coat to cover his body. The Hindus have discovered that the Absolute can only be realized, or thought of, or stated, through the relative, and that the images, crosses, and crescents are simply so many symbols, so many pegs to hang spiritual ideas on. It is not that this help is necessary for everyone; but those that do not need it have no right to say that it is wrong. Nor is it compulsory in Hinduism.

One thing I must tell you. Idolatry in India does not mean anything horrible. It is not the "mother of harlots." On the contrary, it is the attempt of undeveloped minds to grasp high spiritual truths. The Hindus have their faults; they sometimes have their exceptions. But mark this: they are always for punishing their own bodies, and never for cutting the throats of their neighbours. If the Hindu fanatic burns himself on the pyre, he never lights the fire of the Inquisition. And even his self-immolation cannot be laid at the door of his religion any more than the burning of witches can, at the door of Christianity.

To the Hindu, then, the whole world of religions is only a travelling, a coming up, of different men and women, through various conditions and circumstances, to the same goal. Every religion is only the evolving of a God out of the material man; and the same God is the inspirer of all of them. Why, then, are there so many contradictions? They are only apparent, says the Hindu. The contradictions come from the same truth's adapting itself to the varying circumstances of different natures.

It is the same light coming through glasses of different colours. And these little variations are necessary for purposes of adaptation. But in the heart of everything the same truth reigns. The Lord has declared to the Hindu, in His incarnation as Krishna: "I am in every religion, like the thread through a string of pearls. Wherever thou seest extraordinary holiness and extraordinary power raising and purifying humanity, know thou that I am there." And what has been the result? I challenge the world to find, throughout the whole system of Sanskrit philosophy, any such expression as that the Hindu alone will be saved and not others. Says Vyāsa, "We find perfect men also beyond the pale of our caste and creed."

One thing more. How, then, can the Hindu, whose whole fabric of thought centres in God, believe in Buddhism, which is agnostic, or in Jainism, which is atheistic?

The Buddhists and the Jains do not depend upon God; but the whole force of their religion is directed to the great central truth in every religion: to evolve a God out of man. They have not seen the Father, but they have seen the Son.[2] And he that hath seen the Son hath seen the Father also.

This, brethren, is a short sketch of the religious ideas of the Hindus. The Hindu may have failed to carry out all his plans. But if there is ever to be a universal religion, it must be one which will have no location in place or time; which will be infinite, like the God it will preach, and whose sun will shine upon the followers of Krishna and of Christ, on saints and sinners, alike; which will not be Brāhminical or Buddhist, Christian or Mohammedan, but the sum total of all these, and still have infinite space for development; which in its catho-

[2] Meaning Buddha in Buddhism and the perfected saints in Jainism; the Buddhists and Jains do not believe in God.

licity will embrace in its infinite arms, and find a place for, every human being, from the lowest grovelling savage, not far removed from the brute, to the highest man, towering by the virtues of his head and heart almost above humanity, making society stand in awe of him and doubt his human nature. It will be a religion which will have no place for persecution or intolerance in its polity, which will recognize divinity in every man and woman, and whose whole scope, whose whole force, will be centred in aiding humanity to realize its own true, divine nature.

Offer such a religion and all the nations will follow you. Aśoka's council was a council of the Buddhist faith. Akbar's, though more to the purpose, was only a parlour meeting.[3] It was reserved for America to proclaim to all quarters of the globe that the Lord is in every religion.

May He who is the Brahman of the Hindus, the Ahura-Mazda of the Zoroastrians, the Buddha of the Buddhists, the Jehovah of the Jews, the Father in heaven of the Christians, give strength to you to carry out your noble idea! The star arose in the East; it travelled steadily towards the West, sometimes dimmed and sometimes effulgent, till it made a circuit of the world; and now it is again rising on the very horizon of the East, the borders of the Sanpo,[4] a thousandfold more effulgent than it ever was before.

Hail Columbia, motherland of liberty! It has been given to thee, who never dipped thy hand in thy neighbour's blood, who never found out that the shortest way of becoming rich was by robbing one's neighbours—it has been given to thee to march in the vanguard of civilization with the flag of harmony.

[3] Both Aśoka, the great Buddhist emperor (*circa* 274-237 B.C.), and Akbar, the great Moghul emperor (A.D. 1556-1605), were known for their liberal outlook in religious matters. They made serious efforts to establish harmony among different faiths.

[4] The Brahmaputra river, whose source is Lake Manasarovar in Tibet. The part of the river that flows through Tibet is called the Sanpo.

RELIGION NOT THE CRYING NEED
OF INDIA

(September 20, 1893)

CHRISTIANS MUST ALWAYS be ready for good criticism, and I hardly think you will mind if I make a little criticism. You Christians, who are so fond of sending out missionaries to save the souls of the heathen—why do you not try to save their bodies from starvation? In India, during the terrible famines, thousands died from hunger, yet you Christians did nothing. You erect churches all through India, but the crying need in the East is not religion—they have religion enough; it is bread that the suffering millions of burning India cry out for with parched throats. They ask us for bread, but we give them stones. It is an insult to starving people to offer them religion; it is an insult to a starving man to teach him metaphysics. In India a priest that preached for money would lose caste and be spat upon by the people. I came here to seek aid for my impoverished people, and I fully realized how difficult it was to get help for the heathen from Christians in a Christian land.

BUDDHISM: THE FULFILMENT OF HINDUISM

(September 26, 1893)

I AM NOT a Buddhist, as you have heard, and yet I am. If China or Japan or Ceylon follows the teachings of the great Master, India worships him as God incarnate on earth. You have just now heard that I am going to criticize Buddhism. But by that I wish you to understand only this: Far be it from me to criticize him whom I worship as God incarnate on earth; but our views about Buddha are that he was not understood properly by his disciples.

The relation between Hinduism—by Hinduism I mean the religion of the Vedas—and what is called Buddhism at the present day is nearly the same as that between Judaism and Christianity. Jesus Christ was a Jew, and Śākya Muni was a Hindu. The Jews rejected Jesus Christ, nay, crucified him, and the Hindus have accepted Śākya Muni as God and worship him. But the real difference that we Hindus want to show between modern Buddhism and what we should understand as the teachings of Lord Buddha lies principally in this: Śākya Muni came to preach nothing new. He, like Jesus, came to fulfil and not to destroy. Only, in the case of Jesus, it was his contemporaries, the Jews, who did not understand him, while in the case of Buddha, it was his own followers who did not realize the import of his teachings. As the Jews did not understand the fulfilment of the Old Testament, so the Buddhists did not understand the fulfilment of the truths of the Hindu religion. Again I repeat, Śākya Muni came not to destroy, but he was the fulfilment, the logical conclusion, the logical development, of the religion of the Hindus.

The religion of the Hindus is divided into two parts: the ceremonial and the spiritual. The spiritual portion is studied especially by the monks. In that, there is no caste. A man from the highest caste and a man from the lowest may become monks in India and the two castes become equal. In religion there is no caste; caste is simply a social institution. Śākya Muni himself was a monk, and it was his glory that he had the large-heartedness to bring out the truths hidden in the Vedas and scatter them broadcast all over the world. He was the first being in the world who brought missionizing into practice—nay, he was the first to conceive the idea of proselytizing.

The great glory of the Master lay in his wonderful sympathy for everybody, especially for the ignorant and the poor. Some of his disciples were brāhmins. When Buddha was teaching, Sanskrit was no longer the spoken language in India. It was then used only by scholarly people. Some of Buddha's brāhmin disciples wanted to translate his teachings into Sanskrit, but he distinctly told

195

them, "I am for the poor, for the people; let me speak in the tongue of the people." And so to this day the great bulk of his teachings is in the vernacular of that day in India.

Whatever may be the position of philosophy, whatever may be the position of metaphysics, so long as there is such a thing as death in the world, so long as there is such a thing as weakness in the human heart, so long as there is a cry going out of the heart of man in his very weakness, there will be faith in God.

On the philosophic side the disciples of the great Master dashed themselves against the eternal rocks of the Vedas and could not crush them, and on the other side they took away from the nation that eternal God to which everyone, man or woman, clings so fondly. And the result was that Buddhism had to die a natural death in India. At the present day there are very few in India, the land of its birth, who call themselves Buddhists.

But at the same time, Brāhminism lost something—that reforming zeal, that wonderful sympathy and charity for everybody, that wonderful leaven which Buddhism had brought to the masses and which had rendered Indian society so great that a Greek historian who wrote about the India of that time was led to say that no Hindu was known to tell an untruth and no Hindu woman was known to be unchaste.

Hinduism cannot live without Buddhism, nor Buddhism without Hinduism. The separation has shown us that the Buddhist cannot stand without the brain and philosophy of the brāhmin, nor the brāhmin without the heart of the Buddhist. This separation between the Buddhists and the brāhmins is the cause of the downfall of India. That is why India is populated by three hundred millions of beggars, and that is why India has been the slave of conquerors for the last thousand years. Let us, then, join the wonderful intellect of the brāhmin with the heart, the noble soul, the wonderful humanizing power of the great Master.

ADDRESS AT THE FINAL SESSION

(September 27, 1893)

THE WORLD'S PARLIAMENT of Religions has become an accomplished fact, and the merciful Father has helped those who laboured to bring it into existence, and crowned with success their most unselfish labour.

My thanks to those noble souls whose large hearts and love of truth first dreamt this wonderful dream and then realized it. My thanks to those who showered the liberal sentiments that have overflowed this platform. My thanks to this enlightened audience for their uniform kindness to me and for their appreciation of every thought that tends to smooth the friction between religions. A few jarring notes were heard from time to time in this harmony. My special thanks to those who have uttered them; for they have, by their striking contrast, made the general harmony the sweeter.

Much has been said of the common ground of religious unity. I am not going just now to venture my own theory. But if anyone here hopes that this unity will come by the triumph of any one of the religions and the destruction of the others, to him I say, "Brother, yours is an impossible hope." Do I wish that the Christian would become Hindu? God forbid. Do I wish that the Hindu or Buddhist would become Christian? God forbid.

The seed is put in the ground; earth and air and water are supplied to it. Does the seed become the earth or the air or the water? No. It becomes a plant; it develops after the law of its own growth, assimilates the air, the earth, and the water, converts them into plant substance, and grows into a plant.

Thus also it is with religion. The Christian is not to become a Hindu or a Buddhist, nor is a Hindu or a Buddhist to become a Christian. But each must assimilate the spirit of the others and yet preserve his individuality and grow according to his own law of growth.

If the Parliament of Religions has shown anything to the world, it is this: It has proved to the world that holiness, purity, and charity are not the exclusive possessions of any church in the world, and that every system has produced men and women of the most exalted character. In the face of this evidence, if anybody dreams of the exclusive survival of his own religion and the destruction of the others, I pity him from the bottom of my heart and point out to him that upon the banner of every religion will soon be written, in spite of resistance: "Help and not Fight," "Assimilation and not Destruction," "Harmony and Peace and not Dissension."

197

JNĀNA-YOGA

THE NECESSITY OF RELIGION

(Delivered in London)

OF ALL THE FORCES that have worked and are still working to mould the destinies of the human race, none, certainly, is more potent than that whose manifestation we call religion. All social organizations have as a background, somewhere, the workings of that peculiar force, and the greatest cohesive impulse ever brought into play amongst human units has been derived from this power. It is obvious to all of us that in very many cases the bonds of religion have proved stronger than the bonds of race or clime or even of descent. It is a well-known fact that persons worshipping the same God, believing in the same religion, have stood by each other with much greater strength and constancy than people of merely the same descent, or even than brothers.

Various attempts have been made to trace the beginnings of religion. In all the ancient religions which have come down to us at the present day, we find one claim made: that they are all supernatural, that their genesis is not, as it were, in the human brain, but that they have originated somewhere outside it.

Two theories have gained some acceptance amongst modern scholars. One is the spirit theory of religion; the other, the evolution of the idea of the Infinite. One party maintains that ancestor worship is the beginning of religious ideas; the other, that religion originates in the personification of the powers of nature.

Man wants to keep alive the memory of his dead relatives and thinks they are living even when the body is dissolved; he wants to place food for them and, in a certain sense, to worship them. Out of that desire came what we call religion. Studying the ancient religions of the Egyptians, Babylonians, and Chinese, and of many other races, in America and elsewhere, we find very clear traces of this ancestor worship's being the beginning of religion. With the ancient Egyptians the first idea of the soul was that of a double. Every human body contained in itself another being very similar to itself, and when a man died this double went out of the body and yet lived on. But the life of the double lasted only so long as the dead body remained intact; and that is why we find among the Egyptians so much solicitude to keep the body uninjured. And that is why they built those huge pyramids in which they preserved the bodies. For if any portion of the external body was hurt, the double would be correspondingly injured. This is clearly ancestor worship. With the ancient Babylonians we find the same idea of the double, but with a variation. The double lost all sense of love; it frightened the living, to make them give it food and drink and help it in various ways. It even lost all affection for its own children and its own wife. Among the ancient Hindus, also, we find traces of ancestor worship. The basis of religion among the Chinese may also be said to be ancestor worship, and it

201

still permeates the length and breadth of that vast country. In fact, the only religion that can really be said to flourish in China is that of ancestor worship. Thus, on the one hand, it seems that a very strong case has been made for those who hold the theory of ancestor worship as the beginning of religion.

On the other hand, there are scholars who from the ancient Āryan literature show that religion originated in nature worship. Although in India we find proofs of ancestor worship, yet in the oldest records there is no trace of it whatsoever. In the Rig-Veda Samhitā, the most ancient record of the Āryan race, we do not find any trace of it. Modern scholars think it is the worship of nature that they find there. The human mind seems to struggle to get a peep behind the scenes. The dawn, the evening, the hurricane, the stupendous and gigantic forces of nature, and its beauties—all these have exercised the human mind, and it aspires to go beyond, to understand something about them. In the struggle it endows these phenomena with personal attributes, giving them souls and bodies, sometimes beautiful, sometimes transcendental. Every attempt ends by these phenomena's becoming abstractions, whether personalized or not. So also it is found with the ancient Greeks: their whole mythology is simply this abstracted nature worship. So also with the ancient Germans, the Scandinavians, and all the other Āryan races. Thus, on this side too, a very strong case has been made out—that religion has its origin in the personification of the powers of nature.

These two views, though they seem to be contradictory, can be reconciled on a third basis, which to my mind is the real germ of religion, and this I propose to call the struggle to transcend the limitations of the senses. Either a man goes to seek for the spirits of his ancestors, the spirits of the dead—that is, he wants to get a glimpse of what there is after the body is dissolved— or he desires to understand the power working behind the stupendous phenomena of nature. Whichever of these he wants, one thing is certain: that he tries to transcend the limitations of the senses. He cannot remain satisfied with his senses; he wants to go beyond them.

The explanation need not be mysterious. To me it seems very natural that the first glimpse of religion should come through dreams. The first idea of immortality man may well get through dreams. Is not dreaming a most wonderful state? And we know that children and untutored minds find very little difference between dreaming and their awakened state. Even during sleep, when the body is apparently dead, the mind goes on with all its intricate workings. What wonder that men will at once come to the conclusion that, when this body is dissolved for ever, the same working will go on? This, to my mind, would be a more natural explanation of the supernatural. And through this dream idea the human mind rises to higher and higher conceptions.

Of course, in time the vast majority of mankind found out that their dreams are not verified by their waking states, and that during the dream state it is not that a man has a fresh existence, but simply that he recapitulates the experiences of the awakened state. But by this time the search had begun, and the search was inward, and they continued inquiring more deeply into the different stages of the mind and discovered a higher state than either the waking or the dreaming. That state, which we find in all the organized religions of the world, is called either ecstasy or inspiration. In all organized religions, their founders, prophets, and messengers are declared to have gone into a state of mind that was neither waking nor sleeping, in which they came face to face with a new series of facts relating to what is called the spiritual kingdom. They realized things there much more intensely than we realize facts around us in our waking state. Take, for instance, the religion of the Hindus. The Vedas are said to have been written by rishis. These rishis were sages who realized certain facts. The exact definition of the Sanskrit word *rishi* is, a seer of mantras—of the thoughts conveyed in the Vedic hymns. These men declared that they had realized— sensed, if that word can be used with regard to the supersensuous—certain facts, and these facts they proceeded to put on record. We find the same truth declared amongst both the Jews and the Christians.

An exception may be made of the Buddhists as represented by the Southern sect. It may be asked: If the Buddhists do not believe in any God or soul, how can their religion be derived from this supersensuous state of existence? The answer to this is that even the Buddhists find an eternal Moral Law, and that Moral Law was not reasoned out in our sense of the word. But Buddha found it, discovered it, in a supersensuous state. Those of you who have studied the life of Buddha, even as briefly given in that beautiful poem, *The Light of Asia*, may remember that Buddha is represented as sitting under the Bo-tree until he reached that supersensuous state of mind. All his teachings came through this, and not through intellectual cogitation.

Thus, a tremendous statement is made by all the religions: that the human mind at certain moments transcends not only the limitations of the senses but also the power of reasoning. It then comes face to face with facts which it could never have sensed, could never have reasoned out. These facts are the basis of all the religions of the world. Of course, we have the right to challenge these facts, to put them to the tests of reason; nevertheless all the existing religions of the world claim for the human mind this peculiar power of transcending the limits of the senses and the limits of reason; and this power they put forward as a statement of fact.

Apart from the consideration of the question how far these facts claimed by religions are true, we find one characteristic common to them all: They are all abstractions, as contrasted with the concrete discoveries of physics, for instance. And in all the highly organized religions they take the purest form of abstract Unity, as either an abstract Presence, or an omnipresent Being, or an abstract Personality called God, or a Moral Law, or an abstract Essence underlying every existence. In modern times, too, the attempts made to preach religions without appealing to the supersensuous state of the mind have had to take up the old abstractions of the ancients and give different names to them, such as Moral Law, the Ideal Unity, and so forth, thus showing that these abstractions are not in the senses. None of us has yet seen an ideal human being, and yet we are told to believe in him. None of us has yet seen an ideally perfect man, and yet without that ideal we cannot progress.

Thus one fact stands out from all these different religions: that there is an ideal abstract Unity, which is put before us in the form either of a Person, or of an Impersonal Being, or of a Law, or of a Presence, or of an Essence. We are always struggling to raise ourselves up to that ideal. Every human being, who-soever and wheresoever he may be, has an ideal of infinite power. Every human being has an ideal of infinite pleasure. Most of the works that we find around us, the activities displayed everywhere, are due to the struggle for this infinite power or this infinite pleasure.

But a few quickly discover that, although they are struggling for infinite power, it is not through the senses that it can be reached. They find out very soon that this infinite pleasure is not to be got through the senses, or, in other words, that the senses are too limited and the body is too limited to express the Infinite. To manifest the Infinite through the finite is impossible, and sooner or later man learns to give up the attempt to express It through the finite.

This giving up, this renunciation of the attempt, is the background of ethics. Renunciation is the very basis upon which ethics stands. There never was an ethical code preached which has not renunciation for its basis. Ethics always says, "Not I, but thou." Its motto is, "Not self, but non-self." The vain ideas of indi-vidualism to which man clings when he is trying to find that infinite power or that infinite pleasure through the senses—these have to be given up, say the laws of ethics. You have to put yourself last, and others before you. The senses say, "Myself first." Ethics says, "I must hold myself last." Thus all codes of ethics are based upon renunciation: destruction, not construction, of the individual on the material plane. The Infinite will never find expression upon the material plane; it is neither possible nor thinkable. So man has to give up the plane of matter and rise to other spheres, in order to seek a deeper expression of the Infinite. In this way the various ethical laws are being moulded; but all have that one central idea, eternal self-abnegation. Perfect self-annihilation is the ideal of ethics. People are startled if they are asked not to think of their individu-ality. They seem very much afraid of losing what they call their individuality. At the same time, the same men would declare the highest ideals of ethics to be right, never for a moment thinking that the scope, the goal, the idea of all ethics is the destruction, and not the building up, of the individual.

Utilitarian standards cannot explain the ethical relations of men. For, in the first place, we cannot derive any ethical laws from considerations of utility. Without the supernatural sanction, as it is called, or the perception of the superconscious, as I prefer to term it, there can be no ethics. Without the struggle towards the Infinite there can be no ideal. Any system that wants to bind men down to the limits of their own societies is not able to find an explana-tion for the ethical laws of mankind. The utilitarian wants us to give up the struggle after the Infinite, the reaching-out for the supersensuous, as imprac-ticable and absurd, and in the same breath asks us to take up ethics and do good to society. Why should we do good? Doing good is a secondary consideration. We must have an ideal. Ethics itself is not the end, but the means to the end. If the end is not there, why should we be ethical? Why should I do good to other men and not injure them? If happiness is the goal of mankind, why should I not make myself happy and others unhappy? What prevents me?

In the second place, the basis of utility is too narrow. All the current social forms and methods are derived from society as it exists—but what right has the utilitarian to assume that society is eternal? Society did not exist ages ago, possibly will not exist ages hence. Most probably it is one of the passing stages through which we are going towards a higher evolution; and any law that is derived from society alone cannot be eternal, cannot cover the whole ground of man's nature. At best, therefore, utilitarian theories can only work under present social conditions. Beyond that they have no value.

But a morality, an ethical code, derived from religion and spirituality has the whole of infinite man for its scope. It takes up the individual, but its relations are to the Infinite, and it takes up society also—because society is nothing but numbers of these individuals grouped together; and as it applies to the individual and his eternal relations, it must necessarily apply to the whole of society, in whatever condition it may be at any given time. Thus we see that there is always the necessity of spiritual religion for mankind. Man cannot always think of matter, however pleasurable it may be.

It has been said that too much attention to things spiritual disturbs our practical relations in this world. As far back as the days of the Chinese sage Confucius it was said: "Let us take care of this world, and then, when we have finished with this world, we will take care of other worlds." It is all very well that we should "take care" of this world. But if too much attention to the spiritual may affect our practical relations a little, too much attention to the so-called practical hurts us here and hereafter; for it makes us materialistic. Man is not to regard nature as his goal, but something higher.

Man is man so long as he is struggling to rise above nature—and this nature is both internal and external. Not only does it comprise the laws that govern the particles of matter outside us and in our bodies, but also the more subtle nature within, which is, in fact, the motive power governing the external. It is good and very grand to conquer external nature, but grander still to conquer our internal nature. It is grand and good to know the laws that govern the stars and planets; it is infinitely grander and better to know the laws that govern the passions, the feelings, the will, of mankind. This conquering of the inner man, understanding the subtle workings that are within the human mind and knowing its wonderful secrets, belongs entirely to religion.

The human mind—the ordinary human mind, I mean—wants to see big material facts. The ordinary man cannot understand anything that is subtle. Well has it been said that the masses admire the lion that kills a thousand lambs, never for a moment thinking that although it is a momentary triumph for the lion, it is death to the lambs, because the masses find pleasure only in manifestations of physical strength. Thus it is with the ordinary run of mankind. They understand and find pleasure in everything that is external. But in every society there is a section whose pleasures are not in the senses, but beyond, and who now and then catch glimpses of something higher than matter and struggle to reach it. And if we read the history of nations between the lines, we shall always find that the rise of a nation comes with an increase in the number of such men, and the fall begins when this pursuit after the Infinite, however vain the utilitarians may call it, has ceased. That is to say, the mainspring of the strength of every race lies in its spirituality, and the death of the race begins the day that spirituality wanes and materialism gains ground.

Thus, apart from the solid facts and truths that we may learn from religion, apart from the comforts that we may gain from it, religion, as a science, as a study, is the greatest and healthiest exercise that the human mind can have. This pursuit of the Infinite, this struggle to grasp the Infinite, this effort to get beyond the limitations of the senses, out of matter, as it were, and to evolve the spiritual man—this striving day and night to make the Infinite one with our being—this struggle itself is the grandest and most glorious that man can make. Some persons find their greatest pleasure in eating. We have no right to say that they should not. Others find their greatest pleasure in possessing certain things. We have no right to say they should not. But they also have no right to say no to the man who finds his highest pleasure in spiritual thought. The lower the organization, the greater the pleasure in the senses. Very few men can eat a meal with the same gusto as a dog or a wolf. But all the pleasures of the dog or the wolf have gone, as it were, into the senses. The lower types of humanity in all nations find pleasure in the senses, while the cultured and the educated find it in thought, in philosophy, in the arts and sciences.

Spirituality is a still higher plane. The subject being infinite, that plane is the highest, and the pleasure there is the highest for those who can appreciate it. So even if, on utilitarian grounds, man is to seek for pleasure, he should cultivate religious thought; for it is the highest pleasure that exists.

Thus religion, as a study, seems to me to be absolutely necessary. We can see it in its effects. It is the greatest motive power that moves the human mind. No other ideal can put into us the same mass of energy that the spiritual can. So far as human history goes, it is obvious to all of us that this has been the case, and that its powers are not dead. I do not deny that men, on simply utilitarian grounds, can be very good and moral. There have been many great men in this world, perfectly sound, moral, and good, simply on utilitarian grounds. But the world-movers, men who bring, as it were, a mass of magnetism into the world, whose spirit works in hundreds and in thousands, whose life ignites others with a spiritual fire—such men, we always find, have that spiritual background. Their motive power came from religion. Religion is the greatest motive power for realizing that infinite energy which is the birthright and nature of every man. In building up character, in making for everything that is good and great, in bringing peace to others and peace to one's own self, religion is the highest motive power, and therefore ought to be studied from that standpoint.

Religion must be studied on a broader basis than formerly. All narrow, limited, fighting ideas of religion have to go. All sectarian ideas and tribal or national ideas of religion must be given up. That each tribe or nation should have its own particular God, and think that every other is wrong, is a superstition that should belong to the past. All such ideas must be abandoned. As the human mind broadens, its spiritual ideas broaden too. The time has already come when a man cannot record a thought without its reaching to all corners of the earth; by merely physical means we have come in touch with the whole world. So the future religions of the world have to become universal and wide. The religious ideals of the future must embrace all that exists in the world that is good and great, and, at the same time, must have infinite scope for further development. All that was good in the past must be preserved; and the doors must be kept open for future additions to the already existing store. Religions must also be inclusive, and not look down with contempt upon one another because their particular ideals of God are different. In my life I have seen a great many spiritual men, a great many sensible persons, who did not believe in God at all, that is to say, not in our sense of the word. Perhaps they understood God better than we can ever do. The idea of the Personal God, the Impersonal, the Infinite, the Moral Law, the Ideal Man—these all have to come under the definition of religion. And when religions have become thus broadened, their power for good will have increased a hundredfold.

Religions, having tremendous power in them, have often done more injury to the world than good, simply on account of their narrowness and their limitations. Even at the present time we find many sects and societies, with almost the same ideas, fighting each other because one does not want to set forth those ideas in precisely the same way as another. Therefore religions will have to broaden. Religious ideas will have to become universal, vast, and infinite. Then alone shall we have the fullest play of religion; for the power of religion has only just begun to manifest itself in the world. It is sometimes said that religions are dying out, that spiritual ideas are dying out of the world. To me it seems that they have just begun to grow. The power of religion, broadened and purified, is going to penetrate every part of human life. So long as religion was in the hands of a chosen few, or of a body of priests, it was in temples, churches, books, dogmas, ceremonials, forms, and rituals. But when we come to the real, spiritual, universal concept, then, and then alone, will religion become real and living; it will come into our very nature, live in our every movement, penetrate every pore of our society, and be infinitely more a power for good than it has ever been before.

What is needed is a fellow-feeling between the different types of religion, since they all stand or fall together—a fellow-feeling which springs from mutual esteem and mutual respect, and not the condescending, patronizing, niggardly expression of goodwill unfortunately in vogue with many at the present time. And above all, this fellow-feeling is needed between types of religious expression coming from the study of mental phenomena—unfortunately even now laying exclusive claim to the name of religion—and those expressions of religion whose heads, as it were, are penetrating more into the secrets of heaven though their feet are clinging to earth—I mean the so-called materialistic sciences.

To bring about this harmony, both will have to make concessions, sometimes very large, nay more, sometimes painful; but each will find itself the better for the sacrifice and more advanced in truth. And, in the end, the knowledge which is confined within the domain of time and space will meet and become one with that which is beyond them both, where the mind and senses cannot reach—the Absolute, the Infinite, the One without a second.

THE REAL NATURE OF MAN

(Delivered in London)

GREAT IS THE TENACITY with which man clings to the senses. Yet however sub-stantial he may think the external world in which he lives and moves, there comes a time in the lives of individuals and of races when involuntarily they ask, "Is this real?" To the person who never finds a moment to question the creden-tials of his senses, whose every moment is occupied with some sort of sense enjoyment—even to him death comes, and he also is compelled to ask, "Is this real?" Religion begins with this question and ends with its answer. Even in the remote past, where recorded history cannot help us—in the mysterious light of mythology, back in the dim twilight of civilization—we find that the same question was asked: "What becomes of this? What is real?"

One of the most poetical of the Upanishads, the *Katha Upanishad*, begins with the inquiry: "When a man dies, there is a dispute: one party declares that he has gone for ever; the other insists that he is still living. Which is the truth?" Various answers have been given. The whole sphere of metaphysics, philosophy, and religion is really filled with various answers to this question. At the same time, attempts have been made to suppress it, to put a stop to the unrest of the mind, which asks: "What is beyond? What is real?" But so long as death remains, all these attempts at suppression will prove unsuccessful. We may talk about seeing nothing beyond and keeping all our hopes and aspirations confined to the present moment, and struggle hard not to think of anything beyond the world of the senses. And perhaps everything outside may help to keep us limited within its narrow bounds; the whole world may combine to prevent us from broadening out beyond the present. Yet, so long as there is death, the question must come again and again: "Is death the end of all these things to which we are clinging, as if they were the most real of all realities, the most substantial of all substances?" The world vanishes in a moment and is gone. Standing on the brink of a precipice beyond which is the infinite, yawning chasm, every mind, however hardened, is bound to recoil and ask, "Is this real?" The hopes of a lifetime, built up little by little with all the energies of a great mind, vanish in a second. Are they real? This question must be answered. Time never lessens its power; on the contrary it adds strength to it.

Then again, there is the desire to be happy. We run after everything to make ourselves happy; we pursue our mad career in the external world of the senses. If you ask the young man with whom life is successful, he will declare that it is real; and he really thinks so. Perhaps, when the same man grows old and finds fortune ever eluding him, he will then declare that this is the result of fate. He finds at last that his desires cannot be fulfilled. Wherever he goes there

208

is an adamantine wall beyond which he cannot pass. Every sense activity results in a reaction. Everything is evanescent. Enjoyment, misery, luxury, wealth, power, and poverty—even life itself—are all evanescent.

Two positions remain to mankind. One is to believe, with the nihilists, that all is nothing, that we know nothing, that we can never know anything about either the future, the past, or even the present. For we must remember that he who denies the past and the future, and wants to stick to the present, is simply a madman. One may as well deny the father and mother and assert the child. It would be equally logical. To deny the past and future, the present must inevitably be denied also. This is one position, that of the nihilists. I have never seen a man who could really become a nihilist for one minute. It is very easy to talk.

Then there is the other position—to seek for an explanation, to seek for the real, to discover in the midst of this eternally changing and evanescent world whatever is real. In this body, which is an aggregate of molecules of matter, is there anything which is real? This has been the search throughout the history of the human mind. In the very oldest times we often find glimpses of light coming into men's minds. We find men even then going a step beyond this body, finding something which is not this external body, although very much like it, something much more complete, much more perfect, which remains even when this body is dissolved. We read in a hymn of the Rig-Veda addressed to the god of fire, who is burning a dead body: "Carry him, Fire, in your arms gently; give him a perfect body, a bright body. Carry him where the fathers live, where there is no more sorrow, where there is no more death."

The same idea we shall find present in every religion, and with it we get another idea. It is a significant fact that all religions, without one exception, hold that man is a degeneration of what he was, whether they clothe this in mythological words, or in the clear language of philosophy, or in the beautiful expressions of poetry. This is the one fact that comes out of every scripture and every mythology: that man as he is, is a degeneration of what he was. This is the kernel of truth in the story of Adam's fall in the Jewish scripture. This is again and again repeated in the scriptures of the Hindus: the dream of a period which they call the age of truth, when no man died unless he wished to die, when he could keep his body as long as he liked, and his mind was pure and strong. There was no evil, and no misery; and the present age is a corruption of that state of perfection.

Side by side with this, we find everywhere the story of the deluge. That story itself is a proof that this present age is held by every religion to be a corruption of a former age. It went on becoming more and more corrupt until the deluge swept away a large portion of mankind and again the ascending series began. It is going up slowly again, to reach once more that early state of purity. You are all aware of the story of the deluge in the Old Testament. The same story was current among the ancient Babylonians, the Egyptians, the Chinese, and the Hindus.

Manu, a great ancient sage, was praying on the bank of the Ganges, when a little minnow came to him for protection, and he put it into a pot of water he had before him. "What do you want?" asked Manu. The little minnow declared that it was pursued by a bigger fish and wanted protection. Manu carried the little fish home with him. By morning the fish had become as big as the pot and it said, "I cannot live in this pot any longer." Manu put it in a tank, and the next day it was as big as the tank and declared it could not live there any more. So Manu had to take it to a river, and in the morning the fish filled the river. Then Manu put it in the ocean, and it declared: "Manu, I am the Creator of the universe. I have taken this form to come and warn you that I will deluge the world. Build an ark and in it put a pair of every kind of animals, and let your family enter the ark. Out of the water there will project My horn. Fasten the ark to it, and when the deluge subsides, come out and people the earth." So the world was deluged, and Manu saved his own family, and two of every kind of animal, and seeds of every plant. When the deluge subsided he came and peopled the world, and we are all called "man" because we are the progeny of Manu.

Now, human language is the attempt to express the truth that is within. I am fully persuaded that a baby, whose language consists of unintelligible sounds, is attempting to express the highest philosophy; only the baby has not the organs to express it, nor the means. The difference between the language of the highest philosophers and the utterances of babies is one of clarity and not of kind. What you call the most correct, systematic, mathematical language of the present time and the hazy, mystical, mythological language of the ancients differ only in clarity. Both of them have a grand idea behind, which is, as it were, struggling to express itself; and often behind these ancient mythologies are nuggets of truth, while often, I am sorry to say, behind the fine, polished phrases of the moderns is arrant trash. So we need not throw a thing overboard because it is clothed in mythology, because it does not fit in with the notions of Mr. So-and-So or Mrs. So-and-So in modern times. If people should laugh at religion because most religions declared that men must believe in mythologies taught by such and such a prophet, they ought to laugh more at these moderns. In modern times, if a man quotes a Moses or a Buddha or a Christ, he is laughed at; but let him give the name of a Huxley or a Tyndall or a Darwin, and it is swallowed without salt. "Huxley has said it"—that is enough for many. We are free from superstitions indeed! That was a religious superstition, and this a scientific superstition; only in and through that superstition came life-giving ideas of spirituality, whereas in and through this modern superstition come lust and greed. That superstition was worship of God, and this superstition is worship of filthy lucre, of fame, or of power. That is the difference.

To return to mythology. Behind all these stories we find one idea standing supreme: that man is a degeneration of what he was. Coming to the present times, however, we find that modern research seems to repudiate this position absolutely. Evolutionists seem to entirely contradict this assertion. According to them man is the evolution of the mollusc, and therefore what mythology states cannot be true. There is in India, however, a mythology which is able to reconcile both these positions. Indian mythology has a theory of cycles: that all movement is in the form of waves. Every rise is attended by a fall, and that by a rise the next moment, that by a fall the next, and that again by another rise. The motion is in cycles. Certainly it is true, even on the grounds of modern research, that man cannot be simply an evolution. Every evolution presupposes an involution. The modern scientific man will tell you that you can only get the amount of energy out of a machine which you have previously put into it. Something cannot be produced out of nothing. If a man is an evolution of the mollusc, then the perfect man, the Buddha-man, the Christ-man, must have been involved in the mollusc. If it is not so, whence come these gigantic personalities? Something cannot come out of nothing.

Thus we are in a position to reconcile the scriptures with modern light. That energy which manifests itself slowly through various stages until it becomes the perfect man cannot come out of nothing. It existed somewhere. And if the mollusc or the protoplasm is the first point to which you can trace it, then that protoplasm, somehow or other, must have contained the energy.

There is a great discussion going on as to whether the aggregate of materials we call the body is the cause of the manifestation of the force we call the soul, thought, and so on, or whether it is thought that manifests this body. The religions of the world of course hold that the force called thought manifests the body, and not the reverse. There are schools of modern thought which hold that what we call thought is simply the outcome of the adjustment of the parts of the machine which we call the body. Taking the second position—that the soul or the mass of thought, or whatever you may call it, is the outcome of this machine, the outcome of the chemical and physical combinations of matter making up the body and brain—leaves the question unanswered. What makes the body? What force combines the molecules into the body form? What force is there which takes up material from the mass of matter around it and forms my body one way, another body another way, and so on? What makes these infinite distinctions? To say that the force called the soul is the outcome of the combinations of the molecules of the body is putting the cart before the horse. How did the combinations come? Where was the force to make them? If you say that some other force was the cause of these combinations, and the soul, which is now seen to be combined with a particular mass of matter, is itself the result of the combination of these material particles—it is no answer. That theory ought to be taken which explains most, if not all, of the facts, without contradicting other existing theories. It is more logical to say that the force which takes up the matter and forms the body is the same which is manifested through that body.

To say, therefore, that the thought-forces manifested in the body are the outcome of the arrangement of molecules and have no independent existence has no meaning. Nor can force evolve out of matter. Rather it is possible to demonstrate that what we call matter does not exist at all. It is only a certain state of force. Solidity, hardness, or any other state of matter can be proved to be the result of motion. Increase of vortex motion imparted to fluids gives them the force of solids. A mass of air in vortex motion, as in a tornado, becomes solid-like and by its impact breaks or cuts through solids. A thread of a spider's web, if it could be moved at almost infinite velocity, would be as strong as an iron chain and would cut through an oak tree. Looking at it in this way, it would be easier to prove that what we call matter does not exist. But the other way cannot be proved.

What is the force which manifests itself through the body? It is obvious to all of us, whatever that force be, that it is something which takes particles up, as it were, and creates forms out of them—human bodies. None else comes here to manipulate bodies for you and me. I never saw anybody eat food for me. I have to assimilate it, manufacture blood and bones and everything out of that food. What is this mysterious force? Ideas about the future and about the past seem to be terrifying to many. To many they seem to be mere speculation. We will take the present as our theme. What is this force which is now working through us?

We know how in olden times, in all the ancient scriptures, this power, this manifestation of power, was thought to be a bright substance having the form of this body, which remained even after the body fell. Later on, however, we find a higher idea coming: that this bright body did not represent the force. Whatsoever has form, it was discovered, must be the result of combinations of particles and requires something else behind it to move it. If this body requires something which is not the body to manipulate it, the bright body, by the same necessity, will also require something other than itself to manipulate it. That something was called the Soul—the Ātman, in Sanskrit. It was the Ātman which through the bright body, as it were, worked on the gross body outside. The bright body is considered as the receptacle of the mind, and the Ātman is beyond that. It is not even the mind; it works the mind, and through the mind, the body. You have an Ātman, I have another; each one of us has a separate Ātman and a separate fine body, and through that we work on the gross external body. Questions were then asked about this Ātman, about its nature. What is this Ātman, this Soul of man, which is neither the body nor the mind? Great discussions followed. Speculations were made, various shades of philosophic inquiry came into existence. I shall try to place before you some of the conclusions that have been reached about this Ātman.

The different philosophies seem to agree that this Ātman, whatever it may be, has neither form nor shape; and that which has neither form nor shape must be omnipresent. Time begins with mind; space also is in the mind. Causation cannot stand without time—without the idea of succession there cannot be any idea of causation. Time, space, and causation, therefore, are in the mind; and as this Ātman is beyond the mind and formless, it must be beyond time, beyond space, and beyond causation. Now, if it is beyond time, space, and causation, it must be infinite. Then comes the highest speculation in our philosophy. The infinite cannot be two. If the Soul be infinite, there can be only one Soul, and all ideas of various souls—of your having one soul, and I having another, and so forth—are not real. The Real Man therefore is one and infinite, the omnipresent Spirit. And the apparent man is only a limitation of that Real Man. In that sense the mythologies are true in saying that the apparent man, however great he may be, is only a dim reflection of the Real Man, who is beyond. The Real Man, the Spirit, being beyond cause and effect, not bound by time and space, must therefore be free. He was never bound and could not be bound. The apparent man, the reflection, is limited by time, space, and causation, and is therefore bound. Or in the language of some of our philosophers, he appears to be bound but really is not. This is the reality behind our souls, this

omnipresence, this spiritual nature, this infinity. Every soul is infinite. Therefore there is no question of birth and death.

Some children were being examined. The examiner put to them rather hard
questions, and among them was this one: "Why does not the earth fall?" He
wanted to evoke answers about gravitation. Most of the children could not
answer at all; a few answered that it was gravitation or something. One bright
little girl answered it by putting another question: "Where should it fall?"
The first question is nonsense. Where should the earth fall? There is no falling
or rising for the earth. In infinite space there is no up or down; up and down
are only in the relative. Where is any going or coming for the infinite? Whence
should it come and whither should it go?

Thus, when people cease to think of the past or future, when they give up
the idea of body because the body comes and goes and is limited, then they
have risen to a higher ideal. The body is not the Real Man; neither is the mind,
for the mind waxes and wanes. It is the Spirit beyond, which alone can live
for ever. The body and mind are continually changing and are, in fact, only
names of series of changeful phenomena, like rivers whose waters are in a constant state of flux, yet present the appearance of unbroken streams. Every
particle in this body is continually changing; no one has the same body for
many minutes together, and yet we think of it as the same body. So with the
mind: one moment it is happy, another moment unhappy; one moment strong,
another weak—an ever changing whirlpool. That cannot be the Spirit, which
is infinite. Change can only be in the limited. To say that the infinite changes
in any way is absurd; it cannot be. You can move and I can move, as limited
bodies; every particle in this universe is in a state of flux; but taking the
universe as a unit, as one whole, it cannot move, it cannot change. Motion
is always a relative thing. I move in relation to something else. Any particle in
this universe can change in relation to any other particle. But take the whole
universe as one; then in relation to what can it move? There is nothing besides it.
So this infinite Unit is unchangeable, immovable, absolute, and this is the Real
Man. Our reality, therefore, consists in the Universal, and not in the limited.
This is an old delusion, however comfortable it is—to think that we are little
limited beings, constantly changing.

People are frightened when they are told that they are Universal Being, everywhere present. "Through everything you work, through every foot you move,
through every lip you talk, through every heart you feel." People are frightened
when they are told this. They will again and again ask you if they are not going
to keep their individuality. What is individuality? I should like to see it. A baby
has no moustache; when he grows to be a man, perhaps he has a moustache and
beard. His individuality would be lost if it were in the body. If I lose one eye
or if I lose one of my hands, my individuality would be lost if it were in the
body. Then a drunkard should not give up drinking, because he would lose his
individuality. A thief should not be a good man, because he would thereby lose
his individuality. Indeed, no man ought to change his habits, for fear of this.
Nor can individuality be in memory. Suppose, on account of a blow on the head,
I forget all about my past; then I have lost all individuality, I am gone. I do
not remember two or three years of my childhood, and if memory and existence

are one, then whatever I forget is gone. That part of my life which I do not remember, I did not live. That is a very narrow idea of individuality.

There is no individuality except in the Infinite. That is the only condition which does not change. Everything else is in a state of flux. We are not individuals yet. We are struggling towards individuality; and that is the Infinite. That is the real nature of man. He alone lives whose life is in the whole universe; the more we concentrate our lives on limited things, the faster we go towards death. Those moments alone we live when our lives are in the universe, in others; and living this little life is death, simply death, and that is why the fear of death comes. The fear of death can be conquered only when a man realizes that so long as there is one life in this universe, he is living. When he can say, "I am in everything, in everybody; I am in all lives; I am the universe," then alone comes the state of fearlessness. To talk of immortality in constantly changing things is absurd. Says an old Sanskrit philosopher: "It is only the Spirit that is the individual, because It is infinite." Infinity cannot be divided; infinity cannot be broken into pieces. It is the same one undivided unit for ever; and this is the individual man, the Real Man. The apparent man is merely a struggle to express, to manifest, this individuality which is beyond. Evolution is not in the Spirit.

These changes which are going on—the wicked becoming good, the animal becoming man; take them in whatever way you like—are not in the Spirit. They are the evolution of nature and the manifestation of the Spirit. Suppose there is a screen hiding you from me, in which there is a small hole through which I can see some of the faces before me, just a few faces. Now suppose the hole begins to grow larger and larger, and as it does so, more and more of the scene before me reveals itself; when at last the whole screen has disappeared, I stand face to face with you all. You did not change at all; it was the hole that was evolving, and you were gradually manifesting yourselves. So it is with the Spirit. No perfection is going to be attained. You are already free and perfect.

What are these ideas of religion and God and searching for the hereafter? Why does man look for a God? Why does man, in every nation, in every state of society, want a perfect ideal somewhere, either in man, in God, or elsewhere? Because that idea is within you. It was your own heart beating and you did not know; you were mistaking it for something external. It is the God within your own self that is impelling you to seek Him, to realize Him. After long searches here and there, in temples and in churches, on earth and in heaven, at last you come back to your own soul, completing the circle from where you started, and find that He whom you have been seeking all over the world, for whom you have been weeping and praying in churches and temples, on whom you were looking as the mystery of all mysteries, shrouded in the clouds, is the nearest of the near, is your own Self,[1] the reality of your life, body, and soul.

That Self is your own nature. Assert It, manifest It. You are not to become pure; you are pure already. You are not to become perfect; you are that already. Nature is like a screen which is hiding the reality beyond. Every good thought that you think or act upon simply tears the veil, as it were, and the Purity, the

[1] The word *Self* (spelt with a capital s) conveys the same meaning as *Soul*. See footnote, page 189.

Infinity, the God behind, is manifested more and more. This is the whole history of man. Finer and finer becomes the veil, more and more of the light behind shines forth; for it is its nature to shine.

That Self cannot be known; in vain we try to know It. Were It knowable, It would not be what It is; for It is the eternal Subject. Knowledge is a limitation; knowledge is an objectification. It is the eternal Subject of everything, the eternal Witness of this universe—your own Self. Knowledge is, as it were, a lower step, a degeneration. We are that eternal Subject already; how can we know It?

The infinite Self is the real nature of every man, and he is struggling to express It in various ways. Otherwise, why are there so many ethical codes? Where is the explanation of all ethics? One idea stands out as the centre of all ethical systems, expressed in various forms—namely, doing good to others. The guiding motive of mankind should be charity towards men, charity towards all animals. But these are all various expressions of that eternal truth that "I am the universe; this universe is one." Or else, where is the explanation? Why should I do good to my fellow men? Why should I do good to others? What compels me? It is sympathy, the feeling of sameness everywhere. The hardest hearts sometimes feel sympathy for other beings. Even the man who gets frightened if he is told that this assumed individuality is really a delusion, that it is ignoble to try to cling to this apparent individuality—that very man will tell you that extreme self-abnegation is the centre of all morality. And what is perfect self-abnegation? It means the abnegation of this apparent self, the abnegation of all selfishness.

This idea of "me" and "mine"—ahamkāra and mamatā—is the result of past superstition, and the more this present self passes away, the more the Real Self becomes manifest. This is true self-abnegation, the centre, the basis, the gist of all moral teaching, and whether man knows it or not, the whole world is slowly going towards it, practising it more or less. Only, the vast majority of mankind are doing it unconsciously. Let them do it consciously. Let them make the sacrifice, knowing that this "me" and "mine" is not the Real Self, but only a limitation. But one glimpse of that infinite Reality which is behind, but one spark of that infinite Fire which is the All, represents the present man. The Infinite is his true nature.

What is the utility, the effect, the result of this knowledge? In these days we have to measure everything by utility—by how many pounds, shillings, and pence it represents. What right has a person to ask that truth should be judged by the standard of utility or money? Suppose there is no utility, will it be less true? Utility is not the test of truth. Nevertheless, there is the highest utility in this. Happiness, we see, is what everyone is seeking for; but the majority seek it in things which are evanescent and not real. No happiness was ever found in the senses. There never was a person who found happiness in the senses or in enjoyment of the senses. Happiness is found only in the Spirit. Therefore the highest utility for mankind is to find this happiness in the Spirit.

The next point is that ignorance is the great mother of all misery, and the fundamental ignorance is to think that the Infinite weeps and cries, that It is finite. This is the basis of all ignorance—that we, the immortal, the ever pure, the perfect Spirit, think we are little minds, we are little bodies. It is the mother of all selfishness. As soon as I think I am a little body, I want to preserve it, to protect it, to keep it nice, at the expense of other bodies. Then you and I become separate. As soon as this idea of separation comes, it opens the door to all mischief and leads to all misery. This, then, is the utility of this knowledge —that if a small fractional part of the human beings living today can put aside the idea of selfishness, narrowness, and littleness, this earth will become a paradise tomorrow. But with machines and improvements of material knowledge only, it will never be so. These only increase misery, as oil poured on fire increases the flame all the more. Without the knowledge of the Spirit, all material knowledge is only adding fuel to fire, only giving into the hands of selfish man one more instrument to take what belongs to others, to live upon the life of others instead of giving up his life for them.

Is it practical?—is another question. Can it be practised in modern society? Truth does not pay homage to any society, ancient or modern. Society has to pay homage to truth or die. Societies should be moulded upon truth; truth has not to adjust itself to society. If such a noble truth as unselfishness cannot be practised in society, it is better for a man to give up society and go into the forest. That is the daring man.

There are two sorts of courage. One is the courage of facing the cannon; and the other is the courage of spiritual conviction. An emperor who invaded India was told by his teacher to go and see some of the sages there. After a long search for one, he found a very old man sitting on a block of stone. The emperor talked with him a little and became very much impressed by his wisdom. He asked the sage to go to his country with him. "No," said the sage, "I am quite satisfied with my forest here." Said the emperor: "I will give you money, position, wealth. I am the emperor of the world." "No," replied the man, "I don't care for those things." The emperor replied, "If you do not go, I will kill you." The man smiled serenely and said: "That is the most foolish thing you ever said, Emperor. You cannot kill me. Me the sun cannot dry, fire cannot burn, sword cannot kill; for I am the birthless, the deathless, the ever living, omnipotent, omnipresent Spirit." This is spiritual boldness, while the other is the courage of a lion or a tiger.

During the Mutiny of 1857, there was a Swami, a very great soul, whom a Mohammedan mutineer stabbed severely. The Hindu mutineers caught and brought the man to the Swami, offering to kill him. But the Swami looked up calmly and said, "My brother, thou art He, thou art He!" and expired. This is another instance.

What good is it to talk of the strength of your muscles, of the superiority of your Western institutions, if you cannot make truth square with your society, if you cannot build up a society into which the highest truth will fit? What is the good of this boastful talk about your grandeur and greatness if you stand up and say, "This courage is not practical"? Is nothing practical but pounds, shillings, and pence? If so, why boast of your society? That society is the greatest where the highest truths become practical. That is my opinion. And if society is not fit for the highest truths, make it so—and the sooner, the better.

Stand up, men and women, in this spirit, dare to believe in the truth, dare to practise the truth! The world requires a few hundred bold men and women. Practise that boldness which dares know the truth, which dares show the truth in life, which does not quake before death, nay, welcomes death, makes a man know that he is the Spirit, that in the whole universe nothing can kill him. Then you will be free. Then you will know your real Soul.

"This Ātman is first to be heard of, then thought about, and then meditated upon." There is a great tendency in modern times to talk too much of work and decry thought. Doing is very good, but that comes from thinking. Little manifestations of energy through the muscles are called work. But where there is no thought, there will be no work. Fill the brain, therefore, with high thoughts, with the highest ideals; place them day and night before you, and out of that will come great work. Talk not about impurity, but say that we are pure. We have hypnotized ourselves into this thought that we are little, that we are born and that we are going to die, and into a constant state of fear.

There is a story about a lioness who was big with young. Going about in search of prey, and seeing a flock of sheep, she jumped upon them. She died in the effort and a little baby lion was born, motherless. It was taken care of by the sheep and they brought it up. It grew up with them, ate grass, and bleated like the sheep. And although in time it became a big full-grown lion, it thought it was a sheep. One day another lion came in search of prey and was astonished to find that in the midst of this flock of sheep was a lion, fleeing like the sheep at the approach of danger. He tried to get near the sheep-lion to tell it that it was not a sheep but a lion, but the poor animal fled at his approach. However, he watched his opportunity and one day found the sheep-lion sleeping. He approached it and said, "You are a lion." "I am a sheep," cried the other lion; it could not believe the contrary, but bleated. The lion dragged it towards a lake and said, "Look here: there is my reflection and there is yours." Then came the comparison. The sheep-lion looked at the lion and then at its own reflection, and in a moment came the idea that it was a lion. The lion roared; the bleating was gone.

You are lions; you are the Soul, pure, infinite, and perfect. The might of the universe is within you. "Why weepest thou, my friend? There is neither birth nor death for thee. Why weepest thou? There is no disease or misery for thee. Thou art like the infinite sky: clouds of various colours come over it, play for a moment, then vanish; but the sky is ever the same eternal blue."

Why do we see wickedness? There was a stump of a tree, and in the dark a thief came that way and said, "That is a policeman." A young man waiting for his beloved saw it and thought it was his sweetheart. A child who had been told ghost stories took it for a ghost and began to shriek. But all the time it was the stump of a tree. We see the world as we are. Suppose there is a baby in a room with a bag of gold on the table, and a thief comes and steals the gold. Would the baby know it was stolen? That which we have inside, we see outside. The baby has no thief inside and sees no thief outside. So with all knowledge.

Do not talk of the wickedness of the world and all its sins. Weep that you are bound to see wickedness yet. Weep that you are bound to see sin everywhere. If you want to help the world, do not condemn it. Do not weaken it more. For what is sin and what is misery—what are all these but the results of weakness? The world is made weaker and weaker every day by such teachings. Men are taught from childhood that they are weak and sinners. Teach them that they are all glorious children of immortality, even those who are the weakest in manifestation. Let positive, strong, helpful thoughts enter into their brains from very childhood. Lay yourselves open to these thoughts, and not to weakening and paralysing ones. Say to your own minds, "I am He, I am He." Let it ring day and night in your minds like a song, and at the point of death declare, "I am He." That is the truth. The infinite strength of the world is yours. Drive out the superstition that has covered your minds. Let us be brave. Know the truth and practise the truth. The goal may be distant, but awake, arise, and stop not till the goal is reached.

MĀYĀ

(Delivered in London)

ALMOST ALL OF YOU have heard of the word māyā. Generally it is used, though incorrectly, to denote illusion or delusion or some such thing. But the theory of māyā forms one of the pillars upon which Vedānta rests; it is therefore necessary that it should be properly understood. I ask a little patience of you, for there is a great danger of its being misunderstood.

The oldest use of māyā that we find in Vedic literature is in the sense of delusion; but then the real theory had not been reached. We find such passages as, "Indra through his māyā assumed various forms." Here, it is true, the word māyā means something like magic, and we find various other passages where it always takes the same meaning. The word māyā then dropped out of sight altogether. But in the meantime the idea was developing. Later the question was raised: "Why can't we know the secret of the universe?" And the answer given was very significant: "Because we talk in vain, and because we are satisfied with the things of the senses, and because we are running after desires, therefore we cover the Reality, as it were, with a mist." Here the word māyā is not used at all; but we get the idea that the cause of our ignorance is a kind of mist that has come between us and the truth. Much later on, in one of the latest Upanishads, we find the word māyā reappearing; but by this time a transformation had taken place in it and a mass of new meaning had attached itself to the word. Theories had been propounded and repeated, others had been taken up, until at last the idea of māyā became fixed. We read in the Śvetāśvatara Upanishad: "Know nature to be māyā, and the Ruler of this māyā, the Lord Himself."

Coming to later philosophers, we find that this word māyā was manipulated in various fashions, until we come to the great Śankarāchārya. The theory of māyā was manipulated a little by the Buddhists, too, but in the hands of the Buddhists it became very much like what is called idealism, and that is the meaning which is now generally given to the word māyā.

When the Hindu says the world is māyā, at once people get the idea that the world is an illusion. This interpretation has some basis, as coming through the Buddhist philosophers, because there was one section of those philosophers who did not believe in the external world at all. But the māyā of Vedānta, in its final form, is neither idealism nor realism, nor is it a theory. It is a simple statement of fact—what we are and what we see around us.

As I have told you before, the minds of the people from whom the Vedas came were intent upon following principles, discovering principles. They had no time to work upon details or to wait for them; they wanted to go deep into the heart of things. Something beyond was calling them, as it were, and they could not wait. In the Upanishads we find that the details of subjects which are now dealt with by science are often very erroneous, but at the same time the principles are correct. For instance, the idea of ether, which is one of the latest theories of modern science, is to be found in our ancient literature in a form much more developed than is the modern scientific theory of ether today. But it was only a principle. When the Vedic thinkers tried to demonstrate that principle, they made many mistakes. The theory of the all-pervading life principle, of which all lives in this universe are but differing manifestations, was understood in Vedic times; it is found in the Brāhmanas. There is a long hymn in one of the Samhitās in praise of Prāna, of which all life is but a manifestation. By the bye, it may interest some of you to know that there are theories in the Vedic philosophy about the origin of life on this earth, very similar to those which have been advanced by some modern European scientists. You of course all know that there is a theory that life came from other planets. It was a settled doctrine with some Vedic philosophers that life came, in this way, from the moon.

We find these Vedic thinkers very courageous and wonderfully bold in propounding large and generalized theories. Their solution of the mystery of the universe, from the analysis of the external world, was as satisfactory as it could be. The detailed workings of modern science do not bring the question one step nearer to solution, because the principles propounded by the Vedic thinkers failed. If the theory of ether failed in ancient times to give a solution of the mystery of the universe, working out the details of that ether theory will not bring us much nearer to the truth. If the theory of all-pervading life failed as a theory of this universe, it will not mean anything more if worked out in detail; for the details do not change the principles of the universe. What I mean is that, in their inquiry into the principles, the Hindu thinkers were as bold as, and in some cases much bolder than, the moderns. They made some of the grandest generalizations that have yet been reached, and some of these still remain as theories which modern science has yet to arrive at, even as theories. For instance, they not only arrived at the ether theory, but went beyond and classified mind, also, as a still more rarefied ether. Beyond that, again, they found a still more rarefied ether. Yet that was no solution; it did not solve the problem. No amount of knowledge of the external world could solve the problem.

"But," says the scientist, "we are just beginning to know a little; wait a few thousand years and we shall get the solution." "No," says the Vedāntist; for he has proved beyond all doubt that the mind is limited, that it cannot go beyond certain limits—beyond time, space, and causation. As no man can jump out of his own self, so no man can go beyond the limits that have been put upon him by the laws of time and space. Every attempt to solve the laws of causation, time, and space is futile, because the very attempt can only be made by taking for granted the existence of these three.

What, then, does the statement that the world exists mean? It really means that the world has no existence. What, again, does the statement that the world has no existence mean? It means that it has no absolute existence: it exists only in relation to my mind, to your mind, and to the mind of everyone else. We see this world with the five senses, but if we had another sense, we would see in it something more. If we had yet another sense, it would appear as something still different. It has, therefore, no real existence; it has no unchangeable, immovable, infinite existence. Nor can it be said to have non-existence, since it exists and we have to work in and through it. It is a mixture of existence and non-existence.

Coming from abstractions to the common, everyday details of our lives, we find that our whole life is a mixture of this contradiction of existence and non-existence. There is this contradiction in knowledge: It seems that man can know everything if he only wants to know; but before he has gone a few steps he finds an adamantine wall which he cannot pass. All his work is in a circle, and he cannot go beyond that circle. The problems which are nearest and dearest to him are impelling him on and calling, day and night, for a solution; but he cannot solve them, because he cannot go beyond this intellect. We know that desire is implanted strongly in man. Again, we know that the only good is to be obtained by controlling and checking it. With our every breath, every impulse of our heart asks us to be selfish; at the same time, there is some power beyond us which says that it is unselfishness alone which is good. Every child is a born optimist; he dreams golden dreams. In youth he becomes still more optimistic. It is hard for a young man to believe that there is such a thing as death, such a thing as defeat or degradation. Old age comes, and life is a mass of ruins. Dreams have vanished into the air, and the man becomes a pessimist. Thus we go from one extreme to another, buffeted by nature, without knowing where we are going.

I am reminded of a celebrated song in the *Lalita Vistara*, a biography of Buddha. Buddha was born, says the book, as the Saviour of mankind, but he forgot himself in the luxuries of his palace. Some angels came and sang a song to rouse him. And the burden of the whole song is that we are floating down the river of life, which is continually changing, with no stop and no rest. What, then, are we to do? The man who has enough to eat and drink is an optimist, and he avoids all mention of misery, for it frightens him. Tell not him of the sorrows and the sufferings of the world; go to him and tell that it is all good. "Yes, I am safe," says he. "Look at me, I have a nice house to live in; I do not fear cold and hunger. Therefore do not bring these horrible pictures before me." But on the other hand there are others dying of cold and hunger. If you go and teach *them* that it is all good, they will not hear. How can they wish others to be happy when they are miserable? Thus we are oscillating between optimism and pessimism.

Then there is the tremendous fact of death. The whole world is going towards death. Everything dies. All our progress, our vanities, our reforms, our luxuries, our wealth, our knowledge, have that one end—death. That is all that is certain. Cities come and go, empires rise and fall, planets break into pieces and crumble into dust, to be blown about by the atmospheres of other planets. Thus it has been going on from time without beginning. Death is the end of everything. Death is the end of life, of beauty, of wealth, of power, of virtue too. Saints die and sinners die, kings die and beggars die. They are all going to death. And yet this tremendous clinging to life exists. Somehow, we do not know why, we cling to life; we cannot give it up. And this is māyā.

A mother is nursing her child with great care; all her soul, her life, is in that child. The child grows, becomes a man, and perchance becomes a blackguard and a brute, kicks her and beats her every day; and yet the mother clings to the child, and when her reason awakes, she covers it all up with the idea of love. She little thinks that it is not love, but something else, which has got hold of her nerves and which she cannot shake off. However she may try, she cannot shake off the bondage she is in. And this is māyā.

We are all running after the golden fleece. Every one of us thinks that it will be his. Every reasonable man sees that his chance is perhaps one in twenty millions, yet everyone struggles for it. And this is māyā.

Death is stalking day and night over this earth of ours, but at the same time we think we shall live eternally. A question was once asked of King Yudhishthira: "What is the most wonderful thing on this earth?" And the king replied, "Every day people are dying around us, and yet men think they will never die." And this is māyā.

These tremendous contradictions in our intellect, in our knowledge, indeed, in all the facts of our life, face us on all sides. A reformer arises and wants to remedy the evils existing in a certain nation; and before they have been remedied, a thousand other evils arise in another place. It is like an old house that is falling: you patch it up in one place and the ruin extends to another. In India our reformers cry and preach against the evils of enforced widowhood. In the West, non-marriage is the great evil. Help the unmarried on one side; they are suffering. Help the widows on the other; they are suffering. It is like chronic rheumatism: you drive it from the head and it goes to the body; you drive it from there and it goes to the feet. Reformers arise and preach that learning, wealth, and culture should not be in the hands of a select few; and they do their best to make them accessible to all. These may bring more happiness to some, but perhaps, as culture grows, physical happiness lessens. The knowledge of happiness brings the knowledge of unhappiness. Which way, then, shall we go? The least amount of material prosperity that we enjoy is elsewhere causing the same amount of misery. This is the law. The young, perhaps, do not see it clearly, but those who have lived long enough and those who have struggled enough will understand it. And this is māyā.

These things are going on, day and night, and to find a solution of this problem is impossible. Why should it be so? It is impossible to answer this, because the question cannot be logically formulated. There is neither *how* nor *why* in fact; we only know that it *is* and that we cannot help it. Even to grasp it, to draw an exact image of it in our own mind, is beyond our power. How can we solve it, then?

Māyā is a statement of the fact of this universe, of how it is going on. People generally get frightened when they are told about these things. But bold we must be. Hiding facts is not the way to find a remedy. As you all know, a hare hunted by dogs puts its head down and thinks itself safe. When we take refuge in optimism we act just like the hare. But that is no remedy. There are objections to this idea, but you may remark that they are generally from people who possess many of the good things of life. In this country [England] it is very difficult to become a pessimist. Everyone tells me how wonderfully the world is going on, how progressive it is. But what he himself is, is his own world. The same old questions arise again and again. People assert that Christianity must be the only true religion of the world, because the Christian nations are prosperous! But that assertion contradicts itself, because the prosperity of the Christian nations depends on the misfortune of non-Christian nations. There must be some to prey on. Suppose the whole world were to become Christian; then the Christian nations would become poor, because there would be no non-Christian nations for them to prey upon. Thus the argument kills itself. Animals are living upon plants, men upon animals, and, worst of all, upon one another—the strong upon the weak. This is going on everywhere. And this is māyā.

What solution do you find for this? We hear every day many explanations and are told that in the long run all will be good. Taking it for granted that this is possible, why should there be this diabolical way of doing good? Why cannot good be done through good, instead of through these diabolical methods? The descendants of the human beings of today will be happy; but why must there be all this suffering now? There is no solution. And this is māyā.

Again, we often hear that one of the features of evolution is that it gradually eliminates evil from the world, until evil is completely eliminated, when at last only good will remain. That is very nice to hear; it panders to the vanity of those who have enough of this world's goods, who have no hard struggle to face every day and are not being crushed under the wheel of this so-called evolution. It is very good and comforting indeed to such fortunate ones. The common herd may suffer, but they do not care; let the rest die—they are of no consequence. Very good. Yet this argument is fallacious from beginning to end. It takes for granted, in the first place, that manifested good and evil in this world are two absolute realities. In the second place, it makes a still worse assumption: that the amount of good is an increasing quantity, and the amount of evil is a decreasing quantity. So if evil is being eliminated in this way, by what is called evolution, there will come a time when all this evil will be eliminated and what remains will be all good. Very easy to say, but can it be proved that evil is a lessening quantity?

Take, for instance, the man who lives in a forest, who does not know how to cultivate the mind, cannot read a book, has not heard of such a thing as writing. If he is severely wounded, he is soon all right again, while we die if we get a scratch. Again, machines are making things cheap, making for progress and evolution, but millions are crushed that one may become rich—thousands at the same time become poorer and poorer, and whole masses of human beings are made slaves. That is the way it is going on.

The animal man lives in the senses. If he does not get enough to eat, he is miserable, or if something happens to his body, he is miserable. In the senses both his misery and his happiness begin and end. As soon as this man progresses, as soon as his horizon of happiness increases, his horizon of unhappiness increases proportionately. The man in the forest does not know what it is to be jealous, to be in the law-courts, to pay taxes, to be blamed by society, and to be ruled over day and night by the most tremendous tyranny that human diabolism ever invented, which pries into the secrets of every human heart. He does not know that man becomes a thousand times more diabolical than any other animal, with all his vain knowledge and with all his pride. Thus it is that, as we emerge out of the senses, we develop higher powers of enjoyment, and at the same time we develop higher powers of suffering too. The nerves become finer and capable of more suffering. In every society we often find that the ignorant common man, when abused, does not feel much, but he feels a good thrashing. But the gentleman cannot bear a single word of abuse: he has become so finely nerved; his misery has increased with his susceptibility to happiness. This does not go far to prove the evolutionist's case.

As we increase our power to be happy we also increase our power to suffer, and sometimes I am inclined to think that if we increase our power to become happy in arithmetical progression, we shall increase, on the other hand, our power to become miserable in geometrical progression. We who are progressing know that the more we progress, the more avenues are opened to pain as well as to pleasure. And this is māyā.

Thus we find that māyā is not a theory for the explanation of the world; it is simply a statement of facts as they exist—that the very basis of our being is contradiction, that everywhere we have to move through this tremendous contradiction, that wherever there is good, there must also be evil, and wherever there is evil there must be some good, wherever there is life, death must follow as its shadow, and everyone who smiles will have to weep, and whoever weeps must smile also. Nor can this state of things be remedied. We may vainly imagine that there will be a place where there will be only good, and no evil, where we shall only smile and never weep. This is impossible in the very nature of things; for the conditions will remain the same. Wherever there is the power of producing a smile in us, there lurks the power of producing tears. Wherever there is the power of producing happiness, there lurks somewhere the power of making us miserable.

Thus the Vedānta philosophy is neither optimistic nor pessimistic. It voices both these views and takes things as they are; it admits that this world is a mixture of good and evil, happiness and misery, and that to increase the one must of necessity increase the other. There will never be a perfectly good or bad world, because the very idea is a contradiction in terms. The great secret revealed by this analysis is that good and bad are not two cut-and-dried, separate existences. There is not one thing in this world of ours which you can label as good, and good alone; and there is not one thing in the universe which you can label as bad, and bad alone. The very same phenomenon which is appearing to be good now may appear to be bad tomorrow. The same thing which is producing misery in one may produce happiness in another. The fire that burns the child may cook a good meal for a starving man. The same nerves that carry the sensations of misery carry also the sensations of happiness.

The only way to stop evil, therefore, is to stop good also; there is no other way. To stop death we shall have to stop life also. Life without death and happiness without misery are contradictions, and neither can be found alone, because both of them are different manifestations of the same thing.

What I thought to be good yesterday, I do not think to be good now. When I look back upon my life and see what were my ideals at different times, I find this to be so. At one time my ideal was to drive a strong pair of horses; at another time I thought if I could make a certain kind of sweetmeat I should be perfectly happy; later I imagined that I should be entirely satisfied if I had a wife and children and plenty of money. Today I laugh at all these ideals as mere childish nonsense. Vedānta says that there must come a time when we shall look back and laugh at the ideas which make us afraid of giving up our individuality. Each one of us wants to keep this body for an indefinite time, thinking he will be very happy; but there will come a time when we shall laugh at this idea.

Now, if such be the truth, we are in a state of hopeless contradiction—neither existence nor non-existence, neither misery nor happiness, but a mixture of them. What, then, is the use of Vedānta and all other philosophies and religions? And above all, what is the use of doing good work? This is a question that comes to the mind. If it is true that you cannot do good without doing evil, and that whenever you try to create happiness there will always be misery, people will ask you, "What is the use of doing good?" The answer is, in the first place, that we must work for lessening misery, for that is the only way to make ourselves happy. Every one of us finds it out sooner or later in life. The bright ones find it out a little earlier, and the dull ones a little later. The dull ones pay very dearly for the discovery, and the bright ones less dearly. In the second place, we must do our part, because that is the only way of getting out of this life of contradiction. The forces of good and evil will keep the universe alive for us until we awake from our dreams and give up this making of mudpies. That lesson we shall have to learn, and it will take a long, long time to learn it.

Attempts have been made in Germany to build a system of philosophy on the basis that the Infinite has become the finite. Such attempts are also made in England. The analysis of the position of these philosophers is this: that the Infinite is trying to express Itself in this universe, and that there will come a time when the Infinite will succeed in doing so. This is all very well, and we have used the words *Infinite* and *manifestation* and *expression*, and so on; but philosophers naturally ask for a logical, irrefutable basis for the statement that the finite can fully express the Infinite. The Absolute or the Infinite can become this universe only by limitation. Everything must be limited that comes through the senses or through the mind or through the intellect; and for the limited to be unlimited is simply absurd; it can never be.

Vedānta, on the other hand, says that it is true that the Absolute or the Infinite is trying to express Itself in the finite, but there will come a time when It will find that it is impossible, and It will then have to beat a retreat; and this beating a retreat means renunciation, which is the real beginning of religion. Nowadays it is very hard even to talk of renunciation. It was said of me in America that I was a man who came out of a land that talked of renunciation and had been dead and buried for five thousand years. So says perhaps the English philosopher. Yet it is true that that is the only path to religion. Renounce and give up. What did Christ say? "He that loseth his life for my sake shall find it." Again and again did he preach renunciation as the only way to perfection.

There comes a time when the mind awakes from this long and dreary dream, the child gives up its play and wants to go back to its mother. It finds the truth of the statement: "Desire is never satisfied by the enjoyment of desires; it only increases the more, like fire when butter is poured upon it." This is true of all sense enjoyments, all intellectual enjoyments, and all the enjoyments of which the human mind is capable. They are nothing; they are within māyā, within this network which we cannot get out of. We may run about therein through infinite time and yet find no escape, and whenever we struggle to get a little enjoyment a mass of misery falls upon us. How awful this is! And when I think of it I cannot but consider that this theory of māyā, this statement that it is all māyā, is the best and only explanation.

What an amount of misery there is in this world! And if you travel among various nations you will find that one nation attempts to cure its evils by one means, and another by another. The very same evil has been taken up by various races, and attempts have been made in various ways to check it; yet no nation has succeeded. If it has been minimized at one point, a mass of evil has been crowded in at another point. Thus it goes.

The Hindus, to keep up a high standard of chastity in the race, have sanctioned child-marriage, which in the long run has degraded the race. At the same time, I cannot deny that this child-marriage makes the race more chaste. What would you have? If you want the nation to be more chaste, you weaken men and women physically by child-marriage. On the other hand, are you in England any better off? No, because chastity is the life of a nation. Do you not find in history that the first death-sign of a nation has been unchastity? When that has entered, the end of the race is in sight. Where shall we get a solution of these miseries, then? If parents select husbands and wives for their children, then this evil is minimized. The daughters of India are more practical than sentimental. But very little of poetry remains in their lives. Again, if people select their own husbands and wives, that does not seem to bring much happiness. The Indian woman is generally very happy; there are not many cases of quarrelling between husband and wife. On the other hand, in the United States, where the greatest liberty obtains, the number of unhappy homes and marriages is large.

Unhappiness is here, there, and everywhere. What does it show? That, after all, not much happiness has been gained by all these ideals. We all struggle for happiness, and as soon as we get a little happiness on one side, on the other side there comes unhappiness.

Shall we not work to do good, then? Yes, with more zest than ever. But what this knowledge will do for us is to break down our fanaticism. The Englishman will no more be a fanatic and curse the Hindu. He will learn to respect the customs of different nations. There will be less of fanaticism and more of real work. Fanatics cannot work; they waste three-fourths of their energy. It is the level-headed, calm, practical man who works. So the power to work will increase from this idea. Knowing that this is the state of things, we shall have more patience. The sight of misery or of evil will not be able to throw us off our balance and make us run after shadows. Patience will come to us, since we know that the world will have to go on in its own way. If, for instance, all men have become good, the animals will have in the meantime evolved into men and will have to pass through the same state, and so with the plants.

But one thing is certain: the mighty river is rushing towards the ocean, and all the drops that constitute the stream will in time be drawn into that boundless ocean. So, in this life, with all its miseries and sorrows, its joys and smiles and tears, one thing is certain: that all things are rushing towards their goal and it is only a question of time when you and I, plants and animals, and every particle of life that exists, must reach the infinite Ocean of Perfection, must attain to Freedom, to God.

Let me repeat once more that the Vedāntic position is neither pessimism nor optimism. It does not say that this world is all evil or all good. It says that our evil is of no less value than our good, and our good of no more value than our evil. They are bound together. This is the world, and knowing this, you work with patience.

What for? Why should we work? If this is the state of things, what shall we do? Why not become agnostics? The modern agnostics also know that there is no solution of this problem, no getting out of this evil of māyā, as we say in our language; therefore they tell us to be satisfied and enjoy life. But here, again, is a mistake, a tremendous mistake, a most illogical mistake. And it is this: What do you mean by life? Do you mean only the life of the senses? In this, every one of us differs only slightly from the brutes. I am sure that no one is present here whose life is only in the senses. Then this present life means something more than that. Our feelings, thoughts, and aspirations are all part and parcel of our life; and is not the struggle towards the great ideal, towards perfection, one of the most important components of what we call life? According to the agnostics we must enjoy life as it is. The agnostic position takes this life, *minus* the ideal of perfection, to be all that exists. That ideal, the agnostic claims, cannot be reached; therefore he must give up the search. But life means, above all, this search after the ideal; the essence of life is going towards perfection. We must have that, and therefore we cannot be agnostics and take the world as it appears.

This nature, this universe, is what is called māyā. All religions are more or less attempts to get beyond nature—the crudest or the most developed, expressed through mythology or symbology, stories of gods or angels or demons, or through stories of saints or seers, great men or prophets, or through the abstractions of philosophy—all have that one object; all are trying to get beyond these limitations. In one word, they are all struggling towards freedom.

Man feels, consciously or unconsciously, that he is bound; he is not what he wants to be. It was taught to him at the very moment he began to look around. That very instant he learnt that he was bound, and he also found that there was something in him which wanted to fly beyond, where the body could not follow, but which was as yet chained down by this limitation. Even in the lowest of religious ideas, where departed ancestors and other spirits, mostly violent and cruel, lurking about the houses of their friends, fond of bloodshed and strong drink, are worshipped—even there we find that one common factor, that of freedom. The man who wants to worship the gods sees in them, above all things, greater freedom than in himself. If a door is closed, he thinks that the gods can get through it, and that walls have no limitations for them. This idea of freedom increases until it comes to the ideal of a Personal God, of which the central concept is that He is a Being beyond the limitations of nature, of māyā.

I see before me, as it were, that in some of the forest retreats this question is being discussed by those ancient sages of India, and that when even the oldest and the holiest among them fail to reach the solution, a young man stands up in the midst of them and declares: "Hear, ye children of immortality! Hear, ye who live in the highest places! I have found the way. By knowing Him who is beyond darkness we can go beyond death."

This māyā is everywhere; it is terrible. Yet we have to work through it. The man who says that he will work when the world has become all good and then he will enjoy bliss is as likely to succeed as the man who sits beside the Ganges and says, "I will ford the river when all the water has run into the ocean." The way is not *with* māyā but *against* it. This is another fact to learn. We are not born as helpers of nature, but as competitors with nature. We are its masters, but we bind ourselves down. Why is this house here? Nature did not build it. Nature says, "Go and live in the forest." Man says, "I will build a house and fight with nature." And he does so. The whole history of humanity is a continuous fight against the so-called laws of nature. And man gains in the end. Coming to the internal world, there too the same fight is going on, the fight between the animal man and the spiritual man, between light and darkness. And here too man becomes victorious. He cuts his way, as it were, out of nature to freedom. We see, then, that beyond this māyā the Vedāntic philosophers find something which is not bound by māyā; and if we can get there, we shall not be bound by māyā. This idea is in some form or other the common property of all religions. But with Vedānta it is only the beginning of religion and not the end. The idea of a Personal God, the Ruler and Creator of this universe, as He has been styled, the Ruler of māyā or nature, is not the end of these Vedāntic ideas; it is only the beginning. The idea grows and grows until the Vedāntist finds that He who, he thought, was standing outside is he himself and is in reality within. He himself is the one who is free, but through limitation he thought he was bound.

MĀYĀ AND THE EVOLUTION OF
THE CONCEPT OF GOD

(Delivered in London, October 20, 1896)

WE HAVE SEEN that the idea of māyā, which forms, as it were, one of the basic doctrines of Advaita Vedānta, is, in its germ, found even in the Samhitās, and that in reality all the ideas which are developed in the Upanishads are to be found already in the Samhitās in some form or other. Most of you are by this time familiar with the idea of māyā and know that it is sometimes erroneously explained as illusion; and hence when the universe is said to be māyā, it also has to be explained as being illusion. The translation of the word is neither happy nor correct. Māyā is not a theory; it is simply a statement of fact about the universe as it exists; and to understand māyā we must go back to the Samhitās and begin with the conception in the germ.

The Samhitās speak of the devas. These devas were at first understood to be only powerful beings, nothing more. Many of us are horrified when reading the old scriptures, whether of the Greeks, the Hebrews, the Persians, or others, to find that the ancient gods sometimes did things which to us are very repugnant. But when we read these books we entirely forget that we are persons of the nineteenth century and that these gods were beings existing thousands of years ago. We also forget that the people who worshipped these gods found nothing incongruous in their characters, found nothing to frighten them, because they were very much like themselves.

I may also remark that that is the one great lesson we have to learn throughout our lives. In judging others we always judge them by our own ideals. That is not as it should be. Everyone must be judged according to his own ideal, and not by that of anyone else. In our dealings with our fellow beings we constantly labour under this mistake, and I am of opinion that the vast majority of our quarrels with one another arise simply from this one cause: that we are always trying to judge others' gods by our gods, others' ideals by our ideals, and others' motives by our motives. Under certain circumstances I might do a certain thing, and when I see another person taking the same course, I think he has also the same motive actuating him, little dreaming that although the effect may be the same, yet many other causes may produce the same thing. He may have performed the action with quite a different motive from that which impelled me to do it. So in judging of those ancient religions we must not take the standpoint to which we incline, but must put ourselves in the position of the thought and life of those early times.

The idea of the cruel and ruthless Jehovah in the Old Testament has frightened many. But why? What right have they to assume that the Jehovah of the ancient Jews must represent the conventional idea of the God of the present day? And at the same time we must not forget that there will come men after us who will laugh at our ideas of religion and God in the same way that we laugh at those of the ancients. Yet through all these various conceptions runs the golden thread of unity. It is the purpose of Vedānta to discover this thread. "I am the thread that runs through all these various ideas, each one of which is like a pearl," says Lord Krishna. And it is the duty of Vedānta to establish this connecting thread, however incongruous or disgusting may seem these ideas when judged according to the conceptions of today.

These ideas, in the setting of past times, were really not hideous; on the contrary, they were harmonious. It is only when we try to take them out of their setting and apply them to our own present circumstances that the hideousness becomes obvious. For the old surroundings are dead and gone. Just as the ancient Jew has developed into the keen, modern, sharp Jew, and the ancient Āryan into the intellectual Hindu, similarly Jehovah has grown, the devas have grown. The great mistake is in recognizing the evolution of the worshippers, while not acknowledging the evolution of the worshipped. He is not credited with the advance that His devotees have made. The truth is that you and I, as representing ideas, have grown; and these gods too, as representing ideas, have grown.

This may seem somewhat curious to you—that God can grow. He cannot. In the same sense the Real Man never grows. We shall see later on that the Real Man, behind each one of these human manifestations, is immovable, unchangeable, pure, and always perfect. As the tangible man is only an appearance, a partial manifestation of the Real Man, so the idea we form of God is a creation of the mind, only a partial manifestation. Behind that is the Real God, who never changes, the Ever Pure, the Immutable. But the manifestation is always changing, revealing more and more the Reality behind. When it reveals more of the fact behind, it is called progression; when it hides more of the fact behind, it is called retrogression. Thus as we grow, so the gods grow. From the ordinary point of view, just as we reveal ourselves, as we evolve, so the gods reveal themselves.

We shall now be in a position to understand the theory of māyā. All the religions of the world raise this question: Why is there disharmony in the universe? Why is there this evil in the universe? We do not find this question at the very inception of primitive religious ideas, because the world did not appear incongruous to the primitive man. Circumstances were not inharmonious for him; there was no clash of opinions; to him there was no antagonism of good and evil. There was merely a feeling in his own heart of something which said yea and something which said nay. The primitive man was a man of impulse. He did what occurred to him; he tried to bring out through his muscles whatever thought came into his mind. He never stopped to judge, and seldom tried to check his impulses. So with the gods: they were also creatures of impulse. Indra comes and shatters the forces of the demons. Jehovah is pleased with one person and displeased with another—for what reason, no one knows or asks; the habit of inquiry had not then arisen, and whatever He did was regarded as right. There was no idea of good or evil. The devas did many wicked things in our sense of the word; again and again Indra and other gods committed very wicked deeds. But to the worshippers of Indra the ideas of wickedness and evil did not occur; so they did not question them.

With the advance of ethical ideas came the struggle. There arose a certain sense in man, called in different languages and nations by different names. Call it the voice of God, or the result of past education, or whatever else you like, but the effect was that it had a checking power upon the natural impulses of man. There is one impulse in our minds which says, Do. Behind it rises another voice which says, Do not. There is one set of ideas in our minds which is always struggling to get outside through the channels of the senses, and behind that, although it may be thin and weak, there is an infinitely small voice which says, Do not go outside. The two beautiful Sanskrit words for these phenomena are pravritti and nivritti, circling forward and circling inward. It is the circling forward which usually governs our actions. Religion begins with the circling inward. Religion begins with this "Do not." Spirituality begins with this "Do not." When the "Do not" is not there, religion has not begun. And this "Do not" came, causing men's ideas to grow, despite the fighting gods whom they had worshipped.

A little love awoke in the hearts of mankind. It was very small indeed, and even now it is not much greater. It was at first confined to a tribe, embracing perhaps members of the same tribe. These gods loved their tribes and each god was a tribal god, the protector of that tribe. And sometimes the members of a tribe would think of themselves as the descendants of their god, just as the clans in different nations think that they are the common descendants of the man who was the founder of the clan. There were in ancient times, and there are even now, some people who claim to be descendants not only of these tribal gods, but also of the sun and the moon. You read in the ancient Sanskrit books of the great heroic emperors of the Solar and the Lunar Dynasty. They were first worshippers of the sun and the moon, and gradually came to think of themselves as descendants of the god of the sun, of the moon, and so forth. So when these tribal ideas began to grow, there came a little love, some slight idea of duty towards each other, a little social organization. Then naturally the idea came: "How can we live together without bearing and forbearing?" How can one man live with another without having some time or other to check his impulses, to restrain himself, to forbear from doing things which his mind would prompt him to do? It is impossible. Thus came the idea of restraint. The whole social fabric is based upon that idea of restraint, and we all know that the man or woman who has not learnt the great lesson of bearing and forbearing leads a most miserable life.

Now, when these ideas of religion came, a glimpse of something higher, more ethical, dawned upon the intellect of mankind. The old gods were found to be incongruous—those boisterous, fighting, drinking, beef-eating gods of the ancients, whose delight was in the smell of burning flesh and libations of strong liquor. Sometimes Indra drank so much that he fell upon the ground and talked unintelligibly. These gods could no longer be tolerated. The notion had arisen of inquiring into motives, and the gods had to come in for their share of inquiry. The reason for such and such actions was demanded, and the reason was wanting. Therefore men gave up these gods, or rather they developed higher ideas concerning them. They took a survey, as it were, of all the actions and qualities of the gods and discarded those which they could not harmonize, and kept those which they could understand, and combined them, labelling them with one name, Deva-deva, the God of gods. The God to be worshipped was no more a simple symbol of power; something more was required than that. He was an ethical God; He loved mankind and did good to mankind. But the idea of God still remained. They increased His ethical significance and increased also His power. He became the most ethical Being in the universe, as well as almost almighty.

But all this patchwork would not do. As the explanation assumed greater proportions, the difficulty it sought to solve did the same. If the virtues of God increased in arithmetical progression, the difficulty and doubt increased in geometrical progression. The difficulty about Jehovah was very little beside the difficulty about the God of the universe. And this question remains to the present day: Why, under the reign of an almighty and all-loving God of the universe, should diabolical things be allowed to remain? Why so much more misery than happiness and so much more wickedness than good?

We may shut our eyes to all these things, but the fact still remains that this world is a hideous world. At best it is the hell of Tantalus. Here we are, with strong impulses and stronger cravings for sense enjoyments, but cannot satisfy them. There rises a wave which impels us forward in spite of our own will, and as soon as we move one step there comes a blow. We are all doomed to live here like Tantalus. Further, ideals come into our heads far beyond the limit of our sense ideals, but when we seek to express them we cannot do so. On the contrary, we are crushed by the surging mass around us. Yet if I give up all idealism and lead a worldly life, my existence becomes that of a brute, and I debase and degrade myself. Neither way is happiness. Unhappiness is the fate of those who are content to live in this world as they are. A thousand times greater misery is the fate of those who dare to stand forth for truth and for higher things, and who dare to ask for something higher than mere brute existence here.

These are facts; but there is no explanation. There cannot be any explanation. But Vedānta shows the way out. You must bear in mind that I have to tell you facts that will frighten you sometimes; but if you remember what I say, think of it, and digest it, it will be yours, it will raise you higher and make you capable of understanding and of living in truth.

Now, it is a fact that this world is a Tantalus' hell. We do not know anything about this universe; yet at the same time we cannot say that we do not know. I cannot assert that this universe exists: when I think, I realize that I do not know anything about it. It may be an entire delusion of my brain. I may be dreaming all the time: I am dreaming that I am talking to you and that you are listening to me. No one can prove that it is not a dream. My brain itself may be a dream; and as to that, no one has ever seen his own brain. We all take it for granted. My own body, too, I take for granted. So it is with everything. At the same time I cannot say that I do not know.

This standing between knowledge and ignorance, in this mysterious twilight,

the mingling of truth and falsehood—and where they meet, no one knows—
is the fate of every one of us. We are walking in the midst of a dream, half
sleeping, half waking, passing all our lives in a haze. This is the fate of all sense
knowledge. This is the fate of all philosophy, of all our boasted science, of all
our boasted human knowledge. This is the universe.

Whether we speak of matter or spirit or mind or anything else, the fact
remains the same: we cannot say that they are; we cannot say that they are
not. We cannot say that they are one; we cannot say that they are many. This
eternal play of light and darkness—indiscriminate, indistinguishable, inseparable
—is always there. Because of it the universe appears real, yet at the same time
not real, and we appear awake, yet at the same time asleep. This is a statement
of fact, and this is what is called māyā.

We are born in this māyā, we live in it, we think in it, we dream in it. We
are philosophers in it, we are spiritual men in it, nay, we are devils in this māyā
and we are gods in this māyā. Stretch your ideas as far as you can, take them
higher and higher, call them infinite or by any other name you please—even
these ideas are within māyā. It cannot be otherwise. The whole of human knowledge is a generalization of this māyā, an attempt to know it as it appears to be.
This is the work of nāma-rupa, name and form. Everything that has form,
everything that calls up an idea in your mind, is within māyā; for everything that
is bound by the laws of time, space, and causation is within māyā.

Let us go back a little to those early ideas of God and see what became
of them. We perceive at once that the idea of some Being who is eternally loving us, eternally unselfish and almighty, ruling this universe, cannot satisfy men.
"What sort of just, merciful God is this?" asks the philosopher. Does He not
see millions and millions of His children perish, in the form of men and animals;
for who can live one moment here without killing others? Can you draw a breath
without destroying thousands of lives? You live because millions die. Every
moment of your life, every breath that you breathe, is death to thousands; every
movement that you make is death to millions. Every morsel that you eat is
death to millions. Why should they die?

There is an old sophism, that they are very low existences. Suppose they are
—which is questionable, for who knows whether the ant is greater than the
man, or the man than the ant? who can prove it one way or the other? Apart
from that question, even taking it for granted that these are very low beings,
still why should they die? If they are low they have more reason to live. Why
not? Because they live more in the senses, they feel pleasure and pain a thousandfold more than you or I can do. Which of us eats a dinner with the same
gusto as a dog or a wolf? None, because our energies are not in the senses; they
are in the intellect, in the spirit. But in animals the whole soul is in the senses;
they become mad after sense pleasure, and enjoy things with an intensity which
we human beings never dream of; and the pain is commensurate with the
pleasure. Pleasure and pain are meted out in equal measure. If the pleasure
felt by animals is so much keener than that felt by man, it follows that the
animals' sense of pain is as keen, if not keener, than man's. So the fact is that
the pain and misery men feel in dying is intensified a thousandfold in animals,
and yet we kill them without troubling about their misery. This is māyā.

If we suppose there is a Personal God like a human being, who made every-thing, these so-called explanations and theories which try to prove that out of evil comes good are not sufficient. Let twenty thousand good things come, but why should they come from evil? On that principle I might cut the throats of others because I want the full pleasure of my five senses. That is no reason. Why should good come through evil? The question remains to be answered, and it cannot be answered. The philosophy of India was compelled to admit this.

Vedānta was—and is—the boldest system of religion. It stopped nowhere, and it had one advantage: There was no body of priests who sought to suppress men who tried to tell the truth. There was always absolute religious free-dom. In India the bondage of superstition is a social one; here in the West society is very free. Social matters in India are very strict, but religious opinion is free. In England a man may dress any way he likes or eat what he likes— no one objects; but if he misses attending church, then Mrs. Grundy is down on him. He has to conform first to what society says on religion, and then he may think of the truth. In India, on the other hand, if a man dines with one who does not belong to his own caste, down comes society with all its terrible power and crushes him then and there. If he wants to dress a little differently from the way in which his ancestors dressed ages ago, he is done for. I have heard of a man who was cast out by society because he went several miles to see the first railway train. Well, we shall presume that that was not true. But in religion we find atheists, materialists, and Buddhists, creeds, opinions, and speculations of every phase and variety, some of a most startling character, living side by side. Preachers of all sects go about teaching and getting adherents, and at the very gates of the temples of gods, the brāhmins—to their credit be it said—allow even materialists to stand and give forth their opinions.

Buddha died at a ripe old age. I remember a friend of mine, a great American scientist, who was fond of reading his life. He did not like the death of Buddha, because he was not crucified. What a false idea! For a man to be great he must be murdered! Such ideas never prevailed in India. This great Buddha travelled all over India, denouncing her gods, and even the God of the universe, and yet he lived to a good old age. For eighty years he lived, and he converted half the country.

Then there were the Chārvākas, who preached horrible things, the most rank, undisguised materialism, such as in the nineteenth century they dare not openly preach. These Chārvākas were allowed to preach, from temple to temple and city to city, that religion was all nonsense, that it was priestcraft, that the Vedas were the words and writings of fools, rogues, and demons, and that there was neither God nor an eternal soul. If there was a soul, why did it not come back after death, drawn by the love of wife and child? Their idea was that if there was a soul it must still love after death and want good things to eat and nice dress. Yet no one hurt these Chārvākas.

You must remember that freedom is the first condition of growth. We in India allowed liberty in spiritual matters, and we have a tremendous power in the realm of religion even today. You grant the same liberty in social matters, and so have a splendid social organization. We have not given any freedom in the expansion of social matters, and ours is a cramped society. You have never given any freedom in religious matters, but with fire and sword have enforced your beliefs; and the result is that religion is a stunted, degenerated growth in the European mind. In India we have to take off the shackles from society; in Europe the chains must be taken from the feet of spiritual progress. Then will come a wonderful growth and development of man. If we discover that there is a unity running through all these developments, spiritual, moral, and social, we shall find that religion, in the fullest sense of the word, must come into society and into our everyday life. In the light of Vedānta you will understand that all sciences are but manifestations of religion, and so is everything that exists in this world.

In society we find two sets of opinions, the one denunciatory and the other positive and constructive. It is a most curious fact that in every society you find them. Suppose there is an evil in society: you will find immediately one group rising up and denouncing it in vindictive fashion; and this sometimes degenerates into fanaticism. There are fanatics in every society, and women frequently join in these outcries, because of their impulsive nature. Every fanatic who gets up and denounces something can secure a following. It is very easy to break down; a maniac can break anything he likes, but it would be hard for him to build up anything. These fanatics may do some good, according to their lights, but they do much more harm. Social institutions are not made in a day, and to change them means removing the cause. Suppose there is an evil: denouncing it will not remove it, but you must go to work at the root. First find out the cause, then remove it, and the effect will be removed also. Mere outcry will not produce any result, unless indeed it produces misfortune.

There are others who have sympathy in their hearts and who understand the idea that we must go deep into the cause. These are the great saints. One fact you must remember: all the great teachers of the world have declared that they came not to destroy but to fulfil. Many times this has not been understood, and their forbearance has been thought to be an unworthy compromise with existing popular opinions. Even now you occasionally hear that these prophets and great teachers were rather cowardly and dared not say and do what they thought was right. But that is not so. Fanatics little understand the infinite power of love in the hearts of these great sages, who looked upon the inhabitants of this world as their children. They were the real fathers, the real gods, filled with infinite sympathy and patience for everyone; they were ready to bear and forbear. They knew how human society should grow, and patiently, slowly, surely, went on applying their remedies, not by denouncing and frightening people, but by gently and kindly leading them upwards, step by step. Such were the writers of the Upanishads. They knew full well that the old ideas of God were not reconcilable with the advanced ethical ideas of the time; they knew full well that what the atheists were preaching contained a good deal of truth, nay, great nuggets of truth; but at the same time they understood that those who wished to sever the thread that bound the beads, who wanted to build a new society in the air, would entirely fail.

We never build anew; we simply rearrange. We cannot have anything new; we only change the position of things. The seed grows into the tree patiently and gently. We must direct our energies towards the truth, and fulfil the truth that exists, not try to make new truths. Thus, instead of denouncing these old ideas of God as unfit for modern times, the ancient sages began to seek out the reality that was in them. The result was the Vedānta philosophy. From the old deities and from the monotheistic God, the Ruler of the universe, they ascended to yet higher and higher ideas. And the highest of them all they called the Impersonal Absolute, in which they beheld the oneness of the universe.

He who sees in this world of manifoldness that One running through all; in this world of death, he who finds that one infinite Life; and in this world of insentience and ignorance, he who finds that one Light and Knowledge—unto him belongs eternal peace, unto none else, unto none else.

MĀYĀ AND FREEDOM

(Delivered in London, October 22, 1896)

"Trailing clouds of glory do we come," says the poet. Not all of us come trailing clouds of glory, however; some of us come trailing black fogs. There can be no question about that. But every one of us comes into this world to fight, as on a battlefield. We come here weeping, to fight our way as well as we can and to make a path for ourselves through this infinite ocean of life. Forward we go, having long ages behind us and an immense expanse beyond. So on we go, till death comes and takes us off the field—victorious or defeated, we do not know. And this is māyā.

Hope is dominant in the heart of childhood. The whole world is a golden vision to the opening eyes of the child; he thinks his will is supreme. As he moves onward, at every step nature stands as an adamantine wall, barring his farther progress. He may hurl himself against it again and again, striving to break through. The farther he goes, the farther recedes the ideal, till death comes and there is release, perhaps. And this is māyā.

A man of science rises. He is thirsting after knowledge. No sacrifice is too great, no struggle too hopeless for him. He moves onward, discovering secret after secret of nature, searching out the secrets from its innermost heart—and what for? What is it all for? Why should we give him glory? Why should he acquire fame? Does not nature do infinitely more than any human being can do? And nature is dull, insentient. Why should it be glorious to imitate the dull, the insentient? Nature can hurl a thunderbolt of any magnitude to any distance. If a man can do one small part as much, we praise him and laud him to the skies. Why? Why should we praise him for imitating nature, imitating death, imitating dullness, imitating insentience? The force of gravitation can pull to pieces the biggest mass that ever existed; yet it is insentient. What glory is there in imitating the insentient? Yet we are all struggling after that. And this is māyā.

The senses drag the human soul out. Man is seeking for pleasure and for happiness where it can never be found. For countless ages we have been taught that this search is futile and vain; there is no happiness here. But we cannot learn; it is impossible for us to do so except through our own experiences. We try them, and a blow comes. Do we learn then? Not even then. Like moths hurling themselves against the flame, we hurl ourselves again and again into sense pleasures, hoping to find satisfaction there. We return again and again with freshened energy; thus we go on till, crippled and cheated, we die. And this is māyā.

So with our intellect. In our desire to solve the mysteries of the universe,

237

we cannot stop our questioning; we feel we must know and cannot believe that no knowledge is ever gained. A few steps, and there arises the wall of beginningless and endless time which we cannot surmount. A few steps, and there appears a wall of boundless space which cannot be surmounted, and the whole is irrevocably bound in by the walls of cause and effect. We cannot go beyond them. Yet we struggle, and still have to struggle. And this is māyā.

With every breath, with every pulsation of the heart, with every one of our movements, we think we are free, and the very same moment we are shown that we are not: we are born slaves, nature's bondslaves, in body, in mind, in all our thoughts, in all our feelings. And this is māyā.

There is never a mother who does not think her child is a born genius, the most extraordinary child that was ever born. She dotes upon her child. Her whole soul is in the child. The child grows up, perhaps becomes a drunkard, a brute, and ill-treats the mother; and the more he ill-treats her, the more her love increases. The world lauds it as the unselfish love of the mother, little dreaming that the mother is a slave; she cannot help herself. She would a thousand times rather throw off the burden, but she cannot. So she covers it with a mass of flowers, which she calls wonderful love. And this is māyā.

We are all like this in the world. A legend tells how once Nārada said to Krishna, "Lord, show me māyā." A few days passed, and Krishna asked Nārada to make a trip with Him towards a forest. After walking several miles Krishna said, "Nārada, I am thirsty; can you fetch some water for Me?" "I will go at once, Sir, and get you water." So Nārada went. At a little distance there was a village. He entered the village in search of water and knocked at a door, which was opened by a most beautiful young girl. At the sight of her he immediately forgot that his Master was waiting for water, perhaps dying for want of it. He forgot everything and began to talk with the girl. Gradually that talk ripened into love. He asked the father for the daughter, and they were married and lived there and had children. Thus twelve years passed. His father-in-law died; he inherited his property. He lived, as he seemed to think, a very happy life with his wife and children, his fields and his cattle, and so forth. Then came a flood. One night the river rose until it overflowed its banks and flooded the whole village. Houses fell, men and animals were swept away and drowned, and everything was floating in the rush of the stream. Nārada had to escape. With one hand he held his wife, and with the other, two of his children; another child was on his shoulders, and he was trying to ford this tremendous flood. After a few steps he found the current was too strong, and the child on his shoulders fell and was borne away. A cry of despair came from Nārada. In trying to save that child, he lost his grasp upon the others, and they also were lost. At last his wife, whom he clasped with all his might, was torn away by the current, and he was thrown on the bank, weeping and wailing in bitter lamentation. Behind him there came a gentle voice: "My child, where is the water? You went to fetch a pitcher of water, and I am waiting for you. You have been gone for quite half an hour." "Half an hour!" Nārada exclaimed. Twelve whole years had passed through his mind, and all these scenes had happened in half an hour! And this is māyā. In one form or another we are all in it. It is a most difficult and intricate state of things to understand. It has been preached in every country, taught everywhere, but only believed in by a few, because until we get the experiences ourselves we cannot believe in it. What does it show? Something very terrible: that it is all futile.

Time, the all-destroyer, comes, and nothing is left. He swallows up the saint and the sinner, the king and the peasant, the beautiful and the ugly; he leaves nothing. Everything is rushing towards that one goal: destruction. Our knowledge, our arts, our sciences—everything is rushing towards it. None can stem the tide, none can hold it back for a minute. We may try to forget it, in the same way that persons in a plague-stricken city try to create oblivion by drinking, dancing, and other vain attempts, and so becoming paralysed. So we are trying to forget, trying to create oblivion by all sorts of sense pleasures. And this is māyā.

Two solutions have been proposed. One, which everyone knows, is very common, and that is: "It is all very true, but do not think of it. 'Make hay while the sun shines,' as the proverb says. It is true that there is suffering; but do not mind it. Seize the few pleasures you can, do what little you can, do not look at the dark side of the picture, but always towards the hopeful, the positive side." There is some truth in this, but there is also a danger. The truth is that it is a good motive power; hope and a positive ideal are very good motive powers for our lives. But there is a certain danger in them. The danger lies in our giving up the struggle in despair, as do those who preach: "Take the world as it is; sit down as calmly and comfortably as you can, and be contented with all these miseries. When you receive blows, say they are not blows but flowers; and when you are driven about like slaves, say that you are free. Day and night tell lies to others and to your own souls, because that is the only way to live happily."

This is what is called practical wisdom, and never was it more prevalent in the world than in this nineteenth century, because never were harder blows hit than at the present time, never was competition keener, never were men so cruel to their fellow men as now; and therefore this consolation must be offered. It is put forward in the strongest way at the present time; but it fails, as it always must fail. We cannot hide carrion with roses; it is impossible. It would not avail long; for soon the roses would fade and the carrion would be worse than before. So with our lives. We may try to cover our old and festering sore with cloth of gold, but there comes a day when the cloth of gold is removed and the sore in all its ugliness is revealed.

Is there no hope, then? True it is that we are all slaves of māyā, are all born in māyā and live in māyā. Is there then no way out, no hope? That we are all miserable, that this world is really a prison, that even our so-called "trailing glory" is but a prison-house, and that even our intellects and minds are prison-houses, has been known for ages upon ages. There has never been a man, there has never been a human soul, who has not felt this some time or other, however he may talk. And the old people feel it most, because in them is the accumulated experience of a whole life, because they cannot be easily cheated by the lies of nature. Is there no way out?

We find that with all this, with this terrible fact before us, in the midst of sorrow and suffering, even in this world where life and death are synonymous, even here a still, small voice has been ringing through all the ages, in every country, and in every heart: "This My māyā is divine, made up of the gunas, and very difficult to cross. Yet those that come unto Me cross the river of māyā." "Come unto Me, all ye that labour and are heavy laden, and I will give you rest." This is the voice that is leading us forward. Man has heard it— and is hearing it—all through the ages. This voice comes to man when everything seems to be lost, and hope has fled, when man's dependence on his own strength has been crushed down, and everything seems to melt away between his fingers, and life is a hopeless ruin. Then he hears it. This is called religion.

On the one side, therefore, is the bold assertion that this is all nonsense, that this is māyā; but along with it there is the hopeful assertion that from this māyā there is a way out. On the other hand, practical men tell us: "Don't bother your heads about such nonsense as religion and metaphysics. Live here; this is a very bad world, indeed, but make the best of it." Which, put in plain language, means: Live a hypocritical, lying life, a life of continuous fraud, covering your old sores in the best way you can; go on putting patch after patch, until everything is lost and you are a mass of patchwork. This is what is called practical wisdom. Those who are satisfied with this patchwork will never come to religion.

Religion begins with a tremendous dissatisfaction with the present state of things, with our lives, and a hatred, an intense hatred, for this patching up of life, an unbounded disgust for fraud and lies. He alone can be religious who dares to say what the mighty Buddha once said under the Bo-tree, when this idea of practicality appeared before him and he saw that it was nonsense, and yet could not find a way out. When the temptation came to him to give up his search after truth, to go back to the world and live the old life of fraud, calling things by wrong names, telling lies to himself and to everybody, he, the giant, conquered it and said: "Death is better than a vegetating ignorant life; it is better to die on the battlefield than to live a life of defeat." This is the basis of religion.

When a man takes this stand he is on the way to find the truth, he is on the way to God. That determination must be the first impulse towards becoming religious. I will hew out a way for myself. I will know the truth or give up my life in the attempt. For on this side it is nothing, it is gone, it is vanishing every day. The beautiful, hopeful young person of today is the veteran of tomorrow. Hopes and joys and pleasures will die like blossoms with tomorrow's frost. That is one side. On the other, there are the great charms of conquest, victories over all the ills of life, victories over life itself, the conquest of the universe. On that side men can stand. Those who dare, therefore, to struggle for victory, for truth, for religion, are on the right path, and that is what the Vedas preach. "Be not in despair; the way is very difficult, like walking on the blade of a razor. Yet despair not; arise, awake, and find the ideal, the goal."

Now, all these various manifestations of religion, in whatever shape or form they have come to mankind, have one common, central basis. It is the preaching of freedom, the way out of this world. They never came to reconcile the world and religion, but to cut the Gordian knot, to establish religion in its own ideal, and not to compromise with the world. That is what every religion preaches; and the duty of Vedānta is to harmonize all these aspirations, to make manifest

the common ground between all the religions of the world, the highest as well
as the lowest. What we call the most arrant superstition and the highest philosophy really have a common aim, in that they both try to show the way out
of the same difficulty; and in most cases this way is through the help of someone who is not himself bound by the laws of nature, in one word, someone
who is free. In spite of all the difficulties and differences of opinion about the
nature of the one free agent, whether he is a Personal God or a sentient being
like man, whether masculine, feminine, or neuter—and the discussions have
been endless—the fundamental idea is the same. In spite of the almost hopeless
contradictions of the different systems, we find the golden thread of unity
running through them all; and in this philosophy, this golden thread has been
traced, revealed little by little to our view; and the first step to this revelation
is the knowledge that we are all advancing towards freedom.

One curious fact present in the midst of all our joys and sorrows, difficulties
and struggles, is that we are surely journeying towards freedom. The question
raised was this: "What is this universe? From what does it arise? Into what
does it go?" And the answer was: "In freedom it rises, in freedom it rests, and
into freedom it melts away." This idea of freedom, you cannot relinquish; your
actions, your very lives, will be lost without it. Every moment nature is proving
us to be slaves and not free. Yet simultaneously rises the other idea, that still
we are free. At every step we are knocked down, as it were, by māyā, and shown
that we are bound; and yet at the same moment, together with this blow,
together with this feeling that we are bound, comes the other feeling that we
are free. Some inner voice tells us that we are free. But if we attempt to realize
that freedom, to make it manifest, we find the difficulties almost insuperable.
Yet in spite of that, it insists on asserting itself inwardly: "I am free, I am free."
And if you study all the various religions of the world you will find this idea
expressed.

Not only religion—you must not take this word in its narrow sense—but the
whole life of society, is the assertion of that one principle of freedom. All movements are the assertion of that one freedom. That voice has been heard by
everyone, whether he knows it or not, that voice which declares, "Come unto
Me, all ye that labour and are heavy laden." It may not be in the same language,
or the same form of speech, but in some form or other that voice calling for
freedom has been with us. Yes, we are born here on account of that voice; every
one of our movements is towards that end. We are all rushing towards freedom,
we are all following that voice, whether we know it or not; as the children of
the village were attracted by the music of the flute-player, so we are all following
the music of the voice without knowing it.

We are ethical when we follow that voice. Not only the human soul, but all
creatures from the lowest to the highest have heard the voice and are rushing
towards it, and in the struggle are either combining with each other or pushing
each other out of the way. Thus come competition, joys, struggles, life, pleasure,
and death; and the whole universe is nothing but the result of this mad struggle
to reach the voice. This is the manifestation of nature.

What happens then? The scene begins to shift. As soon as you know the
voice and understand what it is, the whole scene changes. The same world which

was the ghastly battlefield of māyā is now changed into something good and beautiful. We no longer curse nature or say that the world is horrible and that it is all vain; we need no longer weep and wail. As soon as we understand the voice, we see the reason why this struggle should be here—this fight, this competition, these difficulties, this cruelty, these little pleasures and joys; we see that they are in the nature of things, because without them there would be no going towards the voice, which we are destined to attain, whether we know it or not. All human life, all nature, therefore, is struggling to attain to freedom. The sun is moving towards the goal; so is the earth in circling round the sun; so is the moon in circling round the earth. To that goal the planets are moving and the air is blowing. Everything is struggling towards that. The saint is going towards that voice; he cannot help it; it is no glory to him. So is the sinner. The charitable man is going straight towards that voice, and cannot be hindered. The miser is also going towards the same destination. The greatest worker of good hears the same voice within; he cannot resist it; he must go towards the voice. So is the most arrant idler. One stumbles more than another; him who stumbles more we call bad, and him who stumbles less we call good. Good and bad are never two different things; they are one and the same. The difference is not one of kind, but of degree.

Now, if the manifestation of this power of freedom really governs the whole universe, applying that fact to religion, we find that this idea has been the one assertion of religion throughout. Take the lowest form of religion, where there is the worship of departed ancestors or certain powerful and cruel gods; what is the prominent idea about the gods or ancestors? It is that they are superior to nature, not bound by its restrictions. The worshipper has, no doubt, very limited control of nature. He himself cannot pass through a wall or fly up into the skies, but the gods whom he worships can do these things. What is meant by that, philosophically? That the assertion of freedom is there, that the gods whom he worships are superior to nature as he knows it. So with those who worship still higher beings. As the idea of nature expands, the idea of the soul which is superior to nature also expands, until we come to what we call monotheism, which holds that there is māyā, or nature, and that there is some Being who is the Ruler of this māyā.

Here Vedānta begins, where these monotheistic ideas first appear. But the Vedānta philosophy wants further explanation. This explanation that there is a Being beyond all these manifestations of māyā, who is superior to and independent of māyā and who is attracting us towards Himself, and that we are all going towards Him, is very good, says Vedānta; but yet the perception is not clear, the vision is dim and hazy, although it does not directly contradict reason.

One of your hymns says, "Nearer my God to Thee." The same hymn would be very good to the Vedāntist, only he would change a word and make it "Nearer my God to Me." The idea that the goal is far off, far beyond nature, attracting us all towards it, has to be changed; the goal has to be brought nearer and nearer, without degrading or debasing it. The God of heaven becomes the God in nature, and the God in nature becomes the God who is nature, and the God who is nature becomes the God within this temple of the body, and the God dwelling in the temple of the body at last becomes the temple itself, becomes the soul and man—and there Vedānta reaches the last words it can teach. He whom the sages have been seeking in all these places is in our own hearts; the voice that you heard was right, says Vedānta, but the direction you gave to the voice was wrong. The ideal of freedom that you perceived was correct, but you projected it outside yourself, and that was your mistake. Bring it nearer and nearer, until you find that it was all the time within you, it was the Self of your own self. That freedom was your own nature, and this māyā never bound you.

Nature never had power over you. Like a frightened child you were dreaming that it was throttling you. The release from this fear is the goal: not only to see it intellectually, but to perceive it, actualize it, much more definitely than we perceive this world. Then we shall know that we are free. Then, and then alone, will all difficulties vanish, then will all the perplexities of the heart be smoothed away, all crookedness be made straight; then will vanish the delusion of manifoldness and nature. Māyā, instead of being a horrible, hopeless dream, as it is now, will become beautiful; this earth, instead of being a prison-house, will become our playground; and even dangers and difficulties, even all sufferings, will become deified and show us their real nature, will show us that behind everything, as the substance of everything, He is standing, and that He is our own real Self.

THE ABSOLUTE AND MANIFESTATION

(Delivered in London)

THE ONE QUESTION that is most difficult to grasp in understanding the Advaita philosophy, which will be asked again and again and which will always remain unanswered, is: How has the Infinite, the Absolute, become the finite? I shall now take up this question, and in order to illustrate it I shall use a figure.

Here is the Absolute (a), and this is the universe (b). The Absolute has become the universe. By this is meant not only the material world, but the mental world, the spiritual world—heavens and earth, and in fact everything that exists. Mind is the name of a change, and body the name of another change, and so on, and all these entities compose our universe. This Absolute (a) has become the universe (b) by coming through time, space, and causation (c). This is the central idea of Advaita. Time, space, and causation are the glass through which the Absolute is seen, and when It is seen on the lower side It appears as the universe.

(a) The Absolute
(c)
Time
Space
Causation
(b) The Universe

Now, we at once gather from this that in the Absolute there is neither time, space, nor causation. The idea of time cannot be there, seeing that there is no mind, no thought. The idea of space cannot be there, seeing that there is no external change. What you call motion and causation cannot exist where there is only one. We have to understand this, and impress it on our minds—that what we call causation begins after, if we may be permitted to say so, the degeneration of the Absolute into the phenomenal, and not before; that our will, our desire, and all these things always come after that.

I think Schopenhauer's philosophy makes a mistake in its interpretation of Vedānta; for it seeks to make the will everything. Schopenhauer makes the will stand in place of the Absolute. But the Absolute cannot be presented as will; for will is something changeable and phenomenal, and over the line drawn above time, space, and causation there is no change, no motion; it is only below the line that external motion and internal motion, called thought, begin. There can be no will on the other side, and will, therefore, cannot be the cause of this universe. Coming nearer, we see in our own bodies that will is not the cause of every movement. I move this chair; my will is the cause of this movement, and this will becomes manifested as muscular motion at the other end. But the same power that moves the chair is moving the heart, the lungs, and so on, but not through will. Granted that the power is the same, it becomes will only when it rises to the plane of consciousness, and to call it will before it has risen to this plane is a misnomer. This makes for a good deal of confusion in Schopenhauer's philosophy.

A stone falls and we ask, Why? This question is possible only on the supposition that nothing happens without a cause. I request you to make this very clear in your minds; for whenever we ask why anything happens, we are taking for granted that everything that happens must have a why, that is to say, must have been preceded by something else which acted as the cause. This precedence and succession are what we call the law of causation, which means that everything in the universe is by turn a cause and an effect. An object is the cause of certain things which come after it and is itself the effect of something else which has preceded it. This is called the law of causation and is a necessary condition of all our thinking. We believe that every particle in the universe, whatever it be, is related to every other particle.

There has been much discussion as to how this idea arose. In Europe there have been intuitive philosophers who believed that it was inherent in the human constitution; others have believed that it came from experience. But the question has never been settled. We shall see later on what Vedānta has to say about it. But first of all we have to understand this: that the very asking of the question presupposes that everything around us has been preceded by certain things and will be succeeded by certain other things.

The other belief involved in this question is that nothing in the universe is independent, that everything is acted upon by something outside itself. Interdependence is the law of the whole universe. In asking what caused the Absolute, what an error we are making! To ask this question we have to suppose that the Absolute also is bound by something, that It is dependent on something; and in making this supposition, we drag the Absolute down to the level of the universe. But in the Absolute there is neither time, space, nor causation; it is all one. That which exists by itself alone cannot have any cause. That which is free cannot have any cause, else it would not be free, but bound. That which has relativity cannot be free. Thus we see that the very question as to why the Infinite became the finite is an absurd one, for it is self-contradictory.

Coming from subtleties to the logic of our common plane, to common sense, we can see this from another side when we seek to know how the Absolute has become the relative. Suppose we knew the answer—would the Absolute then remain the Absolute? It would have become the relative. What is meant by knowledge as we generally understand it? Only when something has become limited by our mind do we know it; when it is beyond our mind it is not known. Now if the Absolute becomes limited by the mind, It is no more the Absolute; It has become finite. Everything limited by the mind becomes finite. Therefore to know the Absolute is again a contradiction in terms. That is why this question has never been answered; because if it were answered there would no more be an Absolute. A God known would no more be God: He would have become finite like one of us. He cannot be known; He is always the Unknowable One.

But what Advaita says is that God is more than knowable. This is a great fact to learn. You must not cherish the idea that God is unknowable in the sense in which agnostics use the term. For instance, here is a chair; it is known to us. But what is beyond the ether, or whether people exist there or not, is possibly unknowable. But God is neither known nor unknowable in this sense. He is something higher than known; that is what we understand by God's being unknown and unknowable. The expression is not used in the sense in which it may be said that some questions are unknown and unknowable. God is more than known. This chair is known, but God is known much more intensely, because to know this chair itself we have to know it in and through Him.

He is the Witness, the eternal Witness of all knowledge. Whatever we know we have to know in and through Him. He is the essence of our self. He is the essence of this ego, this I, and we cannot know anything except in and through this I. Therefore you have to know everything in and through Brahman. To know the chair you have to know it in and through God. Thus God is infinitely nearer to us than the chair, but yet He is infinitely higher—neither known nor unknown, but something infinitely higher than either. He is your Self. "Who would live a second, who would breathe a second in this universe, if that Blessed One did not permeate it?"—because in and through Him we breathe, in and through Him we exist. Not that He is standing somewhere and making my blood circulate. What is meant is that He is the Essence of all this, the Soul of my soul. You cannot by any possibility say you know Him; it would be degrading Him. You cannot get out of yourself; so you cannot know Him.

Knowledge is objectification. For instance, in remembering you objectify things, projecting them out of yourself. The memories of all the things which I have seen, and also all those things which I know, are in my mind. The pictures, the impressions of all these things, are in my mind, and when I try to think of them, to know them, the first act of knowledge is to project them outside. This cannot be done with God, because He is the Essence of our souls; we cannot project Him outside ourselves. Here is one of the profoundest passages in Vedānta: "He that is the Essence of your soul, He is the Truth, He is the Self, and thou art That, O Śvetaketu." This is what is meant by "Thou art God." You cannot describe Him by any other language. All attempts of language, calling Him Father, or Brother, or our dearest Friend, are attempts to objectify God, which cannot be done. He is the eternal Subject of everything. As I am the subject of this chair, because I see the chair, so God is the eternal Subject of my soul. How can you objectify Him, the Essence of your soul, the Reality of everything?

Thus, I would repeat to you once more: God is neither knowable nor unknowable, but something infinitely higher than either. He is one with us; and that which is one with us is neither knowable nor unknowable, like our own self. You cannot know your own self, you cannot move it out and make it an object to look at, because you are that and cannot separate yourself from it. Neither is it unknowable; for what is better known than your self? It is really the centre of our knowledge. In exactly the same sense, God is neither unknowable nor known, but infinitely higher than both; for He is our real Self.

First we see, then, that the question "What caused the Absolute to become the relative?" is a contradiction in terms; and secondly, we find that the idea of

God in Advaita is this Oneness, and therefore we cannot objectify Him, for we are always living and moving in Him, whether we know it or not. Whatever we do is always through Him.

Now the question is, What are time, space, and causation? Advaita means non-duality—there are not two, but one. Yet we see that here is a proposition that the Absolute is manifesting Itself as many, through the veil of time, space, and causation. Therefore it seems that here are two: the Absolute and māyā, the sum total of time, space, and causation. It seems apparently very convincing that there are two. To this the Advaitist replies that there cannot be two. To have two, we must have two absolute, independent existences which are uncaused. But time, space, and causation cannot be said to be independent existences. In the first place, time is an entirely dependent existence; it changes with every change of our mind. Sometimes in a dream one imagines that one has lived several years; at other times several months have passed as one second. So time is entirely dependent on our state of mind. Secondly, sometimes the idea of time vanishes altogether. So with space. We cannot know what space is. Yet it is there, indefinable, and cannot exist separate from anything else. So with causation.

The one peculiar attribute we find in time, space, and causation is that they cannot exist separate from other things. Try to think of space without colour or limits or any connexion with the things around—just abstract space. You cannot; you have to think of it as the space between two limits or between three objects. It has to be connected with some object to have any existence. So with time: you cannot have any idea of abstract time, but you have to take two events, one preceding and the other succeeding, and join the two events by the idea of succession. Time depends on two events, just as space has to be related to outside objects. And the idea of causation is inseparable from time and space. This is the peculiar thing about them: they have no independent existence. They have not even the existence which the chair or the wall has. They are like shadows around everything, which you cannot catch. They have no real existence; yet they are not non-existent, seeing that through them all things in this universe are being manifested.

Thus we see, first, that this combination of time, space, and causation has neither existence nor non-existence. Secondly, it sometimes vanishes. To give an illustration: There is a wave in the ocean. The wave is the same as the ocean, certainly, and yet we know it is a wave and, as such, different from the ocean. What makes this difference? The name and the form—that is, the idea in the mind, and the form. Now, can we think of a wave-form as something separate from the ocean? Certainly not. It is always associated with the idea of the ocean. If the wave subsides, the form vanishes in a moment, and yet the form was not a delusion. So long as the wave existed the form was there, and you were bound to see the form. And this is māyā.

The whole of this universe is, as it were, a peculiar form of the Absolute. The Absolute is the ocean, while you and I, and suns and stars, and everything else are various waves of that ocean. And what makes the waves different? Only the form—and that form is nothing but time, space, and causation, which, again, are all entirely dependent on the wave. As soon as the wave goes they vanish.

As soon as the individual gives up this māyā it vanishes for him and he becomes free. The whole struggle is to get rid of this clinging to time, space, and causation, which are always obstacles in our way.

What is the theory of evolution? There are two factors: First, a tremendous potential power is trying to express itself, and secondly, circumstances are holding it down, its environment not allowing it to express itself. So in order to fight with this environment, the power takes new bodies again and again. An amoeba, in the struggle, gets another body and conquers some obstacles, then gets another body, and so on until it becomes man. Now, if you carry this idea to its logical conclusion, there must come a time when the power that was in the amoeba, and that evolved as man, will have conquered all the obstructions that nature can bring before it and will thus escape from all its environments. This idea expressed in metaphysics will take this form: There are two components in every action—the one is the subject, the other the object—and the aim of life is to make the subject master of the object. For instance, I feel unhappy because a man scolds me. My struggle will be to make myself strong enough to conquer the environment, so that he may scold but I shall not feel. That is how we are all trying to conquer nature. What is meant by morality? Making the subject strong by attuning it to the Absolute, so that finite nature ceases to have control over us. It is a logical conclusion of our philosophy, that there must come a time when we shall have conquered all our environments, because nature is finite.

Here is another thing to learn. How do you know that nature is finite? You can know this only through metaphysics. Nature is the Infinite under limitations. Therefore it is finite. So there must come a time when we shall have conquered all environments. And how are we to conquer them? We cannot possibly conquer all the objective environments. We simply cannot. The little fish wants to fly from its enemies in the water. How does it do so? By evolving wings and becoming a bird. The fish does not change the water or the air; the change is in itself. Change is always subjective. All through evolution you find that the conquest of nature comes by change in the subject. Apply this to religion and morality, and you will find that the conquest of evil comes by the change in the subject alone. That is how Advaita gathers its strength, by emphasizing the subjective element in man. To talk of evil and misery is nonsense, because they do not exist outside. If I am inured against all anger, I never feel angry. If I am proof against all hatred, I never feel hatred, because it cannot touch me. This is, therefore, the process by which to achieve that conquest— through the subjective, by perfecting the subjective.

I may make bold to say that the only religion which agrees with and even goes a little farther than modern researches, both on physical and moral lines, is Advaita; and that is why it appeals to modern scientists so much. They find that the old dualistic theories are not enough for them, do not satisfy their necessities. A man must have not only faith, but intellectual faith too. Now, in this latter part of the nineteenth century, such an idea as that religion coming from any other source than one's own hereditary religion must be false shows that there is still weakness left; and such ideas must be given up. I do not mean that such is the case in this country alone; it is so in every country, and nowhere more than in my own. Thus Advaita was never allowed to come to the people. At first some monks got hold of it and took it to the forests, and so it came to be called the "forest philosophy." By the mercy of the Lord, Buddha came and preached it to the masses, and the whole nation became Buddhists. Long after that, when atheists and agnostics had destroyed the nation again, it was found out that Advaita was the only way to save India from materialism.

Thus Advaita has twice saved India from materialism. Before Buddha came, materialism had spread to a fearful extent, and it was of a most hideous kind—not like that of the present day, but of a far worse nature. You see, I myself am a materialist in a certain sense, because I believe that there is only One. That is what the materialist wants you to believe, only he calls it matter and I call it God. The materialists admit that out of this matter all hope and religion and everything have come. I say that all these have come out of Brahman. But the materialism that prevailed before Buddha's time was that crude sort of material-ism which taught: "Eat, drink, and be merry. There is no God, soul, or heaven. Religion is a concoction of wicked priests." It taught the morality that so long as you live you must try to live happily; eat, though you have to borrow money for the food, and never mind about repaying it. That was the old materialism, and that kind of philosophy spread so much that even today it goes by the name of "popular philosophy." Buddha brought Vedānta to light, gave it to the people, and saved India.

A thousand years after his death a similar state of things again prevailed. The mob, the masses, and various races coming from outside had been con-verted to Buddhism; naturally the teachings of Buddha had in time degenerated, because most of the people were very ignorant. Buddhism taught no God, no Ruler of the universe; so gradually the masses brought their gods and devils and hobgoblins out again, and a tremendous hotchpotch was made of Buddhism in India. Again materialism came to the fore, taking the form of license with the higher classes and superstition with the lower. Then Sankarāchārya arose and once more revivified the Vedānta philosophy. He made it a rationalistic philos-ophy. In the Upanishads the arguments are often very obscure. Buddha laid stress upon the moral side of the philosophy, and Sankarāchārya, upon the intellectual. Sankara worked out, rationalized, and placed before men the wonderful, coher-ent system of Advaita.

Materialism prevails in Europe today. You may pray for the salvation of the modern sceptics; but they do not yield; they want reason. The salvation of Europe depends on a rationalistic religion, and Advaita—Non-duality, Oneness, the idea of the Impersonal God—is the only religion that can have any hold on intellectual people. It comes whenever religion seems to disappear and irreligion seems to prevail; and that is why it has taken root in Europe and America.

I would say one thing more in connexion with this philosophy. In the old Upanishads we find sublime poetry; their authors were poets. Plato says that inspiration comes to people through poetry, and it seems as if these ancient rishis, seers of truths, were raised above humanity to show these truths through poetry. They never preached or philosophized or wrote. Music came out of their hearts. In Buddha we had a great, universal heart and infinite patience, making religion practical and bringing it to everyone's door. In Sankarāchārya we saw tremendous intellectual power, throwing the searching light of reason upon everything. We want today that bright sun of intellectuality joined with the heart of Buddha, the wonderful, infinite heart of love and mercy. This union will give us the highest philosophy. Science and religion will meet and shake hands. Poetry and philosophy will become friends. This will be the religion of the future, and if we can work it out, we may be sure that it will be for all times and peoples.

This is the one thing that will prove acceptable to modern science, for it has almost come to it. When a scientist makes the assertion that all objects are the manifestation of one force, does it not remind you of the God of whom you hear in the Upanishads? "As the one fire entering into the universe expresses itself in various forms, even so that one Soul is expressing Itself in every soul and yet is infinitely more besides." Do you not see whither science is tending? The Hindu nation proceeded through the study of the mind, through metaphysics and logic. The European nations start from external nature, and now they too are coming to the same results. We find that, searching through the mind, we at last come to that Oneness, that Universal One, the Internal Soul of everything, the Essence and Reality of everything, the Ever Free, the Ever Blissful, the Ever Existing. Through material science we come to a similar oneness. Science today is telling us that all things are but manifestations of one energy, which is the sum total of everything that exists, and the trend of humanity is towards freedom and not towards bondage. Why should men be moral? Because through morality is the path towards freedom, and immorality leads to bondage.

Another peculiarity of the Advaita system is that from its very start it has been non-destructive. This is its glory, that it has the boldness to preach: "Do not disturb the faith of any, even of those who through ignorance have attached themselves to lower forms of worship." That is what it says: Do not disturb, but help everyone to get higher and higher; include all humanity. This philosophy preaches a God who is the sum total of all things. If you seek a universal religion which can apply to everyone, that religion must not be composed of only specific parts, but it must always be the sum total and include all degrees of religious development. This idea is not clearly found in other religious systems. They represent only parts struggling to attain to the whole. The existence of the part is only for this purpose.

So, from the very first, Advaita had no antagonism against the various sects existing in India. There are dualists existing today, and their number is by far the largest in India, because dualism naturally appeals to less educated minds. It is a very convenient, natural, common-sense explanation of the universe. But with these dualists Advaita has no quarrel. The dualist thinks that God is outside the universe, somewhere in heaven, and the Advaitist, that He is his own Soul and that it would be blasphemy to call Him anything more distant. Any idea of separation would be terrible. He is the nearest of the near. There is no word in any language to express this nearness, except the word Oneness. With any other idea the Advaitist is not satisfied, just as the dualist is shocked with the concept of Advaita and thinks it blasphemous. At the same time the Advaitist knows that these other ideas must remain; so he has no quarrel with the dualist, who is also on the right road. From his own standpoint the dualist has to see the many; it is a constitutional necessity of his standpoint; let him have it. The Advaitist knows that whatever may be the dualist's theories, he is going to the same goal as he himself. There he differs entirely from the dualist, who is forced by his point of view to believe that all other views are wrong.

Dualists all the world over naturally believe in a Personal God who is purely anthropomorphic, who, like a great potentate in this world, is pleased with some and displeased with others. He is arbitrarily pleased with some people or races and showers blessings upon them. Naturally the dualist comes to the conclusion that God has favourites, and he hopes to be one of them. You will find that in almost every religion is the idea: "We are the favourites of our God, and only by believing as we do, can you be taken into favour with Him." Some dualists are so narrow as to insist that only the few that have been predestined to the favour of God can be saved; the rest may try ever so hard, but they cannot be accepted. I challenge you to show me one dualistic religion which has not more or less of this exclusiveness. And therefore, in the nature of things, dualistic religions are bound to fight and quarrel with each other, and this they have ever been doing. Again, these dualists win the popular favour by appealing to the vanity of the uneducated, who like to feel that they enjoy exclusive privileges.

The dualist thinks you cannot be moral until you have a God with a rod in His hand, ready to punish you. The unthinking masses are generally dualists, and they, poor fellows, have been persecuted for thousands of years in every country; and their idea of salvation is, therefore, freedom from the fear of punishment.

But we find that the best and the greatest men that have been born in the world have worked with a high impersonal idea. It is the man who said, "I and my Father are one," whose power has descended unto millions. For two thousand years he has worked for good. And we know that the same man, because he was a non-dualist, was merciful to others. To the masses, who could not conceive of anything higher than a Personal God, he said, "Pray to your Father in heaven." To others, who could grasp a higher idea, he said, "I am the vine and ye are the branches." But to his disciples, to whom he revealed himself more fully, he proclaimed the highest truth, "I and my Father are one."

It was the great Buddha, who never cared for the dualist gods and who has been called an atheist and materialist, who yet was ready to give up his body for a poor goat. That man set in motion the highest moral ideas any nation can have. Wherever there is a moral code, it is a ray of light from that man.

We cannot force the great hearts of the world into narrow limits and keep them there, especially at this time in the history of humanity, when there is a degree of intellectual development such as was never dreamt of even a hundred years ago, when a wave of scientific knowledge has arisen which nobody, even fifty years ago, would have dreamt of. By trying to force people into narrow limits you degrade them into animals and unthinking masses. You kill their moral life. What is now wanted is a combination of the greatest heart with the highest intellectuality, of infinite love with infinite knowledge. The Vedāntist gives no other attributes to God except these three: Infinite Existence, Infinite Knowledge, and Infinite Bliss; and he regards these three as one.

Existence without Knowledge and Love cannot be; Knowledge without Love, and Love without Knowledge, cannot be. What we want is the harmony of Existence, Knowledge, and Bliss Infinite. For that is our goal. We want harmony, not one-sided development. And it is possible to have the intellect of a Śankara with the heart of a Buddha. I hope we shall all struggle to attain to that blessed combination.

GOD IN EVERYTHING

(Delivered in London, October 27, 1896)

WE ARE AWARE that the greater portion of our life must of necessity be filled with evil, however we may resist it, and that this mass of evil is practically infinite for us. We have been struggling to remedy this since the beginning of time; yet everything remains very much the same. The more we discover remedies, the more we find ourselves beset by subtler evils. We have also seen that all religions propose a God as the one way of escaping these difficulties. All religions tell us that if we take the world as it is, as most practical people would advise us to do in this age, then nothing will be left to us but evil. They further assert that there is something beyond this world. This life of the five senses, life in the material world, is not all; it is only a small portion, and merely superficial. Behind and beyond is the Infinite, in which there is no more evil. Some people call It God, some Allah, some Jehovah, Jove, and so on. The Vedāntist calls It Brahman.

The first impression we get of the advice given by religion is that we had better terminate our existence. To the question as to how to cure the evils of life, the answer apparently is, Give up life. It reminds one of an old story. A mosquito settled on the head of a man, and a friend, wishing to kill the mosquito, gave it such a blow that he killed both man and mosquito. The remedy for evil seems to suggest a similar course of action. Life is indeed full of ills; the world is full of evil. That is a fact no one who is old enough to know the world can deny. But what is the remedy proposed by all the religions? That this world is nothing; beyond this world is something which is very real. Here comes the difficulty. The remedy seems to destroy everything. How can that be a remedy? Is there no way out, then?

Vedānta says that what all the religions declare is perfectly true, but it should be properly understood. Often it is misunderstood, because the religions are not very clear in their meaning. What we really want is head and heart combined. The heart is great indeed; it is through the heart that the great inspirations of life come. I would a hundred times rather have a little heart and no brains than be all brains and no heart. Life is possible, progress is possible, for him who has a heart; but he who has no heart and only brains dies of dryness. At the same time we know that he who is carried away by his heart alone has to undergo many ills; for now and then he is liable to tumble into pitfalls. The combination of heart and head is what we want. I do not mean that a man should compromise his heart for his brains or vice versa; but let everyone have an infinite amount of heart and feeling, and at the same time an infinite amount of reason. Is there any limit to what we want in this world? Is not the world

253

infinite? There is room for an infinite amount of feeling, and so also for an infinite amount of knowledge and reason. Let them come together without limit; let them run together, as it were, parallel with each other.

Most of the religions understand this fact, but the error into which they all seem to fall is the same: they are carried away by the heart, the feelings. There is evil in the world; give up the world—that is the great teaching, and the only teaching, no doubt. Give up the world. There cannot be two opinions: to understand the truth every one of us has to give up error. There cannot be two opinions: every one of us, in order to be good, must give up evil. There cannot be two opinions: every one of us, to have life, must give up what is death. And yet, what remains to us if this theory involves giving up the life of the senses, life as we know it? And what else do we mean by life? If we give this up, what remains?

We shall understand this better when, later on, we come to the more philosophical portions of Vedānta. But for the present I beg to state that in Vedānta alone we find a rational solution of the problem. Here I can only lay before you what Vedānta seeks to teach; and that is the deification of the world.

Vedānta does not in reality denounce the world. The ideal of renunciation nowhere attains such a height as in the teachings of Vedānta; but at the same time, no dry suicidal advice is intended. It really means deification of the world: giving up the world as we think of it, as we know it, as it appears to us, and knowing what it really is. Deify it; it is God alone.

We read at the commencement of one of the oldest of the Upanishads: "Whatever exists in this universe is to be covered with the Lord." We have to cover everything with the Lord Himself, not by a false sort of optimism, not by blinding our eyes to evil, but by really seeing God in everything. Thus we have to give up the world. And when the world is given up, what remains? God. What is meant? You can have your wife; you certainly do not have to abandon her; but you are to see God in your wife. Give up your children—what does that mean? To turn them out of doors, as some human brutes do in every country? Certainly not. That is diabolism; it is not religion. But see God in your children. So in everything. In life and in death, in happiness and in misery, the Lord is equally present. The whole world is full of the Lord. Open your eyes and see Him.

This is what Vedānta teaches: Give up the world which you have conjectured, because your conjecture was based upon a very partial experience, upon very poor reasoning, and upon your own weaknesses. Give it up. The world we have been thinking of so long, the world we have been clinging to so long, is a false world of our own creation. Give that up. Open your eyes and see that, as such, it never existed; it was a dream, māyā. What existed was the Lord Himself. It is He who is in the child, in the wife, and in the husband; it is He who is in the good and in the bad. He is in the sin and in the sinner; He is in life and in death.

A tremendous assertion indeed! Yet that is the theme which Vedānta wants to demonstrate, to teach, and to preach. This is just the opening theme.

We avoid the dangers of life and its evils by seeing God in everything. Do not desire anything. What makes us miserable? The cause of all the miseries from which we suffer is desire. You desire something, and the desire is not fulfilled; the result is distress. If there is no desire, there is no suffering. But here, too, there is the danger of my being misunderstood. So it is necessary to explain what I mean by giving up desire and becoming free from all misery. The walls have no desires and they never suffer. True, but they never evolve. This chair has no desires; it never suffers; but it is always a chair. There is a glory in happiness; there is a glory in suffering. If I may say so, there is a utility in evil too. The great lesson in misery we all know. There are hundreds of things we have done in our lives which we wish we had never done, but which, at the same time, have been great teachers. As for me, I am glad I have done something good and many things bad; glad I have done something right, and glad I have committed many errors; because every one of them has been a great lesson. I, as I am now, am the resultant of all I have done, all I have thought. Every action and thought have had their effect, and these effects are the sum total of my progress.

We all understand that desires are wrong; but what is meant by giving up desires? How could life go on? It would be the same suicidal advice, killing the desire and the man too. The solution is this: not that you should not have property, not that you should not have things which are necessary and even things which are luxuries—have all that you want, and more; only know the truth about property: that it does not belong to anybody. Have no idea of proprietorship, possession. You are not anybody, nor am I anybody, nor is anyone else. All belong to the Lord. The opening verse of the Iśa Upanishad tells us to cover everything with the Lord. God is in the wealth that you enjoy. He is in the desire that rises in your mind. He is in the things you buy to satisfy your desire; He is in your beautiful attire, in your beautiful ornaments. This is the line of thought. All will be metamorphosed as soon as you begin to see things in that light. If you put God in your every movement, in your conversation, in your form, in everything, the whole scene will change, and the world, instead of appearing as one of woe and misery, will become a heaven.

"The kingdom of heaven is within you," says Jesus. So says Vedānta and every great teacher. "He that hath eyes to see, let him see, and he that hath ears to hear, let him hear." Vedānta proves that the truth for which we have been searching all this time is present now and was all the time with us. In our ignorance we thought we had lost it, and went about the world crying and weeping, struggling to find the truth, while all along it was dwelling in our own hearts. There alone can we find it.

If we understand the giving up of the world in its old, crude sense, then it would come to this: that we must not work—that we must be idle, sitting like lumps of earth, neither thinking nor doing anything—but must become fatalists, driven about by every circumstance, ordered about by the laws of nature, drifting from place to place. That would be the result. But that is not what is meant. We must work. Ordinary men work, driven by false desires—what do they know of work? If a man is impelled by his impulses, desires, and senses, what does he know about work? He works who is not impelled by his own desires, by any selfishness whatsoever. He works who has no ulterior motive in view. He works who has nothing to gain from work.

Who enjoys a picture—the seller or the seer? The seller is busy with his

accounts, computing what his gain will be, how much profit he will realize from
the picture. His brain is full of that. He is looking at the hammer and watching
the bids. He is intent on hearing how fast the bids are rising. That man is
enjoying the picture who has gone there without any intention of buying or
selling. He looks at the picture and enjoys it. So this whole universe is a picture,
and when these desires have vanished, men will enjoy the world; then this
buying and selling and these foolish ideas of possession will be ended. The
money-lender gone, the buyer gone, the seller gone, this world remains a
picture, a beautiful painting.

I have never read of any more beautiful conception of God than the following: "He is the Great Poet, the Ancient Poet. The whole universe is His poem,
coming in verses and rhymes and rhythms, written in Infinite Bliss." When we
have given up desires, then alone shall we be able to read and enjoy this universe
of God. Then everything will become deified. Nooks and corners, by-ways and
shady places, which we thought dark and unholy, will all be deified. They will
all reveal their true nature, and we shall smile at ourselves and think that all
this weeping and crying has been but child's play, and that we were only standing by, watching.

So do your work, says Vedānta. And it advises us how to work: by giving up—
giving up the apparent, illusive world. What is meant by that? Seeing God
everywhere. Thus do your work. Desire to live a hundred years; have all earthly
desires, if you wish, only deify them, convert them into heaven. Have the desire
to live a long life of helpfulness, of blissfulness and activity, on this earth. Thus
working, you will find the way out. There is no other way. If a man plunges
headlong into the foolish luxuries of the world without knowing the truth, he
has missed his footing; he cannot reach the goal. And if a man curses the world,
goes into a forest, mortifies his flesh, and kills himself little by little by starvation, makes his heart a barren waste, kills out all feeling, and becomes harsh,
stern, and dried up, that man also has missed the way. These are the two
extremes, the two mistakes at the two ends. Both have lost the way, both have
missed the goal.

So work, says Vedānta, putting God in everything and knowing Him to be
in everything. Work incessantly, holding life as something deified, as God Himself, and knowing that this is all we have to do, this is all we should ask for.
God is in everything; where else shall we go to find Him? He is already in every
work, in every thought, in every feeling. Knowing this, we must work. This is
the only way; there is no other. The effects of work will then not bind us. We
have seen that false desires are the cause of all the misery and evil we suffer
from; but when they are thus deified, purified, through God, they bring no evil,
they bring no misery. Those who have not learnt this secret will have to live in
a demoniacal world until they discover it. Many do not know what an infinite
mine of bliss is in them, around them, everywhere; they have not yet discovered
it. What is a demoniacal world? Ignorance, says Vedānta.

We are dying of thirst sitting on the bank of the mightiest river. We are
dying of hunger sitting near heaps of food. Here is the blissful universe; yet we
do not find it. We are in it all the time and we are always misjudging it. Religion proposes to find this out for us. The longing for this blissful universe is
in all hearts. It has been the search of all nations, it is the one goal of religion,

and this ideal is expressed in various languages in different religions. It is only the difference of language that makes all these apparent divergences: one expresses a thought in one way, another a little differently, yet perhaps each means exactly what the other is expressing in a different language.

More questions arise in connexion with this. It is very easy to talk. From my childhood I have been told that I should see God everywhere and in everything, and then I could really enjoy the world; but as soon as I mix with the world and get a few blows from it, the idea vanishes. I am walking in the street thinking that God is in every man, and a strong man comes along and gives me a push and I fall flat on the foot-path. Then I rise up quickly with clenched fist, the blood has rushed to my head, and my discrimination goes. Immediately I have become mad. Everything is forgotten; instead of encountering God I see the Devil. Ever since we were born we have been told to see God in all. Every religion teaches that: see God in everything and everywhere. Do you not remember that in the New Testament Christ says so? We have all been taught that; but it is when we come to the practical side that the difficulty begins.

You remember reading in *Aesop's Fables* about a fine stag looking at his form reflected in a lake and saying to his young one: "How powerful I am! Look at my splendid head; look at my limbs. How strong and muscular they are! And how swiftly I can run!" Then he hears the barking of dogs in the distance and immediately takes to his heels; and after he has run several miles he comes back panting. The young one says: "You just told me how strong you were. How was it that when the dogs barked you ran away?" "Yes, my son; but when the dogs bark all my confidence vanishes." Such is the case with us. We think highly of humanity, we feel ourselves strong and valiant, we make grand resolves; but when the dogs of trials and temptations bark, we are like the stag in the fable.

Then, if such is the case, what is the use of teaching all these things? There is the greatest use. The use is this: that perseverance will finally conquer. Nothing can be done in a day.

"This Self is first to be heard about, then to be thought upon, and then meditated upon." Everyone can see the sky; even the very worm crawling upon the earth sees the blue sky—but how very far away it is! So it is with our ideal. It is far away, no doubt, but at the same time we know that we must have it. We must have the highest ideal. Unfortunately, in this world the vast majority of persons are groping in the dark without any ideal at all. If a man with an ideal makes a thousand mistakes, I am sure that the man without an ideal makes fifty thousand. Therefore it is better to have an ideal. And this ideal we must hear about as much as we can, till it enters into our hearts, into our brains, into our very veins, till it tingles in every drop of our blood and permeates every pore in our body. We must meditate upon it. "Out of the fullness of the heart the mouth speaketh," and out of the fullness of the heart the hand works, too.

It is thought which is the propelling force in us. Fill the mind with the highest thoughts, hear them day after day, think them month after month. Never mind failures; they are quite natural. They are the beauty of life, these failures. What would life be without them? It would not be worth having if it were not for struggles. Where would be the poetry of life? Never mind the struggles, the mistakes. I never heard a cow tell a lie; but it is only a cow—

not a man. So never mind these failures, these little backslidings; hold to the ideal a thousand times, and if you fail a thousand times, make the attempt once more. The ideal of man is to see God in everything. But if you cannot see Him in everything, see Him in one thing, in that thing which you like best, and then see Him in another. So on you can go. There is infinite life before the soul. Take your time and you will achieve your end.

"He, the One, who vibrates more quickly than the mind, who attains more speed than the mind can ever attain, whom even the gods reach not, nor thought grasps—He moving, everything moves. In Him all exists. He is moving; He is also immovable. He is near and He is far. He is inside everything, He is outside everything—interpenetrating everything. Whoever sees in every being that same Ātman, and whoever sees everything in that Ātman, he never goes far from that Ātman. When a man sees all life and the whole universe in this Ātman, then he does not become secretive. There is no more delusion for him. Where is any more misery for him who sees this Oneness in the universe?"

This is another great theme of Vedānta, this Oneness of life, this Oneness of everything. We shall see how it demonstrates that all our misery comes through ignorance, and that this ignorance is nothing but the idea of manifoldness, of separation between man and man, between nation and nation, between earth and moon, between moon and sun. Out of this idea of separation between atom and atom comes all misery. But Vedānta says that this separation does not exist; it is not real. It is merely apparent, on the surface. In the heart of things there is unity. If you go below the surface you find that unity between man and man, between race and race, high and low, rich and poor, gods and men, men and animals. If you go deep enough all will be seen as only variations of the One.

He who has attained to this conception of Oneness has no more delusion. What can delude him? He knows the reality of everything, the secret of everything. Where is there any more misery for him? What does he desire? He has traced the reality of everything to the Lord, who is the Centre of all things, and who is Eternal Existence, Eternal Knowledge, Eternal Bliss. Neither death nor disease nor sorrow nor misery nor discontent is there. All is Perfect Union and Perfect Bliss. For whom should he mourn then? In reality there is no death, there is no misery; in reality there is no one to mourn for, no one to be sorry for. He has penetrated everything—He, the Pure One, the Formless, the Bodiless, the Stainless—He, the Knower—He, the Great Poet, the Self-existent —He who gives to everyone what he deserves.

They grope in darkness who worship this material world, the world that is produced out of ignorance, thinking of it as Existence; and those who live their whole lives in this world and never find anything better or higher are groping in still greater darkness. But he who knows the secret of nature, and also That which is beyond nature—through the help of nature he crosses death, and through the help of That which is beyond nature he enjoys Eternal Bliss.

"The door of the Truth is covered by a golden disc. Open it, O Nourisher! Remove it so that I who have been worshipping the Truth may behold It.

"O Nourisher, lone Traveller of the sky! Controller! O Sun, Offspring of Prajāpati! Gather Your rays; withdraw Your light. I would see, through Your grace, that form of Yours which is the fairest. I am indeed He, that Purusha, who dwells there."

REALIZATION

(Delivered in London, October 29, 1896)

I WILL READ TO YOU from one of the simplest but, I think, one of the most poetic of the Upanishads. It is called the *Katha Upanishad*. Some of you, perhaps, have read the translation by Sir Edwin Arnold, called *The Secret of Death*. In a previous lecture we saw how the inquiry which started with the origin of the world and the creation of the universe failed to obtain a satisfactory answer from without, and how it then turned inward. This book psychologically takes up that suggestion, questioning about the internal nature of man. It was first asked who created the external world and how it came into being. Now the question is: What is it in man which makes him live and move, and what becomes of it when he dies?

The first philosophers studied the material world and tried to reach the Ultimate through that. At best they found a Personal Governor of the universe, a human being immensely magnified, but yet to all intents and purposes a human being. But that could not be the whole truth; at best it could only be partial truth. We, as human beings, see this universe, and our God is our explanation of Him from our human reading of the universe. Suppose a cow were philosophical and religious: it would have a cow universe and a cow solution of the problem, and it would not be able to see God as we do. Suppose cats became philosophers: they would see a cat universe and have a cat solution of the problem of the universe, and a cat ruling it. So we see from this that our explanation of the universe is not the whole solution.

Neither does our explanation cover the whole of the universe. It would be a great mistake to accept that tremendously selfish position which man is likely to take. Such a solution of the problem of the universe as we get from the outside labours under this difficulty: that in the first place the universe we see is our own particular universe, our own view of reality. We cannot perceive reality through the senses; we cannot comprehend it. We only know the universe from the point of view of beings with five senses. Suppose we obtain another sense; the whole universe must change for us. Suppose we had a magnetic sense; it is quite possible that we might then find millions and millions of forces in existence which we do not now know and for which we have no present senses or feeling. Our senses are limited, very limited indeed, and within these limitations exists what we call our universe; and our God is the solution of that universe. But that cannot be the solution of the whole problem. Man cannot stop there. He is a thinking being and wants to find a solution which will comprehensively explain the whole of the universe. He wants to see a world which is at once the world of men and of gods and of all possible beings, and to find a solution which will explain all phenomena.

259

We see, then, that we must first find the universe which includes all worlds; we must find something which, by itself, is the material running through all these various planes of existence, whether we apprehend it through the senses or not. If we could possibly find something which we could know as the common property of the lower as well as of the higher worlds, then our problem would be solved. Even if by the sheer force of logic we could understand that there must be one basis of all existence, then our problem might approach some sort of solution. But this solution certainly cannot be obtained only through the world we see and know, because it is only a partial view of the whole.

Our only hope, then, lies in penetrating deeper. The early thinkers discovered that the farther they were from the centre, the more marked were the variations and differentiations, and that the nearer they approached the centre, the nearer they were to unity. The closer we are to the centre of a circle, the closer we are to the common ground in which all the radii meet; and the farther we are from the centre, the more divergent is our radial line from the others. The external world is far away from the centre, and so there is no common ground in it where all the phenomena of existence can meet. At best the external world is but one part of the whole of phenomena. There are other parts: the mental, the moral, and the intellectual—the various planes of existence—and to take up only one and find a solution of the whole out of that one is simply impossible. We first want, therefore, to find somewhere a centre from which, as it were, all the other planes of existence start; and standing there we should try to find a solution. That is the proposition. And where is that centre? It is within us. The ancient sages penetrated deeper and deeper until they found that in the innermost core of the human soul is the centre of the whole universe. All the planes gravitate towards that one point. That is the common ground, and standing there, alone, can we find a common solution. So the question as to who made this world is not very philosophical, nor does its solution amount to anything.

This the *Katha Upanishad* speaks of in very figurative language. There was in olden times a very rich man who performed a certain sacrifice which required that he should give away everything he had. Now this man was not sincere. He wanted to obtain the glory of having performed the sacrifice, but he was only giving things which were of no further use to him—old cows, barren, blind, and lame. He had a boy called Nachiketas. This boy saw that his father was not doing what was right, that he was breaking his vow; but he did not know what to say to him. In India the father and mother are living gods to their children. And so the boy approached the father with the greatest respect and humbly inquired of him: "Father, to whom are you going to give me? For your sacrifice requires that everything should be given away." The father was very much vexed at this question and replied: "What do you mean, boy? A father giving away his own son?" The boy asked the question a second and a third time, and then the angry father answered, "Thee I give unto Death." And the story goes on to say that the boy went to Yama, the god of death.

Yama was the first man who died. He went to heaven and became the governor of the pitris, or manes; all the good people who die go and live with him for a long time. He is a very pure and holy person, chaste and good, as his name Yama implies. So the boy went to Yama's world. But even gods are sometimes not at home, and for three days this boy had to wait there. After the third day Yama returned.

"O learned one," said Yama, "you have been waiting here three days without food, and you are a guest worthy of respect. Salutation to you, O brāhmin! May all be well with me! I am very sorry I was not at home. But for that I will make amends. Ask three boons, one for each day." And the boy said: "My first boon is that my father's anger against me may pass away; that he may be kind to me and recognize me when you allow me to depart." Yama granted this fully. The next boon he asked for was that he might know about a certain sacrifice which took people to heaven.

Now we have seen that the oldest idea in the Samhitā portion of the Vedas was only about heaven, where people had bright bodies and lived with the fathers. Gradually other ideas came, but they were not satisfying; there was still need for something higher. Living in heaven would not be very different from life in this world. At best it would be only a very healthy rich-man's life, with plenty of sense enjoyments and a sound body which knew no disease. It would be this material world, only a little more refined; and we have seen this difficulty: that the external, material world can never solve the problem. So also no heaven can solve it. If this world cannot solve the problem, no multiplication of this world can do so, because, as we must always remember, matter is only an infinitesimal part of the phenomenal universe.

The vast part of the phenomena which we actually see is not matter. For instance, in every moment of our life what a great part is played by thought and feeling, compared with the material phenomena outside! How vast is this internal world with its tremendous activity! Sense phenomena are very limited compared to it. The heaven solution commits this mistake: it insists that the whole of phenomena is only in touch, taste, sight, and so on. So this idea of heaven did not give full satisfaction to all. Yet Nachiketas asks, as the second boon, about some sacrifice through which people might attain to heaven. There was an idea in the Vedas that these sacrifices pleased the gods and took human beings to heaven.

In studying religions you will notice the fact that whatever is old becomes holy. For instance, our forefathers in India used to write on birch bark, but in time they learnt how to make paper. Yet birch bark is still looked upon as very holy. When the utensils in which they used to cook in ancient times were improved upon, the old ones became holy. And nowhere is this idea more kept up than in India. Old methods, which must be nine or ten thousand years old, such as rubbing two sticks together to make fire, are still followed. At the time of sacrifice no other method will do. So with the other branch of the Asiatic Āryans.[1] Their modern descendants still like to obtain fire from lightning, showing that they used to get fire in this way. Even when they learnt other customs, they kept up the old ones, which then became holy. So with the Hebrews. They used to write on parchment. They now write on paper, but

[1] Perhaps Swami Vivekananda referred to the ancient Persians, who formed a branch of the Āryans.

parchment is very holy. So with all nations. Every rite which you now consider holy was simply an old custom, and the Vedic sacrifices were of this nature. In course of time, as men found better methods of life, their ideas were much improved; still these old forms remained, and from time to time they were practised and received a holy significance.

Then a body of men made it their business to carry on these sacrifices. These were the priests, who speculated about the sacrifices; and the sacrifices became everything to them. The gods enjoyed the fragrance of the sacrifices, and it was considered that everything in this world could be got by the power of sacrifices. If certain oblations were made, certain hymns chanted, certain peculiar forms of altars made, the gods would grant everything.

So Nachiketas asked by what form of sacrifice a man could go to heaven. The second boon was also readily granted by Yama, who further promised that this particular sacrifice should henceforth be named after Nachiketas.

Then the third boon comes and with that the Upanishad proper begins. The boy said: "There is this difficulty: when a man dies some say that he is, and others, that he is not. Instructed by you I desire to understand this." Yama realized that the boy was asking about Self-Knowledge, which should be taught only to qualified students. Desirous of testing Nachiketas, he said: "The gods in ancient times were puzzled on this point. This subtle truth is not easy to understand. Choose some other boon, O Nachiketas. Do not press me on this point. Release me from my obligation to you."

But the boy was determined, and said: "What you have said, is true, O Death, that even the gods had doubts on this point, and it is no easy matter to understand. But I cannot obtain another expounder like you, and there is no other boon equal to this."

Death said: "Ask for sons and grandsons who will live one hundred years, many cattle, elephants, gold, and horses. Ask for an empire on this earth, and live as many years as you like. Or choose any other boon which you think equal to these—wealth and long life. Or be the king, O Nachiketas, of the wide earth. I will make you the enjoyer of all your desires. Ask for all those desires which are difficult to satisfy in the world: These heavenly maidens, with chariots and music, which are not to be obtained by man, are yours. Let them serve you, O Nachiketas; but do not question me about what comes after death."

Nachiketas said: "These are merely things of a day, O Death. They wear away the energy of all the sense-organs. Even the longest life is very short. These horses and chariots, dances and songs—let them remain with you. Man cannot be satisfied by wealth. Can we retain wealth for ever when we must some time face you? We shall live only so long as you desire. Only the boon which I have asked is desired by me."

Yama was pleased with this answer and said: "Perfection is one thing and enjoyment another. These two, having different ends, engage men differently. He who chooses perfection becomes pure. He who chooses enjoyment misses his true end. Both perfection and enjoyment present themselves to man. The wise man, having examined both, distinguishes one from the other; he chooses perfection as being superior to enjoyment. But the foolish man chooses enjoyment for the pleasure of his body. O Nachiketas, having thought upon these things which are only apparently desirable, you have wisely abandoned them." Death then proceeded to teach Nachiketas.

We now get a very advanced idea of renunciation and Vedic morality: Until a man has conquered the desire for enjoyment, the truth will not shine in him. So long as these vain desires of our senses are clamouring and, as it were, dragging us outward, every moment making us slaves to everything outside—to a little colour, a little taste, a little touch—notwithstanding all our pretensions, how can the truth express itself in our hearts?

Yama said: "That which is beyond never rises before the mind of a thoughtless child deluded by the folly of riches. 'This world exists, the other does not'—thinking thus he comes again and again under my power." To understand this truth is very difficult; many, even hearing it continually, do not understand it. For the speaker must be wonderful, and so must be the hearer. The teacher must be wonderful, and so must be the taught. Neither is the mind to be disturbed by vain argument; for it is no more a question of argument; it is a question of fact.

We have always heard that every religion insists on our having faith. We have been taught to believe blindly. Well, this idea of blind faith is objectionable, no doubt; but analysing it, we find that behind it is a very great truth. What it really means is what we read now. The mind is not to be ruffled by vain argument, because argument will not help us to know God. It is a question of fact and not of argument.

All argument and reasoning must be based upon certain perceptions. Without these there cannot be any argument. Reasoning is the method of comparison between certain facts which we have already perceived. If these perceived facts are not there already, there cannot be any reasoning. If this is true of external phenomena, why should it not be so of the internal? The chemist combines certain chemicals, and certain results are produced. This is a fact; you see it, sense it, and make that the basis on which to build all your chemical arguments. So with the physicists; so with all other scientists. All knowledge must stand on the perception of certain facts, and upon that we have to build our reasoning.

Yet curiously enough, the vast majority of men—especially modern men—, who are devoid of such perception, indulge in vain argument to understand religion. But we are told by the Upanishad not to disturb the mind by vain argument.

Religion is a question of fact, not of talk. We have to analyse our own souls and find what is there. We have to understand it and realize what is understood. That is religion. No amount of talk will make religion. So the question of whether there is a God or not can never be proved by argument; for the arguments are as much on one side as on the other. But if there is a God, He is in our own hearts. Have you ever seen Him? The question of whether this world exists or not has not yet been decided, and the debate between the idealists and the realists is endless. Yet we know that the world exists, that it goes on. We only change the meaning of the words. So it is with all the questions of life; we must come to facts.

There are certain religious facts which, as in external science, have to be perceived; and upon them religion is to be built. Of course, the extreme claim that you must believe every dogma of a religion is degrading to the human mind. The man who asks you to believe everything, degrades himself, and, if you believe, degrades you too. The sages of the world alone have the right to tell us that they have analysed their minds and have found these facts, and if we do the same we shall also believe, and not before. That is all there is in religion. But you must always remember this: that as a matter of fact ninety-nine and nine-tenths per cent of those who attack religion have never analysed their minds, have never struggled to get at the facts. So their arguments do not affect religion any more than the words of a blind man who cries out, "You are all fools to believe in the sun," would affect us.

This is one great idea to learn and to hold on to, this idea of realization. This turmoil and fight and difference in religions will cease only when we understand that religion is not in books and temples. It is in actual perception. Only the man who has actually perceived God and the soul is religious. There is no real difference between the highest ecclesiastical giant, who can talk by the volume, and the lowest, most ignorant materialist. We are all atheists; let us confess it. Mere intellectual assent does not make us religious.

Be he a Christian or a Mohammedan or a follower of any other religion in the world, any man who truly realizes the truth of the Sermon on the Mount will become perfect immediately. It is said that there are many millions of Christians in the world. But not one in twenty millions is a real Christian. So, in India, there are said to be three hundred millions of Vedāntists. But if there were one in a thousand who had actually realized religion, this world would soon be greatly changed. We are all atheists, and yet we try to fight the man who admits being one. We are all in the dark; religion is to us mere intellectual assent, mere talk, mere nothing.

We often consider a man religious who can talk well. But this is not religion. "Wonderful methods of joining words, rhetorical powers, and explaining the texts of the books in various ways," says Śankarāchārya, "are only for the enjoyment of the learned; they are not religion." Religion begins only when actual realization begins in our own souls. That will be the dawn of religion; and then alone shall we be moral. Now we are not much more moral than the animals. We are only held down by the whips of society. If society said today, "I will not punish you if you steal," we should just make a rush for each other's property. It is the policeman who makes us moral. It is social opinion that makes us moral, but really we are little better than the animals. We understand how much this is so, in the secret of our own hearts. So let us not be hypocrites. Let us confess that we are not religious and have no right to look down on others. We are all brothers, and we shall be truly moral when we have realized religion.

If you have seen a certain country and a man forces you to say you have not seen it, still in your heart of hearts you know you have. So when you see religion and God in a more intense sense than you see this external world, nothing will be able to shake your belief. Then you will have real faith. That is what is meant by the words in your Gospel, "If ye have faith as a grain of mustard seed." Then you will know the truth because you have become the truth.

This is the watchword of Vedānta: Realize religion; no talking will do. But it is done with great difficulty. He has hidden Himself inside the atom, this Ancient One who resides in the inmost recess of every human heart. The sages realized Him through the power of introspection and went beyond both joy and misery, beyond what we call virtue and vice, beyond good and bad deeds, beyond being and non-being. He who has seen Him has seen Reality.

But what, then, about heaven? Heaven is the idea of happiness minus unhappiness. That is to say, what we want is the joys of this life minus its sorrows. This is a very good idea, no doubt; it comes naturally; but it is a mistake throughout, because there is no such thing as absolute good nor any such thing as absolute evil. You have all heard of that rich man in Rome who learnt one day that he had only about a million pounds of his property left. He said, "What shall I do tomorrow?" and forthwith committed suicide. A million pounds were poverty to him.

What is joy and what is sorrow? They are vanishing entities, continually vanishing. When I was a child I thought if I could be a cabman it would be the very acme of happiness for me to drive about. I do not think so now. To what joy will you cling? This is the one point we must all try to understand, and it is one of the last superstitions to leave us. Everyone's idea of pleasure is different. I have seen a man who is not happy unless he swallows a lump of opium every day. He may dream of a heaven where the land is made of opium. That would be a very bad heaven for me. Again and again in Arabian poetry we read of a heaven with beautiful gardens through which rivers run. I have lived much of my life in a country where there is too much water; many villages are flooded and thousands of lives are sacrificed every year. So my heaven would not have gardens through which rivers flow; I would have a land where very little rain falls. Our pleasures are always changing. If a young man dreams of heaven, he dreams of a heaven where he will have a beautiful wife. When that same man becomes old he does not want a wife. It is our necessities which make our heaven, and the heaven changes with the change of our necessities. If we had a heaven like that desired by those to whom sense enjoyment is the very end of existence, then we would not progress. That would be the most terrible curse we could pronounce on the soul.

Is this all we can come to?—a little weeping and dancing, and then to die like a dog! What a curse you pronounce on the head of humanity when you long for these things! That is what you do when you cry after the joys of this world; for you do not know what true joy is. What philosophy insists on is, not to give up joys, but to know what joy really is.

The old Norwegian heaven was a tremendous fighting-place, where all sat before Odin; they had a wild-boar hunt and then they went to war and slashed each other to pieces. But in some way or other, after a few hours of such fighting, the wounds all healed up and they went into a hall where the boar had been roasted, and had a carousal. And then the wild boar took form again, ready to be hunted the next day. That is much the same thing as our heaven— not a whit worse; only our ideas may be a little more refined. We want to hunt wild boars and get to a place where all our enjoyments will continue, just as the Norwegian imagined that the wild boar was hunted and eaten every day and recovered the next day.

Now, philosophy insists that there is a joy which is absolute, which never changes. That joy cannot be like the joys and pleasures we have in this life, and yet Vedānta shows that everything that is joyful in this life is but a particle of that real joy, because that is the only joy there is. Every moment we are really enjoying the Absolute Bliss, though it is covered up, misunderstood, and caricatured. Wherever there is any blessing, blissfulness, or joy, even the joy of the thief in stealing, it is that Absolute Bliss; only it is obscured, muddled up, as it were, with all sorts of extraneous conditions, and misunderstood.

But to understand that, we have to go through negation, and then the positive side will begin. We have to give up ignorance and all that is false, and then the truth will begin to reveal itself to us. When we have grasped the truth, things which we gave up at first will take new shape and form, will appear to us in a new light and become deified. They will be totally sublimated, and then we shall understand them in their true light. But to understand them we have first to get a glimpse of the truth; we must give them up at first, and then we shall get them back again, deified. We have to give up all our miseries and sorrows, all our little joys.

"That which all the Vedas declare, which is aimed at by all penances, seeking which men lead lives of continence, I will tell you in one word. It is Om." You will find this word Om praised very much in the Vedas, and it is held to be very sacred.

Now Yama answers the question, "What becomes of a man when the body dies?" "The knowing Self never dies, is never born. It arises from nothing, and nothing arises from It. Unborn, eternal, everlasting, this Self can never be destroyed with the destruction of the body. If the slayer thinks he can slay, or if the slain thinks he is slain, they both do not know the truth; for the Self neither slays nor is slain." A most tremendous conclusion.

I should like to draw your attention to the adjective in the first line, which is "knowing." As we proceed we shall find that the ideal of Vedānta is that all wisdom and all purity are in the soul already—dimly expressed or better expressed, that is all the difference.

The differences between man and man, and between all things in the whole creation, are not in kind but only in degree. The background, the reality, of everyone is that same eternal, ever blessed, ever pure, and ever perfect One. It is the Ātman, the Soul, in the saint and the sinner, in the happy and the miserable, in the beautiful and the ugly, in men and in animals. It is the same throughout. It is the Shining One. The differences are caused by the degree of expression. In some It is expressed more, in others less; but these differences of expression have no effect upon the Ātman. If one man's dress shows more of his body than another's, it does not make any difference in their bodies; the difference is in their dress.

We had better remember here that throughout the Vedānta philosophy there are no such things as good and bad; they are not two different things; the same thing is good or bad, and the difference is only in degree. The very thing I call pleasurable today, tomorrow, under other circumstances, I may call pain. The fire that warms us can also consume us; it is not the fault of the fire. Thus, the Soul being pure and perfect, the man who does evil is giving the lie unto himself; he does not know his own nature. Even in the murderer the Pure Soul exists. Because of ignorance he does not manifest It; he has covered It up. Nor in the man who thinks that he is killed is the Soul killed; It is eternal. It can never be killed, never destroyed. "Infinitely smaller than the smallest, infinitely larger than the largest, this Lord of all is present in the depths of every human heart. The sinless, bereft of all misery, see Him through the mercy of the Lord. Bodiless, yet dwelling in the body; spaceless, yet seeming to occupy space; infinite, omnipresent—knowing the Soul to be such, the sages never are miserable."

"This Ātman is not to be realized by the power of speech, nor by a vast intellect, nor by the study of the Vedas." This is a very bold utterance. As I told you before, the sages were very bold thinkers and never stopped at anything. You will remember that in India these Vedas are regarded in a much higher light even than that in which the Bible is regarded by the Christians. Your idea of revelation is that it comes through a man inspired by God; but in India the idea is that things exist because they are mentioned in the Vedas. In and through the Vedas the whole creation has come. All that is called knowledge is in the Vedas. Every word is sacred and eternal, eternal as the Soul, without beginning and without end. The whole of the Creator's mind is in this book, as it were. That is the light in which the Vedas are held. Why is this thing moral? Because the Vedas say so. Why is that thing immoral? Because the Vedas say so. In spite of that, look at the boldness of these sages who proclaimed that the truth is not to be found by much study of the Vedas. "With whom the Lord is pleased— to that man He expresses Himself."

But then the objection may be advanced that this is something like partisanship. But Yama explains: "Those who are evil-doers, whose minds are not peaceful, can never see the Light. It is to those who are true in heart, pure in deed, whose senses are controlled, that this Self manifests Itself."

Here is a beautiful figure. Picture the embodied self to be the rider and this body the chariot, the intellect to be the charioteer, the mind the reins, and the senses the horses. He whose horses are well broken in and whose reins are strong and kept well in the hands of the charioteer (the intellect) reaches the goal, which is the supreme state of Him, the Omnipresent. But the man whose horses are not controlled, and whose reins are not well managed, goes to destruction.

This Ātman, hidden in all beings, does not manifest Itself to the eyes or the senses; but those whose minds have become purified and refined realize It. Beyond all sound and all sight, beyond form, immutable, beyond all taste and touch, infinite, without beginning and without end, even beyond nature, and unchangeable—he who thus realizes It frees himself from the jaws of death. But it is very difficult. It is like walking on the edge of a razor; the way is long and perilous—but struggle on, do not despair. Awake, arise, and stop not till the goal is reached.

The one central idea throughout all the Upanishads is that of realization.

About this a great many questions will arise from time to time, and especially to the modern man. There will be the question of utility; there will be various other questions; but in all of them we shall find that we are prompted by our past associations. It is association of ideas that has such a tremendous power over our minds. To those who from childhood have always heard of a Personal God and the individuality of the soul, the ideas of the Upanishads will of course appear very stern and harsh; but if they listen to them and think them over, they will become part of their lives and will no longer frighten them.

The great question that generally arises is the utility of this philosophy. To that there can be only one answer: If on utilitarian grounds it is good for men to seek pleasure, why should not those whose pleasure is in religious speculation seek that? Because sense enjoyments please many, they seek them; but there may be others whom they do not please, who want higher enjoyment. The dog's pleasure is only in eating and drinking. The dog cannot understand the pleasure of the scientist who gives up everything and perhaps dwells on the top of a mountain to observe the position of certain stars. The dog may smile at him and think he is a madman. Perhaps this poor scientist never even had money enough to marry, and lives very simply. Maybe the dog laughs at him. But the scientist says: "My dear dog, your pleasure is only in the senses, which you enjoy and beyond which you know nothing. But I too enjoy my pleasure, and if you have the right to seek your pleasure in your own way, so have I, in mine."

Our mistake is that we want to tie the whole world down to our own plane of thought and make our mind the measure of the whole universe. To you the old sense enjoyments are perhaps the greatest pleasure; but it is not necessary that my pleasure should be the same, and when you insist upon that, I differ with you. That is the difference between the worldly utilitarian and the religious man. The first man says: "See how happy I am. I get money but do not bother my head about religion. It is unsearchable, and I am happy without it." So far, so good—good for all utilitarians. But this world is terrible. If a man gets happiness in any way except by injuring his fellow beings, God speed him; but when this man comes to me and says: "You too must do these things. You will be a fool if you do not," I say: "You are wrong, because the very things which are pleasurable to you have not the slightest attraction for me. If I had to go after a few handfuls of gold, my life would not be worth living. I should die." That is the answer the religious man should make. The fact is that religion is only possible for those who have finished with these lower things. We must have our own experiences, must have our full run. It is only when we have finished this run that the other world opens up.

The enjoyments of the senses sometimes assume another phase, which is dangerous and tempting. You will always hear the idea—in every religion and from the earliest times—that a time will come when all the miseries of life will cease and only its joys and pleasures will remain, and this earth will become a heaven. That I do not believe. This earth will always remain the same. It is a most terrible thing to say; yet I do not see my way out of it. The misery in the world is like chronic rheumatism in the body: drive it from one part and it goes to another; drive it from there and you will feel it somewhere else; whatever you do, it is still there. In olden times people lived in forests and ate each other;

in modern times they do not eat each other's flesh, but they cheat each other. Whole countries and cities are ruined by cheating. That does not show much progress. I do not see that what you call progress in the world is other than the multiplication of desires. If one thing is obvious to me it is this: that desires bring all our misery. It is the state of the beggar, who is always begging for something; unable to see anything without wishing to possess it, he is always longing, longing for more. If the power to satisfy our desires increases in arithmetical progression, our desires increase in geometrical progression.

The sum total of happiness and misery in this world is the same throughout. If a wave rises in the ocean it makes a hollow somewhere. If happiness comes to one man unhappiness comes to another, or perhaps to some animal. Men are increasing in numbers and some animals are decreasing; we are killing them off and taking their land; we are taking all means of sustenance from them. How can we say, then, that happiness is increasing? The strong race eats up the weaker, but do you think that the strong race will be very happy? No; its members will begin to kill each other. I do not see, on practical grounds, how this world can become a heaven. The facts are against it. On theoretical grounds, also, I see that it cannot be.

Perfection is always in the Infinite. We are infinite already and we are trying to manifest our infinity. You and I and all beings are trying to manifest it. So far it is all right. But from this fact some German philosophers have started the peculiar theory that this manifestation will become higher and higher until we attain perfect manifestation, until we have become perfect beings. What is meant by perfect manifestation? Perfection means infinity, and manifestation means limit, and so it means that we shall become unlimited limiteds, which is self-contradictory. Such a theory may please children, but it poisons their minds with lies and is very bad for religion. But we know that this world is a degradation, that man is a degradation of God, and that Adam fell. There is no religion today that does not teach that man is a degradation. We have been degraded down to the animal and are now going up, to emerge out of this bondage. But we shall never be able to entirely manifest the Infinite here. We shall struggle hard, but there will come a time when we shall find that it is impossible to be perfect here, while we are bound by the senses. And then the march back to our original state of infinity will be sounded.

This is renunciation. We shall have to get out of the difficulty by reversing the process by which we got in, and then morality and charity will begin. What is the watchword of all ethical codes? "Not I, but thou." What is this "I"? The Infinite is trying to manifest itself in the outside world. This little "I" is the result, and it will have to go back and join the Infinite, its own nature. Every time you say, "Not I, my brother, but thou," you are trying to go back, and every time you say, "I and not thou," you take the false step of trying to manifest the Infinite through the sense world. That brings struggles and evils into the world; but after a time renunciation must come, eternal renunciation. The little "I" is dead and gone. Why care so much for this little life? All these vain desires of living and enjoying this life, here or in some other place, bring death.

If we are developed from animals, the animals also may be degraded men.

How do you know it is not so? You have seen that the proof of evolution is simply this: you find a series of bodies, from the lowest to the highest, rising in a gradually ascending scale. But from that how can you insist that it is always from the lower upwards, and never from the higher downwards? The argument applies both ways, and if anything is true, I believe it is that the series is repeating itself in going up and down. How can you have evolution without involution? Our struggle for the higher life shows that we have been degraded from a high state. It must be so; only it may vary as to details. I always cling to the idea set forth with one voice by Christ, Buddha, and Vedānta, that we must all come to perfection in time, but only by giving up this imperfection.

This world is nothing. It is at best only a hideous caricature, a shadow of Reality. We must go to that Reality. Renunciation will take us to It. Renunciation is the very basis of our true life: every moment of goodness and real life that we enjoy is when we do not think of ourselves. This little separate self must die. Then we shall find that we are in the Real, and that Reality is God, and He is our own true nature, and He is always in us and with us. Let us live in Him and stand in Him; it is the only joyful state of existence. Life on the plane of the Spirit is the only life. Let us all try to attain to this realization.

UNITY IN DIVERSITY

(Delivered in London, November 3, 1896)

"THE SELF-EXISTENT ONE projected the senses outward and therefore a man looks outward, not within himself. A certain wise one, desiring immortality, turned the senses inward and perceived the Self within." As I have already said, the first inquiry in the Vedas was concerning outward things; and then a new idea came: that the reality of things is not to be found in the external world; it is to be found not by looking outward, but by turning the eyes, as it is expressed literally, inward. And the word used for the Soul is very significant: it is He who has gone inward, the innermost reality of our being, the heart centre, the core from which, as it were, everything comes out; the central Sun, of which the mind, the body, the sense-organs, and everything else that we have are but rays going outward.

"Men of childish intellect, ignorant persons, run after desires, which are external, and enter the trap of far-reaching death; but the wise, understanding immortality, never seek the Eternal in this life of finite things." The same idea is here made clear, that in this external world, which is full of finite things, it is impossible to see and find the Infinite. The Infinite must be sought in that alone which is infinite, and the only thing infinite about us is that which is within us, our own Soul. Neither the body nor the mind, not even our thoughts nor the world we see around us, is infinite. The Seer, He to whom they all belong, the Soul of man, He who is awake in the internal man, alone is infinite; and to seek the infinite Cause of this whole universe we must go *there*. In the infinite Soul alone can we find It.

"What is here is there too, and what is there is also here. He who sees the manifold goes from death to death."

We have seen how at first there was the desire to go to heaven. When the ancient Āryans became dissatisfied with the world around them, they naturally thought that after death they would go to some place where there would be all happiness without any misery; these places they called svargas—the word may be translated as heavens—where there would be joy for ever; the body would become perfect, and also the mind, and there they would live with their forefathers.

But as soon as philosophy came men found that this was impossible and absurd. The very idea of something infinite in any place would be a contradiction in terms, as a place must begin and continue in time. Therefore they had to give up that idea. They found out that the gods who lived in these heavens were human beings who through their good works on earth had become gods, and that these various divinities were different states, different positions.

271

None of the gods spoken of in the Vedas are permanent individuals. For instance, Indra and Varuna are not the names of certain persons, but the names of positions as governors and so on. The Indra who lived before is not the same person as the Indra of the present day; he has passed away, and another man from earth has filled his place. So with all the other gods. These are certain positions, which are filled successively by human souls who have raised themselves to the condition of gods; and yet even they die.

In the old Rig-Veda we find the word *immortality* used with regard to these gods; but later it was dropped entirely, for it was found that true immortality, which is beyond time and space, cannot be spoken of with regard to any physical form, however subtle, however fine it may be. It must have had a beginning in time and space; for the necessary factors that enter into the make-up of form are in space. Try to think of having form without space. It is impossible. Space is one of the materials, as it were, which make up the form, and this form is continually changing. Space and time are in māyā, and this idea is expressed in the line: "What is here is there too." If there are these gods they must be bound by the same laws that apply here, and all these laws involve destruction and renewal again and again. These laws are moulding matter into different forms and crushing them out again. Everything born must die; and so if there are heavens, the same laws must hold good there.

In this world we find that all happiness is followed by misery as its shadow. Life has its shadow, death. They must go together, because they are not contradictory, not two separate existences, but different manifestations of the same unit, which appears as both life and death, sorrow and happiness, good and evil. The dualistic conception that good and evil are two separate entities, and that they both continue eternally, is absurd on the face of it. They are the diverse manifestations of one and the same fact, one time appearing as bad and another time as good. The difference is not one of kind but only of degree. They differ from each other in intensity.

We find, as a matter of fact, that the same nerve systems carry good and bad sensations alike, and when the nerves are injured neither sensation comes to us. If a certain nerve is paralysed we do not get the pleasurable feelings that used to come along that wire, and at the same time we do not get the painful feelings either. They are not essentially different. Again, the same thing produces pleasure and pain at different times of life. The same phenomenon will produce pleasure in one and pain in another. The eating of meat produces pleasure in a man, but pain in the animal which is eaten. There has never been anything which gives pleasure to all alike. Some are pleased, others displeased. So it will go on.

Therefore this duality of existence is denied. And what follows? I told you in my last lecture that we can never ultimately have everything good on this earth and nothing bad. It may have disappointed and frightened some of you, but I cannot help it and I am open to conviction if I am shown the contrary; but until that can be proved to me, I cannot accept it.

The general argument against my statement, and apparently a very convincing one, is that in the course of evolution all that is evil in what we see around us is gradually being eliminated, and that if this process of elimination continues for millions of years, a time will come when all the evil will have been extirpated and the good alone will remain. This is apparently a very sound argument. Would to God it were true! But there is a fallacy in it and it is this: It takes for granted that both good and evil are entities that are eternally fixed. It takes for granted that there is a definite mass of evil which may be represented by a hundred, and likewise a definite mass of good, and that this mass of evil is being diminished every day, leaving only the good. But is it so? The history of the world shows that evil, as well as good, is a continuously increasing quantity. Take the lowest man. He lives in the forest. His power of enjoyment is very small, and so also is his power to suffer. His misery is entirely on the sense plane. If he does not get plenty of food he is miserable; but give him plenty of food and freedom to rove and to hunt, and he is perfectly happy. His happiness is only in the senses, and so is his misery. But if that man's knowledge increases, his happiness too will increase, his intellect will develop, and his sense enjoyment will evolve into intellectual enjoyment. He will feel pleasure in reading a beautiful poem, and a mathematical problem will be of absorbing interest to him. But along with this the finer nerves will become more and more susceptible to the miseries of mental pain, about which the savage does not think.

Take another very simple illustration. In certain parts of Tibet there is no marriage as we understand it, and therefore no jealousy; yet we know that marriage is a much higher state. These Tibetans have not known the wonderful joy of chastity, the happiness of being blessed with a chaste, virtuous wife or a chaste, virtuous husband. These people cannot feel that. And similarly they do not feel the intense jealousy of the chaste wife or husband, or the misery caused by unfaithfulness on either side, with all the heart-burnings and sorrows which believers in chastity experience. On one side they gain in happiness, but on the other they suffer misery too.

Take your country, which is the richest in the world, and which is more luxurious than any other, and see how intense is the misery, how much more insanity you have, compared with other races, only because the desires are so keen. A man must keep up a high standard of living, and the amount of money he spends in one year would be a fortune to a man in India. You cannot preach to an Englishman about simple living, because society demands so much of him. The wheel of society is rolling on; it stops not for the widows' tears or the orphans' wails. This is the state of things everywhere. Your power of enjoyment is developed; your society is very much more beautiful than some others. You have so many more things to enjoy. But those who have fewer have much less misery.

You can argue thus throughout. The higher the ideal you have, the greater is your enjoyment and also the more profound your misery. One is like the shadow of the other. That the evils are being eliminated may be true, but if so, the good also must be dying out. But are not the evils multiplying fast, and the good diminishing, if I may so put it? If good increases in arithmetical proportion, evil increases in geometrical proportion. And this is māyā.

This is neither optimism nor pessimism. Vedānta does not take the position that this world is only a miserable one. That would be untrue. On the other hand, it would also be a mistake to say that this world is full of happiness and blessings. So it is useless to tell children that this world is all good, all flowers and milk and honey—which is what we have all dreamt. At the same time it is erroneous to think that because one man has suffered more than another, all is evil. It is this duality, this play of good and evil, that makes our world of experience. Nevertheless, Vedānta says, we should not think that good and evil are two separate entities; for they are one and the same thing appearing in different degrees and in different guises and producing differences of feeling in the same mind. So the first thought of Vedānta is the finding of unity in the external—the One Existence manifesting Itself, however differently It may appear in Its manifestations.

Think of the old theory of the Persians: two gods creating this world, the good god doing everything that is good, and the bad one everything that is bad. On the very face of it, you see the absurdity; for if it is carried out, every law of nature must have two parts, one of which is manipulated by one god, who then goes away while the other god manipulates the other part. There the difficulty comes: both are working in the same world, and these two gods keep in harmony by injuring one portion and doing good to another. This is a crude case, of course, the crudest way of expressing the duality of existence. But take the more advanced, the more abstract theory, that this world is partly good and partly bad. This also is absurd, arguing from the same standpoint. It is the same force that provides us with our food and that kills many through accidents or misadventures.

We find, then, that this world is neither good nor evil; it is a mixture of both. And as we go on we shall see that Vedānta takes the whole blame away from nature and puts it upon our own shoulders. At the same time Vedānta shows the way out—but not by the denial of evil, because it boldly analyses the fact as it is and does not seek to conceal anything. It is not a creed of hopelessness; it is not agnosticism. It has found out a solution of the problem of good and evil, and has placed that solution on such adamantine foundations that it does not gag men, as if they were mere children, and blind their eyes with something which is untrue and which they will find out about in a few days.

I remember when I was young, a young man's father died and left him poorly off, with a large family to support, and he found that his father's friends were unwilling to help him. He had a conversation with a clergyman, who offered this consolation, "Oh, it is all good; all is done for our good." That is the old method of trying to put a piece of gold-leaf on an old sore. It is a confession of weakness, of ignorance. The young man went away, and six months afterwards a son was born to the clergyman, and he gave a thanksgiving party to which the young man was invited. The clergyman prayed, "Thank God for His mercies." And the young man stood up and said, "Stop! This is all misery." The clergyman asked, "Why?" "Because when my father died you said it was good, though apparently evil; so now this is apparently good, but really evil." Is that the way to cure the misery of the world? Do not try to patch it up; nothing will cure this world. Go beyond it.

This is a world of good and evil. Wherever there is good, evil follows; but beyond and behind all these manifestations, all these contradictions, Vedānta finds Unity; and it says, "Give up what is evil and give up what is good." What then remains? Behind good and evil stands something which is yours, the real "you"—beyond every evil, and beyond every good too—and it is that which is manifesting itself as good and evil.

Know that first; then, and then alone, will you be a true optimist, and not before; for then you will be able to control everything. Control these manifestations and you will be at liberty to manifest the real "you." First be master of yourself, stand up and be free, go beyond the pale of these laws; for these laws do not absolutely govern you; they are only part of your being. First find out that you are not the slave of nature, never were and never will be; that this nature, infinite as you may think it, is only finite, a drop in the ocean, and your Soul is the ocean. You are beyond the stars, the sun, and the moon. They are like mere bubbles compared with your infinite Being. Know that, and you will control both good and evil. Then alone will your whole vision change, and you will stand up and say, "How beautiful is good and how wonderful is evil!"

That is what Vedānta teaches. It does not propose any slipshod remedy by covering wounds with gold-leaf, and the more the wound festers, putting on more gold-leaf. This life is a hard fact. Work your way through it boldly, though it may be adamantine. No matter! The soul is stronger. Vedānta lays no responsibility on little gods; for you are the makers of your own fortunes. You make yourselves suffer, you make good and evil, and it is you who put your hands before your eyes and say it is dark. Take your hands away and see the light; you are effulgent, you are perfect already, from the very beginning.

We now understand the verse: "He goes from death to death who sees the many here." See that Oneness and be free. How are we to see it? This mind, so deluded, so weak, so easily led, even this mind can be strong and can catch a glimpse of that Knowledge, that Oneness, which saves us from dying again and again.

As rain falling upon a mountain flows in various streams down the sides of the mountain, so all the energies which you see here are from that one Centre. It has become manifold falling upon māyā. Do not run after the manifold; go towards the One. "He is in all that moves; He is in all that is pure. He fills the universe. He is in the sacrifice; He is the guest in the house; He is in man, in water, in animals, in truth; He is the Great One. As fire coming into this world manifests itself in various forms, even so that one Soul of the universe manifests Himself in all these various forms. As air coming into this universe manifests itself in various forms, even so the one Soul of all souls, of all beings, manifests Himself in all forms." This is true for you when you have understood this Unity, and not before. Then all is optimism, because He is seen everywhere.

The question is: If this be true—that that Pure One, the Self, the Infinite, has entered all this—how is it that He suffers, how is it that He becomes miserable, impure? He does not, says the Upanishad. "As the sun is the cause of the eyesight of every being, yet is not made defective by the defect in any eye, even so the Self of all is not affected by the miseries of the body, or by any misery in the world." I may have some disease and see everything yellow, but the sun is not affected by it.

"He is the One, the Creator of all, the Ruler of all, the Internal Soul of every being, He who makes His Oneness manifold. Thus sages who realize Him as the Soul of their souls—unto them belongs eternal peace; unto none else, unto none else. He who in this world of evanescence finds Him who never changes, he who in this universe of death finds that One Life, he who in this manifold finds that Oneness, he who realizes Him as the Soul of his soul—unto him belongs eternal peace; unto none else, unto none else." How can one find Him in the external world? How can one find Him in the sun or moon or stars? "There the sun cannot shine, nor the moon, nor the stars; the flash of lightning cannot illumine Him, not to speak of this mortal fire. He shining, everything else shines. It is His light that they have borrowed, and He is shining through them."

Here is another beautiful passage from the *Katha Upanishad:* "This is that eternal Aśvattha Tree with its root above and branches below. That root, indeed, is called the Bright; That is Brahman, and That alone is the Immortal. In That all worlds are contained, and none can pass beyond."

Various heavens are spoken of in the Brāhmana portion of the Vedas, but the philosophical teaching of the Upanishads discourages the idea of going to heaven. Happiness is not in this heaven or in that heaven; it is in the soul. Places do not signify anything.

Here is another passage, which shows the different states of realization: "In the heaven of the forefathers, as a man sees things in a dream, so the Real Truth is seen." As in dreams we see things hazy and not distinct, so we see Reality there. There is another heaven, called the Gandharvaloka, in which Reality is seen as a man sees his own reflection in water. The highest heaven of which the Hindus conceive is called Brahmaloka; and there Truth is seen much more clearly, like light and shade, but not yet quite distinctly. But as a man sees his own face in a mirror, perfect, distinct, and clear, so does Truth shine in the soul of man.

The highest heaven, therefore, is in our own souls; the greatest temple of worship is the human soul, greater than all heavens, says Vedānta; for in no heaven, anywhere, can we understand Reality as distinctly and clearly as in this life, in our own soul.

Changing places does not help one much. I thought while I was in India that a cave would give me clearer vision. I found it was not so. Then I thought the forest would do so. Then, Benares. But the same difficulty existed everywhere, because we make our own world. If I am evil, the whole world is evil to me; that is what the Upanishad says. And the same thing applies to all worlds. If I die and go to heaven, I shall find the same; for until I am pure it is no use going to caves or forests or to Benares or to heaven; and if I have polished my mirror, it does not matter where I live; I see Reality just as It is. So it is useless running hither and thither and spending energy in vain, which should be spent only in polishing the mirror. The same idea is expressed again: "None sees Him, none sees His form with the eyes. It is in the mind, in the pure mind, that He is seen, and thus immortality is gained."

Those who were at the summer lectures on rāja-yoga will be interested to know that what was taught then was a different kind of yoga. The yoga which we are now considering consists chiefly in controlling the senses. When the senses are held as slaves by the human soul, when they can no longer disturb the mind, then the yogi has reached the goal. "When all vain desires of the heart have been given up, then this very mortal becomes immortal, then he becomes one with God even here. When all the knots of the heart are cut asunder, then the mortal becomes immortal and he enjoys Brahman here." Here on this earth—nowhere else.

A few words ought to be said here. You will generally hear that this Vedānta philosophy and other Eastern systems look only to something beyond, letting go the enjoyments and struggles of this life. This idea is entirely wrong. It is only ignorant people who do not know anything of Eastern thought and never had brain enough to understand anything of its real teaching, who tell you so. On the contrary, we read in our scriptures that our philosophers do not want us to go to other worlds, but depreciate them as places where people laugh for a little while only and then die. As long as we are weak we shall have to go through these experiences of heaven and hell; but whatever is true is here, and that is the human soul. And this also is insisted upon: by committing suicide we cannot escape the inevitable chain of birth and death. But the right path is hard to find.

The Hindu is just as practical as the Westerner, only they differ in their views of life. The one says, "Build a good house, have good clothes and food, intellectual culture, and so on, for this is the whole of life"; and in that he is immensely practical. But the Hindu says, "True knowledge of the world means knowledge of the soul, metaphysics"; and he wants to enjoy that life.

In America there was a great agnostic, a very noble man, a very good man, and a very fine speaker. He lectured on religion, which he said was of no use; why bother our heads about other worlds? He employed this metaphor: "We have an orange here, and we want to squeeze all the juice out of it." I met him once and said: "I agree with you entirely. I have some fruit and I too want to squeeze out the juice. Our difference lies in the choice of the fruit. You want an orange, and I prefer a mango. You think it is enough to live here and eat and drink and have a little scientific knowledge, but you have no right to say that that will suit all tastes. Such a conception is nothing to me. If I had only to learn how an apple falls to the ground or how an electric current shakes my nerves, I should commit suicide. I want to understand the heart of things, the very kernel itself. Your study is the manifestation of life; mine is life itself. My philosophy says you must know *that* and drive out from your mind all thoughts of heaven and hell and all other superstitions, even though they exist in the same sense that this world exists. I must know the heart of this life, its very essence, what it is—not merely how it works and what are its manifestations. I want the *why* of everything; I leave the *how* to children. It was one of your countrymen who said, 'If I were to write a book about what I feel when I smoke a cigarette, it would be the science of the cigarette.' It is good and great to be scientific. God bless the scientists in their search! But if one says that that is all, one is talking foolishly, not caring to know the meaning of life, never studying existence itself. I can prove that all your knowledge is nonsense, without a basis. You are studying the manifestation of life, and when I ask you what life is, you say you do not know. You are welcome to your study, but leave me to mine."

I am practical, very practical, in my own way. So your idea that only the West is practical is nonsense. You are practical in one way, and I in another. There are different types of men and minds. If in the East a man is told that he will find out the truth by standing on one leg all his life, he will pursue that method. If in the West men hear that there is a gold-mine somewhere in an uncivilized country, thousands will face the dangers there in the hope of getting the gold; and perhaps only one succeeds. The same men have heard that they have souls, but are content to leave the care of them to the church. The Easterner will not go near the savages; he says it may be dangerous. But if we tell him that on the top of a high mountain lives a wonderful sage who can give him knowledge of the soul, he tries to climb up to him, even though he may be killed in the attempt. Both types of men are practical; but the mistake lies in regarding this world as the whole of life. Yours is the evanescent enjoyment of the senses; there is nothing permanent in it; it only brings more and more misery. But mine is eternal peace.

I do not say your view is wrong. You are welcome to it. Great good and blessing come out of it. But do not on that account condemn my view. Mine also is practical in its own way. Let us all work on our own plan. Would to God all of us were equally practical on both sides! I have seen some scientists who are equally practical as scientists and as spiritual men, and it is my great hope that in the course of time the whole of humanity will be efficient in the same manner.

When a kettle of water is coming to the boil, if you watch the phenomenon you find first one bubble rising and then another, and so on, until at last they all join and a tremendous commotion takes place. This world is very similar. Each individual is like a bubble, and the nations resemble many bubbles. Gradually these nations are joining, and I am sure the day will come when separation will vanish and that Oneness to which we are all going will become manifest. A time must come when every man will be as intensely practical in the scientific world as in the spiritual, and then that Oneness, the harmony of Oneness, will pervade the whole world. The whole of mankind will become jivanmuktas—free while living. We are all struggling towards that one end through our jealousies and hatreds, through our love and co-operation. A tremendous stream is flowing towards the ocean, carrying us all along with it; and though, like straws and scraps of paper, we may at times float aimlessly about, in the long run we are sure to join the Ocean of Life and Bliss.

THE FREEDOM OF THE SOUL

(Delivered in London, November 5, 1896)

THE *Katha Upanishad*, which we have been studying, was written much later than that to which we now turn—the *Chhāndogya*; the language of the former is more modern and the thought more organized. In the older Upanishads the language is very archaic, like that of the hymn portion of the Vedas, and one has to wade sometimes through quite a mass of unnecessary things to get at the essential doctrines. The ritualistic literature of the Vedas, about which I have told you, has greatly influenced this old Upanishad, so that more than half of it is still ritualistic. There is, however, one great gain in studying the very old Upanishads. You trace, as it were, the historical growth of spiritual ideas. In the more recent Upanishads the spiritual ideas have been collected and brought into one place; in the Bhagavad Gītā, for instance, which we may perhaps look upon as the last of the Upanishads, you do not find any inkling of these ritualistic ideas. The Gītā is like a bouquet composed of the beautiful flowers of spiritual truths collected from the Upanishads. But in the Gītā you cannot study the growth of the spiritual ideas; you cannot trace them to their source. To do that, as has been pointed out by many, you must study the Vedas.

The idea of great holiness that has been attached to these books has preserved them, more than any other book in the world, from mutilation. In them, thoughts at their highest and at their lowest have all been preserved—the essential and the non-essential. The most ennobling teachings and the simplest matters of detail stand side by side; for nobody has dared to touch them. Commentators came and tried to smooth them down and bring out wonderful new ideas from the old things; they tried to find spiritual ideas in even the most ordinary statements; but the texts remained, and these texts are the most wonderful historical study. We all know that in the scriptures of every religion changes were made to suit the growing spirituality of later times; one word was changed here and another put in there, and so on. This probably has not been done with the Vedic literature, or if ever done, it is almost imperceptible. So we have this great advantage: we are able to study thoughts in their original significance, to note how they developed, how from materialistic ideas finer and finer spiritual ideas evolved, until they attained their greatest height in Vedānta. Descriptions of some of the old manners and customs are also to be found in the Vedic literature; but they do not appear much in the Upanishads, where the language used is a peculiarly terse mnemonic.

The writers of these books simply jotted down these lines as helps to remember certain facts which they supposed were already well known. In a narrative which they are telling, they perhaps take it for granted that it is well known

279

to everyone they are addressing. Thus a great difficulty arises: we scarcely know the real meaning of any one of these stories, because the traditions have nearly died out, and the little that is left of them has been very much exaggerated. Many new interpretations have been put upon them, so that when you find them in the Purānas they have already become lyrical poems.

Just as in the West we find, in the political development of the Western races, the prominent fact that they cannot bear absolute rule, that they are always trying to prevent any one man from ruling over them and are gradually advancing to higher and higher democratic ideas, higher and higher ideas of physical liberty, so, in Indian metaphysics, exactly the same phenomenon appears in the development of the spiritual life. The multiplicity of gods gave place to one God of the universe, and in the Upanishads there is a rebellion even against that one God. The idea was unbearable not only that there should be many governors of the universe ruling their destinies, but also that there should be one person ruling this universe. This is the first thing that strikes us. The idea grows and grows, until it attains its climax. In almost all the Upanishads we find the climax coming at the last, and that is the dethroning of this God of the universe. The personality of God vanishes; impersonality comes. God is no more a person, no more a human being, however magnified and exaggerated, who rules this universe, but He has become an embodied principle in every being, immanent in the whole universe.

It would be illogical to go from the Personal God to the Impersonal and at the same time leave man as a person. So the personal man is broken down, and man as a principle is built up. The person is only a phenomenon; the principle is behind it. Thus from both sides, simultaneously, we find the breaking down of personalities and the approach towards principles, the Personal God approaching the Impersonal, the personal man approaching the impersonal man. Then come the succeeding stages—the gradual convergence of the two advancing lines of the Impersonal God and the impersonal man. And the Upanishads embody the stages through which these two lines at last become one; and the last word of each Upanishad is "Thou art That." There is but one eternally blissful Principle, and that One is manifesting Itself as all this variety.

Then came the philosophers. The work of the Upanishads seems to have ended at that point; the next step was taken by the philosophers. The framework was given them by the Upanishads, and they had to fill in the details. Many questions would naturally arise. Taking for granted that there is but one Impersonal Principle, which is manifesting Itself in all these manifold forms, how is it that the One becomes many? It is another way of putting the same old question which in its crude form comes into the human heart as the inquiry into the cause of evil and so forth. Why does evil exist in the world, and what is its cause? But the same question has now become refined, abstracted. No more is it asked from the sense plane why we are unhappy; but it is asked from the plane of philosophy: Why has this one Principle become manifold? And the answer, as we have seen, the best answer that India has produced, is the theory of māyā, which says that It really has not become manifold, that It really has not lost any of Its real nature. Manifoldness is only apparent. Man is only apparently a person, but in reality he is Impersonal Being. God is a Person only apparently, but really He is Impersonal Being.

But even in the finding out of this answer there have been succeeding stages, and philosophers have varied in their opinions. Not all Indian philosophers have accepted this theory of māyā. Possibly most of them have not. There are dualists, with a crude sort of dualism, who will not allow the question to be asked, but stifle it at the very outset. They say: "You have no right to ask such a question; you have no right to ask for an explanation. It is simply the will of God, and we have to submit to it quietly. There is no liberty for the human soul. Everything is predestined—what we shall do, have, enjoy, and suffer; and when suffering comes it is our duty to endure it patiently. If we do not, we shall be punished all the more. How do we know that? Because the Vedas say so." And thus they quote their texts and give their meanings and they want to enforce them.

There are others who, though not admitting the māyā theory, stand midway. They say that the whole of this creation forms, as it were, the body of God. God is the Soul of all souls and of the whole of nature. In the case of individual souls, contraction comes from evil-doing. When a man does anything evil his soul begins to contract and his power is diminished and goes on decreasing, until he does good works, when it expands again.

One idea seems to be common to all the Indian systems, and I think to all the systems in the world, whether they know it or not, and that is what I should call the divinity of man. There is not one system in the world, not one religion, which does not hold the idea—whether expressed in the language of mythology, allegory, or philosophy—that the human soul, whatever it be, or whatever its relation to God, is essentially pure and perfect. Its real nature is blessedness and power, not weakness and misery. Somehow this present misery has come. The crude systems may speak of a personified evil, a Devil, or an Ahriman, to explain how this misery came. Other systems may try to make a God and a Devil in one, who makes some people miserable and others happy, without any reason whatever. Others again, more thoughtful, bring in the theory of māyā, and so forth. But one thing stands out clearly, and it is with this that we have to deal. After all, these philosophical ideas and systems are but gymnastics of the mind, intellectual exercises. The one great idea that to me seems to be clear and that comes out through masses of superstition in every country and in every religion is the luminous idea that man is divine, that divinity is our nature.

Whatever else comes is a mere superimposition, as Vedānta calls it. Something has been superimposed, but that cannot kill the divine nature. In the most degraded, as well as in the most saintly, it is ever present. It has to be called out and it will work itself out. We have to ask and it will manifest itself. The people of old knew that fire existed in flint and in dry wood, but friction was necessary to call it out. So this fire of freedom and purity is the nature of every soul, and is not a quality, because qualities can be acquired and therefore can be lost.

The soul is one with Freedom, and the soul is one with Existence, and the soul is one with Knowledge. Satchidānanda, Existence-Knowledge-Bliss Absolute, is the nature, the birthright, of the soul, and all the manifestations that we see are Its expressions, dimly or brightly manifesting It. Even death is but a manifestation of that Real Existence. Birth and death, life and decay, degeneration and regeneration, are all manifestations of that Oneness. So knowledge, however it manifests itself, either as ignorance or as learning, is but the manifestation of that same Chit, the Essence of Knowledge; the difference is only in degree and not in kind. The difference in knowledge between the lowest worm that crawls under our feet and the highest genius that the world may produce is only one of degree and not of kind. The Vedāntist thinker boldly says that the enjoyments in this life, even the most degraded joys, are but manifestations of that one Divine Bliss, the Essence of the soul.

This idea seems to be the most prominent in Vedānta, and, as I have said, it appears to me that every religion holds it. I have yet to know the religion which does not. It is the one universal idea working through all religions.

Take the Bible, for instance. You find there the allegorical statement that the first man, Adam, was pure, and that afterwards his purity was obliterated by his evil deeds. It is clear from this allegory that the Hebrews thought that the original nature of man was perfect; the impurities that we see, the weaknesses that we feel, are but superimpositions on that nature. And the subsequent history of the Christian religion shows that the Christians believe in the possibility, nay, the certainty, of regaining that old state. This is the whole history of the Bible, Old and New Testaments together.

So it is with the Mohammedans. They also believe in Adam and the purity of Adam, and hold that through Mohammed the way has been opened to regain that lost state.

So, too, with the Buddhists. They believe in the state called Nirvāna, which is beyond this relative world. It is exactly the same as the Brahman of the Vedāntists; and the whole system of Buddhism is founded upon the idea of regaining that lost state of Nirvāna.

In every system we find this doctrine present—that you cannot get anything which is not yours already. You are indebted to nobody in this universe. You claim your own birthright—as it has been poetically expressed by a great Vedāntist in the title of one of his books, Swārājyasiddhi, The Attainment of Our Own Empire. That empire is ours; we have lost it and we have to regain it. The māyāvādin, however, says that the idea of having lost the empire is a hallucination; you never lost it. This is the only difference.

Although all the systems agree so far—that we had the empire and that we have lost it—they give us varied advice as to how to regain it. One says that we must perform certain ceremonies, worship certain deities in a certain way, eat certain sorts of food, live in a peculiar fashion, to regain that empire. Another says that if we weep and prostrate ourselves and ask pardon of some Being beyond nature, we shall regain that empire. Again, another says that if we love such a Being with all our heart, we shall regain that empire. All this varied advice is in the Upanishads. As I go on, you will find it so.

But the last and the greatest counsel is that we need not weep at all. We need not go through all these ceremonies and need not take any notice of how to regain our empire, because we never lost it. Why should we go about seeking what we never lost? We are pure already, we are free already. If we think we are free, free we are this moment, and if we think we are bound, bound we shall be.

This is a very bold statement, and as I told you at the beginning of these lectures, I shall have to speak to you very boldly. It may frighten you now; but when you think it over and realize it in your own life, then you will come to know that what I say is true. If that freedom is not your nature, by no manner of means can you become free. Or if you were free and in some way you lost that freedom, then you were not free to begin with. Had you been free, what could have made you lose it? The independent can never be made dependent; if it is really dependent, its independence was a hallucination.

Of the two sides, then, which will you take? If you say that the soul was by its own nature pure and free, it naturally follows that there was nothing in this universe which could make it bound or limited. But if there was anything in nature which could bind the soul, it naturally follows that it was not free, and your statement that it was free is a delusion. So if it is possible for us to attain to freedom, the conclusion is inevitable that the soul is by its nature free. It cannot be otherwise.

Freedom means independence of anything outside, and that means that nothing outside itself could work upon it as a cause. The soul is causeless, and from this follow all the great ideas that we have. You cannot establish the immortality of the soul unless you grant that it is by its nature free, or in other words, that it cannot be acted upon by anything outside; for death is an effect produced by some outside cause. I drink poison and I die, thus showing that my body can be acted upon by something outside that is called poison. But if it be true that the soul is free, it naturally follows that nothing can affect it and it can never die. The freedom, immortality, and blessedness of the soul have meaning only if it is beyond the law of causation.

Of these two, which will you take? Either make the first a delusion or make the second a delusion. Certainly I will make the second a delusion. It is more consonant with all my feelings and aspirations. I am perfectly aware that I am free by nature, and I will not admit that this bondage is true and my freedom a delusion.

This discussion goes on, in some form or other, in all philosophies. Even in the most modern philosophies you find the same discussion. There are two parties. One says that there is no soul, that the idea of the soul is a delusion produced by the rapid succession of particles of matter, bringing about the combination which you call the body or the brain; that the impression of freedom is the result of the vibrations and motions and continuous succession of these particles. There were Buddhist sects who held the same view and illustrated it by this example: If you take a torch and whirl it round rapidly, there will be a circle of light. That circle does not really exist, because the torch is changing place every moment. We are but bundles of little particles, which in their rapid whirling produce the delusion of a permanent soul.

The other party states that the rapid succession of thought creates the delusion of matter, which does not really exist. So we see one side claiming that spirit is a delusion, and the other that matter is a delusion. Which side will you take?

Of course we will take the spirit and deny matter. The arguments are similar for both; only on the spirit side the argument is a little stronger. For nobody has ever seen what matter is; we can only feel ourselves. I never knew a man who could feel matter by going outside of himself. Nobody was ever able to jump outside of himself. Therefore the argument is a little stronger on the side of the spirit. Secondly, the spirit theory explains the universe, while materialism does not. Hence the materialistic explanation is illogical. If you boil down all the philosophies and analyse them, you will find that they are reduced to one or other of these two positions.

So here, too, in a more intricate form, in a more philosophical form, we find the same question about freedom and bondage. One side says that the first is a delusion, and the other that the second is a delusion. And of course we side with the second in believing that our bondage is a delusion.

The solution of Vedānta is that we are not bound, we are free already. Not only so, but to say or think that we are bound is dangerous; it is a mistake; it is self-hypnotism. As soon as you say, "I am bound," "I am weak," "I am helpless," woe unto you! You rivet one more chain upon yourself. Do not say it; do not think it. I have heard of a man who lived in a forest and used to repeat day and night, "Śivoham"—"I am the Blessed One"—and one day a tiger fell upon him and dragged him away to kill him. People on the other side of the river saw this and heard the voice, so long as voice remained in him, saying, "Śivoham"—even in the very jaws of the tiger. There have been many such men. There have been men who, while being cut to pieces, have blest their enemies. "I am He, I am He, and so art thou. I am pure and perfect, and so are all my enemies. You are He, and so am I." That is the position of strength. There are, no doubt, great and wonderful things in the religions of the dualists. Wonderful is the idea of the Personal God apart from nature, whom we worship and love. Sometimes this idea is very soothing. But, says Vedānta, that feeling is something like the effect that comes from an opiate; it is not natural. It brings weakness in the long run, and what this world wants today more than it ever did before is strength. It is weakness, says Vedānta, that is the cause of all misery in this world. Weakness is the one cause of suffering. We become miserable because we are weak. We lie, steal, kill, and commit other crimes, because we are weak. We suffer because we are weak. We die because we are weak. Where there is nothing to weaken us, there is no death or sorrow. We are miserable through delusion. Give up the delusion and the whole thing vanishes. It is plain and simple indeed. Through all these philosophical discussions and tremendous mental gymnastics we come to this one religious idea, the simplest in the whole world.

Monistic Vedānta is the simplest form in which you can put the truth. A great mistake was made in India and elsewhere, because people did not look at the ultimate principles, but only thought of the process, which is very intricate indeed. To many these tremendous philosophical and logical propositions were alarming. They thought that these things could not be made universal, could not be followed in everyday practical life, and that under the guise of such a philosophy much laxity of living would arise. But I do not believe at all that monistic ideas preached to the world will produce immorality and weakness. On the contrary, I have reason to believe that they are the only remedy there is. If this be the truth, why let people drink ditch-water when the stream of life is flowing by? If this be the truth, that they are all pure, why not at this moment teach it to the whole world? Why not teach it, with the voice of thunder, to every man that is born, to saints and sinners, men, women, and children, to the man on the throne and to the man sweeping the streets?

It appears to be a very big and a very great undertaking; to many it appears very startling. But that is because of superstition, nothing else. By eating all sorts of bad and indigestible food, or by starving ourselves, we have become incompetent to eat a good meal. We have listened to words of weakness from our childhood. You hear people say that they do not believe in ghosts; but at the same time, there are very few who do not feel a little creepy sensation in the dark. It is simply superstition. So with all religious superstitions. There are people in this country who, if I told them there was no such being as the Devil, would think all religion was gone. Many people have said to me: "How can there be religion without a Devil? How can there be religion without a God to direct us? How can we live without being ruled by somebody? We like to be so treated, because we have become used to it. We are not happy until we feel we have been reprimanded by somebody every day." The same superstition! But however terrible it may seem now, the time will come when we shall look back, each one of us, and smile at every one of those superstitions which covered the pure and eternal Soul, and repeat with gladness, with truth, and with strength: "I am free, and was free, and always will be free."

This monistic idea will come out of Vedānta, and it is the one idea that deserves to live. The scriptures may perish tomorrow. Whether this idea first flashed in the brains of Hebrews or of people living in the Arctic regions, nobody cares. For this is the truth and truth is eternal; and truth itself teaches that it is not the special property of any individual or nation. Men, animals, and gods are all common heirs of this one truth. Let them all receive it. Why make life miserable? Why let people fall into all sorts of superstitions? Not only in this country, but in the land of its very birth, if you tell people this truth they are frightened. They say: "This idea is for sannyāsins, who give up the world and live in forests; for them it is all right. But as for us poor householders, we must all have some sort of fear, we must have ceremonies," and so on. Dualistic ideas have ruled the world long enough, and this is the result. Why not make a new experiment? It may take ages for all minds to receive monism, but why not begin now? If we have told about it to twenty persons in our lives, we have done a great work.

There is one idea which often militates against it. It is this: It is all very well to say, "I am the Pure, the Blessed," but I cannot show it always in my life. That is true; the ideal is always very hard. But would it mend matters to go towards superstition? If we cannot get nectar, would it mend matters for us to drink poison? Would it be any help for us, because we cannot realize Truth immediately, to go into darkness and yield to weakness and superstition?

I have no objection to dualism in many of its forms. I like most of them, but I do have objections to every form of teaching which inculcates weakness. This is the one question that I put to every man, woman, or child who is in

physical, mental, or spiritual training: "How do you feel? Are you any stronger?"
—for I know it is Truth alone that gives strength. I know that Truth alone
gives life, and nothing but approaching Reality will make us strong, and that
none will reach Truth until he is strong. Any system, therefore, which weakens
the mind, which makes one superstitious, makes one mope, makes one desire
all sorts of wild impossibilities, mysteries, and superstitions, I do not like,
because its effect is dangerous. Such systems never bring any good; such things
create morbidity in the mind, make it weak, so weak that in the course of time
it will be almost impossible to receive Truth or live up to it. Strength, therefore,
is the one thing needful. Strength is the medicine for the world's disease.
Strength is the medicine which the poor must have when tyrannized over by
the rich. Strength is the medicine which the ignorant must have when oppressed
by the learned; and it is the medicine which sinners must have when tyrannized
over by other sinners. And nothing gives such strength as this idea of monism;
nothing makes us so moral as this idea of monism; nothing makes us work so
well, at our best and highest, as when all the responsibility is thrown upon
ourselves.

I challenge every one of you. How will you behave if I put a little baby in
your hands? Your life will be changed for the moment. Whatever you may be,
you must become selfless for the time being. You will give up all your criminal
ideas as soon as responsibility is thrown upon you; your whole character will
change. So if the whole responsibility is thrown upon our own shoulders, we
shall be at our highest and best. When we have nobody to grope towards, no
Devil to lay our blame upon, no Personal God to carry our burdens, when we
alone are responsible, then we shall rise to our highest and best. "I am responsible for my fate, I am the bringer of good unto myself, I am the bringer of evil.
I am the Pure and Blessed One." We must reject all thoughts that assert the
contrary. "I have neither death nor fear, I have neither caste nor creed, I have
neither father nor mother nor birth, neither friend nor foe; for I am Existence,
Knowledge, and Bliss Absolute; I am the Blissful One, I am the Blissful One.
I am not bound either by virtue or by vice, by happiness or by misery. Pilgrimages and books and ceremonials can never bind me. I have neither hunger nor
thirst; the body is not mine, nor am I subject to the superstitions and decay
that come to the body. I am Existence, Knowledge, and Bliss Absolute; I am
the Blissful One, I am the Blissful One."

This, says Vedānta, is the only prayer that we should have. This is the only
way to reach the goal: to tell ourselves and to tell everybody else that we are
divine. As we go on repeating this, strength comes. He who falters at first
will get stronger and stronger, and the voice will increase in volume until Truth
takes possession of our hearts and courses through our veins and permeates our
bodies. Delusion will vanish as the light becomes more and more effulgent, load
after load of ignorance will vanish, and then will come a time when all else has
disappeared and the Sun alone shines.

THE COSMOS

The Macrocosm

(Delivered in New York, January 19, 1896)

THE FLOWERS that we see all around us are beautiful, beautiful is the rising of the morning sun, beautiful are the variegated hues of nature. The whole universe is beautiful, and man has been enjoying it since his appearance on earth. Sublime and awe-inspiring are the mountains, the gigantic rushing rivers rolling towards the sea, the trackless deserts, the infinite ocean, the starry heavens; all these are awe-inspiring, sublime, and beautiful indeed. The whole mass of existence which we call nature has been acting on the human mind from time immemorial. It has been acting on the thought of man, and as its reaction has come the question: "What are these? Whence are they?"

As far back as the time of the oldest portion of that most ancient human composition, the Vedas, we find the same question asked: "Whence is this? When there was neither aught nor naught, and darkness was hidden in darkness, who projected this universe? How? Who knows the secret?" And the question has come down to us at the present time. Millions of attempts have been made to answer it, yet millions of times it will have to be answered again. It is not that each answer was a failure; every answer to this question contained a part of the truth, and this truth gathers strength as time rolls on. I will try to present before you the outline of the answer that I have gleaned from the ancient philosophers of India, in harmony with modern knowledge.

We find that in this oldest of questions a few points had been already solved. The first is that there was a time when there was "neither aught nor naught," when this world did not exist; when the planets and luminaries, our mother earth, with the seas and oceans, the rivers and mountains, cities and villages, human beings, animals, plants, and birds—all this infinite variety of creation— had no existence. Are we sure of that? We shall try to trace how this conclusion was arrived at.

What does man see around him? Take a little plant. He puts a seed in the ground and later he finds a plant peep out, lift itself slowly above the ground, and grow and grow till it becomes a gigantic tree. Then it dies, leaving only a seed. It completes the circle, it comes out of the seed, becomes the tree, and ends in the seed again. Look at a bird—how from the egg it springs, lives its life, and then dies, having produced other eggs, seeds of future birds. So with the animals; so with man. Everything in nature begins, as it were, from certain seeds, certain rudiments, certain fine forms, and becomes grosser and

287

grosser, and develops, going on in that way for a certain time, and again goes back to that fine form and subsides.

The raindrop in which the beautiful sunbeam is playing was drawn in the form of vapour from the ocean, went far away into the air, and reached a region where it changed into water and dropped down in its present form—to be converted into vapour again. So with everything in nature by which we are surrounded. We know that the huge mountains are being worked upon by glaciers and rivers, which are slowly but surely pounding them and pulverizing them into sand, which drifts away into the ocean, where it settles down on its bed, layer after layer, becoming hard as rock, once more to be heaped up into mountains in the future. These, again, will be pounded and pulverized, and thus things go on. From sand rise these mountains; unto sand they go.

If it be true that nature is uniform throughout, if it be true—and so far no human experience has contradicted it—that the same method under which a small grain of sand is created works in creating the gigantic suns and stars and all this universe; if it be true that the whole of this universe is built on exactly the same plan as the atom; if it be true that the same law prevails throughout the universe, then if we take up a little plant and study its life, we shall know the universe as it is—as it has been said in the Vedas, "knowing one lump of clay, we know the nature of all the clay in the universe." If we know one grain of sand, we shall know the secret of the whole universe. Applying this type of reasoning to phenomena in general, we find, in the first place, that everything is similar at the beginning and the end. The mountain comes from sand and goes back to sand; the river comes out of vapour and goes back to vapour; plant life comes from the seed and goes back to the seed; human life comes out of the human germ and goes back to the germ. The universe with its stars and planets has come out of a nebulous state and must go back to it. And what do we learn from this? That the manifested or grosser state is the effect, and the finer state, the cause.

Thousands of years ago it was demonstrated by Kapila, the great father of philosophy, that destruction means going back to the cause. If this table here is destroyed it will go back to its cause, to those fine forms and particles which, combined, made this form which we call a table. If a man dies he will go back to the elements which gave him his body; if this earth dies it will go back to the elements which gave it form. This is what is called destruction: going back to the cause. Therefore we learn that the effect is the same as the cause, not different. It is only in another form. This glass is an effect, and it had its cause, and this cause is present in this form. A certain amount of the material called glass plus the force in the hands of the manufacturer are the causes, the material and the instrumental, which, combined, produced this form called a glass. The force which was in the hands of the manufacturer is present in the glass as the power of adhesion, without which the particles would fall apart; and the glass material is also present. The glass is only a manifestation of these fine causes in a new shape; and if it be broken to pieces the force which was present in the form of adhesion will go back and join its own element, and the particles of glass will remain the same until they take new forms. Thus we find that the effect is never different from the cause. It is only a reproduction of the cause in a grosser form.

Next we learn that all these particular forms, whether they are plants, animals, or men, are being repeated *ad infinitum*, rising and falling. The seed produces the tree; the tree produces the seed, which again comes up as another tree; and so on and on. There is no end to it. Water-drops roll down the mountains into the ocean and rise again as vapour, going back to the mountains and again coming down to the ocean. So, rising and falling, the cycle goes on.

So with all lives; so with all existence that we can see, feel, hear, or imagine. Everything that is within the bounds of our knowledge is proceeding in the same way, like breathing in and breathing out in the human body. Everything in creation goes on in this form, one wave rising, another falling, rising again, falling again. Each wave has its hollow; each hollow has its wave.

The same law must apply to the universe taken as a whole, because of its uniformity. This universe must be resolved into its causes; the sun, moon, stars, and earth, the body and mind, and everything in this universe, must return to their finer causes, disappear, be destroyed as it were. But they will live in the causes as fine forms. Out of these fine forms they will emerge again as new earths, suns, moons, and stars.

There is one fact more to learn about this rising and falling. The seed does not immediately become a tree, but has a period of inactivity, or rather, a period of very fine unmanifested action. The seed has to work for some time beneath the soil. It breaks into pieces, degenerates, as it were, and regeneration comes out of that degeneration. In the beginning the whole of this universe has to work likewise, for a period, in that subtle form, unseen and unmanifested, which is called chaos; and out of that comes a new projection. The whole period of one manifestation of this universe—its going back to the finer form, remaining there for some time, and coming out again—is, in Sanskrit, called a kalpa, or cycle.

Next comes a very important question, especially for modern times. We see that the finer forms develop slowly, and slowly and gradually become grosser and grosser. We have seen that the cause is the same as the effect, and the effect is only the cause in another form. Therefore this whole universe cannot have been produced out of nothing. There is nothing which is produced without a cause, and the cause is the effect in another form.

Out of what has this universe been produced, then? From a preceding fine universe. Out of what has man been produced? The preceding fine form. Out of what has the tree been produced? Out of the seed; the whole of the tree was there in the seed. It comes out and becomes manifest. So the whole of this universe has been created out of this very universe existing in a minute form. It has been made manifest now; it will go back to that minute form and again will be made manifest.

Now we find that the fine forms slowly come out and become grosser and grosser until they reach their limit, and when they reach their limit they go back farther and farther, becoming finer and finer again. This coming out of the fine and becoming gross, simply changing the arrangements of the parts, as it were, is in modern times called evolution. This is very true, perfectly true; we see it in our lives. No rational man can possibly quarrel with the evolutionists.

But we have to learn one thing more. We have to go one step farther. And what is that? That every evolution is preceded by an involution. The seed is the father of the tree, but another tree was itself the father of the seed. The seed is the fine form out of which the big tree comes, and that big tree was involved in that seed. The whole of this universe was present in the fine universe. The little cell which afterwards becomes the man is simply the man involved and becomes evolved as a man. If this is accepted, we have no quarrel with the evolutionists; for we see that if they admit this step, instead of destroying religion they will be its greatest supporters.

We see, then, that there is nothing that can be created out of nothing. Everything exists through eternity and will exist through eternity. Only the movement is in succeeding waves and hollows, going back to fine forms and coming out into gross manifestations. Involution and evolution are going on throughout the whole of nature. The whole series of evolution, beginning with the lowest manifestation of life and reaching up to the highest, the most perfect man, must have been the involution of something else. The question is, the involution of what? What was involved? God. The evolutionist will tell you that your idea that it was God is wrong. Why? Because, replies the evolutionist, you say that God is intelligent, but we find that intelligence develops much later in the course of evolution: it is in man and the higher animals that we find intelligence, but millions of years passed in this world before this intelligence was produced.

This objection of the evolutionists, however, does not hold water, as we shall see by applying our theory. The tree comes out of the seed, goes back to the seed; the beginning and the end are the same. The earth comes out of its cause and returns to it. We know that if we can find the beginning we can find the end. Conversely, if we find the end we can find the beginning. If that is so, take this whole evolutionary series, from the protoplasm at one end to the perfect man at the other. This whole series is one life. In the end we find perfection; so in the beginning there must have been the same. Therefore the protoplasm was the involution of the highest intelligence. You may not see it, but that involved intelligence is what is uncoiling itself until it becomes manifested in the most perfect man. And that can be mathematically demonstrated.

If the law of the conservation of energy is true, you cannot get anything out of a machine unless you first put it in. The amount of work you get out of an engine is exactly the same as the amount you have put into it in the form of water and coal—neither more nor less. The work I am doing now is just what I put into me in the shape of air, food, and other things. It is only a question of change and manifestation. There cannot be added in the economy of this universe one particle of matter or one foot-pound of force, nor can one particle of matter or one foot-pound of force be taken out. If that be so, what is this intelligence? If it was not present in the protoplasm, it must have come all of a sudden, something coming out of nothing, which is absurd. It therefore follows absolutely that the perfect man, the free man, the God-man, who has gone beyond the laws of nature and transcended everything, who has no more to go through this process of evolution, through birth and death—that man called the "Christ-man" by the Christians, the "Buddha-man" by the Buddhists, and the "Free Soul" by the yogis—that perfect man who is at one end of the chain of evolution was involved in the protoplasmic cell, which is at the other end of the same chain.

Applying the same sort of reasoning to the whole of the universe, we see that intelligence must be the lord of creation, the cause. What is the most evolved notion that man has of this universe? It is that of intelligence, the adjustment of part to part, the display of intelligence—which notion the ancient design theory attempted to express. The beginning is therefore intelligence. At the beginning that intelligence becomes involved, and in the end that intelligence becomes evolved. The sum total of the intelligence displayed in the universe must therefore be the involved universal intelligence unfolding itself. This universal intelligence is what we call God. Call it by any other name, it is absolutely certain that in the beginning there is that infinite cosmic intelligence. This cosmic intelligence gets involved, and it manifests, evolves itself, until it becomes the perfect man, the "Christ-man," the "Buddha-man." Then it goes back to its own source. That is why all the scriptures say, "In Him we live, and move, and have our being." That is why all the scriptures preach that we come from God and go back to God. Do not be frightened by theological terms; if terms frighten you, you are not fit to be philosophers. This cosmic intelligence is what the theologians call God.

I have been asked many times, "Why do you use that old word God?" Because it is the best word for our purpose. You cannot find a better word than that, because all the hopes, aspirations, and happiness of humanity have been centred in that word. It is impossible now to change the word. Words like this were first coined by great saints, who realized their import and understood their meaning. But as they become current in society, ignorant people take up these words and the result is that they lose their spirit and glory. The word God has been used from time immemorial, and the idea of this cosmic intelligence and all that is great and holy is associated with it. Do you mean to say that because some fool says it is not all right, we should throw it away? Another man may come and say, "Take my word," and another, again, "Take my word." So there will be no end to foolish words. Use the old word, only use it in the true spirit, cleanse it of superstition, and realize fully what this great ancient word means. If you understand the power of the law of association, you will know that these words are associated with innumerable majestic and powerful ideas; they have been used and worshipped by millions of human souls and associated by them with all that is highest and best, all that is rational, all that is lovable, and all that is great and grand in human nature. And they suggest these associations and therefore cannot be given up.

If I had tried to express all this by telling you only that God created the universe, it would have conveyed nothing to you. Yet after all this struggle we have come back to Him, the Ancient and Supreme One.

We now see that all the various forms of cosmic energy, such as matter, thought, force, intelligence, and so forth, are simply the manifestation of that cosmic intelligence, or, as we shall call it henceforth, the Supreme Lord. Everything that you see, feel, or hear—the whole universe—is His creation, or to be a little more accurate, is His projection, or to be still more accurate, is the Lord Himself. It is He who is shining as the sun and the stars. He is mother earth; He Himself is the ocean. He comes as gentle showers, He is the gentle air that we breathe, and He it is who is working as force in the body. He is the speech that is uttered; He is the man who is talking. He is the audience that is here; He is the platform on which I stand; He is the light that enables me to see your faces. It is all He. He Himself is both the material and the efficient cause of this universe, and He it is that becomes involved in the minute cell and evolves at the other end and becomes God again. He it is that comes down and becomes the lowest atom, and slowly unfolding His nature, rejoins Himself.

This is the mystery of the universe. "Thou art the man, Thou art the woman, Thou art the strong man walking in the pride of youth, Thou art the old man tottering on crutches. Thou art in everything, Thou art everything, O Lord." This is the only solution of the cosmos that satisfies the human intellect. In one word, we are born of Him, we live in Him, and unto Him we return.

THE COSMOS

THE MICROCOSM

(Delivered in New York, January 26, 1896)

THE HUMAN MIND naturally wants to get outside, to peer out of the body, as it were, through the channels of the organs. The eye must see, the ear must hear, the senses must sense the external world; and naturally the beauties and sublimities of nature captivate the attention of man first. The first questions that arose in the human soul were about the external world. The solution of the mystery of the sky, of the stars, of the heavenly bodies, of the earth, of the rivers, of the mountains, of the ocean, was asked for; and in all ancient religions we find traces of how the groping human mind at first got hold of everything external. It believed in a river-god, a sky-god, a cloud-god, a rain-god; everything external, all that we now call the forces of nature, became metamorphosed, transfigured into gods, into heavenly powers.

As the inquiry went deeper and deeper, these external manifestations failed to satisfy the human mind, and finally it turned its energy inward and the question was asked about man's own soul. From the cosmos the question was reflected back to the microcosm; from the external world the question was reflected to the internal. From the analysing of external nature, man was led to the analysing of internal nature. This questioning about the internal man comes with a higher state of civilization, with a deeper insight into nature, with a higher state of growth.

The subject of discussion this afternoon is the internal man. No question is so near and dear to man's heart as that of the internal man. How many millions of times, in how many countries, has this question been asked! Sages and kings, rich and poor, saints and sinners, every man, every woman, all have from time to time asked this question: Is there nothing permanent in this evanescent human life? Is there nothing, they have asked, which does not die when the body dies? Does not something endure when the physical frame crumbles into dust? Is there not something which survives the fire which burns the body into ashes? And if there is, what is its destiny? Where does it go? Whence did it come? These questions have been asked again and again, and so long as this creation lasts, so long as there are human brains to think, these questions will have to be asked.

Yet it is not that the answer did not come. Each time the question was raised the answer came; and as time rolls on, the answer will gain more and more strength. In fact the question was answered, once for all, thousands of years

293

ago, and through all subsequent time that answer is being restated, reillustrated, made clearer to our intellect. What we have to do, therefore, is merely to make a restatement of the answer. We do not pretend to throw any new light on these all-absorbing problems, but we shall try to put before you the ancient truth in the language of modern times, to speak the thoughts of the ancients in the language of the moderns, to speak the thoughts of the philosophers in the language of the people, to speak the thoughts of the angels in the language of men, to speak the thoughts of God in the language of poor humanity, so that man will understand them; for the same Divine Essence from which the ideas emanated is ever present in man, and therefore he can always understand them.

I am looking at you. How many things are necessary for this vision? First, the eyes. For if I am perfect in every other way, yet have no eyes, I shall not be able to see you. Secondly, the real organ of vision. For the eyes are not the organs; they are but the instruments of vision, and behind them is the real organ, the nerve-centre in the brain. If that centre be injured, a man may have the clearest pair of eyes, yet he will not be able to see anything. So it is necessary that this centre, or the real organ, be there. Similarly, the external ear is but the instrument for carrying the vibration of sound inward to the centre. Thus with all our senses. Yet that is not sufficient. Suppose in your library you are intently reading a book, and the clock strikes but you do not hear it. The sound is there, the vibrations in the air are there, the ear and the centre are also there, and these vibrations have been carried through the ear to the centre, and yet you do not hear it. What is wanting? The mind is not there. Thus we see that the third thing necessary is that the mind should be there. First there must be the external instrument, then the organ to which this external instrument will carry the sensation, and lastly the organ itself must be joined to the mind. When the mind is not joined to the organ, the organ and the ear may take the impression and yet we shall not be conscious of it. The mind, too, is only the carrier; it has to carry the sensation still farther and present it to the intellect. The intellect is the determinative faculty and decides upon what is brought to it. Still this is not sufficient. The intellect must carry it farther and present the whole thing before the ruler in the body, the human soul, the king on the throne. Before him this is presented, and then from him comes the order as to what to do or what not to do; and the order goes down, in the same sequence, to the intellect, to the mind, to the organs; and the organs convey it to the instruments, and perception is complete.

The instruments are in the external body, the gross body, of man; but the mind and the intellect are not. They are in what is called in Hindu philosophy the fine body, and what in Christian theology you read of as the spiritual body of man—finer, very much finer, than the body, and yet not the soul. The soul is beyond them all. The external body perishes in a few years; any simple cause may disturb and destroy it. The fine body does not perish so easily; yet it sometimes degenerates and at other times becomes strong. We see how, in an old man, the mind loses its strength, how, when the body is vigorous, the mind becomes vigorous, how various medicines and drugs affect it, how everything external acts on it, and how it reacts on the external world. Just as the body has its progress and decadence, so also has the mind, and therefore the mind is not the soul, because the soul can neither decay nor degenerate.

How can we know that? How can we know that there is something behind this mind? Because knowledge, which is self-illuminating and the basis of intelligence, cannot belong to dull, dead matter. Never was seen any gross matter which had intelligence as its own essence. No dull or dead matter can illumine itself. It is intelligence that illumines all matter. This hall is known only through intelligence, because, as a hall, its existence would be unknown unless some intelligence perceived it. This body is not self-luminous; if it were, it would be so in a dead man also. Neither can the mind, nor even the spiritual body, be self-luminous. They are not essentially intelligent. That which is self-luminous cannot decay. The luminosity of that which shines through a borrowed light comes and goes; but that which is light itself—what can make that come and go, flourish and decay? We see that the moon waxes and wanes because it shines through the borrowed light of the sun. If a lump of iron is put into the fire and made red-hot, it glows and shines; but its light will vanish because it is borrowed. So decadence is possible only of that light which is borrowed and is not light in its own essence.

Now we see that the body, the external form, has no light as its own essence, is not self-luminous, and cannot know itself; neither can the mind. Why not? Because the mind waxes and wanes; because it is vigorous at one time and weak at another; because it can be acted upon by anything and everything. Therefore the light which shines through the mind is not its own. Whose is it, then? It must belong to That which has light as Its own essence and, as such, can never decay or die, never become stronger or weaker—to the Soul, which is self-luminous, which is luminosity itself. It cannot be that the Soul knows; It *is* knowledge. It cannot be that the Soul has existence; It *is* existence. It cannot be that the Soul is happy; It *is* happiness. That which is happy has borrowed its happiness; that which has knowledge has received its knowledge; and that which has relative existence has only a reflected existence. Wherever there are qualities, these qualities have been reflected upon the substance. But the Soul does not have knowledge, existence, and blessedness as Its qualities; they are the essence of the Soul.

Again, it may be asked, why should we take this for granted? Why should we admit that the Soul has knowledge, blessedness, and existence as Its essence, and has not borrowed them? It may be argued: Why not say that the Soul's luminosity, the Soul's blessedness, the Soul's knowledge are borrowed in the same way as the luminosity of the body is borrowed from the mind? The fallacy of arguing in this way will be that there will be no limit. From whom were these borrowed? If we say from some other source, the same question will be asked again. So at last we shall have to come to one who is self-luminous. To simplify matters, then, the logical way is to stop where we get self-luminosity, and proceed no farther.

We see, then, that the human being is composed first of this external covering, the body; secondly, of the fine body, consisting of mind, intellect, and ego. Behind them is the real Soul of man. We have seen that all the powers of the gross body are borrowed from the mind, and the mind, the fine body, borrows its powers and luminosity from the Soul standing behind.

A great many questions now arise about the nature of the Soul. If the existence of the Soul is admitted on the basis of the argument that It is self-luminous, that knowledge, existence, and blessedness are Its essence, it naturally follows that this Soul cannot have been created from nothing. A self-luminous existence, independent of any other existence, could never have non-existence for its cause. We have seen that even the physical universe cannot have come from nothing, not to speak of the Soul. It always existed. There was never a time when It did not exist; because if the Soul did not exist, where was time? Time is in the Soul; when the Soul reflects Its powers on the mind and the mind thinks, then time appears. When there was no Soul, certainly there was no thought, and without thought there was no time. How can the Soul, therefore, be said to be existing in time, when time itself exists in the Soul? It has neither birth nor death, but it is passing through all these various stages. It is manifesting Itself slowly and gradually from lower to higher, and so on. It is expressing Its own grandeur, working through the mind on the body, and through the body It is grasping the external world and understanding it. It takes up a body and uses it, and when that body has failed and is used up, It takes another body, and so on It goes.

Here comes a very interesting doctrine, that doctrine which is generally known as the reincarnation of the soul. Sometimes people get frightened at the idea; and superstition is so strong that even thinking men believe that they are the outcome of nothing, and then, with the grandest logic, try to deduce the theory that although they have come out of zero, they will be eternal ever afterwards. Those that come out of zero will certainly have to go back to zero. Neither you nor I nor anyone present has come out of zero, nor will go back to zero. We have been existing eternally, and will exist, and there is no power under the sun, or above the sun, which can undo your or my existence or send us back to zero. Now, this idea of reincarnation is not only not a frightening idea, but most essential for the moral well-being of the human race. It is the only logical conclusion that thoughtful men can arrive at. If you are going to exist in eternity hereafter, it must be that you have existed through eternity in the past; it cannot be otherwise.

I will try to answer a few objections that are generally brought against the theory. Although many of you will think they are very silly objections, still we have to answer them; for sometimes we find that the most learned men are ready to advance the silliest ideas. Well has it been said that there never was an idea so absurd that it did not find philosophers to defend it.

The first objection is: Why do we not remember our past? But do we remember all our past in this life? How many of you remember what you did when you were babies? None of you remember your babyhood; and if upon memory depends your existence, then this argument proves that you did not exist as babies, because you do not remember your babyhood. It is simply unmitigated nonsense to say that our existence depends on our remembering it. How can we remember our past life? That brain is gone, broken into pieces, and a new brain has been manufactured. What has come to this brain is the resultant, the sum total, of the impressions acquired in our past, with which the mind has come to inhabit the new body. I, as I stand here, am the effect, the result, of all the infinite past which is tacked on to me.

Such is the power of superstition that many of those who deny the doctrine of reincarnation believe that we are descended from monkeys. But they do not have the courage to ask why we do not remember our monkey life! When a great ancient sage, a seer or a prophet of old who came face to face with Truth, says something, these modern men stand up and say, "Oh, he was a fool!" But just use another name—Huxley or Tyndall—then it must be true, and they take it for granted. In place of ancient superstitions they have erected modern superstitions; in place of the old popes of religion they have installed modern popes of science.

So we see that this objection as to memory is not valid; and that is about the only serious objection raised against this theory.

Although we have seen that it is not necessary for the acceptance of this theory that there should be the memory of past lives, yet at the same time we are in a position to assert that there are instances which show that this memory does come, and that each one of us will get back this memory at the time of liberation, when we shall find that this world is but a dream. Then alone will you realize in the soul of your soul that you are but actors and the world is a stage; then alone will the idea of non-attachment come to you with the power of thunder; then all this thirst for enjoyment, this clinging to life and this world, will vanish for ever; then the mind will see as clear as daylight how many times all these existed for you—how many millions of times you had fathers and mothers, sons and daughters, husbands and wives, relatives and friends, wealth and power. They came and went. How many times you were on the very crest of the wave, and how many times you were down at the bottom of despair! When memory brings all these to you, then alone will you stand as a hero and smile when the world frowns upon you. Then alone will you stand up and say: "I care not even for thee, O Death! What terrors hast thou for me?" This will come to all.

Are there any arguments, any rational proofs, for the reincarnation of the soul? So far we have been giving the negative side, showing that the opposite arguments to disprove it are invalid. Are there any positive proofs? There are— and most valid ones, too. No other theory except that of reincarnation accounts for the wide divergence that we find between man and man in their power to acquire knowledge. First let us consider the process by means of which knowledge is acquired. Suppose I go into the street and see a dog. How do I know it is a dog? I refer it to my mind, and in my mind are groups of all my past experiences, arranged and pigeon-holed, as it were. As soon as a new impression comes, I take it up and refer it to some of the old pigeon-holes, and as soon as I find a group of the same impressions already existing, I place it in that group and I am satisfied. I know it is a dog because it coincides with impressions already there. And when I do not find the cognates of a new experience inside, I become dissatisfied. When, not finding the cognates of an impression, we become dissatisfied, this state of mind is called ignorance; but when, finding the cognates of an impression already existing, we become satisfied, this is called knowledge. When one apple fell, men became dissatisfied. Then gradually they found out a series of the same impressions, forming, as it were, a chain. What was the chain they found? That all apples fell. They called this gravitation.

Now, we see that without a fund of already existing experiences any new experience would be impossible, for there would be nothing to which to refer the new impression. So if, as some of the European philosophers think, a child came into the world with what they call a *tabula rasa*, such a child would never attain to any degree of intellectual power, because he would have nothing to which to refer his new experiences. We see that the power of acquiring knowledge varies in each individual, and this shows that each one of us has come with his own fund of knowledge. Knowledge can only be got in one way, the way of experience; there is no other way to know. If we have not had the experience in this life, we must have had it in other lives.

How is it that the fear of death is everywhere? A little chicken is just out of the egg and an eagle comes, and the chicken flies in fear to its mother. There is an old explanation (I should hardly dignify it by such a name)—it is called instinct. What makes that little chicken just out of the egg afraid to die? How is it that as soon as a duckling hatched by a hen comes near water it jumps into it and swims? It never swam before nor saw anything swim. People call it instinct. It is a big word, but it leaves us where we were before.

Let us study this phenomenon of instinct. A child begins to play on the piano. At first she must pay attention to every key she is fingering, and as she goes on and on for months and years, the playing becomes almost involuntary, instinctive. What was first done with conscious will does not require later on an effort of the will. This is not yet a complete proof. One half remains, and that is that almost all the actions which are now instinctive can be brought under the control of the will. Each muscle of the body can be brought under control. This is perfectly well known. So the proof is complete, by this double method, that what we now call instinct is the degeneration of voluntary actions. Therefore if the analogy applies to the whole of creation, if all nature is uniform, then what is instinct in lower animals, as well as in men, must be the degeneration of will.

From the study of the macrocosm we discovered that each evolution presupposes an involution, and each involution an evolution. How is instinct explained in the light of this knowledge? What we call instinct is the result of voluntary action. Instinct in men or animals must therefore have been created by their previous voluntary actions. When we speak of voluntary actions, we admit previous experience. This previous experience thus creates instinct. The little chicken's fear of death, the duckling's taking to the water, and all the involuntary actions in the human being, which are the result of past experiences, have now become instinctive.

So far we have proceeded very clearly, and so far the latest science is with us. The latest scientific men are coming back to the ancient sages, and as far as they have done so there is no difficulty. They admit that each man and each animal is born with a fund of experience, and that all the instincts in the mind are the result of past experience. "But what," they ask, "is the use of saying that

that experience belongs to the soul? Why not say it belongs to the body, and the body alone? Why not say it is hereditary transmission?" This is the last question. Why not say that all the experience with which I am born is the resultant of all the past experience of my ancestors? The sum total of the experience from the little protoplasm up to the highest human being is in me, but it has come from body to body in the course of hereditary transmission. Where will the difficulty be?

This question is very nice, and we admit some part of this hereditary transmission. How far? As far as furnishing the material of the body. We, by our past actions, are born in a certain body, and the suitable material for that body comes from the parents who have made themselves fit to have our soul as their offspring. But the simple hereditary theory takes for granted, without any proof, the most astonishing proposition: that mental experience can be recorded in matter, that mental experience can be involved in matter.

When I look at you, in the lake of my mind there is a wave. That wave subsides, but it remains in fine form, as an impression. We understand a physical impression's remaining in the body. But what proof is there for assuming that the mental impression can remain in the body, since the body goes to pieces? What carries it? Even granting that it is possible for each mental impression to remain in the body—that every impression, beginning from the first man down to my father, was in my father's body—how could it be transmitted to me? Through the bioplasmic cell? How could that happen? The father's body does not come to the child in toto. The same parents may have a number of children. Then, from this theory of hereditary transmission, where the impression and the impressed are one, because both are material, it rigorously follows that, by the birth of every child, the parents must lose a part of their own impressions, or, if the parents should transmit the whole of their impressions, then, after the birth of the first child, their minds would be a vacuum.

Again, if in the bioplasmic cell the infinite amount of impressions from all time have entered, where and how can they exist there? This is a most impossible position, and until these physiologists can prove how and where those impressions live in that cell, and what they mean by a mental impression's sleeping in the physical cell, their position cannot be taken for granted.

So far it is clear, then, that these impressions are in the mind, that the mind comes to take birth after birth and uses the material most proper for it, and that the mind which has made itself fit for only a particular kind of body will have to wait until it gets that material. This we understand. The theory then comes to this: There is hereditary transmission so far as furnishing the material to the soul is concerned. But the soul migrates and manufactures body after body; and each thought we think and each deed we do is stored in it in fine forms, ready to spring up again and take a new shape. When I look at you a wave rises in my mind. It goes down, as it were, and becomes finer and finer, but it does not die. It is ready to start up again as a wave in the shape of memory. So all these impressions are in my mind, and when I die the resultant force of them will be upon me. A ball is here, and each one of us takes a mallet in his hands and strikes the ball from all sides; the ball goes from point to point in the room, and when it reaches the door it flies out. What carries it out? The resultant of all these blows. That will give it its direction. So what directs the soul when the body dies? The resultant, the sum total, of all the works it has done, of all the thoughts it has thought. If the resultant is such that it has to manufacture a new body for further experience, it will go to those parents who are ready to supply it with suitable material for that body.

Thus from body to body it will go, sometimes to a heaven, and back again to earth, becoming a man or some lower animal. In this way it will go on until it has finished its experience and completed the circle. It then knows its own nature, knows what it is, and its ignorance vanishes. Its powers become manifest; it becomes perfect. No more is there any necessity for the soul to work through physical bodies, nor is there any necessity for it to work through fine or mental bodies. It shines in its own light and is free—no more to be born, no more to die.

We shall not go now into the particulars of this. But I shall bring before you one more point with regard to this theory of reincarnation: It is the theory that advances the freedom of the human soul. It is the one theory that does not lay the blame for all our weakness upon somebody else, which is a common human failing. We do not look at our own faults. The eyes do not see themselves; they see the eyes of everybody else. We human beings are very slow to recognize our own weakness, our own faults, so long as we can lay the blame upon somebody else. Men in general lay all the blame on their fellow men, or, failing that, on God; or they conjure up a ghost called fate.

Where is fate and what is fate? We reap what we sow. We are the makers of our own fate. None else has the blame, none else the praise. The wind is blowing; those vessels whose sails are unfurled catch it and go forward on their way, but those which have their sails furled do not catch the wind. Is that the fault of the wind? Is it the fault of the merciful Father, whose wind of mercy is blowing without ceasing, day and night, whose mercy knows no decay—is it His fault that some of us are happy and some unhappy?

We make our own destiny. His sun shines for the weak as well as for the strong. His wind blows for saint and sinner alike. He is the Lord of all, the Father of all, merciful and impartial. Do you mean to say that He, the Lord of Creation, looks upon the petty things of our life in the same light as we do? What a degenerate kind of God that would be! We are like little puppies, making life-and-death struggles here and foolishly thinking that even God Himself will take them as seriously as we do. He knows what the puppies' play means. Our attempts to lay the blame on Him, making Him the punisher and the rewarder, are only foolish. He neither punishes nor rewards any. His infinite mercy is open to everyone—at all times, in all places, under all conditions—unfailing, unswerving. Upon us depends how we utilize it. Blame neither man nor God nor anyone in the world. When you find yourselves suffering, blame yourselves and try to do better. This is the only solution of the problem.

Those that blame others—and alas! their number is increasing every day—are generally miserable souls, with helpless brains, who have brought themselves to that pass through their own mistakes. Though they blame others, this does not alter their position. It does not serve them in any way. This attempt to throw the blame upon others only weakens them the more. Therefore blame none for your own faults; stand upon your own feet and take the whole responsibility upon yourselves. Say: "This misery that I am suffering is of my own doing, and that very thing proves that it will have to be undone by me alone. That which I created I can demolish; that which is created by someone else I shall never be able to destroy." Therefore stand up, be bold, be strong. Take the whole responsibility on your own shoulders and know that you are the creator of your own destiny.

All the strength and succour you want is within yourselves. Therefore make your own future. Let the dead past bury its dead. The infinite future is before you, and you must always remember that each word, thought, and deed lays up a store for you, and that as the bad thoughts and bad works are ready to spring upon you like tigers, so also there is the inspiring hope that the good thoughts and good deeds are ready with the power of a hundred thousand angels to defend you always and for ever.

IMMORTALITY

(Delivered in America)

WHAT QUESTION HAS BEEN PONDERED a greater number of times, what idea has led men more to search the universe for an answer, what question is nearer and dearer to the human heart, what question is more inseparably connected with our existence, than this one, the immortality of the human soul? It has been the theme of poets and sages, of priests and prophets. Kings on the throne have discussed it; beggars in the street have dreamt of it. The best of humanity have approached it, and the worst of men have hoped for it. The interest in the theme has not died yet, nor will it die so long as human nature exists.

Various answers have been presented to the world by various minds. Thousands, again, in every period of history have given up the discussion. And yet the question remains fresh as ever. Often in the turmoil and struggle of our lives we seem to forget it; but suddenly someone dies—one, perhaps, whom we loved, one near and dear to our hearts, is snatched away from us—and the struggle, the din, and the turmoil of the world around us cease for a moment, and the soul asks the old question: "What after this? What becomes of the soul?"

All human knowledge proceeds out of experience; we cannot know anything except by experience. All our reasoning is based upon generalized experience; all our knowledge is but harmonized experience. Looking around us, what do we find? A continuous change. The plant comes out of the seed, grows into the tree, completes the circle, and comes back to the seed. The animal is born, lives a certain time, dies, and completes the circle. So does man. The mountains slowly but surely crumble away, the rivers slowly but surely dry up, rain comes out of the sea and goes back to the sea. Everywhere circles are being completed —birth, growth, development, and decay following each other with mathematical precision. This is our everyday experience.

Inside it all, behind all this vast mass of what we call life, of millions of forms and shapes, millions upon millions of varieties, from the lowest atom to the highest spiritual man, we find existing a certain unity. Every day we find that the walls that were thought to divide one thing from another are being broken down; all matter is coming to be recognized by modern science as one substance, manifesting itself in different ways and in various forms—as the one life that runs through all like a continuous chain, of which all these various forms represent the links, link after link, extending almost infinitely, but of the same one chain. This is what is called evolution. It is an old, old idea, as old as human society, only it is getting fresher and fresher as human knowledge progresses.

There is one thing more, which the ancients perceived, but which in modern

302

times is not yet so clearly perceived; and that is involution. The seed becomes the plant; a grain of sand never becomes a plant. It is the father that becomes the child; a lump of clay never becomes a child. From what does this evolution come?—is the question. What was the seed? It was the same as the tree. All the possibilities of a future tree are in that seed; all the possibilities of a future man are in the little baby; all the possibilities of any future life are in the germ. What is this? The ancient philosophers of India called it involution. We find, then, that every evolution presupposes an involution. Nothing can be evolved which is not already there.

Here again modern science comes to our help. You know by mathematical reasoning that the sum total of the energy that is displayed in the universe is the same throughout. You cannot take away one atom of matter or one foot-pound of force. You cannot add to the universe one atom of matter or one foot-pound of force. Evolution, as such, does not come out of zero. Then where does it come from? From previous involution. The child is the man involved, and the man is the child evolved. The seed is the tree involved, and the tree is the seed evolved. All the possibilities of life are in the germ.

The problem becomes a little clearer. Add to it the first idea, that of the continuity of life. In all creatures, from the lowest protoplasm to the most perfect human being, there is really but one life. Just as in one lifetime we have so many various phases of expression, the protoplasm developing into the baby, the child, the young man, the old man, so from the protoplasm up to the most perfect man we get one continuous life, one chain. This is evolution. But we have seen that each evolution presupposes an involution. The whole of this life, which slowly manifests itself, evolves from the lowest protoplasm to the perfected human being, the incarnation of God on earth—the whole of this series is but one life, and the whole of this manifestation must have been involved in that very protoplasm. This whole series, ending in the God-man, was involved in it, and slowly came out, manifesting itself slowly, slowly, slowly. The perfect man must have been there in the germ state, in minute form. Therefore this one force, this whole chain, is the involution of that cosmic life which is everywhere. It is this one mass of intelligence which, from the protoplasm up to the most perfect man, is slowly and slowly uncoiling itself. Not that it grows. Take away all ideas of growth from your mind. With the idea of growth is associated something coming from outside, something extraneous, which would give the lie to the truth that the Infinite, which lies latent in every life, is independent of all external conditions. It can never grow; It is always there, and only manifests Itself.

The effect is the cause manifested. There is no essential difference between the effect and the cause. Take this glass, for instance. There was the material, and that material plus the will of the manufacturer made the glass; these two were its causes and are present in it. In what form? Adhesion. If the force were not here, each particle would fall away. What is the effect, then? It is the same as the cause, only taking a different form, a different composition. When the cause is changed and limited for a time, it becomes the effect. We must remember this. Applying it to our idea of life: The whole of the manifestation of this one series, from the protoplasm up to the most perfect man, must be the very same thing as cosmic life. First it got involved and became finer; and out of that fine something, which was the cause, it has gone on evolving, manifesting itself, and becoming grosser.

But the question of immortality is not yet settled. We have seen that everything in this universe is indestructible. There is nothing new; there will be nothing new. The same series of manifestations are presenting themselves alternately, as if on a wheel, coming up and going down. All motion in this universe is in the form of waves, successively rising and falling. Systems after systems are coming out of fine forms, evolving themselves, and taking grosser forms, again melting down, as it were, and going back to the fine forms. Again they rise out of the fine forms, evolving for a certain period and then slowly going back to the cause. So with all life. Each manifestation of life comes up and then goes down again. What goes down? The form. The form breaks to pieces, but it comes up again.

In one sense even bodies and forms are eternal. How? Suppose we take a number of dice and throw them, and they fall in this order: 6—5—3—4. We take the dice up and throw them again and again. There must be a time when the same number will come again; the same combination must come. Now each particle, each atom, that is in this universe, I take for such a die, and these are being thrown out and combined again and again. All these forms before you are one combination. Here are the forms of a glass, a table, a pitcher of water, and so forth. This is one combination; in time it will all break up. But there must come a time when exactly the same combination will have come again: you will be here and this form will be here, this subject will be talked on, and this pitcher will be here. An infinite number of times this has been repeated, and an infinite number of times this will be repeated. Thus, so far as the physical forms are concerned, what do we find? That even the combination of physical forms is eternally repeated.

A most interesting conclusion that follows from this theory is the explanation of facts such as these: Some of you, perhaps, have seen a man who can read the past life of others and foretell the future. How is it possible for anyone to see what the future will be, unless there is a regulated future? Effects of the past will recur in the future, and we see that it is so. You have seen the big Ferris wheel[1] in Chicago. The wheel revolves and the little carriages in the wheel come regularly one after another; one set of people gets into these, and after they have gone round the circle they get out and a fresh batch of people gets in. Each one of these batches is like one of these manifestations, from the lowest animal to the highest man. Nature is like the chain of the Ferris wheel, endless and infinite, and these little carriages are the bodies or forms, in which fresh batches of souls are riding, going up higher and higher until they become perfect and come out of the wheel. But the wheel goes on. And so long as the bodies are in the wheel, it can be absolutely and mathematically foretold where they will go; but not so of the souls. Thus it is possible to read the past and the future with precision.

We see, then, that there is a recurrence of the same material phenomena at certain periods, and that the same combinations have been taking place

[1] The first Ferris wheel was erected for the Columbian Exposition at Chicago in 1893.

through eternity. But that is not the immortality of the soul. We have observed that no force can die; no matter can be annihilated. What then becomes of the soul? It goes on changing, back and forth, until it returns to the source from which it came. There is no motion in a straight line; everything moves in a circle. A straight line, infinitely produced, becomes a circle. If that is so, there cannot be eternal degeneration for any soul. It cannot be. Everything must complete the circle and come back to its source.

What are you and I and all these souls? In our discussion of evolution and involution, we have seen that you and I must be part of the cosmic conscious-ness, cosmic life, cosmic mind, which got involved, and that we must complete the circle and go back to this cosmic intelligence, which is God. This cosmic intelligence is what people call the Lord, or God, or Christ, or Buddha, or Brah-man; what the materialists perceive as force, and the agnostics, as the infinite, inexpressible Beyond. And we are all parts of that.

This is the second idea. Yet this is not sufficient; there will be still more doubts. It is all very well to say that there is no destruction for any force. But all the forces and forms that we see are combinations. This form before us is a composition of several component parts, and every force that we know is similarly composite. If you take the scientific idea of force, and call every force the sum total, the resultant, of several forces, what becomes of your individuality? Every-thing that is a compound must sooner or later go back to its component parts. Whatever in this universe is the result of the combination of matter or force must sooner or later go back to its components. Whatever is the result of certain causes must die, must be destroyed. It gets broken up, dispersed, and resolved back into its components.

The soul is not a force; neither is it thought. It is the manufacturer of thought, but not thought itself; it is the manufacturer of the body, but not the body. Why so? We see that the body cannot be the soul. Why not? Because it is not intelligent. A corpse is not intelligent, nor a piece of meat in a butcher's shop. What do we mean by intelligence? We mean reactive power. We want to go a little more deeply into this.

Here is a pitcher. I see it. How? Rays of light from the pitcher enter my eyes and make a picture in my retina, which is carried to the brain. Yet there is no vision. What the physiologists call the sensory nerves carry this impression inward. But up to this point there is no reaction. The nerve-centre in the brain carries the impression to the mind, and the mind reacts, and as soon as this reaction comes, the pitcher flashes before me.

Take a more commonplace example. Suppose you are listening to me intently, and a mosquito is sitting on the tip of your nose and giving you that pleasant sensation which mosquitoes alone can give; but you are so intent on hearing me that you do not feel the mosquito at all. What has happened? The mosquito has bitten a certain part of your skin, and certain nerves are there. They have carried a certain sensation to the brain, and the impression is there. But the mind, being otherwise occupied, does not react. So you are not aware of the presence of the mosquito.

When a new impression comes, if the mind does not react we shall not be conscious of it; but when the reaction comes we feel, we see, we hear, and so forth. With this reaction comes illumination, as the Sāmkhya philosophers call it. We see that the body cannot illumine, because in the absence of attention no sensation is possible.

Cases have been known where, under peculiar conditions, a man who had never learnt a particular language was found able to speak it. Subsequent inquiries proved that the man had, when a boy, lived among people who spoke that language and the impressions were left in his brain. These impressions remained stored up there until through some cause the mind reacted and illumination came; and then the man was able to speak the language. This shows that the mind alone is not sufficient, that the mind itself is an instrument in the hands of someone else. The boy's mind contained that language, yet he did not know it; but later there came a time when he did. It shows that there is someone besides the mind; and when the man was a boy that someone did not use the power, but when the boy grew up he took advantage of it and used it.

First, here is the body; second, the mind, or instrument of thought; and third, behind this mind is the Self of man. The Sanskrit word is Ātman. As modern philosophers have identified thought with molecular changes in the brain, they do not know how to explain the case just mentioned, and generally deny it. The mind is intimately connected with the brain, which dies every time the body changes. The Self is the illuminator, and the mind is the instrument in Its hands, and through that instrument It gets hold of the external instruments; and thus comes perception. The external instruments get hold of the impressions and carry them to the organs—for you must remember always that the eyes and ears are only receivers; it is the internal organs, the nerve-centres, that act. In Sanskrit these centres are called indriyas. They carry sensations to the mind, and the mind presents them farther back to another state of the mind, which in Sanskrit is called chitta, and there they are organized into will; and all these present them to the King of kings inside, the Ruler on his throne, the Self of man. He then sees and gives his orders. Then the mind immediately acts on the organs, and the organs on the external body. The real Perceiver, the real Ruler, the Governor, the Creator, the Manipulator of all this, is the Self of man.

We see, then, that the Self of man is not the body, neither is It thought. It cannot be a compound. Why not? Because everything that is a compound can be seen or imagined. That which we cannot imagine or perceive, which we cannot bind together, is not force or matter, cause or effect, and cannot be a compound. The domain of compounds is only so far as our mental universe, our thought universe, extends; beyond this it does not exist. That is as far as law reigns, and if there is anything beyond law, it cannot be a compound at all.

The Self of man, being beyond the law of causation, is not a compound. It is ever free and is the Ruler of everything that is within law. It will never die, because death means going back to the component parts, and that which was never a compound can never die. It is sheer nonsense to say that It dies.

We are now treading on finer and finer ground, and some of you perhaps will be frightened. We have seen that this Self, being beyond the little universe

of matter and force and thought, is a simple, uncompounded entity, and therefore It cannot die. That which does not die cannot live. For life and death are
the obverse and reverse of the same coin. Life is another name for death; and
death, for life. One particular mode of manifestation is what we call life; another
particular mode of manifestation of the same thing is what we call death. When
the wave rises to the top it is life, and when it falls into the hollow it is death.
If anything is beyond death, naturally it must also be beyond life.

I must remind you of the first conclusion, that the Soul of man is part of the
cosmic energy, which is God. We now find that It is beyond life and death.
You were never born and you will never die. What is this birth and death that
we see around us? This belongs to the body only, because the Soul is omnipresent. "How can that be?" you may ask. "So many people are sitting here,
and you say the Soul is omnipresent?" What is there, I ask, to limit anything
that is beyond law, beyond causation? This glass is limited; it is not omnipresent,
because the surrounding matter forces it to take this form, does not allow it to
expand. It is conditioned by everything around it and is therefore limited. But
that which is beyond law and has nothing to act upon it—how can that be
limited? It must be omnipresent. You are everywhere in the universe.

How is it, then, that I am born and I am going to die, and all that? That is
the talk of ignorance, hallucination of the brain. You neither were born nor will
die. You neither have had birth nor will have rebirth nor life nor death nor
anything. What do you mean by coming and going? All shallow nonsense!
You are everywhere. Then what is this coming and going? It is the hallucination produced by the change of the fine body, which you call the mind. That
is what is coming and going—just a little speck of cloud passing before the sky.
As it moves, it may create the illusion that the sky moves. Sometimes you
see a cloud moving before the moon, and you think the moon is moving. When
you are in a train you think the land is flying, or when you are in a boat you
think the water moves. In reality you are neither going nor coming, you have
not been born nor are you going to be reborn; you are infinite, ever present,
beyond all causation, and ever free. How could there be mortality when there
was no birth? Such a question is out of place; it is arrant nonsense.

To come to a logical conclusion we shall have to take one step more. There
is no half-way house. You are metaphysicians, and there is no crying quarter.
If, then, we are beyond all law, we must be omniscient, ever blessed; all knowledge must be in us, and all power and blessedness. Certainly. You are the
omniscient, omnipresent Being of the universe. But of such Beings can there
be many? Can there be a hundred thousand millions of omnipresent Beings?
Certainly not. Then what becomes of us all? You are only one; there is only
one such Self, and that one Self is you. Standing behind this little nature is what
we call the Soul. There is only one Being, one Existence—the Ever Blessed,
the Omnipresent, the Omniscient, the Birthless, the Deathless. "Through His
control the sky expands, through His control the air breathes, through His control the sun shines, and through His control all live. He is the Reality in nature,
He is the Soul of your soul—nay more, you are He, you are one with Him."

Wherever there are two, there is fear, there is danger, there is conflict, there
is strife. When it is all one, who is there to hate, who is there to struggle

with? When it is all He, with whom can you fight? This explains the true nature of life; this explains the true nature of being. This is perfection, and this is God. As long as you see the many, you are under delusion. "In this world of many, he who sees the One, in this ever changing world, he who sees Him who never changes, as the Soul of his own soul, as his own Self—he is free, he is blessed, he has reached the goal."

Therefore know that thou art He; thou art the God of this universe—*Tat tvam asi*. All these various ideas that I am a man or a woman, or sick or healthy, or strong or weak, or that I hate or I love, or have a little power, are but hallucinations. Away with them! What makes you weak? What makes you fear? You are the sole Being in the universe. What frightens you?

Stand up, then, and be free. Know that every thought and word that weakens you in this world is the only evil that exists. Whatever makes men weak, makes men fear, is the only evil that should be shunned. What can frighten you? If the suns come down and the moons crumble into dust and systems after systems are hurled to annihilation, what is that to you? Stand as a rock; you are indestructible. You are the Self, the God of the universe. Say: "I am Existence Absolute, Bliss Absolute, Knowledge Absolute. I am He." And like a lion breaking its cage, break your chain and be free for ever. What frightens you? What holds you down? Only ignorance and delusion; nothing else can bind you. You are the Pure One, the Ever Blessed.

Silly fools tell you that you are sinners, and you sit down in a corner and weep. It is foolishness, wickedness, downright rascality to say that you are sinners! You are all God. See you not God and call Him man? Therefore, if you dare, stand on that, mould your whole life on that. If a man cuts your throat, do not say no, for you are cutting your own throat. When you help a poor man, do not feel the least pride. That is worship for you and not a cause for pride. Is not the whole universe you? Where is there anyone that is not you? You are the Soul of this universe. You are the sun, moon, and stars; it is you that are shining everywhere. The whole universe is you. Whom are you going to hate or fight? Know, then, that you are He, and model your whole life accordingly. He who knows this and models his life accordingly will no more grovel in darkness.

VIVEKANANDA IN AMERICA

VIVEKANANDA IN AMERICA

THE ĀTMAN

(Delivered in Brooklyn, February 2, 1896)

MANY OF YOU perhaps have read Max Müller's book, *Three Lectures on the Vedānta Philosophy*, and some of you may also have read, in German, Professor Deussen's book on the same subject. In what is being written and taught in the West about the philosophical and religious thought of India, one school is principally represented, that which is called Advaita, the monistic side of Indian thought. Sometimes it is believed that all the teachings of the Vedas are comprised in that one system. There are, however, other phases of Indian thought, and perhaps this non-dualistic form is professed by a minority as compared with them.

From the most ancient times there have been various schools of thought in India, and as there never was any formulated or recognized church or body of men to designate the doctrines which should be followed by these schools, people were very free to choose their own form, make their own philosophy, and establish their own sects. We therefore find that from the most ancient times India was full of religious sects. At the present time, I do not know how many hundreds of sects we have in India, and several fresh ones are coming into existence every year. It seems that the religious activity of the nation is simply inexhaustible.

Of these various sects there can be made, in the first place, two main divisions: the orthodox and the unorthodox. Those that believe in the Vedas, the Hindu scriptures, as eternal revelations of truth, are called orthodox, and those that accept other authorities, rejecting the Vedas, are called unorthodox. The chief modern unorthodox sects are the Jains and the Buddhists. Among the orthodox some declare that the scriptures are of much higher authority than reason; others, again, say that only that portion of the scriptures which is rational should be accepted, and the rest rejected. Of the three primary orthodox schools—the Sāmkhyas, the Naiyāikas, and the Mimāmsakas—the first two, although they existed as philosophical schools, failed to form any sect. The one sect that now really covers India is that of the later Mimāmsakas, or the Vedāntists. Their philosophy is called Vedānta.

All the schools of Hindu philosophy start from the Vedānta, or the Upanishads, but the monists took the name to themselves as a specialty, because they wanted to base the whole of their theology and philosophy upon the Upanishads and nothing else. In the course of time the Vedānta philosophy prevailed, and all the various sects of India that now exist can be referred to one or another of its schools. Yet these schools are not unanimous in their doctrines.

We find that there are three principal variations among the Vedāntists. But

309

on one point they all agree, and that is that they all believe in God. All these Vedāntists also believe the Vedas to be the revealed word of God, not exactly in the same sense, perhaps, as the Christians or the Mohammedans believe regarding their scriptures, but in a very peculiar sense. Their idea is that the Vedas are an expression of the Knowledge of God; and since God is eternal, His Knowledge too is eternal, and so are the Vedas.

There is another common ground of belief—that of creation in cycles: that the whole of creation appears and disappears; it is projected and becomes grosser and grosser, and at the end of an incalculable period of time it becomes finer and finer, until it dissolves and subsides, and then comes a period of rest; again it begins to manifest and goes through the same process. The Vedāntists postulate a material substance, which they call ākāśa, which is something like the ether of the modern scientists, and also a force which they call prāna. About this prāna they declare that by its vibration the universe is produced. When a cycle ends, all this manifestation of nature becomes finer and finer and dissolves into ākāśa, which cannot be seen or felt, yet out of which everything is manufactured. All the forces that we see in nature, such as gravitation, attraction, and repulsion, or thought, feeling, and nervous motion—all these various forces resolve into prāna, and then the vibration of prāna ceases. In that state it remains until the beginning of the next cycle. Prāna then begins to vibrate, and that vibration acts upon the ākāśa, and all these forms are projected in regular succession.

The first school I shall tell you about is styled the dualistic school. The dualists believe that God, who is the Creator of the universe and its Ruler, is eternally separate from nature, eternally separate from the human soul. God is eternal; nature is eternal; and so are all souls. Nature and the souls become manifest and change, but God remains the same. According to the dualists, again, this God is personal, in that He has qualities, and not because He has a body. He has human attributes. He is merciful, He is just, He is powerful, He is almighty, He can be approached, He can be prayed to, He can be loved, He loves in return, and so forth. In one word, He is a human God, only infinitely greater than man; He has none of the evil qualities which men have. "He is the repository of an infinite number of blessed qualities"—that is their definition of God. He cannot create without materials, and nature is the material out of which He creates the whole universe.

There are some non-Vedāntic dualists called "Atomists," who believe that nature is nothing but an infinite number of atoms, and it is God's will acting upon these atoms that creates. The Vedāntists deny the atomic theory; they say it is perfectly illogical. The indivisible atoms are like geometrical points, without parts or magnitude; and anything without parts or magnitude, if multiplied an infinite number of times, will remain the same. Anything that has no parts will never make something that has parts; any number of zeros added together will not make one single whole number. So if these atoms are such that they have no parts or magnitude, the creation of the universe out of such atoms is simply impossible. Therefore, according to the Vedāntic dualists, there is what they call indiscrete or undifferentiated nature, and out of that God creates the universe.

The vast mass of Indian people are dualists. Human nature ordinarily cannot conceive of anything higher. We find that ninety per cent of the population of the earth who believe in religion at all are dualists. All the religions of Europe and Western Asia are dualistic; they have to be. The ordinary man cannot think of anything which is not concrete. He naturally likes to cling to that which his intellect can grasp. That is to say, he can only conceive of higher spiritual ideas by bringing them down to his own level. He can only grasp abstract thoughts by making them concrete. This is the religion of the masses all over the world. They believe in a God who is entirely separate from them, a great king, a high, mighty monarch, as it were. At the same time they make Him purer than the monarchs of the earth; they give Him all good qualities and remove the evil qualities from Him—as if it were ever possible for good to exist without evil; as if there could be any conception of light without a conception of darkness!

With all dualistic theories the first difficulty is: How is it possible that, under the rule of a just and merciful God, the repository of an infinite number of good qualities, there can be so many evils in this world? This question arose in all the dualistic religions; but the Hindus never invented a Satan as an answer to it. The Hindus with one accord laid the blame on man, and it was easy for them to do so. Why? Because, as I have just now told you, they did not believe that souls were created out of nothing.

We see in this life that we can shape and form our future; every one of us, every day, is trying to shape the morrow. Today we fix the fate of the morrow; tomorrow we shall fix the fate of the day after; and so on. It is quite logical that this reasoning can be pushed backward too. If by our own deeds we shape our destiny in the future, why not apply the same rule to the past? Suppose there is an infinite chain consisting of two kinds of links, with the links alternating and divided into groups. If one group is explained, we can explain the whole chain. So, from this infinite length of time, if we can cut off one portion and explain that portion and understand it, then, if we assume that nature is uniform, the same explanation must apply to the whole chain of time. If it be true that we are working out our own destiny here within this short space of time, if it be true that everything must have a cause, as we see it now, it must also be true that what we are now is the effect of the whole of our past.

Therefore no other person is necessary to shape the destiny of mankind but man himself. The evils that are in the world are caused by none else but ourselves. We have caused all this evil; and just as we constantly see misery resulting from evil actions, so also we can see that much of the existing misery in the world is the effect of the past wickedness of man. Man alone, therefore, according to this theory, is responsible. God is not to blame. He, the eternally merciful Father, is not to blame at all. "We reap what we sow."

Another important doctrine of the dualists is that every soul must eventually attain salvation. No one will be left out. Through various vicissitudes, through various sufferings and enjoyments, each one of them will come out in the end. Come out of what? The one common idea of all dualistic sects is that every soul has to get out of this physical world; for the world which we see and feel, however glorious it may be, cannot be the right, the real one, because it is a mixture of good and evil. According to the dualists there is beyond this world a place full of happiness and good only, and when that place is reached there will be no more necessity of being born and reborn, of living and dying; and this idea is very dear to them. There will be no more disease and death. There will be eternal happiness, and they will be in the presence of God for all time and enjoy Him for ever. They believe that all beings, from the lowest worm up to the highest angels and gods, will all, sooner or later, attain to that world where there will be no more misery.

But our world will never end; it goes on eternally. Although moving in waves, moving in cycles, it never ends. The number of souls that are to be saved, that are to be perfected, is infinite. Some are in plants, some are in the lower animals, some are in men, some are in gods; but all of them, even the gods, are imperfect, are in bondage. What is the bondage? It is the compulsion of being born and the compulsion of dying. Even the gods die.

What are these gods? They mean certain states, certain offices. For instance, Indra, the king of the gods, means a certain office. Some soul who performed highly meritorious work on earth has gone to fill that post in this cycle, and after this cycle he will be born again as a man and come down to this earth, and a man who is very good in this cycle will take up that post in the next cycle. So with all these gods: they are certain offices which have been filled successively by millions and millions of souls, who, after filling those offices, came down and became men. Those who do good works in this world, and help others, but with an eye to reward, hoping to reach heaven or to get the praise of their fellow men, must, when they die, reap the benefit of those good works. They become gods.

But that is not salvation. Salvation never will come through hope of reward. Whatever a man desires, the Lord gives him. Men desire power, they desire prestige, they desire enjoyments as gods, and they have these desires fulfilled. But no effect of work can be eternal; the effect will be exhausted after a certain length of time—it may be aeons—but after that it will be gone, and these gods must come down again and become men and get another chance for liberation. The lower animals will come up and become men, become gods, perhaps, then become men again, or even become animals, until the time comes when they get rid of all desire for enjoyment, all thirst for life, all clinging to "me" and "mine."

"Me" and "mine" are the very root of all the evil in the world. If you ask a dualist, "Is this child yours?" he will say, "No, it is God's. My property is not really mine, it is God's." Everything should be held as God's.

Now, these dualistic sects in India are great vegetarians, great preachers of non-killing of animals. But their idea about it is quite different from that of the Buddhists. If you ask a Buddhist, "Why do you preach against killing any animal?" he will answer, "We have no right to take any life"; and if you ask a dualist, "Why do you not kill any animal?" he will say, "Because it is the Lord's."

So the dualist says that "me" and "mine" are to be applied to God and God alone; He is the only "me," and everything is His. When a man has come to such a state that he has no "me" and "mine," that everything is given up to God, that he loves everybody and is ready to give up his life even for an animal, without any desire for reward, then his heart will be purified; and when the heart has been purified, into that heart will come the love of God.

God is the centre of attraction for every soul. The dualist says that a needle covered up with clay will not be attracted by a magnet, but as soon as the clay is washed off, it will be attracted. God is the magnet, and the human soul is the needle, and its evil works are the dirt and dust that cover it. As soon as the soul becomes pure it will by natural attraction come to God and remain with Him for ever, though eternally separate.

The perfected soul, if he wishes, can take any form; he is able to take a hundred bodies if he wishes, or have none at all if he so desires. He becomes almost almighty, except that he cannot create a world; that power belongs to God alone. None, however perfect, can manage the affairs of the universe; that function belongs to God. But all souls, when they become perfect, are happy for ever and live eternally with God. This is the religion of the dualists.

One other idea the dualists preach. They protest against the habit of praying to God: "O Lord, give me this, give me that." They assert that this should not be done. If a man must ask for some material gift he should ask inferior beings for it; he should ask one of the gods or angels, or a perfected being, for temporal things. God is only to be loved. It is almost blasphemy to say to God: "Lord, give me this, give me that." According to the dualists, therefore, what a man wants he will get sooner or later by praying to one of the gods; but if he wants salvation he must worship God Himself. This is the religion of the masses of India.

The real Vedānta philosophy begins with those known as qualified non-dualists. They make the statement that the effect is never different from the cause; the effect is but the cause reproduced in another form. If the universe is the effect and God the cause, it must be God Himself; it cannot be anything but that. They start with the assertion that God is both the efficient and the material cause of the universe; that He Himself is the Creator and He Himself is the material out of which the whole of nature is projected. The Sanskrit word for creation has no exact equivalent in your language; there is no sect in India which believes in creation as it is described in the Bible—as something coming out of nothing. It seems that at one time there were a few that had some such idea, but they were very quickly silenced. At the present time I do not know of any sect that believes this. What we mean by creation is projection of that which already existed.

Now, the whole universe, according to the qualified non-dualists, is God Himself. He is the material of the universe. We read in the Vedas: "As the spider spins the thread out of its own body, . . . even so the whole universe has come out of that Being." But if the effect is the cause reproduced, the question is: How is it that we find this dull, unintelligent material universe produced from a God who is not material, but who is eternal intelligence; how, if the cause is pure and perfect, can the effect be quite different?

What do these qualified non-dualists say in reply? Theirs is a very peculiar theory. They say that these three—God, nature, and souls—constitute Reality. God is, as it were, the Soul, and nature and souls are the body of God. Just as I have a body and a Soul, so the whole universe and all souls are the body of God, and God is the Soul of all souls. Thus God is the material cause of the universe.

The body may be changed—may be young or old, strong or weak—but that does not affect the Soul at all. It is the same eternal existence manifesting through the body. Bodies come and go, but the Soul does not change. Even so the whole universe is the body of God, and in that sense it is God. But the change in the universe does not affect God. Out of His body He creates the universe, and at the end of a cycle His body becomes finer and contracts; at the beginning of another cycle it expands again, and out of it evolve all these different worlds.

Now both the dualists and the qualified non-dualists admit that the soul is by its nature pure, but through its own deeds becomes impure. The qualified non-dualists express it more beautifully than the dualists by saying that the soul's purity and perfection become contracted and again become manifest, and that what we are now trying to do is to remanifest the intelligence, the purity, and the power which are natural to the soul. Souls have a multitude of qualities, but not that of almightiness or all-knowingness. Every wicked deed contracts the nature of the soul, and every good deed expands it; and these souls are all parts of God. "As from a blazing fire fly millions of sparks of the same nature, even so from this Infinite Being these souls have come." Each soul has the same goal. Like the God of the dualists, the God of the qualified non-dualists is also a Personal God, the repository of an infinite number of blessed qualities, only He interpenetrates everything in the universe. He is immanent in everything and is everywhere; and when the scriptures say that God is everything, it means that God interpenetrates everything, not that God has become the wall, but that God is in the wall. There is not a particle, not an atom in the universe, where He is not. Again, souls are all limited; they are not omnipresent. When their powers become expanded and they become perfect, there is no more birth and death for them; they live with God for ever.

Now we come to Advaita, the last of the Vedānta schools, and, as we think, the fairest flower of philosophy and religion that any country in any age has produced, where human thought attains its highest expression and even goes beyond the mystery which seems to be impenetrable. This is the Non-dualistic Vedānta. It is too abstruse, too elevated, to be the religion of the masses. Even in India, its birthplace, where it has been ruling supreme for the last three thousand years, it has not been able to permeate the masses.

As we go on we shall find that it is difficult for even the most intelligent man and woman in any country to understand Advaita—we have made ourselves so weak; we have made ourselves so low. We may make a show of strength, but we want to lean on somebody else. We are like little, weak plants, always wanting a support. How many times I have been asked for a "comfortable religion"! Very few men ask for the truth, fewer still dare to learn the truth, and the fewest dare to follow it in all its practical bearings. It is not their fault; it is all weakness of the brain. Any new thought, especially of a high kind, creates a disturbance, tries to make a new channel, as it were, in the brain matter, and that unhinges the system, throws men off their balance. They are used to certain surroundings and have to overcome a formidable mass of superstitions—ancestral superstition, class superstition, city superstition, country superstition—and above all, the innate superstition which makes men forget their divine nature. Yet there are a few brave souls who dare to conceive the truth, who dare to take it up, and who dare to follow it to the end.

What does the Advaitist declare? He says: If there is a God, that God must be both the material and the efficient cause of the universe; not only is He the Creator, but He is also the created; He Himself is this universe.

How can that be? God, the Pure, the Spirit, has become the universe? Yes—apparently so. That which all ignorant people see as the universe does not really exist. What are you and I and all these things we see? Mere self-hypnotism. There is but one Existence, the Infinite, the Ever Blessed One. In that Existence we dream all these various dreams. It is the Ātman, beyond all, the Infinite, beyond the known, beyond the knowable; in and through That we see the universe. It is the only reality. It is this table; It is the audience before me; It is the wall; It is everything—minus the name and form. Take away the form of the table, take away the name; what remains is Ātman.

Vedāntists do not call Ātman either He or She; sex is a mere fiction of the human brain. There is no sex in the Soul. People who are under illusion, who have become like animals, see a woman or a man; Godlike men do not see either. How can they who are beyond everything have any idea of sex? To them everyone is Ātman, the Self—sexless, pure, ever blessed.

It is name and form—created by māyā—which cause all the differences we see in this world between various objects. If you take away name and form the whole universe becomes one. There are not two; there is but one everywhere. You and I are one. There is neither nature, nor God, nor the universe—only that one Infinite Existence, out of which, through name and form, all these are manufactured.

How can you know the Knower? It cannot be known. How can you see your own self? You can only reflect yourself. So all this universe is the reflection of that one Eternal Being, the Ātman; and as the reflection falls upon good or bad reflectors, so good or bad images are created. Thus in the murderer the reflector is bad, not the Self. In the saint the reflector is pure. The Self, the Ātman, is by Its own nature pure. It is the same one Existence, the same Ātman, that is reflecting Itself as the lowest worm and also as the highest and most perfect being.

The whole of this universe is one Unity, one Existence—physically, mentally, morally, and spiritually. We are looking upon this one Existence in different ways and creating all these images upon It. To the being who has limited himself to the condition of man, It appears as the world of man. To the being who is on a higher plane of existence, It may seem like heaven. There is but one Soul in the universe, not two. It neither comes nor goes. It neither is born nor dies nor reincarnates. How can It die? Where can It go after death? All these heavens, all these earths, are vain imaginations of the mind. They do not exist—never existed in the past and never will exist in the future.

I am omnipresent, eternal. Where can I go? Where am I not already? I am reading this book of nature. Page after page I am finishing and turning over, and one dream of life after another goes away. Another page of life is turned over, another dream of life comes, and it goes away, rolling and rolling. And when I have finished my reading I let it all go and stand aside; I throw away the book, and the whole thing is finished.

What does the Advaitist preach? He dethrones all the gods that ever existed or ever will exist in the universe, and puts in their place the Self of man, the Ātman, higher than the sun and the moon, higher than the heavens, greater than this great universe itself. No books, no scriptures, no science, can ever imagine the glory of the Self, which appears as man—the most glorious God that ever was, the only God that ever existed, exists, or ever will exist. I am to worship, therefore, none but my Self. "I worship my Self," says the Advaitist. "To whom shall I bow down? I salute my Self. To whom shall I go for help? Who can help me, the one Infinite Being of the universe?" Do not dream these foolish dreams. Who ever helped anyone? None. Whenever you see a weak man, a dualist, weeping and wailing for help from somewhere above the skies, it is because he does not know that the skies also are in him. He wants help from the skies, and the help comes. We see that it comes; but it comes from within, and he mistakenly thinks it comes from without. It is as when, sometimes, a sick man lying on his bed hears a tap on the door. He gets up and opens it and finds no one there. He goes back to bed, and again he hears a tap. He gets up and opens the door. Nobody is there. At last he finds that it was his own heart-beat, which he fancied to be a knock at the door.

Thus man, after this vain search for various gods outside himself, completes the circle and comes back to the point from which he started—the human soul; and he finds that the God whom he was searching for over hill and dale, whom he was seeking in every brook, in every temple, in every church, the God whom he was even imagining as sitting in heaven and ruling the world, is his own Self. I am He, and He is I. None but I was God; this little I never existed.

Yet how could that perfect God have been deluded? He never was. How could a perfect God have been dreaming? He never dreamt. Truth never dreams. The very question as to where this illusion arose is absurd. Illusion arises from illusion alone. There will be no illusion as soon as Truth is seen. Illusion always rests upon illusion; it never rests upon God, Truth, the Ātman. You are never in illusion; it is illusion that is in you, before you. Suppose a cloud is here; another comes and pushes it aside and takes its place; still another comes and pushes that one away. As there always exists the blue sky, though clouds of various hues and colours appear before it and disappear, even so there exists the eternally pure, eternally perfect Ātman, which is your own Self.

You are the veritable Gods of the universe. Nay, there are not two; there is but One. It is a mistake to say "you" and "I." Say "I." It is I who am eating through millions of mouths; how can I be hungry? It is I who am working through an infinite number of hands; how can I be inactive? It is I who am living the life of the whole universe; where is death for me? I am beyond all life, beyond all death. Where shall I seek for freedom? For I am free by nature. Who can bind me, the God of this universe? The scriptures of the world are but little maps, trying to delineate my glory; I am the only existence. Then what are these books to me?—Thus says the Advaitist.

"Know Truth and be free in a moment." All the darkness will then vanish.

When man has seen himself as one with the Infinite Being of the universe, when all separateness has ceased, when all men and women, all gods and angels, all animals and plants, and the whole universe have melted into that Oneness, then all fear disappears. Can I hurt myself? Can I kill myself? Can I injure myself? Whom shall I fear? Can you fear yourself? Then will all sorrow disappear. What can cause me sorrow? I am the sole Existence. Then will all jealousy disappear. Of whom shall I be jealous? Of myself? Then will all bad feelings disappear. Against whom can I have any bad feeling? Against myself? There is none in the universe but me.

This is the one way, says the Vedāntist, to Knowledge. Kill out this differentiation, kill out this superstition that there are many. "He who in this world of many sees that One; he who in this mass of insentiency sees that one sentient Being; he who in this world of shadows catches that Reality—unto him belongs eternal peace, unto none else, unto none else."

These are the salient points of the three steps which Indian religious thought has taken in regard to Reality. We have seen that it began with the extra-cosmic Personal God. It went from the external to the intra-cosmic God, God immanent in the universe; and it ended in identifying the soul itself with that God, and making one Soul, one Unit, of all these various manifestations in the universe. This is the last word of the Vedas. Indian religious thought begins with dualism, goes through qualified non-dualism, and ends in perfect non-dualism.

We know that very few in this world can come to the last, or even dare to believe in it, and fewer still dare to act according to it. Yet we know that therein lies the explanation of all ethics, all morality, and all spirituality in the universe. Why is it that everyone says, "Do good to others"? Where is the explanation? Why is it that all great men have preached the brotherhood of mankind, and greater men, that of all living beings? Because, from behind all beings, whether they know it or not, shines forth, through all their irrational and personal superstitions, the eternal light of the Self, negating all diversity and asserting that the whole universe is one.

Again, that last word gave us one universe, which through the senses we see as matter, through the intellect as souls, and through the Spirit as God. To the man who puts veils upon himself, which the world calls wickedness and evil, this very universe will change its appearance and become a hideous place; to another man, who wants enjoyment, this very universe will change and become a heaven; and to the perfect man the whole thing will vanish and appear, instead, as his own Self.

Now, as society exists at the present time, all these three stages are necessary. One stage does not deny another; it is simply the fulfilment of the other. The Advaitist or the qualified Advaitist does not say that dualism is wrong; it is a right view, but a lower one. It is on the way to Truth. Therefore let everybody work out his own vision of this universe according to his own ideas. Injure none, deny the position of none. Take a man where he stands, and if you can, lend him a helping hand and put him on a higher level; but do not injure and do not destroy. All will come to Truth in the long run. "When all the desires of the heart are vanquished, then this very mortal will become immortal"; then this very man will become God.

THE ĀTMAN: ITS BONDAGE AND FREEDOM

(Delivered in America)

ACCORDING TO THE Advaita philosophy there is only one thing real in the universe, which it calls Brahman. Everything else is unreal, manifested and manufactured from Brahman by the power of māyā. To reach back to Brahman is our goal. We are, each one of us, that Brahman, that Reality, plus māyā. If we can get rid of this māyā, or ignorance, then we become what we really are. According to this philosophy, each man consists of three parts: the body, the internal organ or mind, and behind that, what is called the Ātman, the Self. The body is the external coating, and the mind is the internal coating, of the Ātman, who is the real perceiver, the real enjoyer, the real Being in the body, who works the body by means of the internal organ, or mind.

The Ātman is the only existence in the human body and is immaterial. Because It is immaterial, It cannot be a compound, and because It is not a compound, It does not obey the law of cause and effect; and so It is immortal. That which is immortal can have no beginning, because everything with a beginning must have an end. It also follows that it must be formless; there cannot be any form without matter. Further, everything that has form must have a beginning and an end. We have none of us seen a form which had no beginning and will have no end.

A form comes out of a combination of force and matter. This chair has a peculiar form, that is to say, a certain quantity of matter is acted upon by a certain amount of force and made to assume a particular shape. The shape is the result of a combination of matter and force. The combination cannot be eternal; there must come to every combination a time when it will dissolve. So all forms have a beginning and an end. We know our body will perish; it had a beginning and it will have an end. But the Self, having no form, cannot have any beginning and end. It has existed for an infinite time.

Secondly, It must be all-pervading. It is only form that is conditioned and limited by space; that which is formless cannot be confined in space. So, according to Advaita Vedānta, the Self, the Ātman, in you, in me, in everyone, is omnipresent. You are as much in the sun now as in this earth, as much in England as in America. But when the Self acts through a particular mind and body, Its action is visible.

Each work we do, each thought we think, produces an impression, called in Sanskrit samskāra, upon the mind, and the sum total of these impressions becomes the tremendous thing called character. The character of a man is what he has created for himself; it is the result of the mental and physical actions

318

that he has done in his life. The sum total of the samskāras is the power which gives a man his next direction after death. A man dies; the body falls away and goes back to the elements; but the samskāras remain, adhering to the mind, which, being made of fine material, does not dissolve, because the finer the material, the more persistent it is. But in the long run the mind also dissolves, and this dissolution of the mind is our goal.

In this connexion, the best illustration that comes to my mind is that of the whirlwind. Different currents of air coming from different directions meet, and at the meeting-point become united and go on rotating; as they rotate they form a column, drawing in dust, bits of paper, straw, and so forth, at one place, only to drop them at another; and thus they continue to rotate, raising and forming bodies out of the materials which are before them. Even so the forces called prāna in Sanskrit come together and form the body and the mind out of matter, and move on until the body falls, when they gather other materials to make another body; and when this falls, still another; and thus the process goes on.

Force cannot travel without matter. So when the body falls, the mind-stuff remains, prāna acting on it, and then it goes on to another point, raises up another whirl from fresh materials, and begins another motion; and so it travels from place to place until the force is all spent, and then it falls down, exhausted. So when the mind comes to an end, is broken to pieces entirely, without leaving any samskāra, we shall be entirely free; and until that time we are in bondage— until then the Ātman is covered by the whirl of the mind and imagines It is being taken from place to place. When the whirl falls down, the Ātman finds that It is all-pervading. It can go where It likes, is entirely free, and is able to manufacture any number of minds or bodies It likes. But until then It can go only with the whirl. This freedom is the goal towards which we are all moving.

Suppose there is a ball in this room, and we each have a mallet in our hands and begin to strike the ball, giving it hundreds of blows, driving it from point to point, until at last it flies out of the room. With what force and in what direction it will go out will be determined by the forces that have been acting upon it all through the room. All the different blows that have been given will have their effects. Each one of our actions, mental and physical, is such a blow, and the human mind is the ball which is being hit. We are being hit about this room of the world all the time, and our passage out of it is determined by the force of all these blows. In each case the speed and direction of the ball are determined by the hits it has received; so all our actions in this world will determine our future birth. Our present birth, therefore, is the result of our past.

Here is an example: Suppose I give you a chain in which a black link alternates with a white link, the two forming a unit, and the chain is without beginning and end. If I ask you about the nature of the chain, you will at first find it difficult to determine, the chain being infinite at both ends. But you will soon discover that this chain is an endless repetition of the unit of black and white links. If you know the nature of one of these units, you know the whole chain, because it is a perfect repetition. Likewise, all our lives— past, present, and future—form, as it were, an infinite chain, without beginning and without end, each unit of which is one life, with two ends: birth and death.

What we are and what we do here in this life is being repeated again and again, with but little variation. So if we know this one unit of life, we shall know all the lives we shall have to pass through in this world. We see, therefore, that our present life in this world has been exactly determined by our previous lives, that is to say, by our own past actions.

Just as we go out of this world with the sum total of our present actions upon us, so we come into it with the sum total of our past actions upon us; that which takes us out is the very same thing which brings us in. What brings us in? Our past deeds. What takes us out? Our own deeds here. And so on and on we go. Like the caterpillar, which takes the thread from its own mouth and builds its cocoon, and at last finds itself caught inside the cocoon, we have bound ourselves by our own actions, we have thrown the network of our actions around ourselves. We have set the law of causation in motion and we find it hard to get out of its control. We have set the wheel in motion and we are being crushed under it. So this philosophy teaches us that we are uniformly being bound by our own actions, good or bad.

The Ātman never comes or goes, never is born or dies. It is nature that moves before the Ātman; and the reflection of this motion is on the Ātman and the Ātman ignorantly thinks that It is moving, and not nature. When the Ātman thinks thus, It is in bondage, but when It comes to find that It never moves, that It is omnipresent, then It is free. The Ātman in bondage is called jiva. Thus you see that when it is said that the Ātman comes and goes, it is said only figuratively. So the jiva, the bound soul, comes to higher or lower states. This is the well-known law of reincarnation, and this law binds all creation.

People in this country think it too horrible that man should become an animal. Why? Are the animals nothing? If we have a soul, so have they, and if they have none, neither have we. It is absurd to say that man alone has a soul, and the animals have none. I have seen men worse than animals.

The human soul has sojourned in lower and higher forms, migrating from one to another according to its samskāras, or impressions; but it is only in the highest form, as man, that it attains to freedom. The man-form is higher even than the god-form; of all forms it is the highest. Man is the highest being in creation because he alone attains to freedom.

All this universe was in Brahman, and it was, as it were, projected out of It and has been moving on, to go back to the source from which it was projected— like electricity, which comes out of the dynamo, completes the circuit, and returns to it. It is the same with the soul. Projected from Brahman, it passed through all sorts of vegetable and animal forms, and at last it is in man; and man is nearest to Brahman.

To go back to Brahman, from which we have been projected, is the great struggle of life. Whether people know it or not does not matter. In the universe, whatever motion or struggle we see—in minerals or plants or animals—is an effort to come back to the centre and be at rest. There was an equilibrium, and that has been destroyed, and all parts—all atoms and molecules—are struggling to find their lost equilibrium again. In this struggle they are combining and re-forming, giving rise to all the wonderful phenomena of nature. All struggles and competitions in animal life, plant life, and everywhere else, all social struggles and wars, are but expressions of the eternal struggle to get back to that equilibrium.

This going from birth to death, this travelling, is what is called samsāra in Sanskrit, literally, the round of birth and death. All creation, passing through this round, will sooner or later become free. The question may be raised: If we all shall come to freedom, why should we struggle to attain it? If everyone is going to be free, why not sit down and wait? If it is true that every being will become free sooner or later and no one will be lost, that nothing will come to destruction and everything must be liberated—if that is so, what is the use of our struggling?

In the first place, the struggle is the only means that will bring us to the centre. And in the second place, we do not know why we struggle; we have to. "Of thousands of men, some are awakened to the idea that they must become free." The vast masses of mankind are content with material things; but there are some who are awake and want to get back, who have had enough of this playing here. These struggle consciously, while the rest do it unconsciously.

The alpha and omega of Vedānta philosophy is to give up the world, give up the unreal and take the real. Those who are enamoured of the world may ask: "Why should we attempt to get out of it, to go back to the centre? Suppose we have all come from God; but we find this world is pleasurable and nice. Then why should we not rather try to get more and more from the world? Why should we try to get out of it?" They say: "Look at the wonderful improvements going on in the world every day—how much luxury is being manufactured for us! This is very enjoyable; why should we go away and strive for something which is not like this?"

The answer is that the world is impermanent and changing, and many times we have had the same enjoyments. All the forms we are seeing now have been manifested again and again, and the world in which we live has been here many times before. I have been here and talked to you many times before. You will see that it must be so; and the very words that you have been listening to now you have heard many times before. And many times more it will be the same. The souls were never different; only the bodies have been constantly dissolving and recurring. Secondly, these things occur periodically. Suppose you have three or four dice, and when you throw them, one comes up five, another four, another three, and another two. If you keep on throwing, there must come times when those very same numbers will recur. Go on throwing, and no matter how long may be the interval, those numbers must come again. It cannot be asserted when they will come again. This is determined by the law of chance. So with souls and their associations. However distant may be the periods, the same combinations and dissolutions will happen again and again. The same birth, eating, and drinking, and then death, come round again and again. Some never find anything higher than the enjoyments of the world; but those who want to soar higher find that these enjoyments are never final, are only by the way.

Every form, let us say, beginning from the little worm and ending in man, is like one of the cars of the Ferris wheel. The car is in motion all the time, but the occupants change. A man gets into the car, moves with the wheel, and comes out. The wheel goes on and on. A soul enters one form, resides in it for a time, then leaves it and goes into another, and quits that again for a third. Thus it goes on, till it comes out of the wheel and becomes free.

Astonishing powers of reading the past and the future of a man's life have been known in every country and every age. The explanation is that so long as the Ātman is within the realm of causation, although its inherent freedom is not entirely lost and can assert itself even to the extent of taking the soul out of the causal chain—as it does in those men who become free—its actions are greatly influenced by the causal law and thus make it possible for men possessed of the insight to trace the sequence of effects, to tell the past and the future.

So long as there is desire or want, it is a sure sign that there is imperfection. A perfect, free being cannot have any desire. God cannot want anything. If He desired, He could not be God; He would be imperfect. So all the talk about God's desiring this and that, and becoming angry and pleased by turns, is babies' talk; it means nothing. Therefore it has been taught by all teachers: "Desire nothing. Give up all desires and be perfectly satisfied."

A child comes into the world crawling and without teeth, and the old man goes out crawling and without teeth. The extremes are alike, but the one has no experience of the life before him, while the other has gone through it all. When the vibrations of the ether are very low, we do not see light; there is darkness. When they are very high, the result is also darkness. The extremes generally appear to be the same, though the one is as distant from the other as the poles. The wall has no desires, and neither has the perfect man. But the wall is not sentient enough to desire, while for the perfect man there is nothing to desire. There are idiots who have no desires in this world, because their brains are imperfect. At the same time, the highest state is reached when we have no desires. But the two are opposite poles of the same existence: one is near to the animal, and the other near to God.

THE REAL AND THE APPARENT MAN

(Delivered in New York, February 16, 1896)

HERE WE STAND, and our eyes look forward, sometimes miles ahead. Man has been doing that since he began to think. He is always looking forward, looking ahead. He wants to know where he goes—even after the dissolution of his body. Various theories have been propounded, system after system has been brought forward, to suggest explanations. Some have been rejected, while others have been accepted, and thus it will go on so long as man is here, so long as man thinks. There is some truth in each of these systems. There is a good deal of what is not truth in all of them. I shall try to place before you the sum and substance, the result, of the inquiries in this line that have been made in India. I shall try to harmonize the various thoughts on the subject as they have come up from time to time among Indian philosophers. I shall try to harmonize the psychologists and the metaphysicians, and if possible, I shall harmonize them with modern scientific thinkers also.

The one theme of the Vedānta philosophy is the search after unity. The Hindu mind does not care for the particular; it is always searching after the general, nay, the universal. "What is that by knowing which everything else becomes known?"—that is the one theme. "As through the knowledge of one lump of clay all that is made of clay is known, similarly, what is that by knowing which this whole universe will be known?"—that is the one search.

One part of this phenomenal universe, according to the Hindu philosophers, can be resolved into a material which they designate as ākāśa. All the things which are around us, and which we see, feel, touch, taste, are simply different manifestations of this ākāśa. It is all-pervading and fine. All that we call solids, liquids, or gases; figures, forms, or bodies; the earth, sun, moon, and stars—all these are composed of ākāśa.

What force is it which acts upon this ākāśa and manufactures this universe out of it? Along with ākāśa exists a universal energy. All forms of energy in the universe—all motion, attraction, nay, even thought—are but differing manifestations of that one energy which the Hindus call prāna. This prāna, acting on ākāśa, creates the whole of the universe. At the beginning of a cycle, prāna sleeps, as it were, in the infinite ocean of ākāśa. This ocean exists motionless in the beginning. Then arises motion in the ākāśa by the action of prāna; and as this prāna begins to move, to vibrate, out of this ocean come the various celestial systems—suns, moons, stars—the earth, human beings, animals, plants, and the manifestations of all the various forces and phenomena. Every manifestation of energy, therefore, according to the Hindus, is prāna. Every manifestation of matter is ākāśa.

When this cycle ends, all that we call solid will melt away into the next finer or the liquid form, that will melt into the gaseous, and that into finer and more uniform heat vibrations; and all will melt back into the original ākāśa. And what we now call attraction, repulsion, and motion will slowly resolve into the original prāna. Then this prāna, it is said, will sleep for a period, again to emerge and throw out all these forms; and when this period ends, the whole thing will subside again. Thus the process of creation is going down and coming up, oscillating backward and forward; in the language of modern science, it becomes static during one period, and during another period it becomes dynamic. At one time it remains potential, and at the next period it becomes active. This alternation has gone on through eternity.

Yet this analysis is only partial. This much has been known even to modern physical science. Beyond that the research of physical science cannot reach. But the inquiry does not therefore stop. We have not yet found that one thing by the knowing of which everything else is known. We have resolved the whole universe into two components, into what are called matter and energy, or what the ancient philosophers of India called ākāśa and prāna. The next step is to resolve ākāśa and prāna into their origin. Both can be resolved into a still higher entity called mind. It is out of mind, mahat, the universally existing thought-power, that these two have been produced. Thought is a finer manifestation than either ākāśa or prāna. It is thought that splits itself into these two. The universal thought existed in the beginning, and that manifested, changed, evolved itself into these two: ākāśa and prāna. By the combination of these two the whole universe has been produced.

We next come to psychology. I am looking at you. The external sensations are brought to me by the eyes; they are carried by the sensory nerves to the brain. The eyes are not the organs of vision; they are but the external instruments; because if the real organ behind, that which carries the sensation to the brain, is destroyed, though I may have twenty eyes I cannot see you. The picture on the retina may be as complete as possible, yet I shall not see you. Therefore the organ is different from its instruments; behind the instruments, the eyes, there must be the organ. So it is with all the sensations. The nose is but the instrument of smell, and behind it is the organ. With every sense we have, there is first the external instrument in the physical body, and behind that, in the same physical body, there is the organ. Yet these are not sufficient.

Suppose I am talking to you, and you are listening to me with close attention. Something happens, say a bell rings; you will not, perhaps, hear the bell ring. The vibrations of that sound come to your ear, strike the tympanum, and the impression is carried by the nerve to the brain; if the whole process is completed when the impression is carried to the brain, why then do you not hear? Something else is wanting: the mind is not attached to the organ. When the mind detaches itself from the organ, the organ may bring any news to it, but the mind will not receive it. When it attaches itself to the organ, then alone is it possible for the mind to receive the news.

Yet even that does not explain perception. The instruments may bring the sensation from outside, the organs may carry it inside, the mind may attach itself to the organ, and yet the perception may not be complete. One more factor is necessary: there must be a reaction within. With this reaction comes knowledge. That which is outside sends, as it were, the current of news into my brain. My mind takes it up and presents it to the intellect, which groups it in relation to pre-received impressions and sends a current of reaction; and with that reaction comes perception. Here, then, is the will. The state of mind which reacts is called the buddhi, the intellect. Yet even this does not complete the process. One step more is required.

Suppose that here is a camera[1] and there a sheet of cloth, and I want to throw a picture on that sheet. What must I do? I must guide various rays of light from the camera to fall upon the sheet and be focused there. Something that does not move is needed upon which to throw the picture. I cannot form a picture upon something which is moving; that something must be stationary, because the rays of light which I throw on it are moving, and these moving rays of light must be gathered, unified, co-ordinated, and completed, upon something stationary. So it is with the sensations which these organs of ours are carrying inside and presenting to the mind, and which the mind in its turn is presenting to the intellect. This process will not be completed unless there is something permanent in the background, upon which the picture, as it were, may be formed, upon which we may unify all the different impressions.

What is it that gives unity to the many changes of our being? What is it that keeps up the identity of the thing called individuality, moving from moment to moment? What is it by which all our different impressions are pieced together, and where the perceptions, as it were, come together, blend, and form a united whole? We have seen that there must be something to serve this end, and we also know that, relative to the body and mind, that something must be motionless. The sheet of cloth upon which the camera throws the picture is, relative to the rays of light, motionless; else there will be no picture. That is to say, the perceiver must be an individual. This something upon which the mind is painting all these pictures, this something upon which our sensations, carried by the mind and intellect, are placed and grouped and formed into a unity, is what is called the soul of man.

We have seen that it is the universal cosmic mind that splits itself into ākāśa and prāna, and beyond this mind we have found the soul in us. In the universe, behind the universal mind, there is also a Soul, and it is called God. In the individual it is the soul of man. In this universe, in the cosmos, just as the universal mind becomes evolved into ākāśa and prāna, even so we find that the Universal Soul Itself becomes evolved as mind. Is it really so with the individual man? Is his mind the creator of his body, and his soul the creator of his mind? That is to say, are his body, his mind, and his soul three different existences, or are they three in one, or are they different states of existence of one and the same entity? We shall try to find answers to these questions.

The first step that we have now gained is this. Here is this external body; behind this external body are the organs, the mind, the intellect; and behind these is the soul. At the first step we have found, as it were, that the soul is separate from the body, separate from the mind itself. Opinions in the religious world become divided at this point, and the division is this: All those religious

[1] Perhaps the Swami refers to a magic lantern.

views which generally pass under the name of dualism hold that the soul is conditioned; that it has various qualities; that all feelings of enjoyment, pleasure, and pain really belong to the soul. The non-dualists deny that the soul has any such qualities; they say it is unconditioned.

Let me first take up the dualists and try to present to you their position with regard to the soul and its destiny; next, the system that contradicts them; and lastly, let us try to find the harmony which non-dualism will bring us.

This soul of man, because it is separate from the mind and body, because it is not composed of ākāśa and prāna, must be immortal. Why? What do we mean by mortality? Decomposition. And that is only possible for things that are the result of composition. Anything that is made of two or three ingredients must become decomposed. That alone which is not the result of composition can never become decomposed and therefore can never die. It must be immortal. It must have existed throughout eternity. It must be uncreate. Every item of creation is simply a composition; no one ever saw creation come out of nothing. All that we know of creation is the combination of already existing things into newer forms. That being so, the soul of man, being simple, must have been existing for ever, and must go on existing for ever.

When this body falls off, the soul lives on. According to the dualists, when the body dissolves, the vital forces of the man go back to his mind and the mind becomes dissolved, as it were, into the prāna, and that prāna enters into the soul of man, and the soul of man comes out, clothed with what they call the fine body, the mental body, or the spiritual body, as you may prefer to call it.

In this body lie the samskāras of the man. What are the samskāras? This mind is like a lake, and every thought is like a wave upon that lake. Just as, in a lake, waves rise and then fall and disappear, so these thought-waves are continually rising in the mind-stuff and then disappearing. But they do not disappear for ever. They become finer and finer, but they are all there, ready to start up at another time, when called upon to do so. Memory is simply the calling back into wave-form of some of those thoughts which have gone into that finer state of existence. Thus everything that we have thought, every action that we have done, is lodged in the mind; it is all there in fine form; and when a man dies, the sum total of these impressions use the fine body as a medium. The soul, clothed, as it were, with these impressions and the fine body, passes out, and its destiny is guided by the resultant of all the different forces represented by the different impressions.

According to the dualists there are three different goals for the soul. Those who are very spiritual, when they die follow the solar rays and reach what is called the solar sphere; through that they reach what is called the lunar sphere; and through that they reach what is called the sphere of lightning. There they meet with another soul, who is already blessed, and he guides the new-comers forward to the highest of all spheres, which is called Brahmaloka, the sphere of Brahmā. There these souls attain to omniscience and omnipotence, become almost as powerful and all-knowing as God Himself; and they reside there for ever, according to the dualists; or, according to the non-dualists, they become one with the Universal Soul at the end of the cycle.

The next class of persons, those who have been doing good work with selfish motives, are carried by the results of their good works, when they die, to what is called the lunar sphere, where there are various heavens, and there they acquire fine bodies, the bodies of gods. They become gods and live there and enjoy the blessings of heaven for a long period; and after that period is finished, the old karma again begins to function and so they fall back to the earth. They come down through the spheres of air and clouds, and all these various regions, and at last reach the earth through raindrops. There on the earth they enter into some cereal, which is eventually eaten by men who are fit to supply them with material to make new bodies.

The last class, namely, the wicked, when they die become ghosts or demons and live somewhere midway between the lunar sphere and this earth. Some of these try to disturb mankind; others are friendly. After living there for some time they also fall back to the earth and become animals. After living for some time in animal bodies they are released and come back again as men, and thus get another chance to work out their salvation.

We see, then, that those who have nearly attained to perfection, in whom only very little of impurity remains, go to Brahmaloka through the rays of the sun. Those, again, who were a middling sort of people, who did some good work here with the idea of going to heaven, go to the lunar sphere and there obtain god-bodies; but they have again to become men in order to have another chance to become perfect. And those who are very wicked become ghosts and demons, and then they may have to become animals; after that they become men again and get another chance to perfect themselves.

This earth is called the karma-bhumi, the sphere of karma. Here alone man performs good or bad karma. When a man wants to go to heaven, and does good works for that purpose, he becomes a god and, as such, does not store up any fresh karma. He just enjoys the effects of the good works he did on earth; and when this good karma is exhausted, there comes upon him the resultant force of all the evil karma he had previously stored up in life, and that brings him down again to this earth. In the same way, those who become ghosts remain in that state without giving rise to fresh karma, but suffering the evil results of their past misdeeds, and later on remain for a time in animal bodies without storing up any fresh karma. When that period is over, they too become men again. The states of reward and punishment due to good and bad karma have no power to generate fresh karma; they are only to be enjoyed or suffered.

If there is an extraordinarily good or an extraordinarily evil karma, it bears fruit very quickly. For instance, if a man who has been doing many evil things all his life, does one very good act, the result of that act will immediately appear; and when that result has been reaped, the evil acts are ready to produce their results also. All men who do certain good and great acts, but the general tenor of whose lives has not been correct, will become gods, and after living for some time in god-bodies, enjoying the powers of gods, will again have to become men. When the effect of the good acts is thus finished, the old evil karma comes up to be worked out. Those who do extraordinarily evil acts have to put on ghost-bodies and devil-bodies, and when the effect of those evil actions is exhausted, the little of good action which remains stored up in them makes them again become men.

The way to Brahmaloka, from which there is no more fall or return, is called the Devayāna, the Way of the Gods; the way to heaven is known as the Pitriyāna, the Way of the Fathers.

Man, therefore, according to dualistic Vedānta, is the greatest being in the universe, and this earth the best place in it, because only here is the greatest and the best chance for him to become perfect. Angels or gods, or whatever you may call them, all have to become men if they want to become perfect. This is the great centre, the wonderful opportunity—this human life.

We come next to another school of philosophy. There are Buddhists who deny the whole theory of the soul that I have just now been propounding. "What use is it," says the Buddhist, "to assume something as the substratum, as the background, of this body and mind? Why may we not allow thought to function? Why admit a third substance, beyond this organism composed of mind and body—a third substance called the soul? What is its use? Is not this organism sufficient to explain itself? Why take a new, a third something?" These arguments are very powerful. This reasoning is very strong. So far as outside research goes, we see that this organism is a sufficient explanation of itself; at least, many of us see it in that light. Why, then, need there be a soul as substratum, a something which is neither mind nor body but stands as a background for both mind and body? Let there be only mind and body. Body is the name of a stream of matter continuously changing. Mind is the name of a stream of consciousness or thought similarly changing. How does one explain the apparent unity in the body and the mind? This unity does not really exist. Take, for instance, a lighted torch. If you whirl it rapidly, you see a circle of fire. The circle does not really exist, but because the torch is continually moving, it creates the appearance of a circle. So there is no unity in this body; it is a mass of matter continually rushing on, and this stream of matter you may call one unity, if you like. So it is with the mind. Each thought is separate from every other thought; it is only the rushing current that leaves behind the illusion of unity; there is no need of a third substance. This universal phenomenon of body and mind is all that really is; do not posit something behind it.

You will find that this Buddhist thought has been taken up by certain sects and schools in modern times, and all of them claim that it is new—their own invention. This has been the central idea of most of the Buddhist philosophies: that this world is itself all-sufficient; that you need not ask for any background at all. All that is, is this sense universe; what is the use of thinking of something as a support for this universe? Everything is the aggregate of qualities; why should there be a hypothetical substance in which they inhere? The idea of substance comes from the rapid succession of qualities, not from something unchangeable which exists behind them.

We see how wonderful some of these arguments are; and they appeal easily to the ordinary experience of men. In fact, not one in a million can think of anything other than phenomena. To the vast majority of men nature appears to be only a whirling, combining, mingling mass of change. Few of us ever have a glimpse of the calm sea behind. For us it is always lashed into waves; this universe appears to us only as a tossing mass of waves.

Thus we find these two opinions: One is that there is something behind both body and mind which is an unchangeable and immovable substance; and the other is that there is no such thing as immovability or unchangeability in the universe; it is all change and nothing but change.

The solution of this difference comes in the next step of thought, namely, the non-dualistic. It says that the dualists are right in finding something behind all as a background which does not change; we cannot conceive change without there being something unchangeable. We can only conceive something changeable by knowing something which is less changeable, and this also must appear more changeable in comparison with something else which is less changeable; and so on and on, until we are bound to admit that there must be something which never changes at all. The whole of this manifestation must have been in a state of non-manifestation, calm and silent, being the balance of opposing forces, so to say, when no force operated, because force acts when a disturbance of the equilibrium comes in. This universe is ever hurrying on to return to that state of equilibrium again. If we are certain of any fact whatsoever, we are certain of this. When the dualists claim that there is something which does not change, they are perfectly right; but their analysis that it is something which is neither the body nor the mind, something separate from them both but underlying them, is wrong. Again, so far as the Buddhists say that the whole universe is a mass of change, they are perfectly right; for, so long as I am separate from the universe, so long as I stand back and look at something before me, so long as there are two things, the looker-on and the thing looked upon, it will appear always that the universe is one of change, that it is continuously changing. But the truth of the matter is that there are both change and changelessness in this universe. It is not true that the soul and the mind and the body are three separate existences. It is the same thing which appears as the body, as the mind, and as the thing beyond mind and body; but it is not at the same time all these. He who sees the body does not even see the mind; he who sees the mind does not see that which he calls the soul; and he who sees the soul—for him the body and mind have vanished. He who sees only motion never sees absolute calm, and he who sees absolute calm—for him motion has vanished. A rope is taken for a snake. He who sees the rope as the snake—for him the rope has vanished; and when the delusion ceases and he looks at the rope, the snake has vanished.

There is, then, but one all-comprehending Existence, and that Existence appears as manifold. This Self, or Soul, or Substance, is all that exists in the universe. This Self, or Soul, or Substance, is, in the language of non-dualism, Brahman, and It appears to be manifold by the interposition of name and form. Look at the waves in the sea. Not one wave is really different from the sea; but what makes the wave apparently different? Name and form—the form of the wave and the name which we give to it: "wave." That is what makes it different from the sea. When name and form go, it is the same sea. Who can find any real difference between the wave and the sea? So this whole universe is that one Existence; name and form have created all these various differences.

When the sun shines upon millions of globules of water, upon each particle is seen a most perfect representation of the sun. So the one Soul, the one Self, the one Existence of the universe, being reflected on all these numerous globules of varying names and forms, appears to be various; but It is in reality only one. There is no "I" or "you"; it is all one. It is either all "I" or all "you."

This idea of duality, of two, is entirely false, and the whole universe, as we ordinarily know it, is the result of this false knowledge. When discrimination comes, and man finds there are not two but one, he finds that he is himself this universe. It is I who am this universe as it now exists, a continuous mass of change. It is I who am beyond all changes, beyond all qualities, eternally perfect, eternally blessed.

There is, therefore, but one Ātman, one Self, eternally pure, eternally perfect, unchangeable, unchanged. It has never changed. And all these various changes in the universe are but appearances in that one Self.

Upon It name and form have painted all these dreams; it is the form that makes the wave different from the sea. Suppose the wave subsides; will the form remain? No; it will vanish. The existence of the wave was entirely dependent upon the existence of the sea, but the existence of the sea was not at all dependent upon the existence of the wave. The form remains so long as the wave remains; but as soon as the wave leaves it, the form vanishes; it cannot remain.

Name and form are the outcome of what is called māyā. It is this māyā that creates individuals, making one appear different from another. Yet it has no existence. Māyā cannot be said to exist. Form cannot be said to exist, because it depends upon the existence of another thing. At the same time, it cannot be said not to exist, seeing that it makes all this difference. According to the Advaita philosophy, then, this māyā or ignorance—or name and form; or, as it has been called in Europe, "time, space, and causality"—is showing us, out of this one Infinite Existence, the manifoldness of the universe. As substance this universe is one. So long as a man thinks that there are two ultimate realities, he is mistaken. When he has come to know that there is but one, he is right.

This is being proved to us every day—on the physical plane, on the mental plane, and also on the spiritual plane. Today it has been demonstrated that you and I, the sun, the moon, and the stars are but the different names of different spots in the same ocean of matter, and that this matter is continuously changing in its configuration. The particle of matter that was in the sun several months ago may be in the human being now; tomorrow it may be in an animal; the day after tomorrow it may be in a plant. It is ever coming and going. It is all one unbroken, infinite mass of matter, merely differentiated by names and forms. One point is called the sun; another, the moon; another, the stars; another, a man; another, an animal; another, a plant—and so on. And all these names are fictitious; they have no reality, because the whole is a continuously changing mass of matter. This very same universe, from another standpoint, is an ocean of thought, where each one of us is a point called a particular mind. You are a mind, I am a mind, everyone is a mind. And the very same universe viewed from the standpoint of Knowledge, when the eyes have been cleared of delusions, when the mind has become pure, appears as the unbroken Absolute Being, ever pure, unchangeable, immortal.

What, then, becomes of all this threefold eschatology of the dualist—that when a man dies he goes to heaven, or goes to this or that sphere, and that wicked persons become ghosts or animals, and so forth? None comes and none goes, says the non-dualist. How can you come and go? You are infinite; where is the place for you to go?

In a certain school a number of little children were being examined. The examiner had foolishly put all sorts of difficult questions to the little children. Among others there was this question: "Why does the earth not fall?" His intention was to bring out the idea of gravitation or some other intricate scientific truth from these children. Most of them could not even understand the question, and so they gave all sorts of wrong answers. But one bright little girl answered it with another question: "Where should it fall?" The very question of the examiner was nonsense on the face of it. There is no up and down in the universe; the idea is only relative. So it is with regard to the Soul: the very question of birth and death in regard to It is utter nonsense. Who goes and who comes? Where are you not? Where is the heaven that you are not in already? Omnipresent is the Self of man. Where is It to go? Where is It not to go? It is everywhere. So all this childish dream, this puerile illusion of birth and death, of heavens and higher heavens, and of lower worlds, all vanishes immediately for the perfect; and for the nearly perfect it vanishes after showing them the several scenes up to Brahmaloka. It continues for the ignorant.

How is it that the whole world believes in going to heaven and in dying and being born? I am studying a book; page after page is being read and turned over. Another page comes and is turned over. Who changes? Who comes and goes? Not I, but the book. The whole of nature is a book before the Soul. Chapter after chapter is being read and turned over, and every now and then a scene opens. That is read and turned over; a fresh one comes; but the Soul is ever the same—eternal. It is nature that is changing, not the Soul of man. This never changes. Birth and death are in nature, not in you. Yet the ignorant are deluded: just as we think, under delusion, that the sun is moving, and not the earth, in exactly the same way we think that we are dying, and not nature. These are all, therefore, hallucinations. Just as it is a hallucination when we think that the fields are moving and not the railway train, exactly in the same manner are birth and death a hallucination.

When men are in a certain frame of mind, they see this very existence as the earth, the sun, the moon, the stars; and all those who are in the same state of mind see the same things. Between you and me there may be millions of beings on different planes of existence. They will never see us, nor we them; we see only those who are in the same state of mind and on the same plane with us. Those musical instruments respond which have the same attunement of vibration, as it were. If the state of vibration which may be called the "man-vibration" should be changed, no longer would men be seen here; the whole man-universe would vanish, and instead of that, other scenery would come before us, perhaps gods and the god-universe, or perhaps, for the wicked man, devils and the diabolic world. But all would be only different views of the one universe. It is this universe which, from the human plane, is seen as the earth, the sun, the moon, the stars, and all such things. It is this very universe which, seen from the plane of wickedness, appears as a place of punishment; and this very universe is seen as heaven by those who want to see it as heaven. Those who have been dreaming of going to a God who is sitting on a throne, and of standing there praising Him all their lives, when they die will merely see a vision of what they have in their minds. This very universe will simply change into a vast heaven, with all sorts of winged beings flying about, and a God sitting on a throne. These heavens are all of man's own making.

So what the dualist believes is true, says the non-dualist, but it is all simply of his own making. These spheres and devils and gods and reincarnations and transmigrations are all mythology. So also is this human life. The great mistake that men always make is to think that this life alone is real; they understand it well enough when other things are called mythologies, but are never willing to admit the same of their own position. The whole thing as it appears is mere mythology, and the greatest of all lies is to say that we are bodies, which we never were nor ever can be. It is the greatest of all lies to say that we are mere men. We are the God of the universe. In worshipping God we have always been worshipping our own hidden Self. The worst lie that you can ever tell yourself is that you were born a sinner or a wicked man. He alone is a sinner who sees a sinner in another man. Suppose there is a baby here, and you place a bag of gold on the table, and then a robber comes and takes the gold away. To the baby it is all the same: because there is no robber inside, he sees no robber outside. To sinners and vile men there is vileness outside; but not to good men. So the wicked see this universe as hell, and the partially good see it as heaven, while perfect beings realize it as God Himself. Only when a man sees this universe as God does the veil fall from his eyes; then that man, purified and cleansed, finds his whole vision changed. The bad dreams that have been torturing him for millions of years all vanish, and he who had thought of himself as either a man or a god or a demon, he who had thought of himself as living in low places, in high places, on earth, in heaven, and so on, finds that he is really omnipresent; that all time is in him, and he is not in time; that all the heavens are in him, and he is not in any heaven; that all the gods that man ever worshipped are in him, and he is not in any one of those gods. He was the manufacturer of gods and demons, of men and plants and animals and stones. And the real nature of man now stands unfolded to him as being higher than heaven, more perfect than this universe of ours, more infinite than infinite time, more omnipresent than the omnipresent ether.

Thus alone does a man become fearless and free. Then all delusions cease, all fears come to an end for ever. Birth goes away and with it death; pains fly and with them fly away pleasures; earth vanishes and with it vanishes heaven; the body vanishes and with it vanishes the mind also. For that man, disappears the whole universe, as it were. This surging, moving, continuous struggle of forces stops for ever, and that which was manifesting itself as force and matter, as the struggles of nature, as nature itself, as heavens and earths and plants and animals and men and angels—all that becomes transfigured into one infinite, unbreakable, unchangeable Existence; and the knowing man finds that he is one with that Existence. "Even as clouds of various colours come before the sky, remain there for a moment, and then vanish away," even so before this Soul come all these visions—of earth and heaven, of the moon and the gods, of pleasures and pains; but they all pass away, leaving behind the infinite, unchangeable Spirit. The sky never changes; it is the clouds that change. It is a mistake to think that the Spirit changes. It is a mistake to think that we are impure, that we are limited, that we are separate. The real man is the one Existence.

Two questions now arise. The first is: "Can one ever realize this truth? So far it is doctrine, philosophy; but is it possible to realize it?" It is. There are men still living for whom delusion has vanished for ever. The second is: "Do they immediately die after such realization?" Not so soon as we should think. Two wheels joined by one pole are running together. If, with an axe, I cut the pole asunder and get hold of one of the wheels, it stops. But in the other wheel is its past momentum; so it runs on a little and then falls down. This pure and perfect Being, the Soul, is one wheel, and this external hallucination of body and mind is the other wheel, and they are joined together by the pole of work, of karma. Knowledge is the axe which will sever the bond between the two, and the wheel of the Soul will stop—stop thinking that It is coming and going, living and dying, stop thinking that It is a part of nature and has wants and desires—and will find that It is perfect, desireless. But in the other wheel, that of the body and mind, will be the momentum of past acts. So it will live for some time, until that momentum of past work is exhausted, until that momentum is worked out. Then the body and mind will fall, and the Soul be free. No more is there any going to heaven and coming back, not even any going to Brahmaloka or to any of the higher spheres; for where is the Soul to come from or to go to?

The man who has in this life attained to this state, for whom, for a minute at least, the ordinary vision of the world has changed and the reality has been apparent—he is called "free while living." This is the goal of the Vedāntist, to attain freedom in life.

Once in Western India I was travelling in the desert country. For days and days I travelled on foot through the desert; but to my surprise I saw every day beautiful lakes, with trees all round them, and the reflections of the trees upside down and vibrating there. "How wonderful it looks—and they call this a desert country!" I said to myself. Nearly a month I travelled, seeing these wonderful lakes and trees and plants. One day I was very thirsty and wanted to have a drink of water; so I started to go to one of these clear, beautiful lakes. But as I approached, it vanished; and with a flash the idea came to me, "This is the mirage, about which I have read all my life." And with that came also the idea that throughout the whole of that month, every day, I had been seeing the mirage and did not know it. The next morning I began my march. There was the lake again, but with it came also the idea that it was a mirage and not a true lake.

So is it with this universe. We are all travelling in this mirage of the world, day after day, month after month, year after year, not knowing that it is a mirage. One day it will disappear; but it will come back again. The body has to remain under the power of past karma, and so the mirage will come back. This world will come back to us so long as we are bound by karma: men, women, animals, plants, our attachments and duties, all will come back to us. But not with the same power; under the influence of the new knowledge the strength of karma will be broken, its poison will be lost. It will become transformed, for along with it will come the idea that we understand it now, that the sharp distinction between the reality and the mirage has been known. This world will not then be the same world as before.

There is, however, a danger here. We often see people taking up this philosophy and saying, "I am beyond all virtue and vice; so I am not bound by any moral laws; I may do anything I like." You can find many fools in this country at the present time saying, "I am not bound; I am God Himself; let me do anything I like." This is not right, although it is true that the Soul is beyond all laws, physical, mental, or moral. Within law is bondage; beyond law is freedom. It is also true that freedom is the nature of the Soul; it is Its birthright. That real freedom of the Soul shines through the veils of matter in the form of the apparent freedom of man. Every moment of your life you feel that you are free. We cannot live, talk, or breathe for a moment without feeling that we are free. But at the same time, a little thought shows us that we are like machines and not free. What is true, then? Is this idea of freedom a delusion? One party holds that the idea of freedom is a delusion; another says that the idea of bondage is a delusion. How does this happen?

Man is really free; the real man cannot but be free. It is when he comes into the world of māyā, into name and form, that he becomes bound. Free will is a misnomer. The will can never be free. How can it be? It is only when the real man has become bound that his will comes into existence, and not before. The will of man is bound, but that which is the foundation of that will is eternally free. So even in the state of bondage which we call human life or god-life, on earth or in heaven, there yet remains to us that recollection of the freedom which is ours by divine right. And consciously or unconsciously we are all struggling towards it.

When a man has attained his inner freedom, how can he be bound by any law? No law in this universe can bind him; for this universe itself is his. He is the whole universe. Either say he is the whole universe or say that to him there is no universe. How, then, can he have all these little ideas about sex and about country? How can he say, "I am a man," "I am a woman," "I am a child"? Are these not fantasies? He knows they are. How can he say that these are man's rights and these others are woman's rights? Nobody has rights; nobody exists separately. There is neither man nor woman; the Soul is sexless, eternally pure. It is a lie to say that I am a man or a woman or to say that I belong to this country or that. All the world is my country, the whole universe is mine, because I have clothed myself with it as my body.

Yet we see that there are people in this world who proclaim these doctrines and at the same time go on doing things which we should call filthy. And if we ask them why they do so, they tell us that we are deluded and that they can do nothing wrong. What is the test by which they are to be judged? The test is here. Though evil and good are both conditioned manifestations of the Soul, yet evil is the more external coating, and good is the inner coating of the Real Man, the Self. Unless a man cuts through the layer of evil he cannot reach the layer of good, and unless he has passed through both the layers, of good and of evil, he cannot reach the Self. He who reaches the Self—what remains attached to him? A little karma, a little bit of the momentum of his past life;

but it is all good momentum. Until the bad momentum is entirely worked out and the past impurities are entirely burnt up, it is impossible for any man to see and realize Truth.

So what is left attached to the man who has reached the Self and seen Truth is the remnant of the good impressions of his past life, the good momentum. Even if he lives in the body and works incessantly, he works only to do good; his lips speak only benediction to all; his hands do only good works; his mind can think only good thoughts; his presence is a blessing wherever he goes. He is himself a living blessing. Such a man will, by his very presence, change even the most wicked persons into saints. Even if he does not speak, his very presence will be a blessing to mankind. Can such men do any evil? Can they do wicked deeds?

There is, you must remember, all the difference of pole from pole between realization and mere talking. Any fool can talk. Even parrots talk. Talking is one thing, and realizing is another. Philosophies and doctrines and arguments and books and theories and churches and sects and all such things are good as far as they go; but when realization comes these things drop away. For instance, maps are good, but when you see the country itself and look again at the maps, what a great difference you find! So those who have realized Truth do not require the ratiocinations of logic or any other gymnastics of the intellect to make them understand Truth; it is to them the life of their lives, concretized, made more than tangible. It is, as the sages of the Vedānta say, "even as a fruit in your hand": you can stand up and say, "It is here." So those who have realized Truth will stand up and say, "Here is the Self." You may argue with them by the year, but they will smile at you; they will regard it all as a child's prattle; they will let the child prattle on. They have realized Truth and are satisfied. Suppose you have seen a country, and a man comes and tries to argue with you that that country never existed. He may go on arguing indefinitely, but your only attitude of mind towards him will be to hold that the man is fit for a lunatic asylum. So the man of realization says, "All this talk in the world about its little religions is but prattle; realization is the soul, the very essence, of religion." Religion can be realized. Are you ready? Do you want it? You will get the realization if you do, and then you will be truly religious. Until you have attained realization there is no difference between you and the atheists. The atheists are sincere, but the man who says that he believes in religion and never attempts to realize it is not sincere.

The next question is to know what comes after realization. Suppose we have realized this oneness of the universe, suppose we know that we are that one Infinite Being; and suppose we have realized that this Self is the only Existence, and that it is the same Self which is manifested in all these various phenomenal forms—what becomes of us after that? Shall we become inactive, get into a corner and sit down there and die? "What good will it do to the world?"—that old question! In the first place why should it do good to the world? Is there any reason that it should? What right has anyone to ask the question, "What good will it do to the world?" What is meant by that? A baby likes candies. Suppose you are conducting investigations in connexion with some aspect of electricity and a baby asks you, "Does it buy candies?" "No," you answer. "Then what good will it do?" says the baby. So men stand up and say: "What good will this do to the world? Will it give us money?" "No." "Then what good is there in it?" That is what men mean by doing good to the world.

Yet religious realization does the greatest good to the world. People are afraid that when they attain to it, when they realize that there is but One, the fountains of love will be dried up, everything in life will go away, and all that they love will vanish for them, as it were, in this life and in the life to come. People never stop to think that the greatest workers in the world have been those who bestowed the least thought on their own individualities. Then alone does a man love when he finds that the object of his love is not any low, little, mortal thing. Then alone does a man love when he finds that the object of his love is not a clod of earth, but is the veritable God Himself. The wife will love the husband the more when she thinks that the husband is God Himself. The husband will love the wife the more when he knows that the wife is God Himself. That mother will love her children more who thinks that the children are God Himself. That man will love his greatest enemy who knows that that very enemy is God Himself. That man will love a holy man who knows that the holy man is God Himself, and that very man will also love the unholiest of men because he knows that the background of that unholiest of men is even He, the Lord. Such a man becomes a world-mover. For him the little self is dead and God stands in its place; for him the whole universe becomes transfigured. That which is painful and miserable will all vanish; struggles will all depart. Instead of being a prison-house, where every day we struggle and fight and compete for a morsel of bread, this universe will then be to us a playground. Beautiful will be this universe then! Such a man alone has the right to stand up and say, "How beautiful is this world!" He alone has the right to say that it is all good.

This will be the great good to the world resulting from such realization: If all mankind today realizes only a bit of that great truth, the aspect of the whole world will be changed; in place of fighting and quarrelling there will be a reign of peace. This indecent and brutal hurry which forces us to go ahead of everyone else will then vanish from the world. With it will vanish all fighting, with it will vanish all hate, with it will vanish all jealousy; all evil will vanish away for ever. Gods will live then upon this earth. This very earth will become heaven—and what evil can there be when gods are playing with gods, when gods are working with gods, and gods are loving gods? That is the great utility of divine realization. Everything that you see in society will be changed and transfigured then. No more will you think of man as evil; and that is the first great gain. No more will you stand up and sneeringly cast a glance at a poor man or woman who has made a mistake. No more, ladies, will you look down with contempt upon the poor woman who walks the street in the night, because you will see even there God Himself. No more will you think of jealousy and punishments. They will all vanish; and love, the great ideal of love, will be so powerful that no whip and cord will be necessary to guide mankind aright.

If one millionth part of the men and women who live in this world simply sit down and for a few minutes say: "You are all God, O ye men and O ye animals and living beings! You are all the manifestations of the one living Deity!" the whole world will be changed in half an hour. Instead of throwing tremendous bomb-shells of hatred into every corner, instead of projecting currents of jealousy and of evil thought, in every country people will think that it is all He. He is all that you see and feel. How can you see evil unless there is evil in you? How can you see the thief unless he is there, sitting in your heart of hearts? How can you see the murderer unless you are yourself a murderer? Be good, and evil will vanish for you. The whole universe will thus be changed. This is the great gain to society. This is the great gain to humanity.

These thoughts were thought out, worked out, amongst individuals in ancient times in India. For various reasons, such as the exclusiveness of the teachers and foreign conquest, those thoughts were not allowed to spread. Yet they are grand truths, and wherever they have been working man has become divine. My whole life has been changed by the touch of one of these divine men, about whom I am going to speak to you next Sunday. The time is coming when these thoughts will be cast abroad over the whole world. Instead of living in monasteries, instead of being confined to books of philosophy to be studied only by the learned, instead of being the exclusive possession of sects and of a few of the learned, they will all be sown broadcast over the whole world, so that they may become the common property of the saint and the sinner, of men and women and children, of the learned and of the ignorant. They will then permeate the atmosphere of the world, and the very air that we breathe will say with every one of its vibrations, "Thou art That." And the whole universe, with its myriads of suns and moons, through everything that speaks, with one voice will say, "Thou art That."

PRACTICAL VEDĀNTA

Part I

(Delivered in London, November 10, 1896)

I HAVE BEEN ASKED to say something about the practical position of the Vedānta philosophy. As I have told you, theory is very good indeed; but how are we to carry it into practice? If it is absolutely impracticable, no theory is of any value whatever, except as intellectual gymnastics. Vedānta therefore, as a religion, must be intensely practical. We must be able to carry it out in every part of our lives. And not only this. The fictitious differentiation between religion and the life of the world must vanish; for Vedānta teaches Oneness—one life throughout. The ideals of religion must cover the whole field of life; they must enter into all our thoughts, and more and more into practice. I shall gradually take up the practical side as we proceed. But this series of lectures is intended to be a basis, and so we must first apply ourselves to theories and understand how they can be worked out, not only in forest caves but also in busy cities. And one peculiar feature we shall find is that many of these thoughts, instead of being the outcome of retirement into the forest, have emanated from persons whom we expect to lead the busiest lives—from ruling monarchs.

Śvetaketu was the son of Āruni, a sage, most probably a recluse. He was brought up in the forest, but he went to the city of the Pānchālas and appeared at the court of King Pravāhana Jaivali. The king asked him, "Do you know how beings depart hence at death?" "No, sir." "Do you know how they return hither?" "No, sir." "Do you know the Way of the Fathers and the Way of the Gods?" "No, sir." Then the king asked other questions. Śvetaketu could not answer them. So the king told him that he knew nothing. The boy went back to his father and the father admitted that he himself could not answer these questions. It was not that he was unwilling to answer these questions; it was not that he was unwilling to teach the boy. But he did not know these things. So Śvetaketu returned to the king with his father and they both asked to be taught these secrets. The king said that these things had hitherto been known only among kings; the priests never knew them. He proceeded, however, to teach them what they desired to know.

In various Upanishads we find that this Vedānta philosophy is not the outcome of meditation in the forest only, but the very best parts of it were thought out and expressed by those brains which were busiest in the everyday affairs of life. We cannot conceive of any man busier than an absolute monarch, a man who rules over millions of people; and yet some of these rulers were deep thinkers.

338

Everything goes to show that this philosophy is very practical. Later on, when we come to the Bhagavad Gitā—most of you, perhaps, have read it; it is the best commentary we have on the Vedānta philosophy—curiously enough the scene is laid on a battlefield, where Krishna teaches this philosophy to Arjuna. And the doctrine which stands out luminously on every page of the Gitā is that of intense activity, but in the midst of it, eternal calmness.

This is the secret of work, to attain which is the goal of Vedānta. Inactivity as we understand it, in the sense of passivity, certainly cannot be the goal. Were it so, then the walls around us would be the wisest of things; for they are inactive. Clods of earth, stumps of trees, would be the greatest sages in the world; for they are inactive. Nor does inactivity become activity when it is combined with passion. Real activity, which is the goal of Vedānta, is that which is combined with eternal calmness, the calmness which cannot be ruffled, the balance of mind which is not disturbed, no matter what happens. And we all know from experience that that is the best attitude for work.

I have been told many times that we cannot work if we do not have the passion which men generally feel for work. I also thought in that way years ago, but as I am growing older, getting more experience, I find it is not true. The less passion there is, the better we work. The calmer we are, the better it is for us and the greater is the amount of work we can do. When we let loose our feelings we waste so much energy, shatter our nerves, disturb our minds, and accomplish very little work. The energy which ought to have gone into work is spent as mere feeling, which counts for nothing. It is only when the mind is very calm and collected that the whole of its energy is spent in doing good work. And if you read the lives of the great workers the world has produced, you will find that they were wonderfully calm men. Nothing, as it were, could throw them off their balance. That is why the man who becomes angry never does a great amount of work, and the man whom nothing can make angry accomplishes so much. The man who gives way to anger or hatred or any other passion cannot work; he only breaks himself to pieces and does nothing practical. It is the calm, forgiving, equable, well balanced mind that does the greatest amount of work.

Vedānta preaches the ideal, and the ideal, as we know, is always far ahead of the real, of the practical, as we may call it. There are two tendencies in human nature: one to reconcile the ideal with life and the other to elevate life to the ideal. It is a great thing to understand this; for we are often tempted by the former. I think that I can do a certain kind of work. Most of it, perhaps, is bad; most of it, perhaps, has a motive power of passion behind it—anger, or greed, or selfishness. Now, if any man comes to preach to me a certain ideal, the first step towards which is to give up selfishness, to give up self-enjoyment, I think that that is impractical. But when a man brings an ideal which can be reconciled with my selfishness, I am glad and at once jump at it. That is the ideal for me. As the word orthodox has been manipulated into various forms, so has the word practical. "My doxy is orthodoxy; your doxy is heterodoxy." So with practicality. What I think is practical is to me the only practicality in the world. If I am a shopkeeper, I think shopkeeping the only practical pursuit in the world If I am a thief, I think stealing is the best means of being practical;

others are not practical. You see how we all use this word *practical* for things that we like and can do. Therefore I ask you to understand that Vedānta, though it is intensely practical, is always so in the sense of the ideal. It does not preach an impossible ideal, however high it may be, and it is high enough for an ideal.

In one word, this ideal is that you are divine. "Thou art That." This is the essence of Vedānta. After all its ramifications and intellectual gymnastics, you know the human soul to be pure and omniscient; you see that such superstitions as birth and death are entire nonsense when spoken of in connexion with the soul. The soul was never born and will never die, and all these ideas that we are going to die and are afraid to die are mere superstitions. And all such ideas as that we can do this, or cannot do that, are superstitions. We can do everything. Vedānta teaches men to have faith in themselves first. As certain religions of the world say that a man who does not believe in a Personal God outside himself is an atheist, so Vedānta says that a man who does not believe in himself is an atheist. Not believing in the glory of our own soul is what Vedānta calls atheism.

To many this is, no doubt, a terrible ideal, and most of us think that this ideal can never be reached; but Vedānta insists that it can be realized by everyone. One may be either man or woman or child; one may belong to any race— nothing will stand as a bar to the realization of this ideal, because, as Vedānta shows, it is realized already, it is already there. All the powers in the universe are already ours. It is we who have put our hands before our eyes and cry that it is dark. Know that there is no darkness around you. Take your hands away and there is the light which was from the beginning. Darkness never existed; weakness never existed. We who are fools cry that we are weak; we who are fools cry that we are impure. Thus Vedānta insists not only that the ideal is practical, but that it has been so always, and that this ideal, this Reality, is our own nature. Everything else that you see is false, untrue. As soon as you say, "I am a little mortal being," you are saying something which is not true, you are giving the lie to yourselves, you are hypnotizing yourselves into something vile and weak and wretched. Vedānta recognizes no sin; it recognizes only error. And the greatest error, it says, is to think that you are weak, that you are a sinner, a miserable creature, and that you have no power and cannot do this or that. Every time you think in that way, you rivet, as it were, one more link in the chain that binds you down, you add one more layer of hypnotism upon your soul. Therefore whosoever thinks he is weak is wrong, whosoever thinks he is impure is wrong, and is throwing a bad thought into the world.

This we must always bear in mind: In Vedānta there is no attempt at reconciling the present life, the hypnotized life, this false life which we have assumed, with the ideal; but this false life must go, and the real life, which has always existed, must manifest itself, must shine out. No man becomes purer and purer; it is a matter of greater manifestation of the perfection that has always been in him. The veil drops away, and the native purity of the soul begins to manifest itself. Everything is ours already—infinite purity, freedom, love, and power.

Vedānta also says that this can be realized not only in the depths of forests or in caves, but by men in all possible conditions of life. We have seen that the people who discovered these truths were neither living in caves or forests nor following the ordinary vocations of life, but were men who, we have every reason to believe, led the busiest of lives, men who had to command armies, to sit on thrones and look to the welfare of millions—and all this in the days of absolute monarchy, and not in these days when a king is to a great extent a mere figurehead. Yet they could find time to think out all these thoughts, to realize them, and to teach them to humanity. How much more, then, should they be practical for us, whose lives, compared with theirs, are lives of leisure! That we cannot realize them is a shame to us, seeing that we are comparatively free all the time and have very little to do. My requirements are as nothing compared with those of an ancient absolute monarch. My wants are as nothing compared with the demands of Arjuna on the battlefield of Kurukshetra, commanding a huge army; and yet he could find time in the midst of the din and turmoil of battle to talk the highest philosophy and to carry it into his life. Surely we ought to be able to do as much in this life of ours, comparatively free, easy, and comfortable. Most of us here have more time than we think we have, if we really want to use it for good. With the amount of freedom we have, we can attain to two hundred ideals in this life, if we will. But we must not degrade the ideal to the actual. Here is a great danger. There are persons who teach us how to make special excuses for all our foolish wants and foolish desires; and we think that their ideal is the only ideal we need have. But it is not so. Vedānta teaches no such thing. The actual should be reconciled to the ideal; the present life should be made to coincide with life eternal.

For you must always remember that the central ideal of Vedānta is Oneness. There are no two in anything—no two lives or even two different kinds of life for the two worlds. You will find the Vedas speaking, at first, of heavens and things like that; but later on, when they come to the highest ideals of their philosophy, they brush away all these things. There is but one Life, one World, one Existence. Everything is that One; the differences are of degree and not of kind. The differences between our lives are not of kind. Vedānta entirely denies such ideas as that animals are essentially separate from men and that they were made and created by God to be used for our food.

Some people have been kind enough to start an anti-vivisection society. I asked a member, "Why do you think, my friend, that it is quite lawful to kill animals for food, and not to kill one or two for scientific experiments?" He replied, "Vivisection is most horrible, but animals have been given to us for food."

Oneness includes all animals. If man is immortal, so also are the animals. The differences are only of degree and not of kind. The amoeba and I are the same; the difference is only one of degree; and from the standpoint of the highest life, all differences vanish. A man may see a great deal of difference between grass and a little tree, but if he mounts very high, the grass and the biggest tree will appear much the same. So, from the standpoint of the highest ideal, the lowest animal and the highest man are the same. If you believe there is a God, then to Him the animals and the highest creatures must be the same. A God who is partial to His children called men, and cruel to His children called brute beasts, is worse than a demon. I would rather die a hundred times than worship such a God. My whole life would be a fight with such a God. But there is no difference from the standpoint of God; and those who say that there is are irresponsible, heartless people, who do not know.

Here, then, is a case of the word *practical* used in a wrong sense. We eat meat not because animals have been given to us for food, but because we want to. I myself may not be a very strict vegetarian, but I understand the ideal. When I eat meat I know it is wrong. Even if I am bound to eat it under certain circumstances, I know it is cruel. I must not drag my ideal down to the actual and give excuses for my weak conduct. The ideal is not to eat flesh, not to injure any being; for all animals are my brothers. If you can think of them as your brothers, you have made a little headway towards the brotherhood of all souls, not to speak of the brotherhood of man! But to carry this out is no child's play. You generally find that this is not very acceptable to many, because it teaches them to give up the actual and go towards the ideal. But if you bring out a theory which can be reconciled with their present conduct, they regard it as entirely practical.

There is a strongly conservative tendency in human nature; we do not like to move one step forward. I think of mankind as being like those I have read about who have become frozen in the snow. All such, they say, want to go to sleep, and if you try to drag them out, they say: "Let me sleep. It is so beautiful to sleep in the snow"; and they die there in that sleep. So is our nature. That is what we are doing all our life—getting frozen from the feet upwards and yet wanting to sleep. Therefore you must struggle towards the ideal; and if a man comes who wants to bring that ideal down to your level and teach a religion which does not carry out that highest ideal, do not listen to him. To me that is an impracticable religion. But if a man teaches a religion which presents the highest ideal, I am ready for him.

Beware when anyone is trying to give excuses for sense vanities and sense weaknesses. If anyone wants to preach that way to us—poor, sense-bound clods of earth that we have made ourselves—by following that teaching we shall never progress. I have seen many of these things; I have had some experience of the world; and my country is the land where religious sects grow like mushrooms. Every year new sects arise. But one thing I have marked: that it is only those who never want to reconcile the man of flesh with the man of truth who make progress. Wherever there is this false idea of reconciling fleshly vanities with the highest ideals, of dragging down God to the level of man, there comes decay. Man should not be degraded to worldly slavery, but should be raised up to God.

At the same time, there is another side to the question. We must not look down with contempt on others. All of us are going towards the same goal. The difference between weakness and strength is one of degree. The difference between virtue and vice is one of degree. The difference between heaven and hell is one of degree. The difference between life and death is one of degree. All differences in this world are of degree, and not of kind, because Oneness is the secret of everything. All is the One, and the One manifests Itself either as thought or life or soul or body. This being so, we have no right to look down with contempt upon those who are not developed exactly in the same degree as we are. Condemn none. If you can stretch out a helping hand, do so; if you cannot, fold your hands, bless your brothers, and let them go their own way. Dragging down and condemning is not the way to work. Never is work accomplished in that way. We spend our energies in condemning others. Criticism and condemnation are a vain way of spending our energies; for in the long run we come to learn that all are seeking the same thing, are more or less approaching the same ideal, and that most of our differences are merely differences of expression.

Take the idea of sin. I was telling you just now the Vedāntic idea of it. The other view is that man is a sinner. They are practically the same, only the one takes the positive and the other the negative side. One shows man his strength, and the other, his weakness. There may be weakness, says Vedānta, but never mind, we want to grow. Disease existed in man as soon as he was born. Everyone knows his disease; it requires no one to tell us what our diseases are. But thinking all the time that we are diseased will not cure us. Medicine is necessary. In our heart of hearts we all know our weaknesses. But, says Vedānta, being reminded of weakness does not help much. Give strength. And strength does not come by thinking of weakness all the time. The remedy for weakness is not brooding over weakness, but thinking of strength. Teach men of the strength that is already within them. Instead of telling them that they are sinners, Vedānta takes the opposite position and says, "You are pure and perfect, and what you call sin does not belong to you." Sins are very low degrees of Self-manifestation; manifest the Self in a high degree. That is the one thing to remember. All of us can do that. Never say no; never say, "I cannot"; for you are infinite. Even time and space are as nothing compared with your nature. You can do anything and everything; you are almighty.

These are the principles of ethics; but we shall now come down lower and work out the details. We shall see how Vedānta can be carried into our everyday life—the city life, the country life, the national life, and the home life of every nation. For if a religion cannot help a man wherever he may be, wherever he stands, it is not of much use; it will remain only a theory for the chosen few. A religion, to help mankind, must be ready and able to help a man in whatever condition he may be—in servitude or in freedom, in the depths of degradation or on the heights of purity. Everywhere, equally, it should be able to come to his aid. The ideal of Vedānta, the ideal of religion—or whatever you may prefer to call it—will be fulfilled only if it is capable of performing this great and noble function.

The ideal of faith in ourselves is of the greatest help to us. If faith in ourselves had been more extensively taught and practised, I am sure a very large portion of the evils and miseries that we have would have vanished. Throughout the history of mankind, if any one motive power has been more potent than others in the lives of great men and women, it is that of faith in themselves. Born with the consciousness that they were to be great, they became great. Let a man go down as low as possible, yet there must come a time when out of sheer desperation he will take an upward curve and learn to have faith in himself. But it is better for us that we should know it from the very first. Why should we have all these bitter experiences in order to gain faith in ourselves? We can see that all the difference there is between man and man is due to the existence or non-existence of faith in himself. Faith in ourselves will do everything. I have experienced it in my own life, and am still doing so, and as I grow older that faith is becoming stronger and stronger. He is an atheist who does not believe in himself. The old religions said that he who did not believe in God was the atheist. The new religion says that he is the atheist who does not believe in himself. But it is not selfish faith, because Vedānta, again, is the doctrine of Oneness. It means faith in all because you are all. Love for yourself means love for all—love for animals, love for everything; for you are all. This is the great faith which will make the world better. I am sure of that.

He is the highest man who can say with truth, "I know all about myself." Do you know how much energy, how many powers, how many forces, are still lurking within that frame of yours? What scientist has known all that is in man? Millions of years have passed since man first came here, and yet but one infinitesimal part of his powers has been manifested. Therefore you must not say that you are weak. How do you know what possibilities lie behind that degradation on the surface? You know but little of that which is within you. For behind you is the Ocean of infinite power and blessedness.

"This Ātman is first to be heard of." Hear day and night that you are that Soul. Repeat it to yourselves day and night till it enters into your very veins, till it tingles in every drop of blood, till it is in your flesh and bone. Let the whole body be full of that one idea: "I am the birthless, the deathless, the blissful, the omniscient, the omnipotent, ever glorious Soul." Think of it day and night; think of it till it becomes part and parcel of your life. Meditate upon it. And out of that will come work. "Out of the fullness of the heart the mouth speaketh," and out of the fullness of the heart the hand worketh also. Action will come. Fill yourselves with the ideal; remember it well before you take up any work. Then all your actions will be glorified, transformed, deified, by the very power of this thought. If matter is powerful, thought is omnipotent. Bring this thought to bear upon your life, fill yourselves with the thought of your almightiness, your majesty, and your glory.

Would to God no superstitions had been put into your head! Would to God we had not been surrounded from our birth by all these superstitious influences and paralysing ideas of our weakness and vileness! Would to God that mankind had had an easier path through which to attain to the noblest and highest truths! But man has to pass through all this; do not make the path more difficult for those who come after you.

These are sometimes terrible doctrines to teach. I know people who get frightened at these ideas; but for those who want to be practical, this is the first thing to learn. Never tell yourselves or others that you are weak. Do good if you can, but do not injure the world. You know in your inmost heart that many of your limited ideas—this humbling of yourself, and praying and weeping to imaginary beings—are superstitions. Tell me one case where these prayers have been answered from outside. All the answers came from your own hearts. You know there are no ghosts, but no sooner are you in the dark than you feel a little creepy sensation. That is because in your childhood you have had all these fearful ideas put into your heads. But do not teach these things to others—

through fear of society and public opinion, or for fear of incurring the hatred of friends, or for fear of losing cherished superstitions. Be masters of all these. What is there to be taught in religion more than the oneness of the universe, and faith in oneself? All the efforts of mankind for thousands of years past have been directed towards this one goal, and mankind is yet to work it out. It is your turn now and you already know the truth. For it has been taught on all sides. Not only philosophy and psychology, but the materialistic sciences have declared it. Where is the scientific man today who fears to acknowledge the truth of this oneness of the universe? Who is there who dares talk of many worlds? All these are superstitions.

There is only one Life, one World; and this one Life, this one World, appears to us to be manifold. This manifoldness is like a dream. When you dream, one dream passes away and another comes. None of your dreams are real. The dreams come one after another; scene after scene unfolds before you. So it is in this world of ninety per cent misery and ten per cent happiness. Perhaps after a while it will appear as ninety per cent happiness, and we shall call it heaven. But a time comes to the sage when the whole thing vanishes and this world appears as God Himself, and his own soul as that God. It is not true that there are many worlds; it is not true that there are many lives. All this manifoldness is the manifestation of that One. That One is manifesting Himself as many—as matter, spirit, mind, thought, and everything else. Therefore the first step for us to take is to teach the truth to ourselves and to others. Let the world resound with this ideal and let superstitions vanish. Tell it to men who are weak, and persist in telling it.

"You are the Pure One. Awake and arise, Almighty One! This sleep does not become you. Awake and arise; it does not befit you. Think not that you are weak and miserable. Almighty One, arise and awake, and manifest your true nature. It is not fitting that you think yourself a sinner. It is not fitting that you think yourself weak." Say that to the world, say it to yourselves, and see what a practical result follows; see how with an electric flash the truth is manifested, how everything is changed. Tell it to men and show them their power. Then they will learn how to apply it in their daily lives.

To be able to use what we call viveka, discrimination, to learn how, in every moment of our lives, in every one of our actions, to discriminate between right and wrong, true and false, we shall have to know the test of truth, which is purity, oneness. Everything that makes for oneness is truth. Love is truth and hatred is falsehood, because hatred makes for multiplicity. It is hatred that separates man from man; therefore it is wrong and false. It is a disintegrating power; it separates and destroys. Love unites; love makes for that oneness. You become one—the mother with the child, families with the city; human beings become one with the animals. For love is Existence, God Himself, and all this is the manifestation of that one Love, more or less expressed. The differences are only of degree; it is the manifestation of that one Love throughout. Therefore in all our actions we have to judge whether our act is making for diversity or for oneness. If it makes for diversity, we have to give it up, but if for oneness, we may be sure it is good. So with our thoughts; we have to decide whether they make for disintegration, multiplicity, or for oneness, binding soul to soul and thus generating a great force. If they do this, we will take them up, and if not, we will throw them off as wicked.

The whole idea of Vedāntic ethics is that it does not depend on anything unknowable, nor does it teach anything unknown. On the contrary, it teaches, in the language of St. Paul: "Whom therefore ye ignorantly worship, him declare I unto you." It is through the Self that you know everything. I see this chair; but to see the chair, first I have to perceive myself and then the chair. It is in and through the Self that the chair is perceived. It is in and through the Self that you are known to me, that the whole world is known to me; and therefore to say that this Self is unknown is sheer nonsense. Take away the Self and the whole universe vanishes. In and through the Self all knowledge comes. Therefore It is the best known of all. It is yourself—that which you call "I." You may wonder how this "I" of me can be the "I" of you. You may wonder how this limited "I" can be the unlimited Infinite. But it is so. The limited "I" is a mere fiction. The Infinite has been covered up, as it were, and a little of It is being manifested as the "I." Limitation can never come upon the unlimited; it is a fiction. The Self is known, therefore, to every one of us—man, woman, or child—and even to animals. Without knowing It we can neither live nor move nor have our being; without knowing this Lord of all we cannot breathe or live a second. The God of Vedānta is the most known of all and is not the outcome of imagination.

If this is not preaching a practical God—how else could you preach a practical God? Where is there a more practical God than Him whom I see before me, a God omnipresent, in every being, more real than anything we see through our senses? For you are He, the omnipresent God Almighty, and if I say you are not, I tell an untruth. I know it, whether at all times I realize it or not. He is the Oneness, the Unity of all, the Reality of all life and all existence.

These ideas of the ethics of Vedānta have to be worked out in detail, and therefore you must have patience. As I have told you, we want to take the subject in detail and work it out thoroughly to see how these ideas have grown from a very low level and how the one great idea of oneness has developed and become shaped into the Universal Love. We ought to study all these in order to avoid dangers.

The world cannot find time to work it out from the lowest steps. But what is the use of our standing on higher steps if we cannot give the truth to others coming afterwards? Therefore it is better to study it in all its workings; and first it is absolutely necessary to clear the intellectual portion, although we know that intellectuality is almost nothing; for it is the heart that is of most importance. It is through the heart that the Lord is seen, and not through the intellect. The intellect is a street-cleaner, cleansing the path for us, a secondary worker, a policeman. But the policeman is not a positive necessity for the workings of society; he is only to stop disturbances, to check wrong-doing. And that is all the work required of the intellect. When you read intellectual books, you feel when you have mastered them, "Bless the Lord that I am out of them!" because the intellect is blind and cannot move of itself; it has neither hands nor feet. It is feeling that works, that moves with speed infinitely superior to that of electricity or anything else. Do you feel?—that is the question. If you do, you will see the Lord. The feeling that you have today will be intensified, deified, raised to the highest level, till you feel the oneness in everything, till you feel God in yourself and in others. The intellect can never do that. "Different methods of speaking words, different methods of explaining the texts of books—these are for the enjoyment of the learned, not for the salvation of the soul."

Those of you who have read Thomas à Kempis know how on every page he insists on this, and almost every holy man in the world has insisted on it. Intellect is necessary; for without it we fall into crude errors and make all sorts of mistakes. Intellect checks these. But beyond that do not try to build anything upon it. It is an inactive, secondary help; the real help is feeling, love. Do you feel for others? If you do, you are growing in oneness. If you do not feel for others, you may be the greatest intellectual giant ever born, but you will be nothing; you are but dry intellect and you will remain so. And if you feel, even if you cannot read any book and do not know any language, you are on the right way. The Lord is yours.

Do you not know, from the history of the world, where the power of the prophets lay? Where was it? In the intellect? Did any of them write a fine book on philosophy, on the most intricate ratiocinations of logic? Not one of them. They only spoke a few words. Feel like Christ and you will be a Christ; feel like Buddha and you will be a Buddha. It is feeling that is the life, the strength, the vitality, without which no amount of intellectual activity can reach God. Intellect is like limbs without the power of locomotion. It is only when feeling enters and gives the intellect motion that it moves and works on others. That is so all over the world, and it is a thing which you must always remember. It is one of the most practical things in Vedāntic morality; for it is the teaching of Vedānta that you are all prophets and that you all must be prophets.

Scripture is not the proof of your conduct, but you are the proof of scripture. How do you know that a book teaches truth? Because you are truth and feel it. That is what Vedānta says. What is the proof of the Christs and Buddhas of the world? That you and I feel like them. That is how you and I understand that they were true. Our prophet soul is the proof of their prophet soul. Your godhead is the proof of God Himself. If you are not a prophet there never has been anything true of God. If you are not God there never was any God and never will be.

This, says Vedānta, is the ideal to follow. Every one of us will have to become a prophet. You are that already; only know it. Never think there is anything impossible for the soul. It is the greatest heresy to think so. If there is sin, this is the only sin: to say that you are weak or others are weak.

PRACTICAL VEDĀNTA

PART II

(Delivered in London, November 12, 1896)

I WILL RELATE TO YOU a very ancient story from the *Chhāndogya Upanishad*, which tells how knowledge came to a boy. The story itself is crude, but we shall find that it contains a principle.

A young boy said to his mother: "I am going to study the Vedas. Tell me the name of my father and my caste." The mother was not a married woman, and in India the child of a woman who has not been married is considered an outcaste; he is not recognized by society and is not entitled to study the Vedas. So the poor mother said: "My child, I do not know your family name. I used to serve different people. You were born when I was in service. I do not know who your father is. But my name is Jabālā and your name is Satyakāma."

The boy went to a sage and asked to be taken as a student. The sage asked him, "What is the name of your father, and what is your caste?" The boy repeated to him what he had heard from his mother. The sage at once said: "None but a brāhmin could speak such a damaging truth about himself. You are a brāhmin and I will teach you. You have not swerved from truth." So he kept the boy with him and educated him.

Now we come to some of the peculiar methods of education in ancient India. This teacher gave Satyakāma four hundred lean, weak cows to take care of and sent him to the forest. There he went and lived for some time. The teacher had told him to come back when the herd had increased to one thousand. After a few years, one day Satyakāma heard a big bull in the herd saying to him: "We are a thousand now; take us back to your teacher. I will teach you a little of Brahman." "Go on, sir," said Satyakāma. Then the bull said: "The East is a part of the Lord; so is the West; so is the South; so is the North. The four cardinal points are the four parts of Brahman. Fire will also teach you something of Brahman."

In those days fire was worshipped as a special symbol of Brahman, and every student had to light the sacrificial fire and make offerings. So on the following day Satyakāma started for his guru's house, and when in the evening he had offered his oblation and worshipped the fire, and was sitting near it, he heard a voice come from the fire: "O Satyakāma!" "Speak, Lord," said Satyakāma. (Perhaps you remember a very similar story in the Old Testament: how Samuel heard a mysterious voice.) The fire said: "O Satyakāma, I will teach you a little of Brahman. This earth is a portion of that Brahman. The sky and heaven are

348

portions of It. The ocean is a part of that Brahman." Then the fire said that a certain bird would also teach him something.

Satyakāma continued his journey, and on the next day, when he had performed his evening sacrifice, a swan came to him and said: "I will teach you something about Brahman. This fire which you worship, O Satyakāma, is a part of that Brahman. The sun is a part, the moon is a part, lightning is a part of that Brahman. A bird called Madgu will tell you more about It." The next evening that bird came, and a similar voice was heard by Satyakāma: "I will tell you something about Brahman. Breath is a part of Brahman, sight is a part, hearing is a part, the mind is a part."

Then the boy arrived at his teacher's place and presented himself before him with due reverence. No sooner had the teacher seen him than he said: "Satyakāma, your face shines like the face of a knower of Brahman! Who, then, has taught you?" "Creatures other than men," replied Satyakāma. "But I wish that you should teach me, sir. For I have heard from men like you that knowledge learnt from a guru alone leads to the supreme good." Then the sage taught him the same knowledge that he had received from the others. "And nothing was left out, yea, nothing was left out."

Now, apart from the allegories in what the bull, the fire, and the birds taught, we see the tendency of the thought and the direction in which it was going in those days. The great idea of which we here see the germ is that all these voices are inside ourselves. As we understand these truths better, we find that the voice is in our own heart. The student understood that all the time he was hearing the truth; but his explanation was not correct. He was interpreting the voice as coming from the external world, while all the time it was within him.

The second idea that we get is that of making the knowledge of Brahman practical. The world is always seeking the practical possibilities of religion, and we find in these stories how it was becoming more and more practical every day. The truth was shown through everything with which the students were familiar. The fire they were worshipping was Brahman, the earth was a part of Brahman, and so on.

The next story refers to Upakosala Kamalāyana, a disciple of this Satyakāma, who wanted to be taught by him and dwelt with him for some time. Now, Satyakāma went away on a journey, and the student became very downhearted; and when the teacher's wife came and asked him why he was not eating, the boy said, "I am too unhappy to eat." Then a voice came from the fire he was worshipping, and said: "Life is Brahman; Brahman is ākāśa; Brahman is happiness. Know Brahman." "I know, sir," the boy replied, "that life is Brahman, but that It is ākāśa and happiness I do not know." Then the voice explained that the two words ākāśa and happiness signified one thing in reality, that is, Pure Intelligence, which resides in the heart. So it taught him that Brahman is life and the ākāśa in the heart. Next the fire taught: "This earth, food, fire, and the sun, which you worship, are forms of Brahman. The Person who is seen in the sun—I am He. He who knows this and meditates on Him—all his sins vanish and he has long life and becomes happy. He who lives in the cardinal points, the moon, the stars, and water—I am He. He who lives in this life, the ākāśa, the heavens, and lightning—I am He."

Here too we see the same idea of practical religion. The things which they were worshipping, such as fire, the sun, the moon, and so forth, and with which they were familiar, form the subject of the stories, which explain them and give them a higher meaning. And this is the real, practical side of Vedānta. It does not destroy the world, but it explains it; it does not destroy the person, but it explains him; it does not destroy the individuality, but it explains it by showing the real individuality. It does not show that this world is vain and does not exist, but it says, "Understand what this world is, so that it may not hurt you."

The voice did not say to Satyakāma that the fire which he was worshipping, or the sun, or the moon, or the lightning, or anything else, was all wrong; but it showed him that the same Spirit which was inside the sun and moon and lightning and fire and the earth was in him, so that everything became transformed, as it were, in the eyes of Satyakāma. The fire, which before had been merely a material fire in which to make oblations, assumed a new aspect and became God. The earth became transformed, life became transformed, the sun, the moon, the stars, lightning, everything became transformed and deified. Their real nature was known. The theme of Vedānta is to see the Lord in everything, to see things in their real nature, not as they appear to be.

Then another lesson is taught in the Upanishads: "He who shines through the eyes is Brahman. He is the Beautiful One. He is the Shining One. He shines in all these worlds." A certain peculiar light, a commentator says, which radiates from the eyes of the pure man, is what is meant by the light in the eyes; and it is said that when a man is pure such a light will shine in his eyes, and that light belongs really to the Soul within, which is everywhere. It is the same light that shines in the planets, in the stars, and in the sun.

I will now read to you some other doctrines of these ancient Upanishads, about birth and death and so on. Perhaps they will interest you. Śvetaketu went to the king of the Pānchālas, and the king asked him: "Do you know where people go when they die? Do you know how they come back? Do you know why the earth is neither full nor empty?" The boy replied that he did not know. Then he went to his father and asked him the same questions. The father said, "I do not know," and they both returned to the king. The king said that this knowledge was never known to the priests; it was known only to the kings, and that was why kings ruled the world. They both served the king for some time, and at last the king said he would teach them. "The other world, O Gautama, is the fire. The sun is its fuel, the rays are the smoke, the day is the flame, the moon is the embers, and the stars are the sparks. In this fire the gods pour the libation of faith, and from this libation King Soma is born." So on he goes. The gist of the teaching is this: "You need not make oblation in that little fire; the whole world is the fire, and this oblation, this worship, is continually going on. The gods and the angels and everybody are worshipping it. Man is the greatest symbol of fire—the body of man."

Here also we see the ideal becoming practical. Brahman is seen in everything. The principle that underlies all these stories is that invented symbolism may be good and helpful, but symbols better than any we can invent already exist. You may invent an image through which to worship God, but a better image already exists—the living man. You may build a temple in which to worship

God, and that may be good, but a better one, a much higher one, already exists —the human body.

You remember that the Vedas have two parts: the ceremonial and the philosophical. In time, ceremonies had multiplied and become so intricate that it was almost hopeless to disentangle them; and so in the Upanishads the ceremonies are almost discarded, but gently, by having their deeper meaning explained. We see that in olden times people had had these oblations and sacrifices. Then the philosophers came, and instead of snatching away the symbols from the hands of the ignorant, instead of taking the negative position which we unfortunately find so general among modern reformers, they gave them something in their place. "Here is the symbol of fire," they said. "Very good. But here is another symbol of fire—the earth, where sacrifice is going on day and night. What a grand symbol! Here is this little temple. But the whole universe is a temple; a man can worship anywhere. There are altars made by men; but here is the greatest of altars, the living, conscious human body; and worship at this altar is far higher than the worship of any dead symbols."

We now come to a peculiar doctrine. I do not understand much of it myself. I shall describe it to you and see if you can make something out of it. When a man who has by meditation purified himself and got knowledge dies, he first goes to light, then from light to day, from day to the bright half of the moon, from there to the six months when the sun goes to the north, from there to the year, from the year to the sun, from the sun to the moon, from the moon to lightning, and when he comes to the sphere of lightning he meets a person who is not human, and that person leads him to the conditioned Brahman. This is the Way of the Gods. When sages and wise persons die they go that way and they do not return. What is meant by this month and year and all these things, no one understands clearly. Each one gives his own meaning, and some say it is all nonsense. What is meant by going to the world of the moon and of the sun, and by this person who comes to help the soul after it has reached the sphere of lightning, no one knows.

There is an idea among the Hindus that the moon is a place where life exists, and we shall see how life has come from there. When those who have not attained to knowledge, but have done good work in this life, die, they first go through smoke, then to night, then to the dark half of the moon, then to the six months when the sun goes to the south, and from there to the region of their forefathers, then to the ākāśa, then to the region of the moon, and there become the food of the gods, and later are born as gods and live there so long as their good works permit. This is called the Way of the Fathers. And when the effect of the good works is finished they come back to earth by the same route. They first become ākāśa, and then air, and then smoke, and then mist, and then cloud, and then they fall upon the earth as raindrops; then they get into food, which is eaten by human beings, and finally become their children. Those whose works have been very good are born in good families, and those whose works have been bad are born in bad families, and even in animal bodies. Again, those who do not travel either by the Way of the Gods or the Way of the Fathers— those who have done vile deeds—become insects, being born and dying almost instantly. That is why the earth is neither full nor empty.

We can get several ideas from this also, and later on perhaps we shall be able to understand it better and speculate a little upon what it means. The last part, which deals with how those who have been in heaven return, is clearer perhaps than the first part; but the whole idea seems to be that there is no true immortality without realizing God. Some people who have not realized God, but have done good work in this world with a view to enjoying the results, go, when they die, through this and that place until they reach heaven, and there they are born in the same way as we are here, as children of the gods, and they live there so long as their good works permit. Out of this comes one basic idea of Vedānta, namely, that everything which has name and form is transient. This earth is transient, because it has name and form, and so the heavens must be transient, because there also name and form remain. A heaven which was eternal would be a contradiction in terms, because everything that has name and form must begin in time, exist in time, and end in time. These are settled doctrines of Vedānta. And therefore the heavens are given up.

We have seen that in the Samhitās the idea of heaven was that it was eternal —much the same idea as is prevalent among Mohammedans and Christians. The Mohammedans concretize it a little more. They say that it is a place where there are gardens, beneath which rivers run. In the desert of Arabia water is very desirable; so the Mohammedan always conceives his heaven as containing much water. I was born in a country where there are six months of rain every year. I should think of heaven, I suppose, as a dry place, and so also would the English people. These heavens in the Samhitās are eternal, and the departed have beautiful bodies and live with their forefathers and are happy ever afterwards. There they meet with their parents, children, and other relatives, and lead very much the same sort of life as here, only much happier. All the difficulties and obstructions to happiness in this life have vanished, and only its good parts and enjoyments remain.

But however comfortable mankind may consider this state of things, truth is one thing and comfort is another. There are cases where truth is not comfortable until we reach its climax. Human nature is very conservative. It does something, and having once done that, finds it hard to get out of it. The mind will not receive new thoughts, because they bring discomfort.

In the Upanishads we see that a tremendous departure is made. It is declared that these heavens in which men live with their ancestors after death cannot be permanent, seeing that everything which has name and form must die. If there are heavens with form, these heavens must vanish in the course of time; they may last millions of years, but there will come a time when they must go. With this idea comes another: that these souls must come back to earth—that heavens are places where they enjoy the results of their good works, and after these results are exhausted they must come back to this earth-life again.

One thing is clear from this: that mankind had a perception of the philosophy of causation even at that early time. Later on we shall see how our philosophers bring this out in the language of philosophy and logic; but here it is almost in the language of children.

You may remark one thing in reading these books: that it is all internal perception. If you ask me if all this can be practical, my answer is, it was practical first and philosophical next. You can see that these things first were perceived and realized, and then written down. This earth spoke to the early thinkers. Birds spoke to them, animals spoke to them; the sun and moon spoke to them; and little by little they understood things and got into the heart of nature. Not by cogitation, not by the force of logic, not by picking the brains of others and writing a big book, as is the fashion in modern times, not even as I do, by taking up one of their writings and making a long lecture, but by patient investigation and discovery, they found out the truth. Their essential method was practice, and so it must be always. Religion is ever a practical science, and there never was or will be any theoretical religion. It is practice first, and knowledge afterwards.

The idea that souls come back is already there. Those persons who do good work with the idea of a result get the result, but it is not permanent. There we have the idea of causation very beautifully put forward. The effect is only commensurate with the cause. As the cause is, so the effect will be. The cause being finite, the effect must be finite. If the cause is eternal the effect will be eternal; but all these causes—doing good work and all other things—are only finite causes, and as such cannot produce an infinite result.

We now come to the other side of the question. Just as there cannot be an eternal heaven, so, on the same grounds, there cannot be an eternal hell. Suppose I am a very wicked man, doing evil every minute of my life. Still, my whole life here, compared with my eternal life, is nothing. If there were an eternal punishment, it would mean that there was an infinite effect produced by a finite cause, which cannot be. If I do good all my life I cannot have an eternal heaven; it would be making the same mistake.

We have already spoken of the Way of the Gods and the Way of the Fathers. But there is a third course, which applies to those who have known Truth, to those who have realized It. This is the only way to get beyond the veil of māyā—to realize what Truth is. And the Upanishads indicate what is meant by realizing Truth. It means recognizing neither good nor bad, but knowing that all comes from the Self, and that the Self is in everything. It means denying the universe, shutting your eyes to it, seeing the Lord in hell as well as in heaven, seeing the Lord in death as well as in life. This is the line of thought in the passage I have read to you. The earth is a symbol of the Lord, the sky is the Lord—everything is Brahman. And this is to be seen, realized, not simply talked or thought about. We can see as its logical consequence that when the soul has realized that everything is full of the Lord, of Brahman, it will not care whether it goes to heaven or hell or anywhere else, whether it is born again on this earth or in heaven. These things have ceased to have any meaning for that soul, because every place is the same, every place is the temple of the Lord, every place has become holy, and the presence of the Lord is all that it sees in heaven or hell or anywhere else. Neither good nor bad, neither life nor death—only the one infinite Brahman exists.

According to Vedānta, when a man has arrived at that perception he has become free, and he is the only man who is fit to live in this world. Others are not. The man who sees evil—how can he live in this world? His life is a mass of misery. The man who sees dangers—his life is a misery. The man who sees death—his life is a misery. That man alone can live in this world, he alone can say, "I enjoy this life and I am happy in this life," who has seen Truth. And Truth exists in everything.

By the bye, I may tell you that the idea of hell does not occur anywhere in the Vedas. It comes with the Purānas, much later. The worst punishment, according to the Vedas, is coming back to earth, having another life in this world. From the very first we see that the thought is taking an impersonal turn. The ideas of punishment and reward are very material, and they are consonant only with the idea of a Personal God who loves one and hates another just as we do. Punishment and reward are admissible only with the existence of such a God. They had such a God in the Samhitās, and there we find the idea of fear entering; but as soon as we come to the Upanishads, the idea of fear vanishes and the idea of the Impersonal takes its place.

It is naturally the hardest thing for man to understand, this idea of the Impersonal, for he is always clinging to the Personal. Even people who are considered great thinkers get disgusted at the idea of the Impersonal God. But to me it seems absurd to think of God as if He were an embodied man. Which is the higher idea, a living God or a dead God? A God whom nobody sees, nobody knows, or a God known?

The Impersonal God is a living God, a Principle. The difference between Personal and Impersonal God is this: the Personal God is only a man, whereas the Impersonal is angel, man, animal, and yet something more, which we cannot see, because impersonality includes all personalities, is the sum total of everything in the universe, and infinitely more besides. "As the one fire coming into the world manifests itself in so many forms, and yet is infinitely more besides"—even so is the Impersonal.

We want to worship a living God. I have not seen anything but God all my life, nor have you. To see this chair you must first see God and then the chair, in and through Him. He is everywhere, as the "I am." The moment you feel "I am," you are conscious of Existence. Where shall we find God if we cannot see Him in our own hearts and in every living being? "Thou art the man, Thou art the woman, Thou art the girl, and Thou art the boy; Thou art the old man tottering with a stick, Thou art the young man walking in the pride of his strength; Thou art all that exists"—a wonderful, living God who is the only fact in the universe.

This seems to many to be a terrible contradiction of the traditional God, who lives behind a veil somewhere and whom nobody ever sees. The priests only give us an assurance that if we follow them, listen to their admonitions, and walk in the way they mark out for us, then, when we die, they will give us a passport to enable us to see the face of God! What are all these ideas of heaven but simply inventions of this nonsensical priestcraft?

Of course, the idea of the Impersonal is very destructive: it takes away all trade from the priests, churches, and temples. In India there is a famine now, but there are temples in each one of which there are jewels worth a king's ransom. If the priests taught this idea of the Impersonal to the people, their occupation would be gone. Yet we have to teach it unselfishly, without priestcraft. You are God and so am I. Who obeys whom? Who worships whom? You are the highest temple of God; I would rather worship you than any temple, image, or Bible. Why are some people's thoughts so full of contradictions? They say that they are hard-headed practical men. Very good. But what is more practical than worshipping you? I see you, feel you, and I know you are God. The Mohammedan says there is no God but Allah. Vedānta says there is nothing that is not God. It may frighten many of you, but you will understand it by degrees. The living God is within you, and yet you are building churches and temples and believing all sorts of imaginary nonsense. The only God to worship is the human soul in the human body. Of course, all animals are temples too, but man is the highest, the greatest of all temples. If I cannot worship in that, no other temple will be of any advantage. The moment I have realized God sitting in the temple of every human body, the moment I stand in reverence before every human being and see God in him, that moment I am free from bondage, everything that binds vanishes, and I am free.

This is the most practical of all worship; it has nothing to do with theorizing and speculation. Yet it frightens many. They say it is not right. They go on theorizing about old ideas told them by their grandfathers, that a God somewhere in heaven had told someone that he was God. Since that time we have had only theories. This is practicality according to them—and our ideas are impractical! No doubt, Vedānta says, each one must have his own path; but the path is not the goal. The worship of a God in heaven and all these things are not bad; but they are only steps towards the Truth, and not the Truth itself. They are good and beautiful, and some wonderful ideas are there, but Vedānta says at every point: "My friend, Him whom you are worshipping as unknown—I worship Him as you. He whom you are worshipping as unknown and are seeking throughout the universe has been with you all the time. You are living through Him and He is the eternal Witness of the universe." He whom all the Vedas worship, nay more, He who is always present in the eternal "I"—He existing, the whole universe exists. He is the light and life of the universe. If this "I" were not in you, you would not see the sun; everything would be a mass of darkness. He shining, you see the world.

One objection is generally raised, and it is this: that this may lead to a tremendous amount of difficulty. Every one of us will think, "I am God, and whatever I do or think must be good; for God can do no evil." In the first place, even taking this danger of misinterpretation for granted, can it be proved that on the other side the same danger does not exist? Men have been worshipping a God in heaven separate from them and of whom they are much afraid. They have been born shaking with fear, and all their life they will go on shaking. Has the world been made much better by this? Those who have understood and worshipped a Personal God, and those who have understood and worshipped an Impersonal God—which of these have been the great workers of the world? On which side have been the gigantic workers, gigantic moral powers? Certainly on the side of the Impersonal. How can you expect morality to be developed through fear? It can never be. "When one sees another, when one hears another, that is māyā. When one does not see another, when one does not hear another, when everything has become Ātman, who sees whom, who perceives whom?" It is all He and all I at the same time. The soul has become pure.

Then and then alone do we understand what love is. Love cannot come through fear. Its basis is freedom. When we really begin to love the world, then we understand what is meant by the brotherhood of mankind, and not before.

So it is not right to say that the idea of the Impersonal will lead to a tremendous amount of evil in the world, as if the other doctrine never lent itself to works of evil; as if it did not lead to sectarianism, deluging the world with blood and causing men to tear each other to pieces. "My God is the greatest God; if anyone disagrees, let us decide it by a free fight"—that is the outcome of dualism all over the world. Come out into the broad, open light of day; come out from the little narrow paths. For how can the infinite Soul rest content to live and die in small ruts? Come out into the universe of light. Everything in the universe is yours. Stretch out your arms and embrace it with love. If you ever felt you wanted to do that, you have felt God.

You remember that passage in the sermon of Buddha: how he sent a thought of love towards the south, the north, the east, and the west, above and below, until the whole universe was filled with this love, so grand, great, and infinite. When you have that feeling you have true personality; for the whole universe is one Person. Let little things go. Give up the small for the Infinite; give up small enjoyments for Infinite Bliss. It is all yours, for the Impersonal includes the personal. So God is personal and impersonal at the same time. And Man— the infinite Impersonal Man—is manifesting Himself as a person. We, the Infinite, have limited ourselves, as it were, into small parts.

Vedānta says that infinity is our true nature; it will never vanish; it will abide for ever. But we limit ourselves by our karma, which like a chain round our necks has dragged us into this limitation. Break that chain and be free. Trample law under your feet. No law can bind man's true nature—no destiny, no fate. How can there be law in infinity? Freedom is its watchword. Freedom is its nature, its birthright. Be free and then have any number of personalities you like. Then we shall play like the actor who comes upon the stage and plays the part of a beggar. Contrast him with the actual beggar walking in the streets. The scene is perhaps the same in both cases; the words are perhaps the same; but yet what a difference! The one enjoys his beggary, while the other is suffering misery from it. And what makes this difference? The one is free and the other is bound. The actor knows that his beggary is not true, but that he has assumed it for the play, while the real beggar thinks that it is his own natural state and he has to bear it whether he will or not; for this is the law.

So long as we have no knowledge of our real nature, we are beggars, jostled about by every force in nature and made slaves of by everything in nature. We cry all over the world for help, but help never comes to us. We cry to imaginary beings and yet it never comes. But still we hope help will come; and thus in weeping, wailing, and hoping, this life is passed and the same play goes on and on.

Be free. Hope for nothing from anyone. I am sure if you look back upon your lives you will find that you were always vainly trying to get help from others which never came. All the help that ever came was from within yourselves. You had the fruits only of what you yourselves worked for, and yet you were strangely hoping all the time for help from others. A rich man's parlour is always full; but, if you notice, you do not find the same people there. The visitors are always hoping that they will get something from the wealthy man; but they never do. So are our lives spent in hoping, hoping, hoping, to which there is no end. Give up hope, says Vedānta. Why should you hope? You *have* everything, nay, you *are* everything. What are you hoping for? If a king goes mad and runs about trying to find the king of his country, he will never find him, because he is the king himself. He may go through every village and city in his own country, seeking in every house, weeping and wailing, but he will never find him, because he is the king himself. It is better that we know we are God and give up this fool's search after Him. Knowing we are God, we become happy and contented.

Give up all these mad pursuits and then play your part in the universe as an actor on the stage. The whole scene will change, and instead of an eternal prison this world will appear a playground; instead of a land of competition it will be a land of bliss, where perpetual spring exists, flowers bloom, and butterflies flit about. This very world, which formerly was a hell, will be a heaven. To the eyes of the bound it is a tremendous place of torment, but to the eyes of the free it is quite otherwise. This very life is the Universal Life. Heavens and all those places are here; all the gods are here, the so-called prototypes of man. The gods did not create man after their image, but man created the gods. And here are the prototypes; here is Indra, here is Varuna, and all the gods of the universe. We have been projecting our little doubles, and we are the originals of these gods; we are the real, the only gods to be worshipped.

This is the view of Vedānta, and this is its practicality. When we have become free, we need not go crazy and give up society and rush off to die in the forest or in a cave. We shall remain where we are, only we shall understand the whole thing. The same phenomena will remain, but with a new meaning.

We do not know the world yet; it is only through freedom that we shall see what it is and understand its nature. We shall see then that this so-called law, or fate, or destiny, touched only a small fraction of our nature. It was only one side, but on the other side there was freedom all the time. We did not know this, and that is why we tried to save ourselves from evil by hiding our faces in the ground, like hunted hares. Through delusion we tried to forget our nature, and yet we could not; it was always calling to us, and all our search after God or the gods or external freedom was a search after our real nature. We mistook the voice. We thought it came from the fire or from a god, or from the sun or moon or stars. But at last we have found that it is from within ourselves. Within ourselves is this eternal voice speaking of eternal freedom; its music is eternally going on. Part of this music of the Soul has become the earth, the law, this universe; but it was always ours and always will be.

In one word, the ideal of Vedānta is to know man as he really is; and this is its message: If you cannot worship your brother man, the manifested God, how can you worship a God who is unmanifested? Do you not remember what the Bible says: "If you cannot love your brother whom you have seen, how can you love God whom you have not seen?" If you cannot see God in the human face, how can you see Him in the clouds or in images made of dull, dead matter, or in the mere fictions of your brain? I shall call you religious from the day you begin to see God in men and women. Then you will understand what is meant by turning the left cheek to the man who strikes you on the right. When you see man as God, everything, even the tiger, will be welcome. Whatever comes to us is but the Lord, the Eternal, the Blessed One, appearing to us in various forms—as our father and mother and friend and child. They are our own Soul playing with us.

As our human relationships can thus be made divine, so our relationship with God may take any of these forms, and we can look upon Him as our Father or Mother or Friend or Beloved. Calling God Mother is a higher ideal than calling God Father, and to call Him Friend is still higher; but the highest is to regard Him as the Beloved. The culmination of all is to see no difference between lover and beloved. You may remember, perhaps, the old Persian story of how a lover came and knocked at the door of his beloved and was asked, "Who are you?" He answered, "It is I," and there was no response. A second time he came and exclaimed, "I am here," but the door was not opened. A third time he came, and the voice asked from inside, "Who is there?" He replied, "I am thyself, my beloved," and the door opened. So is the relation between God and ourselves. He is in everything; He is everything. Every man and woman is the palpable, blissful, living God. Who says God is unknown? Who says He is to be searched after? We have known God eternally. We have been living in Him eternally. Everywhere He is eternally known, eternally worshipped.

Then comes another idea: that other forms of worship are not errors. This is one of the great points to be remembered: that those who worship God through ceremonials and forms, however crude we may think them, are not in error. It is the journey from truth to truth, from lower truth to higher truth. Darkness means less light; evil means less good; impurity means less purity. It must always be borne in mind that we should see others with eyes of love, with sympathy, knowing that they are going along the same path that we have trodden. If you are free, you must know that all will be so sooner or later; if you are free, how can you see anyone in bondage? If you are really pure, how do you see the impure? For what is within is without. We cannot see impurity without having it inside ourselves.

This is one of the practical sides of Vedānta, and I hope that we shall all try to carry it into our lives. Our whole life here is an opportunity to carry this into practice. But our greatest gain is that we shall work with satisfaction and contentment instead of with discontent and dissatisfaction; for we know that Truth is within us, we have It as our birthright, and we have only to manifest It and make It tangible.

PRACTICAL VEDĀNTA

PART III

(Delivered in London, November 17, 1896)

IN THE Chhāndogya Upanishad we read that a sage named Nārada comes to another named Sanatkumāra and asks him various questions, one of which is concerning the cause of things as they are. And Sanatkumāra leads him, as it were, step by step, telling him that there is something higher than this earth and something higher than that, and so on, till he comes to ākāśa. Ākāśa is higher than light, because in ākāśa exist the sun and the moon, lightning, and the stars; in ākāśa we live and in ākāśa we die. Then the question arises whether there is anything higher than that, and Sanatkumāra tells him of prāna. This prāna, according to Vedānta, is the principle of life. It is, like ākāśa, an omnipresent principle; and all motion, either in the body or anywhere else, is the work of prāna. It is higher than ākāśa, and through it everything lives. Prāna is in the mother, in the father, in the sister, in the teacher; prāna is the knower.

I will read another passage, where Śvetaketu asks his father about Truth. The father teaches him different things and concludes by saying: "That which is the subtle cause of all these things—of It are all these things made. That is the All; That is Truth. Thou art That, O Śvetaketu." And then he gives various examples: "As a bee, O Śvetaketu, gathers honey from different flowers, and as the different honeys do not know that they come from various trees and from various flowers, so all of us, having come from that Existence, know not that we have done so. Now, That which is that subtle essence—in It all that exists has its Self. It is the True; It is the Self. And thou, O Śvetaketu, art That." He gives another example, of the rivers running down to the ocean: "As rivers coming from various sources ultimately flow into the ocean but do not know where they have come from, even so, though we have come out of that Existence, we do not know that we are That. O Śvetaketu, thou art That." So he goes on with his teachings.

Now, there are two principles of knowledge. The one principle is that we can know only by referring the particular to the general, and the general to the universal; and the second is that anything of which the explanation is sought, is to be explained as far as possible from its own nature. Taking up the first principle, we see that all our knowledge really consists of classifications, going higher and higher. When something happens once, we are, as it were, dissatisfied. When it can be shown that the same thing happens again and again, we are satisfied and call it law. When we find that one apple falls, we are dissatisfied; but when we find that all apples fall, we call it the law of gravitation and are satisfied. The fact is that from the particular we deduce the general.

When we want to study religion, we should apply this scientific process. The same principle also holds good here; and as a matter of fact we find that that has been the method throughout. In reading these books from which I have been translating to you, the earliest idea that I can trace is this principle of going from the particular to the general. We see how the gods, the "bright ones," become merged into a principle; and likewise, in their ideas of the cosmos, we find the ancient thinkers going higher and higher—from the fine elements they go to finer and more embracing elements, and from these particulars they come to one omnipresent ākāśa, and even from that they go to an all-embracing force, or prāna. And through all this runs the principle that one is not separate from the others. It is the very ākāśa that exists in the higher form of prāna; or the higher form of prāna is concretized, so to say, and becomes ākāśa, and that ākāśa becomes still grosser, and so on.

The generalization of the Personal God is another case in point. We have seen how this generalization was reached, and how the Personal God was called the sum total of all consciousness. But a difficulty arises: it is an incomplete generalization. We take up only one side of the facts of nature, the fact of consciousness, and upon that we generalize; but the other side, namely, inert nature, is left out. So in the first place it is a defective generalization.

There is another insufficiency about the Personal God, and it relates to the second principle, namely, that everything should be explained from its own nature. There may have been people who ascribed the falling of apples to ghosts; but the scientific explanation is the law of gravitation. And although we know it is not a perfect explanation, yet it is much better than the other, because it is derived from the nature of the thing itself, while the other posits an extraneous cause. So throughout the whole range of our knowledge: the explanation which is based upon the nature of the thing itself is a scientific explanation, and the explanation which brings in an outside agent is unscientific.

So the explanation of a Personal God as the Creator of the universe has to stand that test. If that God is said to be outside nature, having nothing to do with nature, and if nature is said to be the outcome of the command of that God and to have been produced from nothing, then it is a very unscientific theory. This has been the weak point of every theistic religion throughout the ages. These two defects we find in what is generally called the theory of monotheism, the theory of a Personal God, endowed with all the qualities of a human being multiplied very much, who by His will created this universe out of nothing and yet is separate from it.

This, as we have seen, leads us into two difficulties: It is not a sufficient generalization, and secondly, it is not an explanation of nature from within itself. It holds that the effect is not the cause, that the cause is entirely separate from the effect. Yet all human knowledge shows that the effect is but the cause in another form. To this idea the discoveries of modern science are tending every day, and the latest theory, which has been accepted on all sides, is the theory of evolution, the principle of which is that the effect is but the cause in another form, a readjustment of the cause, and that the cause takes the form of the effect.

The theory of creation out of nothing would be laughed at by modern scientists.

Now, can religion stand these tests? If there be any religious theories which can stand these two tests, they will be acceptable to the modern mind, to the thinking mind. Any other theory which we ask the modern man to believe—on the authority of priests or churches or books—he is unable to accept, and the result is a hideous mass of unbelief. Even those in whom there is an external display of belief have in their hearts a tremendous amount of unbelief. The rest of the people shrink away from religion; they give it up, regarding it as priestcraft only.

Religion in modern times has been reduced to a sort of national affair: It is one of our very best social remnants; so let it remain. But the real need which our grandfathers felt for it is gone; we no longer find it satisfactory to our reason. The idea of such a Personal God and such a creation, the idea generally known as monotheism in every religion, cannot hold its own any longer. In India it could not hold its own because of the Buddhists; and that was the very point where they gained their victory in ancient times. They showed that if we admit that nature is possessed of infinite power, and that nature can work out all its wants, it is simply unnecessary to insist that there is something besides nature. Even the soul is unnecessary.

The discussion about substance and qualities is very old, and you will sometimes find that the old superstition lives even at the present day. Most of you have read how, during the middle ages, and, I am sorry to say, even much later, this was one of the subjects of discussion: whether qualities inhere in substance, whether length, breadth, and thickness inhere in the substance which we call dead matter, or whether the substance can exist whether the qualities are there or not. To this our Buddhist says: "You have no ground for maintaining the existence of such a substance. The qualities are all that exist. You do not see beyond them." This is just the position of most of our modern agnostics. For it is this fight about substance and qualities that, on a higher plane, takes the form of the fight about noumenon and phenomenon. There is the phenomenal world, the universe of continuous change, and there is something behind which does not change; and this duality of existence—noumenon and phenomenon—some hold to be real, while others, with better reason, claim that you have no right to admit the two, for what we see, feel, and think of is only the phenomenon. You have no right, they say, to assert that there is anything beyond the phenomenon; and apparently there has been no answer to this.

But the monistic school of Vedānta has given the answer. According to it, one thing alone exists, and that one thing is either phenomenon or noumenon. It is not true that there are two: something changing, and, in and through that, something which does not change; but it is one and the same thing which appears as changing and is in reality unchangeable. We have come to think of the body and mind and soul as separate, but really there is only one; and that one appears through these various forms. Take the well-known illustration of the monists: the rope appearing as the snake. Some people, in the dark or for some other reason, mistake a rope for a snake; but when knowledge comes, the snake vanishes and it is found to be a rope. By this illustration we see that when the snake exists in the mind, the rope has vanished, and when the rope exists, the snake has gone. When we see the phenomenon, and the phenomenon only, around us, the noumenon has vanished; but when we see the noumenon, the unchangeable, it naturally follows that the phenomenon has vanished.

Now we understand better the position of both the realist and the idealist. The realist sees the phenomenon only, and the idealist looks at the noumenon. For the idealist, the really genuine idealist, who has truly acquired that power of perception whereby he can get away from all ideas of change—for him the changeful universe has vanished, and he has the right to say that it is all delusion and there is no change. The realist, at the same time, looks at the changeful phenomenon. For him the unchangeable has vanished, and he has the right to say that the phenomenon alone is real.

What is the outcome of this discussion? It is that the idea of a Personal God is not sufficient. We have to get to something higher, to the idea of the Impersonal. It is the only logical step that we can take. Not that the idea of the Personal God will be destroyed by that, not that we have proved that the Personal God does not exist; but we must go to the Impersonal for the explanation of the Personal God, for the Impersonal is a much higher generalization. Only the Impersonal can be infinite; the Personal is limited. Thus we preserve the Personal God and do not destroy Him. Often the doubt comes to us that if we hold to the idea of the Impersonal God, the Personal God may be destroyed; if we hold to the idea of the Impersonal Man, the personal man may be lost. But the Vedāntic idea is not the destruction of the individual, but its real vindication. We cannot prove the existence of the individual except by referring to the universal, by proving that the individual is really the universal. If we think of the individual as separate from everything else in the universe, it cannot stand a minute. Such a thing never existed.

Secondly, by the application of the other principle, that the explanation of everything must come out of the nature of the thing, we are led to a still bolder idea and one more difficult to understand. It is nothing less than this: The Impersonal Being, our highest generalization, is in ourselves and we are That. "O Śvetaketu, thou art That." You are that Impersonal Being; that God for whom you searched all over the universe has been all the time you yourself —yourself not in the personal sense but in the impersonal. The man we know now, the manifested, is personalized, but the reality in him is the Impersonal. To understand the personal we have to refer it to the Impersonal; the particular must be referred to the general. And that Impersonal is the true Self of man.

There will be various questions in connexion with this, and I shall try to answer them as we go on. Many difficulties will arise. But first let us clearly understand the position of monism. As manifested beings we appear to be separate, but our reality is One, and the less we think of ourselves as separate from that One, the better for us. The more we think of ourselves as separate from the whole, the more miserable we become.

From this monistic principle we get at the basis of ethics, and I venture to say that we cannot get any ethics from anywhere else. We know that the oldest idea of ethics was that it was based on the will of some particular being or beings; but few are ready to accept that now, because it would be only a partial generalization. The Hindus say we must not do this and must do that because the Vedas say so; but the Christian is not going to obey the authority of the Vedas. The Christian says you must do this and not do that because the Bible says so. That will not be binding on those who do not believe in the Bible. But we must have a theory which is large enough to take in all these various viewpoints. Just as there are millions of people who are ready to believe in a Personal Creator, there have also been thousands of the brightest minds in this world who have felt that such ideas were not sufficient for them and wanted something higher; and wherever religion was not broad enough to include all these minds, the result was that the brightest minds in society remained outside religion. Never was this so marked as at the present time, especially in Europe.

Therefore religion must become broad enough to include these minds. Everything it claims must be judged from the standpoint of reason. Why religions should claim that they are not bound to abide by reason no one knows. If one does not take the standard of reason there cannot be any true judgement, even in religion. One religion may ordain something very hideous. For instance, the Mohammedan religion allows Mohammedans to kill all who are not of their religion. It is clearly stated in the Koran: "Kill the infidels if they do not become Mohammedans." They must be put to fire and sword. Now, if we tell a Mohammedan that this is wrong, he will naturally ask: "How do you know that? How do you know it is not good? My book says it is." If you point out that your book is older, the Buddhist will come and say, "My book is much older still." Then will come the Hindu and say, "My books are the oldest of all." Therefore referring to books will not do. Where is the standard by which you can compare? You will say, "Look at the Sermon on the Mount," and the Mohammedan will reply, "Look at the ethics of the Koran." The Mohammedan will say, "Who is the arbiter as to which is the better of the two?" Neither the New Testament nor the Koran can be the arbiter in a quarrel between them. There must be some independent authority, and that cannot be any book, but something that is universal. And what is more universal than reason?

It has been said that reason is not always strong enough to help us to get at the truth; many times it makes mistakes; and therefore the conclusion is that we must believe in the authority of a church! That was said to me by a Roman Catholic, but I could not see the logic of it. On the other hand, I should say, if reason is so weak, a body of priests would be weaker, and I am not going to accept their verdict, but I will abide by my reason, because with all its weakness there is some chance of my getting at the truth through it, while by the other means there is no such hope at all.

We should therefore follow reason, and also we should sympathize with those who, following reason, do not come to any sort of belief. For it is better that mankind should become atheists by following reason than blindly believe in two hundred millions of gods on the authority of somebody. What we want is progress, development, realization. No theories ever made men higher. No amount of books can help us to become purer. The only power is in realization, and that lies in ourselves and comes from thinking. Let men think. A clod of earth never thinks; but it remains only a clod of earth. The glory of man is that he is a thinking being. It is the nature of man to think, and therein he differs from animals. I believe in reason and follow reason, having seen enough of the evils of authority; for I was born in a country where people have gone to the extreme in authority.

The Hindus believe that creation has come out of the Vedas. How do you know there is a cow? Because the word cow is in the Vedas. How do you know there is a man? Because the word man is there. If it had not been, there would have been no man in the world. That is what they say. Authority with a vengeance! Some of the most powerful minds have taken this idea up and spun out wonderful logical theories round it. They have reasoned it out, and there it stands, a whole system of philosophy; and thousands of the brightest intellects have been dedicated through hundreds of years to the working out of this idea. Such has been the power of authority, and great are the dangers thereof. It stunts the growth of humanity, and we must not forget that we want growth. In all our attempts to find out relative truth, what we want, even more than the truth itself, is the exercise of the mind. That exercise is, indeed, our life.

The monistic theory has this merit: It is the most rational of all the religious theories that we can conceive of. Every other theory, every conception of God which is partial and petty and personal, is not rational. And yet monism is so grand that it embraces all these partial conceptions of God as being necessary for many. Some people say that though this personal explanation is irrational, it is consoling. They want a consoling religion, and we understand that it is necessary for them. The clear light of truth very few in this life can bear, much less live up to. It is necessary, therefore, that this comfortable religion should exist; it helps many souls to find a better one. Small minds, whose circumference is very limited and who require little things to build them up, never venture to soar high in thought. Their conceptions, even if only of little gods and symbols, are very good and helpful to them.

But you have to understand the Impersonal, for it is in and through That alone that these others can be explained. Take, for instance, the idea of the Personal God. A man who understands and believes in the Impersonal—John Stuart Mill, for example—may say that a Personal God is impossible and cannot be proved. I agree with him that a Personal God cannot be demonstrated. But He is the highest reading of the Impersonal that can be reached by the human intellect; and what else is the universe but various readings of the Absolute? It is like a book before us, and each one has brought his intellect to read It, and each one has to read It for himself. There is something which is common to the intellects of all men; therefore certain things appear to be the same to all. That you and I see a chair proves there is something common to both our minds. If a being comes with another sense, he will not see the chair at all. But all beings similarly constituted will see the same things. Thus this universe itself is the Absolute, the Unchangeable, the noumenon; and the reading thereof constitutes the phenomenon. For you will find that all phenomena are finite; every phenomenon that we can see, feel, or think of is finite, limited by our knowledge. And the Personal God, as we conceive of Him, is in fact a phenomenon. The very idea of causation exists only in the phenomenal world, and God as the cause of this universe must naturally be thought of as limited;

and yet He is the same Impersonal God. This phenomenal universe, as we have seen, is the same Impersonal Being read by our intellect. Whatever is real in the universe is that Impersonal Being, and the forms and names are given by our intellects. Whatever is real in this table is that Being, and the table form and all else are given by our intellects.

Now, motion, for instance, which is a necessary adjunct of the phenomenal, cannot be predicated of the universal. Every particle, every atom in the universe, is in a constant state of change and motion, but the universe as a whole is unchangeable, because motion or change is a relative thing; we can think of something in motion only in comparison with something which is not moving. There must be two things in order to understand motion. The whole mass of the universe, taken as a unit, cannot move. In regard to what will it move? It cannot be said to change. In regard to what will it change? So the whole is the Absolute; but within It every particle is in a constant state of flux and change. It is unchangeable and changeable at the same time, impersonal and personal in one. This is our conception of the universe, of motion, and of God.

Thus we see that the Impersonal, instead of doing away with the Personal—the Absolute, instead of pulling down the relative—only explains it to the full satisfaction of our reason and heart. The Personal God and all that exists in the universe are the same Impersonal Being seen through our minds. When we shall be rid of our minds, our little personalities, we shall become one with It. This is what is meant by "Thou art That." We must know our true nature, the Absolute.

The finite, manifested man forgets his source and thinks himself to be an entirely separate entity. We, as personalized, differentiated beings, forget our reality, and the teaching of monism is not that we must give up these differentiations, but that we must learn to understand what they are. We are in reality that Infinite Being, and our personalities represent so many channels through which this Infinite Reality is manifesting Itself; and the whole mass of changes which we call evolution is brought about by the soul's trying to manifest more and more of its infinite energy. We cannot stop anywhere on this side of the Infinite; our power and blessedness and wisdom cannot but grow into the Infinite. Infinite power and existence and blessedness are ours, and we do not have to acquire them; they are our own and we have only to manifest them.

This is the central idea of monism, and one that is very hard to understand. From my childhood everyone around me taught me weakness; I have been told ever since I was born that I was a weak thing. It is very difficult for me now to realize my own strength; but by analysis and reasoning I gain knowledge of my own strength, I realize it. All the knowledge that we have in this world—where does it come from? It is within us. What knowledge is outside? None. Knowledge is not in matter; it is in man all the time. Nobody ever creates knowledge; man brings it from within. It is lying there. The whole of the big banyan tree which covers acres of ground is in a little seed which is perhaps no bigger than one-eighth of a mustard seed; all that mass of energy is confined there. The gigantic intellect, we know, lies coiled up in the protoplasmic cell; and why should not infinite energy? We know that it is so. It may seem like a paradox, but it is true. Each one of us comes out of a protoplasmic cell, and all the powers we possess are coiled up there. You cannot say they come from food; for if you heap up food mountain high, what power comes out of it? The energy is in the cell, potentially no doubt, but still there.

So infinite power is in the soul of man, whether he knows it or not. Its manifestation is only a question of being conscious of it. Slowly this infinite giant is, as it were, waking up, becoming conscious of his power, and arousing himself; and with his growing consciousness, more and more of his bonds are breaking, his chains are bursting asunder, and the day is sure to come when, with the full consciousness of his infinite power and wisdom, the giant will rise to his feet and stand erect. Let us all help to hasten that glorious consummation.

PRACTICAL VEDĀNTA

Part IV

(Delivered in London, November 18, 1896)

So FAR WE HAVE BEEN DEALING mostly with the universal. This morning I shall try to place before you the Vedāntic ideas of the relation of the particular to the universal. As we have seen, in the earlier, dualistic form of the Vedic doctrines, there was a clearly defined particular and limited soul for every being. There have been a great many theories about this particular soul in each individual, but the main discussion was between the ancient Vedāntists and the ancient Buddhists, the former believing in the individual soul as complete in itself, the latter denying *in toto* the existence of such an individual soul. As I told you the other day, it is pretty much the same discussion you have in Europe as to substance and qualities, one party holding that behind the qualities there is something known as substance, in which the qualities inhere, and the other denying the existence of such a substance, as being unnecessary, for the qualities may exist by themselves.

The most ancient theory of the soul, of course, is based upon the argument of self-identity—"I am I": that the "I" of yesterday is the "I" of today, and the "I" of today will be the "I" of tomorrow; that in spite of all the changes that are happening to the body, I yet believe that I am the same "I." This seems to have been the central argument with those who believed in a limited, and yet perfectly complete, individual soul.

On the other hand, the ancient Buddhists denied the necessity of such an assumption. They brought forward the argument that all that we know and all that we possibly can know are simply these changes. The positing of an unchangeable and unchanging substance is simply superfluous, and even if there were any such unchangeable thing, we could never understand it, nor should we ever be able to cognize it in any sense of the word.

The same discussion you will find going on at the present time in Europe between the religionists and the idealists on the one side, and the modern positivists and agnostics on the other—one set believing that there is something which does not change (of whom the latest representative is your Herbert Spencer), and that we catch a glimpse of something which is unchangeable; and the other being represented by the modern Comtists and modern agnostics. Those of you who were interested a few years ago in the discussions between Herbert Spencer and Frederick Harrison might have noticed that it was the same old difficulty, the one party standing for a substance behind the changeful,

367

and the other party denying the necessity for such an assumption. One party says we cannot conceive of changes without conceiving of something which does not change. The other party brings out the argument that this is superfluous; we can only conceive of something which changes, and as to the unchanging, we can neither know, feel, nor sense it.

In India this great question did not find its solution in very ancient times, because, as we have seen, the assumption of a substance behind the qualities which is not the qualities can never be substantiated. Nay, even the argument from self-identity, from memory—that I am the "I" of yesterday because I remember it, and therefore I have been a continuous something—cannot be substantiated. The other quibble that is generally put forward is a mere delusion of words. For instance, a man may take a long series of such sentences as "I do," "I go," "I dream," "I sleep," "I move," and here you will find it claimed that the doing, going, dreaming, and so forth, have been changing, but what remained constant was that "I." Therefore they conclude that the "I" is something constant, and an individual in itself, but all these changes belong to the body. This, though apparently very convincing and clear, is based upon mere play on words. The "I" and the doing, going, and dreaming may be separate in black and white, but no one can separate them in his mind. When I eat, I think of myself as eating—I am identified with eating. When I run, I and the running are not two separate things. Thus the argument from personal identity does not seem to be very strong.

The other argument, the argument from memory, is also weak. If the identity of my being is represented by my memory, then it will have to be admitted that I did not exist at those times which I have forgotten. And we know that people under certain conditions forget their whole past. In many cases of lunacy a man thinks of himself as made of glass or as being an animal. If the existence of that man depended on his memory, then he should have been made of glass—which not being so, we cannot make the identity of the self depend on such a flimsy thing as memory. Thus we see that the soul as a limited, yet complete and continuing identity cannot be established as separate from qualities. We cannot establish a narrowed-down, limited existence to which is attached a bundle of qualities.

On the other hand, the argument of the ancient Buddhists seems to be stronger—that we do not know, and cannot know, anything that is beyond this bundle of qualities. According to them the soul consists of certain qualities called sensations and feelings. An aggregate of these is what is called the soul, and this aggregate is continually changing.

The Advaitist theory of the soul reconciles both these positions. The position of the Advaitist is that it is true that we cannot think of the substance as separate from the qualities; we cannot think of change and not-change at the same time. It would be impossible. But the very thing which is called the substance is also the qualities; substance and qualities are not two things. It is the unchangeable that is appearing as the changeable. The unchangeable substance of the universe is not something separate from it. The noumenon is not something different from the phenomenon, but it is the very noumenon which has become the phenomenon. There is a Soul, which is unchanging, and what we call feelings and perceptions, nay, even the body, are that very Soul seen from another point of view. We have got into the habit of thinking that we have bodies and souls, and so forth, but properly speaking, there is only one. When I think of myself as the body, I am only a body; it is meaningless to say I am something else. And when I think of myself as the Soul, the body vanishes; the perception of the body does not remain. None can have the perception of the Soul unless his perception of the body has vanished; none can have the perception of the substance unless his perception of the qualities has vanished.

The ancient illustration of Advaita, of a rope being taken for a snake, may elucidate the point a little more. When a man mistakes the rope for a snake, the rope has vanished, and when he takes it for a rope, the snake has vanished and only the rope remains. The ideas of dual or treble existence come from reasoning on insufficient data, and we read of them in books or hear about them until we come under the delusion that we really have a dual perception of the Soul and the body; but such a perception never really exists. The perception is either of the body or of the Soul. It requires no arguments to prove it; you can verify it in your own minds.

Try to think of yourself as the Soul, as something disembodied. You will find it to be almost impossible, and those few who are able to do so will find that at the time when they realize themselves as the Soul they have no idea of the body. You have heard of, or perhaps have seen, persons who on particular occasions have been in peculiar states of mind brought about by deep meditation, self-hypnotism, hysteria, or drugs. From their experience you may gather that when they were perceiving something internally, the external had vanished for them. This shows that whatever exists is one. That unity is appearing in these various forms, and all these various forms give rise to the relation of cause and effect. The relation of cause and effect is one of evolution—the one becomes the other, and so on. Sometimes the cause vanishes, as it were, and in its place leaves the effect. If the Soul is the cause of the body, the Soul, as it were, vanishes for the time being and the body remains, and when the body vanishes, the Soul remains. This theory meets the arguments of the Buddhists that were levelled against the assumption of the dualism of body and Soul, by denying the duality and showing that the substance and the qualities are one and the same thing appearing in various forms.

We have also seen that this idea of the unchangeable can be established only as regards the whole, but never as regards the part. The very idea of parts comes from the idea of change or motion. Everything that is limited we can understand and know, because it is changeable; and the whole must be unchangeable, because there is no other thing besides it in relation to which change would be possible. Change is always in regard to something which does not change, or which changes relatively less. According to Advaita, therefore, the idea of the Soul as universal, unchangeable, and immortal can be demonstrated. The difficulty would be as regards the particular. What shall we do with the old dualistic theories, which have such a hold upon us and which we all have to pass through—these beliefs in limited, little, individual souls?

We have seen that we are immortal as the whole; but the difficulty is that we desire so much to be immortal as *parts* of the whole. We have seen that we are the Infinite, and that That is our real individuality; but we want so much to make these little souls individual. What becomes of them when we find in our everyday experience that these little souls are individuals with only the reservation that they are continuously growing individuals? They are the same, yet not the same. The "I" of yesterday is the "I" of today, and yet not so; it is changed somewhat.

Now, by getting rid of the dualistic conception that in the midst of all these changes there is something that does not change, and taking the most modern of conceptions, that of evolution, we find that the "I" is a continuously changing, expanding entity. If it be true that man is the evolution of a mollusc, the mollusc individual is the same as the man, only it has become expanded a great deal. From mollusc to man it has been a continuous expansion towards infinity. Therefore the limited soul can be styled an individual who is continuously expanding towards the Infinite Individual. Perfect individuality will be reached only when it has reached the Infinite, but on this side of the Infinite it is a continuously changing, growing personality.

One of the remarkable features of the Advaita system of Vedānta is that it harmonized the preceding systems. Our ancient philosophers knew what you call the theory of evolution—that growth is gradual, step by step; and the recognition of this led them to harmonize all the preceding systems. Thus not one of these preceding steps was rejected. The fault of the Buddhist faith was that it had neither the faculty nor the perception of this continual, expansive growth, and for this reason it never even made an attempt to harmonize itself with the pre-existing steps towards the ideal. They were rejected as useless and harmful.

This tendency in religion is itself most harmful. A man gets a new and better idea and then he looks back on those he has given up, and forthwith decides that they were mischievous and unnecessary. He never thinks that, however crude they may appear from his present point of view, they were very useful to him, that they were necessary if he was to reach his present state, and that every one of us has to grow in a similar fashion, living first on crude ideas, deriving benefit from them, and then arriving at a higher standard. With the oldest theories, therefore, Advaita is friendly. Dualism and all the systems that preceded it are accepted by Advaita, not in a patronizing way, but with the conviction that they are true, being manifestations of the same Truth, and that they all lead to the same conclusion that Advaita has reached.

With blessings, and not with curses, should be preserved all these various steps through which humanity had to pass. Therefore all these dualistic systems have never been rejected or thrown out, but have been kept intact in Vedānta, and the dualistic conception of an individual soul, limited, yet complete in itself, finds its place in Vedānta. According to dualism man dies and goes to other worlds, and so forth, and these ideas are kept in Vedānta in their entirety. For with the recognition of growth, in the Advaita system, these theories are given their proper place by admitting that they represent only a partial view of Truth.

From the dualistic standpoint this universe can only be looked upon as a creation of matter or force, can only be looked upon as the play of a certain will; and that will, again, can only be looked upon as separate from the universe. Thus, from such a standpoint, a man has to see himself as composed of a dual nature—body and soul; and this soul, though limited, is individually complete in itself. Such a man's ideas of immortality and of the future life will necessarily accord with his idea of the soul. These phases have been kept in Vedānta, and it is therefore necessary for me to present to you a few of the popular ideas of dualism.

According to this theory we have a body, of course, and behind the body there is what is called a fine body. This fine body is also made of matter, only very fine. It is the receptacle of all our karma, of all our actions and impressions, which are ready to spring up into visible forms. Every thought that we think, every deed that we do, after a certain time becomes fine, goes into seed form, so to speak, and lives in the fine body in a potential form; and after a time it emerges again and bears its results. These results condition the life of man. Thus he moulds his own life. Man is not bound by any other laws except those which he makes for himself. Our thoughts, our words, and our deeds are the threads of the net which we throw round ourselves, for good or for evil. Once we set in motion a certain power, we have to take the full consequences of it. This is the law of karma.

Behind the subtle body lives the jiva, or individual soul of man. There are various discussions about the form and the size of this individual soul. According to some it is very small, like an atom; according to others it is not so small as that; according to still others it is very big, and so on. This jiva is a part of the universal substance, and it is also eternal; from time immemorial it has existed, and for time without end it will exist. It is passing through all these forms in order to manifest its real nature, which is purity. Every action that retards this manifestation is called an evil action; so also with thoughts. And every action and every thought that helps the jiva to expand, to manifest its real nature, is good. One theory that is held in common in India by the crudest dualists as well as by the most advanced non-dualists is that all the possibilities and powers of the soul are within it and do not come from any external source. They are in the soul in potential form, and our task is simply to manifest those potentialities.

The dualists also have the theory of reincarnation, which says that after the dissolution of this body, the jiva will have another, and after that has been dissolved, it will again have another, and so on, either here or in some other world. But this world is given the preference, since it is considered the best of all worlds for our purpose. Other worlds are conceived of as worlds where there is very little misery; but for that very reason, they argue, there is less chance of thinking of higher things there. Living in this world, which contains some happiness and a good deal of misery, the jiva some time or other gets awakened, as it were, and thinks of freeing itself. But just as very rich persons in this world have the least chance of thinking of higher things, so the jiva in heaven has little chance of progress; for its condition is the same as that of a rich man, only intensified. It has a very fine body, which knows no disease and is under no necessity of eating or drinking, and all its desires are fulfilled. The jiva lives there, having enjoyment after enjoyment, and so forgets all about its real nature.

But there are some souls in these higher worlds which, in spite of all the enjoyments, can evolve still further Some dualists conceive of the goal as the highest heaven, where souls will live with God for ever. They will have beautiful bodies and will know neither disease nor death nor any other evil, and all their desires will be fulfilled. From time to time some of them will come back to this earth and take another body to teach human beings the way to God; and the great teachers of the world have been such. They were already free and were living with God in the highest sphere; but their love and sympathy for suffering humanity were so great that they incarnated themselves again to teach mankind the way to heaven.

Of course, we know that Advaita holds that this cannot be the goal or the ideal. Bodilessness must be the ideal. The ideal cannot be a finite existence. Anything short of the Infinite cannot be the ideal, and there cannot be an infinite body. That would be impossible, for the body comes from limitation. There cannot be infinite thought, because thought comes from limitation. We have to go beyond the body and beyond thought too, says Advaita. And we have also seen that, according to Advaita, this freedom is not to be attained; it is already ours. We only forget it and deny it. Perfection is not to be attained; it is already within us. Immortality and bliss are not to be acquired; we possess them already. They have been ours all the time. If you dare to declare that you are free, free you are this moment. If you say you are bound, bound you will remain. This is what Advaita boldly declares. I have told you the ideas of the dualists and other schools of philosophers. You can take whichever you like.

The highest ideal of Vedānta is very difficult to understand, and people are always quarrelling about it; and the greatest difficulty is that when they get hold of certain ideas they deny and fight other ideas. Take up what suits you and let others take up what they need. If you are desirous of clinging to this little individuality, to this limited manhood, remain in it, fulfil all these desires, and be content and pleased with them. If your experience of human life has been very good and nice, retain it as long as you like. And you can do so, for you are the makers of your own fortunes; none can compel you to give up your human life. You will be men as long as you like; none can prevent you. If you want to be angels, you will be angels. That is the law. But there may be others who do not even want to be angels. What right have you to think that theirs is a horrible notion? You may be frightened to lose a hundred pounds; but there may be others who would not even wink if they lost all the money they had in the world. There have been such men and there still are. Why do you dare to judge them according to your standards? You may cling to your limitations, and these little worldly ideas may be your highest ideal. You are welcome to them. It will be to you as you wish. But there are others who have seen the truth and cannot rest in these limitations, who have finished with these things and want to get beyond. The world with all its enjoyments is a mere mud-puddle for them. Why do you want to bind them down to your ideas? You must get rid of this tendency once for all. Accord a place to everyone.

I once read a story about some ships that were caught in a cyclone in the South Sea Islands, and there was a picture of them in the *Illustrated London News*. All of them were wrecked except one English vessel, which weathered the storm. The picture showed the men who were going to be drowned, standing on the decks and cheering the people who were sailing through the storm.[1] Be brave and generous like that. Do not drag others down to where you are.

Another foolish notion is that if we lose our little individuality there will be no morality, no hope for humanity. As if everybody had been dying for humanity all the time! God bless you! If in every country there were two hundred men and women really wanting to do good to humanity, the millennium would come in five days. We know how we are dying for humanity. This is all tall talk, and nothing else. The history of the world shows that those who never thought of their little individuality were the greatest benefactors of the human race, and that the more men and women think of themselves, the less they are able to do for others. One is unselfishness, and the other selfishness. Clinging to little enjoyments and desiring the continuation and repetition of this state of things are utter selfishness. They arise not from any desire for truth; their genesis is not in kindness for other beings, but in the utter selfishness of the human heart, in the idea, "I will have everything and do not care for anyone else." This is as it appears to me.

I should like to see more moral men in the world like some of those grand old prophets and sages of ancient times, who would have given up a hundred lives if by so doing they could benefit one little animal. Talk of morality and doing good to others! Silly talk of the present time! I should like to see moral men like Gautama Buddha, who did not believe in a Personal God or a personal soul, never asked about them, and was a perfect agnostic, and yet was ready to lay down his life for anyone, and worked all his life for the good of all, and thought only of the good of all. Well has it been said by his biographer, in describing his birth, that he was born for the good of the many, as a blessing to the many. He did not go to the forest to meditate for his own salvation; he felt that the world was burning and that he must find a way out. "Why is there so much misery in the world?"—was the one question that dominated his whole life. Do you think we are as moral as Buddha?

The more selfish a man, the more immoral he is. And so also with races. That race which has been the most self-centred has also been the most cruel and the most wicked in the whole world. There has not been a religion which has clung to dualism more intensely than that founded by the Prophet of Arabia, and there has not been a religion which has shed more blood and been more cruel to others. In the Koran there is the doctrine that a man who does not believe its teachings should be killed—it is merciful to kill him! And the surest way to get to heaven, where there are beautiful houris and all sorts of sense enjoyments, is to kill these unbelievers. Think of the bloodshed there has been in consequence of such beliefs!

In the religion of Christ there was little of crudeness; there is very little difference between the pure religion of Christ and that of Vedānta. You find there the idea of Oneness. But Christ also preached dualistic ideas to the people in order to give them something tangible to take hold of, to lead them up to the highest ideal. The same Prophet who preached, "Our Father which art in

---

[1] H.M.S. *Calliope* and several American men-of-war at Samoa, in the Pacific Ocean.

heaven," also preached, "I and my Father are one," and the same Prophet knew that through the "Father in heaven" lies the way to "I and my Father are one." There was only blessing and love in the religion of Christ. But as soon as crudeness crept in, it was degraded into something not much better than the religion of the Prophet of Arabia. It was crudeness indeed, this fight for the little self, this clinging to the "I," this desire not only for its preservation in this life, but also for its continuance even after death. This they declare to be unselfishness; this, the foundation of morality! Lord help us, if this be the foundation of morality! And strangely enough, men and women who ought to know better think that all morality will be destroyed if these little selves go, and stand aghast at the idea that morality can be based only on their destruction.

The watchword of all well-being, of all moral good, is "Not I but thou." Who cares whether there is a heaven or a hell, who cares if there is a soul or not, who cares if there is an Unchangeable or not? Here is the world, and it is full of misery. Go out into it as Buddha did and struggle to lessen its misery or die in the attempt. Forget yourselves—this is the first lesson to be learnt, whether you are a theist or an atheist, whether you are an agnostic or a Vedāntist, a Christian or a Mohammedan. The one lesson taught by all is the destruction of the little self and the building up of the Real Self.

Two forces have been working side by side in parallel lines. The one says "I," the other says "not I." Their manifestation is not only in man but in animals, not only in animals but in the smallest worms. The tigress that plunges her fangs into the warm blood of a human being would give up her own life to protect her cubs. The most depraved man, who thinks nothing of taking the lives of his brother men, will perhaps sacrifice himself without any hesitation to save his starving wife and children. Thus throughout creation these two forces are working side by side. Where you find the one, you find the other too. The one is selfishness; the other is unselfishness. The one is acquisition; the other is renunciation. The one takes; the other gives. From the lowest to the highest, the whole universe is the playground of these two forces. It does not require any demonstration; it is obvious to all.

What right has any section of the community to say that the working and the evolution of the universe are based upon one of these two factors alone—upon competition and struggle? What right has it to say that the whole working of the universe is based upon passion and fighting, upon competition and struggle? That these exist we do not deny; but what right has anyone to deny the working of the other force? Can any man deny that love—this "not I," this renunciation—is the only positive power in the universe? The other is only the misguided employment of the power of love. The wrong use of love brings competition; the real genesis of competition is in love. The real genesis of evil is in unselfishness. The creator of evil is good, and the end is also good. It is only misdirection of the power of good. A man who murders another is perhaps moved to do so by love of his own child. His love has become limited to that one little baby, to the exclusion of the millions of other human beings in the universe. Yet, limited or unlimited, it is the same love.

Thus the motive power of the whole universe, in whatever way it manifests itself, is that one wonderful thing, unselfishness, renunciation, love—the real, the only living force in existence. Therefore the Vedāntist insists upon oneness. We insist upon this explanation because we cannot admit two causes of the universe. If we simply hold that by limitation the same beautiful, wonderful love appears to be evil or vile, we find the whole universe explained by the one force of love. If not, two causes of the universe have to be taken for granted, one good and the other evil, one love and the other hatred. Which is more logical? Certainly the one-force theory.

Let us now pass on to things which do not possibly belong to dualism. I cannot stay longer with the dualists, I am afraid. My idea is to show that the highest ideal of morality and unselfishness goes hand in hand with the highest metaphysical conception, and that you need not lower your conception to get ethics and morality, but on the contrary, to reach a real basis of morality and ethics you must have the highest philosophical and scientific conceptions. Human knowledge is not antagonistic to human well-being. Indeed, it is knowledge alone that will save us in every department of life. Knowledge is worship. The more we know, the better for us.

Vedānta says that the cause of all that is apparently evil is the limitation of the Unlimited. The love which gets limited into little channels and seems to be evil eventually comes out at the other end and manifests itself as God. Vedānta also says that the cause of all this apparent evil is in ourselves. Do not blame any supernatural being; neither be hopeless and despondent, nor think we are in a place from which we can never escape unless someone comes and lends us a helping hand. That cannot be, says Vedānta. We are like silk-worms. We make the thread out of our own substance, and spin the cocoon, and in the course of time are imprisoned inside. But this cannot be for ever. We shall develop spiritual realization in that cocoon and, like the butterfly, come out free. We have woven this network of karma around ourselves, and in our ignorance we feel as if we are bound, and weep and wail for help. But help does not come from without; it comes from within ourselves.

Cry to all the gods in the universe. I cried for years, and in the end I received help. But the help came from within myself; and I had to undo what I had done by mistake. That is the only way. I had to cut the net which I had thrown round myself; and the power to do this is within. Of this I am certain: that not one aspiration in my life, well guided or ill guided, has been in vain, but I am the resultant of all my past, both good and evil. I have committed many mistakes in my life, but mark you, I am sure that without every one of those mistakes, I should not be what I am today; and so I am quite satisfied to have made them. I do not mean that you are to go home and wilfully commit mistakes; do not misunderstand me in that way. But do not mope because of the mistakes you have committed, but know that in the end all will come out straight. It cannot be otherwise, because goodness is our nature, purity is our nature, and that nature can never be destroyed. Our essential nature always remains the same.

What we must understand is that what we call mistakes, or evil, we commit because we are weak, and we are weak because we are ignorant. I prefer to call them mistakes. The word *sin*, although originally a very good word, has a certain flavour about it that frightens me. Who makes us ignorant? We ourselves.

We put our hands over our eyes and weep because it is dark. Take the hands away and there is light; the light exists always for us, the self-effulgent nature of the human soul. Do you not hear what your modern scientific men say? What is the cause of evolution? Desire. The animal wants to do something, but does not find the environment favourable and therefore develops a new body. Who develops it? The animal itself—its will. You have developed from the lowest amoeba. Continue to exercise your will and it will take you higher still. The will is almighty. If it is almighty, you may say, why can I not do everything I like? But you are thinking only of your little self. Look back on yourselves from the state of the amoeba to the human being. Who made all that? Your own will. Can you deny, then, that will is almighty? That which has made you come up so high can make you go higher still. What you want is character, strengthening of the will.

If I teach you, therefore, that your nature is evil, that you should go home and sit in sackcloth and ashes and weep your lives out because you took certain false steps, it will not help you, but will weaken you all the more, and I shall be showing you the road to more evil than good. If this room has been full of darkness for thousands of years and you come in and begin to weep and wail, "Oh, the darkness!"—will the darkness vanish? Strike a match and light comes in a moment. What good will it do you to think all your lives, "Oh, I have done evil; I have made many mistakes"? It requires no ghost to tell us that. Bring in the light and the evil goes in a moment. Build up your character and manifest your real nature, the Effulgent, the Resplendent, the Ever Pure, and call it up in everyone that you see.

I wish that every one of us had come to such a state that even in the vilest of human beings we could see the Real Self within, and instead of condemning them, say: "Rise, Thou Effulgent One! Rise, Thou who art always pure! Rise, Thou Birthless and Deathless One! Rise, Almighty One! and manifest Thy true nature. These little manifestations do not befit Thee." This is the highest prayer that Advaita teaches. This is the only prayer—to remember our true nature, the God who is always within us, thinking of it always as infinite, almighty, ever good, ever beneficent, selfless, bereft of all limitations; and to remember that because that nature is selfless, it is strong and fearless; for only to the selfish comes fear. He who has nothing to desire for himself—whom does he fear and what can frighten him? What fear has death for him? What fear has evil for him? So if we are Advaitists, we must think from this moment that our old self is dead and gone. The old Mr., Mrs., and Miss So-and-so are gone. They were mere superstitions; and what remains is the Ever Pure, the Ever Strong, the Almighty, the All-knowing—That alone remains for us. And then all fear vanishes from us. Who can injure us, the Omnipresent? All weakness has vanished from us; and our only work is to arouse this knowledge in our fellow beings. We see that they too are the same Pure Self, only they do not know it. We must teach them; we must help them to rouse up their infinite nature. This is what I feel to be absolutely necessary all over the world.

These doctrines are old—older, possibly, than many mountains. All truth is eternal. Truth is nobody's property; no race, no individual, can lay exclusive claim to it. Truth is the nature of all souls. Who can lay special claim to it?

But it has to be made practical, to be made simple (for the highest truths are always simple), so that it may penetrate every pore of human society and become the property of the highest intellects and the commonest minds, of man, woman, and child at the same time. All these ratiocinations of logic, all these bundles of metaphysics, all these theologies and ceremonies, may have been good in their own time. But let us try to make things simpler and bring about the golden days when every man will be a worshipper, and the Reality in every man will be the object of worship.

THE WAY TO THE REALIZATION OF
THE UNIVERSAL RELIGION

(Delivered in the Universalist Church, Pasadena, California, January 28, 1900)

No SEARCH HAS BEEN DEARER to the human heart than that which brings to us light from God. No study has taken so much human energy, whether in times past or present, as the study of the soul, of God, and of human destiny. However deeply immersed we are in our daily occupations, in our ambitions, in our work, sometimes in the midst of the greatest of our struggles there comes a pause; the mind stops and wants to know something beyond this world. Sometimes it catches glimpses of a realm beyond the senses, and a struggle to get at it is the result. Thus it has been throughout the ages in all countries. Man has wanted to look beyond, wanted to expand himself; and all that we call progress, evolution, has always been measured by that one search, the search for human destiny, the search for God.

As our social struggles are represented, among different nations, by different social organizations, so man's spiritual struggles are represented by various religions. And as different social organizations are constantly quarrelling, are constantly at war with each other, so these spiritual organizations have been constantly at war with each other, constantly quarrelling. Men belonging to a particular social organization claim that the right to live belongs only to them, and so long as they can, they want to exercise that right at the cost of the weak. We know that just now there is a fierce struggle of that sort going on in South Africa.[1] Similarly each religious sect has claimed the exclusive right to live. And thus we find that though nothing has brought man more blessings than religion, yet at the same time there is nothing that has brought him more horror than religion. Nothing has made more for peace and love than religion; nothing has engendered fiercer hatred than religion. Nothing has made the brotherhood of man more tangible than religion; nothing has bred more bitter enmity between man and man than religion. Nothing has built more charitable institutions, more hospitals for men and even for animals, than religion; nothing has deluged the world with more blood than religion.

We know, at the same time, that there has always been an opposing undercurrent of thought; there have always been parties of men, philosophers, students of comparative religion, who have tried and are still trying to bring about harmony in the midst of all these jarring and discordant sects. As regards certain countries these attempts have succeeded, but as regards the whole world they have failed.

---

[1] A reference to the Boer War.

Then again, there are some religions, which have come down to us from the remotest antiquity, imbued with the idea that all sects should be allowed to live—that every sect has a meaning, a great idea, imbedded in it, and therefore all sects are necessary for the good of the world and ought to be helped. In modern times the same idea is prevalent, and attempts are made from time to time to reduce it to practice. But these attempts do not always come up to our expectations, up to the required efficiency. Nay, to our great disappointment, we sometimes find that we are quarrelling all the more.

Now, leaving aside dogmatic study and taking a common-sense view of the thing, we find at the start that there is a tremendous life-power in all the great religions of the world. Some may say that they are unaware of this; but ignorance is no excuse. If a man says, "I do not know what is going on in the external world, therefore the things that are said to be going on there do not exist," that plea is inexcusable. Now, those of you who are watching the movement of religious thought all over the world are perfectly aware that not one of the great religions of the world has died. Not only so; each one of them is progressing. The Christians are multiplying, the Mohammedans are multiplying, and the Hindus are gaining ground; the Jews also are increasing in numbers, and as a result of their activities all over the world, the fold of Judaism is constantly expanding.

Only one religion of the world—an ancient, great religion—is dwindling away, and that is the religion of Zoroastrianism, the religion of the ancient Persians. After the Mohammedan conquest of Persia, about a hundred thousand of these people came to India and took shelter there, and some remained in Persia. Those who were in Persia, under the constant persecution of the Mohammedans, dwindled till there are at most only ten thousand. In India there are about eighty thousand of them, but they do not increase. Of course, there is an initial difficulty: they do not convert others to their religion. And then, this handful of persons living in India, with the pernicious custom of cousin-marriage, does not multiply. With this single exception, all the great religions are living, spreading, and increasing.

We must remember that all the great religions of the world are very ancient—not one has been formed at the present time—and that every religion of the world had its origin in the region between the Ganges and the Euphrates. Not one great religion has arisen in Europe; not one in America—not one. Every religion is of Asiatic origin and belongs to that part of the world. If what the modern scientists say is true, that the survival of the fittest is the test, these religions prove by their still being alive that they are yet fit for some people. And there is a reason why they should live: they bring good to many. Look at the Mohammedans, how they are spreading in some places in southern Asia, and spreading like wildfire in Africa. The Buddhists are spreading over central Asia all the time. The Hindus, like the Jews, do not convert others; still, gradually other races are coming within Hinduism and adopting the manners and customs of the Hindus and falling into line with them. Christianity, you all know, is spreading—though I am not sure that the results are equal to the energy put forth. The Christians' attempt at propaganda has one tremendous defect, and that is the defect of all Western institutions: the machine consumes ninety per cent of the energy; there is too much machinery. Preaching has always been the business of the Asiatics. The Western people are grand in organization—social institutions, armies, governments, and so forth. But when it comes to preaching religion, they cannot come near the Asiatics, whose business it has been all the time—and they know it, and do not use too much machinery.

This, then, is a fact in the present history of the human race: that all these great religions exist and are spreading and multiplying. Now, there is a meaning, certainly, to this; and had it been the will of an all-wise and all-merciful Creator that one of these religions should alone exist and the rest die, it would have become a fact long, long ago. If it were a fact that only one of these religions was true and all the rest were false, by this time it would have covered the whole world. But this is not so; not one has gained all the ground. All religions sometimes advance, sometimes decline. Now, just think of this: in your own country there are more than sixty millions of people, and only twenty-one millions profess a religion of some sort. So it is not always progress. In every country, probably, if the statistics were taken, you would find that the religions sometimes progress and sometimes go back. Sects are multiplying all the time. If the claim of any one religion that it has all the truth, and that God has given it all that truth in a certain book, be true, why then are there so many sects? Not fifty years pass before there are twenty sects founded upon the same book. If God has put all the truth in certain books, He does not give us those books in order that we may quarrel over texts. That seems to be the fact. Why is this? Even if a book were given by God which contained all the truth about religion, it would not serve the purpose, because nobody could understand the book. Take the Bible, for instance, and all the sects that exist among the Christians. Each one puts its own interpretation upon the same text, and each says that it alone understands that text and all the rest are wrong. So with every religion. There are many sects among the Mohammedans and among the Buddhists, and hundreds among the Hindus.

Now, I place these facts before you in order to show you that any attempt to bring all humanity to one method of thinking in spiritual things has been a failure and always will be a failure. Every man who starts a theory, even at the present day, finds that if he goes twenty miles away from his followers they will make twenty sects. You see that happening all the time. You cannot make all conform to the same ideas; that is a fact, and I thank God that it is so. I am not against any sect. I am glad that sects exist, and I only wish they may go on multiplying more and more. Why? Simply because of this: If you and I and all who are present here were to think exactly the same thoughts, there would be no thoughts for us to think. We know that two or more forces must come into collision in order to produce motion. It is the clash of thought, the differentiation of thought, that awakens thought. Now, if we all thought alike, we should be like Egyptian mummies in a museum, looking vacantly at one another's faces—no more than that. Whirls and eddies occur only in a rushing, living stream. There are no whirlpools in stagnant, dead water.

When religions are dead, there will be no more sects; it will be the perfect peace and harmony of the grave. But so long as mankind thinks, there will be sects. Variation is the sign of life, and it must be there. I pray that sects may multiply so that at last there will be as many sects as human beings and each one will have his own method, his individual method of thought, in religion.

Such a situation, however, exists already. Each one of us is thinking in his own way. But this natural thinking has been obstructed all the time and is still being obstructed. If the sword is not used directly, other means are used. Just hear what one of the best preachers in New York says. He preaches that the Filipinos should be conquered because that is the only way to teach Christianity to them! They are already Catholics; but he wants to make them Presbyterians, and for this he is ready to lay all this terrible sin of bloodshed upon his race. How terrible! And this man is one of the greatest preachers of this country, one of the best informed men. Think of the state of the world when a man like that is not ashamed to stand up and utter such arrant nonsense; and think of the state of the world when an audience cheers him. Is this civilization? It is the old blood-thirstiness of the tiger, the cannibal, the savage, coming out once more under new names in new circumstances. What else can it be? If such is the state of things now, think of the horrors through which the world passed in olden times, when every sect was trying, by every means in its power, to tear to pieces the other sects. History shows that the tiger in us is only asleep; it is not dead. When opportunities come it jumps up and, as of old, uses its claws and fangs. And apart from the sword, apart from material weapons, there are weapons still more terrible: contempt, social hatred, and social ostracism.

Now, these afflictions that are hurled against persons who do not think exactly in the same way we do are the most terrible of all afflictions. And why should everybody think just as we do? I do not see any reason. If I am a rational man, I should be glad that they do not think just as I do. I do not want to live in a grave-like land. I want to be a man in a world of men. Thinking beings must differ; difference is the first sign of thought. If I am a thoughtful man, certainly I ought to like to live among thoughtful persons, where there are differences of opinion.

Then arises the question: How can all this variety be true? If one thing is true, its negation is false. How can contradictory opinions be true at the same time? This is the question which I intend to answer. But I shall first ask you: Are all the religions of the world really contradictory? I do not mean the external forms in which great thoughts are clad. I do not mean the different buildings, languages, rituals, books, and so forth, employed in various religions, but I mean the internal soul of every religion. Every religion has a soul behind it, and that soul may differ from the soul of another religion; but are they contradictory? Do they contradict or supplement each other?—that is the question.

I took up this question when I was quite a boy, and have been studying it all my life. Thinking that my conclusion may be of some help to you, I place it before you. I believe that they are not contradictory; they are supplementary. Each religion, as it were, takes up one part of the great, universal truth and spends its whole force in embodying and typifying that part of the great truth. It is therefore addition, not exclusion. That is the idea. System after system arises, each one embodying a great ideal; ideals must be added to ideals. And this is how humanity marches on.

Man never progresses from error to truth, but from truth to truth—from lesser truth to higher truth, but never from error to truth. The child may develop more than the father; but was the father inane? The child is the father plus something else. If your present stage of knowledge is much higher than the stage you were in when you were a child, would you look down upon that earlier stage now? Will you look back and call it inanity? Your present stage is the knowledge of childhood plus something more.

Then again, we know that there may be almost contradictory points of view of a thing, but they all point to the same thing. Suppose a man is journeying towards the sun and as he advances he takes a photograph of the sun at every stage. When he comes back, he has many photographs of the sun, which he places before us. We see that no two are alike; and yet who will deny that all these are photographs of the same sun, from different standpoints? Take four photographs of this church from different corners. How different they would look! And yet they would all represent this church. In the same way, we are all looking at truth from different standpoints, which vary according to our birth, education, surroundings, and so on. We are viewing truth, getting as much of it as these circumstances will permit, colouring it with our own feelings, understanding it with our own intellects, and grasping it with our own minds. We can know only as much of truth as is related to us, as much of it as we are able to receive. This makes the difference between man and man and sometimes even occasions contradictory ideas. Yet we all belong to the same great, universal truth.

My idea, therefore, is that all these religions are different forces in the economy of God, working for the good of mankind, and that not one can become dead, not one can be killed. Just as you cannot kill any force in nature, so you cannot kill any one of these spiritual forces. You have seen that each religion is living. From time to time it may retrogress or go forward. At one time it may be shorn of a good many of its trappings; at another time it may be covered with all sorts of trappings. But all the same, the soul is ever there; it can never be lost. The ideal which every religion represents is never lost, and so every religion is intelligently on the march.

And that universal religion about which philosophers and others have dreamt in every country already exists. It is here. As the universal brotherhood of man already exists, so also does the universal religion. Which of you that have travelled far and wide have not found brothers and sisters in every nation? I have found them all over the world. Brotherhood already exists; only there are numbers of persons who fail to see this and upset it by crying for new brotherhoods. The universal religion, too, already exists. If the priests and other people who have taken upon themselves the task of preaching different religions simply cease preaching for a few moments, we shall see it is there. They are disturbing it all the time, because it is to their interest.

You see that the priests in every country are very conservative. Why is this so? There are very few priests who lead the people; most of them are led by the people and are their slaves and servants. If you say it is dry, they say it is dry; if you say it is black, they say it is black. If the people advance, the priests must advance. They cannot lag behind. So before blaming the priests—it is the fashion to blame the priests—you ought to blame yourselves. You get only what you deserve. What would be the fate of a priest who wanted to give you new and advanced ideas and lead you forward? His children would probably starve and he would be clad in rags. He is governed by the same worldly laws that you are governed by. If you move on, he says, "Let us march."

Of course, there are exceptional souls, not cowed by public opinion. They see the truth, and truth alone they value. Truth has got hold of them, has got possession of them, as it were, and they cannot but march ahead. They never look backward. And they do not pay heed to people. God alone exists for them; He is the light before them and they are following that light.

I met a Mormon gentleman in this country who tried to convert me to his faith. I said: "I have great respect for your opinions, but in certain points we do not agree. I belong to a monastic order, and you believe in marrying many wives. But why don't you go to India to preach?" He was simply astonished. He said, "Why, you don't believe in any marriage at all, and we believe in polygamy, and yet you ask me to go to your country!" I said: "Yes. My countrymen will hear any religious thought, wherever it may come from. I wish you would go to India. First, because I am a great believer in sects. Secondly, there are many men in India who are not at all satisfied with any of the existing sects, and on account of this dissatisfaction they will not have anything to do with religion; and possibly you might get some of them."

The greater the number of sects, the more chance of people's becoming religious. In a hotel, where there are all sorts of food, everyone has a chance to have his appetite satisfied. So I want sects to multiply in every country, that more people may have a chance to be spiritual.

Do not think that people do not like religion. I do not believe that. The preachers cannot give them what they need. The same man who may have been branded as an atheist, as a materialist, or what not, may meet a man who gives him the truth needed by him, and he may turn out to be the most spiritual man in the community. We can eat only in our own way. For instance, we Hindus eat with our fingers. Our fingers are suppler than yours; you cannot use your fingers the same way. Not only should the food be supplied; it should also be taken in your own particular way. Not only must you have the spiritual ideas; they must also come to you according to your own method. They must speak your own language, the language of your soul, and then alone will they satisfy you. When the man comes who speaks my language and gives me the truth in my language, I at once understand it and receive it for ever. This is a great fact.

Now, from this we see that there are various grades and types of human minds—and what a task the religions take upon themselves! A man brings forth two or three doctrines and claims that his religion ought to satisfy all humanity. He goes out into the world, God's menagerie, with a little cage in hand, and says: "Man and the elephant and everybody have to fit into this. Even if we have to cut the elephant into pieces, he must go in." Again, there may be a sect with a few good ideas. It says, "All men must come in!" "But there is no room for them." "Never mind! Cut them to pieces; get them in anyhow; if they don't get in, why, they will be damned." No preacher, no sect, have I ever met that paused and asked, "Why is it that people do not listen to us?" Instead they curse them and say, "The people are wicked." They never ask: "How is it that people do not listen to my words? Why can I not make them see the truth? Why can I not speak in their language? Why can I not open their eyes?" Surely they ought to know better, and when they find that people do not listen to them, if they curse anybody it should be themselves. But it is always the people's fault! They never try to make their sect large enough to embrace everyone.

Therefore we at once see why there has been so much narrow-mindedness, the part always claiming to be the whole, the little, finite unit always laying claim to the infinite. Think of little sects, born only a few hundred years ago, out of fallible human brains, making this arrogant claim of knowing the whole of God's infinite truth! Think of the arrogance of it! If it shows anything, it shows how vain human beings are. And it is no wonder that such claims have always failed, and by the mercy of the Lord are always destined to fail. In this line the Mohammedans were the best off. Every step forward was made with the sword—the Koran in the one hand and the sword in the other: "Take the Koran, or you must die. There is no other alternative!" You know from history how phenomenal was their success; for six hundred years nothing could resist them. And then there came a time when they had to cry halt. So will it be with other religions if they follow the same methods.

We are such babies! We always forget human nature. When we begin life we think that our fate will be something extraordinary, and nothing can make us disbelieve that. But when we grow old we think differently. So with religions. In their early stages, when they spread a little, they get the idea that they can change the minds of the whole human race in a few years, and they go on killing and massacring to make converts by force. Then they fail and begin to understand better. These religions did not succeed in what they started out to do, which was a great blessing. Just think! If one of those fanatical sects had succeeded all over the world, where would man be today? The Lord be blessed that they did not succeed! Yet each one represents a great truth; each religion represents a particular excellence, something which is its soul.

There is an old story which comes to my mind: There were some ogresses who used to kill people and do all sorts of mischief; but they themselves could not be killed until someone should find out that their souls were in certain birds and so long as the birds were alive nothing could destroy the ogresses. So each one of us has, as it were, such a bird, where his soul is—has an ideal, a mission to perform in life. Every human being is an embodiment of such an ideal, such a mission. Whatever else you may lose, so long as that ideal is not lost and that mission is not hurt, nothing can kill you. Wealth may come and go, misfortunes may be piled mountain high, but if you have kept the ideal pure, nothing can kill you. You may have grown old, even a hundred years old, but if that mission is fresh and young in your heart, what can kill you? But when that ideal is lost and that mission is forgotten, nothing can save you. All the wealth, all the power of the world will not save you.

And what are nations but multiplied individuals? So each nation has a mission of its own to perform in this harmony of races, and so long as a nation keeps to that ideal, nothing can kill that nation. But if the nation gives up its mission and goes after something else, its life becomes short and ultimately it vanishes.

And so with religions. The fact that all these old religions are living today proves that they must have kept that mission intact. In spite of all their mistakes, in spite of all difficulties, in spite of all quarrels, in spite of all the incrustation of forms and rituals, the heart of every one of them is sound—it is a throbbing, beating, living heart. They have not lost, any of them, the great mission they came for. And it is splendid to study that mission. Take Mohammedanism, for instance. Christian people hate no religion in the world so much as Mohammedanism. They think it is the very worst form of religion that ever existed. But as soon as a man becomes a Mohammedan, the whole of Islām receives him as a brother with open arms, without making any distinction, which no other religion does. If one of your American Indians became a Mohammedan, the Sultan of Turkey would have no objection to dining with him. If he had brains, no position would be barred to him. In this country I have never yet seen a church where the white man and the Negro can kneel side by side to pray. Just think of that: Islām makes its followers all equal. So that, you see, is the peculiar excellence of Mohammedanism. In many places in the Koran you find very sensual ideals of life. Never mind. What Mohammedanism comes to preach to the world is this practical brotherhood of all belonging to their faith. That is the essential part of the Mohammedan religion; and all the other ideas, about heaven and life and so forth, are not real Mohammedanism. They are accretions.

With the Hindus you will find one great idea: spirituality. In no other religion, in no other sacred books in the world, will you find so much energy spent in defining the idea of God. They tried to describe God in such a way that no earthly touch might mar Him. The Spirit must be divine; and Spirit, as such, must not be identified with the physical world. The idea of unity, of the realization of God, the Omnipresent, is preached throughout. They think it is nonsense to say that God lives in heaven, and all that. That is a mere human, anthropomorphic idea. All the heaven that ever existed is now and here. One moment in infinite time is quite as good as any other moment. If you believe in a God, you can see Him even now. We Hindus think that religion begins when you have realized something. It is not believing in doctrines or giving intellectual assent or making declarations. If there is a God, have you seen Him? If you say no, then what right have you to believe in Him? If you are in doubt whether there is a God, why do you not struggle to see Him? Why do you not renounce the world and spend the whole of your life for this one object? Renunciation and spirituality are the two great ideals of India, and it is because India clings to these ideals that all her mistakes count for so little.

With the Christians, the central idea that has been preached by them is the same: "Watch and pray, for the kingdom of heaven is at hand"—which means: Purify your minds and be ready. You recollect that the Christians, even in the darkest days, even in the most superstitious Christian countries, have always tried to prepare themselves for the coming of the Lord by trying to help others, building hospitals, and so on. So long as the Christians keep to that ideal, their religion lives.

Now, an ideal presents itself to my mind. It may be only a dream. I do not know whether it will ever be realized in this world; but sometimes it is better to dream a dream than to die on hard facts. Great truths, even in a dream, are good—better than bad facts. So let us dream a dream.

You know that there are various grades of mind. You may be a matter-of-fact, common-sense rationalist. You do not care for forms and ceremonies; you want intellectual, hard, ringing facts, and they alone will satisfy you. Then there are the Puritans and the Mohammedans, who will not allow a picture or a statue in their place of worship. Very well. But there is another man who is more artistic. He wants a great deal of art—beauty of lines and curves, colours, flowers, forms; he wants candles, lights, and all the insignia and paraphernalia of ritual, that he may see God. His mind grasps God in those forms, as yours grasps Him through the intellect. Then there is the devotional man, whose soul is crying for God; he has no other idea but to worship God and praise Him. Then again, there is the philosopher, standing outside all these things, mocking at them. He thinks: "What nonsense they are! What ideas about God!"

They may laugh at each other, but each one has a place in this world. All these various minds, all these various types, are necessary. If there is ever going to be an ideal religion, it must be broad and large enough to supply food for all these minds. It must supply the strength of philosophy to the philosopher, the devotee's heart to the worshipper; to the ritualist it must give all that the most marvellous symbolism can convey; to the poet it must give as much of heart as he can absorb, and other things besides. To make such a broad religion, we shall have to go back to the very source and take them all in.

Our watchword, then, will be acceptance and not exclusion. Not only toleration; for so-called toleration is often blasphemy and I do not believe in it. I believe in acceptance. Why should I tolerate? Toleration means that I think that you are wrong and I am just allowing you to live. Is it not blasphemy to think that you and I are allowing others to live? I accept all the religions that were in the past and worship with them all; I worship God with every one of them, in whatever form they worship Him. I shall go to the mosque of the Mohammedan; I shall enter the Christian church and kneel before the Crucifix; I shall enter the Buddhist temple, where I shall take refuge in Buddha and his Law. I shall go into the forest and sit down in meditation with the Hindu, who is trying to see the Light which enlightens the hearts of everyone.

Not only shall I do all this, but I shall keep my heart open for all the religions that may come in the future. Is God's Book finished? Or is revelation still going on? It is a marvellous Book—these spiritual revelations of the world. The Bible, the Vedas, the Koran, and all other sacred books are but so many pages, and an infinite number of pages remain yet to be unfolded. I shall leave my heart open for all of them. We stand in the present, but open ourselves to the infinite future. We take in all that has been in the past, enjoy the light of the present, and open every window of the heart for all that will come in the future. Salutation to all the prophets of the past, to all the great ones of the present, and to all that are to come in the future!

THE IDEAL OF A UNIVERSAL
RELIGION

(Delivered in New York, January 12, 1896)

WHERESOEVER OUR SENSES REACH or whatsoever our minds imagine, we find therein the action and reaction of two forces, the one counteracting the other and thus causing the constant play of the mixed phenomena which we see around us or which we feel in our minds. In the external world, the action of these opposite forces expresses itself as attraction and repulsion, or as the centripetal and centrifugal forces; and in the internal, as love and hatred, good and evil. We repel some things; we attract others. We are attracted by one; we are repelled by another. Many times in our lives we find that without any reason whatsoever, we are, as it were, attracted towards certain persons; at other times, similarly, we are repelled by others. This is patent to all; and the higher the field of action, the more potent, the more remarkable, are the influences of these opposite forces.

Religion is the highest plane of human thought and life, and herein we find that the workings of these two forces have been most marked. The intensest love that humanity has ever known has come from religion, and the most diabolical hatred that humanity has known has also come from religion. The noblest words of peace that the world has ever heard have come from men on the religious plane, and the bitterest denunciation that the world has ever known has been uttered by religious men. The higher the goal of any religion and the finer its organization, the more remarkable are its activities. No other human motive has deluged the world with so much blood as religion; at the same time, nothing has brought into existence so many hospitals and asylums for the poor, no other human influence has taken such care, not only of humanity, but also of the lowest of animals, as religion. Nothing makes us so cruel as religion, and nothing makes us so tender as religion. This has been so in the past and will also, in all probability, be so in the future.

Yet out of the midst of this din and turmoil, this strife and struggle, this hatred and jealousy of religions and sects, there have arisen, from time to time, potent voices drowning all this noise—making themselves heard from pole to pole, as it were—proclaiming peace and harmony.

Will it ever come? Is it possible that there should ever reign unbroken harmony in this plane of mighty religious struggle? The world is exercised in the latter part of this century by the question of harmony. In society various plans are being proposed, and attempts are made to carry them into practice. But we know how difficult it is to do so. People find that it is almost impossible to mitigate the fury of the struggle of life, to tone down the tremendous nervous tension that is in man. Now, if it is so difficult to bring harmony and peace on the physical plane of life—the external and gross side of it—then it must be a thousand times more difficult to bring harmony and peace to rule over the internal nature of man.

I would ask you for the time being to come out of the network of words. We have all been hearing from childhood of such things as love, peace, charity, equality, and universal brotherhood; but they have become to us mere words without meaning, words which we repeat like parrots; and it has become quite natural for us to do so. We cannot help it. Great souls, who first felt these great ideas in their hearts, created these words; and at that time many understood their meaning. Later on, ignorant people took up those words to play with them, and they made religion a mere play with words and not a thing to be carried into practice. It has become "my father's religion," "our nation's religion," "our country's religion," and so forth. It has become part of patriotism to profess a certain religion; and patriotism is always partial.

To bring harmony into religion must always be difficult. Yet we shall consider this problem of the harmony of religions.

We see that in every religion there are three parts—I mean in every great and recognized religion. First, there is the philosophy, which presents the whole scope of that religion, setting forth its basic principles, its goal, and the means of reaching that goal. The second part is mythology, which is philosophy made concrete. It consists of legends relating to the lives of men or of supernatural beings, and so forth. It is abstract philosophy made concrete through the more or less imaginary lives of men and supernatural beings. The third part is ritual. This is still more concrete and is made up of forms and ceremonies, various physical attitudes, flowers and incense, and many other things that appeal to the senses.

You will find that all recognized religions have these three elements. Some lay more stress on one, some on another.

Let us now take into consideration the first part, philosophy. Is there one universal philosophy? Not yet. Each religion brings out its own doctrines and insists upon them as being the only true ones. And not only does it do that, but it thinks that he who does not believe in them must go to some horrible place. Some will even draw the sword to compel others to believe as they do. This is not through wickedness, but through a particular disease of the human brain, called fanaticism. They are very sincere, these fanatics, the most sincere of human beings; but they are quite as irresponsible as other lunatics in the world. This disease of fanaticism is one of the most dangerous of all diseases. All the wickedness of human nature is roused by it. Anger is stirred up, nerves are strung high, and human beings become like tigers.

Is there any mythological similarity, any mythological harmony, any universal mythology accepted by all religions? Certainly not. All religions have their own mythology; only each of them says, "My stories are not mere myths." Let us try to understand the matter through an illustration. I simply mean to illustrate; I do not mean to criticize any religion.

The Christian believes that God took the shape of a dove and came down to earth; to him this is history and not mythology. The Hindu believes that God is manifested in the cow. Christians say that to believe so is mere mythology, and not history; that it is superstition. The Jews think that if an image is made in the form of a box or a chest, with an angel on either side, then it may be placed in the Holy of Holies; it is sacred to Jehovah. But if the image is made in the form of a beautiful man or woman, they say, "This is a horrible idol; break it down!" This is our unity in mythology! Again, if a man stands up and says, "My prophet did such and such a wonderful thing," others will say, "That is only superstition." But at the same time they say that their own prophet did still more wonderful things, which they hold to be historical. Nobody in the world, as far as I have seen, is able to make out the fine distinction between history and mythology as it exists in the brains of these persons. All such stories, to whatever religion they may belong, are really mythological— mixed up occasionally, it may be, with a little history.

Next come the rituals. One sect has one particular form of rituals and thinks that they are holy whereas the rituals of another sect are simply arrant superstition. If one sect worships a peculiar sort of symbol, another sect says, "Oh, it is horrible." Take for instance a common Hindu symbol: the phallus. This is certainly a sex symbol; but gradually that aspect of it has been forgotten, and it stands now as a symbol of the Creator. Those Hindus who use this as their symbol never connect it with sex; to them it is just a symbol, and there it ends. But a man from another race or creed sees in it nothing but the phallus, and condemns it; yet at the same time he may be doing something which to the so-called phallus-worshippers appears most horrible. Let me take two cases for illustration: the phallus symbol and the sacrament of the Christians. To the Christians the phallus is horrible, and to the Hindus the Christian sacrament is horrible. They say that the Christian sacrament, the killing of a man and the eating of his flesh and the drinking of his blood to get the good qualities of that man, is cannibalism. This is what some of the savage tribes do. If a man is brave, they kill him and eat his heart, because they think that it will give them the qualities of courage and bravery possessed by that man. Even such a devout Christian as Sir John Lubbock admits this and says that the origin of this Christian symbol is in this primitive idea. Most Christians, of course, do not admit this view of its origin, and what it originally implied never comes to their minds. It stands for a holy thing, and that is all they care about. So even in rituals there is no universal symbol which can command general recognition and acceptance.

Where, then, is there any universality in religion? How is it possible, then, to have a universal form of religion? I am convinced, however, that that form of religion already exists. Let us see what it is.

We all hear about universal brotherhood, and how societies spring up especially to preach it. I remember an old story. In India, wine-drinking is considered very bad. There were two brothers who one night wished to drink wine secretly; and their uncle, who was a very orthodox man, was sleeping in a room quite close to theirs. So before they began to drink they said to each other, "We must be very quiet, or Uncle will wake up." When they were drinking they continued repeating to each other, "Silence! Uncle will wake up," each trying to shout the other down. And as the shouting increased, the uncle woke up, came into the room, and discovered the whole thing.

Now, we all shout like these drunken men: "Universal brotherhood! We are all equal; therefore let us make a sect." As soon as you make a sect you protest against equality, and equality is no more. Mohammedans talk of universal brotherhood; but what comes out of that in reality? Why, that anybody who is not a Mohammedan will not be admitted into the brotherhood; he will more likely have his throat cut. Christians talk of universal brotherhood; but anyone who is not a Christian must go to that place where he will be eternally barbecued. And so we go on in this world in our search after universal brotherhood and equality.

When you hear such talk in the world, I would ask you to be a little reticent, to take care of yourselves, for behind all this talk is often the intensest selfishness. "In the winter sometimes a thunder-cloud comes up; it roars and roars, but it does not rain. But in the rainy season the clouds speak not, but deluge the world with water." So those who are real workers and who really feel at heart the universal brotherhood of man do not talk much, do not make little sects for universal brotherhood; but their acts, their movements, their whole life, show clearly that they in truth possess the feeling of brotherhood for mankind, that they have love and sympathy for all. They do not speak; they do and they live. This world is too full of blustering talk. We want a little more earnest work and less talk.

So far we see that it is hard to find any universal features in regard to religion; and yet we know that they exist. We are all human beings, but are we all equal? Certainly not. Who says we are equal? Only the lunatic. Are we all equal in our brains, in our powers, in our bodies? One man is stronger than another; one man has more brain-power than another. If we are all equal, why is there this inequality? Who made it? We ourselves. Because we have more or less powers, more or less brains, more or less physical strength, these must make a difference between us. Yet we know that the doctrine of equality appeals to our hearts. We are all human beings; but some are men and some are women. Here is a black man, there is a white man; but all are men, all belong to one humanity. Various are our faces; I see no two alike; yet we are all human beings. Where is this one humanity? I find a man or a woman either dark or fair; and among all these faces, I know that there is an abstract humanity common to all. I may not find it when I try to grasp it, perceive it, and actualize it, yet I know for certain that it is there. If I am sure of anything, it is of this humanity which is common to us all. It is through this common entity that I see you as a man or a woman.

So it is with this universal religion which runs through all the various religions of the world in the form of God; it must and does exist through eternity. "I am the thread that runs through all these pearls," and each pearl is a religion or even a sect thereof. These are the different pearls, and the Lord is the thread that runs through all of them; only the majority of mankind are entirely unconscious of it.

Unity in variety is the plan of the universe. We are all men, and yet we are all distinct from one another. As a part of humanity I am one with you, and as Mr. So-and-so I am different from you. As a man you are separate from woman; as a human being you are one with woman. As a human being you are separate from the animals; but as living beings man, woman, and animal are all one. And as existence you are one with the whole universe. That universal existence is God, the ultimate Unity in the universe. In Him we are all one. At the same time, in manifestation these differences must always remain. In our work, in our energies as they are being manifested outside, these differences must always remain.

We find, then, that if by the idea of a universal religion it is meant that one set of doctrines should be believed in by all mankind, it is wholly impossible; it can never be. There can never be a time when all faces will be the same. Again, if we expect that there will be one universal mythology, that also is impossible; it cannot be. Neither can there be one universal ritual. Such a state of things can never come into existence. If it ever did, the world would be destroyed, because variety is the first principle of life.

What makes us beings endowed with forms? Differentiation. Perfect balance would be destruction. Take, for instance, the heat in this room, whose tendency is towards equal diffusion; suppose it gets that kind of diffusion; then for all practical purposes that heat will cease to be. What makes motion possible in this universe? Lost balance. Complete sameness can come only when this universe is destroyed; otherwise such a thing is impossible. Not only so; it would be dangerous to have it. We must not wish that all of us should think alike. There would then be no thought to think; we should all be alike, as the Egyptian mummies in a museum are, looking at each other without a thought to think. It is this difference, this differentiation, this losing of sameness between us, which is the very soul of our progress, the soul of all our thought. This must always be.

What, then, do I mean by the ideal of a universal religion? I do not mean any one universal philosophy or any one universal mythology or any one universal ritual held alike by all; for I know that this world must go on working, wheel within wheel, this intricate mass of machinery, most complex, most wonderful. What can we do then? We can make it run smoothly, we can lessen the friction, we can grease the wheels, as it were. How? By recognizing the natural necessity of variation. Just as we have recognized unity as our very nature, so we must also recognize variation. We must learn that truth may be expressed in a hundred thousand ways, and that each of these ways is true as far as it goes. We must learn that the same thing can be viewed from a hundred different standpoints and yet be the same thing. Take for instance the sun. Suppose a man standing on the earth looks at the sun when it rises in the morning; he sees a big ball. Suppose he starts on a journey towards the sun and takes a camera with him, taking photographs at every stage of his journey until he reaches the sun. The photographs of each stage will be seen to be different from those of the other stages; in fact, when he gets back, he brings with him so many photographs of so many different suns, as it would appear; and yet we know that the same sun was photographed by the man at the different stages of his progress.

Even so is it with the Lord. Through high philosophy or low, through the most exalted mythology or the grossest, through the most refined ritualism or arrant fetishism, every sect, every soul, every nation, every religion, consciously or unconsciously is struggling upward towards God; every vision of truth that man has is a vision of Him and of none else. Suppose we all go with vessels in our hands to fetch water from a lake. One has a cup, another a jar, another a bucket, and so forth, and we all fill our vessels. The water in each case naturally takes the form of the vessel carried by each of us. He who brought the cup has the water in the form of a cup; he who brought the jar—his water takes the shape of a jar; and so forth. But in every case, water, and nothing but water, is in the vessel. So it is with religion. Our minds are like these vessels, and each one of us is trying to arrive at the realization of God. God is like that water filling these different vessels, and in each vessel the vision of God takes the form of the vessel. Yet He is One. He is God in every case. This is the only recognition of universality that we can get.

So far it is all right theoretically; but is there any way of practically working out this harmony in religions? We find that this recognition that all the various views of religion are true is very, very old. Hundreds of attempts have been made in India, in Alexandria, in Europe, in China, in Japan, in Tibet, and lastly in America, to formulate a harmonious religious creed to make all religions come together in love. They have all failed, because they did not adopt any practical plan. Many have admitted that all the religions of the world are right; but they show no practical way of bringing them together so as to enable each of them to maintain its own individuality in the conflux. That plan alone is practical which does not destroy the individuality of any man in religion and at the same time shows him a point of union with all others. But so far all the plans of religious harmony that have been tried, while proposing to take in all the various views of religion, have in practice tried to bind them all down to a few doctrines, and so have produced more new sects, fighting, struggling, and pushing against each other.

I have also my little plan. I do not know whether it will work or not; and I want to present it to you for discussion. What is my plan? In the first place I would ask mankind to recognize this maxim: "Do not destroy." Iconoclastic reformers do no good to the world. Break not, pull not anything down; but build. Help, if you can; if you cannot, fold your hands and stand by and see things go on. Do not injure if you cannot render help. Say not a word against any man's convictions so far as they are sincere. Secondly, take a man where he stands, and from there give him a lift. If it is true that God is the centre of all religions and that each of us is moving towards Him along one of these radii, then it is certain that all of us must reach that centre; and at the centre, where all the radii meet, all our differences will cease. But until we reach it, differences there must be. All these radii converge upon the same centre. One, according to his nature, travels along one of these lines, and another along another; and if we all push onward along our own lines, we shall surely come to the centre, because "all roads lead to Rome."

Each of us is naturally growing and developing according to his own nature; each will in time come to know the highest truth; for after all, men must teach themselves. What can you and I do? Do you think you can teach even a child? You cannot. The child teaches himself. Your duty is to afford opportunities and to remove obstacles. A plant grows. Do you make the plant grow? Your duty is to put a hedge round it and see that no animal eats it up; and there your duty ends. The plant grows of itself. So is it in regard to the spiritual growth of every man. None can teach you; none can make a spiritual man of you. You have to teach yourself; your growth must come from inside. What can an external teacher do? He can remove the obstructions a little; and there his duty ends. Therefore help, if you can; but do not destroy. Give up all ideas that you can make men spiritual. It is impossible. There is no other teacher for you than your own soul. Recognize this.

What comes of it? In society we see so many different natures. There are thousands and thousands of varieties of minds and inclinations. A thorough generalization of them is impossible, but for our practical purpose it is sufficient to have them divided up into four classes. First, there is the active man, the worker; he wants to work, and there is tremendous energy in his muscles and his nerves. His aim is to work—to build hospitals, do charitable deeds, make streets, plan and organize. Then there is the emotional man, who loves the sublime and the beautiful to an excessive degree. He loves to think of the beautiful, to enjoy the aesthetic side of nature, to love and adore the God of Love. He loves with his whole heart the great souls of all times, the prophets of religion, and the Incarnations of God on earth. He does not care whether reason can or cannot prove that Christ or Buddha existed. He does not care for the exact date when the Sermon on the Mount was preached, or for the exact moment of Krishna's birth. What he cares for is their personalities, their lovable figures. Such is his ideal. This is the nature of the lover, the emotional man. Then there is the mystic, whose mind wants to analyse its own self, to understand the workings of the human mind—what the forces are that are working inside—and how to know, manipulate, and obtain control over them. This is the mystical mind. And finally there is the philosopher, who wants to weigh everything and use his intellect even beyond the possibilities of human thinking.

Now, a religion, to satisfy the largest portion of mankind, must be able to supply food for all these various types of minds; and where this capability is wanting, the existing sects all become one-sided. Suppose you go to a sect which preaches love and emotion. They sing and weep, and preach love. But as soon as you say: "My friend, that is all right, but I want something stronger than this, a little reason and philosophy; I want to understand things step by step and more rationally"—"Get out!" they say, and they not only ask you to get out but would send you to the other place if they could. The result is that that sect can only help people of an emotional turn of mind. They not only do not help others, but try to destroy them. And the most wicked part of the whole thing is that they not only will not help others, but do not believe in their sincerity. Again, there are philosophers who talk of the wisdom of India and the East and use big psychological terms, fifty syllables long; but if an ordinary man like me goes to them and says, "Can you tell me anything to make me spiritual?" the first thing they will do will be to smile and say: "Oh, you are too far below us in your reason. What can you understand about spirituality?" These are high-up philosophers. They simply show you the door. Then there are the mystical sects, who speak all sorts of things about different planes of existence, different states of mind, and what the power of the mind can do, and so on. If you are an ordinary man and say: "Show me something good that I can do. I am not much given to speculation; can you give me anything that will suit me?" they will smile, and say: "Listen to that fool! He knows nothing; his existence is for nothing." And this is going on everywhere in the world. I should like to get extreme exponents of all these different sects and shut them up in a room and photograph their beautiful derisive smiles! This is the existing condition of religion, the existing condition of things.

What I want to propagate is a religion that will be equally acceptable to all minds. It must be equally philosophic, equally emotional, equally mystical, and equally conducive to action. If professors from the colleges come—or scientific men and philosophers—they will court reason. Let them have it as much as they want. There will be a point beyond which they will discover they cannot go without breaking with reason. If they say, "These ideas of God and salvation are superstitions; give them up," I shall reply: "Mr. Philosopher, this body of yours is a bigger superstition. Give it up. Don't go home to dinner or to your philosophic chair. Give up the body, and if you cannot, cry quarter and sit down." Religion must be able to show us how to realize the knowledge that teaches that this world is one, that there is but one Existence in the universe. Similarly, if the mystic comes, we must welcome him, be ready to teach him the science of mental analysis, and practically demonstrate it before him. If emotional people come, we must sit with them and laugh and weep in the name of the Lord; we must "drink the cup of love and become mad." And if the energetic worker comes, we must work with him with all the energy that we have. And this combination will be the ideal, the nearest approach to a universal religion.

Would to God that all men were so constituted that in their minds all these elements—of philosophy, mysticism, emotion, and work—were equally present in full! That is the ideal, my ideal of a perfect man. Everyone who has only one or two of these elements I consider partial and one-sided. This world is almost full of such one-sided men, who possess knowledge of that one road only in which they move, and to whom anything else is dangerous and horrible. To become harmoniously balanced in all these four directions is my ideal of religion. And this ideal is attained by what we in India call yoga—union. To the worker, it is union between himself and the whole of humanity; to the mystic, union between his lower self and Higher Self; to the lover, union between himself and the God of Love; and to the philosopher, the unity of all existence. That is what is meant by yoga. This is a Sanskrit term, and these four divisions of yoga have, in Sanskrit, different names. The man who seeks after this kind of union is called a yogi. The worker is called a karma-yogi. He who seeks union through love is called a bhakti-yogi. He who seeks it through mysticism is called a rāja-yogi. And he who seeks it through philosophy is called a jnāna-yogi. So this word yogi comprises them all.

Now, first of all let me take up rāja-yoga. What is this rāja-yoga, this controlling of the mind? In this country you associate all sorts of hobgoblins with the word *yoga*. I am afraid, therefore, I must start by telling you that it has nothing to do with such things. Not one of these yogas gives up reason; not one of them asks you to be hoodwinked or to deliver your reason into the hands of priests of any type whatsoever. Not one of them asks that you should give your allegiance to any superhuman messenger. Each one of them tells you to cling to your reason, to hold fast to it.

We find in all living beings three instruments of knowledge. The first is instinct, which you find most highly developed in animals; this is the lowest instrument of knowledge. What is the second instrument of knowledge? Reasoning. You find that most highly developed in man. Now, in the first place, instinct is an inadequate instrument; to animals the sphere of action is very limited, and within that limit instinct acts. When you come to man, you see instinct largely developed into reason. The sphere of action also has here become enlarged. Yet even reason is insufficient. Reason can go only a little way and then it stops. It cannot go any farther; and if you try to push it, the result is helpless confusion; reason itself becomes unreasonable. Logic becomes argument in a circle. Take, for instance, the very bases of our perception: matter and force. What is matter? That which is acted upon by force. And force? That which acts upon matter. You see the complication, what the logicians call a "see-saw," one idea depending on the other, and this again depending on that. Thus you find a mighty barrier before reason, beyond which reasoning cannot go. Yet it always feels impatient to get into the region of the Infinite Beyond. This world, this universe, which our senses feel or our mind thinks about, is but one atom, so to say, of the Infinite, projected on to the plane of consciousness. Within that narrow limit defined by the network of consciousness works our reason, and not beyond. Therefore there must be some other instrument to take us beyond; and that instrument is called inspiration.

So instinct, reason, and inspiration are the three instruments of knowledge. Instinct belongs to animals, reason to man, and inspiration to God-men. But in all human beings are to be found in a more or less developed condition the germs of all these three instruments of knowledge. To have these mental instruments evolve, the germs must be there. And this must also be remembered: one instrument is a development of another and therefore does not contradict it. It is reason that develops into inspiration; and therefore inspiration does not contradict reason, but fulfils it. Things which reason cannot get at are brought to light by inspiration, and they do not contradict reason. The old man does not contradict the child, but fulfils the child.

Therefore you must always bear in mind that the great danger lies in mistaking the lower form of instrument for the higher. Many times instinct is presented before the world as inspiration, and then come all the spurious claims to the gift of prophecy. A fool or a semi-lunatic thinks that the confusion going on in his brain is inspiration, and he wants men to follow him. The most contradictory, irrational nonsense that has been preached in the world is simply the instinctive jargon of confused lunatic brains trying to pass for the language of inspiration. The first test of true instruction is that it does not contradict reason.

You can see that this is the basis of all these yogas. Take, for instance, rāja-yoga, the psychological yoga, the psychological way to union. It is a vast subject, and I can only point out to you now the central idea of this yoga. We have but one method of acquiring knowledge. From the lowest man to the highest yogi, all have to use the same method; and that method is what is called concentration. The chemist who works in his laboratory concentrates all the powers of his mind, brings them into one focus, and throws them on the elements, and the elements stand analysed; and thus his knowledge comes. The astronomer also concentrates the powers of his mind and brings them into one focus; he throws them on objects through his telescope, and stars and various heavenly systems roll forward and yield their secrets. So it is in every case—with the professor in his chair, the student with his book, with every man who is working to know. You are hearing me, and if my words interest you, your mind will become concentrated on them. Then suppose a clock strikes; you will not hear it, on account of this concentration. And the more you are able to concentrate your mind, the better you will understand me; and the more I concentrate my love and powers, the better I shall be able to give expression to what I want to convey to you.

The more there is of this power of concentration, the more knowledge is acquired, because this is the one and only method of acquiring knowledge. Even the lowest shoeblack, if he gives more concentration, will black shoes better; the cook with concentration will cook a meal all the better. In making money or in worshipping God or in doing anything, the stronger is the power of concentration, the better will that thing be done. This is the one call, the one knock, which opens the gates of nature and lets out floods of light. This, the power of concentration, is the only key to the treasure-house of knowledge.

The system of rāja-yoga deals almost exclusively with this concentration. In the present state of our body and mind we are much distracted; the mind is frittering away its energies upon a hundred sorts of things. As soon as I try to calm my thoughts and concentrate my mind upon any one object of knowledge, thousands of undesired impulses rush into the brain, thousands of thoughts rush into the mind and disturb it. How to check them and bring the mind under control is the whole subject of study in rāja-yoga.

Now take karma-yoga, the attainment of God through work. It is evident that in society there are many persons who seem to be born for some sort of activity or other, whose minds cannot be concentrated on the plane of thought alone, and whose principal idea is to express themselves through work visible and tangible. There must be a science for this kind of mind too. Each one of us is engaged in some work or other, but the majority of us fritter away a great portion of our energy because we do not know the secret of work. Karma-yoga explains this secret and teaches where and how to work, how to employ to the greatest advantage the largest part of our energies in the work that is before us.

But with this secret we must take into consideration the great objection against work, namely, that it causes pain. All misery and pain come from attachment. I want to do work, I want to do good to a human being; and it is ninety to one that that human being whom I have helped will prove ungrateful and go against me. And the result to me is pain. Such things deter mankind from working; this fear of pain and misery wastes a good portion of the work and energy of mankind. Karma-yoga teaches us how to work for work's sake, unattached, without caring who is helped and why. The karma-yogi works because it is his nature to work, because he feels that it is good for him to do so; and he has no object beyond that. His position in this world is that of a giver; he never cares to receive anything. He knows that he is giving, and does not ask for anything in return, and there he eludes the grasp of misery. Pain, whenever it comes, is the result of attachment.

Then there is bhakti-yoga for the man of emotional nature, the lover. He wants to love God; he relies upon and uses all sorts of rituals, flowers, incense, beautiful buildings, forms, and all such things. Do you mean to say that these are wrong? One fact I must tell you. It is good for you to remember, in this country especially, that the world's great spiritual giants have all been produced by religious sects which have been in possession of a very rich mythology and ritual. All sects that have attempted to worship God without any form or cere-mony have crushed without mercy everything that is beautiful and sublime in religion. Their religion is fanaticism—at best a dry thing. The history of the world is a standing witness to this fact. Therefore do not decry these rituals and mythologies. Let people have them; let those who so desire have them. Do not exhibit that unworthy derisive smile and say, "They are fools; let them have it." For it is not so. The greatest men I have seen in my life, the most wonderfully developed in spirituality, have all come through the discipline of these rituals. I do not hold myself worthy to sit at their feet; it would be shameful for me to criticize them. How do I know how these ideas act upon the human mind, which of them I am to accept and which to reject? We are apt to criticize everything in the world without sufficient warrant. Let people have all the mythology they want, with its beautiful inspirations; for you must always bear in mind that emotional natures do not care for abstract definitions of the truth. God to them is something tangible, the only thing that is real. They feel, hear, and see Him, and they love Him. Let them have their God. Your rationalist seems to them to be like the fool who, when he sees a beautiful statue, wants to break it to find out what material it is made of.

Bhakti-yoga teaches them how to love without any ulterior motives, loving God and loving the good because it is good to do so—not in order to go to heaven or to get children, wealth, or anything else. It teaches them that love itself is the highest recompense of love—that God Himself is Love. It teaches them to pay all kinds of tribute to God as the Creator, the omnipresent, omniscient, almighty Ruler, the Father and Mother.

The best phrase that can express Him, the highest idea that the human mind can conceive about Him, is that He is the God of Love. Wherever there is love, it is He. "Wherever there is any love, it is He; the Lord is present there." Where the husband kisses the wife, He is there in the kiss; where the mother kisses the child, He is there in the kiss; where friends clasp hands, He, the Lord, is present as the God of Love. When a great man loves and wishes to help mankind, He is there giving freely of His bounty out of His love for mankind. Wherever the heart expands, He is there manifested. This is what bhkati-yoga teaches.

We lastly come to the jnāna-yogi, the philosopher, the thinker, he who wants
to go beyond the visible. He is the man who is not satisfied with the little things
of this world. His idea is to go beyond the daily routine of eating, drinking,
and so on. Not even the teachings of thousands of books will satisfy him. Not
even all the sciences will satisfy him. At best they only explain this little world
to him. What else, then, will give him satisfaction? Not even myriads of
systems of worlds will satisfy him; they are to him but drops in the ocean
of existence. His soul wants to go beyond all that into the very heart of Being,
by seeing Reality as It is—by realizing It, by being It, by becoming one with
that Universal Being. That is the philosopher. To say that God is the Father
or Mother, the Creator of this universe, its Protector and Guide, is to him quite
inadequate to express Him. To him, God is the Life of his life, the Soul of his
soul. God is his own Self. Nothing else exists which is other than God. All
the mortal parts of him become pulverized by the weighty strokes of philosophy
and are brushed away. What at last truly remains is God Himself.

Upon the same tree there are two birds, one on the top, the other below.
The one on the top is calm, silent, and majestic, immersed in his own glory;
the one on the lower branches, eating sweet and bitter fruits by turns, hopping
from branch to branch, becomes happy and miserable by turns. After a time
the lower bird eats a very bitter fruit and becomes disgusted. Then he looks
up and sees the other bird, that wondrous one of golden plumage, who eats
neither sweet nor bitter fruit, who is neither happy nor miserable, but is calm,
Self-centred, and sees nothing beyond his Self. The lower bird longs for this
condition, but soon forgets it and again begins to eat the fruit. In a little
while he eats another exceptionally bitter fruit, which makes him feel miserable, and again he looks up and tries to get nearer to the upper bird. Once
more he forgets, and after a time looks up; and so on he goes, again and again,
until he comes very near to the beautiful bird and sees the reflection of light
from his plumage playing around his own body, and he feels a change and
seems to melt away. Still nearer he comes, and everything about him melts
away, and at last he understands this wonderful phenomenon. The lower bird
was, as it were, only a substantial-looking shadow, a reflection of the higher;
he himself was in essence the upper bird all the time. This eating of fruits, sweet
and bitter, and this lower little bird, weeping and happy by turns, were a vain
chimera, a dream; all along, the real bird was there above, calm and silent,
glorious and majestic, beyond grief, beyond sorrow.

The upper bird is God, the Lord of this universe; and the lower bird is the
human soul, eating the sweet and bitter fruits of this world. Now and then
comes a heavy blow to the soul. For a time he stops eating and goes towards
the unknown God, and a flood of light comes. He thinks that this world is a
vain show. Yet again the senses drag him down, and he begins as before to eat
the sweet and bitter fruits of the world. Again an exceptionally hard blow
comes. His heart becomes open again to the divine light. Thus gradually he
approaches God; and as he gets nearer and nearer he finds his old self melting
away. When he has come near enough he sees that he is none other than God
Himself, and he exclaims: "He whom I have described to you as the Life of

this universe, present in the atom and in suns and moons—He is the basis of
our own life, the Soul of our soul. Nay, thou art That."

This is what jñāna-yoga teaches. It tells man that he is essentially divine.
It shows mankind the real unity of being: that each one of us is the Lord God
Himself manifested on earth. All of us, from the lowest worm that crawls under
our feet to the highest being to whom we look up with wonder and awe, all
are manifestations of the same Lord.

Lastly, it is imperative that all these various yogas should be carried out in
practice. Mere theories about them will not do any good. First we have to hear
about them; then we have to think about them. We have to reason the thoughts
out, impress them on our minds, and meditate on them, realize them, until at
last they become our whole life. No longer will religion remain a bundle of
ideas or theories, or an intellectual assent; it will enter into our very self. By
means of intellectual assent we may subscribe today to many foolish things,
and change our minds altogether tomorrow. But true religion never changes.
Religion is realization—not talk or doctrines or theories, however beautiful they
may be. It is being and becoming—not hearing or acknowledging. It is the
whole soul's becoming changed into what it believes. That is religion.

BHAKTI-YOGA

INVOCATION

"He is the Soul of the universe. He is the Immortal. His is the Rulership. He is the All-knowing, the All-pervading, the Protector of the universe, the Eternal Ruler. None else is there efficient to govern the world eternally.

"He who at the beginning of creation projected Brahmā and who delivered the Vedas unto Him—seeking liberation, I go for refuge unto that Effulgent One, whose light turns the understanding towards the Ātman."—Śvetāśvatara Upanishad VI. 17-18.

Vivekananda in America

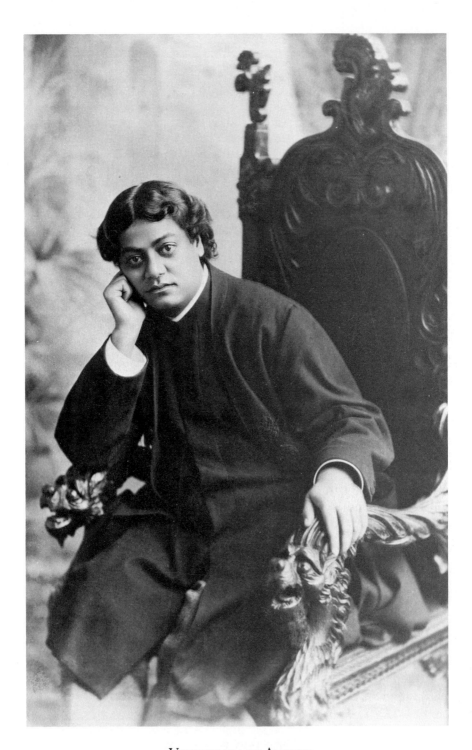

VIVEKANANDA IN AMERICA

DEFINITION OF BHAKTI

Bhakti-yoga is a real, genuine search after the Lord, a search beginning, continuing, and ending in love. One single moment of the madness of extreme love of God brings us eternal freedom. "Bhakti is intense love of God," says Nārada in his bhakti aphorisms. "When a man gets it he loves all, hates none; he becomes satisfied for ever." "This love cannot be reduced to any earthly benefit"—because so long as worldly desires last that kind of love does not arise. "Bhakti is greater than karma, greater than jnāna, and greater than yoga," because these have in view the attainment of an object, while bhakti is its own fruition, "its own means, and its own end."

Bhakti has been the one constant theme of our sages. Apart from the special writers on bhakti such as Śāndilya or Nārada, the great commentators on the Vyāsa Sutras, evident advocates of jnāna, have also something very suggestive to say about love. Even when those commentators are anxious to explain many, if not all, of the texts so as to make them import a sort of dry knowledge, the sutras, in the chapter on worship especially, do not lend themselves to be easily manipulated in that fashion.

There is not really so much difference between jnāna and bhakti as people sometimes imagine. We shall see, as we go on, that in the end they converge and finally meet in the same point. So also is it with rāja-yoga, which, when pursued as a means to attain liberation and not (as unfortunately it has frequently become in the hands of charlatans and mystery-mongers) as an instrument to hoodwink the unwary, leads us to the same goal.

The one great advantage of bhakti is that it is the easiest and the most natural way to reach the great divine end in view. Its great disadvantage is that in its lower forms it oftentimes degenerates into hideous fanaticism. The fanatical crew in Hinduism or Mohammedanism or Christianity have always been almost exclusively recruited from these worshippers on the lower planes of bhakti. That singleness of attachment (nishthā) to a loved object, without which no genuine love can grow, is very often also the cause of the denunciation of everything else. All the weak and undeveloped minds in every religion or country have only one way of loving their own ideal, and that is to hate every other ideal. Herein is the explanation of why the same man who is so lovingly attached to his own ideal of God, so devoted to his own ideal of religion, becomes a howling fanatic as soon as he sees or hears anything of any other ideal. This kind of love is somewhat like the canine instinct of guarding the master's property from intruders; only the instinct of the dog is better than the reason of man, for the dog never mistakes its master for an enemy, in whatever dress he may come before it. Again, the fanatic loses all power of judgement. Personal considerations are in his case of such absorbing interest that to him it is no question at all of what a man says—whether it is right or wrong; but the one thing he is always particularly careful to know is, who says it. The same man who is kind, good, honest, and loving to people of his own opinion will not hesitate to do the vilest deeds against persons beyond the pale of his own religious brotherhood.

But this danger exists only in that stage of bhakti which is called the gauni or preparatory stage. When bhakti has become ripe and has passed into that form which is called the parā or supreme, no more is there any fear of these hideous manifestations of fanaticism. That soul which is overpowered by this higher form of bhakti is too near the God of Love to become an instrument for the diffusion of hatred.

It is not given to all of us to be harmonious in the building up of our characters in this life; yet we know that that character is of the noblest type in which all these three—knowledge and love and rāja-yoga—are harmoniously fused. Three things are necessary for a bird to fly: the two wings, and the tail as a rudder for steering. Jnāna is the one wing, bhakti is the other, and rāja-yoga is the tail that maintains the balance. For those who cannot pursue all these three forms of worship together in harmony, and take up, therefore, bhakti alone as their way, it is necessary always to remember that forms and ceremonials, though absolutely necessary for the progressing soul, have no other value than to lead us on to that state in which we feel the most intense love of God.

There is a little difference in opinion between the teachers of knowledge and those of love, though both admit the power of bhakti. The jnānis hold bhakti to be an instrument of liberation; the bhaktas look upon it as both the instrument and the thing to be attained. To my mind this is a distinction without much difference. In fact, bhakti, when used as an instrument, really means a lower form of worship; and when this lower form is further cultivated it becomes inseparable from the higher form of bhakti. Each seems to lay great stress upon his own peculiar method of discipline, forgetting that with perfect love true knowledge is bound to come unsought, and that, at the end, true love is inseparable from perfect knowledge.

Bearing this in mind, let us try to understand what the great Vedāntic commentators have to say on the subject. In explaining an aphorism of the Vedānta Sutras, Śankara says: "Thus people say, 'He is devoted to the king' or 'He is devoted to the guru.' They say this of him who follows his king or his guru, and does so, having that following as the one end in view. Similarly they say, 'The loving wife meditates on her loving husband away in a foreign land.' Here also a kind of eager and continuous remembrance is meant." This is devotion according to Śankara.

Bhagavān Rāmānuja, in his commentary on the first aphorism of the Vedānta Sutras, says:

"Meditation, again, is a constant remembrance [of the thing meditated upon], flowing like an unbroken stream of oil poured from one vessel to another. When this kind of remembering has been attained [in relation to God], all bondages break. Thus it is said in the scriptures regarding constant remembering as a means to liberation. This remembering, again, is of the same form as seeing, because it has the same meaning, as in the passage: 'When He who is far and near is seen, the bonds of the heart are broken, all doubts vanish, and all effects of work disappear.' He who is near can be seen, but he who is far can only be remembered. Nevertheless the scriptures say that we have to see Him who is near as well as far, thereby indicating to us that the above kind of remembering is as good as seeing. This remembrance, when exalted, assumes the same form as seeing. . . . Worship is constant remembering, as may be seen from the principal texts of the scriptures. Knowing, which is the same as repeated worship, has been described as constant remembering. . . . Thus the memory which has attained to the height of what is as good as direct perception is spoken of in the Śruti as a means of liberation. 'This Ātman is not to be reached through various sciences, nor by intellect, nor by much study of the Vedas. Whomsoever this Ātman desires—by him is Ātman attained; unto him Ātman reveals Itself.' Here, after saying that mere hearing, thinking, and meditating are not the means of attaining this Ātman, the Śruti says: 'Whomsoever this Ātman desires—by him is Ātman attained.' The extremely beloved is desired. He by whom this Ātman is extremely beloved becomes the most beloved of the Ātman. So that this beloved may attain the Ātman, the Lord Himself helps. For it has been said by the Lord: 'Those who are constantly attached to Me and worship Me with love—I give that direction to their will by which they come to Me.' Therefore it is said that he to whom this remembering, which is of the same nature as direct perception, is very dear, because it is dear to the object of such memory perception—he is desired by the Supreme Ātman and by him the Supreme Ātman is attained. This constant remembrance is denoted by the word *bhakti*."

In commenting on the sutra of Patanjali, "Or by the worship of the Supreme Lord," Bhoja says: "Pranidhāna ('worship') is that sort of bhakti in which, without one's seeking results, such as sense enjoyments and so forth, all works are dedicated to the Lord, who is the Teacher of teachers." Bhagavān Vyāsa also, when commenting on the same sutra, defines pranidhāna as "the form of bhakti by which the mercy of the Supreme Lord comes to the yogi and blesses him by granting him his desires." According to Śāndilya, "bhakti is intense love of God." The best idea of bhakti, however, is given by the king of bhaktas, Prahlāda: "May that intense and deathless love which ignorant people have for the fleeting objects of the senses not slip away from my heart as I keep meditating on Thee!"

Love for whom? For the Supreme Lord Iśvara. Love for any other being, however great, cannot be bhakti; for, as Rāmānuja says in his Śri Bhāshya, quoting an ancient āchārya, or great teacher: "From Brahmā to a clump of grass, all things that live in the world are slaves of birth and death caused by karma; therefore they cannot be helpful as objects of meditation, because they are all in ignorance and subject to change." In commenting on the word *anurakti* used by Śāndilya, the commentator Svapneśvara says that it means *anu*, after, and *rakti*, attachment; that is to say, the attachment which comes after the knowledge of the nature and glory of God—else a blind attachment to anyone, such as wife or children, would be bhakti. We plainly see, therefore, that bhakti is a series or succession of mental efforts at religious realization, beginning with ordinary worship and ending in a supreme intensity of love for Iśvara.

THE PHILOSOPHY OF IŚVARA

WHO IS IŚVARA? "From whom are the birth, continuation, and dissolution of the universe"—He is Iśvara, "the Eternal, the Pure, the Ever Free, the Almighty, the All-knowing, the All-merciful, the Teacher of all teachers." And above all, "He is the Lord, whose nature is inexpressible Love."

These certainly are the definitions of a Personal God. Are there then two Gods—the "Not this, not this," the Satchidānanda, the Existence-Knowledge-Bliss, of the philosopher, and this God of Love of the bhakta? No, it is the same Satchidānanda who is also the God of Love—impersonal and personal in one. It has always to be understood that the Personal God worshipped by the bhakta is not separate or different from Brahman. All is Brahman, the One without a second; only Brahman, as Unity or the Absolute, is too much of an abstraction to be loved and worshipped. So the bhakta chooses the relative aspect of Brahman, that is, Iśvara, the Supreme Ruler. To use a metaphor: Brahman is the clay or substance out of which an infinite variety of articles are fashioned. As clay, they are all one; but form or manifestation differentiates one from another. Previously they had all been potentially in the clay; and of course, they are identical in substance. But when formed, and so long as the form remains, they are separate and different. The clay mouse can never become a clay elephant, because, as manifestations, form alone makes them what they are, though as unformed clay they are all one. Iśvara, the Personal God, is the highest manifestation of Absolute Reality, or, in other words, the highest possible reading of the Absolute by the human mind. Creation is eternal and so also is Iśvara.

In the fourth pāda of the fourth chapter of his *Sutras*, after saying that almost infinite power and knowledge will come to the liberated soul after the attainment of moksha, Vyāsa states, in an aphorism, that none, however, will get the power of creating, ruling, and dissolving the universe, because that belongs to God alone. In explaining the sutra it is easy for the dualistic commentators to show how it is ever impossible for a subordinate soul, or jiva, to have the infinite power and total independence of God. The thoroughly dualistic commentator Madhvāchārya deals with this passage in his usual summary method by quoting a verse from the *Varāha Purāna*.

In explaining this aphorism the commentator Rāmānuja says: "This doubt being raised, whether among the powers of the liberated soul is included that unique power of the Supreme One, that is, of creating, ruling, and dissolving the universe, and even the Lordship of all, or whether, without that, the glory of the liberated consists only in the direct perception of the Supreme One, we meet with the following objection: 'It is reasonable that the liberated soul should obtain the Lordship of the universe, because the *Mundaka Upanishad* says

408

(III. i. 3.) that the liberated soul, free from sin, attains extreme sameness, which means that it attains oneness with the Supreme Spirit. It is further stated elsewhere in the scriptures that all the desires of the liberated are realized. Now, this extreme sameness and the realization of all desires are not possible without possession of the power of ruling the universe, which is the unique power of the Supreme Spirit. Therefore if it is said that the liberated soul attains the realization of all desires and extreme sameness, it must be admitted that it obtains the power of ruling the whole universe.'

"To this we reply that the liberated soul gets all the powers except that of ruling the universe. Ruling the universe means guiding the form and the life and the desires of all sentient and non-sentient beings. The liberated soul, from whom all that veils its true nature has been removed, only enjoys the unobstructed perception of Brahman, but does not possess the power of ruling the universe. This is proved from the scriptural text: 'From whom all these things are born, by whom all that are born live, unto whom they, departing, return— ask about It. That is Brahman.' If this quality of ruling the universe be common also to the liberated, then this text would not apply to Brahman as Its definition; but Brahman is defined as the Ruler of the universe. It is the uncommon attributes which define a thing. Therefore in texts like: 'My beloved boy, there existed in the beginning only the One without a second. That saw and reflected: I will give birth to the many. That projected heat'; 'Brahman, indeed, alone existed in the beginning. That One evolved. That projected a blessed form, the Kshatra. All these gods are Kshatras: Varuna, Soma, Rudra, Parjanya, Yama, Mrityu, Iśāna'; 'Ātman alone, indeed, existed in the beginning; nothing else vibrated. He thought of projecting the world; He projected the world afterwards'; 'Nārāyana alone existed—neither Brahmā nor Iśāna, nor the Dyāvāprithivi, nor the stars nor water nor fire, nor soma nor the sun. He did not take pleasure in being alone. He, after His meditation, created one daughter and the ten organs,' and so forth, and in others, such as: 'Who living in the earth is separate from the earth, who living in the Ātman,' and so forth—the Śrutis speak of the Supreme One as responsible for the work of ruling the universe. Nor in these descriptions of the ruling of the universe is there any reference to the liberated soul by which such a soul may have the ruling of the universe ascribed to it."

In explaining the next sutra, Rāmānuja says: "If you (the opponent) say it is not so, because there are direct texts in the Vedas in evidence to the contrary, we state in reply that these texts refer to the glories of the liberated dwelling in the spheres of the subordinate deities." This also is an easy solution of the difficulty. Although the system of Rāmānuja admits the unity of the total, within that totality of existence there are, according to him, eternal differences. Therefore, for all practical purposes, this system also being dualistic, it was easy for Rāmānuja to keep the distinction between the personal soul and the Personal God very clear.

We shall now try to understand what Śankara, the great teacher of the Advaita school, has to say on the point. We shall see how the Advaita system maintains intact all the hopes and aspirations of the dualist and at the same time propounds its own solution of the problem in consonance with the high destiny of humanity. Those who aspire to retain their individual minds even after liberation, and to remain distinct, will have ample opportunity of realizing their aspirations and will enjoy the blessing of Brahman with attributes. These are they who have been spoken of in the *Bhāgavata Purāna* thus: "O King, such are the glorious qualities of the Lord that the sages whose only pleasure is in the Self, from whom all fetters have fallen—even they love the Omnipresent with a love that is for love's sake." These are they who are spoken of by Sāmkhya as merged in nature. After having attained perfection in this cycle, these souls are born in the next as Lords of world systems. But none of these ever becomes equal to Iśvara. Those, however, who attain to that state where there is neither creation nor created nor Creator, where there is neither knower nor knowable nor knowledge, where there is neither "I" nor "thou" nor "he," where there is neither subject nor object nor relation ("there, who is seen and by whom?")—such persons have gone beyond everything, to "where words cannot go nor mind," gone to that which the Śrutis declare as "Not this, not this." But for those who cannot or will not reach this state, there will inevitably remain the triune vision of the one undifferentiated Brahman as nature, soul, and the interpenetrating sustainer of both—Iśvara.

So, when Prahlāda forgot himself in meditation on the Lord, he found neither the universe nor its cause; all was to him one Infinite, undifferentiated by name and form. But as soon as he remembered that he was Prahlāda, there was the universe before him, and with it the Lord of the universe, "the repository of an infinite number of blessed qualities." So it was with the blessed gopis. So long as they had lost the sense of their own personal identity and individuality, they were all Krishnas, and when they began again to think of Him as the One to be worshipped, then they were gopis, and immediately "unto them appeared Krishna with a smile on His lotus face, clad in yellow robes and adorned with garlands, the veritable conqueror [in beauty] of the god of love." (*Bhāgavata Purāna* X. xxxii. 2.)

Now to go back to our Āchārya Śankara: "Suppose," he says, "some by worshipping Brahman with attributes attain conjunction with the Supreme Ruler, preserving their own minds; is their glory limited or unlimited? This doubt arising, the opponent argues: Their glory should be unlimited, because of the scriptural texts: 'They attain their own Kingdom'; 'To him all the gods offer worship'; and 'Their desires are fulfilled in all the worlds.' As an answer to this, Vyāsa says: 'Without the power of ruling the universe.' Barring the power of creating, ruling, and dissolving the universe, the other powers, such as animā and the rest, are acquired by the liberated. As to ruling the universe, that belongs to the eternally perfect Iśvara. Why? Because He is referred to in all the scriptural texts concerning creation and so forth, and the liberated souls are not mentioned therein in any connexion whatsoever. The Supreme Lord, indeed, is alone engaged in ruling the universe. The texts as to creation and so forth all point to Him. Besides there is given the epithet *ever perfect*. Also the scriptures say that the powers—such as animā and the rest—of the liberated are derived from the search after and the worship of God. Therefore they have no place in the ruling of the universe. Again, on account of their possessing their own minds, it is possible that their wills might differ and that while one desired

to create, another might desire to destroy. The only way of avoiding this conflict is to make all wills subordinate to some one will. Therefore the conclusion
is that the wills of the liberated are dependent on the will of the Supreme
Ruler."

Bhakti, then, can be directed towards Brahman only in Its personal aspect.
"The ideal of the Unmanifest is hard to attain for those who are identified with
their bodies." Bhakti enables us to float on smoothly with the current of our
nature. True it is that we cannot have any idea of Brahman which is not
anthropomorphic; but is it not equally true of everything we know? The greatest
psychologist the world has ever known, Kapila, demonstrated ages ago that
human consciousness is one of the elements in the make-up of all the objects
of our perception and conception, internal as well as external. So we see that,
beginning with our own bodies and going up to Iśvara, every object of our
perception is this consciousness plus something else, whatever that may be.
And this unavoidable mixture is what we ordinarily think of as reality. Indeed
it is, and ever will be, all of reality that it is possible for the human mind to
know. Therefore to say that Iśvara is unreal because He is anthropomorphic
is sheer nonsense. It sounds very much like the Occidental squabble on idealism
and realism, which fearful-looking quarrel has for its foundation a mere play on
the word real. The idea of Iśvara covers all the ground denoted and connoted
by the word real, and Iśvara is as real as anything else in the universe. After all,
the word real means nothing more than what has just been pointed out. Such
is our philosophical conception of Iśvara.

SPIRITUAL REALIZATION: THE
AIM OF BHAKTI-YOGA

To THE BHAKTA these dry details are necessary only to strengthen his will. Beyond that they are of no use to him; for he is treading on a path which is fitted to lead him very soon beyond the hazy and turbulent regions of reason to the realm of realization. He soon, through the mercy of the Lord, reaches a plane where pedantic and powerless reason is left far behind, and the mere intellectual groping through the dark gives place to the daylight of direct perception. He no longer reasons and believes; he almost perceives. He no longer argues; he senses. And is not this seeing God and feeling God and enjoying God higher than everything else? Nay, bhaktas have not been wanting who have maintained that it is higher even than moksha, liberation. And is it not also the highest utility? There are people in the world—and a good many of them too—who are convinced that only that is of use to man which brings him creature comforts. Even religion, God, eternity, the soul—none of these is of any use to them, since they do not bring them money or physical comfort. To such, all those things which do not go to gratify the senses and appease the appetites are of no use. In every mind, utility, however, is conditioned by its own peculiar wants. To men, therefore, who never rise higher than eating, drinking, begetting progeny, and dying, the only gain is in sense enjoyment; and they must wait and go through many more births and reincarnations to learn to feel even the faintest necessity for anything higher. But those to whom the eternal interests of the soul are of much higher value than the fleeting interests of this mundane life, to whom the gratification of the senses is but the thoughtless play of the baby— to them, God and the love of God form the highest and the only utility of human existence. Thank God, there are some such still living in this world of too much worldliness.

Bhakti-yoga, as we have said, is divided into the gauni or preparatory stage, and the parā or supreme stage. We shall find, as we go on, how in the preparatory stage we unavoidably stand in need of many concrete helps to enable us to make progress. And indeed, the mythological and symbolical parts of all religions are natural growths which early environ the aspiring soul and help it Godward. It is also a significant fact that spiritual giants have been produced only in those systems of religion where there is an exuberant growth of rich mythology and ritualism. The dry, fanatical forms of religion, which attempt to eradicate all that is poetical, all that is beautiful and sublime, all that gives a firm grasp to the infant mind tottering on its Godward way—the forms which attempt to break down the very ridge-poles of the spiritual roof, and in their ignorant and superstitious conceptions of truth try to drive away all that is life-giving, all that furnishes the formative material to the spiritual plant growing in the human soul—such forms of religion too soon find that all that is left to them is but an empty shell, a contentless frame of words and sophistry, with perhaps a little flavour of a kind of social scavengering or the so-called spirit of reform.

The vast mass of those whose religion is like this are conscious or unconscious materialists—the aim of their lives here and hereafter being material enjoyment, which, indeed, is to them the alpha and omega of human life. Ishtāpurta —work like street-cleaning and scavengering intended for the material comfort of man—is, according to them, the be-all and end-all of human existence. And the sooner the followers of this curious mixture of ignorance and fanaticism come out in their true colours and join, as they well deserve to do, the ranks of atheists and materialists, the better it will be for the world. One ounce of the practice of righteousness and of spiritual self-realization outweighs tons and tons of frothy talk and nonsensical sentiments. Show us one, but one, gigantic spiritual genius growing out of all this dry dust of ignorance and fanaticism; and if you cannot, close your mouths, open the windows of your hearts to the clear light of truth, and sit like children at the feet of those who know what they are talking about—the sages of India. Let us, then, listen attentively to what they say.

THE NEED OF A GURU

EVERY SOUL IS DESTINED to be perfect, and every being, in the end, will attain the state of perfection. Whatever we are now is the result of our acts and thoughts in the past, and whatever we shall be in the future will be the result of what we think and do now. But this, the shaping of our own destinies, does not preclude our receiving help from outside; nay, in the vast majority of cases such help is absolutely necessary. When it comes, the higher powers and possibilities of the soul are quickened, spiritual life is awakened, growth is animated, and in the end man becomes holy and perfect.

This quickening impulse cannot be derived from books. The soul can receive impulses only from another soul, and from nothing else. We may study books all our lives, we may become very intellectual, but in the end we find that spiritually we have not developed at all. It is not true that a high order of intellectual development always goes hand in hand with a proportionate development of 'the spiritual side in man. In studying books we are sometimes deluded into thinking that thereby we are being spiritually helped; but if we analyse the effect of the study of books on ourselves, we shall find that, at the utmost, it is only our intellect that derives profit from such studies, and not our inner spirit. This inadequacy of books to quicken spiritual growth is the reason why, although almost every one of us can *speak* most wonderfully on spiritual matters, when it comes to action and the *living* of a truly spiritual life, we find ourselves so awfully deficient. To quicken the spirit, the impulse must come from another soul.

The person from whose soul such an impulse comes is called the guru, the teacher; and the person to whose soul the impulse is conveyed is called the śishya, the student. To convey such an impulse to any soul, in the first place, the soul from which it proceeds must possess the power of transmitting it, as it were, to another; and in the second place, the soul to which it is transmitted must be fit to receive it. The seed must be a living seed, and the field must be ready ploughed; and when both these conditions are fulfilled a wonderful growth of genuine religion takes place. "The true preacher of religion has to be of wonderful capabilities, and clever shall his hearer be"; and when both of these are really wonderful and extraordinary, then will result a splendid spiritual awakening, and not otherwise. Such alone are the real teachers, and such alone are also the real students, the real aspirants. All others are only playing with spirituality. They have just a little curiosity awakened, just a little intellectual aspiration kindled in them, and are merely standing on the outward fringe of the horizon of religion. There is, no doubt, some value even in that, since it may, in course of time, result in the awakening of a real thirst for religion; and it is a mysterious law of nature that as soon as the field is ready, the seed must

414

and does come; as soon as the soul earnestly desires to have religion, the transmitter of the religious force must and does appear to help that soul. When the power which attracts the light of religion in the receiving soul is full and strong, the power which answers to that attraction and sends in light does come as a matter of course.

There are, however, certain great dangers in the way. There is, for instance, the danger to the receiving soul of its mistaking momentary emotions for real religious yearning. We may see this in ourselves. Many a time in our lives somebody dies whom we loved. We receive a blow; we feel that the world is slipping between our fingers, that we want something surer and higher, that we must become religious. In a few days that wave of feeling passes away, and we are left stranded exactly where we were before. All of us often mistake such impulses for real thirst after religion; but as long as these momentary emotions are thus mistaken, that continuous, real craving of the soul for religion will not come, and we shall not find the true transmitter of spirituality. So whenever we are tempted to complain that our search after the truth that we desire so much is proving vain—instead of so complaining, our first duty is to look into our own souls and find whether the craving in the heart is real. Then, in the vast majority of cases, it will be discovered that we were not fit to receive the truth, that there was no real thirst for spirituality.

There are still greater dangers in regard to the transmitter, the guru. There are many who, though immersed in ignorance, yet, in the pride of their hearts, fancy they know everything and not only do not stop there, but offer to take others on their shoulders; and thus, the blind leading the blind, both fall into the ditch. "Fools dwelling in darkness, wise in their own conceit and puffed up with vain knowledge, go round and round, staggering to and fro, like blind men led by the blind." (Mundaka Upanishad I. ii. 8.) The world is full of these. Everyone wants to be a teacher; every beggar wants to make a gift of a million dollars! Just as such beggars are ridiculous, so are such teachers.

QUALIFICATIONS OF THE ASPIRANT
AND THE TEACHER

How, THEN, ARE WE TO KNOW a teacher? The sun requires no torch to make it visible; we need not light a candle in order to see it. When the sun rises, we instinctively become aware of the fact, and when a teacher of men comes to help us, the soul will instinctively know that truth has already begun to shine upon it. Truth stands on its own evidence; it does not require any other testimony to demonstrate it. It is self-effulgent. It penetrates into the innermost corners of our nature, and in its presence the whole universe stands up and says, "This is truth." Those teachers whose wisdom and truth shine like the light of the sun are the very greatest the world has known, and they are worshipped as God by the major portion of mankind. But we may get help from comparatively lesser teachers also; only we ourselves do not possess intuition enough to judge properly of the man from whom we receive teaching and guidance. So there ought to be certain tests, certain conditions, for the teacher to satisfy, as also for the taught.

The conditions necessary for the taught are purity, a real thirst after knowledge, and perseverance. No impure soul can be really religious. Purity in thought, speech, and act is absolutely necessary for anyone to be religious. As to the thirst after knowledge, it is an old law that we all get only what we want. None of us can get anything other than what we fix our hearts upon. To pant for religion is truly a very difficult thing; it is not as easy as we generally imagine. Hearing religious talks, reading religious books, is no proof yet of a real want felt in the heart. There must be a continuous struggle, a constant fight, an unremitting grappling with our lower nature, till the higher want is actually felt and the victory is achieved. It is not a question of one or two days, of years, or of lives; the struggle may have to go on for hundreds of lifetimes. Success may sometimes come immediately, but we must be ready to wait patiently even for what may look like an infinite length of time. The student who sets out with such a spirit of perseverance will surely find success and realization at last.

With regard to the teacher, we must see that he knows the spirit of the scriptures. The whole world reads Bibles, Vedas, and Korans; but they are all only words, syntax, etymology, philology—the dry bones of religion. The teacher who deals too much in words and allows the mind to be carried away by the force of words loses the spirit. It is knowledge of the spirit of the scriptures, alone, that characterizes the true religious teacher. The network of the words of the scriptures is like a huge forest, in which the human mind often loses itself and finds no way out. "The network of words is a big forest; it is the cause of aimless wandering of the mind." "The various methods of joining words, the various methods of speaking in beautiful language, the various methods of

416

explaining the diction of the scriptures, are only for the disputations and enjoyment of the learned; they do not conduce to the development of spiritual perception." Those who employ such methods to impart religion to others are only desirous to show off their learning, so that the world may praise them as great scholars. You will find that not one of the great teachers of the world ever went into these various explanations of the texts; there is with them no attempt at "text-torturing," no eternal playing upon the meaning of words and their roots. Yet they taught nobly, while others who have nothing to teach have taken up a word, sometimes, and written a three-volume book on its origin, on the man who used it first, and on what that man was accustomed to eat and how long he slept, and so on.

Bhagavān Ramakrishna used to tell a story about some men who went into a mango orchard and busied themselves in counting the leaves, the twigs, and the branches, examining their colour, comparing their size, and noting down everything most carefully, and who then got up a learned discussion on each of these topics, which were undoubtedly highly interesting to them. But another man, more sensible than they, did not care for all these things and instead began to eat the mangoes. And was he not wise? So leave this counting of leaves and twigs and this note-taking to others. This kind of work has its proper place, but not here in the spiritual domain. You never see a strong spiritual man among these "leaf-counters." Religion, the highest aim, the highest glory of man, does not require so much labour. If you want to be a bhakta, it is not at all necessary for you to know whether Krishna was born in Mathurā or in Vraja, what He did, or the exact date on which He imparted the teachings of the Gītā. You only need to feel the craving for the beautiful lessons about duty and love in the Gītā. All the other particulars about it and its author are for the enjoyment of the learned. Let them have what they desire. Say, "Śāntih, śāntih!" to their learned controversies, and you yourself "eat the mangoes."

The second condition necessary in the teacher is sinlessness. The question is often asked: "Why should we look into the character and personality of a teacher? We have only to judge of what he says and take that up." This is not right. If a man wants to teach me something of dynamics or chemistry or any other physical science, he may be anything he likes, because what the physical sciences require is merely an intellectual equipment; but in the spiritual sciences it is impossible from first to last that there should be any spiritual light in the soul that is impure. What religion can an impure man teach? The *sine qua non* of acquiring spiritual truth for oneself, or for imparting it to others, is purity of heart and soul. A vision of God or a glimpse of the beyond never comes until the soul is pure. Hence, with the teacher of religion, we must see first what he *is* and then what he says. He must be perfectly pure, and then alone will his words come to have value, because he is only then a true transmitter. What can he transmit if he has no spiritual power in himself? There must be a worthy vibration of spirituality in the mind of the teacher so that it may be sympathetically conveyed to the mind of the taught. The function of the teacher is indeed an affair of the transference of something, and not one of mere stimulation of the existing intellectual or other faculties in the taught. Something real and appreciable as an influence comes from the teacher and goes to the taught. Therefore the teacher must be pure.

The third condition is with regard to the motive. The teacher must not teach with any ulterior, selfish motive—for money, name, or fame; his work must be simply out of love, out of pure love for mankind at large. The only medium through which spiritual force can be transmitted is love. Any selfish motive, such as the desire for gain or for name, will immediately destroy this conveying medium. God is love, and only he who has known God as love can be a teacher of godliness and God to man.

When you see that in your teacher these conditions are all fulfilled, you are safe. If they are not, it is unsafe to allow yourself to be taught by him; for there is the great danger that, if he cannot convey goodness to your heart, he may convey wickedness. This danger must by all means be guarded against. "He who is learned in the scriptures, sinless, unpolluted by lust, and is the greatest knower of Brahman" is the real teacher.

From what has been said, it naturally follows that we cannot be taught to love, appreciate, and assimilate religion everywhere, by everybody. "Sermons in stones, books in the running brooks, and good in everything"—is all very true as a poetical figure; but nothing can impart to a man a single grain of truth unless he has the undeveloped germ of it in himself. To whom do the stones and brooks preach sermons? To that human soul the lotus of whose holy inner shrine is already about to open. And the light which causes the beautiful opening of this lotus comes always from the good and wise teacher. When the heart has thus been opened, it becomes fit to receive teaching from the stones or the brooks, the stars or the sun or the moon, or from anything that exists in our divine universe; but the unopened heart will see in them nothing but mere stones or mere brooks. A blind man may go to a museum, but he will not profit by it in any way; his eyes must be opened first, and then alone will he be able to learn what the things in the museum can teach.

This eye-opener of the aspirant after religion is the teacher. With the teacher, therefore, our relationship is the same as that between a descendant and his ancestor. Without faith, humility, submission, and veneration in our hearts towards our religious teacher, there cannot be any growth of religion in us. It is a significant fact that where this kind of relation between the teacher and the taught prevails, there alone do gigantic spiritual men grow, while in those countries which have neglected to keep up this kind of relation, the religious teacher has become a mere lecturer—the teacher expecting his five dollars and the person taught expecting his brain to be filled with the teacher's words, and each going his own way after this much has been done. Under such circumstances spirituality becomes almost an unknown quantity. There is none to transmit it and none to have it transmitted to. Religion with such people becomes a business; they think they can obtain it with their dollars. Would to God that religion could be obtained so easily! But unfortunately it cannot be.

Religion, which is the highest knowledge and the highest wisdom, cannot be bought, nor can it be acquired from books. You may thrust your head into all the corners of the world, you may explore the Himālayas, the Alps, and the

Caucasus, you may sound the bottom of the sea and pry into every nook of Tibet and the desert of Gobi, but you will not find it anywhere until your heart is ready to receive it and your teacher has come. And when that divinely appointed teacher comes, serve him with childlike confidence and simplicity, freely open your heart to his influence, and see in him God manifested. Those who come to seek the truth with such a spirit of love and veneration—to them the Lord of Truth reveals the most wonderful things regarding truth, goodness, and beauty.

INCARNATIONS

Wherever His name is spoken, that very place is holy. How much more so is the man who speaks His name, and with what veneration ought we to approach that man out of whom comes to us spiritual truth! Such great teachers of spiritual truth are indeed very few in number in this world; but the world is never altogether without them. They are always the fairest flowers of human life—"an ocean of mercy without any motive." "Know the guru to be Me," says Śri Krishna in the *Bhāgavata*. The moment the world is absolutely bereft of these, it becomes a hideous hell and hastens on to its destruction.

Higher and nobler than all ordinary teachers in the world is another set of teachers, the Avatāras of Iśvara. They can transmit spirituality with a touch, even with a mere wish. At their command the lowest and most degraded characters become saints in one second. They are the Teachers of all teachers, the highest manifestations of God through man. We cannot see God except through them. We cannot help worshipping them. And indeed they are the only ones whom we are bound to worship.

No man can really see God except through these human manifestations. If we try to see God otherwise, we make for ourselves a hideous caricature of Him and believe the caricature to be as good as the original. There is a story of an ignorant man who was asked to make an image of the god Śiva, and who, after days of hard struggle, manufactured only the image of a monkey. So whenever we try to think of God as He is in His absolute perfection, we invariably meet with the most miserable failure; because as long as we are men we cannot conceive Him as being anything higher than a man. The time will come when we shall transcend our human nature and know Him as He is; but as long as we are men we must worship Him in man and as a man.

Talk as you may, try as you may, you cannot think of God except as a man. You may deliver great intellectual discourses on God and on all things under the sun, become great rationalists, and prove to your satisfaction that all these accounts of the Avatāras of God as men are nonsense. But let us come for a moment to practical common sense. What is there behind this kind of remarkable intellect? Zero, nothing, simply so much froth. When next you hear a man delivering a great intellectual lecture against this worship of the Avatāras of God, get hold of him and ask him what *his* idea of God is, what he understands by "omnipotence," "omnipresence," and all such terms, beyond the spelling of the words. He really means nothing by them; he cannot formulate as their meaning any idea unaffected by his own human nature. He is no better off in this matter than the man in the street who has not read a single book. That man in the street, however, is quiet and does not disturb the peace of the world, while this big talker creates disturbance and misery among mankind. Religion is, after all, realization, and we must make the sharpest distinction between

talk and intuitive experience. What we experience in the depths of our souls
is realization. Nothing indeed is so uncommon as common sense in regard to
this matter.

By our present constitution we are limited and bound to see God as a man. If,
for instance, the buffaloes want to worship God, they will, in keeping with their
own nature, see Him as a huge buffalo; if the fish want to worship God, they
will have to form an idea of Him as a big fish; and men have to think of Him
as a man. And these various conceptions are not due to a morbidly active imagination. Man, buffalo, and fish all may be supposed to represent so many different
vessels, so to say. All these vessels go to the sea of God to get filled with water,
each according to its own shape and capacity. In the man, the water takes
the shape of a man, in the buffalo, the shape of a buffalo, and in the fish, the
shape of a fish. In each of these vessels there is the same water of the sea of
God. When men see Him, they see Him as a man, and the animals, if they have
any conception of God at all, must see Him as an animal, each according to his
own ideal. So we cannot help seeing God as a man; and therefore we are bound
to worship Him as a man. There is no other way.

Two kinds of men do not worship God as a man: the human brute, who has
no religion, and the paramahamsa, who has risen beyond all the weaknesses of
humanity and has transcended the limits of his own human nature. To him
all nature has become his own Self. He alone can worship God as He is. Here
too, as in all other cases, the two extremes meet. The extreme of ignorance and
the other extreme of knowledge—neither of these goes through acts of worship.
The human brute does not worship because of his ignorance, and the jivanmuktas, the free souls, do not worship because they have realized God in themselves. If anyone between these two poles of existence tells you that he is not
going to worship God as a man, kindly beware of that person. He is, not to use
any harsher term, an irresponsible talker; his religion is for unsound and empty
brains.

God understands human failings and becomes man to do good to humanity.
"Whenever virtue subsides and wickedness prevails I manifest Myself. To establish virtue, to destroy evil, to save the good, I embody Myself in every yuga."
"Fools deride Me who have assumed the human form, without knowing My
real nature as the Lord of the universe." Such is Śri Krishna's declaration, in the
Gitā, on the Incarnation. "When a huge tidal wave comes," says Bhagavān Śri
Ramakrishna, "all the little brooks and ditches become full to the brim without any effort or consciousness on their own part; so when an Incarnation
comes, a tidal wave of spirituality breaks upon the world, and people feel spirituality in the very air."

THE MANTRA: OM

But we are now considering not these Mahāpurushas, the great Incarnations, but only the siddha-gurus, the teachers who have attained the goal. They, as a rule, have to convey the germs of spiritual wisdom to the disciple by means of mantras, or words to be meditated upon. What are these mantras?

The whole of this universe has, according to Indian philosophy, both name and form as its conditions of manifestation. In the human microcosm there cannot be a single wave in the mind-stuff which is not conditioned by name and form. If it be true that nature is built throughout on the same plan, this kind of conditioning by name and form must also be the plan of the building of the whole of the cosmos. "As, one lump of clay being known, all things of clay are known," so the knowledge of the microcosm must lead to the knowledge of the macrocosm. Now, the form is the outer crust, and the name or the idea is the inner essence or kernel. The body is the form, and the mind, or antahkarana, is the name; and sound-symbols are universally associated with the names in all beings having the power of speech. In the individual man the thought-waves rising in the limited mahat, known as the chitta or mind-stuff, must manifest themselves first as words and then as the more concrete forms.

In the universe, Brahmā (Hiranyagarbha or the cosmic mahat) first manifested Himself as name and then as form, that is to say, as this universe. All this expressed, sensible universe is the form, and behind it stands the eternal, inexpressible Sphota, the manifester, as Logos or Word. This eternal Sphota, the essential and eternal material of all ideas or names, is the power through which the Lord creates the universe. Nay, the Lord first becomes conditioned as the Sphota and then evolves Himself as the yet more concrete sensible universe. This Sphota has one word as its only possible symbol, and this is Om. And as we can by no possible means of analysis separate the word from the idea, Om and the eternal Sphota are inseparable; and therefore it is out of this holiest of all holy words, the mother of all names and forms, the eternal Om, that the whole universe may be supposed to have been created.

But it may be said that, although thought and word are inseparable, yet as there may be various word-symbols for the same thought, it is not necessary that this particular word Om should be the word representative of the thought out of which the universe has become manifested. To this objection we reply that this Om is the only possible symbol which covers the whole ground, and there is none other like it. The Sphota is the material of all words; yet it is not any definite word in its fully formed state. That is to say, if all the peculiarities which distinguish one word from another be removed, then what remains will be the Sphota. Therefore this Sphota is called the Nāda-Brahman, the Sound-Brahman. Now, as every word-symbol intended to express the inexpressible Sphota will so particularize it that it will no longer be the Sphota, that symbol which particularizes it the least and at the same time most approximately expresses its nature will be the truest symbol thereof. This is Om, and Om only, because these three letters—A, U, M—pronounced in combination as Om, may well be the generalized symbol of all possible sounds. The letter A is the least differentiated of all sounds; therefore Krishna says in the Gītā, "I am A among the letters." Again, all articulate sounds are produced in the space within the mouth, beginning with the root of the tongue and ending in the lips. The throat sound is A, and M is the last lip sound, and U exactly represents the rolling forward of the impulse, which begins at the root of the tongue and ends in the lips. If properly pronounced, this Om will represent the whole phenomenon of sound-production; and no other word can do this. This, therefore, is the fittest symbol of the Sphota, which is the real meaning of Om. And as the symbol can never be separated from the thing signified, Om and the Sphota are one. Furthermore, as the Sphota, being the finer side of the manifested universe, is nearer to God and is indeed the first manifestation of Divine Wisdom, this Om is the true symbol of God.

Again, just as the non-dual Brahman, the Akhanda Satchidānanda, the undivided Existence-Knowledge-Bliss, can be conceived by imperfect human souls only from particular standpoints and associated with particular qualities, so this universe, Its body, has also to be thought of according to the particular trend of the thinker's mind. This direction of the worshipper's mind is guided by its prevailing elements, or tattvas. As a result, the same Reality will be seen in various manifestations as the possessor of various predominant qualities, and the same universe will appear full of manifold forms. Even as in the case of the least differentiated and most universal symbol Om, thought and sound-symbol are seen to be inseparably associated with each other, so also this law of their inseparable association applies to the many differentiated views of God and the universe. Each of them, therefore, must have a particular word-symbol to express it. These word-symbols, evolved out of the deepest spiritual perceptions of sages, symbolize and express as nearly as possible the particular view of God and the universe they stand for. As Om represents the Akhanda, the undifferentiated Brahman, so the others represent the khanda or differentiated views of the same Being; and they are all helpful to divine meditation and the acquisition of true knowledge.

WORSHIP OF SUBSTITUTES AND IMAGES

THE NEXT POINTS to be considered are the worship of pratikas, or things more or less satisfactory as substitutes for God, and the worship of pratimās, or images. What is the worship of God through a pratika? It means "joining the mind with devotion to what is not Brahman, taking it to be Brahman," says Bhagavān Rāmānuja. Śankara says, "Worship of the mind as Brahman—this is worship with regard to the internal; and of the ākāśa as Brahman—this is with regard to the gods." The mind is an internal pratika; ākāśa is an external one; and both have to be worshipped as substitutes for God. Similarly: " 'The sun is Brahman; this is the command'; 'He who worships name as Brahman'—in all such passages a doubt arises as to the worship of pratikas," says Śankara. The word *pratika* means "going towards"; and worshipping a pratika means worshipping, as a substitute, something which is, in one or more respects, like Brahman, but is not Brahman. Along with the pratikas mentioned in Śruti there are various others to be found in the Purānas and the Tantras. In this kind of pratika-worship may be included all the various forms of pitri-worship and deva-worship.

Now, worshipping Iśvara, and Him alone, is bhakti; the worship of anything else—deva or pitri or any other being—cannot be bhakti. The various kinds of worship of the various devas are all included in ritualistic karma, which gives to the worshipper only a particular result in the form of some celestial enjoyment, but can neither give rise to bhakti nor lead to mukti. One thing therefore has to be carefully borne in mind. If, as it may happen in some cases, the highly philosophic ideal, the Supreme Brahman, is dragged down by pratika-worship to the level of the pratika and the pratika itself is taken to be the Ātman of the worshipper, his Antaryāmin, then the worshipper becomes entirely misled; for no pratika can really be the Ātman of the worshipper. But where Brahman Himself is the object of worship, and the pratika stands only as a substitute or a suggestion thereof, that is to say, where, through the pratika, the omnipresent Brahman is worshipped, the pratika itself being idealized into the cause of all, or Brahman—the worship is positively beneficial. Nay, it is absolutely necessary for all mankind until they have got beyond the primary or preparatory state of the mind with regard to worship.

When, therefore, any gods or other beings are worshipped in and for themselves, such worship is only ritualistic karma; and as a vidyā, a science, it gives us only the fruit belonging to that particular vidyā. But when the devas or any other beings are looked upon as Brahman and worshipped, the result obtained is the same as that obtained by the worshipping of Iśvara.

This explains how in many cases, both in the Śrutis and in the Smritis, a god or a sage or some other extraordinary being is taken up and lifted, as it were, out of his own nature and idealized into Brahman, and is then worshipped. Says the Advaitist, "Is not everything Brahman when the name and the form have been removed from it?" "Is not He, the Lord, the innermost Self of everyone?" says the Viśishtādvaitist. "The fruition of even the worship of the Ādityas, and so forth, Brahman Himself bestows, because He is the Ruler of all." Says Śankara, in his *Brahma Sutra* Bhāshya: "Here, in this way, Brahman becomes the object of worship, because He, as Brahman, is superimposed on the pratikas, just as Vishnu, and so forth, are superimposed upon images."

The same ideas apply to the worship of the pratimās as to that of the pratikas. That is to say, if the image stands for a god or a saint, the worship does not result in bhakti and does not lead to liberation; but if it stands for the one God, the worship thereof will bring both bhakti and mukti. Of the principal religions of the world, we see Vedānta, Buddhism, and certain forms of Christianity freely using images; only two religions, Mohammedanism and Protestantism, refuse such help. Yet the Mohammedans use the graves of their saints and martyrs almost in the place of images; and the Protestants, in rejecting all concrete helps to religion, are drifting away every year farther and farther from spirituality, till at present there is scarcely any difference between the advanced Protestants and the followers of Auguste Comte, or the agnostics, who preach ethics alone. Again, in Christianity and Mohammedanism whatever exists of image worship is made to fall under that category in which the pratika or the pratimā is worshipped in itself, but not as a help to the vision of God. Therefore it is at best only of the nature of ritualistic karma and cannot produce either bhakti or mukti. In this form of image worship, the allegiance of the soul is given to other things than Iśvara, and therefore such use of images or graves, of temples or tombs, is real idolatry. It is in itself neither sinful nor wicked. It is a rite, a karma, and worshippers must and will get the fruit thereof.

THE CHOSEN IDEAL

THE NEXT THING to be considered is what we know as Ishta-nishthā, or devotion to the "Chosen Ideal."

One who aspires to be a bhakta must know that "so many opinions are so many ways." He must know that all the various sects of the different religions are the various manifestations of the glory of the same Lord. "They call You by so many names; they divide You, as it were, by different names; yet in each one of these is to be found Your omnipotence. . . . You reach the worshipper through all of these; there is no special time for Your worship so long as the soul has intense love for You. You are so easy of approach; it is my misfortune that I cannot love You." Not only this. The bhakta must take care not to hate, or even criticize, those radiant sons of light who are the founders of various sects; he must not even hear them spoken ill of.

Very few, indeed, are those who are at once the possessors of an extensive sympathy and power of appreciation as well as of an intense love. We find, as a rule, that liberal and sympathetic sects lose the intensity of religious feeling, and in their hands religion is likely to degenerate into a kind of politico-social club life. On the other hand, intensely narrow sectarians, while displaying a very commendable love for their own ideals, are seen to have acquired every particle of that love by hating everyone who is not of exactly the same opinion as themselves. Would to God that this world were full of men who were as intense in their love as they were world-wide in their sympathies! But such are few and far between. Yet we know that it is practicable to educate large numbers of human beings in the ideal of a wonderful blending of both the breadth and the intensity of love; and the way to do that is by this path of Ishta-nishthā.

Every sect of every religion presents only one ideal of its own to mankind; but the eternal Vedāntic religion opens to mankind an infinite number of doors for ingress into the inner shrine of Divinity, and places before humanity an almost inexhaustible array of ideals, there being in each of them a manifestation of the Eternal One. With the kindest solicitude Vedānta points out to aspiring men and women the numerous roads hewn out of the solid rock of the realities of human life by the glorious sons, or human manifestations, of God in the past and in the present, and stands with outstretched arms to welcome all—to welcome even those that are yet to be—to that Home of Truth and that Ocean of Bliss wherein the human soul, liberated from the net of māyā, may transport itself with perfect freedom and with eternal joy.

Bhakti-yoga, therefore, lays on us the imperative command not to hate or deny any one of the various paths that lead to salvation. Yet the growing plant must be hedged round to protect it until it has grown into a tree. The tender plant of spirituality will die if exposed too early to the action of a constant change of ideas and ideals. Many people, in the name of what may be called religious liberalism, may be seen feeding their idle curiosity with a continuous succession of different ideals. With them, hearing new things grows into a kind of disease, a sort of religious drink-mania. They want to hear new things just by way of getting a temporary nervous excitement, and when one such exciting influence has had its effect on them, they are ready for another. Religion is with these people a sort of intellectual opium-eating, and there it ends. "There is another sort of man," says Bhagavān Ramakrishna, "who is like the pearl-oyster of the story. The pearl-oyster leaves its bed at the bottom of the sea and comes up to the surface to catch the rain-water when the star Svāti is in the ascendant. It floats about on the surface of the sea with its shell wide open until it has succeeded in catching a drop of the rain-water, and then it dives deep down to its sea-bed and there rests until it has succeeded in fashioning a beautiful pearl out of that raindrop." This is indeed the most poetical and forcible way in which the theory of Ishta-nishthā has ever been put.

Eka-nishthā, or devotion to one ideal, is absolutely necessary for the beginner in the practice of religious devotion. He must say with Hanumān in the Rāmāyana: "Though I know that the Lord of Śri and the Lord of Jānaki[1] are both manifestations of the same Supreme Being, yet my All in all is the lotus-eyed Rāma." Or, as was said by the sage Tulsidās: "Take the sweetness of all, sit with all, take the name of all, say yea, yea—but keep your seat firm." Then, if the devotional aspirant is sincere, out of this little seed will come a gigantic tree, like the Indian banyan, sending out branch after branch and root after root to all sides, till it covers the entire field of religion. Thus will the true devotee realize that He who was his own ideal in life is worshipped in all ideals, by all sects, under all names, and through all forms.

[1] Referring to Vishnu and Rāma respectively.

HOW TO CULTIVATE BHAKTI

With regard to the method and the means of bhakti-yoga we read in the commentary of Bhagavān Rāmānuja on the *Vedānta Sutras:* "The attaining of bhakti comes through discrimination, controlling the passions, practice, sacrificial work, purity, strength, and suppression of excessive joy." Viveka, or discrimination, is, according to Rāmānuja, discriminating, among other things, pure food from impure. According to him, food becomes impure for three reasons: (1) from the nature of the food itself, as with garlic and so forth, (2) from its coming from wicked and accursed persons, and (3) from physical impurities, such as dirt or hair and the like. Śruti says: "When the food is pure the sattva element gets purified and the memory becomes unwavering"; and Rāmānuja quotes this from the *Chhāndogya Upanishad.*

The question of food has always been one of the most vital questions with the bhaktas. Apart from the extravagance into which some of the bhakti sects have run, there is a great truth underlying this question of food. We must remember that, according to the Sāmkhya philosophy, sattva, rajas, and tamas, which in the state of equilibrium form the undifferentiated prakriti, and in the disturbed condition form the visible universe, are both the substance and the qualities of prakriti. As such they are the materials out of which every human form has been manufactured. And the predominance of sattva material is what is absolutely necessary for spiritual development. The materials which we receive through food into our body structure go a great way to determine our mental constitution; therefore the food we eat has to be particularly taken care of. In this matter as in others, however, the fanaticism into which the disciples invariably fall is not to be laid at the door of the masters.

And this discrimination of food is, after all, of secondary importance. The very same passage quoted above is explained by Śankara in his Bhāshya on the Upanishad in a different way, by giving an entirely different meaning to the word āhāra, generally translated as "food." According to him: "That which is gathered in is āhāra. The knowledge of the various sensations, such as sound and the rest, is gathered in for the enjoyment of the embodied self; the purification of this knowledge received through sense perception is called the purification of the food (āhāra). The purification of the food means the acquiring of the knowledge of sensations untouched by the defects of attachment, aversion, and delusion. Therefore such knowledge, or āhāra, being purified, the sattva material of its possessor—the internal organ—will become purified, and the sattva being purified, an unbroken memory of the Infinite One, who has been known in His real nature from the scriptures, will result."

These two explanations are apparently conflicting; yet both are true and necessary. The manipulating and controlling of what may be called the finer body, that is to say, the mind, are no doubt higher functions than the controlling of the grosser body of flesh. But the control of the grosser is absolutely necessary to enable one to arrive at the control of the finer. The beginner, therefore, must pay particular attention to all such dietetic rules as have come down from the line of the accredited teachers. But the extravagant, meaningless fanaticism which has driven religion entirely to the kitchen, as may be noticed in many of our sects—without any hope that the noble truth of that religion will ever come out into the sunlight of spirituality—is a peculiar sort of pure and simple materialism. It is neither jnāna nor bhakti nor karma; it is a special kind of lunacy, and those who pin their souls to it are more likely to go to lunatic asylums than to Brahmaloka. So it stands to reason that discrimination in the choice of food is necessary for the attainment of this higher state of mind, which cannot be easily obtained otherwise.

Controlling the passions is the next thing to be attended to. To restrain the indriyas, or organs, from going towards the objects of the senses, to control them and bring them under the guidance of the will, is the very central virtue in religious culture. Then comes the practice of self-restraint and self-denial. The immense possibilities of divine realization in the soul cannot become actualized without struggle and without such practice on the part of the aspiring devotee. "The mind must always think of the Lord." It is very hard at first to compel the mind to think of the Lord always; but with every new effort the power to do so grows stronger in us. "By practice, O son of Kunti, and by non-attachment is yoga attained," says Śri Krishna in the Gitā. And then as to sacrificial work, it is understood that the "five great sacrifices"[1] have to be performed as usual.

Purity is absolutely the basic discipline, the bedrock upon which the building of bhakti rests. Cleansing the external body and discriminating about food are both easy, but without internal cleanliness and purity these external observances are of no value whatsoever. In the list of the qualities conducive to purity, as given by Rāmānuja, there are enumerated satya, truthfulness; ārjava, sincerity; dayā, doing good to others without any gain to oneself; ahimsā, not injuring others by thought, word, or deed; anabhidhyā, not coveting others' goods, not thinking vain thoughts, and not brooding over injuries received from another.

In this list, the one idea that deserves special notice is ahimsā, non-injury to others. This duty of non-injury is, so to say, obligatory on us in relation to all beings. It does not simply mean, as with some, the non-injuring of human beings and mercilessness towards the lower animals; nor does it mean, as with

[1] Every householder commits inevitably the fivefold sin of killing, which results from the use of the pestle and mortar, the grinding-stone, the oven, the water-jar, and the broom. He is absolved from this sin by the performance of the five obligatory duties known as yajna, or sacrifice. The five sacrifices are: devayajna (the offering of sacrifices to the gods), brahmayajna (the teaching and reciting of the scriptures), pitriyajna (the offering of libations of water to the ancestors), nriyajna (the feeding of the hungry), and bhutayajna (the feeding of the lower animals). The performance of these five daily sacrifices, or duties, spiritualizes life and establishes concord and harmony between the living and the dead, as well as between the superhuman, human, and subhuman worlds. The selfish life is transformed into an unselfish one. The individual becomes aware of the interdependence of all beings.

some others, the protecting of cats and dogs and the feeding of ants with sugar, with liberty to injure brother man in every possible way. It is remarkable that almost every good idea in this world can be carried to a disgusting extreme. A good practice carried to an extreme and worked out according to the letter of the law becomes a positive evil. The stinking monks of certain religious sects, who do not bathe lest the vermin on their bodies should be killed, never think of the discomfort and disease they bring to their fellow human beings. They do not, however, belong to the religion of the Vedas.

The test of ahimsā is absence of jealousy. Any man may do a good deed, or make a good gift on the spur of the moment or under the pressure of some superstition or priestcraft; but the real lover of mankind is he who is jealous of none. The so-called great men of the world are seen to become jealous of each other for a small name, for a little fame, and for a few bits of gold. So long as this jealousy exists in a heart, it is far away from the perfection of ahimsā. The cow does not eat meat, nor does the sheep. Are they great yogis, great non-injurers? Any fool may abstain from eating this or that; surely that gives him no more distinction than the herbivorous animals. The man who will mercilessly cheat widows and orphans, and do the vilest deeds for money, is worse than any brute, even if he lives entirely on grass. The man whose heart never cherishes even the thought of injury to anyone, who rejoices at the prosperity of even his greatest enemy—that man is a bhakta, he is a yogi, he is the guru of all, even though he lives every day of his life on the flesh of swine.

Therefore we must always remember that external practices have value only as they help to develop internal purity. It is better to have internal purity alone, when minute attention to external observances is not practicable. But woe unto the man and woe unto the nation that forgets the real, internal, spiritual essentials of religion and mechanically clutches with death-like grasp all external forms and never lets them go! The forms have value only so far as they are the expressions of the life within. If they have ceased to express life, crush them out without mercy.

The next means to the attainment of bhakti is strength, or anavasāda. "This Ātman is not to be attained by the weak," says Śruti. Both physical weakness and mental weakness are meant here. "The strong, the hardy," are the only fit students. What can puny little decrepit things do? They will break to pieces whenever the mysterious forces of the body and mind are even slightly awakened by the practice of any of the yogas. It is "the young, the healthy, the strong," that can score success. Physical strength, therefore, is absolutely necessary. It is the strong body alone that can bear the shock of the reaction resulting from the attempt to control the organs. He who wants to become a bhakta must be strong, must be healthy. When the miserably weak attempt any of the yogas, they are likely to get some incurable malady or weaken their minds. Voluntarily weakening the body is really no prescription for spiritual enlightenment.

The mentally weak also cannot succeed in attaining Ātman. The person who aspires to be a bhakta must be cheerful. In the Western world the idea of a religious man is that he never smiles, that a dark cloud must always hang over his face, which, again, must be long-drawn, with the jaws almost collapsed. People with emaciated bodies and long faces are fit subjects for the physician;

they are not yogis. It is the cheerful mind that can persevere. It is the strong mind that hews its way through a thousand difficulties. And this, the hardest task of all, the cutting of our way out of the net of māyā, is the work reserved only for giant wills.

Yet at the same time excessive mirth, or anuddharsha, should be avoided. Excessive mirth makes us unfit for serious thought. It also fritters away the energies of the mind in vain. The stronger the will, the less the yielding to the sway of the emotions. Excessive hilarity is quite as objectionable as too much of sad seriousness. Religious realization is possible only when the mind is in a steady, peaceful condition of harmonious equilibrium.

It is thus that one may begin to learn how to love the Lord.

THE PREPARATORY RENUNCIATION

WE HAVE FINISHED the consideration of what may be called the preparatory bhakti and shall now enter on the study of parā-bhakti, or supreme devotion. We have to speak of the preparations for the practice of this parā-bhakti. All such preparations are intended only for the purification of the soul. The repetition of names, the rituals, the forms, and the symbols—all these various things are for the purification of the soul.

The greatest purifier among all such things, a purifier without which no one can enter the regions of the higher devotion, is renunciation. This frightens many; yet without it there cannot be any spiritual growth. In all the yogas renunciation is necessary. This is the stepping-stone and the real centre, the real heart, of all spiritual culture—renunciation. This is religion—renunciation. When the human soul draws back from the things of the world and tries to go into deeper things; when man, the Spirit, which has here somehow become concretized and materialized, understands that he is going to be destroyed and reduced almost to mere matter, and turns his face away from matter—then begins renunciation, then begins real spiritual growth.

The karma-yogi's renunciation takes the shape of giving up all the fruits of his actions. He is not attached to the results of his labours; he does not care for any reward here or hereafter. The rāja-yogi knows that the whole of nature is intended as a means for the soul to acquire experience, and that the result of all the experiences of the soul is that it becomes aware of its eternal separateness from nature. The human soul has to understand and realize that it has been Spirit, and not matter, through eternity, and that this conjunction of it with matter is and can be only for a time. The rāja-yogi learns the lesson of renunciation through his own experience of nature. The jnāna-yogi has the harshest of all renunciations to go through, for he has to realize from the very first that the whole of this solid-looking nature is an illusion. He has to understand that any kind of manifestation of power in external nature belongs to the soul and not to nature. He has to know, from the very start, that all knowledge and all experience are in the soul and not in nature; so he has at once and by the sheer force of rational conviction to tear himself away from all bondage to nature. He lets nature and all that belongs to it go; he lets them vanish and tries to stand alone.

Of all renunciations, the most natural, so to say, is that of the bhakti-yogi. Here there is no violence, nothing to give up, nothing to tear off, as it were, from ourselves, nothing from which we have to separate ourselves violently. The bhakta's renunciation is easy, smooth-flowing, and as natural as the things around us. We see the manifestation of this sort of renunciation, although more or less in the form of caricatures, every day around us. A man begins to love a woman; after a while he loves another, and he lets the first woman go. She drops out of his mind smoothly, gently, without his feeling the want of her at all. A woman loves a man; she then begins to love another man, and the first one drops out of her mind quite naturally. A man loves his own city; then he begins to love his country, and the intense love for his little city drops off smoothly, naturally. Again, a man learns to love the whole world; his love for his country, his intense, fanatical patriotism, drops off without hurting him, without any manifestation of violence. An uncultured man loves the pleasures of the senses intensely; as he becomes cultured, he begins to love intellectual pleasures, and his sense enjoyments become less and less intense. No man can enjoy a meal with the same gusto or pleasure as does a dog or a wolf; but those pleasures which a man gets from intellectual experiences and achievements, the dog can never enjoy.

At first, pleasure is associated with the lower sense-organs; but as soon as an animal reaches a higher plane of existence, the lower pleasure becomes less intense. In human society, the nearer a man is to the animal, the stronger is his pleasure in the senses; and the higher and the more cultured a man is, the greater is his pleasure in intellectual and other such finer pursuits. So, when a man goes even higher than the plane of the intellect, higher than that of mere thought, when he reaches the plane of spirituality and of divine inspiration, he finds there a state of bliss compared with which all the pleasures of the senses, or even of the intellect, are as nothing. When the moon shines brightly all the stars become dim, and when the sun shines the moon itself becomes dim. The renunciation necessary for the attainment of bhakti is not obtained by killing anything; it comes naturally, just as, in the presence of an increasingly stronger light, less intense lights become dimmer and dimmer until they vanish away completely.

So this love of the pleasures of the senses and of the intellect is all made dim and thrown aside and cast into the shade by the love of God Himself. That love of God grows and assumes a form called parā-bhakti, or supreme devotion. Forms vanish, rituals fly away, books are superseded; images, temples, churches, religions and sects, countries and nationalities—all these little limitations and bondages fall away naturally from him who knows this love of God. Nothing remains to bind him or fetter his freedom. A ship all of a sudden comes near a magnetic rock, and its iron bolts and bars are all attracted and drawn out, and the planks are loosened and float freely on the water. Divine grace thus loosens the binding bolts and bars of the soul, and it becomes free. So in this renunciation auxiliary to devotion there is no harshness, no dryness, no struggle, no repression or suppression. The bhakta has not to suppress any single one of his emotions; he only strives to intensify them and direct them to God.

THE BHAKTA'S RENUNCIATION
RESULTS FROM LOVE

WE SEE LOVE everywhere in nature. Whatever in society is good and great and sublime is the working out of that love; whatever in society is very bad, nay, diabolical, is also the ill-directed working out of the same emotion of love. It is this same emotion that gives us not only the pure and holy conjugal love between husband and wife, but also the sort of love which goes to satisfy the lowest forms of animal passion. The emotion is the same, but its manifestation is different in different cases. It is the same feeling of love, well or ill directed, that impels one man to do good and to give all he has to the poor, and makes another man cut the throats of his brethren and take away all their possessions. The former loves others as much as the latter loves himself. The direction of the love is bad in the latter case, but is right and proper in the other. The same fire that cooks a meal for us may burn a child, and it is no fault of the fire if it does so; the difference lies in the way in which it is used. Therefore love—the intense longing for association, the strong desire on the part of two to become one, and, it may be after all, of all to become merged in one—is being manifested everywhere in higher or lower forms as the case may be.

Bhakti-yoga is the science of higher love. It shows us how to direct it; it shows us how to control it, how to manage it, how to use it, how to give it a new aim, as it were, and from it obtain the highest and most glorious results, that is, how to make it lead us to spiritual blessedness. Bhakti-yoga does not say, "Give up"; it only says, "Love—love the Highest." And everything low naturally falls away from him, the object of whose love is this Highest.

"I cannot tell anything about Thee except that Thou art my love. Thou art beautiful—oh, Thou art beautiful! Thou art beauty itself." What is really required of us in this yoga is that our thirst after the beautiful should be directed to God. What is the beauty in the human face, in the sky, in the stars, and in the moon? It is only the partial manifestation of the real, all-embracing Divine Beauty. "He shining, everything shines. It is through His light that all things shine." Take this high position of bhakti, which makes you forget at once all your little personalities. Take yourself away from all the world's little selfish clingings. Do not look upon humanity as the centre of all your human or higher interests. Stand as a witness, and observe and study the phenomena of nature. Have the feeling of non-attachment with regard to man, and see how this mighty feeling of love is working itself out in the world. Sometimes a little friction is produced, but that is only in the course of the struggle to attain the higher, real love. Sometimes there is a little fight or a little fall; but it is all only by the way. Stand aside and freely let these frictions come. You feel the frictions only when you are in the current of the world;

434

but when you are outside it, simply as a witness and as a student, you will be able to see that there are millions and millions of channels through which God is manifesting Himself as love.

"Wherever there is any bliss, even though it is of the most sensual kind, there is a spark of that Eternal Bliss which is the Lord Himself." Even in the lowest kinds of attraction there is the germ of divine love. One of the names of the Lord, in Sanskrit, is Hari, and this means "He who attracts all things to Himself." His is in fact the only attraction felt by human hearts. Who can really attract a soul? Only He. Do you think dead matter can truly attract the soul? It never did and never will. When you see a man going after a beautiful face, do you think it is the handful of arranged material molecules which really attracts the man? Not at all. Behind those material particles there must be and is the play of divine influence and divine love. The ignorant man does not know it; but yet, consciously or unconsciously, he is attracted by it and it alone. So even the lowest forms of attraction derive their power from God Himself. "None, O beloved, ever loves the husband for the husband's sake; it is the Ātman, the Lord who is within, for whose sake the husband is loved." Loving wives may know this or they may not; it is true all the same. "None, O beloved, ever loves the wife for the wife's sake; but it is the Self in the wife that is loved." Similarly, no one loves a child or anything else in the world except on account of Him who is within. The Lord is the great magnet, and we are all like iron filings; we are being constantly attracted by Him, and all of us are struggling to reach Him. All this struggling of ours in this world is surely not intended for selfish ends. Fools do not know what they are doing: the goal of their life is, after all, to approach the great magnet. All the tremendous struggling and fighting in life is intended to make us ultimately go to Him and be one with Him.

The bhakti-yogi, however, knows the meaning of life's struggles; he understands it. He has passed through a long series of these struggles and knows what they mean, and earnestly desires to be free from the friction thereof. He wants to avoid the clash and go direct to the centre of all attraction, the great Hari. This is the renunciation of the bhakta. This mighty attraction in the direction of God makes all other attractions vanish for him; this mighty, infinite love of God which enters his heart leaves no place for any other love to live there. How can it be otherwise? Bhakti fills his heart with the divine waters of the Ocean of Love, which is God Himself; there is no place there for little loves. That is to say, the bhakta's renunciation is that vairāgya, or non-attachment for all things that are not God, which results from anurāga, or great attachment to God.

This is the ideal preparation for the attainment of the supreme bhakti. When this renunciation comes, the gate opens for the soul to pass through and reach the lofty regions of supreme devotion, or parā-bhakti. Then it is that we begin to understand what parā-bhakti is; and the man who has entered into the inner shrine of parā-bhakti alone has the right to say that all forms and symbols are useless to him as aids to religious realization. He alone has attained that supreme state of love commonly called the brotherhood of men. The rest only talk. He sees no distinctions; the mighty Ocean of Love has entered into him, and he sees not man in man, but beholds his Beloved everywhere. Through every face shines to him his Hari. The light in the sun or the moon is all His manifestation. Wherever there is beauty or sublimity, to him it is all His. Such bhaktas are still living; the world is never without them. Though bitten by a serpent, they only say that a messenger came to them from their Beloved. Such men alone have the right to talk of universal brotherhood. They feel no resentment; their minds never react in the form of hatred or jealousy. The external, the sensuous, has vanished for them for ever. How can they be angry, when, through their love, they are always able to see the Reality behind the scenes?

THE NATURALNESS OF BHAKTI-YOGA
AND ITS CENTRAL SECRET

"THOSE WHO WITH constant attention always worship You, and those who worship the Undifferentiated, the Absolute—of these which are the greater yogis?" asked Arjuna of Śri Krishna. The answer was: "Those who, concentrating their minds on Me, worship Me with eternal constancy and are endowed with the highest faith—they are My best worshippers, they are the greatest yogis. Those who worship the Absolute, the Indescribable, the Undifferentiated, the Omnipresent, the Unthinkable, the All-comprehending, the Immovable, and the Eternal, by controlling their organs and having the conviction of sameness with regard to all things—they too, being engaged in doing good to all beings, come to Me alone. But for those whose minds have been devoted to the unmanifested Absolute, the difficulty of the struggle along the way is much greater; for it is indeed with great difficulty that the path of the unmanifested Absolute is trodden by any embodied being. Those who, having offered up all their work unto Me, with entire reliance on Me, meditate on Me and worship Me without any attachment to anything else—them I soon lift up from the ocean of ever recurring births and deaths, since their minds are wholly attached to Me."

Jnāna-yoga and bhakti-yoga are both referred to here. Both may be said to have been defined in the above passage. Jnāna-yoga is grand; it is high philosophy; and almost every human being thinks, curiously enough, that he can surely do everything required of him by this philosophy. But it is really very difficult to live truly the life of a jnāni. We are liable to run into great danger in trying to guide our life by jnāna. This world may be said to contain both persons of demoniacal nature, who think that taking care of the body is the be-all and end-all of existence, and persons of godly nature, who realize that the body is simply a means to an end, an instrument intended for the culture of the soul. The Devil can and indeed does quote the scriptures for his own purpose; and thus the way of knowledge appears to offer justification for what the bad man does, as much as it offers inducements for what the good man does. This is the great danger in jnāna-yoga. But bhakti-yoga is natural, sweet, and gentle; the bhakta does not take such high flights as the jnāna-yogi, and therefore he is not liable to have such big falls. Until the bondages of the soul pass away, it cannot of course be free, whatever may be the nature of the path that the religious man takes.

Here is a passage showing how, with regard to one of the blessed gopis, the soul-binding chains of both merit and demerit were broken: "The intense pleasure of meditating on God took away the binding effects of her good deeds.

437

Then her intense misery of soul in not attaining unto Him washed off all her sinful propensities. And then she became free."

In bhakti-yoga the central secret is, therefore, to know that the various passions and feelings and emotions in the human heart are not wrong in themselves; only they have to be carefully controlled and given a higher and higher direction, until they attain the very highest condition of excellence. The highest direction is that which takes us to God; every other direction is lower. We find that pleasure and pain are very common and oft-recurring feelings in our lives. When a man feels pain because he has no wealth or some such worldly thing, he is giving a wrong direction to the feeling. Still, pain has its uses. Let a man feel pain because he has not reached the Highest, because he has not reached God, and that pain will lead to his salvation. When you become glad that you have a handful of coins, you give a wrong direction to the faculty of joy. It should be given a higher direction; it should be made to serve the highest ideal. Pleasure in that kind of ideal must surely be our highest joy. This same thing is true of all our other feelings. The bhakta says that not one of them is wrong; he takes hold of them all and points them unfailingly towards God.

FORMS OF LOVE-MANIFESTATION

HERE ARE SOME of the forms in which love manifests itself. First, reverence. Why do people feel reverence for temples and holy places? Because God is worshipped there and His presence is associated with all such places. Why do people in every country pay reverence to teachers of religion? It is natural for the human heart to do so, because all such teachers preach the Lord. At bottom, reverence grows out of love; none of us can revere one whom we do not love. Then comes priti, or pleasure in God. What an immense pleasure men take in the objects of the senses! They go anywhere, run through any danger, to get the thing which they love, the thing which their senses crave. What is wanted of the bhakta is this very kind of intense love, which has, however, to be directed to God. Then there is the sweetest of pains, viraha, the intense misery due to the absence of the beloved. When a man feels intense misery because he has not attained to God, has not known that which is the only thing worthy to be known, and becomes in consequence very dissatisfied and almost mad, then there is viraha; and this state of mind makes him feel disturbed in the presence of anything other than the Beloved. In earthly love we see how often this viraha comes. Again, when men are really and intensely in love with women, or women with men, they feel a kind of natural annoyance in the presence of all those whom they do not love. Exactly the same state of impatience with regard to things that are not loved comes to the mind when parā-bhakti holds sway over it. Even to talk about things other than God becomes distasteful then. "Think of Him, think of Him alone, and give up all vain words." The bhakta feels friendly towards those who talk of Him alone; while those who talk of anything else appear to him to be unfriendly.

A still higher stage of love is reached when life is maintained only for the sake of the one ideal of love, when life is considered beautiful and worth living only on account of that love. Without it, life would not endure even for a moment. Life is sweet because one thinks of the Beloved. Tadiyatā, "Hisness," comes when a man becomes perfect according to bhakti—when he has become blessed, when he has attained God, when he has touched the feet of God, as it were. Then his whole nature is purified and completely changed. All his purpose in life then becomes fulfilled. Yet many such bhaktas live on solely to worship Him. That is the bliss, the only pleasure in life, which they will not give up. "O king, such is the blessed quality of Hari that even those who have become satisfied with the Self, all the knots of whose hearts have been cut asunder, even they love the Lord for love's sake"—the Lord, "whom all the gods worship, all the lovers of liberation and all the knowers of Brahman." Such is the power of love. When a man has forgotten himself altogether and does not feel that anything belongs to him, then he acquires the state of

439

tadiyatā. Everything is sacred to him because it belongs to the Beloved. Even with regard to earthly love, the lover thinks that everything belonging to his beloved is sacred and very dear to him. He loves even a piece of the cloth belonging to the darling of his heart. In the same way, when a person loves the Lord the whole universe becomes dear to him, because it is all His.

UNIVERSAL LOVE

How can we love the vyashti, the particular, without first loving the samashti, the universal? God is the samashti, the generalized and abstract universal whole; and the universe that we see is the vyashti, the particularized entity. To love the visible universe is possible only by way of loving the samashti, the universal, which is, as it were, the one unity in which are to be found millions and millions of smaller unities. The philosophers of India do not stop at particulars; they cast a hurried glance at the particulars and immediately start to find the generalized forms which will include all the particulars. The search after the universal is the one search of Indian philosophy and religion. The jnāni aims at the wholeness of things, at that one absolute and generalized Being by knowing which he knows everything. The bhakta wishes to realize that one generalized abstract Person, in loving whom he loves the whole universe. The yogi wishes to have possession of that one generalized form of power by controlling which he controls this whole universe. The Indian mind, throughout its history, has been directed to this kind of singular search after the universal in everything —in science, in psychology, in love, in philosophy. So the conclusion to which the bhakta comes is that if you go on merely loving one person after another, you may go on loving them for an infinite length of time without being in the least able to love the world as a whole. When at last, however, one arrives at the central idea that the sum total of all love is God, that the sum total of the aspirations of all the souls in the universe, whether they be free or bound or struggling towards liberation, is God, then alone does it become possible for one to manifest universal love.

God is the samashti, and this visible universe is God differentiated and made manifest. If we love the sum total, we love everything. Loving the world and doing good to it will all come easily then. But we have to obtain this power by loving God first; otherwise it is no easy matter to do good to the world. "Everything is His and He is my Lover. I love Him," says the bhakta. In this way everything becomes sacred to the bhakta, because all things are His. All are His children, His body, His manifestation. How then can we hurt anyone? How then can we dislike anyone? With love of God will come, as a sure effect, love of everyone in the universe. The nearer we approach God, the more do we begin to see that all things are in Him.

When the soul succeeds in enjoying the bliss of this supreme love, it also begins to see Him in everything. Our heart thus becomes an eternal fountain of love. And when we reach even higher states of this love, all the little differences between the things of the world are entirely lost. A man is seen no more as a man, but only as God; an animal is seen no more as an animal, but as God; even the tiger is no more a tiger, but a manifestation of God. Thus, in this

441

intense state of bhakti, worship is offered to everyone—to every life and to every being. "Knowing that Hari, the Lord, is in every being, the wise have thus to manifest unswerving love towards all beings." As a result of this kind of intense, all-absorbing love comes the feeling of perfect self-surrender, the conviction that nothing that happens is against us. Then the loving soul is able to say, if pain comes, "Welcome, pain!" If misery comes, it will say, "Welcome, misery! You are also from the Beloved." If a serpent comes, it will say, "Welcome, serpent!" If death comes, such a bhakta will welcome it with a smile. "Blessed am I that they all come to me," he will say. "They are all welcome." The bhakta in this state of perfect resignation, arising out of intense love of God and of all that are His, ceases to distinguish between pleasure and pain in so far as they affect him. He does not know what it is to complain of pain or misery; and this kind of uncomplaining resignation to the will of God, who is all love, is indeed a worthier acquisition than all the glory of grand and heroic per-formances.

To the vast majority of mankind the body is everything. The body is all the universe to them; bodily enjoyment is their all in all. This demon of the worship of the body and of the things of the body has entered into us all. We may indulge in tall talk and take very high flights on the wings of thought, but we are like vultures all the same: our minds are directed to the piece of carrion down below. Why should our body be saved, say, from a tiger? Why may we not give it up to the tiger? The tiger will thereby be pleased, and that is not, after all, so very far from self-sacrifice and worship.

Can you reach the realization of such an idea, in which the sense of self is completely lost? It is a dizzy height, the very pinnacle of the religion of love, and few in this world have ever climbed up to it; but until a man reaches that highest point of ever ready and ever willing self-sacrifice, he cannot become a perfect bhakta. We may all manage to maintain our bodies more or less satis-factorily and for longer or shorter intervals of time. Nevertheless our bodies have to go; there is no permanence about them. Blessed are they whose bodies are destroyed in the service of others. "Wealth, and even life itself, the sage always holds ready for the service of others. In this world, there being one thing certain, namely, death, it is far better that this body die in a good cause than in a bad one." We may drag our life on for fifty years or a hundred years; but after that, what is it that happens? Everything that is the result of com-bination must be dissolved and die. There must and will come a time for it to be decomposed. Jesus and Buddha and Mohammed are all dead; all the great prophets and teachers of the world are dead. "In this evanescent world, where everything is falling to pieces, we have to make the highest use of what we have," says the bhakta; and really the highest use of life is to hold it at the service of all beings.

It is the horrible idea of the body that breeds all the selfishness in the world—just this one delusion that we are wholly the body we own, and that we must by all possible means try our very best to preserve and to please it. If you know that you are positively other than your body, you have then none to fight with or struggle against; you are dead to all ideas of selfishness. So the bhakta declares that we have to hold ourselves as if we are altogether dead to all the things of the world; and that is indeed self-surrender. Let things come as they may. This is the meaning of "Thy will be done"—not going about fighting and struggling, and thinking all the while that God wills all our own weaknesses and worldly ambitions. It may be that good comes even out of our selfish struggles; that is, however, God's look-out. The perfected bhakta's idea must be never to will and work for himself. "Lord, they build high temples in Your name; they make large gifts in Your name. I am poor; I have nothing. So I take this body of mine and place it at Your feet. Do not give me up, O Lord"—such is the prayer proceeding out of the depths of the bhakta's heart.

To him who has experienced it, this eternal sacrifice of the self unto the beloved Lord is higher by far than all wealth and power, even than all soaring thoughts of renown and enjoyment. The peace of the bhakta's calm resignation is a peace that passeth all understanding and is of incomparable value. His self-surrender is a state of the mind in which it has no selfish interests and naturally knows nothing that is opposed to it. In this state of sublime resignation everything in the shape of attachment goes away, except that one all-absorbing love for Him in whom all things live and move and have their being. This attachment of love for God is, indeed, one that does not bind the soul but effectively breaks all its bondages.

THE ONENESS OF THE HIGHER
KNOWLEDGE AND THE HIGHER LOVE

THE UPANISHADS distinguish between a higher knowledge and a lower knowledge; and to the bhakta there is really no difference between this higher knowledge and his higher love, or parā-bhakti. The *Mundaka Upanishad* says: "The knowers of Brahman declare that there are two kinds of knowledge worthy to be known, namely, the higher (parā) and the lower (aparā). Of these, the lower knowledge consists of the Rig-Veda, the Yajur-Veda, the Sāma-Veda, the Atharva-Veda, śikshā (the science dealing with pronunciation and accent), kalpa (the sacrificial liturgy), grammar, nirukta (the science dealing with etymology and the meaning of words), prosody, and astronomy; and the higher knowledge is that by which the Unchangeable is known." The higher knowledge is thus clearly shown to be the Knowledge of Brahman. The *Devi-Bhāgavata* gives us the following definition of the higher love (parā-bhakti): "As oil poured from one vessel to another falls in an unbroken line, so, when the mind in an unbroken stream thinks of the Lord, we have what is called parā-bhakti, or supreme love." This kind of undisturbed and ever steady direction of the mind and heart to the Lord, with an inseparable attachment, is indeed the highest manifestation of man's love for God. All other forms of bhakti are only preparatory to the attainment of this highest form thereof, namely, parā-bhakti, which is also known as rāgānugā, the love that comes after attachment. When this supreme love once comes into a man's heart, his mind will continuously think of God and remember nothing else. He will give no room to thoughts other than those of God; his soul will be unconquerably pure and will break all the bonds of mind and matter and become serenely free. He alone can worship the Lord in his own heart; to him forms, symbols, books, and doctrines are all unnecessary and are incapable of proving serviceable in any way.

It is not easy to love the Lord thus. Ordinarily human love is seen to flourish only in places where it is returned. Where love is not returned for love, cold indifference is the natural result. There are, however, rare instances in which we may notice love exhibiting itself even where there is no return of love. We may compare this kind of love, for purposes of illustration, to the love of the moth for the fire: the insect loves the fire, falls into it, and dies. It is indeed in the nature of this insect to love so. To love because it is the nature of love to love is undeniably the highest and the most unselfish manifestation of love that can be seen in the world. Such love working itself out on the plane of spirituality necessarily leads to the attainment of parā-bhakti.

THE TRIANGLE OF LOVE

We may represent love as a triangle, each of the angles of which corresponds to one of its inseparable characteristics. There can be no triangle without its three angles, and there can be no true love without its three following characteristics. The first angle of our triangle of love is that love knows no bargaining. Wherever there is any seeking for something in return, there cannot be any real love; it becomes a mere matter of shopkeeping. So long as there is in us 'any idea of deriving this or that favour from God in return for our respect and allegiance to Him, there can be no true love growing in our hearts. Those who worship God because they wish Him to bestow favours on them are sure not to worship Him if those favours are not forthcoming. The bhakta loves the Lord because He is lovable; there is no other motive originating or directing this divine emotion of the true devotee.

We have heard it said that a great king once went into a forest and there met a sage. He talked with the sage a little and was very much pleased with his purity and wisdom. The king then wanted the sage to oblige him by receiving a present from him. The sage refused to do so, saying: "The fruits of the forest are enough food for me; the pure streams of water flowing down from the mountains give enough of drink for me; the bark of the trees supplies me with enough of covering; and a cave in the mountains forms my home. Why should I take any present from you or from anybody?" The king said, "Just to benefit me, sir, please take something from my hands and please come with me to the city and to my palace." After much persuasion the sage at last consented to do as the king desired, and went with him to his palace. Before offering the gift to the sage the king prayed to God repeatedly: "Lord, give me more children. Lord, give me more wealth. Lord, give me more territory. Lord, keep my body in better health"—and so on. Before the king finished saying his prayers the sage got up and quietly walked out of the room. On seeing this the king became perplexed and began to follow him, crying aloud: "Sir, you are going away! You have not received my gifts." The sage turned round and said to him: "I do not beg of beggars. You are yourself nothing but a beggar; and how can you give me anything? I am no fool to think of taking anything from a beggar like you. Go away. Do not follow me."

In this story is well brought out the distinction between mere beggars and the real lovers of God. Begging is not the language of love. To worship God even for the sake of salvation or any other reward is equally degenerate. Love knows no reward. Love is always for love's sake. The bhakta loves because he cannot help loving. When you see some beautiful scenery and fall in love with it, you do not demand anything in the way of a favour from the scenery; nor does the scenery demand anything from you. Yet the vision of it brings you

445

to a blissful state of mind: it tones down all the friction in your soul; it makes you calm, almost raises you, for the time being, beyond your mortal nature, and places you in a condition approaching divine ecstasy. This nature of real love is the first angle of our triangle. Ask not anything in return for your love; let your position be always that of the giver. Give your love unto God, but do not ask anything in return from Him.

The second angle of the triangle of love is that love knows no fear. Those who love God through fear are the lowest of devotees—not fully developed men. They worship God from fear of punishment. To them He is a great Being with a whip in one hand and a sceptre in the other. They are afraid that if they do not obey Him they will be whipped. It is a degradation to worship God through fear of punishment; such worship is, if worship at all, the crudest form of worship through love. So long as there is any fear in the heart, how can there be love also? Love conquers all fear naturally. Think of a young mother in the street, and a dog barking at her; she is frightened and flies into the nearest house. But suppose the next day she is in the street with her child, and a lion springs upon the child. Where will she be now? Of course, in the very mouth of the lion, protecting her child. Love conquers all fear. Fear comes from the selfish idea of cutting oneself off from the universe. The smaller and the more selfish I make myself, the greater is my fear. If a man thinks he is a mere nothing, fear will surely come upon him. And the less you think of yourself as an insignificant person, the less fear will there be for you. So long as there is the least spark of fear in you there can be no love. Love and fear are incompatible; God is never to be feared by those who love Him. The commandment, "Do not take the name of the Lord thy God in vain," the true lover of God laughs at. How can there be any blasphemy in the religion of love? The more you take the name of the Lord, the better for you, in whatever way you may do it. You are only repeating His name because you love Him.

The third angle of the triangle of love is that love knows no rival, for in it is always embodied the lover's highest ideal. True love never comes until the object of our love becomes to us our highest ideal. It may be that in many cases human love is misdirected and misplaced; but to the person who loves, the thing he loves is always his highest ideal. One man may see his ideal in the vilest of beings, and another in the highest of beings; nevertheless in every case it is the ideal alone that is truly and intensely loved. The highest ideal of every man is called God. Ignorant or wise, saint or sinner, man or woman, educated or uneducated, cultivated or uncultivated—to every human being the highest ideal is God. The synthesis of all the highest ideals of beauty, of sublimity, and of power gives us the completest conception of the loving and lovable God. These ideals exist naturally, in some shape or other, in every mind; they form part and parcel of all our minds. All the active manifestations of human nature are struggles of those ideals to become realized in practical life. All the various movements that we see around us in society are caused by the various ideals, in various souls, trying to come out and become concretized; what is inside presses on to come outside. This perennially dominant influence of the ideal is the one force, the one motive power, that may be seen to be constantly working in the midst of mankind.

It may be after hundreds of births, after struggling through thousands of years, that a man finds it is vain to try to make the inner ideal completely mould external conditions and square well with them. After realizing this he no longer tries to project his own ideal on the outside world, but worships the ideal itself as ideal, from the highest standpoint of love. This ideally perfect ideal embraces all lower ideals. Everyone admits the truth of the saying that a lover sees Helen's beauty on an Ethiop's brow. The man who is standing aside as a looker-on sees that love is here misplaced; but the lover sees his Helen all the same, and does not see the Ethiop at all. Helen or Ethiop, the objects of our love are really the centres round which our ideals become crystallized. What is it that the world commonly worships? Certainly not the all-embracing, ideally perfect ideal of the supreme devotee and lover. That ideal which men and women commonly worship is what is in themselves; every person projects his or her own ideal on the outside world and kneels before it. That is why we find that men who are cruel and bloodthirsty conceive of a bloodthirsty God, because they can love only their own highest ideal. That is why good men have a very high ideal of God, and why their ideal is indeed so very different from that of others.

THE GOD OF LOVE IS HIS OWN PROOF

WHAT IS THE IDEAL of the lover who has quite passed beyond the idea of selfishness, of bartering and bargaining, and who knows no fear? Even to the great God such a man will say: "I will give You my all, and I do not want anything from You. Indeed there is nothing I can call my own." When a man has acquired this conviction, his ideal becomes one of perfect love, one of perfect fearlessness born of love. The highest ideal of such a person has no narrowness of particularity about it; it is love universal, love without limits and bonds, love itself, absolute love. This grand ideal of the religion of love is worshipped and loved absolutely as such without the aid of any symbols or suggestions. This is the highest form of parā-bhakti, the worship of such an all-comprehending ideal as the ideal; all the other forms of bhakti are only stages on the way to reach it. All our failures and all our successes in following the religion of love are on the road to the realization of that one ideal. Object after object is taken up, and the inner ideal is successively projected on them all; and all such external objects are found inadequate as expressions of the ever expanding inner ideal and are naturally rejected one after another. At last the aspirant begins to think that it is vain to try to realize the ideal in external objects—that all external objects are as nothing when compared to the ideal itself. And in the course of time he acquires the power of realizing the highest and most generalized abstract ideal entirely as an abstraction that is to him quite alive and real.

When the devotee has reached this point, he is no longer impelled to ask whether God can be demonstrated or not, whether He is omnipotent and omniscient or not. To him He is only the God of Love. He is the highest ideal of love, and that is sufficient for all his purposes. He, as love, is self-evident; it requires no proofs to demonstrate the existence of the beloved to the lover. The magistrate-Gods of other forms of religion may require a good deal of proof to prove them; but the bhakta does not and cannot think of such Gods at all. To him God exists entirely as love. "None, O beloved, loves the husband for the husband's sake; it is for the sake of the Self who is in the husband that the husband is loved. None, O beloved, loves the wife for the wife's sake; it is for the sake of the Self who is in the wife that the wife is loved."

It is said by some that selfishness is the only motive power behind all human activities. That also is love, though it has been lowered by being particularized. When I think of myself as comprehending the Universal, there can surely be no selfishness in me; but when, by mistake, I think that I am something little, my love becomes particularized and narrowed. The mistake consists in making the sphere of love narrow and contracted. All things in the universe are of

448

divine origin and deserve to be loved. It has to be borne in mind, however, that the love of the whole includes the love of the parts.

This whole is the God of the bhaktas; and all the other Gods, Fathers in Heaven, Rulers, or Creators, and all theories and doctrines and books, have no purpose and no meaning for them, seeing that they have through their supreme love and devotion risen above those things altogether. When the heart is purified and cleansed and filled to the brim with the divine nectar of love, all other ideas of God become simply puerile and are rejected as being inadequate or unworthy. Such is indeed the power of parā-bhakti, or supreme love. The perfected bhakta no longer goes to see God in temples and churches; he knows no place where he will not find Him. He finds Him outside the temple as well as in the temple. He finds Him in the wicked man's wickedness as well as in the saint's saintliness, because he has Him already seated in glory in his own heart, as the one almighty, inextinguishable light of love, which is ever shining and eternally present.

HUMAN REPRESENTATIONS OF
DIVINE LOVE

IT IS IMPOSSIBLE to express the nature of this supreme and absolute ideal of love in human language. Even the highest flight of human imagination is incapable of comprehending it in all its infinite perfection and beauty. Nevertheless the followers of the religion of love in its higher as well as its lower forms, in all countries, have all along had to use inadequate human language to comprehend and to define their own ideal of love. Nay, human love itself, in all its varied forms, has been made to typify this inexpressible divine love. Man can think of divine things only in his own human way; to us the Absolute can be expressed only in our relative language. The whole universe is to us a writing of the Infinite in the language of the finite. Therefore bhaktas make use, in relation to God and His worship through love, of all the common terms associated with the common love of humanity.

Some of the great writers on parā-bhakti have tried to understand and experience this divine love in a number of different ways. The lowest form in which this love is apprehended is what they call the peaceful, the śānta. When a man worships God without the fire of love in him, without its madness in his brain, when his love is just the calm, commonplace love, a little higher than mere forms and ceremonies and symbols, but not at all characterized by the madness of intensely active love, it is said to be śānta. We see some people in the world who like to move on slowly, and others who come and go like the whirlwind. The śānta-bhakta is calm, peaceful, gentle.

The next higher type is that of dāsya, servantship. It comes when a man thinks he is the servant of the Lord. The attachment of the faithful servant to the master is his ideal.

The next type of love is sakhya, friendship—"Thou art our beloved friend." Just as a man opens his heart to his friend and knows that the friend will never chide him for his faults, but will always try to help him; just as there is the idea of equality between him and his friend—so equal love flows in and out between the worshipper and his friendly God. Thus God becomes our friend, the friend who is near, the friend to whom we may freely tell all the tales of our lives, before whom we may place the innermost secrets of our hearts with the greatest assurance of safety and support. He is the friend whom the devotee accepts as an equal. God is viewed here as our playmate.

We may well say that we are all playing in this universe. Just as children play their games, just as the most glorious kings and emperors play their own games, so is the beloved Lord Himself playing in this universe. He is perfect. He does not want anything. Why should He create? Activity, with us, is always for the fulfilment of a certain want; and want always presupposes imperfection.

God is perfect. He has no wants. Why should He go on with this incessant work of creation? What purpose could He have in view? The stories of God's creating the world for some end or other that we imagine, are good as stories, but not otherwise. It is all really sport; the universe is merely His play. The whole universe must after all be a big piece of pleasing fun to Him. If you are poor enjoy being poor, as fun; if you are rich enjoy the fun of being rich; if dangers come it is also good fun; if happiness comes there is more good fun. The world is just a playground, and we are here having good fun, having a game; and God is playing with us all the while, and we are playing with Him. God is our eternal playmate. How beautifully He is playing! The play is finished when the cycle comes to an end. There is rest for a shorter or longer time; again all come out and play.

It is only when you forget that it is all play and that you are also helping in the play—it is only then that misery and sorrows come, that the heart becomes heavy, that the world weighs upon you with tremendous power. But as soon as you give up your serious belief in the reality of the changing incidents of the three minutes of life, and know it to be but a stage on which you are playing, helping Him to play, at once misery ceases for you. He plays in every atom. He is playing when He is building up earths and suns and moons. He is playing with the human heart, with animals, with plants. We are His chessmen: He puts the chessmen on the board and shakes them up. He arranges us first in one way and then in another, and we consciously or unconsciously help in His play. And oh, bliss! we are His playmates.

The next type of love is what is known as vātsalya, loving God not as our father but as our child. This may seem peculiar, but it is a discipline to enable us to detach all ideas of power from the concept of God. The idea of power brings with it awe. There should be no awe in love. The ideas of reverence and obedience are necessary for the formation of character; but when character is formed, when the lover has tasted the calm peaceful love and tasted also a little of love's intense madness, then he need talk no more of ethics and discipline. The lover says he does not care to conceive of God as mighty, majestic, and glorious, as the Lord of the universe or as the God of gods. It is to avoid this association with God of the fear-creating sense of power that he worships God as his own child. The mother and the father are not moved by awe in relation to the child. They cannot have any reverence for the child. They cannot think of asking any favour of him. The child's position is always that of the receiver; and out of love for him the parents will give up their bodies a hundred times over. A thousand lives they will sacrifice for that one child of theirs. And therefore God is loved as a child.

This idea of loving God as a child comes into existence and grows naturally among those religious sects which believe in the incarnation of God. For the Mohammedans it is impossible to have this idea of God as a child; they would shrink from it with a kind of horror. But the Christians and the Hindus can realize it easily, because they have the Baby Jesus and the Baby Krishna. The women in India often look upon themselves as Krishna's mother. Christian mothers also may take up the idea that they are Christ's mother; and it will bring to the West the knowledge of God's divine Motherhood, which they so much need. The superstitions of awe and reverence in relation to God are deeply rooted in our heart of hearts, and it takes long years to sink entirely in love our ideas of reverence and veneration, of awe and majesty and glory, with regard to God.

There is one more human representation of the divine ideal of love. It is known as the madhura, the sweetheart relationship, and is the highest of all such representations. It is indeed based on the highest manifestation of love in this world, and this love is also the strongest known to man. What love shakes the whole nature of man, what love runs through every particle of his being, makes him mad, makes him forget his own nature, transforms him, makes him either a god or a demon, as does the love between man and woman? In this sweet representation of divine love God is our husband. We are all women; there are no men in this world. There is but one Man, and that is He, our Beloved. All that love which man gives to woman, or woman to man, has here to be given to the Lord.

All the different kinds of love which we see in the world, and with which we are more or less merely playing, have God as the one goal. But unfortunately man does not know the infinite Ocean into which this mighty river of love is constantly flowing, and so, foolishly, he often tries to direct it to little dolls of human beings. The tremendous love for the child that is in human nature is not for the little doll of a child. If you bestow it blindly and exclusively on the child, you will suffer in consequence. But through such suffering will come the awakening by which you are sure to find out that the love which is in you, if it is given to any human being, will sooner or later bring pain and sorrow as the result. Our love must therefore be given to the Highest One, who never dies and never changes, to Him in the ocean of whose love there is neither ebb nor flow. Love must reach its right destination; it must go unto Him who is really the infinite Ocean of Love. All rivers flow into the ocean. Even the drop of water coming down from the mountain-side cannot stop its course after reaching a brook or a river, however big; at last even that drop somehow does find its way to the ocean.

God is the one goal of all our passions and emotions. If you want to be angry, be angry with Him. Chide your Beloved; chide your Friend. Whom else can you safely chide? Mortal man will not patiently put up with your anger; there will be a reaction. If you are angry with me, I am sure to react quickly, because I cannot patiently put up with your anger. Say unto the Beloved: "Why do You not come to me? Why do You leave me thus alone?" Where is there any enjoyment but in Him? What enjoyment can there be in little clods of earth? It is the crystallized essence of infinite enjoyment that we have to seek—and that is in God. Let all our passions and emotions go up unto Him. They are meant for Him, for if they miss their mark and go lower, they become vile. When they go straight to the mark, to the Lord, even the lowest of them becomes transfigured; all the energies of the human body and mind, howsoever they may express themselves, have the Lord as their one goal. All loves and all passions of the human heart must go to God. He is the Beloved. Whom else can this heart love? He is the most beautiful, the most sublime; He is beauty itself, sublimity itself. Who in this universe is more beautiful than He? Who in this universe is more fit to become the husband than He? Who in this universe is more fit to be loved than He? So let Him be the Husband; let Him be the Beloved.

Often it so happens that divine lovers who sing of this divine love accept the language of human love in all its aspects as adequate to describe it. Fools do not understand this; they never will. They look at it only with the physical eye. They do not understand the mad throes of this spiritual love. How can they? "Oh, for one kiss of Thy lips, Beloved! One who has been kissed by Thee—his thirst for Thee increases for ever, all his sorrows vanish, and he forgets all things except Thee alone." Aspire after that kiss of the Beloved, that touch of His lips which makes the bhakta mad, which makes of man a god. To him who has been blessed with such a kiss, the whole of nature changes, worlds vanish, suns and moons die out, and the universe itself melts away into that one infinite Ocean of Love. That is the perfection of the madness of love.

Ay, the true spiritual lover does not rest even there; even the love of husband and wife is not mad enough for him. The bhaktas take up also the idea of illegitimate love, because it is so strong. The impropriety of it is not at all the thing they have in view. The nature of this love is such that the more obstructions there are to its free play, the more passionate it becomes. The love between husband and wife is smooth; there are no obstructions there. So the bhaktas take up the idea of a girl who is in love with a man—and her mother or father or her husband objects to that love, and the more anybody obstructs the course of her love, the more her love tends to grow in strength. Human language cannot describe how madly the ever blessed gopis loved Krishna in the groves of Vrindā, how at the sound of His flute they rushed out to meet Him, forgetting everything, forgetting this world and its ties, its duties, its joys and its sorrows.

Man, O man! you speak of divine love and at the same time are able to attend to all the vanities of this world. Are you sincere? "Where Rāma is, there is no room for any desire; where desire is, there is no room for Rāma. These never co-exist. Like light and darkness they are never together."

CONCLUSION

WHEN THIS HIGHEST IDEAL of love is reached, philosophy is thrown away. Who will then care for it? Freedom, salvation, Nirvāna—all are thrown away. Who cares to become free while in the enjoyment of divine love? "Lord, I do not want wealth, or friends, or beauty, or learning, or even freedom. Let me be born again and again, and be Thou ever my Love. Be Thou ever and ever my Love." "Who cares to become sugar?" says the bhakta. "I want to taste sugar." Who will then desire to become free and one with God? "I may know that I am He; yet I will take myself away from Him and become different, so that I may enjoy the Beloved." That is what the bhakta says. Love for love's sake is his highest enjoyment. Who would not be bound hand and foot a thousand times over to enjoy the Beloved?

No bhakta cares for anything except love—except to love and be loved. His motiveless love is like the tide rushing up the river. The lover goes up the river, against the current. The world calls him mad. I know one whom the world used to call mad, and this was his answer: "My friends, the whole world is a lunatic asylum. Some are mad after worldly love, some after name, some after fame, some after money, some after salvation and going to heaven. In this big lunatic asylum I am also mad—I am mad after God. If you are mad after money, I am mad after God. You are mad; so am I. I think my madness is after all the best." The true bhakta's love is this burning madness, before which everything else vanishes for him. The whole universe is to him full of love and love alone; that is how it seems to the lover. So when a man has this love in him, he becomes eternally blessed, eternally happy. He has drawn near to God; he has thrown off all those vain desires with which he was filled before. And with his desires, selfishness has vanished. This blessed madness of divine love alone can cure for ever the disease of the world that is in us.

We all have to begin as dualists in the religion of love. God is to us a separate Being, and we feel ourselves to be separate beings also. Love then comes between, and man begins to approach God; and God also comes nearer and nearer to man. Man takes up all the various relationships of life—such as father, mother, son, friend, master, lover—and projects them on his ideal of love, on his God. To him God exists as all these. And the last point of his progress is reached when he feels that he has become absolutely merged in the object of his worship.

We all begin with love for ourselves, and the unfair claims of the little self make even love selfish. At last, however, comes the full blaze of light, in which this little self is seen to have become one with the Infinite. Man himself is transfigured in the presence of this light of love, and he realizes at last the beautiful and inspiring truth that love, the lover, and the Beloved are one.

454

KARMA-YOGA

KARMA AND ITS EFFECT ON CHARACTER

THE WORD karma is derived from the Sanskrit kri, "to do." All action is karma. Technically this word also means the effects of actions. In connexion with metaphysics it sometimes means the effects of which our past actions were the causes. But in karma-yoga we have simply to do with the word karma as meaning work.

The goal of man is knowledge. That is the one great ideal placed before us by Eastern philosophy. Not pleasure, but knowledge, is the goal of man. Pleasure and happiness come to an end. It is a mistake to suppose that pleasure is the goal; the cause of all the miseries we have in the world is that men foolishly think pleasure to be the ideal to strive for. After a time a man finds that it is not happiness, but knowledge, towards which he is going, and that both pleasure and pain are great teachers, and that he learns as much from pain as from pleasure. As pleasure and pain pass before his soul, they leave upon it different pictures, and the result of these combined impressions is what is called a man's "character." If you take the character of any man, it really is but the aggregate of tendencies, the sum total of the inclinations of his mind; you will find that misery and happiness are equal factors in the formation of that character. Happiness and misery have an equal share in moulding character, and in some instances misery is a better teacher than happiness. Were one to study the great characters the world has produced, I dare say it would be found, in the vast majority of cases, that misery taught them more than happiness, poverty taught them more than wealth, blows brought out their inner fire more than praise.

Now knowledge, again, is inherent in man. No knowledge comes from outside; it is all inside. What we say a man "knows" should, in strict psychological language, be what he discovers or unveils; what a man "learns" is really what he discovers by taking the cover off his own soul, which is a mine of infinite knowledge. We say that Newton discovered gravitation. Was it sitting anywhere in a corner waiting for him? It was in his own mind. The right time came and he found it out. All the knowledge that the world has ever received comes from the mind; the infinite library of the universe is in your own mind. The external world is simply the suggestion, the occasion, which sets you to studying your own mind; but the object of your study is always your own mind. The falling of an apple gave the suggestion to Newton, and he studied his own mind; he rearranged all the previous links of thought in his mind and discovered a new link among them, which we call the law of gravitation. It was not in the apple nor in anything in the centre of the earth. All knowledge, therefore, secular or spiritual, is in the human mind. In many cases it is not discovered, but remains covered. When the covering is being slowly taken off we say that we are "learning," and the advance of knowledge is made by the advance of this process of uncovering. The man from whom this veil is being lifted is the knowing man; the man upon whom it lies thick is ignorant; and the man from whom it has entirely gone is all-knowing, omniscient. There have been omniscient men, and, I believe, there will be yet; there will be many of them in years to come.

Like fire in a piece of flint, knowledge exists in the mind. Suggestion is the friction which brings it out. So with all our feelings and actions. Our tears and our smiles, our joys and our griefs, our weeping and our laughter, our curses and our blessings, our praises and our blamings—every one of these we shall find, if we calmly study our own selves, to have been brought out from within ourselves by so many blows. The result is what we are. All these blows taken together are called karma—work, action. Every mental and physical blow that is given to the soul, by which, as it were, fire is struck from it, and by which its own power and knowledge are discovered, is karma, using the word in its widest sense. Thus we are all doing karma all the time. I am talking to you: that is karma. You are listening: that is karma. We breathe: that is karma. We walk: that is karma. Everything we do, physical or mental, is karma, and it leaves its marks on us.

There are certain works which are, as it were, the aggregate, the sum total, of a large number of smaller works. If we stand near the seashore and hear the waves dashing against the shingle, we think it is a great noise. And yet we know that one wave is really composed of millions and millions of minute waves: Each one of these is making a noise, and yet we do not hear it; it is only when they become the big aggregate that we hear them. Similarly every pulsation of the heart is work. Certain kinds of work we feel and they become tangible to us; they are, at the same time, the aggregate of a number of small works. If you really want to judge the character of a man, do not look at his great performances. Every fool can act as a hero at one time or another. Watch a man do his most common actions; those are indeed the things which will tell you the real character of a great man. Great occasions rouse even the lowest of human beings to some kind of greatness; but he alone is the really great man whose character is great always, the same wherever he may be.

Karma in its effect on character is the most tremendous power that man has to deal with. Man is, as it were, a centre and is attracting all the powers of the universe towards himself, and in this centre is fusing them all and again sending them off in a big current. Such a centre is the real man, the almighty and the omniscient. He draws the whole universe towards him; good and bad, misery and happiness, all are running towards him and clinging round him. And out of them he fashions the mighty stream of tendency called character and throws it outwards. As he has the power of drawing in anything, so has he the power of throwing it out.

All the actions that we see in the world, all the movements in human society, all the works that we have around us, are simply the display of thought, the manifestation of the will of man. Machines, instruments, cities, ships, men-of-war—all these are simply the manifestation of the will of man; and this will is caused by character, and character is manufactured from karma. As is the karma, so is the manifestation of the will. The men of mighty will the world has produced have all been tremendous workers—gigantic souls with wills powerful enough to overturn worlds, wills they got by persistent work through ages and ages. Such a gigantic will as that of a Buddha or a Jesus could not be obtained in one life, for we know who their fathers were. It is not known that their fathers ever spoke a word for the good of mankind. Millions and millions of carpenters like Joseph had come and gone; millions are still living. Millions and millions of petty kings like Buddha's father had been in the world. If it was only a case of hereditary transmission, how do you account for the fact that this petty prince, who was not, perhaps, obeyed by his own servants, produced a son whom half the world worships? How do you explain the gulf between the carpenter and his son, whom millions of human beings worship as God? It cannot be solved by the theory of heredity. The gigantic will which manifested Buddha and Jesus—whence did it come? Whence came this accumulation of power? It must have been there through ages and ages, continually growing bigger and bigger until it burst on society as Buddha or Jesus, and it is rolling down even to the present day.

All this is determined by karma, work. No one can get anything unless he earns it; this is an eternal law. We may sometimes think it is not so, but in the long run we become convinced of it. A man may struggle all his life for riches; he may cheat thousands; but he finds at last that he does not deserve to become rich and his life becomes a trouble and a nuisance to him. We may go on accumulating things for our physical enjoyment, but only what we earn is really ours. A fool may buy all the books in the world, and they will be in his library; but he will be able to read only those that he deserves to. This deserving is produced by karma. Our karma determines what we deserve and what we can assimilate. We are responsible for what we are; and whatever we wish ourselves to be, we have the power to make ourselves. If what we are now has been the result of our own past actions, it certainly follows that whatever we wish to be in the future can be produced by our present actions. So we have to know how to act. You will say: "What is the use of learning how to work? Everyone works in some way or other in this world." But there is such a thing as frittering away our energies. Karma-yoga, the Bhagavad Gītā says, is doing work with cleverness and as a science. By knowing how to work one can obtain the greatest results. You must remember that the aim of all work is simply to bring out the power of the mind which is already there, to wake up the soul. The power is inside every man; and so is knowledge. Different works are like blows to bring them out, to cause these giants to wake up.

Man works with various motives; there cannot be work without motive. Some people want to get fame and they work for fame. Others want money and they work for money. Some want to have power and they work for power. Others want to get to heaven and they work for that. Still others want to earn a name for their ancestors, as in China, where no man gets a title until he is dead; and that is a better way, after all, than ours. When a man does something very good there, they give a title of nobility to his dead father or grandfather. Some people work for that. Some of the followers of certain Mohammedan sects work all their lives to have a big tomb built for them when they die. I know sects among whom, as soon as a child is born, a tomb is started; that is among them the most important work a man has to do; and the bigger and the finer the tomb, the happier the man is supposed to be. Others work as a penance; they do all sorts of wicked things and then erect a temple or give something to the priests to buy them off and obtain a passport to heaven. They think that this kind of beneficence will clear them and that they will go scot-free in spite of their sinfulness. Such are some of the various motives for work.

Now let us consider work for work's sake. There are some who are really the salt of the earth, who work for work's sake, who do not care for name or fame or even to go to heaven. They work just because good will come of it. There are others who do good to the poor and help mankind from still higher motives, because they believe in doing good and they love good. As a rule, the desire for name and fame seldom brings quick results; they come to us when we are old and have almost done with life. If a man works without any selfish motive, does he not gain something? Yes, he gains the highest benefit. Unselfishness is more paying; only people have not the patience to practise it. It is more paying from the point of view of health also. Love, truth, and unselfishness are not merely figures of speech used by moralists, but they form our highest ideal, because in them lies such a manifestation of power. In the first place, a man who can work for five days, or even five minutes, without any selfish motive whatever, without thinking of the future, of heaven, of punishment, or anything of the kind, has in him the capacity to become a powerful moral giant. It is hard to do it, but in our heart of hearts we know its value and the good it brings.

It is the greatest manifestation of power, this tremendous restraint; self-restraint is a manifestation of greater power than any selfish action. A carriage with four horses may rush down a hill unrestrained, or the coachman may curb the horses. Which is the greater display of power—to let the horses go or to hold them? A cannon-ball flying through the air goes a long distance and falls. Another is cut short in its flight by striking against a wall, and the impact generates intense heat. All outgoing energy following from a selfish motive is frittered away; it will not cause power to return to you; but if selfishness is restrained, it will result in the development of power. This self-control will tend to produce a mighty will, a character which makes a Christ or a Buddha. Foolish men do not know this secret; they nevertheless want to rule mankind. Even a fool may rule the whole world if he works and waits. Let him wait a few years, restrain that foolish idea of governing, and when that idea is wholly gone, he will be a power in the world. The majority of us cannot see beyond a few years, as some animals cannot see beyond a few steps. Just a little narrow circle—that is our world. We have not the patience to look beyond, and thus we become immoral and wicked. This is our weakness, our powerlessness.

Even the lowest forms of work are not to be despised. Let the man who knows no better work for selfish ends, for name and fame; but everyone should always try to move towards higher and higher motives and to understand them. "To work we have the right, but not to the fruits thereof." Leave the fruits alone. Why care for results? If you wish to help a man, never think what that man's attitude should be towards you. If you want to do a great or a good work, do not trouble to think what the result will be.

There arises a difficult question in this ideal of work. Intense activity is necessary; we must always work. We cannot live a minute without work. What then becomes of rest? Here is one side of life: struggle and work by which we are whirled rapidly round. And here is the other: calm, retiring renunciation—everything is peaceful around, there is very little of noise and show, only nature with her animals and flowers and mountains. Neither of them is a perfect picture. A man used to solitude, if brought in contact with the surging whirlpool of the world, will be crushed by it, just as the fish that lives in deep-sea water, as soon as it is brought to the surface, breaks into pieces, deprived of the weight of water on it that kept it together. Can a man who has been used to the turmoil and the rush of life live at ease if he comes to a quiet place? He suffers and perchance may lose his mind. The ideal man is he who in the midst of the greatest silence and solitude finds the intensest activity, and in the midst of the intensest activity, the silence and solitude of the desert. He has learnt the secret of restraint; he has controlled himself. He goes through the streets of a big city with all its traffic, and his mind is calm as if he were in a cave where not a sound could reach him; but he is intensely working all the time. That is the ideal of karma-yoga; and if you have attained to that you have really learnt the secret of work.

But we have to start from the beginning, to take up works as they come to us and slowly make ourselves more unselfish every day. We must do the work and find out the motive that prompts us; and in the first years we shall find that almost without exception our motives are selfish. But gradually this selfishness will melt through persistence, and at last will come the time when we shall be able to do really unselfish work. We may all hope that some day or other, as we struggle through the paths of life, there will come a time when we shall become perfectly unselfish; and the moment we attain to that, all our powers will be concentrated and the knowledge which is ours will be manifest.

EACH IS GREAT IN HIS OWN PLACE

ACCORDING TO THE Sāmkhya philosophy, nature is composed of three forces called, in Sanskrit, sattva, rajas, and tamas. These, as manifested in the physical world, are what we may call equilibrium, activity, and inertness. Tamas typifies darkness or inactivity; rajas is activity, expressed as attraction or repulsion; and sattva is the equilibrium of the two.

In every man there are these three forces. Sometimes tamas prevails and we become lazy, we cannot move; we are inactive, bound down by certain set ideas or by mere dullness. At other times activity prevails, and at still other times the calm balancing of both. Again, in different men, one of these forces is generally predominant. The characteristic of one man is inactivity, dullness, and laziness; that of another, activity, power, manifestation of energy; and in still another we find sweetness, calmness, and gentleness, which are due to the balancing of both action and inaction. So in all created beings—in animals, plants, and men—we find more or less typical manifestations of these different forces. Karma-yoga has especially to deal with these three factors. By teaching what they are and how to employ them it helps us to do our work better.

Human society is a graded organization. We all know about morality and we all know about duty, but at the same time we find that in different countries the significance of morality varies greatly. What is regarded as moral in one country may in another be considered perfectly immoral. For instance, in one country cousins may marry; in another this is thought to be very immoral; in one, men may marry their sisters-in-law; in another, that is regarded as immoral; in one country people may have only one wife; in another, many wives; and so forth. Similarly, in all other departments of morality we find that the standard varies greatly; yet we feel that there must be a universal standard of morality.

So it is with duty. The idea of duty varies much among different nations. In one country, if a man does not do certain things, people will say he has acted wrongly, while in another country, if he does those very things, people will say he has acted wrongly; and yet we know that there must be some universal idea of duty. In the same way, one class of society thinks that certain things are among its duties, while another class thinks quite the opposite and would be horrified if it had to do those things. Two ways are left open to us: the way of the ignorant, who think that there is only one way to truth and that all the rest are wrong; and the way of the wise, who admit that, according to our mental constitution or the different circumstances in which we dwell, duty and morality may vary. The important thing is to know that there are gradations of duty and of morality—that the duty of one state of life, in one set of circumstances, will not and cannot be that of another.

For example, all great teachers have taught: "Resist not evil"—that non-resistance is the highest moral ideal. But we also know that if even a small number of us tried to put that maxim fully into practice, the whole social fabric would fall to pieces, the wicked would take possession of our properties and our lives, and would do whatever they liked with us. Even if for only one day such non-resistance were practised it would lead to disaster. Yet intuitively, in our heart of hearts, we feel the truth of the teaching, "Resist not evil." This seems to us to be the highest ideal; yet to teach only this doctrine would be equivalent to condemning a vast portion of mankind. Not only so; it would make many feel that they were always doing wrong, cause in them scruples of conscience in all their actions; it would weaken them, and that constant self-disapproval would breed more vice than any other weakness would. To the man who has begun to hate himself, the gate to degeneration has already opened; and the same is true of a nation. Our first duty is not to hate ourselves; to advance we must have faith in ourselves first and then in God. He who has no faith in himself can never have faith in God. Therefore the only alternative remaining to us is to recognize that duty and morality vary under different circumstances. The man who resists evil is not necessarily doing what is always and in itself wrong, but under the circumstances in which he is placed it may even become his duty to resist evil.

In reading the Bhagavad Gītā, many of you in Western countries may have felt astonished at the second chapter, wherein when Arjuna refuses to fight or offer resistance, because his adversaries are his friends and relatives, and makes the plea that non-resistance is the highest ideal of love, Śri Krishna calls him a hypocrite and a coward. There is a great lesson for us all to learn— that in all matters the two extremes are alike. The extreme positive and the extreme negative are always similar. When the vibrations of light are too low we do not see them, nor do we see them when they are too intense. So with sound: when it is very low in pitch we do not hear it, when very high we do not hear it either. Of like nature is the difference between resistance and non-resistance. One man does not resist because he is weak and lazy, and he will not because he cannot; the other man knows that he can strike an irresistible blow if he likes; yet he not only does not strike, but blesses his enemies. The one who from weakness resists not commits a sin and hence cannot receive any benefit from the non-resistance; while the other would commit a sin by offering resistance. Buddha gave up his throne and renounced his position; that was true renunciation. But there cannot be any question of renunciation in the case of a beggar who has nothing to renounce. So we must always be careful about what we really mean when we speak of non-resistance and ideal love. We must first take care to understand whether we have the power of resistance or not. Then, having the power, if we renounce it and do not resist, we are doing a grand act of love; but if we cannot resist, and yet, at the same time, try to deceive ourselves into the belief that we are actuated by motives of the highest love, we are doing the exact opposite. Arjuna became a coward at the sight of the mighty array against him; his "love" made him forget his duty towards his country and king. That is why Śri Krishna told him that he was a hypocrite: "Thou talkest like a wise man, but thy actions betray thee to be a coward; therefore stand up and fight!"

Such is the central idea of karma-yoga. The karma-yogi is the man who understands that the highest ideal is non-resistance, and who also knows that this non-resistance is the highest manifestation of power; but he knows, too, that what is called the resisting of evil is a step on the way towards the manifestation of this highest power, namely, non-resistance. Before reaching this highest ideal man's duty is to resist evil. Let him work, let him fight, let him strike straight from the shoulder. Then only, when he has gained the power to resist, will non-resistance be a virtue.

I once met a man in my country whom I had known before as a very stupid, dull person, who knew nothing and had not the desire to know anything and was living the life of a brute. He asked me what he should do to know God, how he was to get free. "Can you tell a lie?" I asked him. "No," he replied. "Then you must learn to do so. It is better to tell a lie than to be a brute or a log of wood. You are inactive; you have certainly not reached the highest state, which is beyond all action, calm and serene. You are too dull even to do something wicked." That was an extreme case, of course, and I was joking with him; but what I meant was that a man must be active in order to pass through activity to perfect calmness. Inactivity should be avoided by all means. Activity always means resistance. Resist all evils, mental and physical; and when you have succeeded in resisting, then calmness will come.

It is very easy to say, "Hate nobody, resist not evil," but we know what that kind of advice generally means in practice. When the eyes of society are turned towards us we may make a show of non-resistance, but in our hearts there is canker all the time. We feel the utter want of the calm of non-resistance; we feel that it would be better for us to resist. Further, if you desire wealth, and know at the same time that the whole world regards him who aims at wealth as a very wicked man, you will perhaps not dare to plunge into the struggle for wealth; yet your mind will be running day and night after money. This is hypocrisy and will serve no purpose. Plunge into the world, and then, after a time, when you have suffered and enjoyed all that is in it, will renunciation come, then will calmness come. So fulfil your desire for power and everything else; and after you have fulfilled the desire, will come the time when you shall know that they are all very little things. But until you have fulfilled this desire, until you have passed through that activity, it is impossible for you to come to the state of calmness, serenity, and self-surrender. These ideas of serenity and renunciation have been preached for thousands of years; everybody has heard of them from childhood; and yet we see very few in the world who have really realized them. I do not know if I have seen twenty persons in my life who are really calm and non-resisting, and I have travelled over half the world.

Every man should take up his own ideal and endeavour to accomplish it; that is a surer way of progressing than taking up other men's ideals, which he can never hope to accomplish. For instance, we take a child and at once give him the task of walking twenty miles; either the little one dies or one in a thousand crawls the twenty miles to reach the end exhausted and half dead. That is what we generally try to do with the world. Not all the men and women in any society are of the same mind, capacity, or power to do things; they must have different ideals, and we have no right to sneer at any ideal. Let everyone do the best he can to realize his own ideal. Nor is it right that I should be judged by your standard or you by mine. The apple tree should not be judged by the standard of the oak, nor the oak by that of the apple. To judge the apple tree you must take the apple standard; and to judge the oak, its own standard.

Unity in variety is the plan of creation. However men and women may vary individually, there is unity in the background. The different individual characters and classes of men and women are natural variations in creation. Hence we ought not to judge them by the same standard or put the same ideal before them. Such a course only creates an unnatural struggle, and the result is that a man begins to hate himself and is hindered from becoming religious and good. Our duty is to encourage everyone in his struggle to live up to his own highest ideal, and strive at the same time to make that ideal as near as possible to the truth.

In the Hindu system of morality we find that this fact has been recognized from very ancient times; and in the Hindu scriptures and books on ethics different rules are laid down for the different classes of men—the student, the householder, the vānaprasthin, and the sannyāsin.

The life of every individual, according to the Hindu scriptures, has its peculiar duties apart from those which are common to humanity. The Hindu begins life as a student; then he marries and becomes a householder; in old age he retires; and lastly he gives up the world and becomes a sannyāsin. To each of these stages of life certain duties are attached. One of these stages is not intrinsically superior to another; the life of the married man is quite as great as that of the celibate who has devoted himself to religious work. The scavenger in the street is quite as great and glorious as the king on his throne. Take the king off his throne, make him do the scavenger's work, and see how he fares. Put the scavenger on the throne and see how he rules. It is useless to say that the man who lives outside the world is a greater man than he who lives in the world; it is much more difficult to live in the world and worship God than to give it up and live a free and easy life. The four stages of life in India have in later times been reduced to two: the life of the householder and that of the monk. The householder marries and carries on his duties as a citizen; the duty of the other is to devote his energies wholly to religion, to preach and to worship God. I shall present to you a few ideas from the Mahānirvāna Tantra which treat of this subject, and you will see that it is a very difficult task for a man to be a householder and perform all his duties perfectly:

The householder should be devoted to God; knowledge of God should be the goal of his life. Yet he must work constantly, perform all his duties; he must give up the fruits of his actions to God.

It is the most difficult thing in this world to work and not care for the result, to help a man and never think that he ought to be grateful, to do good work and at the same time never look back to see whether it brings you name or fame or nothing at all. Even the most arrant coward becomes brave when the world praises him. A fool can do heroic deeds when he receives the approbation of society; but to constantly do good without caring for the approbation of his fellow men is indeed the highest sacrifice a man can perform.

The great duty of the householder is to earn a living, but he must take care that he does not do it by telling lies or by cheating or by robbing others; and he must remember that his life is for the service of God and the poor.

Knowing that his mother and father are the visible representatives of God, the householder always and by all possible means must please them. If his mother is pleased, and his father, then God is pleased with that man. That child is really a good child who never speaks harsh words to his parents. Before one's parents one must not utter jokes, must not show restlessness, must not show anger or temper. Before his mother or father a child must bow down low; he must stand up in their presence and must not take a seat until they order him to sit.

If the householder enjoys food and drink and clothes without first seeing that his mother and father, his children, his wife, and the poor are supplied with them, he is committing a sin. The mother and father are the causes of this body; so a man must undergo a thousand troubles in order to do good to them.

Even so is his duty to his wife. No man should scold his wife, and he must always maintain her as if she were his own mother. And even when he is in the greatest difficulties and troubles, he must not renounce his wife if she is chaste and devoted to him.

He who cherishes another woman besides his wife—if he touches her even with his mind, that man goes to a dark hell.

Before women a man must not use improper language, and must never brag of his powers. He must not say, "I have done this, and I have done that."

The householder must always please his wife with money, clothes, love, faith, and words like nectar, and must never do anything to disturb her. That man who has succeeded in getting the love of a chaste wife has succeeded in his religion and has all the virtues.

The following are a man's duties towards his children:

A son should be lovingly reared up to his fourth year; he should be educated till he is sixteen. When he is twenty years of age he should be employed in some work; he should then be treated affectionately by his father as his equal. Exactly in the same manner the daughter should be brought up, and she should be educated with the greatest care. When she marries, the father ought to give her jewels and wealth.

Then there is the duty of a man towards his brothers and sisters, and towards the children of his brothers and sisters, if they are poor, and towards his other relatives, his friends, and his servants. Further, there are his duties towards the people of the same village, and the poor, and anyone that comes to him for help. If the householder, having sufficient means, does not care to help his relatives and the poor, know him to be only a brute; he is not a human being.

Excessive attachment to food, clothes, and the tending of the body and the dressing of the hair should be avoided. The householder must be pure in heart and clean in body, always active and always ready for work.

To his enemies the householder must be a hero. When threatened by them he must resist. That is the duty of the householder. He must not sit down in a corner and weep, and talk nonsense about non-resistance. If he does not show himself a hero to his enemies, he has not done his duty. And to his friends and relatives he must be as gentle as a lamb.

It is the duty of the householder not to pay reverence to the wicked, because if he reverences the wicked people of the world, he patronizes wickedness. And it will be a great mistake if he disregards those who are worthy of respect, the good people. He must not be gushing in his friendship; he must not go out of his way to make friends everywhere; he must watch the actions of the men he wants to make friends with, and their dealings with other men, reflect upon them, and then make friends.

These three things he must not talk of: He must not talk in public of his own fame, or preach his own name or his own powers; he must not talk of his wealth; and he must not talk of anything that has been told him privately.

A man must not say that he is poor or that he is wealthy; he must not brag of his wealth. Let him keep his own counsel; this is his religious duty. This is not mere worldly wisdom; if a man does not do so, he may be held to be immoral.

The householder is the basis, the prop, of the whole of society; he is the principal earner. The poor, the weak, and the women and children, who do not work—all live upon the householder. So he has certain duties towards them, and these duties should be such as to make him feel strong while performing them, and not make him think that he is doing things beneath his ideal. Therefore if he has done something unworthy or has made some mistake, he must not say so in public; and if he is engaged in some enterprise and knows he is sure to fail in it, he must not speak of it. Such self-exposure is not only uncalled for but also unnerves the man and makes him unfit for the performance of his legitimate duties in life. At the same time, he must struggle hard to acquire two things: first, knowledge, and second, wealth. This is his duty, and if he does not do his duty he is nobody. A householder who does not struggle to get wealth is immoral. If he is lazy and content to lead an idle life, he is immoral, because upon him depend hundreds. If he gets riches, hundreds of others will be thereby supported.

If there were not in this city hundreds who had striven to become rich, and who had acquired wealth, where would all this civilization and these almshouses and mansions be? Going after wealth in such a case is not bad, because that wealth is for distribution. The householder is the centre of life and society. It is a kind of worship for him to acquire and spend wealth nobly; for the householder who struggles to become rich by good means and for good purposes is doing practically the same thing for the attainment of salvation as the anchorite does in his cell when he prays; for in them we see only different aspects of the same virtue of self-surrender and self-sacrifice prompted by the feeling of devotion to God and to all that is His.

The householder must struggle to acquire a good name; he must not gamble; he must not move in the company of the wicked; he must not tell lies and must not be the cause of trouble to others.

Often people enter into things they have not the means to accomplish, with the result that they cheat others to attain their own ends. Then there is in all things the time factor to be taken into consideration; what at one time might be a failure would perhaps at another time be a very great success.

The calm householder must speak the truth and speak gently, using words which people like, which will do good to others; and he should not boast about himself or criticize other men.

The householder, by digging wells, by planting trees along the roadsides, by establishing rest-houses for men and animals, by making roads and building bridges, goes towards the same goal that the greatest yogi attains.

This is one part of the doctrine of karma-yoga—activity, the duty of the householder. There is a passage later on where the *Mahānirvāna Tantra* says: "If the householder dies in battle, fighting for his country or his religion, he comes to the same goal that the yogi attains through meditation," showing thereby that what is duty for one is not duty for another. At the same time, it does not say that the former duty is lowering, and the latter, elevating; each duty has its own place, and according to the circumstances in which we are placed must we perform our duties.

One idea comes out of all this: the condemnation of all weakness. This is a particular idea in all our teachings which I like, whether in philosophy or in religion or in work. If you read the Vedas you will find one word always repeated: "fearlessness." Fear nothing. Fear is a sign of weakness. A man must go about his duties without taking notice of the sneers and the ridicule of the world.

If a man retires from the world to worship God, he must not think that those who live in the world and work for the good of the world are not worshipping God. Neither must those who live in the world, working for the good of wife and children, think that those who give up the world are low vagabonds. Each is great in his own place. This thought I will illustrate by a story.

A certain king used to inquire of all the sannyāsins that came to his country, "Which is the greater man—he who gives up the world and becomes a sannyāsin or he who lives in the world and performs his duties as a householder?" Many wise monks sought to solve the problem. Some asserted that the sannyāsin was the greater, upon which the king demanded that they prove their assertion. When they could not do so, he ordered them to marry and become householders. Then others came and said, "The householder who performs his duties is the greater man." Of them, too, the king demanded proofs. When they could not give them, he made them also settle down as householders.

At last there came a young sannyāsin, and the king asked him the same question. He said, "Each, O King, is great in his own place." "Prove this to me," demanded the king. "I will prove it to you," said the sannyāsin, "but you must come and live with me for a few days, that I may be able to prove to you what I say." The king consented. He followed the sannyāsin out of his own territory and they passed through many other countries until they came to a great kingdom. In the capital of that kingdom a ceremony was going on. The king and the sannyāsin heard the noise of drums and music, and heard also the criers; the people were assembled in the streets in gala dress, and a proclamation was being made. The king and the sannyāsin stood there to see what was going on. The crier was proclaiming loudly that the princess, daughter of the king of that country, was about to choose a husband from among those assembled before her.

It was an old custom in India for princesses to choose husbands in this way. Each princess had certain ideas of the sort of man she wanted for a husband.

Some wanted the handsomest man, others wanted only the most learned, others again the richest, and so on. All the princes of the neighbourhood would put on their best attire and present themselves before her. Sometimes they too had their own criers to enumerate their virtues—the reasons why they hoped the princess would choose them. The princess would be taken round on a throne, in the most splendid array, and would look at them and hear about them. If she was not pleased with what she saw and heard, she would say to her bearers, "Move on," and would take no more notice of the rejected suitor. If, however, the princess was pleased with any one of them, she would throw a garland of flowers over him and he became her husband.

The princess of the country to which our king and the sannyāsin had come was having one of these interesting ceremonies. She was the most beautiful princess in the world, and her husband would be ruler of the kingdom after her father's death. The idea of this princess was to marry the handsomest man, but she could not find one to please her. Several such meetings had taken place, but the princess had been unable to select a husband. This meeting was the most splendid of all; more people than ever before attended it. The princess came in on a throne, and the bearers carried her from place to place. She did not seem to care for anyone, and everyone was disappointed, thinking that this meeting also was going to be a failure.

Just then a young man, a sannyāsin, radiant as if the sun had come down to the earth, came and stood in one corner of the assembly, watching what was going on. The throne with the princess came near him, and as soon as she saw the beautiful sannyāsin, she stopped and threw the garland over him. The young sannyāsin seized the garland and threw it off, exclaiming: "What nonsense is this? I am a sannyāsin. What is marriage to me?" The king of that country thought that perhaps this man was poor and so dared not marry the princess, and said to him, "With my daughter goes half my kingdom now, and the whole kingdom after my death!" and put the garland on the sannyāsin again. The young man threw it off once more, saying, "Nonsense! I do not want to marry," and walked quickly away from the assembly.

Now, the princess had fallen so much in love with this young man that she said, "I must marry this man or I shall die"; and she went after him to bring him back. Then our other sannyāsin, who had brought the king there, said to him, "King, let us follow this pair." So they went after them, but at a good distance behind. The young sannyāsin who had refused to marry the princess walked out into the country for several miles. When he came to a forest and entered it, the princess followed him, and the other two followed also. Now this young sannyāsin was well acquainted with that forest and knew all the intricate paths in it. He suddenly entered one of these and disappeared, and the princess could not discover him. After vainly trying for a long time to find him, she sat down under a tree and began to weep, for she did not know the way out. Then our king and the other sannyāsin came up to her and said: "Do not weep. We shall show you the way out of this forest, but it is too dark for us to find it now. Here is a big tree; let us rest under it, and in the morning we shall show you the road."

Now, a little bird and his wife and their three young ones lived in that tree, in a nest. This little bird looked down and saw the three people under the tree and said to his wife: "My dear, what shall we do? Here are some guests in the house, and it is winter, and we have no fire." So he flew away and got a bit of burning firewood in his beak and dropped it before the guests, to which they added fuel and made a blazing fire. But the little bird was not satisfied. He said again to his wife: "My dear, what shall we do? There is nothing to give these people to eat, and they are hungry. We are householders; it is our duty to feed anyone who comes to the house. I must do what I can; I will give them my body." So he plunged into the fire and perished. The guests saw him falling and tried to save him, but he was too quick for them.

The little bird's wife saw what her husband did, and she said: "Here are three persons and there is only one little bird for them to eat. It is not enough; it is my duty as a wife not to let my husband's effort go in vain. Let them have my body also." Then she fell into the fire and was burnt to death.

Then the three baby birds, when they saw what was done and that there was still not enough food for the three guests, said: "Our parents have done what they could and still it is not enough. It is our duty to carry on the work of our parents. Let our bodies go." And they too dashed down into the fire.

Amazed at what they saw, the three people could not of course eat these birds. They passed the night without food, and in the morning the king and the sannyāsin showed the princess the way, and she went back to her father.

Then the sannyāsin said to the king: "King, you have seen that each is great in his own place. If you want to live in the world, live like those birds, ready at any moment to sacrifice yourself for others. If you want to renounce the world, be like that young man, to whom the most beautiful woman and a kingdom were as nothing. If you want to be a householder, hold your life as a sacrifice for the welfare of others; and if you choose the life of renunciation, do not even look at beauty and money and power. Each is great in his own place, but the duty of the one is not the duty of the other."

THE SECRET OF WORK

HELPING OTHERS PHYSICALLY, by removing their physical needs, is indeed great; but the help is greater according as the need is greater and the help more far-reaching. If a man's wants can be removed for an hour, it is helping him indeed; if his wants can be removed for a year, it will be rendering him more help; but if his wants can be removed for ever, it is surely the greatest help that can be given him.

Spiritual knowledge is the only thing that can destroy our miseries for ever; any other knowledge removes wants only for a time. It is only with the knowledge of the Spirit that the root cause of want is destroyed for ever; so helping man spiritually is the highest help that can be given him. He who gives man spiritual knowledge is the greatest benefactor of mankind, and we always find that they are the most powerful who help man in his spiritual needs, because spirituality is the true inspiration of all our activities. A spiritually strong and sound man will be strong in every other respect, if he so wishes. Until there is spiritual strength in a man, even physical needs cannot be well satisfied.

Next to spiritual comes intellectual help. The gift of knowledge is a far higher gift than that of food and clothes; it is even higher than giving life to a man, because the real life of man consists in knowledge. Ignorance is death; knowledge is life. Life is of very little value if it is a life in the dark, groping through ignorance and misery.

Next in order comes, of course, helping a man physically. Therefore, in considering the question of helping others, we must always strive not to commit the mistake of thinking that physical help is the only help that can be given. It is not only the last but the least, because it cannot give any permanent satisfaction. The misery that I feel when I am hungry is satisfied by eating, but hunger returns; my misery can cease for ever only when I am beyond all physical wants. Then hunger will not make me miserable; no distress, no sorrow, will be able to move me. So that help which tends to make us strong spiritually is the highest, next to it comes intellectual help, and after that physical help.

The miseries of the world cannot be cured by physical help only; until a man's nature changes, these physical needs will always arise and miseries will always be felt, and no amount of physical help will cure them completely. The only lasting solution is to give man spiritual wisdom. Ignorance is the mother of all the evil and all the misery we see. Let men have light, let them be pure and spiritually strong and educated; then alone will misery cease in the world, and not before. We may convert every house in the country into a charity asylum; we may fill the land with hospitals; but the misery of man will continue to exist until man's character changes.

We read in the Bhagavad Gītā again and again that we must all work inces-

471

santly. All work is by nature composed of good and evil. We cannot do any work which will not do some good somewhere; there cannot be any work which will not cause some harm somewhere. Every work must necessarily be a mixture of good and evil. Yet we are commanded to work incessantly. Good and evil will both have their results, will bear their fruit. Good action will produce good effects; bad action, bad. But good and bad are both bondages of the soul. The solution reached in the Gītā in regard to the bondage-producing nature of work is that, if we do not attach ourselves to the work we do, it will not have any binding effect on our soul. This is the one central idea in the Gītā: work incessantly, but be not attached. We shall try to understand what is meant by non-attachment to work.

The word *samskāra* can be translated very nearly by "inherent tendency." To use the simile of a lake for the mind: a ripple or a wave that rises in the mind does not die out entirely when it subsides, but leaves a mark and a future possibility of its coming back. This mark, with the possibility of the wave's reappearing, is what is called a samskāra.

Every work we do, every movement of our body, every thought we think, leaves such an impression on the mind-stuff; and even when these impressions are not obvious on the surface, they are sufficiently strong to work beneath the surface, subconsciously. What we are every moment is determined by the sum total of these impressions in the mind. What I am just at this moment is the effect of the sum total of all the impressions of my past. This is really what is meant by character; each man's character is determined by the sum total of these impressions. If good impressions prevail, the character becomes good; if bad, it becomes bad. If a man continually hears bad words, thinks bad thoughts, does bad deeds, his mind will be full of bad impressions; and they will influence his thought and work without his being conscious of the fact. These bad impressions are always working, and their resultant must be evil; and that man will be a bad man; he cannot help it. The sum total of these impressions in him will create a strong motive power for doing bad deeds, he will be like a tool in the hands of his impressions, and they will force him to do evil. Similarly, if a man thinks good thoughts and does good works, the sum total of these impressions will be good; and they, in a similar manner, will force him to do good even in spite of himself. When a man has done much good work and thought many good thoughts, there is created in him an irresistible tendency to do good. His mind, controlled by the sum total of his good tendencies, will not then allow him to do evil even if he wishes to do so. The tendencies will turn him back; he is completely under the influence of the good tendencies. When such is the case, a man's good character is said to be established.

When the tortoise tucks its head and feet inside its shell, you may kill it and break the shell to pieces, and yet the head and feet will not come out; even so the character of that man who has control over his motives and organs is unchangeably established. He controls his own inner forces, and nothing can draw them out against his will. Through the continuous reflex action of good thoughts and good impressions moving over the surface of the mind, the tendency for doing good becomes strong, and as a result we feel able to control the indriyas—the sense-organs, the nerve-centres. Thus alone is character established; then alone does a man attain to truth. Such a man is safe for ever; he cannot do any evil. You may place him in any company; there will be no danger for him.

There is a still higher state than having this good tendency, and that is the desire for liberation. You must remember that freedom of the soul is the goal of all the yogas, and all of them lead to the same result. By work alone men may get to where Buddha got largely by meditation or Christ by prayer. Buddha was a working jnāni; Christ was a bhakta; but the same goal was reached by both of them. The difficulty is here: Liberation means entire freedom—freedom from the bondage of good as well as from the bondage of evil. A golden chain is as much a chain as an iron one. Suppose there is a thorn in my finger. I use another to take the first one out, and when I have done so I throw both of them away; I have no need to keep the second thorn, because both are thorns after all. So the bad tendencies are to be counteracted by the good ones; the bad impressions in the mind should be removed by the waves of good impressions, until all that is evil almost disappears, or is subdued and held in control in a corner of the mind. But after that the good tendencies also have to be conquered. Thus the "attached" will become the "unattached." Work, but let not the action or the thought of it produce a deep impression on the mind. Let the ripples come and go; let huge actions proceed from the muscles and the brain, but let them not make any deep impression on the soul.

How can this be done? We see that the impression of any action to which we attach ourselves remains. I may meet hundreds of persons during the day, and among them see also one whom I love; and when I retire at night and try to think of all the faces I saw, the only face that comes before my mind is the face that I saw perhaps only for one minute and that I loved. All the others have vanished. My attachment to this particular person caused a very deep impression on my mind. Physiologically, the impressions have all been the same; every one of the different faces that I saw was pictured on the retina, and the brain took the picture in, and yet there was no similarity of effect upon the mind. Most of the faces, perhaps, were entirely new faces, about which I had never thought before; but that one face of which I got only a glimpse found associations inside. Perhaps I had pictured the person in my mind for years, knew hundreds of things about him, and this vision of him awakened hundreds of sleeping memories in my mind; this one impression, having been repeated perhaps a hundred times more than those of the different faces together, produced a great effect on the mind.

Therefore be unattached. Let things work; let the brain centres work; work incessantly, but let not a ripple conquer the mind. Work as if you were a stranger in this land, a sojourner. Work incessantly, but do not bind yourselves; bondage is terrible. This world is not our habitation, but only a stage through which we are passing. Remember that great saying of the Sāmkhya philosophy: "The whole of nature is for the soul, not the soul for nature." The very reason for nature's existence is the education of the soul; it has no other meaning. It is there because the soul must have knowledge, and through knowledge free itself. If we remember this always, we shall never be attached to nature; we shall know that nature is a book which we are to read, and that when we have gained the required knowledge the book is of no more value to us. Instead of that, however, we identify ourselves with nature; we think that the soul is for nature, that the spirit is for the flesh, and, as the common saying has it, we think that man "lives to eat," not "eats to live." We are continually making this mistake; we regard nature as the self and become attached to it; and as soon as this attachment comes, there is created in the soul a deep impression, which binds us down and makes us work, not through freedom but like slaves.

The whole gist of this teaching is that you should work as a master, not as a slave; work incessantly, but do not do slave's work. Do you not see how everybody works? Nobody can be altogether at rest. Ninety-nine per cent of mankind work like slaves, and the result is misery; it is all selfish work. Work through freedom! Work through love! The word *love* is very difficult to understand. Love never comes until there is freedom. There is no true love possible in the slave. If you buy a slave and tie him down in chains and make him work for you, he will work like a drudge, but there will be no love in him. So when we ourselves work as slaves for the things of the world, there can be no love in us, and our work is not true work. This is true of work done for relatives and friends, and it is true of work done for our own selves. Selfish work is slave's work. And here is a test: Every act of love brings happiness; there is no act of love which does not bring peace and blessedness as its reaction. Real Existence, real Knowledge, and real Love are eternally connected with one another—the three in one. Where one of them is, the others also must be; they are the three aspects of the One without a second, Existence-Knowledge-Bliss. When that Existence becomes relative, we see it as the world; that Knowledge becomes in its turn modified into the knowledge of the things of the world; and that Bliss forms the foundation of all the love known to the heart of man. Therefore true love can never react so as to cause pain either to the lover or to the beloved. Suppose a man loves a woman. He wishes to have her all to himself and feels extremely jealous about her every movement; he wants her to sit near him, to stand near him, and to eat and move at his bidding. He is a slave to her and wishes to have her as his slave. That is not love; it is a kind of morbid affection of the slave, insinuating itself as love. It cannot be love, because it is painful; if she does not do what he wants, it brings him pain. With love there is no painful reaction; love brings only a reaction of bliss. If it does not, it is not love; it is a mistaking of something else for love. When you have succeeded in loving your husband, your wife, your children, the world, the whole universe, in such a manner that there is no reaction of pain or jealousy, no selfish feeling, then you are in a fit state to be unattached.

Krishna says: "Look at Me, Arjuna! If I stop working for one moment the whole universe will die. I have nothing to gain from work; I am the sole Lord. But why do I work? Because I love the world." God is unattached because He loves. That real love makes us unattached. Wherever there is attachment, the clinging to the things of the world, you must know that it is all physical attraction between particles of matter—something that attracts two bodies nearer and nearer all the time, and, if they cannot get near enough, produces pain. But where there is real love it does not rest on physical attraction at all.

Such lovers may be a thousand miles away from one another, but their love will be there all the same; it does not die and will never produce any painful reaction.

To attain this non-attachment is almost a life-work; but as soon as we have reached this point we have attained the goal of love and become free. The bondage of nature falls away from us, and we see nature as it is; it forges no more chains for us. We stand entirely free and do not take the results of work into consideration. Who then cares what the results may be?

Do you ask anything of your children in return for what you have given them? It is your duty to work for them, and there the matter ends. In whatever you do for a particular person, city, or state, assume the same attitude towards it as you do towards your children—expect nothing in return. If you can invariably take the position of a giver, in which everything given by you is a free offering to the world, without any thought of return, then your work will bring you no attachment. Attachment comes only where we expect a return.

If working as slaves results in selfishness and attachment, working as masters of our own minds gives rise to the bliss of non-attachment. We often talk of right and justice, but we find that in the world right and justice are mere baby's talk. There are two things which guide the conduct of men: might and mercy. The exercise of might is invariably the exercise of selfishness. Men and women generally try to make the most of whatever power or advantage they have. Mercy is heaven itself; to be good we have all to be merciful. Even justice and right should stand on mercy. All thought of obtaining a return for the work we do hinders our spiritual progress; nay, in the end it brings misery.

There is another way in which this idea of mercy and selfless charity can be put into practice; that is by looking upon work as worship, if we believe in a Personal God. Here we give up all the fruits of our work unto the Lord; and worshipping Him thus, we have no right to expect anything from mankind for the work we do. The Lord Himself works incessantly and is ever without attachment. Just as water cannot wet the lotus leaf, so work cannot bind the unselfish man by giving rise to attachment to results. The selfless and unattached man may live in the very heart of a crowded and sinful city; he will not be touched by sin.

This idea of complete self-sacrifice is illustrated by the following story:

After the battle of Kurukshetra the five Pāndava brothers performed a great sacrifice and made very large gifts to the poor. All the people expressed amazement at the greatness and splendour of the sacrifice and said that such a sacrifice the world had never seen before. But after the ceremony there came a little mongoose; half his body was golden and the other half was brown; and he began to roll on the floor of the sacrificial hall. He said to those present: "You are all mistaken. This was no sacrifice." "What!" they exclaimed. "You say this was no sacrifice! Do you not know how money and jewels were poured out to the poor and everyone became rich and happy? This was the most wonderful sacrifice any man ever performed."

But the mongoose said: "There was once a little village, and in it there dwelt a poor brāhmin with his wife, his son, and his son's wife. They were very poor and lived on small gifts made to them for preaching and teaching. There came in that land a three years' famine, and the poor brāhmin suffered more than ever. At last, when the family had starved for days, the father brought home one morning a little barley flour, which he had been fortunate enough to obtain, and he divided it into four parts, one for each member of the family. They prepared it for their meal, and just as they were about to eat there was a knock at the door. The father opened it, and there stood a guest." (Now, in India a guest is a sacred person; he is like a god for the time being and must be treated as such.) "So the brāhmin said, 'Come in, sir; you are welcome.' He set before the guest his own portion of food. After quickly eating it the guest said: 'Oh, sir, you have almost killed me! I have been starving for ten days, and this little bit has but increased my hunger.' Then the wife said to her husband, 'Give him my share.' But the husband said, 'Not so.' The wife however insisted, saying: 'Here is a poor man. It is our duty as householders to see that he is fed, and it is my duty as a wife to give him my portion, seeing that you have no more to offer him.' Then she gave her share to the guest, after eating which he said he was still burning with hunger. So the son said: 'Take my portion also. It is the duty of a son to help his father to fulfil his obligations.' The guest ate that, but remained still unsatisfied; so the son's wife gave him her portion also. That was sufficient, and the guest departed, blessing them. That night those four people died of starvation. A few grains of that flour had fallen on the floor, and when I rolled my body on them half of it became golden, as you see. Since then I have been travelling all over the world, hoping to find another sacrifice like that. But nowhere have I found one; not even here has the other half of my body been turned into gold. That is why I say this was no sacrifice."

This idea of charity is going out of India; great men are becoming fewer and fewer. When I was first learning English I read an English story-book in which there was a story about a dutiful boy who had gone out to work and given some of his money to his old mother, and this act was praised for three or four pages. I was puzzled. No Hindu boy can ever understand the moral of that story. Now I understand it when I hear the Western idea, "every man for himself." And some men take everything for themselves, and fathers and mothers and wives and children go to the wall. That should never and nowhere be the ideal of the householder.

Now you see what karma-yoga means: even at the point of death to help anyone, without asking questions. Be cheated millions of times and never ask a question, and never think that you are doing good. Never vaunt of your gifts to the poor or expect their gratitude, but rather be grateful to them for giving you the occasion of practising charity towards them. Thus it is plain that to be an ideal householder is a much more difficult task than to be an ideal sannyāsin; the true life of action is indeed as hard as, if not harder than, the true life of renunciation.

WHAT IS DUTY?

It is necessary in the study of karma-yoga to know what duty is. If I have to do something, I must first know that it is my duty, and then I can do it. The idea of duty, again, is different in different nations. The Mohammedan says that what is written in his book, the Koran, is his duty; the Hindu says that what is in the Vedas is his duty; and the Christian says that what is in the Bible is his duty. We find that there are varied ideas of duty, differing according to different states in life, different historical periods, and different nations.

The term duty, like every other universal, abstract term, is impossible to define clearly; we can only get an idea of it by knowing its practical operations and results. When certain things occur before us, we feel a natural or trained impulse to act in a certain manner towards them; when this impulse comes, the mind begins to think about the situation; sometimes it thinks that it is good to act in a particular manner under the given conditions, at other times it thinks that it is wrong to act in the same manner even in the very same circumstances. The ordinary idea of duty everywhere is that every good man follows the dictates of his conscience. But what is it that makes an act a duty? If a Christian finds a piece of beef before him and does not eat it to save his own life, or will not give it to save the life of another man, he is sure to feel that he has not done his duty. But if a Hindu dares to eat that piece of beef or to give it to another Hindu, he is equally sure to feel that he too has not done his duty; the Hindu's training and education make him feel that way. In the last century there was a notorious band of robbers in India called Thugs. They thought it their duty to kill any man they could and take away his money; the larger the number of men they killed, the better they thought they were. Ordinarily, if a man goes out into the street and shoots down another man, he is apt to feel sorry for it, thinking that he has done wrong. But if the very same man, as a soldier in his regiment, kills not one but twenty, he is certain to feel glad and think that he has done his duty remarkably well.

Therefore we see that it is not the thing done that defines a duty. To give an objective definition of duty is thus impossible. Yet one can define duty from the subjective side. Any action that makes us go Godward is a good action and is our duty; any action that makes us go downward is evil and is not our duty. From the subjective standpoint we may see that certain acts have a tendency to exalt and ennoble us, while certain other acts have a tendency to degrade and brutalize us. But it is not possible to make out with certainty which acts have which kind of tendency in relation to all persons, of all sorts and conditions. There is, however, only one idea of duty which has been universally accepted by all mankind, of all ages and sects and countries, and it has been summed up

477

in a Sanskrit aphorism thus: "Not injuring any living being is virtue; injuring any being is sin."

The Bhagavad Gītā frequently alludes to duties as dependent upon birth and position in life. Birth and also position in life and society largely determine the mental and moral attitude of individuals towards the various activities of life. It is therefore our duty to do that work which will exalt and ennoble us in accordance with the ideals and activities of the society in which we are born. But it must be particularly remembered that the same ideals and activities do not prevail in all societies and countries; our ignorance of this is the main cause of much of the hatred of one nation towards another. An American thinks that whatever an American does in accordance with the customs of his country is the best thing to do, and that whoever does not follow his customs must be a very wicked man. A Hindu thinks that his customs are the only right ones and are the best in the world, and that whoever does not obey them must be the most wicked man living. This is quite a natural mistake, which all of us are apt to make. But it is very harmful; it is the cause of half the uncharitableness found in the world.

When I came to this country[1] and was going through the Chicago Fair, a man from behind pulled at my turban. I looked back and saw that he was a very gentlemanly-looking man, neatly dressed. I spoke to him and when he found that I knew English he became very much abashed. On another occasion in the same Fair a man gave me a push. When I asked him the reason, he also was ashamed and stammered out an apology saying, "Why do you dress that way?" The sympathies of these men were limited within the range of their own language and their own fashion of dress. Much of the dislike felt by powerful nations for weaker ones is caused by this kind of prejudice, which dries up their fellow-feeling for others. That very man who asked me in Chicago why I did not dress as he did and wanted to ill-treat me because of my dress may have been a very good man, a good father and a good citizen; but the kindliness of his nature died out as soon as he saw a man in different dress. Foreigners are exploited in all countries, because they do not know how to defend themselves; thus they carry home false impressions of the peoples they have seen. Sailors, soldiers, and traders behave in foreign lands in very queer ways, although they would not dream of doing so in their own country; perhaps this is why the Chinese call Europeans and Americans "foreign devils." They would not do this if they saw the good, the kindly side, of Western life.

Therefore the one point we ought to remember is that we should always try to see the duty of others through their own eyes and never judge the customs of other peoples by our own standard. I am not the standard of the universe. I have to accommodate myself to the world; the world does not have to adjust itself to me. So we see that environments change the nature of our duties, and doing the duty which is ours at any particular time is the best thing we can do in this world. Let us do the duty which is ours by birth; and when we have done that, let us do the duty which is ours by our position in life and in society. There is, however, one great danger in human nature—that is, that man never

[1] The United States of America.

examines himself. He thinks he is quite as fit to be on the throne as the king. Even if he is, he must first show that he has done his duty in his own position; and then higher duties will come to him. When we begin to work earnestly in the world, nature gives us blows right and left and soon enables us to find out our position. No man can long occupy satisfactorily a position for which he is not fit. There is no use in grumbling against nature's adjustment. He who does the lower work is not therefore a lower man. No man is to be judged by the mere nature of his duties, but all should be judged by the manner and the spirit in which they perform them.

Later on we shall find that even this idea of duty undergoes change, and that the greatest work is done only when there is no selfish motive to prompt it. Yet it is work through the sense of duty that leads us to work without any idea of duty. Then work becomes worship—nay, something higher; then work is done for its own sake. We shall find that the goal of duty, either from the standpoint of ethics or of love, is the same as in all the other yogas, namely, to attenuate the lower self so that the Higher Self may shine forth, and to lessen the frittering away of energies on the lower plane of existence so that the soul may manifest them on the higher planes. This is accomplished by the constant denial of low desires, which duty rigorously requires. The whole organization of society has thus been developed consciously or unconsciously by means of action and experience. By limiting selfishness, we open the way to an unlimited expansion of the real nature of man.

Duty is seldom sweet. It is only when love greases its wheels that it runs smoothly; otherwise it is a continuous friction. How else could parents do their duties to their children, husbands to their wives, and vice versa? Do we not meet with cases of friction every day in our lives? Duty is sweet only through love, and love shines alone in freedom. Yet is it freedom to be a slave to the senses, to anger, to jealousies, and to a hundred other petty things that occur every day in human life? In all these little roughnesses that we meet with in life the highest expression of freedom is to forbear. Women who are slaves to their own irritable, jealous tempers are apt to blame their husbands and assert their own "freedom"—as they think—not knowing that thereby they only prove that they are slaves. So it is with husbands who eternally find fault with their wives.

Chastity is the first virtue in man or woman, and the man who, however he may have strayed away, cannot be brought to the right path by a gentle and loving and chaste wife is indeed very rare. The world is not yet as bad as that. We hear much about brutal husbands all over the world and about the impurity of men, but is it not true that there are quite as many brutal and impure women as men? If all women were as good and pure as their own constant assertions would lead one to believe, I am perfectly satisfied that there would not be one impure man in the world. What brutality is there which purity and chastity cannot conquer? A good, chaste wife, who thinks of all men except her own husband as her children and has the attitude of a mother towards them, can grow so great in the power of her purity that there will not be a single man, however brutal, who will not breathe an atmosphere of holiness in her presence. Similarly, every husband must look upon all women, except his own wife, as he looks on his own mother or daughter or sister. That man, again, who wants to be a teacher of religion must look upon every woman as his mother and always behave towards her as such.

The position of the mother is the highest in the world, for it is the one place in which to learn and exercise the greatest unselfishness. The love of God is the only love that is higher than a mother's love; all other forms of love are lower. It is the duty of the mother to think of her children first and then of herself. But instead of that, if the parents are always thinking of themselves first, the result is that the relation between parents and children becomes the same as that between birds and their offspring; as soon as the latter are fledged, they do not recognize their parents. Blessed, indeed, is the man who can look upon woman as the representative of the Motherhood of God. Blessed, indeed, is the woman to whom man represents the Fatherhood of God. Blessed are the children who look upon their parents as Divinity manifested on earth.

The only way to grow is to do the duty near at hand, and thus go on gathering strength till the highest state is reached. A young sannyāsin went to a forest. There he meditated, worshipped, and practised yoga for a long time. After much hard work and practice, he was one day sitting under a tree, when some dry leaves fell upon his head. He looked up and saw a crow and a crane fighting on the top of the tree, which made him very angry. He said, "What! How dare you throw these dry leaves upon my head?" As with these words he angrily looked at them, a flash of fire went out—such was the yogi's power—and burnt the birds to ashes. He was very glad, almost overjoyed, at this development of power: he could burn the crow and the crane by a look! After a time he had to go to the town to beg his bread. He stood at a door and called out, "Mother, give me food." A voice came from inside the house: "Wait a little, my son." The young man thought: "You wretched woman, how dare you make me wait? You do not yet know my power." While he was thinking thus the voice said again: "Boy, don't be thinking too much of yourself. Here is neither crow nor crane." He was astonished. Still he had to wait. At last the woman came, and he humbly said to her, "Mother, how did you know that?" She said: "My boy, I do not know your yoga or your other practices. I am a simple, ordinary woman. I made you wait because my husband is ill and I was nursing him. All my life I have struggled to do my duty. When I was unmarried, I did my duty to my parents; now that I am married, I do my duty to my husband. That is all the yoga I practise. But by doing my duty I have become illumined; thus I could read your thoughts and know what you had done in the forest." She further told him that if he wanted to know something higher, he should go to the market of a certain town, where he would find a vyādha² who would tell him something that he would be very glad to learn. The sannyāsin thought, "Why should I go to that town, and to a vyādha?" But after what he had seen, his mind had opened a little; so he went. When he came to the town he found the market, and there saw, at a distance, a big fat vyādha cutting meat with a big knife, talking and bargaining with different people. The young man said: "Lord help me! Is this the man from whom I am going to learn? He is the incarnation of a demon, if he is anything." In the meantime the man looked up

² One belonging to the lowest class of people, who were hunters and butchers.

and said: "O Swami, did a lady send you here? Take a seat until I have done my business." The sannyāsin thought, "What comes to me here?" He took a seat, however. The man went on with his work, and after he had finished he took his money and said to the sannyāsin, "Come, sir; come to my home." On reaching home the vyādha gave him a seat, saying, "Wait here," and went into the house. He then bathed his old father and mother, fed them, and did all he could to please them, after which he came to the sannyāsin and said: "Now, sir, you have come here to see me. What can I do for you?" The sannyāsin asked him a few questions about the soul and about God, and the vyādha gave him a lecture which forms a part of the Mahābhārata called the Vyādha Gītā. It contains one of the highest flights of Vedānta. When the vyādha finished his teaching the sannyāsin felt astonished. He said: "Why are you in that body? With such knowledge as yours, why are you in a vyādha's body, and doing such filthy, ugly work?" "My son," replied the vyādha, "no duty is ugly, no duty is impure. My birth placed me in these circumstances and this environment. In my boyhood I learnt the trade. I am unattached and I try to do my duty well as a householder; I do all I can to make my father and mother happy. I neither know your yoga, nor have become a sannyāsin, nor have I gone out of the world into a forest; nevertheless all that I know has come to me through the unattached doing of the duty which belongs to my position."

There is a sage in India, a great yogi, one of the most wonderful men I have ever seen in my life.[3] He is a peculiar man; he will not teach anyone. If you ask him a question he will not answer. He hesitates to take up the position of a teacher; he will not do it. If you ask a question and wait for some days, in the course of conversation he will bring up the subject, and wonderful light will he throw on it. He told me once the secret of work: "Let the end and the means be one." When you are doing any work, do not think of anything beyond. Do it as worship, as the highest worship, and devote your whole life to it for the time being. The vyādha and the woman in the story did their duty with cheerfulness and whole-heartedness; and the result was that they became illumined, thus clearly showing that the right performance of the duties of any station in life, without attachment to results, leads us to the realization of the perfection of the soul.

It is the worker attached to results who grumbles about the nature of the duty which has fallen to his lot; to the unattached worker all duties are equally good and form efficient instruments with which selfishness and sensuality may be killed and the freedom of the soul secured. We are all apt to think too highly of ourselves. Our duties are determined by our deserts to a much larger extent than we are willing to grant. Competition rouses envy, and it kills the kindliness of the heart. To the grumbler all duties are distasteful; nothing will ever satisfy him, and his whole life is doomed to failure. Let us work on, doing whatever happens to be our duty, and be ever ready to put our shoulders to the wheel. Then surely we shall see the Light.

[3] A reference to Pavhari Baba, whom Swami Vivekananda knew well. (See page 42.)

WE HELP OURSELVES, NOT
THE WORLD

BEFORE CONSIDERING further how devotion to duty helps us in our spiritual progress, let me place before you in brief another aspect of what we in India mean by karma. In every religion there are three parts: philosophy, mythology, and ritual. Philosophy, of course, is the essence of every religion; mythology explains and illustrates it by means of the more or less legendary lives of great men, stories and fables of wonderful things, and so on; ritual gives to that philosophy a still more concrete form, so that everyone may grasp it—ritual is in fact concretized philosophy. This ritual is karma. It is necessary in every religion, because most of us cannot understand abstract spiritual things until we grow a great deal spiritually.

It is easy for men to think that they can understand everything, but when it comes to actual experience they find that abstract ideas are often very hard to comprehend. Therefore symbols are of great help and we cannot dispense with the symbolical method of understanding abstract philosophical ideas. From time immemorial all kinds of symbols have been used by religions. In one sense we cannot think except in symbols; words themselves are symbols of thought. In another sense everything in the universe may be looked upon as a symbol; the whole universe is a symbol and God is the essence behind. This kind of symbology is not simply the creation of man. Certain people belonging to a religion did not sit down together and think out certain symbols, and bring them into existence out of their own minds. The symbols of religion have a natural growth. Otherwise, why is it that certain symbols are associated with certain ideas in the minds of almost everyone?

Certain symbols are universally prevalent. Many of you may think that the cross first came into existence as a symbol in connexion with the Christian religion; but as a matter of fact it existed before Christianity, before Moses was born, before the Vedas were revealed, even before there was any record of human things. There is evidence that the cross was used by the Aztecs and the Phoenicians; every race seems to have had the cross. Again, the symbol of the crucified Saviour, of a man crucified upon a cross, appears to have been known to almost every nation. The circle has been a great symbol throughout the world. Then there is the most universal of all symbols, the swastika. At one time it was thought that the Buddhists carried it all over the world with them; but it has been found out that ages before Buddhism it was used by various nations. In Babylon and in Egypt it was also in use. What does this show? It shows that all these symbols could not have been purely conventional. There must be some reason for their use, some natural association between them and the human mind.

482

Language is not the result of convention; it is not a fact that people ever agreed to represent certain ideas by certain words. There never was an idea without a corresponding word or a word without a corresponding idea. Ideas and words are in their nature inseparable. The symbols to represent ideas may be sound-symbols or colour-symbols. Deaf-and-dumb people have to think with other than sound-symbols. Every thought in the mind has a form as its counterpart; this is called in Sanskrit philosophy nāma-rupa—"name and form." It is as impossible to create by convention a system of symbols as it is to create a language.

In the world's ritualistic symbols we have an expression of the religious thought of humanity. It is easy to say that there is no use for rituals and temples and all such paraphernalia; every baby says that in modern times. But it must be easy for all to see that those who worship inside a temple are in many respects different from those who will not worship there. Therefore the association of particular temples, rituals, and other concrete forms with particular religions has a tendency to bring into the minds of the followers of those religions the thoughts for which those concrete things stand as symbols; and it is not wise to ignore rituals and symbology altogether. The study and practice of these things naturally form a part of karma-yoga.

There are many other aspects of this science of work. One among them is to know the relation between thought and word, and what can be achieved by the power of the word. In every religion the power of the word is recognized —so much so that in some of them creation itself is said to have come out of the Word. The external aspect of the thought of God is the Word, and because God thought and willed before He created, creation came out of the Word.

In this stress and hurry of our materialistic life our nerves lose sensitivity and become hardened. The older we grow and the longer we are knocked about in the world, the more callous we become; and we are apt to neglect even things that happen persistently and prominently around us. Human nature, however, asserts itself sometimes and we are led to inquire into and wonder at some of these common occurrences. Wondering is thus the first step in the acquisition of wisdom. Apart from the higher philosophic and religious value of the Word, we can see that sound-symbols play a prominent part in the drama of human life. I am talking to you. The vibrations of the air caused by my speaking go into your ears; they touch your nerves and produce effects in your minds. You cannot resist this. What could be more wonderful than this? One man calls another a fool, and this other stands up and clenches his fist and lands a blow on his nose. Look at the power of words! There is a woman weeping and miserable; another woman comes along and speaks a few gentle words to her; the doubled-up frame of the weeping woman becomes straight at once; her sorrow is gone and soon she begins to smile. Think of the power of the words! They are as great a force in common life as they are in higher philosophy. Day and night we manipulate this force without thought and without inquiry. To know the nature of this force and to use it well is also a part of karma-yoga.

Our duty to others means helping others, doing good to the world. Why should we do good to the world? Apparently to help the world, but really to help ourselves. We should always try to help the world. That should be the highest motive in us. But if we consider well, we find that the world does not require our help at all. This world was not made that you or I should come and help it. I once read a sermon in which it was said: "All this beautiful world is very good, because it gives us time and opportunity to help others." Apparently this is a very beautiful sentiment; but is it not blasphemy to say that the world needs our help? We cannot deny that there is much misery in it; to go out and help others is, therefore, the best thing we can do, although, in the long run, we shall find that by helping others we only help ourselves. As a boy I had some white mice. They were kept in a little box in which there were little wheels, and when the mice tried to cross the wheels, the wheels turned and turned, and the mice never got anywhere. So it is with the world and our helping it. The only gain is that we get moral exercise.

This world is neither good nor evil; each man manufactures a world for himself. If a blind man thinks of the world, he will think of it as soft or hard, cold or hot. We are a mass of happiness or misery; we have seen that hundreds of times in our lives. As a rule the young are optimistic and the old pessimistic. The young have life before them; the old complain that their day is gone; hundreds of desires, which they cannot fulfil, struggle in their hearts. Both are foolish nevertheless. Life is good or evil according to the state of mind in which we look at it; it is neither in itself. Fire, in itself, is neither good nor evil. When it keeps us warm we say, "How beautiful fire is!" When it burns our fingers we curse it. Still, in itself it is neither good nor bad; according as we use it, it produces in us the feeling of good or bad. So also is this world. It is perfect. By perfection I mean that it is perfectly fitted to meet its ends. We may all be perfectly sure that it will go on beautifully without us, and we need not bother our heads with wishing to help it.

Yet we must do good; the desire to do good is the highest motive power we have. But we must remember that it is a privilege to help others. Do not stand on a high pedestal and take five cents in your hand and say, "Here, my poor man!" But be grateful that the poor man is there, so that by making a gift to him you are able to help yourself. It is not the receiver that is blessed, but it is the giver. Be thankful that you are allowed to exercise your power of benevolence and mercy in the world, and thus become pure and perfect. All good acts tend to make us pure and perfect. What can we do at best? Build a hospital, make roads, or erect charity asylums! We may organize a charity and collect two or three millions of dollars, build a hospital with one million, with the second give balls and drink champagne, and of the third let the officers steal half, and leave the rest finally to reach the poor—but what are all these? One mighty wind in five minutes can break all your buildings up. What shall we do then? One volcanic eruption may sweep away all our roads and hospitals and cities and buildings. Let us give up all this foolish talk of doing good to the world. It is not waiting for your or my help. Yet we must work and constantly do good, because it is a blessing to ourselves. That is the only way we can become perfect. No beggar whom we have helped has ever owed a single cent to us; we owe everything to him, because he has allowed us to exercise our charity on him. It is entirely wrong to think that we have done, or can do, good to the world, or to think that we have helped certain people. It is a foolish thought, and all foolish thoughts bring misery. We think that we have helped some man and expect him to thank us; and because he does not, unhappiness comes to us. Why should we expect anything in return for what we do? Be grateful to the man you help. Think of him as God. Is it not a great privilege to be allowed to worship God by helping our fellow man? If we were really unattached, we should escape all this pain of vain expectation and could cheerfully do good work in the world. Never will unhappiness or misery come through work done without attachment. The world will go on with its happiness and misery through eternity.

There was a poor man who wanted some money, and someone had told him that if he could get hold of a ghost, he might command him to bring money or anything else he liked; so he was very anxious to get hold of a ghost. He went about searching for a man who would give him a ghost; and at last he found a sage with yogic powers, and besought his help. The sage asked him what he would do with a ghost. "I want a ghost to work for me. Teach me how to get hold of one, sir; I desire it very much," replied the man. But the sage said, "Don't disturb yourself; go home." The next day the man went again to the sage and began to weep and pray, "Give me a ghost; I must have a ghost, sir, to help me." At last the sage was disgusted and said: "Here is a magic word for you. Repeat it and a ghost will come; and whatever you say to him he will do. But beware; these ghosts are terrible beings and must be kept continually busy. If you fail to give them work they will take your life." The man replied, "That is easy; I can give him enough work for his whole life." Then he went to a forest and repeated the magic word for a long while, when a huge ghost appeared before him and said: "I am a ghost. I have been conquered by your magic; but you must keep me constantly employed. The moment you fail to give me work I will kill you." The man said, "Build me a palace," and the ghost said, "It is done; the palace is built." "Bring me money," said the man. "Here is your money," said the ghost. "Cut this forest down and build a city in its place." "That is done," said the ghost; "anything more?" Now the man began to be frightened and thought, "I can give him nothing more to do; he does everything in a trice." The ghost said, "Give me something to do or I will eat you up." The poor man could find no further occupation for him and was frightened. So he ran and ran and at last reached the sage, and said, "Oh, sir, save my life!" The sage asked him what the matter was, and the man replied: "I have nothing to give the ghost to do. Everything I tell him to do he does in a moment, and he threatens to eat me up if I do not give him work." Just then the ghost arrived, saying, "I'll eat you up," and he was about to swallow the man. The man began to tremble, and begged the sage to save his life. The sage said: "I will find you a way out. Do you see that dog with a curly tail? Draw your sword quickly and cut his tail off and give it to the ghost to straighten out." The man cut off the dog's tail and gave it to the ghost, saying, "Straighten that out for me." The ghost took it and slowly and carefully straightened it out, but as soon as he let it go, it instantly curled up again. Once more he laboriously straightened it out, only to find that again it curled up as soon as he let it go. Once more he patiently straightened it out, but as soon as he let it go it curled up again. So he went on for days and days, until he was exhausted and said: "I was never in such trouble before in my life. I am an old, veteran ghost, but never before was I in such trouble. I will make a compromise with you. You let me off and I will let you keep all I have given you and will promise not to harm you." The man was much pleased and accepted the offer gladly.

This world is like a dog's curly tail, and people have been striving to straighten it out for hundreds of years; but when they let it go, it curls up again. How could it be otherwise? When we know that this world is like a dog's curly tail and will never be straightened, we shall not become fanatics. One must first know how to work without attachment; then one will not be a fanatic. If there were no fanaticism in the world it would make much more progress than it does now. It is a mistake to think that fanaticism can make for the progress of mankind. On the contrary, it is a retarding element, creating hatred and anger, causing people to fight each other, and making them unsympathetic. We think that whatever we do or possess is the best in the world, and what we do not do or possess is of no value. So always remember the instance of the dog's curly tail whenever you have a tendency to become a fanatic. You need not worry or make yourself sleepless about the world; it will go on without you. When you have avoided fanaticism, then alone will you work well. It is the level-headed man, the calm man of good judgement and cool nerves, of great sympathy and love, who does good work and so does good to himself. The fanatic is foolish and has no sympathy; he can never straighten out the world, nor can he himself become pure and perfect.

To recapitulate the chief points in today's lecture: First, we have to bear in mind that we are all debtors to the world and that the world does not owe us anything. It is a great privilege for all of us to be allowed to do anything for the world. In helping the world we really help ourselves. The second point is that there is a God in this universe. It is not true that this universe is drifting and stands in need of help from you and me. God is ever present therein; He is undying and eternally active and infinitely watchful. When the whole universe sleeps He sleeps not; He is working incessantly; all the changes in the world are caused by Him. Thirdly, we ought not to hate anyone. This world will always continue to be a mixture of good and evil. Our duty is to sympathize with the weak and to love even the wrongdoer. The world is a grand moral gymnasium wherein we all have to take exercise so that we shall become stronger and stronger spiritually. Fourthly, we ought not to be fanatics of any kind, because fanaticism is opposed to love. You hear fanatics glibly saying, "I do not hate the sinner; I hate the sin"; but I am prepared to go any distance to see the face of that man who can really make a distinction between the sin and the sinner. It is easy to say so. If we can distinguish well between quality and substance we may become perfect men. It is not easy to do this. And further, the calmer we are and the less disturbed our nerves, the more shall we love and the better will our work be.

NON-ATTACHMENT IS COMPLETE
SELF-ABNEGATION

JUST AS EVERY ACTION that emanates from us comes back to us as reaction, even so our actions may act on other people and theirs on us. Perhaps all of you have observed that when persons do evil actions they become more and more evil, and that when they begin to do good they become better and better and learn to do good at all times. This intensification of the influence of action cannot be explained on any other ground than that we act and react upon each other. When I am doing a certain action, my mind may be said to be in a certain state of vibration; all minds which are in a similar state will have the tendency to be affected by my mind. To take an illustration from physical science: Suppose there are different musical instruments tuned alike in one room; you may have noticed that when one is struck the others have a tendency to vibrate so as to give the same note. So all minds that have the same tension, so to say, will be equally affected by the same thought. Of course, this influence of thought on mind will vary, according to distance and other causes, but the mind is always open to being affected. Suppose I am doing an evil act; my mind is in a certain state of vibration, and all minds in the universe which are in a similar state have a tendency to be affected by the vibration of my mind. So, when I am doing a good action, my mind is in another state of vibration, and all minds similarly strung have a tendency to be affected by my mind; and this power of mind upon mind is greater or less according as the force of the tension is greater or less.

Following this simile further, it is quite possible that, just as light-waves may travel for millions of years before they reach any object, so thought-waves too may travel hundreds of years before they meet an object with which they will vibrate in unison. It is quite possible, therefore, that this atmosphere of ours is full of such thought-vibrations, both good and evil. Every thought projected from every brain goes on vibrating, as it were, until it meets an object fit to receive it. Any mind which is capable of receiving some of these impulses will take them immediately. So when a man is doing evil actions he has brought his mind to a certain state of tension, and all the waves corresponding to that state of tension, which may be said to be already in the atmosphere, will struggle to enter into his mind. That is why an evil-doer generally goes on doing more and more evil. His actions become intensified. Such, also, is true of the doer of good; he will open himself to all the good waves that are in the atmosphere, and his good actions also will become intensified. We run, therefore, a two-fold danger in doing evil: first, we open ourselves to all the evil influence surrounding us; secondly, we create evil which will affect others perhaps hundreds of years hence. In doing evil we injure ourselves and others also. In doing good we do good to ourselves and to others as well; and like all other forces in man, these forces of good and evil also gather strength from outside.

According to karma-yoga, the action one has done cannot be destroyed until it has borne fruit; no power in nature can stop it from yielding its results. If I do an evil deed I must suffer for it; there is no power in this universe to stop or stay it. Similarly, if I do a good deed there is no power in the universe which can stop its bearing good results. The cause must have its effect; nothing can prevent or restrain this.

Now comes a very fine and serious point in karma-yoga, namely, that these actions of ours, both good and evil, are intimately connected with each other. We cannot draw a line of demarcation and say that one action is entirely good and another entirely evil. There is no action which does not bear good and evil fruits at the same time. To take the nearest example: I am talking to you, and some of you, perhaps, think I am doing good; and at the same time I am surely killing thousands of microbes in the atmosphere. I am thus doing evil to something else. When an action affects, in a good manner, those whom we know and who are very dear to us, we say that it is a very good action. For instance, you may call my speaking to you very good, but the microbes will not; the microbes you do not see, but yourselves you do see. The way in which my talk affects you is obvious to you, but how it affects the microbes is not so obvious. And so, too, if we analyse our evil actions, we may find that some good possibly results from them somewhere. He who sees that in good action there is something evil, and that in evil action there is some good somewhere, has known the secret of work.

But what follows from this? That howsoever we may try, there cannot be any action which is perfectly pure or any which is perfectly impure, taking purity and impurity in the sense of injury and non-injury. We cannot breathe or live without injuring others, and every bit of the food we eat is taken away from another's mouth; our very lives are crowding out other lives. It may be men or animals or microbes, but some one or other of these we have to crowd out. That being the case, it naturally follows that perfection can never be attained by work. We may work through all eternity, but there will be no way out of this intricate maze. You may work on and on and on; there will be no end to this inevitable association of good and evil in the results of work.

The second point to consider is: What is the end of work? We find that the vast majority of people in every country believe that there will be a time when this world shall become perfect, when there shall be no disease or death or unhappiness or wickedness. That is a very good idea, a very good motive power to inspire and uplift the ignorant; but if we think for a moment, we shall find on the very face of it that it cannot be so. How can it be, seeing that good and evil are the obverse and reverse of the same coin? How can you have good without evil at the same time? What is meant by perfection? A perfect life is a contradiction in terms. Life itself is a state of continuous struggle between ourselves and everything outside. Every moment we are actually fighting with external nature, and if we are defeated our life must go. There is, for instance, a continual struggle for food and air. If food or air fails we die. Life is not a simple and smoothly flowing thing; it is a complex affair. This struggle between something inside and the external world is what we call life. So it is clear that when this struggle ceases there will be an end of life. What is meant by ideal happiness is this: the cessation of struggle. But then life too will cease, for the struggle can cease only when life itself has ceased.

We have seen already that in helping the world we help ourselves. The main effect of work done for others is that it purifies us. By means of the constant effort to do good to others we are attempting to forget ourselves; this forgetfulness of self is the one great lesson we have to learn in life. Man foolishly thinks that through selfish action he can make himself happy; but after years of struggle he finds out at last that true happiness consists in killing selfishness and that no one can make him happy except himself. Every act of charity, every thought of sympathy, every act of help, every good deed, takes so much of self-importance away from our little selves and makes us think of ourselves as the lowest and the least; and therefore they are all good. Here we find that jnāna, bhakti, and karma all come to one point. The highest idea is eternal and entire self-abnegation, where there is no "I," but all is "Thou"; and whether he is conscious or unconscious of it, karma-yoga leads man to that end. A religious preacher may become horrified at the idea of an Impersonal God; he may insist on a Personal God and wish to maintain his own identity and individuality, whatever he may mean by that. But his ideas of ethics, if they are really good, cannot but be based on the highest self-abnegation. This is the basis of all morality. You may extend it to men or animals or angels; it is the one basic idea, the one fundamental principle, running through all ethical systems.

You will find various classes of men in this world. First, there are the godly men, whose self-abnegation is complete and who do only good to others even at the sacrifice of their own lives. These are the highest of men. If there are a hundred of such in any country, that country need never despair. But they are unfortunately too few. Then there are the good men, who do good to others so long as it does not injure themselves. And there is a third class, who, to do good to themselves, injure others. It is said by a Sanskrit poet that there is a fourth unnameable class of people, who injure others merely for injury's sake. Just as there are at one pole of existence supremely good men, who do good for the sake of doing good, so, at the other pole, there are men who injure others just for the sake of the injury. They do not gain anything thereby, but it is their nature to do evil.

Here are two Sanskrit words. The one is pravritti, which means "revolving towards," and the other is nivritti, which means "revolving away from." The "revolving towards" is what we call the world: the "me" and "mine." It includes all those things which are always pampering that "me" by wealth and position and power and name and fame, and which are of a grasping nature, always tending to accumulate everything in one centre, that centre being "myself." That is pravritti, the natural tendency of every human being—taking everything from everywhere and heaping it around one centre, that centre being man's own sweet self. When this tendency begins to break and is replaced by nivritti, or "revolving away from," then begin morality and religion. Both pravritti and nivritti are of the nature of work: the former is evil work, and the latter is good work.

Nivritti is the fundamental basis of all morality and religion; and the very culmination of it is entire self-abnegation, readiness to sacrifice mind and body and everything for another being. When a man has reached that state he has attained to the perfection of karma-yoga. This is the highest result of good works. Although a man has not studied a single system of philosophy, although he does not believe in any God and never has believed, although he has not prayed even once in his whole life, if the simple power of good actions has brought him to that state where he is ready to give up his life and all else for others, he has arrived at the same point to which the religious man will come through his prayers and the philosopher through his knowledge. So you find that the philosopher, the worker, and the devotee all meet at one point, that one point being self-abnegation.

However much the various systems of philosophy and religion may differ, all mankind stands in reverence and awe before the man who is ready to sacrifice himself for others. Here it is not at all a question of creed or doctrine. Even men who are very much opposed to all religious ideas feel, when they see one of these acts of complete self-sacrifice, that they must revere it. And have you not seen even a most bigoted Christian, when he reads Edwin Arnold's *The Light of Asia*, stand in reverence of Buddha, who preached no God, preached nothing but self-sacrifice? The only thing is that the bigot does not know that his own end and aim in life is exactly the same as that of those with whom he differs.

The worshipper, by keeping constantly before him the idea of God and living in holy surroundings, comes to the same point at last and says, "Thy will be done"; he keeps nothing for himself. That is self-abnegation. The philosopher, with his knowledge, sees that the seeming self is a delusion and easily gives it up. That too is self-abnegation. So karma, bhakti, and jnāna all meet here; and this is what was meant by all the great preachers of ancient times when they taught that God is not the world. The world is one thing and God is another; and this distinction is very true. What they mean by the world is selfishness. Unselfishness is God. One man may be living on a throne, in a golden palace, and be perfectly unselfish; then he is in God. Another may live in a hut and wear rags and have nothing in the world; yet if he is selfish, he is an intensely worldly man.

To come back to one of our main points: We say that we cannot do good without at the same time doing some evil, or do evil without doing some good. Knowing this, how can we work? There have therefore been sects in this world which have in an astoundingly preposterous way preached slow suicide as the only means to get out of the world; because if a man lives he has to kill poor little animals and plants or do injury to something or someone. So, according to them, the only way out of the world is to die. The Jains have preached this doctrine as their highest ideal and it seems to be very logical. But the true solution is found in the Gitā. It is the doctrine of non-attachment—to be at-tached to nothing while doing our duty in life. Know that you are separated entirely from the world; that you are in the world but not of it, and that what-ever you may be doing in it you are not doing for your own sake. Any action that you do for yourself will bring its effect to bear upon you. If it is a good action, you will have to take the good result, and if a bad action, you will have to take the bad result; but any action that is not done for your own sake, whatever it be, will not affect you. There is to be found a very expressive sentence in our scriptures, embodying this idea: Even if a man kills the whole universe or is himself killed, he is neither the killer nor the killed, when he knows that he is not acting for himself at all.

Therefore karma-yoga teaches: "Do not give up the world. Live in the world, imbibe its ideas as much as you can." But are these for your own enjoyment's sake? Certainly not. Enjoyment should not be the goal. First kill your self and then regard the whole world as yourself. "The old man must die," as the Christians used to say. This "old man" is the selfish idea that the whole world is made for our enjoyment. Foolish parents teach their children to pray, "O Lord, Thou hast created this sun for me and this moon for me"—as if the Lord had nothing else to do than to create everything for these babies. Do not teach your children such nonsense. Then again, there are people who are foolish in another way: They teach us that all these animals were created for us to kill and eat, and that this universe is for the enjoyment of men. That is all fool-ishness. A tiger may say, "Man was created for me," and complain: "Lord, how wicked are these men, who do not come and place themselves before me to be eaten! They are breaking Your law." If the world is created for us we are also created for the world. That this world is created for our enjoyment is the most wicked idea that holds us down. This world is not for our sake. Millions pass out of it every year; the world does not feel it; millions of others take their place. Just as much as the world is created for us, so also are we created for the world.

To work properly, therefore, you have first to give up the idea of attachment. Secondly, do not mix in the fray; hold yourself as a witness and go on work-ing. My Master used to say, "Look upon your children as a nurse does." The nurse will love your baby and fondle it and play with it and behave towards it as gently as if it were her own child; but as soon as you give her notice to quit, she is ready to start off with bag and baggage from the house—everything in the shape of attachment is forgotten. It will not give the ordinary nurse the least pang to leave your children and take care of other children. Even so should be your attitude towards all that you consider your own. You are like the nurse; if you believe in God, believe that all these things which you consider yours are really His.

The greatest weakness often insinuates itself as the greatest good and strength. It is a weakness to think that anyone is dependent on me and that I can do good to another. This belief is the mother of all our attachment, and through this attachment comes all our pain. We must inform our minds that no one in this universe depends upon us; not one beggar depends on our charity, not one soul on our kindness, not one living thing on our help. All are helped on by nature and would be so helped even though millions of us were not here. The course of nature will not stop for such as you and me; it is, as already pointed out, only a blessed privilege to you and to me that we are allowed, through helping others, to educate ourselves. This is a great lesson to learn in life, and when we have learnt it fully we shall never be unhappy; we can go and mix without harm in society anywhere and everywhere. You may have wives or husbands, and regiments of servants, and kingdoms to govern; but if you act on the principle that the world is not for you and does not inevitably need you, they can do you no harm. This very year some of your friends may have died. Has the world stopped moving? Is it waiting for their coming back? Is everything standing still? No, it is not. So drive out of your mind the idea that you have to do something for the world; the world does not require any help from you. It is sheer nonsense on the part of any man to think that he is born to help the world. It is simply vanity; it is selfishness insinuating itself in the form of virtue.

When you have trained your mind and your nerves to realize this idea of the world's non-dependence on you or on anybody, there will then be no reaction in the form of pain resulting from work. When you give something to a man and expect nothing—do not even expect the man to be grateful—his ingratitude will not tell upon you, because you never expected anything, never thought you had any right to anything in the way of a return. You gave him what he deserved; his own karma got it for him; your karma made you the carrier of it. Why should you be proud of having given away something? You were the bearer who carried the money or other kind of gift, and the man deserved it by his own karma. Where then is the reason for pride in you? There is nothing very great in what you give to the world. When you have acquired the feeling of non-attachment, there will then be neither good nor evil for you. It is only selfishness that causes the difference between good and evil.

It is a very hard thing to understand, but you will come to learn in time that nothing in the universe has power over you until you allow it to exercise such power. Nothing has power over the Self of man until the Self becomes a fool and loses independence. So by non-attachment you overcome and deny the power of anything to act upon you. It is very easy to say that nothing has the right to act upon you until you allow it to do so; but what is the true sign of the man who really does not allow anything to work upon him, who is neither happy nor unhappy when acted upon by the external world? The sign· is that good or ill fortune causes no change in his mind; in all conditions he remains the same.

There was a great sage in India named Vyāsa. This Vyāsa is known as the author of the Vedānta Sutras and was a holy man. His father had tried to become a very perfect man and had failed. His grandfather had also tried and failed. His great-grandfather had likewise tried and failed. He himself did not succeed fully, but his son, Śuka, was born perfect. Vyāsa taught his son wisdom, and after teaching him the knowledge of Truth himself, he sent him to the court of King Janaka. Janaka was a great king and was called Janaka Videha. Videha means "without a body." Although a king, he had entirely forgotten that he had a body; he felt all the time that he was Spirit. The boy Śuka was sent to be taught by him. The king knew that Vyāsa's son was coming to him to learn wisdom; so he made certain arrangements beforehand. When the boy presented himself at the gate of the palace, the guards took no notice of him whatsoever. They only gave him a seat, and he sat there for three days and nights, nobody speaking to him, nobody asking him who he was or whence he came. He was the son of a very great sage; his father was honoured by the whole country; and he himself was a most respectable person; yet the low, vulgar guards of the palace would take no notice of him. Then, suddenly, the ministers of the king and all the great officials came and received him with the greatest honours. They conducted him in and showed him into splendid rooms, gave him the most fragrant baths and wonderful dress, and for eight days they kept him there in all kinds of luxury. The solemnly serene face of Śuka did not change even to the smallest extent by the change in the treatment accorded to him; he was the same in the midst of this luxury as when waiting at the door. Then he was brought before the king. The king was on his throne, music was playing, and dancing and other amusements were going on. The king gave him a cup of milk, full to the brim, and asked him to go seven times round the hall without spilling even a drop. The boy took the cup and proceeded in the midst of the music and the attraction of the beautiful faces. As the king had asked, seven times did he go round, and not a drop of the milk was spilt. The boy's mind could not be attracted by anything in the world unless he allowed it to affect him. And when he brought the cup to the king, the king said to him: "What your father has taught you, and what you have learnt yourself, I can only repeat. You have known the Truth. Go home."

Thus the man who has practised control over himself cannot be acted upon by anything outside; there is no more slavery for him; his mind has become free. Such a man alone has earned the right to live well in the world. We generally find men holding two opinions regarding the world. Some are pessimists and say: "How horrible this world is! How wicked!" Others are optimists and say: "How beautiful this world is! How wonderful!" To those who have not controlled their own minds, the world is either full of evil or at best a mixture of good and evil. This very world will become to us a happy world when we become masters of our own minds. Nothing will then work upon us as good or evil; we shall find everything to be in its proper place, to be harmonious. Often men who begin by saying that the world is a hell end by saying that it is a heaven, when they succeed in the practice of self-control. If we want to be karma-yogis and wish to train ourselves for the attainment of this state, wherever we may begin we are sure to end in perfect self-abnegation; and as soon as this seeming self has gone, the whole world, which at first appears to us to be filled with evil, will appear to be heaven itself and full of blessedness. Its very atmosphere will be blessed; every human face there will be good. Such is the end and aim of karma-yoga, and such is its perfection in practical life.

Our various yogas do not conflict with each other; each of them leads us to the same goal and makes us perfect; only each has to be strenuously practised. The whole secret is in practising. First you have to hear, then think, and then practise. This is true of every yoga. You have first to hear about it and understand what it is; and many things which you do not understand will be made clear to you by constant hearing and thinking. It is hard to understand everything at once. The explanation of everything is after all in yourself. No one is ever really taught by another; each of us has to teach himself. The external teacher offers only the suggestion, which arouses the internal teacher, who helps us to understand things. Then things will be made clearer to us by our own power of perception and thought, and we shall realize them in our own souls; and that realization will grow into intense power of will. First it is feeling, then it becomes willing, and out of that willing comes tremendous force for work, which will go through every vein and nerve and muscle, until the whole mass of the body is changed into an instrument of the yoga of unselfish work, and the desired result of perfect self-abnegation and utter unselfishness is duly attained. This attainment does not depend on any dogma or doctrine or belief. Whether one is Christian or Jew or Hindu, it does not matter. Are you unselfish? That is the question. If you are, you will be perfect without reading a single religious book, without going into a single church or temple. Each one of our yogas is fitted to make men perfect even without the help of the others, because they all have the same goal in view. The yogas of work, wisdom, and devotion are all capable of serving as direct and independent means for the attainment of moksha. "Fools alone say that work and philosophy are different, not the learned." The learned know that, though apparently different from each other, they at last lead to the same goal of human perfection.

FREEDOM

We have stated that in addition to meaning work, psychologically the word *karma* also implies causation. Any word, any action, any thought, that produces an effect is called a karma. Thus the law of karma means the law of causation, of inevitable cause and sequence. Wheresoever there is a cause, there an effect must be produced; this necessity cannot be resisted; and this law of karma, according to our philosophy, is true throughout the whole universe. Whatever we see or feel or do, whatever action there is anywhere in the universe, while being on the one hand the effect of past work, becomes, on the other, a cause in its turn and produces its own effect.

It is necessary, together with this, to consider what is meant by the word *law*. By law is meant the tendency of a series to repeat itself. When we see one event followed by another, or sometimes happening simultaneously with another, we expect this sequence or coexistence to recur. Our old logicians and philosophers of the Nyāya school call this law by the name of vyāpti. According to them all our ideas of law are due to association. A series of phenomena becomes associated with certain things in our mind in a sort of invariable order; so whatever we perceive at any time is immediately referred to similar facts in the mind. Any one idea or, according to our psychology, any one wave that is produced in the mind-stuff, or chitta, must always give rise to many similar waves. This is the psychological idea of association, and causation is only an aspect of this grand pervasive principle of association. This pervasiveness of association is what is, in Sanskrit, called vyāpti. In the external world the idea of law is the same as in the internal—the expectation that a particular phenomenon will be followed by another and that the series will repeat itself. Strictly speaking, therefore, law does not exist in nature. It is really an error to say that gravitation exists in the earth or that there is any law existing objectively anywhere in nature. Law is the method, the manner, in which our mind grasps a series of phenomena; it is all in the mind. Certain phenomena, happening one after another, or together, and followed by the conviction of the regularity of their recurrence, thus enabling our minds to grasp the method of the whole series, are explained by what we call law.

The next question for consideration is what we mean by law's being universal. Our universe is that portion of Existence which is conditioned by what the Sanskrit philosophers call deśa-kāla-nimitta, or what is known to European philosophy as space, time, and causation. This universe is only a part of Infinite Existence, thrown into a peculiar mould composed of space, time, and causation. It necessarily follows that law is possible only within this conditioned universe; beyond it there cannot be any law. When we speak of the universe we mean only that portion of Existence which is limited by our minds—the universe of the senses, which we can see, feel, touch, hear, think of, imagine. This alone is under law; but beyond it, Existence cannot be subject to law, because causation does not extend beyond the world of our minds. Anything beyond the range of the mind and the senses is not bound by the law of causation, because there is no mental association of things in the region beyond the senses, and no causation is possible without association of ideas. It is only when Being or Existence becomes moulded into name and form that it obeys the law of causation and is said to be subject to law—because all law has its essence in causation.

Therefore we see at once that there cannot be any such thing as free will; the very words are a contradiction, because the will is something that we know, and everything that we know is within our universe, and everything within our universe is moulded by the conditions of space, time, and causation. Everything that we know, or can possibly know, must be subject to causation, and that which obeys the law of causation cannot be free. It is acted upon by other agents and becomes a cause in its turn. But that which has become converted into the will, which was not the will before, but which, when it fell into this mould of space, time, and causation, became converted into the human will, is free; and when this will gets out of the mould of space, time, and causation, it will be free again. From freedom it comes, and it falls into the mould of bondage, and it gets out and goes back to freedom again.

The question has been raised as to whence this universe comes, in what it rests, and whither it goes; and the answer has been given that from freedom it comes, in bondage it rests, and into that freedom it goes back again. So when we speak of man as no other than the Infinite Being, which is manifesting Itself through him, we mean that only one very small part thereof is man; this body and this mind which we see are only one part of the whole, only one speck in the Infinite Being. This whole universe is only one speck in the Infinite Being; and all our laws, our bondages, our joys and our sorrows, our happinesses and our expectations, are only within this small universe; all our progression and regression are within its small compass. So you see how childish it is to expect a continuation of this universe—the creation of our minds—and to expect to go to heaven, which after all must mean only a repetition of this world that we know. You see at once that it is an impossible and childish desire to make the whole of Infinite Existence conform to the limited and conditioned existence which we know. When a man says that he will have again and again this same thing which he is having now, or, as I sometimes put it, when he asks for a comfortable religion, you may know that he has become so degenerate that he cannot think of anything higher than what he is now, anything beyond his insignificant present surroundings. He has forgotten his infinite nature, and his whole idea is confined to these little joys and sorrows and heart-jealousies of the moment. He thinks that this finite thing is the Infinite; and not only so, but he will not let this foolishness go. He clings desperately to trishnā, the thirst after life, what the Buddhists call tanhā and trissā. There may be millions of kinds of happiness and beings and laws and progress and causation, all acting outside the little universe that we know; and after all, the whole of this comprises but one section of our infinite nature.

To acquire freedom we have to get beyond the limitations of this universe; it cannot be found here. Perfect equilibrium, or what the Christians call the peace that passeth all understanding, cannot be had in this universe, nor in heaven, nor in any place where our minds and thoughts can go, where the senses can feel, or of which the imagination can conceive. No such place can give us that freedom, because all such places would be within our universe, and it is limited by space, time, and causation. There may be places that are more ethereal than this earth of ours, where enjoyments are keener; but even those places must be in the universe, and therefore in bondage to law. So we have to go beyond, and real religion begins where this little universe ends. These little joys and sorrows and this knowledge of things end there, and Reality begins. Until we give up the thirst after life, the strong attachment to this our transient, conditioned existence, we have no hope of catching even a glimpse of that infinite freedom beyond. It stands to reason then that there is only one way to attain to that freedom, which is the goal of all the noblest aspirations of mankind, and that is to give up this little life, give up this little universe, give up this earth, give up heaven, give up the body, give up the mind, give up everything that is limited and conditioned. If we give up our attachment to this little universe of the senses and of the mind, we shall be free immediately. The only way to come out of bondage is to go beyond the limitation of law, to go beyond causation.

But it is a most difficult thing to give up the clinging to this universe; few ever attain to that. There are two ways to do it mentioned in our books. One is called "Neti, neti" ("Not this, not this"); the other is called "Iti" ("This"); the former is the negative, and the latter is the positive, way. The negative way is the more difficult. It is only possible for men of the very highest, exceptional minds and gigantic wills, who simply stand up and say, "No, I will not have this," and the mind and body obey their will, and they come out successfully. But such people are very rare. The vast majority of mankind choose the positive way, the way through the world, making use of their bondage in order to break that very bondage. This is also a kind of giving up; only it is done slowly and gradually, by knowing things, enjoying things, and thus obtaining experience and knowing the nature of things until the mind lets them all go at last and becomes unattached. The former way of obtaining non-attachment is by reasoning, and the latter way is through work and experience. The first is the path of jnāna-yoga, characterized by the refusal to do any work; the second is that of karma-yoga, in which there is no cessation from work. Almost everyone in the universe must work. Only those who are perfectly satisfied with the Self, whose desires do not go beyond the Self, whose minds never stray out of the Self, to whom the Self is all in all—only those do not work. The rest must work.

A current of water, rushing down of its own nature, falls into a hollow and makes a whirlpool, and after turning around a little there, it emerges again in the form of the free current to go on unchecked. Each human life is like that current. It gets into the whirl, becomes involved in this world of space, time, and causation, whirls round a little, crying out, "my father, my brother, my name, my fame," and so on, and at last emerges out of it and regains its original freedom. The whole universe is doing that. Whether we know it or not, whether we are conscious or unconscious of it, we are all working to get out of the whirl of the world. The aim of man's experience in the world is to enable him to get out of its whirlpool.

What is karma-yoga? The knowledge of the secret of work. We see that the whole universe is working. For what? For salvation, for liberty. From the atom to the highest being, working for the one end: liberty of the mind, of the body, of the spirit. All things are always trying to get freedom, to fly away from bondage. The sun, the moon, the earth, the planets, all are trying to fly away from bondage. The centrifugal and centripetal forces function throughout the whole universe. Instead of being knocked about in this universe and, after long delay and thrashing, getting to know things as they are, we learn from karma-yoga the secret of work, the method of work, the organizing power of work. A vast mass of energy may be spent in vain if we do not know how to utilize it. Karma-yoga makes a science of work; you learn by it how best to utilize all the activities in this world. Work is inevitable; it must be so. But we should work to the highest purpose. Karma-yoga makes us realize that this world is a world of five minutes, that it is something we have to pass through, and that freedom is not here, but is only to be found beyond. To find the way out of the bondages of the world we have to go through it slowly and surely. There may be exceptional persons, such as those about whom I just spoke, who can stand aside and give up the world as a snake casts off its skin and looks at it as a witness. There are, no doubt, these exceptional beings; but the rest of mankind have to go slowly through this world. Karma-yoga shows the process, the secret and method of doing it to the best advantage.

What does it say? Work incessantly, but give up all attachment to work. Do not identify yourself with anything. Hold your mind free. All that you see, the pains and the miseries, are but the necessary conditions of this world. Poverty and wealth and happiness are but momentary; they do not belong to our real nature at all. Our nature is far beyond misery and happiness, beyond every object of the senses, beyond the imagination. And yet we must go on working all the time. Misery comes through attachment, not through work. As soon as we identify ourselves with the work we do, we feel miserable; but if we do not identify ourselves with it, we do not feel that misery. If a beautiful picture belonging to another is burnt, a man does not generally become miserable; but when his own picture is burnt how miserable he feels! Why? Both were beautiful pictures, perhaps copies of the same original; but in one case very much more misery is felt than in the other. It is because in one case he identifies himself with the picture, and in the other he does not.

This feeling of "I and mine" causes the whole misery. With the sense of possession comes selfishness, and selfishness brings on misery. Every act of selfishness or thought of selfishness makes us attached to something, and immediately we are made slaves. Each wave in the chitta that says "I and mine" immediately puts a chain round us and makes us slaves; and the more we say "I and mine," the more the slavery grows, the more the misery increases. Therefore karma-yoga tells us to enjoy the beauty of all the pictures in the world, but not to identify ourselves with any of them. Never say "mine." Whenever we say a thing is ours, misery immediately comes. Do not say "my child" even in your mind. If you do, then will come misery. Do not say "my house," do not say "my body." The whole difficulty is there. The body is neither yours, nor mine, nor anybody's. These bodies are coming and going by the laws of nature, but the Soul is free, standing as the witness. This body is no more free than a picture or a wall. Why should we be attached so much to a body? Suppose somebody paints a picture; why should he be attached to it? He will have to part with it at death. Do not project that tentacle of selfishness, "I must possess it." As soon as that is done, misery will begin.

So karma-yoga says: First destroy the tendency to project this tentacle of selfishness, and when you have the power of checking it, hold it in and do not allow the mind to get into the wave of selfishness. Then you may go out into the world and work as much as you like. Mix everywhere; go where you please; you will never be contaminated by evil. There is the lotus leaf in the water; the water cannot moisten or stick to it; so will you live in the world. This is called vairāgya, "dispassion" or "non-attachment." I believe I have told you that without non-attachment there cannot be any kind of yoga. Non-attachment is the basis of all the yogas. The man who gives up living in houses, wearing fine clothes, and eating good food, and goes into the desert, may be a most attached person. His only possession, his own body, may become everything to him; and while he lives he will struggle day and night to preserve his body. Non-attachment does not mean anything that we may do in relation to our external body; it is all in the mind. The binding link of "me and mine" is in the mind. If we have not this link with the body and with the things of the senses, we are non-attached, wherever and whatever we may be. A man may be on a throne and perfectly non-attached; another man may be in rags and still very much attached. First we have to attain this state of non-attachment, and then we have to work incessantly. Karma-yoga teaches us the method that will help us in giving up all attachment, though it is indeed very hard.

Here are the two ways of giving up all attachment. One way is for those who do not believe in God or in any outside help. They are left to their own devices; they have simply to work with their own will, with the powers of their mind and discrimination, thinking, "I must be non-attached." For those who believe in God there is another way, which is much less difficult. They give up the fruits of work unto the Lord; they work but never feel attached to the results. Whatever they see, feel, hear, or do is for Him. Whatever good work we may do, let us not claim any praise or benefit for it. It is the Lord's; give up the fruits unto Him. Let us stand aside and think that we are only servants obeying the Lord, our Master, and that every impulse for action comes from Him every moment. Whatever worship you offer, whatever you perceive, whatever you do—give up all unto Him and be at rest. Let us give up our whole body and mind and everything as an eternal sacrifice unto the Lord and be at peace, perfect peace, with ourselves. Instead of pouring oblations into the fire, as in a sacrifice, perform this one great sacrifice day and night—the sacrifice of your little self. "I searched for wealth in this world; Thou art the only wealth I have found; I sacrifice myself unto Thee. I searched for someone to love; Thou art the only beloved I have found; I sacrifice myself unto Thee."

Let us repeat this day and night, and say: "Nothing for me. No matter
whether the thing is good, bad, or indifferent, I do not care for it. I sacrifice
all unto Thee." Day and night let us renounce our seeming self until renunciation becomes a habit with us, until it gets into the blood, the nerves, and the
brain, and the whole body is every moment obedient to this idea of self-
renunciation. Go then into the battlefield, amidst the roaring cannon and the
din of war, and you will find yourself free and at peace.

Karma-yoga teaches us that the ordinary idea of duty is on the lower plane;
nevertheless all of us have to do our duty. Yet we may see that this peculiar
sense of duty is very often a great cause of misery. Duty becomes a disease
with us; it drags us on for ever. It catches hold of us and makes our whole
life miserable. It is the bane of human life. This duty, this idea of duty, is the
midday summer sun, which scorches the innermost soul of mankind. Look at
those poor slaves to duty! Duty leaves them no time to say prayers, no time to
bathe; duty is ever on them. They go out and work; duty is on them. They
come home and think of the work for the next day; duty is on them. It is
living a slave's life, and at last dropping down in the street and dying in
harness, like a horse. This is duty as it is understood. The only true duty is to
be unattached and to work as free beings, to give up all work unto God. All
our duties are His. Blessed are we that we are sent here. We serve our time;
whether we do it ill or well, who knows? If we do it well, we shall not think of
the fruits. If we do it ill, we shall not worry. Let us be at rest, be free, and work.
This kind of freedom is very hard to attain. How easy it is to interpret slavery as
duty—the morbid attachment of flesh for flesh as duty! Men go out into the
world and struggle and fight for money or for some other thing. Ask them why
they do it, and they will say, "It is my duty." But it is only the absurd greed for
gold and gain, and they try to cover it with a few flowers.

What is this duty after all? It is really attachment—the impulsion of the
flesh. And when an attachment has become established, we call it duty. For
instance, where there is no marriage, there is no duty between husband and
wife. When marriage comes, husband and wife live together on account of
attachment; and that kind of living together becomes accepted after generations; and when it becomes so accepted, it becomes a duty. It is, so to say, a sort
of chronic disease. When attachment becomes chronic, we baptize it with the
high-sounding name of duty. We strew flowers upon it, trumpets sound for it,
and sacred texts are said over it. The whole world fights and men earnestly rob
each other for this duty's sake.

Duty is good to the extent that it checks brutality. To the lowest kinds of
men, who cannot have any other ideal, it is of some good; but those who want
to be karma-yogis must throw this idea of duty overboard. There is no duty
for you and me. Whatever you have to give to the world do give by all means,
but not as a duty. Do not take any more thought of it. Be not compelled. Why
should you be compelled? Everything that you do under compulsion goes to
build up attachment. Why should you have any duty? Resign everything unto
God. In this tremendous fiery furnace where the fire of duty scorches everybody, drink this nectar of resignation and be happy. We are all simply working
out His will and have nothing to do with rewards and punishments. If you want

the reward you must also have the punishment; the only way to get out of the punishment is to give up the reward. The only way to get out of misery is to give up the idea of happiness, because these two are linked to each other. On one side there is happiness; on the other there is misery. On one side there is life; on the other there is death. The only way to get beyond death is to give up the love of life. Life and death are the same thing looked at from different points. So the idea of happiness without misery, or of life without death, is very good for schoolboys and children; but the thinker sees that it is all a contradiction in terms and gives up both. Seek no praise, no reward, for anything you do. No sooner do we perform a good action than we begin to desire credit for it. No sooner do we give money to some charity than we want to see our names blazoned in the papers. Misery must come as the result of such desires.

The greatest men in the world have passed away unknown. The Buddhas and the Christs that we know are but second-rate heroes in comparison with the greatest men, of whom the world knows nothing. Hundreds of these unknown heroes have lived in every country, working silently. Silently they live and silently they pass away; and in time their thoughts find expression in Buddhas or Christs, and it is these latter who become known to us. The highest men do not seek any name or fame from their knowledge. They leave their ideas to the world; they put forth no claims for themselves and establish no schools or systems in their name. Their whole nature shrinks from such a thing. They are the pure sāttvikas, who never make any stir but only melt down in love. I have seen one such yogi,[1] who lives in a cave in India. He is one of the most wonderful men I have ever seen. He has so completely lost the sense of his own individuality that we may say that the man in him is entirely gone, leaving behind only the all-comprehending sense of the Divine. If an animal bites one of his arms, he is ready to give it his other arm also and say that it is the Lord's will. Everything that comes to him is from the Lord. He does not show himself to men, and yet he is a magazine of love and of true and sweet ideas.

Next in order come the men with more rajas, or activity—combative natures, who take up the ideas of the perfect ones and preach them to the world. The highest men silently collect true and noble ideas, and others—the Buddhas and Christs—go from place to place preaching them and working for them. In the life of Gautama Buddha we notice his constantly saying that he is the twenty-fifth Buddha. The twenty-four before him are unknown to history, although the Buddha known to history must have built upon foundations laid by them. The highest men are calm, silent, and unknown. They are the men who really know the power of thought; they are sure that even if they go into a cave and close the door and simply think five true thoughts and then pass away, those five thoughts of theirs will live through eternity. Indeed, such thoughts will penetrate through the mountains, cross the oceans, and travel through the world. They will enter deep into human hearts and brains and raise up men and women who will give them practical expression in the workings of human life. These sāttvika men are too near the Lord to be active and to fight, to be working, struggling, preaching, and doing good to humanity,

[1] A reference to Pavhari Baba.

as they say, here on earth. The active workers, however good, have still a little remnant of ignorance left in them. Only while our nature has yet some impurities left in it can we work. It is in the nature of work to be impelled ordinarily by motive and by attachment. In the presence of an ever active Providence, who notes even the sparrow's fall, how can man attach any importance to his own work? Is it not blasphemy to do so when we know that He is taking care of the minutest things in the world? We have only to stand in awe and reverence before Him, and say, "Thy will be done."

The highest men cannot work, for in them there is no attachment. Those who rejoice in the Self and are satisfied with the Self and are content in the Self alone—for them there is no work to do. Such are indeed the highest among men; but apart from them everyone has to work. In working we should never think that we can help even the least thing in this universe. We cannot. We only help ourselves in this gymnasium of the world. This is the proper attitude for work. If we work in this way, if we always remember that our present opportunity to work thus is a privilege which has been given to us, we shall never be attached to anything. Millions like you and me think that we are great people in the world; but we all die and in five minutes the world forgets us. But the life of God is infinite. "Who can live a moment, breathe a moment, if this All-powerful One does not will it?" He is the ever active Providence. All power is His and within His command. Through His command the winds blow, the sun shines, the earth moves, and death stalks upon the earth. He is the All in all; He is all and in all. We can only worship Him. Give up all fruits of work; do good for its own sake; then alone will come perfect nonattachment. The bonds of the heart will thus break, and we shall realize perfect freedom. This freedom is indeed the goal of karma-yoga.

THE IDEAL OF KARMA-YOGA

THE GRANDEST IDEA in the religion of Vedānta is that we may reach the same goal by different paths; and these paths I have generalized into four, namely, those of work, love, psychology, and knowledge. But you must remember, at the same time, that these divisions are not well marked and quite exclusive of each other. Each blends into the other. It is not a fact that you can find men who have no other faculty than that of work, or that you can find men who are devoted worshippers only, or that there are men who cultivate nothing but knowledge. These divisions are made in accordance with the type or the tendency that may be seen to prevail in a man. We have found that, in the end, all these four paths converge and become one. All religions and all spiritual disciplines lead to one and the same goal.

I have already tried to point out that goal. It is, as I understand it, freedom. Everything that we perceive around us is struggling towards freedom, from the atom to man, from the insentient, lifeless particle of matter to the highest existence on earth, the human soul. The world process in fact reveals this struggle for freedom. In all combinations every particle is trying to go its own way, to fly from the other particles; but the others are holding it in check. Our earth is trying to fly away from the sun, and the moon from the earth. Everything has a tendency to infinite dispersion. All that we see in the universe has for its basis this one struggle towards freedom. It is under the impulse of this tendency that the saint prays and the robber robs. When the line of action taken is not a proper one we call it evil, and when the manifestation of it is proper and high we call it good. But the impulse is the same: the struggle towards freedom. The saint is oppressed with the knowledge of his bondage, and he wants to get rid of it; so he worships God. The thief is oppressed with the idea that he does not possess certain things, and he tries to get rid of that want, to obtain freedom from it; so he steals. Freedom is the one goal of all nature, sentient or insentient. And, consciously or unconsciously, everything is struggling towards that goal. The freedom which the saint seeks is very different from that which the robber seeks; the freedom loved by the saint leads him to the enjoyment of infinite, unspeakable bliss, while that on which the robber has set his heart only forges other bonds for his soul.

There is to be found in every religion the manifestation of this struggle towards freedom. It is the groundwork of all morality, of unselfishness, which means getting rid of the idea that men are the same as their little bodies. When we see a man doing good work, helping others, we know that he cannot be confined within the limited circle of "me and mine." There is no limit to this getting out of selfishness. All the great systems of ethics preach absolute unselfishness as the goal. Supposing this absolute unselfishness can be reached by a

503

man, what becomes of him? He is no more the little Mr. So-and-so; he has
acquired infinite expansion. That little personality which he had before is now
lost to him for ever; he has become infinite; and the attainment of this infinite
expansion is indeed the goal of all religions and of all moral and philosophical
teachings. The personalist, when he hears this idea expressed philosophically,
feels frightened. At the same time, if he preaches morality, he after all teaches
the very same idea himself. He puts no limit to the unselfishness of man.
Suppose a man becomes perfectly unselfish under the personalistic system, how
are we to distinguish him from the perfected ones of other systems? He has
become one with the universe, and to become that is the goal of all; only the
poor personalist has not the courage to follow out his own reasoning to its right
conclusion. Karma-yoga is the attaining through unselfish work of that freedom
which is the goal of all human nature. Every selfish action, therefore, retards our
reaching the goal, and every unselfish action takes us towards the goal. That is
why the only definition that can be given of morality is this: That which is
selfish is immoral, and that which is unselfish is moral.

But if you come to details, you will see that the matter is not quite so simple.
For instance, as I have already mentioned, environment often makes the details
different. The same action under one set of circumstances may be unselfish, and
under another set quite selfish. So we can give only a general definition and
must leave the details to be worked out by taking into consideration the differences in time, place, and circumstances. In one country one kind of conduct
is considered moral, and in another the very same is immoral, because the circumstances differ. The goal of all nature is freedom, and freedom is to be
attained only by perfect unselfishness; every thought, word, or deed that is
unselfish takes us towards the goal, and as such is called moral. That definition,
you will find, holds good in every religion and every system of ethics. In some
religious systems, morality is derived from a superior Being—God. If you
ask the followers of these systems why a man ought to do this and not that,
their answer is: "Because such is the command of God." But whatever be the
source from which it is derived, their code of ethics also has the same central
idea—not to think of self but to give up self.

And yet some persons, in spite of professing this high ethical idea, are frightened at the thought of having to give up their little personalities. We may ask
those who cling to the idea of little personalities to consider the case of a
person who has become perfectly unselfish, who has no thought for himself,
who does no deed for himself, who speaks no word for himself—and then to
say where his "himself" is. That "himself" is known to him only so long as he
thinks, acts, or speaks for himself. If he is only conscious of others, of the
universe, and of all, where is his "himself"? It is gone for ever.

Karma-yoga, therefore, is a system of discipline aiming at the attainment
of freedom through unselfishness and good works. The karma-yogi need not
believe in any religious doctrine whatever. He need not believe even in God,
may not ask what his soul is or think of any metaphysical speculation. He has his
own special aim of realizing selflessness; and he has to work it out himself.
Every moment of his life must be realization, because he has to solve by mere

work, without the help of doctrine or theory, the very same problem to which the jnāni applies his reason and inspiration and the bhakta his love.

Now comes the next question: What is this work? What is this doing good to the world? Can we do good to the world? In an absolute sense, no; in a relative sense, yes. No permanent or everlasting good can be done to the world; if it could be done, the world would not be this world. We may satisfy the hunger of a man for five minutes, but he will be hungry again. Every pleasure with which we supply a man may be seen to be momentary. No one can permanently cure this ever recurring fever of pleasure and pain. Can any permanent happiness be given to the world? In the ocean a wave cannot arise without causing a hollow somewhere else. The sum total of the good things in the world has been the same throughout in its relation to man's need. It cannot be increased or decreased. Take the history of the human race, as we know it today. Do we not always find the same miseries and the same happinesses, the same pleasures and pains, the same differences in position? Are not some rich, some poor, some high, some low, some healthy, some unhealthy? All this was just the same with the Egyptians, the Greeks, and the Romans in ancient times as it is with the Americans today. So far as history is known, it has always been the same. Yet at the same time we find that along with all these incurable differences of pleasure and pain there has ever been the struggle to alleviate them. Every period of history has given birth to thousands of men and women who have worked hard to smooth the passage of life for others. And how far have they succeeded? We can only play at driving the ball from one place to another. We take away pain from the physical plane and it goes to the mental one. It is like that picture in Dante's hell where the misers were given a mass of gold to roll up a hill. Every time they rolled it up a little, it rolled down again. All our discussions of the millennium are very nice as schoolboys' stories, and they are no better than that. All nations that dream of the millennium also think that they, of all the peoples in the world, will then have the best of it for themselves. This is the wonderfully unselfish idea of the millennium.

We cannot add happiness to this world; similarly, we cannot add pain to it either. The sum total of pleasure and pain displayed here on earth will be the same throughout. We just push it from this side to the other side, and from that side to this; but it will remain the same, because to remain so is its very nature. This ebb and flow, this rising and falling, is in the world's very nature; it would be as logical to hold otherwise as to say that we may have life without death. This is complete nonsense, because the very idea of life implies death and the very idea of pleasure implies pain. The lamp is constantly burning out, and that is its life. If you want to have life you have to die every moment. Life and death are only different expressions of the selfsame thing; they are the same thing looked at from different standpoints; they are the rising and the falling of the same wave, and the two form one whole. One looks at the "fall" side and becomes a pessimist; another looks at the "rise" side and becomes an optimist. When a boy is going to school and his father and mother are taking care of him, everything seems blessed to him; his wants are simple; he is a great optimist. But the old man, with his varied experience, becomes calmer and is sure to have his warmth considerably cooled down. So old nations, with signs of decay all around them, are apt to be less hopeful than new nations. There is a proverb in India: "A thousand years a city, and a thousand years a forest." This change of city into forest and vice versa is going on everywhere, and it makes people optimists or pessimists according to the side they see of it.

The next idea we take up is that of equality. The idea of the millennium has been a great incentive for work. Many religions preach this as one of their ideals—that God is coming to rule the universe and that then there will be no difference at all among men. The people who preach this doctrine are mere fanatics, and fanatics are indeed the sincerest of mankind. Christianity was preached precisely on the basis of the fascination of this fanaticism, and that is what made it so attractive to the Greek and Roman slaves. They believed that under this millennial religion there would be no more slavery, that there would be plenty to eat and drink; and therefore they flocked round the Christian standard. Those who preached the idea were of course ignorant fanatics, but very sincere. In modern times this millennial aspiration is voiced through the slogans of liberty, equality, and fraternity. This also is fanaticism. True equality has never been and never can be on earth. How can we all be equal here? This impossible kind of equality implies total death. What makes this world what it is? Lost balance. In the primal state, which is called chaos, there was perfect balance. How, then, do you explain the diverse forces in the universe? Through struggle, competition, conflict. Suppose that all the particles of matter were held in equilibrium; would there be then any process of creation? We know from science that it is impossible. Disturb a sheet of water, and you will find every particle of the water trying to become calm again, one rushing towards another; and in the same way all the phenomena which we call the universe—all things therein—are struggling to get back to the state of perfect balance. Again a disturbance comes, and again we have combination and creation. Inequality is the very basis of creation. At the same time, the forces struggling to obtain equality are as much a necessity for creation as those which destroy it.

Absolute equality, which means a perfect balance of all the struggling forces in all the planes, can never be had in this world. Before you attain that state, the world will have become quite unfit for any kind of life, and no one will be here. We find, therefore, not only that all these ideas of the millennium and of absolute equality are impossible, but also that, if we try to carry them out, they will surely lead us to the day of destruction. What makes the difference between man and man? It is largely the difference in the brain. Nowadays no one but a lunatic will say that we are all born with the same brain-power. We come into the world with unequal endowments; we come as greater men or as lesser men, and there is no getting away from that pre-natally determined condition. The American Indians were in this country for thousands of years, and a mere handful of your ancestors came to their land. What a difference they have caused in the appearance of the country! Why did not the Indians make improvements and build cities, if all were equal? With your ancestors a different sort of brain-power came into the land; different bundles of past impressions came, and they manifested themselves. Absolute non-differentiation is death. So long as this world lasts, differentiation there will and must be, and the millennium of perfect equality will come only when a cycle of creation comes to its end. Before that, equality cannot be. Yet this idea of realizing the millennium is a great incentive. Just as inequality is necessary for creation, so the struggle to limit it is also necessary. If there were no struggle to become free and return to God, there would be no creation either. It is the difference between these two forces that determines the nature of the motives of men. There will always be these motives for work, some tending towards bondage and others towards freedom.

This world's wheels within wheels are a terrible mechanism. As soon as we put our hands in it, we are caught and we are gone. We all think that when we have done a certain duty we shall be at rest; but before we have done a part of that duty another is already waiting. We are all being dragged along by this mighty, complex world-machine. There are only two ways out of it. One is to give up all concern with the machine and stand aside—that is, to give up all desires. That is very easy to say, but almost impossible to do. I do not know whether in twenty millions of men one can do that. The other way is to plunge into the world and learn the secret of work, and that is the way of karma-yoga. Do not fly away from the wheels of the world-machine, but stand inside it and learn the secret of work. Through proper work done inside, it is also possible to come out. Through this machine itself is the way out.

We have now seen what work is. It is a part of nature's scheme, and it goes on always. Those who believe in God understand this better, because they know that God is not such an incapable being as will need our help. Although this world will go on always, we must remember that our goal is freedom; and according to karma-yoga that goal is to be reached through work. All ideas of making the world perfectly happy may be good as motives for fanatics; but we must know that fanaticism brings forth as much evil as good. The karma-yogi asks why you require any motive for work other than the inborn love of freedom. Go beyond the so-called "worthy" motives. "To work you have the right, but not to the fruits thereof." Man can train himself to know and to practise that, says the karma-yogi. When the idea of doing good becomes a part of his very being, then he will not seek any motive from outside. Let us do good because it is good to do good; he who does good work even in order to get to heaven binds himself down, says the karma-yogi. Any work that is done with even the least selfish motive, instead of making us free, forges one more chain for our feet.

So the only way is to give up all the fruits of work, to be unattached to them. Know that this world is not we, nor are we this world; that we are really not the body; that we really do not work. We are the Self, eternally at rest and at peace. Why should we be bound by anything? It is very good to say that we should be perfectly non-attached; but what is the way to be so? Every good work we do without any ulterior motive, instead of forging a new link, will break one of the links in the existing chain. Every good thought we send to the world, without thinking of any return, will be stored up and break one link in the chain, and make us purer and purer, until we become the purest of mortals. Yet all this may seem to be rather quixotic and too philosophical, more theoretical than practical. I have read many arguments against the teachings of the Bhagavad Gītā, and many have said that without motives men cannot work. They have never seen unselfish work except under the influence of fanaticism, and therefore they speak in that way.

Let me tell you in conclusion a few words about one man who actually carried this teaching of karma-yoga into practice. That man is Buddha. He is the one man who has carried it into perfect practice. All the prophets of the world, except Buddha, had external motives to move them to unselfish action. The prophets of the world, with this single exception, may be divided into two groups, one holding that they are Incarnations of God come down on earth, and the other holding that they are Messengers from God; and both draw their impetus for work from outside and expect reward from outside, however highly spiritual may be the language they use. But Buddha is the only prophet who said: "I do not care to know your various theories about God. What is the use of discussing all the subtle doctrines about the soul? Do good and be good, and this will take you to freedom and to whatever truth there is." He was, in the conduct of his life, absolutely without personal motives; and what man worked more than he? Show me one character in history who has soared so high above all. The whole human race has produced but one such character, such high philosophy, such wide sympathy. This great philosopher preached the highest philosophy, and yet had the deepest sympathy for the lowest of animals and never put forth any claims for himself. He is the ideal karma-yogi, acting entirely without motive, and the history of humanity shows him to have been the greatest man ever born—beyond compare the greatest combination of heart and brain that ever existed, the greatest soul-power that has ever been manifested. He is the greatest reformer the world has seen. He was the first who dared to say: "Believe not because some old manuscripts are quoted; believe not because it is your national belief, because you have been made to believe it from your childhood; but reason it all out, and after you have analysed it and found out that it will do good to one and all, then believe it, live up to it, and help others to live up to it."

He works best who works without any motive—neither for money, nor for fame, nor for anything else. And when a man can do that, he will be a Buddha and out of him will come the power to work in such a manner as will transform the world. This man represents the very highest ideal of karma-yoga.

INSPIRED TALKS

VIVEKANANDA COTTAGE AT THOUSAND ISLAND PARK

(The open upper window in the left-hand wing belonged to Vivekananda's room. The upper porch was where the evening talks were given, and the Swami's seat was at the end near his room. The morning instruction embodied in *Inspired Talks* was given in the room to the left of the lower porch.)

VIVEKANANDA AT THOUSAND ISLAND PARK

INSPIRED TALKS

Wednesday, June 19, 1895.

(This day marks the beginning of the regular teaching given daily by Swami Vivekananda to his disciples at Thousand Island Park.[1] He opened the Bible at the Book of John, saying that since the students were all Christians, it was proper that he should begin with the Christian scriptures.)

"IN THE beginning was the Word, and the Word was with God, and the Word was God." The Hindu calls this māyā, the manifestation of God, because it is the power of God.[2] The Absolute reflecting through māyā is what we call nature. The Word has two manifestations: the general one of nature, and the special one of the great Incarnations of God—Krishna, Buddha, Jesus, and Ramakrishna. Christ, the special manifestation of the Absolute, is known and knowable. The Absolute cannot be known. We cannot know the Father; we can only know the Son. We can only see the Absolute through the "tint of humanity," through Christ.

In the first five verses of John is the whole essence of Christianity; each verse is full of the profoundest philosophy.

The Perfect never becomes imperfect. It is in the darkness but is not affected by the darkness. God's mercy goes to all but is not affected by man's wickedness. The sun is not affected by any disease of our eyes which makes us see it distortedly. In the twenty-ninth verse, "taketh away the sin of the world" means that Christ will show us the way to become perfect. God became Christ to show man his true nature—that we too are God. We are human coverings over the Divine; but as the Divine Man, Christ and we are one.

The Trinitarian Christ is elevated above us; the Unitarian Christ is merely a moral man. Neither can help us. The Christ who is the Incarnation of God, who has not forgotten his divinity—that Christ can help us; in him there is no imperfection. These Incarnations are always conscious of their own divinity; they know it from their birth. They are like the actors whose play is over, but who, after their work is done, return to please others. These great ones are untouched by aught of earth. They assume our form and our limitations for a time in order to teach us; but in reality they are never limited, they are ever free.

*　　　*　　　*

Good is near Truth but is not yet Truth. After learning not to be disturbed

---

[1] For a description of Thousand Island Park and Swami Vivekananda's stay there, see page 79 ff.

[2] Māyā is the Śakti, or power, of the Supreme Lord, which appears to hide His Reality and project the names and forms of the relative universe.

by evil, we have to learn not to be made happy by good. We must find that we are beyond both evil and good; we must study their adjustment and see that they are both necessary.

The idea of dualism comes from the ancient Persians.[3] Really good and evil are one and the same,[4] and are in our own mind. When the mind is tranquil neither good nor evil affects it. Be perfectly free; then neither can affect you, and you will enjoy freedom and bliss. Evil is the iron chain; good is the gold one. Both are chains. Be free, and know once for all that there is no chain for you. Lay hold of the gold chain to loosen the hold of the iron one; then throw both away. The thorn of evil is in our flesh; take another thorn from the same bush and extract the first thorn, and then throw away both and be free.

* * *

In the world take always the position of the giver. Give everything and look for no return. Give love, give help, give service, give any little thing you can, but keep out barter. Make no conditions and none will be imposed. Let us give out of our own bounty, just as God gives to us.

The Lord is the only giver; all men in the world are only shopkeepers. Get His cheque and it will be honoured everywhere.

God is the inexplicable, inexpressible essence of love—to be known but never defined.

* * *

In our miseries and struggles the world seems to us a very dreadful place. But just as when we watch two puppies playing and biting we do not concern ourselves at all—realizing that it is only fun and that even a sharp nip now and then will do no actual harm—so all our struggles are but play in God's eyes. This world is all for play and only amuses God; nothing in it can make God angry.

* * *

Mother, in the sea of life my bark is sinking!
The whirlwind of illusion, the storm of attachment, is growing every moment;
My five oarsmen[5] are foolish, and the helmsman[6] is weak;
My bearings are lost, my boat is sinking.
O Mother, save me!

"Mother, Thy light stops not for the saint or the sinner; it animates the lover and the murderer."

Mother is ever manifesting through all. The light is not polluted by what it

[3] I.e. the Parsees. They are the followers of Zoroaster, who taught that the whole creation has come out of two primary principles, one being called Ahura Mazda (the principle of good), and the other Ahriman (the principle of evil).
[4] Because, as products of māyā, they are both chains binding men to the relative world.
[5] The sense-organs.
[6] The mind.

shines on, nor benefited by it. The light is ever pure, ever changeless. Behind every creature is the Mother—pure, lovely, never changing.

"Mother, manifested as light in all beings, we bow down to Thee." She is equally in suffering, hunger, pleasure, sublimity.

"When the bee sucks honey, the Lord is eating." Knowing that the Lord is everywhere, the sages give up praising and blaming.

Know that nothing can hurt you. How can it? Are you not free? Are you not the Ātman? He is the life of our lives, the hearing of our ears, the sight of our eyes.

We go through the world like a man pursued by a policeman and see the barest glimpses of the beauty of it. All this fear that pursues us comes from believing in matter. Matter gets its whole existence from the presence of mind behind it. What we see is God percolating through nature.[7]

Sunday, June 23.

Be brave and be sincere; then follow any path with devotion and you must reach the Lord. Lay hold of one link of the chain, and the whole chain must come by degrees. Water the roots of the tree—that is, reach the Lord— and the whole tree is watered. Getting the Lord, we get all.

One-sidedness is the bane of the world. The more sides you develop, the more varied will be your enjoyment of the universe. You will enjoy it as a jnāni, a bhakta, and in all other ways. Determine your own nature and stick to it. Nishthā is the only method for the beginner; but with devotion and sincerity it will lead to all. Churches, doctrines, forms, are the hedges to protect the tender plant, but they must later be broken down that the plant may become a tree. So the various religions, Bibles, Vedas, dogmas, all are just pots for little plants; but they must get out of the pots. Nishthā is, in a manner of speaking, placing the plant in the pot, shielding the struggling soul on its chosen path.

* * *

Look at the ocean and not at the wave; see no difference between ant and angel. Every worm is the brother of the Nazarene. How can you say one is greater and one less great? Each is great in his own place.

We are in the sun and in the stars as much as here. Spirit is beyond space and time, and is everywhere. Every mouth praising the Lord is my mouth; every eye seeing is my eye. We are confined nowhere. We are not the body; the universe is our body. We are magicians waving magic wands and creating scenes before us at will.

We are a spider in a huge web, who can go on the varied strands wheresoever he desires. The spider is now conscious only of the spot where he is; but he will in time become conscious of the whole web. We too are conscious of our existence only where our body is; we can use only one brain. But when we reach ultraconsciousness we know all, we can use all brains. Even now we can "give the push" to consciousness and it will go beyond and act in the super-conscious.

[7] Here nature means matter and mind.

We are striving to "be" and nothing more; there will not even be "I"—just pure crystal, reflecting all, but itself ever the same. When that state is reached there is no more doing; the body becomes a mere mechanism, pure without our trying for purity; it cannot become impure.

Know you are the Infinite; then fear will die. Say ever, "I and my Father are one."

*   *   *

In time to come Christs will be born in numbers like bunches of grapes on a vine; then the play will be over and all will pass out—as water in a kettle beginning to boil shows first one bubble, then another, then more and more, until all is in ebullition and passes out as steam. Buddha and Christ are the two biggest "bubbles" the world has yet produced. Moses was a tiny bubble; greater and greater ones came. Sometime, however, all will be bubbles and escape. But creation, ever new, will bring new water to go through the process all over again.

Monday, June 24.

(The reading today was from the Bhakti Sutras by Nārada.)

"Extreme love of God is bhakti; and this love is the real immortality, getting which a man becomes perfectly satisfied, sorrows for no loss, and is never jealous; knowing which a man becomes mad."

My Master used to say: "This world is a huge lunatic asylum where all men are mad—some after money, some after women, some after name or fame, and a few after God. I prefer to be mad after God. God is the philosophers' stone that turns us to gold in an instant: the form remains, but the nature is changed; the human form remains, but no more can we hurt or sin."

"Thinking of God, some weep, some sing, some laugh, some dance, some say wonderful things—but all speak of nothing but God."

Prophets preach, but the Incarnations—Jesus, Buddha, Ramakrishna—can give religion. One glance, one touch, is enough. That is the power of the Holy Ghost, the "laying on of hands." The power was actually transmitted to the disciples by the Master—the "chain of guru-power." That, the real baptism, has been handed down for untold ages.

"Bhakti cannot be used to fulfil any desires, itself being the check to all desires." Nārada gives these as the signs of love: "When all thoughts, all words, and all deeds are given up unto the Lord, and the least forgetfulness of God makes one intensely miserable, then love has begun."

"This is the highest form of love, because in it there is no desire for reciprocity, which desire is found in all human love."

"A man who has gone beyond social and scriptural usage is a sannyāsin. When the whole soul goes to God, when we take refuge only in God, then we know that we are about to get this love."

Obey the scriptures until you are strong enough to do without them; then go beyond them. Books are not final. Verification is the only proof of religious truth. Each must verify for himself; and no teacher who says, "I have seen, but you cannot" is to be trusted—only that one who says, "You can see, too." All scriptures and all truths, of all times and of all countries, are Vedas because these truths are to be *seen* and anyone may discover them.

"When the sun of love begins to break on the horizon, we want to give up all our actions unto God, and when we forget Him for a moment, it grieves us greatly."

Let nothing stand between God and your love for Him. Love Him, love Him, love Him—and let the world say what it will. Love is of three sorts: one demands, but gives nothing; the second is exchange; and the third is love without thought of return, love like that of the moths for the light.

"Love is higher than works, than yoga, than knowledge."

Work is merely a schooling for the doer; it can do no good to others. We must work out our own problem; the prophets only show us how to work. "What you think, you become." So if you throw your burden on Jesus, you will have to think of him; thus you become like him and you love him.

"Extreme love and the highest knowledge are one."

But theorizing about God will not do. We must love and work. Give up the world and all worldly things, especially while the "plant" is tender. Day and night think of God, and as far as possible think of nothing else. The daily necessary thoughts can all be thought through God. Eat to Him, drink to Him, sleep to Him, see Him in all. Talk of God to others—this is most beneficial.

Get the mercy of God and of His greatest children; these are the two chief ways to God. The company of these children of Light is very hard to get. Five minutes in their company will change a whole life, and if you really want it enough, one will come to you. The presence of those who love God makes a place holy, such is the glory of the children of the Lord. They are He, and when they speak, their words are scriptures. The place where they have been becomes filled with their vibrations, and those going there feel them and have a tendency to become holy also.

"To such lovers there is no distinction of caste, learning, beauty, birth, wealth, or occupation, because all are His."

Give up all evil company, especially at the beginning. Avoid worldly company; that will distract your mind. Give up all thought of "me and mine." To him who has nothing in the universe the Lord comes. Cut the bondage of all worldly affections; go beyond laziness and also beyond all worry as to what will become of you.

Never turn back to see the result of what you have done. Give all to the Lord, and work, and think not of it. When the whole soul pours in a continuous current to God, when there is no time to seek money or name or fame, no time to think of anything but God, then will come into your heart that infinite, wonderful bliss of love. All desires are but beads of glass. True love of God increases every moment and is ever new—it is to be known only by feeling it. Love is the easiest of all disciplines. It waits for no logic; it is natural. We need no demonstration, no proof. Reasoning is limiting something by our own minds. We throw a net and catch something, and then say that we have demonstrated it. But never, never can we catch God in a net.

Love should be motiveless. Even when we love wrongly, it is an expression of the true love, of the true bliss. The power is the same, use it as we may. Its very nature is peace and bliss. The murderer, when he kisses his baby, forgets for an instant all but love. Give up all self, all egotism; get out of anger and lust; give all to God. "Not I, but Thou. The old man is all gone; only Thou remainest." "I am Thou." Blame none. If evil comes, know that the Lord is playing with you and be exceeding glad.

Love is beyond time and space. It is absolute.

Tuesday, June 25.

After every happiness comes misery; they may be far apart or near. The more advanced the soul, the more quickly does the one follow the other. What we want is neither happiness nor misery. Both make us forget our true nature; both are chains—one iron, one gold. Behind both is the Ātman, who knows neither happiness nor misery. These are states, and states must ever change; but the nature of the Soul is bliss, peace—unchanging. We have not to get it; we have it. Only wash away the dross and see it.

Stand upon the Self; then only can you truly love the world. Take a very, very high stand. Knowing our universal nature, we must look with perfect calmness upon all the panorama of the world. It is but baby's play, and we know that, so cannot be disturbed by it. If the mind is pleased with praise it will be displeased with blame. All pleasures of the senses or even of the mind are evanescent; but within ourselves is the one true unrelated pleasure, dependent upon nothing. It is perfectly free. It is bliss. The more we enjoy inner bliss, the more spiritual we are. The pleasure of the Self is what is called religion.

The internal universe, the real, is infinitely greater than the external, which is only a shadowy projection of the true one. This world is neither true nor untrue; it is the shadow of truth. It is imagination—the gilded shadow of truth—says the poet.

We enter into creation, and then for us it becomes living. Things are dead in themselves; only we give them life and then, like fools, we turn around and are afraid of them or run after them. But be not like certain fishwives who, caught in a storm on their way home from market, took refuge in the house of a florist. They were lodged for the night in a room next to the garden, where the air was full of the fragrance of flowers. In vain did they try to rest, until one of their number suggested that they wet their fish-baskets and place them near their heads. As soon as they got the smell of fish, they all fell into a sound sleep.

The world is our fish-basket. We must not depend upon it for enjoyment. Those who do are the tāmasikas, the bound. Then there are the rājasikas, the egotistical, who talk always about "I," "I." They do good work sometimes and may become spiritual. But the highest are the sāttvikas, the introspective, those who live only in the Self. These three qualities—tamas, rajas, and sattva—are in everyone, and different ones predominate at different times.

Creation is not a "making" of something; it is the struggle to regain equilibrium—as when bits of cork, thrown to the bottom of a pail of water, rush to the top, singly or in clusters. Life is and must be accompanied by evil. A little evil is the source of life. The little wickedness that is in the world is very good; for when the balance is regained, the world will end, because sameness and destruction are one. As long as this world exists, good and evil exist with it;

but when we can transcend this world, we get rid of both good and evil and have bliss.

There is no possibility of ever having pleasure without pain, good without evil; for life itself is just lost equilibrium. What we want is freedom—not life, nor pleasure, nor good. Creation is infinite, without beginning and without end, the ever moving ripple in an infinite lake. There are, however, unreached depths in this lake, where equilibrium has been regained; but the ripple on the surface is always there; the struggle to regain the balance is eternal. Life and death are only different names for the same fact, the two sides of the one coin. Both are māyā, the inexplicable state of striving at one time to live, and a moment later having to die. Beyond this is our true nature, the Ātman. What we call God is really only the Self, from which we have separated ourselves and which we worship as outside us; but it is our true Self, all the time, the one and only God.

To regain the balance we must counteract tamas by rajas, then conquer rajas by sattva, the calm, beautiful state that will grow and grow until all else is gone. Give up bondage, become a son of God, be free, and then you can "see the Father" as did Jesus. Infinite strength is religion and God. Avoid weakness and slavery. You are the Soul only if you are free; there is immortality for you only if you are free; there is a God only if He is free.

*   *   *

The world is for me—I am not for the world. Good and evil are our slaves, not we theirs. The brute's nature is to remain where he is. It is the nature of man to seek good and avoid evil; it is the nature of God to seek neither, but just to be eternally blissful. Let us be God! Make the heart like an ocean; go beyond all the trifles of the world. Be mad with joy even at evil; see the world as a picture and then enjoy its beauty, knowing that nothing affects you. Do you know what good is? It is like glass beads that children find in a mud-puddle. Look at the world with calm complacency. See good and evil as the same; both are merely God's "play." Enjoy all.

*   *   *

My Master used to say: "All is God, but tiger-God is to be shunned. All water is water, but we avoid dirty water for drinking."

The whole sky is God's votive tray, on which the sun and moon burn as lamps. What other temple is needed? All eyes are Thine, yet Thou hast not an eye; all hands are Thine, yet Thou hast not a hand.

Neither seek nor avoid: take what comes. This is freedom—to be affected by nothing. Do not merely endure; be unattached. Remember the story of the bull. A mosquito sat long on the horn of a certain bull. Then his conscience troubled him and he said: "Mr. Bull, I have been sitting here a long time; perhaps I annoy you. I am sorry. I will go away." But the bull replied: "Oh no, not at all! Bring your whole family and live on my horn. What can you do to me?"

Wednesday, June 26.

Our best work is done, our greatest influence is exerted, when we are without thought of self. All great geniuses know this. Let us open ourselves to the one

Divine Actor and let Him act; let us do nothing ourselves. "O Arjuna! I have no duty in the whole world," says Krishna. Be perfectly resigned, perfectly unconcerned; then alone can you do any true work. No eyes can see the real forces behind the work; we can only see the results. Put out self, lose it, forget it. Just let God work; it is His business. We have nothing to do but stand aside and let God work. The more we go away, the more God comes in. Get rid of the little "I" and let only the great "I" live.

We are what our thoughts have made us; so take care about what you think. Words are secondary. Thoughts live; they travel far. Each thought we think is tinged with our own character; so even the jests or abuse of a pure and holy man will bear a trace of his own love and purity and do good.

Desire nothing. Think of God and look for no return. It is desireless work that brings results. The begging monks carry religion to every man's door; but they think that they do nothing, they claim nothing, their work is unconsciously done. If they should eat of the tree of knowledge, they would become egotists and all the good they do would fly away. As soon as we say "I" we are fooled. And what we call "knowledge" is only going round and round like a bullock tied to an oil-mill. The Lord has hidden Himself best and His work is best; so he who hides himself best accomplishes most. Conquer yourself and the whole universe is yours.

In the state of sattva we see the very nature of things; we go beyond the senses and beyond reason. The adamantine wall that shuts us in is egotism. We refer everything to ourselves, thinking I do this, that, or the other. Get rid of this puny "I"; kill this diabolism in us. "Not I, but Thou"—say it, feel it, live it. Until we give up the world manufactured by the ego, never can we enter the kingdom of heaven. None ever did, none ever will. To give up the world is to forget the ego, to know it not at all—being in the body, but not of it. This rascal ego must be obliterated. Bless men when they revile you. Think how much good they are doing you. If anyone is hurt it is only themselves. Go where people hate you; let them thrash the ego out of you and you will get nearer to the Lord. Like the mother monkey,[8] we hug our baby, the world, as long as we can; but at last, when we are driven to put it under our feet and step on it, then we are ready to come to God. Blessed it is to be persecuted for the sake of righteousness. Blessed are we if we cannot read; we have less to take us away from God.

Enjoyment is the million-headed serpent that we must tread underfoot. We renounce and go onward; then, perhaps, we find nothing and we despair. But hold on, hold on. The world is a demon.

The world is a kingdom of which the puny ego is king. Put it away and stand firm. Give up lust and gold and fame and hold fast to the Lord, and at last you will reach a state of perfect indifference. The idea that the gratification of the senses constitutes enjoyment is purely materialistic. There is not one spark of real enjoyment there: all the joy there is, is a mere reflection of the true bliss.

Those who give themselves up to the Lord do more for the world than all

[8] The mother monkey is very fond of her young one in times of safety; but when danger comes, she does not scruple to throw it down and trample on it, if necessary, to save herself.

the so-called workers. One man who has thoroughly purified himself accomplishes more than a regiment of preachers. Out of purity and silence comes the power of the word.

Be like a lily: stay in one place and expand your petals, and the bees will come of themselves. There was a great contrast between Keshab Chandra Sen and Śri Ramakrishna. The second never recognized any sin or misery in the world, no evil to fight against. The first was a great ethical reformer, a leader of the Brāhmo Samāj. After twelve years of discipline the quiet prophet of Dakshineswar worked a revolution, not only in India, but in the world. The power is with the silent ones, who only live and love and then leave the world. They never say "me" and "mine"; they feel blessed in being instruments. Such men are the Christs and Buddhas, ever living, fully identified with God, ideal existences, asking nothing and not consciously doing anything. They are the real world-movers, the jivanmuktas, absolutely selfless; their little personality is entirely blown away, and their ambition is non-existent. They are all principle, no personality.

Thursday, June 27.

(The Swami brought the New Testament this morning and talked again on the Book of John.)

Mohammed claimed to be the Comforter that Christ promised to send. He considered it unnecessary to claim a supernatural birth for Jesus. Such claims have been common in all ages and in all countries. All great men have claimed gods for their fathers.

Knowing is only relative: we can be God, but never *know* Him. Knowledge is a lower state. Adam's fall occurred when he came to know. Before that he was God, he was truth, he was purity. We certainly are not other than our own faces, but we can see only a reflection, never the real thing. We are love, but when we think of it we have to use a phantasm,[9] which proves that matter is only externalized thought.

Nivritti means turning aside from the world. Hindu mythology says that the four first-created beings[10] were warned by a swan—God Himself—that manifestation was only secondary; so they lived without procreating. The meaning of this is that manifestation is degeneration, because the spirit can only be expressed by the letter, and "the letter killeth."[11] Yet the principle is bound to be clothed in matter, though we know that later we lose sight of the real in the covering. Every great teacher understands this. And that is why a continual succession of prophets has to come to show us the principle and give it a new form suited to the times. My Master taught that religion is one. All prophets teach the same thing; but they can only present the principle in a form, and so they take it out of the old form and put it before us in a new one.

When we free ourselves from name and form, especially from a body— when we need no body, good or bad—then only do we escape from bondage. Eternal progression is eternal bondage; annihilation of form is to be preferred.

[9] That is to say, an external object of love.
[10] Namely, Sanaka, Sanandana, Sanātana, and Sanatkumāra.
[11] New Testament, II Cor. 3:6.

We must get free from all bodies, even a god-body. God is the only real Existence; there cannot be two.[12] There is but one Soul and I am That.

Good works are valuable only as a means of becoming free. They do good to the doer, never to any other.

*   *   *

Knowledge is mere classification. When we find many things of the same kind, we give them a name and are satisfied. We discover events, never why they happen. We take a circuit in a wider field of darkness and think we know something. No "why" can be answered in this world; for that we must go to God.

We can never know the real Knower, by whom all things are known. A salt doll wanted to know the depth of the ocean. The moment it touched the water, it merged in it.

Differentiation creates; homogeneity or sameness is God. Get beyond differentiation; then you will conquer life and death and reach eternal sameness, and will be in God, will be God. Get freedom even at the cost of life. All our lives belong to us as leaves to a book; but we are the unchanged Witness, upon whom the impression is made—as when the impression of a circle is made upon the eyes when a firebrand is rapidly whirled round and round. The Soul is the unity of all our personalities, and because It is at rest, eternal, unchangeable, It is God, Ātman. It is not life, but It is coined into life. It is not pleasure, but It gives rise to pleasure.

*   *   *

Today God is being abandoned by the world because He does not seem to be doing enough for the world. So we hear, "Of what good is He?" Shall we look upon God as a mere municipal authority?

All we can do is to put down all desires, hates, differences. We must put down the lower self, commit mental suicide, as it were. Keep the body and mind pure and healthy, but only as instruments to help us to God—that is their only true use.

Seek truth for truth's sake alone; look not for bliss. It may come, but do not let that be your incentive. Have no motive except God. Dare to come to truth even through hell.

Friday, June 28.

(*The entire household went on a picnic for the day, and although the Swami taught constantly, as he did wherever he was, no notes were taken this day and no record, therefore, of what he said remains. As he began his breakfast before setting out, however, he made the following remark.*)

Be thankful for food. It is Brahman.[13] The universal energy of Brahman is transmuted into our individual energy, and helps us in all that we do.

----

[12] The body is a limitation. Hence the formless must be limitless or infinite. Since there cannot be two infinites, God or the Soul, who is formless, must be one.

[13] Brahman (neuter) is the impersonal, beginningless Supreme Spirit. Brahmā (masculine) is the First Person of the Hindu Trinity (Brahmā, Vishnu, and Śiva) and is the Creator of the universe.

Saturday, June 29.

(The Swami came this morning with the Gītā in his hand.)

Krishna, the "Lord of souls," talks to Arjuna, or Gudākeśa, the "lord of sleep" —he who has conquered sleep. Dharmakshetra, the "field of virtue"—the battle-field—is this world; the five brothers—representing righteousness—fight the hundred other brothers—the worldly objects that we are attached to and have to contend against. The most heroic brother, Arjuna—the awakened soul—is the general. We have to fight all sense-delights, the things to which we are most attached, and kill them. We have to be detached. We are Brahman; all other ideas must be merged into this one.

Krishna did everything, but without any attachment; he was *in* the world but not *of* it. Do all work, but without attachment. Work for work's sake, never for yourself.

*   *   *

Freedom can never belong to name and form. As, by means of name and form, pots are made out of clay, so are we made out of Brahman. But then Brahman becomes limited and is not free. Freedom can never belong to the relative. A pot can never say, "I am free"—as a pot; only as it loses all idea of form does it become free. The whole universe is only the Self with variations, one tune made bearable by variations. Sometimes there are discords, but they only make the subsequent harmony more perfect. In the universal melody three ideas stand out: freedom, strength, and sameness.

If your freedom hurts others, you are not truly free. You must not hurt others.

"To be weak is miserable," says Milton. Work and result are inseparably joined. "To work you have the right—not to the fruits thereof."

*   *   *

Evil thoughts, from the physical standpoint, are the disease bacilli. Each thought is a little hammer-blow on the lump of iron which is our body, making it into what we want it to be. We are heirs to all the good thoughts of the universe, if we open ourselves to them.

The book is in us. "Fool, hearest thou not? In thine own heart day and night is singing that eternal music: 'Satchidānanda, Soham, Soham'—'Existence-Knowledge-Bliss Absolute, I am He, I am He.'"

The fountain of all knowledge is in every one of us—in the ant as in the highest angel. Real religion is one, but we quarrel about the forms, the symbols, the illustrations. The millennium exists already for those who find it; we have lost ourselves and then think the world is lost.

Perfect strength has no activity in this world. It only *is*; it does not act.

While real perfection is only one, relative perfections may be many.

Sunday, June 30.

To try to think without imagery is to try to make the impossible possible. We cannot think "mammalia" without a concrete example. So with the idea of God.

The highest of abstractions in the world is what we call God.

Each thought has two parts: the idea and the word; and we must have both. Neither idealists nor materialists are right; we must take both idea and expression.

All knowledge is of the reflected, just as we can only see our face in a mirror. No one will ever know his own Self or God; but we are that Self, we are God.

In Nirvāna you are when you are not. Buddha said, "You are best, you are real, when you are not"—when the little self is gone.

The Light Divine within is obscured in most people. It is like a lamp in a cask of iron: no gleam of light can shine through. Gradually, by purity and unselfishness, we can make the obscuring medium less and less dense, until at last it becomes as transparent as glass. Śri Ramakrishna is the iron cask transformed into a glass cask, through which the Inner Light can be seen as it is. We are all on the way to becoming the cask of glass and even higher and higher mediums of reflection. As long as there is a cask at all, we must think through material means. No impatient one can ever succeed.

*   *   *

Great saints are illustrations of the Principle. But the disciples make the saint the Principle and then they forget the Principle in the person.

The result of Buddha's constant inveighing against a Personal God was the introduction of idols into India. In the Vedas they knew them not, because they saw God everywhere. But the reaction against the loss of God as Creator and Friend was the introduction of idols; and Buddha became an idol—so too, Jesus. The range of idols is from wood and stone to Jesus and Buddha; but we must have idols.

*   *   *

Violent attempts at reform always end by retarding reform. Do not say, "You are bad"; say only, "You are good, but be better."

Priests are an evil in every country, because they denounce and criticize, pulling at one string to mend it until two or three others are out of place. Love never denounces, but ambition does. There is no such thing as "righteous" anger or justifiable killing.

If you do not allow a man to become a lion, he will become a fox. Woman is a power; only now it is more for evil because man oppresses her. She is a fox, but when she is no longer oppressed she will become a lion.

Ordinarily speaking, spiritual aspiration ought to be balanced through the intellect; otherwise it may degenerate into mere sentimentality.

*   *   *

All theists agree that behind the changeable there is an Unchangeable, though they differ in their conception of the Ultimate. Buddha denied this *in toto*. "There is no Brahman, no Ātman, no soul," he said.

As a character Buddha was the greatest the world has ever seen; next to him, Christ. But the teachings of Krishna as given in the Gītā are the grandest the world has ever known. He who wrote that wonderful poem was one of those rare souls whose lives send a wave of regeneration through the world. The human race will never again see such a brain as his.

*　　*　　*

There is only one Power, manifesting as evil or good. God and the Devil are the same river with the water flowing in opposite directions.

Monday, July 1.

(*Śri Ramakrishna Deva.*)

Śri Ramakrishna was the son of very orthodox brāhmins, who would even refuse a gift from any but a special caste of brāhmins. Neither might such brāhmins work, nor even be priests in a temple, nor sell books, nor serve anyone. They could only have "what fell from the skies," that is to say, alms, and even then it must not come through a "fallen" brāhmin.

Temples have no hold on the Hindu religion; if they were all destroyed, Hinduism would not be affected a bit. A man can build a house for "God and guests"; to build for himself would be selfish. Therefore he erects temples as dwelling-places for God.

Owing to the extreme poverty of his family, Śri Ramakrishna was obliged to become in his boyhood a priest in a temple dedicated to the Divine Mother, also called Prakriti or Kāli, represented by a female figure standing with her feet on a male figure—indicating that until māyā lifts we can know nothing. Brahman is neuter, unknown and unknowable; but to be objectified It covers Itself with a veil of māyā, becomes the Mother of the universe, and so brings forth the creation. The prostrate male figure is Śiva, or Brahman. Being covered by māyā, He has become a corpse, śava. The jnāni, or non-dualist, says, "I will uncover God by force"; but the dualist says, "I will uncover God by praying to Mother, begging Her to open the door to which She alone has the key."

The daily service of Mother Kāli gradually awakened such intense devotion in the heart of the young priest that he could no longer carry on the regular temple worship; so he abandoned his duties and retired to a small woodland in the temple compound, where he gave himself up entirely to meditation. These woods were on the bank of the river Ganges, and one day the swift current bore to his very feet just the necessary materials to build him a little hut. In this hut he stayed and wept and prayed, taking no thought for the care of his body or for aught except his Divine Mother. A relative fed him once a day and watched over him. Later came a woman sannyāsin, or ascetic, to help him find the Mother. Whatever teachers he needed came to him unsought; from every sect some holy saint came and offered to teach him, and to each he listened eagerly. But he worshipped only Mother; all to him was Mother.

Śri Ramakrishna never spoke a harsh word against anyone. So beautifully tolerant was he that every sect thought that he belonged to them. He loved everyone. To him all religions were true. He found a place for each one. He was free—but free in love, not in "thunder." The mild type creates; the thundering type spreads. Paul was the thundering type to spread the light.

The age of St. Paul, however, is gone. We are to be the new lights for this age. A self-adjusting organization is the great need of our time. When we can get one, that will be the last religion of the world. The wheel of the world must revolve, and we should help it, not hinder.

The waves of religious thought rise and fall, and on the topmost wave stands the Prophet of the period. Ramakrishna came to teach the religion of today— constructive, not destructive. He had to go afresh to nature to ask for facts, and he got scientific religion, which never says "Believe," but "See"—"I see, and you too can see." Use the same means and you will reach the same vision. God will come to everyone; harmony is within the reach of all. Sri Ramakrishna's teachings are the gist of Hinduism; they were not peculiar to him. Nor did he claim that they were; he cared naught for name or fame.

He began to preach when he was about forty; but he never went out to do so. He waited for those who wanted his teachings to come to him. In accordance with Hindu custom, he had been married by his parents in early youth to a little girl of five, who lived at home with her family in a distant village, unconscious of the great struggle through which her young husband was passing. When she reached maturity he was already deeply absorbed in religious devotion. She travelled on foot from her home to the temple at Dakshineswar, where he was then living, and as soon as she saw him she recognized what he was; for she herself was a great soul, pure and holy, who only desired to help his work, never to drag him down to the level of the grihastha, the householder.

Sri Ramakrishna is worshipped in India as one of the great Incarnations, and his birthday is celebrated there as a religious festival.

*   *   *

A round stone with special marks is the emblem of Vishnu, the Omnipresent, worshipped in the shrine. Each morning a priest comes in, bathes the image, clothes it, and puts his own Divine Spirit into it to "make it alive." Then he worships it with flowers and other offerings, waves incense before it, and finally puts it to bed, apologizing to God for worshipping Him in that way because of his inability to conceive Him without the help of an image or some other material object.

*   *   *

There is a sect which says, "It is weakness to worship only the good and the beautiful; we ought also to love and worship the hideous and the evil." This sect prevails all over Tibet, and its members do not marry. In India they cannot work openly, but organize secret societies. No decent men will belong to them except sub rosa. Thrice communism was tried in Tibet and thrice it failed. They use tapas and with immense success as far as power is concerned.

Tapas means, literally, "to burn." It is a kind of penance to "heat" the higher nature. It is sometimes in the form of a sunrise to sunset vow, such as repeating Om all day incessantly. Such a discipline produces a certain power that you can convert into any form you wish, spiritual or material. This idea of tapas pervades the whole of the Hindu religion. The Hindus even say that God practised tapas to create the world. It is a mental instrument with which to do anything. "Everything in the three worlds can be attained by tapas."

People who report about sects with which they are not in sympathy are either conscious or unconscious liars. A staunch believer in one sect can rarely see truth in others.

*   *   *

A great bhakta, Hanumān, once said, when asked what day of the month it was, "God is my eternal date; no other date I care for."

Tuesday, July 2.

(The Divine Mother.)

The Śāktas worship the Universal Energy as Mother; it is the sweetest name they know. The mother is the highest ideal of womanhood in India. When God is worshipped as Mother, the Hindus call such worship the "right-hand" way; and it leads to spirituality but never to material prosperity. When God is worshipped in His terrible aspect, that is, in the "left-hand" way, it leads usually to great material prosperity but rarely to spirituality; and eventually it leads to degeneration and the obliteration of the race that practises it.

Mother is the first manifestation of power and is considered a higher idea than Father. The name of Mother brings the idea of Śakti, Divine Energy and Omnipotence: the baby believes its mother to be all-powerful, able to do anything. The Divine Mother is the Kundalini sleeping in us; without worshipping Her we can never know ourselves. All-merciful, all-powerful, omnipresent—these are attributes of the Divine Mother. She is the sum total of the energy in the universe. Every manifestation of power in the universe is Mother. She is life, She is intelligence, She is love. She is in the universe, yet separate from it. She is a Person and can be seen and known—as Śri Ramakrishna saw and knew Her. Established in the idea of Mother, we can do anything. She quickly answers prayer.

She can show Herself to us in any form at any moment. The Divine Mother can have form, rupa, and name, nāma, or name without form; and as we worship Her in these various aspects, we can rise to Pure Being, having neither form nor name.

The sum total of all the cells in an organism is the person; each soul is like one cell, and the sum of them is God. And beyond that is the Absolute. The sea calm is the Absolute; the same sea in waves is the Divine Mother. She is time, space, and causation. Mother is the same as Brahman and has two natures: the conditioned and the unconditioned. As the former She is God, nature, and soul. As the latter She is unknown and unknowable. Out of the Unconditioned came the trinity: God, nature, and soul—the triangle of existence. This is the Viśishtādvaita idea.

A bit of Mother, a drop, was Krishna; another was Buddha; another was Christ. The worship of even one spark of Mother in our earthly mother leads to greatness. Worship Her if you want love and wisdom.

Wednesday, July 3.

Generally speaking, man's religion begins with fear. "The fear of the Lord is the beginning of wisdom." But later comes the higher idea: "Perfect love casteth out fear." Traces of fear will remain with us until we get Knowledge, know what God is. Christ, being man, had to see impurity and denounced it; but God, infinitely higher, does not see iniquity and cannot be angry. Denunciation is never the highest. David's hands were smeared with blood; he could not build the temple.

The more we grow in love and virtue and holiness, the more we see love and virtue and holiness outside. All condemnation of others really condemns ourselves. Adjust the microcosm—which it is in your power to do—and the macrocosm will adjust itself for you. It is like the hydrostatic paradox: one drop of water can balance the universe. We cannot see outside what we are not inside. The universe is to us what a huge engine is to a miniature engine; an indication of any error in the tiny engine leads us to imagine trouble in the huge one.

Every step that has been really gained in the world has been gained by love. Criticizing can never do any good; it has been tried for thousands of years. Condemnation accomplishes nothing.

A real Vedāntist must sympathize with all. Monism, or absolute oneness, is the very soul of Vedānta. Dualists naturally tend to become intolerant, to think theirs the only way. The Vaishnavas in India, who are dualists, are a most intolerant sect. Among the Śaivas, another dualistic sect, the story is told of a devotee by the name of Ghantākarna, the Bell-eared, who was so fanatical a worshipper of Śiva that he did not wish even to hear the name of any other deity; so he wore two bells tied to his ears in order to drown the sound of any voice uttering other divine names. At the sight of his intense devotion, Śiva wanted to teach him that there was no difference between Himself and Vishnu; so He appeared before him as half Vishnu and half Śiva. At that moment the devotee was waving incense before Him; but so great was the bigotry of Ghantākarna that when he saw the fragrance of the incense entering the nostril of Vishnu, he thrust his finger into it to prevent the Deity from enjoying the sweet smell.

*   *   *

The meat-eating animal, like the lion, gives one blow and becomes still, but the patient bullock goes on all day, eating and sleeping as it walks. The "live Yankee" cannot compete with the rice-eating Chinese coolie. While military power dominates, meat-eating will prevail; but with the advance of science fighting will grow less, and then the vegetarians will come in.

*   *   *

We divide ourselves into two to love God—myself loving my Self. God has created me and I have created God. We create God in our image. It is we who create Him to be our Master; it is not God who makes us His servants. When we know that we are one with God, that we and He are friends, then come equality and freedom. So long as you hold yourself separated by a hair's breadth from this Eternal One, fear cannot go.

Never ask that foolish question: What good will our love of God do the world? Let the world go. Love and ask nothing; love and look for nothing further. Love and forget all the "isms." Drink the cup of love and become mad. Say, "Thine, O Thine for ever, O Lord!" and plunge in, forgetting all else. The very essence of God is love. Seeing a cat loving her kittens, stand and pray. God has become manifest there—literally believe this. Repeat, "I am Thine, I am Thine"; for we can see God everywhere. Do not seek Him; just see Him.

May the Lord—the Light of the world, the Soul of the universe—ever protect you!

*   *   *

The Absolute cannot be worshipped; so we must worship a manifestation, such a one as has our nature. Jesus had our nature; he became the Christ. So can we and so must we. Christ and Buddha were the names of a state to be attained; Jesus and Gautama were the persons to attain it. Mother is the first and highest manifestation of the Absolute; next, the Christs and Buddhas.

We make the prison of our own environment and we strike the fetters off. The Ātman is fearless. When we pray to a God outside, it is good, only we do not know what we do. When we know the Self, we understand. The highest expression of love is unification.

> There was a time when I was a woman and he was a man;
> Still love grew until there was neither he nor I.
> Only I remember faintly there was a time when there were two;
> But love came between and made them one.[14]

Knowledge exists eternally and is coexistent with God. The man who discovers a spiritual law is inspired and what he says is revelation; but revelation too is eternal, not to be crystallized as final and then blindly followed. The Hindus have been criticized so many years by their conquerors that they—the Hindus—dare to criticize their religion themselves; and this makes them free-thinkers. Their foreign rulers struck off their fetters without knowing it. The most religious people on earth, the Hindus have actually no sense of blasphemy; to speak of holy things in any way is to them in itself a sanctification. Nor have they any artificial respect for prophets or the scriptures, or for hypocritical piety.

The Church tries to fit Christ into it, not the Church into Christ; so only those writings were preserved that suited its purpose in hand. Thus the scriptures are not to be depended upon. Book-worship is the worst kind of idolatry to bind our feet. All has to conform to the book—science, religion, philosophy. It is the most horrible tyranny, this tyranny of the Protestant Bible. Every man in Christian countries has a huge cathedral on his head, and on top of that a book, and yet man lives and grows! Does this not prove that man is God?

Man is the highest being that exists, and this is the greatest world. We can have no conception of a God higher than man; so our God is man and man is God. When we rise and go beyond and find something higher, we have to jump out of the mind, out of the body and the imagination, and leave this world; when we rise to the Absolute, we are no longer in this world. Man is the apex of the only world we can ever know. All we know of animals is only by analogy: we judge them by what we do and feel ourselves.

[14] From a Persian Sufi poem.

The sum total of knowledge is ever the same; only sometimes it is more manifested and sometimes less. The only source of it is within; there alone is it found.

*   *   *

All poetry, painting, and music are feeling expressed through words, through colour, through sound.

*   *   *

Blessed are those upon whom their sins are quickly visited: their account is the sooner balanced! Woe to those whose punishment is deferred: it will be the greater!

Those who have attained sameness are said to be living in God. All hatred is "killing the Self by the self"; therefore love is the law of life. To rise to this is to be perfect; but the more perfect we are, the less work—so-called—can we do. The sāttvikas see and know that all is mere child's play and do not trouble themselves about anything.

It is easy to strike a blow, but tremendously hard to stay the hand, stand still, and say, "In Thee, O Lord, I take refuge," and then wait for Him to act.

Friday, July 5.

Until you are ready to change any minute for the sake of truth, you can never see truth; but you must hold fast and be steady in the search for truth.

*   *   *

The Chārvākas, a very ancient sect in India, were rank materialists. They have died out now and most of their books are lost. They claimed that the soul, being the product of the body and its forces, died with it, and that there was no proof of its further existence. They denied inferential knowledge, accepting only the knowledge that comes through the senses.

*   *   *

Samādhi is the state in which the Divine and the human become one; it means "the attaining of sameness."

*   *   *

Materialism says: The voice of freedom is a delusion. Idealism says: The voice that tells of bondage is a delusion. Vedānta says: You are free and not free at the same time—never free on the earthly plane, but ever free on the spiritual. Go beyond both freedom and bondage.

We are Śiva: we are immortal Knowledge beyond the senses.

Infinite power is back of everyone; pray to Mother and it will come to you.

"O Mother, Giver of vāk, eloquence! Thou Self-existent One, come as vāk upon my lips."[15]

"Mother, whose voice is in the thunder, manifest Thyself in me! Kālī, Thou time eternal, Thou force irresistible—Śakti, Power!"

[15] A Hindu invocation.

Saturday, July 6.

(Today we heard Śaṅkarāchārya's commentary on Vyāsa's Vedānta Sutras.)

Om Tat Sat. According to Śaṅkara there are two phases of the universe: one is "I" and the other "thou"—and they are as contrary as light and darkness. So it goes without saying that neither can be derived from the other. On the subject, the object has been superimposed; the subject is the only reality, the other a mere appearance. The opposite view is untenable. Matter and the external world are but certain states of the Soul; in reality there is only one.

All our world comes from truth and untruth coupled together. Samsāra, life, is the result of the contradictory forces acting upon us, like the diagonal motion of a ball in a parallelogram of forces. The world is God and is real; but that is not the way we see it. Just as we see silver in the mother-of-pearl where it does not exist, so we see the relative world in God. This is what is known as adhyāsa, or superimposition, that is, a relative existence dependent upon a real one—as when we recall a scene we have seen before. For the time it exists for us; but that existence is not real. Or some say that it is as when we imagine water to be hot. Heat does not belong to water; it is something which has been superimposed. Thus adhyāsa means "taking a thing for what it is not." We see Reality, but distorted by the medium through which we see It.

You can never know yourself except as objectified. When we mistake one thing for another, we always take the thing before us as the real—never the unseen. Thus we mistake the object for the subject. The Ātman never becomes the object. The mind is the internal sense; the outer senses are its instruments. In the subject is a trifle of the objectifying power, which enables him to know, "I am"; but the subject is the object of his own self, never of the mind or the senses. You can, however, superimpose one idea on another idea, as when we say, "The sky is blue." We are superimposing the idea of blueness on the idea of sky.

Science and nescience are all that there is; but the Self is never affected by nescience. Relative knowledge is good, because it leads to Absolute Knowledge; but neither the knowledge of the senses, nor that of the mind, nor even that of the Vedas is Truth, since they are all within the realm of relative knowledge. First get rid of the delusion "I am the body"; then only will you want real knowledge. Man's knowledge is only a degree higher than brute knowledge.

*   *   *

One part of the Vedas deals with karma—forms and ceremonies. The other part deals with the Knowledge of Brahman and discusses spirituality. The Vedas in this part teach of the Self, and because they do, their teaching approaches real Knowledge. Knowledge of the Absolute depends upon no book, upon nothing; it is absolute in itself. No amount of study will give this Knowledge. It is not theory; it is realization. Cleanse the dust from the mirror, purify your own mind, and in a flash you will know that you are Brahman.

God alone exists—not birth or death, nor pain, nor misery, nor murder, nor change, nor good, nor evil. All is Brahman. We take the "rope for the serpent"; the error is ours.

We can do good only when we love God. The murderer too is God; only the mask of "murderer" is superimposed upon him. Take him by the hand and tell him the truth.

The Soul has no caste and to think It has is a delusion; neither has It life or death, or any motion or quality. The Ātman never changes, never goes or comes. It is the eternal Witness of all Its own manifestations, but we take It for the manifestation—an eternal illusion, without beginning or end, ever going on. The Vedas, however, have to come down to our level; for if they told us the highest truth in the highest way, we could not understand it.

Heaven is a mere superstition arising from desire, and desire is ever a yoke, a degeneration. Never approach anything except as God; for if we do not approach things as God, we see evil. We throw a veil of delusion over what we look at and then we see evil. Get free from these illusions. Be blessed. Freedom is to be rid of all illusions.

In one sense Brahman is known to every human being: he knows, "I am." But man does not know himself as he is. We all know *that* we are, but not *what* we are. All lower explanations are partial truths; but the flower, the essence, of the Vedas is that the Self in each of us is Brahman.

Every phenomenon is limited by birth, growth, and death—appearance, continuance, and disappearance.

Our own realization is beyond the Vedas, because even the Vedas depend, for their proof, upon realization. The highest Vedānta is the philosophy of the Beyond.

To say that creation has any beginning is to lay the axe at the root of all philosophy.

Māyā is the energy in the universe, both potential and kinetic. Until māyā, the Mother, releases us, we cannot get free.

The universe is ours to enjoy. But want nothing: to want is weakness. Want makes us beggars, and we are sons of the king—not beggars.

Sunday morning, July 7.

Infinite manifestation dividing itself into portions still remains infinite, and each portion is infinite.[16]

Brahman is the same though appearing in two forms: changeable and unchangeable, expressed and unexpressed. Know that the knower and the known are one. The trinity of the knower, the known, and knowing is manifesting itself as this universe. The God that the yogi sees in meditation he sees through the power of his own Self.

What we call nature or fate is simply God's will.

So long as enjoyment is sought, bondage remains. Only the imperfect being can enjoy, because enjoyment is the fulfilling of desire. The human soul enjoys nature. The underlying reality of nature, soul, and God is Brahman; but Brahman is unseen until we bring It out. It may be brought out by pramantha, friction, just as we can produce fire by friction. The body is the lower piece of wood, Om is the upper piece, and meditation is the friction. Through friction, that is to say, meditation, that light which is the Knowledge of Brahman will

---

[16] Because the very idea of division is māyā.

burst forth in the soul. Seek it through tapas. Holding the body upright, sacrifice the organs of sense in the mind. The sense-centres are within, the organs without. So drive them into the mind and through dhāranā, concentration, fix the mind in dhyāna, meditation.[17] Brahman permeates the universe, as butter permeates milk; but friction makes it manifest in one particular place. As churning brings out the butter, so dhyāna leads to the realization of Brahman in the soul.

All Hindu philosophy declares that there is a sixth sense, the superconscious, and through it comes inspiration.

*   *   *

The universe is motion, and friction will eventually bring everything to an end. Then comes a rest, and after that all begins again.

*   *   *

So long as the "skin sky" surrounds a man, that is, so long as he identifies himself with his body, he cannot see God.

Sunday afternoon.

There are six schools of philosophy in India that are regarded as orthodox, and this is because they believe in the Vedas.

Vyāsa's philosophy is *par excellence* that of the Upanishads. He wrote in sutra form, that is, in brief algebraic symbols without nominative or verb. This caused so much ambiguity that out of the *Vedānta Sutras* came dualism, qualified non-dualism, and monism, or the "roaring lion of Vedānta"; and all the great commentators of these different schools were at times conscious liars in order to make the texts suit their philosophy.

The Upanishads contain very little history of the doings of any man; but nearly all other scriptures are largely personal histories. The Upanishads deal almost entirely with philosophy. Religion without philosophy runs into superstition; philosophy without religion becomes dry atheism.

Viśishtādvaita is qualified Advaita, qualified non-dualism. Its expounder was Rāmānuja. He says, "Out of the ocean of milk of the Vedas, Vyāsa has churned this butter of philosophy in order to help mankind." He says again: "All virtues and all qualities belong to Brahmā, the Lord of the universe. He is the greatest Purusha." Madhva is a thoroughgoing dualist, or Dvaitist. He claims that even women may study the Vedas. He quotes chiefly from the Purānas. He says that Brahman means Vishnu, not Śiva at all, because there is no salvation except through Vishnu.

Monday, July 8.

There is no place for reasoning in Madhva's explanation; it is all taken on the authority of the Vedas.

Rāmānuja says that the Vedas are the holiest study. Let the sons of the three upper castes receive the sacred thread at eight, ten, or eleven years of age and

[17] When the thought-current is interrupted, it is called concentration; when the flow is uninterrupted, it is called meditation.

begin their study, which means going to a guru and learning the Vedas word for word, with perfect intonation and pronunciation.

Japa is repeating the holy name. Through this the devotee rises to the Infinite. The boat of sacrifices and ceremonies is very frail; we need more than that to know Brahman, the knowledge of which alone is freedom. Freedom is nothing more than the destruction of ignorance, and that can only go when we know Brahman. It is not necessary to go through all these ceremonials to reach the meaning of Vedānta. Repeating Om is enough.

Seeing difference is the cause of all misery; and ignorance is the cause of seeing difference. That is why ceremonials are not needed. They increase the idea of inequality. You practise them to get rid of something or to obtain something.

Brahman is without action; Ātman is Brahman, and we are Ātman—knowledge like this takes away all error. This must be heard, apprehended intellectually, and finally realized. Reflection is applying reason and establishing this knowledge in ourselves by reason. Realizing is making it a part of our lives by constant thinking of it. This constant thought, dhyāna, is like the unbroken flow of oil as it is poured from vessel to vessel; dhyāna holds the mind to this thought day and night and so helps us to attain to liberation. Think always, "Soham, Soham"; this is almost as good as liberation. Say it day and night; realization will come as the result of this continuous cogitation. This absolute and continuous remembrance of the Lord is what is meant by bhakti.

Bhakti is indirectly helped by good works. Good thoughts and good works create less differentiation than bad ones; so indirectly they lead to freedom. Work, but give up the results to the Lord. Knowledge alone can make us perfect. He who follows the God of Truth with devotion—to him the God of Truth reveals Himself.

*   *   *

We are like a lamp and its burning is what we call life. When the supply of oxygen gives out, then the lamp must go out. All we can do is keep the lamp clean. Life is a product, a compound, and as such must resolve itself into its elements.

Tuesday, July 9.

Man, as Ātman, is really free; as man he is bound, changed by every physical condition. As man, he is a machine with an idea of freedom; but this human body is the best body and the human mind the highest mind there is. When a man attains to the Ātman he can take a body, making it to suit himself; he is above law. This is a statement and must be proved. Each one must prove it for himself. We may satisfy ourselves but we cannot satisfy another.

Rāja-yoga is the only science of religion that can be demonstrated, and only what I myself have proved by experience do I teach. The full ripeness of reason is intuition, but intuition cannot antagonize reason.

Work purifies the heart and so leads to vidyā, wisdom. The Buddhists said that doing good to men and to animals were the only works; the brāhmins said that worship and all ceremonials were equally work and purified the mind.

Śankara declares that all works, good and bad, are against knowledge. Actions tending to ignorance are sins, not directly, but as causes, because they tend to increase tamas and rajas. With sattva only comes wisdom. Virtuous deeds take off the veil from Knowledge, and Knowledge alone can make us see God.

Knowledge can never be created; it can only be discovered; and every man who makes a great discovery is inspired. When it is a spiritual truth that he brings, we call him a prophet, and when it is a truth on the physical plane, we call him a scientific man; and we attribute more importance to the former, although the source of all truth is one.

Śankara says that Brahman is the essence, the reality, of all knowledge, and that all manifestations—such as knower, knowing, and known—are mere imaginings in Brahman. Rāmānuja attributes consciousness to God; the real monists attribute nothing, not even existence—whatever meaning we may attach to it. Rāmānuja declares that God is the essence of conscious knowledge. Undifferentiated consciousness, when differentiated, becomes the world.

*   *   *

Buddhism, one of the most philosophical religions in the world, spread all through the populace, the common people of India. What a wonderful culture there must have been among the Āryans twenty-five hundred years ago, if they were able to grasp such ideas!

Buddha was the only great Indian philosopher who would not recognize caste; and not one of his followers remains in India. All the other philosophers pandered more or less to social prejudices; no matter how high they soared, still a bit of the vulture remained in them. As my Master used to say: "The vulture soars high out of sight in the sky, but his eye is ever on a bit of carrion on the earth."

*   *   *

The ancient Hindus were wonderful scholars, veritable living encyclopaedias. They said, "Knowledge in books and money in other people's hands are like no money and no knowledge at all."

Śankara was regarded by many as an Incarnation of Śiva.

Wednesday, July 10.

There are sixty-five million Mohammedans in India, some of them Sufis. The Sufis identify man with God, and through them this idea came into Europe. They say, "I am that Truth"; but they have an esoteric as well as an exoteric doctrine, although Mohammed himself did not hold it.

The word *assassin* has been derived from Hashashin,[18] because an old sect of Mohammedans killed non-believers as a part of their creed.

[18] The name of a militant religious order existing in Syria in the eleventh century, famous for the number of secret murders committed by its members in obedience to the will of their chief. The literal meaning of the word is "hashish-eater" and was applied to the order because of their habitual use of this special drug to fortify the murderers for their task.

The Mohammedans, at the time of worship, must have a pitcher of water as a symbol of God's filling the universe.

The Hindus believe that there are ten Divine Incarnations. Nine have been and the tenth is still to come.

*   *   *

Śankara sometimes resorts to sophistry in order to prove that the ideas in the Vedas go to uphold his philosophy. Buddha was more brave and sincere than any teacher. He said: "Believe no book; the Vedas are all humbug. If they agree with me, so much the better for the books. I am the greatest book. Sacrifice and prayer are useless." Buddha was the first human being to give to the world a complete system of morality. He did good for good's sake; he loved for love's sake.

Śankara says that God is to be reasoned about because the Vedas say so. Reason helps inspiration; the scriptures and one's own realization are both proofs of God's existence. The Vedas are, according to him, a sort of embodiment of universal knowledge. The proof of the Vedas is that they were brought forth by Brahman, and the proof of Brahman is that Brahman alone could give out such wonderful books. The Vedas are the mine of all knowledge and they have come out of Brahman as the breath comes out of a man. Therefore we know that He is infinite in power and knowledge. He may or may not have created the world—that is a trifle. To have produced the Vedas is more important! The world has come to know God through the Vedas. No other way there is. And so universal is this belief, held by Śankara, in the all-inclusiveness of the Vedas that there is even a Hindu proverb that if a man loses his cow, he goes to the Vedas to look for her!

Śankara further affirms that obedience to ceremonial is not Knowledge. Knowledge of God is independent of moral duty or sacrifice or ceremonial, or what we think or do not think, just as the stump is not affected when one man takes it for a ghost and another sees it as it is.

The Knowledge of Vedānta is necessary because neither reasoning nor books can show us God. He is to be realized only by superconscious perception, and Vedānta teaches how to attain that. You must go beyond the Personal God, or Iśvara, and reach the Absolute. Brahman alone is perceived by every being. It is all there is to be perceived. That which says "I" is Brahman; but although we day and night perceive It, we do not know that we are perceiving It. As soon as we become aware of this truth, all misery goes. So we must get the Knowledge of Truth. Reach unity; no more will duality come. But Knowledge does not come through sacrifice, but by seeking, worshipping, knowing the Ātman.

*   *   *

Brahmavidyā, the Knowledge of Brahman, is the Higher Knowledge; the lower knowledge is science. This is the teaching of the *Mundaka Upanishad*, or the Upanishad for sannyāsins. There are two sorts of knowledge: principal and secondary. The unessential is that part of the Vedas which deals with worship and ceremonial, also all secular knowledge. The essential is that by which we reach the Absolute. The Absolute creates everything from Itself; there is no other cause, nothing outside. Brahman is all energy; It is all there is. He who makes all sacrifices to the Self, the Ātman, he alone knows Brahman. Fools think external worship the highest; fools think works can give us God. Only those who go through the Sushumnā, the path of the yogis, reach the Ātman. They must go to a guru to learn. Each part has the same nature as the whole; all springs from the Ātman. The soul is the arrow, and Om is the bow, which speeds the arrow to its mark, the Ātman. As finite beings, we can never express the Infinite; but we are the Infinite. Knowing this we argue with no one.

Divine wisdom is to be got by devotion, meditation, and chastity. "Truth alone triumphs, and not untruth." Through truth alone the way is spread to Brahman, where dwell love and truth.

Thursday, July 11.

Without mother love no creation could continue. Nothing is entirely physical, nor yet entirely metaphysical; one presupposes the other and explains the other. All theists agree that there is a background to this visible universe; they differ as to the nature or character of that background. Materialists say there is no background.

In all religions the superconscious state is identical. Hindus, Christians, Mohammedans, Buddhists, and even those of no creed, all have the very same experience when they transcend the body.

*   *   *

The purest Christianity in the world was established in India by the Apostle Thomas about twenty-five years after the death of Jesus. This was while the Anglo-Saxons were still savages, painting their bodies and living in caves. The Christians in India once numbered about three millions, but now there are about one million.

Christianity is often propagated by the sword. How surprising that the disciples of such a gentle soul should kill so much! The three missionary religions are Buddhism, Mohammedanism, and Christianity. The three older ones —Hinduism, Judaism, and Zoroastrianism—never sought to make converts. The Buddhists never killed, but at one time converted three-quarters of the world by pure gentleness.

The Buddhists were the most logical agnostics. You can really stop nowhere between nihilism and non-dualism. The Buddhists were intellectually all-destroyers, carrying their theory to its logical conclusion. The Advaitists also worked out their theory to its logical conclusion and reached the Absolute, the one, homogeneous, unitary Substance out of which all phenomena are being manifested. Both Buddhists and Advaitists have a feeling of identity and non-identity at the same time. One of these feelings must be false and the other true. The Buddhist nihilist describes non-identity[19] as reality; the Advaitist describes identity[20] as reality; and this is the fight which occupies the whole world. This is the tug-of-war.

[19] I.e. unrelated sensations.
[20] I.e. the oneness of existence.

The Advaitist asks: How does the nihilist get any idea of identity?[21] How does the revolving light appear as a circle? A state of rest alone explains motion. The existence of an indivisible reality behind phenomena must be admitted. The nihilist calls this a delusion, but can never explain the genesis of the delusion. Neither can the Advaitist explain how the One becomes the many. The explanation can come only from beyond the sense plane. We must rise to the superconscious, to a state entirely beyond sense perception. That inexplicable power by which we can go beyond phenomena, the Advaitist alone can use. He can experience the Absolute. The man Vivekananda can resolve himself into the Absolute and then come back to the man again. For him, then, the problem is solved, and secondarily for others; for he can show the way to others. Religion begins where philosophy ends.

The good to the world, through such realization, is that what is now the superconscious will in ages to come be the conscious for all. Religion is therefore the highest task the world has; and because man has unconsciously felt this, he has clung through all the ages to the idea of religion.

Religion, the great milch cow, has given many kicks; but never mind—it also gives a great deal of milk. The milkman does not mind the kick of the cow which gives much milk.

The Sanskrit drama *Prabodhachandrodaya* records the fight between two kings, Delusion and Discrimination. King Discrimination could not gain a complete victory. At last he was reunited with the goddess Upanishad. A son was born to them called Prabodha, Knowledge. Through the influence of this boy they could not look upon anyone as an enemy. Consequently they spent their days in great happiness. We too must beget a glorious son like Prabodha, Knowledge. We must nourish him and help him to grow. Thus he will become a great hero.

Love concentrates all the power of the will without effort, as when a man and woman fall in love. The path of devotion is natural and pleasant. Philosophy is taking the mountain stream back to its source by force. It is a quicker method, but very hard. Philosophy says, "Control everything." Devotion says, "Float with the stream; have total self-surrender." It is a longer way, but easier and happier.

"Thine am I for ever. Henceforth whatever I do, it is Thou doing it; no more is there any 'me' or 'mine' "—thus says the devotee. Further:

"Having no money to give, no brains to learn with, no time to practise yoga, to Thee, O Sweet One, I give myself—to Thee my body and mind."

No amount of ignorance or wrong ideas can put a barrier between the soul and God. Even if there be no God, still hold fast to love. It is better to die seeking God than to live as a dog, seeking only carrion. Choose the highest ideal and give your life up to that. Death being certain, it is the highest thing to give up life for a great purpose.

[21] The Buddhist idealist (called nihilist by Śankara) accepts sensations alone as real. He gives the example of a stick, one end of which is burning; when the stick is whirled about, the point of fire creates the illusion of a circle. Likewise, sensations, moved by the wind of desire, create the illusion of names and forms.

Love will painlessly lead to philosophy; then, after knowledge, comes parā-bhakti, supreme devotion.

Knowledge is critical and makes a great fuss over everything; but love says, "God will show His real nature to me," and accepts all.

> Rabbia, sick upon her bed,
> By two saints was visited—
>
> Holy Malik, Hassan wise,
> Men of mark in Moslem eyes.
>
> Hassan said, "Whose prayer is pure
> Will God's chastisements endure."
>
> Malik from a deeper sense
> Uttered his experience:
>
> "He who loves his Master's choice
> Will in chastisement rejoice."
>
> Rabbia saw some selfish will
> In their maxims lingering still,
>
> And replied, "O men of grace,
> He who sees his Master's face
>
> Will not in his prayers recall
> That he is chastised at all."[22]

Friday, July 12.

(*Śankara's Commentary.*)

Fourth Vyāsa sutra: "Ātman, or Brahman, is the purport of all Vedāntic texts."

Iśvara is to be known from the Vedānta; all the Vedas point to Him, who is the Cause—the Creator, Preserver, and Destroyer. Iśvara is the unification of the Trinity, known as Brahmā, Vishnu, and Śiva, who stand at the head of the Hindu pantheon.

The Vedas cannot show you Brahman. You are That already. They can only help to take away the veil that hides the truth from your eyes. The first veil to vanish is ignorance; and when that is gone, sin goes; next desire ceases, selfishness ends, and all misery disappears. This cessation of ignorance can come only when I know that God and I are one. In other words, identify yourself with the Ātman, not with human limitations. Disidentify yourself with the body and all pain will cease. This is the secret of healing. The universe is a case of hypnotization; dehypnotize yourself and cease to suffer.

In order to be free we have to pass through vice to virtue, and then get rid of both. Tamas is to be conquered by rajas; both are to be submerged in sattva. Then go beyond the three qualities. Reach a state where your very breathing is a prayer.

Whenever you learn, that is to say, gain anything, from another man's words,

[22] Persian poem.

know that you had the experience in a previous existence, because experience is the only teacher.

With powers comes misery; so kill desire. Fulfilling any desire is like putting a stick into a hornets' nest. Vairāgya is finding out that desires are but gilded balls of poison.

"Mind is not God," says Śankara. "Tat tvam asi," "Aham Brahmāsmi"— "That thou art," "I am Brahman." When a man realizes this, all the knots of his heart are cut asunder, all his doubts vanish. Fearlessness is not possible as long as we have even God over us; we must be God. What is disjoined will remain for ever disjoined; if you are separate from God, you can never be one with Him, and vice versa. If by virtue you are joined to God, when that ceases, disjunction will come. The junction of God and man is eternal and virtue only helps to remove the veil. We are āzād, free; we must realize it.

The Upanishad says, "The Self is only attained by him whom the Self chooses." This means that we are the Self and we choose ourselves.

Does seeing depend upon our own efforts or does it depend upon something outside? It depends upon ourselves: our efforts take off the dust; the mirror does not change.

There is neither knower, knowing, nor known. "He who knows that he does not know, knows It." He who has only a theory knows nothing.

The idea that we are bound is indeed an illusion.

Religion is not of this world; it is heart-cleansing and its effect on this world is secondary. Freedom is inseparable from the nature of the Ātman, which is ever pure, ever perfect, ever unchangeable. This Ātman you can never know. We can say nothing about the Ātman but "Not this, not this."

"Brahman is that which we can never drive out by any power of mind or imagination."[23]

*   *   *

The universe is thought, and the Vedas are the words expressing this thought. We can create and uncreate this whole universe. Through the repetition of words, the unseen thought is aroused and as a result a seen effect is produced— this is the claim of a certain sect of karmis. They think that each one of us is a Creator. Pronounce the words, and the thought which corresponds to them will arise and the result will become visible. "Thought is the power of the word; the word is the expression of the thought," say the Mimāmsakas, a Hindu philosophical sect.

Saturday, July 13.

Everything we know is a compound, and all sense knowledge comes through analysis. To think that the mind is simple, single, or independent is dualism. Philosophical wisdom is not obtained through studying books; the more you read, the more muddled you become. Superficial philosophers thought that the mind was an uncompounded substance, and this led them to believe in free will. Psychology, which analyses the mind, shows the mind to be a compound; and every compound must be held together by some outside force;

[23] Śankarāchārya.

so the will, which is an aspect of the mind, is held together by a combination of outside forces. Man cannot even will to eat unless he is hungry. The will is subject to desire. Still we are free, and everyone feels it.

The agnostic says that this idea of freedom is a delusion. But how do you prove the world? Its only proof is that we all see it and feel it. So, just as much, we all feel freedom. If the universal consensus affirms this world, it also affirms freedom. But freedom is not of the will as we see it. The inherent belief of man in freedom is the basis of all reasoning. Freedom means freedom of the will as it was before it became bound. The idea of free will is demonstrated every moment by man's struggle against bondage. That alone can be free which is one—the Unconditioned, the Infinite, the Unlimited. Freedom in man is now a mere memory, an attempt towards freedom.

Everything in the universe is struggling to complete a circle, to return to its source, to return to its only real source, the Ātman. The search for happiness is a struggle to find the balance, to restore the equilibrium. Morality is the struggle of the bound will to get free and is the proof that we have come from perfection.

*   *   *

The idea of duty is the midday sun of misery scorching the very soul. "O king, drink this one drop of nectar and be happy." ("I am not the doer"—this is the nectar.)

Let there be action without reaction. Action is pleasant; all misery is reaction. The child puts its hand in the flame. That is pleasure. But when its body reacts, then comes the pain of burning. When we can stop that reaction, then we have nothing to fear. Control the brain and do not let it read the record; be the witness and do not react. Only thus can you be happy. The happiest moments we ever know are when we entirely forget ourselves. Work of your own free will, not from duty. We have no duty. This world is just a gymnasium in which we play; our life is an eternal holiday.

The whole secret of existence is to have no fear. Never fear what will become of you; depend on no one. Only the moment you reject all help are you free and fully perfect. The full sponge can absorb no more.

*   *   *

Even fighting in self-defense is wrong, though it is higher than fighting in aggression. There is no "righteous" indignation, because indignation comes from not recognizing sameness in all things.

Sunday, July 14.

Philosophy in India means that through which we see God; it is the rationale of religion; so no Hindu would ever ask for a link between religion and philosophy.

Concrete, generalized, and abstract are the three stages in the process of philosophy. The highest abstraction, in which all things are harmonized, is the One. In religion we have, first, symbols and forms, next, mythology, and last,

philosophy. The first two serve a temporary purpose. Philosophy is the underlying basis of all, and the others are only stepping-stones in the struggle to reach
the Ultimate.

In Christianity the idea is that without the New Testament and Christ
there could be no religion; and a similar belief exists in Judaism with regard
to Moses and the Prophets—because these religions are dependent upon
mythology only. Real religion, the highest, rises above mythology; it can never
rest upon that. Modern science has really made the foundations of religion
strong. That the whole universe is one is scientifically demonstrable. What
the metaphysician calls "being," the physicist calls "matter"; but there is
no real fight between the two, for they are one. Though an atom is invisible,
unthinkable, yet in it are the whole power and potency of the universe. That
is exactly what the Vedāntist says of the Ātman. All sects are really saying the
same thing in different words.

Vedānta and modern science both posit a self-evolving cause. In it exist all
subsidiary causes. Take, for example, a potter shaping a pot. The potter is the
primal cause, the clay the material cause, and the wheel the instrumental cause;
but the Ātman is all three. The Ātman is cause and manifestation too. The
Vedāntist says that the universe is not real, it is only apparent. Nature is God
seen through the veil of nescience. The pantheists say that God has become
nature, or this world; the Advaitists affirm that God is appearing as this world,
but He is not this world.

We can only know an experience as a mental process, a fact in the mind as
well as a mark in the brain. We cannot push the brain back or forward, but we
can the mind; it can stretch over all time—past, present, and future—and so
facts in the mind are eternally preserved. All facts are already generalized in
mind, which is omnipresent.[24]

Kant's great achievement was the discovery that time, space, and causation
are modes of thought; but Vedānta taught this ages ago and called it "māyā."
Schopenhauer stands on reason only and rationalizes the Vedas.

Śankara maintained the orthodoxy of the Vedas.

"Treeness," or the idea of tree, discovered by looking at trees, is knowledge,
and the highest knowledge is the knowledge of the One.

The Personal God is the last generalization of the universe—only hazy, not
clear-cut and philosophic.

Unity is self-evolving; out of it everything comes.

Physical science wants to find out facts; metaphysics is the thread to bind
these flowers of facts into a bouquet. Every abstraction is metaphysical; even
putting manure at the root of a tree involves a process of abstraction.

Religion includes the concrete, the more generalized, and the ultimate Unity.
Do not stick to particularizations. Get to the principle, to the One.

---

[24] Since the entire creation existing in space, time, and causation can never exist beyond
mind or memory, manifesting itself as thinking, feeling, and willing, therefore the whole
of space, time, and causation must exist in it. Hence mind is omnipresent. The individual mind is a portion of the omnipresent or universal mind, almost shut up in a
body, like a gulf or a bit of the ocean mostly surrounded by land, with only a narrow
opening which joins it to the ocean.

Devils are machines of darkness; angels are machines of light; but both are machines. Man alone is not a machine. Destroy the machine idea; feel you are superior to both angels and devils; then alone can you become free. This is the only world where man can work out his salvation.

"Whom the Self chooses" is true. Election is true; but explain it as an inner experience. As an external and fatalistic doctrine it is horrible.

Monday, July 15.

Where there is polyandry, as in Tibet, the women are physically stronger than the men. When the English go there, these women carry large men up the mountains.

In Malabar, although naturally polyandry does not exist there, the women lead in everything. Exceptional cleanliness is apparent everywhere, and there is the greatest impetus to learning. When I myself was in that country, I met many women who spoke good Sanskrit, while in the rest of India not one woman in a million can speak it. Freedom elevates and servitude debases. Malabar has never been conquered either by the Portuguese or by the Mussulmans.

The Dravidians were a non-Āryan race of Central Asia who preceded the Āryans, and those of Southern India were the most civilized. Women with them stood higher than men. They subsequently divided, some going to Egypt, others to Babylonia, and the rest remaining in India.

Tuesday, July 16.

(Śankara.)

Adrishtam, the "unseen cause,"[25] leads to the performance of sacrifice and worship, which in turn produce seen results. But in order to attain liberation, we must first hear about Brahman, then think or reason, and then meditate upon Brahman.

The result of works and the result of knowledge are two different things. "Do" and "Do not do" are the foundation of all morality, but they really belong only to the body and the mind. All happiness and misery are inextricably connected with the senses, and the body is necessary to experience them. The higher the body, the higher the standard of virtue. Up to Brahmā all have bodies. As long as there is a body, there must be pleasure and pain; only when one has got rid of the body can one escape them. "The Ātman is bodiless," says Śankara.

No law can make you free. You are free. Nothing can give you freedom if you have it not already. The Ātman is self-illumined; cause and effect do not reach there. And this luminosity is freedom. Beyond what was or is or is to be is Brahman. As an effect, freedom would have no value; it would be a compound, and as such would contain the seeds of bondage. Freedom is the one real thing—not to be attained, but the real nature of the soul.

Work and worship, however, are necessary to take away the veil, to lift off the bondage and illusion. They do not give us freedom; but all the same, with-

[25] According to the Vedic mystics, the oblations offered at the sacrifice are transformed into adrishtam or an unseen factor, which produces a tangible result.

out effort on our own part we do not open our eyes and see what we are. Śankara says further that Advaita Vedānta is the crowning glory of the Vedas;
but the other systems of Vedānta are also necessary, because they teach work
and worship, and through these many come to the Lord. Some may come without any help but Advaita. Work and worship lead to the same result as Advaita.

The books cannot teach God, but they can destroy ignorance; their action is
negative. To have held to the books and at the same time opened the way to
freedom was Śankara's great achievement. But to accomplish this he had to
indulge in hair-splitting arguments. Give man first the concrete; then raise him
to the highest by slow degrees. This is the effort of the various religions, and
justifies their existence and explains how each is suited to some stage of
development. The very books are a part of the ignorance they help to dispel.
Their duty is to drive out the ignorance that has come upon knowledge. "Truth
shall drive out untruth." You are free; you cannot be made so.

So long as you have a creed, you have no God. "He who knows he knows,
knows nothing." Who can know the Knower? There are two eternal facts in
existence: God and the universe—the former unchangeable, the latter changeable. The world exists eternally. Where your mind cannot grasp the amount
of change, you call it eternity.

You see the stone or the bas-relief on it, but not both at once. Yet both
are one.

*   *   *

Can you make yourself at rest even for a second? All yogis say that you can.

The greatest sin is to think yourself weak. No one is greater. Realize that you
are Brahman. Nothing has power except what you give it. We are beyond the
sun, the stars, the universe. Teach the Godhood of man. Deny evil, create none.
Stand up and say, "I am the master, the master of all." We forge the chain
and we alone can break it.

No action can give you freedom; only knowledge can make you free. Knowledge is irresistible: the mind cannot take it or reject it. When it comes, the
mind has to accept it. So it is not a work of the mind; but its expression comes
through the mind.

Work or worship brings you back to your own nature. Through illusion the
Self is identified with the body; so even while living in the body we can be
free. The body has nothing in common with the Self. Illusion means to take
the unreal for the real, not "nothing at all."

Wednesday, July 17.

Rāmānuja divides the universe into chit, achit, and Iśvara—soul, nature, and
God; conscious, subconscious, and superconscious. Śankara, on the contrary,
says that chit, the soul, is the same as God. God is Truth, is Knowledge, is
Infinity; these are not qualities. Any thought of God is a qualification, and all
that can be said of Him is: "Om Tat Sat."

Śankara further asks: Can you see existence separate from everything else?
Where is the differentiation between two objects? Not in sense perception, else
all would be one in it. We have to perceive in sequence. In order to know what

a thing is, we also have to know what it is not. The differentiae are in the memory and are known by comparison with what is stored there. Difference is not in the nature of a thing; it is in the brain. Homogeneous oneness is outside; differentiae are inside—in the mind. So the idea of the many is the creation of the mind.

Differentiae become qualities when they are separate but joined in one object. We cannot say positively what differentiation is. All that we see and feel about things is pure and simple existence, "isness." All else is in us. Being is the only positive proof we have of anything. All differentiation is really secondary reality, like the snake in the rope—because the serpent too has a certain reality, in that something is seen, although misapprehended. When the knowledge of the rope becomes negative, the knowledge of the snake becomes positive, and vice versa; but the fact that you see only one of them does not prove that the other is non-existent. The idea of the world is an obstruction covering the idea of God, and is to be removed; but it does have an existence.

Śankara says, again, that perception is the final proof of existence. It is self-effulgent and self-luminous, because to go beyond the senses we should still need perception. Perception is independent of the senses and all other instruments; it is unconditioned. There can be no perception without consciousness. Perception has self-luminosity, whose partial manifestation is called consciousness. Not one act of perception can be unconscious; in fact, consciousness is the nature of perception. Existence and perception are one thing, not two things joined together. That which needs no cause is infinite; so as perception is the final proof of itself, it is infinite. It is always subjective: perception itself is its own perceiver. Perception is not in the mind, but perception creates mind. It is absolute, the only Knower; so perception is really the Ātman. Perception itself perceives; but the Ātman cannot be a knower, because a knower becomes such by the action of knowledge. But Śankara says that this Ātman is not the "I," because the consciousness of "I am," or aham, is not in the Ātman. We are but the reflections of that Ātman; and Ātman and Brahman are one.

When you talk and think of the Absolute, you have to do it in the relative; all these logical arguments apply there. In yoga, perception and realization are one. Viśishtādvaita, of which Rāmānuja is the exponent, means seeing partial unity and is a step towards Advaita. Viśishta means differentiation. Prakriti is the nature of the world, and change comes upon it. Changeful thoughts expressed in changeful words can never prove the Absolute. You reach only something that is minus certain qualities, not Brahman Itself—only a verbal unification, the highest abstraction, but not the non-existence of the relative.

Thursday, July 18.

(The lesson today was mainly about Śankara's argument against the conclusions of the Sāmkhya philosophy.)

Sāmkhya says that consciousness is a compound, and beyond that, the last analysis gives us the Purusha, the Witness; but there are many Purushas—each of us is one. Advaita, on the contrary, affirms that the Purusha can be only one. That Purusha cannot be conscious or unconscious or have any qualifica-

tion; for these qualities would bind It and they would eventually cease. So
the One must be without any qualities, even knowledge; and It cannot be the
cause of the universe or of anything. "In the beginning there was Existence only,
One and without a second," say the Vedas.

*   *   *

The presence of sattva with knowledge does not prove that sattva is the
cause of knowledge; on the contrary, sattva calls out what was already existing in
man, as fire heats an iron ball placed near it by arousing the heat latent in it—
not by entering into the ball.

Śankara says that knowledge is not a bondage, because it is the nature of
God. The world ever is, whether manifested or unmanifested; so an eternal
object exists.

God is jnāna-bala-kriyā—knowledge, power, activity. He does not need form,
because only the finite needs form to interpose as an obstruction to catch and
hold infinite knowledge; but God really needs no such help. There is no trans-
migrating soul; there is only one Ātman. The jiva, the individual soul, is the
conscious ruler of this body, in whom the five life principles are unified; and
yet that very jiva is the Ātman, because all is the Ātman. What you think
about it is your delusion and is not in the jiva. You are God, and whatever else
you may think is wrong. You must worship the Self in Krishna, not Krishna
as Krishna. Only by worshipping the Self can freedom be won. Even the
Personal God is but the Self objectified. "An intense search after one's own
reality is bhakti," says Śankara.

All the means we take to reach God are true; it is only like trying to find
the pole-star by locating it through the stars that are around it.

*   *   *

The Bhagavad Gitā is the best authority on Vedānta.

Friday, July 19.

So long as I am conscious of "I" and "you," I have the right to speak of a
God protecting us. So long as I see differentiation, I must take all the consequences. If I admit the existence of "I" and "you," I must also admit the
existence of a third, the ideal, which stands between us. That ideal is the apex
of the triangle. The vapour becomes snow, then water, then the Ganges; but
when it is vapour, there is no Ganges, and when it is water, we think of no
vapour in it. The idea of creation or change is inseparably connected with will.
So long as we perceive this world in motion, we have to conceive a will behind
it. Physics proves the utter delusion of the senses; nothing really is as we see,
hear, feel, smell, or taste it. Certain vibrations producing certain results affect
our senses; we know only relative truth.

The Sanskrit word for truth is Sat, "isness." From our present standpoint
this world appears to us as will and consciousness. The Personal God is as real
as we are ourselves, and no more. God can also be seen as a form, just as we are
seen. As men we must have a God; as God we need no one. This is why Śri
Ramakrishna constantly saw the Divine Mother present with him, more real
than any other thing around him; but in samādhi all disappeared but the

Self. The Personal God comes nearer and nearer until He melts away and there
is no more Personal God and no more "I"; all is merged in the Self.

The argument from design claims that intelligence precedes form; but if
intelligence is the cause of anything, it itself is in its turn an effect. This is
māyā. God creates us and we create God; and this is māyā. The circle is
unbroken: mind creates body and body creates mind; the egg brings forth the
chicken, the chicken the egg; the tree the seed, the seed the tree. The world
is neither entirely differentiated nor yet entirely homogeneous. Man is free
and must rise above both sides. Both are right in their place; but to know
truth, "isness," we must transcend all that we now know of existence, will,
consciousness, doing, going, knowing.

There is no real individuality of the jiva, the embodied soul; as a compound,
it will eventually go to pieces. Only that which is beyond further analysis is
simple, and that alone is truth, freedom, immortality, bliss. All struggles for
the preservation of this illusive individuality are really vices. All struggles to
lose this individuality are virtues. Everything in the universe is trying to break
down this individuality, either consciously or unconsciously. All morality is
based upon the destruction of separateness or false individuality, because that
is the cause of all sin. Morality exists first; later religion codifies it. Customs
come first and then mythology follows to explain them. While things are happening they come by a higher law than reasoning; reasoning arises later in the
attempt to understand them. It is not the cause; it is merely "chewing the cud"
afterwards. Reason is the historian of the actions of the human being.

*   *   *

Buddha was a great Vedāntist—for Buddhism was really only an offshoot of
Vedānta—and Śankara is often called a "hidden Buddhist." Buddha made the
analysis; Śankara made the synthesis out of it. Buddha never bowed down to
anything—neither Vedas nor caste nor priest nor custom. He fearlessly reasoned
so far as reason could take him. Such a fearless search for truth and such love
for every living thing the world has never seen. Buddha was the Washington
of the religious world: he conquered a throne only to give it to the world, as
Washington did to the American people. He sought nothing for himself.

Saturday, July 20.

Perception is our only knowledge, our real religion. Talking about our soul for
ages will never make us know it. There is no difference between theories and
atheism. In fact, the atheist is the truer man. Every step I take in the light is
mine for ever. When you go to a country and see it, then it is yours. We have
each to see for ourselves. Teachers can only bring the food; we must eat it to
be nourished. Argument can never prove God's existence save as a logical
conclusion.

It is impossible to find God outside ourselves. Our own souls contribute all
the divinity that is outside us. We are the greatest temple. The objectification
is only a faint imitation of what we see within ourselves.

Concentration of the powers of the mind is our only instrument to help us
see God. If you know one soul—your own—you know all souls, past, present,
and to come. The will concentrates the mind; certain things excite and control

this will, such as reason, love, devotion, and breathing. The concentrated mind is a lamp that shows us every corner of the soul.

No one method can suit all. These different methods are not steps necessary to be taken one after another. Ceremonials are the lowest form, next God external, and after that God internal. In some cases gradation may be needed, but in many only one way is required. It would be the height of folly to say to everyone, "You must pass through karma and bhakti before you can reach · jnāna."

Stick to your reason until you reach something higher; and you will know it to be higher because it will not jar with reason. The stage beyond consciousness is inspiration (samādhi); but never mistake hysterical trances for the real thing. It is a terrible thing to claim this inspiration falsely, to mistake instinct for inspiration. There is no external test for inspiration; we know it ourselves. Our guard against mistake is negative: the voice of reason. All religion means going beyond reason; but reason is the only guide to get there. Instinct is like ice, reason is like water, and inspiration is like the subtlest form or vapour; one follows the other. Everywhere is this eternal sequence: unconsciousness, consciousness, intelligence; matter, body, mind; and to us it seems as if the chain begins with the particular link we first lay hold of. According to some, the body creates the mind; according to others, the mind, the body. The arguments on both sides are of equal weight and both are true. We must go beyond both, to where there is neither the one nor the other. These successions are all māyā.

Religion is above reason—supernatural. Faith is not belief; it is the grasp on the Ultimate, an illumination. First hear; then reason and find out all that reason can give about the Ātman, let the flood of reason flow over It; then take what remains. If nothing remains, thank God you have escaped a superstition. When you have determined that nothing can take away the Ātman, that It stands every test, hold fast to this and teach it to all. Truth cannot be your monopoly; it is for the good of all. Finally, in perfect peace, meditate upon It, concentrate your mind upon It, make yourself one with It. Then no speech is needed; silence will carry the truth. Do not spend your energy in talking, but meditate in silence; and do not let the rush of the outside world disturb you. When your mind is in the highest state, you are unconscious of it. Accumulate power in silence and become a dynamo of spirituality. What can a beggar give? Only a king can give, and he only when he wants nothing himself.

*   *   *

Hold your money merely as a custodian for what is God's. Have no attachment to it. Let name and fame and money go; they are a terrible bondage. Feel the wonderful atmosphere of freedom. You are free, free, free! "Oh, blessed am I! Freedom am I! I am the Infinite! In my Soul I can find no beginning and no end. All is my Self." Say this unceasingly.

Sunday, July 21.

(Patanjali's Yoga Aphorisms.)

Yoga is the science of restraining the chitta, mind, from breaking into vrittis, modifications. The mind is a mixture of sensations and feelings, or action and reaction; so it cannot be permanent. The mind has a fine body, and through this it works on the gross body. Vedānta says that behind the mind is the real Self. It accepts the other two, the body and the mind, but posits a third, the Eternal, the Ultimate, the final conclusion of analysis, the indivisible Unit, where there is no further compound. Birth is re-composition, death is de-composition, and the final analysis is where the Ātman is found. There being no further division possible, the perdurable is reached.

The whole ocean is present at the back of each wave, and all manifestations are waves—some very big, some small. Yet all are the ocean in their essence—the whole ocean; but as waves each is a part. When the waves are stilled, then all is one—"a spectator without a spectacle," says Patanjali. When the mind is active, the Ātman is mixed up with it.

The repetition of old forms in quick succession is memory.

Be unattached. Knowledge is power: when you get knowledge you get power. By knowledge you can even banish the material world. When you can mentally get rid of one quality after another from any object, until all are gone, you can at will make the object itself disappear from your consciousness.

Those who are ready advance very quickly and can become yogis in six months. The less developed may take several years; and anyone, by faithful work and by giving up everything else and devoting himself solely to practice, can reach the goal in twelve years. Bhakti will bring you there without any of these mental gymnastics; but it is a slower way.[26]

Iśvara is the Ātman as seen or grasped by the mind. His highest name is Om; so repeat it, meditate on it, and think of its wonderful nature and attributes. Repeating Om continually is the only true worship. It is not a word; it is God Himself.

Religion gives you nothing new; it only takes off obstacles and lets you see your Self. Sickness is the first great obstacle: a healthy body is the best instrument. Melancholy is an almost insuperable barrier. If you have once known Brahman, never again can you be melancholy. Doubt, want of perseverance, and mistaken ideas are other obstacles.

*   *   *

The prānas are subtle energies, sources of motion. There are ten in all, five primary and five secondary. One great current flows upward, and the others downward. Prānāyāma means controlling the prānas through breathing. Breath is the fuel, prāna is the steam, and the body is the engine. Prānāyāma has three parts: puraka or in-breathing, kumbhaka or holding the breath, and rechaka or out-breathing.

The guru is the conveyance through which the spiritual influence is brought to you. Anyone can teach, but the spirit is transmitted only by the guru to the śishya, the disciple, and that will fructify. The relation between śishyas is that of brotherhood, and this is actually accepted by law in India. The guru passes

---

[26] Here by bhakti the Swami does not mean intense or undivided love for God. He has already taught, "Extreme love and the highest knowledge are one"; and again, in defining it, he says, "This absolute and continuous remembrance of the Lord is what is meant by bhakti." So by bhakti he means, here, love which is not yet whole-souled.

the thought-power, the mantra, that he has received from those before him; and nothing can be done without a guru—in fact, great danger ensues. Usually without a guru these yoga practices lead to lust; but with one this seldom happens. Each Ishta has a mantra. The Ishta is the ideal peculiar to the particular worshipper; the mantra is the external word to express it. Constant repetition of the word helps to fix the ideal firmly in the mind. This method of worship prevails among religious devotees all over India.

Tuesday, July 23.

(Bhagavad Gītā: karma-yoga.)

To attain liberation through work, join yourself to work but without desire, looking for no result. Such work leads to knowledge, which in turn brings emancipation. To give up work before you know, leads to misery. Work done for the Self creates no bondage. Neither desire pleasure nor fear pain from work. It is the mind and body that work—not I. Tell yourself this unceasingly and realize it. Try not to feel that you work.

Do all as a sacrifice or offering to the Lord. Be in the world, but not of it, like the lotus leaf, whose roots are in the mud but which remains always pure. Let your love go to all, whatever they may do to you.

A blind man cannot see colour; so how can we see evil unless it is in us? We compare what we see outside with what we find in ourselves and pronounce judgement accordingly. If we are pure, we cannot see impurity. It may exist, but not for us. See only God in every man, woman, and child; see it by the antarjyoti, the inner light. Seeing that, you can see naught else.

Do not want this world, because what you desire you get. Seek the Lord and the Lord only.

The more power there is, the more bondage, the more fear. How much more afraid and miserable are we than the ant! Get out of it all and come to the Lord. Seek the science of the Maker and not that of the made.

"I am the doer and the deed."

"He who can stem the tide of lust and anger is a great yogi."

"Only by practice and non-attachment can we conquer the mind."

*   *   *

Our Hindu ancestors sat down and thought about God and morality, and so have we brains to use for the same ends; but in the rush of trying to get material gain, we are likely to lose them.

*   *   *

The body has in it a certain power of curing itself, and many things can rouse this curative power into action, such as mental conditions or medicine or exercise. As long as we are disturbed by physical conditions, so long we need the help of physical agencies. Not until we have got rid of bondage to the nerves can we disregard them.

There is unconscious mind, but it is below consciousness, which is just one part of the human organism. Philosophy is guess-work about the mind. Religion is based upon perception, upon seeing, the only basis of knowledge. What comes in contact with the superconscious mind is fact. Āptas are those who have "sensed" religion. The proof is that if you follow their method, you too will see. Each science requires its own particular method and instruments. An astronomer cannot show you the rings of Saturn by the aid of all the pots and pans in the kitchen. He needs a telescope. So, to see the great facts of religion, the method of those who have already seen must be followed. The greater the science, the more varied the means of studying it.

Before we came into the world God provided the means to get out; so all we have to do is to find the means. But do not fight over the methods. Look only for realization and choose the best method you can find to suit you. "Eat the mangoes" and let the rest quarrel over the basket. See Christ—then you will be a Christian. All else is talk. The less talking the better.

The message makes the messenger; the Lord makes the temple—not vice versa.

Learn until the glory of the Lord shines through your face, as it shone through the face of Śvetaketu.

Guess against guess makes fight; but talk of what you have seen and no human heart can resist it. Paul was converted, against his will, by realization.

Tuesday afternoon.

(After dinner there was a short conversation in the course of which the Swami made the following remarks.)

Delusion creates delusion. Delusion creates itself and destroys itself—such is māyā. All knowledge (so-called), being based on māyā, is a vicious circle, and in time that very knowledge destroys itself. "Let go the rope of māyā"; delusion cannot touch the Ātman. When we lay hold of the rope—identify ourselves with māyā—it has power over us. Let go of it, be a witness only; then you can admire the picture of the universe undisturbed.

Wednesday, July 24.

The powers acquired by the practice of yoga are not obstacles for the yogi who is perfect, but are apt to be so for the beginner, through the wonder and pleasure excited by their exercise. Siddhis are the powers which mark success in the practice, and they may be produced by various means, such as the repetition of a mantra, yoga disciplines, meditation, fasting, or even the use of herbs and drugs. The yogi who has conquered all interest in the powers acquired and who renounces all virtue arising from his actions attains the "cloud of virtue"—the name of one of the states of samādhi—and radiates holiness as a cloud rains water.

Concentration means holding the mind to a particular object; meditation is an unbroken flow of awareness towards that object.

The mind is cognized by the Ātman; it is not self-illuminated. The Ātman cannot be the cause of anything. How can It be? How can the Purusha join Itself to prakriti, nature? It does not; It is only mistakenly thought to do so.

*   *   *

Learn to help without pitying or feeling that there is any misery. Learn to be the same to enemy and to friend. Then, when you can do that and no longer have any desires, the goal is attained.

Cut down the banyan tree of desire with the axe of non-attachment and it will vanish utterly. It is all illusion. "He from whom grief and delusion have fallen, he who has conquered the evil of attachment—he alone is āzād, free." To love anyone especially is bondage. Love all alike; then all desires fall off.

Time, the "eater of everything," comes and all has to go. Why try to improve the earth, to paint the evanescent butterfly? It all has to go at last. Do not be mere white mice in a cage with a treadmill, busy always and never accomplishing anything. Every desire is fraught with evil, whether the desire itself be good or evil. It is like a dog's jumping for a piece of meat which is ever receding from his reach, and dying a dog's death at last. Do not be like that. Cut off all desire.

* * *

Paramātman ruling māyā is Iśvara; the same Paramātman under māyā is jivātman. Māyā is the sum total of manifestation and will one day utterly vanish.

Tree-nature is māyā; it is really God-nature, which we see under the veil of māyā. The "why" of anything is in māyā. To ask why māyā came is a useless question, because the answer can never be given in māyā, and beyond māyā who will ask it? Evil creates "why," not "why" the evil; and it is evil that asks "why?" Illusion destroys illusion. Reason itself, being based upon contradiction, is a circle and has to kill itself. Sense perception is an inference, and yet all inference comes from perception.

Ignorance reflecting the light of God is seen; but by itself it is zero. The cloud would not appear except as the sunlight falls on it.

There were four travellers who came to a high wall. The first one climbed with difficulty to the top and, without looking back, jumped over. The second clambered up the wall, looked over, and with a shout of delight disappeared. The third in his turn climbed to the top, looked where his companions had gone, laughed with joy, and followed them. But the fourth one came back to tell what had happened to his fellow travellers. The sign to us that there is something beyond is the laugh that rings back from those great ones who have plunged from māyā's wall.

* * *

Separating ourselves from the Absolute and attributing certain qualities to It gives us Iśvara. He is the Reality of the universe as seen through our mind. The Devil is the misery of the world seen through the minds of the superstitious.

Thursday, July 25.

(*Patanjali's Yoga Aphorisms.*)

"Things may be done, caused to be done, or approved of," and the effect upon us is nearly equal.

Complete continence gives great intellectual and spiritual power. The brahmachārin must be sexually pure in thought, word, and deed. Lose regard for the body; get rid of the consciousness of it so far as possible.

Āsana, posture, must be steady and pleasant; and constant practice, identifying the mind with the Infinite, will make it so.

Continuous attention to one object is contemplation.

When a stone is thrown into still water, many circles are made, each distinct but all interacting. So with our minds; only in us the action is unconscious, while in the yogi it is conscious. We are spiders in a web, and yoga practice will enable us, like the spider, to pass along any strand of the web we please. Non-yogis are bound to the particular spots where they are.

*   *   *

To injure another creates bondage and hides the truth. Negative virtues are not enough; we have to conquer māyā and then it will follow us. We only deserve things when they have ceased to bind us. When the bondage ceases, really and truly, all things come to us. Only those who want nothing are masters of nature.

Take refuge in some soul who has already broken his bondage, and in time he will free you through his mercy. Higher still is to take refuge in the Lord, or Iśvara; but it is most difficult. Only once in a century can one be found who has really done it. Feel nothing, know nothing, do nothing, have nothing, give up all to God and say utterly, "Thy will be done." We only dream this bondage. Wake up and let it go. Take refuge in God; only so can we cross the desert of māyā. "Let go thy hold, sannyāsin bold! Say, 'Om Tat Sat, Om!' "

It is our privilege to be allowed to be charitable; for only so can we grow. The poor man suffers that we may be helped. Let the giver kneel down and give thanks; let the receiver stand up and permit. See the Lord back of every being and give to Him. When we cease to see evil, the world will end for us, because to rid us of that mistake is its only object. To think there is any imperfection creates it. Thoughts of strength and perfection alone can cure it. Do what good you can, some evil will inhere in it; but do all without regard to personal result, give up all results to the Lord, and then neither good nor evil will affect you.

Doing work is not religion; but work done rightly leads to freedom. In reality all pity is ignorance, because who is there to pity? Can you pity God? And is there anything else? Thank God for giving you this world as a moral gymnasium to help your development; but never imagine you can help the world. Be grateful to him who curses you; for he gives you a mirror to show what cursing is, also a chance to practise self-restraint. So bless him and be glad. Without exercise power cannot come out; without the mirror we cannot see ourselves.

Unchaste imagination is as bad as unchaste action. Controlled desire leads to the highest result. Transform the sexual energy into spiritual energy, but do not emasculate, because that will be throwing away the power. The stronger this force, the more can be done with it. Only a powerful current of water can do hydraulic mining.

What we need today is to know that there is a God and that we can see and feel Him here and now. A Chicago professor says: "Take care of this world. God will take care of the next." What nonsense! If we can take care of this world, what need of a gratuitous Lord to take care of the other?

Friday, July 26.

(Brihadāranyaka Upanishad.)

Love all things only through and for the Self. Yājnavalkya said to Maitreyi, his wife, "Through the Ātman we know all things." The Ātman can never be an object of knowledge, nor can the Knower be known. He who knows he is the Ātman—he is a law unto himself. He knows he is the universe and its Creator.

*   *   *

Perpetuating old myths in the form of allegories and giving them undue importance fosters superstition and is really weakness. Truth must have no compromise. Teach truth and make no apology for any superstition; neither drag truth down to the level of the listener.

Saturday, July 27.

(Katha Upanishad.)

Learn not the truth of the Self save from one who has realized it; in all others it is mere talk. Realization is beyond virtue and vice, beyond future and past, beyond all the pairs of opposites. "The stainless one sees the Self, and an eternal calm comes to his soul." Talking, arguing, and reading books, the highest flights of the intellect, the Vedas themselves—all these cannot give the Knowledge of the Self.

In us are the two: the God-soul and the man-soul. The sages know that the latter is but the shadow, that the former is the only real Sun.

Unless we join the mind to the senses, we get no report from eyes, nose, ears, and so forth. The external organs are used by the power of the mind. Do not let the senses go outside; then you can get rid of the body and the external world.

This very "x," which we see here as the external world, the departed see as heaven or hell according to their own mental states. Here and hereafter are two dreams, the latter modelled on the former. Get rid of both. All is omnipresent; all is now. Nature, body, and mind go to death—not we; we never go nor come. The man Swami Vivekananda is in nature, is born and dies; but the Self, which we see as Swami Vivekananda, is never born and never dies. It is the eternal and unchangeable Reality.

The power of the mind is the same whether we divide it into five senses or whether we see only one. A blind man says, "Everything has a distinct echo; so I clap my hands and get that echo and then I can tell everything that is around me." So in a fog the blind man could safely lead the seeing man. Fog or darkness makes no difference to him.

Control the mind, cut off the senses; then you are a yogi. After that all the rest will come. Refuse to hear, to see, to smell, to taste; take away the mental power from the external organs. You continually do it unconsciously, as when your mind is absorbed; so you can learn to do it consciously. The mind can put the senses where it pleases. Get rid of the fundamental superstition that we are obliged to act through the body. We are not. Go into your own room and get the Upanishads out of your own Self. You are the greatest book that ever was or ever will be, the infinite depository of all that is. Until the inner teacher awakens, all outside teaching is in vain. It must lead to the opening of the book of the heart to have any value.

The will is the "still, small voice," the real Ruler who says "Do" and "Do not." It has done all that binds us. The ignorant will leads to bondage; the knowing will can free us. The will can be made strong in thousands of ways. Every way is a kind of yoga; but the systematized yoga accomplishes the work more quickly. Bhakti-yoga, karma-yoga, rāja-yoga, and jnāna-yoga get over the ground more effectively. Employ all powers—philosophy, work, prayer, meditation. Crowd on all sail, put on full steam, and reach the goal. The sooner, the better.

* * *

Baptism is external purification symbolizing the internal. It is of Buddhist origin.

The Eucharist is a survival of a very ancient custom of savage tribes. They sometimes killed their great chiefs and ate their flesh in order to obtain in themselves the qualities that made their leaders great. They believed that in such a way the characteristics that made the chiefs brave and wise would become theirs and make the whole tribe brave and wise, instead of only one man. Human sacrifice was also a Jewish idea and one that clung to the Jews despite many chastisements from Jehovah. Jesus was gentle and loving, but to fit him into Jewish beliefs the idea of human sacrifice in the form of atonement, that is to say, of a human scapegoat, had to come in. This cruel idea made Christianity depart from the teachings of Jesus himself and develop a spirit of persecution and bloodshed.

* * *

Say it is your "nature" to do it; never say it is your "duty" to do anything whatever.

"Truth alone triumphs, not untruth." Stand upon Truth and you have got God.

* * *

From the earliest times in India the brāhmins have held themselves beyond all law; they claim to be gods. They are poor, but their weakness is that they seek power. Here are about sixty millions of people who are good and moral and hold no property, and they are what they are because from their birth they are taught that they are above law, above punishment. They feel themselves to be "twice-born," to be sons of God.

Sunday, July 28.

(Avadhuta Gitā, or Song of the Purified, by Dattātreya.)[27]

"All knowledge depends upon calmness of mind."

"He who has filled the universe, He who is Self in self—how shall I salute Him?"

[27] Dattātreya was a sage, the son of Atri and Anasuyā, and was an Incarnation of Brahmā, Vishnu, and Śiva.

To know the Ātman as my nature is both knowledge and realization. "I am He; there is not the least doubt about it."

"No thought, no word, no deed, creates a bondage for me. I am beyond the senses; I am Knowledge and Bliss."

There is neither existence nor non-existence: all is the Ātman. Shake off all ideas of relativity; shake off all superstitions. Let caste and birth and devas and all else vanish. Why talk of being and becoming? Give up talking of dualism and Advaitism. When were you two, that you talk of two or one? The universe is this Holy One and He alone. Talk not of yoga to make you pure; you are pure by your very nature. None can teach you.

Men like him who wrote this *Gitā* keep religion alive. They have actually realized the Self; they care for nothing, feel nothing done to the body, care not for heat or cold or danger or anything. They sit still and enjoy the bliss of the Ātman even while red-hot coals burn their body, and they feel them not.

"When the threefold bondage of knower, knowledge, and known ceases, then one realizes the Ātman."

"When the delusion of bondage and freedom ceases, one realizes the Ātman."

"What if you have controlled the mind? What if you have not? What if you have money? What if you have not? You are the Ātman ever pure. Say: 'I am the Ātman. No bondage ever came near me. I am the changeless sky: clouds of belief may pass over me, but they do not touch me.'"

"Burn virtue; burn vice. Freedom is baby-talk. I am that immortal knowledge. I am that purity."

"No one was ever bound; none was ever free. There is none but me. I am the Infinite, the Ever Free. Do not try to teach me! What can change me, the essence of Knowledge? Who can teach? Who can be taught?"

Throw argument, throw philosophy, into the ditch.

"Only a slave sees slaves; the deluded, delusion; the impure, impurity."

Space, time, causation are all delusions. It is your disease that you think you are bound and will be free. You are the Unchangeable. Talk not. Sit down and let all things melt away; they are but dreams. There is no differentiation, no distinction; it is all superstition. Therefore be silent and know what you are.

"I am the essence of Bliss."

Follow no ideal: you are all there is. Fear naught: you are the essence of Existence. Be at peace. Do not disturb yourself. You never were in bondage; you never were virtuous or sinful. Get rid of all these delusions and be at peace. Who is there to worship? Who worships? All is the Ātman. To speak, to think, is superstition. Repeat over and over: "I am Ātman, I am Ātman." Let everything else go.

Monday, July 29.

We sometimes indicate a thing by describing its surroundings. When we say "Satchidānanda"—"Existence-Knowledge-Bliss," we are merely indicating the shores of an indescribable Beyond. Not even can we say "is" about It, for that too is relative. Any imagination, any concept, is in vain. "Neti, neti"—"Not this, not this," is all that can be said; for even to think is to limit and so to lose.

The senses cheat you day and night. Vedānta found that out ages ago;

modern science is just discovering the same fact. A picture has only length and breadth, and the painter copies nature in its cheating by artificially giving the appearance of depth. No two people see the same world. The highest knowledge will show you that there is no motion, no change in anything; that the very idea of it is all māyā.

Study nature as a whole; that is, study motion. Mind and body are not our real Self: both belong to nature. But eventually we can know the *Ding an sich*. Then, mind and body being transcended, all that they conceive goes. When you cease utterly to know and see the world, then you realize the Ātman. The superseding of relative knowledge is what we want. There is no infinite mind or infinite knowledge, because both mind and knowledge are limited. We are now seeing through a veil; then we reach the "x," which is the reality of all our knowing.

If we look at a picture through a pin-hole in a cardboard, we get an utterly mistaken notion; yet what we see is really the picture. As we enlarge the hole, we get a clearer and clearer idea. Out of the reality we manufacture different views in conformity with our mistaken perceptions of name and form. When we throw away the cardboard, we see the same picture, but we see it as it is. We put in all the attributes, all the errors; the picture itself is unaltered thereby—because the Ātman is the reality of all. All we see is the Ātman; but It is not rightly seen through name and form; they are in the veil, in māyā.

They are like spots in the object-glass of a telescope; yet it is the light of the sun that shows us the spots. We could not even see the illusion save for the background of Reality, which is Brahman. Vivekananda, the man, is just a speck on the object-glass. But truly I am the Ātman, real, unchangeable; and that Reality alone enables me to see Vivekananda. The Ātman is the essence behind every hallucination. The sun is never identified with the spots on the glass; neither is the Ātman, with name and fame. Our actions, evil or good, increase or decrease the spots, but never affect the Self. Cleanse the mind of spots and you will instantly see: "I and my Father are one."

We first perceive, and we reason later. We must have perception as a fact; and this is called religion. No matter if one never heard of creed or prophet or book; let him get realization and he will need nothing more. Cleanse the mind—this is the whole of religion; and until we ourselves clean off the spots, we cannot see Reality as It is.

The baby sees no sin; he has not yet in himself the means to measure it. Get rid of the defects which are within yourself and you will not see any without. A baby sees robbery done and it means nothing to him. Once you find the hidden object in a puzzle picture, you see it always; so when once you are free and stainless, you see only freedom and purity in the world around. That moment all the knots of the heart are cut asunder, all crooked places are made straight, and this world vanishes as a dream. And when we awake, we wonder how we ever came to dream such trash!

We must realize Him, "getting whom, misery mountain high has no power to move the soul."

With the axe of knowledge sever the wheels of mind and body from the Ātman, and It will stand free, even though the old momentum carries on the wheels of mind and body. But the wheels can now only go straight, can only do good. If that body or mind does anything bad, know that the man is not a jivanmukta; he lies if he makes that claim. It is only when the wheels have got a good straight motion—from cleansing the mind—that the axe can be applied. All purifying action deals delusion conscious or unconscious blows. Good action done ignorantly produces the same result and helps to break the bondage. To call another a sinner is the worst thing you can do.

To identify the sun with the spots on the object-glass is the fundamental error. Know the sun, the "I," to be ever unaffected by anything, and devote yourself to cleaning off the spots. Man is the greatest being that ever can be. The highest worship is to worship a man like Krishna, Buddha, or Christ.

What you want, you create. Get rid of desire.

*   *   *

The angels and the departed are all here, seeing this world as heaven. The same "x" is seen by all according to their mental attitude. The best vision to be had of the "x" is here on this earth. Never want to go to heaven: that is the worst delusion. Even here, too much wealth and grinding poverty are both bondages and hold us back from religion.

There are three rare things. First, a human body. (The human mind is the nearest reflection of God; we are His own image.) Second, the desire to be free. Third, a noble soul who has crossed the ocean of delusion, as teacher. When you have these three, bless the Lord. You are sure to be free.

What you only grasp intellectually may be overthrown by a new argument; but what you realize is yours for ever. Talking, talking religion, does but little good. Put God behind everything—man, animal, food, work; make this a habit.

Ingersoll once said to me, "I believe in making the most of this world, in squeezing the orange dry, because this world is all we are sure of." I replied: "I know a better way to squeeze the orange of this world than you do, and I get more out of it. I know I cannot die; so I am not in a hurry. I know there is no fear; so I enjoy the squeezing. I have no duty, no bondage of wife and children and property. I can love all men and women. Everyone is God to me. Think of the joy of loving man as God! Squeeze your orange this way and get ten thousandfold more out of it. Get every single drop."

That which seems to be the will is really the Ātman; It is free.

Monday afternoon.

Jesus was imperfect because he did not live up fully to his own ideal and above all because he did not give woman a place equal to man's. Women did everything for him and yet he was so bound by Jewish custom that not one was made an Apostle. Still he was the greatest character next to Buddha, who in his turn was not fully perfect. Buddha, however, recognized woman's right to an equal place in religion, and one of his first and greatest disciples was his own wife, who became the head of the whole Buddhist movement among the women of India. But we ought not to criticize these great ones; we should only look upon them as far above ourselves. Nonetheless we must not pin our faith on any man, however great; we too must become Buddhas and Christs.

No man should be judged by his defects. The great virtues a man has are his own; but his errors are the common weaknesses of humanity and should never be counted in estimating his character.

*   *   *

Vira, the Sanskrit word for heroic, is the origin of the word *virtue;* in ancient times the best fighter was regarded as the most virtuous man.

Tuesday, July 30.

Christs and Buddhas are simply occasions upon which to objectify our own inner powers. We really answer our own prayers.

It is blasphemy to think that if Jesus had never been born, humanity would not have been saved. It is horrible to thus forget the divinity in human nature, a divinity that must come out. Never forget the glory of human nature. We are the greatest God that ever was or ever will be. Christs and Buddhas are but waves on the boundless ocean which *I am.* Bow down to nothing but your own higher Self. Until you know that you are that very God of gods, there will never be any freedom for you.

All our past actions are really good, because they lead us to what we ultimately become. Of whom shall I beg? I am the real Existence, and all else is a dream. I am the whole ocean. Do not call the little wave you have made "I"; know it for nothing but a wave. Satyakāma heard the inner voice telling him: "You are the Infinite; the Universal is in you. Control yourself and listen to the voice of your true Self."

The great prophets who do the fighting have to be less perfect than those who live silent lives of holiness, thinking great thoughts and so helping the world. These men, passing out one after another, produce as their final result the man of power who preaches.

*   *   *

Knowledge exists; man only discovers it. The Vedas are the Eternal Knowledge through which God created the world. They preach high philosophy—the highest—and make this tremendous claim.

*   *   *

Tell the truth boldly, whether it hurts or not. Never pander to weakness. If truth is too much even for the intelligent and sweeps them away, let them go. The sooner, the better. Childish ideas are for babies and savages—and these are not all in the nursery and the forests; some of them have fallen into the pulpits.

It is bad to stay in the church after you are grown up spiritually. Come out and die in the open air of freedom.

All progression is in the relative world. The human form is the highest, and man is the greatest being, because here and now we can get rid of the relative world entirely, can actually attain freedom. And this is the goal. Not only can we reach perfection, but some have reached it. So no matter what finer bodies men may assume after death, they will still be on the relative plane and can do no more than we; for to attain freedom is the highest.

The angels never do wicked deeds; so they never get punished and also never get saved. Blows are what awaken us and help to break the dream. They show us the insufficiency of this world and make us long to escape, to have freedom.

A thing dimly perceived we call by one name; the same thing when fully perceived we call by another. The higher the moral nature, the subtler the perception and the stronger the will.

Tuesday afternoon.

The reason for the harmony between thought and matter is that they are two sides of one thing—call it "x"—which divides itself into the internal and the external.

The English word *paradise* comes from the Sanskrit *para-deśa*, which was taken over into the Persian language and means, literally, "beyond the land" or "the land beyond," that is to say, the other world. The old Āryans always believed in a soul, and never that man was the body. Their heavens and hells were all temporary, because no effect can outlast its cause and no cause is eternal; therefore all effects must come to an end.

The whole of the Vedānta philosophy is in this parable: Two birds of golden plumage sat on the same tree—the one above, serene, majestic, immersed in his own glory; the one below, restless and eating the fruits of the tree, now sweet, now bitter. Once the lower bird ate an exceptionally bitter fruit; then he paused and looked up at the majestic bird above. But he soon forgot about the other bird and went on eating the fruits of the tree as before. Again he ate a bitter fruit, and this time he hopped up a few boughs nearer to the bird at the top. This happened many times until at last the lower bird came to the place of the upper bird and lost himself in him. He found all at once that there had never been two birds, but that all the time he was that upper bird, serene, majestic, and immersed in his own glory.

Wednesday, July 31.

Luther drove a nail into the coffin of religion when he took away renunciation and gave us morality instead. Atheists and materialists can have ethics, but only believers in the Lord can have religion.

The wicked pay the price of the great soul's holiness. Think of that when you see a wicked man, and do not despise him. Just as the poor man's labour pays for the rich man's luxury, so is it in the spiritual world. The terrible degradation of the masses in India is the price she pays for the production of great souls like Mirābāi, Buddha, and so forth.[28]

"I am the holiness of the holy." "I am the root; each uses it in his own way, but all is I." "I do everything; you are but the occasion."

Do not talk much, but feel the Spirit within you; then you are a jnāni. This is Knowledge; all else is ignorance. All that is to be known is Brahman. It is the All.

---

[28] Most people in society cannot follow an ideal if it is very high; in trying to do so they fail and generally become wicked. But the ideal cannot be preserved without their participation. It is like one hundred soldiers attacking a fort: eighty die and only twenty succeed. The fact cannot be denied that the eighty, by their deaths, paid the price for the success of the twenty.

Sattva binds through the search for happiness and knowledge; rajas binds through desire: tamas binds through wrong perception and laziness. Conquer the lower two by sattva, and then give up all to the Lord and be free.

The bhakti-yogi very soon goes beyond the three qualities and realizes Brahman.

The will, consciousness, the senses, desire, the passions—all these combined make what we call the embodied soul.

There is, first, the apparent self, or the physical body; second, the mental self, which mistakes the body for itself; and third, the Ātman, the Absolute, the Ever Pure and Ever Free. Seen partially, the Ātman is nature; when It is seen wholly, all nature disappears—even the memory of it is lost. First, there is the changing, or the mortal; next, the eternally changing, or nature; and lastly, the Unchangeable, or the Ātman.

*   *   *

Give up hope completely; that is the highest state. What is there to hope for? Burst asunder the bonds of hope, stand on your Self, and be at rest. Never mind what you do; give up all to God, but have no hypocrisy about it.

Svastha, the Sanskrit word for "standing on your own Self," is used colloquially in India to inquire: "Are you well? Are you happy?" And when Hindus would express the idea "I saw a thing," they say, "I saw a word-meaning (padārtha)." Even this universe is a "word-meaning," that is, an idea denoted by a word.

*   *   *

A perfect man's body mechanically does right; it can do only good because it is fully purified. The past momentum that carries on the wheel of the body is all good. All evil tendencies are burnt out.

*   *   *

"That day is indeed a bad day when we do not speak of the Lord—not a stormy day."

Only love for the Supreme Lord is true bhakti. Love for any other being, however great, is not bhakti. The Supreme Lord here means Iśvara, the concept of which transcends what you in the West mean by the Personal God. "He from whom this universe proceeds, in whom it rests, and to whom it returns—He is Iśvara, the Eternal, the Pure, the All-merciful, the Almighty, the Ever Free, the All-knowing, the Teacher of all teachers, the Lord, who of His own nature is inexpressible Love."

Man does not manufacture God out of his own brain; but he can only see God in the light of his own capacity, and he attributes to Him the best of all he knows. Each attribute is the whole of God, and this signifying of the whole by one quality is the metaphysical explanation of the Personal God. Iśvara is without form yet has all forms, is without qualities yet has all qualities. As human beings we have to see the trinity of existence: God, man, nature. We cannot do otherwise.

But to the bhakta all these philosophical distinctions are mere idle talk. He cares nothing for argument, he does not reason; he senses, he perceives. He wants to lose himself in pure love of God. And there have been bhaktas who maintain that this is more to be desired than liberation, and who say: "I do not want to be sugar; I want to taste sugar. I want to love and enjoy the Beloved."

In bhakti-yoga the first essential is to want God honestly and intensely. We want everything but God, because our ordinary desires are fulfilled by the external world. So long as our needs are confined within the limits of the physical universe, we do not feel any need for God. It is only when we have had hard blows in our lives and are disappointed with everything here that we feel the need for something higher; and then we seek God.

Bhakti is not destructive; it teaches that all our faculties may become means to reach salvation. We must turn them all towards God and give to Him that love which is usually wasted on the fleeting objects of sense.

Bhakti differs from your Western idea of religion in that bhakti admits no element of fear, no Being to be appeased or propitiated. There are even bhaktas who worship God as their own child, so that there may remain no feeling even of awe or reverence. There can be no fear in true love, and so long as there is the least fear, bhakti cannot even begin. In bhakti there is also no place for begging or bargaining with God. The idea of asking God for anything is sacrilege to a bhakta. He will not pray for health or wealth or even to go to heaven.

One who wants to love God, to be a bhakta, must make a bundle of all these desires and leave them outside the door, and then enter. He who wants to enter the realm of light must make a bundle of all shopkeeping religion and cast it away before he can pass the gates. It is not that you do not get what you pray for; you get everything; but it is low, vulgar—a beggar's religion. "A fool indeed is he who, living on the bank of the Ganges, digs a little well for water." A fool indeed is the man who, coming to a diamond mine, begins to search for glass beads. These prayers for health and wealth and material prosperity are not bhakti. They are the lowest form of karma. Bhakti is a higher thing. We are striving to come into the presence of the King of kings. We cannot get there in a beggar's dress. If we wanted to enter the presence of an emperor, would we be admitted in a beggar's rags? Certainly not. The lackey would drive us out of the gates. This is the Emperor of emperors, and never can we come before Him in a beggar's garb. Shopkeepers never have admission there; buying and selling will not do there at all. You read in the Bible that Jesus drove the buyers and sellers out of the temple.

So it goes without saying that the first task in becoming a bhakta is to give up all desires for heaven and so on. Such a heaven would be like this place, this earth, only a little better. The Christian idea of heaven is a place of intensified enjoyment. How can that take the place of God? All this desire to go to heaven is a desire for enjoyment. This has to be given up. The love of the bhakta must be absolutely pure and unselfish, seeking nothing for itself either here or hereafter.

Giving up the ideas of pleasure and pain, gain and loss, worship God day and night; not a moment is to be spent in vain.

Giving up all other thoughts, with the whole mind day and night worship God. Thus being worshipped day and night, He reveals Himself and makes His worshippers feel His presence.

Thursday, August 1.

The real guru is the one through whom we have our spiritual descent. He is the channel through which the spiritual current flows to us, the link which joins us to the whole spiritual world. Too much faith in personality has a tendency to produce weakness and idolatry. But intense love for the guru makes rapid growth possible; he connects us with the internal guru. Adore your guru if there be real truth in him; that guru-bhakti, devotion to the teacher, will quickly lead you to the highest.

Śri Ramakrishna's purity was that of a baby. He never touched money in his life, and lust was absolutely annihilated in him. Do not go to great religious teachers to learn physical science; their whole energy has gone to the spiritual. In Śri Ramakrishna Paramahamsa the man was all dead and only God remained. He actually could not see sin; his eyes were so pure that he literally could not behold iniquity. The purity of these few paramahamsas is all that holds the world together. If they should all die and leave the world, it would go to pieces. They do good by simply being, and they know it not; they just are.

*   *   *

Books suggest the inner light and the method of bringing it out; but we can understand them only when we have earned the knowledge ourselves. When the inner light has flashed for you, let the books go and look only within. You have in you all that is in the books, and a thousand times more. Never lose faith in yourself; you can do anything in this universe. Never weaken; all power is yours.

If religion and life depend upon books or upon the existence of any prophet whatsoever, then perish all religion and books! Religion is in us. No books or teachers can do more than help us to find it, and even without them we can get all truth within. Yet be grateful to books and teachers without bondage to them; and worship your guru as God, but do not obey him blindly. Love him as much as you will, but think for yourself. No blind belief can save you. Work out your own salvation. Remember that God is our eternal help.

Freedom and the highest love must go together; then neither can become a bondage. We can give nothing to God; He gives all to us. He is the Guru of gurus. Then we find that He is the Soul of our souls, our very Self. No wonder we love Him; He is the Soul of our souls. Whom else or what else can we love? We want to be the "steady flame burning without smoke."

To whom can you do good, when you see only God? You cannot do good to God. All doubt goes; all is "sameness." If you do good at all, you do it to yourself; feel that the receiver is the higher one. You serve the other because you are lower than he, not because he is low and you are high. Give as the rose gives perfume—because it is its own nature—utterly unconscious of giving.

The great Hindu reformer, Rājā Rammohan Roy, was a wonderful example of this unselfish work. He devoted his whole life to helping India. It was he who stopped the burning of widows. It is usually believed that this reform was due entirely to the English; but it was Rājā Rammohan Roy who started the agitation against the custom and succeeded in obtaining the support of the

Government in suppressing it. Until he began the movement the English did nothing. He also founded the important religious society called the Brāhmo Samāj, and subscribed one hundred thousand dollars to found a university. He then stepped out and told them to go ahead without him. He cared nothing for fame or for results to himself.

Thursday afternoon.

The phenomenal world unceasingly goes on through endless series of manifestations—like a merry-go-round. Individual souls ride in it and finally get out. But the machine goes on. Events repeat themselves eternally; and that is how one's past and future can be read—because all is really present. When the soul is in a certain chain, it has to go through the experiences of that chain. From one series the soul goes to another; from some series it escapes for ever, through Self-Knowledge. By getting hold of one prominent event in a chain and holding on to it, you can drag in the whole chain and read it. This power is easily acquired; but it is of no real value, and to practise it takes just so much from our spiritual forces. Go not after these things. Worship God.

Friday, August 2.

Nishthā, devotion to one ideal, is the beginning of realization. Take the honey out of all flowers; sit and be friendly with all, pay reverence to all. Say to all, "Yes, brother; yes, brother"; but keep firm in your own way. A higher stage is actually to take the position of the other. If I am all, why can I not really and actively sympathize with my brother and see with his eyes? While I am weak, I must stick to one course, I must practise nishthā; but when I am strong, I can feel with all others and perfectly sympathize with their ideas.

The old way was to develop one idea at the expense of all the rest. The modern way is harmonious development. A third way is to develop the mind and control it, then put it where you will; the result will come quickly. This is developing yourself in the truest way. Learn concentration and use it in any direction. Thus you lose nothing. He who gets the whole must have the parts too. Dualism is included in Advaita, or monism.

*   *   *

"I first saw him and he saw me; there was a flash of eye from me to him and from him to me." This went on until the two souls became so closely united that they actually became one.

There are two kinds of samādhi. The one is called savikalpa. In it one feels a trace of duality, of distinction between subject and object. The other kind is called nirvikalpa. In that samādhi one effaces, in the depths of meditation, all distinction between the knower and the goal of knowledge.

You must be able to sympathize fully with each ideal, then at once jump back to the highest monism. After having perfected yourself, you limit yourself voluntarily. Take the whole power into each action. Be able to become a dualist for the time being and forget Advaita, yet be able to take it up again at will.

The cause-and-effect relationship is māyā, and we shall grow to understand that all we see is as disconnected as the child's fairy tales now seem to us. There is really no such thing as cause and effect, and we shall come to know it. Then, if you can, lower your intellect to let any allegory pass through your mind without questioning about the connexion. Develop love of imagery and beautiful poetry and then enjoy all mythologies as poetry. Come not to mythology with ideas of history and reasoning. Let it flow as a current through your mind; let it be whirled as a candle before your eyes, without asking who holds the candle, and you will get the circle; the residuum of truth will remain in your mind.

The writers of all mythologies wrote in symbols what they saw and heard; they painted flowing pictures. Do not try to pick out the themes and so destroy the pictures; take them as they are and let them act on you. Judge them only by the effect and get the good out of them.

Your own will is all that answers prayer; only it appears differently, under the guise of different religious conceptions, to each mind. We may call it Buddha, Jesus, Krishna, Jehovah, Allah—but it is only the Self, the "I."

*   *   *

Concepts grow, but there is no historical value in the allegories which present them. Moses' visions are more likely to be wrong than ours are, because we have more knowledge and are less likely to be deceived by illusions.

Books are useless to us until our inner book opens; then all other books are good so far as they confirm our book. It is the strong that understands strength; it is the elephant that understands the lion—not the rat. How can we understand Jesus until we are his equals? Only grandeur appreciates grandeur; only God realizes God. It is all in the dream, in māyā—to feed five thousand with two loaves, or to feed two with five loaves; neither is real and neither affects the other. The dream is not different from the dreamer; it has no other basis. The dream is not one thing and the dreamer another.

The keynote running through the music is "I am He, I am He"; all other notes are but variations and do not affect the real theme. We are the living books, and books are but the words we have spoken. Everything is the living God, the living Christ; see it as such. Read man: he is the living poem. We are the light that illumines all the Bibles and Christs and Buddhas that ever were. Without that, these would be dead for us, not living.

Stand on your own Self.

The dead body resents nothing; let us make our bodies dead and cease to identify ourselves with them.

Saturday, August 3.

Individuals who are to get freedom in this life have to live thousands of years in one lifetime. They have to be ahead of their times; but the masses can only crawl. Thus we have Christs and Buddhas.

*   *   *

There was once a Hindu queen who so much desired that all her children should attain freedom in this life that she herself took all the care of them;

and as she rocked them to sleep, she sang always the one song to them: "Tat tvam asi, Tat tvam asi"—"That thou art, That thou art." Three of them became sannyāsins, but the fourth was taken away to be brought up elsewhere to become a king. As he was leaving home, his mother gave him a piece of paper, which he was to read when he grew to manhood. On that piece of paper was written: "God alone is true. All else is false. The soul never kills or is killed. Live alone or in the company of holy ones." When the young prince read this, he too at once renounced the world and became a sannyāsin.

Give up. Renounce the world. Now we are like dogs that have strayed into a kitchen, eating a piece of meat and looking round in fear lest at any moment someone may come and drive them out. Instead of that be a king and know you own the world. This never comes until you give up the world and it ceases to bind. Give up mentally, if you cannot physically. Give up from your heart of hearts. Have vairāgya, renunciation. This is the real sacrifice, and without it, it is impossible to attain spirituality. Do not desire; for what you desire you get and with it comes terrible bondage. It is nothing but "bringing noses upon us," as it was in the case of the man who had three boons to ask.[29] We never get freedom until we are satisfied with the Self. "Self is the Saviour of Self—none else."

Learn to feel yourself in other bodies, to know that we are all one. Throw all other nonsense to the winds. Spit out your actions, good or bad, and never think of them again. What is done is done. Throw off superstition. Have no weakness even in the face of death. Do not repent, do not brood over past deeds, and do not remember your good deeds. Be āzād, free. The weak, the fearful, the ignorant, will never reach the Ātman. You cannot undo the past; the effect must come. Face it, but be careful never to do the same thing again. Give up the burden of all deeds to the Lord. Give all, both good and bad; do

---

[29] A poor man was once able to propitiate a certain god, who gave him some dice and said to him that he should ask for three boons along with three throws of the dice. The happy man went home and communicated the news of this piece of good luck to his wife, who, full of joy, at once told him to cast first for wealth. Thereupon the man replied: "We both have very ugly little noses, for which people laugh at us. Let us first cast for beautiful aquiline noses. Wealth cannot remove the deformity of our persons." But the wife was for the wealth first and so she caught hold of his hand to prevent him from throwing the dice. The man hastily snatched his hand away and at once threw the dice, exclaiming, "Let us both have beautiful noses and nothing but noses." All at once both their bodies were covered over with many beautiful noses; but they proved such a great nuisance to them that both of them agreed to throw for the second time asking for their removal. It was done, and by that they also lost their own little noses and were left completely noseless. Thus they had lost two boons, and in utter dismay they did not know what to do. There was only one boon more to ask. Having lost their noses they looked more ugly than before. They could not even dream of going out in that plight. They wanted to have two beautiful noses, but they feared to be questioned about their transformation lest they should be regarded by all as two big fools who could not mend their circumstances even with the help of three boons. So both of them agreed to get back their ugly little noses and the dice were accordingly cast. This story illustrates the sentence: "Do not desire; for what you desire you get and with it comes terrible bondage."

not keep the good and give only the bad. God helps those who do *not* help themselves.

"Drinking the cup of desire, the world becomes mad." As day and night never come together, so desire and the Lord can never come together. Give up desire.

*　　*　　*

There is a vast difference between saying "Food, food!" and eating it, between saying "Water, water!" and drinking it. So by merely repeating "God! God!" we cannot hope to attain realization. We must strive and practise.

Only when a wave falls back into the sea can it become unlimited; never can it be so as a wave. Then after it has become the sea, it can become a wave again and as big a one as it pleases. Break your identification with the wave and know that you are free.

True philosophy is the systematizing of certain perceptions. Intellect ends where religion begins. Inspiration is much higher than reason, but it must not contradict it. Reason is the rough tool to do the hard work; inspiration is the bright light which shows us all truth. The will to do a thing is not necessarily inspiration.

*　　*　　*

Progression in māyā is a circle that brings you back to the starting-point, with the difference that you start ignorant and come to the end with knowledge. Worship of God, worship of the holy ones, concentration and meditation, and unselfish work—these are the ways of breaking away from māyā's net. But we must first have the strong desire to get free. The flash of light that will illumine the darkness for us is in us; it is the Knowledge that is our nature. (There is no such thing as our "birthright": we were never born.) All that we have to do is to drive away the clouds that cover it.

Give up all desire for enjoyment on earth or in heaven. Control the organs of the senses and control the mind. Bear every misery without even knowing that you are miserable. Think of nothing but liberation. Have faith in your guru, in his teachings, and in the surety that you can get free. Say, "Soham, Soham," "I am He, I am He," whatever comes. Tell yourself this even in eating, walking, suffering. Tell the mind this incessantly—that what we see never existed; that there is only "I." Flash!—the dream will break. Think day and night, "This universe is zero; only God is." Have intense desire to get free.

All relatives and friends are but "old dry wells"; we fall into them and have dreams of duty and bondage, and there is no end. Do not create illusion by believing you can help anyone. If you are a dualist, you are a fool to try to help God. If you are a monist, you know that you are God—where find duty? You have no duty to husband, child, friend. Take things as they come; lie still, and wherever your body floats, go: rise with the rising tide, fall with the falling tide. Let the body die; this idea of the body is but a worn-out fable. "Be still and know that I am God."

The present is the only existence. There is no past or future even in thought, because to think it you have to make it the present. Give up everything and

let the body float where it will. This world is all a delusion; do not let it fool
you again. You have known it for what it is not; now know it for what it is.
If the body is dragged anywhere, let it go; do not care where the body is. This
tyrannical idea of duty is a terrible poison and is destroying the world.

Do not wait to have a harp in heaven and rest by and by. Why not take a
harp and begin here? Why wait for heaven? Make it here. In heaven there is no
marrying or giving in marriage. Why not begin at once and have none here? The
yellow robe of the sannyāsin is the sign of the free. Give up the beggar's dress
of the world; wear the flag of freedom, the ochre robe.

Sunday, August 4.

"Whom therefore ye ignorantly worship, him declare I unto you."

This one and only God is the knownest of the known. He is the one thing
we see everywhere. All know their own Self; all know, "I am"—even animals.
All we know is the projection of the Self. Teach this to the children; they can
grasp it. Every religion has worshipped the Self, even though unconsciously,
because there is nothing else.

This indecent clinging to life as we know it here is the source of all evil. It
causes all this cheating and stealing. It makes money a god, and all vices and
fears ensue. Value nothing material, and do not cling to anything. If you cling to
nothing, not even to life, then there will be no fear. "He goes from death to
death who sees many in this world." There can be no physical death for us and
no mental death when we see that all is one. All bodies are mine; so even my
body is eternal, because the tree, the animal, the sun, the moon, the universe
itself is my body. Then how can it die? Every mind, every thought is mine.
Then how can death come? The Self is never born and never dies. When we
realize this all doubts vanish. "I am, I know, I love"—these can never be
doubted. There is no hunger, for all that is eaten is eaten by me. If a hair falls
out, we do not think we die; so if one body dies, it is but a hair falling.

*   *   *

The superconscious is God—beyond speech, beyond thought, beyond consciousness. There are three states: brutality, or tamas; humanity, or rajas;
and divinity, or sattva. Those attaining the highest state simply are. Duty dies
there; they only love, and like a magnet draw others to them. This is freedom.
No more do you do moral acts, but whatever you do is moral. The Brahmavit,
the knower of God, is higher than all the gods. The angels came to worship
Jesus when he had conquered delusion and had said, "Get thee behind me,
Satan." None can help a Brahmavit; the universe itself bows down before him.
His every desire is fulfilled; his spirit purifies others. Therefore worship the
Brahmavit if you wish to attain the highest. When we have the three great
gifts of God—a human body, an intense desire to be free, and the help of a
great soul to show us the way—then liberation is certain for us. Mukti is ours.

*   *   *

Death of the body for ever is Nirvāna. It is the negative side and says, "I am
not this, nor this, nor this." Vedānta takes the further step and asserts the

positive side—mukti, or freedom. "I am Existence Absolute, Knowledge Absolute, Bliss Absolute; I am He"—this is Vedānta, the cap-stone of the perfect arch.

The great majority of the adherents of Northern Buddhism believe in mukti and are really Vedāntists. Only the Ceylonese accept Nirvāna as annihilation.

No belief or disbelief can kill the "I." That which comes with belief and goes with disbelief is only a delusion. Nothing touches the Ātman. "I salute my own Self." "Self-illumined, I salute myself; I am Brahman." The body is a dark room. When we enter it, it becomes illumined, it becomes alive. Nothing can ever affect the illumination; it cannot be destroyed. It may be covered, but can never be destroyed.

* * *

At the present time God should be worshipped as Mother, the Infinite Energy. This will lead to purity, and tremendous energy will come here in America. Here no temples weigh us down, no one suffers as do those in poorer countries. Woman has suffered for aeons and has thus acquired infinite patience and infinite perseverance. She holds on to an idea. It is this which makes her the support of even superstitious religions and of the priests in every land, and it is this that will free her. We have to become Vedāntists and live this grand thought. The masses must get it, and only in free America can this be done. In India these ideas were taught by individuals like Buddha, Śankara, and others, but the masses did not retain them. The new cycle must see the masses living Vedānta, and this will have to come through women.

Keep the beloved, beautiful Mother in your heart of hearts with all care.
Let no evil counsellors enter; let you and me, my heart, alone see Mother.
Throw out everything but the tongue; keep that to say, "Mother, Mother!"

Thou art beyond all that lives!
Moon of my life! Soul of my soul!

Sunday afternoon.

Mind is an instrument in the hands of the Ātman, just as body is an instrument in the hands of mind. Matter is motion outside; mind is motion inside. All change begins and ends in time. If the Ātman is unchangeable, It must be perfect; if perfect, It must be infinite; and if It is infinite, It must be only one—there cannot be two infinites. So the Ātman, the Self, can be only one. Though It seems to be various, It is really one. If a man were to go towards the sun, at every step he would see a different sun, and yet it would be the same sun after all.

Asti, "isness," is the basis of all unity, and just as soon as the basis is found, perfection ensues. If all colour could be resolved into one colour, painting would cease. Perfect oneness is rest. We refer all manifestations to one Being. Taoists, Confucianists, Buddhists, Hindus, Jews, Mohammedans, Christians, and Zoroastrians all preached the golden rule and in almost the same words; but only the Hindus have given the rationale, because they saw the reason. Man must love others because those others are himself. There is but one.

Of all the great religious teachers the world has known, only Lao-tze, Buddha, and Jesus transcended the golden rule and said: "Do good to your enemies. Love them that hate you."

Principles exist: we do not create them, we only discover them.

Religion consists solely in realization. Doctrines are methods, not religion. All the different religions are but applications of the one Religion, adapted to suit the requirements of different nations. Theories only lead to fighting; thus the name of God, which ought to bring peace, has been the cause of half the bloodshed of the world. Go direct to the source. Ask God what He is. Unless He answers, He is not. But every religion teaches that He does answer.

Have something to say for yourself; else how can you have any idea of what others have said? Do not cling to old superstitions; be ever ready for new truths. "Fools are they who would drink brackish water from a well that their forefathers have digged and would not drink pure water from a well that others have digged." Until we realize God for ourselves we can know nothing about Him. Each man is perfect by nature; prophets have manifested this perfection, but it is potential in us. How can we understand that Moses saw God unless we too see Him?

If God ever came to anyone He will come to me. I will go to God direct; let Him talk to me. I cannot take belief as a basis; that is atheism and blasphemy. If God spoke to a man in the deserts of Arabia two thousand years ago, He can also speak to me today; else how can I know that He has not died?

Come to God any way you can; only come. But in coming do not push anyone down.

The knowing ones must have pity on the ignorant. One who knows is willing to give up his body even for an ant, because he knows that the body is nothing.

Monday, August 5.

The question is: Is it necessary to pass through all the lower stages to reach the highest, or can a plunge be taken at once? The modern American boy takes twenty-five years to attain that which his forefathers took hundreds of years to attain. The Hindu gets in twenty years to the height reached in eight thousand years by his ancestors. On the physical side, the embryo goes from the amoeba to man in the womb. These are the teachings of modern science. Vedānta goes farther and tells us that we not only have to live the life of all past humanity, but also the future life of all humanity. The man who does the first is the educated man; the second is the jivanmukta, ever free.

Time is merely the measure of our thoughts, and thought being inconceivably swift, there is no limit to the speed with which we can live the life ahead. So it cannot be stated how long it would take to live all future life. It might be in a second, or it might take fifty lifetimes. It depends on the intensity of the desire. The teaching must therefore be modified according to the needs of the taught. The consuming fire is ready for all; even water and chunks of ice are quickly consumed. Fire a mass of bird-shot; one at least will strike. Give a man a whole museum of truths; he will at once take what is suited to him. Past lives have moulded our tendencies; give to the taught in accordance with his tendency. Intellectual, mystical, devotional, practical—make one the basis, but teach the others with it. Intellect must be balanced with love, the mystical nature with reason, while the practical must form part of every method. Take everyone where he stands and push him forward. Religious teaching must always be constructive, not destructive.

Each tendency shows the life-work of the past, the line or radius along which that man must move. All radii lead to the centre. Never even attempt to disturb anyone's tendencies; to do that retards both teacher and taught. When you teach jnāna, you must become a jnāni and stand mentally exactly where the taught stands. Similarly in every other yoga. Develop every faculty as if it were the only one that exists; this is the true secret of so-called harmonious development. That is, get extensity with intensity, but not at its expense. We are infinite. There is no limitation in us. We can be as intense as the most devoted Mohammedan and as broad as the most roaring atheist.

The way to do this is not to put the mind on any one subject, but to develop and control the mind itself; then you can turn it on any side you choose. Thus you keep intensity and extensity. Feel jnāna as if it were all there is; then do the same with bhakti, with rāja, with karma. Give up the waves and go to the ocean; then you can have the waves as you please. Control the lake of your own mind; else you cannot understand the lake of another's mind.

The true teacher is one who can throw his whole force into the tendency of the taught. Without real sympathy we can never teach well. Give up the notion that every man is a responsible being; only the perfect man is responsible. The ignorant have drunk deep of the cup of delusion and are not sane. You, who know, must have infinite patience with these. Have nothing but love for them and find out the disease that has made them see the world in a wrong light; then help them to cure it and see aright. Remember always that only the free have free will; all the rest are in bondage and are not responsible for what they do. Will as will is bound. The water when melting on the top of the Himālayas is free, but becoming the river, it is bound by the banks; yet the original impetus carries it to the sea and it regains its freedom. The first is the fall of man; the second is the resurrection. Not one atom can rest until it finds its freedom.

Some imaginations help to break the bondage of the rest. The whole universe is imagination, but one set of imaginations will cure another set. Those which tell us that there is sin and sorrow and death in the world are terrible; but the other set, which says ever: "I am holy. There is a God. There is no pain"—these are good and help to break the bondage of the others. The highest imagination, which can break all the links of the chain, is that of the Personal God.

"Om Tat Sat" is the only thing beyond māyā; but the Personal God exists eternally. As long as Niagara Falls exists, the rainbow will exist; but the water continually flows away. The Falls are the universe, and the rainbow is the Personal God, and both are eternal. While the universe exists, God must exist. God creates the universe and the universe creates God, and both are eternal. Māyā is neither existence nor non-existence. Both Niagara Falls and the rainbow are eternally changing—Brahman seen through māyā. The Persians and the Christians split māyā into two and call the good half God and the bad half the Devil. Vedānta takes māyā as a whole and sees beyond it the non-dual Brahman.

*   *   *

Mohammed found that Christianity was straying from the Semitic fold, and his teachings were to show what Christianity ought to be as a Semitic religion— that it should hold to one God. The Āryan idea "I and my Father are one" disgusted and terrified him. In reality the conception of the Trinity was a great advance over the dualistic idea of Jehovah, who was for ever separate from man. The theory of the Incarnation is the first link in the chain of ideas leading to the recognition of the oneness of God and man. God first appearing in one human form, then reappearing at different times in other human forms, is at last recognized as being in every human form, in all men. The monistic is the highest stage; the monotheistic is a lower stage. Imagination will lead you to the highest even more rapidly and easily than reasoning.

Let a few stand out and live for God alone and save religion for the world. Do not pretend to be like Janaka when you are only the progenitor of delusions. (The word *Janaka* means progenitor; it is also the name of a king who, although he still held his kingdom for the sake of his people, had given up everything mentally.) Be honest and say, "I see the ideal but I cannot yet approach it"; but do not pretend to give up when you do not. If you give up, stand fast. If a hundred fall in the fight, seize the flag and carry it on. God is true for all that, no matter who falls. Let him who falls hand on the flag to another to carry on; it must never fall.

The Bible says: Seek first the kingdom of heaven and everything else will be added unto you. But when I am washed and clean, why should impurity be added unto me? Be only too glad to get rid of it. Give up and know that success will follow, even if you never see it. Jesus left twelve fishermen and yet those few blew up the Roman Empire.

Sacrifice on God's altar earth's purest and best. He who struggles is better than he who never attempts. Even to look on one who has given up has a purifying effect. Stand up for God; let the world go. Make no compromise. Give up the world; then alone are you loosened from the body. When it dies, you are āzād, free. Be free. Death alone can never free us. Freedom must be attained by our own efforts during life; then, when the body falls, there will be no rebirth.

Truth is to be judged by truth and by nothing else. Doing good is no test of truth; the sun needs no torch by which to see it. Even if truth destroys the whole universe, still it is truth; stand by it.

Practising the concrete forms of religion is easy. It attracts the masses. But really there is nothing in the external.

"As the spider throws her web out of herself and draws it in, even so this universe is thrown out and drawn in by God."

Tuesday, August 6.

Without the "I" there can be no "you" outside. From this some philosophers came to the conclusion that the external world did not exist save in the subject; that the "you" existed only in the "I." Others have argued that the "I" can be known only through the "you"—and with equal logic. These two views are partial truths, each wrong in part and each right in part. Thought is as much material and as much in nature as the body is. Both matter and mind exist in a third, a unity, which divides itself into the two. This unity is the Ātman, the real Self.

There is Being, "x," which is manifesting Itself as both mind and matter. Its movements in the tangible world are along certain fixed lines called law. As a unity It is free; as many It is bound by law. Still, with all this bondage, the idea of freedom is ever present, and this is nivritti, or "turning from attachment." The materializing forces, which, through desire, lead us to take an active part in worldly affairs, are called pravritti.

That action is moral which frees us from the bondage of matter, and vice versa. This world appears infinite because all things move in a circle—they return whence they came. So there is no rest or peace here. We must get out. Mukti is the sole end to be attained.

*   *   *

Evil changes in form but remains the same in quality. In ancient times force ruled; today it is cunning. The misery in India is not so bad as in America, because the poor man here sees a greater contrast to his own bad condition.

Good and evil are inextricably combined, and one cannot be had without the other. The sum total of energy in this universe is like a lake: every wave inevitably leads to a corresponding depression. The sum total is absolutely the same; so to make one man happy is to make another unhappy. External happiness is material and the supply is fixed; so not one grain can be had by one person without taking from another. Only bliss beyond the material world can be had without loss to any. Material happiness is but a transformation of material sorrow.

Those who are born in the wave and keep in it do not see the depression and what is there. Never think you can make the world better and happier. The bullock in the oil-mill never reaches the wisp of hay tied in front of him; he only grinds out the oil. So we chase the will-o'-the-wisp of happiness, which always eludes us, and we only grind nature's mill, then die merely to begin again. If we could get rid of evil, we should never catch a glimpse of anything higher; we should be satisfied and never struggle to get free. When man finds that all searching for happiness in matter is nonsense, then religion begins. All human knowledge is but part of religion. In the human body the balance between good and evil is so even that there is a chance for man to wish to free himself from both.

The free Soul never became bound. To ask how It did is an illogical question. Where no bondage is, there is no cause and effect. "I became a fox in a dream and a dog chased me." Now how can I ask why the dog chased me? The fox was a part of the dream and the dog followed as a matter of course; but both belong to the dream and have no existence outside. Science and religion are both attempts to help us out of bondage; only religion is the more ancient and we

Vivekananda

have the superstition that it is the more holy. In a way it is, because it makes morality a vital point and science does not.

"Blessed are the pure in heart, for they shall see God." This sentence alone would save mankind if all the books and prophets were lost. This purity of heart will bring the vision of God. It is the theme of the whole music of this universe. In purity there is no bondage. When we remove the veil of ignorance by purity, then we manifest ourselves as we really are and know that we were never in bondage. The seeing of many is the great sin of all the world. See all as the Self and love all; let all ideas of separateness go.

*   *   *

The diabolical man is a part of my body, as a wound or a burn is. We have to nurse a wound or a burn to help it get better; so continually nurse and help the diabolical man until he heals and is once more happy and healthy.

While we think on the relative plane, we have the right to believe that as bodies we can be hurt by relative things and equally that we can be helped by them. This idea of help, abstracted, is what we call God. The sum total of all ideas of help is God.

God is the abstract compound of all that is merciful and good and helpful: that should be the sole idea. As Ātman we have no body; so to say "I am God and poison does not hurt me" is an absurdity. While there is a body and we see it, we have not realized God. Can the little whirlpool remain after the river vanishes?

Cry for help and you will get it, and at last you will find that the one crying for help has vanished and so also the Helper, and the play is over: only the Self remains. This once done, come back and play as you will. This body can then do no evil, because it is not until the evil forces are all burnt out that liberation comes. When that state has been attained, the dross has been burnt out; all that remains is "flame without smoke," "fire without fuel." The past momentum carries on the body, but it can only do good, because the bad was all gone before freedom came.

The dying thief on the cross reaped the effects of his past actions. He had been a yogi and had slipped; then he had to be born again. Again he slipped and became a thief. But the past good he had done bore fruit, and he met Jesus in the moment when liberation could come, and one word made him free.

Buddha set his greatest enemy free because, by hating Buddha so much, he kept constantly thinking of him. That thought purified his mind and he became ready for freedom. Therefore think of God all the time and you will be purified.

(Thus ended the inspired talks of Swami Vivekananda. The following day, blessing the Thousand Islands, he left Thousand Island Park and returned to New York.)

RĀJA-YOGA

Each soul is potentially divine. The goal is to manifest this divinity within by controlling nature: external and internal. Do this either by work, or worship, or psychic control, or philosophy—by one, or more, or all of these—and be free. This is the whole of religion. Doctrines, or dogmas, or rituals, or books, or temples, or forms, are but secondary details.

VIVEKANANDA

A Symbolic Representation of the Kundalini Rising
through the Different Centres in the Sushumnā
to the Thousand-petalled Lotus in the Brain

AUTHOR'S PREFACE

SINCE THE DAWN OF HISTORY various extraordinary phenomena have been recorded as happening amongst human beings. Witnesses are not wanting in modern times to attest such events even in societies living under the full blaze of modern science. The vast mass of such evidence is unreliable, coming as it does from ignorant, superstitious, or fraudulent persons. In many instances the so-called miracles are imitations. But what do they imitate? It is not the sign of a candid and scientific mind to throw overboard anything without proper investigation. Surface scientists, unable to explain the various extraordinary mental phenomena, strive to ignore their very existence. They are therefore more culpable than those who think that their prayers are answered by a being or beings above the clouds, or than those who believe that their petitions will make such beings change the course of the universe. The latter have the excuse of ignorance, or at least of a defective system of education, which has taught them dependence upon such beings, a dependence which has become a part of their degenerate nature. The former have no such excuse.

For thousands of years such phenomena have been studied, investigated, and generalized; the whole ground of the religious faculties of man has been analysed; and the practical result is the science of Rāja-yoga. Rāja-yoga does not, after the unpardonable manner of some modern sciences, deny the existence of facts which are difficult to explain; on the contrary, it gently, yet in no uncertain terms, tells the superstitious that miracles and answers to prayer and powers of faith, though true as facts, are not rendered comprehensible through superstitious explanations attributing them to the agency of a being or beings above the clouds. It declares that each man is only a conduit for the infinite ocean of knowledge and power that lies behind mankind. It teaches that desires and wants are in man, that the power of supply is also in man, and that wherever and whenever a desire, a want, or a prayer has been fulfilled, it was out of this infinite magazine that the fulfilment came, and not from any supernatural being. The idea of supernatural beings may rouse to a certain extent the power of action in man, but it also brings spiritual decay. It brings dependence; it brings fear; it brings superstition. It degenerates into a horrible belief in the natural weakness of man. There is no supernatural, says the yogi, but there are in nature gross manifestations and subtle manifestations. The subtle are the causes, the gross the effects. The gross can be easily perceived by the senses; not so the subtle. The practice of rāja-yoga will lead to the acquisition of the subtle perceptions.

All the orthodox systems of Indian philosophy have one goal in view: the liberation of the soul through perfection. The method is yoga. The word yoga covers an immense ground. Both the Sāmkhya and the Vedānta schools point to yoga in some form or other.

The subject of the present book is that form of yoga known as Rāja-yoga.[1] The aphorisms of Patanjali are the highest authority on Rāja-yoga and form its text-book. The other philosophers, though occasionally differing from Patanjali in some philosophical points, have, as a rule, accorded to his method of practice a decided consent. The first part of this book comprises several lectures delivered by the present writer to his classes in New York. The second part is a rather free translation of the *Aphorisms (Sutras)* of Patanjali, with a running commentary. An effort has been made to avoid technicalities as far as possible, and to keep to the free and easy style of conversation. In the first part some simple and specific directions are given for students who want to practise; but all such are especially and earnestly warned that, with few exceptions, Rāja-yoga can be safely learnt only by direct contact with a teacher. If these conversations succeed in awakening a desire for further information on the subject, the teacher will not be wanting.

The system of Patanjali is based upon the system of Sāmkhya, the points of difference being very few. The two most important differences are, first, that Patanjali admits the Personal God in the form of the First Teacher, while the only God that Sāmkhya concedes is a nearly perfected being, temporarily in charge of a cycle of creation. Second, a yogi holds the mind to be equally all-pervading as the Soul, or Purusha, and Sāmkhya does not.

VIVEKANANDA

---

[1] Throughout this volume the editor has followed the policy of spelling *Rāja-yoga* with a capital r when the word refers to the well-known system of Yoga philosophy, and with a small r when it denotes the spiritual discipline generally known as yoga. But in practice it has not always been possible to maintain this distinction. The word Yoga, too, has been spelt with capital y and small y to denote the Yoga philosophy and the yogic discipline respectively.

INTRODUCTION

ALL OUR KNOWLEDGE is based upon experience. What we call inferential knowledge, in which we go from the particular to the general or from the general to the particular, has experience as its basis. In what are called the exact sciences people easily find the truth, because it appeals to the specific experiences of every human being. The scientist does not ask you to believe in anything blindly; but he has got certain results, which have come from his own experiences, and when, reasoning on them, he wants us to believe in his conclusions, he appeals to some universal experience of humanity. In every exact science there is a basis which is common to all humanity, so that we can at once see the truth or the fallacy of the conclusions drawn therefrom. Now, the question is: Has religion any such basis or not? I shall have to answer the question both in the affirmative and in the negative.

Religion, as it is generally taught all over the world, is found to be based upon faith and belief, and in most cases consists only of different sets of theories; and that is why we find religions quarrelling with one another. These theories, again, are based upon belief. One man says there is a great Being sitting above the clouds and governing the whole universe, and he asks me to believe that solely on the authority of his assertion. In the same way I may have my own ideas, which I am asking others to believe; and if they ask for a reason, I cannot give them any. This is why religion and religious philosophy have a bad name nowadays. Every educated man seems to say: "Oh, these religions are only bundles of theories without any standard to judge them by, each man preaching his own pet ideas." Nevertheless there is a basis of universal belief in religion, governing all the different theories and all the varying ideas of different sects in different countries. Going to this basis, we find that they too are based upon universal experiences.

In the first place, if you analyse the various religions of the world, you will find that they are divided into two classes: those with a book and those without a book. Those with a book are stronger and have a larger number of followers. Those without books have mostly died out, and the few new ones have very small followings. Yet in all of them we find one consensus of opinion: that the truths they teach are the results of the experiences of particular persons. The Christian asks you to believe in his religion, to believe in Christ and to believe in him as the Incarnation of God, to believe in a God, in a soul, and in a better state of that soul. If I ask him for the reason, he says that he believes in them. But if you go to the fountainhead of Christianity, you will find that it is based upon experience. Christ said that he saw God, the disciples said that they felt God, and so forth. Similarly, in Buddhism, it is Buddha's experience. He experienced certain truths, saw them, came in contact with them, and preached them to the world. So with the Hindus: in their books the writers, who are called rishis, or sages, declare that they have experienced certain truths, and these they preach.

Thus it is clear that all the religions of the world have been built upon that one universal and adamantine foundation of all our knowledge—direct experience. The teachers all saw God; they all saw their own souls, they saw their souls' future and their eternity; and what they saw they preached. Only there is this difference: By most of these religions, especially in modern times, a peculiar claim is made, namely, that these experiences are impossible at the present day; they were possible only to a few men, who were the founders of the religions that subsequently bore their names. At the present time these experiences have become obsolete, and therefore we now have to take these religions on faith.

This I entirely deny. If there has been one experience in this world in any particular branch of knowledge, it absolutely follows that that experience has been possible millions of times before and will be repeated eternally. Uniformity is the rigorous law of nature: what once happened can happen always.

The teachers of the science of Rāja-yoga, therefore, declare not only that religion is based upon the experiences of ancient times, but also that no man can be religious until he has had the same experiences himself. Rāja-yoga is the science which teaches us how to get these experiences. It is not much use to talk about religion until one has felt it. Why is there so much disturbance, so much fighting and quarrelling, in the name of God? There has been more bloodshed in the name of God than for any other cause, because people never went to the fountainhead; they were content to give only a mental assent to the customs of their forefathers, and wanted others to do the same. What right has a man to say that he has a soul if he does not feel it, or that there is a God if he does not see Him? If there is a God we must see Him; if there is a soul we must perceive it; otherwise it is better not to believe. It is better to be an outspoken atheist than a hypocrite.

The modern idea, on the one hand, with the "learned" is that religion and metaphysics and all search after a Supreme Being are futile; on the other hand, with the semi-educated the idea seems to be that these things really have no basis, their only value consisting in the fact that they furnish a strong motive power for doing good to the world. If men believe in a God, they may become good and moral, and so make good citizens. We cannot blame them for holding such ideas, seeing that all the teaching these men get is simply to believe in an eternal rigmarole of words, without any substance behind them. They are asked to live upon words. Can they do it? If they could, I should not have the least regard for human nature. Man wants truth, wants to experience truth for himself. When he has grasped it, realized it, felt it within his heart of hearts, then alone, declare the Vedas, will all doubts vanish, all darkness be scattered, and all crookedness be made straight. "Ye children of immortality, even those who live in the highest sphere, the way is found. There is a way out of all this darkness, and that is by perceiving Him who is beyond all darkness. There is no other way."

The science of Rāja-yoga proposes to put before humanity a practical and scientifically worked out method of reaching this truth. In the first place, every science must have its own method of investigation. If you want to become an astronomer, and sit down and cry, "Astronomy! astronomy!" you will never become one. It is the same with chemistry. A certain method must be followed. You must go to a laboratory, take different substances, mix them, examine them, experiment with them; and out of that will come a knowledge of chemistry. If you want to be an astronomer you must go to an observatory, take a telescope, and study the stars and planets. And then you will become an astronomer. Each science must have its own methods. I could preach you thousands of sermons, but they would not make you religious until you followed the method. This truth has been preached by sages of all countries, of all ages, by men pure and unselfish who had no motive but to do good to the world. They all declare that they have found certain truths higher than what the senses can bring us, and they invite verification. They ask us to take up the discipline and practise honestly. Then, if we do not find this higher truth, we shall have the right to say that there is no truth in the claim; but before we have done that, we are not rational in denying the truth of their assertions. So we must work faithfully, using the prescribed methods, and light will come.

In acquiring knowledge we make use of generalization, and generalization is based upon observation. We first observe facts, then generalize, and then draw conclusions or formulate principles. The knowledge of the mind, of the internal nature of man, of thought, can never be had until we have first developed the power of observing what is going on within. It is comparatively easy to observe facts in the external world, for many instruments have been invented for the purpose; but in the internal world we have no instrument to help us. Yet we know that we must observe in order to have a real science. Without proper analysis any science will be hopeless, mere theorizing; and that is why the psychologists have been quarrelling among themselves since the beginning of time, except those few who found out the means of observation.

The science of Rāja-yoga proposes, in the first place, to give us such a means of observing the internal states. The instrument is the mind itself. The power of attention, when properly guided and directed towards the internal world, will analyse the mind and illumine facts for us. The powers of the mind are like rays of light dissipated; when they are concentrated they illumine. This is our only means of knowledge. Everyone is using it, both in the external and in the internal world; but, for the psychologist, the same minute observation has to be directed to the internal world which the scientific man directs to the external; and this requires a great deal of practice. From childhood onward we have been taught to pay attention only to things external, but never to things internal; hence most of us have nearly lost the faculty of observing the internal mechanism. To turn the mind, as it were, inside, stop it from going outside, and then to concentrate all its powers and throw them upon the mind itself, in order that it may know its own nature, analyse itself, is very hard work. Yet that is the only way to anything which will be like a scientific approach to the subject.

What is the use of such knowledge? In the first place, knowledge itself is the highest reward of knowledge, and secondly, there is also utility in it. It will take away all our misery. When, by analysing his own mind, a man comes face to face, as it were, with something which is never destroyed, something which is, by its own nature, eternally pure and perfect, he will no more be miserable, no more be unhappy. All misery comes from fear, from unsatisfied desire. When a man finds that he never dies, he will then have no more fear of death. When he knows that he is perfect, he will have no more vain desires. And both these causes being absent, there will be no more misery; there will be perfect bliss, even in this body.

There is only one method by which to attain this knowledge, and that is concentration. The chemist in his laboratory concentrates all the energies of his mind into one focus and throws them upon the materials he is analysing, and thus finds out their secrets. The astronomer concentrates all the energies of his mind and projects them through his telescope upon the skies; and the stars, the sun, and the moon give up their secrets to him. The more I can concentrate my thoughts on the matter on which I am talking to you, the more light I can throw upon it. You are listening to me, and the more you concentrate your thoughts, the more clearly you will grasp what I have to say.

How has all the knowledge in the world been gained but by the concentration of the powers of the mind? The world is ready to give up its secrets if we only know how to knock, how to give it the necessary blow. The strength and force of the blow come through concentration. There is no limit to the power of the human mind. The more concentrated it is, the more power is brought to bear on one point. That is the secret.

It is easy to concentrate the mind on external things; the mind naturally goes outward. But it is not so in religion or psychology or metaphysics, where the subject and the object are one. The object is internal: the mind itself is the object. It is necessary to study the mind itself; the mind studies the mind. We know that there is a power of the mind called reflection. I am talking to you; at the same time I am standing aside, like a second person, and knowing and hearing what I am saying. You work and think at the same time, while a portion of your mind stands by and sees what you are thinking. The powers of the mind should be concentrated and turned back upon it; and as the darkest places reveal their secrets before the penetrating rays of the sun, so will the concentrated mind penetrate into its own innermost secrets. Thus we shall come to the basis of belief, to the real religion. We shall perceive for ourselves whether or not we have souls, whether or not life lasts for five minutes or for eternity, whether or not there is a God. All this will be revealed to us.

This is what Rāja-yoga proposes to teach. The goal of all its teaching is to show how to concentrate the mind; then how to discover the innermost recesses of our own minds; then how to generalize their contents and form our own conclusions from them. It never asks what our belief is—whether we are deists, or atheists, whether Christians, Jews, or Buddhists. We are human beings, and that is sufficient. Every human being has the right and the power to seek religion; every human being has the right to ask the reason why and to have his question answered by himself—if he only takes the trouble.

So far, then, we see that in the study of Rāja-yoga no faith or belief is necessary. Believe nothing until you find it out for yourself; that is what it teaches us.

Truth requires no prop to make it stand. Do you mean to say that the facts of our awakened state require any dreams or imaginings to prove them? Certainly not. The study of Rāja-yoga takes a long time and constant practice. A part of this practice is physical, but in the main it is mental. As we proceed we shall find how intimately the mind is connected with the body. If we believe that the mind is simply a finer part of the body, and that the mind acts upon the body, then it stands to reason that the body must react upon the mind. If the body is sick, the mind becomes sick also. If the body is healthy, the mind remains healthy and strong. When one is angry, the mind becomes disturbed; and when the mind is disturbed, the body also becomes disturbed. With the majority of mankind the mind is greatly under the control of the body, their minds being very little developed. The vast mass of humanity is very little removed from the animals; for in many instances their power of control is little higher than that of the animals. We have very little command of our minds. Therefore to acquire that command, to get that control over body and mind, we must take certain physical helps; when the body is sufficiently controlled we can attempt the manipulation of the mind. By manipulating the mind, we shall be able to bring it under our control, make it work as we like, and compel it to concentrate its powers as we desire.

According to the rāja-yogi, the external world is but the gross form of the internal, or subtle. The fine is always the cause, and the gross, the effect. So the external world is the effect, and the internal, the cause. Therefore the external forces are simply the grosser parts of that of which the internal forces are the finer. The man who has discovered and learnt how to manipulate the internal forces will get the whole of nature under his control. The yogi proposes to himself no less a task than to master the whole universe, to control the whole of nature. He wants to arrive at the point where what we call nature's laws will have no influence over him, where he will be able to go beyond them all. He will be the master of the whole of nature, internal and external. The progress and civilization of the human race simply mean controlling nature.

Different races take to different processes of controlling nature. Just as in the same society some individuals want to control external nature, and others internal, so, amongst races, some want to control external nature, and others internal. Some say that by controlling internal nature we control everything; others, that by controlling external nature we control everything. In the end both are right, because in nature you will not find any such division as internal or external. These are fictitious limitations that never existed. The externalists and the internalists are destined to meet at the same point, when both reach the limits of their knowledge. Just as a physicist, when he pushes his knowledge to its limits, finds that his knowledge melts into metaphysics, so a metaphysician finds that what he calls mind and matter are but apparent distinctions, which will ultimately disappear.

The end and aim of all science is to find the Unity, the One, out of which the manifold is manufactured, the One appearing as many. Rāja-yoga proposes to start from the internal world, study internal nature, and through that, control the whole—both internal and external. It is a very old attempt. India has been its special stronghold, but it has also been attempted by other nations. In Western countries it was regarded as occultism, and people who wanted to practise it were either burnt or killed as witches and sorcerers. In India, for various reasons, it fell into the hands of persons who destroyed ninety per cent of the knowledge and tried to make a great secret of the remainder. In modern times, in the West, one finds many so-called teachers, but these are worse than those of India, because the latter knew something, ʾ ⸱ile these modern exponents know nothing.

Anything that is secret and mysterious in this system of Yoga should be at once rejected. The best guide in life is strength. In religion, as in all other matters, discard everything that weakens you; have nothing to do with it. Mystery-mongering weakens the human brain. It has wellnigh destroyed Yoga, one of the grandest of sciences. From the time it was discovered, more than four thousand years ago, Yoga was perfectly delineated, formulated, and preached in India. It is a striking fact that the more modern the commentator, the greater the mistakes he makes, while the more ancient the writer, the more rational he is. Most of the modern writers talk of all sorts of mysteries. Thus Yoga fell into the hands of a few persons who made it a secret, instead of letting the full blaze of daylight and reason fall upon it. They did so that they might have the powers to themselves.

In the first place there is no mystery in what I shall teach. What little I know I will tell you. So far as I can reason it out I will do so; but as to what I do not know, I will simply tell you what the books say. It is wrong to blindly believe. You must exercise your own reason and judgement; you must learn from experience whether these things happen or not. Just as you would take up any other science, exactly in the same manner you should take up this science for study. There is neither mystery nor danger in it. So far as it is true it ought to be preached in the public streets in broad daylight. Any attempt to mystify these things is productive of great danger.

Before proceeding farther, I will tell you a little of the Sāmkhya philosophy, upon which the whole of Rāja-yoga is based. According to the Sāmkhya philosophy, the genesis of perception is as follows: The impressions of external objects are carried by the outer instruments to their respective brain centres, or organs; the organs carry the impressions to the mind; the mind, to the determinative faculty; from this the Purusha, the Soul, receives them, when perception results. Next the Purusha gives the order back to the motor centres to do the needful. With the exception of the Purusha, all of these are material; but the mind is much finer matter than the external instruments. That material of which the mind is composed becomes grosser and forms the tanmātras. These become still more gross and form external matter. That is the psychology of Sāmkhya. So between the intellect and the gross matter outside there is only a difference in degree. The Purusha is the only thing which is intelligent. The mind is an instrument, as it were, in the hands of the Soul, through which the Soul perceives external objects.

The mind is constantly changing—running from one object to another. Sometimes it attaches itself to several organs, sometimes to one, and sometimes to none. For instance, if I listen to the clock with great attention, I may not see anything although my eyes are open, showing that the mind was not attached to the organ of vision while it was to the organ of hearing. The mind sometimes attaches itself to all the organs simultaneously. But again, it has the reflexive power of looking back into its own depths. This power the yogi wants to attain; by concentrating the powers of the mind and turning them inward, he seeks to know what is happening inside. There is in this no question of belief; it is the result of the analysis made by certain philosophers. Modern physiologists tell us that the eyes are not the organ of vision, but that the organ is in one of the nerve centres of the brain, and so with all the senses. They also tell us that these centres are formed of the same material as the brain itself. Sāmkhya also tells us the same thing. The former is a statement on the physical side, and the latter on the psychological side; yet both are the same.

Our field of research lies beyond this. The yogi proposes to attain that fine state of perception in which he can perceive all the different mental states. There must be mental perception of all of them. One can perceive how, as soon as an external organ comes in contact with an object, there arises a sensation, how the sensation is carried by a particular nerve to the nerve centre, how the mind receives it, how it is presented to the determinative faculty, and how this last conveys it to the Purusha. All these different steps are to be observed, one by one. As each science requires certain preparations and has its own method, which must be followed before it can be understood, so it is with Rāja-yoga.

Certain regulations as to food are necessary: we must use that food which brings us the purest state of mind. If you go to a menagerie you will find this demonstrated at once. You see the elephants: huge animals, but calm and gentle; and if you go towards the cages of the lions and tigers you find them restless—showing how much difference has been made by food. All the forces that are working in the body have been produced out of food; we see that every day. If you begin to fast, first your body will get weak, the physical forces will suffer. Then, after a few days, the mental forces will suffer also: first memory fails; then comes a point when you are not able to think, much less to pursue any course of reasoning. We have therefore to take care what sort of food we eat at the beginning; and when we have got strength enough, when our practice is well advanced, we need not be so careful in this respect. While the plant is growing it must be hedged round, lest it should be injured; but when it becomes a tree the hedges are taken away; it is then strong enough to withstand all assaults.

A yogi must avoid the two extremes of luxury and austerity. He must not fast or torture his flesh. He who does so, says the Gitā, cannot be a yogi; he who fasts, he who keeps awake, he who sleeps much, he who works too much, he who does no work—none of these can be a yogi.

THE FIRST STEPS

Rāja-yoga is divided into eight steps. The first is yama, which consists of non-killing, truthfulness, non-stealing, continence, and non-receiving of gifts. Next is niyama, consisting of cleanliness, contentment, austerity, study, and self-surrender to God. Then come āsana, or posture; prānāyāma, or control of the prāna; pratyāhāra, or restraint of the senses from their objects; dhāranā, or fixing the mind on a spot; dhyāna, or meditation; and samādhi, or superconscious experience. Yama and niyama are moral training, without which no practice of yoga will succeed. As the yogi becomes established in these, he will begin to realize the fruits of his practice; without them it will never bear fruit. A yogi must not injure anyone by thought, word, or deed. Mercy must not be for men alone, but must go beyond and embrace the whole world.

The next step is āsana, posture. A series of exercises, physical and mental, is to be gone through every day until certain higher states are reached. Therefore it is quite necessary that we should find a posture in which we can remain for a long time. That posture which is the easiest should be the one chosen. For thinking, a certain posture may be very easy for one man, while for another it may be very difficult. We shall find later on that during the study of these psychological matters a good deal of activity goes on in the body. Nerve currents will have to be displaced and given a new channel. New sorts of vibrations will begin; the whole constitution will be remodelled, as it were. But the main part of the activity will lie along the spinal column; so the one thing necessary for the posture is to hold the spinal column free, sitting erect, holding the three parts—the chest, neck, and head—in a straight line. Let the whole weight of these three be supported by the ribs, and then you will have an easy, natural posture with the spine straight. You will easily see that you cannot think very high thoughts with the chest in.

This portion of yoga is a little similar to hatha-yoga, which deals entirely with the physical body, its aim being to make the physical body very strong. We have nothing to do with it here, because its practices are very difficult and cannot be learnt in a day, and, after all, do not lead to much spiritual growth. Many of these practices—such as placing the body in different postures—you will find in the teachings of Delsarte and others. The object in these is physical, not spiritual. There is not one muscle in the body over which a man cannot establish perfect control: the heart can be made to stop or go on at his bidding, and each part of the organism can be similarly controlled.

The result of hatha-yoga is simply to make men live long; health is the chief idea, the one goal of the hatha-yogi. He is determined not to fall sick, and he never does. He lives long. A hundred years is nothing to him; he is quite young and fresh when he is one hundred and fifty, without one hair turned grey. But that is all. A banyan tree lives sometimes five thousand years, but it is a banyan tree and nothing more. So if a man lives long, he is only a healthy animal. But one or two ordinary lessons of the hatha-yogis are very useful. For instance, some of you may find it a good thing for headaches to drink cold water through the nose as soon as you get up in the morning; the whole day your brain will feel very cool, and you will never catch cold. It is very easy to do: put your nose into the water, draw it up through the nostrils, and make a pump action in the throat.

After one has learnt to have a firm, erect seat, one has to perform, according to certain schools, a practice called the purification of the nerves. This part has been rejected by some as not belonging to Rāja-yoga; but since so great an authority as the commentator Śankarāchārya advises it, I think it fitting that it should be mentioned, and I will quote his own directions from his commentary on the *Svetāśvatara Upanishad*: "The mind whose dross has been cleared away by prānāyāma becomes fixed in Brahman; therefore prānāyāma is taught. First the nerves are to be purified; then comes the power to practise prānāyāma. Stopping the right nostril with the thumb, draw in air through the left nostril according to capacity; then, without any interval, eject the air through the right nostril, closing the left one. Again inhaling through the right nostril according to capacity, eject through the left. Practising this three or five times at four periods of the day—before dawn, during midday, in the evening, and at midnight—one attains purity of the nerves in fifteen days or a month. Then begins prānāyāma."

Practice is absolutely necessary. You may sit down and listen to me by the hour every day, but if you do not practise, you will not get one step farther. It all depends on practice. We never understand these things until we experience them. We have to see and feel them for ourselves. Simply listening to explanations and theories will not do.

There are several obstructions to practice. The first obstruction is an unhealthy body; if the body is not fit, the practice will be obstructed. Therefore we have to keep the body in good health; we have to take care about what we eat and drink, and what we do. Always use a mental effort, what is usually called Christian Science, to keep the body strong. That is all; nothing further about the body. We must not forget that health is only a means to an end. If health were the end we would be like animals; animals rarely become unhealthy.

The second obstruction is doubt. We always feel doubtful about things we do not see. Man cannot live upon words, however he may try. So doubt comes to us as to whether there is any truth in these things or not; even the best of us will doubt sometimes. With practice, within a few days, a little glimpse will come, enough to give one encouragement and hope. As a certain commentator on Yoga philosophy says: "When one proof is obtained, however little that may be, it will give us faith in the whole teaching of Yoga." For instance, after the first few months of practice you will begin to find you can read another's thoughts; they will come to you in picture form. Perhaps you will hear something happening at a long distance when you concentrate your mind with a wish to hear. These glimpses will come, by little bits at first, but enough to give you faith and strength and hope. For instance, if you concentrate your thoughts on the tip of your nose, in a few days you will begin to smell a most wonderful fragrance, which will be enough to show you that there are certain mental perceptions which one can experience without the contact of physical objects. But we must always remember that these are only the means; the aim, the end, the goal, of all this training is liberation of the soul. Absolute control of nature, and nothing short of it, must be the goal. We must be the masters, and not the slaves, of nature; neither body nor mind must be our master, nor must we forget that the body is ours, and not we the body's.

A god and a demon went to learn about the Self from a great sage. They studied with him for a long time. At last the sage told them, "You yourselves are the Being you are seeking." Both of them thought that their bodies were the Self. The demon went back to his people quite satisfied and said, "I have learnt everything that was to be learnt: eat, drink, and be merry; we are the Self; there is nothing beyond us." The demon was ignorant by nature; so he never inquired any further, but was perfectly contented with the idea that he was God and that by the Self was meant the body.

The god had a purer nature. He at first committed the mistake of thinking, "I, this body, am Brahman; so let me keep it strong and healthy, and well dressed, and give it all sorts of enjoyments." But soon he found out that that could not be the meaning of the sage, their master; there must be something higher. So he came back and said: "Sir, did you teach me that this body was the Self? If so, I see that all bodies die; but the Self should not die." The sage said: "Find it out yourself. Thou art That." Then the god thought that the vital forces which work the body were what he meant by the Self. But after a time he found that if he ate, these vital forces remained strong, but if he starved, they became weak. The god then went back to the sage and said, "Sir, do you mean that the vital forces are the Self?" The sage said: "Find out for yourself. Thou art That." The god returned home once more, thinking that it was the mind, perhaps, that was the Self. But in a short while he saw that his thoughts were extremely various—now good, again bad; the mind was too changeable to be the Self. He went back to the sage and said: "Sir, I do not think that the mind is the Self. Did you mean that?" "No," replied the sage; "thou art That. Find out for yourself." The god went home and at last found the true Self, beyond all thought, one, without birth or death, whom sword cannot pierce or fire burn, whom the air cannot dry or water melt, the beginningless and endless, the immovable, the intangible, the omniscient, the omnipotent Being— neither the body nor the mind, but beyond them both. So he was satisfied; but the poor demon, owing to his fondness for the body, did not get the truth.

This world has a good many of these demoniac natures, but there are some gods too. If one proposes to teach a science to increase the power of sense enjoyment, one finds multitudes ready for it. If one undertakes to show the supreme goal, one finds few to listen. Very few have the power to grasp the highest, fewer still the perseverance to attain to it. But there are a few who know that even if the body can be made to live for a thousand years, the result in the end will be the same. When the forces that hold it together cease to function, the body must fall. No man was ever born who could stop his body from changing. The body is the name of a series of changes. As in a river the masses of water are changing before you every moment, and new masses are coming, taking similar form, so is it with this body. Yet the body must be kept strong and healthy; it is the best instrument we have.

This human body is the greatest body in the universe, and the human being, the highest being. Man is higher than all the animals, than all the angels; none is greater than man. Even the devas, the gods, will have to come down again and attain to salvation through a human body. Man alone realizes perfection, not even the devas. According to the Jews and Mohammedans, God created man after creating the angels and everything else, and after creating man He asked the angels to come and salute him, and all did so except Iblis; so God cursed him and he became Satan. Behind this allegory is the great truth that this human birth is the greatest birth we can have. The lower creation, the animal, is dull and manufactured mostly out of tamas. Animals cannot have any high thoughts; nor can the angels or devas attain to direct freedom without human birth. In human society, in the same way, too much wealth or too much poverty is a great impediment to the higher development of the soul. It is from the middle classes that the great ones of the world come. Here the forces are equally adjusted and balanced.

Returning to our subject, we come next to prānāyāma, control of the breathing. What has that to do with concentrating the powers of the mind? The breath is like the fly-wheel of this machine, the body. In a big machine you find the fly-wheel moving first, and that motion is conveyed to finer and finer parts until the most delicate and finest mechanism in the machine is in motion. The breath is that fly-wheel, supplying and regulating the motive power to everything in this body.

There was once a minister to a great king. He fell into disgrace. As a punishment, the king ordered him to be shut up in the top of a very high tower. This was done, and the minister was left there to perish. He had a faithful wife, however, who came to the tower at night and called to her husband at the top to know what she could do to help him. He told her to return to the tower the following night and bring with her a long rope, some stout twine, packthread, silk thread, a beetle, and a little honey. Wondering much, the good wife obeyed her husband and brought him the desired articles. The husband directed her to attach the silk thread firmly to the beetle, then to smear its horns with a drop of honey and set it free on the wall of the tower with its head pointing upward. She obeyed all these instructions, and the beetle started on its long journey. Smelling the honey ahead it slowly crept onward, in the hope of reaching the honey, until at last it reached the top of the tower, when the minister grasped the beetle and got possession of the silk thread. He told his wife to tie the other end to the packthread, and after he had drawn up the packthread, he repeated the process with the stout twine, and lastly with the rope. Then the rest was easy. The minister descended from the tower by means of the rope and made his escape. In this body of ours the motion of the breath is the silk thread; by laying hold of and learning to control it we grasp the packthread of the nerve currents, and from these the stout twine of our thoughts, and lastly the rope of the prāna, controlling which we reach freedom.

We do not know anything about our own bodies. We cannot know. At best we can take a dead body and cut it in pieces; and there are some who can take a live animal and cut it in pieces in order to see what is inside the body. Still that has nothing to do with our own bodies. We know very little about them. Why is that? Because our attention is not discriminating enough to catch the very fine movements that are going on within. We can know of them only when the mind becomes more subtle and enters, as it were, deeper into the body. To get that subtle perception we have to begin with the grosser perceptions. We have to get hold of that which is setting the whole engine in motion; that is the prāna, the most obvious manifestation of which is the breath. Then, along with the breath, we shall slowly enter into the body, and thus be able to find out about the subtle forces, the nerve currents, which are moving all through the body. As soon as we perceive and learn to feel them, we shall begin to get control over them and over the body. The mind is also set in motion by these different nerve currents; so at last we shall reach the state of perfect control over the body and the mind, making both our servants. Knowledge is power. We have to get this power; so we must begin at the beginning, with prānāyāma, restraining the prāna. This prānāyāma is a long subject, and it will take several lessons to explain it thoroughly. We shall take it up part by part.

We shall gradually see the reasons for each exercise and also what forces in the body are set in motion. All these things will come to us. But it requires constant practice; and the proof will come from practice. No amount of reasoning which I can give you will be proof to you until you have demonstrated it for yourselves. As soon as you begin to feel these currents in motion all over you, doubts will vanish; but it requires hard practice every day. You must practise at least twice every day, and the best times are towards the morning and the evening. When night passes into day, and day into night, a state of relative calmness ensues. The early morning and the early evening are the two periods of calmness. Your body will have a like tendency to become calm at those times. We should take advantage of that natural condition and begin to practise then. Make it a rule not to eat until you have practised; if you do this the sheer force of hunger will break your laziness. In India they teach children never to eat until they have practised or worshipped, and it becomes natural to them after a time; a boy will not feel hungry until he has bathed and practised the disciplines of yoga.

Those of you who can afford it should have a room where you can practise alone. Do not sleep in that room; it must be kept holy. You must not enter the room until you have bathed and are perfectly clean in body and mind. Place flowers in that room always—they are the best surroundings for a yogi— and pictures that are pleasing. Burn incense morning and evening. Have no quarrel or anger or unholy thought in that room. Only allow those persons to enter it who are of the same thought as you. Then gradually there will be an atmosphere of holiness in the room, so that when you are miserable, sorrowful, or doubtful, or when your mind is disturbed, if you then enter the room you will feel inner peace. This was the real idea behind the temple and the church; and in some temples and churches you will find it even now; but in the majority of them this idea has been lost. The fact is that by preserving spiritual vibrations in a place you make it holy. Those who cannot afford to have a room set apart can practise anywhere they like.

Sit in a straight posture. The next thing to do is to send a current of holy thought to all creation. Mentally repeat: "Let all beings be happy; let all beings be peaceful; let all beings be blissful." So do to the east, south, north, and west. The more you practise this, the better you will feel. You will find at last that the easiest way to make ourselves healthy is to see that others are healthy, and the easiest way to make ourselves happy is to see that others are happy. After doing that, those who believe in God should pray—not for money, not for health, nor for heaven. Pray for knowledge and light; every other prayer is selfish. Then the next thing to do is to think that your body is firm, strong, and healthy; for it is the best instrument you have. Think of it as being as strong as adamant, and that with the help of this body you will cross the ocean of life. Freedom is never to be reached by the weak; throw away all weakness. Tell your body that it is strong, tell your mind that it is strong, and have unbounded faith and hope in yourself.

PRĀNA

PRĀNĀYĀMA IS NOT, as many think, concerned solely with the breath; breath indeed has very little to do with it. Breathing is only one of the many exercises through which we get to the real prānāyāma. Prānāyāma means the control of prāna.

According to the philosophers of India, the universe is composed of two entities, one of which they call ākāśa, and the other, prāna. Ākāśa is the all-penetrating existence. Everything that has form, everything that is the result of combination, is evolved out of ākāśa. It is ākāśa that becomes the air, that becomes the liquids, that becomes the solids; it is ākāśa that becomes the sun, the earth, the moon, the stars, the comets; it is ākāśa that becomes the human body, the animal body, the plants, every form that we see, everything that can be sensed, everything that exists. It cannot be perceived; it is so subtle that it is beyond all ordinary perception; it can only be seen when it has become gross and has taken a form. At the beginning of creation there is only ākāśa; at the end of the cycle the solids, the liquids, and the gases all melt into ākāśa again, and the next creation similarly proceeds out of ākāśa.

By what power is ākāśa manufactured into this universe? By the power of prāna. Just as ākāśa is the infinite, omnipresent material of this universe, so is prāna the infinite, omnipresent manifesting power of this universe. At the beginning and at the end of a cycle all tangible objects resolve back into ākāśa, and all the forces in the universe resolve back into prāna. In the next cycle, out of this prāna is evolved everything that we call energy, everything that we call force. It is prāna that is manifesting as motion; it is prāna that is manifesting as gravitation, as magnetism. It is prāna that is manifesting as the actions of the body, as the nerve currents, as thought-force. From thought down to physical force, everything is but the manifestation of prāna. The sum total of all forces in the universe, mental or physical, when resolved back to their original state, is called prāna. "When there was neither aught nor naught, when darkness covered darkness, what existed then? That ākāśa existed without motion." The physical motion of prāna was stopped, but it existed all the same. At the end of a cycle the energies now displayed in the universe quiet down and become potential. At the beginning of the next cycle they start up, strike upon ākāśa, and thus out of ākāśa evolve these various forms; and as ākāśa changes, prāna changes also into all these manifestations of energy. The knowledge and control of prāna is really what is meant by prānāyāma.

This opens to us the door to almost unlimited power. Suppose, for instance, a man understood prāna perfectly and could control it; what power on earth would not be his? He would be able to move the sun and stars out of their places, to control everything in the universe, from the atoms to the biggest

592

suns. This is the end and aim of prānāyāma. When the yogi becomes perfect there will be nothing in nature not under his control. If he orders the gods or the souls of the departed to come, they will come at his bidding. All the forces of nature will obey him as slaves. When the ignorant see these powers of the yogi they call them miracles.

One peculiarity of the Hindu mind is that it always inquires first for the highest possible generalization, leaving the details to be worked out afterwards. The question is raised in the Vedas: "What is that, knowing which we shall know everything?" Thus all books and philosophies have been written for the purpose of demonstrating that one thing by the knowing of which everything is known. If a man wants to know this universe bit by bit he must know every individual grain of sand, which requires infinite time; he cannot know all of them. Then how can there be any knowledge? How can a man know all through knowing particulars? The yogis say that behind this particular manifestation there is a generalization. Behind all particular ideas stands a generalized, abstract principle. Grasp it and you have grasped everything. Just as this whole universe has been generalized, in the Vedas, into that one Absolute Existence, and he who has grasped that Existence has grasped the whole universe, so all forces have been generalized into prāna, and he who has grasped prāna has grasped all the forces of the universe, mental and physical. He who has controlled prāna has controlled his own mind and all the minds that exist. He who has controlled prāna has controlled his body and all the bodies that exist, because prāna is the source of all energy.

How to control prāna is the sole idea of prānāyāma. All the trainings and exercises in this regard are for that one end. Each man must begin where he stands, must learn how to control the things that are nearest to him. This body is very near to us, nearer than anything in the external universe; and the mind is nearer than the body. But the prāna which is working this mind and body is the nearest. It is a part of the prāna that moves the universe. In the infinite ocean of prāna, this little wave of prāna which represents our own energies, mental and physical, is the nearest to us. If we can succeed in controlling that little wave, then alone can we hope to control the whole of prāna. The yogi who has done this gains perfection; no longer is he under any power. He becomes almost almighty, almost all-knowing.

We see in every country sects that have attempted the control of prāna. In this country there are mind-healers, faith-healers, spiritualists, Christian Scientists, hypnotists, and so on. If we examine these different sects, we shall find at the back of each the control of prāna, whether they know it or not. If you boil all their theories down the residuum will be that. It is one and the same force that they are manipulating, only unknowingly. They have stumbled on the discovery of a force and are using it unconsciously without knowing its nature; but it is the same as what the yogi uses, and it comes from prāna.

The vital force in every being is prāna. Thought is the finest and highest manifestation of this prāna. Conscious thought, again, as we see it, is not the whole of thought. There is also what we call instinct, or unconscious thought, the lowest plane of thought. If a mosquito bites me, my hand will strike it automatically, instinctively. This is one expression of thought. All reflex actions of the body belong to this plane of thought. There is, again, the other plane of thought, the conscious: I reason, I judge, I think, I see the pros and cons of certain things. Yet that is not all. We know that reason is limited. Reason can go only to a certain length; beyond that it cannot reach. The circle within which it runs is very, very limited indeed. Yet at the same time we find that facts rush into this circle, like comets coming into the earth's orbit. It is plain that they come from outside, although our reason cannot go beyond. The causes of these phenomena which intrude into this small circle are outside it. Yogis say that even this cannot be the limit of knowledge; the mind can function on a still higher plane, the superconscious. When the mind has attained that state, which is called samādhi—perfect concentration—it goes beyond the limits of reason and comes face to face with facts which no instinct or reason can ever know. All manipulations of the subtle forces of the body, different manifestations of prāna, give a push to the mind, help it to go up higher and become superconscious, from where it acts.

In this universe there is one continuous substance on every plane of existence. Physically this universe is one: there is no difference between the sun and you. The scientist will tell you that to say otherwise is without meaning. There is no real difference between this table and me: the table is one point in the mass of matter, and I am another point. Each form represents, as it were, one whirlpool in the infinite ocean of matter. The whirlpools are ever changing. Just as in a rushing stream there may be millions of whirlpools, the water in each of which is different every moment, turning round and round for a few seconds and then passing out, replaced by a fresh quantity, so the whole universe is one constantly changing mass of matter, in which all forms of existence are so many whirlpools. A mass of matter enters into one whirlpool, say a human body, stays there for a period, becomes changed, and goes out into another, say an animal body this time, from which again, after a few years, it enters into another whirlpool, perhaps a lump of mineral. There is constant change. Not one body remains the same. There is no such thing as my body or your body, except in words. Of the one huge mass of matter, one point is called a moon, another a sun, another a man, another the earth, another a plant, another a mineral. Not one is constant, but everything is changing, matter eternally forming and disintegrating.

So it is with the inner world. Matter is represented by the ether;[1] when the action of prāna is most subtle, this ether, in a finer state of vibration, will represent the mind, and there it will be still one unbroken mass. If you can create in yourself that subtle vibration, you will see and feel that the whole universe is composed of subtle vibrations. Sometimes certain drugs have the power to take us to a supersensuous state where we can feel those vibrations. Many of you may remember the celebrated experiment of Sir Humphry Davy, when the laughing-gas overpowered him—how, during the lecture, he remained motionless, stupefied, and how, after that, he said that the whole universe was made up of ideas. For the time being the gross vibrations had ceased and only the

---

[1] During the last part of the nineteenth century the concept of ether was much in vogue among certain scientists.

subtle vibrations, which he called ideas, were present to him. He could see only the subtle vibrations round him; everything had become thought; the whole universe was an ocean of thought, and he and everyone else had become little thought whirlpools.

Thus even in the universe of thought we find unity; and at last, when we get to the Self, we know that that Self can only be one. Beyond the vibrations of matter in its gross and subtle forms, beyond motion, there is but one. Even in manifested motion there is only unity. These facts can no longer be denied. Modern physics has demonstrated that the sum total of the energies in the universe is the same throughout. It has also been proved that this sum total of energy exists in two forms. It becomes potential, unmanifested, and next it becomes manifested as all these various forces; again it goes back to the quiet state, and again it manifests. Thus it goes on evolving and becoming involved through eternity. The control of this prāna, as before noted, is what is called prānāyāma.

As I have already stated, prānāyāma has very little to do with breathing. But the control of the breath is a means to the real practice of prānāyāma. The most obvious manifestation of prāna in the human body is the motion of the lungs. If that stops, as a rule all other manifestations of force in the body will immediately stop. But there are persons who can train themselves in such a manner that the body will live on, even when this motion has stopped. There are some persons who can bury themselves for days and yet live without breathing. To reach the subtle we must take the help of the gross, and slowly travel towards the most subtle until we gain our objective.

Prānāyāma really means controlling the motion of the lungs, and this motion is associated with the breath. Not that the breath produces it; on the contrary, it produces the breath. This motion draws in the air by pump action. Prāna moves the lungs; the movement of the lungs draws in the air. So prānāyāma is not breathing, but controlling that muscular power which moves the lungs. That muscular power which is transmitted through the nerves to the muscles and from them to the lungs, making them move in a certain manner, is the prāna we have to control through the practice of prānāyāma. When this prāna has become controlled, then we shall immediately find that all the other actions of prāna in the body will slowly come under control. I myself have seen men who have controlled almost every muscle of the body—and why not? If I can control certain muscles, why not every muscle and nerve of the body? What is impossible about that? At present we have lost that control and the motion has become automatic. We cannot move the ears at will, but we know that animals can. We do not have that power because we do not exercise it.

Again, we know that motion which has become latent can be made manifest. By hard work and practice certain motions of the body which are beyond our control can be brought under perfect control. Reasoning in this manner, we find that it is not at all impossible, but on the contrary very probable, that each part of the body can be brought under perfect control. This the yogi does through prānāyāma.

Perhaps some of you have read that in prānāyāma, when drawing in the breath, you must fill your whole body with prāna. In the English translation *prāna* is given as breath, and you are inclined to ask how that is to be done. The fault is with the translator. Every part of the body can be filled with prāna, the vital force; and when you are able to do that, you can control the whole body. All the sickness and misery felt in the body will be perfectly controlled. Not only so, but you will be able to control another's body. Everything is infectious in this world—good or bad. If your body is in a certain state of tension, it will have a tendency to produce the same tension in others. If you are strong and healthy, those who live near you will also have a tendency to become strong and healthy; but if you are sick and weak, those around you will have a tendency to become the same. In the case of one man's trying to heal another, the first step is simply to transfer his own health to the other. This is the primitive sort of healing. Consciously or unconsciously, health can be transmitted. A very strong man, living with a weak man, will make him feel a little stronger, whether he knows it or not. When consciously done this action becomes quicker and better. Next come those cases in which a person, though he may not be very healthy himself, yet can bring health to another. The first man, in such a case, has a little more control over his prāna, and for the time being can rouse his prāna to a certain state of vibration and transmit it to another person.

There have been cases where this process has been carried on at a distance. But in reality there is no distance which admits of gaps. Where is the distance with such gaps? Is there any gap between you and the sun? There is a continuous mass of matter, the sun being one part, and you another. Is there a gap between one part of a river and another? If not, then why cannot force travel? There is no reason why it cannot. Cases of healing from a distance are perfectly true. Prāna can be transmitted to a very great distance; but for one genuine case there are hundreds of frauds. This process of healing is not so easy as it is thought to be. In the most ordinary cases of such healing you will find that the healers simply take advantage of the naturally healthy state of the human body. An allopath comes and treats cholera patients and gives them his medicines; the homoeopath comes and gives his medicines, and cures perhaps more than the allopath cures, because the homoeopath does not disturb his patients, but allows nature to deal with them. The faith-healer cures still more, because he brings the strength of his mind to bear upon the patient and rouses, through faith, his dormant prāna.

There is a mistake constantly made by faith-healers; they think that faith directly heals a man. But faith alone does not do all the healing. There are diseases where the worst symptom is that the patient never thinks that he has the disease. That tremendous faith of the patient is itself a symptom of the disease and usually indicates that he will die quickly. In such a case the principle that faith cures does not apply. If faith alone cured, these patients also would be cured. It is prāna that really does the curing. The pure-souled man who has controlled his prāna has the power to bring it into a certain state of vibration which can be conveyed to others, arousing in them a similar vibration. You see that in our everyday actions. I am talking to you. What am I trying to do? I am, in reality, bringing my mind to a certain state of vibration, and the more I succeed in bringing it to that state, the more you will be affected by what I say. All of you know that the day I am more enthusiastic, you enjoy the lecture more, and when I am less enthusiastic you feel a lack of interest.

The world-movers, endowed with gigantic will-power, can bring their prāna into a high state of vibration; and it is so great and powerful that it affects others in a moment, and thousands are drawn towards them, and half the world think as they do. The great prophets of the world had the most wonderful control of their prāna, which gave them tremendous will-power; they had brought their prāna to the highest state of vibration, and this is what gave them power to sway the world. All manifestations of power arise from this control. Men may not know the secret, but this is the explanation.

Sometimes in your own body the supply of prāna gravitates more or less to one part; the balance is disturbed, and when the balance of prāna is disturbed, what we call disease is produced. To take away the superfluous prāna, or to supply the prāna that is wanting, will be to cure the disease. To perceive when there is more or less prāna in one part of the body than there should be is also a part of prānāyāma. The perception will be so subtle that the mind will feel that there is less prāna in the toe or the finger than there should be and will possess the power to supply it. These are among the various functions of prānāyāma. They have to be learnt slowly and gradually; and as you see, the whole scope of Rāja-yoga is really to teach the control and direction of prāna in different ways. When a man has concentrated his energies he masters the prāna that is in his body. When a man is meditating he is also controlling his prāna.

In an ocean there are huge waves, like mountains, then smaller waves, and still smaller, down to little bubbles; but back of all these is the infinite ocean. The ocean is connected with the bubble at one end, and with the huge wave at the other end. One man may be a gigantic wave, and another a little bubble, but each is connected with that infinite ocean of energy which is the common birthright of every being that exists. Wherever there is life, the storehouse of infinite energy is behind it. Starting as some fungus, some very minute, microscopic bubble, and all the time drawing from that infinite storehouse of energy, a form changes slowly and steadily, until, in the course of time, it becomes a plant, then an animal, then a man, and ultimately God. This is attained through millions of aeons. But what is time? An increase of speed, an increase of struggle, is able to bridge the gulf of time. That which naturally takes a long time to accomplish can be shortened by the intensity of the action, says the yogi. A man may go on slowly drawing in this energy from the infinite mass that exists in the universe, and perhaps he will require a hundred thousand years to become a deva, and then perhaps five hundred thousand years to become still higher, and perhaps five million years to become perfect. Given rapid growth, the time will be lessened. Why is it not possible, with sufficient effort, to reach this very perfection in six years or six months? There is no limit. Reason shows that. If an engine, with a certain amount of coal, runs two miles an hour, it will run the distance in less time with a greater supply of coal. Similarly, why should not the soul, by intensifying its action, attain perfection in this very life? All beings will at last attain to that goal, we know. But who cares to wait all these millions of aeons? Why not reach it immediately, even in this body, in this human form? Why should I not get that infinite knowledge, infinite power, now?

The ideal of the yogi, the whole science of Yoga, is directed to the end of teaching men how, by intensifying the power of assimilation, to shorten the time for reaching perfection instead of slowly advancing from point to point and waiting until the whole human race has become perfect. All the great prophets, saints, and seers of the world—what did they do? In one span of life they lived the whole life of humanity, traversed the whole length of time that it takes an ordinary man to come to perfection. In one life they perfected themselves; they had no thought for anything else, never lived a moment for any other idea, and thus the way was shortened for them. This is what is meant by concentration: intensifying the power of assimilation, thus shortening the time. Rāja-yoga is the science which teaches us how to gain the power of concentration.

What has prānāyāma to do with spiritualism? Spiritualism is also a manifestation of prānāyāma. If it be true that the departed spirits exist, only we cannot see them, it is quite probable that there are hundreds and millions of them about us that we can neither see, feel, nor touch. We may be continually passing and repassing through their bodies, and they do not see or feel us. It is plane within plane, universe within universe. We have five senses, and we represent prāna in a certain state of vibration. All beings in the same state of vibration will see one another; but if there are beings who represent prāna in a higher state of vibration, they will not be seen. We may increase the intensity of a light until we cannot see it at all, but there may be beings with eyes so powerful that they can see such a light. Again, if its vibrations are very low we do not see a light, but there are animals that can see it, such as cats and owls. Our range of vision is only one plane of the vibrations of prāna. Take the atmosphere, for instance: it is piled up layer on layer, but the layers nearer the earth are denser than those above, and as you go higher the atmosphere becomes finer and finer. Or take the ocean: as you go deeper and deeper the pressure of the water increases, and the animals which live at the bottom of the sea can never come up, or they will be broken into pieces.

Think of the whole universe as an ocean of ether, vibrating under the action of prāna and consisting of plane after plane of varying degrees of vibration. In the more external the vibrations are slower, and nearer the centre they are quicker. Think of the whole thing as a circle, the centre of which is perfection. The farther you move from the centre, the slower are the vibrations. Matter is the outermost plane; next comes mind; and Spirit is the centre. Now, it is clear that those who live on a certain plane of vibration will have the power to recognize each other but will not recognize those above or below them. Yet, just as by the telescope and the microscope we can increase the scope of our vision, similarly by yoga we can bring ourselves to the state of vibration of another plane and thus enable ourselves to see what is going on there.

Suppose this room is full of beings whom we do not see. They represent prāna in a certain state of vibration, while we represent another. Suppose they represent a quick one, and we the opposite. Prāna is the material of which they are composed, as well as we. We are all parts of the same ocean of prāna, and we differ only in the rate of vibration. If I can bring myself to the quick vibration, this plane will immediately change for me; I shall not see you any more; they will appear. Some of you, perhaps, know this to be true. All this bringing of the mind into a higher state of vibration is included in one word in Yoga: samādhi. All these states of higher vibration, superconscious vibrations of the mind, are indicated by that one word samādhi; and the lower states of samādhi give us visions of these supernatural beings. In the highest kind of samādhi we see the real thing, we see the material out of which all these classes of beings are composed. One lump of clay being known, we know all the objects made of clay in the universe.

Thus we see that prānāyāma includes all that is true even of spiritualism. Similarly, you will find that wherever any sect or body of people is trying to discover anything occult, mysterious, or hidden, they are really practising some sort of yoga, attempting to control their prāna. You will find that wherever there is any extraordinary display of power, it is the manifestation of prāna. Even the physical sciences can be included in prānāyāma. What moves the steam-engine? Prāna acting through the steam. What are all these phenomena of electricity and so forth but prāna? What is physical science? The science of prānāyāma by external means. Prāna, manifesting itself as mental power, can only be controlled by mental means. That part of prānāyāma which attempts to control the physical manifestations of prāna by physical means is called physical science, and that part which tries to control the manifestations of prāna as mental force, by mental means, is called Rāja-yoga.

THE PSYCHIC PRĀNA

ACCORDING TO THE YOGIS there are two nerve currents in the spinal column called the Pingalā and the Idā, and a hollow canal called the Sushumnā running through the spinal cord. At the lower end of the canal is what the yogis call the "lotus of the Kundalini." They describe it as triangular in form. In it, in the symbolical language of the yogis, there is coiled up a power called the Kundalini. When the Kundalini awakes, it tries to force a passage through this hollow canal; and as it rises step by step, as it were, layer after layer of the mind opens up and many different visions and wonderful powers come to the yogi. When it reaches the brain, the yogi becomes perfectly detached from the body and mind; the soul realizes its freedom.

We know that the spinal cord is shaped in a peculiar manner. If we take the figure eight horizontally (∞), we see two parts, which are connected in the middle. Now if you pile up a number of eights, one on top of another, that will represent the spinal cord. The left side is the Idā, the right is the Pingalā, and that hollow canal which runs through the centre of the spinal cord is the Sushumnā. Where the spinal cord ends in some of the lumbar vertebrae, a fine fibre issues downwards, and the canal runs even through that fibre, only much finer. The canal is closed at the lower end, situated near what is called the sacral plexus, which, according to modern physiology, is triangular in form. The different plexuses that have their centres in the spinal canal can very well stand for the different "lotuses" of the yogi.

The yogi describes several centres, beginning with the Mulādhāra, the basic, and ending with the Sahasrāra, the thousand-petalled lotus in the brain. So if we take the different plexuses as representing these lotuses, the idea of the yogi can be understood very easily in the language of modern physiology. We know that there are two sorts of actions in the nerve currents: one afferent, and the other efferent; one sensory, and the other motor; one centripetal, and the other centrifugal. One carries the sensations to the brain, and the other, from the brain to the outer parts of the body. In the long run these vibrations are all connected with the brain.

There are several other facts which we have to remember in order to clear the way for the explanation which is to come. The spinal cord, at the brain, ends in a sort of bulb in the medulla, which is not attached to the brain but floats in a fluid in the brain, so that if there is a blow on the head the force of that blow will be dissipated in the fluid and will not hurt the bulb. This is an important fact to remember. Secondly, we have also to remember that, of all the centres, three are particularly important: the Mulādhāra (the basic), the Sahasrāra (the thousand-petalled lotus in the brain), and the Manipura (the lotus at the navel).

Next we shall take one fact from physics. We all hear of electricity and various other forces connected with it. What electricity is no one knows, but so far as it is known, it is a sort of motion. There are various other motions in the universe. What is the difference between them and electricity? Suppose that this table moves and that the molecules which compose this table are moving in different directions; but if they are all made to move in the same direction, then this motion will be electricity. Electricity becomes manifest when the molecules of a body move in the same direction. If all the air molecules in a room are made to move in the same direction, that will make a gigantic battery of electricity of the room.

Another point we must remember—from physiology—is that the nerve centre which regulates the respiratory system, the breathing system, has a controlling action over the whole system of nerve currents. Now we can see why rhythmical breathing is practised. In the first place, from it comes a tendency of all the molecules in the body to move in the same direction. When the mind, by nature distracted, becomes one-pointed and thus is changed into a strong will, the nerve currents, too, change into a motion similar to electricity; for the nerves have been proved to show polarity under the action of electric currents. This shows that when the will is transformed into the nerve currents it changes into something like electricity. Therefore when all the motions of the body have become perfectly rhythmical, the body becomes a gigantic battery of will. This tremendous will is exactly what the yogi wants to acquire. This is, therefore, the physiological explanation of prāṇāyāma; it tends to bring a rhythmic action in the body, and helps us, through the respiratory centre, to control the other centres. The aim of prāṇāyāma is to rouse the coiled-up power in the Mulādhāra, called the Kundalini.

Everything that we see or imagine or dream, we have to perceive in space. This is the ordinary space, called the mahākāśa, or physical space. When a yogi reads the thoughts of other men or perceives supersensuous objects, he sees them in another sort of space, called the chittākāśa, the mental space. When perception has become objectless and the Soul shines in Its own nature, it is called the Chidākāśa, or Knowledge space. When the Kundalini is aroused and enters the canal of the Sushumnā, all the perceptions are in the mental space. When it has reached that end of the canal which opens out into the brain, the objectless perception is in the Knowledge space.

Taking the analogy of electricity, we find that man can send a current only along a wire,[1] but nature requires no wires to send her tremendous currents. This proves that the wire is not really necessary; only our inability to dispense with it compels us to use it. Similarly, all the sensations and motions of the body are being sent into the brain, and sent out of it, through these wires of the nerve fibres. The columns of the sensory and motor fibres in the spinal cord are the Iḍā and Pingalā of the yogis. They are the main channels through which the afferent and efferent currents travel. But why should not the mind send news without any wire or react without any wire? We see this done in

---

[1] The reader should remember that this was said before the discovery of wireless telegraphy.

nature. The yogi says that if you can do that you have got rid of the bondage of matter. How can you do it? If you can make the current pass through the Sushumnā, the canal in the middle of the spinal column, you have solved the problem. The mind has made this network of the nervous system, and it has to break it so that no wires will be required to work through. Then alone will all knowledge come to us—no more bondage of the body. That is why it is so important that we should get control of the Sushumnā. If we can send the mental current through that hollow canal without any nerve fibres to act as wires, the yogi says, the problem is solved. And he also says it can be done. This Sushumnā is in ordinary persons closed up at the lower extremity; no current comes through it. The yogi proposes a practice by which it can be opened and the nerve currents made to travel through it.

When a sensation is carried to a centre, the centre reacts. This reaction, in the automatic centres, is followed by motion; in the conscious centres it is followed first by perception and secondly by motion. All perception is the reaction to action from outside. How, then, do perceptions in dreams arise? There is then no action from outside. The sensations must therefore have been coiled up somewhere. For instance, I see a city. The perception of that city is from my reaction to the sensations brought from outside objects comprising that city. That is to say, a certain motion in the brain molecules has been set up by the motion in the in-carrying nerves, which, again, are set in motion by external objects in the city. Now, even after a long time I can remember the city. Dreams are exactly the same phenomena, only in a milder form. But whence is the action that set up even the milder form of similar vibrations in the brain? Certainly not from the primary sensations. Therefore it must be that the sensations are coiled up somewhere, and by their action bring out the mild reaction which we call dream perception.

Now, the centre where all these residual sensations are, as it were, stored up, is called the Mulādhāra, the root receptacle, and the coiled-up energy of action is the Kundalini, the "coiled up." It is very probable that the residual motor energy is also stored up in the same centre, since, after deep study or meditation on external objects, the part of the body where the Mulādhāra centre is situated—probably the sacral plexus—gets heated. Now, if this coiled-up energy is roused and made active and then consciously made to travel up the Sushumnā canal, as it acts upon centre after centre, a tremendous reaction will set in. When a minute portion of energy travels along a nerve fibre and causes a reaction from the centres, the perception is either dream or imagination. But when by the power of long internal meditation the vast mass of energy stored up travels along the Sushumnā and strikes the centres, the reaction is tremendous, immensely superior to the reaction of dream or imagination, immensely more intense than the reaction of sense perception. It is supersensuous perception. And when it reaches the metropolis of all sensations, the brain, the whole brain, as it were, reacts, and the result is the full blaze of illumination, the perception of the Self. As this Kundalini force travels from centre to centre, layer after layer of the mind, as it were, opens up, and the universe is perceived by the yogi in its fine, or causal, form. Then alone are the causes of the universe, both as sensation and as reaction, known as they are; and hence comes all knowledge. The causes being known, the knowledge of the effects is sure to follow.

Thus the rousing of the Kundalini is the one and only way to the attaining of divine wisdom, superconscious perception, realization of the Spirit. The rousing may come in various ways: through love for God, through the mercy of perfected sages, or through the power of the analytic will of the philosopher. Wherever there has been any manifestation of what is ordinarily called super-natural power or wisdom, there a little current of the Kundalini must have found its way into the Sushumnā. Only, in the vast majority of such cases, the people had ignorantly stumbled on some practice which set free a minute portion of the coiled-up Kundalini. All worship, consciously or unconsciously, leads to this end. The man who thinks that he is receiving a response to his prayers does not know that the fulfilment comes from his own nature, that he has succeeded, by the mental attitude of prayer, in waking up a bit of this infinite power which is coiled up within himself. Thus what men ignorantly worship under various names, through fear and tribulation, the yogi declares to the world to be the real power coiled up in every being, the Mother of eternal happiness. And Rāja-yoga is the science of religion, the rationale of all worship, all prayers, forms, ceremonies, and miracles.

THE CONTROL OF THE PSYCHIC PRĀNA

WE HAVE NOW to deal with the exercises in prāṇāyāma. We have seen that the first step, according to the yogis, is to control the motion of the lungs. What we want to do is to feel the finer motions that are going on in the body. Our minds have become externalized and have lost sight of the fine motions inside. If we can begin to feel them, we can also begin to control them. These nerve currents flow all through the body, bringing life and vitality to every muscle; but we do not feel them. The yogi says that we can learn to do so. How? It is by controlling the motion of the lungs. When we have done that for a sufficient length of time we shall be able to control the finer motions in the body.

We now come to the exercises in prāṇāyāma. Sit upright; the body must be kept straight. The spinal cord, although not attached to the vertebral column, is yet inside it. If you sit crookedly you disturb the spinal cord; so let it be free. Any time that you sit crookedly and try to meditate you do yourself an injury. The three parts of the body—the chest, the neck, and the head—must always be held straight, in one line. You will find that by a little practice this will come to you as easily as breathing. The second thing is to get control of the nerves. We have said that the nerve centre that controls the respiratory organs has a sort of controlling effect on the other nerves, and rhythmical breathing is therefore necessary. The way we generally breathe should not be called breathing at all; it is very irregular. Then there are some natural differences of breathing between men and women.

The first lesson is to breathe, in a measured way, in and out. That will harmonize the system. When you have practised this for some time, you may repeat along with your breathing the word Om, or any other sacred word. In India we use certain symbolical words to measure the periods of inhalation and exhalation, instead of counting one, two, etc. That is why I advise you to mentally repeat a sacred word while you practise. Let the word flow in and out with the breath, rhythmically, and you will find that the whole body is becoming rhythmical. Then you will enjoy real rest. Compared with it, sleep is no rest. Once this rest comes, the most tired nerves will be calmed down and you will find that you have never before really rested.

The first effect of this practice is perceived in a change of expression in one's face. Harsh lines disappear; with calm thought, calmness comes over the face. Next comes a beautiful voice. I never saw a yogi with a croaking voice. These signs come after a few months' practice.

After practising the above-mentioned breathing for a few days, you should take up a higher one. Slowly fill the lungs with breath through the left nostril, and at the same time concentrate the mind on the Iḍā, the left nerve current. You are, as it were, sending the nerve current down the spinal column and striking violently the last plexus, the basic lotus, which is triangular in form, the seat of the Kundalini. Then hold the current there for some time. Next imagine that you are slowly drawing that nerve current, with the breath, through the other side, the Pingalā; then slowly exhale it through the right nostril. This you will find a little difficult. The easiest way is to stop the right nostril with the thumb and then slowly draw in the breath through the left; then close both nostrils with thumb and forefinger, and imagine that you are sending that current down and striking the base of the Sushumnā; then take the thumb off and let the breath out through the right nostril. Next inhale slowly through that nostril, keeping the other closed with the forefinger; then close both, as before.

The way the Hindus practise this would be very difficult for the people of this country, because they do it from their childhood and their lungs are prepared for it. Here it is well to begin with four seconds and slowly increase. Draw in for four seconds, hold in for sixteen seconds, then exhale in eight seconds. This makes one prānāyāma. At the same time think of the basic lotus, triangular in form; concentrate the mind on that centre. The imagination can help you a great deal.

The next exercise is slowly to draw the breath in and then immediately exhale it slowly, and then stop the breath altogether, using the same numbers. The only difference is that in the first case the breath is held in, and in the second, held out. This last is the easier one. The exercise in which you hold the breath in the lungs must not be practised too much. Do it only four times in the morning and four times in the evening. Then you can slowly increase the time and number. You will find that you have the power to do so and that you take pleasure in it. So, very carefully and cautiously increase the number, as you feel that you have the power, to six instead of four. It may injure you if you practise it irregularly.

Of the three processes for the control of prāna, described above, the first and the last are neither difficult nor dangerous. The more you practise the first one, the calmer you will be. Repeat Om as you breathe; you can practise even while you are sitting at your work. You will be all the better for it. Some day, if you practise hard, the Kundalini will be aroused. For those who practise once or twice a day, just a little calmness of body and mind will ensue, and a beautiful voice. Only for those who can go on farther with it will the Kundalini be aroused. Then the whole of nature will begin to change and the door of knowledge will open. No more will you need to go to books for knowledge; your own mind will have become your book, containing infinite knowledge.

I have already spoken of the Idā and Pingalā currents, flowing through either side of the spinal column, and also of the Sushumnā, the passage through the centre of the spinal cord. These three are present in every animal—whatever creature has a spinal column. But the yogis claim that in ordinary beings the Sushumnā is closed, its action is not evident, while that of the other two carries power to different parts of the body.

For the yogi alone the Sushumnā opens. When the current begins to rise through the Sushumnā, we go beyond the senses, and our minds become supersensuous, superconscious; we go beyond even the intellect, where reasoning cannot reach. To open the Sushumnā is the prime object of the yogi. According to him, along the Sushumnā are ranged the centres, or, in the figurative language of Yoga, lotuses. The lowest one is at the bottom of the spinal cord and is called the Mulādhāra, the next higher is called the Svādhisthāna, the third the Manipura, the fourth the Anāhata, the fifth the Viśuddha, the sixth the Ājnā, and the last, which is in the brain, is called the Sahasrāra, or "thousand-petalled." Of these we have to take cognizance just now of two centres only: the lowest, the Mulādhāra, and the highest, the Sahasrāra. All the energy has to be taken up from its seat in the Mulādhāra and brought to the Sahasrāra.

The yogis claim that, of all the energies that are in the human body, the highest is what they call ojas. Now, this ojas is stored up in the brain, and the more ojas a man has, the more powerful he is, the more intellectual, the more spiritually strong. One man may express beautiful thoughts in beautiful language, but cannot impress people. Another man may not be able to give beautiful expression to his thoughts, yet his words charm; every movement of his is powerful. That is the power of ojas.

Now, in every man there is stored up more or less of this ojas. The highest form of all the forces that are working in the body is ojas. You must remember that it is only a question of transformation of one force into another. The same force which is working outside as electricity or magnetism will be changed into inner force; the same force that is working as muscular energy will be changed into ojas. The yogis say that that part of the human energy which is expressed through sexual action and sexual thought, when checked and controlled, easily becomes changed into ojas; and since the Mulādhāra guides these, the yogi pays particular attention to that centre. He tries to convert all his sexual energy into ojas. It is only the chaste man or woman who can create ojas and store it in the brain; that is why chastity has always been considered the highest virtue. A man feels that if he is unchaste, his spirituality goes away; he loses mental vigour and moral stamina. That is why, in all the religious orders in the world which have produced spiritual giants, you will always find absolute chastity insisted upon. That is why there came into existence monks, who gave up marriage. There must be perfect chastity in thought, word, and deed. Without it the practice of rāja-yoga is dangerous and may lead to insanity. If people practise rāja-yoga and at the same time lead an impure life, how can they expect to become yogis?

PRATYĀHĀRA AND DHĀRANĀ

THE NEXT STEP is called pratyāhāra. What is this? You know how perceptions arise. First of all there are the external instruments, then the internal organs, functioning in the body through the brain centres, and last there is the mind. When these join together and attach themselves to some external object, then we perceive it. At the same time it is very difficult to concentrate the mind and attach it to one organ only; the mind is a slave of physical objects.

We hear "Be good," "Be good," "Be good," taught all over the world. There is hardly a child born in any country in the world who has not been told, "Do not steal," "Do not tell a lie"; but nobody tells the child how he can avoid stealing or lying. Talking will not help him. Why should he not become a thief? We do not teach him how not to steal; we simply tell him, "Do not steal." Only when we teach him how to control his mind do we really help him.

All actions, internal and external, occur when the mind joins itself to certain centres, called organs. Willingly or unwillingly people join their minds to the centres, and that is why they do foolish deeds and feel miserable. But if the mind were under control they would not do so. What would be the result of controlling the mind? It then would not join itself to the centres of perception, and naturally feeling and willing would be under control. It is clear so far. But is this possible? Certainly it is; you see it practised in modern times. The faith-healers teach people to deny misery and pain and evil. Their philosophy is rather roundabout, but it is a part of yoga upon which they have somehow stumbled. Where they succeed in making a person throw off suffering by denying it, they really use a part of pratyāhāra, for they make the mind of the person strong enough to ignore the senses. The hypnotists, in a similar manner, by their suggestion excite in the patient a sort of morbid pratyāhāra for the time being. So-called hypnotic suggestion can act only upon a weak mind; and until the operator, by means of fixed gaze or something else, has succeeded in putting the mind of the subject in a sort of passive, morbid condition, his suggestions never work.

Now, the control of the centres which for a time is established in a patient, whether by a hypnotist or by a faith-healer, is reprehensible, because it leads to ultimate ruin. It is not really controlling the brain centres by the power of the patient's own will, but it is, as it were, stunning his mind for a time by sudden blows which another's will delivers to it. It is not checking the mad career of a fiery team by means of reins and muscular strength, but rather by asking another to deliver heavy blows on the heads of the horses in order to stun them for a time into gentleness. By each one of these processes the man operated upon loses a part of his mental energies, till at last his mind, instead

607

of gaining the power of perfect control, becomes a shapeless, powerless mass and the only destination of the patient is the lunatic asylum.

Every attempt at control which is not voluntary, not made with the individual's own will, not only is disastrous but defeats its own end. The goal of each soul is freedom, mastery—freedom from the slavery of matter and thought, mastery of external and internal nature. Instead of leading towards that, every will-current from another, in whatever form it comes, either directly controlling the organs or forcing one to control them while under a morbid condition, only rivets one more link to the already existing heavy chain of the bondage of past thoughts, past superstitions. Therefore beware how you allow yourselves to be acted upon by others. Beware how you unknowingly bring another to ruin. True, some succeed in doing good to many, for a time, by giving a new trend to their propensities; but at the same time they bring ruin to millions by the unconscious suggestions they throw around, rousing in men and women that morbid, passive, hypnotic condition which makes them at last almost soulless.

Whosoever asks anyone to believe blindly, or drags people behind him by the controlling power of his superior will, does an injury to humanity, though he may not intend it. Therefore use your own minds, control body and mind yourselves, and remember that unless you are a diseased person no extraneous will can work upon you. Avoid everyone, however great and good he may be, who asks you to believe blindly.

All over the world there have been dancing and jumping and howling sects, whose influence spreads like infection as they sing and dance and preach; they too are a sort of hypnotists. They exercise a singular control for the time being over sensitive persons—alas! often, in the long run, to degenerate whole races. Ay, it is healthier for the individual or the race to remain wicked than to be made apparently good by such morbid, extraneous control. One's heart sinks to think of the amount of injury done to humanity by such irresponsible yet well-meaning religious fanatics. They little know that the minds which attain to sudden spiritual upheaval under their suggestions, with music and prayers, are simply making themselves passive, morbid, and powerless and opening themselves to any other suggestion, be it ever so evil. Little do these ignorant, deluded persons dream that, while they are congratulating themselves upon their miraculous power to transform human hearts, which power they think was poured upon them by some Being above the clouds, they are sowing the seeds of future decay, of crime, of lunacy, and of death. Therefore beware of everything that takes away your freedom. Know that it is dangerous and avoid it by all the means in your power.

He who has succeeded in attaching or detaching his mind to or from the centres at will has succeeded in pratyāhāra, which means "gathering towards," checking the outgoing powers of the mind, freeing it from the thraldom of the senses. When we can do this we shall really possess character. Then we shall have taken a long step towards freedom; before that we are mere machines.

How hard it is to control the mind! Well has it been compared to the maddened monkey in the story. There was a monkey, restless by his own nature, as all monkeys are. As if that were not enough, someone made him drink freely of wine, so that he became still more restless. Then a scorpion stung him. When a man is stung by a scorpion he jumps about for a whole day; so the poor monkey found his condition worse than ever. To complete his misery a demon entered into him. What language can describe the uncontrollable restlessness of the monkey? The human mind is like that monkey. Incessantly active by its own nature, it then becomes drunk with the wine of desire, thus increasing its turbulence. After desire has taken possession, comes the sting of the scorpion of jealousy at the success of others; and last of all the demon of pride enters the mind, making it think itself all-important. How hard to control such a mind!

The first lesson, then, is to sit for some time and let the mind run on. The mind is bubbling up all the time. It is like that monkey jumping about. Let the monkey jump as much as he can; you simply wait and watch. Knowledge is power, says the proverb, and that is true. Until you know what the mind is doing you cannot control it. Give it the rein. Many hideous thoughts may come into it; you will be astonished that it was possible for you to harbour such thoughts; but you will find that each day the mind's vagaries are becoming less and less violent, that each day it is becoming calmer. In the first few months you will find that the mind has a great many thoughts; later you will find that they have somewhat decreased, and in a few more months they will be fewer and fewer, until at last the mind is under perfect control. But you must patiently practise every day. As long as the steam is there, the engine must run; as long as things are before us, we must perceive them. So a man, to prove that he is not a machine, must demonstrate that he is under the control of nothing. This controlling of the mind and not allowing it to join itself to the centres is pratyāhāra. How is this practised? It is a tremendous work; it cannot be done in a day. Only after a patient, continuous struggle for years can we succeed.

After you have practised pratyāhāra for a time, take the next step, dhāranā, holding the mind to certain points. What is meant by holding the mind to certain points? Forcing the mind to feel certain parts of the body to the exclusion of others. For instance, try to feel only the hand, to the exclusion of other parts of the body. When the chitta, or mind-stuff, is confined and limited to a certain place, it is dhāranā. This dhāranā is of various sorts, and along with it, it is better to have a little play of the imagination. For instance, the mind should be made to think of one point in the heart. That is very difficult; an easier way is to imagine a lotus there. That lotus is full of light— effulgent light. Put the mind there. Or think of the lotus in the brain as full of light, or of the different centres in the Sushumnā mentioned before.

The yogi must always practise. He should try to live alone; the companionship of different sorts of people distracts the mind. He should not speak much, because to speak distracts the mind; not work much, because too much work distracts the mind; the mind cannot be controlled after a whole day's hard work. One observing the above rules becomes a yogi.

Such is the power of yoga that even the least of it will bring a great amount of benefit. It will not hurt anyone but will benefit everyone. First of all, it will calm down nervous excitement, bring peace, enable us to see things more clearly. The temperament will be better and the health will be better. Sound health will be one of the first signs, and a beautiful voice. Defects in the voice will be changed. This will be among the first of the many effects that will come. Those who practise hard will get many other signs. Sometimes there will be sounds, as of a peal of bells heard at a distance, commingling and falling on the ear as one continuous sound. Sometimes things will be seen—little specks of light floating and becoming bigger and bigger; and when these things appear, know that you are progressing fast. Those who want to be yogis and to practise hard must be careful about their diet at first. But those who want only a little practice for an everyday, business sort of life—let them not eat too much; otherwise they may eat whatever they please.

For those who want to make rapid progress and to practise hard a strict diet is absolutely necessary. They will find it advantageous to live only on milk and cereals for some months. As the bodily organization becomes finer and finer, it will be found in the beginning that the least irregularity throws one out of balance. One bit of food more or less will disturb the whole system, until one gets perfect control, and then one will be able to eat whatever one likes. When one begins to concentrate, the dropping of a pin will seem like a thunderbolt going through the brain. As the organs get finer, the perceptions get finer. These are stages through which we have to pass, and all those who persevere will succeed. Give up all argumentation and other distractions. Is there anything in dry, intellectual jargon? It only throws the mind off its balance and disturbs it. The things of the subtler planes have to be realized. Will talking do that? So give up all vain talk. Read only those books which have been written by persons who have had spiritual experiences.

Be like the pearl-oyster. There is a pretty Indian fable to the effect that if it rains when the star Svāti is in the ascendant, and a drop of rain falls into an oyster, that drop becomes a pearl. The oysters know this; so they come to the surface when that star appears, and wait to catch the precious raindrops. When the drops fall into them, quickly the oysters close their shells and dive down to the bottom of the sea, there patiently to develop the raindrops into pearls. You should be like that. First hear, then understand, and then, leaving all distractions, shut your minds to outside influences and devote yourselves to developing the truth within you. There is a danger of frittering away your energies by taking up an idea only for its novelty and then giving it up for another that is newer. Take one thing up and follow it, and see the end of it, and before you have seen the end, do not give it up. He who can become mad with an idea, he alone sees the light. Those who only take a nibble here and a nibble there will never attain anything. They may titillate their nerves for a moment, but there it will end. They will be slaves in the hands of nature and will never go beyond the senses.

Those who really want to be yogis must give up, once for all, this nibbling at things. Take up one idea; make that one idea your life. Think of it, dream of it, live on that idea. Let the brain, muscles, nerves, every part of your body, be full of that idea, and just leave all other ideas alone. This is the way to success and this is the way great spiritual giants are produced. Others are mere talking-machines. If we really want to be blessed and make others blessed, we must go deeper.

The first step is not to disturb the mind, not to associate with persons whose ideas are disturbing. All of you know that certain persons, certain places, certain foods, repel you. Avoid them; and those who want to realize the highest must avoid all company, good or bad. Practise hard; whether you live or die does not matter. You have to plunge in and work without thinking of the result. If you are brave enough, in six months you will be a perfect yogi. But those who take up just a bit of it and a little of everything else make no progress. It is of no use simply to take a course of lessons. To those who are full of tamas, ignorant and dull—those whose minds never get fixed on any idea, who only crave for something to amuse them—religion and philosophy are simply objects of entertainment. These are the unpersevering. They hear a talk, think it very nice, and then go home and forget all about it. To succeed you must have tremendous perseverance, tremendous will. "I will drink the ocean," says the persevering soul, "and at my will mountains will crumble." Have that sort of energy, that sort of will, work hard, and you will reach the goal.

DHYĀNA AND SAMĀDHI

WE HAVE TAKEN a cursory view of the different steps in Rāja-yoga except the finer ones, the training in concentration, which is the goal to which Rāja-yoga will lead us. We see, as human beings, that all our knowledge which is called rational is referred to consciousness. My consciousness of this table and of your presence makes me know that the table and you are here. At the same time, there is a very great part of my existence of which I am not conscious: all the different organs inside the body, the different parts of the brain—nobody is conscious of these.

When I eat food I do it consciously; when I assimilate it I do it unconsciously; when the food is manufactured into blood, it is done unconsciously; when out of the blood all the different parts of my body are strengthened, it is done unconsciously. And yet it is I who am doing all this; there cannot be twenty people in this one body. How do I know that I do it, and nobody else? It may be urged that my business is only to eat and assimilate the food, and that the strengthening of the body by the food is done for me by somebody else. That cannot be; because it can be demonstrated that almost every action of which we are now unconscious can be brought up to the plane of consciousness. The heart is beating apparently without our control; none of us can control the heart; it goes on its own way. But by practice men can bring even the heart under control, until it will just beat at will, slowly or quickly, or almost stop. Nearly every part of the body can be brought under control. What does this show? That the functions which are beneath consciousness are also performed by us, only we are performing them unconsciously. We have, then, two planes in which the human mind works. First is the conscious plane, in which all work is always accompanied by the feeling of "I." Next comes the unconscious plane, where the work is unaccompanied by the feeling of "I." That part of the mind's work which is unaccompanied by egoity is unconscious work, and that part which is accompanied by egoity is conscious work. In the lower animals this unconscious work is called instinct. In higher animals, and in the highest of all animals, man, what is called conscious work prevails.

But the matter does not end here. There is a still higher plane on which the mind can work. It can go beyond consciousness. Just as unconscious work is beneath consciousness, so there is another sort of work which is above consciousness and which also is not accompanied by egoity. The feeling of "I" is only on the middle plane. When the mind is above or below that plane, there is no feeling of "I," and yet the mind works. When the mind goes beyond the plane of self-consciousness, it experiences samādhi, or superconsciousness. But how do we know that a man in samādhi has not gone below consciousness, has not degenerated instead of going higher? In both cases the experience is unaccompanied by the feeling of "I." The answer is that by the effects, by the results of the work, we know which is below and which is above. When a man goes into deep sleep he enters a plane beneath consciousness. His body functions all the time: he breathes, perhaps he moves the body in his sleep, without any accompanying feeling of "I"; he is unconscious, and when he returns from his sleep he is the same man who went into it. The sum total of the knowledge which he had before he went to sleep remains the same; it does not increase at all. No enlightenment comes. But when a man goes into samādhi, if he goes into it a fool, he comes out a sage.

What makes the difference? From one state a man comes out the very same man that went in, and from the other state the man comes out enlightened: a sage, a prophet, a saint—his whole character changed, his life changed, illumined. These are two different effects. Now that being so, the causes must be different. As this illumination with which a man comes back from samādhi is much higher than can be got from unconsciousness, or much higher than can be got by reasoning in a conscious state, it must therefore be superconsciousness, and so samādhi is called the superconscious state.

This, in short, is the idea of samādhi. What is its application? The application is here. The field of reason, or of the conscious working of the mind, is narrow and limited. There is a little circle within which human reason must move. It cannot go beyond. Every attempt to go beyond is futile. Yet it is beyond this circle of reason that there lies all that humanity holds most dear. All these questions—whether there is an immortal Soul, whether there is a God, whether there is any supreme Intelligence guiding this universe, or not—are beyond the field of reason. Reason can never answer these questions. What does reason say? It says, "I am an agnostic; I do not know either yea or nay." Yet these questions are very important to us. Without a proper answer to them human life will be purposeless.

All our ethical theories, all our moral attitudes, all that is good and great in human nature, have been moulded by answers that have come from beyond the circle. It is very important, therefore, that we should have answers to these questions. If life is only a short play, if the universe is only a "fortuitous combination of atoms," then why should I do good to another? Why should there be mercy, justice, or fellow-feeling? The best thing for men in this world would be to make hay while the sun shines, each man for himself. If there is no hope, why should I love my brother and not cut his throat? If there is nothing beyond, if there is no freedom, but only rigorous, dead law, I should only try to make myself happy here. You will find people saying, nowadays, that they make utility the basis of morality. What is this basis? The procuring of the greatest amount of happiness for the greatest number. Why should I do this? Why should I not procure the greatest unhappiness for the greatest number, if that serves my purpose? How will utilitarians answer this question? How do you know what is right or what is wrong? I am impelled by my desire for happiness; I fulfil it because it is my nature to do so; I know nothing beyond. I have these desires and must fulfil them. Why should you complain? Whence come all these truths about human life, about morality, about the immortal Soul, about God, about love and sympathy, about being good, and above all, about being unselfish?

All ethics, all human action, and all human thought hang upon this one idea of unselfishness; the whole ideal of human life can be put into that one word unselfishness. Why should we be unselfish? Where is the necessity, the force, the power, that compels me to be unselfish? You call yourself a rational man, a utilitarian, but if you do not show me a reason for your utility, I say you are irrational. Show me the reason why I should not be selfish. To ask one to be unselfish may be good as poetry; but poetry is not the reason. Show me the reason: Why should I be unselfish, and why good? Because Mr. and Mrs. So-and-so say this does not weigh with me. Where is the utility in my being unselfish? If utility means the greatest amount of happiness, for me utility means to be selfish. What is the answer? The utilitarian can never give it. Where did those who preached unselfishness and taught it to the human race get this idea from? We know it is not instinctive; the animals, which act through instinct, do not know it. Neither has it come from reason; reason does not know much about such ideas. Whence, then, did they come?

We find, in studying history, that one fact is held in common by all the great teachers of religion the world has ever had: they all claim to have got their truths from beyond; only many of them did not know where they got them from. For instance, one would say that an angel came down, in the form of a human being with wings, and said to him: "Hear, O man! This is the message." Another says that a deva, a bright being, appeared to him. A third says that he dreamt that his ancestor came and told him certain things; he did not know anything beyond that. But this is common: all claim that this knowledge has come to them from beyond, not through their reasoning power. What does the science of Yoga teach? It teaches that they were right in claiming that all this knowledge came to them from beyond reasoning, but also that it came from within themselves.

The yogi teaches that the mind itself has a higher state of existence, beyond reason, a superconscious state, and that when the mind rises to that state, then this knowledge, which is beyond reason, comes—metaphysical and transcendental knowledge comes to that man. This state of going beyond reason, beyond ordinary human knowledge, may sometimes come by chance to a man who does not understand its science; he stumbles upon it, as it were. When he stumbles upon it, he generally interprets it as coming from outside. So this explains why an inspiration, or transcendental knowledge, may be the same in different countries, but in one country it will seem to come through an angel, and in another through a deva, and in a third through God. What does it mean? It means that the mind brought out the knowledge from within itself and that the manner of finding it was interpreted according to the beliefs and education of the person through whom it came. The real fact is that these various men stumbled, as it were, upon this superconscious state.

The yogi says that there is a great danger in stumbling upon this state. In a good many cases there is the danger of the brain's being deranged; and as a rule you will find that all those men, however great they were, who stumbled upon this superconscious state without understanding it groped in the dark and generally had, along with their knowledge, some quaint superstitions. They opened themselves to hallucinations. Mohammed claimed that the Angel Gabriel came to him in a cave one day and took him on the heavenly horse Harak to visit the heavens. But with all that, Mohammed spoke some wonderful truths. If you read the Koran, you find the most wonderful truths mixed with superstitions. How will you explain it? The man was inspired, no doubt, but that inspiration was, as it were, stumbled upon. He was not a trained yogi and did not know the reason for what he was doing. Think of the good Mohammed did to the world, and think of the great evil that has been done through his fanaticism! Think of the millions massacred through his teachings— mothers bereft of their children, children made orphans, whole countries destroyed, millions upon millions of people killed!

So we see this danger when we study the life of a great teacher like Mohammed: Whenever a prophet got into the superconscious state by heightening his emotional nature, he brought away from it not only some truths but some fanaticism also, some superstition which injured the world as much as the greatness of the teaching helped it. Yet we find, at the same time, that all the great teachers were inspired. To get any meaning out of the mass of incongruity we call human life, we have to transcend our reason; but we must do it scientifically, slowly, by regular practice, and we must cast off all superstition. We must take up the study of the superconscious state just like any other science. On reason we must lay our foundation. We must follow reason as far as it leads, and when reason fails, reason itself will show us the way to the highest plane. When you hear a man say, "I am inspired," and then talk irrationally, reject him. Why? Because these three states—instinct, reason, and superconsciousness, or the unconscious, conscious, and superconscious—belong to one and the same mind. There are not three minds in one man, but one state of the mind develops into the others. Instinct develops into reason, and reason into the transcendental consciousness; therefore not one of the states contradicts the others. Real inspiration never contradicts reason, but fulfils it. Just as the great prophets "come not to destroy but to fulfil," so inspiration always comes to fulfil reason and is in harmony with it.

All the different steps in yoga are intended to bring us scientifically to the superconscious state, or samādhi. Furthermore, this is a most vital point to understand: Inspiration is as much in every man's nature as it was in that of the ancient prophets. These prophets were not unique; they were men such as you or I. They were great yogis. They had gained this superconsciousness, and you and I also can gain the same. They were not peculiar people. The very fact that one man ever reached that state proves that it is possible for every man to do so. Not only is it possible, but every man must eventually reach that state—and that is religion. Experience is the only teacher we have. We may talk and reason all our lives, but we shall not understand a word of truth until we experience it ourselves. You cannot hope to make a man a surgeon by simply giving him a few books. You cannot satisfy my curiosity to see a country by showing me a map; I must have actual experience. Maps can only create curiosity in us to get more perfect knowledge. Beyond that, they have no value whatever. Clinging to books only degenerates the human mind. Was there ever a more horrible blasphemy than the statement that all the knowledge of God is confined to this or that book? How dare men call God infinite and yet try to compress Him within the covers of a little book! Millions of people have been killed because they did not believe what the books said, because they would not see all the knowledge of God within the covers of a book. Of course, all this killing and murdering has gone by; but the world is still tremendously bound up in a belief in books.

In order to reach the superconscious state in a scientific manner, it is necessary to pass through the various steps of Rāja-yoga I have been teaching. After pratyāhāra and dhāranā, we come to dhyāna, meditation. When the mind has been trained to remain fixed on a certain internal or external object, there comes to it the power of flowing in an unbroken current, as it were, towards that object. This state is called dhyāna. When one has so intensified the power of dhyāna as to be able to reject the external part of the perception and meditate only on the internal part, the meaning, that state is called samādhi. The three—dhāranā, dhyāna, and samādhi—together are called samyama. To explain: If the mind can first concentrate upon an object, and then is able to continue in that concentration for a length of time, and then, by continued concentration, can dwell only on the internal part of the perception, of which the object was the effect, or gross part, everything comes under its control.

This meditative state is the highest state of existence. So long as there is desire no real happiness can come. It is only the contemplative, witness-like study of objects that brings us real enjoyment and happiness. The animal has its happiness in the senses, man in his intellect, and the god in spiritual contemplation. It is only to the soul that has attained this contemplative state that the world really becomes beautiful. To him who desires nothing and does not mix himself up with the world the manifold changes of nature are one panorama of beauty and sublimity.

These ideas have to be understood in studying dhyāna, or meditation. We hear a sound. First there is the external vibration; second, the nerve motion that carries it to the mind; third, the reaction from the mind, along with which flashes the knowledge of the object which was the external cause of these different changes, from the ethereal vibrations to the mental reaction. These three are called, in yoga, sabda (sound), artha (meaning), and jnāna (knowledge). In the language of physiology they are called the ethereal vibration, the motion in the nerve and brain, and the mental reaction. Now these, though distinct processes, have become mixed up in such a fashion as to become quite indistinguishable. In fact, we cannot now perceive any of these; we perceive only their combined effect, what we call the external object. Every act of perception includes these three, and there is no reason why we should not be able to distinguish them.

When, by the previous preparations, the mind has become strong and controlled, and gained the power of finer perception, it should be employed in meditation. This meditation must begin with gross objects and slowly rise to finer, until it becomes objectless. The mind should first be employed in perceiving the external causes of sensations, then the internal motions, and then its own reaction. When it has succeeded in perceiving the external causes of sensations by themselves, the mind will acquire the power of perceiving all fine material existences, all fine bodies and forms. When it thus succeeds in perceiving the motions inside by themselves, it will gain the control of all mental waves, in itself or in others, even before they have translated themselves into physical energy. And when the yogi's mind is able to perceive the mental reaction by itself, it will acquire the knowledge of everything, since every sensible object and every thought is the result of this reaction. Then the yogi will have seen the very foundations of his mind, and it will be under his perfect control. Different powers will come to the yogi; if he yields to the temptations of any one of these the road to his farther progress will be barred—such is the evil of running after enjoyments. But if he is strong enough to reject even these miraculous powers, he will attain to the goal of yoga, the complete suppression of the waves in the ocean of the mind. Then the glory of the Soul, undisturbed by distractions of the mind or motions of the body, will shine in its full effulgence, and the yogi will find himself, as he is and as he always was, the Essence of Knowledge, the Immortal, the All-pervading.

Samādhi is the property of every human being—nay, of every animal. From the lowest animal to the highest angel, some time or other each one will have to come to that state; and then, and then alone, will real religion begin for him. Until then we only struggle towards that stage. There is no difference now between us and those who have no religion, because we have no experience. What is concentration good for, save to bring us to this experience? Each one of the steps to attain samādhi has been reasoned out, properly adjusted, and scientifically organized. When faithfully practised, they will surely lead to the desired end. Then will all sorrows cease, all miseries vanish. The seeds of action will be burnt, and the Soul will be free for ever.

RĀJA-YOGA IN BRIEF

THE FOLLOWING is a summary of Rāja-yoga freely translated from the Kurma Purāna:

The fire of yoga burns the cage of sin which imprisons a man. Knowledge becomes purified and Nirvāna is directly obtained. From yoga comes knowledge; knowledge, again, helps the yogi to obtain freedom. He who combines in himself both yoga and knowledge—with him the Lord is pleased. Those who practise mahā-yoga either once a day, or twice, or thrice, or always—know them to be gods. Yoga is divided into two parts: one is called abhāva-yoga, and the other, mahā-yoga. That in which one's self is meditated upon as a void and without qualities is called abhāva-yoga. That in which one sees one's self as blissful, bereft of all impurities, and as one with God is called mahā-yoga. The yogi, by either of these, realizes the Self. The other yogas that we read and hear of do not deserve to be ranked with mahā-yoga, in which the yogi finds himself and the whole universe to be God. This is the highest of all yogas.

Yama, niyama, āsana, prānāyāma, pratyāhāra, dhāranā, dhyāna, and samādhi are the steps in Rāja-yoga. Non-injury, truthfulness, non-covetousness, chastity, and not receiving anything from another are called yama, which purifies the mind, the chitta. Never producing pain in any living being, by thought, word, or deed, is what is called ahimsā, non-injury. There is no virtue higher than non-injury. There is no happiness higher than what a man obtains by this attitude of non-offensiveness to all creation. By truthfulness we attain the fruits of work. Through truth everything is attained; in truth everything is established. Relating facts as they are—this is truthfulness. Not taking others' goods by stealth or by force is called asteyam, non-covetousness. Chastity in thought, word, and deed, always and in all conditions, is what is called brahmacharya. Not receiving any present from anybody, even when one is suffering terribly, is what is called aparigraha. The idea is that when a man receives a gift from another, his heart becomes impure, he becomes low, he loses his independence, he becomes bound and attached.

The following are helps to success in yoga and are called niyama, or regular habits and observances: tapas (austerity), svādhyāya (study), santosha (contentment), śaucham (purity), and Iśvara-pranidhāna (worshipping God). Fasting or in other ways controlling the body is called physical tapas. Repeating the Vedas and other mantras, by which the sattva material in the body is purified, is called study, svādhyāya. There are three sorts of repetitions of these mantras. One is called verbal, another semi-verbal, and the third mental. The verbal or audible is the lowest, and the inaudible is the highest of all. Repetition which is loud is the verbal; in the next one only the lips move, but no sound is heard. The inaudible repetition of the mantra, accompanied by the thinking of its meaning, is called mental repetition and is the highest. The sages have said that there are two sorts of purification: external and internal. The purification of the body by water, earth, or other materials is the external purification; bathing is an example. Purification of the mind by truthfulness, and by the other virtues, is what is called the internal purification. Both are necessary for the practice of yoga. It is not enough for a man to be internally pure and externally dirty. When only one is attainable, the internal purity is to be preferred; but no one will be a yogi until he has both. God is worshipped by praise, by thought, and by devotion.

We have spoken about yama and niyama. The next is āsana, posture. The only thing to understand about it is to leave the body free, holding the chest, shoulders, and head straight. Then comes prāṇāyāma. Prāṇa means the vital force in one's own body, and the word āyāma means control. There are three sorts of prāṇāyāma: the very simple, the middle, and the very high. It is further divided into three parts: filling, restraining, and emptying. When you begin with twelve seconds it is the lowest prāṇāyāma; when you begin with twenty-four seconds it is the middle prāṇāyāma; the prāṇāyāma which begins with thirty-six seconds is the best. In the lowest kind of prāṇāyāma there is perspiration; in the medium kind, quivering of the body; and in the highest prāṇāyāma, levitation of the body and influx of great bliss. There is a mantra called the Gāyatri, a very holy verse of the Vedas. It reads: "We meditate on the glory of that Being who has produced this universe; may He enlighten our minds." Om is joined to it at the beginning and the end. In one prāṇāyāma repeat three Gāyatris. All the books speak of prāṇāyāma's being divided into rechaka (rejecting or exhaling), puraka (inhaling), and kumbhaka (restraining or stationary).

The indriyas, the organs of the senses, are turned outward and come in contact with external objects. Bringing them under the control of the will is what is called pratyāhāra, or gathering towards oneself.

Fixing the mind on the lotus of the heart or on the centre in the head is what is called dhāranā. Confined to one spot as the base, certain mental waves arise; these waves, not swallowed up by other kinds of waves, by degrees become prominent, while the latter recede and finally disappear. Next the multiplicity of the original waves gives place to unity and one wave only is left in the mind. This is dhyāna, meditation.

When no basis is necessary, when the whole of the mind has become one wave, has attained one-formedness, it is called samādhi. Bereft of all association with places and centres, only the meaning of the wave is present. If the mind can be fixed on a centre for twelve seconds it will be a dhāranā; twelve such dhāranās will be a dhyāna; and twelve such dhyānas will be a samādhi.

Where there is apprehension of fire or water, where the ground is strewn with dry leaves, where there are many ant-hills, where there is danger from wild animals, where four streets meet, where there is too much noise, where there are many wicked persons—there yoga must not be practised. This applies more particularly to India. Do not practise when the body feels very lazy or ill, or when the mind is very miserable and sorrowful. Go to a place which is well hidden and where people do not come to disturb you. Do not choose dirty places.

Rather choose beautiful scenery or a room in your own house which is beautiful. When you practise, first salute all the ancient yogis and your own guru and God, and then begin.

Dhyāna having been explained, a few examples are given of what to meditate upon. Sit straight and look at the tip of your nose. Later on we shall come to know how that helps to concentrate the mind, how by controlling the two optic nerves one advances a long way towards the control of the arc of reaction, and so to the control of the will. Here is one specimen of meditation: Imagine a lotus upon the top of the head, several inches up, with virtue as its centre and knowledge as its stalk. The eight petals of the lotus are the eight powers of the yogi. Inside, the stamens and pistils are renunciation. If the yogi refuses the external powers he will come to salvation. So the eight petals of the lotus are the eight powers, but the internal stamens and pistils are extreme renunciation, the renunciation of all these powers. Inside that lotus, think of the Golden One, the Almighty, the Intangible, whose name is Om, the Inexpressible, surrounded with effulgent light. Meditate on that. Another meditation is given: Think of a space in your heart, and think that in the midst of that space a flame is burning. Think of that flame as your own soul. Inside the flame is another effulgent light, and that is the Soul of your soul, God. Meditate upon that in the heart.

Chastity, non-injury, forgiving even the greatest enemy, truthfulness, and faith in the Lord—these are all different vows. Be not afraid if you are not perfect in all of these. Work and you will succeed. He who has given up all attachment, all fear, and all anger, he whose whole soul has gone unto the Lord, he who has taken refuge in the Lord, whose heart has become purified—with whatsoever desire he comes to the Lord, He will grant that to him. Therefore worship Him through knowledge, love, and renunciation.

"He who hates none, who is the friend of all, who is merciful to all, who has nothing of his own, who is free from egotism, who is even-minded in pain and pleasure, who is forbearing, who is always satisfied, who is ever devoted to yoga, whose self has become controlled, whose will is firm, whose mind and intellect are given unto Me—such a one is My beloved bhakta. He from whom comes no disturbance, who cannot be disturbed by others, who is free from joy, fear, and anxiety—such a one is My beloved. He who does not depend on anything, who is pure and active, who does not care whether good comes or evil, and never becomes miserable, who has given up all efforts for himself, who is the same in praise or in blame, silent and thoughtful, pleased with what little comes his way, homeless, having the whole world for his home, and steady in his mind—such a one is My beloved bhakta."[1] Such a one becomes a yogi.

*   *   *

There was a great god-sage called Nārada. Just as there are sages among men, great yogis, so there are great yogis among the gods. Nārada was a great yogi, and renowned. He travelled everywhere. One day he was passing through a forest and saw a man who had been meditating until the white ants

[1] Bhagavad Gītā XII. 13-20.

had built a huge mound around his body—he had been sitting in that position so long. He said to Nārada, "Where are you going?" Nārada replied, "I am going to heaven." "Then ask God when He will be merciful to me, when I shall attain freedom." Farther on Nārada saw another man. He was jumping about, singing and dancing, and said, "O Nārada, where are you going?" His voice and his gestures were wild. Nārada said, "I am going to heaven." "Then ask when I shall be free." Nārada went on. In the course of time he came again by the same road, and there was the man who had been meditating with the ant-hill around him. He said, "O Nārada, did you ask the Lord about me?" "Oh, yes." "What did He say?" "The Lord told me that you would attain freedom in four more births." Then the man began to weep and wail, and said, "I have meditated until an ant-hill has grown around me, and I have yet four more births!" Nārada went to the other man. "Did you ask my question?" "Oh, yes. Do you see this tamarind tree? I have to tell you that you shall be born as many times as there are leaves on that tree, and then you shall attain freedom." The man began to dance for joy, and said, "Ah, I shall have freedom after such a short time!" A voice came, "My child, you will have freedom this minute." That was the reward for his perseverance. He was ready to work through all those births; nothing discouraged him. But the first man felt that even four more births were too long. Only perseverance like that of the man who was willing to wait aeons brings about the highest result.

INTRODUCTION TO
PATANJALI'S YOGA APHORISMS

BEFORE GOING INTO the *Yoga Aphorisms* I shall try to discuss one great question, upon which, for the yogis, rests the whole theory of religion. It seems to be the consensus of the great minds of the world, and it has been nearly demonstrated by researches into physical nature, that we are the outcome and manifestation of an absolute condition, which lies behind our present relative condition, and that we shall return to that absolute condition. This being granted, the question is, which is better, the absolute state or this present state? There are not wanting people who think that the manifested state is the higher state of man. Thinkers of great calibre are of the opinion that we are manifestations of undifferentiated being, and that the differentiated state is higher than the absolute. They imagine that in the absolute state there cannot be any quality; that it must be insensate, dull, and lifeless; that only this life can be enjoyed, and therefore we must cling to it.

First of all let us inquire into other solutions of life. There was an old solution that man remained the same after death, that all his good qualities, minus his evil ones, remained for ever. Logically stated, this means that man's goal is the world; this world carried a stage higher, and purified of its evils, is the state called heaven. The theory, on the face of it, is absurd and puerile, because such a state cannot exist. There cannot be good without evil, or evil without good. A world where there is all good and no evil is what Indian logicians call a "castle in the air."

Another theory in modern times has been presented by several schools: that man's destiny is to go on always improving, always struggling towards, but never reaching, the goal. This statement, though apparently very nice, is also absurd, because there is no such thing as motion in a straight line. Every motion is in a circle. If you take up a stone and throw it into space, and then live long enough, that stone, if it meets with no obstruction, will come back exactly to your hand. A straight line, infinitely projected, must end in a circle. Therefore this idea that the destiny of man is to progress ever forward and forward, without ever stopping, is absurd. Although it is extraneous to the subject, I may remark that the idea of motion's being in a circle explains the ethical theory that you must not hate, but must love. Just as, according to the modern theory, the electric current leaves the dynamo, completes the circle, and comes back to the dynamo, so also hate and love: they must come back to the source. Therefore do not hate anybody, because that hatred which goes out from you must in the long run come back to you. If you love, that love will come back to you, completing the circle. It is as certain as can be that every bit of hatred that

622

goes out of the heart of a man comes back to him in full force; nothing can stop it. Similarly every impulse of love comes back to him.

On other and more practical grounds we see that the theory of eternal progression is untenable; for destruction is the end of everything earthly. All our struggles and hopes and fears and joys—what will they lead to? We shall all end in death. Nothing is so certain as this. Where, then, is this motion in a straight line, this infinite progression? It only means going out to a distance and coming back to the centre from which one started. See how from nebulae the sun, moon, and stars are produced, and then dissolve and go back to nebulae. The same is happening everywhere. The plant takes its substance from the earth, decays, and gives it back to the earth. Every form in this world is taken out of surrounding atoms and goes back to these atoms. It cannot be that the same law acts differently in different places. Law is uniform; nothing is more certain than that. If this is the law of nature, it also applies to the mind. The mind will dissolve and go back to its origin. Whether we will or no, we shall have to return to our origin, which is called God, or the Absolute. We have all come from God and we are all bound to go back to God; call it by any name you like—God, the Absolute, or nature—the fact remains the same. "From whom all this universe comes out, in whom all that is born lives, and to whom all returns." This is one fact that is certain. Nature works on the same plan; what is being worked out in one sphere is repeated in millions of spheres. What you see in the planets, the same will be with this earth, with men, and with all. The huge wave consists of small waves, maybe millions of them. Likewise, the life of the whole world is compounded of the lives of millions of little beings, and the death of the whole world is compounded of the deaths of these millions of little beings.

Now the question arises, is going back to God the higher state, or not? The philosophers of the Yoga school emphatically answer that it is. They say that man's present state is a degeneration; there is not one religion on the face of the earth which says that man is an improvement. The idea is that his beginning is perfect and pure, then he degenerates until he cannot degenerate further, and finally there must come a time when he shoots upward again to complete the circle; the circle must be described. However low he may go, he must ultimately take the upward curve and go back to the original source, which is God. Man comes from God in the beginning, in the middle he becomes man, and in the end he goes back to God. This is the way of putting it in the dualistic form. The monistic form is that man is God and becomes God again. If our present state is the higher one, then why is there so much horror and misery, and why is there an end to it? If this is the higher state, why does it end? That which corrupts and degenerates cannot be the highest state. Why should it be so diabolical, so unsatisfying? It is only excusable inasmuch as, through it, we are able to reach a higher stage; we have to pass through it in order to become regenerate. Put a seed into the ground and it disintegrates, dissolves, after a time; and out of that dissolution comes a splendid tree. Every soul must disintegrate in order that it may become God. So it follows that the sooner we get out of this state we call manhood, the better for us. Is it by committing suicide that we get out of this state? Not at all. That would be making it worse. Torturing ourselves or condemning the world is not the way to get out. We have to pass through the Slough of Despond, and the sooner we are through, the better. It must always be remembered that manhood is not the highest state.

The really difficult part to understand is that the Absolute, which has been called the highest state, is not, as some fear, that of the zoophyte or the stone. According to them there are only two states of existence: one, that of the stone, and the other, that of thought. What right have they to limit existence to these two? Is there not something infinitely superior to thought? The vibrations of light, when they are very low, we do not see. When they become a little more intense they become light to us. When they become still more intense we do not see them; it is dark to us. Is the darkness in the end the same darkness as that in the beginning? Certainly not; they are different as the poles. Is the absence of thought in the stone the same as the absence of thought in God? Certainly not. God does not think; He does not reason. Why should He? Is anything unknown to Him, that He should reason? The stone *cannot* reason; God *does* not. That is the difference. These philosophers think it is awful if we go beyond thought; they find nothing beyond thought. But there is a much higher state of existence than reasoning. It is really beyond the intellect that the first state of religious life is to be found. When you step beyond thought and intellect and all reasoning, then you have made the first step towards God; and that is the beginning of life. What is commonly called life is but an embryo state.

The next question will be: What proof is there that the state beyond thought and reasoning is the highest state? In the first place, all the great men of the world, much greater than those who only talk—men who move the world, men who never think of any selfish ends whatever—declare that this life is but a little stage on the way towards Infinity, which is beyond. In the second place, they not only say so, but show the way to everyone, explain their methods, that all may follow in their steps. In the third place, there is no other way left. There is no other explanation. Taking it for granted that there is no higher state, why are we going through this circle all the time? What can explain the world's existence? If we cannot go farther, if we must not ask for anything more, our knowledge will be limited to the sensible world. This is what is called agnosticism. But what reason is there to believe the testimony of the senses? I would call that man a true agnostic who would stand still in the street and die. If reason is all in all, then we must accept nihilism and shall have no place to stand. If a man is agnostic about everything but money, fame, and name, he is only a fraud. Immanuel Kant has said, no doubt, that we cannot penetrate beyond the tremendous dead wall called reason. But that we can go beyond reason is the very first idea upon which all Indian thought takes its stand; it dares to seek, and succeeds in finding, something higher than reason, where alone the explanation of the present state is to be found. This is the value of the study of Yoga, which will take us beyond the world. "Thou art our Father, who takest us to the other shore of this ocean of ignorance." This going beyond ignorance, and nothing else, is the goal of religion.

CONCENTRATION: ITS SPIRITUAL USES

1

Now yoga is explained.

2

Yoga is the restraining of the mind-stuff (chitta) from taking various forms (vrittis).

A good deal of explanation is necessary here. We have to understand what the chitta is and what the vrittis are. I have eyes. The eyes do not really see. Take away the nerve centre which is in the brain; the eyes will still be there, with the retinae complete, as also the pictures of objects on them, and yet the eyes will not see. So the eyes are only a secondary instrument, not the organ of vision. The organ of vision is in a nerve centre in the brain. The two eyes will not be sufficient. Sometimes a man is asleep with his eyes open. The light is there and the picture is there, but a third thing is necessary: the mind must be joined to the organ. So the eye is merely the external instrument; we need also the centre in the brain and the agency of the mind. Carriages roll down a street and you do not hear them. Why? Because your mind has not attached itself to the organ of hearing. First there is the instrument, second, the organ, and third, the mind's attachment to these two. The mind takes the impression farther in and presents it to the determinative faculty, or buddhi, which reacts. Along with this reaction flashes the idea of ego. Then this mixture of action and reaction is presented to the Purusha, the real Soul, which perceives an object in this mixture.

The organs (indriyas), the mind (manas), the determinative faculty (buddhi), and egoity (ahamkāra)—all these together form the group called the antah-karana, the internal instrument. They are but various processes in the mind-stuff, or chitta. The waves of thought in the chitta are called vrittis (literally, whirlpools).

What is thought? Thought is a force, as is gravitation or repulsion. From the infinite storehouse of force in nature, the instrument called the chitta takes hold of some, absorbs it, and sends it out as thought. Force is supplied to us through food, and out of that food the body obtains the power of motion, and so forth. Others, the finer forces, it sends out as what we call thought. So we see that the mind is not intelligent; yet it appears to be intelligent. Why so? Because the intelligent Soul is behind it. The Soul is the only sentient being; the mind is merely the instrument through which It perceives the external world. Take this book: as a book it does not exist outside; what exists outside is unknown and unknowable. The unknowable furnishes the suggestion that gives a blow to the mind, and the mind gives out the reaction in the form of a book, just as when a stone is thrown into the water, the water is thrown against it in the form of waves. The real universe is the occasion of the reaction of the mind. A book form or an elephant form or a man form is not outside; all that we know is our mental reaction from the outer suggestion. "Matter is the permanent possibility of sensations," said John Stuart Mill. It is only the suggestion that is outside. Take an oyster for example. You know how pearls are made. A parasite gets inside the shell and causes irritation, and the oyster throws a sort of enamelling round it, and this makes the pearl. The universe of experience is our own enamel, so to say, and the real universe is the parasite serving as nucleus. The ordinary man will never understand it, because when he tries to do so, he throws out an enamel and sees only his own enamel.

Now we understand what is meant by these vrittis. The real man is behind the mind; the mind is the instrument in his hands. It is his intelligence that is percolating through the mind. It is only when you stand behind the mind that it becomes intelligent. When you give it up it falls to pieces and becomes nothing. Thus you understand what is meant by the chitta. It is the mind-stuff, and the vrittis are the waves and ripples rising in it when external causes impinge on it. These vrittis are our universe.

The bottom of a lake we cannot see, because its surface is covered with ripples. It is only possible for us to catch a glimpse of the bottom when the ripples have subsided and the water is calm. If the water is muddy, or is agitated all the time, the bottom will not be seen. If it is clear and there are no waves, we shall see the bottom. The bottom of the lake is our own true Self; the lake is the chitta, and the waves are the vrittis. Again, the mind has three states, one of which is darkness, called tamas, found in brutes and idiots; it only acts to injure. No other idea comes into that state of mind. Then there is the active state of mind, rajas, whose chief motives are power and enjoyment: "I will be powerful and rule others." Then there is the state called sattva, serenity, calmness, in which the waves cease and the water of the mind-lake becomes clear. It is not inactive; rather, it is intensely active. It is the greatest manifestation of power to be calm. It is easy to be active. Let the reins go and the horses will run away with you. Anyone can do that; but he who can stop the plunging horses is the strong man. Which requires the greater strength, letting go or restraining? The calm man is not the man who is dull. You must not mistake sattva for dullness or laziness. The calm man is the one who has control over the mind's waves. Activity is the manifestation of inferior strength; calmness, of superior.

The chitta is always trying to get back to its natural pure state, but the organs draw it out. To restrain it, to check this outward tendency, and to start it on the return journey to the Essence of Intelligence is the first step in yoga, because only in this way can the chitta get into its proper state.

Although the chitta exists in every animal, from the lowest to the highest, it is only in the human being that we find it as the intellect. Until the mind-stuff can take the form of intellect, it is not possible for it to return through all these steps and liberate the soul. Immediate salvation is impossible for the cow or the dog, although they have minds, because their chitta cannot as yet take that form which we call intellect.

The chitta manifests itself in the following forms: scattering, darkening, gathering, one-pointed, and concentrated. The "scattering" form is activity. Its tendency is to manifest itself in the form of pleasure or of pain. The "darkening" form is dullness, which tends to injury. The commentator says that the first form is natural to the devas, the gods, and the second to the demons. The "gathering" form functions when the chitta struggles to draw itself to its centre; the "one-pointed" form, when it tries to concentrate. And the "concentrated" form brings us to samādhi.

3

At that time (i.e. the time of concentration) the Seer (Purusha) rests in His own [unmodified] state.

As soon as the waves have stopped and the lake has become quiet, we see its bottom. So with the mind: when it is calm, we see what our own nature is; we do not mix ourselves with the modifications of the mind, but remain our own selves.

4

At other times (i.e. when not concentrating) the Seer is identified with the modifications.

For instance, someone blames me; this produces a modification, vritti, in my mind, and I identify myself with it, and the result is misery.

5

There are five classes of modifications, [some] painful and [others] not painful.

6

[These are] right knowledge, indiscrimination, verbal delusion, sleep, and memory.

7

Direct perception, inference, and competent evidence constitute right knowledge, or proof.

When two of our perceptions do not contradict each other we call it a proof. I hear something, and if it contradicts something already perceived, I do not believe it and begin to fight it out. There are three kinds of proof. Direct perception, pratyaksha, whatever we see and feel, is its own proof, if there has been nothing to delude the senses. I see the world; that is sufficient proof that it exists. Secondly, anumāna, inference: you see a sign, and from the sign you come to the thing signified. Thirdly, āptavākya, the direct perception of the yogis, of those who have seen Truth. We are all of us struggling towards knowledge. You and I have to struggle hard and come to knowledge through a long, tedious process of reasoning; but the yogi, the pure one, has gone beyond all this. To him the past, the present, and the future alike are one book for his mind to read; he does not have to go through the tedious processes for obtaining knowledge that we have to; his words are their own proof, because he sees knowledge in himself. These, for instance, are the authors of the sacred scriptures; therefore the scriptures are their own proof. If any such persons are living now their words will be their own proof. Other philosophers go into long discussions about āptavākya and they ask, "What is the proof of their words?" The proof is their direct perception. Because whatever I see is its own proof, and whatever you see is its own proof, if it does not contradict any past knowledge. There is knowledge beyond the senses, and whenever it does not contradict reason and past human experience, that knowledge is its own proof. Any madman may come into this room and say that he sees angels around him; that would not be sufficient proof. In the first place, it must be true knowledge, and secondly, it must not contradict past knowledge, and thirdly, it must depend upon the character of the man who gives it out. I hear it said that the character of the man is not of so much importance as what he may say; we must first hear what he says. This may be true in other things: a man may be wicked and yet make an astronomical discovery; but in religion it is different, because no impure man will ever have the power to reach the truths of religion.

Therefore we have first of all to see that the man who declares himself to be an āpta is a perfectly unselfish and holy person; secondly, that he has gone beyond the senses; and thirdly, that what he says does not contradict the past knowledge of humanity. Any new discovery of truth must not contradict past truth, but must fit into it. And fourthly, we have to see that that truth has a possibility of verification. If a man says, "I have seen a vision," and tells me that I cannot see it, I will not believe him. Everyone must have the power to see it for himself. Further, no one who sells his knowledge is an āpta. All these conditions must be fulfilled: You must first see that the man is pure and that he has no selfish motive, that he has no thirst for gain or fame; secondly, he must show that he has had superconscious experience; thirdly, he must give us something which we cannot get from our senses and which is for the benefit of the world. And we must see that it does not contradict other truths; if it contradicts them we must reject it at once. Fourthly, the man should never be an exception; he should represent only what all men can attain. The three sorts of proof are, then, direct sense perception, inference, and the words of an āpta. I cannot translate this word into English. It is not "one who is inspired," because inspiration is believed to come from outside, while this knowledge comes from the man himself. The literal meaning is "one who has attained."

<h3 style="text-align:center">8</h3>

Indiscrimination is false knowledge not based on the real nature [of an object].

The next class of vrittis that arises is the mistaking of one thing for another, as a piece of mother-of-pearl is mistaken for a piece of silver.

<h3 style="text-align:center">9</h3>

Verbal delusion follows from words having no [corresponding] reality.

There is another class of vrittis called vikalpa. A word is uttered, and we do not wait to consider its meaning; we jump to a conclusion immediately.

It is a sign of weakness of the chitta. Now you can understand the importance of restraint. The weaker the man, the less he has of restraint. Examine yourselves always by that test. When you are about to become angry or miserable, reason it out and see how some news that has come to you is throwing your mind into vrittis.

10

Sleep is a vritti which embraces the feeling of voidness.

The next class of vrittis is called sleep, comprising dream and deep sleep. When we awake we know that we were sleeping; we can only have memory of perception. That which we do not perceive we never can have any memory of. Every reaction is a wave in the lake. Now if, during sleep, the mind had no waves, it would have no perceptions, positive or negative, and therefore we should not remember them. The very reason of our remembering sleep is that during sleep there was a certain class of waves in the mind. Memory is another class of vrittis; it is called smriti.

11

Memory arises when [the vrittis of] perceived objects do not slip away [and through impressions come back to consciousness].

Memory can come from direct perception, false knowledge, verbal delusion, and sleep. For instance, you hear a word. That word is like a stone thrown into the lake of the chitta; it causes a ripple, and that ripple rouses a series of ripples. This is memory. So it is in sleep. When the peculiar kind of ripple called sleep throws the chitta into a ripple of memory, it is called a dream. Dreaming is another form of the ripple which in the waking state is called memory.

12

These [vrittis] are controlled by practice and non-attachment.

The mind, to have non-attachment, must be clear, good, and rational. Why should we practise? Because actions are like the vibrations quivering over the surface of the lake. The vibrations die out, and what is left? The samskāras, the impressions. When a large number of these impressions is left on the mind, they coalesce and become a habit. It is said that habit is second nature. It is first nature also, and the whole nature of man; everything that we are is the result of habit. That gives us consolation; for if it is only habit, we can make and unmake it at any time. The samskāras are left by these vibrations, which pass out of our mind, each one of them leaving its result. Our character is the sum total of these impressions, and according as a particular wave prevails one takes that tone. If good prevails, one becomes good; if wickedness, one becomes wicked; if joyfulness, one becomes happy. The only remedy for bad habits is counter-habits; all the bad habits that have left their impressions are to be controlled by good habits. Go on doing good, thinking holy thoughts, continuously; that is the only way to suppress base impressions. Never say any man is hopeless, because he only represents a character, a bundle of habits, which can be checked by new and better ones. Character is repeated habits, and repeated habits alone can reform character.

13

Continuous struggle to keep them (the vrittis) perfectly restrained is practice.

What is practice? It is the attempt to keep the mind under restraint, to prevent its going out into waves.

14

It becomes firmly grounded by long and constant efforts with great love [for the end to be attained].

Restraint does not come in a day, but by long continued practice.

15

The subjugation of the thirst for objects seen or heard of is non-attachment.

The motive powers of our actions are two: what we see ourselves, and the experience of others. These two forces throw the mind, the lake, into various waves. Non-attachment is the power of battling against these forces and holding the mind in check. The renunciation of these is what we want. I am passing through a street, and a man comes and takes away my watch. That is my own experience. I see it myself, and it immediately throws my chitta into a wave, taking the form of anger. Do not allow that to come. If you cannot prevent it, you are nothing; if you can, you have vairāgya. Again, the experience of the worldly-minded tells us that sense enjoyments are the highest ideal. These are tremendous temptations. To deny them and not allow the mind to break into waves with regard to them is renunciation; to control the twofold motive powers arising from my own experience and from the experience of others, and thus prevent the chitta from being governed by them, is vairāgya. These should be controlled by me, and not I by them. This sort of mental strength is called renunciation. Vairāgya is the only way to freedom.

16

That is extreme non-attachment which gives up even the thirst for the gunas, and which comes from the knowledge of [the real nature of] the Purusha.

The highest manifestation of the power of vairāgya occurs when it takes away even our attraction towards the gunas. We have first to understand what the Purusha, the Self, is, and what the gunas are. According to the Yoga philosophy the whole of nature consists of three gunas, that is to say, factors or forces; one is called tamas, another rajas, and the third sattva. These three gunas manifest themselves in the physical world as darkness or inactivity, attraction or repulsion, and the equilibrium of the two. Everything that is in nature, all manifestations, are combinations and recombinations of these three forces. Nature has been divided into various categories by the Sāmkhya philosophy; the Self of man is beyond all these, beyond nature. It is effulgent, pure, and perfect. Whatever intelligence we see in nature is but the reflection of this Self upon nature. Nature itself is insentient. You must remember that the word *nature* also includes the mind. Mind is in nature; thought is in nature; from thought down to the grossest form of matter, everything is in nature, is the manifestation of nature. This nature has covered the Self of man, and when nature takes away the covering, the Self appears in Its own glory. Non-attachment, described in aphorism 15 as being the subjugation of the thirst for objects, or nature, is the greatest help towards manifesting the Self. The next aphorism defines samādhi, perfect concentration, which is the goal of the yogi.

17

The samādhi endowed with right knowledge is that which is attended by reasoning, discrimination, bliss, and unqualified ego.

Samādhi is divided into two kinds: one is called samprajnāta, and the other, asamprajnāta. In samprajnāta samādhi come all the powers of controlling nature. It is of four varieties. The first variety is called savitarka, when the mind meditates upon an object again and again, by isolating it from other objects. There are two sorts of objects for meditation in the twenty-five categories of Sāmkhya: the twenty-four insentient categories of nature, and the one sentient Purusha. This part of Yoga is based entirely on Sāmkhya philosophy, about which I have already told you. As you will remember, ego and will and mind have a common basis, the chitta or mind-stuff, out of which they are all manufactured. This mind-stuff takes in the forces of nature and projects them as thought. There must be something, again, where both force and matter are one. This is called avyakta, the unmanifested state of nature before creation, to which, after the end of a cycle, the whole of nature returns, and from which it comes out again at the time of the next creation. Beyond that is the Purusha, the Essence of Intelligence.

Knowledge is power, and as soon as we begin to know a thing we get power over it; so also, when the mind begins to meditate on the different elements it gains power over them. That sort of meditation where the external gross elements are the objects is called savitarka. Vitarka means "question"; savitarka, "with question." This samādhi implies the questioning of the elements, as it were, that they may yield their powers to the man who meditates upon them. There is no liberation in getting powers. It is a search after worldly enjoyments, and there is no real enjoyment in this life. All search for enjoyment is vain; this is the old, old lesson which man finds so hard to learn. When he does learn it, he gets out of the universe and becomes free. The possession of what are called occult powers only intensifies worldliness, and, in the end, intensifies suffering. Though as a scientist Patanjali is bound to point out the possibilities of his science, he never misses an opportunity to warn us against these powers.

Again, in the very same meditation, when one struggles to take the elements out of time and space, and thinks of them as they are, it is called nirvitarka samādhi, "samādhi without question." When the meditation goes a step higher and takes the tanmātras as its object, and thinks of them as within time and space, it is called savichāra samādhi, "samādhi with discrimination"; and when in the same meditation one eliminates time and space and thinks of the fine elements as they are, it is called nirvichāra samādhi, "samādhi without discrimination."

In the next step the elements, both gross and fine, are given up and the object of meditation is the interior organ, the thinking organ. When the thinking organ is thought of as bereft of the qualities of activity and dullness, then follows the sānanda or blissful samādhi. When the mind itself, free from the impurity of rajas and tamas, is the object of meditation, when meditation becomes very ripe and concentrated, when all ideas of the gross and fine materials are given up, when only the sattva state of the ego remains, but differentiated from all other objects, it is called asmitā samādhi. Even in this state one does not completely transcend the mind. The man who has attained it is called in the Vedas videha, or "bereft of body." He can think of himself as without his gross body; but he will have to think of himself as having a fine body. Those who in this state get merged in nature without attaining the goal are called prakritilinas; but those who do not stop even here reach the goal, which is freedom.

18

There is another samādhi, which is attained by constant practice of the cessation of all mental activity, and in which the chitta retains only the unmanifested impressions.

This is the perfect superconscious asamprajnāta samādhi, the state which gives us freedom. The first state does not give us freedom, does not liberate the soul. A man may attain all the powers and yet fall again. There is no safeguard until the soul goes beyond nature. It is very difficult to do so although the method seems easy. The method is to meditate on the mind itself, and whenever any thought comes, to strike it down, allowing no thought to come into the mind, thus making it an entire vacuum. When we can really do this, that very moment we shall attain liberation. When persons without training and preparation try to make their minds vacant, they are likely to succeed only in covering themselves with tamas, the material of ignorance, which makes the mind dull and stupid and leads them to think that they are making a vacuum of the mind. To be able to really do that is to manifest the greatest strength, the highest control.

When this state, asamprajnāta, or superconsciousness, is reached, the samādhi becomes seedless. What is meant by that? In a concentration where there is consciousness, where the mind succeeds only in quelling the waves in the chitta and holding them down, the waves remain in the form of tendencies. These tendencies, or seeds, become waves again when the opportunity comes. But when you have destroyed all these tendencies, almost destroyed the mind, then the samādhi becomes seedless; there are no more seeds in the mind out of which to manufacture again and again this plant of life, this ceaseless round of birth and death.

You may ask what that state would be in which there is no mind, no knowledge. What we call knowledge is a lower state than the one beyond knowledge. You must always bear in mind that the extremes look very much alike. If a very low vibration of ether is taken as darkness, and an intermediate state as light, a very high vibration will be darkness again. Similarly, ignorance is the lowest state, knowledge is the middle state, and beyond knowledge is the highest state; the two extremes seem the same. Knowledge itself is a manufactured something, a combination; it is not Reality.

What is the result of constant practice of this higher concentration? All old tendencies of restlessness and dullness will be destroyed, as well as the tendencies of goodness too. The case is similar to that of the chemicals used to take the dross from gold ore. When the ore is smelted, the dross is burnt along with the chemicals. So this constant controlling power will destroy the previous bad tendencies, and eventually the good ones also. Those good and evil tendencies will destroy each other, leaving alone the Soul in Its own splendour, untrammelled by either good or bad, omnipresent, omnipotent, and omniscient. Then the man will know that he had neither birth nor death nor need of heaven or earth. He will know that he neither came nor went; it was nature which was moving, and that movement was reflected upon the Soul. The form of the light reflected by a glass upon the wall moves, and the wall foolishly thinks it is moving. So with all of us: it is the chitta that is constantly moving, making itself into various forms, and we think that we are these various forms. All these delusions will vanish. When that free Soul commands—not prays or begs, but commands—then whatever It desires will be immediately fulfilled; whatever It wants It will be able to do.

According to the Sāmkhya philosophy there is no God. It says that there can be no God of this universe, because if there were one, He must be a soul, and a soul must be either bound or free. How can the soul that is bound by nature, or controlled by nature, create? It is itself a slave. On the other hand, why should the Soul, which is free, create and manipulate all these things? It has no desires; so it cannot have any need to create. Secondly, it says that the theory of God is an unnecessary one; nature explains all. What is the use of any God? But Kapila teaches that there are many souls, who, though nearly attaining perfection, fall short because they cannot completely renounce all powers. Their minds for a time merge in nature, to re-emerge as its masters. These souls are called gods. Such gods there are. We shall all become gods, and according to Sāmkhya, the God spoken of in the Vedas really means one of these free souls. Beyond them there is not an eternally free and blessed Creator of the universe.

On the other hand, the yogis say: "Not so. There is a God; there is one Soul separate from all other souls, and He is the eternal Master of all creation, the Ever Free, the Teacher of all teachers." The yogis admit that those whom Sāmkhya calls the "merged in nature" also exist. They are yogis who have fallen short of perfection; though for a time debarred from attaining the goal, they remain as rulers of parts of the universe.

19

[This samādhi, when not followed by extreme non-attachment,] becomes the cause of the remanifestation of the gods and of those who become merged in nature.

The gods in the Indian systems of philosophy represent certain high offices which are filled successively by various souls. But none of them is perfect.

20

By others [this samādhi] is attained through faith, energy, memory, concentration, and discrimination of the real [from the unreal].

The aphorism refers to those who do not want the position of gods or even that of rulers of cycles; they attain to liberation.

21

Success is speedy for the extremely energetic.

22

The success of yogis differs according as the means they adopt are mild, medium, or intense.

23

Or [this samādhi is attained] by devotion to Iśvara.

24

Iśvara (the Supreme Ruler) is a special Purusha, untouched by misery, actions and their results, and desires.

We must again remember that Patanjali's Yoga philosophy is based upon the Sāmkhya philosophy, the difference being that in the latter there is no place for God, while with the yogis God has a place. The yogis, however, do not associate with God the idea of creating or preserving the universe. God as the Creator of the universe is not what is meant by the Iśvara of the yogis. According to the Vedas, Iśvara is the Creator of the universe; because it is harmonious, it must be the manifestation of one will. The yogis, too, want to establish a God, but they arrive at Him in a peculiar fashion of their own. They say:

25

In Him becomes infinite that all-knowingness which in others is [only] a germ.

The mind always travels between two extremes. You can think of a limited space, but that very idea gives you also unlimited space. Close your eyes and think of a little circle; at the same time that you perceive the little circle, you perceive a circle round it of unlimited dimensions. It is the same with time. Try to think of a second; you will have, with the same act of perception, to think of time which is unlimited. So with knowledge. Knowledge is only a germ in man; but you will have to think of infinite knowledge around it. So the very constitution of our minds shows us that there is unlimited knowledge, and the yogis say that that unlimited knowledge belongs to God.

26

He is the Teacher of even the ancient teachers, not being limited by time.

It is true that all knowledge is within ourselves; but this has to be called forth by another knowledge. Although the capacity to know is within us, this capacity must be awakened. The inner knowledge can be called forth, a yogi maintains, only through another knowledge. Dead, insentient matter can never call forth knowledge; it is the power of knowledge that brings out knowledge. Knowing beings must help us to awaken what is in us; so these teachers are always necessary. The world has never been without them, and no knowledge can be had without them. God is the Teacher of all teachers, because these teachers, however great they may have been—even gods or angels—are all bound and limited by time, while God is not.

There are two peculiar deductions of the yogis. The first is that in thinking of the limited, the mind must also think of the unlimited, and that if one part of that perception is true, so also must the other be, for the reason that their value as perceptions of the mind is equal. The very fact that man has a little knowledge shows that God has unlimited knowledge. If I am to take one, why not the other? Reason forces me to take both or reject both. If I believe that there is a man with a little knowledge, I must also admit that there is Someone behind him with unlimited knowledge. The second deduction is that no knowledge can come without a teacher. It is true, as the modern philosophers say, that there is something in man which evolves out of him. All knowledge is in man; but certain environments are necessary to call it out. We cannot find any knowledge without teachers. Yet though there are men teachers, god teachers, and angel teachers, they are all limited. Who was the teacher before them? We are forced to admit, finally, one Teacher who is not limited by time; and that Teacher, of infinite knowledge and without beginning or end, is called God.

27

The word that manifests Him is Om.

Every thought that you have in the mind has a counterpart in a word; the word and the thought are inseparable. The external part of a thing is what we call word, and the internal part of that same thing is what we call thought. No man can, by analysis, separate thought from word. The idea that language was created by men, certain men sitting together and deciding upon words, has been proved to be wrong. So long as man has existed there have been words and language.

What is the connexion between a thought and a word? Although we see that there must always be a word with a thought, it is not necessarily true that the same thought requires the same word. The thought may be the same in twenty different countries, yet the language is different. We must have a word to express each thought, but these words need not necessarily have the same sound. Sounds will vary in different nations. A commentator says: "Although the relation between thought and word is perfectly natural, yet it does not mean a rigid connexion between a thought and a sound." The sounds vary, yet the relation between the sounds and the thoughts is a natural one. The connexion between thoughts and sounds is good only if there is a real connexion between the thing signified and the symbol; until then that symbol will never come into general use. The symbol is the manifester of the thing signified, and if the thing

signified is already existing, and if, by experience, we know that the symbol
has expressed that thing many times, then we are sure that there is a real relation
between them. Even if the thing is not present, there will be thousands who
will know it by its symbol. There must be a natural connexion between
the symbol and the thing signified; then, when that symbol is pronounced, it
recalls the thing signified.

Patanjali says that the word that manifests God is Om. Why does he emphasize this word? There are hundreds of words for God. One thought is connected
with a great many words; the idea of God is connected with hundreds of words,
and each one stands as a symbol for God. Very good. But there must be a
generalization among all these words, some substratum, some common ground
of all these symbols; and that which is the common symbol will be the best and
will really represent them all. In making a sound we use the larynx and the
palate as a sounding-board. Is there any articulate sound of which all other
sounds are manifestations, one which is the most natural sound? Om (Aum)
is such a sound, the basis of all sounds. The first letter, A,[1] is the root
sound, the key, pronounced without touching any part of the tongue or palate;
M represents the last sound in the series, being produced with closed lips, and
the U rolls from the very root to the end of the sounding-board of the mouth.
Thus Om represents the whole phenomenon of sound-production. As such, it
must be the natural symbol, the matrix of all the various sounds. It denotes
the whole range and possibility of all the words that can be uttered.

Apart from these speculations, we see that around this word Om are centred
all the different religious ideas in India; all the various religious ideas of the
Vedas have gathered themselves around this word. What has that to do with
America and England, or any other country? Simply this: that the word has
been retained at every stage of religious growth in India and has been manipulated to mean all the various ideas about God. Monists, dualists, mono-dualists,
separatists, and even atheists have taken up this Om. Om has become the one
symbol for the religious aspiration of the vast majority of human beings. Take,
for instance, the English word God. It covers only a limited function; and if you
go beyond it you have to add adjectives to make it the Personal or Impersonal
or Absolute God. So with the words for God in every other language; their
signification is very limited. This word Om, however, has around it all the various significances. As such it should be accepted by everyone.

28

The repetition of this (Om) and meditating on its meaning [is the way].

Why should there be repetition? We have not forgotten the theory of
samskāras: that the sum total of impressions lives in the mind. They may
become more and more latent, but they remain there, and as soon as they get
the right stimulus they come out. Atomic vibration never ceases. When this
universe is destroyed, all the massive vibrations disappear; the sun, moon, stars,
and earth melt down; but the vibrations remain in the atoms. Each atom performs the same function as the big worlds do. So even when the vibrations of

---

[1] Pronounced like *aw* in *dawn*.

the chitta subside, its atomic vibrations go on; and when they get the impulse, they come out again.

We can now understand what is meant by repetition. It is the greatest stimulus that can be given to the spiritual samskāras. "One moment of company with the holy builds a ship to cross this ocean of life"—such is the power of association. So this repetition of Om and thinking of its meaning are the same as keeping good company in your own mind. Study and then meditate on what you have studied. Thus light will come to you; the Self will become manifest. But one must think of Om and of its meaning too.

Avoid evil company, because the scars of old wounds are in you and evil company is just the thing necessary to call them out. In the same way, we are told that good company will call out the good impressions which are in us but have become latent. There is nothing holier in the world than to keep good company, because the good impressions will then tend to come to the surface.

29

From that is gained introspection and the destruction of obstacles.

The first effect of the repetition and thinking of Om is that the introspective power will manifest itself more and more; all the mental and physical obstacles will begin to vanish. What are the obstacles for the yogi?

30

Disease, mental laziness, doubt, lack of enthusiasm, lethargy, clinging to sense enjoyments, false perception, non-attaining of concentration, and falling away from concentration when attained—these are the obstructing distractions.

Disease: This body is the boat which will carry us to the other shore of the ocean of life. It must be taken care of. Unhealthy persons cannot be yogis. *Mental laziness* makes us lose all lively interest in the subject, without which there will be neither the will nor the energy to practise. *Doubts* will arise in the mind about the truth of the science of Yoga, however strong one's intellectual conviction may be, until certain peculiar psychic experiences come, such as hearing or seeing at a distance. These glimpses strengthen the mind and make the student persevere. *Falling away from concentration when attained:* Some days or weeks, when you are practising, the mind will be calm and easily concentrated and you will find yourself progressing fast. All of a sudden, one day, the progress will stop and you will find yourself, as it were, stranded. But persevere. All progress proceeds by such rise and fall.

31

Grief, mental distress, tremor of the body, and irregular breathing accompany non-retention of concentration.

Concentration will bring perfect repose to mind and body every time it is practised. When the practice has been misdirected or the mind not well controlled, these disturbances come. Repetition of Om and self-surrender to the Lord will strengthen the mind and bring fresh energy. The nervous shakings will come to almost everyone. Do not mind them at all, but keep on practising. Practice will cure them and make the seat firm.

32

To remedy this [one should] practise on one object.

Making the mind take the form of one object for some time will destroy these obstacles. This is general advice. In the following aphorisms it will be expanded and particularized. As one practice cannot suit everyone, various methods will be advanced, and everyone by actual experience will find out that which helps him most.

33

The feelings of friendship, mercy, gladness, and indifference, in regard to objects happy, unhappy, good, and evil, respectively, pacify the chitta.

We must have these four kinds of attitudes. We must have friendship for all; we must be merciful towards those that are in misery; when people are happy we ought to be happy; and to the wicked we must be indifferent. So with all objects that come before us. If the object is a good one, we must feel friendly towards it; if the object of thought is one that is miserable, we must be merciful towards the object. If it is good we must be glad; and if it is evil we must be indifferent. These attitudes of mind towards the different objects that come before it will make the mind peaceful. Most of our difficulties in our daily lives come from our being unable to hold down our minds in this way. For instance, if a man does evil to us, instantly we want to react with evil. Every reaction in the form of evil shows that we are not able to hold the chitta down; it comes out in waves towards the object, and we lose our mental power. Every reaction in the form of hatred or evil is so much loss to the mind, and every evil thought or deed of hatred, or any thought of reaction, if it is controlled, will be laid up in our favour. Not that we lose anything by thus restraining ourselves; rather we gain infinitely more than we suspect. Each time we suppress hatred or a feeling of anger, it is so much good energy stored up in our favour; that energy will be converted into the higher powers.

34

By expelling and restraining the breath [the chitta is pacified].

The word used is prāna. Prāna is not exactly breath; it is the name for the energy that pervades the universe. Whatever you see in the universe, whatever moves or works or has life, is a manifestation of prāna. The sum total of the energy displayed in the universe is called prāna. This prāna, when a cycle ends, remains in an almost motionless state, and when the next cycle begins, it gradually manifests itself. It is prāna that is manifested as motion, as the nervous motion in human beings and animals; and the same prāna is manifested as thought, and so on. The whole universe is a combination of prāna and ākāśa; so is the human body. Out of ākāśa you get the different materials that you feel and see, and out of prāna all the various forces. Now, the expelling and restraining of the prāna is what is called prānāyāma.

Patanjali, the father of the Yoga philosophy, does not give very many partic- ular directions about prānāyāma; but later on other yogis found out various things about prānāyāma and made of it a great science. With Patanjali it is one of the many ways; but he does not lay much stress on it. He means that you simply expel the air, and draw it in, and hold it for some time—that is all; and by that the mind will become a little calmer. But you will find that out of this, later on, was evolved a particular science called prānāyāma. We shall study a little of what these later yogis have to say. Some of this I have told you before, but a little repetition will serve to fix it in your minds.

First, you must remember that prāna is not the breath; but that which causes the motion of the breath, that which is the vitality of the breath, is prāna. Again, the word *prāna* is used for all the senses; they are all called prānas; and the mind is called a prāna. We have also seen that prāna is force. And yet we cannot call it force, because force is only the manifestation of it. It is that which manifests itself as force and everything else in the shape of motion. The chitta, the mind-stuff, is an engine which draws in prāna from its surroundings and manufactures out of prāna the various vital forces—those that keep the body in preservation—and thought, will, and all other powers. By the above-mentioned process of breathing we can control all the various motions in the body, and the various nerve currents that are flowing through the body. First we begin to recognize them, and then we slowly get control over them.

Now, according to the later yogis, there are three main currents of prāna in the human body. One they call the Iḍā, another the Pingalā, and the third the Sushumnā. The Pingalā, according to them, is on the right side of the spinal column, and the Iḍā on the left, and in the middle of the spinal column is the Sushumnā, a hollow canal. The Iḍā and the Pingalā, according to them, are currents working in every man, and through these currents we perform all the functions of life. Though the Sushumnā is present in all, it is not active; it functions only in the yogi. You must remember that yoga changes the body; as you go on practising your body changes; it is not the same body that you had before the practice. That is very rational and can be explained. Every new thought that we entertain must make, as it were, a new channel through the brain. This explains the tremendous conservatism of human nature. Human nature likes to run through the ruts that are already there, because it is easy. If we think, just for example's sake, that the mind is like a needle, and the brain substance a soft lump before it, then each thought that we have makes a channel, as it were, in the brain. This channel would close up, but for the grey matter, which comes in and makes a lining to keep it open. If there were no grey mat- ter there would be no memory, because memory means going over these old channels, retracing a thought, as it were. Now, perhaps you have noticed that when a man talks on subjects in which he takes up a few ideas that are familiar to everyone, and combines and recombines them, it is easy to follow him, because these channels are present in everyone's brain, and it is only necessary to refer to them. But whenever a new subject comes, new channels have to be made; so it is not readily understood. And that is why the brain (it is the brain, and not the people themselves) unconsciously refuses to be acted upon by new ideas. It resists. Prāna tries to make new channels, and the brain will not allow it. This is the secret of conservatism. The fewer channels there are in the brain and the less the needle of prāna has made these passages, the more conservative will be the brain and the more it will struggle against new thoughts. The more thoughtful the man, the more complicated will be the channels in his brain and the more easily he will take to new ideas and understand them. So with every fresh idea we make a new impression in the brain, cut new channels through the brain-stuff; and that is why we find that in the practice of yoga—consisting, as it does, of an entirely new set of thoughts and motives—there is so much physical resistance at first. That is why we find that the part of religion which deals with the external side of nature can be so widely accepted, while the other part, the philosophy or the psychology, which deals with the inner nature of man, is so frequently neglected.

We must remember the definition of this world of ours: it is only the Infinite Existence projected into the plane of consciousness. A little of the Infinite is projected into consciousness, and that we call our world. So there is an Infinite Beyond, and religion has to deal with both—with the little lump we call our world and with the Infinite Beyond. Any religion which deals with one only of these two will be defective. It must deal with both. That part of religion which deals with the part of the Infinite which has come into the plane of conscious-ness and got itself caught, as it were, in the plane of consciousness, in the cage of time, space, and causation, is quite familiar to us, because we are in it already, and ideas about this plane have been with us almost from time immemorial. The part of religion which deals with the Infinite Beyond comes to us entirely new, and our effort to understand produces new channels in the brain, disturb-ing the whole system. That is why you find that in the practice of yoga ordinary people are at first turned out of their grooves. In order to lessen these disturb-ances as much as possible, all these methods have been devised by Patanjali. We may practise any one which is best suited to us.

35

Those forms of concentration which bring extraordinary sense perceptions cause perseverance of the mind.

This naturally comes with dhāranā, concentration. The yogis say that if the mind is concentrated on the tip of the nose, after a few days one begins to smell wonderful perfumes. If it is concentrated on the root of the tongue, one begins to hear sounds; if on the tip of the tongue, one begins to taste wonder-ful flavours; if on the middle of the tongue, one feels as if one were coming in contact with some object. If one concentrates the mind on the palate one begins to see strange things. If a man whose mind is disturbed wants to take up some of these practices of yoga, yet doubts the truth of them, he will have his doubts set at rest when, after a little practice, these things come to him, and he will persevere.

36

Or [the chitta is pacified by meditation on] the Effulgent Light, which is beyond all sorrow.

This is another sort of concentration. Think of the lotus of the heart, with petals downward, and running through it, the Sushumnā. Take in the breath, and while expelling it imagine that the petals are turned upward and that inside the lotus is an effulgent light. Meditate on that.

37

Or [by meditation on] the heart that has given up all attachment to sense-objects.

Take some holy person, some great person whom you revere, some saint whom you know to be perfectly non-attached, and think of his heart. That heart has become non-attached. Meditate on that heart and it will calm the mind. If you cannot do that, there is the next way.

38

Or [by meditation on] the knowledge that comes in dreams or the happiness experienced in deep sleep.

Sometimes a man dreams that he sees angels and talks to them, and that he is in an ecstatic condition and hears music floating through the air. All this makes a deep impression on him when he awakes. Let him think of that dream as real and meditate upon it.

39

Or by meditation on anything that appeals to one as good.

This does not mean a wicked subject, but anything good that you like: the place that you like best, the scenery that you like best, the idea that you like best—anything that will concentrate the mind.

40

The yogi's mind, thus meditating, becomes unobstructed from the atomic to the infinite.

The mind, by this practice, easily contemplates the most minute as well as the biggest thing. Thus the waves of the mind become fainter.

41

The yogi whose vrittis have thus become powerless (i.e. controlled) obtains, in the receiver, [the instrument of] receiving, and the received (i.e. the soul, the mind, and external objects), concentratedness and sameness, like a crystal [before different coloured objects].

What results from this constant meditation? We must remember how, in a previous aphorism, we took up the various states of meditation: the first was on gross objects, the second on fine, and from them we proceeded to still finer objects. The result is that we can meditate as easily on fine as on gross objects. While meditating thus the yogi sees three things: the receiver, the received, and the receiving instrument, corresponding to the soul, external objects, and the mind. There are three objects of meditation given us: first, gross things, such as bodies or material objects; second, fine things, such as the mind, the chitta; and third, the Purusha qualified—not the Purusha Itself, but the ego. By practice the yogi gets established in all these meditations. Whenever he meditates he can keep out all other thoughts; he becomes identified with that on which he meditates. When he meditates he is like a piece of crystal. Before flowers the crystal becomes almost identified with the flowers: if the flower is red, the crystal looks red, and if the flower is blue, the crystal looks blue.

42

[The samādhi in which] sound, meaning, and the resulting knowledge are mixed is [called] "samādhi with question."

Sound here means vibration; meaning, the nerve currents which conduct it; and knowledge, the reaction. All the various meditations we have discussed so far, Patanjali calls savitarka, "with question." Later on he gives us higher and higher meditations. In these that are called "with question," we keep the duality of subject and object, which results from the mixture of word, meaning, and knowledge. There is first the external vibration, the word; this, carried inward by the nerve currents, is the meaning. After that there comes a reactionary wave in the chitta, which is knowledge; but the mixture of these three makes what we call knowledge. In all the meditations up to this we get this mixture as objects of meditation. The next samādhi is higher.

43

The samādhi called "without question" [is attained] when the memory is purified, or becomes devoid of qualities, expressing only the meaning [of the object meditated on].

It is by the practice of meditation on these three that we come to the state where these three are not mixed. We can get rid of them. We shall first try to understand what these three are. Here is the chitta. You should always remember the comparison of the mind-stuff to a lake, and the vibration, the word, the sound, to a wave coming over it. You have that calm lake in you, and I pronounce a word, "cow." As soon as it enters through your ears there is a wave produced in your chitta along with it. So that wave represents the idea of the cow—the form or the meaning as we call it. The apparent cow that you know is really the wave in the mind-stuff that comes as a reaction to the internal and external sound vibrations. With the sound, the wave dies away; it can never exist without a word. You may ask what happens when we only think of the cow and do not hear the sound. At such times you make that sound yourself. You are saying "cow" inaudibly in your mind, and with that comes the wave. There cannot be any wave without this impulse of sound, and when it is not from outside it is from inside; and when the sound dies, the wave dies. What remains? The result of the reaction—and that is knowledge. These three are so closely combined in our minds that we cannot separate them. When the sound comes, the senses vibrate, and the wave rises as a reaction; they follow so closely upon one another that there is no discerning one from the other. When this meditation has been practised for a long time, the memory, the receptacle of all impressions, becomes purified, and we are able to distinguish them clearly from one another. This is called nirvitarka, samādhi "without question."

44

By this process [the samādhis] "with discrimination" and "without discrimination," whose objects are finer, are [also] explained.

A process similar to the preceding is applied again; but the objects to be taken up in the former meditations are gross, whereas in this they are fine.

45

The finer objects end with the pradhāna.

The gross objects are only the elements, and everything manufactured out of them. The fine objects begin with the tanmātras, or fine particles. The organs, the mind,[2] ego, the mind-stuff (the cause of all manifestation), the state of equilibrium of sattva, rajas, and tamas—called the pradhāna (the chief), prakriti (nature), or avyakta (the unmanifest)—are all included within the category of fine objects, the Purusha (the Soul) alone being excepted.

46

These samādhis are "with seed."

These do not destroy the seed of past actions and thus cannot give liberation; but what they bring to the yogi is stated in the following aphorism.

47

When the yogi becomes established in the samādhi "without discrimination," his chitta becomes firmly fixed.

48

The knowledge attained through it is called "filled with Truth."

The next aphorism will explain this.

49

The knowledge that is gained from testimony and inference is about ordinary objects. That from the samādhi just mentioned is of a much higher order, being able to penetrate where inference and testimony cannot go.

The idea is that we obtain our knowledge of ordinary objects by direct perception, by inference therefrom, and through the testimony of people who are competent. By people who are competent the yogis always mean the rishis, the seers of the thoughts recorded in the scriptures, the Vedas. According to them, the only proof of the scriptures is that they were the testimony of competent persons; yet they say that the scriptures cannot take us to realization. We may read all the Vedas and yet not realize anything; but when we practise

[2] The mind, or common sensory, the aggregate of all the senses.

their teachings, then we shall attain to that state in which we realize what the scriptures say, which penetrates where neither reason nor perception nor inference can go, and where the testimony of others is of no avail. This is what is meant by the aphorism. Realization is the real religion; all the rest is only preparation—hearing lectures, or reading books, or reasoning, is merely preparing the ground; this is not religion. Intellectual assent and intellectual dissent are not religion.

The central idea of the yogis is that just as we come in direct contact with the objects of the senses, so also we can directly perceive religion itself, though in a far more intense sense. The truths of religion, such as God or the Soul, cannot be perceived by the external senses. I cannot see God with my eyes, nor can I touch Him with my hands. We also know that neither can we reason beyond the senses. Reason leaves us at a point quite indecisive. We may reason all our lives, as the world has been doing for thousands of years, but the only result will be that we shall find we are incompetent to prove or disprove the facts of religion. What we perceive directly we take as a basis, and upon that basis we reason. So it is obvious that reasoning has to run within the bounds of perception; it can never go beyond. The whole scope of realization, therefore, is beyond sense perception. The yogis say that man can go beyond his direct sense perception and beyond his reason also. Man has in him the faculty, the power, of transcending even his intellect—a power which is in every being, every creature. By the practice of yoga that power is aroused, and then a man transcends the ordinary limits of reason and directly perceives things which are beyond all reason.

50

The resulting impression from this samādhi obstructs all other impressions.

We have seen in the foregoing aphorism that the only way of attaining to superconsciousness is through samādhi, and we have also seen that the past samskāras, or impressions, are what hinder the mind from achieving samādhi. All of you have observed that when you are trying to concentrate your mind, your thoughts wander. When you are trying to think of God, that is the very time these samskāras appear. At other times they are not so active, but when you do not want them they are sure to be there, trying their best to crowd into your mind. Why should that be so? Why should they be much more potent at the time of concentration? It is because you are repressing them and they react with all their force. At other times they do not react. How countless these old past impressions must be, all lodged somewhere in the chitta, ready, waiting like tigers, to jump up! These have to be suppressed that the one idea which we want may arise, to the exclusion of the others. Instead they are all struggling to come up at the same time. Such is the power of the various samskāras in hindering concentration of the mind. So this samādhi which has just been given is the best to be practised, on account of its power of suppressing the samskāras. The samskāra raised by this sort of concentration will be so powerful that it will hinder the action of the others and hold them in check.

51

By the restraint of even this [impression, which obstructs all other impressions], all being restrained, comes the seedless samādhi.

You remember that our goal is to perceive the Soul Itself. We cannot perceive the Soul because It has got mixed up with nature, with the mind, with the body. The ignorant man thinks his body is the Soul. The learned man thinks his mind is the Soul. But both of them are mistaken. What makes the Soul get mixed up with all this? Different waves that rise in the chitta and cover the Soul. We see only a little reflection of the Soul through these waves; so if the wave is one of anger, we think the Soul is angry—"I am angry," we say. If it is one of love, we see ourselves reflected in that wave and say we love. If that wave is one of weakness, and the Soul is reflected in it, we think we are weak. These various ideas come from these impressions, these samskāras, covering the Soul. The real nature of the Soul is not perceived as long as there is one single wave in the lake of the chitta; this real nature will never be perceived until all the waves have subsided. So first Patanjali teaches us the meaning of these waves; secondly, the best way to repress them; and thirdly, how to make one wave so strong as to suppress all other waves, fire eating fire, as it were. When only one remains, it will be easy to suppress that also, and when that is done, the samādhi or concentration that follows is called "seedless." It leaves nothing, and the Soul is manifested just as It is, in Its own glory. Then alone do we know that the Soul is not a compound; It is the only eternally simple substance in the universe; and as such, It cannot be born, It cannot die. It is immortal, indestructible, the ever living essence of intelligence.

CONCENTRATION: ITS PRACTICE

1

Mortification, study, and the surrender of the fruits of work to God are called kriyā-yoga.

Those samādhis with which the first chapter ended are very difficult to attain; so we must take them up slowly. The first step, the preliminary step, is called kriyā-yoga. Literally, this means practising yoga through work. The organs are the horses, the mind is the reins, the intellect is the charioteer, the soul is the rider, and the body is the chariot. If the horses are very strong and do not obey the reins, and if the charioteer has no discrimination, then the rider comes to grief. But if the horses, the organs, are well controlled by the reins, the mind, and the charioteer possesses discrimination, then the rider, the soul, reaches the goal.

What is meant, in this case, by "mortification"? It means holding the reins firmly while guiding the body and the organs; not letting them do everything they like, but keeping them both under proper control.

What is meant by "study"? Not study of novels or story-books, but study of those works which teach the liberation of the soul. Then again, this study does not mean controversial studies at all. The yogi is supposed to have finished his period of controversy. He has had enough of that and has become satisfied. He studies only to intensify his convictions. Vāda and siddhānta are the two kinds of scriptural knowledge: vāda, the argumentative, and siddhānta, the decisive. When a man is entirely ignorant he takes up the first of these, the argumentative, fighting and reasoning pro and con; and when he has finished that he takes up the siddhānta, the decisive, arriving at a conclusion. Simply arriving at this conclusion will not do. It must be realized. Books are infinite in number, and time is short; therefore the secret of knowledge is to take only what is essential. Take what is essential and try to live up to it. There is an old Indian legend that if you place a cup of milk and water before a rāja-hamsa, a swan, he will take all the milk and leave the water. In that way we should take what is of value in knowledge and leave the dross. Intellectual gymnastics are necessary at first; we must not go blindly into anything. But the yogi has passed the argumentative stage and has come to a conclusion, which is immovable, like the rocks. The only thing he now seeks to do is to intensify that conclusion. Do not argue, he says; if anyone forces arguments upon you, be silent. Do not answer any argument, but go away calmly, because arguments only disturb the mind. The only use of argument is to train the intellect. When that is accomplished, what is the use of disturbing it further? The intellect is but a weak instrument and can only give us knowledge limited by the senses. The yogi wants to go beyond the senses; therefore the intellect is of no ultimate use to him. He is certain of this and therefore is silent and does not argue. Every argument throws his mind out of balance, creates a disturbance in the chitta; and a disturbance is a drawback. Argumentation and reasoning are only preliminary stages; there are things beyond them. The whole of life is not for schoolboy fights and debating societies.

The "surrender of the fruits of work to God" means to take to ourselves neither credit nor blame, but to give both up to the Lord and be at peace.

2

[Kriyā-yoga leads to] samādhi and attenuates the pain-bearing obstructions.

Most of us are like spoilt children, who allow the mind to do whatever it wants. Therefore it is necessary that kriyā-yoga should be constantly practised, in order to gain control of the mind and bring it into subjection. The obstructions to yoga arise from lack of control and cause us pain. They can be removed only by controlling the mind and holding it in check through kriyā-yoga.

3

The pain-bearing obstructions are ignorance, egoity, attachment, aversion, and clinging to life.

These are the five kinds of pain, the fivefold tie that binds us down. Of them, ignorance is the cause, and the other four are the effects. It is the only cause of all our misery. What else can make us miserable? The nature of the Soul is eternal bliss. What can make It sorrowful except ignorance, hallucination, delusion? All pain in the Soul is simply delusion.

4

Ignorance is the productive field of all those that follow, whether they are dormant, attenuated, overpowered, or expanded.

Ignorance is the cause of egoity, attachment, aversion, and clinging to life. These impressions exist in different states. They are sometimes dormant. You often hear the expression "innocent as a baby"; yet in the baby may be the nature of a demon, which will come out by degrees. In the yogi, these impressions, the samskāras left by past actions, are "attenuated," that is, their power is much weakened; and he can control them and not allow them to become manifest. "Overpowered" means that sometimes one set of impressions is held down for a while by those that are stronger; but they come out when that repressing cause is removed. The last state is the "expanded," when the samskāras, having helpful surroundings, attain to great activity, either as good or evil.

5

Ignorance is to take what is non-eternal, impure, painful, and not-Self, for what is eternal, pure, happy and the Ātman, or Self [respectively].

All the different sorts of impressions have one source: ignorance. We have first to learn what ignorance is. Every one of us thinks: "I am the body, and not the Self, the pure, the effulgent, the ever blissful"—and that is ignorance. We think of the Self and see It as the body. This is the great delusion.

6

Egoity is the identification of the Seer with the instrument of seeing.

The Seer is really the Self, the Pure One, the Ever Holy, the Infinite, the Immortal. This is the Self of man. And what are the instruments? The chitta, or mind-stuff, the buddhi, or determinative faculty, the manas, or mind, and the indriyas, or sense-organs. These are Its instruments for seeing the external world; and the identification of the Self with the instruments is what is called egoity, which results from ignorance. We say: "I am the mind," "I am unhappy," "I am angry," or "I am happy." How can we be angry and how can we hate? We should identify ourselves with the Self; That cannot change. If It is unchangeable, how can It be one moment happy and one moment unhappy? It is formless, infinite, omnipresent. What can change It? It is beyond all law. What can affect It? Nothing in the universe can produce an effect on It; yet, through ignorance, we identify ourselves with the mind-stuff and think we feel pleasure or pain.

7

Attachment is that which dwells on pleasure.

We find pleasure in certain things, and the mind, like a current, flows towards them; and this following the centre of pleasure, as it were, is what is called attachment. We are never attached to that in which we do not find pleasure. We find pleasure in very queer things, sometimes, but the principle remains that whatever object we find pleasure in, to that we are attached.

8

Aversion is that which dwells on pain.

That which gives us pain we immediately seek to get away from.

9

Abiding in its own nature [due to the past experience of death], and established even in the learned, is the clinging to life.

This clinging to life you see manifested in every living being. Upon it attempts have been made to build the theory of a future life, because men are so fond of life that they desire a future life also. Of course, it goes without saying that this argument is without much value; but the most curious part of it is that in Western countries the idea that this clinging to life indicates a possibility of future life applies only to men but does not include animals.

In India this clinging to life has been one of the arguments to prove past experience and existence. For instance, if it is true that all our knowledge has come from experience, then it is sure that that which we never experienced we cannot imagine or understand. As soon as chickens are hatched they begin to pick up food. Many times it has been seen that, when ducks have been hatched by a hen, they run to the water as soon as they come out of the eggs, and the mother hen thinks they will drown. If experience is the only source of knowledge, where do chickens learn to pick up food, or ducklings learn that water is their natural element? If you say it is instinct, it means nothing; it is simply giving a word, but is no explanation. What is this instinct? We have many instincts in ourselves. For instance, those of you who play the piano can remember, when you first were learning, how carefully you had to put your fingers on the black and the white keys, one after the other, but now, after long years of practice, you can talk with your friends while your fingers play mechanically. Your playing has become instinctive. So with every work: by practice it becomes instinctive and automatic, and so far as we know, all the cases which we now regard as automatic are degenerated reason. In the language of the yogi, instinct is involved reason. Discrimination becomes involved and gets to be automatic samskāras. Therefore it is perfectly logical to think that all that we call instinct in this world is simply involved reason. As reason cannot come without experience, all instinct is, therefore, the result of past experience. Chickens fear the hawk, and ducklings love the water; these are both the results of past experience.

Then the question is whether that experience belongs to a particular soul or simply to the body, whether this experience which comes to the duck is the duck's forefathers' experience or the duck's own experience. Modern scientific men hold that it belongs to the body; but the yogis hold that it is the experience of the mind, transmitted through the body. This is called the theory of reincarnation. We have seen that all our knowledge, whether we call it perception or reason or instinct, must come through that one channel called experience, and that all that we now call instinct is the result of past experience, degenerated into instinct, and that instinct regenerates into reason again. And this is so throughout the universe. Upon this, in India, has been built one of the chief arguments for reincarnation.

The recurring experience of various fears produces, in course of time, this clinging to life. That is why the child is instinctively afraid; the past experience of pain is there in it. Even in the most learned men, who know that this body will die and who say: "Never mind. We have had hundreds of bodies; the Soul cannot die"—even in them, with all their intellectual conviction, we still find this clinging to life. Why is there this clinging to life? We have seen that it has become instinctive. In the psychological language of the yogis it has become a samskāra. The samskāras, fine and hidden, are sleeping in the chitta. All these past experiences of death, all that we call instinct, are experiences become subconscious. They live in the chitta; and they are not inactive, but work underneath.

The chitta-vrittis, the mind-waves, which are gross, we can appreciate and feel; they can be more easily controlled. But what about the finer instincts? How can they be controlled? When I am angry my whole mind becomes a huge wave of anger. I feel it, see it, handle it, can easily manipulate it, can fight with it; but I shall not succeed completely in the fight until I can get down to its causes. A man says something very harsh to me, and I begin to feel that I am getting heated; and he goes on till I am totally angry, till I forget myself and identify myself with anger. When he first began to abuse me, I thought, "I am going to be angry"; the anger was one thing and I was another. But when I became angry, I was the anger. These feelings have to be controlled in the germ, the root, in their fine forms, even before we have become conscious that they are acting on us. With the majority of mankind the fine states of these passions are not even known—the states below consciousness from which they slowly emerge. When a bubble is rising from the bottom of the lake we do not see it, nor even when it has nearly come to the surface; it is only when it bursts and makes a ripple that we know it is there. We shall only be successful in grappling with the waves when we can get hold of them in their fine forms; until we can get hold of them and subdue them before they become gross, there is no hope of conquering any passion perfectly. To control our passions we have to control them at their very root; then alone shall we be able to burn out their seeds. As fried seeds sown in the ground will never come up, so these passions will never arise.

10

The fine samskāras are to be conquered by resolving them into their causal state.

The samskāras are the subtle impressions which remain even when the mental waves are destroyed by meditation. How can these samskāras be controlled? By resolving the effect into the cause. When the chitta, which is an effect, is resolved, through samādhi, into its cause, asmitā or "I-consciousness," then only do the fine impressions die along with it.

11

By meditation their [gross] modifications are to be rejected.

Meditation is one of the effective means of controlling the rise of these waves. By meditation you can subdue these mental waves; and if you go on practising meditation for days and months and years—until it has become a habit, until it comes in spite of yourself—anger and hatred will be completely controlled and checked.

12

The "receptacle of works" has its roots in the aforesaid pain-bearing obstructions, and the experience of the latter is in this visible (present) life or in the unseen (next) life.

By the "receptacle of works" is meant the sum total of samskāras. Any work we do throws the mind into a wave; and after the work is finished we think the wave is gone. It is not so; the wave has only become fine; it is still there. When we try to remember the work, it comes up again and becomes a wave. So it was there; if not, there would not have been memory. Thus every action, every thought, good or bad, goes into the deepest level of the mind, becomes fine, and remains stored up there. Both happy and unhappy thoughts are called "pain-bearing obstructions," because, according to the yogis, in the long run both bring pain. All happiness which comes from the senses will eventually bring pain. All enjoyment will make us thirst for more, and that brings pain as its result. There is no limit to man's desire; he goes on desiring, and when he comes to a point where desire cannot be fulfilled, the result is pain. Therefore the yogis regard the sum total of the impressions, good or evil, as pain-bearing obstructions; they obstruct the way to the freedom of the Soul.

The samskāras, the fine roots of all our works, should be regarded as causes which will bring effects either in this life or in the lives to come. In exceptional cases, when these samskāras are very strong, they bear fruit quickly; exceptional acts of wickedness or of goodness bring their fruits even in this life. The yogis hold that men who are able while living to acquire a tremendous power of good samskāras do not have to die, but even in this life can change their bodies into god bodies. There are several such cases mentioned by the yogis in their books. These men change the very material of their bodies; they rearrange the molecules in such a fashion that they have no more sickness, and what we call death does not come to them. Why should this not be? Physiologically, the eating of food means assimilation of energy from the sun. The energy first enters the plant, the plant is eaten by an animal, and the animal by a man. This means, in the language of science, that we take an amount of energy from the sun and make it part of ourselves. If that be so, why should there be only one way of assimilating energy? The plant's way is not the same as ours; the earth's process of assimilating energy differs from our own. But all assimilate energy in some way or other. The yogis contend that they are able to assimilate energy by the power of the mind alone, that they can draw in as much of it as they desire without recourse to the ordinary methods. As a spider makes its web out of its own substance, and becomes bound by it, and cannot go anywhere except along the lines of that web, so we have projected out of the material of our bodies this network called the nerves, and now we cannot work except through the channels of those nerves. The yogis say that we need not be bound by them.

To give another example, we can send electricity to any part of the world, but we have to send it by means of wires. Nature can send a vast mass of electricity without any wires at all. Why cannot we do the same? We can send mental electricity everywhere. What we call mind is very much the same as electricity. It is clear that the nerve fluid has some amount of electricity, because it is polarized and has all the characteristics of electricity. We can now send our electricity only through these nerve channels. Why can we not send mental electricity without this aid? The yogis say that it is perfectly possible and practicable, and that when you can do that you will work all over the universe. You will be able to work with any body anywhere, without the help of the nervous system. When the soul is acting through these nerve channels we say that a man is living, and when it ceases to work through them a man is said to be dead. But when a man can act either with or without these channels, birth and death will have no meaning for him. All the bodies in the universe are made up of tanmātras; their difference lies in the arrangement of the latter. If you are the arranger you can arrange a body in one way or another. Who makes up this body but

you? Who eats the food? If another ate the food for you, you would not live
long. Who makes the blood out of the food? You, certainly. Who purifies the
blood and sends it through the veins? You. We are the masters of the body
and we live in it. Only we have lost the knowledge of how to rejuvenate it;
we have become automatic, degenerate; we have forgotten the process of arranging its molecules. So what we do automatically has to be done knowingly. We
are the masters and we have to regulate that arrangement, and as soon as we
can do that we shall be able to rejuvenate ourselves just as we like, and then we
shall have neither birth nor disease nor death.

13

**The roots being there, the fruition comes in [the form of] species, longevity,
and experience of pleasure and pain.**

The roots, the causes, the samskāras being there, in the mind, they manifest
themselves and form the effects. The cause dying down becomes the effect; the
effect getting subtler becomes the cause of the next effect. A tree bears a seed,
which becomes the cause of another tree, and so on. All our present works are
the effects of past samskāras; again, these works, becoming samskāras, will be
the causes of future actions, and thus we go on. So this aphorism says that, the
causes being there, the fruit must come in the form of species of beings: one
will be a man, another an angel, another an animal, another a demon. Then
there are different effects of karma on longevity: one man lives fifty years, another a hundred, another dies in two years and never attains maturity. All these
differences in longevity are regulated by past karma. One man is born, as it were,
for pleasure; if he buries himself in a forest, pleasure will follow him there.
Another man, wherever he goes, is followed by pain; everything becomes painful
for him. It is all the result of their own past. According to the philosophy of the
yogis, all virtuous actions bring pleasure and all vicious actions bring pain. Any
man who does wicked deeds is sure to reap their fruit in the form of pain.

14

They (i.e. actions) bear fruit as pleasure or pain, caused by virtue or vice.

15

**To the discriminating, all is, as it were, painful because everything brings
pain, either as consequence or as anticipation of loss of happiness or as fresh
craving arising from impressions of happiness, and also because the gunas counteract one another.**

The yogis say that the man who has the power of discrimination, the man
of good sense, sees through all that is called pleasure or pain and knows that
they come to all, and that one follows and melts into the other. He sees that
men follow an ignis fatuus all their lives and never succeed in fulfilling their
desires. The great king Yudhishthira once said that the most wonderful thing
in life is that every moment we see people dying around us and yet we think
we shall never die. We think that, though surrounded by fools on every side,
we are the only exceptions, the only learned men. Though everywhere we
experience fickleness, we think our love is the only lasting love. How can that

be? Even love is selfish; and the yogi says that in the end we shall find that even the love of husbands and wives and children and friends slowly decays. Decadence seizes everything in this life. It is only when everything, even love, fails that, in a flash, man finds out how vain, how dreamlike, is this world. Then he catches a glimpse of vairāgya, renunciation, catches a glimpse of the Beyond. It is only by giving up this world that the other is seen—never through holding on to this one. Never yet was there a great soul who had not to reject sense pleasures and enjoyments to acquire his greatness. The cause of misery is the clash between the different forces (gunas) of nature, one dragging one way and another dragging another, rendering permanent happiness impossible.

16

The misery which has not yet come is to be avoided.

Some karma we have worked out already, some we are working out in our present life, and some is waiting to bear fruit in a future life. The first kind is past and gone. The second we shall have to work out. It is only that which is waiting to bear fruit in the future that we can conquer and control; and towards this end all our forces should be directed. This is what Patanjali means when he says (II. 10.) that the samskāras are to be controlled by resolving them into their causal state.

17

The cause of that [misery] which is to be avoided is the junction of the Seer and the seen.

Who is the Seer? The Self of man, the Purusha. What is the seen? The whole of nature, from the mind down to gross matter. All pleasure and pain arise from the joining of the Purusha and the mind. The Purusha, you must remember, according to this philosophy is pure; when joined to nature, and reflected therein, It appears to feel pleasure or pain.

18

The seen, which is composed of elements and organs, and characterized by illumination, action, and inertia, is for the purpose of experience and release [of the Seer].

Nature, or the seen, is composed of gross and fine elements and the organs—that is to say, the sense-organs, the mind, and so forth—and is characterized by illumination (sattva), action (rajas), and inertia (tamas). What is the whole purpose of the seen, or nature? It is to give the Purusha experience. The Purusha has, as it were, forgotten Its mighty, godlike nature. There is a story that the king of the gods, Indra, once became a pig wallowing in mire; he had a she-pig and a lot of baby pigs and was very happy. Then some gods saw his plight and came to him and said, "You are the king of the gods; you have all the gods under your command; why are you here?" But Indra said: "Never mind. I am all right here; I do not care for heaven while I have this sow and these little pigs." The poor gods were at their wits' end. After a time they decided to slay

all the pigs one after another. When all were dead, Indra began to weep and
mourn. Then the gods ripped his pig body open, and he came out of it and
began to laugh when he realized what a hideous dream he had had—he, the king
of the gods, to have become a pig and to have thought that that pig life was the
only life! Not only so, but to have wanted the whole universe to join him in the
pig life!

Likewise, the Purusha, when identified with nature, forgets that It is pure and
infinite. The Purusha does not love; It is love itself. It does not exist; It is
existence itself. The Soul does not know; It is knowledge itself. It is a mistake
to say that the Soul loves, exists, or knows. Love, existence, and knowledge are
not the qualities of the Purusha, but Its essence. When they are reflected upon
something, you may call them the qualities of that thing. They are not the
qualities but the essence of the Purusha, the great Ātman, the Infinite Being,
without birth or death, established in Its own glory. It appears to have become
so degenerate that if you come and tell It, "You are not a pig," It begins to
squeal and bite.

Thus is it with us all in this māyā, this dream-world, where it is all misery,
weeping, and crying, where a few golden balls are rolled and the world scrambles
after them. You were never bound by laws; nature never put a bond on you.
That is what the yogi tells you. Have patience to learn it. And the yogi shows
how, by junction with nature, by identifying Itself with the mind and the world,
the Purusha thinks Itself miserable. Then he goes on to show you that the way
out is through experience. You have to get all this experience; but finish it
quickly. We have placed ourselves in this net and we shall have to get out.
We have got ourselves caught in the trap, and we shall have to work out our
freedom. So get this experience of husbands and wives and friends and little
loves; you will pass through them safely if you never forget what you really are.
Never forget that this is only a momentary state and that you have to pass
through it. Experience is the one great teacher—experience of pleasure and pain
—but know that it is only momentary. It leads step by step to that state where
all things become small, and the Purusha so great that the whole universe seems
as a drop in the ocean and falls off by its own nothingness. We have to go
through different experiences, but let us never forget the ideal.

19

**The states of the gunas are the defined (the gross elements), the undefined
(the subtle elements), the merely indicated (the cosmic intelligence), and the
signless (prakriti).**

The system of Yoga is built entirely on the philosophy of Sāmkhya, as I told
you before; and here again I shall remind you of the cosmology of the Sāmkhya
philosophy. According to Sāmkhya, nature is both the material and the efficient
cause of the universe. In nature there are three gunas, or elements: sattva, rajas,
and tamas. Tamas is all that is dark, all that is ignorant and heavy; rajas is
activity; and sattva is calmness, light. Nature, before creation, is called avyakta,
undefined or indiscrete—that is, the state in which there is no distinction of form
or name, in which these three gunas are held in perfect balance. Then the

balance is disturbed, the three gunas begin to mingle in various fashions, and the result is the universe.

In every man, also, these three gunas exist. When sattva prevails, knowledge comes; when rajas, activity; and when tamas, darkness, lassitude, idleness, and ignorance. According to the Sāmkhya theory, the highest manifestation of nature, consisting of these three gunas, is called mahat, or intelligence, universal intelligence, of which the human intellect is a part. In the Sāmkhya psychology there is a sharp distinction between the function of the manas, or mind, and the function of the buddhi, or intellect. The mind's function is simply to collect outer impressions and present them to the buddhi, the individual mahat, which decides about them. Out of mahat comes egoity, from which, again, come the subtle elements. The subtle elements combine and become the gross materials, the external universe. The claim of the Sāmkhya philosophy is that, from the intellect down to a block of stone, all things are the products of one substance, differing only as finer or grosser states of existence. The finer are the causes, and the grosser are the effects. According to the Sāmkhya philosophy, beyond the whole of nature is the Purusha, which is not material at all. The Purusha is not similar to anything else, either the buddhi or the mind or the tanmātras or the gross materials. It is not akin to any one of these; It is entirely separate, entirely different in Its nature; and further, it is argued that the Purusha must be immortal, because It is not the result of combination. That which is not the result of combination cannot die. According to Sāmkhya, Purushas are infinite in number.

Now we shall understand the aphorism when it says that the states of the gunas are the defined, the undefined, the merely indicated, and the signless. By the "defined" are meant the gross elements, which we can sense. By the "undefined" are meant the very fine materials, the tanmātras, which cannot be sensed by ordinary men. If you practise yoga, however, says Patanjali, after a while your perceptions will become so fine that you will actually see the tanmātras. For instance, you have heard that every man sheds a certain light about him; every living being emits a certain light, and this, the yogi says, can be seen by him. We do not all see it, but we all throw out these tanmātras, just as a flower continuously sends out the fine particles which enable us to smell it. Every day of our lives we throw out a mass of good or evil, and everywhere we go the atmosphere is full of these materials. That is how there came to the human mind, unconsciously, the idea of building temples and churches. Why should men build churches in which to worship God? Why not worship Him anywhere? Even if they did not know the reason, men found that a place where people worshipped God became full of good tanmātras. Every day people go there, and the more they go the holier they get and the holier that place becomes. If any man who has not much sattva in him goes there, the place will influence him and arouse his sattva quality. Here, therefore, is the significance of all temples and holy places; but you must remember that their holiness depends on holy people's congregating there. The difficulty with man is that he forgets the original meaning and puts the cart before the horse. It was men who made these places holy, and then the effect became the cause and made men holy. If the wicked alone were to go there it would become as bad as any other place.

It is not the building, but the people, that make a church; and that is what we always forget. That is why sages and holy persons, who have much of this sattva quality, can send it out and exert a tremendous influence day and night on their surroundings. A man may be so pure that his purity will become tangible. Whosoever comes in contact with him will become pure.

Next, the "merely indicated" means the cosmic buddhi, the cosmic intellect. It is the first manifestation of nature; from it all other manifestations proceed.

Last, the "signless," or nature. There seems to be a great difference between modern science and the religions at this point. Every religion says that the universe comes out of intelligence. The theory of God, taking the word in its psychological significance, apart from all ideas of personality, is that intelligence comes first in the order of creation and that out of intelligence comes what we call gross matter. Modern philosophers say that intelligence is the last to come. They say that unintelligent things slowly evolve into animals, and animals into men. They claim that instead of everything's coming out of intelligence, intelligence itself is the last to come. Both the religious and the scientific statements, though seeming to be directly opposed to each other, are true. Take an infinite series: A—B—A—B—A—B and so on. The question is: Which is first, A or B? If you take the series as A—B, you will say that A is first; but if you take it as B—A, you will say that B is first. It depends upon the way you look at it. Intelligence undergoes modification and becomes gross matter; this again merges into intelligence; and thus the process goes on. The followers of Sāmkhya, and other religious people, put intelligence first, and the series becomes intelligence, and then matter. The scientific man puts his finger on matter and says that first comes matter, and then intelligence. They both indicate the same chain. Hindu philosophy, however, goes beyond both intelligence and matter, and finds a Purusha, or Self, which is beyond intelligence, and of which intelligence is but the borrowed light.

20

The Seer is intelligence only, and though pure, sees through the colouring of the intellect.

This is again Sāmkhya philosophy. We have seen from the same philosophy that, from the lowest form up to intelligence, all is nature; beyond nature are Purushas, which have no qualities. Then how does a Purusha appear to be happy or unhappy? By reflection. If a red flower is put near a piece of pure crystal, the crystal appears to be red. Similarly, the appearance of happiness or unhappiness in the Soul is but a reflection; the Soul Itself has no colouring. The Soul is separate from nature; nature is one thing, the Soul another, eternally separate. Sāmkhya says that intelligence is a compound, that it grows and wanes, that it changes just as the body changes, and that its nature is nearly the same as that of the body. As a finger-nail is to the body, so is the body to intelligence. The nail is a part of the body, but it can be pared off hundreds of times and the body will still last. Similarly, intelligence lasts aeons, while this body can be pared off, thrown off. Yet intelligence cannot be immortal, because it changes, growing and waning. Anything that changes cannot be immortal. Certainly intelligence is manufactured; and that very fact shows us that there must be something beyond it. It cannot be free; everything connected with matter is in nature, and therefore bound for ever. Who is free? The free must certainly be beyond cause and effect.

If you say that the idea of freedom is a delusion, I shall say that the idea of bondage is also a delusion. Two facts come into our consciousness and stand or fall with each other. These are our notions of bondage and freedom. If we want to go through a wall, and our heads bump against it, we see that we are limited by that wall. At the same time, we find that we have a will-power and think we can direct our will everywhere. At every step these contradictory ideas come to us. We have to believe that we are free, yet at every moment we find we are not free. If one idea is a delusion, the other is also a delusion, and if one is true, the other also is true, because both stand upon the same basis: experience.

The yogi says that both are true—that we are bound as regards intelligence, but that we are free so far as the Soul is concerned. The real nature of the Soul, or Purusha, is beyond the law of causation. Its freedom is percolating through layers of matter in various forms, through intelligence, mind, and so forth. It is Its light that is shining through all. Intelligence has no light of its own. Each organ has a particular centre in the brain. There is not just one centre for all the organs; each organ is separate. Why do all perceptions harmonize? Where do they get their unity? If it were in the brain, it would be necessary for all the organs—the eyes, the nose, the ears, and so forth—to have one centre only; whereas we know for certain that there are different centres for each. But a man can see and hear at the same time; so there must be a unity at the back of intelligence. Intelligence is connected with the brain, but behind even intelligence stands the Purusha, the Unit, where all the different sensations and perceptions join and become one. The Soul Itself is the centre where all the different perceptions converge and become unified. That Soul is free, and it is Its freedom that tells you every moment that you are free, and not bound. But you mistakenly identify that freedom with intelligence and mind. You try to attribute that freedom to the intellect, and immediately find that the intellect is not free; you attribute that freedom to the body, and immediately nature tells you that you are again mistaken. That is why there is this mingled sense of freedom and bondage at the same time. The yogi analyses both what is free and what is bound, and his ignorance vanishes. He finds that the Purusha is free, is the essence of that knowledge which, coming through the buddhi, becomes intelligence and, as such, is bound.

21

The [transformation that takes place in the] nature of the seen (i.e. prakriti) is for Him (i.e. the Purusha).

Prakriti has no power of its own. As long as the Purusha is near it, it appears to have power; but the power is borrowed, just as the moon's light is borrowed. According to the yogis, the whole manifested universe has come from prakriti itself; but prakriti has no purpose except to free the Purusha.

22

Though destroyed for him whose goal has been gained, yet prakriti is not destroyed for others, being common to them.

The whole activity of nature is to make the Soul know that It is entirely separate from nature. When the Soul knows this, nature has no more attractions for It. But the whole of nature vanishes only for that man who has become free. There will always remain an infinite number of others for whom nature will go on working.

23

Junction [of prakriti and the Purusha] is the cause of the realization of the nature of the powers of both the seen and its Lord.

According to this aphorism, the powers of both Soul and nature (i.e. the experiencer and the experienced) become manifest when they (i.e. the Soul and nature) are in conjunction. It is then that the manifestation of the phenomenal universe occurs. Ignorance is the cause of this conjunction. We see every day that the cause of our pain or pleasure is always our joining ourselves with the body. If I were perfectly certain that I am not this body, I should take no notice of heat and cold, or anything of the kind. This body is a combination. It is only a fiction to say that I have one body, you another, and the sun another. The whole universe is one ocean of matter, and you are the name of a little particle, and I of another, and the sun of a third. We know that this matter is continuously changing. What forms the sun one day, the next day may form the material of our bodies.

24

Ignorance is its cause.

Through ignorance we have joined ourselves with particular bodies and thus opened ourselves to misery. This idea of the body is simply a superstition. It is superstition that makes us happy or unhappy; it is superstition caused by ignorance that makes us feel heat and cold, pain and pleasure. It is our duty to rise above this superstition; and the yogi shows us how we can do this. It has been demonstrated that under certain mental conditions a man may be burnt and yet feel no pain. But this sudden exaltation of the mind comes like a whirlwind one minute and goes away the next. If, however, we gain it through yoga, we shall permanently achieve the separation of the Self from the body.

25

There being absence of that (i.e. ignorance), there is absence of junction. This is the destruction of ignorance, and this is the independence of the Seer.

According to the Yoga philosophy, it is through ignorance that the soul has been joined with nature. The aim is to get rid of nature's control over us. That is the goal of all religions. Each soul is potentially divine. The goal is to manifest this divinity within by controlling nature: external and internal. Do this either by work, or worship, or psychic control, or philosophy—by one, or more, or all of these—and be free. This is the whole of religion. Doctrines, or dogmas, or rituals, or books, or temples, or forms, are but secondary details.

The yogi tries to reach this goal through psychic control. Until we can free ourselves from nature we are slaves; as it dictates so we must do. The yogi claims that he who controls mind controls matter also. Internal nature is much subtler than external, and much more difficult to grapple with, much more difficult to control. Therefore he who has conquered internal nature controls the whole universe; it becomes his servant. Rāja-yoga propounds the methods of gaining this control. Forces subtler than any we know in physical nature will have to be subdued. This body is just the external crust of the mind. They are not two different things; they are just like the oyster and its shell. They are but two aspects of one thing. The internal substance of the oyster takes up matter from outside and manufactures the shell. In the same way the internal, fine forces which constitute the mind take up gross matter from outside and from that manufacture this external shell, the body. If, then, we have control of the internal, it is very easy to have control of the external. Then again, these forces are not different. It is not that some forces are physical, and some mental; the physical forces are but the gross manifestations of the fine forces, just as the physical world is but the gross manifestation of the fine world.

26

The means of destruction of ignorance is unbroken practice of discrimination.

This is the real goal of practice: discrimination between the real and the unreal, knowing that the Purusha is not nature, that It is neither matter nor mind, and that because It is not nature, It cannot possibly change. It is only nature which changes, combining and recombining, dissolving continually. When through constant practice we begin to discriminate, ignorance will vanish and the Purusha will begin to shine in Its real nature, omniscient, omnipotent, omnipresent.

27

His knowledge is attained in seven supreme steps.

When this knowledge comes, it comes, as it were, in seven steps, one after another; as we attain one of these we know that we are getting knowledge. The first step will make us feel that we have known what is to be known. The mind will cease to be dissatisfied. As long as we are aware of a thirst after knowledge we seek it here and there, wherever we think we can get some truth, and failing to find it we become dissatisfied and seek in a fresh direction. All search is vain until we begin to perceive that knowledge is within ourselves, that no one can help us, that we must help ourselves. When we begin to develop the power of discrimination, the first sign that we are getting near truth will be that this dissatisfied state will vanish. We shall feel quite sure that we have found the truth and that it cannot be anything else but the truth. Then we may know that the sun is rising, that the morning is breaking for us; and taking courage, we must persevere until the goal is reached.

The second step will be the absence of all pain. It will be impossible for anything in the universe, external or internal, to give us pain. The third will be the attainment of full knowledge. Omniscience will be ours. The fourth will be the attainment, through discrimination, of the end of all duties. Next will come what is called freedom of the chitta. We shall realize that all difficulties and struggles, all vacillations of the mind, have fallen away, just like a stone rolling from the mountain top into the valley and never coming up again. The next will be that the chitta will realize that it can melt away into its causes whenever we so desire.

Lastly, we shall find that we are established in our true Self, that the Self in us has been alone throughout the universe, and that neither body nor mind has ever been related, much less joined, to It. They were working their own way, and we, through ignorance, joined the Self to them. But we have been alone, omnipotent, omnipresent, ever blessed; our own Self was so pure and perfect that we required none else. We required none else to make us happy, for we are happiness itself. We shall find that this knowledge does not depend on anything else. Throughout the universe there can be nothing that will not become effulgent before this knowledge. This will be the last step, and the yogi will become peaceful and calm, never to feel any more pain, never again to be deluded, never to be touched by misery. He will know that he is ever blessed, ever perfect, almighty.

28

Through the practice of the different parts of yoga the impurities are destroyed and knowledge is kindled, leading up to discrimination.

Now come the practical disciplines. What we have just been speaking about is very difficult; it is far above our heads. But it is the ideal. The first thing necessary is to obtain control of the body and mind. Then the realization of the ideal will become steady. The ideal being known, what now remains is to practise the method of reaching it.

29

Yama, niyama, āsana, prānāyāma, pratyāhāra, dhāranā, dhyāna, and samādhi are the eight limbs of yoga.

30

Non-killing, truthfulness, non-stealing, continence, and non-receiving [of gifts] are called yama.

A man who wants to be a perfect yogi must give up the idea of sex. The Soul has no sex; why should It degrade Itself with ideas of sex? Later on we shall understand better why these ideas must be given up. The mind of the man who receives gifts is acted on by the mind of the giver; so the receiver is likely to become degenerate. The receiving of gifts tends to destroy the independence of the mind and make us slavish. Therefore receive no gifts.

31

These, unbroken by time, place, purpose, or caste-rules, are universal, great vows.

These disciplines—non-killing, truthfulness, non-stealing, chastity, and non-receiving—are to be practised by every yogi—man, woman, or child; by everyone, irrespective of nation, country, or position.

32

Internal and external purification, contentment, mortification, study, and worship of God are the niyamas.

External purification means keeping the body pure; a dirty man will never be a yogi. There must be internal purification also. That is obtained through the practice of the virtues named in I. 33. Of course, the internal purity is of greater value than the external; but both are necessary, and the external purity, without the internal, is of no value.

33

When thoughts obstructive to yoga arise, contrary thoughts should be employed.

That is the way to practise the virtues that have been mentioned. For instance, when a big wave of anger has come into the mind, how are we to control it? By raising an opposing wave. Think of love. Sometimes a mother is very angry with her husband, and while she is in that state, the baby comes in and she kisses the baby; the old wave dies out and a new wave arises—love for the child. That suppresses the other one. Love is the opposite of anger. Similarly, when the idea of stealing comes, non-stealing should be thought of; when the idea of receiving gifts comes, replace it by a contrary thought.

34

The obstructions to yoga are killing, falsehood, and so forth—whether committed, caused, or approved—either through avarice, anger, or ignorance—whether slight, middling, or great; they result in infinite ignorance and misery: this is [the method of] thinking the contrary.

To tell a lie, or cause another to tell one, or to approve of another's doing so—it is all equally sinful. A very mild lie is still a lie. Every vicious thought will rebound, every thought of hatred which you may have cherished, even in a cave, is stored up and will one day come back to you with tremendous power in the form of some misery here. If you project hatred and jealousy, they will rebound on you with compound interest. No power can avert them; when once you have put them in motion you will have to bear their fruit. Remembering this will prevent you from doing wicked things.

35

When the yogi is established in non-killing, all enmities [in others] cease in his presence.

If a man realizes the ideal of not injuring others, before him even animals which are by nature ferocious will become peaceful. The tiger and the lamb will play together before that yogi. When you have come to this state, then alone will you understand that you have become firmly established in non-injury.

36

By being established in truthfulness, the yogi gets the power of attaining for himself and others the fruits of work without the work.

When this power of truth is established within you, then you will never tell an untruth even in a dream. You will be true in thought, word, and deed. Whatever you say will be truth. You may say to a man, "Be blessed," and that man will be blessed. If a man is diseased and you say to him, "Be thou cured," he will be cured immediately.

37

By being established in non-stealing, the yogi obtains all wealth.

The more you fly from nature, the more it follows you; and if you do not care for it at all, it becomes your slave.

38

By being established in continence, the yogi gains energy.

The chaste person has tremendous energy and gigantic will-power. Without chastity there can be no spiritual strength. Continence gives wonderful control over mankind. The spiritual leaders of men have been continent, and this is what gave them power. Therefore the yogi must be continent.

39

When the yogi is established in non-receiving he gets the memory of past life.

When a man does not receive presents, he is not beholden to others but remains independent and free. His mind becomes pure. With every gift, he is likely to receive the evils of the giver. If he does not receive gifts, his mind is purified, and the first power he gets is memory of past life. Then alone does the yogi become perfectly fixed in his ideal. He sees that he has been coming and going many times; so he becomes determined that this time he will be free, that he will no more come and go and be the slave of nature.

40

When he is established in internal and external cleanliness, there arises in him disgust for his own body and desire for non-intercourse with others.

When there is real purification of the body, external and internal, there arises neglect of the body; the idea of keeping it nice vanishes. A face which others call most beautiful will appear to the yogi as merely an animal face if the Spirit is not behind it. What the world calls a very common face he will regard as heavenly if the Spirit shines behind it. The thirst after the body is the great bane of human life. So the first sign of the attainment of purity is that you do not care to think you are a body. It is only when purity comes that we get rid of the idea of the body.

41

There also arise purification of the sattva, cheerfulness of the mind, concentration, conquest of the organs, and fitness for the realization of the Self.

Through the practice of cleanliness the sattva material prevails and the mind becomes concentrated and cheerful. The first sign of your becoming religious is that you are cheerful. Gloominess may be a sign of dyspepsia, but it is surely not religion. A pleasurable feeling is the nature of the sattva. Everything is pleasurable to the sāttvika man; and when this comes, know that you are progressing in yoga. All pain is caused by tamas; so you must get rid of it. Moroseness is one of the results of tamas. The strong, the well-knit, the young, the healthy, the daring alone are fit to be yogis. To the yogi everything is bliss, every human face that he sees brings cheerfulness to him, That is the sign of a virtuous man. Misery is caused by sin, and by nothing else. What business have you with clouded faces? It is terrible. If you have a clouded face do not go out that day; shut yourself up in your room. What right have you to carry this disease out into the world? When your mind has become controlled you have control over the whole body; instead of being a slave to this machine, you make the machine your slave. Instead of this machine's being able to drag the soul down, it becomes its greatest helpmate.

42

From contentment comes superlative happiness.

43

The mortification of the organs and the body, through the destruction of their impurities, brings powers to them.

The results of mortification are seen immediately, sometimes in heightened powers of vision, sometimes in the hearing of things at a distance, and so on.

44

By the repetition of the mantra comes the realization of the Chosen Deity.[1]

The higher the being that you want to realize, the harder the practice.

45

Through the sacrificing of all to Iśvara comes samādhi.

By resignation to the Lord, samādhi becomes perfect.

[1] That aspect of the Godhead which the aspirant accepts as his Chosen Ideal.

46

Posture is that which is firm and pleasant.

Now comes āsana, posture. Until you acquire a firm posture you cannot practise the breathing and other exercises. Firmness of posture means that you do
not feel the body at all. Generally speaking, you will find that as soon as you sit
for a few minutes you feel all sorts of bodily disturbances. But when you have
gone beyond the idea of a gross, physical body, you will lose all sense of the
body. You will feel neither pleasure nor pain. And when you again become aware
of it you will feel completely rested. This is the only real rest that you can give
to the body. When you have succeeded in controlling the body and keeping it
firm, your practice will be steady; but while you are disturbed by the body, your
nerves become disturbed and you cannot concentrate the mind.

47

**Through the lessening of the natural tendency [for activity, caused by identi-
fication with the body,] and through meditation on the Infinite, [posture becomes firm and pleasant].**

We can make the posture firm by thinking of the Infinite. We cannot actually think of the transcendental Infinite, but we can think of the infinite sky.

48

Posture being conquered, the dualities do not obstruct.

The dualities—good and bad, heat and cold, and all the pairs of opposites—
will not then disturb you.

49

Control of the motion of exhalation and inhalation follows after this.

When posture has been conquered, the motion of the prāna is then to be
broken—that is, stopped—and then controlled. Thus we come to prānāyāma,
the controlling of the vital forces of the body. Prāna is not the breath, though
it is usually so translated. It is the sum total of the cosmic energy. It is also
the energy that is in each body, and its most apparent manifestation is the
motion of the lungs. This motion is caused by prāna drawing in the breath, and
it is what we seek to control by prānāyāma. We begin by controlling the breath
as the easiest way of getting control of the prāna.

50

**Its modifications are threefold, namely, external, internal, and motionless;
they are regulated by place, time, and number; and further, they are either long
or short.**

There are three kinds of motion in prānāyāma: one by which we draw the
breath in, another by which we expel it, and a third by which the breath is held
in the lungs or stopped from entering the lungs. These, again, vary according

to place and time. "Regulated by place" refers to some particular part of the body the prāna is to be held. "Regulated by time" refers to how long the prāna should be confined to a certain place; and so we are told how many seconds to keep up one motion and how many seconds another. The result of prānāyāma is udghāta, or the awakening of the Kundalini.

51

The fourth is the restraining of the prāna by directing it either to external or to internal objects.

This is the fourth kind of prānāyāma. The prāna can be directed either inside or outside.

[The above aphorism has also been translated and interpreted in the following manner: "The fourth prānāyāma is that which discards both the external and the internal movement of the prāna."

When the external and the internal breathing, regulated by place, time, and number, etc., as described in the preceding aphorism, has been discarded, there then follows the fourth kind of prānāyāma. It consists in the gradual stopping of the course of both exhalation and inhalation; the difference between the one described in the preceding aphorism and the present one is that in the latter the stopping of exhalation and inhalation is affected by objects and is attained by stages. It is characterized by the absence of all movement of the breath, following upon the complete cessation of inhalation and exhalation. Needless to say, these exercises, like the others in rāja-yoga, should be practised under the guidance of a teacher.]

52

By that, the covering of the light of the chitta is attenuated.

The chitta, by its own nature, is endowed with all knowledge. It is made of sattva particles, but is covered by rajas and tamas particles; and by prānāyāma this covering is removed.

53

The mind becomes fit for dhāranā.

After this covering has been removed we are able to concentrate the mind.

54

Pratyāhāra, or the drawing in of the organs, is effected by their giving up their own objects and taking, as it were, the form of the mind-stuff.

The organs are separate states of the mind-stuff. I see a book: the form is not in the book; it is in the mind. Something is outside which calls that form up; but the real form is in the chitta. The organs identify themselves with, and take the forms of, whatever comes to them. If you can restrain the mind-stuff from taking these forms, the mind will remain calm. This is called pratyāhāra.

55

Thence arises supreme control of the organs.

When the yogi has succeeded in preventing the organs from taking the forms of external objects, and in making them remain one with the mind-stuff, then comes perfect control of the organs. When the organs are perfectly under control, every muscle and nerve will be under control, because the organs are the centres of all sensations and of all actions. These organs are divided into organs of action and organs of sensation. When the organs are controlled, the yogi can control all feeling and doing; the whole of the body comes under his control. Then alone does one begin to feel joy in being born. Then one can truthfully say, "Blessed am I that I was born." When that control of the organs is obtained we feel how wonderful this body really is.

THE POWERS

We have now come to the chapter in which the powers of yoga are described.

1

Dhāraṇā is the holding of the mind to some particular object.

When the mind holds on to some object, either in the body or outside the body, and keeps itself in that state, it has attained dhāraṇā, concentration.

2

An unbroken flow of knowledge about that object is dhyāna.

When the mind tries to think of one object, to hold itself to one particular spot, such as the top of the head, or the heart, and succeeds in receiving sensations only through that part of the body, and no other part, it has attained dhāraṇā; and when the mind succeeds in keeping itself in that state for some time, it has attained dhyāna, meditation.

3

When that (i.e. dhyāna), giving up all forms, reveals only the meaning, it is samādhi.

This comes when in meditation the form or the external part is given up. Suppose I am meditating on a book; I have gradually succeeded in concentrating the mind on it, and then in perceiving only the internal sensations, the meaning, unexpressed in any form. That state of dhyāna is called samādhi.

4

[These] three, [when practised] in regard to one object, constitute samyama.

When a man can direct his mind to any particular object and fix it there, and then keep it there for a long time, separating the object from the internal part, this is samyama—that is to say, dhāraṇā, dhyāna, and samādhi, one following the other and all three being directed to one object. The form of the thing has vanished and only its meaning remains in the mind.

5

Through the attainment of that (i.e. samyama) comes the light of knowledge.

When one has succeeded in practising samyama, all the powers come under one's control. This is the great instrument of the yogi. The objects of knowledge

667

are infinite, and they are divided into gross, grosser, grossest, and fine, finer, finest, and so on. Samyama should be first applied to gross things, and when one begins to get knowledge of the gross, slowly, by stages, it should be applied to finer things.

6

That (i.e. samyama) should be practised in stages.

This is a note of warning not to attempt to go too fast.

7

These three disciplines are more internal than those that precede.

We have described pratyāhāra, prānāyāma, āsana, yama, and niyama before; they are more external than dhāranā, dhyāna, and samādhi. When a man has attained to these latter he may attain to such powers as omniscience and omnipotence, but that is not salvation. These three do not make the mind nirvikalpa, free from modifications, but leave the seeds of future embodiment. Only when the seeds are, as the yogi says, fried, do they lose the possibility of producing further plants. These powers cannot fry the seed.

8

But even they (i.e. dhāranā, dhyāna, and samādhi) are external to the seedless [samādhi].

Compared with that seedless samādhi, therefore, even these are external. We have not yet reached the real samādhi, the highest; we are in a lower stage, in which the universe still exists as we see it and in which lie all the powers described in the present chapter.

9

By the suppression of the disturbing impressions of the mind, and by the rise of impressions of control, the mind which persists in that state of control is said to attain the controlling modifications.

That is to say, in the first state of samādhi the modifications of the mind have been controlled, but not perfectly, because if they were, there would be no modifications. If there is a modification which impels the mind to rush out through the senses, and the yogi tries to control it, that very control will be another modification. One wave will be checked by another wave; so it will not be the real samādhi, in which all the waves subside, since the control itself will remain as a wave. Yet this lower samādhi is very much nearer to the higher samādhi than when the mind bubbles up.

10

Its flow becomes steady by habit.

The flow of this continuous control of the mind becomes steady when practised day after day, and the mind obtains the faculty of constant concentration.

11

Taking in all sorts of objects and concentrating upon one object are two modifications of the mind. When the first of these is suppressed and the other manifested, the chitta acquires the modification called samādhi.

The mind generally takes up various objects, runs into all sorts of things. That is the lower state. There is a higher state of the mind, when it takes up one object and excludes all others. The result of this is samādhi.

12

The modification called one-pointedness of the chitta is acquired when the impression that is past and that which is present are similar.

How are we to know that the mind has become concentrated? The idea of time will vanish. The greater the amount of time that passes unnoticed, the more deeply concentrated we are. In everyday life we see that when we are interested in a book we do not note the time at all, and when we leave the book we are often surprised to find how many hours have passed. All time will have a tendency to be unified in the one present. So the definition is given: when the past and present become one, the mind is said to be concentrated.[1]

13

In this way (i.e. by the three modifications mentioned above) is explained the threefold transformation as to form, time, and state in matter and in the organs.

Aphorisms 9, 11, and 12 have explained the threefold transformation in the mind-stuff, or chitta. In like manner are explained the transformations in matter and in the organs. Suppose there is a lump of earth. When it is transformed into a pot, it gives up the form of the lump and takes that of the pot. This is called "transformation as to form." Concerning "transformation as to time," there are three aspects of time: past, present, and future. One can view the pot in any of these three aspects. Lastly, the pot may be thought of as new, old, or as it is going to be. This is called "transformation as to state." Now, referring to aphorisms 9, 11, and 12, the mind-stuff changes into vrittis. This is transformation as to form. When it passes through past, present, and future moments of time, it is transformation as to time. And lastly, when the disturbing impressions of the mind-stuff are strong and the controlling impressions are weak (see aphorism 9), and vice versa, it is transformation as to state. Since the mind is an organ, thus is explained transformation of the organs as to form, time, and state, as mentioned in the text. The similar transformation of matter

---

[1] The difference between the three kinds of concentration mentioned in aphorisms 9, 11, and 12 is as follows: In the first, the disturbed impressions are merely held back, but not altogether obliterated by the impressions of control, which have just come in; in the second, the former are completely suppressed by the latter, which stand in bold relief; while in the third, which is the highest, there is no question of suppressing, but only similar impressions succeed each other in a stream.

has been explained above. The concentrations taught in the preceding aphorisms give the yogi a voluntary control over the transformations of his mind-stuff, which alone enables him to practise samyama as described in III. 4. It should be noted that all entities except the Purusha, or Self, are subject to the threefold transformation mentioned in the text.

14

That which is acted upon by transformations, either past, present, or yet to be manifested, is the substance qualified.

That is to say, the "substance qualified" is the substance which is being acted upon by time and by the samskāras, and is always getting changed and being manifested.

15

The succession of changes is the cause of manifold evolution.

16

Through the practice of samyama on the three sorts of changes comes the knowledge of the past and future.

We must not lose sight of the definition of samyama. When the mind has attained to that state in which it identifies itself with the internal impression of the object, leaving the external, and when, by long practice, that is retained by the mind, and the mind can get into that state in a moment, that is samyama. If a man in that state wants to know the past and future, he has to practise samyama on the changes in the samskāras (III. 13). Some are working themselves out at present, some have already worked themselves out, and some are waiting to work; so by practising samyama on these he knows the past and future.

17

Through samyama on word, meaning, and knowledge, which are ordinarily confused, comes the knowledge of all animal sounds.

"Word" represents the external cause; "meaning" represents the internal vibration, which travels to the brain through the channels of the indriyas, conveying the external impression to the mind; and "knowledge" represents the reaction of the mind, with which comes perception. These three, confused, make up our sense-objects. Suppose I hear a word. There is first the external vibration, next the internal sensation carried to the mind by the organ of hearing; then the mind reacts and I know the word. The word I know is a mixture of these three: vibration, sensation, and reaction. Ordinarily they are inseparable; but by practice the yogi can separate them. When a man has attained to this, if he practises samyama on any sound, he understands the meaning which that sound was intended to express, whether it was made by a human being or by any other animal.

18

Through the perceiving of the impressions [comes] the knowledge of past life.

Each experience that we have comes in the form of a wave in the chitta; this subsides and becomes finer and finer, but is never lost. It remains there in a subtle form, and if we can bring this wave up again, it becomes a memory. So if the yogi can practise samyama on these past impressions in the mind, he will begin to remember all his past lives.

19

Through the practice of samyama on the signs on another's body comes knowledge of his mind.

Each man has particular signs on his body, which differentiate him from others; when the yogi practises samyama on these signs on anyone, he knows the nature of that person's mind.

20

But not its contents, that not being the object of the samyama.

By practising samyama on the body he would not know the contents of the mind. That would require a twofold samyama: first on the signs on the body and then on the mind itself. The yogi would then know everything in that mind.

21

Through the practice of samyama on the form of the body, the power of perceiving forms being obstructed and the power of manifestation in the eye being separated [from the form], the yogi's body becomes unseen.

A yogi standing in the middle of this room can apparently vanish. He does not really vanish, but he will not be seen by anyone. The form and the body are, as it were, separated. You must remember that this can only be done when the yogi has attained to that power of concentration when the form and the thing formed have been separated. Then he practises samyama on that form, and the power to perceive forms is obstructed, because the power of perceiving forms comes from the junction of the forms and the things formed.

22

In this manner the disappearance or concealment of words which are being spoken, and other such things, are also explained.

23

Karma is of two kinds: some to be fructified soon and some to be fructified later. By practising samyama on these, or on the signs called arishta, portents, the yogis know the exact time of their separation from their bodies.

When a yogi practises samyama on his own karma, upon those impressions in his mind which are now working themselves out and those which are just waiting to work, he knows, by those that are waiting, exactly when his body will fall. He knows when he will die—at what hour, even at what minute. The Hindus think very highly of this knowledge or consciousness of the nearness of death, because it is taught in the Gītā that the thoughts at the moment of departure have great influence in determining the next life.

24

By practising samyama on friendship, mercy, and so forth [I. 33] the yogi excels in these respective qualities.

25

Through samyama on the strength of the elephant, and other creatures, their respective strength comes to the yogi.

When a yogi has attained to samyama and wants strength, he practises samyama on the strength of the elephant and gets it. Infinite energy is at the disposal of everyone, if he only knows how to obtain it. The yogi has discovered the science of obtaining it.

26

Through samyama on the effulgent light [I. 36] comes the knowledge of the fine, the obstructed, and the remote.

When the yogi practises samyama on the effulgent light in the heart, he sees things which are very remote, things, for instance, which are happening in a distant place and which are obstructed by mountain barriers, and also things which are very fine.

27

Through samyama on the sun [comes] knowledge of the world.

28

On the moon, knowledge of the cluster of stars.

29

On the pole-star, knowledge of the motion of the stars.

30

[Through samyama] on the navel circle [comes] knowledge of the constitution of the body.

31

On the hollow of the throat, cessation of hunger.

When a man is very hungry, if he can practise samyama on the hollow of the throat, hunger ceases.

32

On the nerve called the kurma, fixity of the body.

When he is practising disciplines the body is not disturbed.

33

On the light emanating from the top of the head, sight of the siddhas.

The siddhas are beings a little above ghosts. When the yogi concentrates his mind on the top of his head he sees these siddhas. The word *siddhas* does not here refer to those men who have become free, a sense in which it is often used.

34

Or by the power of pratibhā [comes] all knowledge.

All these can come without any samyama to the man who has the power of pratibhā, spontaneous enlightenment through purity. When a man has risen to a high state of pratibhā he has that great light. All things are apparent to him. Everything comes to him naturally without practising samyama.

35

[Through samyama] on the heart [comes] knowledge of minds.

36

Enjoyment comes through the non-discrimination of the Soul and the sattva (buddhi), which are totally different. This enjoyment is for the sake of the Soul. There is another state of the sattva, called svārtha (its own pure state). The practice of samyama on this state gives the knowledge of the Purusha.

The Purusha and the sattva, or buddhi, which is a modification of prakriti, are totally different from each other. But the Purusha is reflected in the buddhi and identifies Itself with the different states of the buddhi, such as happiness or misery, and thus regards Itself as happy or miserable. These experiences of the buddhi are not for its own sake but for that of another, namely, the Soul. But there is another state of the buddhi, which serves its own purpose. In that state it is free from the sense of "me and mine." Devoid of impurities, the buddhi becomes pervaded by the light of the Purusha; it reflects the Purusha alone. Becoming introspective, it is related only to the Purusha and becomes independent of all other relations. When one concentrates on this aspect of the buddhi, one attains the knowledge of the Purusha. The reason for practising samyama on the purified buddhi is that the Purusha Itself can never be the object of knowledge, since It is the knower.

37

From that arises the knowledge of [supernatural] hearing, touching, seeing, tasting, and smelling, which belong to pratibhā.

38

These are obstacles to samādhi, but they are powers in the worldly state.

To the yogi, knowledge of the enjoyments of the world comes by the junction of the Purusha and the mind. If he wants to practise samyama on the knowledge that they are two different things, nature and Self, he gets knowledge of the Purusha. From that arises discrimination. When he has got that discrimination he gets the pratibhā, the light of supreme knowledge. The powers which the yogi obtains, however, are obstructions to the attainment of the highest goal, the knowledge of the Pure Self, or freedom. These are to be met on the way, and if the yogi rejects them he attains the highest. If he is tempted to acquire these, his farther progress is barred.

39

When the cause of bondage has become loosened, the yogi, by his knowledge of the channels of activity of the chitta (i.e. the nerves), enters another's body.

The yogi can enter a dead body and make it get up and move, even while he himself is working in his own body. Or he can enter a living body and hold that man's mind and organs in check, and for the time being act through the body of that man. This the yogi does by discriminating between the Purusha and nature. If he wants to enter another's body he practises samyama on that body and enters it, because not only is his Self omnipresent, but also his mind, as Yoga teaches. It is one bit of the universal mind. At first, however, it can work only through the nerve currents in his own body; but when the yogi has loosened himself from these nerve currents, he can work through other bodies.

40

When he has conquered the current called the udāna, the yogi does not sink in water or in swamps, he can walk on thorns and so forth, and can die at will.

The udāna is the nerve current that governs the lungs and all the upper parts of the body, and when the yogi has mastered it he becomes light in weight. He does not sink in water, he can walk on thorns and sword blades and stand in fire, and can depart from this life whenever he likes.

41

Through the conquest of the current called the samāna he is surrounded by a blaze of light.

Whenever he wishes, light flashes from his body.

42

Through samyama on the relation between the ear and ākāśa comes divine hearing.

There is ākāśa, ether, and there is also the instrument, the ear. By practising samyama on them the yogi gets supernormal hearing; he hears anything he wants to. He can hear sounds uttered miles away.

43

By practising samyama on the relation between ākāśa and the body and

regarding himself to be as light as cotton-wool, and so forth, the yogi can go through the skies.

Ākāśa is the material of this body; the body is only ākāśa in a certain form. If the yogi practises samyama on this material of his body, it acquires the lightness of ākāśa and he can go anywhere through the air.

44

Through samyama on the real modifications of the mind, outside the body, called great disembodiedness, comes disappearance of the covering to light.

The mind in its foolishness thinks that it is working in one body. Why should I be bound by one system of nerves and limit the ego to only one body, if the mind is omnipresent? There is no reason why I should. The yogi wants to feel the ego wherever he likes. The mental waves which arise in the absence of egoity in the body are called "real modifications" or "great disembodiedness." When he has succeeded in practising samyama on these modifications, all the covering to light goes away and all darkness and ignorance vanish. Everything appears to him to be full of knowledge.

45

Through samyama on the gross and fine forms of the elements, their essential traits, the inherence of the gunas in them, and their contributing to the experience of the Soul comes mastery of the elements.

The yogi practises samyama on the elements, first on the gross and then on the fine. This samyama is taken up mostly by a sect of Buddhists. They take a lump of clay and practise samyama on that, and gradually they begin to see the fine materials of which it is composed; and when they have known all the fine materials in it, they get power over those elements. So with all the elements. The yogi can conquer them all.

46

From that come minuteness and the rest of the powers, glorification of the body, and indestructibility of the bodily qualities.

This means that the yogi has attained the eight supernatural powers. He can make himself as minute as an atom or as huge as a mountain, as heavy as the earth or as light as air; he can reach anything he likes, he can rule everything he wants, he can conquer everything he wants, and so on. A lion sits at his feet like a lamb, and all his desires are fulfilled at will.

47

"Glorification of the body" means beauty, complexion, strength, adamantine hardness.

The body becomes indestructible. Nothing can injure it. Nothing can destroy it until the yogi wishes. "Breaking the rod of time, he lives in this universe in his body." In the Vedas it is written that for such a man there is no more disease, death, or pain.

48

Through samyama on the perception, by the organs, of external objects, the knowledge that follows, the "I-consciousness" that accompanies this knowledge, the inherence of the gunas in all of these, and their contributing to the experience of the Soul comes the conquest of the organs.

In the perception of external objects the organs leave their places in the mind and go towards the objects; this process is followed by knowledge. Ego also is present in the act. When the yogi practises samyama on these and the other two, by gradation, he conquers the organs. Take up anything that you see or feel—a book, for instance: first concentrate the mind on it, then on the knowledge that is in the form of a book, and then on the ego that sees the book, and so on. By this practice all the organs will be conquered.

49

From that come to the body the power of rapid movement like that of the mind, power of the organs independent of the body, and the conquest of nature.

Just as by the conquest of the elements comes a glorified body, so from the conquest of the organs come the above-mentioned powers.

50

Through samyama on the discrimination between the sattva and the Purusha come omnipotence and omniscience.

When nature has been conquered, and the difference between the Purusha and nature realized—that the Purusha is indestructible, pure, and perfect, and nature, Its opposite—then come omnipotence and omniscience.

51

Through the giving up of even these powers comes the destruction of the very seed of evil, and this leads to kaivalya (isolation).

The yogi attains aloneness and becomes free. When one gives up even the ideas of omnipotence and omniscience, there comes the entire rejection of enjoyment, of the temptations from celestial beings. When the yogi has seen all these wonderful powers and rejected them, he reaches the goal. What are all these powers? Simply manifestations. They are no better than dreams. Even omnipotence is a dream. It depends on the mind. So long as there is a mind it can be omnipotent; but the goal is beyond even the mind.

52

The yogi should not feel allured or flattered by the overtures of celestial beings, for fear of evil again.

There are other dangers too: gods and other beings come to tempt the yogi. They do not want anyone to be perfectly free. They are jealous, just as we are, and are even worse than us sometimes. They are very much afraid of losing their positions. Those yogis who do not reach perfection become gods after death; leaving the direct road, they go into one of the side-streets and get these powers. Then they have to be born again. But he who is strong enough to withstand these temptations, and goes straight to the goal, becomes free.

53

Through samyama on a particle of time and that which precedes and succeeds it comes discrimination.

How are we to avoid all these things—these devas and heavens and powers? By discrimination, by knowing good from evil. Therefore a samyama is prescribed by which the power of discrimination can be strengthened. This is done through samyama on a particle of time and the time preceding and following it.

54

Those things which cannot be differentiated by species, sign, or place—even they will be differentiated by the above samyama.

The misery we suffer from is the result of ignorance, of non-discrimination between the real and the unreal. We all take the bad for the good, the dream for the reality. The Self is the only reality, and we have forgotten It. The body is an unreal dream, and we all think we are bodies. This non-discrimination is the cause of misery. It is caused by ignorance. When discrimination comes it brings strength. Then alone can we avoid all these various ideas of body, heavens, and gods. We differentiate between objects by means of species, sign, and place. For instance, take a cow. The cow is differentiated from the dog by species. Even with cows alone, how do we make the distinction between one cow and another? By signs. If two objects are exactly similar, they can be distinguished if they are in different places. When objects are so mixed up that even these differentiae will not help us, the power of discrimination acquired by the above-mentioned practice will give us the ability to distinguish them. The highest philosophy of the yogi is based upon this fact: that the Purusha is pure and perfect and is the only simple substance that exists in this universe. The body and mind are compounds, and yet we are for ever identifying ourselves with them. This is the great mistake—that the distinction has been lost. When the power of discrimination has been attained, a man sees that everything in this world, mental and physical, is a compound, and, as such, cannot be the Purusha.

55

The saving knowledge is that knowledge of discrimination which simultaneously covers all objects in all their variations.

This knowledge is called "saving" because it takes the yogi across the ocean of birth and death. The whole of prakriti in all its states, subtle and gross, is within the grasp of this knowledge. There is no succession in perception of this knowledge; it takes in all things simultaneously, at a glance.

56

By the similarity of purity between the sattva and the Purusha comes kaivalya.

When the Purusha realizes that It depends on nothing in the universe, from the gods to the lowest atom, It attains the state of kaivalya, or perfection. Kaivalya is the goal. When the Self attains this state, It realizes that It has always been alone and "isolated," and that It did not require anything to make It happy. As long as we want somebody or something else for our happiness, so long we are slaves. When the Purusha knows that freedom is Its very nature and that It does not need anything to attain perfection, when It knows that nature is transitory and really meaningless, that very moment the Purusha attains liberation and becomes "isolated" from nature. This state is attained when the mixture of purity and impurity called the sattva, that is to say, the intellect, has been made as pure as the Purusha Itself; then the sattva reflects only the unqualified essence of purity, which is the Purusha.

INDEPENDENCE

1

The siddhis, or powers, are attained through birth, chemical means, the power of words, mortification, or concentration.

Sometimes a man is born with the siddhis, or powers; of course these he had earned in his previous incarnation. This time he is born, as it were, to enjoy their fruits. It is said of Kapila, the great father of the Sāmkhya philosophy, that he was a born siddha, which means, literally, a man who has attained to success.

The yogis claim that these powers can also be gained by chemical means. All of you know that chemistry originally began as alchemy; men began to search for the philosophers' stone and elixirs of life, and so forth. In India there was a sect called the Rasāyanas. According to them, subtle theories, knowledge, spirituality, and religion were all very good, but the body was the only instrument by which to attain them. If the body came to an end every now and again, it would take so much more time to attain the goal. For instance, a man wants to practise yoga or wants to become spiritual. Before he has advanced very far he dies. Then he takes another body and begins again, then dies, and so on. In this way much time is lost in dying and being born again. If the body could be made strong and perfect, so that it could free itself from birth and death, we should have so much more time to become spiritual.

So these Rasāyanas said that we should first make the body very strong. They claimed that this body could be made immortal. Their idea was that if the mind manufactured the body, and if it was true that each mind is only one outlet of the infinite energy, there should be no limit to each outlet's getting power from outside. Therefore why should it be impossible to keep our bodies alive all the time? We have to manufacture all the bodies that we ever have. As soon as this body dies we shall have to manufacture another. If we can do that, why cannot we do it just here and now, without getting out of the present body? The theory is perfectly correct. If it is possible for us to live after death and make other bodies, why is it impossible for us to make bodies here, without entirely dissolving this body—simply changing it continually? They also thought that in mercury and sulphur was hidden a most wonderful power, and that by certain preparations of these a man could keep the body alive as long as he liked. Others believed that certain drugs could bring powers, such as flying through the air. Many of the most wonderful medicines of the present day we owe to the Rasāyanas, notably the use of metals in medicine. Certain sects of yogis claim that many of their principal teachers are still living in their old bodies. Patanjali, the great authority on Yoga, does not deny this.

The power of words: There are certain sacred words, called mantras, which, when repeated under proper conditions, are able to produce these extraordinary powers. We are living in the midst of such a mass of miracles, day and night, that we do not think anything of them. There is no limit to man's power: the power of words and the power of mind.

Mortification: You find that every religion prescribes such disciplines as mortification and asceticism. In matters like these the Hindus always go to extremes. You will find men holding their hands up all their lives, until their hands wither and die. Men keep standing, day and night, until their feet swell, and if they live, the legs become so stiff in this position that they can no more bend them, but have to stand all their lives. I once saw a man who had kept his hands raised in this way, and I asked him how he felt when he did it first. He said it was awful torture. It was such torture that he had to go to a river and put himself in water, and that allayed the pain for a little while. After a month he did not suffer much. Through such practices the powers, or siddhis, can be attained.

Concentration: This is yoga proper; this is the principal theme of this science, and it is the highest discipline. The preceding ones are only secondary, and we cannot attain to the goal through them. Samādhi is the means through which we can gain anything and everything—mental, moral, and spiritual.

2

The change into another species is effected by the filling in of nature.

Patanjali has advanced the proposition that these powers come by birth or by chemical means or through mortification. He also has said that the body can be kept alive for any length of time. Now he goes on to state what is the cause of the change of the body into another species. He says that this is done by the filling in of nature, which he explains in the next aphorism.

3

Good and bad deeds are not the direct causes of the transformations of nature, but they act as breakers of obstacles to its evolutions—as a farmer breaks the obstacles to the course of water, which then flows down by its own nature.

The water for irrigating the fields is already in the canal, only held back by gates. The farmer opens these gates and the water flows in by itself, by the law of gravitation. So all progress and power are already in man. Perfection is man's very nature; only it is barred off and so prevented from taking its proper course. If anyone can take the bar away, in rushes nature. Then the man attains the powers which are his already. Those whom we call wicked become saints as soon as the bar is broken and nature rushes in. It is nature that is driving us towards perfection, and eventually it will bring everyone there. All these practices and struggles to become religious are only negative work, to take off the bars and open the doors to that perfection which is our birthright, our nature.

Today the evolution theory of the ancient yogis will be better understood in the light of modern research. But the theory of the yogis is a better explanation. The two causes of evolution advanced by the moderns, namely, sexual selection and the survival of the fittest, are inadequate. Suppose human knowledge has advanced so much that it has eliminated competition as a factor in the acquiring both of physical sustenance and of a mate; then, according to the moderns, human progress will stop and the race will die. The result of this theory is to furnish every oppressor with an argument to calm the qualms of conscience. Men are not lacking who, posing as philosophers, would kill out all weak and incompetent persons—they are, of course, the only judges of competency— and thus preserve the human race. But the great ancient evolutionist Patanjali declares that the true goal of evolution is the manifestation of the perfection which is already in every being; that this perfection has been barred off, and the infinite tide is struggling to express itself. All this struggle and competition is but the result of our ignorance, because we do not know the proper way to unlock the gate and let the water in. This infinite tide behind must express itself; it is the cause of all manifestation. Competition for survival or sex-gratification is only a momentary, unnecessary, extraneous factor caused by ignorance. Even when all competition has ceased, this perfect nature in us will make us go forward until everyone has attained perfection. Therefore there is no reason to believe that competition is necessary to progress. In the animal the man was suppressed, but as soon as the door was opened, out rushed man. So, too, in man there is the potential god, kept in by the locks and bars of ignorance. When knowledge breaks these bars the god becomes manifest.

4

A yogi can create many minds from his egoity.

The theory of karma is that we experience the results of our good or bad deeds, and the whole scope of philosophy is to help us realize the glory of man. All the scriptures sing the glory of man, of the Soul, and then, in the same breath, they preach karma. A good deed brings one result, and a bad deed another. But if the Soul can be acted upon by a good or bad deed, It amounts to nothing. Bad deeds simply put a bar to the manifestation of the nature of the Purusha; good deeds take the obstacles off, and the glory of the Purusha becomes manifest. The Purusha Itself is never changed. Whatever you do never destroys your own glory, your own nature, because the Soul cannot be acted upon by anything; only a veil is spread before It, hiding Its perfection.

With a view to exhausting their karma quickly, yogis create kāya-vyuha, or groups of bodies, in which to work it out. For all these bodies they create minds from egoity. These are called "created minds" in contradistinction to their original minds.

5

Though the activities of the different created minds are various, the one original mind is the controller of them all.

These different minds, which act in the different bodies, are called "created minds," and the bodies, "created bodies"—that is, manufactured bodies and minds. Matter and mind are like two inexhaustible storehouses. When you become a yogi you learn the secret of their control. It was yours all the time, but you had forgotten it. When you become a yogi you recollect it. Then you can do anything with it, manipulate it in any way you like. The material out of which a created mind is made is the very same material which is used for the macrocosm. It is not that mind is one thing and matter another; they are different aspects of the same thing. Asmitā, egoity, is the material, the fine state of existence, out of which these "created minds" and "created bodies" of the yogi are manufactured. Therefore when the yogi has found the secret of these energies of nature, he can manufacture any number of bodies or minds out of the substance known as egoity.

6

Among the various minds, that which is attained by samādhi is desireless.

Among all the various minds that we see in various men, that mind which has attained to samādhi, perfect concentration, is the highest. A man who has attained certain powers through medicines, or through mantras, or through mortifications, still has desires; but he who has attained to samādhi through concentration is free from all desires.

7

Works are neither black nor white for the yogis; for others they are three-fold: black, white, and mixed.

When the yogi has attained perfection, his actions, and the results produced by those actions, do not bind him, because he is free from desire. He just works on. He works to do good, and he does good; but he does not care for the results, and they will not come to him. But for ordinary men, who have not attained to that highest state, works are of three kinds: black, or evil, white, or good, and mixed.

8

From these threefold works are manifested in each state only those desires [which are] fitting to that state alone. [The others are held in abeyance for the time being.]

Suppose that I have performed the three kinds of karma—good, bad, and mixed—and suppose that I die and become a god in heaven. The desires in a god body are not the same as the desires in a human body. The god body neither eats nor drinks. What becomes of my past unfulfilled karmas, which should produce as their effect the desire to eat and drink? Where do these karmas go when I become a god? The answer is that desires can only manifest themselves in proper environments. Only those desires become active for which the environment is fitted; the rest will remain stored up. In this life we have many godly desires, many human desires, many animal desires. If I take a god body, only the good desires will function, because for them the environment is suitable. And if I take an animal body, only the animal desires will become active, and the good desires will wait. What does this show? It shows that by means of environment we can check desires. Only that karma which is suited to and fitted for the environment will come out. This shows that the power of environment is a great check to control even karma itself.

9

There is consecutiveness in desires, even though separated by species, space, and time, there being identification of memory and impressions.

Experiences becoming fine become impressions; impressions revivified become memory. The word memory here includes unconscious co-ordination of past experiences, reduced to impressions, with present conscious action. In each body, only the group of impressions acquired in a similar body becomes the cause of action in that body. The experiences of a dissimilar body are held in abeyance. Each body acts as if it were the descendant of a series of bodies of that species only; thus consecutiveness of desires is not broken.

10

Thirst for happiness being eternal, desires are without beginning.

All experience is preceded by desire for happiness. There is no beginning of experience, since each fresh experience is built upon the tendency generated by past experience; therefore desire is without beginning.

11

[Desire] being held together by cause, effect, support, and objects, in the absence of these it is absent.

Desires are held together by cause and effect;[1] if a desire has been raised, it does not die without producing its effect. Then again, the mind-stuff is the great storehouse, the receptacle of all past desires reduced to samskāra form; until they have worked themselves out they will not die. Moreover, so long as the senses receive external objects, fresh desires will arise. If it is possible to get rid of the cause, effect, support, and objects of desire, then alone will it vanish.

12

The past and future exist in their own nature, their difference being due to the differences in the gunas.

The idea is that existence never comes out of non-existence. The past and future, though not existing in a manifested form, exist in a fine form.

13

They are manifested or fine, the gunas being their inmost nature.

The gunas are the three substances—sattva, rajas, and tamas—whose gross state is the tangible universe. Past and future arise from the different modes of manifestation of these gunas.

[1] The causes are the "pain-bearing obstructions" (II. 3) and works (IV. 7), and the effects are "species, longevity, and experience of pleasure and pain" (II. 13).

14

The unity in things follows from the unity in changes [of the gunas].

Though there are three substances, their changes being co-ordinated, all objects manifest a unity.

15

Since perception and desire vary with regard to the same object, mind and object are of different nature.

That is, there is an objective world independent of our minds. This is a refutation of Buddhist idealism. Since different people look at the same thing differently, it cannot be a mere imagination of any particular individual.[2]

16

Things are known or unknown to the mind, being dependent on the colouring which they give to the mind.

17

The states of the mind are always known, because the Lord of the mind, the Purusha, is unchangeable.

The whole gist of this theory is that the universe is both mental and material. Both matter and mind are in a state of flux. What is this book? It is a combination of molecules in constant change: one lot is going out, and another coming in. It is like a whirlpool. But what makes the unity? What makes it the same book? The changes are rhythmical; in harmonious order they are sending impressions to my mind, and these pieced together make a continuous picture, although the parts are continuously changing. The mind, too, is continuously changing. Mind and body are like two layers in the same substance, moving at different rates of speed. One being slower and the other quicker, we can distinguish between the two motions. For instance, a train is in motion and a carriage is moving alongside of it. It is possible to determine the motion of both of them, to a certain extent. But still something else is necessary. Motion can only be perceived when there is something else which is not moving. But when two or three things are moving relative to one another, we first perceive the motion of the faster one, and then that of the slower ones. How can the mind perceive? It too is in a flux. Hence another thing is necessary which moves more slowly; then you must think of something in which the motion is still slower, and so on; and you will find no end. Therefore logic compels you to stop somewhere. You must complete the series by knowing something which never changes. Behind

[2] There is an additional aphorism here in some editions:

"The object cannot be said to be dependent on a single mind. There being no proof of its existence, [if the mind did not perceive it,] it would then become non-existent."

If the perception of an object were the only criterion of its existence, then, when a man's mind was absorbed in something or was in samādhi, that object would not be perceived by anybody and might as well be said to be non-existent. This is an undesirable conclusion.

this never-ending chain of motion is the Purusha, changeless, colourless, pure. All these impressions are merely reflected upon It, as a magic lantern throws images upon a screen without in any way staining it.

18

The mind is not self-luminous, being an object.

Tremendous power is manifested everywhere in nature, but it is not self-luminous, not essentially intelligent. The Purusha alone is self-luminous, and It gives Its light to everything. It is the power of the Purusha that is percolating through all matter and energy.

19

On account of its being unable to cognize both at the same time, [the mind is not self-luminous].

If the mind were self-luminous it would be able to cognize itself and its objects at the same time, which it cannot. When it cognizes objects it cannot reflect on itself. Therefore the Purusha is self-luminous and the mind is not.

20

Another cognizing mind being assumed, there will be no end to such assumptions, and confusion of memory will be the result.

Let us suppose that there is another mind which cognizes the ordinary mind; there will then have to be still another to cognize the former, and so there will be no end to it. The result will be confusion of memory; there will be no store-house of memory.

21

The Essence of Knowledge (the Purusha) is unchangeable; when the mind takes Its form, it becomes conscious.

Patanjali says this to make it more clear that knowledge is not a quality of the Purusha. When the mind comes near the Purusha, the latter is reflected, as it were, upon the mind, and the mind, for the time being, becomes knowing and seems as if it were itself the Purusha.

22

Coloured by the Seer and the seen, the mind is able to understand everything.

On one side of the mind the external world, the seen, is being reflected, and on the other, the Seer is being reflected; thus comes to the mind the power of knowing everything.

23

The mind, though variegated on account of innumerable desires, acts for another (i.e. the Purusha), because it acts in combination.

The mind is a compound of various things and therefore cannot work for itself. Everything that is a combination in this world serves the purpose of another entity for which that combination has been made. So this combination of the mind is for the Purusha.

24

For the discriminating the perception of the mind as Ātman ceases.

Through discrimination the yogi knows that the Purusha is not the mind.

25

Then, bent on discriminating, the mind attains the state preliminary to kaivalya, isolation.

[There is another reading: "Then the mind becomes deep in discrimination and gravitates towards kaivalya."]

Thus the practice of yoga leads to the power of discriminating, to clearness of vision. The veil drops from the eyes and we see things as they are. We find that nature is a compound and is showing its panorama for the satisfaction of the Purusha, who is the witness; that nature is not the Lord, that all the combinations of nature are simply for the sake of showing these phenomena to the Purusha, the enthroned King within. When discrimination comes by long practice, fear ceases and the mind attains isolation.

26

The thoughts that arise [from time to time] as obstructions to that come from impressions.

All the various ideas that arise, making us believe that we require something external to make us happy, are obstructions to that perfection. The Purusha is happiness and blessedness by Its own nature. But that knowledge is covered over by past impressions. These impressions have to work themselves out.

27

Their destruction is in the same manner as that of ignorance, egoity, and so forth, as said before (II. 10).

28

Even when arriving at the right discriminative knowledge of the essences, he who gives up its fruits—unto him comes, as the result of perfect discrimination, the samādhi called the "cloud of virtue."

When the yogi has attained to discrimination, all the powers mentioned in the last chapter come to him; but the true yogi rejects them all. Unto him comes a peculiar knowledge, a particular light, called the dharmamegha, the "cloud of virtue." All the great prophets of the world whom history has recorded had this. They had found the whole foundation of knowledge within themselves. Truth to them had become real. Peace and calmness and perfect purity became their own nature after they had given up the vanities of powers.

29

From that comes the cessation of pain and works.

When that "cloud of virtue" has come, then no more is there fear of falling; nothing can drag the yogi down. No more will there be evil for him; no more will there be pain.

30

Then knowledge, bereft of covering and impurities, becomes infinite and the knowable becomes small.

Knowledge itself is there; its covering is gone. One of the Buddhist scriptures defines the Buddha—which is the name of a state—as infinite knowledge, infinite as the sky. Jesus attained to that and became the Christ. All of you will attain to that state. Knowledge becoming infinite, the knowable becomes small. The whole universe, with all its objects of knowledge, becomes as nothing before the Purusha. The ordinary man thinks himself very small, because to him the knowable seems to be infinite.

31

Then are finished the successive transformations of the gunas, they having attained their end.

Then all these various transformations of the gunas, which change from species to species, cease for ever.

32

The changes that exist in relation to moments, and which are perceived at the other end (i.e. at the end of a series), are what is meant by succession.

Patanjali here defines the word *succession*: the changes that exist in relation to moments. While I think, many moments pass, and with each moment there is a change of idea; but I only perceive these changes at the end of a series. This is called succession. But for the mind that has realized omnipresence there is no succession. Everything has become present for it. To it the present alone exists; the past and future are lost. Time stands controlled; all knowledge is there in one second. Everything is known in a flash.

33

The resolution of the gunas in the inverse order, when they are bereft of any motive of action for the Purusha, is kaivalya (isolation or freedom); or kaivalya is the establishment of the Power of Knowledge in Its own nature.

Nature's task is done, this unselfish task which our sweet nurse, nature, has imposed upon herself. She gently takes the self-forgetting soul by the hand, as it were, and shows it all the experiences in the universe, all manifestations, bringing it higher and higher through various bodies, till its lost glory comes back and it remembers its own nature. Then the kind mother goes back the same way she came, for others who also have lost their way in the trackless desert of life. Thus is she working, without beginning and without end; and thus, through pleasure and pain, through good and evil, the infinite river of souls is flowing into the ocean of perfection, of Self-realization.

Glory unto those who have realized their own nature! May their blessings be on us all!

APPENDIX

REFERENCES TO YOGA

Śvetāśvatara Upanishad

Chapter II

6

Where the fire is kindled by rubbing, where the air is controlled, where the soma flows over, there a [perfect] mind is created.

8

Placing the body in a straight posture, with the chest, the neck, and the head held erect, making the organs and the mind enter the heart, the sage crosses all the fearful currents by means of the raft of Brahman.

9

The man of well regulated endeavours controls the prāna, and when it has become quieted, breathes out through the nostrils. The wise man undistractedly holds his mind, as a charioteer restrains restive horses.

10

In [lonely] places, such as mountain caves, where the floor is even, free from pebbles or sand, free from fire, where there are no disturbing noises from men or waterfalls, in places pleasing to the mind and not painful to the eyes, yoga is to be practised.

11

When yoga is practised, the forms which appear first and which gradually manifest Brahman are those of snowflakes, smoke, sun, wind, fire, fire-flies, lightning, crystal, and the moon.

12

When the perceptions of smell, taste, touch, form, and sound, arising from earth, water, air, fire, and ākāśa, as described in yoga, have taken place, then yoga has begun. Unto him disease does not come, nor old age nor death, who has got a body purified by the fire of yoga.

13

The first signs of entering yoga are lightness, health, absence of desire, a good complexion, a beautiful voice, an agreeable odour of the body, and slight excretions.

14

As a lump of gold or silver covered with earth shines brightly when well cleaned, so the embodied man, realizing the truth of Ātman, attains Non-duality and becomes sorrowless and blessed.

Yājnavalkya, Quoted by Śankara

"After practising the postures as desired, according to the rules, O Gārgi, a man who has conquered the postures will practise prāṇāyāma.

"Seated in an easy posture, on a [deer or tiger] skin placed on kuśa grass, worshipping Ganapati with fruits and sweetmeats, placing the right palm on the left, holding the neck and head in the same line, the lips closed and firm, facing the east or the north, the eyes fixed on the tip of the nose, avoiding too much food or fasting, the nāḍis should be purified, without which the practice will be fruitless. Thinking of [the seed-word] *Hum*, at the junction of the Pingalā and the Idā (the right and the left nostrils), the Idā should be filled with external air in twelve seconds; then the yogi meditates on fire in the same place, with the word *Rung*, and while meditating thus, slowly ejects the air through the Pingalā. Again filling in, through the Pingalā, the air should be slowly ejected through the Idā in the same way. This should be practised for three or four years, or three or four months, according to the directions of a guru, in secret (alone in a room), in the early morning, at midday, in the evening, and at midnight [until] the nerves become purified. Lightness of body, clear complexion, good appetite, and hearing of the Nāda are the signs of the purification of the nerves. Then should be practised prāṇāyāma, composed of rechaka (exhalation), kumbhaka (retention), and puraka (inhalation). Joining the prāna with the apāna is prāṇāyāma.

"After filling the body from the head to the feet in sixteen seconds, the prāna is to be expelled in thirty-two seconds, and for sixty-four, kumbhaka should be practised.

"There is another prāṇāyāma, in which kumbhaka should first be made for sixty-four seconds, then the prāna should be expelled in sixteen, and the body next filled in sixteen seconds.

"By prāṇāyāma the impurities of the body are expelled; by dhāraṇā, the impurities of the mind; by pratyāhāra, the impurities of attachment; and by samādhi is taken off everything that hides the lordship of the Soul."

Sāmkhya Philosophy

Book III

29

Through intensity of meditation there come to the Purusha all the powers of nature.

30

Meditation is the destruction of attachment.

31

It is perfected by the suppression of the modifications.

32

It is perfected by dhāranā, posture, and performance of one's duties.

33

Restraint of the prāna is effected by means of expulsion and retention.

34

Posture is that which is steady and easy.

36

Meditation is also perfected by non-attachment and practice.

74

By reflection on the principles of nature and by giving them up as "not this, not this," discrimination is perfected.

Book IV

3

The student should repeatedly hear instruction [from the scriptures and the teacher].

5

As the hawk becomes unhappy if his food is taken away from him and happy if he gives it up himself, [so he who gives up everything voluntarily is happy].

6

As the snake is happy in giving up his old skin, [so he who gives up everything voluntarily is happy].

8

That which is not a means of liberation is not to be thought of; it becomes a cause of bondage, as in the case of Bharata.[1]

9

Association with many persons creates passion, aversion, and so forth, and is an obstruction to meditation, as with the shell bracelets on the virgin's hand.[2]

10

It is the same even with two [persons].

11

The renouncers of hope are happy, like the girl Pingalā.[3]

13

Though an aspirant should show devotion to many scriptures and teachers, he must take from all of them the essence only, as a bee takes the essence from many flowers.

14

One whose mind has become concentrated like an arrow-maker's is not disturbed in his samādhi.

15

As great harm is done in a worldly undertaking when the prescribed rules are violated, so it is also with meditation.

19

Through continence, reverence, and devotion to the guru, success is attained after a long time [as in the case of Indra].

20

There is no law as to time, as in the case of Vāmadeva.[4]

[1] According to the story, King Bharata on his death-bed brooded over his pet deer and consequently was reborn as a deer.

[2] A maiden, who wore a number of bracelets on her wrists, was massaging her father in order to put him to sleep. But the friction of the bracelets made a noise, disturbing his rest.

[3] The prostitute Pingalā, eagerly awaiting the arrival of her paramour, felt extremely unhappy because he did not come. Suddenly giving up all thought of him, she went to her room and spent the night free from anxiety.

[4] It is said that Vāmadeva attained Knowledge while still in his mother's womb.

24

Or [success is attained] through association with one who has attained perfection.

27

As the sage Sauvari [who practised yoga for a long time] could not appease his desires through enjoyments, so it is also with others.

Book V

128

As recovery through medicines, and so forth, cannot be denied, so neither can the siddhis attained through yoga.

Book VI

24

Any posture which is easy and steady is an āsana; there is no injunction [about any particular posture].

Vyāsa Sutras

Chapter IV, Section i

7

Worship is possible in a sitting posture. [Therefore one should be seated while worshipping.]

8

Because of meditation.[5]

9

Because the meditating [person] is compared to the immovable earth.

[5] When we see a man seated without moving his limbs, we say that he is meditating. Therefore meditation is possible for a person who is seated.

10

Also because the Smritis say so.

11

There is no law of place [for meditation]; wherever the mind is concentrated, meditation should be practised.

These several extracts give an idea of what other systems of Indian philosophy have to say about Yoga.

MISCELLANEOUS LECTURES

Vivekananda at Colombo (1897)

VIVEKANANDA

MY MASTER

(Delivered in New York)

"Whenever virtue subsides and vice prevails, I come down to help mankind," declares Krishna in the Bhagavad Gītā. Whenever this world of ours, on account of growth and of additional circumstances, requires a new adjustment, a wave of power comes; and as man is acting on two planes, the spiritual and the material, the wave of adjustment comes on both planes. On the one side, on the material plane, Europe has mainly been the basis of the adjustment during modern times, and on the other side, on the spiritual plane, Asia has been the basis of the adjustment throughout the history of the world. Today man requires one more adjustment on the spiritual plane. Today, when material ideas are at the height of their glory and power, today, when man is likely to forget his divine nature through his growing dependence on matter, and is likely to be reduced to a mere money-making machine, an adjustment is necessary. And the voice has spoken; the power is coming to drive away the clouds of gathering materialism. The power has been set in motion which, at no distant date, will bring unto mankind once more the memory of its real nature, and again the place from which this power has started is Asia. This world of ours is built on the plan of the division of labour. It is vain to say that one nation shall possess everything. Yet how childish we are! The baby, in his childishness, thinks that his doll is the only possession that is to be coveted in this whole universe. So a nation which is great in the possession of material power thinks that this is all that is to be coveted, that this is all that is meant by progress, that this is all that is meant by civilization, and if there are other nations which do not care to possess, and do not possess this power, they are not fit to live, their whole existence is useless. On the other hand, another nation may think that mere material civilization is utterly useless. From the Orient came the voice which once told the world that if a man possessed everything that is under the sun or above it, and did not possess spirituality, it availed him nothing. This is the Oriental type; the other is the Occidental type.

Each of these types has its grandeur, each has its glory. The present adjustment will be the harmonizing, the blending, of these two ideals. To the Oriental, the world of the Spirit is as real as to the Occidental is the world of the senses. In the spiritual, the Oriental finds everything he wants or hopes for; in it he finds all that makes life real to him. To the Occidental he is a dreamer. To the Oriental, the Occidental is a dreamer, playing with dolls that last only for five minutes, and he laughs to think that grown-up men and women should make so much of a handful of matter which they will have to leave sooner or

697

later. Each calls the other a dreamer. But the Oriental ideal is as necessary for the progress of the human race as the Occidental, and I think it is more necessary. Machines never made mankind happy, and never will. He who tries to make us believe this, claims that happiness is in the machine; but it is always in the mind. The man who is lord of his mind alone can be happy, and none else.

But what, after all, is this power of the machine? Why should a man who can send a current of electricity through a wire be called a very great and a very intelligent man? Does not nature do a million times more than that every moment? Why not then fall down and worship nature? What matters it if you have power over the whole of the world, if you have mastered every atom in the universe? That will not make you happy unless you have the power of happiness in yourself, until you have conquered yourself. Man is born to conquer nature, it is true, but the Occidental means by "nature" only the physical or external nature. It is true that external nature is majestic, with its mountains and oceans and rivers, and with its infinite power and variety. Yet there is a more majestic, internal nature of man, higher than the sun, moon, and stars, higher than this earth of ours, higher than the physical universe, transcending these little lives of ours; and it affords another field of study. There the Orientals excel, just as the Occidentals excel in the other. Therefore it is fitting that, whenever there is a spiritual adjustment, it should come from the Orient. It is also fitting that when the Oriental wants to learn about machine-making, he should sit at the feet of the Occidental and learn from him. When the Occident wants to learn about the Spirit, about God, about the soul, about the meaning and the mystery of this universe, he must sit at the feet of the Orient.

I am going to present before you the life of a man who has put in motion a spiritual wave in India. But before going into the life of this man, I will try to present before you the secret of India, what India stands for. If those whose eyes have been blinded by the glamour of material things, whose whole life is dedicated to eating and drinking and enjoying, whose whole ideal of possession is lands and gold, whose whole ideal of pleasure is in the senses, whose God is money, and whose goal is a life of ease and comfort in this world and death after that, whose minds never look forward, and who rarely think of anything higher than the sense-objects in the midst of which they live—if such as these go to India, what do they see? Poverty, squalor, superstition, darkness, hideousness everywhere. Why? Because to their minds enlightenment means dress, education, social politeness. Whereas Occidental nations have used every effort to improve their material position, India has done differently. There lives the only race in the world who, in the whole history of humanity, never went beyond their frontiers to conquer anyone, who never coveted that which belonged to anyone else, and whose only fault was that their lands were so fertile, and their wits so keen, that they accumulated wealth by the hard labour of their hands and so tempted other nations to come and despoil them. They are content to be despoiled, and to be called barbarians, and in return they want to send to this world visions of the Supreme, to lay bare for the world the secrets of human nature, to rend the veil that conceals the real man, because they know that all this is a dream, because they know that behind matter lives the real, divine nature of man, which no sin can tarnish, no crime can spoil, no lust can kill; which fire cannot burn, nor water wet, which heat cannot dry, nor death kill; and to them this true nature of man is as real as is any material object to the senses of an Occidental.

Just as you are brave enough to jump into the mouth of a cannon with a hurrah, brave enough, in the name of patriotism, to stand up and give up your lives for your country, so they are brave in the name of God. There it is that when a man declares that this is a world of ideas, that it is all a dream, he casts off clothes and property to demonstrate that what he believes and thinks is true. There it is that a man sits on the bank of a river, when he has known that life is eternal, and is willing to give up his body as if it were nothing, just as you would give up a bit of straw. Therein lies his heroism; he is ready to face death as a brother because he is convinced that there is no death for the soul. Therein lies the strength that has made India invincible through hundreds of years of oppression and foreign invasions and foreign tyranny. The nation lives today, and in that nation, even in the days of the direst disaster, spiritual giants have never failed to arise. Asia produces giants in spirituality, just as the Occident produces giants in politics, giants in science.

In the beginning of the present century, when Western influence began to pour into India, when Western conquerors, swords in hand, came to demonstrate to the children of the sages that they were mere barbarians, a race of dreamers, that their religion was but mythology, and God and soul and everything they had been struggling for were mere words without meaning, that the thousands of years of struggle, the thousands of years of endless renunciation, had all been in vain—at that time certain questions began to agitate young men at the universities: whether their whole national existence up to then had been a failure, whether they must begin anew on the Occidental plan, tear up their old books, burn their philosophies, drive away their preachers, and break down their temples. Did not the Occidental conqueror, the man who demonstrated his religion with sword and gun, say that all the old ways were mere superstition and idolatry? Children brought up and educated in the new schools started on the Occidental plan drank in these ideas from their childhood, and it is not to be wondered at that doubts assailed their minds. But instead of throwing away superstition and making a real search after truth, they asked: "What does the West say?" This, for them, became the test of truth. The priests must go, the Vedas must be burnt, because the West said so. Out of the feeling of unrest thus produced there arose a wave of so-called reform in India.

If you wish to be a true reformer, you must possess three things. The first is to feel. Do you really feel for your brothers? Do you really feel that there is so much misery in the world, so much ignorance and superstition? Do you really feel that all men are your brothers? Does this idea permeate your whole being? Does it run in your blood? Does it tingle in your veins? Does it course through every nerve and filament of your body? Are you full of that idea of sympathy? If you are, that is only the first step. Next you must ask yourself if you have found any remedy. The old ideas may be all superstition, but in and around these masses of superstition are nuggets of truth. Have you discovered means by which to keep that truth alone, without any of the dross? If you have done that, that is only the second step; one thing more is necessary. What is your motive? Are you sure that you are not actuated by greed for gold, by thirst for fame or power? Are you really sure that you can stand up for your ideals and work on, even if the whole world wants to crush you down? Are you sure that you know what you want and will perform your duty, and that alone, even if your life is at stake? Are you sure that you will persevere so long as life endures, so long as one pulsation is left in the heart? Then you are a real reformer, you are a teacher, a master, a blessing to mankind. But man is so impatient, so shortsighted! He has not the patience to wait, he has not the power to see. He wants to rule, he wants results immediately. Why? He wants to reap the fruits himself and does not really care for others. Duty for duty's sake is not what he wants. "To work you have the right, but not to the fruits thereof," says Krishna. Why cling to results? Ours is to do our duties. Let the fruits take care of themselves. But man has no patience; he takes up any scheme that will produce quick results; and the majority of reformers all over the world can be classed under this heading.

As I have said, an intense desire for reform came to India, and it seemed as if the wave of materialism that had invaded her shores would sweep away the teachings of the sages. But the nation had borne the shocks of a thousand such waves of change. This one was mild in comparison. Wave after wave had flooded the land, breaking and crushing everything for hundreds of years; the sword had flashed and "Victory unto Allah!" had rent the skies of India; but these floods subsided, leaving the national ideals unchanged.

The Indian nation cannot be killed. Deathless it stands, and it will stand so long as that spirit shall remain as the background, so long as her people do not give up their spirituality. Beggars they may remain, poor and poverty-stricken; dirt and squalor may surround them perhaps throughout all time; but let them not give up their God, let them not forget that they are the children of the sages. Just as, in the West, even the man in the street wants to trace his descent from some robber-baron of the Middle Ages, so in India, even an emperor on the throne wants to trace his descent from some beggar-sage in the forest, from a man who wore the bark of a tree, lived upon the fruits of the forest, and communed with God. That is the type of heritage we want, and so long as holiness is thus supremely venerated, India cannot die.

Many of you, perhaps, have read the article by Prof. Max Müller in a recent issue of the Nineteenth Century, entitled "A Real Mahātman." The life of Śri Ramakrishna is deeply interesting; for it is a living illustration of the ideas that he preached. Perhaps it will seem a little romantic to you who live in the West, in an atmosphere entirely different from that of India; for the methods and manners in the busy rush of life in the West differ utterly from those of India. Yet perhaps it will be all the more interesting for that, because it will bring into a new light things about which many of you have heard.

It was while reforms of various kinds were being inaugurated in India that a child was born of poor brāhmin parents on the eighteenth of February, 1836, in one of the remote villages of Bengal. The father and mother were very orthodox people. The life of an orthodox brāhmin is one of continuous renunciation. Very few things can he do to earn a living, and beyond these the orthodox brāhmin must not occupy himself with any secular business. At the same time he must not receive gifts from everybody. You may imagine how rigorous that life becomes. You have heard of the brāhmins and their priest-craft many times, but very few of you have ever stopped to ask what makes this wonderful band of men the rulers of their fellows. They are the poorest of all the classes in the country, and the secret of their power lies in their renunciation. They never covet wealth. Theirs is the poorest priesthood in the world, and therefore the most powerful. Even in this poverty, a brāhmin's wife will never allow a poor man to pass through the village without giving him something to eat. That is considered the highest duty of the mother in India; and because she is the mother it is her duty to be served last; she must see that everyone is served before her turn comes. That is why the mother is regarded as God in India. This particular woman, the mother of the child we are talking about, was an ideal Hindu mother.

The higher the caste, the greater the restrictions. The people of the lowest caste can eat and drink anything they like, but as men rise in the social scale, more and more restrictions come, and when they reach the highest caste, the brāhmin, the hereditary priesthood of India, their lives, as I have said, are very much circumscribed. Judged by Western standards, their lives are lives of continuous asceticism. But they have great steadiness. When they get hold of an idea they carry it out to its very conclusion, and they keep hold of it generation after generation until they make something out of it. Once you have given them an idea, it is not easy to take it back again; but it is hard to make them grasp a new idea.

The orthodox Hindus, therefore, are very exclusive, living entirely within their own horizon of thought and feeling. Their lives are laid down in our old books in every little detail, and the least detail is grasped by them with almost adamantine firmness. They would starve rather than eat a meal cooked by the hands of a man not belonging to their own small sub-caste. But withal, they have intensity and tremendous earnestness. That force of intense faith and religious life is often found among the orthodox Hindus, because their very orthodoxy comes from a tremendous conviction that it is right. We may not all think that what they hold on to with such perseverance is right; but to them it is.

Now, as our books say, a man should always be charitable, even if it means extreme suffering. If a man starves to death in order to help another man, to save that man's life, it is all right; it is even held that a man ought to do that. And it is expected of a brāhmin to carry this idea out to the very extreme. Those who are acquainted with the literature of India will remember a beautiful old story about this extreme charity, as related in the *Mahābhārata*: how a whole family starved themselves to death and gave their last meal to a beggar. This is not an exaggeration, for such things still happen.

The character of the father and the mother of my Master was very much like that. Very poor they were, and yet many a time the mother would starve herself a whole day to help a poor man. Of them this child was born, and he was a peculiar child from his very babyhood. He remembered his past from his birth and knew for what purpose he had come into the world, and all his powers were devoted to the fulfilment of that purpose.

While he was quite young his father died and the boy was sent to school. A brāhmin's boy must go to school; the caste restricts him to a learned profession only. The indigenous system of education in India, especially of the orthodox type, still prevalent in many parts of the country, was very different from the modern system. The students did not have to pay for their education. It was thought that knowledge is so sacred that no man ought to sell it. Knowledge must be given freely. The teachers used to take students without charge; and not only so, but most of them gave their students food and clothes. To support these teachers the wealthy families on certain occasions, such as a marriage festival or the ceremonies for the dead, made gifts to them. They were considered the first and foremost claimants to such gifts, and they in their turn had to maintain their students.

Now, this boy about whom I am speaking had an elder brother, a learned professor, who took him to Calcutta to study with him. After a short time the boy became convinced that the aim of all secular learning was mere material advancement, and he resolved to give up study and devote himself solely to the pursuit of spiritual knowledge. The father being dead, the family was very poor, and the boy had to make his own living. He went to a place near Calcutta and became a temple priest. To become a temple priest is thought very degrading to a brāhmin. Our temples are not churches in your sense of the word; they are not places for public worship; for, properly speaking, there is no such thing as public worship in India. Temples are erected mostly by rich persons as a meritorious religious act.

If a man has much property he wants to build a temple. In that temple he puts a symbol of God or an image of an Incarnation and dedicates it in the name of God. The worship is akin to that which is conducted in Roman Catholic churches, very much like the Mass, the priest reading certain sentences from the sacred books, waving a light before the image, and treating the image in every respect as we treat a great man. This is all that is done in the temple. The man who goes to a temple is not considered thereby a better man than he who never goes. Rather, the latter is often considered the more religious, for in India religion is to each man his own private affair, and all his worship is conducted in the privacy of his own home.

It has been held from the most ancient times in our country that to be a temple priest is degrading. The idea is that temple priests, like school-teachers, but in a far more intense sense, make merchandise of sacred things by taking fees for their work. So you may imagine the feelings of this boy when he was forced through poverty to take up the only occupation open to him, that of a temple priest.

There have been various poets in Bengal whose songs have passed down to the people and are sung in the streets of Calcutta and in every village. Most of these are religious songs, and their one central idea, which is perhaps peculiar to the religions of India, is the idea of realization. There is not a book in India on religion which does not breathe this idea. Man must realize God, feel God, see God, talk to God. That is religion. The Indian atmosphere is full of stories of saintly persons who have had visions of God. Such ideas form the basis of their religion; and all these ancient books and scriptures are the writings of persons who came into direct contact with spiritual facts. These books were not written to appeal to the intellect, nor can any reasoning understand them; they were written by men who saw the things of which they wrote, and they can be understood only by men who have raised themselves to the same height. They declare that there is such a thing as realization even in this life, and it is open to everyone, and religion begins with the opening of this faculty—if I may call it so. This is the central idea in all religions. And this is why, in India, we find that one man, with the most finished oratorical powers or the most convincing logic, may preach the highest doctrines and yet is unable to get people to listen to him, while another, a poor man who scarcely can speak the language of his own motherland, is yet worshipped as God by half the nation in his own lifetime. When the idea somehow or other gets abroad that a man has raised himself to a high state of realization—that religion is no more a matter of conjecture to him, that he is no longer groping in the dark about such momentous questions of religion as the immortality of the soul and God—people come from all quarters to see him, and gradually they begin to worship him.

In the temple was an image of the "Blissful Mother." The boy had to conduct the worship morning and evening, and by and by this one idea filled his mind: "Is there any reality behind this image? Is it true that there is a Blissful Mother of the universe? Is it true that She is living and guides this universe, or is it all a dream? Is there any reality in religion?" This kind of doubt comes to almost every Hindu aspirant—Is this that we are doing real? And theories will not satisfy us, although there are ready at hand almost all the theories that have ever been made with regard to God and the soul. Neither books nor dogmas can satisfy us; the one idea that gets hold of thousands of our people is this idea of realization. Is it true that there is a God? If it be true, can I see Him? Can I realize the Truth? The Western mind may think all this very unpractical, but to us it is intensely practical. For this idea men will give up their lives. For this idea thousands of Hindus every year give up their homes, and many of them die through the hardships they have to undergo. To the Western mind this must seem most visionary, and I can see the reason for this point of view. But after years of residence in the West, I still think this idea the most practical thing in life.

Life is but momentary, whether you are a toiler in the streets or an emperor ruling millions. Life is but momentary, whether you have the best of health or the worst. There is but one solution of life, say the Hindus, and that solution is what they call God and religion. If God and religion are real, then life becomes explained, life becomes bearable, becomes enjoyable. Otherwise life is but a useless burden. That is our idea. But no amount of reasoning can demonstrate religion; it can only make it probable, and there it rests. Facts are based only upon experience, and we have to experience religion to demonstrate it to ourselves. We have to see God to be convinced that there is a God. Nothing but our own realization can make religion real to us. That is the Hindu conception.

This idea of realization took possession of the boy, and his whole life became concentrated upon it. Day after day he would weep and say: "Mother, is it true that Thou dost exist, or is it all poetry? Is the Blissful Mother an imagination of poets and misguided people, or is there such a Reality?" We have seen already that of education in our sense of the word he had none; therefore so much the more natural, so much the more healthy, was his mind, so much the purer his thoughts, undiluted by the drinking in of the thoughts of others. Because he never went to a university, he was able to think for himself. Well has Prof. Max Müller said, in the article I have just referred to, that he was a clean, original man, and that the secret of his originality was that he was not brought up within the precincts of a university.

Now this thought—whether God can be realized—which was uppermost in his mind gained in strength every day until he could think of nothing else. He could no longer conduct the worship properly, could no more attend to the various details in all their minuteness. Often he would forget to place the food offering before the image, sometimes he would forget to wave the light, at other times he would wave the light for hours and forget everything else.

At last it became impossible for the boy to serve in the temple. He gave up the worship and spent most of his time in meditation in a wood near by. About this part of his life he told me many times that he could not tell when the sun rose or set, or how he lived. He lost all thought of himself and forgot to eat. During this period he was lovingly watched over by a relative who put into his mouth food which he mechanically swallowed.

Days and nights thus passed with the boy. At the end of the day, towards evening, when the peals of bells and the singing in the temples would reach the wood, it would make him very sad, and he would cry: "Another day is gone in vain, Mother, and Thou hast not come. One more day of this short life has gone and I have not known the Truth." In the agony of his soul, sometimes he would rub his face against the ground and weep.

This is the tremendous thirst that seizes the devotee's heart. Later on, this very man said to me: "My child, suppose there is a bag of gold in one room, and a robber is in the next room. Do you think that robber can sleep? He cannot. His mind will be always thinking how to get into that room and obtain possession of the gold. Do you think, then, that a man firmly persuaded that there is a Reality behind all these appearances, that there is a God, that there is One who never dies, One whose nature is infinite Bliss, compared to which these pleasures of the senses are simply playthings—can rest contented without struggling to attain Him? Can he cease his efforts for a moment? No. He will become mad with longing." This divine madness seized the boy. At that time he had no teacher, nobody to tell him anything, and everyone thought he was out of his mind. This is the ordinary condition of things: If a man throws aside the vanities of the world, we hear him called mad. But such men are the salt of the earth. Out of such madness have come the powers that have moved this world of ours, and out of such madness alone will come the powers of the future that are going to move the world.

So days, weeks, months passed in the continuous struggle of his soul to arrive at Truth. The boy began to see visions, to see wonderful things; the secrets of his nature were beginning to open up to him. Veil after veil was, as it were, being taken off. Mother Herself became the teacher and initiated the boy into the truths he sought. At this time there came to the place a woman beautiful to look at, learned beyond compare. Later on this saint used to say about her that she was not learned, but was the embodiment of learning; she was learning itself in human form. There too you find the peculiarity of the Indian nation. In the midst of the ignorance in which the average Hindu woman lives, in the midst of what is called in Western countries her lack of freedom, there could arise a woman of supreme spirituality. She was a sannyāsini; for women also give up the world, renounce their property, do not marry, and devote themselves to the worship of the Lord. She came, and when she heard of this boy's yearning she offered to go and see him; and hers was the first help he received. At once she recognized what his trouble was, and she said to him: "My son, blessed is the man upon whom such madness comes. All men in this world are mad: some are mad for wealth, some for pleasure, some for fame, some for a hundred other things. But blessed are they who are mad after God. Such men are very few." This woman remained near the boy for years, taught him various religious disciplines, and initiated him into the different practices of yoga.

Later, there came to the same temple a sannyāsin, one of the begging friars of India, a learned man, a philosopher. He was an unusual man; he was an idealist. He did not believe that this world existed in reality, and to demonstrate that, he would never live under a roof; he would always live out of doors, in storm and sunshine alike. This man began to teach the boy the philosophy of the Vedas, and he found very soon, to his astonishment, that the pupil was in some respects wiser than the master. He spent several months with the boy, after which he initiated him into the order of sannyāsins, and finally he departed.

Previously, when his extraordinary conduct as a temple priest had made people think him mad, his relatives had taken him home and married him to a girl of five, thinking that that would restore the balance of his mind. But he had come back and only merged deeper in his madness. Sometimes, in our country, children are married by their parents without having any voice in the matter. Of course such a marriage is little more than a betrothal. When they are married they still continue to live with their parents, and the real marriage takes place when the wife grows older, at which time it is customary for the husband to bring his bride home. In this case, however, the husband, absorbed in worship, had entirely forgotten that he had a wife. In her far-off home the girl had heard that her husband had become a religious enthusiast and that he was even considered insane by many. She resolved to learn the truth for herself; so she set out and walked to the place where her husband was. When at last she stood in her husband's presence, he at once admitted her rights as his wife—although in India any person, man or woman, who embraces a monastic life is thereby freed from all worldly obligations. The young man said to her: "As for me, the Mother has shown me that She resides in every woman, and so I have learnt to look upon every woman as Mother. But if you wish to draw me into the world, since I have been married to you, I am at your service."

The maiden was a pure and noble soul and was able to understand her husband's aspirations and sympathize with them. She quickly told him that she had no wish to drag him down to the life of worldliness, but that all she desired was to remain near him, to serve him, and to learn from him. She became one of his most devoted disciples, always revering him as a divine being. Thus through his wife's consent the last barrier was removed and he was free to lead the life he had chosen.

The next desire that seized upon the soul of this man was to know the truth about the various religions. Up to that time he had not known any religion but his own. He wanted to understand what other religions were like. So he sought teachers of different religions. By a teacher you must always remember what we mean in India: not a book-worm, but a man of realization, one who knows truth at first hand and not through an intermediary. He found a Mohammedan saint and underwent the disciplines prescribed by him. To his astonishment he found that, when faithfully carried out, these devotional methods led him to the same goal he had already attained. He gathered a similar experience from following the religion of Jesus Christ. He went to all the sects he could find, and whatever he took up he went into with his whole heart. He did exactly as he was told, and in every instance he arrived at the same result. Thus from actual experience he came to know that the goal of every religion is the same, that each is trying to teach the same thing, the difference being largely in method and still more in language. At the core, all sects and all religions have the same aim; they only quarrel for their own selfish purposes.

He then set about to learn humility, because he had found that the common idea in all religions is "Not I, but Thou," and that the Lord fills the heart of him who says, "Not I." The less of this little "I," the more of God there is in him. This, he found, was taught by every religion in the world, and he set himself to realize it. As I have told you, whenever he wanted to do anything he never confined himself to theories, but would enter into the practice immediately. Now, there was a family of pariahs living near the temple. The pariahs number several millions in the whole of India, and are so low in society that some of our books say that if a brāhmin, on coming out of his house, sees the face of a pariah, he has to fast that day and recite certain prayers before he becomes holy again. In the dead of night, when all were sleeping, my Master would enter the house of the pariahs and cleanse the dirty places there, saying, "O Mother, make me the servant of the pariah, make me feel that I am even lower than the pariah."

There were various other disciplines, which would take a long time to relate, and I want to give you just a sketch of his life.

Then came to him the conviction that to be perfect, the idea of sex must go, because the soul has no sex, the soul is neither male nor female. It is only in the body that sex exists, and the man who desires to reach the Spirit cannot at the same time hold to sex distinctions. Having been born in a masculine body, this man wanted to bring the feminine idea into everything. He began to think that he was a woman: he dressed like a woman, spoke like a woman, behaved like a woman, and lived as a member of the household among the women of a good family, until, after months of this discipline, his mind became changed and he entirely forgot the idea of sex. Thus his whole view of life became changed.

We hear in the West about worshipping woman, but this is usually for her youth and beauty. This man meant by worshipping woman that to him every woman's face was that of the Blissful Mother, and nothing but that. I myself have seen him standing, bathed in tears, before those women whom society would not touch, and saying with utmost humility: "Mother, in one form Thou art in the street, and in another form Thou art the universe. I salute Thee, Mother, I salute Thee." Think of the blessedness of that life from which all carnality has vanished, which can look upon every woman with that love and reverence, to which every woman's face becomes transfigured and only the face of the Divine Mother, the Blissful One, the Protectress of the human race, shines instead! That is what we want. Do you mean to say that the divinity back of woman can ever be cheated? It never was and never will be. It always asserts itself. Unfailingly it detects fraud, it detects hypocrisy; unerringly it feels the warmth of truth, the light of spirituality, the holiness of purity. Such purity is absolutely necessary if real spirituality is to be attained.

This rigorous, unsullied purity came into the life of my Master; all the struggles which we have in our lives were past for him. The hard-earned jewels of spirituality, for which he had given three-quarters of his life, were now ready to be given to humanity; and then began his work. His teaching and preaching were peculiar: he would never take the position of a teacher. In our country a teacher is a most highly venerated person; he is regarded as God Himself. We have not even the same respect for our father and mother. Our father and mother give us our body, but the teacher shows us the way to salvation. We are his children; we are born in the spiritual line of the teacher. All Hindus come to pay respect to an extraordinary teacher; they crowd around him. And here was such a teacher. But the teacher had no thought whether he was to be respected or not; he had not the least idea that he was a great teacher; he thought that it was the Mother who was doing everything, and not he. He always said: "If any good comes from my lips, it is the Mother who speaks. What have I to do with it?" That was his one idea about his work, and to the day of his death he never gave it up. This man sought no one. His principle was: first form character, first earn spirituality, and results will come of themselves. His favourite illustration was: "When the lotus opens, the bees come of their own accord to seek the honey. So let the lotus of your character be full-blown, and the results will follow." This is a great lesson to learn. My Master taught me this lesson hundreds of times, yet I often forget it.

Few understand the power of thought. If a man goes into a cave, shuts himself in, and thinks one really great thought and dies, that thought will penetrate the walls of the cave, vibrate through space, and at last permeate the whole human race. Such is the power of thought.

Be in no hurry, therefore, to give your thoughts to others. First have something to give. He alone teaches who has something to give. For teaching is not talking, teaching is not imparting doctrines; it is communicating. Spirituality can be communicated just as directly as I can give you a flower. This is true in the most literal sense. This idea is very old in India and finds illustration in the

West in the theory of apostolic succession. Therefore first form character: that is your highest duty. Know truth for yourself, and there will be many to whom you can teach it afterwards. They will all come.

This was the attitude of my Master. He criticized no one. For years I lived with that man, but never did I hear those lips utter one word of condemnation for any sect. He had the same sympathy for all sects; he had found the inner harmony of religions. A man may be intellectual or devotional or mystical or active: the various religions represent one or other of these types. Yet it is possible to combine all the four in one man, and this is what future humanity is going to do. That was his idea. He condemned no one, but saw the good in all.

People came by thousands to see and hear this wonderful man, who spoke in a *patois* every word of which was forceful and instinct with light. For it is not what is spoken, much less the language in which it is spoken, but the personality of the speaker, which dwells in everything he says, that carries weight. Every one of us feels this at times. We hear most splendid orations, most wonderfully reasoned-out discourses, and we go home and forget everything. At other times we hear a few words in the simplest language, and they remain with us all the rest of our lives, become part and parcel of ourselves and produce lasting results. The words of a man who can put his personality into them take effect; but he must have tremendous personality. All teaching means giving and taking: the teacher gives and the taught receives; but the one must have something to give, and the other must be open to receive.

This man lived near Calcutta, the capital of India, the most important university town in our country, which was sending out sceptics and materialists by the hundreds every year; yet great men from the colleges—many of them sceptics and agnostics—used to come and listen to him. I heard of this man, and I went to see him. He looked just like an ordinary man, with nothing remarkable about him. He used the most simple language, and I thought, "Can this man be a great teacher?" I crept near him and asked him the question I had been asking others all my life: "Do you believe in God, sir?" "Yes," he replied. "Can you prove it, sir?" "Yes." "How?" "Because I see Him just as I see you here, only much more intensely."

That impressed me at once. For the first time I found a man who dared to say that he saw God, that religion was a reality—to be felt, to be sensed in an infinitely more intense way than we can sense the world. I began to go to that man day after day, and I actually saw that religion could be given. One touch, one glance, can change a whole life. I had read about Buddha and Christ and Mohammed, about all those different luminaries of ancient times, and how they would stand up and say, "Be thou whole," and men became whole. I now found it to be true; and when I myself saw this man, all scepticism was brushed aside. It could be done. As my Master used to say: "Religion can be given and taken more tangibly, more directly, than anything else in the world." Be therefore spiritual first; have something to give, and then stand before the world and give it.

Religion is not talk or doctrines or theories, nor is it sectarianism. Religion cannot live in sects and societies. It is the relation between the soul and God. How can it be fitted into a society? It would then degenerate into business, and wherever there are business and business principles in religion, spirituality dies. Religion does not consist in erecting temples or building churches or attending public worship. It is not to be found in books or in words or in lectures or in organizations. Religion consists in realization. We all know as a fact that nothing will satisfy us until we realize the Truth for ourselves. However we may argue, however much we may hear, but one thing will satisfy us, and that is our own realization; and such an experience is possible for every one of us, if we will only try.

The first idea in this attempt to realize religion is that of renunciation. As far as we can, we must give up. Darkness and light, enjoyment of the world and enjoyment of God, will never go together. "Ye cannot serve God and Mammon."

The second idea that I learnt from my Master, which is perhaps the most vital, is the wonderful truth that the religions of the world are not contradictory or antagonistic; they are but various phases of one Eternal Religion. There never was my religion or yours, my national religion or your national religion. There never existed many religions; there is only one Religion. One infinite Religion has existed all through eternity and will ever exist, and this Religion is expressing itself in various countries in various ways. Therefore we must respect all religions and we must try to accept them all as far as we can.

Religions manifest themselves not only according to race and geographical position, but according to individual powers. In one man, religion is manifesting itself as intense activity, as work; in another, it is manifesting itself as intense devotion; in yet another, as mysticism; in others, as philosophy, and so forth. It is wrong when we say to others, "Your methods are not right." To learn this central secret that the Truth may be one and yet many at the same time, that we may have different visions of the same Truth from different standpoints, is exactly what must be done. Then, instead of feeling antagonism towards anyone, we shall have infinite sympathy for all. Knowing that there are different natures born into this world and that they will require different applications of the same religious truths, we shall understand why we should bear with each other. Just as in nature there is unity in variety—an infinite variation in the phenomenal, and behind all these variations, the Unchangeable, the Absolute—so it is with every human being. The microcosm is but a miniature repetition of the macrocosm. In spite of all these variations, in and through them all runs this eternal harmony, and we have to recognize this. This idea, above all other ideas, I find to be the crying necessity of the day.

Born in a country which is a hotbed of religious sects—through good fortune or ill fortune, everyone who has a religious idea wants to send an advance guard there—I have been acquainted from my childhood with the various sects of the world. Even the Mormons came to preach in India. Welcome to them all! That is the place to preach religion. There it takes deeper root than in any other country. If you teach politics to the Hindus they will not understand, but if you preach religion, however curious it may be, you will have hundreds and thousands of followers in no time, and you have every chance of becoming a living god in your lifetime. I am glad that it is so; for it shows that one thing we prize in India is God.

The sects among the Hindus are various, almost innumerable, and some of them apparently hopelessly contradictory. Yet the Hindus will tell you that they are but different manifestations of one Religion. "As different rivers, taking their start from different mountains, running crooked or straight, all finally mingle their waters in the ocean, so the different sects, with their different points of view, at last all come unto Thee." This is not a theory. This has to be recognized—but not in that patronizing way in which some people do, when they say, "Oh yes, there are some very good things in them." Some even have the most wonderfully liberal idea that while other religions are remnants of a prehistoric evolution, "ours is the fulfilment of things." One man says that because his is the oldest religion it is the best; another makes the same claim because his is the latest. We have to recognize that each one of them has the same saving power as every other. The same God helps all, and it is not you or I or any body of men that is responsible for the safety and salvation of the least little bit of the soul. I do not understand how people declare themselves to be believers in God, and at the same time think that God has handed over to a little body of men all truth, and that they are the guardians of the rest of humanity.

Do not try to disturb the faith of any man. If you can give him something better, if you can get hold of a man where he stands and give him a push upward, do so; but do not destroy what he has. The only true teacher is he who can convert himself, as it were, into a thousand persons at a moment's notice. The only true teacher is he who can immediately come down to the level of the student and transfer his soul to the student's soul and see through the student's eyes and hear through his ears and understand through his mind. Such a teacher can really teach, and none else. All these negative, destructive teachers that are in the world can never do any good.

In the presence of my Master I found out that a man could be perfect even in this body. Those lips never cursed anyone, never even criticized anyone. Those eyes were beyond the possibility of seeing evil, that mind had lost the power of thinking evil. He saw nothing but good. That tremendous purity, that tremendous renunciation, is the one secret of spirituality. "Neither through wealth nor through progeny, but through renunciation alone, is immortality to be reached," say the Vedas. "Sell all that thou hast and give to the poor, and follow me," says Christ. So all great saints and prophets have expressed it and have carried it out in their lives. How can great spirituality come without that renunciation? Renunciation is the background of all religious thought, wherever it be; and you will always find that the more this idea of renunciation diminishes, the more the senses will creep into the field of religion and spirituality will decrease.

That man was the embodiment of renunciation. In our country it is necessary for a man who wants to realize God to give up all wealth and position; and this condition my Master carried out literally. There were many who would have felt themselves blest if he would only have accepted a present from them; who would gladly have given him thousands of rupees if he would have taken them; but these were the only men from whom he would turn away. He was a triumphant example, a living realization of the complete conquest of lust and of desire for money. He was beyond all ideas of either. Such men are necessary for this century. Such renunciation is necessary in these days when men have begun to think that they cannot live a month without what they call their "necessities," which they are increasing out of all proportion. It is necessary in a time like this that someone should arise to demonstrate to the sceptics of the world that there yet breathes a man who does not care a straw for all the gold or all the fame that is in the universe. And there are such men.

The third idea I learnt from my Master was intense love for others. The first part of his life was spent in acquiring spirituality, and the remaining years in distributing it.

Men came in crowds to hear him and he would talk twenty hours out of twenty-four, and that not for one day, but for months and months, until at last the body broke down under the pressure of this tremendous strain. His intense love for mankind would not let him refuse to help even the humblest of the thousands who sought his aid. Gradually there developed a fatal throat disorder, and yet he could not be persuaded to refrain from these exertions. As soon as he heard that people were asking to see him, he would insist upon having them admitted and would answer all their questions. When expostulated with, he replied: "I do not care. I will give up twenty thousand such bodies to help one man. It is glorious to help even one man." There was no rest for him. Once a man asked him, "Sir, you are a great yogi; why do you not put your mind a little on your body and cure your disease?" At first he did not answer, but when the question had been repeated, he gently said: "My friend, I thought you were a sage, but you talk like other men of the world. This mind has been given to the Lord; do you mean to say that I should take it back and put it upon the body, which is but a mere cage of the soul?"

So he went on preaching to people. When the news spread that his body was about to pass away, people began to flock to him in greater crowds than ever. You cannot imagine the way they come to these great religious teachers in India, how they crowd round them and make gods of them while they are yet living. Thousands wait simply to touch the hem of their garments. It is through this appreciation of spirituality in others that spirituality is produced. Whatever man wants and appreciates, he will get; and it is the same with nations. If you go to India and deliver a political lecture, however grand it may be, you will scarcely find people to listen to you; but just go and teach religion, *live* it, not merely talk it, and hundreds will crowd just to look at you, to touch your feet. When the people heard that this holy man was likely to go from them soon, they began to come to him more than ever before, and my Master went on teaching them without the least regard for his health. We could not prevent this. Many of the people came from long distances, and he would not rest until he had answered their questions. "While I can speak I must teach them," he would say, and he was as good as his word. One day he told us that he would lay down the body that day, and repeating the most sacred word of the Vedas he entered into samādhi and passed away.

His thoughts and his message were known to very few capable of giving them out. Among others, he left a few young boys who had renounced the world and were ready to carry on his work. Attempts were made to crush them; but they stood firm, having the inspiration of that great life before them. Having had the contact of that blessed life for years, they stood their ground. These young men lived as sannyāsins, begging through the streets of the city where they were born, although some of them came from well-known families. At first they met with great antagonism, but they persevered and went on from day to day spreading all over India the message of that great man, until the whole country was filled with the ideas he had preached. This man, from a remote village of Bengal, without education, by the sheer force of his own determination, realized the truth and gave it to others, leaving only a few young boys to keep it alive.

Today the name of Śri Ramakrishna Paramahamsa is known all over India, with its millions of people. Nay, the power of that man has spread beyond India, and if there has ever been a word of truth, a word of spirituality, that I have spoken anywhere in the world, I owe it to my Master. Only the mistakes are mine.

This is the message of Śri Ramakrishna to the modern world: "Do not care for doctrines, do not care for dogmas or sects or churches or temples. They count for little compared with the essence of existence in each man, which is spirituality; and the more a man develops it, the more power he has for good. Earn that first, acquire that, and criticize no one; for all doctrines and creeds have some good in them. Show by your lives that religion does not mean words or names or sects, but that it means spiritual realization. Only those can understand who have felt. Only those who have attained to spirituality can communicate it to others, can be great teachers of mankind. They alone are the powers of light."

The more such men are produced in a country, the more that country will be raised; and that country where such men do not exist is simply doomed; nothing can save it. Therefore my Master's message to mankind is: "Be spiritual and realize Truth for yourself." He would have you give up all for the sake of your fellow beings. He would have you cease talking about love for your brothers and set to work to prove your words. The time has come for renunciation, for realization, and then you will see the harmony in all the religions of the world. You will know that there is no need of any quarrel; and then only will you be ready to help humanity. To proclaim and make clear the fundamental unity underlying all religions was the mission of my Master. Other teachers have taught special religions which bear their names, but this great teacher of the nineteenth century made no claim for himself. He left every religion undisturbed because he had realized that, in reality, they are all part and parcel of one Eternal Religion.

CHRIST, THE MESSENGER

A WAVE RISES in the ocean, and then there is a hollow. Again another wave rises, perhaps bigger than the first, only to fall again, and again to rise, driving onward. Similarly, in the march of events, we may notice the same rise and fall; but we generally look towards the rise, forgetting the fall. Both are necessary and both are great. This is the nature of the universe. Whether in the world of our thoughts or in the world of our relations, in society or in our spiritual affairs, this same succession of movements, of rises and falls, is going on. Hence, in the march of events, liberal ideals move forward, afterwards to sink down in order to gather strength once more for a new rise and a greater one.

The history of nations, also, has been ever like this. The great soul, the Messenger whom we are to study this afternoon, came at a period in the history of His race which we may well designate as a great fall. We can catch but little glimpses here and there of the stray records that have been kept of His sayings and doings, for it has been well said that the sayings and doings of that great soul would have filled the world, could they all have been written down. And the three years of His ministry were like one compressed and concentrated age, which it has taken nineteen hundred years afterwards to unfold, and may yet take who knows how much longer? Little men like you and me are reservoirs of just a little energy. A few minutes, a few hours, a few years at best, are enough to spend it all, to stretch it out, as it were, to its fullest strength, and then we are gone for ever. But mark this giant. Centuries and ages pass, yet the energy that He left upon the world is not yet stretched out, not yet expended to its full. It goes on gaining new vigour as the ages roll on.

Now what you see in the life of Christ is the life of all the past. The life of every man is, in a manner, the life of the past. It comes to him through heredity, through his surroundings, through education, through his own reincarnations— the past of the whole race. In a way the past of the earth, the past of the whole world, stands impressed upon every soul. What are we, in the present, but a result, an effect, of the infinite past of the world? What are we but floating wavelets in the eternal current of events, irresistibly moved forward and onward and incapable of rest? But you and I are only little things, bubbles. There are always some giant waves in the ocean of the world. In you and me the past life of the race may have been embodied only a little; but there are giants who embody, as it were, almost the whole of the past and stretch out their hands over the future also. They are the sign-posts, here and there, directing the march of humanity; they are verily giants, their shadows covering the earth; they stand undying, eternal. As was said by the same Messenger: "No man hath seen God at any time, but through the Son." It is true. For where should we see God but in the Son? It is true that you and I, and the poorest and meanest

713

of us, embody that God, even reflect that God. The vibration of light is every-where, omnipresent; but we see it most vividly in a lamp. Likewise God is omnipresent; but He can be seen most vividly when He is reflected in some one of these giant lamps of the earth—the Prophets, the man-Gods, the Incarnations, the embodiments of God.

We all know that God exists, and yet we do not see Him, we do not under-stand Him. Take one of these great Messengers of Light, and compare His character with the highest ideal of God that you ever formed, and you will find that your ideal falls short of Him, and that the character of the Prophet exceeds your imagination. You cannot even imagine a higher ideal of God than what He actually embodied, practically realized, and set before us as an example. Is it wrong, therefore, to worship these as God? Is it a sin to fall at the feet of these man-Gods and worship them as the only divine beings in the world? If they are really, actually, higher than all our conceptions of God, what harm is there in worshipping them? Not only is there no harm, but it is the only possible and positive way of worship. However much you may try, by struggle, by abstraction, by whatsoever method you like, still so long as you are a man in the world of men, your world is human, your religion is human, and your God is human. And that must be so. Who is not practical enough to take up an actually existing thing and give up an idea which is only an abstrac-tion that he cannot grasp, and which is difficult of approach except through a concrete medium? Therefore these Incarnations of God have been worshipped in all ages and in all countries.

We are now going to study a little of the life of Christ, the Incarnation of the Jews. When Christ was born, the Jews were in that state which I call a con-dition of fall between two waves: a state of conservatism, a state where the human mind is, as it were, tired for the time being of moving forward and is taking care only of what it has already won; a state when the attention is more bent upon particulars, upon details, than upon the great and vital problems of life; a state of stagnation, rather than of forging ahead; a state of suffering more than of achieving. Mark you, I do not blame this state of things; we have no right to criticize it. Because had it not been for this fall, the next rise, which was embodied in Jesus of Nazareth, would have been impossible. The Pharisees and Sadducees might have been insincere, they might have been doing things which they ought not to have done; they might even have been hypocrites; but whatever they were, these factors were the very cause of which the Messenger was the effect. The Pharisees and Sadducees at one end were the very impetus which came out at the other end as the gigantic brain of Jesus of Nazareth.

The attention to forms, to formulas, to the everyday details of religion, and to rituals may sometimes be laughed at, but nevertheless within them is strength. Many times in our rushing forward we lose much vigour. It is a fact that the fanatic is stronger than the liberal man. Even the fanatic, therefore, has one great virtue: he conserves energy, a tremendous amount of it. As with the individual, so with the race, energy is gathered to be conserved. Hemmed in by external enemies, driven back upon its own centre by the Roman might, by the Hellenic tendencies in the world of intellect, by waves of thought from Persia, India, and Alexandria—hemmed in physically, mentally, and morally—

there stood the Jewish race, with an inherent, conservative, tremendous strength, which their descendants have not lost even today. That race was forced to concentrate and focus all its energies upon Jerusalem and Judaism; and, like all power when once gathered, it cannot remain collected; it must expand and expend itself. There is no power on earth which can be kept long confined within too narrow a limit. No power can be kept compressed very long without its expanding at a subsequent period.

It was the concentrated energy of the Jewish race which found expression, at the next period, in the rise of Christianity. The small streams formed into rivers. Gradually all the rivers joined together and became one vast, surging river. On the top of one of its mighty waves we see standing Jesus of Nazareth. In this way every Prophet is the creation of His times; created by the past of His race, He Himself is the creator of the future. The movement of today is the effect of the past and the cause of the future. In this position stands the Messenger. In Him is embodied all that is the best and greatest in His own race—the meaning, the life, for which that race has struggled for ages— and He Himself is the impetus for the future, not only for His own race, but also for unnumbered other races of the world.

We must bear in mind another fact: that my view of the great Prophet of Nazareth is necessarily from the standpoint of the Orient. Many times you forget that the Nazarene was an Oriental of Orientals. Notwithstanding all your attempts to paint Him with blue eyes and yellow hair, the Nazarene is still an Oriental. All the similes, all the imaginery, with which the Bible is filled—the scenes, the locations, the attitudes, the groups, the poetry and symbolism—speak to you of the Orient: of the bright sky, of the heat, of the sun, of the desert, of thirsty men and animals, of women coming with pitchers on their heads to fill them at the wells, of the flocks, of the ploughmen, of the cultivation that is going on all around, of the water-mill and the wheel of the mill-pond, of the millstones. All these are to be seen today in Asia.

The voice of Asia is the voice of religion, and the voice of Europe is the voice of politics. Each is great in its own sphere. The voice of Europe is the voice of ancient Greece. To the mind of the Greek, his immediate society was all in all; beyond that lived barbarians. None but the Greek had the right to live. Whatever the Greek did was right and correct; whatever else might exist in the world was neither right nor correct, nor should it be allowed to live. Here was a mind intensely human in its sympathies, intensely natural, and therefore intensely artistic. The Greek lived entirely in this world. He did not care to dream. Even his poetry was practical. His gods and goddesses were not only human beings but intensely human, with almost the same human passions and feelings as we have. He loved what was beautiful, but mind you, it was always external nature. The beauty of the hills, of the snows, of the flowers; the beauty of forms and of figures; the beauty in the human face and, more often, in the human form—that is what the Greeks loved. And the Greeks being the teachers of all subsequent Europeans, the voice of Europe is Greek.

There is another type in Asia. Think of that vast continent, whose mountain-tops rise beyond the clouds, almost touching the canopy of heaven's blue; whose deserts roll on for miles upon miles, where not a drop of water can be found, neither will a blade of grass grow; think of its interminable forests and its gigantic rivers rushing down to the sea. In the midst of such surroundings, the Oriental love of the beautiful and of the sublime developed in quite another direction. It looked within and not without. Here also there was the same thirst for nature, the same thirst for power, there was the same thirst for excellence—the common idea of the Greek and the Oriental. But here it extended over a wider circle. In Asia, even today, birth or colour or language never alone makes a race. That which makes a race is its religion: we are all Christians; we are all Mohammedans; we are all Hindus or all Buddhists. No matter if the Buddhists be a Chinaman and a man from Persia, they will both think of themselves as brothers, because of their professing the same religion. Religion is the supreme tie in the uniting of humanity. And then again, the Oriental, for the same reason, is a visionary, is a born dreamer. The ripples of water-falls, the songs of birds, the beauties of the sun and moon and stars and the whole earth, are pleasant enough; but they are not sufficient for the Oriental. He wants to dream a dream of the Beyond. He wants to go beyond the present. The present is, as it were, nothing to him.

The Orient has been the cradle of the human race for ages, and all the vicissitudes of fortune have been there: kingdoms succeeding kingdoms; empires succeeding empires; human power, glory, and wealth, all rolling on the ground— a Golgotha of power and learning. That is the Orient: a Golgotha of power, of kingdoms, of learning. No wonder the Oriental mind looks with contempt upon the things of this world and seeks to see something which changes not, something which dies not, something which in the midst of this world of misery and death is eternal, blissful, undying. An Oriental Prophet never tires of insisting upon these ideals; and as for Prophets, you may also remember that, without one exception, all of them were Orientals.

We see, therefore, in the life of this great Messenger of light, the first watchword: "Not this life, but something higher." And like a true son of the Orient, He is practical in that. You people of the West are practical in your own department, in military affairs and in managing politics and other similar things. Perhaps the Oriental is not practical in those matters; but he is practical in his own field; he is practical in religion. If he preaches a philosophy, tomorrow there will be hundreds who will struggle their utmost to make it practical in their lives. If a man preaches that standing on one foot will lead to salvation, he will immediately get five hundred to stand on one foot. You may call it ludicrous; but mark you, behind that is the secret of religion: intense practicality. In the West, plans of salvation mean intellectual gymnastics, plans which are never worked out, never brought into practical life. In the West, the preacher who talks the best is the greatest preacher.

So in the first place we find Jesus of Nazareth to be a true son of the Orient, intensely practical. He has no faith in this evanescent world and its various belongings. No need of text-torturing, as is the fashion in the West in modern times, no need of stretching out texts until they will not stretch any more. Texts are not india-rubber, and even that has its limits. Now, please do not make religion pander to the vanity of the present day! Let us all, mark you, be honest. If we cannot follow the ideal, let us confess our weakness, but let us not degrade it. Let us not try to pull it down. One gets sick at heart at the different accounts of the life of the Christ that Western people give. I do not know what He was or what He was not! One would make Him a great politician; another, perhaps, would make of Him a great military general; another, a great patriotic Jew, and so on. Is there any warrant in the Bible for all such assumptions? The best commentary on the life of a great Teacher is His own life. "The foxes have holes, the birds of the air have nests, but the Son of man hath not where to lay his head." That is what Christ says is the only way to salvation. He lays down no other way.

Let us confess in sackcloth and ashes that we cannot do that. We still have a fondness for "me" and "mine." We want property, power, wealth. Woe unto us! Let us confess and not put to shame that great Teacher of humanity! He had no family ties. Do you think that that man had any physical ideas in Him? Do you think that this mass of light, this God and not man, came down to earth to be a brother of animals? And yet people make Him preach all sorts of things. He had no sex-ideas. He was the Soul—nothing but the Soul, just working through a body for the good of men; and that was all His relation to the body. In the Soul there is no sex. The disembodied Soul has no relationship to the animal, no relationship to the body. The ideal may be far beyond us; but never mind; keep to the ideal. Let us confess that it is our ideal, but we cannot approach it yet.

He had no other idea of Himself, no other except that He was Spirit. He was disembodied, unfettered, unbound Spirit. And not only so, but He, with his marvellous vision, had found that every man and woman, whether Jew or Gentile, whether rich or poor, whether saint or sinner, was the embodiment of the same undying Spirit as Himself. Therefore the one work of His whole life was calling upon them to realize their own spiritual nature. Give up, He says, these superstitious dreams that you are low and that you are poor. Think not that you are trampled upon and tyrannized over as if you were slaves; for within you is something that can never be tyrannized over, never be trampled upon, never be troubled, never be killed. You are all sons of God, Immortal Spirit. "Know ye," He declared, "the kingdom of heaven is within you." "I and my Father are one." Dare not only to stand up and say, "I am the son of God," but also to find in your heart of hearts: "I and my Father are one." That was what Jesus of Nazareth said. He never talks of this world and of this life. He has nothing to do with it, except that He wants to get hold of the world as it is, give it a push, and drive it forward and onward until the whole world has reached to the effulgent Light of God, until everyone has realized his spiritual nature, until death is vanquished and misery banished.

We have read the different stories that have been written about Him; we know the scholars and their writings, and the higher criticism; and we know all that has been achieved by study. We are not here to discuss how much of the New Testament is true; we are not here to discuss how much of that life is historical. It does not matter at all whether the New Testament was written within five hundred years of His birth; nor does it even matter how much of that life is true. But there is something behind it, something we want to imitate. To tell a lie, you have to imitate a truth, and that truth is a fact. You cannot imitate that which never existed. You cannot imitate that which you have never perceived. There must have been a nucleus through which has come down a tremendous power, a marvellous manifestation of spiritual power —and of that we are speaking. It stands there. Therefore we are not afraid of the criticisms of the scholars. If I, as an Oriental, am to worship Jesus of Nazareth, there is only one way left to me: that is to worship Him as God and nothing else. Do you mean to say that we have no right to worship Him in that way? If we bring Him down to our own level and simply pay Him a little respect as a great man, why should we worship at all? Our scriptures say: "These great Children of Light, who manifest the Light themselves, who are Light themselves, they being worshipped, become one with us, and we become one with them."

For there are three ways in which man perceives God. First, the undeveloped intellect of the uneducated man sees God as being far away, up in the heavens somewhere, sitting on a throne as a great Judge. He looks upon Him with fear, as a terror. Now, that is good; there is nothing bad in it. You must remember that humanity travels not from error to truth, but from truth to truth—it may be, if you like it better, from lower truth to higher truth; but never from error to truth. Suppose you start from here and travel towards the sun in a straight line. From here the sun looks small. Suppose you go forward a million miles; it will surely seem much larger. At every stage it will become bigger and bigger. Suppose that twenty thousand photographs are taken of the same sun, all from different standpoints; these twenty thousand photographs will all certainly differ from one another. But can you deny that each is a photograph of the same sun? So all forms of religion, high or low, are just different stages in the upward journey towards that eternal Light, which is God Himself. Some embody a lower view, some a higher, and that is all the difference. Therefore the religions of the unthinking masses all over the world teach, and have always taught, of a God who is outside the universe, who lives in heaven, who governs from that place, who is the punisher of the bad and the rewarder of the good, and so on. As man advances spiritually, he begins to feel that God is omnipresent, that He must be in him, that He must be everywhere, that He is not a distant God, but clearly the Soul of all souls. As my soul moves my body, even so is God the mover of my soul—the Soul within the soul. And a few individuals of pure heart and highly developed mind go still farther, and at last find God. As the New Testament says: "Blessed are the pure in heart, for they shall see God." And they find at last that they and the Father are one.

You will find that these three stages are taught by the great Teacher in the New Testament. Note the common prayer He taught: "Our Father which art in heaven, hallowed be Thy name," and so on; a simple prayer, mark you, a child's prayer. It is indeed the "common prayer" because it is intended for the uneducated masses. To a higher circle, to those who had advanced a little more, He gave a more elevated teaching: "I am in my Father, and ye in me, and I in you." Do you remember that? And then, when the Jews asked Him who He was, he declared that He and His Father were one; and the Jews thought that that was blasphemy. What did He mean by that? But the same thing had been taught by the Jewish Prophets: "Ye are gods; and all of you are children of the Most High." Mark the same three stages. You will find that it is easier for you to begin with the first and end with the last.

The Messenger came to show the path: that the Spirit is not in forms; that it is not through all sorts of vexatious and knotty problems of philosophy that you know the Spirit. Better that you had had no learning; better that you had never read a book in your life. These are not at all necessary for salvation—neither wealth nor position nor power, nor even learning. But what is necessary is that one thing, purity: "Blessed are the pure in heart," for the Spirit in Its own nature is pure. How can It be otherwise? It is of God; It has come from God. In the language of the Bible, "It is the Breath of God." In the language of the Koran, "It is the Soul of God." Do you mean to say that the Spirit of God can ever be impure? But alas, It has been covered over, as it were, with the dust and dirt of ages, through our own actions, good and evil; various works which were not correct, which were not true, have covered the Spirit with the dust and dirt of the ignorance of ages. It is only necessary to clear away the dust and dirt, and then the Spirit shines immediately. "Blessed are the pure in heart, for they shall see God." "The kingdom of heaven is within you." Where goest thou to seek for the kingdom of God?—asks Jesus of Nazareth, when it is there within you. Cleanse your spirit and find it there. It is already yours. How can you get what is not yours? It is yours by right. You are the heirs of immortality, sons of the Eternal Father.

This is the great lesson of the Messenger; another lesson, forming the basis of all religions, is renunciation. How can you make your spirit pure? By renunciation. A rich young man asked Jesus, "Good Master, what shall I do that I may inherit eternal life?" And Jesus said unto him, "One thing thou lackest: go thy way, sell whatsoever thou hast, and give to the poor, and thou shalt have treasure in heaven: and come, take up thy cross, and follow me." And the man was sad at that saying, and went away grieved; for he had great possessions. We are all more or less like that. The Voice is ringing in our ears day and night. In the midst of our joys and pleasures, in the midst of worldly things, in the midst of the world's turmoil, we forget it; then comes a moment's pause, and the Voice rings in our ears: "Give up all that thou hast and follow me. Whosoever will save his life shall lose it; and whosoever shall lose his life for my sake shall find it." For whoever gives up this life for His sake finds the life immortal. In the midst of all our weakness there is a moment of pause and the Voice rings: "Give up all that thou hast; give it to the poor and follow me." This is the one ideal He preaches, and this has been the ideal preached by all the great Prophets of the world: renunciation. What is meant by renunciation? Unselfishness. That is the only ideal in morality. The ideal is perfect unselfishness. When a man is struck on the right cheek, he is to turn the left also. When a man's coat is carried off, he is to give his cloak in addition.

We should work in the best way we can, without dragging the ideal down. Here is the ideal: When a man has no more of self in him, no possession, nothing to call "me" or "mine," has given himself up to God, destroyed himself, as it were—in that man God is manifest; for in him self-will is gone, crushed out, annihilated. That is the ideal man. We cannot reach that state yet; nevertheless, let us worship the ideal and slowly struggle to reach the ideal, though it may be with faltering steps. It may be tomorrow, or it may be a thousand years hence, but that ideal has to be reached. For it is not only the end, but also the means. To be unselfish, perfectly selfless, is salvation itself; for the man within dies and God alone remains.

One more point. All the Teachers of humanity are unselfish. Suppose Jesus of Nazareth was teaching, and a man came and told Him: "What you teach is beautiful. I believe that it is the way to perfection and I am ready to follow it; but I do not care to worship you as the only-begotten Son of God." What would be the answer of Jesus of Nazareth? "Very well, brother, follow the ideal and advance in your own way. I do not care whether you give me the credit for the teaching or not. I am not a shopkeeper; I do not trade in religion. I teach truth only and truth is nobody's property. Nobody can patent truth. Truth is God Himself. Go forward." But what the disciples say nowadays is: "No matter whether you practise the teachings or not, do you give credit to the Man? If you credit the Master, you will be saved; if not, there is no salvation for you." And thus the whole teaching of the Master has degenerated and all the struggle and fight is about the personality of the Man. They do not know that in emphasizing that difference they are, in a manner, bringing shame to the very Man they want to honour, the very Man who would have shrunk with shame from such an idea. What did He care if there was one man in the world that remembered Him or not? He had to deliver His message, and He gave it. And if He had twenty thousand lives, He would give them all up for the poorest man in the world. If He had to be tortured millions of times, for a million despised Samaritans, and if for each one of them the sacrifice of His own life would be the only condition of salvation, he would have given His life. And all this without wishing to have His name known even to a single person. Quiet, unknown, silent, would He work, just as the Lord works. Now, what will the disciple say? He will tell you that you may be a perfect man, perfectly unselfish, but unless you give the credit to his Teacher, to his Saint, it is of no avail. Why? What is the origin of this superstition, this ignorance? The disciple thinks that the Lord can manifest Himself only once: there lies the whole mistake. God manifests Himself to you in man. But in nature, what happens once must have happened before and must happen in the future. There is nothing in nature which is not bound by law, and that means that whatever happened once must have been going on ever since.

In India they have the same idea of the Incarnation of God. One of their great Incarnations, Krishna, whose grand sermon, the Bhagavad Gita, some of you may have read, says: "Though I am unborn, of changeless nature, and Lord of beings, yet subjugating My prakriti (nature), I come into being by My own māyā. Whenever virtue subsides and immorality prevails I body Myself forth. For the protection of the good, for the destruction of the wicked, and for the establishment of dharma, I assume a body in every age." Whenever the world goes down, the Lord comes to help it forward; and so He comes from age to age, in place after place. In another passage He speaks to this effect: "Wherever thou findest a great soul of immense power and purity struggling to raise humanity, know that He is born of My splendour, that I am there working through Him."

Let us, therefore, find God not only in Jesus of Nazareth, but in all the Great Ones who preceded Him, in all who have come after Him, and all who are yet to come. Our worship is unbounded and free. They are all manifestations of the same infinite God. They are all pure and unselfish; they suffer and give up their lives for us poor human beings. They each and all suffer vicarious atonement for every one of us, and also for all who are to come hereafter.

In a sense, you are all Prophets; every one of you is a Prophet, bearing the burden of the world on your own shoulders. Have you ever seen a man, have you ever seen a woman, who is not quietly, patiently, bearing his or her little burden of life? The great Prophets were giants: they bore the whole world on their shoulders. Compared with them we are pigmies, no doubt; yet we are doing the same task. In our little circles, in our little homes, we are bearing our little crosses. There is no one so evil, no one so worthless, but he has to bear his own cross. But with all our mistakes, with all our evil thoughts and evil deeds, there is a bright spot somewhere, there is still somewhere the golden thread through which we are always in touch with the Divine. For know for certain that the moment the touch of the Divine was lost there would be annihilation; and because none can be annihilated, there is always somewhere in our heart of hearts, however low and degraded we may be, a little circle of light which is in constant touch with the Divine.

Our salutations go to all the past Prophets, whose teachings and lives we have inherited, whatever their race, clime, or creed. Our salutations go to all those God-like men and women who are working at present to help humanity, whatever their birth, colour, or race. Our salutations go to those who are coming in the future—living Gods—to work unselfishly for our descendants.

THE VEDĀNTA PHILOSOPHY[1]

THE VEDĀNTA PHILOSOPHY, as it is generally called at the present day, is really professed by all the various sects that now exist in India. Thus there have been different interpretations; and to my mind they have been progressive, beginning with the Dualistic, or Dvaita, and ending with the Non-dualistic, or Advaita. The word Vedānta means, literally, "the end of the Vedas"—the Vedas being the scriptures of the Hindus.[2] Sometimes, in the West, by the Vedas are meant only the hymns and rituals of the Vedas. But at the present time these parts have almost gone out of use, and usually by the word Vedas, in India, Vedānta is meant. All our commentators, when they want to quote a passage from the scriptures, as a rule quote from Vedānta, which has another technical name with the commentators: the Śrutis.[3] Now the books known by the name of Vedānta were not all written after the ritualistic portions of the Vedas. For instance, one of them—the Iśa Upanishad—forms the fortieth chapter of the Yajur-Veda, that being the oldest part of the Vedas. There are other Upanishads[4] which form portions of the Brāhmanas, or ritualistic writings; and the rest of the Upanishads are independent, not comprised in any of the Brāhmanas or other parts of the Vedas. But there is no reason to suppose that they were wholly independent of the other parts; for, as we well know, many of these

---

[1] This lecture was delivered by Swami Vivekananda on March 25, 1896, at the Graduate Philosophical Society, before professors and graduates of Harvard University. The lecture and the discussion that followed it were published in America by Mr. J. P. Fox with a note by himself and an introduction by Dr. C. C. Everett, of Harvard University. The four following footnotes were added by Swami Vivekananda.

[2] The Vedas are divided into two main portions: the Karmakānda and the Jnānakānda, the work portion and the knowledge portion. To the Karmakānda belong the famous hymns and the rituals, or Brāhmanas. Those books which treat of spiritual matters apart from ceremonials are called Upanishads. The Upanishads generally belong to the Jnānakānda, or knowledge portion of the Vedas. Not all the Upanishads, however, are included in the Jnānakānda. Some are interspersed among the rituals, and at least one is in the Samhitā, or hymn portion. Sometimes the term Upanishad is applied to books which are not included in the Vedas—e.g. the Gītā; but as a rule it is applied to the philosophical treatises scattered through the Vedas. These treatises have been collected and are called Vedānta.

[3] The term Śruti—meaning "that which is heard"—though including the whole of the Vedic literature, is chiefly applied by the commentators to the Upanishads.

[4] The Upanishads are said to be one hundred and eight in number. Their dates cannot be fixed with accuracy; but it is certain that they are older than the Buddhist movement. Though some of the minor Upanishads contain allusions indicating a later date, yet that does not prove the later date of the treatise, since, in very many cases in Sanskrit literature, the substance of a book, though of very ancient date, has received a coating, as it were, of later events at the hands of sectarians, to exalt their particular sect.

have been lost entirely, and many of the Brāhmanas have become extinct. So it is quite possible that the independent Upanishads belonged to Brāhmanas which in course of time fell into disuse, while the Upanishads remained. These Upanishads are also called Forest Books, or Āranyakas.

Vedānta, then, practically forms the scriptures of the Hindus, and all systems of philosophy that are orthodox have to take it as their foundation. Even the Buddhists and Jains, when it suits their purposes, will quote a passage from Vedānta as authority. All the schools of philosophy in India, although they claim to have been based upon the Vedas, took different names for their systems. The last one, the system of Vyāsa, took its stand upon the doctrines of the Vedas more than the previous systems did, and made an attempt to harmonize the preceding philosophies, such as the Sāmkhya and the Nyāya, with the doctrines of Vedānta. So it is especially called the Vedānta philosophy; and the *Sutras*, or *Aphorisms*, of Vyāsa are, in modern India, the basis of the Vedānta philosophy. Again, these *Sutras* of Vyāsa have been variously explained by different commentators. In general there are three classes of commentators[5] in India now; and from their interpretations have arisen three systems of philosophy and sects. One is the Dualistic, or Dvaita; the second is the Qualified Non-dualistic, or Viśishtādvaita; and the third is the Non-dualistic, or Advaita. Of these, the Dualistic and the Qualified Non-dualistic include the largest number of the Indian people. The Non-dualists are comparatively few in number.

Now I shall try to lay before you the ideas that are contained in all these three sects. But before going on I shall make one remark: that these different Vedānta systems have one common psychology, and that is the psychology of the Sāmkhya system. This Sāmkhya psychology is very much like the psychologies of the Nyāya and Vaiśeshika systems, differing only in minor particulars.

All the Vedāntists agree on three points. They believe in God, in the Vedas as revelation, and in cycles. We have already considered the Vedas. The belief about cycles is as follows: All matter throughout the universe is the outcome of one primal matter called ākāśa; and all force, whether gravitation, attraction

---

[5] The commentaries are of various kinds—such as the Bhāshya, Tikā, Tippani, Churni, etc.—of which all except the Bhāshya are explanations of the text or difficult words in the text. The Bhāshya is not properly a commentary, but the elucidation of a system of philosophy out of the texts, the object being not to explain the words, but to bring out the philosophy. So the writer of a Bhāshya expands his own system, taking the texts as authority for his system.

There have been various commentaries on Vedānta. Its doctrines found their final expression in the philosophical aphorisms of Vyāsa. This treatise, called the *Uttara Mimāmsā*, is the standard authority on Vedānta—nay, is the most authoritative exposition of the Hindu scriptures. The most antagonistic sects have been compelled, as it were, to take up the texts of Vyāsa and harmonize them with their own philosophy. Even in very ancient times the commentators on the Vedānta philosophy formed themselves into the three celebrated Hindu sects of Dualists, Qualified Non-dualists, and Non-dualists. The ancient commentaries are perhaps lost; but later on they were revived by the post-Buddhist commentators Śankara, Rāmānuja, and Madhva. Śankara revived the Non-dualistic form, Rāmānuja the Qualified Non-dualistic form, of the ancient commentator Bodhāyana, and Madhva the Dualistic form. In India the sects differ mainly in their philosophy; the difference in rituals is slight.

or repulsion, or life, is the outcome of one primal force called prāna. Prāna acting on ākāśa creates or projects[6] the universe. At the beginning of a cycle, ākāśa is motionless, unmanifested. Then prāna begins to act, gradually creating grosser and grosser forms out of ākāśa—plants, animals, men, stars, and so on. After an incalculable time this evolution ceases and involution begins, everything being resolved back through finer and finer forms into the original ākāśa and prāna, when a new cycle follows. Now, there is something beyond ākāśa and prāna. Both can be resolved into a third thing called mahat, the cosmic mind. This cosmic mind does not create ākāśa and prāna, but changes itself into them.

We shall now take up the beliefs about mind, soul, and God. According to the universally accepted Sāmkhya psychology, in perception—in the case of vision, for instance—there is, first of all, the instrument, or kārana, of vision: the eye. Behind the instrument—the eye—is the organ, or indriya, of vision: the optic nerve and its centre—which is not the external instrument, but without which the eye will not see. More still is needed for perception. The mind, or manas, must come and attach itself to the organ. And besides this, the sensation must be carried to the intellect, or buddhi—the determinative, reactive state of the mind. When the reaction comes from the buddhi, along with it flash the external world and the ego. Here, then, is the will; but everything is not complete. Just as the pictures in a magic lantern, composed of successive impulses of light, must be united on something stationary to form a whole, so all the ideas in the mind must be gathered and projected on something that is stationary, relative to the body and mind—that is, on what is called the Soul or Purusha or Ātman.

According to the Sāmkhya philosophy, the reactive state of the mind, called buddhi, or intellect, is the outcome, the change, or a certain manifestation, of mahat, the cosmic mind. Mahat becomes changed into vibrating thought; and that becomes in one part changed into the organs, and in another part into ākāśa and prāna. Out of the combination of all these, the whole of this universe, from mahat down to the grossest objects, is produced. Behind even mahat, Sāmkhya conceives of a certain state which is called avyakta, or the unmanifested, where even the manifestation of mind is not present, but only the causes exist. It is also called prakriti. Beyond this prakriti, and eternally separate from it, is the Purusha, the Soul in Sāmkhya, which is without attributes and omnipresent. The Purusha is not the doer but the witness. The illustration of a crystal is used to explain the Purusha. The latter is said to be like a crystal without any colour, before which different colours are placed; and then it seems to be coloured by all the colours before it, but in reality it is not.

The Vedāntists reject the Sāmkhya ideas of the Soul (Purusha) and nature (prakriti). They claim that between the Soul and nature there is a gulf to be bridged over. On the one hand the Sāmkhya system refers to nature, and then at once jumps over to the other side and refers to the Soul, which is entirely

[6] "The Sanskrit word for creation has no exact equivalent in your language; there is no sect in India which believes in creation as it is described in the Bible—as something coming out of nothing. . . . What we mean by creation is projection of that which already existed." (*From Swami Vivekananda's lecture "The Ātman."*)

separate from nature. How can prakriti, the Vedāntists ask, act on the Soul, which by its nature is independent? So the Vedāntists, from the very first, affirm that the Soul and nature are one.[7] Even the Dualistic Vedāntists admit that Ātman, or God, is not only the efficient cause of this universe but also the material cause. But what they say is only so many words; they do not really mean it; for they try to escape from their conclusions in this way.

The Dualistic Vedāntists say there are three existences in this universe: God, soul, and nature. Nature and soul are, as it were, the body of God, and in this sense it may be said that God and the whole universe are one. But nature and all these various souls remain different from each other through all eternity. At the beginning of a cycle they become manifest, and when the cycle ends they become fine and remain in a fine state.

The Advaita Vedāntists—the Non-dualists—reject this theory of the soul and, having nearly the whole range of the Upanishads in their favour, build their philosophy entirely upon them. All the Upanishads have one subject, one task before them—to answer the following question: "As by knowing one lump of clay we know all the clay in the universe—what is that by knowing which we know everything in the universe?"[8] The idea of the Advaitists is to generalize the whole universe into One—that Something which is really the whole of this universe. And they claim that this whole universe is one, that it is one Being manifesting Itself in all these various forms. They admit that what Sāmkhya calls nature exists, but they say that nature is God. It is this Being, or Sat, that has become converted into all this—the universe, men, souls, and everything that exists. Mind and mahat are but manifestations of that one Sat.

But then the difficulty arises that this would be pantheism. How does the Sat, which is unchangeable, become changed into that which is changeable and perishable? The Advaitists here have a theory which they call vivartavāda, or apparent manifestation. According to the Dualists and the followers of Sāmkhya, the whole of this universe is the evolution of primal nature. According to some of the Advaitists and some of the Dualists, the whole of this universe is evolved from God. And according to the Advaitists proper, the followers of Śankarāchārya, the universe is only an apparent evolution of God. God is the material cause of this universe—but not really, only apparently. The celebrated illustration used is that of the rope and the snake, where the rope appears to be a snake, but is not really so. The rope does not really change into the snake. Even so this whole universe as it exists is that Being. It is unchanged, and all the changes we see in It are only apparent. These changes are caused by deśa, kāla, and nimitta—time, space, and causation—or, according to a higher metaphysical generalization, by nāma and rupa—name and form. It is by name and form that

---

[7] The Vedānta and Sāmkhya philosophies are very little opposed to each other. Vedānta's God developed out of Sāmkhya's Purusha. All the systems accept the psychology of Sāmkhya. Both Vedānta and Sāmkhya believe in an infinite Soul, but Sāmkhya believes there are many Souls. According to Sāmkhya, this universe does not require any explanation from outside. The Vedāntists believe there is one Soul, which appears as many; and they build on Sāmkhya's analysis. (From Swami Vivekananda's talk of March 24, 1896.)

[8] Compare Chhāndogya Upanishad VI. 1-4 and Mundaka Upanishad I. i. 3.

one thing is differentiated from another. The name and the form alone cause
the difference. In reality they are one and the same.

Again, it is not, the Vedāntists say, that there is something known as phenomenon and something else as noumenon. The rope is changed into the snake
only apparently; and when the delusion ceases, the snake vanishes. When a
man is in ignorance, he sees the phenomenon and does not see God. When he
sees God, the universe vanishes entirely.

Ignorance, or māyā, as it is called, is the cause of all this phenomenon—the
Absolute, the Unchangeable, being taken as this manifested universe. This
māyā is not absolute zero, not non-existence. It is defined as neither existence
nor non-existence. It cannot be said that it is existence, because that can be
said only of the Absolute, the Unchangeable, and in this sense māyā is non-
existence. Again, it cannot be said that it is non-existence; for if it were, it
could never produce the phenomenon. So it is something that is neither. In
the Vedānta philosophy it is called anirvachaniya, or inexpressible. Māyā, then,
is the real cause of this universe. Māyā gives the name and form to that for
which Brahman, or God, gives the material; and the latter seems to have been
transformed into all this.

The Advaitists have no place for the individual soul. They say individual souls
are created by māyā. In reality they cannot exist. If there is only one existence
throughout, how can it be that I am one, and you are another, and so on? We
are all one; and the cause of evil is the perception of duality. As soon as I begin
to feel that I am separate from this universe, first comes fear and then comes
misery. "Where one hears another, sees another—that is small. Where one
does not see another, where one does not hear another—that is the greatest,
that is God. In the greatest is perfect happiness; in small things there is no
happiness."⁹

According to the Advaita philosophy, then, these material objects, these
phenomena, for a time hide, as it were, the real nature of man. But the latter
really does not change at all. In the lowest worm, as well as in the highest
human being, the same divine nature is present. The worm form is the lower
form, in which the divinity has been greatly obscured by māyā; and that
indeed is the highest form in which it has been least obscured. Behind
everything the same divinity exists; and out of this comes the basis of morality.
Do not injure another. Love everyone as your own self, because the whole
universe is one. In injuring another, I am injuring myself; in loving another, I
am loving myself.

From this also springs that principle of Advaita morality which has been
summed up in one word: self-abnegation. The Advaitist says that this little
personalized self is the cause of all my misery. This individualized self, which
makes me different from all other beings, brings hatred and jealousy and
misery and friction and all other evils. When this idea has been got rid of,
all friction will cease, all misery vanish. So this is to be given up. We must
always hold ourselves ready to give up even our lives for the lowest beings.
When a man has become ready to give up even his life for a little insect, he
has reached the perfection that the Advaitist wants to attain; and at that

⁹ *Chhāndogya Upanishad* VII. xxiv. 1.

moment when he has become thus ready, the veil of ignorance will be taken away from him and he will feel his true nature. Even in this life he will feel that he is one with the universe. For a time, as it were, the whole phenomenal world will disappear for him, and he will realize what he is. But so long as the karma of this body remains, he will have to live. This state, when the veil has vanished and yet the body remains for some time, is what the Vedāntists call jivanmukti, freedom while one is living in the body. Suppose a man has been deluded by a mirage for some time, and one day he understands his mistake; though it may return the next day or some other time, he will not be deluded again. Before the true nature of the mirage is known, the man cannot distinguish between the reality and the deception. But when it is recognized, as long as he has organs and eyes, he will have to see the mirage, but he will no longer be deluded. He has known the difference between the actual world and the mirage, and the mirage cannot delude him any more. So when the Vedāntist has realized his own nature, the whole world has vanished for him. It will come back again, but never more as the same world of misery. The prison of misery has become changed into Sat, Chit, Ānanda—Existence Absolute, Knowledge Absolute, Bliss Absolute—and the attainment of this is the goal of the Advaita philosophy.

WHAT IS RELIGION?

A HUGE LOCOMOTIVE rushes down the tracks, and a small worm that has been creeping upon one of the rails saves its life by crawling out of the path of the locomotive. Yet this little worm, so insignificant that it can be crushed in a moment, is a living something, while the locomotive, so huge, so immense, is only an engine, a machine. You see, the one has life and the other is only dead matter, and all its power and strength and speed are only those of a dead machine, a mechanical contrivance. The poor little worm which moves upon the rail and which the least touch of the engine would surely deprive of its life is a majestic being compared to that huge locomotive. It is a small part of the Infinite and therefore it is greater than the powerful engine. Why should that be so? How do we know the living from the dead? The machine mechanically performs all the movements its maker made it to perform; its movements are not those of life. How can we make the distinction between the living and the dead, then? In the living there is freedom, there is intelligence; in the dead all is bound and no freedom is possible, because there is no intelligence. This freedom that distinguishes us from mere machines is what we are all striving for. To be more free is the goal of all our efforts; for only in perfect freedom can there be perfection. This effort to attain freedom underlies all forms of worship, whether we know it or not.

If we were to examine the various sorts of worship all over the world, we would see that the crudest of mankind are worshipping ghosts, demons, and the spirits of their forefathers. Serpent-worship, worship of tribal gods, and worship of the departed ones—why do they practise all this? Because they feel that in some unknown way these beings are greater, more powerful, than themselves and so limit their freedom. They therefore seek to propitiate these beings in order to prevent them from molesting them—in other words, to get more freedom. They also seek to win favour from these superior beings, to get as a gift what ought to be earned by personal effort.

On the whole, this shows that the world is expecting a miracle. This expectation never leaves us, and however we may try, we are all running after the miraculous and extraordinary. What is mind but that ceaseless inquiry into the meaning and mystery of life? We may say that only uncultivated people are going after all these things; but the question still is there—why should it be so? The Jews were asking for a miracle. The whole world has been asking for the same thing these thousands of years.

There is, again, the universal dissatisfaction: we take up an ideal, but we have rushed only half the way after it when we take up a new one. We struggle hard to attain a certain goal and then discover we do not want it. This dissatisfaction we are experiencing time after time; and what is there in life if there is to

728

be only dissatisfaction? What is the meaning of this universal dissatisfaction? It indicates that freedom is every man's goal. He seeks it ever; his whole life is a struggle after it. The child rebels against law as soon as it is born. Its first utterance is a cry, a protest against the bondage in which it finds itself. This longing for freedom produces the idea of a Being who is absolutely free. The concept of God is a fundamental element in the human constitution. Satchidānanda, Existence-Knowledge-Bliss, is, in Vedānta, the highest concept of God possible to the mind. It is by its nature the Essence of Knowledge and the Essence of Bliss. We have been stifling that inner voice, seeking to follow law and suppress our true nature; but there is that human instinct to rebel against nature's laws.

We may not understand what all this means; but there is that unconscious struggle of the human with the spiritual, of the lower with the higher mind, and through this struggle we attempt to preserve our separate life, what we call our "individuality." Even hell illustrates this miraculous fact that we are born rebels. Against the inevitable facts of life we rebel and cry out, "No law for us!" As long as we obey the laws we are like machines; and the universe goes on and we cannot change it. Laws become man's nature. The first inkling of life on its higher level is in seeing this struggle within us to break the bonds of nature and to be free. "Freedom, oh, freedom! Freedom, oh, freedom!" is the song of the soul. Bondage, alas—to be bound in nature—seems its fate.

Why should there be serpent-worship or ghost-worship or demon-worship and all the various creeds and forms for the obtaining of miracles? Why do we say that there is life, there is being, in anything? There must be a meaning in all this search, this endeavour to understand life, to explain being. It is not meaningless and vain. It is man's ceaseless endeavour to become free. The knowledge which we now call science has been struggling for thousands of years in its attempt to gain freedom, and people still ask for freedom. Yet there is no freedom in nature. It is all law. Still the struggle goes on. Nay, the whole of nature, from the very sun down to the atoms, is under law, and even for man there is no freedom. But we cannot believe it. We have been studying laws from the beginning and yet cannot—nay, will not—believe that man is under law. The soul cries ever, "Freedom, oh, freedom!"

With the conception of God as a perfectly free Being, man cannot rest eternally in this bondage. Higher he must go, and were the struggle not for freedom he would think it too severe. Man says to himself: "I am a born slave, I am bound; nevertheless there is a Being who is not bound by nature. He is free and the Master of nature." The conception of God, therefore, is as essential and as fundamental a part of the mind as is the idea of bondage. Both are the outcome of the idea of freedom. There cannot be life, even in the plant, without the idea of freedom. In the plant or in the worm, life has to rise to the concept of individuality; it is there, unconsciously working. The plant lives in order to preserve a principle; it is not simply nature. The idea of nature's controlling every step onward overrules the idea of freedom. Onward goes the material world, onward moves the idea of freedom. Still the fight goes on. We are hearing about all the quarrels of creeds and sects; yet creeds and sects are just and proper; they must be there. They no doubt lengthen the chain, and naturally the struggle increases; but there will be no quarrels if we only know that we are all striving to reach the same goal.

The embodiment of freedom, the Master of nature, is what we call God. You cannot deny Him. No, because you cannot move or live without the idea of freedom. Would you come here if you did not believe you were free? It is quite possible that the biologist can and will give some explanation of this perpetual effort to be free. Taking all that for granted, still the idea of freedom is there. It is a fact, as much so as the other fact that you cannot apparently get over, the fact of being under nature.

Bondage and liberty, light and shadow, good and evil, must be there; but the very fact of the bondage shows also this freedom hidden there. If one is a fact, the other is equally a fact. There must be this idea of freedom. While now we cannot see that this idea of bondage, in uncultivated man, is his struggle for freedom, yet the idea of freedom is there. The consciousness of the bondage of sin and impurity in the uncultivated savage is very slight; for his nature is only a little higher than that of the animal. What he struggles against is the bondage of physical nature, the lack of physical gratification; but out of this lower consciousness grows and broadens the higher conception of a mental or moral bondage and a longing for spiritual freedom. Here we see the divine dimly shining through the veil of ignorance. The veil is very dense at first, and the light may be almost obscured, but it is there, ever pure and undimmed—the radiant light of freedom and perfection. Man personifies this as the Ruler of the universe, the one free Being. He does not yet know that the universe is all one, that the difference is only in the concept and not in things themselves.

The whole of nature is worship of God. Wherever there is life there is this search for freedom, and that freedom is the same as God. Necessarily freedom gives us mastery over all nature and is impossible without knowledge. The more we know, the more we become masters of nature. Mastery alone makes us strong; and if there be some being who is entirely free and a master of nature, that being must have a perfect knowledge of nature, must be omnipresent and omniscient. Freedom must go hand in hand with these; and only that being who has acquired these will be beyond nature.

Blessedness, eternal peace, arising from perfect freedom, is the highest concept of religion, underlying all the ideas of God in Vedānta: absolutely free existence, not bound by anything—no change, no nature, nothing that can produce a change in Him. This same freedom is in you and in me and is the only real freedom.

God is always established upon His own majestic changeless Self. You and I try to be one with Him, but find ourselves diverted by nature, by the trifles of daily life, by money, by fame, by human love, and all these changing forms which make for bondage. When nature shines, upon what depends its shining? Upon God, and not upon the sun or the moon or the stars. Wherever anything shines, whether it is the light in the sun or in our own consciousness, it is He. He shining, all shines after Him.

Now, we have seen that this God is self-evident, impersonal, omniscient, the Knower and Master of nature, the Lord of all. He is behind all worship, and all worship is directed to Him whether we know it or not. I go one step farther:

That which we call evil is His worship too. This too is a part of freedom. When you are doing evil, the impulse behind is that of freedom. It may be misguided and misled, but it is there, and there cannot be any life or any impulse unless that freedom is behind it. Freedom throbs in the heart of the universe. Such is the conception of the Lord in the Upanishads.

Sometimes it rises even higher, presenting to us an ideal before which at first we stand aghast: that we are in essence one with God. He who is the colouring in the wings of the butterfly and the blossoming of the rose-bud is the power that is in the plant and in the butterfly. He who gives us life is the power within us. Out of His power comes life, and the direst death is also His power. He whose shadow is death—His shadow is immortality also.

Take a still higher conception; see how we are flying like hunted hares from all that is terrible, and like them hiding our heads and thinking we are safe. See how the whole world is flying from everything terrible. Once when I was in Benares, I was passing through a place where there was a large reservoir of water on one side and a high wall on the other. There were many monkeys around that place. The monkeys of Benares are huge brutes and are sometimes surly. They now took it into their heads not to allow me to pass through their street; so they howled and shrieked and clutched at my feet as I passed. As they pressed closer, I began to run; but the faster I ran, the faster came the monkeys, and they began to bite at me. It seemed impossible to escape. But just then I met a stranger, who called out to me, "Face the brutes." I turned and faced the monkeys and they fell back and finally fled. That is a lesson for all life: face the terrible, face it boldly. Like the monkeys, the hardships of life fall back when we cease to flee before them. If we are ever to gain freedom, it must be by conquering nature, never by running away. Cowards never win victories. We have to fight fear and troubles and ignorance if we expect them to flee before us.

What is death? What are terrors? Do you not see the Lord's face in them? Fly from evil and terror and misery and they will follow you. Face them and they will flee. The whole world worships ease and pleasure, and very few dare to worship what is painful. To rise above both is the ideal of freedom. Unless a man passes through pleasure and pain he is not free. We have to face them. We strive to worship the Lord, but the body comes between, nature comes between Him and us and blinds our vision. We must learn how to worship and love Him in the thunderbolt, in shame, in sorrow, in sin. All the world has ever been preaching the God of virtue. I preach a God of virtue and a God of sin in one. Take Him if you dare. That is the one way to salvation. Then alone will come to us the Truth Ultimate which comes from the idea of Oneness. Then will be lost the idea that one is greater than another. The nearer we approach the ideal of freedom, the more shall come under the Lord and troubles will vanish. Then we shall not differentiate the door of hell from the gate of heaven, nor differentiate between men and say, "I am greater than any other being in the universe." Until we see nothing in the world but the Lord Himself, all these evils will beset us and we shall make all these distinctions; for it is only in the Lord, in the Spirit, that we are all one, and until we see God everywhere, this unity will not exist for us.

The man who is groping through sin, through misery, the man who is choosing the path through hell, will reach freedom, but it will take time. We cannot help him. Some hard knocks on his head will make him turn to the Lord. The path of virtue, purity, unselfishness, spirituality, he will know at last, and what he has been doing unconsciously he will do consciously. The idea is expressed by St. Paul: "Whom therefore ye ignorantly worship, Him declare I unto you." This is the lesson for the whole world to learn. What have these philosophies and theories of nature to do, if not to help us to attain this one goal in life? Let us come to that consciousness of the identity of everything and let man see himself in everything. Let us be no more the worshippers of creeds or sects with small, limited notions of God, but see Him in everything in the universe. If you are knowers of God, you will everywhere find the same worship as in your own heart.

Get rid, in the first place, of all these limited ideas and see God in every person—working through all hands, walking through all feet, and eating through every mouth. In every being He lives, through all minds He thinks. He is self-evident, nearer unto us than ourselves. To know this is religion, is faith. May it please the Lord to give us this faith! When we shall feel that Oneness we shall be immortal. We are immortal even physically: one with the universe. So long as there is one that breathes throughout the universe, I live in that one. I am not this limited little being; I am the Universal. I am the life of all the Sons of God. I am the soul of Buddha, of Jesus, of Mohammed. I am the soul of all the teachers, and I am the soul of all the robbers that robbed and of all the murderers that were hanged. Stand up then! This is the highest worship. You are one with the universe. That alone is humility—not crawling upon all fours and calling yourself a sinner. That is the highest evolution when this veil of differentiation is torn off. The highest creed is Oneness. I am So-and-so— is a limited idea, not true of the real "I." I am the Universal: stand upon that and ever worship the Highest through the highest form; for God is Spirit and should be worshipped in Spirit and in Truth. Through lower forms of worship man's materialistic thoughts rise to spiritual worship, and the universal Infinite One is at last worshipped in and through the Spirit. That which is limited is material. The Spirit alone is infinite. God is Spirit, is infinite; man is Spirit and therefore infinite; and the Infinite alone can worship the Infinite. We will worship the Infinite; that is the highest spiritual worship. How grand these ideas are, and how difficult to realize! I theorize, talk, philosophize, and the next moment I come up against something and I unconsciously become angry; I forget there is anything in the universe but this little limited self. I forget to say: "I am the Spirit, what is this trifle to me? I am the Spirit." I forget it is all myself playing. I forget God; I forget freedom.

Sharp as the blade of a razor, long and difficult and hard to cross, is the way to freedom. The sages have declared this again and again. Yet do not let these weaknesses and failures deter you. The Upanishads have declared: "Arise! Awake! and stop not until the goal is reached." We shall then certainly cross the path, sharp as it is, like the razor, and long and distant and difficult though it be. Man becomes the master of gods and demons. No one is to blame for our miseries but ourselves. Do you think there is only a dark cup of poison if man goes to look for nectar? The nectar is there and is for every man who strives to reach it. The Lord Himself tells us: "Give up all these paths and struggles. Do thou take refuge in Me. I will take thee to the other shore; be not afraid." We hear that from all the scriptures of the world that have come to us.

The same voice teaches us to say, "Thy will be done on earth as it is in heaven, for Thine is the kingdom and the power and the glory." It is difficult, all very difficult. I say to myself this moment: "I will take refuge in Thee, O Lord; unto Thy love I will sacrifice all, and on Thine altar I will place all that is good and virtuous. My sins, my sorrows, my actions, good and evil, I will offer unto Thee; do Thou take them and I will never forget." One moment I say, "Thy will be done," and the next moment something comes to try me and I spring up in a rage. The goal of all religions is the same, but the language of the teachers differs. The goal is to kill the false "I" so that the real "I," the Lord, will reign. "I, the Lord, am a jealous God. Thou shalt have no other God but Me," say the Hebrew scriptures. We must cherish God alone. We must say, "Not I, but Thou," and then we should give up everything but the Lord. He, and He alone, should reign. Perhaps we struggle hard and yet the next moment our feet slip, and then we try to stretch out our hands to Mother. We find we cannot stand alone. Life is infinite, one chapter of which is, "Thy will be done," and unless we realize all the chapters we cannot realize the whole.

"Thy will be done"—every moment the traitor mind rebels against it; yet it must be said again and again if we are to conquer the lower self. We cannot serve a traitor and yet be saved. There is salvation for all except the traitor, and we stand condemned as traitors—traitors against our own selves, against the majesty of God—when we refuse to obey the voice of our higher Self. Come what will, we must give our bodies and minds up to the Supreme Will. Well has it been said by the Hindu philosopher, "If man says twice, 'Thy will be done,' he commits sin." "Thy will be done"—what more is needed? Why say it twice? What is good is good. No more shall we take it back. "Thy will be done on earth as it is in heaven, for Thine is the kingdom and the power and the glory for evermore."

REASON AND RELIGION

(Delivered in England)

A SAGE CALLED NĀRADA went to another sage named Sanatkumāra to learn about Truth, and Sanatkumāra inquired what he had studied already. Nārada answered that he had studied the Vedas, astronomy, and various other things, yet he had got no satisfaction. Then there was a conversation between the two, in the course of which Sanatkumāra remarked that all this knowledge of the Vedas, of astronomy, and of philosophy was but secondary; sciences were but secondary. That which made us realize Brahman was the supreme, the highest knowledge. This idea we find in every religion, and that is why religion has always laid claim to the supreme knowledge. Knowledge of the sciences covers, as it were, only a part of our lives, but the knowledge which religion brings to us is eternal, as infinite as the Truth it preaches. Claiming this superiority, religions have many times looked down, unfortunately, on all secular knowledge, and not only so, but many times have refused to justify themselves by the aid of secular knowledge. In consequence, all the world over there have been fights between secular knowledge and religious knowledge, the latter claiming infallible authority as its guide, refusing to listen to anything that secular knowledge has to say on the point, and the former, with its shining sword of reason, wanting to cut to pieces everything religion could bring forward. This fight was and is still being waged in every country.

The worship of the goddess of reason during the French Revolution was not the first manifestation of that phenomenon in the history of humanity; it was a re-enactment of what had happened in ancient times. But in modern times it has assumed greater proportions. The physical sciences are better equipped now than formerly, and the religions have become less and less well equipped. The foundations have all been undermined, and modern man, whatever he may say in public, knows in the privacy of his heart that he can no more "believe." Believing certain things because an organized body of priests tells him to believe, believing because it is written in certain books, believing because his people like him to believe, the modern man knows to be impossible for him. There are, of course, a number of people who seem to acquiesce in the so-called popular faith; but we also know for certain that they do not think. Their idea of belief may be better defined as unthinking carelessness. This fight cannot last much longer without breaking to pieces the whole building of religion.

The question is: Is there a way out? To put it in a more concrete form: Can religion justify itself through reason, by means of which every other science justifies itself? Are the same methods of investigation which we apply to physical science and knowledge to be applied to the science of religion? In my opinion this can be done, and I am also of opinion that the sooner it is done, the better. If a religion is destroyed by such investigations, it was then all the time useless, unworthy superstition, and the sooner it goes, the better. I am thoroughly convinced that its destruction would be the best thing that could happen. All that is dross will be taken off, no doubt, but the essential parts of religion will emerge triumphant out of this investigation. Not only will it be made scientific —as scientific, at least, as any of the conclusions of physics or chemistry—but it will have greater strength, because physics or chemistry has no internal mandate to vouch for its truth, which religion has.

People who deny the efficacy of any rationalistic investigation into religion seem to me somewhat to contradict themselves. For instance, the Christian claims that his religion is the only true one, because it was revealed to So-and-so. The Mohammedan makes the same claim for his religion: his is the only true one, because it was revealed to So-and-so. But the Christian says to the Mohammedan: "Certain parts of your ethics do not seem to be right. For instance, your books say, my Mohammedan friend, that an infidel may be converted to the religion of Mohammed by force, and if he will not accept the Mohammedan religion he may be killed, and any Mohammedan who kills such an infidel will get a sure entry into heaven, whatever may have been his sins or misdeeds." The Mohammedan will retort by saying: "It is right for me to do so, because my book enjoins it. It will be wrong on my part not to do so." The Christian says, "But my book does not say so." The Mohammedan replies: "I do not know; I am not bound by the authority of your book. My book says, 'Kill all the infidels.' How am I to know which is right and which is wrong? Surely what is written in my book is right, and what your book says, 'Do not kill,' is wrong. You also say the same thing, my Christian friend. You say that what Christ declared to the Christians is right, and what he forbade them to do is wrong. But I say, Allah declared in my book that certain things should be done and that certain things should not be done, and that is all the test of right and wrong."

In spite of that the Christian is not satisfied; he insists on a comparison of the morality of the Sermon on the Mount with the morality of the Koran. How is this to be decided? Certainly not by the books, because the books, disagreeing among themselves, cannot be the judges. Decidedly, then, we have to admit that there is something more universal than these books, something higher than all the ethical codes that are in the world, something which can judge the strength of the inspirations of different nations. Whether we declare it boldly, clearly, or not, it is evident that here we appeal to reason.

Now, the question arises whether this light of reason is able to judge between inspiration and inspiration and whether this light can uphold its standard when the quarrel is between prophet and prophet, whether it has the power of understanding anything whatsoever of religion. If it has not, nothing can settle the hopeless fight of books and prophets which has been going on through the ages; and it will mean that all religions are mere lies, hopelessly contradictory, without any consistent idea of ethics.

The proof of religion depends on the truth of the constitution of man, and not on any books. These books are the outgoings, the effects of man's constitution; man made these books. We are yet to see the books that made man.

Reason is equally an effect of that common cause, the constitution of man, to which we must appeal. And yet, since reason alone is directly connected with this constitution, it should be resorted to as long as it follows it faithfully. What do I mean by resorting to reason? I mean what every educated man or woman is wanting to do at the present time: to apply the principles of secular knowledge to religion.

The first principle of reasoning is that the particular is explained by the general, the general by the more general, until we come to the universal. For instance, we have the idea of law. If something happens and we believe that it is the effect of such and such a law, we are satisfied; that is an explanation for us. What we mean by that explanation is that it is proved that this one effect, which had dissatisfied us, is only one instance in a general mass of occurrences which we designate by the word *law*. When one apple fell, Newton was evidently disturbed, but when he found that all apples fell, he explained this by the law of gravitation, and was satisfied. This is one principle of human knowledge. I see a particular being, a human being, in the street; I refer him to the bigger concept of man, and I am satisfied: I know he is a man by referring him to the more general. So the particular is to be referred to the general, the general to the more general, and all things at last to the universal, the last concept that we have—Existence. Existence is the ultimate concept.

We are all human beings; that is to say, each one of us is, as it were, a particular part of the general concept called humanity. A man and a cat and a dog are all animals. These particular examples, such as man or dog or cat, are parts of a bigger and more general concept: animals. The man, the cat, the dog, the plant, and the tree all come under the still more general concept: life. Again, all animals, all plants, and all material entities come under the one concept of existence; for all are included in it. This explanation merely means referring the particular to a higher concept, finding more of its kind. The mind has stored up numerous classes of such generalizations. It is full of pigeon-holes, as it were, where all these ideas are grouped together, and whenever we find a new thing the mind immediately tries to find out its type in one of these pigeon-holes. If we find it we put the new thing in there and are satisfied, and we are said to have known the thing. This is what is meant by knowledge. And if we do not find that there is something like that thing, we are dissatisfied and have to wait until we find a further classification for it, already existing in the mind. Therefore, as I have already pointed out, knowledge is more or less classification.

There is something more. A second explanation of knowledge is that the explanation of a thing must come from inside and not from outside. There had been a belief that when a man threw up a stone and it fell, some demon dragged it down. Many occurrences which are really natural phenomena are attributed by people to supernatural beings. That a ghost dragged down the stone was an explanation that was not in the thing itself; it was an explanation from outside. But the second explanation, that of gravitation, is something in the nature of the stone; the explanation comes from inside.

This tendency you will find throughout modern thought; in one word, what is meant by science is that the explanations of things are in their own nature, and that no external beings or existences are required to explain what is going on in the universe. The chemist never requires demons or ghosts or anything of that sort to explain his phenomena. The physicist never requires any one of these to explain the things he knows, nor does any other scientist. And this is one of the features of science which I mean to apply to religion. In this religions are found wanting, and that is why they are crumbling into pieces. Every science wants its explanation from inside, from the very nature of things, and the religions are not able to supply this.

There is an ancient theory of a Personal Deity entirely separate from the universe, which has been believed in from the very earliest times. The arguments in favour of this have been repeated again and again: how it is necessary to have a God entirely separate from the universe, an extra-cosmic Deity, who has created the universe out of His will and is conceived by religion to be its Ruler. We find, apart from all these arguments, the Almighty God painted as the All-merciful; but at the same time inequalities remain in the world. These things do not convince the philosopher at all; he says the heart of the thing is wrong; it is an explanation from outside, and not inside. What is the cause of the universe? Something outside of it, some being who is moving this universe! And just as an external being was found insufficient to explain the phenomenon of the falling stone, so an extra-cosmic Deity was found insufficient to explain the world. And religions are falling to pieces because they cannot give a better explanation than that.

Another idea connected with this, a manifestation of the same principle, that the explanation of everything comes from inside it, is the modern law of evolution. The whole meaning of evolution is simply this: that the nature of a thing is reproduced, that the effect is nothing but the cause in another form, that all the potentialities of the effect are present in the cause, that the whole of creation is but an evolution and nothing else. That is to say, every effect is a reproduction of a preceding cause, changed only by the circumstances; and this law applies throughout the universe. And we need not go outside the universe to seek the causes of these changes; they are within. It is unnecessary to seek for any cause outside. This also is breaking down religion. What I mean by breaking down religion is that religions that have held on to the idea of an extra-cosmic Deity, who is a very big man and nothing else, can no more stand on their feet; they have been pulled over, as it were.

Can there be a religion satisfying these two principles? I think there can be. In the first place we have seen that we have to satisfy the principle of generalization. The generalization principle ought to be satisfied along with the principle of evolution. We have to come to an ultimate generalization, not only one which will be the most universal of all generalizations, but one out of which everything else must come. It will be of the same nature as the lowest effect; the primal cause must be identical with the most insignificant effect. The Brahman of Vedānta fulfils that condition, because Brahman is the last generalization to which we can come. It has no attributes, but is Absolute Existence, Knowledge, and Bliss. Existence, we have seen, is the very last generalization which the human mind can come to. Knowledge does not mean empirical knowledge, but the essence of that which is expressing itself in the course of evolution, in human beings or in other animals, as knowledge. It means the essence of that knowledge, the ultimate fact beyond—if I may be allowed to say so—even consciousness. That is what is meant by Knowledge—what we see in the universe as the essential unity of things.

To my mind, if modern science is proving anything again and again, it is this: that we are one—mentally, spiritually, and physically. It is wrong to say we are different even physically. Supposing we are materialists, for argument's sake, we shall have to come to this: that the whole universe is simply an ocean of matter, in which you and I are like little whirlpools. Masses of matter are coming into each whirlpool, taking the whirlpool form, and coming out as matter again. The matter that is in my body may have been in yours a few years ago, or in the sun, or may have been the matter in a plant, and so on, in a continuous state of flux. What is meant by your body and my body? All bodies are one. So with thought. It is all an ocean of thought, one infinite mass, in which your mind and my mind are like whirlpools. Are you not seeing this even now—how my thoughts are entering into yours, and yours into mine? We are one even in thought. Coming to a still higher generalization, we find that the essence of matter and thought is Spirit. This Spirit, from which all things have come, must be essentially one. We are absolutely one; we are physically one, we are mentally one, and it goes without saying that as Spirit we are one, if we believe in Spirit at all.

This oneness is the one fact that is being proved every day by modern science. To proud man it is told: "You are the same as that little worm there. Think not that you are something enormously different from it; you are the same. You have been that in a previous incarnation; the worm has crawled up to this man state of which you are so proud." This grand preaching, the oneness of things, making us one with everything that exists, is the great lesson to learn; for most of us are very glad to be made one with higher beings, but nobody wants to be made one with lower beings. Such is human ignorance that if among our ancestors were men whom society honoured, even if they were brutish, if they were robbers, or robber barons, every one of us would be proud to trace his ancestry to them; but if among our ancestors were poor, honest gentlemen, none of us would want to trace his ancestry to them. But the scales are falling from our eyes; truth is beginning to manifest itself more and more; and that is a great gain to religion. That is exactly the teaching of Advaita. The Self is the essence of this universe, the essence of all souls; It is the essence of your own life, nay, "Thou art That." You are one with this universe. He who says he is different from others, even by a hair's breadth, immediately becomes miserable. Happiness belongs to him who knows this oneness, who knows he is one with this universe.

Thus we see that Vedānta can satisfy the demands of the scientific world in regard to both the law of the highest generalization and the law of evolution. That the explanation of a thing comes from within itself is still more completely satisfied by Vedānta. There is nothing outside Brahman, the God of Vedānta—nothing at all. All this indeed is He. He is in the universe; He Himself is the universe. "Thou art the man, Thou art the woman, Thou art the young man walking in the pride of youth, Thou art the old man tottering on his staff." He is here. Him we see and feel; in Him we live and move and have our being. You have that conception in the New Testament. It is that idea: God immanent in the universe, the very essence, the heart, the soul of things. He manifests Himself, as it were, in this universe. You and I are little bits, little points, little channels, little expressions, all living inside that infinite ocean of Existence, Knowledge, and Bliss.

The difference between man and man, between angels and man, between man and animals, between animals and plants, between plants and stones, is not of kind—because every one, from the highest angel to the lowest particle of matter, is but an expression of that one infinite ocean—but the difference is only of degree. I am a low manifestation; you may be a higher; but in both the essence is the same. You and I are both outlets of the same ocean, and that is God; as such, your nature is God, and so is mine. You are of the same nature as God by your birthright, and so am I. You may be an angel of purity, and I may be the blackest of demons; nevertheless my birthright is that infinite ocean of Existence, Knowledge, and Bliss, and so is yours. You have manifested your power. Wait. I shall manifest mine, for I have it all within me.

No extraneous explanation is asked for; none is given. The sum total of this whole universe is God Himself. Is God then matter? No, certainly not, for matter is that God perceived by the five senses. That God as perceived through the intellect is mind, and as perceived through Spirit is Spirit. He is not matter, but whatever is real in matter is He. Whatever is real in this chair is He. The chair requires two things to make it what it is. Something was outside which my senses brought to me and to which my mind contributed something else, and the combination of these two is the chair. That which existed eternally, independent of the senses and of the intellect, was the Lord Himself. Upon Him the senses are painting chairs and tables and rooms and houses and worlds and moons and suns and stars, and everything else.

How is it, then, that we all see this same chair, that we are all alike painting these various things on the Lord, on this Existence, Knowledge, and Bliss? It need not be that all paint the same way, but those who paint the same way are on the same plane of existence and therefore they see one another's paintings as well as one another. There may be millions of beings between you and me who do not paint the Lord in the same way, and them and their paintings we do not see. On the other hand, as you all know, modern physical researches are tending more and more to demonstrate that what is real is the finer; the gross is simply appearance.

However that may be, we have seen that if any theory of religion can stand the test of modern reasoning, it is Advaita, because it fulfils its requirements. It gives the highest generalization, even beyond personality, a generalization which is common to every being. A generalization ending in the Personal God can never be universal; for, first of all, to conceive of a Personal God we must say that He is all merciful, all good. But this world is a mixed thing—somewhat good and somewhat bad. We cut off what we like and generalize that into a Personal God! Just as you say a Personal God is this and that, so you have also to say that He is not this and not that. And you will always find that the idea of a Personal God has to carry with it that of a personal Devil. So, we clearly see, the idea of a Personal God is not a true generalization. We have to go beyond, to the Impersonal. In That the universe exists, with all its joys and miseries; for whatever exists in it has all come from the Impersonal.

What sort of God can He be to whom we attribute evil and other things? The fact is that both good and evil are different aspects, or manifestations, of the same thing. The idea that they were two was a very wrong idea from the first, and it has been the cause of a good deal of the misery in this world of ours—the idea that right and wrong are two separate things, cut and dried, independent of each other, that good and evil are two eternally separable or separate things. I should be very glad to see a man who could show me something which is good all the time and something which is bad all the time—as if one could stand and gravely define some occurrences in this life of ours as good and good alone, and some others as bad and bad alone. That which is good today may be evil tomorrow. That which is bad today may be good tomorrow. What is good for me may be bad for you. The conclusion is that, as in everything else, there is an evolution of good and evil too. There is something which from one standpoint we call good, and from another, evil. The storm that kills my friend, I call evil; but it may have saved the lives of hundreds of thousands of people by killing the bacilli in the air. They call it good, but I call it evil. So both good and evil belong to the relative world, to phenomena. The Impersonal God we propose is not a relative God; therefore it cannot be said that It is either good or bad. It is something beyond, because It is neither good nor evil. Good, however, is a nearer manifestation of It than evil.

What is the effect of accepting such an Impersonal Being, an Impersonal Deity? What shall we gain? Will religion stand as a factor in human life, our consoler, our helper? What becomes of the desire of the human heart to pray for help to some Being? That will all remain. The Personal God will remain, but on a better basis. He will be strengthened by the Impersonal. We have seen that without the Impersonal, the Personal cannot remain. If you mean to say there is a Being entirely separate from this universe, who has created this universe just by His will, out of nothing, that cannot be proved. Such a state of things cannot be. But if we understand the idea of the Impersonal, then the idea of the Personal can remain also. This universe in its various forms is but various readings of the Impersonal. When we read It with the five senses we call It the material world. If there be a being with more senses than five, he will read It as something else. If one of us gets the electrical sense, he will see It as something else again. There are various forms of that same Oneness, of which all these various ideas of the world are but different readings; and the Personal God is the highest reading of that Impersonal that can be attained to by the human intellect.

So the Personal God is true as much as this chair is true, as much as this world is true, but no more. He is not absolute truth. That is to say, the Personal God, as such, is true and not true at the same time, just as I, as a human being, am true and not true at the same time. It is not true that I am what you see me to be; you can satisfy yourself on that point. I am not the being that you take me to be. You can satisfy your reason as to that, because light and various vibrations or conditions of the atmosphere, and all sorts of motions inside me, have contributed to my being looked upon by you as you see me. If any one of these conditions changes, I become different. You may satisfy yourself by taking a photograph of the same man under different conditions of light. So I am as I appear in relation to your senses; and yet, in spite of all these facts, there is an unchangeable something of which all these manifestations are different appearances—the impersonal "me," of which thousands of "me's" are different appearances. I was a child, then I was young, now I am getting older. Every day of my life my body and thoughts are changing. But in spite of all these changes, the sum total of them constitutes a unit which is a constant quantity. That is the impersonal "me," of which all these manifestations form, as it were, parts.

Similarly, the sum total of this universe is immovable, we know; but everything pertaining to this universe consists of motion, everything is in a constant state of flux, everything changing and moving. At the same time, we see that the universe as a whole is immovable, because motion is a relative term. I move with regard to the chair, which does not move. There must be at least two to make motion. If this whole universe is taken as a unit there is no motion; with regard to what should it move? Thus the Absolute is unchangeable and immovable, and all the movements and changes are only in the phenomenal world, the limited. That whole is the Impersonal, and within this Impersonal are all these various persons, from the smallest atom up to God, the Personal God, the Creator, the Ruler of the universe, to whom we pray, to whom we kneel, and so on.

Such a Personal God can be established with a great deal of logic. Such a Personal God is explicable as the highest manifestation of the Impersonal. You and I are very low manifestations, and the Personal God is the highest that we can conceive. Nor can you or I become that Personal God. When Vedānta says that you and I are God, it does not mean the Personal God. To take an example: Out of a mass of clay a huge elephant of clay is manufactured, and out of the same clay a little mouse is made. Would the clay mouse ever be able to become the clay elephant? No. But put them both in water and they are formless clay; as clay they are one, but as mouse and elephant there will be an eternal difference between them. The Infinite, the Impersonal, is like the clay in the example. We and the Ruler of the universe are one; but as manifested beings, men, we are His eternal slaves, His worshippers. Thus we see that the Personal God remains. Everything else in this relative world remains, as well, and religion is made to stand on a better foundation. Therefore it is necessary that we first know the Impersonal in order to understand the Personal. As we have seen, the law of reason says that the particular is known only through the general; so all these particulars, from man to God, are known only through the Impersonal, the highest generalization.

Prayers will remain, only they will get a better meaning. All those senseless forms of prayer used by worldly people, which simply give expression to all sorts of silly desires in their minds, will perhaps have to go. In all sensible religions they never allow prayers to God; they allow prayers to gods. That is quite natural. The Roman Catholics pray to the saints. That is quite good. But to pray to God is senseless. To ask God to give you a breath of air, to send down a shower of rain, to make fruits grow in your garden, and so on, is quite unnatural. The saints, however, who were little beings like ourselves, may help us. But to pray to the Ruler of the universe, prating about every little need of ours and from our childhood saying "O Lord, I have a headache; let it go," is ridiculous. There have been millions of pious souls that have died in this world, and they are all here; they have become gods and angels; let them come to your help. But do not call upon God for that. Unto Him we must go for higher things. A fool indeed is he who, living on the bank of the Ganges, digs a little well for water; a fool indeed is he who, living near a diamond mine, digs for bits of crystal.

And indeed we shall be fools if we go to the Father of all mercy, the Father of all love, for trivial earthly things. Unto Him, therefore, we shall go for light, for strength, for love. But so long as there is weakness and a craving for servile dependence in us, there will be these little prayers and ideas of the worship of the Personal God. But those who are highly advanced do not care for such little helps; they have wellnigh forgotten all about this seeking things for themselves, wanting things for themselves. The predominant idea in them is "Not I, but thou, my brother." Those are the fit persons to worship the Impersonal God. And what is the worship of the Impersonal God? No slavery there—"O Lord, I am nothing; have mercy on me." You know the old Persian poem: A man came to see his beloved. The door was closed. He knocked and a voice came from inside, "Who art thou?" He told his name. The door was not opened. A second time he came and knocked. He was asked the same question and gave the same answer. The door did not open. He came a third time and the same question was asked. But now he answered, "I am thou, my love," and the door opened.

Worship of the Impersonal God is through the truth. And what is the truth? I am He. When I say that I am not Thou, it is not true. When I say I am separate from you it is a lie, a terrible lie. I am one with this universe—born one. It is self-evident to my senses that I am one with the universe. I am one with the air that surrounds me, one with heat, one with light, eternally one with the whole Universal Being, who is called this universe, who is mistaken for the universe; for it is He and nothing else, the Eternal Subject in the heart, who says "I am" with every heart-beat—the Deathless One, the Sleepless One, ever awake, the Immortal, whose glory never dies, whose powers never fail. I am one with That.

This is the worship of the Impersonal. And what is the result? The whole life of man will be changed. Strength, strength it is that we want in this life; for what we call sin and sorrow have all one cause, and that is our weakness. With weakness comes ignorance, and with ignorance comes misery. The Impersonal will make us strong. Then miseries will be laughed at, then the vileness of the vile will be smiled at, and the ferocious tiger will reveal, behind its tiger's nature, my own Self. That will be the result. That soul is strong that has become one with the Lord; none else is strong. In your own Bible, what do you think was the cause of the strength of Jesus of Nazareth, that immense, infinite strength which laughed at traitors and blessed those that were willing to murder him?

It was the knowledge that "I and my Father are one"; it was that prayer: "Father, just as I am one with Thee, so make them all one with me." That is the worship of the Impersonal God. Be one with the universe, be one with Him.

And this Impersonal God requires no demonstrations, no proofs. He is nearer to us even than our senses, nearer to us than our own thoughts; it is in and through Him that we see and think. To see anything, I must first see Him. To see this wall I first see Him, and then the wall; for He is the eternal subject. Who is seeing whom? He is here in our heart of hearts. Bodies and minds change; misery, happiness, good and evil, come and go; days and years roll on; life comes and goes; but He dies not. The same voice, "I am, I am," is eternal, unchangeable. In Him and through Him we know everything. In Him and through Him we see everything. In Him and through Him we sense, we think, we live, and we are. And that "I," which we mistake to be a little, limited "I," is not only my "I," but yours also, the "I" of everyone—of the animals, of the angels, of the lowest of the low. That "I" is the same in the murderer as in the saint, the same in the rich as in the poor, the same in man as in woman, the same in man as in animals. From the lowest amoeba to the highest angel, He resides in every soul and eternally declares, "I am He, I am He."

When we have understood that voice eternally present there, when we have learnt this lesson, the whole universe will have expressed its secret; nature will have given up its secret to us. Nothing more remains to be known. Thus we find the truth for which all religions search: that all this knowledge of the material sciences is but secondary; for that is the only true knowledge which makes us one with the Impersonal God, the Lord of the universe.

STEPS TO REALIZATION

(A class lecture delivered in America)

FIRST AMONG the qualifications required of the aspirant for jnāna, or wisdom, come śama and dama, which may be taken together. They mean the keeping of the organs in their own centres without allowing them to stray out. I shall explain to you first what the word *organ* means. Here are the eyes. The eyes are not the organs of vision, but only the instruments. Unless the organs also are present, I cannot see, even if I have eyes. But given both the organs and the instruments, unless the mind attaches itself to these two, no vision takes place. So in each act of perception three things are necessary: first the external instrument, then the internal organ, and lastly the mind. If any one of them is absent, then there will be no perception. Thus the mind acts through two agencies—one external and the other internal. When I see things, my mind goes out, becomes externalized. But suppose I close my eyes and begin to think; the mind does not go out; it is internally active. But in either case there is activity of the organs. When I look at you and speak to you, both the organs and the instruments are active. When I close my eyes and begin to think, the organs are active, but not the instruments. Without the activity of these organs there will be no thought. You will find that none of you can think without some symbol. Even a blind man has to think through some figure. The organs of sight and hearing are generally very active. You must bear in mind that by the word *organ* is meant the nerve centre in the brain. The eyes and ears are only the instruments of seeing and hearing, and the organs are inside. If the organs are somehow destroyed, even though the eyes or the ears are there, we shall not see or hear. So in order to control the mind we must first be able to control these organs. To restrain the mind from wandering outward or inward and keep the organs in their respective centres is what is meant by the words śama and dama. Śama consists in not allowing the mind to externalize, and dama, in checking the external instruments.

Then comes the next preparation—(It is a hard task to be a philosopher!)—titikshā, the most difficult of all. It is nothing less than ideal forbearance: "Resist not evil." This requires a little explanation. We may not resist an evil but at the same time we may feel very miserable. A man may say very harsh things to me, and I may not outwardly hate him for it, may not answer him back, and may restrain myself from apparently getting angry; but anger and hatred may be in my mind, and I may feel very badly towards that man. That is not non-resistance. I should be without any feeling of hatred or anger, without any thought of resistance; my mind must be as calm as if nothing had happened. Only when I have got to that state have I attained to non-resistance, and

744

not before. The bearing of all misery, without any thought of resisting or driving it out, without even any painful feeling in the mind or any remorse—this is titikshā. Suppose I do not resist, and some great evil comes thereby; if I have titikshā, I should not feel any remorse for not having resisted. When the mind has attained to that state it has become established in titikshā. People in India do extraordinary things in order to practise this titikshā. They bear tremendous heat and cold without caring; they do not even care for snow, because they take no thought for the body; it is left to itself as if it were a foreign thing.

Now comes uparati, which consists in not thinking of the things of the senses. Most of our time is spent in thinking about sense-objects, things which we have seen or we have heard, which we shall see or shall hear, things which we have eaten or are eating or shall eat, places where we have lived, and so on. We think of them or talk of them most of the time. One who wishes to be a Vedāntist must give up this habit.

The next qualification required is śraddhā, faith. One must have tremendous faith in religion and God. Until one has it, one cannot aspire to be a jnāni. A great sage once told me that not one in twenty millions in this world believed in God. I asked him why, and he told me: "Suppose there is a thief in this room, and he comes to know that there is a mass of gold in the next room, and only a very thin partition between the two rooms. What will be the condition of that thief?" I answered: "He will not be able to sleep at all. His brain will be actively thinking of some means of getting at the gold, and he will think of nothing else." Then he replied: "Do you believe that a man could believe in God and not go mad to realize Him? If a man sincerely believes that there is an immense, infinite mine of Bliss, and that it can be reached, will not that man go mad in his struggles to reach it?" Strong faith in God and the consequent eagerness to reach Him constitute śraddhā.

Then comes samādhāna, or constant practice to hold the mind on God. Nothing is done in a day. Religion cannot be swallowed in the form of a pill. It requires hard and constant practice. The mind can be conquered only by slow and steady practice.

Next is mumukshutvam, the intense desire to be free. Those of you who have read Edwin Arnold's *Light of Asia* remember his translation of the first sermon of Buddha, where Buddha says:

> Ye suffer from yourselves. None else compels.
> None other holds you that ye live and die,
> And whirl upon the wheel, and hug and kiss
> Its spokes of agony,
> Its tire of tears, its nave of nothingness.

All the misery we have is of our own choosing; such is our nature. The old Chinaman who, having been kept in prison for sixty years, was released on the coronation of a new emperor, exclaimed, when he came out, that he could not live; he must go back to his horrible dungeon among the rats and mice. He could not bear the light. So he asked them to kill him or send him back to the prison, and he was sent back. Exactly similar is the condition of all men. We run headlong after all sorts of misery and are unwilling to be freed from it.

Every day we run after pleasure, and before we reach it, we find it is gone, it has slipped through our fingers; still we do not cease from our mad pursuit, but on and on we go, blinded fools that we are.

In some oil-mills in India bullocks are used to grind the oil-seed. They are made to go round and round. There is a yoke on the bullock's neck. A piece of wood protrudes from the yoke, and on that is fastened a wisp of straw. The bullock is blindfolded in such a way that it can only look forward, and so it stretches its neck to get at the straw; and in doing so, it pushes the piece of wood out a little farther; and it makes another attempt with the same result, and yet another, and so on. It never catches the straw, but goes round and round in the hope of getting it, and in so doing, grinds out the oil. In the same way you and I, who are born slaves to nature, money, and wealth, to wives and children, are always chasing a wisp of straw, mere chimeras, and go through an innumerable round of lives without obtaining what we seek. The great dream is love: we are all going to love and be loved, we are all going to be happy and never meet with misery. But the more we go towards happiness, the more it goes away from us. Thus the world is going on, society goes on, and we, blinded slaves, have to pay for it without knowing. Study your own lives and find how little of happiness there is in them, and how little in truth you have gained in the course of this wild-goose chase of the world.

Do you remember the story of Solon and Croesus? The king said to the great sage that Asia Minor was a very happy place. And the sage asked him: "Who is the happiest man? I have not seen anyone very happy." "Nonsense," said Croesus, "I am the happiest man in the world." "Wait, sir, till the end of your life; don't be in a hurry," replied the sage and went away. In the course of time the king was conquered by the Persians and they ordered him to be burnt alive. The funeral pyre was prepared and when poor Croesus saw it, he cried aloud, "Solon! Solon!" On being asked to whom he referred, he told his story, and the Persian emperor was touched and saved his life.

Such is the life-story of each one of us; such is the tremendous power of nature over us. It repeatedly kicks us away, but still we pursue it with feverish excitement. We are always hoping against hope. This hope, this chimera, maddens us. We are always hoping for happiness.

There was a great king in ancient India who was once asked four questions, of which one was: "What is the most wonderful thing in the world?" "Hope," was the answer. This is the most wonderful thing: Day and night we see people dying around us, and yet we think we shall not die; we never think that we shall die or that we shall suffer. Each man thinks that success will be his, hoping against hope, against all odds, against all mathematical reasoning. Nobody is ever really happy here. If a man is wealthy and has plenty to eat, his digestion is out of order and he cannot eat. If a man's digestion is good, and he has the digestive power of a cormorant, he has nothing to put into his mouth. If he is rich, he has no children. If he is hungry and poor, he has a whole regiment of children and does not know what to do with them. Why is it so? Because happiness and misery are the obverse and reverse of the same coin: he who takes happiness must take misery also. We all have this foolish idea that we can have happiness without misery, and it has taken such possession of us that we have no control over the senses.

When I was in Boston a young man came up to me and gave me a scrap of paper on which he had written a name and address, followed by these words: "All the wealth and all the happiness of the world are yours if you only know how to get them. If you come to me I will teach you how to get them. Charge, five dollars." He gave me this and said, "What do you think of this?" I said, "Young man, why don't you get the money to print this? You haven't even enough money to get this printed!" He did not understand this. He was infatuated with the idea that one could get immense wealth and happiness without any trouble.

There are two extremes to which men are running: one is extreme optimism, when everything is rosy and nice and good; the other, extreme pessimism, when everything seems to be against them. The majority of men have more or less undeveloped brains. One in a million we see with a well developed brain; the rest either have peculiar idiosyncrasies or are monomaniacs. Naturally we run to extremes. When we are healthy and young we think that all the wealth of the world will be ours, and when later we get kicked about by society like footballs and get older, we sit in a corner and croak, and throw cold water on the enthusiasm of others. Few men know that with pleasure there is pain, and with pain, pleasure; and as pain is disgusting, so is pleasure, since it is the twin brother of pain.

It is derogatory to the glory of man that he should be going after pain, and equally derogatory that he should be going after pleasure. Both should be turned aside by men whose reason is balanced. Why will not men seek freedom from being played upon? This moment we are whipped, and when we begin to weep, nature gives us a dollar; again we are whipped, and when we weep, nature gives us a piece of gingerbread and we begin to laugh again. The sage wants liberty; he finds that sense-objects are all vain and that there is no end to pleasures and pains.

How the rich people in the world want to find fresh pleasures! All pleasures are old—and they want new ones. Do you not see how many foolish things they are inventing every day just to titillate the nerves for a moment, and that done, how there comes a reaction? The majority of people are just like a flock of sheep. If the leading sheep falls into a ditch, all the rest follow and break their necks. In the same way, what one leading member of society does, all the others do without thinking what they are doing.

When a man begins to see the vanity of worldly things, he will feel he ought not to be thus played upon or borne along by nature. That is slavery. If a man hears a few kind words said to him, he begins to smile, and when he hears a few harsh words, he begins to weep. He is a slave to a bit of bread, to a breath of air; a slave to dress, a slave to patriotism, to country, to name and fame. He is thus in the midst of slavery, and the real man has become buried within through his bondage. What you call man is a slave. When one realizes all this slavery, then comes the desire to be free; an intense desire comes. If a piece of burning charcoal is placed on a man's head, see how he struggles to throw it off. Similar will be the struggle for freedom of a man who really understands that he is a slave of nature.

We have now seen what mumukshutvam, or the desire to be free, is. The next discipline is also a very difficult one: nityānityaviveka—discriminating between that which is true and that which is untrue, between the eternal and the transitory. God alone is eternal; everything else is transitory. Everything dies: the angels die, men die, animals die, earths die, sun, moon, and stars all die; everything undergoes constant change. The mountains of today were oceans yesterday and will be oceans tomorrow. Everything is in a state of flux; the whole universe is a mass of change. But there is One who never changes, and that is God. And the nearer we get to Him, the less will be the change for us, the less will nature be able to work on us; and when we reach Him and stand with Him, we shall conquer nature, we shall be masters of these phenomena of nature, and they will have no effect on us.

You see, if we really have undergone the above discipline, we certainly do not require anything else in this world. All knowledge is within us; all perfection is there already in the soul. But this perfection has been covered up by nature; layer after layer of nature has covered this purity of the soul. What have we to do? Really we do not develop our souls at all; what can develop the perfect? We simply take the veil off, and the soul manifests itself in its pristine purity, its natural, innate freedom.

Now comes the question: Why is discipline so necessary? It is because religion is not attained through the ears, nor through the eyes, nor even through the brain. No scriptures can make us religious; we may study all the books in the world, yet we may not understand a word of religion or of God. We may talk all our lives and yet may not be the better for it; we may be the most intellectual people the world ever saw, and yet we may not come to God at all. Have you not seen what irreligious men have been produced from the most intellectual training? It is one of the evils of your Western civilization that you are after intellectual education alone, and take no care of the heart. It only makes men ten times more selfish, and that will be your destruction. When there is a conflict between the heart and the brain, let the heart be followed, because intellect has only one faculty, reason, and through it intellect works; it cannot get beyond. It is the heart that takes one to the highest plane, which intellect can never reach. It goes beyond intellect and reaches what is called inspiration. The intellect can never become inspired; only the heart, when it is enlightened, becomes inspired. An intellectual, heartless man never becomes an inspired man. It is always the heart that speaks in the man of love; it discovers a greater instrument than intellect can give you, the instrument of inspiration. Just as the intellect is the instrument of knowledge, so is the heart the instrument of inspiration. In a lower state the heart is a much weaker instrument than the intellect. An ignorant man knows nothing, but he is emotional by nature; compare him with a great professor—what wonderful power the latter possesses! But the professor is bound by his intellect and he can be a devil and an intellectual man at the same time. The man of heart can never be a devil; no man with emotion was ever a devil. Properly cultivated, the heart can be changed and will go beyond intellect; it will function through inspiration.

Man will have to go beyond intellect in the end. The knowledge of man, his powers of perception, of reasoning and intellect and heart, all are busy churning this milk of the world. Out of long churning comes butter, and this butter is God. Men of heart get the butter, and the buttermilk is left for the intellectual.

These are all preparations for the heart—for that love, for that intense sympathy appertaining to the heart. It is not at all necessary to be educated or learned to realize God. A sage once told me: "To kill others one must be equipped with swords and shields, but to commit suicide a needle is sufficient." So to teach others, much intellect and learning are necessary, but not so for your own illumination. Are you pure? If you are pure you will reach God. "Blessed are the pure in heart, for they shall see God." If you are not pure, and you know all the sciences in the world, that will not help you at all. You may be buried in all the books you read, but that will not be of much use. It is the heart that reaches the goal. Follow the heart. A pure heart sees beyond the intellect. It becomes inspired; it knows things that reason can never know. Whenever there is conflict between the pure heart and the intellect, always side with the pure heart, even if you think what your heart is doing is unreasonable. When it is desirous of doing good to others, your brain may tell you that it is not politic to do so, but follow your heart and you will find that you make fewer mistakes than by following your intellect. The pure heart is the best mirror for the reflection of truth. So all these disciplines are for the purification of the heart; and as soon as it is pure, all truths flash upon it in a minute. All the truth in the universe will be manifest in your heart if you are sufficiently pure.

The great secrets about atoms and the finer elements, and the fine perceptions of men, were discovered ages ago by men who never saw a telescope or a microscope or a laboratory. How did they know all these things? It was through the heart; they purified the heart. It is open to us to do the same today. It is the culture of the heart, really, and not that of the intellect that will lessen the misery of the world. The intellect has been cultured with the result that hundreds of sciences have been discovered; and their effect has been that the few have made slaves of the many—that is all the good that has been done. Artificial wants have been created; and every poor man, whether he has money or not, desires to have those wants satisfied, and when he cannot, he struggles, and dies in the struggle. This is the result. Through the intellect is not the way to solve the problem of misery, but through the heart. If all this vast amount of effort had been spent in making men purer, gentler, more forbearing, this world would have a thousandfold more happiness than it has today. Always cultivate the heart; through the heart the Lord speaks, and through the intellect you yourself speak.

You remember where Moses was told, in the Old Testament, "Take off thy shoes from off thy feet, for the place whereon thou standest is holy ground." We must always approach the study of religion with that reverent attitude. He who comes with a pure heart and a reverent attitude will have his heart opened; the doors will open for him and he will see the truth. If you come with intellect only, you can have a little intellectual gymnastics, intellectual theories, but not truth. Truth has such a face that anyone who sees that face becomes convinced.

The sun does not require any torch to show it: the sun is self-effulgent. If truth requires evidence, what will evidence that evidence? If something is necessary as a witness for truth, where is the witness for that witness? We must approach religion with reverence and with love, and our hearts will stand up and say, this is truth and this is untruth.

The field of religion is beyond our senses, even beyond our consciousness. We cannot sense God. Nobody has seen God with his eyes or ever will see; nobody knows God in his consciousness. I am not conscious of God, nor you, nor anybody. Where is God? Where is the field of religion? It is beyond the senses, beyond consciousness. Consciousness is only one of the many planes in which we work. You will have to transcend the field of consciousness, go beyond the senses, approach nearer and nearer to your own centre; and as you do that, you will approach nearer and nearer to God. What is the proof of God? Direct perception, pratyaksha. The proof of this wall is that I perceive it. God has been perceived that way by thousands before, and will be perceived by all who want to perceive Him. But this perception is not sense perception at all; it is supersensuous, superconscious; and all this training is needed to take us beyond the senses.

Because of all sorts of past work and attachment we are being dragged downward; the disciplines just described will purify us. Our bonds will fall off by themselves, and we shall be buoyed up beyond this plane of sense perception to which we are tied down; and then we shall see and hear and feel things which men in the three ordinary states—waking, dreaming, and sleep—neither feel nor see nor hear. Then we shall speak a strange language, as it were, and the world will not understand us, because it does not know anything but the senses.

True religion is entirely transcendental. Every being that is in the universe has the potentiality of transcending the senses; even the little worm will one day transcend the senses and reach God. No life will be a failure; there is no such thing as failure in the universe. A hundred times man will hurt himself, a thousand times he will tumble, but in the end he will realize that he is God. We know there is no progress in a straight line. Every soul moves, as it were, in a circle and will have to complete it; and no soul can go so low but there will come a time when it will have to go upward. No one will be lost. We are all projected from one common centre, which is God. The highest as well as the lowest life God ever projected will come back to the Father of all lives. "From whom all beings are projected, in whom all live, and unto whom they all return—He is God."

VEDĀNTA AND PRIVILEGE

(Delivered in London)

WE HAVE NEARLY finished the metaphysical portion of Advaita. One point, perhaps the most difficult one to understand, remains. We have seen so far that, according to the Advaita theory, all we see around us, and the whole universe in fact, is the evolution of the one Absolute. It is called, in Sanskrit, Brahman. The Absolute has become changed into the whole of nature. But here comes a difficulty. How is it possible for the Absolute to change? What made the Absolute change? By Its very definition the Absolute is unchangeable. Change of the unchangeable would be a contradiction. The same difficulty is faced by those who believe in a Personal God. For instance, how did this creation arise? It could not have arisen out of nothing; that would be a contradiction; something coming out of nothing can never be. The effect is the cause in another form. Out of the seed, the big tree grows; the tree is the seed, plus the air and water that are taken in. And if there were any method of testing the amount of the air and water taken to make the body of the tree, we should find that it is exactly the same as the effect, the tree. Modern science has proved beyond doubt that it is so, that the effect is the cause in another form. An adjustment of the parts produces a change in the cause, and it becomes the effect. So we have to avoid this difficulty of having a universe without a cause, and we are bound to admit that God has become the universe.

But we have avoided one difficulty and landed in another. In every theory, the idea of God is associated with the idea of unchangeability. We have traced historically how the one idea which we have always in mind in our search for God, even in its crudest form, is the idea of freedom; and the idea of freedom and of unchangeability is one and the same. Only that which is free never changes, and the unchangeable alone is free; for change is produced by something exterior to a thing, or within itself, which is more powerful than the surroundings. Everything which can be changed is necessarily bound by a certain cause or causes, which cannot be unchangeable. Suppose God has become this universe; then God is here and has changed. And suppose the Infinite has become this finite universe; then so much of the Infinite has gone, and therefore what remains is the infinite God minus the universe. A changeable God would be no God.

To avoid the doctrine of pantheism, there is the bold theory of Vedānta: It is that this universe, as we know and think of it, does not exist, that the unchangeable has not changed, that the whole of this universe is mere appearance and not reality, that this idea of parts, and little beings, and differentiations, is only apparent, not the nature of the thing itself. God has not changed

751

at all and has not become the universe. We see God as the universe because we have to see it through time, space, and causation. It is time, space, and causation that make this differentiation—apparently, but not really. This is a very bold theory indeed.

Now, this theory ought to be explained a little more clearly. It does not mean idealism in the sense in which it is generally understood. It does not say that this universe does not exist; it exists, but at the same time, it is not what we take it for. To illustrate this, the example given by the Advaita philosophy is well known. In the darkness of night, a stump of a tree is looked upon as a ghost by some superstitious person, as a policeman by a robber, as a friend by someone waiting for his companion. In all these cases the stump of the tree did not change, but there were apparent changes, and these changes were in the minds of those who saw it. From the subjective side we can understand it better through psychology. There is something outside of ourselves, the true nature of which is unknown and unknowable to us; let us call it x. And there is something inside, which is also unknown and unknowable to us; let us call it y. The knowable is a combination of x plus y; and everything that we know, therefore, must have two parts, the x outside and the y inside; and x plus y is the thing we know. So every form in the universe is partly our creation and partly something outside. Now what Vedānta holds is that this x and this y are one and the same.

A very similar conclusion has been arrived at by certain Western philosophers, especially by Herbert Spencer and some other modern philosophers. It has been said that the same power which is manifesting itself in the flower is welling up in my own consciousness; the Vedāntists of India want to preach the very same idea: that the reality of the external world and the reality of the internal world are one and the same. Even the ideas of internal and external exist only apparently and do not exist in the things themselves. For instance, if we develop another sense, the whole world will change for us, showing that it is the subject which changes the object. If I change, the external world changes.

The theory of Vedānta therefore comes to this: that you and I and everything in the universe are the Absolute—not parts, but the whole. You are the whole of that Absolute, and so are all others, because the idea of parts cannot come into it. These divisions, these limitations, are only apparent, not in the thing itself. I am complete and perfect, and I was never bound. Boldly preaches Vedānta, if you think you are bound, bound you will remain; if you know that you are free, free you are. Thus the end and aim of this philosophy is to let us know that we have been free always and shall remain free for ever. We never change, we never die, and we are never born. What are all these changes, then? What becomes of this phenomenal world? This world is admitted as an apparent world, bound by the laws of time, space, and causation; and this is called the vivartavāda in Vedānta: illusory superimposition of names and forms upon the Absolute. The Absolute does not change. In the little amoeba that infinite perfection is latent. It is called amoeba from its amoeba covering. And from the amoeba to the perfect man the change is not in what is inside; that remains the same, unchangeable; but the change occurs in the covering.

There is a screen here. and some beautiful scenery outside. There is a small hole in the screen through which we can catch only a glimpse of it. Suppose this hole begins to increase; as it grows larger and larger, more and more of the scenery comes into view; and when the screen has vanished, we come face to face with the whole of the scenery. This scene outside is the Soul, and the screen between us and the scenery is māyā—time, space, and causation. There is a little hole somewhere, through which I can catch only a glimpse of the Soul. As the hole grows bigger, I see more and more, and when the screen has vanished, I know that I am the Soul.

So the changes in the universe are not in the Absolute, but in nature. Nature evolves more and more until the Absolute is fully manifest. In everyone It exists; in some It is manifested more than in others. The whole universe is really one. From the standpoint of the Soul, to say that one person is superior to another is meaningless. From the same standpoint, to say that man is superior to the animal or the plant is meaningless. In plants the obstacle to Soul-manifestation is very great; in animals, a little less; in man, still less; in cultured, spiritual men, still less; and in perfect men it has vanished altogether. All our struggles, exercises, pains, pleasures, tears, and smiles—all that we do and think—tend towards that goal, the tearing up of the screen by making the hole bigger, the thinning of the layers that remain between the manifestation and the Reality behind. Our work, therefore, is not to make the Soul free, but to get rid of the bondage. The sun is covered by layers of clouds but remains unaffected by them. The work of the wind is to drive the clouds away, and the more the clouds disappear, the more the light of the sun appears. There is no change whatsoever in the Soul—infinite, absolute, eternal Knowledge, Bliss, and Existence.

Neither can there be birth or death for the Soul. Dying and being born, reincarnation, and going to heaven cannot be for the Soul. These are different appearances, different mirages, different dreams. If a man who is dreaming of this world now, dreams of wicked thoughts and wicked deeds, after a certain time the thought of that very dream will produce the next dream; he will dream that he is in a horrible place, being tortured. The man who is dreaming good thoughts and good deeds, after that period of dream is over will dream he is in a better place. And so on from dream to dream.

But the time will come when the whole of this dream will vanish. To every one of us there must come a time when the whole universe will be found to have been a dream, when we shall find that the Soul is infinitely more real than its surroundings. In this struggle through what we call our environments, there will come a time when we shall find that these environments were almost zero in comparison with the power of the Soul. It is only a question of time, and time is nothing compared to the Infinite. It is as a drop in the ocean. We can afford to wait and be calm.

Consciously or unconsciously, therefore, the whole universe is going towards that goal. The moon is struggling to get out of the sphere of attraction of other bodies, and will come out of it in the long run. But those who consciously strive to get free shorten the time. One practical benefit from this theory, we see, is that the idea of a real universal love is possible only from this point of view. All are our fellow travellers. All living things—plants, animals, and men;

not only my brother man, but my brother brute, my brother plant; not only my brother the good man, but my brother the evil, my brother the spiritual man and my brother the wicked—they all are going to the same goal. All are in the same stream; each is hurrying towards that infinite freedom. We cannot stay the course; none can stay it, none can go back, however he may try; he will be driven forward and finally will attain to freedom. The cosmic process means the struggle to get back to freedom, the centre of our being, from whence we have been thrown off, as it were. The very fact that we are here shows that we are going towards the centre, and the manifestation of this attraction towards the centre is what we call love.

The question is asked: From what does this universe come, in what does it remain, to what does it go back? And the answer is: From love it comes, in love it remains, back it goes unto love. Thus we are in a position to understand that, whether one likes it or not, there is no holding back for anyone. Everyone has to get to the centre, however he may struggle to hold back. Yet if we struggle consciously, knowingly, it will smooth the passage; it will lessen the jar and quicken the time.

Another conclusion we naturally arrive at from this is that all knowledge and all power are within and not without. What we call nature is a reflecting-glass; the only use of nature is to reflect, and all knowledge is a reflection of the internal on the glass of nature. What we call secrets of nature and powers are all within. In the external world is only a series of changes. There is no knowledge in nature; all knowledge comes from the human soul. Man manifests knowledge—discovers it within himself—which has existed through eternity. Everyone is the embodiment of Knowledge, everyone is the embodiment of eternal Bliss and eternal Existence.

The effect of this theory is the same, as we have seen elsewhere, with regard to equality. The idea of privilege is the bane of human life. Two forces, as it were, are constantly at work, the one making caste and the other breaking caste; in other words, the one making for privilege and the other breaking down privilege. And whenever privilege is broken down, more and more light and progress come to a race. This struggle we see all around us. Of course there is first the brutal idea of privilege: that of the strong over the weak. There is the privilege of wealth: if a man has more money than another, he wants a little privilege over those who have less. There is the still subtler and more powerful privilege of intellect: because one man knows more than others he claims more privilege. And the last of all, and the worst, because the most tyrannical, is the privilege of spirituality: if some persons think they know more of spirituality, of God, they claim a privilege over everyone else; they say, "Come and worship us, ye common herd; we are the messengers of God, and you have to worship us."

None can be Vedāntists and at the same time sanction privilege for anyone, either mental, physical, or spiritual. There should be absolutely no privilege for anyone. The same power is in every man, one manifesting more, another less; the same potentiality is in all. Where then is the claim to privilege? All knowledge is in every soul, even in the most ignorant; he has not manifested it, but perhaps he has not had the opportunity; his environment was not, perhaps, suitable to him; when he gets the opportunity he will manifest it. The idea that one man is born superior to another has no meaning in Vedānta; that between two nations one is superior and the other inferior has no meaning whatsoever. Put them in the same circumstances and see whether the same intelligence comes out or not. Before that you have no right to say that one nation is superior to another.

And as to spirituality, no privilege should be claimed there. It is a privilege to serve mankind; for this is the worship of God. God is here in all these human souls. He is the soul of man; what privilege can men ask? There are no special messengers of God, never were, and never can be. All beings, great or small, are equally manifestations of God; the difference is only in the degree of manifestation. The same eternal message, which has been eternally given, comes to them all. That eternal message has been written in the heart of every being; it is there already, and all are struggling to express it. Some, in suitable circumstances, express it a little better than others; but as bearers of the message they are all one. What claim to superiority is there? The most ignorant man, the most ignorant child, is as great a messenger of God as any that ever existed and as great as any that is yet to come. For the infinite message is there, imprinted once for all in the heart of every being. Wherever there is a being, that being contains the infinite message of the Most High. It is there.

The task of Advaita, therefore, is to break down all these privileges. It is the hardest work of all; and curious to say, in the land of its birth Advaita has been less active than anywhere else. If there is any land of privilege, it is the land which gave birth to this philosophy—privilege for the spiritual man as well as for the man of birth. In India there is not so much the privilege of money (that is one of the benefits, I think); but the privilege of birth and spirituality is everywhere.

Once a gigantic attempt was made in India to preach Vedāntic ethics, which succeeded to a certain extent for several hundred years; and we know historically that those years were the best times for the country. I mean the Buddhist attempt to break down privilege. Some of the most beautiful epithets addressed to Buddha that I remember are: "Thou the breaker of castes, destroyer of privileges, preacher of equality to all beings." He preached this one idea of equality. Its power has been misunderstood to a certain extent in the brotherhood of Śramaṇas, where we find that hundreds of attempts have been made to form them into a church, with superiors and inferiors. You cannot make much of a church when you tell people they are all gods. One of the good effects of Vedānta has been freedom of religious thought, which India has enjoyed throughout its history. It is something to glory in, that it is the land where there was never a religious persecution, where people are allowed perfect freedom in religion.

This practical side of Vedāntic morality is necessary as much today as it ever was—more necessary, perhaps, than it ever was; for all this privilege-claiming has become tremendously intensified with the extension of knowledge. The idea of God and the Devil, or Ahura Mazda and Ahriman, has a good deal of poetry in it. The difference between God and the Devil is in nothing except in unselfishness and selfishness. The Devil knows as much as God, is as powerful as

God, only he has no holiness: that makes him the Devil. Apply the same idea to the modern world: excess of knowledge and power, without holiness, makes human beings devils. Tremendous power is being acquired through machines and other appliances, and privilege is claimed today by those in power as it never has been claimed in the history of the world. That is why Vedānta wants to preach against it, to break down this tyrannizing over the souls of men.

Those of you who have studied the Gitā will remember the memorable passages: "He who looks upon the learned brāhmin, upon the cow, the elephant, the dog, or the outcaste, with the same eye, he indeed is the sage and the wise man." "Even in this life he has conquered relative existence whose mind is firmly fixed on sameness; for the Lord is one and the same to all, and the Lord is pure. Therefore those who feel this sameness for all and are pure are said to be living in God." This is the gist of Vedāntic morality, this sameness for all. We have seen that it is the subjective world that rules the objective. Change the subject, and the object is bound to change; purify yourself, and the world is bound to be purified. This one thing requires to be taught now more than ever before. We are becoming more and more busy about our neighbours, and less and less about ourselves. The world will change if we change; if we are pure the world will become pure. The question is why I should see evil in others. I cannot see evil unless I am evil. I cannot be miserable unless I am weak. Things that used to make me miserable when I was a child do not do so now. The subject changed, and so the object was bound to change—so says Vedānta. All these things which we call causes of misery and evil, we shall laugh at when we arrive at that wonderful state of equality, that sameness. This is what is called in Vedānta attaining to freedom. The sign of approaching that freedom is the realization of more and more of this sameness and equality. In misery and happiness the same, in success and defeat the same—such a mind is nearing the state of freedom.

But the mind cannot be easily conquered. Minds that rise into waves at the approach of every little thing, at the slightest provocation or danger, in what a state they must be! How talk of greatness or spirituality when these changes come over the mind? This unstable condition of the mind must be changed. We must ask ourselves how far we can be acted upon by the external world, and how far we can stand on our own feet in spite of all the forces outside us. When we have succeeded in preventing all the forces in the world from throwing us off our balance, then alone have we attained to freedom, and not before. That is salvation. It is here and nowhere else, this very moment.

Out of this idea, out of this fountainhead, two beautiful streams of thought have flowed upon the world, generally misunderstood in their expression, apparently contradicting each other. We find hosts of brave and wonderfully spiritual souls, in every nation, taking to caves or forests for meditation, severing their connexion with the external world. This is the one idea. And on the other hand, we find bright, illustrious beings coming into society, trying to raise their fellow men, the poor, the miserable. Apparently these two methods are contradictory. The man who lives in a cave, apart from his fellow beings, smiles contemptuously upon those who are working for the regeneration of their fellow men. "How foolish!" he says. "What work is there to do? The world of māyā will always remain the world of māyā; it cannot be changed."

If I ask one of our priests in India, "Do you believe in Vedānta?" He says: "That is my religion; I certainly do. That is my life." "Very well, do you admit the equality of all life, the sameness of everything?" "Certainly I do." The next moment, when a low-caste man approaches this priest, he jumps to one side of the street to avoid that man. "Why did you jump?" "Because his very touch would have polluted me." "But you were just saying we are all the same, and you admit there is no difference in souls." He says, "Oh, that does not apply to householders; when I become a monk, then I shall look upon everyone as the same." You ask one of your great men in England, of great birth and wealth, if he believes as a Christian in the brotherhood of mankind, since all came from God. He answers in the affirmative; but in five minutes he shouts something uncomplimentary about the common herd. Thus it has been only a theory for several thousand years, and has never come into practice. All understand it, declare it as the truth, but when you ask them to practise it, they say it will take millions of years.

There was a certain king who had a large number of courtiers, and each one of these courtiers declared that he was ready to sacrifice his life for his master and that he was the most sincere being ever born. In the course of time a sannyāsin came to the king. The king said to him that there never was a king who had so many sincere courtiers as he had. The sannyāsin smiled and said that he did not believe it. The king said that the sannyāsin could test it if he liked. So the sannyāsin declared that he would perform a great sacrifice by which the king's reign would be extended very long; as an accessory of the sacrifice, he wanted a small pond into which, in the dark of night, each one of his courtiers should pour a pitcher of milk. The king smiled and said, "Is this the test?" And he asked his courtiers to come to him and told them what was to be done. They all expressed their joyful assent to the proposal and returned. In the dead of night they came and emptied their pitchers into the pond. But in the morning it was found full of water only. The courtiers were assembled and questioned about the matter. Each one of them had thought there would be so many pitchers of milk that his water would not be detected. Unfortunately most of us have the same idea, and we do our share as did the courtiers in the story.

There is so much talk of equality, says the priest, that my little privilege will not be detected. So say our rich men; so say the tyrants of every country. There is more hope for those tyrannized over than for the tyrants. It will take a very long time for tyrants to arrive at freedom, but less time for the others. The cruelty of the fox is much more terrible than the cruelty of the lion. The lion strikes a blow and is quiet for some time afterwards; but the fox, persistently following his prey, never misses an opportunity to harass it. Priestcraft is in its nature cruel and heartless. That is why religion goes down where priestcraft arises. Vedānta says that we must give up the idea of privilege; then religion will come. Before that there is no religion at all.

Do you accept what Christ says? "Go and sell that thou hast, and give to the poor." Practical equality there—no trying to torture the texts, but taking the truth as it is. Do not try to torture texts. I have heard it said that that was preached only to the handful of Jews who listened to Jesus. The same argument will apply to other things also. Do not torture texts. Dare to face truth as it is. If we cannot reach it, let us confess our weakness, but let us not destroy the ideal. Let us hope that we shall attain to it sometime, and let us strive for it. There it is: "Sell that thou hast, and give to the poor, and follow me." Thus, trampling on every privilege and everything in us that works for privilege, let us work for that knowledge which will bring the feeling of sameness towards all mankind. You think that because you use a little more polished language you are superior to the man in the street. Remember that when you are thinking this, you are not going towards freedom, but are forging a fresh chain for your feet. And above all, if the pride of spirituality enters into you, woe unto you. It is the most awful bondage that ever existed. Neither can wealth nor any other bondage of the human heart bind the soul so much as this. "I am purer than others" is the most awful idea that can enter into the human heart. In what sense are you pure? The God in you is the God in all. If you have not known this, you have known nothing. How can there be difference? It is all one. Every being is the temple of the Most High; if you can see that, good; if not, spirituality has yet to come to you.

THE FREE SOUL

(Delivered in New York, 1896)

THE ANALYSIS of the Sāmkhya philosophers stops with the duality of existence: nature and souls. There is an infinite number of souls, which, being simple, cannot die and must therefore be separate from nature. Nature of itself changes and manifests all these phenomena, and the soul, according to Sāmkhya, is inactive. It is a simple substance in itself, and nature works out all these phenomena for the liberation of the soul; and liberation consists in the soul's discerning that it is not nature. At the same time, we have seen that the Sāmkhya philosophers had to admit that every soul is omnipresent. Being a simple substance, the soul cannot be limited, because all limitation comes either through time, space, or causation. The soul, being entirely beyond these, cannot have any limitation. To have any limitation one must be in space, which means in a body, and that which is in a body must be in nature. If the soul had form, it would be identified with nature. Therefore the soul is formless; and that which is formless cannot be said to exist here, or there, or anywhere. It must be omnipresent. Beyond this the Sāmkhya philosophy does not go.

The first argument of the Vedāntists against this analysis is that it is not a perfect one. If nature is absolute and the soul also is absolute, there will be two absolutes, and all the arguments that apply in regard to the soul to show that it is omnipresent will apply in regard to nature, and nature too will be beyond all time, space, and causation; and as a result there will be no change or manifestation. Then will come the difficulty of having two absolutes, which is impossible. What is the solution of the Vedāntist? His solution is that— just as the Sāmkhya philosophers say—it requires some sentient Being as the power behind, to make the mind think and nature work, because nature in all its modifications, from gross matter up to mahat, or the cosmic mind, is simply insentient. Now, the Vedāntist says that this sentient Being which is behind the whole universe is what we call God, and that this universe is not different from Him. It is He Himself who has become this universe. He is not only the instrumental cause of this universe, but also the material cause. Cause is never different from effect; the effect is but the cause reproduced in another form. We see that every day. So this Being is the cause of nature.

All the forms and phases of Vedānta, either dualistic or qualified-monistic or monistic, first take the position that God is not only the instrumental but also the efficient cause of the universe, and that everything that exists is He. The second step in Vedānta is that these souls are also parts of God, sparks of that infinite fire. "As from a mass of fire millions of particles fly, even so from this Ancient One have come all these souls."

759

So far, so good; but it does not yet satisfy. What is meant by a part of the Infinite? The Infinite is indivisible; there cannot be parts of the Infinite. The Absolute cannot be divided. What is meant therefore by saying that all these sparks are from Him? The Advaitist, the non-dualistic Vedāntist, solves the problem by maintaining that there is really no part; that each soul is really not a part of the Infinite, but actually is the infinite Brahman. Then how can there be so many? The sun reflected from millions of globules of water appears to be millions of suns, and in each globule is a miniature picture of the sun; so all these souls are but reflections, and are not real. They are not the real "I," which is the God of this universe, the one undivided Being of the universe. And all these different little beings—men, animals, and so on—are but reflections, and are not real. They are simply illusory reflections upon nature. There is but one infinite Being in the universe, and that Being appears as you and as I; but this appearance of division is after all a delusion. He has not been divided, but only appears to be divided, This apparent division is caused by looking at Him through the network of time, space, and causation.

When I look at God through the network of time, space, and causation, I see Him as the material world. When I look at Him from a little higher plane, yet through the same network, I see Him as an animal, a little higher as a man, a little higher as a god; but still He is the one infinite Being of the universe, and that Being we are. I am He and you are He—not parts of Him but the whole of Him. "He is the eternal Knower standing behind the whole of phenomena; He Himself is the phenomena." He is both the subject and the object; He is the "I" and the "you." How is this? "How can one know the Knower?" The Knower cannot know Himself; I see everything but cannot see myself. The Knower, the Lord of all, the real Being, the Self, is the cause of all the seeing that is in the universe; but it is impossible for It to see Itself or know Itself except through reflection. You cannot see your own face except in a mirror; and just so the Self cannot see Its own nature until It is reflected; and this whole universe therefore is the Self trying to realize Itself. This reflection is thrown back first from the protoplasm, then from plants and animals, and so on and on from better and better reflectors, until the best reflector, the perfect man, is reached; just as a man who, wanting to see his face, looks first in a little pool of muddy water, and sees just an outline, then comes to clear water and sees a better image, then to a piece of shining metal and sees a still better image, and at last to a looking-glass and sees himself reflected as he is. Therefore the perfect man is the highest reflection of that Being, who is both subject and object.

You now find why perfect men are instinctively worshipped as God in every country. You may talk as you like, but it is they who are bound to be worshipped. That is why men worship Incarnations such as Christ or Buddha. They are the most perfect manifestations of the eternal Self. They are much higher than all the conceptions of God that you or I can have. A perfect man is much higher than such conceptions. In him the circle becomes complete, the subject and the object become one. For him all delusions vanish, and in their place comes the realization that he has always been that perfect Being.

How came this bondage then? How was it possible for this perfect Being to degenerate into the imperfect? How was it possible for the free to become bound? The Advaitist says he was never bound, but was always free. Various clouds of different colours come before the sky. They remain there a minute and then pass away. It is the same eternal blue sky stretching there for ever. The sky never changes; it is the cloud that is changing. So you are always perfect, eternally perfect. Nothing ever changes your nature or ever will. All these ideas that I am imperfect, I am a man or a woman, or a sinner, or I am the mind, I have thought, I will think—all are hallucinations. You never think; you never had a body; you never were imperfect. You are the blessed Lord of this universe, the one Almighty Ruler of everything that is or ever will be, the one mighty Ruler of these suns and stars and moons and earths and planets, and all the little bits of our universe. It is through you that the sun shines and the stars shed their lustre and the earth becomes beautiful. It is through your blessedness that they all love and are attracted to each other. You are in all and you are all. Whom shall you avoid, and whom shall you accept? You are all in all. When this knowledge comes, delusion immediately vanishes.

I was once travelling in a desert in India. I travelled for over a month and always found the most beautiful landscapes before me, beautiful lakes and all that. One day I was very thirsty and I wanted to have a drink at one of these lakes, but when I approached that lake it vanished. Immediately with a blow came into my brain the idea that this was a mirage, about which I had read all my life; and as I remembered, I smiled at my folly, realizing that for the last month all the beautiful landscapes and lakes I had been seeing had been this mirage, but I could not distinguish them then. The next morning I again began my march. There was the lake and the landscape, but immediately came the idea, "All this is a mirage." Once known it lost its power to delude. So this illusion of the universe will break one day. The whole of this will vanish, melt away. This is realization. Philosophy is no joke or talk. It must be realized. This body will vanish, this earth and everything will vanish, this idea that I am the body or the mind will vanish. If one's karma is ended the body will never come back; but if part of the karma remains, the body, even after the delusion has vanished, will continue to function for some time—like a potter's wheel, which goes on moving from the past momentum even after the pot has been moulded. Again this world will come, men and women and animals will come, just as the mirage came the next day, but not with the same force; along with it will come the idea that I know its nature now, and it will cause no bondage, no more pain or grief or misery. Whenever anything miserable comes, the mind will be able to say, "I know it is a hallucination."

When a man has reached that state he is called jivanmukta, "living-free," free even while living. The aim and end of this life for the jnāna-yogi is to become jivanmukta. He is jivanmukta who can live in this world without being attached. He is like the lotus leaves in water, which are never wetted by the water. He is the highest of human beings, nay, the highest of all beings; for he has realized his identity with the Absolute, he has realized that he is one with God.

So long as you think there is the least difference between you and God, fear will seize you; but when you have known that you are He, that there is no difference, entirely no difference, that you are He, all of Him, the whole of Him, all fear ceases. "There who sees whom? Who worships whom? Who talks to whom? Who hears whom? Where one sees another, where one talks to another, where one hears another, that is little. Where one does not see another, where one does not speak to another, that is the Highest, that is the Great, that is Brahman." Being That, you are always That.

What will become of the world then? What good shall we do to the world? Such questions do not arise. "What becomes of my gingerbread if I become old?" says the baby. "What becomes of my marbles if I grow up; so I will not grow up," says the boy. "What will become of my dolls if I grow old?" says the little child. It is the same question in connexion with this world. The world has no existence in the past, present, or future. If we have known Ātman as It is, if we have known that there is nothing else but this Ātman, that everything else is but a dream, with no existence in reality, then this world with its poverty, its miseries, its wickedness, and its goodness will cease to disturb us. If they do not exist, for whom and for what shall we take trouble? This is what the jnāna-yogis teach.

Therefore dare to be free, dare to go as far as your thought leads and dare to carry that out in your life. It is very hard to attain jnāna. It is for the bravest and most daring, who dare to smash all idols, not only intellectual but physical also. This body is not I; it must go. All sorts of curious things may come out of this philosophy. A man may say, "I am not the body; therefore my headache must be cured"; but where is the headache if not in his body? Let a thousand headaches and a thousand bodies come and go. What is that to me? I have neither birth nor death; father or mother I never had; friends and foes I have none, because they are all I. I am my own friend and I am my own enemy; I am Existence-Knowledge-Bliss Absolute; I am He, I am He. If in a thousand bodies I am suffering from fever and other ills, in millions of bodies I am healthy. If in a thousand bodies I am starving, in another thousand bodies I am feasting. If in thousands of bodies I am suffering, in thousands of bodies I am happy. Who shall blame whom, who shall praise whom? Who is there to seek, who to avoid? I seek none, nor avoid any, for I am all the universe. I praise myself, I blame myself, I suffer for myself, I am happy according to my own will; I am free. This is the jnāni, the brave and daring. Let the whole universe tumble down; he smiles and says it never existed; it was all a hallucination. He sees the universe tumble down. Where was it? Where has it gone?

Before going into the practical part, we shall take up one more intellectual question. So far the logic is tremendously rigorous. If a man reasons, there is no place for him to stand until he comes to this: that there is but one Existence, that everything else is nothing. There is no other way left for rational mankind but to take this view. But how is it that what is infinite, ever perfect, ever blessed, Existence-Knowledge-Bliss Absolute, has come under these delusions? It is the same question that has been asked all the world over. In the vulgar form the question becomes, "How did sin come into this world?" This is the most vulgar and sensuous form of the question, and the other is the more philosophic form; but the answer is the same. The same question has been asked in various grades and fashions, but in its lower form it finds no solution, because the stories of apples and serpents and women do not give the explanation. In that state the question is childish and so is the answer. But the question has assumed very high proportions now: "How did this illusion come?" The answer is that we cannot expect any answer to an impossible question. The very question is impossible the way it is asked. You have no right to ask that question. Why so? What is perfection? That which is beyond time, space, and causation. That is the perfect. Then you ask how the perfect became imperfect. In logical language the question may be put in this form: "How did that which is beyond causation become caused?" You contradict yourself. You first admit that it is beyond causation and then ask what causes it. This question can only be asked within the limits of causation. As far as time and space and causation extend, so far can this question be asked. But beyond that it will be nonsense to ask it, because the question is illogical. Within time, space, and causation it can never be answered, and what answer may lie beyond these limits can only be known when we have transcended them; therefore the wise will let this question rest. When a man is ill, he devotes himself to curing his disease, without insisting that he must first learn how he came to have it.

There is another answer to the question as to what caused this delusion: maybe more practical and understandable. Can any reality produce delusion? Certainly not. We see that one delusion produces another, and so on. It is delusion always that produces delusion. It is disease that produces disease, and not health that produces disease. The wave is the same thing as the water; the effect is the cause in another form. The effect is delusion, and therefore the cause must be delusion. What produced this delusion? Another delusion. And so on without beginning. The only question that remains for you to ask is: Does this not destroy your monism, because you get two existences in the universe—one the Self, and the other the delusion? The answer is: Delusion cannot be called existence. Thousands of dreams come into your life but do not form any part of your life. Dreams come and go; they have no existence. To call delusion existence will be sophistry. Therefore there is only one indivisible Existence in the universe, ever free and ever blessed, and that is what you are. This is the last conclusion reached by the Advaitists.

It may then be asked: What becomes of all these various forms of worship? They will remain. They are simply a groping in the dark for light; and through this groping light will come.

We have just seen that the Self cannot see Itself. Our knowledge is within the network of māyā, unreality, and beyond that is freedom. Within the network there is slavery; it is all under law. Beyond that there is no law. So far as the universe is concerned, existence is ruled by law; and beyond that is freedom. As long as you are in the network of time, space, and causation, to say you are free is nonsense, because in that network all is under rigorous law: antecedent and consequent. Every thought that you think is caused, every feeling has been caused; to say that the will is free is sheer nonsense. It is only when the infinite Existence comes, as it were, into this network of māyā that it takes the form of will. Will is a portion of that Being, caught in the network of māyā; and therefore free will is a misnomer. It means nothing; it is sheer nonsense. And so is all this talk about freedom. There is no freedom in māyā. Everyone is as much bound in thought, word, deed, and mind as a piece of stone or this table. That I talk to you now is as rigorously in causation as that you listen to me. There is no freedom until you go beyond māyā. That is the real freedom of the soul.

Men, however sharp and intellectual they may be, however clearly they may see the force of the logic that nothing here can be free, are all compelled to think they are free; they cannot help it. No work can be done unless we think we are free. This simply means that the freedom we talk about is a glimpse of the blue sky through the clouds, and that the real freedom—the blue sky itself—is behind. True freedom cannot exist in the midst of this delusion, this hallucination, this nonsense of the world, this universe of the senses, body, and mind. All these dreams, without beginning or end, uncontrolled and uncontrollable, ill-adjusted, broken, inharmonious, form our idea of this universe. In a dream, when you see a giant with twenty heads chasing you, and you are flying from him, you do not think it is inharmonious; you think it is proper and right. So it is with law. All that you call law is simply chance without meaning. In this dream state you call it law. Within māyā, so far as this law of time, space, and causation exists, there is no freedom; and all the various forms of worship are within this māyā. The idea of God and the ideas of brute and of man are within this māyā, and as such are equally hallucinations; all of them are dreams.

But you must take care not to argue like some extraordinary men of whom we hear at the present time. They say the idea of God is a delusion, but the idea of this world is true. But both ideas stand or fall by the same logic. He alone has the right to be an atheist who denies this world as well as God. The same argument applies to both. The same mass of delusion extends from God to the lowest animal, from a blade of grass to the Creator. They stand or fall by the same logic. The same person who sees falsity in the idea of God ought also to see it in the idea of his own body or his own mind. When God vanishes, then also vanish the body and mind, and when both vanish, that which is the real Existence remains for ever. "There the eyes cannot go, nor the speech, nor the mind. We cannot see It, neither can we know It." And we now understand that so far as speech and thought and knowledge and intellect go, it is all within māyā, within bondage. Beyond that is Reality. There neither thought nor mind nor speech can reach.

So far it is intellectually all right; but then comes the practice. The real work is in the practice. Are any practices necessary to realize this Oneness? Most decidedly so. It is not that you become this Brahman. You are already That. It is not that you are going to become God or be perfect; you are already perfect, and whenever you think you are not, it is a delusion. The delusion that says you are Mr. So-and-so or Mrs. So-and-so can be got rid of by another delusion, and that is practice. Fire will eat fire, and you can use one delusion to conquer another delusion. One cloud will come and brush away another cloud, and then both will go away. What are these practices then? We must always bear in mind that we are not going to be free, but are free already. Every idea that we are bound is a delusion. Every idea that we are happy or unhappy is a tremendous delusion; and another delusion will come—that we have got to work and worship and struggle to be free; and this will chase out the first delusion, and then both will stop.

The fox is considered very unholy by the Mohammedans and by the Hindus. Also, if a dog touches any bit of food it has to be thrown out; it cannot be eaten by any man. A fox entered a certain Mohammedan's house and took a little bit of food from the table, ate it up, and fled. The man was a poor man and had prepared a very nice feast for himself, and that feast was made unholy and he could not eat it. So he went to a mullāh, a priest, and said: "This has happened to me: a fox came and took a mouthful out of my meal. What can be done? I had prepared a feast and wanted so much to eat it, and now comes this fox and spoils the whole thing." The mullāh thought for a minute and then found the solution and said: "The only way is for you to get a dog and make him eat a bit out of the same plate, because dogs and foxes are eternally quarrelling. The food that was left by the fox will go into your stomach, and that left by the dog will go there too, and their impurities will cancel each other." We are very much in the same predicament. This idea that we are imperfect is a hallucination, and we take up another: that we have to practise disciplines to become perfect. Then one will chase out the other, just as we can use one thorn to extract another and then throw both away. There are people for whom it is sufficient knowledge to hear, "Thou art That." With a flash this universe goes away and their real nature shines; but others have to struggle hard to get rid of this idea of bondage.

The first question is: Who are fit to become jnāna-yogis? Those who are equipped with certain prerequisites. First, renunciation of all fruits of work and of all enjoyments in this life or another life. If you are the Creator of this universe, whatever you desire you will have, because you will create it for yourself; it is only a question of time. Some get it immediately; with others the past samskāras, impressions, stand in the way of their having their desires fulfilled. We give the first place to desires for enjoyment, either in this or in another life. But if you want to be a jnāna-yogi, you must deny there is any life at all, because life is only another name for death. Deny that you are a living being. Who cares for life? Life is a hallucination, and death is its counterpart. Joy is a hallucination, and misery is its counterpart, and so on. What have you to do with life or death? These are all creations of the mind. Thinking thus, we give up desires for enjoyment either in this life or in another.

Then comes controlling the mind, calming it so that it will not break into waves and have all sorts of desires, holding the mind steady, not allowing it to get into waves from external or internal causes, controlling the mind perfectly just by the power of the will. The jnāna-yogi does not take any one of the physical helps or external helps; simply philosophic reasoning, knowledge, and his own will—these are the instruments he believes in. Next comes titikshā, forbearance, bearing all miseries without murmuring, without complaining. When an injury comes, do not mind it. If a tiger comes, stand there. There are men who practise titikshā and succeed in it. There are men who sleep on the sandy banks of the Ganges in the midsummer sun of India and in winter float in the waters of the Ganges for a whole day; they do not care. Men sit in the snow of the Himālayas and do not care to wear any garment. What is heat? What is cold? Let things come and go; what is that to me? I am not the body. It is hard to believe this in these Western countries; but it is good to know that it is done. Just as your people are brave enough to jump into the mouth of a cannon or into the midst of the battlefield, so our people are brave enough to think and act out their philosophy. They give up their lives for it. "I am Existence-Knowledge-Bliss Absolute; I am He, I am He." Just as the Western ideal is to keep up luxury in practical life, so ours is to keep up the highest form of spirituality, to demonstrate that religion is not merely frothy words but can be carried out, every bit of it, in this life. This is titikshā, to bear everything, not to complain of anything. I myself have seen men who say: "I am the Soul; what is the universe to me? Neither pleasure nor pain, nor virtue nor vice, nor heat nor cold, is anything to me." That is titikshā—not running after the enjoyments of the body.

What is religion? To pray, "Give me this and that"? Foolish ideas of religion! Those who believe in them have no true idea of God and the soul. As my Master used to say, the vulture rises higher and higher until he becomes a speck, but his eye is always on a piece of rotten carrion on the earth. After all, what is your idea of religion? To cleanse the streets and have more bread and clothes? Who cares for bread and clothes? People are born and die every minute. Who cares? Why care for the joys and vicissitudes of this little world? Go beyond that if you dare; go beyond law, let the whole universe vanish; stand alone and say: "I am Existence Absolute, Knowledge Absolute, Bliss Absolute; I am He, I am He."

RELIGION: ITS METHODS AND PURPOSE

(Delivered in England)

IN STUDYING THE RELIGIONS of the world we generally find two methods of procedure. The one is from God to man. That is to say, we have the Semitic group of religions, in which the idea of God comes almost from the very first, and, strangely enough, without any idea of the soul. It is very remarkable that the ancient Hebrews, until a very recent period in their history, never evolved a definite idea of the soul. Man was composed of certain mental and material particles, and that was all. With death everything ended. But on the other hand, there was a most wonderful idea of God evolved by the same race. This is one of the methods of procedure. The other is from man to God. The second is peculiarly Indo-Āryan and the first is peculiarly Semitic. The Indo-Āryan first began with the soul. His ideas of God were hazy, not very clear; but as his idea of the human soul began to be clearer, his idea of God began to be clearer in the same proportion. So the inquiry in the Vedas was always through the soul. All the knowledge the Indo-Āryans got of God was through the soul; and as such, the peculiar stamp that has been left upon their whole cycle of philosophy is that introspective search after Divinity.

The Indo-Āryan man was always seeking Divinity inside himself. It became, in the course of time, a natural characteristic of his thinking. It is evident in his art and in his commonest dealings. But even at the present time, if we take a European picture of a man in a religious attitude, the painter always makes his subject point his eyes upward, looking outside nature for God, looking up into the skies. In India, on the other hand, the religious attitude is always presented by making the subject close his eyes. He is, as it were, looking inward.

These are the two subjects of study for man: external and internal nature; and though at first these seem to be contradictory, yet external nature must be entirely composed of internal nature, the world of thought. The majority of philosophies in every country, especially in the West, have started with the assumption that these two, matter and mind, are contradictory existences; but in the long run we shall find that they converge towards each other, and in the end unite and form an indivisible whole. So by this analysis I do not imply a higher or lower standpoint with regard to the subject. I do not mean that those who want to search after truth through external nature are wrong, nor that those who want to search after truth through internal nature are right. These are the two modes of procedure. Both of them must remain; both of them must be studied; and in the end we shall find that they meet. We shall see that neither is the body antagonistic to the mind, nor the mind to the body, although we find many persons who think that this body is nothing. In olden times, every country was full of people who thought this body was only a disease, a sin, or something of that kind. Later on, however, we see how, as it was taught in the Vedas, this body melts into the mind and the mind into the body.

You must remember the one theme that runs through all the Vedas: "What is that by the knowing of which we know everything else?" This, expressed more or less clearly, is the theme of all human knowledge. It is the finding of a Unity towards which we are all going. Every action of our lives—the most material, the grossest, as well as the finest, the highest, the most spiritual—is alike tending towards this one ideal, the finding of Unity. A man is single. He marries. Apparently it may be a selfish act, but at the same time, the impulse, the motive behind, is to find Unity. He has children, he has friends, he loves his country, he loves the world, and ends by loving the whole universe. Irresistibly we are impelled towards that perfection which consists in finding Unity, killing this little self and making ourselves broader and broader. This is the goal, the end towards which the universe is rushing. Every atom here is trying to join itself to the next atom. Atoms after atoms combine, making huge balls—the earths, the suns, the moons, the stars, the planets. They in their turn are trying to rush towards each other; and we know that at last the whole universe, mental and material, will be fused into one.

The process that is going on in the cosmos, on a large scale, is the same as is going on in the microcosm, on a smaller scale. Just as this universe has its existence in separation, in distinction, and all the while is rushing towards Unity, non-separation, so in our little worlds each soul is born, as it were, cut off from the rest of the world. The more ignorant, the more unenlightened the soul, the more it thinks that it is separate from the rest of the universe. The more ignorant the person, the more he thinks about his birth and death, and all such ideas that are an expression of this separateness. But we find that, as knowledge comes, man grows, morality is evolved, and the idea of non-separateness begins. Whether men understand it or not, they are impelled by that power behind to become unselfish. That is the foundation of all morality. It is the quintessence of all ethics preached in any language or in any religion or by any prophet in the world: "Be thou unselfish." "Not I, but thou"—that is the background of all ethical codes. And what is meant by this is the recognition of non-individuality: that you are a part of me, and I of you; the recognition that in hurting you I hurt myself and in helping you I help myself; the recognition that there cannot possibly be death for me when you live. When one worm lives in this universe, how can I die? For my life is in the life of that worm. At the same time this idea teaches us that we cannot leave one of our fellow beings without helping him, that in his good lies our good.

This is the theme that runs through the whole of Vedānta, and that runs through all religions. For every religion, you must remember, generally is divided into three parts. There is the first part, consisting of the philosophy, the essence, the principles of religion. These principles find their expression in mythology—lives of saints or heroes, demi-gods, or gods, or divine beings, and the whole idea behind mythology is that of power; and in the lower class of mythologies, the primitive, the expression of this power is in the muscles—their heroes are strong, gigantic. One hero conquers the whole world. As man advances he must find an expression for his energy in something higher than the muscles; so his heroism also finds expression in something higher. The higher mythologies have heroes who are gigantic moral men. Their strength is manifested in becoming moral and pure. They are detached; they can beat back the surging tide of selfishness and immorality. The third portion of all religions is symbolism, which you call ceremonials and forms. Even the expression through mythology, the lives of heroes, is too high for many. There are undeveloped minds. Like children, they must have their kindergarten of religion, and so these symbols are used as concrete examples which they can handle and grasp and understand, which they can see and feel as something material.

So in every religion you find there are the three stages: philosophy, mythology, and ceremonial. There is one advantage which can be pleaded for Vedānta: that in India, fortunately, these three stages have been sharply defined. In other religions the principles are so interwoven with the mythology that it is very hard to distinguish the one from the other. The mythology stands supreme, swallowing up the principles; and in the course of centuries the principles are lost sight of. The explanation, the illustration of the principle, swallows up the principle. People see only the explanation: the prophet, the preacher. The principles have almost gone out of existence—so much so that even today, if a man dares to preach the principles of Christianity apart from Christ, they will attack him, thinking that he is wrong and is dealing blows at Christianity. In the same way, if a man wants to preach the principles of Mohammedanism, Mohammedans will think likewise; because concrete ideas, the lives of great men and prophets, have entirely overshadowed the principles.

In Vedānta the chief advantage is that it was not the work of one single man, and therefore, naturally, unlike Buddhism or Christianity or Mohammedanism, the prophet or teacher did not entirely swallow up or overshadow the principles. In Vedānta the principles play an important part, and the prophets occupy a secondary position. The Upanishads do not mention any particular prophet but they speak of various prophets and prophetesses. The old Hebrews had something of that idea; yet we find Moses occupying much of the space of the Hebrew literature. Of course I do not mean that it is bad that these prophets should exercise an influence upon a nation; but it certainly is very injurious if the whole field of principles is lost sight of. We can very well agree as to principles, but not so well as to persons. The persons appeal to our emotions, and the principles to something higher, to our calm judgement. Principles must prevail in the end, for they appeal to man's reason. Emotions many times drag us down to the level of animals. Emotions have more connexion with the senses than with the faculty of reason; and therefore when principles are entirely lost sight of and emotions prevail, religions degenerate into fanaticism and sectarianism. They are no better than party politics and such things. The most horribly ignorant notions will be taken up, and for these ideas thousands will be ready to cut the throats of their brethren. This is the reason that, though these great personalities and prophets are tremendous motive powers for good, at the same time their lives are altogether dangerous when they lead to the disregard of the principles they represent. That has always led to fanaticism and has deluged the world in blood. Vedānta can avoid this difficulty because it has not one special prophet. It has many seers, who are called rishis, or sages. Seers—that is the literal translation—are those who see these truths, which are known as mantras.

The word *mantra* means "thought out," cogitated by the mind, and the word *rishi* signifies the seer of these thoughts. These thoughts are not the monopoly of any particular race, nor of any man or woman, however great he or she may be—not even the exclusive property of the greatest spirits whom the world has produced, the Buddhas or Christs. They are as much the property of the lowest of the low as they are the property of a Buddha, and as much the property of the smallest worm that crawls as of a Christ, because they are universal principles. They are never created. These principles have existed throughout time, and they will continue to exist. They are uncreate: not created by any laws which science teaches us today. They remain covered and become discovered, but exist through all eternity in nature. If Newton had not been born, the law of gravitation would have remained all the same and would have worked all the same. It was Newton's genius which discovered it, brought it into consciousness, formulated it, made the human race conscious of it. Similar are these religious laws, the grand truths of spirituality. They are working all the time. If all the Vedas and Bibles and Korans did not exist at all, if seers and prophets had never been born, yet these laws would exist. They would only remain unknown, and slowly but surely would work to raise the human race, to raise human nature. But the prophets see them, discover them; such prophets are discoverers in the field of spirituality. As Newton and Galileo were prophets of physical science, so are they prophets of spirituality. They can claim no exclusive right to any one of these laws, which are the common property of all humanity.

The Vedas, as the Hindus say, are eternal. We now understand what they mean by calling them eternal: it is that the laws have neither beginning nor end, just as nature has neither beginning nor end. Earth after earth, system after system, will evolve, run for a certain time, and then dissolve back again into chaos; but the universe remains the same. Millions and millions of systems are being born, while millions are being destroyed. The universe remains the same. The beginning and the end of time can be told as regards a certain planet; but as regards the universe they have no meaning at all. So are the laws of nature— the physical laws, the mental laws, the spiritual laws—without beginning and without end; and it is within a few years, comparatively speaking, a few thousand years at best, that man has tried to reveal them. But the infinite mass of them remains before us. Therefore the one great lesson that we learn from the Vedas, at the start, is that religion has just begun. The infinite ocean of spiritual truth lies before us to be worked on, to be discovered, to be brought into our lives. The world has seen thousands of prophets and it has yet to see millions.

There were times in olden days when prophets were many in every society. The time is to come when prophets will walk through every street in every city in the world. In olden times certain peculiar persons were, so to speak, selected by the operations of the laws of society to become prophets. The time is coming when we shall understand that to become religious means to become a prophet, that none can become religious until he or she becomes a prophet.

We shall come to understand that the secret of religion is being able not merely to think and say all these thoughts, but, as the Vedas teach, to realize them, to realize newer and higher ones than have ever been realized, to discover them, bring them to society; and the study of religion should be the training to make prophets. The schools and colleges should be training-grounds for prophets. All men must become prophets; and until a man becomes a prophet, religion is a mockery and an empty word to him. We must see religion, feel it, realize it, in a thousand times more intense a way than that in which we see this wall.

But there is one principle which underlies all these various manifestations of religion and which has been already mapped out for us. Every science must end where it finds a unity, because we cannot go any farther; when a perfect unity is reached, that science has nothing more of principles to tell us. Take any science—chemistry, for example. Suppose we find one element out of which we can manufacture all the other elements. Then chemistry, as a science, will have become perfect. What will remain for us is to discover every day new combinations of that one material, and the application of those combinations for all the purposes of life. So it is with religion. The gigantic principles, the scope, the plan, of religion, were already discovered ages ago, when man found the last words, as they are called in the Vedas, "I am He"—the truth that there is One in whom this whole universe of matter and mind finds its unity, whom he calls God or Brahman or Allah or Jehovah, or by any other name. We cannot go beyond that. The grand principle has been already mapped out for us; all that the different religions have to do is to work out the details. Our work lies in filling it in, working it out, applying it to every part of our lives. We have to work now so that everyone will become a prophet. That is the great work before us.

In olden times many did not understand what a prophet meant. They thought it was something that happened by chance—that just by the fiat of will of some higher intelligence a man gained superior knowledge. In modern times we are prepared to demonstrate that this knowledge is the birthright of every living being, whosoever and wheresoever he be, and that there is no such thing as chance in this universe. Every man who, as we think, gets something by chance has been working for it slowly and surely through ages; and the whole question devolves upon us: do we want to be prophets? If we do, we shall be.

This, the training of prophets, is the great work that lies before us, and consciously or unconsciously all the great systems of religion are working towards this one great goal, only with the difference that in many religions you will find they declare that direct perception of spirituality is not to be had in this life, that man must die, and that after his death there will come a time in another world when he will have visions of spirituality, when he will realize things which now he must believe. But Vedānta will ask all people who make such assertions: "Then how do you know that spirituality exists?" And they will have to answer that there must always have been certain particular people who, even in this life, somehow got a glimpse of things which are unknown and unknowable.

Even this creates a difficulty. If they were peculiar people, having this power simply by chance, we have no right to believe in them. It would be a sin to believe in anything that happened by chance, because we cannot know it. What is meant by knowledge? Destruction of peculiarity. Suppose a man goes into the street or to a menagerie and sees a peculiarly shaped animal. He does not know what it is. Then he goes to a country where there are hundreds like it and he is satisfied; he knows what the species is. Our knowledge is knowing the principle. Our non-knowledge is finding the particular without reference to the principle. When we find one case or a few cases separate from the principle, without any reference to the principle, we are in darkness and do not know. Now, if these prophets, as they say, were peculiar persons who alone had the right to catch a glimpse of that which is beyond, and no one else has the right, we should not believe in these prophets, because they are peculiar cases without any reference to a principle. We can only believe in them if we ourselves become prophets.

All of you hear the various jokes that get into the newspapers about the sea-serpent; and why should it be so? Because a few persons, at long intervals, came and told their stories about the sea-serpent, and others never see it. They have no particular principle to which to refer, and therefore the world does not believe. If a man comes to me and says a prophet disappeared into the air or went through it, I have the right to see it. I ask him: "Did your father or grandfather see it?" "Oh, no," he replies, "but five thousand years ago such a thing happened"—and if I do not believe it, I have to be barbecued through eternity.

What a mass of superstition this is! And its effect is to degrade man from his divine nature to that of the brutes. Why was reason given us if we have to believe? Is it not tremendously blasphemous to believe against reason? What right have we not to use the greatest gift that God has given to us? I am sure God will pardon a man who uses his reason and cannot believe, rather than a man who believes blindly instead of using the faculties He has given him. Such a man degrades his nature and sinks to the level of the beasts, degrades his senses and dies. We must reason, and when reason proves to us the truth of these prophets and great men about whom the ancient books speak in every country, we shall believe in them. We shall believe in them when we see such prophets among ourselves. We shall then find that they were not peculiar men, but only illustrations of certain principles. They worked, and that principle expressed itself naturally, and we shall have to work to express that principle in us. We shall believe that they were prophets when we become prophets. That they were seers of things divine, that they could go beyond the bounds of the senses and catch a glimpse of that which is beyond, we shall believe when we are able to do all this ourselves, and not before.

That is the one principle of Vedānta. Vedānta declares that religion is here and now, because the question of this life and that life, of life and death, of this world and that world, is merely one of superstition and prejudice. There is no break in time beyond what we make. What real difference is there between ten and twelve o'clock, except in certain changes we observe in nature? Time flows on the same. So what is meant by this life and that life? It is only a question of time, and what is lost in time may be made up by speed in work. So, says Vedānta, religion is to be realized now. And for you to become religious means that you will start without any religion, work your way up, and realize things, see things for yourself. When you have done that, then, and then alone, are you religious. Before that you are no better than atheists, or rather you are worse, because the atheist is sincere; he stands up and says, "I do not know about these things," while those others do not know but go about the world saying, "We are very religious people." What religion they have no one knows; they have only swallowed some grandmother's story, and priests have asked them to believe these things—if they do not, then let them take care. That is how it is going on.

Realization is the only way. Each one of us will have to discover the Truth. Of what use are these books, then, these Bibles of the world? They are of great use, just as maps of a country are. I had seen maps of England all my life before I came here, and they were of great help to me in forming some sort of conception of England. Yet when I arrived in this country, what a difference between the maps and the country itself! So is the difference between realization and the scriptures. These books are only the maps, the experiences of past men, and they are useful as an incentive to us to dare to have the same experiences and make discoveries in the same, or even a better, way.

This is the first principle of Vedānta: that realization is religion. He who realizes Truth is the religious man, and he who does not is no better than he who says, "I do not know," if he is not actually worse, because the other says, "I do not know," and is sincere. In this realization, again, we shall be helped very much by the books, because they give instructions and exercises; for every science has its own particular method of investigation. You will find many persons in this world who say, "I wanted to become religious, I wanted to realize these things, but I have not been able, so I do not believe in anything." If you say to a chemist, "I do not believe anything about chemistry, because all my life I have tried to become a chemist and have not succeeded," he will ask, "When did you try?" "When I went to bed, I repeated, 'O chemistry, come to me,' and it never came." The chemist will laugh at you and say: "Oh, that is not the way. Why did you not go to the laboratory and get all the acids and alkalis and burn your hands from time to time? That alone would have taught you." Do you take the same trouble with religion?

Every science has its own method of learning, and religion is to be learnt the same way. It has its own methods; and here is something we can learn, and must learn, from all the ancient prophets of the world, from everyone who has found something, who has realized religion. They will give us the methods, the particular methods, through which alone we shall be able to realize the truths of religion. They struggled all their lives, discovered particular methods of mental culture, brought their minds to a certain state of fine perception, and through that they perceived the truths of religion. To become religious, to perceive religion, to feel it, to become a prophet, we must follow these methods and practise them; and then if we find nothing, we shall have the right to say: "There is nothing in religion, for I have tried and failed."

This is the practical side of all religions. You will find it in every Bible in the world. All the scriptures teach disciplines, and you will find these followed by saints and prophets. And though it is not expressly laid down as a rule of conduct, you will always find in the lives of these prophets that they some-times regulated even their eating and drinking. Their whole living—their food, their drink, everything—was different from that of the masses who surrounded them. These were the causes that gave them the higher light, the vision of the Divine; and we, if we want to have this vision, must be ready to take up these methods. It is practice, work, that will bring us to that vision. The plan of Vedānta, therefore, is first to lay down the principles, map out for us the goal, and then to teach us the method by which to arrive at the goal, to understand and realize religion.

Again, these methods must be different. Seeing that we are so different in our natures, the same method can scarcely be applied to any two of us in the same manner. We have idiosyncrasies in our minds, each one of us; so the method ought to be varied. Some, you will find, are very emotional by nature; some, very philosophical, rational; others cling to all sorts of ritualistic forms and want things which are concrete. You will find that one man does not care for any ceremony or form or anything of the sort; they are like death to him. And another man carries a load of amulets all over his body; he is so fond of these symbols. Another man, who is emotional in nature, wants to show acts of charity to everyone; he weeps, he loves, and so on. And all of these certainly cannot have the same method. If there were only one method to arrive at Truth, it would be death for everyone else who was not similarly constituted. Therefore the methods should be various. Vedānta understands that and lays before the world different methods through which we can work. Take up any one you like, and if one does not suit you, another may.

From this standpoint we see how glorious it is that there are so many religions in the world, how good it is that there are so many teachers and prophets, instead of there being only one, as many persons would like to have it. The Mohammedans want the whole world to be Mohammedan; the Christians, Christian; and the Buddhists, Buddhist; but Vedānta says: "Let each person in the world be separate, if you will; but the one principle, the unity, will be behind. The more prophets there are, the more books, the more seers, the more methods, the better it is for the world." Just as in social life the greater the number of occupations in every society, the better it is for that society—the more chance there is for everyone in that society to make a living—so it is in the world of thought and of religion. How much better it is today when we have so many divisions of science—how much more possible for everyone to have great mental culture with this great variety before us! How much better it is, even on the physical plane, to have the opportunity of so many various things spread before us, so that we may choose any one we like, the one which suits us best! So it is with the world of religion. It is a most glorious dispensa-tion of the Lord that there are so many religions in the world; and would to God that these would increase every day until every man had a religion unto himself!

Vedānta understands this and therefore preaches the one principle and admits various methods. It has nothing to say against anyone; whether you are a Christian or a Buddhist or a Jew or a Hindu, no matter what mythology you believe in, whether you owe allegiance to the prophet of Nazareth or of Mecca or of India or of anywhere else, or even if you yourself are a prophet, it has nothing to say. It only preaches the principle which is the background of every religion and of which all the prophets and saints and seers are but illustrations and manifestations. Multiply your prophets if you like; it has no objection. It only preaches the principle, and the methods it leaves to you. Take any path you like; follow any prophet you like; but have only that method which suits your own nature, so that you will be sure to progress.

REINCARNATION[1]

"Both you and I have passed through many births.
You know them not; I know them all."
— Bhagavad Gītā.

OF THE MANY RIDDLES that have perplexed the intellect of man in all climes
and times, the most intricate is himself. Of the myriad mysteries that have called
forth his energies to struggle for their solution, from the very dawn of history,
the most mysterious is his own nature. It is at once the most insoluble enigma
and the problem of all problems. As the starting-point and the repository of
all we know and feel and do, there never has been, nor will be, a time when
man's own nature will cease to demand his best and foremost attention.

Though through hunger after that truth which of all others has the most
intimate connexion with his very existence; though through an all-absorbing
desire for an inward standard by which to measure the outward universe;
though through the absolute and inherent necessity of finding a fixed point
in a universe of change, man has sometimes clutched at handfuls of dust for
gold, and even when urged on by a voice higher than reason or intellect has
many times failed to interpret rightly the meaning of the divinity within—
still there never has been a time, since the search began, when some race or
some individuals did not hold aloft the lamp of truth.

Taking a one-sided, cursory, and prejudiced view of the surroundings and
the unessential details, sometimes disgusted also with the vagueness of many
schools and sects, and often, alas, driven to the opposite extreme by the violent
superstitions of organized priestcraft, men have not been wanting, especially
among advanced intellects, in either ancient or modern times, who not only
have given up the search in despair, but have declared it fruitless and useless.
Philosophers may fret and sneer, and priests ply their trade even at the point
of the sword; but truth comes to those alone who worship at her shrine for her
sake only, without fear and without shopkeeping.

Light comes to individuals through the conscious efforts of their intellects;
it comes slowly, though, to the whole race, through unconscious percolation.
The philosophers show the volitional struggles of great minds. History reveals
the silent process of permeation through which truth is absorbed by the masses.

Of all the theories that have been held by man about himself, that of a soul
entity, separate from the body and immortal, has been the most widespread.
And among those that have held the belief in such a soul, the majority of the
thoughtful have always believed also in its pre-existence. At present the greater
portion of the human race with an organized religion believes in it; and many

[1] Contributed to the *Metaphysical Magazine*, New York, March 1895.

of the best thinkers in the most favoured lands, though nurtured in religions avowedly hostile to every idea of the pre-existence of the soul, have endorsed it. Hinduism and Buddhism have it for their foundation; the educated classes among the ancient Egyptians believed in it; the ancient Persians arrived at it; some of the Greek philosophers made it the corner-stone of their philosophy; the Pharisees among the Hebrews accepted it; and the Sufis, among the Mohammedans, almost universally acknowledged its truth.

There must be peculiar surroundings which generate and foster certain forms of belief among nations. It required ages for the ancient races to arrive at any idea about something apart from the body which survives after death. It took ages more to come to any rational idea about this something which persists and lives apart from the body. It was only when the idea was reached of an entity whose connexion with the body was only for a time, and only among those nations who arrived at such a conclusion, that the unavoidable question arose: Whither? Whence?

The ancient Hebrews never disturbed their equanimity by questioning themselves about the soul. With them death ended all. Karl Heckel justly says: "Though it is true that in the Old Testament, preceding the exile, the Hebrews distinguish a life principle, different from the body, which is sometimes called 'Nephesh,' or 'Ruakh,' or 'Neshama,' yet all these words correspond rather to the idea of breath, than to that of spirit or soul. Also, in the writings of the Palestinian Jews, after the exile, no mention is ever made of an individual immortal soul, but always only of a life-breath emanating from God, which, after the body is dissolved, is reabsorbed into the divine 'Ruakh.' "

The ancient Egyptians and the Chaldeans had peculiar beliefs of their own about the soul; but their ideas about this soul living after death must not be confused with those of the ancient Hindu, the Persian, the Greek, or any other Āryan race. There was from the earliest times a broad distinction between the Āryans and the non-Sanskrit-speaking mlechchas in the conception of the soul. Externally it was typified by their disposal of the dead—the mlechchas mostly trying their best to preserve the dead bodies either by careful burial or by the more elaborate processes of mummifying, and the Āryans generally burning their dead. Herein lies the key to a great secret: the fact that no mlechcha race, whether Egyptian, Assyrian, or Babylonian, ever attained to the idea of the soul as a separate entity which can live independent of the body, without the help of the Āryans, especially of the Hindus.

Although Herodotus states that the Egyptians were the first to conceive the idea of the immortality of the soul, and states, as a doctrine of the Egyptians, that "the soul after the dissolution of the body enters again and again into a creature that comes to life; then, that the soul wanders through all the animals of the land and the sea and through all the birds, and finally, after three thousand years, returns to a human body," yet modern researches into Egyptology have hitherto found no trace of metempsychosis in the popular Egyptian religion. On the contrary, the most recent researches of Maspero, A. Erman, and other eminent Egyptologists tend to confirm the supposition that the doctrine of palingenesis was not at home with the Egyptians.

With the ancient Egyptians the soul was only a double, having no individu-

ality of its own and never able to break its connexion with the body. It persisted
only so long as the body lasted, and if by chance the corpse was destroyed,
the departed soul suffered a second death and annihilation. The soul after
death was allowed to roam freely all over the world, but it must always return
at night to where the corpse was, feeling always miserable, always hungry and
thirsty, always extremely desirous to enjoy life once more, and never being able
to fulfil the desire. If any part of its old body was injured, the soul was also
invariably injured in its corresponding part, and this idea explains the solicitude
of the ancient Egyptians to preserve their dead.

At first the deserts were chosen as the burial-place, because the dryness of
the air did not allow the body to perish soon, thus granting to the departed
soul a long lease of existence. In the course of time one of the gods discovered
the process of making mummies, through which the devout hoped to preserve
the dead bodies of their ancestors for an almost infinite length of time, thus
securing immortality to the departed ghost, however miserable it might be.

The perpetual regret for the world, in which the soul could take no further
interest, never ceased to torture the deceased. "O my brother," exclaims the
departed, "withhold not thyself from drinking and eating, from drunkenness,
from love, from all enjoyment, from following thy desire by night and by day;
put not sorrow within thy heart; for what are the years of man upon earth?
The west is a land of sleep and of heavy shadows, a place wherein the inhabitants, when once installed, slumber on in their mummy forms, never more
waking to see their brethren, never more to recognize their fathers and mothers,
with hearts forgetful of their wives and children. The living water which earth
giveth to all who dwell upon it is for me stagnant and dead; that water floweth
to all who are on earth, while for me it is but liquid putrefaction, this water
that is mine. Since I came into this funeral valley I know not where nor what
I am. Give me to drink of running water, . . . let me be placed by the edge
of the water with my face to the north, that the breeze may caress me and my
heart be refreshed from its sorrow."[2]

Among the Chaldeans also, although they did not speculate so much as the
Egyptians as to the condition of the soul after death, the soul was still a double
and was bound to its sepulchre. They also could not conceive of a state without
this physical body, and expected a resurrection of the corpse again to life; and
though the goddess Ishtar, after great perils and adventures, procured the
resurrection of her shepherd husband Dumuzi, the son of Ea and Damkina,
"the most pious votaries pleaded in vain from temple to temple for the resurrection of their dead friends."

Thus we find that the ancient Egyptians and Chaldeans never could entirely
dissociate the idea of the soul from the corpse of the departed or from the
sepulchre. The state of earthly existence was best after all, and the departed
were always longing to have a chance once more to renew it; and the living were
fervently hoping to help them in prolonging the existence of the miserable
double and striving the best they could to help them.

This is not the soil out of which any higher knowledge of the soul can spring.

[2] This text has been translated into German by Brugsch, Die Egyptische Gräberwelt,
pp. 39-40, and into French by Maspero, Études Égyptiennes, Vol. I, pp. 181-190.

In the first place the whole idea is grossly materialistic, and even then it is one of terror and agony. Frightened by the almost innumerable powers of evil, and making hopeless, agonized efforts to avoid them, the souls of the living, like their ideas of the souls of the departed—wander all over the world though they might—could never get beyond the sepulchre and the crumbling corpse.

We must turn now for the source of the higher ideas of the soul to another race, whose God was an all-merciful, all-pervading Being manifesting Himself through various bright, benign, and helpful devas; the first of all the human race who addressed their God as Father: "Oh, take me by the hands even as a father takes his dear son"; with whom life was a hope and not a despair; whose religion was not the intermittent groans escaping from the lips of an agonized man during the intervals of a life of mad excitement, but whose ideas come to us redolent with the aroma of the field and forest; whose songs of praise—spontaneous, free, joyful, like the songs which burst forth from the throats of the birds when they hail this beautiful world illuminated by the first rays of the lord of the day—come down to us even now, through the vista of eighty centuries, as fresh calls from heaven. We turn to the ancient Āryans.

"Place me in that deathless, undecaying world where is the light of heaven and everlasting lustre shines"; "Make me immortal in that realm where dwells King Vivasvān's son, where is the secret shrine of heaven"; "Make me immortal in that realm where they move even as they list"; "In the third sphere of the inmost heaven, where the worlds are full of light, make me immortal in that realm of bliss"—these are the prayers of the Āryans in their oldest record, the Rig-Veda Samhitā.

We find at once a whole world of difference between the mlechcha and the Āryan ideals. To the one, this body and this world were all that were real and all that were desirable. A little life-fluid which flew off from the body at death, to feel torture and agony at the loss of the enjoyments of the senses, could, they fondly hoped, be brought back if the body was carefully preserved; and thus the corpse became more of an object of care than the living man. The other found out that that which left the body was the real man, and when separated from the body it enjoyed a state of bliss higher than it ever enjoyed when in the body; and they hastened to annihilate the corrupted corpse by burning it.

Here we find the germ out of which a true idea of the soul could come. Here it was—where the real man was not the body, but the soul; where all ideas of an inseparable connexion between the real man and the body were utterly absent—that a noble idea of the freedom of the soul could arise. And it was when the Āryans penetrated even beyond the shining cloth of the body with which the departed soul was enveloped, and found its real nature, a formless, individual principle, that the question inevitably arose: Whence?

It was in India and among the Āryans that the doctrine of the pre-existence, the immortality, and the individuality of the soul first arose. Recent researches in Egypt have failed to show any trace of the doctrines of an independent and individual soul existing before and after the earthly phase of existence. Some of the mysteries were no doubt in possession of this idea, but in those it has been traced to India.

"I am convinced," says Karl Heckel, "that the deeper we enter into the study of the Egyptian religion, the more clearly it is shown that the doctrine of metempsychosis was entirely foreign to the popular Egyptian religion, and that even that which single mysteries possessed of it was not inherent in the Osiris teachings, but derived from Hindu sources."

Later on we find the Alexandrian Jews imbued with the doctrine of an individual soul; and the Pharisees of the time of Jesus, as already stated, not only had faith in an individual soul, but believed in its wanderings through various bodies; and thus it is easy to find how Christ was recognized as the incarnation of an older prophet, and Jesus himself directly asserted that John the Baptist was the prophet Elias come back again. "If ye will receive it, this is Elias, which was for to come." (Matt. 11:14.)

The idea of a soul and of its individuality, among the Hebrews, evidently came through the higher mystical teachings of the Egyptians, who in their turn had derived it from India. And that it should come through Alexandria is significant, since the Buddhist records clearly show Buddhist missionary activity in Alexandria and Asia Minor.

Pythagoras is said to have been the first Greek who taught the doctrine of palingenesis among the Hellenes. As an Āryan race, already burning their dead and believing in the doctrine of an individual soul, it was easy for the Greeks to accept the doctrine of reincarnation, through the Pythagorean teachings. According to Apuleius, Pythagoras had gone to India, where he had been instructed by the brāhmins.

So far we have learnt that wherever the soul was held to be an individual, the real man, and not a vivifying part of the body only, the doctrine of its pre-existence inevitably came, and that those nations that believed in the independent individuality of the soul almost always signified it externally by burning the bodies of the departed; though one of the ancient Āryan races, the Persian, developed at an early period, and without any Semitic influence, a peculiar method of disposing of the bodies of the dead; the very name by which they call their "towers of silence" comes from the Sanskrit root *daha*, to burn.

In short, the races who did not pay much attention to the analysis of their own nature never went beyond the material body as their all in all; and even when driven by higher light to penetrate beyond, they only came to the conclusion that somehow or other, at some distant period of time, this body will become incorruptible. On the other hand, that race which spent the best part of its energies in the inquiry into the nature of man as a thinking being—the Indo-Āryan—soon found out that beyond this body, beyond even the shining body which their forefathers longed for, is the real man, the principle, the individual who clothes himself with this body and then throws it off when worn out.

Was such a principle created? If creation means something coming out of nothing, the answer is a decisive no. This soul is without birth and without death. It is not a compound or combination, but an independent individual, and as such it cannot be created or destroyed; it is only travelling through various states.

Naturally, the question arises: Where was it all this time? The Hindu philosophers say that in the physical sense it was passing through different bodies, or, really and metaphysically speaking, passing through different mental planes.

Are there any proofs, apart from the teachings of the Vedas, upon which the doctrine of reincarnation has been founded by the Hindu philosophers? There are; and we hope to show later on that there are grounds as valid for it as for any universally accepted doctrine. But first we shall see what some of the greatest of modern European thinkers have thought about reincarnation.

Schopenhauer, in his book *Die Welt als Wille und Vorstellung*, speaking about palingenesis, says:

"What sleep is for the individual, death is for the 'will.' It would not endure to continue the same actions and sufferings throughout an eternity without true gain, if memory and individuality remained to it. It flings them off, and this is Lethe, and through this sleep of death it reappears fitted out with another intellect as a new being; a new day tempts to new shores. These constant new births, then, constitute the succession of the life-dreams of a will which in itself is indestructible, until, instructed and improved by so much and such various successive knowledge in a constantly new form, it abolishes and abrogates itself. . . . It must not be neglected that even empirical grounds support a palingenesis of this kind. As a matter of fact, there does exist a connexion between the birth of the newly appearing beings and the death of those that are worn out. It shows itself in the great fruitfulness of the human race which appears as a consequence of devastating diseases. When in the fourteenth century the Black Death had for the most part depopulated the Old World, a quite abnormal fruitfulness appeared among the human race, and twin-births were very frequent. The circumstance was also remarkable that none of the children born at this time obtained their full number of teeth; thus nature, exerting itself to the utmost, was niggardly in details. This is related by F. Schnurrer in his *Chronik der Seuchen*, 1825. Casper also, in his *Über die Wahrscheinliche Lebensdauer des Menschen*, 1835, confirms the principle that the number of births in a given population has the most decided influence upon the length of life and mortality in it, as this always keeps pace with mortality; so that always and everywhere the deaths and the births increase and decrease in like proportion, which he places beyond doubt by an accumulation of evidence collected from many lands and their various provinces. And yet it is impossible that there can be a physical, causal connexion between my early death and the fruitfulness of a marriage with which I have nothing to do, or conversely. Thus here the metaphysical appears undeniable, and in a stupendous manner, as the immediate ground of explanation of the physical. Every new-born being comes fresh and blithe into the new existence, and enjoys it as a free gift; but there is and can be nothing freely given. Its fresh existence is paid for by the old age and death of a worn-out existence which has perished, but which contained the indestructible seed out of which the new existence has arisen; they are one being."

The great English philosopher Hume, nihilistic though he was, says in the sceptical essay on immortality: "The metempsychosis is therefore the only system of this kind that philosophy can listen to." The philosopher Lessing, with a deep poetical insight, asks: "Is this hypothesis so laughable merely because it is the oldest? because the human understanding, before the sophistries of the schools had dissipated and debilitated it, lighted upon it at once? . . . Why should not I come back as often as I am capable of acquiring fresh knowledge, fresh experience? Do I bring away so much from one life that there is nothing to repay the trouble of coming back?"

The arguments for and against the doctrine of a pre-existing soul reincarnating through many lives have been many, and some of the greatest thinkers of all ages have taken up the gauntlet to defend it; and so far as we can see, if there is an individual soul, that it existed before seems inevitable. If the soul is not an individual, but a combination of skandhas, or notions, as the Mādhyamikas among the Buddhists insist, still they find pre-existence absolutely necessary to explain their position.

The argument showing the impossibility of an infinite existence's beginning in time is unanswerable, though attempts have been made to ward it off by appealing to the power of God to do anything, however contrary to reason it may be. We are sorry to find this most fallacious argument proceeding from some of the most thoughtful persons.

In the first place, God being the universal and common cause of all phenomena, the question was to find the natural causes of certain phenomena in the human soul, and the *deus ex machina* theory is therefore quite irrelevant. It amounts to nothing more than confession of ignorance. We can give that answer to every question asked in every branch of human knowledge, and stop all inquiry, and therefore knowledge, altogether.

Secondly, this constant appeal to the omnipotence of God is only a word-puzzle. The cause, as cause, is and can only be known to us as sufficient for the effect, and nothing more. As such we have no more idea of an infinite effect than of an omnipotent cause. Moreover, all our ideas of God are limited; even the idea of cause limits our idea of God. Thirdly, even taking the position for granted, we are not bound to allow any such absurd theories as "something coming out of nothing" or "infinity beginning in time" so long as we can give a better explanation.

A so-called strong argument is made against the idea of pre-existence by asserting that the majority of mankind are not conscious of it. To prove the validity of this argument, the person who offers it must prove that the whole of the soul of man is bound up in the faculty of memory. If memory be the test of existence, then all that part of our lives which is not now in it must be non-existent, and every person who in a state of coma, or otherwise, loses his memory must be non-existent also.

The premises from which the inference is drawn of a previous existence, and that, too, on the plane of conscious action, as adduced by the Hindu philosophers, are chiefly these:

First, how else do you explain this world of inequalities? Here is one child born in the providence of a just and merciful God, with every circumstance conducing to his becoming a good and useful member of the human race, and perhaps at the same instant and in the same city another child is born, under circumstances every one of which is against his becoming good. We see children born to suffer, perhaps all their lives, and that owing to no fault of theirs. Why should it be so? What is the cause? Of whose ignorance is it the result? If not the child's, why should it suffer? For its parents' actions?

It is much better to confess ignorance than try to evade the question by the allurements of future enjoyments in proportion to the evil here, or by posing "mysteries." Not only undeserved suffering forced upon us by any agent is immoral—not to say unjust—but even the future-making-up theory has no legs to stand upon. How many of the miserably born struggle towards a higher life, and how many more succumb to the circumstances they are placed under? Should those who grow worse and more wicked by being forced to be born under evil circumstances be rewarded for the wickedness of their lives in the future? In that case, the more wicked the man is here, the better will be his deserts hereafter.

There is no other way to vindicate the glory and the liberty of the human soul and to reconcile the inequalities and the horrors of this world than to place the whole burden upon the legitimate cause: our own independent actions, or karma. Not only so, but every theory of the creation of the soul from nothing inevitably leads to fatalism and preordination, and instead of a merciful Father, places before us a hideous, cruel, and ever angry God to worship. And so far as the power of religion for good or evil is concerned, this theory of a created soul, leading to its corollaries of fatalism and predestination, is responsible for the horrible idea prevailing among Christians and Mohammedans that the heathen are the lawful victims of their swords, and for all the horrors that have followed and are following it still.

But an argument which the philosophers of the Nyāya school have always advanced in favour of reincarnation, and which to us seems conclusive, is this: Our experiences cannot be annihilated. Our actions (karma), though apparently disappearing, remain still unperceived (adrishtam), and reappear again in their effect as tendencies (pravrittis). Even little babies come with certain tendencies: fear of death, for example.

Now, if a tendency is the result of repeated actions, the tendencies with which we are born must be explained on that ground too. Evidently we could not have got them in this life; therefore we have to seek for their genesis in the past. Now, it is also evident that some of our tendencies are the effects of the self-conscious efforts peculiar to man; and if it is true that we are born with such tendencies, it rigorously follows that their causes were conscious efforts in the past—that is, we must have been on the same mental plane which we call the human plane before this present life.

So far as explaining the tendencies of the present life by past conscious efforts goes, the reincarnationists of India and the latest school of evolutionists are at one; the only difference is that the Hindus, being spiritual, explain them by the conscious efforts of individual souls, and the materialistic school of evolutionists, by hereditary physical transmission. The schools which hold to the theory of creation out of nothing are entirely out of court.

The issue has to be fought out between the reincarnationists, who hold that all experiences are stored up as tendencies in the subject of those experiences, the individual soul, and are transmitted by reincarnation of that unbroken individuality, and the materialists, who hold that the brain is the subject of all actions and accept the theory of transmission through cells.

Thus the doctrine of reincarnation assumes an infinite importance to our mind; for the fight between reincarnation and mere cellular transmission is, in reality, the fight between spirituality and materialism. If cellular transmission is the all-sufficient explanation, materialism is inevitable and there is no necessity for the theory of a soul. If it is not a sufficient explanation, the theory of an individual soul bringing into this life the experiences of the past is as absolutely true. There is no escape from the alternative, reincarnation or materialism. Which shall we accept?

BUDDHA'S MESSAGE TO THE WORLD

(Delivered in San Francisco, March 18, 1900)

BUDDHISM IS HISTORICALLY the most important religion—historically, not philo-sophically—because it was the most tremendous religious movement that the world ever saw, the most gigantic spiritual wave ever to burst upon human society. There is no civilization on which its effect has not been felt in some way or other.

The followers of Buddha were most enthusiastic and very missionary in spirit. They were the first among the adherents of the various religions not to remain content with the limited sphere of their mother church. They spread far and wide; they travelled east and west, north and south. They reached into darkest Tibet; they went into Persia, Asia Minor; they went into Russia, Poland, and many other countries of the Western world. They went into China, Korea, Japan; they went into Burma, Siam, the East Indies, and beyond. When Alexander the Great, through his military conquests, brought the Mediterranean world in contact with India, the wisdom of India at once found a channel through which to spread over vast portions of Asia and Europe. Buddhist priests went out teaching among the different nations, and as they taught, superstition and priestcraft began to vanish like mist before the sun.

To understand this movement properly you should know what conditions prevailed in India when Buddha was born, just as to understand Christianity you have to grasp the state of Jewish society at the time of Christ. It is necessary that you have an idea of Indian society six hundred years before the birth of Christ, by which time Indian civilization had already completed its growth.

When you study the civilization of India you find that it has died and revived several times; this is its peculiarity. Most races rise once and then decline for ever. There are two kinds of peoples: those who grow continually and those whose growth comes to an end. The peaceful nations, India and China, fall down, yet rise again. But the others, once they go down, do not come up; they die. Blessed are the peacemakers, for they shall enjoy the earth.

At the time Buddha was born, India was in need of a great spiritual leader, a prophet. There was already a most powerful body of priests. You will under-stand the situation better if you remember the history of the Jews—how they had two types of religious leaders: priests and prophets, the priests keeping the people in ignorance and grinding superstitions into their minds. The methods of worship the priests prescribed were only a means by which they could dominate the people. All through the Old Testament you find the prophets challenging the superstitions of the priests. The outcome of this fight was the triumph of the prophets and the defeat of the priests.

Priests believe that there is a God, but that this God can be approached and known only through them. People can enter the holy of holies only with the permission of the priests. You must pay them, worship them, place everything in their hands. Throughout the history of the world this priestly desire for power has asserted itself; this tremendous thirst for power, this tiger-like thirst, seems a part of human nature. The priests dominate you, lay down a thousand rules for you. They describe simple truths in roundabout ways. They tell you stories to support their own superior position. If you want to thrive in this life or go to heaven after death, you have to pass through their hands. You have to perform all kinds of ceremonies and rituals. All this has made life so complicated and has so confused the brain that if I give you plain words you will go home unsatisfied. You have become thoroughly befuddled. The less you understand, the better you feel! The prophets have been giving warnings against the priests and their superstitions and machinations; but the vast mass of people have not yet learnt to heed these warnings; they must be educated about this.

Men must have education. They speak of democracy, of the equality of all men, these days. But how will a man know he is equal with all? He must have a strong brain, a clear mind free of nonsensical ideas; he must pierce through the mass of superstitions encrusting his mind to the pure truth that is in his inmost self. Then he will know that all perfections, all powers, are already within himself; that these have not to be given him by others. The moment he realizes this truth he becomes free, he achieves equality. He also realizes that everyone else is just as perfect as he, and that he does not have to exercise any power—physical, mental, or moral—over his brother men. He abandons the idea that there was ever any man who was lower than himself. Then he can talk of equality—not until then.

Now, as I was telling you, among the Jews there was a continuous struggle between the priests and the prophets, and the priests sought to monopolize power and knowledge, till they themselves began to lose them and the chains they had put on the feet of the people were on their own feet. The masters always become slaves before long. The culmination of the struggle was the victory of Jesus of Nazareth. This triumph is the history of Christianity; Christ at last succeeded in overthrowing the mass of priestcraft. This great prophet killed the dragon of priestly selfishness, rescued from its clutches the jewel of truth, and gave it to all the world, so that whosoever desired to possess it would have absolute freedom to do so and would not have to wait on the pleasure of any priest or priests.

The Jews were never a very philosophical race; they had not the subtlety of the Indian brain nor did they have the Indian's psychic power. The priests in India, the brāhmins, possessed great intellectual and psychic power. It was they who began the spiritual development of India, and they accomplished wonderful things. But the time came when the free spirit of development that had at first actuated the brāhmins disappeared. They began to arrogate powers and privileges to themselves. If a brahmin killed a man he would not be punished. The brāhmin, by his very birth, is the lord of the universe. Even the most wicked brāhmin must be worshipped.

But while the priests were flourishing, there existed also the poet-prophets called sannyāsins. All Hindus, whatever their caste may be, must, if they want to attain freedom, give up the world and prepare for death. No more is the world to be of any interest to them. They must go out and become sannyāsins. The sannyāsins have nothing to do with the two thousand ceremonies that the priests have invented—sanctifying them with certain words, ten syllables, twenty syllables long, and so on! All these things are nonsense.

So these poet-prophets of ancient India repudiated the ways of the priests and declared the pure truth. They tried to break the power of the priests and they succeeded a little. But in two generations their disciples went back to the superstitious, roundabout ways of the priests and became priests themselves: "You can get truth only through us." Truth became crystallized again, and again prophets came to break the encrustations and free the truth, and so it went on. Yes, there must always be prophets in the world; otherwise humanity will perish.

You wonder why there have to be all these roundabout methods of the priests. Why can you not come directly to the truth? Are you ashamed of God's truth, that you have to hide it behind all kinds of intricate ceremonies and formulas? Are you ashamed of God, that you cannot confess His truth before the world? Do you call that being religious and spiritual? The priests are the only people fit for the truth! The masses are not fit for it! It must be diluted! Water it down a little!

Take the Sermon on the Mount and the Gītā: they are simplicity itself. Even the man in the street can understand them. How grand! In them you find the truth clearly and simply revealed. But no, the priests will not agree that truth can be found so directly. They speak of two thousand heavens and two thousand hells. If people follow their prescriptions they will go to heaven! If they do not obey the rules they will go to hell!

But people must know the truth. Some are afraid that if the full truth is given to all, it will hurt them. They should not be given the unqualified truth, they say. But the world is not much better off by compromising truth. How much worse can it be than it is already? Bring the truth out! If it is real, it will do good. When people protest and propose other methods, they only make apologies for priestcraft.

India was full of it in Buddha's day. Masses of people were debarred from all knowledge. If just a word of the Vedas entered the ears of a low-caste man, terrible punishment was visited upon him. The priests had made a secret of the Vedas—the Vedas, which contained the spiritual truths discovered by the ancient Hindus!

At last one man could bear it no more. He had the brain, the power, and the heart—a heart as infinite as the broad sky. He saw how the masses were being led by the priests and how the priests were glorying in their power, and he wanted to do something about it. He did not want any power over anyone, and he wanted to break the mental and spiritual bonds of men. His heart was large. The heart, many around us may have, and we also want to help others. But we do not have the brain; we do not know the ways and means by which help can be given. But this man had the brain to discover the means of breaking the bondage of souls. He learnt why men suffer and he found the way out of suffering. He was a man of accomplishment; he worked everything out. He taught one and all without distinction, and made them realize the peace of enlightenment. This was the man Buddha.

You know from Arnold's poem *The Light of Asia* how Buddha was born a prince and how the misery of the world struck him deeply; how, although brought up and living in the lap of luxury, he could not find comfort in his personal happiness and security; how he renounced the world, leaving his princess and new-born son behind; how he wandered searching for truth from teacher to teacher; and how he at last attained to enlightenment. You know about his long mission, his disciples, his organizations. You all know these things.

Buddha was the triumph in the struggle that had been going on between the priests and the prophets in India. One thing can be said for these Indian priests: they were not and never are intolerant of religion; they never have persecuted religion. Any man was allowed to preach against them—such was their catholicity. They never molested anyone for his religious views. But they suffered from the peculiar weaknesses of all priests: they sought power; they also promulgated rules and regulations and made religion unnecessarily complicated, and thereby undermined the strength of those who followed their religion.

Buddha cut through all these excrescences. He preached the most tremendous truths. He taught the very gist of the philosophy of the Vedas to one and all without distinction; he taught it to the world at large, because one of his great messages was the equality of man. Men are all equal. No concession there to anybody. Buddha was the great preacher of equality. Every man and woman has the same right to attain spirituality—that was his teaching. The difference between the priests and the other castes he abolished. Even the lowest were entitled to the highest attainments; he opened the door of Nirvāna to one and all. His teaching was bold even for India. No amount of preaching can ever shock the Indian soul; but it was hard for India to swallow Buddha's doctrine. How much harder it must be for you!

His doctrine was this: Why is there misery in our life? Because we are selfish. We desire things for ourselves—that is why there is misery. What is the way out? The giving up of the self. The self does not exist; the phenomenal world, all this that we perceive, is all that exists. There is nothing called soul underlying the cycle of life and death. There is a stream of thought, one thought following another in succession, each thought coming into existence and becoming non-existent at the same moment. That is all. There is no thinker of the thought, no soul. The body is changing all the time; so is mind, consciousness. The self therefore is a delusion. All selfishness comes of holding on to the self, to this illusory self. If we know the truth that there is no self, then we shall be happy and make others happy.

This was what Buddha taught. And he did not merely talk; he was ready to give up his own life for the world. He said, "If sacrificing an animal is good, sacrificing a man is better," and he offered himself as a sacrifice. He said: "This animal sacrifice is another superstition. God and soul are the two big superstitions. God is only a superstition invented by the priests. If there is a God, as these brāhmins preach, why is there so much misery in the world? He is just like me, a slave to the law of causation. If He is not bound by the law of causation, then why does He create? Such a God is not at all satisfactory. If there is a Ruler in heaven who rules the universe according to His sweet will and leaves us all here to die in misery—He never has the kindness to look at us for a moment. Our whole life is continuous suffering. But this is not sufficient punishment: after death we must go to places where we have other punishments. Yet we continually perform all kinds of rites and ceremonies to please this Creator of the world!"

Buddha said: "These ceremonials are all wrong. There is but one ideal in the world. Destroy all delusions; what is true will remain. As soon as the clouds are gone, the sun will shine." How is one to kill the self? Be perfectly unselfish; be ready to give up your life even for an ant. Give up all superstition; work not to please God, to get any reward, but work because you are seeking your own release by killing your self. Worship and prayer and all that—these are all nonsense. You all say, "I thank God"—but where does He live? You do not know and yet you are all going crazy because of your belief in God.

The Hindus can give up everything except their God. To deny God is to cut the very ground from under the feet of devotion. Devotion and God the Hindus must cling to. They can never relinquish these. And here, in the teaching of Buddha, are no God and no soul—simply work. What for? Not for the self, for the self is a delusion. We shall be free when this delusion has vanished. Very few are there in the world that can rise to that height and work for work's sake.

Yet the religion of Buddha spread fast. It was because of the marvellous love which, for the first time in the history of humanity, overflowed a large heart and devoted itself to the service not only of all men but of all living things—a love which did not care for anything except to find a way of release from suffering for all beings.

Man was loving God and had forgot all about his brother man. The man who in the name of God could give up his life could also turn around and kill his brother man in the name of the same God. That was the state of the world. Men would sacrifice their sons for the glory of God, would rob nations for the glory of God, would kill thousands of beings for the glory of God, would drench the earth with blood for the glory of God. Buddha was the first to turn their minds to the other God—man. It was man that was to be loved. Buddha set in motion the first wave of intense love for all men, the first wave of true, unadulterated wisdom, which, starting from India, gradually inundated country after country—north, south, east, west.

This teacher wanted to make truth shine as truth. No softening, no compromise, no pandering to the priests and the powerful kings. No bowing before superstitious traditions, however hoary; no respect for forms and books just because they came down from the distant past. He rejected all scriptures, all forms of religious practice. Even the very language, Sanskrit, in which religion had been traditionally taught in India, he rejected, so that his followers would not have any chance to imbibe the superstitions which were associated with it.

There is another way of looking at the truth we have been discussing: the Hindu way. We claim that Buddha's great doctrine of selflessness can be better understood if it is looked at in our way. In the Upanishads there was already the great doctrine of Ātman and Brahman. Ātman, the Self, is the same as Brahman, the Lord. This Self is all that is; It is the only Reality. Māyā, delusion, makes us see It as differentiated. There is one Self, not many. That one Self shines in various forms. Man is man's brother because all men are one. A man is not only my brother, say the Vedas, but he is myself. Hurting any part of the universe, I only hurt myself. I am the universe. It is a delusion to think that I am Mr. So-and-so.

The more you approach your Self, the more quickly delusion vanishes. The more all differences and divisions disappear, the more you realize all as the one Divinity. God exists, but He is not a man sitting upon a cloud. He is pure Spirit. Where does He reside? Nearer to you than your very self. He is the Soul. How can you perceive God as separate and different from yourself? When you think of Him as someone separate from yourself, you do not know Him. He is you yourself. That was the doctrine of the prophets of India.

It is selfishness to think that you are Mr. So-and-so and all the world is different from you. You believe that you are different from me. You do not take any thought of me. You go home and have your dinner and sleep. If I die you still eat, drink, and are merry. But you cannot really be happy when the rest of the world is suffering. We are all one. It is the delusion of separateness that is the root of misery. Nothing exists but the Self. There is nothing else.

Buddha's idea was that there was no God, but only man. He repudiated the mentality which underlay the prevalent ideas of God. He found they made men weak and superstitious. If God gives you everything you pray for, why then do you go out and work? God comes to those who work. God helps them that help themselves. An opposite idea of God weakens our nerves, softens our muscles, makes us dependent. Only the independent are happy; and the dependent are miserable. Man has infinite power within himself and he can realize it—he can realize himself as the one, infinite Self. It can be done; but you do not believe it. You pray to God and keep your powder dry all the time.

Buddha taught the opposite. Do not let men weep. Let them have none of this praying and all that. God is not keeping shop. With every breath you are praying to God. I am talking—that is a prayer. You are listening—that is a prayer. Is there ever any movement of yours, mental or physical, in which you do not make use of the infinite Divine Energy? It is all a constant prayer. If you call only a set of words prayer, you make prayer superficial. Such prayers are not much good; they can scarcely bear any real fruit. Is prayer a magic formula by repeating which, even if you do not work hard, you gain miraculous results? No. All have to work hard; all have to reach the depths of that Infinite Energy. Behind the poor, behind the rich, there is the same Infinite Energy. It is not true that while one man works hard, another by repeating a few words achieves the same results. This universe is a constant prayer. If you take prayer in this sense, I am with you. Words are not necessary. Better is silent prayer.

The vast majority of people do not understand the meaning of this doctrine. In India any compromise regarding the Self means that we have given power into the hands of the priests and have forgotten the great teachings of the prophets. Buddha knew this; so he brushed aside all the priestly doctrines and practices and made man stand on his own feet. It was necessary for him to go against the accustomed ways of the people; he had to bring about revolutionary changes. As a result this sacrificial religion passed away from India for ever and was never revived.

Buddhism apparently has passed away from India, but really it has not. There was an element of danger in the teaching of Buddha: it was a reforming religion. In order to bring about the tremendous spiritual change he did, he had to give many negative teachings. But if a religion emphasizes the negative side too much, it is in danger of eventual destruction. Never can a reforming sect survive if it is only reforming; the positive elements alone—the real impulse, that is, the principles—live on and on. After a reform has been brought about it is the positive side that should be emphasized; after the building is finished the scaffolding must be taken away.

It so happened in India that as time went on the followers of Buddha emphasized the negative aspect of his teachings too much and thereby caused the eventual downfall of their religion. The positive aspects of truth were suffocated by the forces of negation, and thus India repudiated the destructive tendencies that flourished in the name of Buddhism. That was the decree of the Indian national thought.

The negative ideas of Buddhism—that there is no God and no soul—died out. I can say that God is the only Being that exists; it is a very positive statement. He is the one Reality. When Buddha says there is no soul, I say, "Man, thou art one with the universe; thou art all things." How positive! The reformative element died out, but the formative element has lived through all time. Buddha taught kindness towards lower beings, and since then there has not been a sect in India that has not taught charity to all beings, even to animals. This kindness, this mercy, this charity—greater than any doctrine—are what Buddhism left to us.

The life of Buddha has an especial appeal. All my life I have been very fond of Buddha, but not of his doctrine. I have more veneration for that character than for any other—that boldness, that fearlessness, and that tremendous love. He was born for the good of men. Others may seek God, others may seek truth for themselves; he did not even care to know truth for himself. He sought truth because people were in misery. How to help them—that was his only concern. Throughout his life he never had a thought for himself. How can we ignorant, selfish, narrow-minded human beings ever understand the greatness of this man?

And consider his marvellous brain. No emotionalism. That giant brain never was superstitious. "Believe not because an old manuscript has been produced, because it has been handed down to you from your forefathers, because your friends want you to—but think for yourself; search out truth for yourself; realize it yourself. Then if you find it beneficial to one and all, give it to people." Soft-brained men, weak-minded, chicken-hearted, cannot find the truth. One has to be free and as broad as the sky. One has to have a mind that is crystal clear; only then can truth shine in it. We are so full of superstitions! Even in

your country, where you think you are highly educated, how full of narrow-
nesses and superstitions you are! Just think, with all your claims to civilization
in this country, on one occasion I was refused a chair to sit on, because I was
a Hindu!

Six hundred years before the birth of Christ, at the time when Buddha lived,
the people of India must have had wonderful education. Extremely free-minded
they must have been. Great masses followed him. Kings gave up their thrones;
queens gave up their thrones. People were able to appreciate and embrace his
teaching—so revolutionary, so different from what they had been taught by
the priests through the ages. Their minds must have been unusually free and
broad.

And consider his death. If he was great in life, he was also great in death.
He ate food offered to him by a member of a race similar to your American
Indians. Hindus do not touch these people because they eat indiscriminately.
He told his disciples: "Do not eat this food, but I cannot refuse it. Go to the
man and tell him he has done me one of the greatest services of my life: he
has released me from the body." An old man came and sat near him—he had
walked miles and miles to see the Master—and Buddha taught him. When
he found a disciple weeping, he reproved him, saying: "What is this? Is this
the result of all my teaching? Let there be no false bondage, no dependence on
me, no false glorification of this passing personality. The Buddha is not a person;
he is a state of realization. Work out your own salvation."

Even when dying he would not claim any distinction for himself. I worship
him for that. What you call Buddhas and Christs are only the names of certain
states of realization. Of all the teachers of the world, he was the one who
taught us most to be self-reliant, who freed us not only from the bondage of
our false selves but from dependence on the invisible Being or beings called
God or gods. He invited everyone to enter into that state of freedom which
he called Nirvāna. All must attain to it one day, and that attainment is the
complete fulfilment of man.

DISCIPLESHIP

(Delivered in San Francisco, March 29, 1900)

My subject is "Discipleship." I do not know how you will take what I have to say. It will be rather difficult for you to accept it: the idea of teacher and disciple in this country differs so much from that in ours. An old proverb of India comes to my mind: "There are hundreds of thousands of teachers, but it is hard to find one disciple." It seems to be true. The one important thing in the attainment of spirituality is the attitude of the pupil. When the right attitude is there, illumination comes easily.

What does the disciple need in order to receive the truth? The great sages say that to attain truth takes but the twinkling of an eye: it is just a question of knowing. The dream breaks—how long does it take? In a second the dream is gone. When the illusion vanishes, how long does it take? Just the twinkling of an eye. When I know the truth, nothing happens except that the falsehood vanishes away. I took the rope for a snake, and now I see it is a rope. It is only a question of half a second and the whole thing is done. Thou art That; Thou art Reality—how long does it take to know this? If we are God and always have been so, not to know this is most astonishing. To know this is the only natural thing. It should not take ages to find out what we have always been and what we now are.

Yet it seems difficult to realize this self-evident truth. Ages and ages pass before we begin to catch a faint glimpse of it. God is life; God is truth—we write about this; we feel in our inmost heart that this is so, that everything else but God is nothing—here today, gone tomorrow. And yet most of us remain the same all through life. We cling to untruth and we turn our backs upon truth. We do not want to attain truth. We do not want anyone to break our dream. You see, teachers are not wanted. Who wants to learn? But if anyone wants to realize the truth and overcome illusion, if he wants to receive the truth from a teacher, he must be a true disciple.

It is not easy to be a disciple: great preparations are necessary; many conditions have to be fulfilled. Four principal conditions are laid down by the Vedāntists.

The first condition is that the student who wants to know the truth must give up all desires for gain in this world or in the life to come.

The truth is not what we see. We do not see the truth as long as any desire creeps into the mind. God is true and the world is not true. So long as there is in the heart the least desire for the world, truth will not come. Let the world fall to ruin before my eyes—I do not care. So with the next life: I do not care to go to heaven. What is heaven? Only the continuation of this earth. We would be better off and the little foolish dreams we are dreaming would break sooner if there were no heaven, no continuation of this silly life on earth. By going to heaven we only prolong the miserable illusions.

What do you gain in heaven? You become gods, drink nectar, and get rheumatism! There is less misery there than on earth, but also less truth. The very rich can understand truth much less than the poorer people. "It is easier for a camel to go through the eye of a needle than for a rich man to enter into the kingdom of God." The rich man has no time to think of anything beyond his wealth and power, his comforts and indulgences. The rich rarely become religious. Why? Because they think if they become religious they will have no more fun in life. In the same way, there is very little chance to become spiritual in heaven. There is too much comfort and enjoyment there; the dwellers in heaven are disinclined to give up their fun.

They say there will be no more weeping in heaven. I do not trust the man who never weeps; he has a big block of granite where his heart should be. It is evident that the heavenly people have not much sympathy. There are vast masses of them over there, and we are miserable creatures suffering in this horrible place. They could pull us all out of it, but they do not. They do not weep. There is no sorrow or misery there; therefore they do not care for anyone's misery. They drink their nectar; dances go on—beautiful wives and all that.

Going beyond these things, the disciple should say: "I do not care for anything in this life nor for all the heavens that have ever existed. I do not care to go to any of them. I do not want the sense life in any form—this identification of myself with the body. As I feel now, I am this body—this mass of flesh; this is what I feel I am. But I refuse to accept that as the final truth."

The world and the heavens, all these are bound up with the senses. You do not care for the world if you do not have any senses. Heaven also is in the world. Earth, heaven, and all that is between have but one name: the world. Therefore the disciple, knowing the past and the present and thinking of the future, knowing what prosperity means, what happiness means, gives up all these and seeks to know truth and truth alone. This is the first condition.

The second condition is that the disciple must be able to control the internal and the external senses and must be established in several other spiritual virtues.

The external senses are the visible organs situated in different parts of the body; the internal senses are intangible. We have the external eyes, ears, nose, and so on, and we have the corresponding internal senses. We are continually at the beck and call of both these groups of senses. Corresponding to the senses are sense-objects. If any sense-objects are near by, the senses compel us to perceive them; we have no choice or independence. There is the big nose. A little fragrance is there: I have to smell it. If there were a bad odour, I would say to myself, "Do not smell it." But the nose says, "Smell," and I smell it. Just think what we have become! We have bound ourselves. I have eyes. Anything going on, good or bad, I must see. It is the same with hearing. If anyone speaks unpleasantly to me, I must hear it. My sense of hearing compels me to do so, and how miserable I feel! Curse or praise man has got to hear. I have seen many deaf people who do not usually hear; but anything about themselves they always hear!

All these senses, external and internal, must be under the disciple's control.

By hard practice he has to arrive at the stage where he can assert himself against the senses, against the commands of his mind. He must be able to say to his mind, "You are mine; I order you, do not see or hear anything," and the mind will not see or hear anything—no form or sound will react on the mind. In that state the mind has become free of the domination of the senses, has become separated from them. No longer is it attached to the senses and the body; external things cannot order the mind now; the mind refuses to attach itself to them. There is a beautiful fragrance. The disciple says to the mind, "Do not smell," and the mind does not perceive the fragrance. When you have arrived at that point, you are just beginning to be a disciple. That is why when everybody says, "I know the truth," I say, "If you know the truth, you must have self-control, and if you have control of yourself, show it by controlling the organs."

Next, the mind must be made to quiet down. It is rushing about. Just as I sit down to meditate, all the vilest ideas in the world come up. The whole thing is nauseating. Why should the mind think thoughts I do not want it to think? I am as it were a slave to the mind. No spiritual knowledge is possible so long as the mind is restless and out of control. The disciple has to learn to control the mind. Yes, it is the function of the mind to think. But it must not think if the disciple does not want it to; it must stop thinking when he commands it to. To qualify as a disciple, this state of the mind is very necessary.

Also, the disciple must have great power of endurance. You will find the mind behaving well when everything goes right with you and life seems comfortable. But if something goes wrong, your mind loses its balance. That is not good. Bear all evil and misery without the slightest murmur, without one thought of unhappiness, resistance, remedy, or retaliation. That is true endurance, and that you must acquire.

Good and evil there always are in the world. Many forget there is any evil—at least they try to forget—and when evil comes upon them they are overwhelmed by it and feel bitter. There are others who deny that there is any evil at all and consider everything good. That also is a weakness; that also proceeds from a fear of evil. If something is evil-smelling, why sprinkle it with rose-water and call it fragrant? Yes, there are good and evil in the world. God has put evil in the world. But you do not have to whitewash it. Why there is evil is none of your business. Have faith and keep quiet.

When my Master, Śri Ramakrishna, fell ill, a brāhmin suggested to him that he apply his tremendous mental power to cure himself; he said that if my Master would only concentrate his mind on the diseased part of the body, it would heal. Śri Ramakrishna answered, "What! Bring down the mind that I've given to God to this little body!" He refused to think of body and illness. His mind was continually conscious of God; it was dedicated to Him utterly. He would not use it for any other purpose.

This craving for health, wealth, long life, and the like—the so-called good—is nothing but delusion. To devote the mind to them in order to secure them only strengthens the delusion. We have these dreams and illusions in life, and we want to have more of them in the life to come, in heaven. More and more illusion!

Resist not evil. Face it. You are higher than evil. There is this misery in the world; it has to be suffered by someone. You cannot act without creating evil for somebody. And when you seek worldly good you only avoid an evil which must be suffered by somebody else. Everyone is trying to put it on someone else's shoulders. The disciple says: "Let the miseries of the world come to me; I shall endure them all. Let others go free."

Remember the man on the Cross? He could have brought legions of angels to win him the victory. But he did not resist; he blessed those who crucified him. He endured every humiliation and suffering. He took the burden of all upon himself: "Come unto me, all ye that labour and are heavy laden, and I will give you rest." Such is true endurance. How very high he was above this life, so high that we cannot understand it, we slaves! No sooner does a man slap me in the face than my hand hits back: bang, it goes! How can I understand the great-ness and blessedness of the Crucified One? How can I see his glory?

But I will not drag the ideal down. I feel I am the body, resisting evil. If I get a headache, I go all over the world to have it cured. I drink two thousand bottles of medicine. How can I understand these marvellous minds? I can see the ideal—but how much of that ideal? None of this consciousness of the body, of the little self, of its pleasures and pains, its hurts and comforts—none of these can touch that ideal. By thinking only of the Spirit and keeping the mind out of matter all the time, I can catch a glimpse of that ideal. Material thought and forms of the sense-world have no place in that ideal. Put them away and fix the mind upon the Spirit. Forget your life and death, your pains and pleasures, your name and fame, and realize that you are neither body nor mind, but pure Spirit.

When I say "I," I mean this Spirit. Close your eyes and see what picture appears when you think of your "I." Is it the picture of your body that comes, or of your mental nature? If so, you have not realized your true "I" yet. The time will come, however, when as soon as you say "I" you will see the universe, the Infinite Being. Then you will have realized your true Self and found that you are the Infinite. That is the truth. You are the Spirit; you are not matter. There is such a thing as illusion; on account of it one thing is taken for another —matter is taken for Spirit, the body for the Soul. That is the tremendous illusion. It has to go.

The next qualification is that the disciple must have faith in the guru, the teacher. In the West the teacher simply gives intellectual knowledge; that is all. In India the relationship with the teacher is the greatest in life. My guru is my nearest and dearest relative in life; next, my mother; then my father. My first reverence is to my guru. If my father says, "Do this," and my guru says, "Do not do this," I do not do it. The guru frees my soul. The father and mother give me this body, but the guru gives me rebirth in the Spirit.

We have certain peculiar beliefs. One of these is that there are some souls, a few exceptional ones, who are already free and who are born here for the good of the world, to help the world. They are free already. They do not care for their own salvation; they want to help others. They do not require to be taught anything. From their childhood they know everything; they may speak the highest truth even when they are mere babies.

Upon these free souls depends the spiritual growth of mankind. They are like the first lamps from which other lamps are lighted. True, the light is in everyone; but in most men it is hidden. The great souls are shining lamps from their very birth. Those who come in contact with them get, as it were, their own lamps lighted. By this the first lamps do not lose anything, yet they communicate their light to other lamps. A million lamps are lighted, but the first lamps go on shining with undiminished light. One such first lamp is the guru, and the lamp lighted from it is the disciple. The second in turn becomes a guru, and so on. Those great ones whom you call Incarnations of God are mighty spiritual giants. They come and set in motion a tremendous spiritual current by transmitting their power to their immediate disciples, and through them to generation after generation of disciples.

A bishop in the Christian Church, by the laying on of hands, claims to transmit the power which he is supposed to have received from the preceding bishops. The bishop says that Jesus Christ transmitted his power to his immediate disciples, and they to others, and that that is how Christ's power has come to him. We hold that every one of us, not bishops only, ought to have such power. There is no reason why each of you cannot be a vehicle of the mighty current of spirituality.

But first you must find a teacher, a true teacher, and you must remember that he is not just a man. You may get a teacher in the body, but the real teacher is not in the body. He is not the physical man; he is not as he appears to your eyes. It may be that the teacher will come to you as a human being, and you will receive the power from him. Sometimes he will come in a dream and transmit the spiritual ideal to you. The power of the teacher may come to us in many ways. But for us ordinary mortals a human teacher must come, and our preparation must go on till he comes.

We attend lectures and read books, argue and reason about God and soul, religion and salvation. This is not spirituality, because spirituality does not exist in books or in theories or in philosophies. It is not in learning or reasoning, but in actual inner growth. Even parrots can learn things by heart and repeat them. If you become learned, what of it? Asses can carry whole libraries. So when real light comes there will be no more of this learning from books—no book-learning. The man who cannot write even his own name can be perfectly religious, and the man with all the libraries of the world in his head may fail to be so. Learning is not a condition of spiritual growth; scholarship is not a condition. The touch of the guru, the transmittal of spiritual energy, will quicken your heart. Then will begin the growth. That is the real baptism by fire. No more stopping; you go on and on.

Some years ago one of your Christian teachers, a friend of mine, said, "You believe in Christ?" "Yes," I answered, "but perhaps with a little more reverence." "Then why don't you be baptised?" How could I be baptised? By whom? Where is the man who can give true baptism? What is baptism? Is it sprinkling some water over you or dipping you in water, while muttering formulas?

Baptism is the direct introduction into the life of the Spirit. If you receive the real baptism, you know you are not the body but the Spirit. Give me that baptism if you can, or else you are not a Christian teacher. Even after the so-called baptism which you received, you have remained the same. What is the sense of merely saying you have been baptised in the name of Christ? Mere talk —only disturbing the world with your foolishness! "Ever steeped in the darkness of ignorance, yet considering themselves wise and learned, fools go round and round, staggering to and fro like the blind led by the blind." Therefore do not say you are Christians, do not brag about baptism and things of that sort.

Of course there is true baptism. There was baptism in the beginning when Christ came to the earth and taught. The illumined souls, the great ones that come to earth from time to time, have the power to reveal the supernal vision to us. This is true baptism. You see, before the forms and ceremonies of any religion come into being, there exists in it the germ of universal truth. In the course of time this truth becomes forgotten; it becomes strangled, as it were, by forms and ceremonies. The forms alone remain—we find only the casket with the spirit gone. You have the form of baptism, but few can evoke the living spirit of baptism. The form will not suffice. If we want to gain the living knowledge of the living truth, we have to be truly initiated into it. That is the ideal.

The guru must teach me and lead me into light, make me a link in that chain of which he himself is a link. The man in the street cannot claim to be a guru. The guru must be a man who has known, has actually realized the Divine Truth, has perceived himself as the Spirit. A mere talker cannot be a guru. A talkative fool like me can talk much, but cannot be a guru. A true guru will tell the disciple, "Go and sin no more," and no more can he sin—no more has the person the power to sin.

I have seen such men in this life. I have read the Bible and all such books; they are wonderful. But the living power you cannot find in books. The power that can transform life in a moment can be found only in living illumined souls, those shining lights who appear among us from time to time. They alone are fit to be gurus. You and I are only hollow talkers, not teachers. We are disturbing the world by talking, making bad vibrations. Let us hope and pray and struggle on, and the day will come when we shall arrive at the truth, and we shall not have to speak.

"The teacher was a boy of sixteen; he taught a man of eighty. Silence was the method of the teacher, and the doubts of the disciple vanished for ever." That is the guru. Just think: if you find such a man, what faith and love you ought to have for that person! Why, he is God Himself, nothing less than that. That is why Christ's disciples worshipped him as God. The disciple must worship the guru as God Himself. All a man can know is the living God, God as embodied in man, until he himself has realized God. How else would he know God?

Here is a man in America, born nineteen hundred years after Christ, who does not even belong to the same race as Christ, the Jewish race. He has not seen Jesus or his family. He says: "Jesus was God. If you do not believe it, you will go to hell." We can understand how the disciples believed it—that Christ was God; he was their guru and they must have believed he was God. But what has this American got to do with the man born nineteen hundred years ago? This young man tells me that I do not believe in Jesus and therefore I shall have to go to hell. What does he know of Jesus? He is fit for a lunatic asylum. This kind of belief won't do. He will have to find his guru.

Jesus may be born again, may come to you. Then, if you worship him as God, you are all right. We must all wait till the guru comes, and the guru must be worshipped as God. He is God; he is nothing less than that. As you look at him, the guru gradually melts away—and what is left? The picture of the guru gives place to God Himself. The guru is the bright mask which God wears in order to come to us. As we look steadily on him, gradually the mask falls off and God is revealed.

"I bow to the guru, who is the embodiment of the Bliss Divine, the personification of the highest Knowledge, and the giver of the greatest beatitude; who is pure, perfect, one and without a second, eternal, beyond pleasure and pain, beyond all thought and all qualification, transcendental." Such is in reality the guru. No wonder the disciple looks upon him as God Himself and trusts him, reveres him, obeys him, follows him unquestioningly. This is the relation between the guru and the disciple.

The next condition the disciple must fulfil is to conceive an extreme desire to be free.

We are like moths, plunging into the flaming fire of the senses, though fully knowing that it will burn us. Sense enjoyment only enhances our desire. Desire is never satiated by enjoyment; enjoyment only increases desire, as butter fed into fire increases the fire. Desire is increased by desire. Knowing all this, people still plunge into it all the time. Life after life they have been going after the objects of desire, suffering extremely in consequence; yet they cannot give up desire. Even religion, which should rescue them from this terrible bondage to desire, they have made a means of satisfying desire. Rarely do they ask God to free them from bondage to the body and senses, from slavery to desire. Instead they pray to Him for health and prosperity, for long life: "O God, cure my headache, give me some money or something!" The circle of vision has become so narrow, so degraded, so beastly, so animal! None is desiring anything beyond this body. Oh, the terrible degradation, the terrible misery of it! Of what little consequence are the flesh, the five senses, the stomach!

What is the world but a combination of stomach and sex? Look at the millions of men and women—that is what they are living for. Take these away from them and they will find their life empty, meaningless, and intolerable. Such are we—and such is our mind. It is continually hankering for ways and means to satisfy the hunger of the stomach and sex. All the time this is going on. There is also endless suffering. These desires of the body bring only momentary satisfaction and endless suffering. It is like drinking a cup of which the surface layer is nectar, while underneath all is poison. But we still hanker for all these things.

What can be done? Renunciation of the senses and of desire is the only way out of this misery. If you want to be spiritual, you must renounce. This is the real test. Give up the world—this nonsense of the senses. There is only one real desire: to know what is true, to be spiritual. No more of materialism, no more of this egoism. I must become spiritual. Strong, intense, must be the desire.

If a man's hands and feet were so tied that he could not move, and then if a burning piece of charcoal were placed on his body, he would struggle with all his power to throw it off. When I shall have that sort of extreme desire, that restless struggle to throw off this burning world, then the time will have come for me to glimpse the Divine Truth.

Look at me. If I lose my little pocketbook with two or three dollars in it, I go twenty times into the house to find that pocketbook. The anxiety, the worry, and the struggle! If one of you curses me, I remember it twenty years; I cannot forgive and forget it. For the little things of the senses I can struggle like that. Who is there that struggles for God that way? "Children forget everything in their play. The young are mad after the enjoyment of the senses; they do not care for anything else. The old are brooding over their past misdeeds." They are thinking of their past enjoyments—old men who cannot have any enjoyment. Chewing the cud—that is the best they can do. None crave for the Lord in the same intense spirit in which they crave for the things of the senses.

They all say that God is the Truth, the only thing that really exists; that Spirit alone is, not matter. Yet the things they seek of God are rarely Spirit. They ask always for material things. In their prayers Spirit is not separated from matter. Degradation—that is what religion has turned out to be. The whole thing is becoming a sham; and the years are rolling on and nothing spiritual is being attained. But man should hunger for one thing alone, the Spirit, because Spirit alone is real. That is the ideal. If you cannot attain it now, say, "I cannot do it; that is the ideal, I know, but I cannot follow it yet." But that is not what you do. You degrade religion to your low level and seek matter in the name of Spirit. You are all atheists. You do not believe in anything except the senses. "So-and-so said such-and-such a thing—there may be something to it. Let us try it out and have the fun. Possibly some benefit will come; possibly my broken leg will get straight."

Miserable are the diseased people; they are great worshippers of the Lord, for they hope that if they pray to Him He will heal them. Not that that is altogether bad—if such prayers are honest and if they remember that that is not religion. Śrī Krishna says in the Gītā: "Four classes of people worship Me: the distressed, the seeker of material things, the inquirer, and the knower of Truth." People who are in distress approach God for relief. If they are ill they worship Him to be healed; if they lose their wealth they pray to Him to get it back. There are other people who ask Him for all kinds of things, because they are full of desires—for name, fame, wealth, position, and so on. They will say: "O Virgin Mary, I will make an offering to you if I get what I want. If you are successful in granting my prayer, I will worship God and give you a part of everything." Men not so material as that, but still with no faith in God, feel inclined to know about Him. They study philosophies, read scriptures, listen to lectures, and so on. They are the inquirers. The last class are those who worship God and know Him. All these four classes of people are good, not bad. All of them worship Him.

But we are trying to be disciples. Our sole concern is to know the highest Truth. Our goal is the loftiest. We have said big words to ourselves—absolute realization and all that. Let us measure up to the words. Let us worship the Spirit in

Spirit, standing on Spirit. Let the foundation be Spirit; the middle, Spirit; the culmination, Spirit. There will be no world anywhere. Let it go and whirl into space—who cares? Stand thou upon the Spirit! That is the goal. We know we cannot reach it yet. Never mind. Do not despair, and do not drag the ideal down. The important thing is how much less you think of the body, of yourself, as matter, as dead, dull, insentient matter; how much more you think of yourself as shining, immortal Being. The more you think of yourself as shining, immortal Spirit, the more eager you will be to be absolutely free of matter, body, and senses. This is the intense desire to be free.

The fourth and last condition of discipleship is the discrimination of the Real from the unreal. There is only one thing that is real: God. All the time the mind must be drawn to Him, dedicated to Him. God exists; nothing else exists. Everything else comes and goes. Any desire for the world is illusion, because the world is unreal. More and more the mind must become conscious of God alone, until everything else appears as it really is: unreal.

These are the four conditions which one who wants to be a disciple must fulfil. Without fulfilling them he will not be able to come in contact with a true guru. And even if he is fortunate enough to find one, he will not be quickened by the power that the guru may transmit. There cannot be any compromising of these conditions. With the fulfilment of these conditions—with all these preparations—the lotus of the disciple's heart will open and the bee will come. Then the disciple knows that the real guru was within the body, within himself. He unfolds. He realizes the Spirit. He crosses the ocean of life, goes beyond. He crosses this terrible ocean, and in mercy, without a thought of gain or praise, he in his turn helps others to cross.

WORK AND ITS SECRET

(Delivered at Los Angeles, January 4, 1900)

ONE OF THE GREATEST lessons I have learnt in my life is to pay as much attention to the means of work as to its end. He was a great man from whom I learnt it, and his own life was a practical demonstration of this great principle. I have always been learning great lessons from that one principle; and it appears to me that all the secret of success is there: to pay as much attention to the means as to the end.

Our great defect in life is that we are too much drawn to the ideal; the goal is so much more enchanting, so much more alluring, so much bigger in our mental horizon, that we lose sight of the details altogether. But whenever failure comes, if we analyse it critically, in ninety-nine per cent of cases we shall find that it was because we did not pay attention to the means. Proper attention to the finishing, strengthening, of the means is what we need. With the means all right, the end must come. We forget that it is the cause that produces the effect; the effect cannot come by itself; and unless the causes are exact, proper, and powerful, the effect will not be produced. Once the ideal is chosen and the means determined, we may almost let go the ideal; because we are sure it will be there when the means are perfected. When the cause is there, there is no more difficulty about the effect; the effect is bound to come. If we take care of the cause, the effect will take care of itself. The realization of the ideal is the effect. The means are the cause. Attention to the means, therefore, is the great secret of work. We also read this in the Gītā and learn that we have to work, constantly work with all our power, put our whole mind in the work, whatever it be, that we are doing. At the same time we must not be attached; that is to say, we must not be drawn away from the work by anything else; still, we must be able to quit the work whenever we like.

If we examine our own lives, we find that the greatest cause of sorrow is this: we take up something and put our whole energy into it; perhaps it is a failure—and yet we cannot give it up. We know that it is hurting us, that any further clinging to it will simply bring misery upon us; still we cannot tear ourselves away from it. A bee came to sip honey, but its feet stuck to the honey-pot and it could not get away. Again and again we find ourselves in that state. That is the whole story of life. Why are we here? We came here to sip the honey, and we find our hands and feet sticking to it. We are caught though we came to catch. We came to enjoy; we are being enjoyed. We came to rule; we are being ruled. We came to work; we are being worked. All the time we find that. And this is seen in every detail of our life. We are being worked upon by other minds, though we are always struggling to work

802

on those minds. We want to enjoy the pleasures of life, and they eat into our vitals. We want to get everything from nature, but we find in the long run that nature takes everything from us—depletes us and casts us aside.

Had it not been for this, life would have been all sunshine. Never mind! With all its failures and successes, with all its joys and sorrows, life can still be one succession of sunshine if only we are not caught.

That is the one cause of misery: we are attached, we are being caught. Therefore says the Gītā: Work constantly; work but be not attached, be not caught. Reserve unto yourself the power of detaching yourself from everything, however beloved, however much the soul might yearn for it; no matter how great the pangs of misery you would feel if you were going to leave it, still reserve the power of leaving it whenever you want. The weak have no place here, in this life or in any other life. Weakness leads to slavery. Weakness leads to all kinds of misery, physical and mental. Weakness is death. There are hundreds of thousands of microbes surrounding us, but they cannot harm us unless we become weak, until the body is ready and predisposed to receive them. There may be a million microbes of misery floating about us. Never mind! They dare not approach us; they have no power to get a hold on us until the mind is weakened. This is the great fact: strength is life; weakness is death. Strength is felicity, life eternal, immortal; weakness is constant strain and misery; weakness is death.

Attachment is the source of all our pleasures now. We are attached to our friends, to our relatives; we are attached to our intellectual and spiritual work; we are attached to external objects; and so we get pleasure from them. What, again, brings misery but this very attachment? We have to detach ourselves to earn joy. If only we had the power to detach ourselves at will, there would not be any misery. That man alone will be able to get the best of nature who, having the power to attach himself to a thing with all his energy, has also the power to detach himself when he should do so. But it is difficult to cultivate an equal power of attachment and detachment. There are men who are never attracted by anything: they can never love; they are hard-hearted and apathetic; and they escape most of the miseries of life. But a wall never feels misery; a wall never loves, is never hurt; yet it is a wall, after all. Surely it is better to be attached and caught than to be a wall. Therefore the man who never loves, who is hard and stony, escaping most of the miseries of life, escapes also its joys. We do not want that. That is weakness; that is death. That soul has not been awakened that never feels attachment, never feels misery; that is a callous state. We do not want that.

At the same time, not only do we want this mighty power of love, this mighty power of attachment, the power of throwing our whole soul upon a single object, losing ourselves and letting ourselves be annihilated, as it were, for other souls, which is the power of the gods, but we want to be higher even than the gods. The perfect man can focus his whole soul upon that one point of love; yet he is unattached. How does this come about? There is another secret to learn.

The beggar is never happy. The beggar only gets a dole, with pity and scorn behind it—at least with the thought behind it that the beggar is a low object. He never really enjoys what he gets.

We are all beggars. Whatever we do, we want a return. We are all traders. We are traders in life, we are traders in virtue, we are traders in religion. And alas! we are also traders in love.

If you come to trade, if it is a question of give-and-take, if it is a question of buy-and-sell, abide by the laws of buying and selling. There is a bad time and there is a good time; there is a rise and there is a fall in prices; always expect the blow to come. It is like looking in the mirror. Your face is reflected: you make a grimace—there is one in the mirror; if you laugh, the mirror laughs. This is buying and selling, giving and taking.

We get caught. How? Not by what we give, but by what we expect. We get misery in return for our love, not from the fact that we love, but from the fact that we want love in return. There is no misery where there is no want. Desire, want, is the father of all misery. Desires are bound by the laws of success and failure. Desires must bring misery.

The great secret of true success, of true happiness, then, is this: the man who asks for no return, the perfectly unselfish man, is the most successful. It seems to be a paradox. Do we not know that every man who is unselfish in life gets cheated, gets hurt? Yes, apparently he does. Christ was unselfish, and yet he was crucified. True; but we also know that his unselfishness is the reason, the cause, of a great victory: the crowning of millions upon millions of lives with the blessing of true success.

Ask nothing; want nothing in return. Give what you have to give; it will come back to you—but do not think of that now. It will come back multiplied a thousandfold, but the attention must not be on that. Yet have the power to give; give, and let it end there. Learn that the whole of life is giving, that nature will force you to give; so give willingly. Sooner or later you must give up. You come into the world to accumulate. With clenched hands you want to take; but nature puts a hand on your throat and makes them open. Whether you will or no, you have to give. The moment you say, "I will not," the blow comes; you are hurt. None is there who will not be compelled, in the long run, to give up everything; and the more one struggles against this law, the more miserable one feels. It is because we dare not give, because we are not resigned enough to accede to this grand demand of nature, that we are miserable. The forest is gone, but we get heat in return. The sun takes up water from the ocean, to return it in showers. You are a machine for taking and giving: you take in order to give. Ask, therefore, nothing in return; but the more you give, the more will come to you. The quicker you can empty the air out of this room, the quicker it will be filled up by fresh air; and if you close all the doors and every aperture, that which is within will remain, but that which is outside will never come in, and that which is within will stagnate, degenerate, and become poisoned. A river is continually emptying itself into the ocean and is continually filling up again. Bar not the exit into the ocean. The moment you do that, death seizes you.

Be therefore not a beggar; be unattached. This is the most difficult task in life. We do not calculate the dangers on the path. Even by intellectually recognizing the difficulties, we really do not know them until we feel them. From a distance we may get a general view of a park: well, what of that? We feel and really know it when we are in it. Even if our every attempt is a failure and we bleed and are torn asunder, yet through all this we have to preserve our heart; we must assert our godhead in the midst of all these difficulties. Nature wants us to react, to return blow for blow, cheating for cheating, lie for lie, to hit back with all our might. It requires a super-divine power not to hit back, to keep control, to be unattached.

Every day we renew our determination to be unattached. We cast our eyes back and look at the past objects of our love and attachment, and feel how every one of them made us miserable. We went down into the depths of despondency because of our love. We found ourselves mere slaves in the hands of others; we were dragged down and down. And we make a fresh determination: "Henceforth I will be master of myself; henceforth I will have control over myself." But the time comes and it is the same story once more. Again the soul is caught and cannot get out. The bird is in a net, struggling and fluttering. This is our life.

I know the difficulties. They are tremendous; and ninety per cent of us become discouraged and lose heart, and in the end often become pessimists and cease to believe in sincerity, love, and all that is grand and noble. So we find that men who in the freshness of their lives have been forgiving, kind, simple, and guileless become in old age lying masks of men. Their minds are a mass of intricacy. Their lives exhibit a good deal of prudence, perhaps: they are not hot-headed; they do not speak out. But it would be better for them to speak out; their hearts are dead and therefore they do not do so. They do not curse or become angry; but it would be better for them to be able to be angry, a thousand times better to be able to curse. They cannot. There is death in the heart, for cold hands have seized upon it and it can no more act, even to utter a curse, even to use a harsh word.

All this we have to avoid. Therefore I say we require super-divine power. Superhuman power is not enough. Super-divine strength is the thing necessary, the one way out. By it alone can we pass through all these intricacies, through these showers of miseries, unscathed; we may be cut to pieces, torn asunder, yet our hearts must grow nobler and nobler all the time.

It is very difficult; but we can overcome the difficulty by constant practice. We must learn that nothing can happen to us unless we make ourselves susceptible to it. As I have just said, no disease can come to me until the body is ready; it does not depend alone on the germs, but upon a certain predisposition which is already in the body. We get only that for which we are fitted. Let us give up our pride and understand this: that misery never is undeserved. There never has been a blow undeserved; there never has been an evil for which I did not pave the way with my own hands. We ought to know that. Analyse yourselves and you will find that every blow you have received came to you because you prepared yourselves for it. You did half and the external world did the other half: that is how the blow came. That will sober us down. At the same time, from this very analysis will come a note of hope, and the note of hope is this: "I have no control over the external world; but that which is in me and nearer unto me, my own world, is under my control. If the two together are required to make a failure, if the two together are necessary to give me a blow, I will not contribute the one which is in my control—and how then can the blow come? If I get real control of myself, the blow will never come."

From our childhood, all the time we have been trying to lay the blame upon something outside ourselves. We are always standing up to set right other people, and not ourselves. If we are miserable, we say, "Oh, the world is a devil's world." We curse others and say, "What ungrateful fools!" But why should we be in such a world if we really are so good? If this is a devil's world, we must be devils also; why else should we be here? "Oh, the people of the world are so selfish!" True enough; but why should we be found in that company if we are better? Just think of that.

We get only what we deserve. It is a lie to say that the world is bad and we are good. It can never be so. It is a terrible lie we tell ourselves.

This is the great lesson to learn: be determined not to curse anything outside, not to lay the blame upon anyone outside, but be a man, stand up, lay the blame on yourself. You will find that that is always right. Get hold of yourself.

Is it not a shame that at one moment we talk of our manhood, of our being gods, of our being able to know everything, do everything, of our being blameless, spotless, the most unselfish people in the world—and the next moment a little stone hurts us, a little anger from a little Jack wounds us, any fool in the street makes us—these "gods"—miserable! Could this happen if we were really such gods? Is it true that the world is to blame? Could God, who is the purest and the noblest of souls, be made miserable by any of our tricks? If you are really so unselfish, you are like God. How can the world hurt you? You will go through the seventh hell unscathed, untouched. But the very fact that you complain and want to lay the blame upon the external world shows that you feel the external world; the very fact that you feel, shows that you are not what you claim to be. You only make your offence greater by heaping misery upon misery, by imagining that the external world is hurting you, and crying out: "Oh, this devil's world! This man hurts me; that man hurts me!" and so forth. It is adding lies to misery.

We have to take care of ourselves—that much we can do—and give up minding others for a time. Let us perfect the means; the end will take care of itself. For the world can be good and pure only if our lives are good and pure. It is an effect, and we are the means. Therefore let us purify ourselves. Let us make ourselves perfect.

THE POWERS OF THE MIND

(Delivered at Los Angeles, January 8, 1900)

ALL OVER THE WORLD there has been a belief in the supernatural, throughout the ages. All of us have heard of extraordinary happenings, and many of us have had some personal experience of them. I should like to introduce the subject by telling you certain facts which have come within my own experience.

I once heard of a man who, if anyone went to him with questions in his mind, would answer them immediately; and I was also informed that he foretold events. I was curious and went to see him with a few friends. Each one of us had something in his mind to ask; and to avoid mistakes, each of us wrote down his question and put it in his pocket. As soon as the man saw us, he repeated our questions and gave the answers to them. Then he wrote something on a piece of paper, which he folded up and asked me to sign on the back, and said: "Don't look at it; put it in your pocket. This will be your next question; and here is the answer." And so to each one of us. He next told us about some events that would happen to us in the future. Then he said, "Now think of a word or a sentence from any language you like." I thought of a long sentence from Sanskrit, a language of which he was entirely ignorant. "Now take out the paper from your pocket," he said. The Sanskrit sentence was written there! He had written it an hour before, with the remark, "In confirmation of what I have written, this man will think of this sentence." It was correct. Another of us who had been given a similar paper, which he had signed and placed in his pocket, was also asked to think of a sentence. He thought of a sentence in Arabic, which it was still less possible for the man to know; it was some passage from the Koran. And my friend found this written down on the paper. Another of us was a physician. He thought of a sentence from a German medical book. It was written on his paper.

Several days later I went to this man again, thinking possibly I had been deluded somehow before. I took other friends, and on this occasion also he came out wonderfully triumphant.

Another time, I was in the city of Hyderabad in India, and I was told of a brāhmin there who could produce numbers of things from nobody knew where. This man was in business there; he was a respectable gentleman. And I asked him to show me his tricks. It so happened that this man had fever; and in India there is a general belief that if a holy man puts his hand on a sick man he will be well. This brāhmin came to me and said, "Sir, put your hand on my head, so that my fever may be cured." I said, "Very good; but you show me your tricks." He promised. I put my hand on his head as desired, and later he came to fulfil his promise. He had only a strip of cloth about his loins; we took

807

everything else off him. I had a blanket, which I gave him to wrap round himself because it was cold, and made him sit in a corner. Twenty-five pairs of eyes were looking at him. And he said, "Now look here; write down anything you want." We all wrote down names of fruits that never grew in that locality— bunches of grapes, oranges, and so on. And we gave him those bits of paper. And there came from under his blanket bushels of grapes, oranges, and so on— so much that if all that fruit had been weighed it would have been twice as heavy as the man. He asked us to eat the fruit. Some of us objected, thinking it was hypnotism; but the man himself began eating; so we all ate. It was all right.

He ended by producing a mass of roses. Each flower was perfect, with dewdrops on the petals, not one crushed, not one injured. And masses of them! When I asked the man for an explanation, he said, "It is all sleight-of-hand."

Whatever it was, it seemed to be impossible that it could be sleight-of-hand merely. Where could he have got such large quantities of things?

Well, I have seen many things like that. Going about India, you find hundreds of similar things in different places. These happen in every country. Even in this country you will find some such wonderful things. Of course there is a great deal of fraud, no doubt; but then, whenever you see fraud, you have also to say that that fraud is an imitation. There must be some truth somewhere that is being imitated; you cannot imitate nothing. Imitation must be of something substantially true.

In very remote times in India, thousands of years ago, these things used to happen even more than they do today. It seems to me that when a country becomes very thickly populated, psychical power deteriorates. Given a vast country, thinly inhabited, there will perhaps be more of psychical power there. These facts the Hindus, being analytically minded, took up and investigated. And they came to certain remarkable conclusions; that is, they made a science of them. They found out that all these happenings, though extraordinary, are also natural; there is nothing supernatural about them. They are under laws just as any other physical phenomena are. It is not a freak of nature that a man is born with such powers. They can be systematically studied and acquired. This science they call the science of Rāja-yoga. There are thousands of people who practise it.

The conclusion of Rāja-yoga is that all these extraordinary powers are in the mind of man. This mind is a part of the universal mind. Each mind is connected with every other mind; and each mind, wherever it is located, is in actual communication with the whole world.

Have you ever noticed the phenomenon that is called thought-transference? A man here is thinking something and that thought is manifested in somebody else, in some other place. With preparations—not by chance—a man wants to send a thought to another mind at a distance, and this other mind knows that a thought is coming, and he receives it exactly as it is sent out. Distance makes no difference. The thought goes and reaches the other man, and he understands it. If your mind were an isolated something here, and my mind were an isolated something there, and there were no connexion between the two, how would it be possible for my thought to reach you? In ordinary cases it is not my thought that is reaching you direct; but my thought has got to be dissolved into ethereal vibrations, and those ethereal vibrations go into your brain, and they have to be resolved again into your own thoughts. Here is a dissolution of thought, and there is a resolution of thought. It is a roundabout process. But in telepathy there is no such thing; it is direct.

This shows that there is a continuity of mind, as the yogis call it. The mind is universal. Your mind, my mind, all these little minds, are fragments of that universal mind, little waves in the ocean; and on account of this continuity, we can convey our thoughts directly to one another.

You see what is happening all around us. The world is one of influence. Part of our energy is used up in the preservation of our own bodies; beyond that, every particle of our energy is day and night being used in influencing others. Our bodies, our virtues, our intellect, and our spirituality—all these are continuously influencing others; and so, conversely, we are being influenced by them. This is going on all around us. Now, to take a concrete example: A man comes. You know he is very learned, his language is beautiful, and he speaks to you by the hour—but he does not make any impression. Another man comes, and he speaks a few words, not well arranged, ungrammatical perhaps; all the same, he makes an immense impression. Many of you have seen that. So it is evident that words alone cannot always produce an impression. Words, even thoughts, contribute only one-third of the influence in making an impression; the man, two-thirds. What you call the personal magnetism of the man—that is what goes out and impresses you.

Each family has a head; some heads of families are successful, others are not. Why? We accuse others for our failures. The moment I am unsuccessful, I say that So-and-so is the cause of the failure. In failures, one does not like to confess one's own faults and weaknesses. Each person tries to hold himself faultless and lay the blame upon somebody or something else, or even on bad luck. When the head of a family fails he should ask himself why it is that some persons manage their families so well and he cannot. Then it will be apparent that the difference is owing to the man—his personality.

Coming to great leaders of mankind, we always find that it was the personality of the man that counted. Now, take all the great authors of the past, the great thinkers. Really, how many original thoughts have they thought? Take all the writings that have been left to us by the past leaders of mankind; take each one of their books and appraise them. The real thoughts, new and genuine, that have been thought in this world up to this time amount to only a handful. Read in their books the thoughts they have left to us. The authors do not appear to be giants to us, and yet we know that they were great giants in their day. What made them so? Not simply the thoughts they thought, neither the books they wrote, nor the speeches they made; it was something else that is now gone, and that is their personality. As I have already remarked, the personality of the man is two-thirds, and his intellect, his words, are but one-third. It is the real man, the personality of the man, that influences us.

Our actions are but effects; actions must come when the man is there; the effect is bound to follow the cause. The ideal of all education, all training, should be this man-making. But instead of that, we are always trying to polish up the outside. What use is there in polishing up the outside when there is no inside? The aim of all training should be to make the man grow. The man who influences, who throws his magic, as it were, upon his fellow beings, is a dynamo of power, and when that man is ready, he can do anything and everything he likes; that personality, handling anything, will make it work.

Now, we see that though this is a fact, no physical laws that we know of will explain it. How can we explain it by the laws of chemistry and physics? How much of oxygen, hydrogen, carbon, how many molecules in different positions, and how many cells, and so on, can explain this mysterious personality? And still we see it is a fact; and not only that, it is the real man; and it is that man that lives and moves and works; it is that man that influences, moves his fellow beings, and passes away; and his intellect and books and works are but traces left behind. Think of this. Compare the great teachers of religion with intellectual philosophers. The latter scarcely influenced anybody's inner self, and yet they wrote most marvellous books. The religious teachers, on the other hand, moved countries in their lifetime. The difference was made by personality. In the philosopher it is a faint personality that influences; in the great prophets it is a tremendous one. In the former we touch the intellect; in the latter we touch life. In the one case it is simply a chemical process, putting certain chemical ingredients together which may gradually combine and, under proper circumstances, bring out a flash of light, or may fail. In the other, it is like a torch that goes round quickly lighting others.

The science of Yoga claims that it has discovered the laws which develop this personality, and by proper attention to those laws and methods each one can grow and strengthen his personality. This is one of the great practical things and this is the secret of all education. It has a universal application: in the life of the householder, in the life of the poor, the rich, the man of business, the spiritual man—in everyone's life—it is a great thing, the strengthening of this personality. As we know, there are laws, very fine, which are behind the physical laws. That is to say, there are no such realities as a physical world, a mental world, a spiritual world. Whatever is, is one. Let us say, it is a sort of tapering existence: the thickest part is here; it tapers and becomes finer and finer. The finest is what we call Spirit; the grossest, the body. And just as it is here, in the microcosm, exactly so is it in the macrocosm. This universe of ours is exactly like that: the thickest part is the gross, external world, and it tapers into something finer and finer until it becomes God.

We also know that the greatest power is lodged in the fine, not in the gross. We see a man take up a huge weight: we see his muscles swell, and all over his body we see signs of exertion; and we think the muscles are powerful things. But it is the thin, thread-like wires, the nerves, which bring power to the muscles; the moment one of these threads is cut off from reaching the muscles, they are not able to work at all. These tiny nerves bring the power from something still finer; and that again in its turn brings it from something finer still— thought; and so on. So it is the fine that is really the seat of power. Of course, we can see the movements in the gross; but when the fine movements take place we cannot see them. When a gross thing moves, we catch it, and thus we naturally identify movement with things which are gross. But all the power is really in the fine.

We do not see any movement in the fine, perhaps because the movement is so intense that we cannot perceive it. But if by any science, any investigation, we are helped to get hold of these finer forces which are the cause of the gross manifestation, the gross itself will be under control. There is a little bubble coming from the bottom of a lake: we do not see it coming all the time; we see it only when it bursts on the surface. So we can perceive thoughts only after they develop a great deal or after they become actions.

We constantly complain that we have no control over our actions, over our thoughts. But how can we have it? If we can get control over the fine movements, if we can get hold of thought at the root, before it has become thought, before it has become action, then it will be possible for us to control the whole. Now, if there is a method by which we can analyse, investigate, understand, and finally grapple with those finer powers, the finer causes, then alone is it possible to have control over ourselves. And the man who has control over his own mind assuredly will have control over every other mind. That is why purity and morality have always been the object of religion. A pure, moral man has control of himself. And all minds are the same—different parts of one Mind. He who knows one lump of clay has known all the clay in the universe. He who knows and controls his own mind knows the secret of every mind and has power over every mind.

Now, we can get rid of a good deal of our physical evil if we have control over the fine parts; we can throw off a good many worries if we have control over the fine movements; a good many failures can be averted if we have control over these fine powers. So far is its utility. Yet beyond there is something higher.

Now I shall tell you a theory. I shall not argue about it, but simply place before you the conclusion. Each man in his childhood runs through the stages through which his race has come up; only the race took thousands of years to do it, while the child takes a few years. The child is first the old savage man and, like a savage, he crushes a butterfly under his feet. He is like a primitive ancestor of his race. As he grows, he passes through different stages until he reaches the development of his race; only he does it swiftly and quickly. Now, take the whole of humanity as a race, or take the whole of the animal creation— man and the lower animals as one whole. There is an end towards which the whole is moving. Let us call it perfection. Some men and women there are who anticipate the whole progress of mankind. Instead of waiting and being born over and over again for ages until the whole human race has attained to that perfection, they rush through them, as it were, in the few short years of their life. And we know that we can hasten these processes if we be true to ourselves. If a number of men without any culture are left to live upon an island and are given barely enough food, clothing, and shelter, they will in the course of time evolve higher and higher stages of civilization. But we know also that this growth can be hastened by additional means. We help the growth of trees, do we not? Left to nature they would have grown, only they would have taken longer. We help them to grow in a shorter time than they would otherwise have taken. We are doing all the time the same thing—hastening the growth of things by artificial means.

Why cannot we hasten the growth of man? We can do that as a race. Why are teachers sent to other countries? Because by these means we can hasten the growth of races. Now, cannot we hasten the growth of individuals? We can. Can we put a limit to the hastening process? We cannot say how much a man can grow in one life. You have no reason to say that this much a man can do and no more. Circumstances can hasten his growth wonderfully. Can there be any limit then, till he comes to perfection?

So what comes of this principle? A perfect man, that is to say, the type that is to come of his race perhaps millions of years hence—that man can come today. And this is what the yogis say: that all great Incarnations and prophets are such men; that they reached perfection in this one life. We have had such men at all periods of the world's history and at all times. Quite recently there was such a man who lived the life of the whole human race and reached the end in this very life. Even this hastening of the growth must be under laws. Suppose we investigate these laws and understand their secrets and apply them to our own needs; it follows that we grow. We hasten our growth, we hasten our development, and we become perfect even in this life.

This is the higher part of life, and the science of the study of the mind and its powers has this perfection as its real end. Helping others with money and other material things and teaching them how to go on smoothly in their daily life are secondary. The purpose of this science is to bring out the perfect man and not let him wait and wait for ages, just a plaything in the hands of the physical world, like a log of drift-wood carried from wave to wave and tossing about in the ocean. This science wants you to be strong, to take the work in your own hands instead of leaving it in the hands of nature, and get beyond this little life. That is the great idea.

Man is growing in knowledge, in power, in happiness. Continuously we are growing as a race. We see that is true, perfectly true. Is it true of individuals? To a certain extent, yes. But yet, again comes the question: Where do you fix the limit? I can see only for a distance of so many feet. But I have seen a man close his eyes and see what is happening in another room. If you say you do not believe it, perhaps in three weeks that man can make you do the same. It can be taught to anybody. Some persons, in five minutes even, can be made to read what is happening in another man's mind. These facts can be demonstrated.

Now, if these things are true, where can we put a limit? If a man can read what is happening in another's mind in the corner of this room, why not in the next room? Why not anywhere? We cannot say why not. We dare not say that it is not possible. We can only say that we do not know how it happens. Physical scientists have no right to say that things like this are not possible; they can only say, "We do not know." Science has to collect facts, generalize upon them, deduce principles, and state the truth—that is all. But if we begin by denying the facts, how can there be a science?

There is no end to the power a man can obtain. This is the peculiarity of the Indian mind: when anything interests it, it gets absorbed in it and other things are neglected. You know how many sciences had their origin in India. Mathematics began there. You are even today counting one, two, three, and

so on, to zero, after Sanskrit figures, and you all know that algebra also originated in India, and that gravitation was known to the Indians centuries before
Newton was born.

You see the peculiarity. At a certain period of Indian history this one subject
of man and his mind absorbed all the interest of the Hindus. And it was so
enticing because it seemed the easiest way to achieve their ends. Now, the
Hindus became so thoroughly persuaded that the mind could do anything and
everything according to law that its powers became the great object of study.
There was nothing extraordinary about charms, magic, and other powers. They
were regularly taught, just like the physical sciences they had taught before that.
Such a conviction about these things came upon the race that the physical
sciences nearly died out. This one thing claimed their attention. Different
sects of yogis began to make all sorts of experiments. Some made experiments
with light, trying to find out how lights of different colours produced changes
in the body. They wore clothes of a certain colour, ate foods of a certain colour,
and used things of a certain colour. All sorts of experiments were made in this
way. Others made experiments with sound, by stopping and unstopping their
ears. And still others experimented with the sense of smell and so on. The
whole idea was to reach the source, to reach the fine aspect of the thing. And
some of them really attained most marvellous results.

Many of them tried to float in the air or pass through it. I shall tell you a
story which I heard from a great scholar in the West. It was told him by
a Governor of Ceylon, who saw the performance. A girl was brought forward
and seated cross-legged upon a stool made of sticks crossed. After she had been
seated for a time, the showman began to take out these cross-bars one after
another; and when all were taken out, the girl was left floating in the air. The
Governor thought there was some trick; so he drew his sword and violently
passed it under the girl. Nothing was there. Now, what was this? It was not
magic or something supernatural. That is the peculiarity. No one in India
will tell you that things like this do not exist. To the Hindus it is a matter
of course. You know what the Hindus would often say when they had to fight
their enemies: "Oh, one of our yogis will come and drive them all out!"
Perhaps it is going to the extreme. But be that as it may, what power is there
in the hand or the sword? The power is all in the Spirit.

If this is true, it is temptation enough for the mind to exert its highest. But
just as it is very difficult to make any great achievement in other sciences,
so also in this—nay, much more. Yet most people think that these powers
can be easily gained. How many are the years you take to make a fortune? Think
of that. First, how many years do you take to learn electrical science or engi-
neering? And then you have to work all the rest of your life.

Again, most of the other sciences deal with things that do not move, that are
fixed. You can analyse a chair; the chair does not fly from you. But this science
deals with the mind, which moves all the time; the moment you want to study
it, it slips away. Now the mind is in one mood; the next moment, perhaps,
it is different—changing, changing all the time. In the midst of all this change it
has to be studied, understood, grasped, and controlled. How much more difficult then is this science! It requires rigorous training. People ask me why I

do not give them practical lessons. Why, it is no joke. I stand upon this platform talking to you, and you go home and find no benefit; nor do I. Then you say, "It is all bosh." It is, because you wanted to make bosh of it. I know very little of this science; but the little that I gained I worked for for thirty years of my life, and for six years I have been telling people the little that I know. It took me thirty years to learn it—thirty years of hard struggle. Sometimes I worked at it twenty hours during the twenty-four; sometimes I slept only one hour in the night; sometimes I worked whole nights. Sometimes I lived in places where there was hardly a sound, hardly a breath; sometimes I had to live in caves. Think of that. And yet I know little or nothing; I have barely touched the hem of the garment of this science. But I can understand that it is true and vast and wonderful.

Now, if there is anyone among you who really wants to study this science, he will have to start with that sort of determination, the same as, nay, even more than, that which he puts into any business of life. And what an amount of attention does business require, and what a rigorous taskmaster it is! Even if the father, the mother, the wife, or the child dies, the business cannot stop. Even if the heart is breaking, we still have to go to our place of business, when every hour of work is a pang. That is business; and we think that it is just, that it is right.

This science calls for more application than any business can ever require. Many men can succeed in business, very few in this, because so much depends upon the particular constitution of the person studying it. As in business all may not make a fortune, but everyone can make something, so in the study of this science each one can get a glimpse which will convince him of its truth and of the fact that there have been men who have realized it fully.

This is an outline of this science. It stands upon its own feet and in its own light and challenges comparison with any other science. There have been charlatans, there have been magicians, there have been cheats, and more here than in any other field. Why? For the simple reason that the more profitable the business, the greater the number of charlatans and cheats. But that is no reason why the business should not be good. And one thing more: It may be a good intellectual gymnastic to listen to all the arguments and an intellectual satisfaction to hear of wonderful things. But if any one of you really wants to learn something beyond that, merely attending lectures will not do. This cannot be taught in lectures, for it is life; and only life can convey life. If there are any among you who are really determined to learn it, I shall be very glad to help you.

THE GREAT TEACHERS OF THE WORLD

(Delivered at the Shakespeare Club, Pasadena, California, February 3, 1900)

THE UNIVERSE, according to a philosophical theory of the Hindus, is moving in cycles of wave form. It rises, reaches its zenith, and then falls and remains in the hollow, as it were, for some time, once more to rise, and so on in wave after wave. What is true of the universe is true of every part of it. The march of human affairs is like that; the history of nations is like that: they rise and they fall. After the rise comes a fall; again, out of the fall comes a rise, with greater power. This movement is always going on.

In the religious world the same movement exists. In every nation's spiritual life there is a fall as well as a rise. The nation goes down and everything seems to go to pieces. Then again it gains strength and rises. A huge wave comes—sometimes a tidal wave; and always on the crest of that tidal wave is a shining soul, a Messenger. Creator and created by turns, he is the impetus that makes the wave rise, the nation rise; at the same time, he is created by the same forces which make the wave, acting and interacting by turns. He puts forth his tremendous power upon society, and society makes him what he is. These are the great world thinkers; these are the Prophets, the Messengers, the Incarnations of God.

Men have an idea that there can be only one religion, that there can be only one Prophet, that there can be only one Incarnation; but that idea is not true. By studying the lives of all these great Messengers, we find that each was destined to play a part, as it were, and a part only; that the true harmony consists in the sum total and not in one note. It is the same in the life of races: no race is born to alone enjoy the world. None dare say so. Each race has a part to play in this divine harmony of nations; each race has its mission to perform, its duty to fulfil. The sum total is the great harmony.

So not one of these Prophets is born to rule the world for ever. None has yet succeeded and none is going to succeed in the future. Each only contributes a part; and he will control the world and its destinies as far as that part is concerned.

Most of us are born believers in a Personal God. We talk of principles, we think of theories, and that is all right; but every thought and every movement, every one of our actions, shows that we can only understand a principle when it comes to us through a person. We can only grasp an idea when it comes to us through a concrete ideal person. We can only understand the precept through the example. Would to God that all of us were so developed that we did not require any example, did not require any persons. But that we

815

are not; and naturally the vast majority of mankind have put their souls at the feet of these extraordinary personalities, the Prophets, the Incarnations of God —Incarnations worshipped by the Christians, by the Buddhists, and by the Hindus. The Mohammedans from the beginning stood out against any such worship. They would have nothing to do with worshipping the Prophets or the Messengers, or paying any homage to them; but practically, instead of one Prophet, thousands upon thousands of saints are being worshipped. We cannot go against facts. We are bound to worship personalities, and it is good. Remember the answer of your great Prophet to the prayer, "Lord, show us the Father" —"He that hath seen me hath seen the Father." Which of us can have a better idea of God than that He is a man? We can see Him only in and through humanity. The vibration of light is everywhere in this room; why cannot we see it everywhere? You can see it only in the lamp. God is an omnipresent Principle—everywhere; but we are so constituted at present that we can see Him, feel Him, only in and through a human God.

When these great Lights come, then man realizes God. And they come in a different way from the way we come. We come as beggars; they come as emperors. We come here like orphans, as people who have lost their way and do not know it. What are we to do? We do not know what is the meaning of our lives. We cannot realize it. Today we are doing one thing, tomorrow another. We are like little bits of straw drifting to and fro in water, like feathers blown about in a hurricane. But in the history of mankind you will find that these Messengers come, and that from their very birth their mission is found and formed. The whole plan is there, laid down, and you see them swerving not one inch from it.

Because they come with a mission, they come with a message. They do not want to reason. Did you ever hear or read of these great Teachers or Prophets reasoning out what they taught? No; not one of them has done so. They speak direct. Why should they reason? They see the Truth. And not only do they see It, but they show It. If you ask me, "Is there any God?" and I say "Yes," you immediately ask my grounds for saying so, and poor me has to exercise all his powers to provide you with some reason. If you had come to Christ and said, "Is there any God?" he would have said, "Yes"; and if you had asked, "Is there any proof?" he would have replied, "Behold the Lord!" And thus, you see, it is a direct perception, and not at all the ratiocination of logic. There is no groping in the dark; but there is the strength of direct vision. I see this table; no amount of reason can take that faith from me. It is a direct perception. Such is their faith—faith in their ideals, faith in their mission, above all else faith in themselves. The great Shining Ones believe in themselves as nobody else ever does.

The people say: "Do you believe in God? Do you believe in a future life? Do you believe in this doctrine or that dogma?" But here the base is wanting: this belief in oneself. Ay! the man who cannot believe in himself, how can they expect him to believe in anything else? I am not sure of my own existence. One moment I think that I am existing and nothing can destroy me; the next moment I am quaking in fear of death. One minute I think I am immortal; the next minute a spook appears, and then I don't know what I am or where

I am; I don't know whether I am living or dead. One moment I think that I am spiritual, that I am moral; and the next moment a blow comes, and I am thrown flat on my back. And why? I have lost faith in myself; my moral backbone is broken.

But in these great Teachers you will always find this sign: that they have intense faith in themselves. Such intense faith is unique and we cannot understand it. That is why we try to explain away in various ways what these Teachers speak of themselves; and people invent twenty thousand theories to explain what they say about their realization. We do not think of ourselves in the same way, and naturally we cannot understand them.

Then again, when they speak the world is bound to listen. When they speak each word is direct; it bursts like a bombshell. What is in the word unless it has the power behind? What matters it what language you speak and how you arrange your language? What matters it whether or not you speak with correct grammar and fine rhetoric? What matters it whether your language is ornamental or not? The question is whether or not you have anything to give. It is a question of giving and taking, and not of listening. Have you anything to give?—that is the first question. If you have, then give. Words but convey the gift; they are but one of the many modes.

Sometimes they do not speak at all. There is an old Sanskrit verse which says: "I saw the teacher sitting under a tree. He was a young man of sixteen and the disciple was an old man of eighty. The preaching of the teacher was in silence, and the doubts of the doubter departed." Thus, though they do not speak at all, yet they can convey the truth from mind to mind. They come to give. They command—they, the Messengers; you have to obey the command. Do you not remember in your own scriptures the authority with which Jesus speaks? "Go ye therefore, and teach all nations. . . . Teaching them to observe all things whatsoever I have commanded you. . . ." It runs through all his utterances, that tremendous faith in his own message. That you find in the life of all these great giants whom the world worships as its Prophets.

These great teachers are the living Gods on this earth. Whom else should we worship? I try to get an idea of God in my mind, and I find what a false little thing I conceive; it would be a sin to worship that as God. I open my eyes and look at the actual life of these great ones of the earth. They are higher than any conception of God that I could ever form. For what idea of mercy could be formed by a man like me, who would go after a man if he steals anything from me and send him to jail? And what can be my highest idea of forgiveness? Nothing beyond myself. Which of you can jump out of his own body? Which of you can jump out of his own mind? Not one of you. What idea of divine love can you form except what you actually feel? What we have never experienced we can form no idea of. So all my best attempts at forming an idea of God will fail in every case. And here are plain facts and not ideas— actual facts of love, of mercy, of purity, of which I cannot even have any conception. What wonder that I should fall at the feet of these men and worship them as God? And what else can anyone do? I should like to see the man who can do anything else, however much he may talk. Talking is not actuality. Talking about God and the Impersonal, and this and that, is all very good; but these man-Gods are the real Gods of all nations and all races. These divine men have been worshipped and will be worshipped so long as man is man. Therein is our faith, therein is our hope. Of what avail is a mere mystical principle?

The purpose and intent of what I have to say to you is this: that I have found it possible in my life to worship all of them and to be ready for all that are yet to come. A mother recognizes her son in any dress in which he may appear before her; and if she does not do so, I am sure that she is not the mother of that man. Now, as regards those of you who think you understand Truth and Divinity and God in only one Prophet in the world, and not in any other, naturally, the conclusion which I draw is that you do not understand Divinity in anybody; you have simply swallowed words and identified yourself with one sect, just as you would in party politics, as a matter of opinion. But that is no religion at all. There are some fools in this world who use brackish water although there is excellent sweet water near by, because, they say, the brackish-water well was dug by their father. Now, in my little experience I have collected this knowledge: that for all the devilry that religion is blamed for, religion is not at all at fault. No religion ever persecuted men, no religion ever burnt witches, no religion ever did any of these things. What then incited people to do these things? Politics, but never religion; and if such politics takes the name of religion, whose fault is that?

So when a man stands up and says, "My Prophet is the only true Prophet," he is not right; he knows not the A B C of religion. Religion is neither talk nor theory nor intellectual consent. It is realization in our heart of hearts; it is touching God; it is feeling, realizing that I am a spirit related to the Universal Spirit and all Its great manifestations. If you have really entered the house of the Father, how can you have seen His children and not know them? And if you do not recognize them, you have not entered the house of the Father. The mother recognizes her child in any dress and knows him however disguised. Recognize all the great spiritual men and women in every age and country and see that they are not really at variance with one another.

Wherever there has been actual religion—this touch of the Divine, the soul coming in direct contact with the Divine—there has always been a broadening of the mind which has enabled it to see the light everywhere. Now, the Mohammedans are the crudest in this respect, and the most sectarian. Their watchword is: "There is one God and Mohammed is His Prophet." Everything beyond that not only is bad but must be destroyed forthwith; at a moment's notice every man or woman who does not exactly believe in that must be killed; everything that does not belong to this worship must be immediately broken; every book that teaches anything else must be burnt. From the Pacific to the Atlantic, for five hundred years, blood ran all over the world. That is Mohammedanism. Nevertheless, among these Mohammedans, wherever there was a philosophic man he was sure to protest against these cruelties. In that he showed the touch of the Divine and realized a fragment of the truth; he was not playing with his religion—for it was not his father's religion he was talking about—but spoke the truth direct, like a man.

Side by side with the modern theory of evolution there is another thing:

atavism. There is a tendency in us to revert to old ideas in religion. Let us think something new, even if it be wrong. It is better to do that. Why should we not try to hit the mark? We become wiser through failures. Time is infinite. Look at the wall. Did the wall ever tell a lie? It is always the wall. Man tells a lie—and becomes a god, too. It is better to do something; never mind even if it proves to be wrong. It is better than doing nothing. The cow never tells a lie, but she remains a cow all the time. Do something. Think some thought; it doesn't matter whether you are right or wrong. But think something. Because my forefathers did not think this way, shall I sit down quietly and gradually lose my sense of feeling and my own thinking faculty? I may as well be dead. And what is life worth if we have no living ideas, no convictions of our own, about religion? There is some hope for the atheists, because though they differ from others, they think for themselves. The people who never think anything for themselves are not yet born into the world of religion; they have a mere jelly-fish existence. They will not think; they do not care for religion. But the disbeliever, the atheist, cares and he is struggling. So think something. Struggle Godwards. Never mind if you fail, never mind if you get hold of a queer theory. If you are afraid to be called queer, keep it in your own mind; you need not go out and preach it to others. But do something. Struggle Godwards. Light must come. If a man feeds me every day of my life, in the long run I shall lose the use of my hands. Spiritual death is the result of following others as in a flock of sheep. Death is the result of inaction. Be active; and wherever there is activity there must be difference. Difference is the sauce of life; it is the beauty, it is the art, of everything: difference makes all beautiful here. It is variety that is the source of life, the sign of life. Why should we be afraid of it?

Now we are coming into a position to understand about the Prophets. We see that the historical evidence is—apart from the jelly-fish acceptance of dogmas—that where there has been any real thinking, any real love of God, the soul has grown Godwards and has got, as it were, a glimpse now and then, has attained direct perception, even for a second, even once in its life. Immediately "all doubts vanish for ever, all the crookedness of the heart is made straight, all bondage vanishes, and the results of past actions fly away; for He is seen who is the nearest of the near and the farthest of the far." That is religion; that is all of religion. The rest is mere theory, dogma, so many ways of going to that state of direct perception. Now we are fighting over the basket and the fruits have fallen into the ditch.

If two men quarrel about religion, just ask them the question: "Have you seen God? Have you seen spiritual things?" One man says that Christ is the only Prophet. Well, has he seen Christ? "Has your father seen him?" "No, sir." "Has your grandfather seen him?" "No, sir." "Have you seen him?" "No, sir." "Then what are you quarrelling for? The fruits have fallen into the ditch and you are quarrelling over the basket!" Sensible men and women should be ashamed to go on quarrelling in that way.

These Messengers and Prophets were great and true. Why so? Because each one came to preach a great idea. Take the Prophets of India, for instance. They are the oldest of the founders of religion. We take, first, Krishna. You who have read the Gitā know that the one idea all through the book is non-attachment. Remain unattached. The heart's love is due to only One. To whom? To Him who never changes. Who is that One? He is God. Do not make the mistake of giving the heart to anything that is changing, because that is misery. You may give it to a man; but if he dies, misery is the result. You may give it to a friend; but tomorrow he may become your enemy. If you give it to your husband, he may one day quarrel with you. You may give it to your wife, and she may die the day after tomorrow. Now, this is the way the world is going on. So says Krishna in the Gitā. The Lord is the only one who never changes. His love never fails. Wherever we are and whatever we do, He is ever and ever the same merciful, the same loving Spirit. He never changes, He is never angry, whatever we do.

How can God be angry with us? Your baby does many mischievous things: are you angry with that baby? Does not God know what we are going to be? He knows we are all going to be perfect sooner or later. He has patience, infinite patience. We must love Him and, only in and through Him, everyone that lives. This is the keynote. You must love your wife, but not for your wife's sake. "Never, O Beloved, is the husband loved on account of the husband, but because the Lord is in the husband." The Vedānta philosophy says that even in the love of husband and wife, although the wife is thinking that she is loving the husband, the real attraction is the Lord, who is present there. He is the only attraction; there is no other. But the wife in most cases does not know that it is so; yet ignorantly she is doing the right thing, which is loving the Lord. Only, when one does it ignorantly it may bring pain. If one does it knowingly, that is salvation. This is what our scriptures say. Wherever there is love, wherever there is a spark of joy, know that to be a spark of His presence, because He is Joy, Blessedness, and Love itself. Without Him there cannot be any love.

This is the trend of Krishna's instruction all through. He has implanted that in his race; therefore, when a Hindu does anything, even when he drinks water, he says, "If there is virtue in it, let it go to the Lord." The Buddhist says, if he does any good deed, "Let the merit of the good deed belong to the world; if there is any virtue in what I do, let it go to the world, and let the evils of the world come to me." The Hindu—he is a great believer in God—the Hindu says that God is omnipotent and that He is the Soul of all souls everywhere. So he says, "If I give all my virtues unto Him, that is the greatest sacrifice, and they will go to the whole universe."

Now, this is one message. And what is another message of Krishna? "Whosoever lives in the midst of the world, and works, giving up all the fruit of his action unto the Lord, is never touched by the evils of the world. The lotus, born under the water, rises up and blossoms above the water; even so is the man who is engaged in the activities of the world, giving up all the fruit of his activities unto the Lord."

Krishna strikes still another note as a teacher of intense activity. Work, work, day and night, says the Gitā. You may ask: "Then where is peace? If all through life I am to work like a cart-horse and die in harness, what am I here for?" Krishna says: "Yes, you will find peace. Flying from work is never the way to find peace." Throw off your duties if you can and go to the top of a mountain; even there the mind keeps on going—whirling, whirling, whirling. Someone asked a sannyāsin: "Sir, have you found a nice place? How many years have you been travelling in the Himālayas?" "For forty years," replied the sannyāsin. "There are many beautiful spots to select from and to settle down in; why did you not do so?" "Because for these forty years my mind would not allow me to." We all say, "Let us find peace," but the mind will not allow us to do so.

You know the story of the man who caught a Tartar. A soldier was outside the town, and he cried out when he came near the barracks, "I have caught a Tartar." A voice called out, "Bring him in." "He won't come in, sir." "Then you come in." "He won't let me come in, sir!" So, in this mind of ours, we have "caught a Tartar": neither can we quiet it down nor will it let us be quieted down. We have all "caught Tartars." We all say: Be quiet and peaceful and so forth. But every baby can say that and thinks he can do it. However, that is very difficult. I have tried. I threw overboard all my duties and fled to the tops of mountains; I lived in caves and deep forests; but all the same, I had "caught a Tartar," because I had my world with me all the time. The "Tartar" is what I have in my own mind; so we must not blame poor people outside. "These circumstances are good, and these are bad," so we say, while the "Tartar" is here within. If we can quiet him down, we shall be all right.

Therefore Krishna teaches us not to shirk our duties, but to take them up manfully and not think of the result. The servant has no right to question. The soldier has no right to reason. Go forward and do not pay too much attention to the nature of the work you have to do. Ask your mind if you are unselfish. If you are, never mind anything; nothing can resist you. Plunge in. Do the duty at hand. And when you have done this, by degrees you will realize the truth: "Whosoever in the midst of intense activity finds intense peace, whosoever in the midst of the greatest peace finds the greatest activity, he is a yogi, he is a great soul, he has arrived at perfection."

Now you can see that the result of this teaching is that all the duties of the world are sanctified. There is no duty in this world which we have any right to call menial; and each man's work is quite as good as that of an emperor on his throne.

Listen to Buddha's message—a tremendous message. It has a place in our heart. Says Buddha: Root out selfishness and everything that makes you selfish. Have neither wife, child, nor family. Be not of the world; become perfectly unselfish. A worldly man thinks he will be unselfish, but when he looks at the face of his wife it makes him selfish. The mother thinks she will be perfectly unselfish, but she looks at her baby and immediately selfishness comes. So with everything in this world. As soon as selfish desires arise in a man, as soon as he follows some selfish pursuit, immediately the real man is gone; he becomes like a brute, he is a slave, he forgets his fellow men. No more does he say, "You first and me afterwards," but it is "Me first and let every one else look out for himself."

We find that Krishna's message has a place for us. Without that message we cannot move at all. We cannot conscientiously, and with peace, joy, and happiness, take up any duty of our lives without listening to the message of

Krishna: "Be not afraid even if there is evil in your work, for there is no work which has no evil." "Leave it unto the Lord, and do not look for the results."

On the other hand, there is a corner in the heart for the other message: Time flies. This world is finite and all misery. With your good food, nice clothes, and your comfortable home, O sleeping man and woman, do you ever think of the millions that are starving and dying? Think of the great fact that it is all misery, misery, misery! Note the first utterance of the child: when it enters into the world, it weeps. That is the fact: the child weeps. This is a place for weeping. If we listen to Buddha, we shall not be selfish.

Behold another Messenger, he of Nazareth. He teaches: "Be ready, for the kingdom of heaven is at hand." I have pondered over the message of Krishna, and am trying to work without attachment; but sometimes I forget. Then, suddenly, comes to me the message of Buddha: "Take care, for everything in the world is evanescent, and there is always misery in this life." I listen to that and I am uncertain which to accept. Then again comes, like a thunderbolt, the message: "Be ready, for the kingdom of heaven is at hand. Do not delay a moment. Leave nothing for tomorrow. Get ready for that final event, which may overtake you immediately, even now." That message, also, has a place, and we acknowledge it. We salute the Christ; we salute the Lord.

And then comes Mohammed, the Messenger of equality. You ask, "What good can there be in his religion?" If there were no good, how could it live? The good alone lives; that alone survives. Because the good alone is strong, therefore it survives. How long does the influence of an impure man endure? Is it not a fact that the pure man's influence lasts much longer? Without doubt, for purity is strength, goodness is strength. How could Mohammedanism have lived had there been nothing good in its teaching? There is much good. Mohammed was the Prophet of equality, of the brotherhood of man, the brotherhood of all Mussulmans.

So we see that each Prophet, each Messenger, has a particular message. When you first listen to that message, and then look at his life, you see his whole life stand explained, radiant.

Now, ignorant fools start twenty thousand theories and put forward, according to their own mental development, explanations to suit their own ideas, and ascribe them to these great teachers. They take their teachings and put their misconstruction upon them. With every great Prophet his life is the only commentary. Look at his life: what he did will bear out the texts. Read the Gītā, and you will find that it is exactly borne out by the life of the Teacher.

Mohammed by his life showed that among Mohammedans there should be perfect equality and brotherhood. There was no question of race, caste, creed, colour, or sex. The Sultan of Turkey may buy a Negro from the mart of Africa and bring him in chains to Turkey; but should he become a Mohammedan and have sufficient merit and abilities, he might even marry the daughter of the Sultan. Compare this with the way in which the Negroes and the American Indians are treated in this country. And what do Hindus do? If one of your missionaries chanced to touch the food of an orthodox person, he would throw it away. Notwithstanding our grand philosophy, you note our weakness in practice; but there you see the greatness of Islām beyond other faiths, showing itself in equality, perfect equality, regardless of race or colour.

Will other and greater Prophets come? Certainly they will come in this world. But do not look forward to that. I should better like that each one of you become a Prophet of this real New Testament, which is made up of all the Old Testaments. Take all the old messages, supplement them with your own realizations, and become a Prophet unto others. Each one of these Teachers has been great; each has left something for us. They have been our Gods. We salute them; we are their servants. And at the same time we salute ourselves; for if they have been Prophets and children of God, we are Prophets also. They reached their perfection and we are going to attain ours now. Remember the words of Jesus: "The kingdom of heaven is at hand." This very moment let every one of us make a staunch resolution: "I will become a Prophet, I will become a Messenger of Light, I will become a child of God, nay, I will become God Himself."

WOMEN OF INDIA

(Delivered at the Shakespeare Club, Pasadena, California, January 18, 1900)

SWAMI VIVEKANANDA: "Some persons desire to ask questions about Hindu philosophy before the lecture and also general questions about India after the lecture, but the chief difficulty is I do not know what I am to lecture on. I would be very glad to lecture on any subject, either on Hindu philosophy or on anything concerning the race, its history, or its literature. If you ladies and gentlemen will suggest anything, I shall be very glad."

QUESTIONER: "I would like to ask, Swami, what special principle in Hindu philosophy you would have us Americans, who are a very practical people, adopt, and what that would do for us beyond what Christianity can do."

SWAMI VIVEKANANDA: "That is very difficult for me to decide. It rests upon you. If you find anything which you think you ought to adopt, and which will be helpful, you should take that. You see, I am not a missionary and I am not going about converting people to my ideas. My principle is that all religious ideas are good and great; some of your ideas may suit some people in India, and some of our ideas may suit some people here. So ideas must be broadcast all over the world."

QUESTIONER: "We would like to know the result of your philosophy: has your philosophy and religion lifted your women above our women?"

SWAMI VIVEKANANDA: "You see, that is a very invidious question. I like our women and your women too."

QUESTIONER: "Well, will you tell us about your women, their customs and education, and the position they hold in the family?"

SWAMI VIVEKANANDA: "Oh, yes. Those things I would be very glad to tell you. So you want to know about Indian women tonight, and not philosophy and other things?"

THE LECTURE

I must begin by saying that you may have to bear with me a good deal, because I belong to an order of people who never marry; so my knowledge of women in all their relations—as mother, as wife, as daughter, as sister—must necessarily not be so complete as may be the knowledge of others. And then, India, I must remind you, is a vast continent, not merely a country, and is inhabited by many different races. The nations of Europe are nearer to each other, more similar to each other, than the races of India. You may get just a rough idea of it if I tell you that there are eight different languages in all India: different languages—not dialects—each having a literature of its own. The Hindi language, alone, is spoken by one hundred million people; the Bengali, by about sixty million; and so on. Then again, the four North Indian languages differ more from the South Indian languages than any two European languages from each other. They are entirely different—as different as your language is from the Japanese language; you will be astonished to know that when I go to Southern India, unless I meet some people who can talk Sanskrit, I have to speak to them in English. Furthermore, these various races differ from each other in manners, customs, food, dress, and in their methods of thought.

Then again, there is caste. Each caste has become, as it were, a separate racial unit. If a man lives long enough in India, he will be able to tell from the features what caste a man belongs to. Then, between castes, the manners and customs are different. And all these castes are exclusive; that is to say, they would meet socially, but they would not eat or drink together, nor intermarry. In these things they remain separate. They would meet and be friends with each other, but there it would end.

Although I have had more opportunities than many other men to know women in general, from my position and my occupation as a preacher, continually travelling from one place to another and coming in contact with all grades of society—and women, even in Northern India, where they do not appear before men, in many places would break this law for religion and would come to hear us preach and talk to us—still it would be hazardous on my part to assert that I know everything about the women of India. So I will try to place before you the ideal.

In each nation, man or woman represents the conscious or unconscious working out of an ideal. The individual is the external expression of an ideal. The sum total of such individuals is the nation, which also represents a great ideal: towards that it is moving. And therefore it is rightly assumed that to understand a nation you must first understand its ideal; for a nation refuses to be judged by any other standard than its own.

All growth, progress, well-being, or degradation is but relative. It refers to a certain standard, and each man, to be understood, has to be referred to his own standard of perfection. You see this more markedly in nations: what one nation thinks is good might not be so regarded by another nation. Cousin-marriage is quite permissible in this country. Now, in India it is illegal. Not only so; it would be classed with the most horrible incest. Widow-marriage is perfectly legitimate in this country. Among the higher castes in India it would be the greatest degradation for a woman to marry twice. So, you see, we work through such different ideas that to judge one people by another's standard would be neither just nor practicable. Therefore we must know what the ideal is that a nation has placed before itself.

When speaking of different nations, we start with a general idea that there are one code of ethics and one kind of ideal for all races. Practically, however, when we come to judge others, we think what is good for us must be good for everybody: what we do is the right thing; what we do not do would, of course, in others be outrageous. I don't mean to say this as a criticism, but just to bring the truth home. When I hear Western women denounce the confining of the feet of Chinese ladies, they never seem to think of the corsets which are doing far more injury to their own race. This is just one example. For you must know that cramping the feet does not do one millionth part of the injury to the human form that the corset has done and is doing—when every organ is displaced and the spine is curved like a serpent. When measurements are taken, you can note the curvatures. I do not mean that as a criticism, but I want to point out to you the situation: As you stand aghast at the women of other races, thinking that you are superior, so the very fact that they have not adopted your manners and customs shows that they also stand aghast at you. Therefore there is misunderstanding on both sides.

There is a common platform, a common ground, a common humanity, which must be the basis of our understanding. We ought to find out that complete and perfect human nature which is only functioning partially here and there. It has not been given to one man to have everything in perfection. You have a part to play; I, in my humble way, another. Here is one who plays his little part; there, another, who plays his. Just as with individuals, so with races. The perfection is the combination of all these parts. Each race has a part to play; each race has one side of human nature to develop; and we have to take all these together. And possibly, in the distant future, all these marvellous individual perfections attained by the different races will blend together and find expression through a new race, the like of which the world has not yet dreamt of. Beyond saying that, I have no criticism to offer about anybody. I have travelled not a little in my life; I have kept my eyes open; and the more I go about the more my mouth remains closed. I have no criticism to offer.

Now, the ideal woman in India is the mother—the mother first and the mother last. The word *woman* calls up, to the mind of the Hindu, the idea of motherhood. God is addressed as Mother.

In the West the ideal woman is the wife. The ideal of womanhood is concentrated there in the wife. To the ordinary man in India, the whole force of womanhood is concentrated in motherhood. In the Western home the wife rules. In an Indian home the mother rules. If a mother comes into a Western home, she has to be subordinate to the wife: to the wife belongs the home. A mother always lives in our homes; the wife must be subordinate to her. See how different our ideas are.

Now, I only suggest comparisons; I would state facts so that we may compare the two sides. Make this comparison. If you ask, "Where is the Indian woman as wife?" the Indian retorts: "Where is the American woman as mother?" Where, in your society, is she, the all-glorious, who gave me this body? Where is she who kept me in her body for nine months? Where is she who would give me twenty times her life, if I needed it? Where is she whose love never dies, however wicked, however vile I am? Where does she stand, in your society, in comparison with her who goes to the divorce court the moment she is treated a little badly? O American women, where is she, the mother? I do not find her in your country. I have not found the son who thinks that his mother comes first. When we are dying, even then, we do not want our wives and our children to take her place. Our mother!—we want to die with our head on her lap once more, if we die before her. Where is she in America? Is woman a name to be coupled with the physical body only? Ay, the Hindu mind fears all those ideals which say that the flesh must cling unto the flesh. No, no! Woman, thou shalt not be coupled with anything connected with the flesh. The name has been called holy once and for ever, for what name is there which no lust can ever approach, no carnality ever come near, save the one word *mother?* That is the ideal of India.

I belong to an order which is very much like that of the mendicant friars of the Catholic Church; that is to say, we have to go about without very much in the way of dress and beg from door to door, live thereby, preach to people when they want it, and sleep wherever we can find a place. That is the way we have to follow. And the rule is that the members of this order have to call every woman "mother"; to every woman and little girl we have to say "mother." That is the custom. Coming to the West, that old habit remained and I would say to ladies, "Yes, mother," and they would be horrified. I couldn't understand why they should be horrified. Later on I discovered the reason: because that would mean that they were old. The ideal of womanhood in India is motherhood—that marvellous, unselfish, all-suffering, ever forgiving mother. The wife walks behind—the shadow. She must imitate the life of the mother; that is her duty. But the mother is the ideal of love. She rules the family; she possesses the family. It is the father in India who thrashes the child when something wrong has been done by him, and always the mother puts herself between the father and the child. You see, it is just the opposite here. It has become the mother's business to spank the children in this country, and poor father comes in between. You see, the ideals are different. I don't mean this as any criticism. It is all good—this that you do. But our way is what we have been taught for ages. You never hear of a mother cursing her child; she is forgiving, always forgiving. Instead of "Our Father in heaven," we say "Mother" all the time. That idea and that word are ever associated in the Hindu mind with infinite love, the mother's love being the nearest approach to God's love in this mortal world of ours. "Mother, O Mother, be merciful; I am wicked! Many children have been wicked, but there never was a wicked mother"—so says the great saint Rāmprasād.

There she is, the Hindu mother. The son's wife comes in as her daughter. Just as the mother's own daughter married and went out, so her son married and brought in another daughter, and she has to fall in line under the government of the queen of queens, of his mother. Even I, who never married, belonging to an order that never marries, would be disgusted if my wife, supposing I had married, dared to displease my mother. I would be disgusted. Why? Don't I worship my mother? Why should not her daughter-in-law? If I can worship, why not she? Who is she, then, that would try to ride over my head and govern my mother? She has to wait till her womanhood is fulfilled, and the one thing that fulfils womanhood, that is womanliness in woman, is motherhood. Wait till she becomes a mother; then she will have the same right. That, according to the Hindu mind, is the great mission of woman—to become a mother.

But oh, how different it is here! Oh, how different! My mother fasted and prayed, for years and years, so that I would be born. Parents pray for every child before it is born. Says our great lawgiver, Manu, giving the definition of an Āryan: "He is the Āryan who is born through prayer." Every child not born through prayer is illegitimate, according to the great lawgiver. The child must be prayed for. Those children that come with curses, that slip into the world, just in a moment of inadvertence, because that could not be prevented—what can we expect of such progeny? Mothers of America, think of that! Think in your heart of hearts—are you ready to be mothers? Not any question of race or country, or that false sentiment of national pride. Who dares to be proud in this mortal life of ours, in this world of woes and miseries? What are we before this infinite force of God? But I ask you the question tonight: "Do you all pray for the children to come? Are you thankful to be mothers, or not? Do you think that you are sanctified by motherhood, or not?" Ask that of your minds. If you don't, your marriage is a lie, your womanhood is false, your education is superstition, and your children, if they come without prayer, will prove a curse to humanity.

See the different ideals now coming before us. From motherhood comes tremendous responsibility. There is the basis; start from that. Well, why is the mother to be worshipped so much? Because our books teach that it is the prenatal influence that gives the impetus to the child for good or evil. Go to a hundred thousand colleges, read a million books, associate with all the learned men of the world—better off you are when born with the right stamp. You are born for good or evil. The child is a born god or a born demon: that is what our books say. Education and all these things come afterwards—are a mere bagatelle. You are as you are born. Born unhealthful, how many drug-stores, swallowed wholesale, will keep you well all through your life? How many people of good, healthy lives were born of weak parents, were born of sickly, blood-poisoned parents? How many? None—none. We come with a tremendous impetus for good or evil, born demons or born gods. Education or other things are a bagatelle.

Thus say our books: direct the prenatal influence. Why should the mother be worshipped? Because she made herself pure. She underwent harsh penances, sometimes, to keep herself as pure as purity can be. For, mind you, no woman in India thinks of giving up her body to any man; it is her own. The English, as a reform, have introduced at present what they call "restitution of conjugal rights"; but no Indian would take advantage of it. When a man comes in physical contact with his wife, she controls the circumstances—through what prayers and through what vows! It is the greatest prayer of a man and wife, the prayer that is going to bring into the world another soul fraught with a tremendous power for good or for evil. Is it a joke? Is it a simple nervous satisfaction? Is it a brute enjoyment of the body? Says the Hindu: no, a thousand times no!

The idea we started with was that the ideal is the love for the mother, who herself is all-suffering, all-forbearing. The worship that is accorded to the mother has its fountain-head there. She was a saint to bring me into the world; she kept her body pure, her mind pure, her food pure, her clothes pure, her imagination pure, for years, because I would be born. Because she did that she deserves worship. And what follows? Linked with motherhood is wifehood.

You Western people are individualistic: I want to do this thing because I like it; I will elbow out everyone. Why? Because I like to. I want my own satisfaction, so I marry this woman. Why? Because I like her. This woman marries me. Why? Because she likes me. There it ends. She and I are the only two persons in the whole, infinite world, and I marry her and she marries me. Nobody else is injured, nobody else responsible. Your Johns and your Janes may go into the forest and there they may live their lives; but when they have to live in society, their marriage means a tremendous amount of good or evil to us. Their children may be veritable demons—burning, murdering, robbing, stealing, drinking—hideous, vile.

So what is the basis of the Indian social order? It is the caste law. I am born for the caste; I live for the caste. I do not mean myself, because, having joined a monastic order, I am outside. I mean those who live in society. Born in the caste, one must live one's whole life according to caste regulation. In other words, in the present-day language of your country, the Western man is born individualistic, while the Hindu is socialistic—entirely socialistic. Now then, the books say, if I allow you freedom to go about and marry any woman you like, and a woman to marry any man she likes, what happens? You fall in love. The father of the woman was, perchance, a lunatic or a consumptive. The girl falls in love with the face of a man whose father was a roaring drunkard. What says the law then? The law lays down that all these marriages shall be illegal. The children of drunkards, consumptives, lunatics, etc. should not be married. The deformed, humpbacked, crazy, idiotic—no marriage for them, absolutely none, says the law.

Our law says that those who are born of the same family, though a hundred degrees distant, must not marry: that is illegitimate; it would deteriorate the race or make it sterile. That must not be, and there it ends. So I have no voice in my marriage, nor does my sister. It is caste that determines all that. We are married sometimes when children. Why? Because caste says that if they have to be married anyway without their consent, it is better that they be married very early, before they have developed love. If they are allowed to grow up apart, the boy may like some other girl, and the girl some other boy, and then something evil will happen. And so, says caste, stop it there. You may say, "Oh, they lose a great deal of enjoyment—those exquisite emotions of a man falling in love with a woman and a woman falling in love with a man. This is a sort of tame thing, loving each other like brothers and sisters, as though they have to." But the Hindu says: "We are socialistic. For the sake of one man's or woman's exquisite pleasure we don't want to load misery on hundreds of others."

There they are—married. Later the wife comes home with her husband; that is called the second marriage. Marriage at an early age is considered the first marriage, and they grow up separately, with their parents. When they have grown up, another ceremony is performed, the second marriage. And then they live together, but under the same roof with his mother and father. When she becomes a mother, she takes her place in turn as queen of the family group.

Now comes another peculiar Indian institution. I have just told you that in the first two or three castes the widows are not allowed to marry. They cannot, even if they would. Of course, it is a hardship for many. There is no denying that not all the widows like it very much, because not marrying imposes upon them the life of a religious student. That is to say, they must not eat meat or fish, or dress except in white clothes, and so on. There are many regulations. We live in a monastic society, always doing penance, and we like it. Now, you see, a woman never eats meat. It was a hardship on us when we were students, but not on the girls. Our women would feel degraded at the idea of eating meat. Men eat meat sometimes in some castes; women never. Still, not being allowed to marry must be a hardship for many. I am sure of that.

But we must go back to the idea that Hindus are intensely socialistic. You will find that the statistics show that in the higher castes of every country the number of women is always much larger than the number of men. Why? Because in the higher castes, for generation after generation, the women have led an easy life. They "neither toil nor spin, yet Solomon in all his glory was not arrayed like one of them." And the poor boys, they die like flies. The girl has a cat's nine lives, they say in India. You will read in the statistics that the girls outnumber the boys in a very short time, except now when they are starting to work as hard as the boys. The number of girls in the higher castes is much larger than in the lower. Conditions are quite opposite in the lower castes. There they all work hard—women a little harder, sometimes, because they have to do the domestic work. But mind you, I never would have thought of that, but one of your American travellers, Mark Twain, writes this about India: "In spite of all that Western critics have said of Hindu customs, I never saw a woman harnessed to a plough with a cow or to a cart with a dog, as is done in some European countries. I saw no woman or girl at work in the fields in India. On both sides and ahead (of the railway train) brown-bodied naked men and boys are ploughing in the fields. But not a woman. In these two hours I have not seen a woman or a girl working in the fields. In India, even the women of the lowest caste never do any hard work. They generally have an easy lot compared to the same class in other nations; and as to ploughing, they never do it."

Now there you are. Among the lower classes the number of men is larger than the number of women; and what would you naturally expect? A woman gets more chances of marriage, the number of men being larger.

Relative to such questions as widows' not marrying: among the first two castes, the number of women is disproportionately large, and here is a dilemma. Either you have the non-marriageable-widow problem, or the non-husband-getting-young-lady problem. We have to face the widow problem or the old-maid problem! There you are—one or the other. Let us go back to the idea that the Indian mind is socialistic. It says: "Now look here! We take the widow problem as the lesser evil." Why? "Because they have had their chance; they were married. If they have lost their chance, at any rate they have had one. Sit down, be calm, and consider these poor old maids; they have not had one chance of marriage." Lord bless them! I remember once in Oxford Street— it was after ten o'clock—all those ladies were coming there, hundreds and thousands of them shopping, and some man, an American, looked around and said, "My Lord! how many of them will ever get husbands?—I wonder." So the Indian mind said to the widows, "Well, you have had your chance, and now we are very, very sorry that such mishaps have come to you, but we cannot help it; others are waiting."

Then, religion comes into the picture. The Hindu religion comes in as a comfort. For mind you, our religion teaches that marriage is ultimately bad; it is meant for the weak. The very spiritual man or woman would not marry at all. So the religious widow says: "Well, the Lord has given me a better chance. What is the use of marrying again? Thank God, I can worship God; what is the use of my loving a man?" Of course, not all of them can put their minds on God. Some find it simply impossible. They have to suffer; but the unmarried women should not suffer for them. Now, I leave this to your judgement; but that is our idea in India.

Next we come to woman as daughter. The great problem in the Indian household is the daughter. The daughter and caste, combined, ruin the poor Hindu, because, you see, she must marry in the same caste, and even inside the caste exactly in the same status; and so the poor man sometimes has to make himself a beggar to get his daughter married. The father of the boy demands a very high dowry for his son, and this poor man sometimes has to sell everything just to get a husband for his daughter. The great problem of the Hindu's life is the daughter. And curiously enough, the word *daughter* in Sanskrit is *duhitā*. The real derivation is this: In ancient times the daughter of the family was accustomed to milk the cows, and so the word *duhitā* comes from *duh*, to milk; and the word *daughter* really means milkmaid. Later on they found a new meaning for that word *duhitā*: she who milks away all the milk of the family. That is the second meaning.

These are the different relations held by our Indian women. As I have told you, the mother is the highest in position, the wife is next, and the daughter comes after them. It is a most intricate and complicated series of gradation. No foreigner can understand it, even if he lives there for years. For instance, we have three forms of the personal pronoun, each one with an appropriate verb. One is very respectful, one is middling, and the lowest is just like *thou* and *thee*. To children and servants the last is addressed. The middling one is used with equals. You see, these are to be applied in all the intricate relations of life. For example, to my elder sister throughout my life I use the pronoun *āpani*, but she never does so in speaking to me; she says *tumi* to me. She should not, even by mistake, say *āpani* to me, because that would mean a curse. Love, the love towards those that are superior, should always be expressed in that form of language. That is the custom. Similarly, I should never dare address my elder sister or elder brother, much less my mother or father, as *tui* or *tumi*. As to calling our mother and father by name—why, we should never do that. Before I knew the customs of this country, I received such a shock when the son, in a very refined family, got up and called his mother by name! However, I got used to that. That is the custom of this country. But with us, we never pronounce the name of our parents when they are present. It is always in the third person plural, even before them.

Thus we see the most complicated mesh-work in the social life of our men and our women and in our degrees of relationship. We don't speak to our wives before our elders; we do so only when we are alone or when inferiors are present. If I were married, I would speak to my wife before my younger sister, my nephews, or my nieces, but not before my elder sister or parents. I cannot talk to my sisters about their husbands at all. The idea is that we are a monastic race. The whole social organization has that one idea before it. Marriage is thought of as something basically impure. Therefore the subject of love must never be talked of. I cannot read a novel before my sister or my brothers or my mother or before my elders. I close the book.

Then again, eating and drinking are both in the same category. There are strict rules about this. Women never eat before men, unless they are children or inferiors. The wife would die rather than, as she says, "munch" before her husband. Sometimes, for instance, brothers and sisters may eat together; and if I and my sister are eating, and her husband comes to the door, my sister stops, and the poor husband flies out.

These are the customs peculiar to the country. A few of these I note in other countries also. As I never married, myself, I am not perfect in all my knowledge about the wife. Mother, sisters—I know what they are; and other people's wives I have seen. What I have gathered from them I have told you.

As to education and culture, it all depends upon the man. That is to say, where the men are highly cultured, there the women are; where the men are not, women are not. Now, from the oldest times, you know, the primary education, according to the old Hindu customs, was a part of the village life. All the land from time immemorial was nationalized, as you say—belonged to the government. There never was any private right in land. The revenue in India came from the land, because every man held his land from the government. This land was held in common by a community—it might be of five, ten, twenty, or a hundred families. They governed the whole of the land, paid a certain amount of revenue to the government, and maintained a physician, a village schoolmaster, and so on.

Those of you who have read Herbert Spencer remember what he calls the "monastery system" of education, which was tried in Europe and which in some parts proved a success. The same system is used in rural India: that is, there is one schoolmaster, whom the village maintains. These primary schools are very primitive, because our methods are so simple. Each boy brings a little mat, and his paper, to begin with, is palm leaves. Palm leaves first; paper is too costly. Each boy spreads his little mat and sits upon it, brings out his inkstand and his books, and begins to write. A little arithmetic, some Sanskrit grammar, a little of language, and accounts—these are taught in the primary school.

A little book on ethics, taught by an old man, we learnt by heart, and I remember one of the lessons:

> For the good of his village, a man ought to give up his family;
> For the good of his country, he ought to give up his village;
> For the good of humanity, he should give up his country;
> For the good of the world, everything.

Such are the verses in the books. We get them by heart, and they are explained by teacher to pupil. These are the things we learn—both boys and girls together. Later on the education differs. The old-type Sanskrit schools are mainly composed of boys. The girls very rarely enter those schools; but there are a few exceptions.

In these modern days there is a general impetus towards higher education on European lines, and the trend of opinion is strong towards women's getting this higher education. Of course, there are some people in India who don't want it; but those who do want it have carried the day. It is a strange fact that Oxford and Cambridge are closed to women today, as are Harvard and Yale; but Calcutta University opened its doors to women more than twenty years ago. I remember that the year I graduated several girls graduated too—the same standard, the same course, the same in everything as the boys; and they did very well indeed. Our religion does not prevent a woman's being educated at all. A girl should be educated in the same way as the boys are trained. In the old books we find that the universities were equally resorted to by both girls and boys; but later the education of the whole nation was neglected. What can you expect under foreign rule? The foreign conqueror is not there to do good to us; he wants his money. I studied hard for twelve years and became a graduate of Calcutta University; now I can scarcely make five dollars a month in my country. Would you believe it? It is actually a fact. So these educational institutions of foreigners are simply to get a lot of useful, practical slaves for a little money—to turn out a host of clerks, postmasters, telegraph operators, and so on. There you are.

As a result, education for both boys and girls is neglected, entirely neglected. There are a great many things that should be done in that land; but you must always remember, if you will kindly excuse me and permit me to use one of your own proverbs, "What is sauce for the goose is sauce for the gander." Your foreign-born ladies are always crying over the hardships of the Hindu woman and never care for the hardships of the Hindu man. They are all weeping salt tears. But who are the little girls married to? Someone, when told that they are all married to old men, asked, "And what do the young men do? What! Are all the girls married to old men, only to old men?" We are born old—perhaps all the men there.

The ideal of the Indian race is freedom of the soul. This world is nothing. It is a vision, a dream. This life is one of many millions like it. The whole of this nature is māyā, is a phantasm, a pest-house of phantasms. That is the philosophy. Babies smile at life and think it so beautiful and good, but in a few years they will have to revert to where they began. They began life crying and they will leave it crying. Nations in the vigour of their youth think that they can do anything and everything: "We are the gods of the earth. We are the chosen people." They think that God Almighty has given them a charter to rule over all the world, to advance His plans, to do anything they like, to turn the world upside down. They have a charter to rob, murder, kill; God has given them this. And they do that because they are only babies. So empire after empire has arisen, glorious and resplendent, and then vanished away—nobody knows where—stupendous, it may be, in its ruin. As a drop of water upon a lotus leaf tumbles about and falls in a moment, even so is this mortal life. Everywhere we turn are ruins. Where the forest stands today was once the mighty empire with huge cities.

That is the dominant idea, the tone, the colour of the Indian mind. We know you Western people have youthful blood coursing through your veins. We know that nations, like men, have their day. Where is Greece? Where is Rome? Where that mighty Spaniard of the other day? Thus they are born and thus they die; they rise and fall. The Hindu as a child knows of the Moghul invader, whose cohorts no power on earth could stop, who has left in your language the terrible word *Tartar*. The Hindu has learnt his lesson. He does not want to prattle like the babies of today. Western people, say what you have to say. This is your day. Onward, go on, babies! Have your prattle out. This is the day of the babies, to prattle. We have learnt our lesson and are quiet. You have a little wealth today and you look down upon us. Well, this is your day. Prattle, babies, prattle—this is the Hindu's attitude.

The Lord of lords is not to be attained by much frothy speech. The Lord of lords is not to be attained by the powers of the intellect. He is not attained even by the power of conquest. That man who knows the secret source of things, who knows that everything else is evanescent—unto him the Lord comes, and unto none else. India has learnt her lesson through ages and ages of experience. She has turned her face towards Him. She has made many mistakes; loads and loads of rubbish there are in India. Never mind—what of that? What are the clearing of rubbish, the cleaning of cities, and all that? Does that give life? Those that have fine institutions, they too die. And what are these institutions, these tin-plate Western institutions, made in five days and broken on the sixth? One of these little nations in the West cannot keep alive for two centuries together. And our institutions have stood the test of ages. Says the Hindu: "Yes, we have buried all the old nations of the earth and stand here to bury all the new races also, because our ideal is not this world, but the other. Just as your ideal is, so shall you be. If your ideal is mortal, if your ideal is of this earth, so shall you be. If your ideal is matter, matter shall you be. Behold! our ideal is the Spirit. That alone exists. Nothing else exists. And like the Spirit we live for ever."

THE RĀMĀYANA

(Delivered at the Shakespeare Club, Pasadena, California, January 31, 1900)

THERE ARE TWO great epics in the Sanskrit language which are very ancient. Of course, there are hundreds of other epic poems. The Sanskrit language and literature have come down to the present day, although for more than two thousand years Sanskrit has ceased to be a spoken language. I am now going to speak to you of the two most ancient epics, called the Rāmāyana and the Mahābhārata. They embody the manners and customs, the state of society, civilization, and so forth, of the ancient Indians. The older of these epics is called the Rāmāyana, the Life of Rāma. There was some poetical literature before this; the greater part of the Vedas, the sacred books of the Hindus, are written in a sort of metre; but this book is held by common consent in India to be the very beginning of poetry.

The author of the poem was the sage Vālmiki. Later on a great many poetical stories were ascribed to this ancient poet, and gradually it became a very general practice to attribute to his authorship verses that were not his. Notwithstanding all these interpolations, the Rāmāyana comes down to us as a very beautiful epic, without equal in the literatures of the world.

There was a young man who could not in any way support his family. He was strong and vigorous, and finally became a highway robber; he attacked persons in the street and robbed them, and with that money he supported his father, mother, wife, and children. This went on continually, until one day a great saint called Nārada was passing by, and the robber attacked him. The sage asked the robber: "Why are you going to rob me? It is a great sin to rob human beings and kill them. What do you incur all this sin for?" The robber said, "Why, I want to support my family with this money." "Now," said the sage, "do you think that they take a share of your sin also?" "Certainly they do," replied the robber. "Very good," said the sage; "make me safe by tying me up here, while you go home and ask your people whether they will share your sin in the same way as they share the money you make." The man accordingly went to his father and asked, "Father, do you know how I support you?" He answered, "No, I do not." "I am a robber, and I kill persons and rob them." "What! you do that, my son? Get away, you outcaste!" He then went to his mother and asked her, "Mother, do you know how I support you?" "No," she replied. "Through robbery and murder." "How horrible it is!" cried the mother. "But do you partake in my sin?" said the son. "Why should I? I never committed a robbery," answered the mother. Then he went to his wife and questioned her, "Do you know how I maintain you all?" "No," she responded.

"Why, I am a highwayman," he rejoined, "and for years have been robbing people; that is how I support and maintain you all. And what I now want to know is whether you are ready to share in my sin." "By no means. You are my husband, and it is your duty to support me."

The eyes of the robber were opened. "That's the world!" he exclaimed. "Even my nearest relatives, for whom I have been robbing, will not share in my sin." He came back to the place where he had left the sage, unfastened his bonds, fell at his feet, recounted everything, and said: "Save me! What must I do?" The sage said: "Give up your present course of life. You see that none of your family really loves you; so give up all delusions about them. They will share your prosperity, but the moment you have nothing they will desert you. There is none who will share in your evil; but they will all share in your good. Therefore worship Him who alone stands by us whether we are doing good or evil. He alone loves us; true love never betrays, knows no barter, no selfishness."

Then the sage taught him how to worship. And this man left everything and went into a forest. There he went on praying and meditating until he forgot himself so entirely that when ants came and built ant-hills around him, he was quite unconscious of them. After many years had passed, a voice came saying, "Arise, O sage!" Thus aroused he exclaimed, "Sage? I am a robber!" "No more a robber," answered the voice, "but a purified sage art thou. Forget thine old name. Since thy meditation was so deep and great that thou didst not remark even the ant-hills which surrounded thee, henceforth thy name shall be Vālmiki, 'he that was born in the ant-hill.' " So he became a sage.

And this is how he became a poet: One day as this sage, Vālmiki, was going to bathe in the holy river Ganges, he saw a pair of doves wheeling round and round and kissing each other. The sage looked up and was pleased at the sight, but in a second an arrow whizzed past him and killed the male dove. As the dove fell down on the ground, the female dove went on whirling round and round the dead body of her companion, in grief. At this sight the sage became miserable, and looking round, he saw the hunter. "Thou art a wretch," he cried, "without the smallest mercy. Thy slaying hand would not even stop for love!" "What is this? What am I saying?" the sage asked himself. "I have never spoken in this way before." And then a voice said to him: "Be not distressed: this is poetry that has come out of your mouth. Write the life of Rāma in poetic language for the benefit of the world." That is how the epic was written. The first verse sprang out of pity, from the mouth of Vālmiki, the first poet. And it was after that that he wrote the beautiful Rāmāyana.

There was in ancient times an Indian town called Ayodhyā; it exists even in modern times. The province in which it is located is called Oudh, and most of you may have noticed it on the map of India. That was the ancient Ayodhyā. There, in olden times, reigned a king called Daśaratha. He had three queens, but no children by any of them; and like all good Hindus, the king and the queens all went on pilgrimages, fasting and praying, that they might have children; and in good time four sons were born. The eldest of them was Rāma.

Now, as it should be, these four brothers were thoroughly educated in all branches of learning. To avoid future quarrels there was in ancient India a custom according to which the king in his own lifetime nominated his eldest son as his successor, the *Yuvarāja*, or "Young King," as he was called.

Now, there was another king, called Janaka, and this king had a beautiful daughter named Sitā. Sitā had been found in a field and was really a daughter of the Earth; she was born without parents. The word *sitā* in old Sanskrit means the furrow made by a plough. In the ancient mythology of India you will find persons born of one parent only, or persons born without parents, born of the sacrificial fire, born in the field, and so on—dropped from the clouds, as it were. All those sorts of miraculous birth were common in the mythological lore of India.

Sitā, being the daughter of the Earth, was pure and immaculate. She was brought up by King Janaka. When she was of a marriageable age, the king wanted to find a suitable husband for her.

There was an ancient Indian custom called svayamvara, by which the princesses used to choose husbands. A number of princes from different parts of the country were invited, and the princess, in splendid array, with a garland in her hand, and accompanied by a crier who enumerated the distinctive claims of each of the royal suitors, would walk in the midst of those assembled before her and select for her husband the prince she liked by throwing the garland of flowers round his neck. They would then be married with much pomp and grandeur.

There were numbers of princes who aspired to the hand of Sitā; the test demanded on this occasion was the breaking of a huge bow, called the Haradhanu. The princes put forth all their strength to accomplish this feat, but failed; finally Rāma took the mighty bow in his hands and with easy grace broke it in twain. Thus Sitā selected Rāma, the son of King Daśaratha, for her husband, and they were wedded with great rejoicings. Then Rāma took his bride home, and his old father thought that the time was now come for him to retire and appoint Rāma as Yuvarāja. Everything was accordingly made ready for the ceremony, and the whole country was jubilant over the affair, when the youngest queen, Kaikeyi, was reminded by one of her maid-servants of two promises made to her by the king long ago. At one time she had pleased the king very much, and he had offered to grant her two boons. "Ask any two things in my power and I will grant them to you," he had said, but she had made no request then. She had forgotten all about it; but the evil-minded maid-servant in her employ began to work upon her jealousy with regard to Rāma's being installed on the throne, and insinuated to her how nice it would be for her if her own son should succeed the king, until the queen was almost mad with jealousy. Then the servant suggested to her to ask from the king the two promised boons: by the one, her own son Bharata would be placed on the throne, and by the other, Rāma would be exiled to the forest for fourteen years.

Now, Rāma was the very life of the old king; but when this wicked request was made to his father, the latter felt he could not go back on his word. So he did not know what to do. But Rāma came to the rescue and willingly offered to give up the throne and go into exile so that his father might not be guilty of falsehood. So Rāma went into exile for fourteen years, accompanied

by his loving wife Sitā and his devoted brother Lakshmana, who would on no
account be parted from him.

The Āryans did not know who the inhabitants of these wild forests were.
In those days they called the forest tribes "monkeys"; and some of the so-called
"monkeys," if unusually strong and powerful, were called "demons."

So into the forest, inhabited by demons and monkeys, Rāma, Lakshmana,
and Sitā went. When Sitā had offered to accompany Rāma, he had exclaimed,
"How can you, a princess, face hardships and follow me into a forest full of
unknown dangers?" But Sitā had replied: "Wherever Rāma goes, there goes
Sitā. How can you talk of 'princess' and 'royal birth' to me? I go with you!"
So Sitā went. And the younger brother also went with them. They penetrated
far into the forest, until they reached the river Godāvari. On the bank of the
river they built little cottages, and Rāma and Lakshmana used to hunt deer
and collect fruits. After they had lived thus for some time, one day there came
a she-monster. She was the sister of the monster-king of Lankā, the island of
Ceylon. Roaming through the forest at will, she came across Rāma, and seeing
that he was a very handsome man, fell in love with him at once. But Rāma
was the purest of men, and also he was a married man; so of course he could
not return her love. In revenge, she went to her brother Rāvana, the monster-
king, and told him all about the beautiful Sitā, the wife of Rāma.

Rāma was the most powerful of mortals; there were no giants or demons,
or anybody else, strong enough to conquer him. So the monster-king had to resort to subterfuge. He got hold of another monster, who was a magician, and had
him change into a beautiful golden deer; the deer went prancing around about the
place where Rāma lived, until Sitā was fascinated by its beauty and asked Rāma
to go and capture it for her. Rāma went into the forest to catch the deer, leaving
his brother in charge of Sitā. Then Lakshmana laid a circle of fire round the
cottage and said to Sitā: "Today I fear that some evil may befall you, and
therefore I tell you not to go outside this magic circle. Some danger may befall
you if you do." Meanwhile Rāma had pierced the magic deer with his arrow,
and immediately the deer changed into the form of the monster and died.

Immediately at the cottage was heard the voice of Rāma, crying, "Oh, Lakshmana, come to my help!" and Sitā said: "Lakshmana, go at once into the forest
to help Rāma!" "That is not Rāma's voice," protested Lakshmana. But at the
entreaties of Sitā, Lakshmana had to go in search of Rāma. As soon as he had
gone away, the monster-king, who had taken the form of a mendicant, stood
at the gate and asked for alms. "Wait awhile," said Sitā, "until my husband
comes back, and I will give you plentiful alms." "I cannot wait, good lady,"
said he; "I am very hungry; give me anything you have." At this, Sitā, who had a
few fruits in the cottage, brought them out. But the mendicant monk, after
much persuading, prevailed upon her to bring the alms to him, assuring her
that she need have no fear since he was a holy person. So Sitā came out of the
magic circle, and immediately the seeming monk assumed his monster body.
Grasping her in his arms, he called his magic chariot and, putting her therein,
fled with the weeping Sitā. Poor Sitā! She was utterly helpless; nobody was there
to come to her aid. As the monster was carrying her away, she took off a few of
the ornaments from her arms and at intervals dropped them to the ground.

She was taken by Rāvana to his kingdom, Lankā. He made proposals to her to become his queen, and tempted her in many ways to accede to his request. But Sitā, who was chastity itself, would not even speak to the monster, and he, to punish her, made her live under a tree day and night, until she should consent to be his wife.

When Rāma and Lakshmana returned to the cottage and found that Sitā was not there, their grief knew no bounds. They could not imagine what had become of her. The two brothers went on seeking, seeking everywhere for Sitā, but could find no trace of her. After long searching, they came across a group of monkeys, and in the midst of them was Hanumān, the "divine" monkey. Hanumān, the best of the monkeys, became the most faithful servant of Rāma and helped him in rescuing Sitā, as we shall see later on. His devotion to Rāma was so great that he is still worshipped by the Hindus as the ideal of a true servant of the Lord. You see, by the monkeys and demons were meant the aborigines of Southern India.

So Rāma at last came to these monkeys. They told him that they had seen flying through the sky a chariot in which was seated a demon who was carrying away a most beautiful lady, and that she was weeping bitterly; and as the chariot passed over their heads she dropped one of her ornaments to attract their attention. Then they showed Rāma the ornament. Lakshmana took the ornament and said: "I do not know whose ornament this is." Rāma took it from him and recognized it at once, saying, "Yes, it is Sitā's." Lakshmana could not recognize the ornament because he had never looked upon the arms and the neck of Sitā—such was the reverence in which he held her, his elder brother's wife. So you see, since it was a necklace he did not know whose it was. There is in this episode a touch of the old Indian custom. Then the monkeys told Rāma who this monster-king was and where he lived, and they all went to seek for him.

Now, the monkey-king Vāli and his younger brother Sugriva were then fighting among themselves for the kingdom. The younger brother was helped by Rāma, and he regained the kingdom from Vāli, who had driven him away; and he in return promised to help Rāma. They searched the country all around, but could not find Sitā. At last Hanumān leapt by one bound from the coast of India to Lanka, the island of Ceylon, and went on looking everywhere for Sitā; but nowhere could he find her.

You see, this monster had conquered the gods, men, and in fact the whole world; and he had collected all the beautiful women and made them his concubines. So Hanumān thought to himself: "Sitā cannot be with them in the palace. She would rather die than be in such a place." So Hanumān went to seek for her elsewhere. At last he found Sitā under a tree, pale and thin, like the new moon that lies low on the horizon. Now Hanumān took the form of a little monkey and settled on the tree; and there he witnessed how giantesses sent by Rāvana tried to frighten Sitā into submission, but she would not even listen to the name of the monster-king.

Then Hanumān came nearer to Sitā and told her how he had become the messenger of Rāma, who had sent him to find out where she was; and Hanumān showed Sitā the signet ring which Rāma had given as a token for establishing his identity. He also informed her that as soon as Rāma knew her whereabouts, he would come with an army and conquer the monster and recover her. He suggested to Sitā, however, that if she wished it he would take her on his shoulders and could with one leap clear the ocean and get back to Rāma. But Sitā could not bear the idea, for she was chastity itself and could not touch the body of any man except her husband. So Sitā remained where she was. But she gave him a jewel from her hair to carry to Rāma; and with that Hanumān returned.

Learning everything about Sitā from Hanumān, Rāma collected an army and with it marched towards the southernmost point of India. There Rāma's monkeys built a huge bridge, called Setu-bandha, connecting India with Ceylon.

Now, Rāma was God incarnate; otherwise how could he have done all these things? In India they believe him to be the seventh Incarnation of God.

The monkeys removed whole hills, placed them in the sea, and covered them with stones and trees, thus making a huge embankment. A little squirrel, so it is said, was there, rolling himself in the sand and running backward and forward on to the bridge and shaking himself. Thus in his small way he was working for the bridge of Rāma by putting in sand. The monkeys laughed, for they were bringing whole mountains, whole forests, huge loads of sand for the bridge; they laughed at the little squirrel rolling in the sand and then shaking himself. But Rāma saw it and remarked, "Blessed be the little squirrel; he is doing his work to the best of his ability, and he is therefore quite as great as the greatest of you." Then he gently stroked the squirrel on the back; and the marks of Rāma's fingers running lengthwise are seen on squirrels' backs to this day.

Now, when the bridge was finished the whole army of monkeys, led by Rāma and his brother, entered Ceylon. Tremendous war and bloodshed followed for several months afterwards. At last the monster-king Rāvana was conquered and killed, and his capital, with all the palaces and everything, which were made of solid gold, was taken. In far-away villages in the interior of India, when I tell them that I have been in Ceylon, the simple folk say, "There, as our books tell, the houses are built of gold." So all these golden palaces fell into the hands of Rāma, who gave them over to Vibhishana, the younger brother of Rāvana, and seated him on the throne in place of his brother, in return for the valuable services rendered by him to Rāma during the war.

Then Rāma and Sitā were about to leave Lankā. But there ran a murmur among the followers. "The test! the test!" they cried. "Sitā has not given the test that she was perfectly pure in Rāvana's household." "Pure! She is chastity itself!" exclaimed Rāma. "Never mind! We want the test," persisted the people. Subsequently a huge sacrificial fire was lighted, into which Sitā had to plunge. Rāma was in agony, thinking that Sitā was lost; but in a moment the god of fire himself appeared, with a throne upon his head, and upon the throne was Sitā. Then there was universal rejoicing and everybody was satisfied.

Early during the period of exile, Bharata, the younger brother, had come and informed Rāma of the death of the old king and earnestly insisted on his occupying the throne. But Rāma had refused. During Rāma's exile Bharata would on no account ascend the throne, and out of respect placed a pair of Rāma's wooden shoes on it as a substitute for his brother.

Rāma now returned to his capital and by the common consent of his people became the king of Ayodhyā.

After Rāma regained his kingdom he took the necessary vows which in olden times the king had to take for the benefit of his people. The king was the servant of his people and had to bow to public opinion, as we shall see later on. Rāma passed a few years in happiness with Sitā, when the people again began to murmur that Sitā had been stolen by a demon and carried across the ocean. They were not satisfied with the former test and clamoured for another test; otherwise she must be banished.

In order to satisfy the demands of the people, Sitā was banished and left alone in the forest, where was the hermitage of the sage and poet Vālmiki. The sage found poor Sitā weeping and forlorn, and hearing her sad story, sheltered her in his āśrama. Sitā was expecting soon to become a mother, and she gave birth to twin boys. The poet never told the children who they were. He brought them up together in the brahmachārin's life. He then composed the poem known as the Rāmāyana, set it to music, and dramatized it.

The drama in India was a very holy thing. Drama and music are themselves held to be religion. Any song—whether it be a love-song or otherwise—if one's whole soul is in that song, leads one to salvation; one has nothing else to do. They say it leads to the same goal as meditation. So Vālmiki dramatized the life of Rāma and taught Rāma's two children how to recite and sing it.

There came a time when Rāma was going to perform a huge sacrifice, or yajna, such as kings of old used to perform. But no ceremony in India can be performed by a married man without his wife; he must have his wife with him, the sahadharmini, the "co-partner"—that is the expression for a wife. The Hindu householder has to perform hundreds of ceremonies, but not one can be duly performed, according to the śāstras, if he has not a wife to complement it with her part in it.

Now, Rāma's wife was not with him then, for she had been banished. So the people asked him to marry again. But Rāma for the first time in his life stood against the wishes of the people. He said: "This cannot be. My life is Sitā's." So, as a substitute, a golden statue of Sitā was made, in order that the ceremony could be accomplished. A dramatic entertainment was even arranged to enhance the religious feeling of this great festival. Vālmiki, the great sage-poet, came with his pupils Lava and Kuśa, the unknown sons of Rāma. A stage had been erected and everything was ready for the performance. Rāma and his brothers, attended by all his nobles and his people, made a vast audience. Under the direction of Vālmiki, the life of Rāma was sung by Lava and Kuśa, who fascinated the whole assembly by their charming voices and appearance. Poor Rāma was nearly maddened, and when in the drama the scene of Sitā's exile came about, he did not know what to do. Then the sage said to him, "Do not be grieved, for I will show you Sitā." Then Sitā was brought upon the stage and Rāma was overjoyed to see his wife. All of a sudden the old murmur arose: "The test! the test!" Poor Sitā was terribly overcome by the repeated cruel slight on her reputation; it was more than she could bear. She appealed to mother earth to testify to her innocence, when the earth opened, and Sitā, exclaiming, "Here is the test!" vanished into the bosom of the earth. The people were taken aback at this tragic end, and Rāma was overwhelmed with grief.

A few days after Sitā's disappearance a messenger came to Rāma from the gods, who intimated to him that his mission on earth was finished and he was to return to heaven. These tidings brought to him the recognition of his own real Self. He plunged into the waters of the Sarayu, the mighty river that laved his capital, and joined Sitā in the other world.

This is the great ancient epic of India. Rāma and Sitā are the ideals of the Indian nation. All children, especially girls, worship Sitā. The height of a woman's ambition is to be like Sitā, the pure, the devoted, the all-suffering. When you study these characters you can at once find out how different is the ideal in India from that of the West. For the race, Sitā stands as the ideal of suffering. The West says, "Do: show your power by doing." India says, "Show your power by suffering." The West has solved the problem of how much a man can have; India has solved the problem of how little a man can have—the two extremes, you see. Sitā is typical of India, the idealized India. The question is not whether she ever lived, whether the story is history or not; for we know that the ideal is there. There is no other ideal that has so permeated the whole nation, so entered into its very life, so tingled in every drop of blood of the race, as this ideal of Sitā. Sitā is the name in India for everything that is good, pure, and holy —everything that in woman we call womanly. If a priest has to bless a woman he says, "Be Sitā!" If he blesses a girl he says, "Be Sitā!" They are all children of Sitā and striving to be like Sitā, the patient, the all-suffering, the ever faithful, the ever pure wife. Through all the suffering she experiences, there is not one harsh word against Rāma. She takes it as her own duty and performs her own part in it. Think of the terrible injustice of her being exiled to the forest! But Sitā knows no bitterness. That is, again, the Indian ideal. Says the prophet Buddha: "When a man hurts you and you turn back to hurt him, that will not cure the first injury; it will only create in the world one more evil." Sitā is a true Indian by nature: she never returns injury.

Who knows which is the truer ideal: the apparent power and strength of the West, or the fortitude in suffering of the East?

The West says, "We minimize evil by conquering it." India says, "We destroy evil by suffering, until evil is nothing to us and becomes positive enjoyment." Well, both are great ideals. Who knows which will survive in the long run? Who knows which attitude will really benefit humanity more? Who knows which will disarm and conquer animality? Will it be suffering or doing?

In the meantime, let us not try to destroy each other's ideals. We are both intent upon the same work, which is the annihilation of evil. You take up your method; let us take up our method. Let us not destroy the ideal. I do not say to the West, "Take up our method." Certainly not. The goal is the same, but the methods can never be the same. And so, after hearing about the ideals of India, I hope that you will say in the same breath to India: "We know the goal is right for us both. You follow your own ideal. You follow your method in your own way, and God speed you!" My mission in life is to ask the East and West not to quarrel over different ideals, but to show them that the goal is the same in both cases, however opposite it may appear. As we wend our way through this mazy vale of life, let us bid each other God-speed.

THE MAHĀBHĀRATA

(Delivered at the Shakespeare Club, Pasadena, California, February 1, 1900)

THE OTHER EPIC, about which I am going to speak to you this evening, is called the Mahābhārata. It contains the story of a race descended from King Bharata, who was the son of Dushyanta and Sakuntalā. Mahā means great, and Bhārata means the descendants of Bharata, from whom India has derived its name, Bhārata. Mahābhārata means the Great India or the story of the great descendants of Bharata. The scene of this epic is the ancient kingdom of the Kurus, and the story is based on the great war which took place between the Kurus and the Pāndavas. So the area covered by the epic is not big. This epic is the most popular one in India; and it exercises the same authority in India as Homer's poems did over the Greeks. As ages went on, more and more matter was added to it, until it became a huge book of about a hundred thousand couplets. All sorts of tales, legends, and myths, philosophical treatises, scraps of history, and various discussions were added to it from time to time, until it became a gigantic mass of literature; and through it all runs the old, original story.

The central story of the Mahābhārata is about a war between two families of cousins—one family called the Kauravas, the other, the Pāndavas—for empire over India.

The Āryans came into India in small tribes. Gradually these tribes began to spread, until at last they became the undisputed rulers of India; and then arose this fight to gain mastery, between two branches of the same family. Those of you that have studied the Gītā know how the book opens with a description of the battlefield, with two armies arrayed one against the other. That is the war of the Mahābhārata.

There were two brothers, sons of an emperor. The elder one was called Dhritarāshtra, and the other was called Pāndu. Dhritarāshtra was born blind. According to Indian law, no blind, halt, maimed, consumptive, or any other constitutionally diseased person can inherit a kingdom. He can only get a maintenance. So Dhritarāshtra could not ascend the throne, though he was the elder son, and Pāndu became the emperor.

Dhritarāshtra had a hundred sons, and Pāndu had only five. After the death of Pāndu at an early age, Dhritarāshtra took charge of the princes and brought up the sons of Pāndu along with his own children. When they grew up they were placed under the tutorship of the great priest-warrior Drona and were well trained in the various martial arts and sciences befitting princes. The education of the princes being finished, Dhritarāshtra put Yudhishthira, the eldest of the sons of Pāndu, on the throne of his father. The sterling virtues of Yudhish-

844

thira and the valour and devotion of his other brothers aroused jealousy in the hearts of the sons of the blind king, and at the instigation of Duryodhana, the eldest of them, the five Pāndava brothers were prevailed upon to visit Vāranā-vata on the pretext of a religious festival that was being held there. They were accommodated in a palace made, under Duryodhana's instructions, of hemp, resin, lac, and other inflammable materials, which were subsequently set fire to secretly. But the good Vidura, the step-brother of Dhritarāshtra, having become cognizant of the evil intentions of Duryodhana and his party, had warned the Pāndavas of the plot, and they managed to escape without anyone's knowledge. When the Kurus saw the house reduced to ashes, they heaved a sigh of relief and thought all obstacles were now removed from their path. Then the children of Dhritarāshtra got hold of the kingdom. The five Pāndava brothers had fled to the forest with their mother, Kunti. They lived there by begging and went about in disguise, giving themselves out as brāhmin students. Many were the hardships and adventures they encountered in the wild forests, but their fortitude of mind and their strength and valour enabled them to conquer all dangers. So things went on until they came to hear of the approaching marriage of the princess of a neighbouring country.

I told you last night of a peculiar form of the ancient Indian marriage. It was called svayamvara, that is, the choosing of a husband by a princess. A great gathering of princes and noblemen assembled, from among whom she would choose her husband. Preceded by her trumpeters and heralds, she would approach, carrying a garland of flowers in her hand. At the throne of each candidate for her hand the praises of that prince and all his great deeds in battle would be declared by the heralds. And when the princess decided which prince she desired to have for her husband, she would signify the fact by throwing the marriage garland round his neck. Then the ceremony would turn into a wedding.

King Drupada was a great king, the king of the Pānchālas, and his daughter, Draupadi, famed far and wide for her beauty and accomplishments, was going to choose a husband. At a svayamvara there was always a great feat of arms or something of the kind. On this occasion a mark in the form of a fish was set up high in the sky; under that fish was a wheel with a hole in the centre, continuously turning round, and on the earth below was a tub of water. A man, looking at the reflection of the fish in the water, was to send an arrow and hit the eye of the fish through the chakra, or wheel, and he who succeeded would be married to the princess. Now, there came kings and princes from different parts of India, all anxious to win the hand of the princess, and one after another they tried their skill, and every one of them failed to hit the mark.

You know, there are four castes in India. The highest caste is that of the hereditary priests, the brāhmins; next is the caste of the kshattriyas, composed of kings and fighters; next come the vaiśyas, the traders or business men; and then, the śudras, the servants. This princess was, of course, a kshattriya, one of the second caste.

When all those princes failed in hitting the mark, the son of King Drupada rose up in the midst of the court and said: "The kshattriya, the kingly caste, has failed; now the contest is open to the other castes. Let a brāhmin, even a śudra, take part in it. Whosoever hits the mark marries Draupadi."

Among the brāhmins were seated the five Pāndava brothers. Arjuna, the third brother, was the hero of the bow. He arose and stepped forward. Now, brāhmins as a caste are very quiet and rather gentle people. According to the law, they must not touch a warlike weapon, they must not wield a sword, they must not go into any enterprise that is dangerous. Their life is one of contemplation, study, and control of the inner nature. Judge, therefore, how quiet and peaceable a people they are. When the brāhmins saw this man get up, they thought he was going to bring the wrath of the kshattriyas upon them and they would all be killed. So they tried to dissuade him. But Arjuna did not listen to them, because he was a soldier. He lifted the bow in his hand, strung it without any effort, and drawing it, sent the arrow right through the wheel and hit the eye of the fish.

Then there was great jubilation. Draupadi, the princess, approached Arjuna and threw the beautiful garland of flowers over his head. But there arose a great cry among the princes, who could not bear the idea that this beautiful princess, who was a kshattriya, should be won by a poor brāhmin from among this huge assembly of kings and princes. So they wanted to fight Arjuna and snatch her from him by force. The brothers had a tremendous fight with the warriors, but held their own and carried off the bride in triumph.

The five brothers now returned home to their mother Kunti with the princess. Brāhmins had to live by begging. So since they were living as brāhmins, they used to go out begging, and what they got they brought home and the mother divided it among them. Thus the five brothers, with the princess, came to the cottage where their mother lived. They shouted out to her jocosely, "Mother, we have brought home the most wonderful alms today." The mother replied, "Enjoy it in common, all of you, my children." Then the mother, seeing the princess, exclaimed: "Oh! What have I said? It is a girl!" But what could be done? The mother's word was spoken once for all. It must not be disregarded. The mother's word must be fulfilled. She could not be made to utter an untruth, for she never had done so. So Draupadi became the common wife of all the five brothers.

Now, you know, in every society there are stages of development. Behind this epic there is a wonderful glimpse of the ancient historic times. The author of the poem mentions the fact of the five brothers' marrying the same woman, but he tries to gloss it over, to find an excuse and a cause for such an act: it was the mother's command, the mother sanctioned this strange betrothal, and so on. You know from history that every race has passed through a stage of development which allowed polyandry; all the brothers of a family would marry one wife in common. Now, this is evidently a glimpse of the past, polyandrous stage.

In the meantime the brother of the princess was perplexed in his mind and thought: "Who are these people? Who is this man whom my sister is going to marry? They have not any chariots, horses, or anything. Why, they go on foot!" So he followed them at a distance and at night overheard their conversation and became fully convinced that they were really kshattriyas. Then King Drupada came to know who they were and was greatly delighted.

Though at first many objections were raised, it was declared by Vyāsa that such a marriage was allowable for these princes, and it was permitted. So King

Drupada had to yield to this polyandrous marriage, and the princess was married to the five sons of Pāndu.

Then the Pāndavas lived in peace and prosperity and became more powerful every day. Though Duryodhana and his party conceived fresh plots to destroy them, King Dhritarāshtra was prevailed upon by the wise counsels of the elders to make peace with the Pāndavas; and so he invited them home amidst the rejoicings of the people and gave them half of the kingdom. The five brothers built for themselves a beautiful city called Indraprastha, and extended their dominions, laying all the people under tribute to them. Then the eldest, Yudhishthira, in order to declare himself emperor over all the kings of ancient India, decided to perform a Rājasuya Yajna, or Imperial Sacrifice, in which the conquered kings would have to come with tribute and swear allegiance, and help in the performance of the sacrifice by personal service. Śri Krishna, who had become their friend and relative, came to them and approved of the idea. But there was one obstacle to its performance. A king, Jarāsandha by name, who intended to offer a sacrifice of a hundred kings, had eighty-six of them kept as captives with him. Śri Krishna counselled an attack on Jarāsandha; so he, Bhima, and Arjuna challenged the king, who accepted the challenge and was finally conquered by Bhima after fourteen days' continuous wrestling. The captive kings were then set free.

Then the four younger brothers went out with armies on a conquering expedition, each in a different direction, and brought all the kings under subjection to Yudhishthira. Returning, they laid all the vast wealth they had secured at the feet of the eldest brother, to meet the expenses of the great sacrifice.

So to this Rājasuya Sacrifice all the liberated kings came, along with those conquered by the brothers, and rendered homage to Yudhishthira. King Dhritarāshtra and his sons were also invited to come and have a share in the performance of the sacrifice. At the conclusion of the sacrifice, Yudhishthira was crowned emperor and declared lord paramount.

This was the sowing of the future feud. Duryodhana came back from the sacrifice filled with jealousy against Yudhishthira and his brothers; for their sovereignty and vast splendour and wealth were more than he could bear; and so he devised plans to effect their fall by guile, since he knew that to overcome them by force was beyond his power. King Yudhishthira loved gambling, and he was challenged in an evil hour to play dice with Śakuni, the crafty gambler and evil genius of Duryodhana.

In ancient India, if a man of the military caste was challenged to fight, he must at any price accept the challenge to uphold his honour. And if he was challenged to play dice, it was also a point of honour to play, and dishonourable to decline the challenge. King Yudhishthira, says the epic, was the incarnation of all virtues. Even he, the great sage-king, had to accept the challenge.

Sakuni and his party played with loaded dice. So Yudhishthira lost game after game, and stung with his losses, he went on with the fatal play, staking everything he had, and losing all, until all his possessions—his kingdom and everything—were lost. The last stage came when, under a further challenge, he had no other resource left but to stake his brothers, and then himself, and last of all, the fair Draupadi—and lost all. Now they were completely at the mercy of the Kauravas, who cast all sorts of insults upon them and subjected Draupadi to most inhuman treatment. At last, through the intervention of the blind king, they got their liberty and were asked to return home and rule their kingdom.

But Duryodhana saw the danger and forced his father to allow one more throw of the dice, the condition being that the party which would lose must retire to the forests for twelve years and then live unrecognized in a city for one year; but if they were found out, the same term of exile would have to be undergone once again, and then only would the kingdom be restored to the exiles.

This last game Yudhishthira lost also, and the five Pāndava brothers retired to the forests with Draupadi, as homeless exiles. They lived in the forests and mountains for twelve years. There they performed many deeds of virtue and valour, and would go out now and then on a long round of pilgrimages, visiting many holy places. That part of the poem is very interesting and instructive, and various are the incidents, tales, and legends with which it is replete. There are in it beautiful and sublime stories of ancient India, religious and philosophical. Great sages came to see the brothers in their exile and narrated to them many telling stories of ancient India, so as to make them bear lightly the burden of their exile. One only I will relate to you here.

There was a king called Aśvapati. The king had a daughter who was so good and beautiful that she was called Sāvitri, which is the name of a sacred prayer of the Hindus. When Sāvitri grew old enough, her father asked her to choose a husband for herself. These ancient Indian princesses were very independent, as you have already seen, and chose their own princely suitors.

Sāvitri consented and travelled in distant regions, mounted in a golden chariot, with her guards and aged courtiers, to whom her father had entrusted her, stopping at different courts and seeing different princes; but not one of them could win the heart of Sāvitri. They came at last to a holy hermitage in one of those forests that in ancient India were reserved for animals, and where no animals were allowed to be killed. The animals lost their fear of man; even the fish in the lakes came and took food out of the hand. For thousands of years no one had killed anything therein. The sages and the aged went there to live among the deer and the birds. Even criminals were safe there. When a man got tired of life, he would go to the forest, and in the company of sages, talking of religion and meditating thereon, he passed the remainder of his life.

Now, it happened that there was a king, Dyumatsena, who had been defeated by his enemies and deprived of his kingdom when he was stricken with old age and had lost his sight. This poor old blind king, with his queen and his son, took refuge in the forest and passed his life in rigid penance. His boy's name was Satyavān.

It came to pass that after having visited all the different royal courts, Sāvitri at last came to this hermitage, or holy place. Not even the greatest king could pass by the hermitages, or āśramas as they were called, without paying his homage to the sages, such were the honour and respect shown to these holy men. The greatest emperor of India would be only too glad to trace his descent to some sage who lived in a forest, subsisting on roots and fruits, and clad in rags.

So Sāvitri came to this hermitage and saw there Satyavān, the hermit's son, and her heart was conquered. She had escaped all the princes of the palaces and the courts, but here in the forest refuge of King Dyumatsena, his son Satyavān stole her heart.

When Sāvitri returned to her father's house, he asked her: "Sāvitri, dear daughter, speak. Did you see anybody whom you would like to marry?" Then softly, with blushes, said Sāvitri, "Yes, father." "What is the name of the prince?" "He is no prince, but the son of King Dyumatsena, who has lost his kingdom—a prince without a patrimony, who lives a monastic life, the life of a sannyāsin, in a forest, collecting roots and herbs, helping and feeding his old father and mother, who live in a cottage."

On hearing this the father consulted the sage Nārada, who then happened to be present there, and he declared it was the most ill-omened choice that was ever made. The king then asked him to explain why it was so. And Nārada said, "Within twelve months from this time the young man will die." Then the king started with terror and spoke: "Sāvitri, this young man is going to die in twelve months and you will become a widow: think of that! Desist from your choice, my child; you shall never be married to a short-lived and fated bridegroom." "Never mind, father; do not ask me to marry another person and sacrifice my chastity of mind, for I love and have accepted in my mind the good and brave Satyavān only as my husband. A maiden chooses only once, and she never departs from her troth." When the king found that Sāvitri was resolute in mind and heart, he complied. Then Sāvitri married Prince Satyavān, and she quietly went from the palace of her father into the forest, to live with her chosen husband and help her husband's parents. Now, though Sāvitri knew the exact date when Satyavān was to die, she kept it hidden from him. Daily he went into the depths of the forest, collected fruits and flowers, gathered faggots, and then came back to the cottage, and she cooked the meals and helped the old people. Thus their lives went on until the fatal day came near, and only three short days remained. She took a severe vow of three nights' penance and holy fasts, and kept her hard vigils. Sāvitri spent sorrowful and sleepless nights with fervent prayers and unseen tears, till the dreaded morning dawned. That day Sāvitri could not bear him out of her sight, even for a moment. She begged permission from his parents to accompany her husband when he went to gather the usual herbs and fuel, and gaining their consent, she went. Suddenly, in faltering accents, he complained to his wife of feeling faint: "My head is dizzy, and my senses reel, dear Sāvitri. I feel sleep stealing over me; let me rest beside thee for a while." In fear and trembling she replied, "Come, lay your head upon my lap, my dearest lord." And he laid his burning head in the lap of his wife, and ere long sighed and expired. Clasping him to her, her eyes flowing with tears, there she sat in the lonesome forest, until the emissaries of death approached to take away the soul of Satyavān. But they could not come near to the place where Sāvitri sat with the dead body of her husband, his head resting in her lap. There was a zone of fire surrounding her, and not one of the emissaries of death could come within it. They all fled back from it, returned to King Yama, the god of death, and told him why they could not obtain the soul of this man.

Then came Yama, the god of death, the judge of the dead. He was the first man that had died—the first man that died on earth—and he had become the presiding deity over all those that die. He judges whether, after a man has died, he is to be punished or rewarded. So he came himself. Of course, he could go inside that charmed circle, for he was a god. When he came to Sāvitri he said: "Daughter, give up this dead body; for know that death is the fate of mortals, and I am the first of mortals who died. Since then everyone has had to die. Death is the fate of man." Thus told, Sāvitri walked off and Yama drew the soul out. Yama, having possessed himself of the soul of the young man, proceeded on his way. Before he had gone far he heard footfalls upon the dry leaves. He turned back. "Sāvitri, daughter, why are you following me? This is the fate of all mortals." "I am not following thee, Father," replied Sāvitri; "but this is also the fate of woman, that she goes where her love takes her, and the eternal law separates not loving man and faithful wife." Then said the god of death: "Ask for any boon except the life of your husband." "If thou art pleased to grant a boon, O Lord of Death, I ask that my father-in-law may be cured of his blindness and made happy." "Let thy pious wish be granted, duteous daughter." And then the king of death travelled on with the soul of Satyavān. Again the same footfalls were heard from behind. He looked round. "Sāvitri, my daughter, you are still following me?" "Yes, my Father. I cannot help doing so; I am trying all the time to go back, but the mind goes after my husband and the body follows. The soul has already gone, for in that soul is also mine; and when you take the soul, the body follows, does it not?" "Pleased am I with your words, fair Sāvitri. Ask yet another boon of me; but it must not be the life of your husband." "Let my father-in-law regain his lost wealth and kingdom, Father, if thou art pleased to grant another supplication." "Loving daughter," Yama answered, "this boon I now bestow; but return home, for living mortal cannot go with King Yama." And then Yama pursued his way. But Sāvitri, meek and faithful, still followed her departed husband. Yama again turned back. "Noble Sāvitri, follow not in hopeless woe." "I cannot choose but follow where thou takest my loved one." "Then suppose, Sāvitri, that your husband was a sinner and has to go to hell. In that case goes Sāvitri with the one she loves?" "Glad am I to follow where he goes, be it life or death, heaven or hell," said the loving wife. "Blessed are your words, my child. Pleased am I with you. Ask yet another boon; but remember that the dead come not to life again." "Since you so permit me, let the line of my father-in-law not be destroyed; let his kingdom descend to Satyavān's sons." And then the god of death smiled: "My daughter, thou shalt have thy desire now. Here is the soul of thy husband; he shall live again. He shall live to be a father and thy children also shall reign in due course. Return home. Love has conquered death! Woman never loved like thee, and thou are the proof that even I, the god of death, am powerless against the power of the true love that abideth."

This is the story of Sāvitri, and every girl in India must aspire to be like Sāvitri, whose love could not be conquered by death, and who through this tremendous love snatched back even from Yama the soul of her husband.

The book is full of hundreds of beautiful episodes like this. I began by telling you that the Mahābhārata is one of the greatest books in the world. It consists of about a hundred thousand verses, in eighteen parvas, or volumes.

To return to our main story. We left the Pāndava brothers in exile. Even there they were not allowed to remain unmolested from the evil plots of Duryodhana; but all of these were futile.

I shall tell you here a story of their forest life. One day the brothers became thirsty in the forest. Yudhishthira bade his brother Nakula go and fetch water. He quickly proceeded in search of a place where there was water and soon came to a lake. He was about to drink of the water, when he heard a voice utter these words: "Stop, my child. First answer my questions, and then drink of this water." But Nakula, who was exceedingly thirsty, disregarded these words, drank of the water, and immediately after dropped down dead. As Nakula did not return, King Yudhishthira told Sahadeva to seek his brother and bring back water with him. So Sahadeva proceeded to the lake and beheld his brother lying dead. Afflicted at the death of his brother, and suffering severely from thirst, he went towards the water, when the same words were heard by him: "My child, first answer my questions, and then drink of the water." He too disregarded these words, and having satisfied his thirst, dropped down dead. Subsequently Arjuna and Bhima were sent, one after the other, on a similar quest, but neither returned, having drunk of the water and dropped down dead. Then Yudhishthira rose up to go in search of his brothers. At length he came to the beautiful lake and saw his brothers lying dead. His heart was full of grief at the sight, and he began to lament. Suddenly he heard the same voice saying: "Do not, my child, act rashly. I am a Yaksha living, as a crane, on tiny fish. It is by me that thy younger brothers have been brought under the sway of the lord of departed spirits. If thou, O Prince, answerest not the questions put by me, even thou shalt become the fifth corpse. Having answered my questions first, do thou, O Kunti's son, drink and carry away as much as thou requirest." Yudhishthira replied: "I shall answer thy questions according to my intelligence. Do thou ask me." The Yaksha then asked him several questions, all of which Yudhishthira answered satisfactorily. One of the questions asked was: "What is the most wonderful fact in this world?" Yudhishthira answered: "We see our fellow beings every moment dying around us, but those who are left think that they will never die. This is the most wonderful fact." Another question was: "How can one know the secret of religion?" And Yudhishthira answered: "By argument nothing can be settled. Doctrines there are many; various are the scriptures, one part contradicting another. There are no two thinkers who do not differ in their opinions. The secret of religion is buried deep, as it were, in dark caves. So the path to be followed is that which the great ones have trodden." Then the Yaksha said: "I am pleased. I am Dharma, the god of justice, in the form of the crane. I came to test thee. Now, thy brothers—see, not one of them is dead. It is all my magic. Since abstention from injury is regarded by thee as higher than both profit and pleasure, therefore let all thy brothers live, O Bull of the Bhārata race." And at these words of the Yaksha, the Pāndavas rose up.

Here is a glimpse of the nature of King Yudhishthira. We can see from his answers that he was more of a philosopher, more of a yogi, than a king.

Now, as the thirteenth year of the exile was drawing nigh, the Yaksha bade them go to Virāt's kingdom and live there in such disguises as they thought best. So after the term of the twelve years' exile had expired, they went to the

kingdom of Virāt in different disguises to spend the remaining year in concealment, and entered into menial service in the king's household. Thus
Yudhishthira became a brāhmin courtier of the king, as one skilled in dice;
Bhima was appointed a cook; Arjuna, dressed as a eunuch, was made a teacher
of dancing and music to Uttarā, the princess, and remained in the inner apart-
ments of the king; Nakula became the keeper of the king's horses; Sahadeva got
the charge of the cows; and Draupadi, disguised as a lady-in-waiting, was also
admitted into the queen's household. Thus concealing their identity, the Pāndava brothers safely spent a year, and the search of Duryodhana to find them
out was of no avail. They were only discovered just when the year was out.

Then Yudhishthira sent an ambassador to Dhritarāshtra and demanded that
half of the kingdom should, as their share, be restored to them. But Duryodhana
hated his cousins and would not consent to their legitimate demands. They
were even willing to accept a single province—nay, even five villages. But the
headstrong Duryodhana declared that he would not yield without a fight even
as much land as a needle's point would hold. Dhritarāshtra pleaded again and
again for peace, but all in vain. Krishna also went and tried to avert the impending war and death of kinsmen, as did the wise elders of the royal court; but all
negotiations for a peaceful partition of the kingdom were futile. So at last preparations were made on both sides for war, and all the warlike nations took part
in it.

In this war the old Indian customs of the kshattriyas were observed. Duryodhana took command of one side; Yudhishthira, of the other. From Yudhishthira
messengers were at once sent to all the surrounding kings, entreating their
alliance, since honourable men would grant the request that first reached them.
So warriors from all parts assembled to espouse the cause of either the
Pāndavas or the Kurus, according to the precedence of their requests; and thus
one brother joined this side, and the other that side, the father was on one
side, and the son on the other. The most curious thing was the code of war
of those days: As soon as the battle for the day ceased and evening came, the
opposing parties were good friends; they visited each other's tents; but when
the morning came, again they proceeded to fight each other. That was the
strange trait that the Hindus carried down to the time of the Mohammedan
invasion. Then again, a man on horseback must not strike one on foot, must
not poison his weapon, must not vanquish the enemy in any unequal fight
or by dishonesty, must never take undue advantage of another, and so on. If
any deviated from these rules he would be covered with dishonour and shunned.
The kshattriyas were trained in that way. And when the foreign invasion came
from Central Asia, the Hindus treated the invaders in the self-same way. They
defeated them several times, and on as many occasions sent them back to their
homes with presents, and so on. The code laid down was that they must not
usurp anybody's country; and when a man was beaten, he must be sent back
to his country with due regard to his position. The Mohammedan conquerors
treated the Hindu kings differently, and when they beat them once, they
destroyed them without remorse.

Mind you, in those days—in the times of our story—the poem says, the
science of arms was not the mere use of plain bows and arrows; it was magic

archery in which the use of mantras, incantations, and so on, played a prominent part. One man could fight millions of men and burn them at will. He could send one arrow, and it would rain thousands of arrows, and thunder; he could make anything burn, and so on. It was all sheer magic. One fact is most curious in both these poems—the *Rāmāyana* and the *Mahābhārata*: along with these magic arrows and all these things going on, you see the cannon already in use. The cannon is an old, old thing, used by the Chinese and the Hindus. Upon the walls of the cities were hundreds of curious weapons made of hollow iron tubes, which, filled with powder and ball, would kill hundreds of men. The people believed that the Chinese, by magic, put the devil inside a hollow iron tube, and when they applied a little fire to a hole, the devil came out with a terrific noise and killed many people.

So in those old days they used to fight with magic arrows. One man would be able to fight millions of others. They had their military arrangements and tactics. There were the foot-soldiers, termed the pada; then the cavalry, the turaga; and two other divisions which the moderns have lost and given up: there was the elephant corps—hundreds and hundreds of elephants, with men on their backs, formed into regiments and protected with huge sheets of iron mail—and these elephants would bear down upon a mass of the enemy. Then there were, of course, the chariots. You have all seen pictures of those old chariots; they were used in every country. These were the four divisions of the army in those old days.

Now, both parties alike wished to secure the alliance of Krishna. But he declined to take an active part and fight in this war, and offered himself as charioteer to Arjuna and as friend and counsellor of the Pāndavas, while to Duryodhana he gave his army of mighty soldiers.

Then was fought on the vast plain of Kurukshetra the great battle in which Bhishma, Drona, Karna, and the brothers of Duryodhana, with the kinsmen on both sides, and thousands of other heroes, fell. The war lasted eighteen days. Indeed, out of the eighteen akshauhinis[1] of soldiers very few men were left. The death of Duryodhana ended the war in favour of the Pāndavas. It was followed by the lament of Gāndhāri, the queen, and the widowed women, and by the funerals of the deceased warriors.

The greatest episode of the war was the marvellous and immortal poem of the Gitā, the Song Celestial. It is the popular scripture of India and the loftiest of all teachings. It consists of a dialogue held by Arjuna with Krishna, just before the commencement of the fight on the battlefield of Kurukshetra. I would advise those of you who have not read this book to read it. If you only knew how much it has influenced even your own country! If you want to know the source of Emerson's inspiration, you will find it in the Gitā. He went to see Carlyle, and Carlyle made him a present of the Gitā, and that little book is responsible for the Concord Movement. All the broad movements in America, in one way or other, are indebted to the Concord group.

The central figure of the Gitā is Krishna. As you worship Jesus of Nazareth as God come down as man, so the Hindus worship many Incarnations of God.

---

[1] An akshauhini is an army division consisting of 21,870 chariots, as many elephants, 65,610 horses, and 109,350 foot-soldiers.

They believe in not one or two only, but in many, who have come down from time to time, according to the needs of the world, for the preservation of dharma and the destruction of wickedness. Each sect has one, and Krishna is one of them. Krishna perhaps has a larger number of followers in India than any other Incarnation of God. His followers hold that he was the most perfect of these Incarnations. Why? "Because," they say, "look at Buddha and other Incarnations: they were only monks, and they had no sympathy for married people. How could they have? But look at Krishna: He was great as a son, as a king, as a father, and all through his life he practised the marvellous teachings which he preached: 'He who in the midst of the greatest activity finds the sweetest peace, and in the midst of the greatest calmness is most active, he has known the secret of life.'" Krishna shows the way to do this: by being non-attached—doing everything but not being identified with anything. You are the Soul, the Pure, the Free, all the time; you are the Witness. Our misery comes, not from work, but from our getting attached to something. Take, for instance, money. Money is a great thing to have; earn it, says Krishna, struggle hard to get money, but don't get attached to it. So with children, with wife, husband, relatives, fame, everything: you have no need to shun them; only don't get attached. There is only one thing that you should be attached to, and that is the Lord. Work for all, love all, do good to all, sacrifice a hundred lives, if need be, for them, but never be attached. Krishna's own life was the exact exemplification of that.

The book which delineates the life and exploits of Krishna is several thousand years old, and some parts of his life are very similar to that of Jesus of Nazareth. Krishna was of royal birth. There was a tyrant king, called Kamśa, who came to hear of a prophecy that one born of a certain family would occupy his throne. So Kamśa ordered all the male children to be massacred. The father and mother of Krishna were cast by King Kamśa into prison, where the child was born. A light suddenly shone in the prison and the child said, "I am the Light of the world, born for the good of the world." You find Krishna, again, symbolically represented with cows—"The Great Cowherd," as he is called. Sages affirmed that God Himself was born, and they went to pay him homage. In other parts of the story the similarity between the two does not continue.

Śri Krishna conquered the tyrant Kamśa, but he never thought of accepting or occupying the throne himself. He had nothing to do with that. He had done his duty and there it ended.

After the conclusion of the Kurukshetra war, the great warrior and venerable grandsire Bhishma, who fought ten days out of the eighteen days' battle, still lay on his death-bed and gave instructions to Yudhishthira on various subjects, such as the duties of the king, the duties of the four castes, the four stages of life, the laws of marriage, the bestowing of gifts, and so on, basing them on the teachings of the ancient sages. He explained the Sāmkhya philosophy and the Yoga philosophy and narrated numerous tales and traditions about saints and gods and kings. These teachings occupy nearly one fourth of the entire work and form an invaluable storehouse of Hindu laws and moral codes, and so on. Yudhishthira had in the meantime been crowned king. But the awful bloodshed and extinction of superiors and relatives weighed heavily on his mind; and then, under the advice of Vyāsa, he performed the Aśvamedha sacrifice.

After the war, for fifteen years Dhritarāshtra dwelt in peace and honour, obeyed by Yudhishthira and his brothers. Then the aged monarch, leaving Yudhishthira on the throne, retired to the forest with his devoted wife and Kunti, the mother of the Pāndava brothers, to pass his last days in asceticism.

Thirty-six years had now passed since Yudhishthira had regained his empire. Then came to him the news that Krishna had left his mortal body. Krishna, the sage, his friend, his prophet, his counsellor, had departed. Arjuna hastened to Dwārakā and came back only to confirm the sad news that Krishna and the Yādavas were all dead. Then the king and the other brothers, overcome with sorrow, declared that the time for them to go, too, had arrived. So they cast off the burden of royalty, placed Parikshit, the grandson of Arjuna, on the throne, and retired to the Himālayas on the Great Journey, the Mahāprasthāna. This was a peculiar form of sannyāsa. It was a custom for old kings to become sannyāsins. In ancient India, when men became very old, they would give up everything; and so did the kings. When a man did not want to live any more, he then went towards the Himālayas, without eating or drinking, and walked on and on till the body failed. All the time thinking of God, he just marched on till the body gave way.

Then came the gods and the sages, and they told King Yudhishthira that he should go to heaven. To go to heaven one has to cross the highest peaks of the Himālayas. Beyond the Himālayas is Mount Meru. On the top of Mount Meru is heaven. None ever went there in the physical body. There the gods reside. And Yudhishthira was called upon by the gods to go there.

So the five brothers and their wife clad themselves in robes of bark and set out on their journey. On the way they were followed by a dog. On and on they went, and they turned their weary feet northward to where the Himālayas lift their lofty peaks, and they saw the mighty Mount Meru in front of them. Silently they walked on in the snow, until suddenly the queen fell, to rise no more. To Yudhishthira, who was leading the way, Bhima, one of the brothers, said, "Behold, O King, the queen has fallen." The king shed tears, but he did not look back. "We are going to meet Krishna," he said. "No time to look back. March on." After a while, again Bhima said, "Behold, our brother Sahadeva has fallen." The king shed tears, but paused not. "March on," he cried.

One after the other, in the cold and snow, all four of his brothers dropped down; but unshaken, though alone, the king moved onward. Looking behind, he saw the faithful dog still following him. And so the king and the dog went on, through snow and ice, over hill and dale, climbing higher and higher till they reached Mount Meru; and there they began to hear the chimes of heaven, and celestial flowers were showered upon the virtuous king by the gods. Then descended the chariot of the gods, and Indra said to him, "Ascend in this chariot, greatest of mortals, thou who alone art permitted to enter heaven without changing the mortal body."

But no; that Yudhishthira would not do without his devoted brothers and his queen. Then Indra explained to him that they had already gone thither before him.

Yudhishthira looked around and said to his dog, "Get into the chariot, child." The god stood aghast. "What! The dog?" he cried. "Do thou cast off this dog. The dog goeth not to heaven. Great King, what dost thou mean? Art thou mad? Thou, the most virtuous of men, thou only canst go to heaven in thy physical body." "But he has been my devoted companion through snow and ice. When all my brothers were dead, my queen dead, he alone never left me. How can I leave him now?" "There is no place in heaven for dogs. This dog has to be left behind. There is nothing unrighteous in this." "I do not go to heaven," replied the king, "without the dog. I shall never give up such a one, who has taken refuge with me, until my own life is at an end. I shall never swerve from righteousness, nay, not even for the joys of heaven or the urging of a god." "Then," said Indra, "on one condition the dog goes to heaven. You have been the most virtuous of mortals and he has been a dog, killing and eating animals; he is sinful; he hunted and took other lives. You can exchange heaven with him." "Agreed," said the king. "Let the dog go to heaven."

At once the scene changed. Hearing these noble words of Yudhishthira, the dog revealed himself as Dharma. Dharma is none other than Yama, the lord of death and justice. And Dharma exclaimed: "Behold, O King, no man was ever so unselfish as thou, willing to exchange heaven with a little dog, for his sake disclaiming all his virtues, and ready to go to hell even for him. Thou art well born, O King of kings. Thou hast compassion for all creatures, O Bhārata, of which this is a bright example. Hence regions of undying felicity are thine. Thou hast won them, O King, and thine is a celestial and high reward."

Then Yudhishthira, with Indra, Dharma, and other gods proceeds to heaven in a celestial car. He undergoes some trials, bathes in the celestial Ganges, and assumes a celestial body. He meets his brothers and his wife, who are now immortals, and all at last is bliss.

Thus ends the story of the Mahābhārata, setting forth in a sublime poem the triumph of virtue and defeat of vice.

In speaking of the Mahābhārata to you, it is simply impossible for me to present the unending array of the grand and majestic characters of the mighty heroes depicted by the genius and master mind of Vyāsa. The internal conflicts between righteousness and filial affection in the mind of the god-fearing yet feeble old blind King Dhritarāshtra; the majestic character of the grandsire Bhishma; the noble and virtuous nature of the royal Yudhishthira and of the other four brothers, as mighty in valour as in devotion and loyalty; the peerless character of Krishna, unsurpassed in human wisdom; and not less brilliant, the characters of the women: the stately Queen Gāndhāri, the loving mother Kunti, the ever devoted and all-suffering Draupadi—these and hundreds of other characters of this epic, and those of the Rāmāyana, have been the cherished heritage of the whole Hindu world for the last several thousands of years and form the basis of its thoughts and of its moral and ethical ideas. In fact, the Rāmāyana and the Mahābhārata are the two encyclopaedias of the ancient Āryan life and wisdom, portraying an ideal civilization which modern society has yet to aspire after.

POEMS

THE SONG OF THE FREE[1]

THE WOUNDED snake its hood unfurls,
The flame stirred up doth blaze,
The desert air resounds the calls
Of heart-struck lion's rage.

The cloud puts forth its deluge strength
When lightning cleaves its breast;
When the soul is stirred to its inmost depth
Great ones unfold their best.

Let eyes grow dim and heart grow faint
And friendship fail and love betray;
Let Fate its hundred horrors send
And clotted darkness block the way—

All nature wear one angry frown
To crush you out—still know, my soul,
You are divine. March on and on,
Nor right nor left, but to the goal.

Nor angel I, nor man nor brute,
Nor body, mind, nor he nor she;
The books do stop in wonder mute
To tell my nature: I am He.

Before the sun, the moon, the earth,
Before the stars or comets free,
Before e'en time had had its birth,
I was, I am, and I will be.

The beauteous earth, the glorious sun,
The calm, sweet moon, the spangled sky,
Causation's laws do make them run;
They live in bonds, in bonds they die.

And mind its mantle, dreamy net,
Casts o'er them all and holds them fast:
In warp and woof of thought are set
Earth, hells, and heavens, or worse or best.

[1] Composed February 15, 1895, in New York.

859

Know these are but the outer crust—
All space and time, effect and cause;
I am beyond all sense, all thought,
The Witness of the universe.

Not two or many, 'tis but One;
And thus in me all me's I have.
I cannot hate, I cannot shun
Myself from me—I can but love.

From dreams awake, from bonds be free.
Be not afraid! This mystery,
My shadow, cannot frighten me.
Know once for all that I am He.

MY PLAY IS DONE[1]

Rising and falling with the waves of time, ever rolling on I go
From fleeting scene to scene ephemeral, with life's currents' ebb and flow.
Oh, I am sick of this ugly farce; these shows that please no more,
This ever running, never reaching, nor e'er a glimpse of shore!

From life to life I am waiting at the gates: they open not.
Dim are my eyes with vain attempts to catch one ray long sought.
Standing on life's high, narrow bridge, heart-struck I see below
The struggling, crying, laughing world, whose mystery none can know.

In front yon gates stand frowning down and say: "No farther way!
This is the limit; tempt not fate. Bear it as best you may.
Go mix with those and drink their cup and be as mad as they.
Who dares to know buys grief. Stop then, and with them stay."

Alas for me! I cannot rest. This fleeting bubble, earth—
Its hollow frame, its hollow name, its hollow death and birth—
For me is nothing. How I yearn to pierce beyond this crust
Of name and form! Oh, ope the gates! To me they open must.

Open the gates, O Mother Divine, to me Thy tired son.
I long, oh, long to return home to Thee! My play is done.
Thou sent'st me out in the dark to play, and wore a hideous mask;
Then hope departed, fear came, and play became a task.

Tossed to and fro, from wave to wave, in this surging, seething sea
Of passions strong and sorrows deep, grief *is*, and joy *to be*,
Where life is living death, and death, alas! who knows but 'tis
Another start afresh of the same old wheel of grief and bliss?
Where children dream their golden dreams, too soon to find them dust,
And age looks back to hopes long lost and life a mass of rust.

Too late, the knowledge age doth gain; and scarce one set is gone,
A fresh set puts their hopeful strength to the wheel, which thus moves on
From day to day and year to year. This dark delusion's toy—
False hope, its motor; desire, its nave; its spokes, both grief and joy.

[1] Composed March 16, 1895, in New York.

I go adrift; oh, take away from me this horrid dream!
Oh, lift me up, Merciful One! from desire's fierce stream.
Turn not to me that awful face; 'tis more than I can bear.
Be merciful and kind to me; my failings, faults, forbear.

Take me, O Mother, to those shores where strifes for ever cease;
Beyond all joy, beyond all pain, where is Nirvāna's peace,
Whose glory neither sun nor moon, nor stars that shine so bright,
Nor flash of lightning can express—they but reflect its light.
Let never more illusive worlds veil off Thy face from me!
My play is done. O break my chains, my Mother! Make me free!

SONG OF THE SANNYĀSIN[1]

WAKE UP the note! the song that had its birth
Far off, where worldly taint could never reach;
In mountain caves and glades of forest deep,
Whose calm no sigh for lust or wealth or fame
Could ever dare to break; where rolled the stream
Of knowledge, truth, and bliss that follows both.
Sing high that note, sannyāsin bold! Say,
  "Om Tat Sat, Om!"

Strike off thy fetters! bonds that bind thee down,
Of shining gold or darker, baser ore—
Love, hate; good, bad; and all the dual throng.
Know slave is slave, caressed or whipped, not free;
For fetters, though of gold, are not less strong to bind.
Then off with them, sannyāsin bold! Say,
  "Om Tat Sat, Om!"

Let darkness go, the will-o'-the-wisp that leads
With blinking light to pile more gloom on gloom.
This thirst for life, for ever quench; it drags
From birth to death, and death to birth, the soul.
He conquers all who conquers self. Know this
And never yield, sannyāsin bold! Say,
  "Om Tat Sat, Om!"

"Who sows must reap," they say, "and cause must bring
The sure effect: good, good; bad, bad; and none
Escape the law—but whoso wears a form
Must wear the chain." Too true; but far beyond
Both name and form is Ātman, ever free.
Know thou art That, sannyāsin bold! Say,
  "Om Tat Sat, Om!"

They know not truth who dream such vacant dreams
As father, mother, children, wife, and friend.
The sexless Self—whose father He? whose child?
Whose friend, whose foe, is He who is but One?
The Self is all in all—none else exists;
And thou art That, sannyāsin bold! Say,
  "Om Tat Sat, Om!"

[1] Composed July 1895, at Thousand Island Park, New York.

There is but One: the Free, the Knower, Self,
Without a name, without a form or stain.
In Him is māyā, dreaming all this dream.
The Witness, He appears as nature, soul.
Know thou art That, sannyāsin bold! Say,
  "Om Tat Sat, Om!"

Where seekest thou? That freedom, friend, this world
Nor that can give. In books and temples, vain
Thy search. Thine only is the hand that holds
The rope that drags thee on. Then cease lament.
Let go thy hold, sannyāsin bold! Say,
  "Om Tat Sat, Om!"

Say: "Peace to all! From me no danger be
To aught that lives. In those that dwell on high,
In those that lowly creep—I am the Self in all.
All life, both here and there, do I renounce,
All heavens and earths and hells, all hopes and fears."
Thus cut thy bonds, sannyāsin bold! Say,
  "Om Tat Sat, Om!"

Heed then no more how the body lives or goes.
Its task is done: let karma float it down.
Let one put garlands on, another kick
This frame: say naught. No praise or blame can be
Where praiser, praised, and blamer, blamed are one.
Thus be thou calm, sannyāsin bold! Say,
  "Om Tat Sat, Om!"

Truth never comes where lust and fame and greed
Of gain reside. No man who thinks of woman
As his wife can ever perfect be;
Nor he who owns the least of things, nor he
Whom anger chains, can ever pass through māyā's gates.
So give these up, sannyāsin bold! Say,
  "Om Tat Sat, Om!"

Have thou no home. What home can hold thee, friend?
The sky thy roof, the grass thy bed, and food
What chance may bring—well cooked or ill, judge not.
No food or drink can taint that noble Self
Which knows Itself. Like rolling river free
Thou ever be, sannyāsin bold! Say,
  "Om Tat Sat, Om!"

Few only know the truth. The rest will hate
And laugh at thee, great one; but pay no heed.
Go thou, the free, from place to place, and help
Them out of darkness, māyā's veil. Without
The fear of pain or search for pleasure, go
Beyond them both, sannyāsin bold! Say,
　　　　"Om Tat Sat, Om!"

Thus, day by day, till karma's powers, spent,
Release the soul for ever. No more is birth,
Nor I, nor thou, nor God, nor man. The "I"
Has All become, the All is "I" and Bliss.
Know thou art That, sannyāsin bold! Say,
　　　　"Om Tat Sat, Om!"

TO AN EARLY VIOLET[1]

WHAT though thy bed be frozen earth,
Thy cloak the chilling blast;
What though no mate to cheer thy path,
Thy sky with gloom o'ercast?

What though e'en love itself doth fail,
Thy fragrance strewed in vain;
What though the bad o'er good prevail
And vice o'er virtue reign?

Change not thy nature, gentle bloom,
Thou violet sweet and pure,
But ever pour thy sweet perfume
Unasked, unstinted, sure!

[1] Written to a Western woman disciple, January 6, 1896, from New York.

PEACE[1]

BEHOLD, it comes in might,
The power that is not power,
The light that is in darkness,
The shade in dazzling light.

It is joy that never spoke,
And grief unfelt, profound,
Immortal life unlived,
Eternal death unmourned.

It is not joy nor sorrow,
But that which is between,
It is not night nor morrow,
But that which joins them in.

It is sweet rest in music
And pause in sacred art,
The silence between speaking;
Between the fits of passion
It is the calm of heart.

It is beauty never lovèd
And love that stands alone;
It is song that lives unsung
And knowledge never known.

It is death between two lives
And lull between two storms,
The void whence rose creation
And that where it returns.

To it the tear-drop goes
To spread the smiling form.
It is the goal of life,
And peace, its only home.

[1] Composed September 21, 1899, at Ridgely Manor, Stone Ridge, New York.

A BENEDICTION[1]

THE MOTHER's heart, the hero's will,
The sweetness of the southern breeze,
The sacred charm and strength that dwell
On Āryan altars, flaming, free—
All these be thine, and many more
No ancient soul could dream before.
Be thou to India's future son
The mistress, servant, friend, in one.

[1] Written to Sister Nivedita, September 22, 1900, at Perros Guirce, Brittany.

THE CUP

This is your cup—the cup assigned to you
From the beginning. Nay, My child, I know
How much of that dark drink is your own brew
Of fault and passion, ages long ago,
In the deep years of yesterday—I know.

This is your road—a painful road and drear.
I made the stones that never give you rest;
I set your friend in pleasant ways and clear,
And he shall come, like you, unto My breast.
But you, My child, must travel here.

This is your task. It has no joy or grace,
But it is not meant for any other hand,
And in My universe has measured place.
Take it: I do not bid you understand.
I bid you close your eyes to see My face.

TO A FRIEND[1]

WHERE DARKNESS is beheld as light,
And sorrow understood as joy;
Where sickness masquerades as health,
And but the new-born infant's cry
Tells one it lives—O wise one, say,
Seekest thou satisfaction here?
Where strife and battle never cease,
And even the father, pitiless,
Turns out his son, and the sole note
Is self and ever self alone,
How dost thou hope, O sage, to find
The mine of everlasting peace?

Who can escape this wretched world,
A very heaven and hell in one?
Say, where can the poor slave, constrained
With karma's fetters round his neck,
Find out at length his freedom here?
Practice of yoga, sense-delight,
Householder's and monastic life,
Prayer, hoarded wealth, austerity,
Dispassion, vows, asceticism—
These I have fathomed through and through,
And so at last have come to know
That not a grain of joy is here;
Embodied life is mockery;
The nobler grows thy heart, be sure,
The more thy share of pain must be.

O selfless lover, great of heart,
Know thou, within this sordid world
There is no room at all for thee:
Could a frail marble bust endure
The blow an anvil's mass will bear?
Be as one slothful, mean, and vile,
With honeyed tongue but poisoned heart,
Empty of truth and self-enslaved—
Then thou wilt find thy place on earth.

[1] Translated from the original Bengali.

For knowledge staking even my life,
I have devoted half my days;
For love, like one insane have I
Clutched often at mere lifeless shades;
And, for religion, countless creeds
Have sought; along the Ganges' banks,
In burning-grounds, by sacred streams,
Or deep in mountain caves have dwelt;
And many a day have passed on alms,
Friendless and clad in common rags,
Begging for food from door to door
To fill my belly, and with frame
Broken by harsh austerities.
But what the treasure I have earned?

Friend, let me speak my heart to thee.
One lesson I have learnt in life:
This dreadful world is tossed with waves,
And one boat only fares across.
Study of scripture, sacred words,
Restraint of breath, conflicting schools,
Dispassion, science, philosophy,
Sense-pleasure, are but freaks of mind.
Love! Love!—that is the only jewel!
In soul and Brahman, man and God,
In ghosts and spirits without shape,
In angels, beasts, birds, insects, worms,
Dwells Love, deep in the hearts of all.

Say, who else is the God of gods?
Say, who else moves this universe?
The mother dies to save her young;
The robber steals; yet are these twain
By the same power of Love impelled.
Beyond both speech and mind concealed,
In grief and happiness Love dwells;
It is that Love Divine that comes
As Kāli, death's embodiment,
Worshipped as Mother by us all.
Grief, sickness, pinching poverty,
Vice, virtue, fruits of deeds alike
Both good and ill, Love's worship are
In varying guise. Say, what is man?
And what can he accomplish here?

Foolish is he who seeks alone
His own delight; mad equally,

Whoever racks his flesh with pain.
Insane is he who longs for death;
Eternal life—a hopeless quest!
However far and far you speed,
Mounting the chariot of the mind,
The selfsame ocean of the world
Spreads out, its waves of bitterness
And pleasure ever plunging on.

Hearken, thou bird bereft of wings!
That way lies no escape for thee.
Times without number beaten back,
Why seek this fruitless task again?
Rely no more on wisdom, prayer,
Offerings to God, or strength of will;
For the sole jewel is selfless Love.
Behold, the insects teach us so
As they embrace the shining flame:
The tiny moth is blinded quite,
Charmed with the beauty of its rays;
So, too, thy heart is mad for Love.
O lover, cast upon the fire
The dross of all thy selfishness!

Say, can a beggar live content?
What good is gleaned from pity's glance?
Give, if within thy heart resides
The slightest treasure fit to share:
Look not behind for recompense!
Ay, to the Infinite born heir
Art thou: within thy bosom swells
The ocean of unbounded Love.
Give! Give! Whoever asks return—
His ocean dwindles to a drop.
From highest Brahman to the worm,
Even to the atom's inmost core,
All things with Love are interfused.
Friend, offer body, mind, and soul
In constant service at their feet.
Thy God is here before thee now,
Revealed in all these myriad forms:
Rejecting them, where seekest thou
His presence? He who freely shares
His love with every living thing
Proffers true service unto God.

LETTERS

To Śri Haridas Viharidas Desai

BOMBAY, 22 May, 1893

DEAR DIWANJI SĀHEB,

Reached Bombay a few days ago and will start off in a few days. . . .

Often and often, we see that even the very best of men are troubled and visited with tribulations in this world. It may be inexplicable; but it is also the experience of my life that the heart and core of everything is good, that however full of waves the surface may be, deep down and underlying everything there is an infinite basis of goodness and love. So long as we do not reach that basis we are troubled; but having once reached that zone of calmness, we may let winds howl and tempests rage; the house which is built on the Rock of Ages cannot shake. I thoroughly believe that a good, unselfish, and holy man like you, whose whole life has been devoted to doing good to others, has already reached this basis of firmness which the Lord Himself has styled as "rest upon Brahman" in the Gitā.

May the blows you have received draw you closer to that Being who is the only one to be loved here and hereafter, so that you may realize Him in everything past, present, and future, and find everything present or lost, in Him and Him alone. Amen.

Yours affectionately,

VIVEKANANDA

To Śri Alasinga Perumal

CHICAGO, 2 November, 1893

DEAR ALASINGA,

I am so sorry that a moment's weakness on my part caused you so much trouble; I was out of pocket at that time. Since then the Lord has sent me friends. At a village near Boston I made the acquaintance of Dr. Wright, Professor of Greek in Harvard University. He sympathized with me very much and urged upon me the necessity of going to the Parliament of Religions, which he thought would give me an introduction to the nation. As I was not acquainted with anybody, the Professor undertook to arrange everything for me, and eventually I came back to Chicago. Here I, together with several Oriental and Occidental delegates to the Parliament of Religions, were all lodged in the house of a gentleman.

On the morning of the opening of the Parliament, we all assembled in a building called the Art Palace, where one huge, and other smaller temporary halls were erected for the sittings of the Parliament. Men from all nations were there. From India were Mazoomdar of the Brāhmo Samāj and Nagarkar of Bombay, Mr. Gandhi representing the Jains, and Mr. Chakravarti representing Theosophy with Mrs. Annie Besant. Of these men, Mazoomdar and I were, of course, old friends, and Chakravarti knew me by name. There was a grand procession, and we were all marshalled on to the platform. Imagine a hall below and a huge gallery above, packed with six or seven thousand men and women representing the best culture of the country, and on the platform learned men of all the nations of the earth. And I, who had never spoken in public in my life, to address this august assemblage!! It was opened in great form with music and ceremony and speeches; then the delegates were introduced one by one, and they stepped up and spoke. Of course my heart was fluttering and my tongue nearly dried up. I was so nervous that I could not venture to speak in the morning. Mazoomdar made a nice speech—Chakravarti a nicer one, and they were much applauded. They were all prepared and came with ready-made speeches. I was a fool and had none, but bowed down to Devi Sarasvati and stepped up, and Dr. Barrows introduced me. I made a short speech. I addressed the assembly as "Sisters and Brothers of America"—a deafening applause of two minutes followed, and then I proceeded, and when it was finished I sat down, almost exhausted with emotion. The next day all the papers announced that my speech was the hit of the day, and I became known to the whole of America. Truly has it been said by the great commentator Śridhara: "Who maketh the dumb a fluent speaker." His name be praised! From that day I became a celebrity, and the day I read my paper on Hinduism, the hall was packed as it had never been before. I quote to you from one of the papers: "Ladies, ladies, ladies, packing every place—filling every corner, they patiently waited and waited while the papers that separated them from Vivekananda were read," etc. You would be astonished if I sent over to you the newspaper cuttings, but you already know that I am a hater of publicity. Suffice it to say that whenever I went on the platform a deafening applause would be raised for me. Nearly all the papers paid high tribute to me, and even the most bigoted had to admit that "this man with his handsome face and magnetic presence and wonderful oratory is the most prominent figure in the Parliament," etc., etc.

And how to speak of their kindness! I have no more wants now. I am well off, and all the money that I require to visit Europe I shall get from here. . . . A boy called —— Acharya has cropped up in our midst. He has been loafing about the city for the last three years. Loafing or no loafing, I like him; but please write to me all about him, if you know anything. He knows you. He came to Europe in the year of the Paris Exhibition.

I am now out of want. Many of the handsomest houses in this city are open to me. All the time I am living as a guest of somebody or other. There is a curiosity in this nation such as you meet with nowhere else. They want to know everything, and their women—they are the most advanced in the world. The average American woman is far more cultivated than the average American man. The men slave all their lives for money, and the women snatch every opportunity to improve themselves. And they are a very kind-hearted, frank people. Everybody who has a fad to preach comes here, and I am sorry to say that most of these are not sound. The Americans have their faults too, and what nation has not? But this is my summing up. Asia laid the germs of civilization, Europe developed man, and America is developing women and the masses. It is the paradise of the woman and the labourer. Now contrast the American masses and women with ours, and you get the idea at once. Americans are fast becoming liberal. Judge them not by the specimens of hard-shelled Christians (it is their own phrase) that you see in India. There are those here, too, but their number is decreasing rapidly, and this great nation is progressing fast towards that spirituality which is the standard boast of the Hindu.

The Hindu must not give up his religion, but must keep religion within its proper limits and give freedom to society to grow. All the reformers in India made the serious mistake of holding religion accountable for all the horrors of priestcraft and degeneration, and went forthwith to pull down the indestructible structure. And what was the result? Failure!! Beginning from Buddha down to Rammohan Roy, everyone made the mistake of holding caste to be a religious institution and trying to pull down religion and caste together, and failed. But in spite of all the ravings of the priests, caste is simply a crystallized social institution, which after doing its service is now filling the atmosphere of India with its stench, and it can only be removed by giving back to the people their lost social individuality. Every man born here knows that he is a man. Every man born in India knows that he is a slave of society. Now, freedom is the only condition of growth; take that away, the result is degeneration. With the introduction of modern competition see how caste is disappearing fast! No religion is now necessary to kill it. The brāhmin shopkeeper, shoemaker, and wine distiller are common in Northern India. And why? Because of competition. No man is prohibited from doing anything he pleases for his livelihood under the present government, and the result is neck-and-neck competition, and thus thousands are seeking and finding the highest level they were born for, instead of vegetating at the bottom.

I must remain in this country at least through the winter, and then go to Europe. The Lord will provide everything for me. You need not disturb yourself about it. I cannot express my gratitude for your love.

Day by day I am feeling that the Lord is with me, and I am trying to follow His direction. His will be done. . . . We will do great things for the world, and that for the sake of doing good and not for name and fame.

"Ours not to reason why, ours but to do and die." Be of good cheer and believe that we are selected by the Lord to do great things, and we will do them. Hold yourself in readiness, i.e. be pure and holy, and love for love's sake. Love the poor, the miserable, the downtrodden, and the Lord will bless you.

See the Rājā of Rāmnād and others now and then, and urge them to sympathize with the masses. Tell them how they are standing on the necks of the poor, and that they are not fit to be called men if they do not try to raise them up. Be fearless! The Lord is with you, and He will yet raise the starving and ignorant millions of India. A railway porter here is better educated than many of your young men and most of your princes. Every American woman has a far better education than can be conceived of by the majority of Hindu women. Why cannot we have the same education? We must.

Think not that you are poor; money is not power—but goodness, holiness. Come and see how it is so all over the world.

Yours etc.,
VIVEKANANDA

P.S.   By the by, —'s paper was the most curious phenomenon I ever saw. It was like a tradesman's catalogue and it was not thought fit to be read in the Parliament. So N— read a few extracts from it in a side hall and nobody understood a word of it. Do not tell him of it. It is a great art to press the largest amount of thought into the smallest number of words. Even —'s paper had to be cut very short. More than a thousand papers were read, and there was no time to give to such wild perorations. I had a good long time given to me over the ordinary half hour, because the most popular speakers were always put down last, to hold the audience. And Lord bless them, what sympathy they have, and what patience! They would sit from ten o'clock in the morning to ten o'clock at night—only a recess of half an hour for a meal, and paper after paper read, most of them very trivial, but they would wait and wait to hear their favourites.

Dharmapala of Ceylon was one of the favourites. . . . He is a very sweet man, and we became very intimate during the Parliament.

A Christian lady from Poona, Miss Sorabji, and the Jain representative, Mr. Gandhi, are going to remain longer in the country and make lecture tours. I hope they will succeed. Lecturing is a very profitable occupation in this country and sometimes pays well.

Mr. Ingersoll gets five to six hundred dollars a lecture. He is the most celebrated lecturer in this country.

V.

To Śri Haridas Viharidas Desai

CHICAGO, 29 January, 1894

DEAR DIWANJI SĀHEB,

Your last letter reached me a few days ago. You have been to see my poor mother and brothers. I am glad you went. But you have touched the softest place in my heart. You ought to know, Diwanji, that I am no hard-hearted brute. If there is any being I love in the whole world, it is my mother. Yet I believed and still believe that without my giving up the world, the great mission which Ramakrishna Paramahamsa, my great Master, came to preach would not see the light; and where would those young men be who have stood as bulwarks against the surging waves of the materialism and luxury of the day? They have done a great amount of good to India, especially to Bengal, and this is only the beginning. With the Lord's help they will do things for which the whole world will bless them for ages. So on the one hand there was my vision of the future of Hinduism and of the whole world, my love for the millions of beings sinking down and down for ages with nobody to help them, nay, nobody with even a thought for them, and on the other, the vision of making my nearest and dearest ones miserable: I chose the former. The Lord will do the rest. He is with me, I am sure of that if of anything. So long as I am sincere, nothing can resist me, because He will be my help. Many and many in India could not understand me; and how could they, poor men? Their thoughts never strayed beyond the everyday routine business of eating and drinking. I know only a few noble souls like yourself who appreciate me. Lord bless your noble self! But appreciation or no appreciation, I am born to organize these young men—nay, hundreds more in every city are ready to join me; and I want to send them rolling like irresistible waves over India, bringing comfort, morality, religion, education, to the doors of the meanest and the most downtrodden. And this I will do or die.

Our people have no idea, no appreciation. On the contrary, that horrible jealousy and that suspicious nature, which is the natural outcome of a thousand years of slavery, make them stand as enemies to every new idea. Still, the Lord is great. . . .

Not only do we tolerate, but we accept every religion, and with the Lord's help I am trying to preach this to the whole world.

Three things are necessary to make every man great, every nation great:
1. Conviction of the power of goodness.
2. Absence of jealousy and suspicion.
3. Helping all who are trying to be and do good.

Why should the Hindu nation, with all its wonderful intelligence and other things, have gone to pieces? I would answer you: *Jealousy.* Never were there people more wretchedly jealous of one another, more envious of one another's fame and name, than this wretched Hindu race. And if you ever come out in the West, the absence of this is the first feeling which you will see in the Western nations.

Three men cannot act in concert together in India for five minutes. Each one struggles for power and in the long run the whole organization comes to grief. Lord! Lord! When will we learn not to be jealous? In such a nation, and especially in Bengal, to create a band of men who are tied and bound together with a most undying love, in spite of differences, is it not wonderful? This band will increase. This idea of wonderful liberality joined with eternal energy and progress must spread over India; it must electrify the whole nation and must enter the very pores of society in spite of the horrible ignorance, spite, caste-feeling, old boobyism, and jealousy which are the heritage of this nation of slaves.

You are one of the few noble natures who stand out like rocks out of water in this sea of universal stagnation. Lord bless you for ever and ever!

Yours ever faithfully,

VIVEKANANDA

To an Indian Disciple

541 DEARBORN AVENUE, CHICAGO
3 March, 1894

DEAR KIDI,

I agree with you so far that faith is a wonderful insight and that it alone can save. But there is the danger in it of breeding fanaticism barring farther progress. Jnāna, philosophical knowledge, is all right, but there is the danger of its becoming dry intellectualism. Love is great and noble, but it may die away in meaningless sentimentalism. A harmony of these two is the thing required. Ramakrishna was such a harmony. Such beings are few and far between; but keeping him and his teachings as the ideal, we can move on. And if, amongst us, each one may not individually attain to that perfection, still we may get it collectively by counteracting, equipoising, adjusting, and fulfilling one another. This would be harmony by a number of persons, and a decided advance on all other forms and creeds.

For a religion to be effective, enthusiasm is necessary. At the same time we must try to avoid the danger of multiplying creeds. We avoid that by being a non-sectarian sect, having all the advantages of a sect and the broadness of a universal religion.

God, though everywhere, can be known to us in and through human character. No character was ever so perfect as Ramakrishna, and that should be the centre round which we ought to rally—at the same time allowing everybody to regard him in his own light, either as God, Saviour, teacher, model, or great man, just as he pleases.

We preach neither social equality nor inequality, but that every being has the same rights, and we insist upon freedom of thought and action in every way. We reject none, neither theist, nor pantheist, monist, polytheist, agnostic, nor atheist; the only condition of being a disciple is modelling a character at once the broadest and the most intense. We do not insist upon particular codes of morality as to conduct or character or eating and drinking; but they must not injure others.

Whatever retards the onward progress or helps the downward fall is vice; whatever helps in coming up and becoming harmonized is virtue.

We leave everybody free to know, select, and follow whatever suits and helps him. Thus, for example, eating meat may help one, eating fruit another. Each is welcome to his own peculiarity, but he has no right to criticize the conduct of others because that would, if followed by him, injure him—much less to insist that others should follow his way. A wife may help some people in this progress; to others she may be a positive obstacle. But the unmarried man has no right to say that the married disciple is wrong, much less to force his own ideal of morality upon his brother.

We believe that every being is divine, is God. Every soul is a sun covered over with clouds of ignorance; the difference between soul and soul is due to the difference in density of these layers of clouds. We believe that this is the conscious or unconscious basis of all religions, and that this is the explanation of the whole history of human progress either in the material, intellectual, or spiritual plane—the same Spirit is manifesting through different planes. We believe that this is the very essence of the Vedas.

We believe that it is the duty of every soul to treat, think of, and behave to other souls as such, i.e. as Gods, and not hate or despise or vilify or try to injure them by any manner of means. This is the duty not only of the sannyāsin but of all men and women.

The soul has neither sex, nor caste, nor imperfection. We believe that nowhere throughout the Vedas, Darśanas, Purānas, and Tantras is it ever said that the soul has any sex, creed, or caste. Therefore we agree with those who say, "What has religion to do with social reforms?" But they must also agree with us when we tell them that religion has no business to formulate social laws and insist on the difference between beings, because its aim and end is to obliterate all such fictions and monstrosities. If it be pleaded that through this difference we would reach the final equality and unity, we answer that the same religion has said over and over again, that mud cannot be washed away with mud. As if a man can be moral by being immoral!

Social laws were created by economic conditions under the sanction of religion. The terrible mistake of religion was to interfere in social matters. But how hypocritically it says and thereby contradicts itself: "Social reform is not the business of religion!" True, what we want is that religion should not be a social reformer, but we insist at the same time that religion has no right to become a social lawgiver. Hands off! Keep yourself to your own bounds and everything will come right.

1. Education is the manifestation of the perfection already in man.

2. Religion is the manifestation of the divinity already in man.

Therefore the only duty of the teacher in both cases is to remove all obstructions from the way. Hands off! as I always say, and everything will be right. That is, our duty is to clear the way. The Lord does the rest.

Especially, therefore, you must bear in mind that religion has to do only with the soul and has no business to interfere in social matters. You must also bear in mind that this applies completely to the mischief which has already been done. It is as if a man after forcibly taking possession of another's property cries through the nose when that man tries to regain it—and preaches the doctrine of the sanctity of human rights!

What business has the priest to interfere (to the misery of millions of human beings) in every social matter?

You speak of the meat-eating kshattriyas. Meat or no meat, it is they who are the fathers of all that is noble and beautiful in Hinduism. Who wrote the Upanishads? Who was Rāma? Who was Krishna? Who was Buddha? Who were the Tirthankaras of the Jains? Whenever the kshattriyas have preached religion, they have given it to everybody, and whenever the brāhmins wrote anything they would deny all rights to others. Read the Gitā and the *Sutras* of Vyāsa, or get someone to read them to you. In the Gitā the way is laid open to all men and women, to all castes and colours, but Vyāsa tries to put meanings upon the Vedas to cheat the poor śudras. Is God a nervous fool like you, that the flow of His river of mercy would be dammed up by a piece of meat? If such be He, His value is not a pie!

Hope nothing from me, but I am convinced, as I wrote to you and have spoken to you, that India is to be saved by the Indians themselves. So you young men of the motherland—can dozens of you become almost fanatics over this new ideal? Take thought, get materials, write a sketch of the life of Ramakrishna, *studiously avoiding all miracles*. The life should be written as an illustration of the doctrines he preached. Only his—do not bring me or any living persons into it. The main aim should be to give to the world what he taught, and the life as illustrating that. I, unworthy though I am, had one commission— to bring out the casket of jewels that was placed in my charge, and make it over to you. Why to you? Because the hypocrites, the jealous, the slavish, and the cowardly, those who believe in matter only, can never do anything. Jealousy is the bane of our national character, natural to slaves. Even the Lord with all His power can do nothing on account of the jealousy. . . .

Think of me as one who has done all his duty and is now dead and gone. Think that the whole work is upon your shoulders. . . . Think that you young men of our motherland were destined to do this. Put yourself to the task. Lord bless you! Leave me, throw me quite out of sight. Preach the new ideal, the new doctrine, the new life. Preach against nobody, against no custom. Preach neither for nor against caste or any other social evil; preach "Hands off," and everything will come right.

With my blessings on you all, my brave, steadfast, and loving souls!

Yours,

VIVEKANANDA

To Śri Haridas Viharidas Desai

CHICAGO, 20 June, 1894

DEAR DIWANJI SĀHEB,

. . . Primarily my coming to America has been to raise funds for an enterprise of my own. Let me tell it all to you again.

The whole difference between the West and the East is in this: they are nations, we are not. That is, civilization, education, here is general; it penetrates into the masses. The higher classes in India and America are the same, but the distance is infinite between the lower classes of the two countries. Why was it so easy for the English to conquer India? It was because they are a nation and we are not. When one of our great men dies, we must sit for centuries to have another—they can produce them as fast as they die. When our Diwanji Sāheb passes away (which may the Lord delay long for the good of my country!), the nation will see the difficulty at once of filling his place—which shows even now why they cannot dispense with your services. It is the dearth of great ones. Why so? Because they have such a big field for recruiting their great ones, and we have such a small one. A nation of three hundred millions has the smallest field for recruiting its great ones, compared with nations of thirty, forty, or sixty millions, because the number of educated men and women in those nations is so great. Now do not forget, my kind friend, that this is the great defect in our nation and must be removed.

Educate and raise the masses—thus alone is a nation possible. Our reformers do not see where the wound is; they want to save the nation by marrying the widows. Do you think that a nation is saved by the number of husbands its widows get? Nor is our religion to blame; for an idol more or less makes no difference. The whole defect is here: the real people, who live in cottages, have forgotten their manhood, their individuality. Trodden under the foot of the Hindu, Mussulman, and Christian, they have come to think that they are born to be trodden under the foot of everybody who has money enough in his pocket. They are to be given back their lost individuality. They are to be educated. Whether idols will remain or not, whether widows will have husbands enough or not, whether caste is good or bad—I do not bother myself with such questions. Everyone must work out his own salvation. Our duty is to put the chemicals together; the crystallization will come through God's laws. Let us put ideas into their heads, and they will do the rest. Now this means educating the masses.

Here are the difficulties. A pauper government cannot, will not, do anything; so no help from that quarter. Even supposing we are in a position to open a free school in each village, still the poor boys would rather go to the plough to earn their living than come to your school. Neither have we the money nor can we make them come to education. The problem seems hopeless. But I have found a way out. It is this: If the mountain does not come to Mahomet, Mahomet must go to the mountain. If the poor cannot come to education, education must reach them at the plough, in the factory, everywhere. How? You have seen my brethren. Now I can get hundreds of such, all over India, unselfish, good, and educated. Let these men go from village to village, bringing not only religion to the door of everyone, but also education. So too I can have a nucleus by organizing the widows as instructors to our women.

Now suppose the villagers after the day's work have come back to the village, and sitting under a tree or somewhere are smoking and talking the time away. Suppose two of these educated sannyāsins get hold of them there, and with a magic lantern show astronomical or other pictures, scenes from different nations, histories, etc. Thus with globes, maps, etc.—and all this orally—how much can be done that way, Diwanji! It is not that the eye is the only door of knowledge; the ear can be the same. So they would have ideas and morality and also hope for improvement. Here our work ends. Let them do the rest.

What would persuade the sannyāsins to make this sacrifice, undertake such a task? Religious enthusiasm. A new religious wave requires a new centre. The old religion can be revivified only by a new centre. Hang your dogmas or doctrines! They never pay. It is a character, a life, a centre, a God-man, that must lead the way, that must be the centre round which all other elements will gather themselves and then fall like a tidal wave upon society, carrying all before them, washing away all impurities. Again, a piece of wood can be easily cut only along the grain. So the old Hinduism can be reformed only through Hinduism and not through the new-fangled reform movements. At the same time, the reformers must be able to unite in themselves the culture of both the East and the West. Now, do you not think that you have already seen the nucleus of such a great movement, that you have heard the low rumblings of the coming tidal wave? That centre, that God-man to lead, was born in India. He was the great Ramakrishna Paramahamsa, and round him this band is slowly gathering. They will do the work. Now, Diwanji Mahārāj, this requires an organization and money—a little at least—to set the wheels in motion. Who would have given us money in India? . . . So, Diwanji Mahārāj, I crossed over to America. You may remember how I begged money from the poor, and the offers of the rich I would not accept because they could not understand my ideas. Now, lecturing for a year in this country, I could not succeed at all (of course, I have no wants for myself) in my plan of raising some funds for setting up my work. First, this year is a very bad year in America: thousands of their poor are without work. Secondly, the missionaries and the ——s try to thwart all my views. Thirdly, a year has rolled by, and our countrymen could not do even so much for me as to say to the American people that I was a real sannyāsin and no cheat, and that I represented the Hindu religion. Even this much, the expenditure of a few words, they could not do! Bravo, my countrymen! I love them, Diwanji Sāheb. Human help I spurn with my foot. He who has been with me through hills and dales, through deserts and forests, will be with me, I hope; if not, some heroic soul will arise some time or other in India, far abler than myself, and carry it out.

So I have told you all about it, Diwanji. Excuse my long letter, my noble friend, one of the few who really feel for me, have real kindness for me. You are at liberty, my friend, to think that I am a dreamer, a visionary; but believe at least that I am sincere to the backbone, and my greatest fault is that I love my country only too, too well. May you and yours be blessed ever and ever, my noble, noble friend! May the shadow of the Almighty ever rest on all those you love. I offer my eternal gratitude to you. My debt to you is immense, not only because you are my friend, but also because you have all your life served the Lord and your motherland so well.

Ever yours in gratitude,
Vivekananda

To H. H. the Mahārājā of Mysore

Chicago, 23 June, 1894

Your Highness:

Śrī Nārāyana bless you and yours! Through Your Highness' kind help it has been possible for me to come to this country. Since then I have become well known here and the hospitable people of this country have supplied all my wants. It is a wonderful country and this is a wonderful nation in many respects. No other nation applies so much machinery in their everyday work as do the people of this country. Everything is machine. Then again, they are only one-twentieth of the whole population of the world, yet they have fully one-sixth of all the wealth of the world. There is no limit to their wealth and luxuries. Yet everything here is so dear. The wages of labour are the highest in the world, yet the fight between labour and capital is constant.

Nowhere on earth have women so many privileges as in America. They are slowly taking everything into their hands, and, strange to say, the number of cultured women is much greater than that of cultured men. Of course, the higher geniuses are mostly from the ranks of the males. With all the criticism of the Westerners against our caste, they have a worse one—that of money. The almighty dollar, as the Americans say, can do anything here. . . .

No country on earth has so many laws, and in no country are they so little observed. On the whole our poor Hindu people are infinitely more moral than any of the Westerners. In religion they practise either hypocrisy or fanaticism. Sober-minded men have become disgusted with their superstitious religions and are looking to India for new light. Your Highness cannot realize, without seeing, how eagerly they take in any little bit of the grand thoughts of the holy Vedas, which resist and are unharmed by the terrible onslaughts of modern science. The theories of creation out of nothing, of a created soul, and of the big tyrant of a God sitting on a throne in a place called heaven, and of the eternal hell-fires, have disgusted all the educated; and the noble thoughts of the Vedas about the eternity of creation and of the soul, and about the God in our own soul, they are imbibing fast in one shape or other. Within fifty years the educated of the world will come to believe in the eternity of both soul and creation, and in God as our highest and perfect nature, as taught in our holy Vedas. Even now their learned priests are interpreting the Bible that way. My conclusion is that they require more spiritual civilization, and we, more material.

The one thing that is at the root of all evils in India is the condition of the poor. The poor in the West are devils; compared with them ours are angels, and it is therefore so much the easier to raise our poor. The only service to be done for our lower classes is to give them education, *to develop their lost individuality.* That is the great task before our people and princes. Up to now nothing has been done in that direction. Priest-power and foreign conquest have trodden them down for centuries, and at last the poor of India have forgotten that they are human beings. They are to be given ideas. Their eyes are to be opened to what is going on in the world around them, and then they will work out their own salvation. Every nation, every man, every woman, must work out their own salvation. Give them ideas—that is the only help they require—and then the rest must follow. Ours is to put the chemicals together; the crystallization comes according to the law of nature. Our duty is to put ideas into their heads; they will do the rest. This is what is to be done in India. It is this idea that has been in my mind for a long time. I could not accomplish it in India, and that was the reason for my coming to this country. The great difficulty in the way of educating the poor is this: Even suppose Your Highness opened a free school in every village, still it would do no good, for the poverty in India is such that the poor boys would rather go to help their fathers in the fields, or otherwise try to make a living, than come to the school. Now, if the mountain does not come to Mahomet, Mahomet must go to the mountain. If the poor boy cannot come to education, education must go to him. There are thousands of single-minded, self-sacrificing sannyāsins in our own country, going from village to village, teaching religion. If a part of them can be organized as teachers of secular things, also, they will go from place to place, from door to door, not only preaching, but teaching also. Suppose two of these men go to a village in the evening with a magic lantern, a globe, some maps, etc. They can teach a great deal of astronomy and geography to the ignorant. By telling stories about different nations, they can give the poor a hundred times more information through the ear than they can get in a lifetime through books. This requires an organization, which again means money. Men enough there are in India to work out this plan, but alas! they have no money. It is very difficult to set a wheel in motion, but when once set, it goes on with increasing velocity. After seeking help in my own country and failing to get any sympathy from the rich, I came over to this country through Your Highness' aid. The Americans do not care a bit whether the poor of India die or live. And why should they, when our own people never think of anything but their own selfish ends?

My noble prince, this life is short, the vanities of the world are transient; but they alone live who live for others. The rest are more dead than alive. One such high, noble-minded, and royal son of India as Your Highness can do much towards raising India on her feet again, and thus leave a name to posterity which shall be worshipped. That the Lord may make your noble heart feel intensely for the suffering millions of India sunk in ignorance is the prayer of

VIVEKANANDA

To the Hale Sisters

541 DEARBORN AVENUE, CHICAGO
26 June, 1894

DEAR SISTERS,

The great Hindi poet Tulsidas, in the benediction to his translation of the *Rāmāyana*, says: "I bow down to both the wicked and the holy—but alas! they are both equally torturers. The wicked begin to torture me as soon as they come in contact with me. The good, alas! take my life away when they *leave me!*"

I say amen to this. To me, for whom the only pleasure left in the world is to love the holy ones of God, it is a mortal torture to separate myself from them. But these things must come. "Thou Music of my Beloved's flute, lead on, I am following." It is impossible to express my pain, my anguish, at being separated from you noble and sweet and generous and holy ones. Oh! how I wish I had succeeded in becoming a stoic!

Hope you are enjoying the beautiful village scenery. "Where the world is awake, there the man of self-control is sleeping. Where the world sleeps, there he is waking." May even the dust of the world never touch you, for after all, the poets say, the world is only a piece of carrion covered over with garlands. Touch it not. If you can, come up, young ones of the bird of Paradise, before your feet touch this cesspool of corruption, this world, and fly upwards. "O, thou that art awake, do not go to sleep again."

"Let the world love its many. We have but one Beloved—the Lord. We care not what they say. We are only afraid when they want to paint our Beloved and give Him all sorts of monstrous qualities. Let them do whatever they please —for us He is only the Beloved—my love, my love, my love, and nothing more." "Who cares to know how much power, how much quality, He has—even that of doing good. We will say once for all, we love not for the long purse. We never sell our love. We want not. We give."

"You, philosopher, come to tell us of His essence, His powers, His attributes —fool! We are here dying for a kiss of His lips. Take your nonsense back to your own home and send me a kiss of my Love—can you?"

"Fool! Whom art thou bending thy tottering knees before in awe and fear? I took my necklace and put it round His neck, and tying a string to it as to a collar, I am dragging Him along with me, for fear He may fly away even for a moment. That necklace is the collar of love, that string the ecstasy of love.

Fool! You know not the secret—the Infinite One comes within my fist under the bondage of love." "Knowest thou not that the Lord of the universe is the bondslave of love? Knowest thou not that the Mover of the universe used to dance to the music of the ringing bracelets of the shepherdesses of Vrindāvan?"

Excuse my mad scribbling—excuse my foolery in trying to express the inexpressible. It is to be felt only.

Ever with blessings, your brother,
VIVEKANANDA

To Mrs. George W. Hale

c/o DR. E. GUERNSEY
FISHKILL LANDING, N. Y.
August 1894

DEAR MOTHER,

I came yesterday to this place. I will remain here a few days. . . .

Our religion teaches that anger is a great sin, even if it is "righteous." And so, you see, it is necessary on my part to try to keep anger down—even "righteous." Each must follow his own religion. I could not for my soul distinguish ever the distinction between "religious anger" and commonplace anger, "religious killing" and commonplace killing, "religious slandering" and irreligious, and so forth. Nor may that "fine" ethical distinction ever enter into the ethics of our nation. Jesting apart, Mother Church,[1] I do not care the least for the gambols these men play,[2] seeing as I do through and through the insincerity, the hypocrisy, and the love of pelf and name that is the *only motive power* in these men. . . .

With sincerest love and respects for you and Father Pope, I remain
Yours,
VIVEKANANDA

To Śri Alasinga Perumal

WASHINGTON, D. C., 27 October, 1894

DEAR ALASINGA,

. . . I am doing here exactly what I used to do in India—always depending on the Lord and making no plans ahead. . . . Moreover you must remember that I have to work incessantly in this country and that I have no time to put together my thoughts in the form of a book—so much so, that this constant rush has worn my nerves, and I am feeling it. I cannot express my obligation to you, and all my friends in Madras, for the most unselfish and heroic work you did for me. I am not an organizer; my nature tends towards scholarship and medita-

[1] Swami Vivekananda often affectionately addressed Mrs. Hale and Mr. Hale as "Mother Church" and "Father Pope," and the Hale girls as "sisters" or "babies."

[2] Referring to certain Presbyterian ministers who had written articles slandering the Swami's character.

tion. I think I have worked enough. Now I want rest and to teach a little to those that have come to me from my Gurudeva. You have known now what you can do, for it is really you young men of Madras that have done all. I am only the figurehead. I am a tyāgi; I only want one thing. I do not believe in a religion or God which cannot wipe the widow's tears or bring a piece of bread to the orphan's mouth. However sublime be the theories, however well spun may be the philosophy, I do not call it religion so long as it is confined to books and dogmas. The eye is in the forehead and not in the back. Move onward and carry into practice that which you are very proud to call your religion, and God bless you!

Look not to me, look to yourselves. I am happy to have been the occasion of rousing an enthusiasm. Take advantage of it, float along with it, and everything will come right. Love never fails, my son. Today or tomorrow or ages after, truth will conquer! Love shall win the victory. Do you love your fellow men? Where should you go to seek for God? Are not all the poor, the miserable, the weak, Gods? Why not worship them first? Why go to dig a well on the bank of the Ganges? Believe in the omnipotent power of love. Who cares for these tinsel puffs of fame? I never keep watch of what the newspapers are saying. Have you love? If so, you are omnipotent. Are you perfectly unselfish? If so, you are irresistible. It is character that pays everywhere. It is the Lord who protects His children in the depths of the sea. Your country requires heroes—be heroes!

Everybody wants me to come over to India. They think they will be able to do more if I come over. They are mistaken, my friend. The present enthusiasm is only a little patriotism; it means nothing. If it is true and genuine, you will find in a short time hundreds of heroes coming forward and carrying on the work. Therefore know that you have really done all, and go on. Look not for me. Here is a grand field. What have I to do with this "ism" or that "ism"? I am the servant of the Lord, and where on earth is there a better field than here for propagating all high ideas?—here, where if one man is against me, a hundred hands are ready to help me—here, where man feels for man, and women are goddesses! Even idiots may stand up to hear themselves praised, and cowards assume the attitude of the brave when everything is sure to turn out well, but the true hero works in silence. How many Buddhas die before one finds expression! My son, I believe in God and I believe in man. I believe in helping the miserable, I believe in going even to hell to save others. Talk of the Westerners —they have given me food, shelter, friendship, protection—even the most orthodox Christians! What do our people do when any of their priests go to India? You do not touch them even; they are mlechchas! No man, no nation, my son, can hate others and live. India's doom was sealed the very day they invented the word mlechcha and stopped from communion with others. Take care how you foster that idea. It is good to talk glibly about the Vedānta, but how hard to carry out even its least precepts!

Ever yours with blessings,
Vivekananda

P.S. Take care about these two things—love of power and jealousy. Cultivate always "faith in yourself."

V.

To Śri Haridas Viharidas Desai

CHICAGO, 15 November, 1894

DEAR DIWANJI SĀHEB,

I have received your kind note. . . . I am glad that there is a good chance of your coming over to Europe. Avail yourself of it by all means. The fact of our isolation from all the other nations of the world is the cause of our degeneration, and its only remedy is getting back into the current of the rest of the world. Motion is the sign of life. America is a grand country. It is a paradise for the poor and women. There are almost no poor in the country, and nowhere else in the world are women so free, so educated, so cultured. They are everything in society.

This is a great lesson. The sannyāsin has not lost a bit of his sannyāsinship, even his mode of living. And in this most hospitable country every home is open to me. The Lord who guided me in India, would He not guide me here? And He has.

You may not understand why a sannyāsin should be in America; but it was necessary. Because the only claim you have to be recognized by the world is your religion, and good specimens of our religious men are required to be sent abroad, to give other nations an idea that India is not dead.

Some representative men must come out of India and go to all the nations of the earth to show at least that you are not savages. You may not feel the necessity of it from your Indian home, but believe me, much depends upon that for your nation. And a sannyāsin who has no idea of doing good to his fellows is a brute, not a sannyāsin.

I am neither a sight-seer nor an idle traveller; but you will see, if you live to see, and bless me all your life.

Mr. Dvivedi's papers were too big for the Parliament, and they had to be cut short.

I spoke at the Parliament of Religions, and with what effect I may quote to you from a few newspapers and magazines ready at hand. I need not be self-conceited, but to you in confidence I am bound to say, because of your love, that no Hindu made such an impression in America, and if my coming has done nothing else, it has done this: that the Americans have come to know that India even today produces men at whose feet even the most civilized nations may learn lessons of religion and morality. Don't you think that is enough to say for the Hindu nation's sending over here their sannyāsin? . . .

These I quote from the journals:

"His culture, his eloquence, and his fascinating personality have given us a new idea of Hindu civilization. . . . He speaks without notes, presenting his facts and his conclusion with the greatest art, the most convincing sincerity, and rising often to rich, inspiring eloquence." New York Critique.

"Vivekananda is undoubtedly the greatest figure in the Parliament of Religions. After hearing him we feel how foolish it is to send missionaries to this learned nation." Herald (the greatest paper here).

I cease from quoting more lest you should think me conceited; but this was necessary for you who have become nearly frogs in the well and will not see how the world is going on elsewhere. I do not mean you personally, my noble friend, but our nation in general.

I am the same here as in India; only here in this highly cultured land there is an appreciation, a sympathy, which our ignorant fools never dream of. There our people grudge us monks a crumb of bread; here they are ready to pay one thousand rupees a lecture and remain grateful for the instruction for ever.

I am appreciated by these strangers more than I ever was in India. I can, if I will, live here all my life in the greatest luxury; but I am a sannyāsin, and "India, with all thy faults I love thee still." So I am coming back after some months, and shall go on sowing the seeds of religion and progress from city to city as I was doing so long, although amongst a people who know not what appreciation and gratefulness are.

I am ashamed of my own nation when I compare their beggarly, selfish, un-appreciative, ignorant ungratefulness with the help, hospitality, sympathy, and respect which the Americans have shown to me, a representative of a foreign religion. Therefore come out of the country; see others and compare.

Now, after these quotations, do you not think it was worth while to send a sannyāsin to America?

Please do not publish this letter. I still hate notoriety in the same manner as I did in India.

I am doing the Lord's work, and wherever He leads I follow. He who makes the dumb eloquent and the lame cross a mountain, He will help me. I do not care for human help. He is ready to help me in India, in America, at the North Pole, if He thinks fit. If He does not, none else can help me. Glory unto the Lord for ever and ever!

Yours with blessings,
VIVEKANANDA

To Śri Alasinga Perumal

NEW YORK, 19 November, 1894

MY BRAVE BOYS,

Push on with the organization. . . . Nothing else is necessary but these—*love, sincerity,* and *patience.* What is life but growth, i.e. expansion, i.e. love? There-fore all love is life, it is the only law of life, all selfishness is death, and this is true here or hereafter. It is life to do good, it is death not to do good to others. Ninety per cent of the human brutes you see are dead, are *ghosts*—for none lives, my boys, but he who loves. Feel, my children, feel: feel for the poor, the ignorant, the downtrodden, feel till the heart stops and the brain reels and you think you will go mad—then pour the soul out at the feet of the Lord, and then will come power, help, and indomitable energy. Struggle, struggle—this was my motto for the last ten years. Struggle, still say I. When all was dark I used to say, struggle; when light is breaking in, I still say, struggle. Be not afraid, my children. Look not up in that attitude of fear towards that infinite starry vault as if it would crush you. Wait! In a few hours more the whole of it will be under your feet. Wait! Money does not pay, nor name; fame does not pay, nor learning. It is love that pays; it is character that cleaves its way through adamantine walls of difficulties.

Now the question before us is this: There cannot be any growth without *liberty*. Our ancestors freed religious thought, and we have a wonderful religion; but they put a heavy chain on the feet of society, and our society is, in a word, *horrid, diabolical*. In the West, society always had freedom, and look at them. On the other hand, look at their religion.

Liberty is the first condition of growth. Just as man must have liberty to think and speak, so he must have liberty in food, dress, and marriage, and in every other thing, so long as he does not injure others.

We talk foolishly against material civilization. The grapes are sour. Even taking all that foolishness for granted, in all India there are, say, a hundred thousand really spiritual men and women. Now, for the spiritualization of these, must three hundred millions be sunk in savagery and starvation? Why should any starve? How was it possible for the Hindus to have been conquered by the Mohammedans? It was due to the Hindus' ignorance of material civilization. The Mohammedans even taught them to wear tailor-made clothes. Would the Hindus had learnt from the Mohammedans how to eat in a cleanly way without mixing their food with the dust of the streets! Material civilization, nay, even luxury, is necessary to create work for the poor. Bread! Bread! I do not believe in a God who cannot give me bread here, giving me eternal bliss in heaven! Pooh! India is to be raised, the poor are to be fed, education is to be spread, and the evil of priestcraft is to be removed. No priestcraft, no social tyranny! More bread, more opportunity for everybody! Our young fools hold meetings to get more power from the English. They only laugh. None deserves liberty who is not ready to give liberty. Suppose the English give over to you all the power. Why, the powers that be, then, will hold the people down and not let them have it. Slaves want power to make slaves.

Now, this is to be brought about slowly and by insisting only on our *religion* and giving liberty to society. Root up priestcraft from the old religion and you get the best religion in the world. Do you understand me? Can you make a European society with India's religion? I believe it is possible and must be. . . . The grand plan is to start a colony in Central India, where you can follow your own ideas independently; and then a little leaven will leaven all. In the meanwhile form a Central Association and go on branching off all over India. Start only on religious grounds now, and do not preach any violent social reform at present; only do not countenance foolish superstitions. Try to revive society on the old grounds of universal salvation and equality as laid down by the old Masters, such as Śankarāchārya, Rāmānuja, and Chaitanya.

Have fire and spread all over. Work, work! Be the servant while leading, be unselfish, and *never listen to one friend in private accusing another*. Have infinite patience and success is yours. . . . Now take care of this: Do not try to "boss" others, as the Yankees say. Because I always direct my letters to you, you need not try to show your consequence over my other friends. I know you never can be such a fool, but still I think it my duty to warn you. This is what kills all organization. Work, work—for to work only for the good of others is life.

I want that there should be no hypocrisy, no Jesuitism, no roguery. I have depended always on the Lord, always on the Truth broad as the light of day. Let me not die with stains on my conscience for having played Jesuitism to get up name or fame, or even to do good. There should not be a breath of immorality or a stain of policy which is bad.

No shilly-shally, no *esoteric blackguardism*, no secret humbug. Nothing should be done in a corner. No special favouritism of the Master; no Master at that, even. Onward, my brave boys—money or no money—men or no men! Have you love? Have you God? Onward, and forward to the breach—you are irresistible.

How absurd! The Theosophical magazines' saying that they prepared the way to my success! Indeed!! Pure nonsense! Theosophists prepared the way!! . . .

Take care! Beware of everything that is untrue; stick to truth and we shall succeed, maybe slowly, but surely. Work on as if I never existed. Work as if on each of you depended the whole work. Fifty centuries are looking on you; the future of India depends on you. Work on. I do not know when I shall be able to come. This is a great field for work. They can at best praise in India, but they will not give a cent for anything; and where shall they get it, *beggars* themselves? Then they have lost the faculty of doing public good for the last two thousand years or more. They are just learning the ideas of nation, public, etc. So I need not blame them. More afterwards.

With blessings, yours,

VIVEKANANDA

To a Friend in Madras

U. S. A., 30 November, 1894

DEAR AND BELOVED,

Your beautiful letter just came to hand. I am so glad that you have come to know Śri Ramakrishna. I am very glad at the strength of your vairāgya, renunciation. It is the one primary necessity in reaching God. I had always great hopes for Madras, and still I have the firm belief that from Madras will come the spiritual wave that will deluge India. I can only say God-speed to your good intentions. But here, my son, are the difficulties. In the first place, no man ought to take a hasty step. In the second place, you must have some respect for the feelings of your mother and wife. True, you may say that we disciples of Ramakrishna have not always shown great deference to the opinions of our parents. I know and know for sure that great things are done only by great sacrifices. I know for certain that India requires the sacrifice of her highest and best, and I sincerely hope that it will be your good fortune to be one of them.

Throughout the history of the world you find that great men make great sacrifices and the masses of mankind enjoy the benefit. If you want to give up everything for your own salvation, it is nothing. Do you want to forgo even your own salvation for the good of the world? Then you are God—think of that. My advice to you is to live the life of a brahmachārin, i.e. give up all sexual enjoyments; for a certain time live in the house of your father. This is the "kutichaka" stage. Try to bring your wife to consent to your great sacrifice for the good of the world. And if you have burning faith and all-conquering love and almighty purity, I do not doubt that you will shortly succeed. Give yourself body and soul to the work of spreading the teachings of Śri Ramakrishna; for work (karma) is the first stage. Study Sanskrit diligently besides practising devotion. For you are to be a great teacher of mankind, and my Guru Mahārājā used to say, "A penknife is sufficient to commit suicide with, but to kill others one requires guns and swords." And in the fullness of time it will be given unto you when to go out and preach to the world His sacred name.

Your determination is holy and good. God-speed to you, but do not take any hasty step. First purify yourself by work and devotion. India has suffered long, the religion eternal has suffered long. But the Lord is merciful. Once more He has come to help His children, once more the opportunity is given to fallen India to rise. India can only rise by sitting at the feet of Śri Ramakrishna. His life and his teachings are to be spread far and wide, are to be made to penetrate every pore of Hindu society. Who will do it? Who are to take up the flag of Ramakrishna and march for the salvation of the world? Who are to stem the tide of degeneration at the sacrifice of name and fame, wealth and enjoyment— nay, of every hope of this or other worlds? A few young men have jumped into the breach, have sacrificed themselves. They are a few. We want a few thousands of such as they, and *they will come*. I am glad that our Lord has put it in your mind to be one of them. Glory unto him on whom falls the Lord's choice! Your determination is good, your hopes are high, your aim is the noblest in the world—to bring millions sunk in darkness to the light of the Lord.

But, my son, here are the drawbacks. Nothing shall be done in haste. Purity, patience, and perseverance are the three essentials for success, and above all, *love*. All time is yours; there should be no indecent haste. Everything will come right if you are pure and sincere. We want hundreds like you bursting upon society and bringing new life and vigour of the Spirit wherever they go. God-speed to you!

Yours with all blessings,
VIVEKANANDA

To Śri Alasinga Perumal

541 DEARBORN AVENUE, CHICAGO
1894

DEAR ALASINGA,

Your letter just to hand. . . . Money can be raised in this country by lecturing for two or three years. I have tried a little; and there is much public appreciation of my work. But it is thoroughly uncongenial and demoralizing to me. . . .

I have read what you say about the Indian papers and their criticisms, which are natural. Jealousy is the central vice of every enslaved race. And it is jealousy and the lack of combination which cause and perpetuate slavery. You cannot feel the truth of this remark until you come out of India. The secret of the

Westerner's success is this power of combination, the basis of which is mutual trust and appreciation. The weaker and more cowardly a nation is, so much the more is this sin visible. . . . But, my son, you ought not to expect anything from a slavish race. The case is almost desperate no doubt, but let me put the case before you all. Can you put life into this dead mass—dead to almost all moral aspiration, dead to all future possibilities—and always ready to spring upon those that would try to do good to them? Can you take the position of a physician who tries to pour medicine down the throat of a kicking and refractory child? . . . An American or a European always supports his countrymen in a foreign country. . . .

Let me remind you again, "Thou hast the right to work, but not to the fruit thereof." Stand firm like a rock. Truth always triumphs. Let the children of Śri Ramakrishna be true to themselves, and everything will be all right. We may not live to see the outcome, but as sure as we live, it will come sooner or later. What India wants is a new, electric power to stir up a fresh vigour in the national veins. This was ever, and always will be, slow work. Be content to work and above all be true to yourself. Be pure, staunch, and sincere to the very backbone and everything will be all right. If you have marked anything in the disciples of Śri Ramakrishna, it is this—they are sincere to the backbone. My task will be done and I shall be quite content to die if I can bring up and launch one hundred such men over India. He, the Lord, knows best. Let ignorant men talk nonsense. We neither seek aid nor avoid it—we are the servants of the Most High. The petty attempts of small men should be beneath our notice. Onward! Through the struggle of ages character is built. Be not discouraged. One word of truth can never be lost; for ages it may be hidden under rubbish, but it will show itself sooner or later. Truth is indestructible, virtue is indestructible, purity is indestructible. Give me a genuine man; I do not want masses of converts. My son, hold fast! Do not look for anybody to help you. Is not the Lord infinitely greater than all human help? Be holy—trust in the Lord, depend on Him always, and you are on the right track; nothing can prevail against you. . . .

Let us pray, "Lead, Kindly Light"—a beam will come through the dark and a hand will be stretched forth to lead us. I always pray for you: you must pray for me. Let each one of us pray day and night for the downtrodden millions in India, who are held fast by poverty, priestcraft, and tyranny—pray day and night for them. I care more to preach religion to them than to the high and the rich. I am no metaphysician, no philosopher, nay, no saint. But I am poor, I love the poor. I see what they call the poor of this country and how many there are who feel for them. What an immense difference in India! Who feels there for the two hundred millions of men and women sunken for ever in poverty and ignorance? Where is the way out? Who feels for them? They cannot find light or education. Who will bring the light to them—who will travel from door to door bringing education to them? Let these people be your God—think of them, work for them, pray for them incessantly—the Lord will show you the way. Him I call a mahātmā whose heart bleeds for the poor; otherwise he is a durātmā. Let us unite our wills in continued prayer for their good. We may die unknown, unpitied, unbewailed, without accomplishing anything—but not one thought will be lost. It will take effect, sooner or later. My heart is too full to express my feeling; you know it, you can imagine it. So long as the millions live in hunger and ignorance, I hold every man a traitor who, having been educated at their expense, pays not the least heed to them. I call those men—who strut about in their finery, having got all their money by grinding the poor—wretches, so long as they do not do anything for those two hundred millions who are now no better than hungry savages. We are poor, my brothers, we are nobodies, but such have always been the instruments of the Most High. The Lord bless you all!

With all love,

VIVEKANANDA

To H. H. the Mahārājā of Khetri

U. S. A., 1894

. . . "It is not the building that makes the home, but it is the wife that makes it," says a Sanskrit poet, and how true it is! The roof that affords you shelter from heat and cold and rain is not to be judged by the pillars that support it—the finest Corinthian columns though they be—but by the real spirit-pillar who is the centre, the real support of the home—the woman. Judged by that standard, the American home will not suffer in comparison with any home in the world.

I have heard many stories about the American home: of liberty running into licence, of unwomanly women smashing under their feet all the peace and happiness of home-life in their mad liberty dance, and much nonsense of that type. And now after a year's experience of American homes, of American women, how utterly false and erroneous that sort of judgement appears! American women! A hundred lives would not be sufficient to pay my deep debt of gratitude to you! I have not words enough to express my gratitude to you. "Oriental hyperbole" alone expresses the depth of Oriental gratitude: "If the black mountain were the ink; the ocean, the ink-pot; the best branch of the Celestial Tree, the pen; the wide earth, the scroll; and if the Goddess Sarasvati went on writing for all time—still all this could not express my gratitude to you!"[1]

Last year I came to this country in summer, a wandering preacher from a far distant country, without name, fame, wealth, or learning to recommend me— friendless, helpless, almost in a state of destitution; and American women befriended me, gave me shelter and food, took me to their homes, and treated me as their own son, their own brother. They stood as my friends even when their own priests were trying to persuade them to give up the "dangerous heathen"—even when, day after day, their best friends had told them not to stand by this "unknown foreigner, maybe of dangerous character." But they

[1] Adapted from a stanza of the famous hymn to Śiva, the "Śiva-mahimnah-stotram," by Pushpadanta.

are better judges of character and soul—for it is the pure mirror that catches the reflection.

And how many beautiful homes I have seen, how many mothers whose purity of character, whose unselfish love for their children, are beyond expression, how many daughters and pure maidens, "pure as the icicle on Diana's temple"— and withal so much culture, education, and spirituality in the highest sense! Is America, then, only full of wingless angels in the shape of women? There are good and bad everywhere, true—but a nation is not to be judged by its weaklings, called the wicked, for they are only the weeds, but by the good, the noble, and the pure, who indicate the national life-current, flowing clear and vigorous.

Do you judge an apple tree and the taste of its fruits by the unripe, unde-veloped, worm-eaten ones that strew the ground, large even though their num-ber be, sometimes? If there is one ripe, developed fruit, that one would indicate the powers, the possibility, and the purpose of the apple tree—and not hundreds that could not develop.

And then the modern American women—I admire their broad and liberal minds. I have seen many liberal and broad-minded men too in this country, some even in the narrowest churches, but here is the difference: there is danger with the men of becoming broad at the cost of religion, at the cost of spiritu-ality—women broaden out in sympathy to everything that is good everywhere without losing a bit of their own religion. They intuitively know that it is a question of positivity and not negativity, a question of addition and not sub-traction. They are every day becoming aware of the fact that it is the affirmative and positive side of everything that shall be stored up, and that this very act of accumulating the affirmative and positive and therefore soul-building forces of nature is what destroys the negative and destructive elements in the world.

What a wonderful achievement was that World's Fair at Chicago! And that wonderful Parliament of Religions, where voices from every corner of the earth expressed their religious ideas! I was also allowed to place my own ideas before it through the kindness of Dr. Barrows and Mr. Bonney. Mr. Bonney is such a wonderful man! Think of that mind that planned and carried out with great success that gigantic undertaking, and he—no clergyman—a lawyer, presiding over the dignitaries of all the churches, the sweet, learned, patient Mr. Bonney, with all his soul speaking through his bright eyes. . . .

Yours etc.,
VIVEKANANDA

To Justice Sir S. Subrahmanya Iyer

541 DEARBORN AVENUE, CHICAGO
3 January, 1895

DEAR SIR,

It is with a heart full of love, gratitude, and trust that I take up my pen to write to you. Let me tell you first that you are one of the few men that I have met in my life who are thorough in their convictions. You have a whole-souled possession of a wonderful combination of feeling and knowledge, and withal a practical ability to bring ideas into realized forms. Above all you are sincere, and as such I confide to you some of my ideas.

The work has begun well in India, and it should not only be kept up but pushed on with the greatest vigour. Now or never is the time. After taking a far and wide view of things, my mind has now been concentrated on the following plan: First, it would be well to open a theological college in Madras, and then gradually extend its scope, so as to give a thorough education to young men in the Vedas and the different bhāshyas and philosophies, including a knowledge of the other religions of the world. At the same time a paper in English and the vernacular should be started as an organ of the college.

This is the first step to be taken, and huge things grow out of small undertakings. . . . Madras just now is following the golden mean by appreciating both the ancient and the modern phases of life.

I fully agree with the educated classes in India that a thorough overhauling of society is necessary. But how to do it? The destructive plans of reformers have failed. My plan is this: We have not done badly in the past; certainly not. Our society is not bad but good, only I want it to be better still. Not from error to truth, nor from bad to good, but from truth to higher truth, from good to better, best. I tell my countrymen that so far they have done well—now is the time to do better.

Now, take the case of caste, in Sanskrit, jāti, i.e. species. Now, this is the first idea of creation. Variation (vichitratā), that is to say, jāti, means creation. "I am one, I will become many." (Vedas.) Unity is before creation, diversity is creation. Now if this diversity stops, creation will be destroyed. So long as any species is vigorous and active it must throw out varieties. When it ceases or is stopped from breeding varieties, it dies. Now the original idea of jāti was this freedom of the individual to express his nature, his prakriti, his jāti, his caste, and so it remained for thousands of years. Not even in the latest books is inter-dining prohibited, nor in any of the older books is inter-marriage forbidden. Then what was the cause of India's downfall? The giving up of this idea of caste. As the Gītā says, with the extinction of caste the world will be destroyed. Now does it not seem true that with the stoppage of these variations the world will be destroyed? The present caste is not the real jāti, but a hindrance to its progress. It really has prevented the free action of jāti, i.e. caste or variation. Any crystallized custom or privilege or hereditary class in any shape really prevents caste (jāti) from having its full sway, and whenever any nation ceases to produce this immense variety, it must die. Therefore what I have to tell you, my countrymen, is this: that India fell because you prevented and abolished caste. Every frozen aristocracy or privileged class is a blow to caste and is not-caste. Let jāti have its sway; break down every barrier in the way of caste, and we shall rise. Now look at Europe. When it succeeded in giving free scope to caste and took away most of the barriers that stood in the way of individuals—each developing his caste—Europe rose. In America there is the best scope for caste (real jāti) to develop, and so the people are great. Every Hindu knows that astrologers try to fix the caste of every boy or girl as soon as he or she is born. That is the real caste, the individuality, and jyotish [astronomy] recognized that. And we can only rise by giving it full sway again. This variety does not mean inequality or any special privilege.

This is my method—to show the Hindus that they have to give up nothing but only to move on in the line laid down by the sages and shake off their inertia, the result of centuries of servitude. Of course we had to stop advancing during the Mohammedan tyranny, for then it was not a question of progress but of life and death. Now that that pressure has gone, we must move forward, not on the lines of destruction directed by renegades and missionaries, but along our own line—our own road. Everything is hideous because the building is unfinished. We had to stop building during centuries of oppression. Now finish the building and everything will look beautiful in its own place. This is all my plan. I am thoroughly convinced of this. Each nation has a main current in life. In India it is religion. Make it strong and the waters on either side must move along with it. This is one phase of my line of thought. In time, I hope to bring them all out, but at present I find I have a mission in this country also. Moreover, I expect help in this country and from here alone. But up to date I could not do anything except spread my ideas. Now I want that a similar attempt be made in India. . . . I do not know when I shall go over to India. I obey the leading of the Lord. I am in His hands.

"In this world I have been searching for wealth; Thou art, O Lord, the greatest jewel I have found. I sacrifice myself unto Thee."

"I have been searching for someone to love; Thou art the One Beloved I have found. I sacrifice myself unto Thee." (Yajur-Veda Samhitā.)

May the Lord bless you for ever and ever!

Yours ever gratefully,
VIVEKANANDA

To Śri G. G. Narasimhachariar

CHICAGO, 11 January, 1895

DEAR G. G.,

Your letter just to hand. . . . The Parliament of Religions was organized with the intention of proving the superiority of the Christian religion over other forms of faith, but the philosophic religion of Hinduism was able to maintain its position notwithstanding. Dr. Barrows and the men of that ilk are very orthodox, and I do not look to them for help. . . . The Lord has sent me many friends in this country and they are always on the increase. . . . The Lord bless them! . . . I have been running all the time between Boston and New York, two great centres of this country, of which Boston may be called the brain, and New York, the purse. In both my success is more than ordinary. I am indifferent to the newspaper reports and you must not expect me to send any of them to you. A little boom was necessary to begin work. We have had more than enough of that.

I have written to Mani Ayer, and I have given you my directions already. Now *show me what you can do.* No foolish talk now, actual work. The Hindus must back their talk with real work; if they cannot, they do not deserve anything, that is all. . . . As for me, I want to teach the truth; I do not care whether here or elsewhere!

In future do not pay any heed to what people say either for or against you or me. Work on, be lions, and the Lord will bless you. I shall work incessantly until I die, and even after death I shall work for the good of the world. Truth is infinitely more weighty than untruth; so is goodness. If you possess these, they will make their way by sheer gravity.

. . . Thousands of the best men do care for me; you know this, so have faith in the Lord. I am slowly exercising an influence in this land greater than all the newspaper blazoning can do for me. . . .

It is the force of character, of purity, and of truth—of personality. So long as I have these things you can feel easy; no one will be able to injure a hair of my head. If they try they will fail, saith the Lord. . . . Enough of books and theories! It is the *life* that is the highest and the only way to stir the hearts of people; it carries the personal magnetism. . . . The Lord is giving me a deeper and deeper insight every day. Work, work, work! . . . A truce to foolish talk; talk of the Lord. Life is too short to be spent in talking about frauds and cranks.

You must always remember that every nation must save itself; so must every man. Do not look to others for help. Through hard work here, I shall be able now and then to send you a little money for your work; but that is all. If you have to look forward to that, better stop work. Know also that this is a grand field for my ideas, and that I do not care whether they are Hindus or Mohammedans or Christians, but those who love the Lord will always command my service.

. . . I like to work on calmly and silently, and the Lord is always with me. Follow me if you will, by being intensely sincere, perfectly unselfish, and above all, by being perfectly pure. My blessings go with you. In this short life there is no time for the exchange of compliments. We can compare notes and compliment each other to our hearts' content after the battle is finished. Now, do not talk; work, work, work! I do not see anything permanent you have done in India—I do not see any centre you have made—I do not see any temple or hall you have erected—I do not see anybody joining hands with you. There is too much talk, talk, talk! We are great, we are great! Nonsense! We are imbeciles; that is what we are! This hankering after name and fame and all other humbugs—what are they to me? What do I care about them? I should like to see hundreds coming to the Lord! Where are they? I want them, I want to see them. You must seek them out. You only spread my name and fame. Have done with name and fame. Now to work, my brave men, to work! You have not caught my fire yet—you do not understand me! You run in the old ruts of sloth and enjoyments. Down with all sloth, down with all enjoyments here or hereafter! Plunge into the fire and bring the people towards the Lord.

That you may catch my fire, that you may be intensely sincere, that you may die heroes' deaths on the field of battle—is the constant prayer of

VIVEKANANDA

P.S.　Tell Alasinga, Kidi, Doctor, Balaji, and all the others not to pin their faith on what Tom, Dick, and Harry say for or against us, but to concentrate all their energy on work.

VIVEKANANDA

To Mrs. Ole Bull

BROOKLYN, 20 January, 1895

DEAR MRS. BULL,

I had a premonition of your father's giving up the old body, and it is not my custom to write to anyone when a wave of would-be inharmonious māyā strikes him. But these are the great turning-points in life, and I know that you are unmoved. The surface of the sea rises and sinks alternately, but to the observant soul, the child of light, each sinking reveals more and more of the depths and the pearl and coral beds at the bottom. Coming and going is a pure piece of delusion. The soul never comes or goes. Where is the place for the soul to go, when all space is in the soul? Where is the time to enter and exit, when all time is in the soul?

The earth is moving, causing the illusion of the movement of the sun; but the sun does not move. So prakriti, or māyā, or nature, is moving, changing, unfolding veil after veil, turning over leaf after leaf of this grand book—while the witnessing soul drinks in all knowledge, unmoved, unchanged. All the souls that have been, that are, that will be, are all in the present tense, and, to use a material simile, all are standing at one geometrical point. Because the idea of space does not occur in the soul. So all that were ours, are ours, will be ours, are always with us, were always with us, and will be always with us. We are in them. They are in us. . . .

The cloud moves over the face of the moon, creating the illusion that the moon is moving. So nature, body, matter, moves on, creating the illusion that the soul is moving. . . .

Each soul is a star, and all stars are set in that infinite azure, the eternal sky—the Lord. There is the root, the reality, the real individuality, of each and all. Religion began with a search after some of the stars which had passed beyond our horizon, and ended in finding them all in God, with ourselves in the same place.

Now the whole secret is that your father has given up the old garment he was wearing, and he is standing where he was through all eternity. Will he put on another garment in this or any other world? I sincerely pray that he may not, unless he does it fully conscious. I pray that none may be dragged anywhere by the unseen power of his own actions. I pray that all may be free, i.e. may know they are free. And if they are to dream again, let us pray that the dreams be all of peace and bliss.

I am to lecture here tonight, and give two other lectures in the next month. I came in only yesterday. Miss Josephine Locke and Mrs. Adams were very,

very kind to me in Chicago, and my debt to Mrs. Adams is simply inexpressible. With my love to Miss Farmer, I remain,

Ever your obedient son,
VIVEKANANDA

To Mrs. Ole Bull

NEW YORK, 24 January, 1895

DEAR MRS. BULL,

. . . This year I am afraid I am getting overworked, as I feel the strain. I want a rest badly. So it is very good, as you say, that the Boston work be taken up in the end of March. By the end of April I will start for England.

Land can be had in large plots in the Catskills for very little money. There is a plot of 101 acres for $200. The money I have ready, only I cannot buy the land in my name. You are the only friend in this country in whom I have perfect trust. If you consent I will buy the land in your name. The students will go there in summer and build cottages or camps as they like, and practise meditation. Later on, if they can collect funds they may build something up.

. . . Tomorrow will be the last Sunday lecture of this month. The first Sunday of next month there will be a lecture in Brooklyn—the rest, three in New York, with which I will close this year's New York lectures.

I have done my best. If there is any truth in my work, it will surely bear fruit. So I have no anxiety about anything. I am also getting tired of lecturing and having classes. After a few months' work in England I will go to India and hide myself absolutely for some years or for ever. I am satisfied in my conscience that I did not remain an idle Swami. I have a note-book which has travelled with me all over the world. I find these words written seven years ago: "Now to seek a corner and lay myself down to die!" Yet all this karma remained. I hope I have worked it out. I hope the Lord will give me freedom from this preaching and adding good bondages.

"If you have known the Ātman as the one existence, and that nothing else exists, for whom, for what desire, do you trouble yourself?" Through māyā all these ideas of doing good entered my brain—now they are leaving me. I get more and more convinced that there is no other object in work except the purification of the soul—to make it fit for knowledge. This world with its good and evil will go on in various forms. Only the evil and good will take new names and new forms. My soul is hankering after peace and rest, eternal, undisturbed.

"Live alone, live alone. He who is alone never comes into conflict with others —never disturbs others, is never disturbed by others." I long, oh, I long for my rags, my shaven head, my sleep under the trees, and my food from begging! India is the only place where, with all its faults, the soul finds its freedom, its God. All this Western pomp is only vanity, only bondage of the soul. Never in my life have I realized more forcibly the vanity of the world. May the Lord break the bondage of all—may all come out of māyā—is the constant prayer of

VIVEKANANDA

To Miss Mary Hale

54 WEST 33RD STREET, NEW YORK
1 February, 1895

DEAR SISTER,

I just received your beautiful note. Very sorry to learn that Mother Church could not go to the concert. Well, sometimes it is a good discipline to be forced to work for work's sake, even to the length of not being allowed to enjoy the fruits of our labour. Sister Josephine Locke writes me a beautiful letter too. I am very glad of your criticisms and am not sorry at all. The other day at Miss Thursby's I had a hot argument with a Presbyterian gentleman, who as usual got very hot, angry, and abusive. However, I was severely reprimanded by Mrs. Bull for it, as such things hinder my work. So, it seems, is your opinion.

I am glad you write about it just now, because I have been giving a good deal of thought to it. In the first place, I am not at all sorry for these things. Perhaps that will disgust you—it may. I know full well how good it is for one's worldly prospects to be sweet. I do everything to be sweet, but when it comes to a horrible compromise with the truth within, there I stop. I do not believe in humility; I believe in samadarśitvam—the same state of mind with regard to all. The duty of the common man is to obey the commands of his "God"—society. The children of light never do it. This is an eternal law. The one accommodates himself to his surroundings and to social opinion and gets all good things from his giver of all good things—society. The other stands alone and drags society up towards him. The accommodating man finds a path of roses—the non-accommodating, one of thorns. But the worshipper of "vox populi" goes to annihilation in a moment—the children of Truth live for ever.

I will compare Truth to a corrosive substance of infinite power. It burns its way in wherever it falls—in a soft substance sooner, in hard granite later—but it must.

What is writ is writ. I am so, so sorry, Sister, that I cannot make myself sweet and accommodating to every black falsehood. But I cannot. I have suffered for it all my life, but I cannot. I have essayed and essayed, but I cannot. The Lord is great. He will not allow me to become a hypocrite. At last I have given it up. Now let what is inside come out. I have not found a way that will please all, and I cannot but be what I am, true to my own self. "Youth and beauty vanish, life and wealth vanish, name and fame vanish—even the mountains are crumbled into dust. Friendship and love vanish. Truth alone abides." God of Truth, be Thou alone my guide. I am too old to change now into milk and honey. Allow me to remain as I am. "Without fear, without shopkeeping, caring for neither friend nor foe, do thou hold on to Truth, sannyāsin." "I from this moment give up this world and the next and all that are to come—their enjoyments and vanities. Truth, be thou my guide." I have no desire for wealth or name or fame or enjoyments, Sister. They are dust unto me. I wanted to help my brethren. I have not the tact to earn money, bless the Lord! What reason is there for me to conform to the vagaries of the world around me and not obey the voice of Truth within? The mind is still weak, Sister. It sometimes mechanically clutches at earthly help. But I am not afraid. Fear is the greatest sin, my religion teaches.

The last fight with the Presbyterian priest and the long fight afterwards with Mrs. Bull showed me in clear light what Manu says to the sannyāsin: "Live alone, walk alone." All friendship, all love, is only limitation. There never was a friendship, especially of women, that was not exacting. O great sage! you were right. He cannot be brave, he cannot be free, he cannot serve the God of Truth who has to look back to somebody. Be still, my soul! Be alone!—and the Lord is with you. Life is nothing. Death is a delusion. All this is not—God is. Fear not, my soul! Be alone. Sister, the way is long, the time is short—evening is approaching. I have to go home soon. I have no time to give my manners a finish. I cannot find time enough to deliver my message. You are good, you are so kind—I will do anything for you. But—be not angry—I see in you all only children.

Dream no more, oh, dream no more, my soul! In one word, I have a message to give; I have no time to be sweet to the world—and every attempt at sweetness makes me a *hypocrite*. I will die a thousand deaths rather than lead the jelly-fish existence of yielding to every requirement of this foolish world—of my own country or a foreign country. You are mistaken, utterly mistaken, if you think I have a *work*, as Mrs. Bull thinks. I have no work under or beyond the sun. I have a message. I will give it after my own fashion. I will neither Hinduize my message nor Christianize it, nor make it any "ize" in the world. I will only *my-ize* it and that is all.

Liberty, mukti, is all my religion, and everything that tries to curb it I will avoid by fight or flight. Pooh! I try to pacify the priests!!!!!! Sister, do not take this amiss. But you are babies, and babies must submit to being taught. You have not yet drunk of that fountain which makes "reason unreason, mortal immortal, this world a zero, and man a God." Come out, if you can, of this network of foolishness they call this world, and I will call you indeed brave and free. If you cannot, cheer those that dare dash this false God, society, unto the earth and trample on its unmitigated hypocrisy. If you cannot even cheer them, pray be silent, but do not try to drag them down again into the mire with such false nonsense as compromise and becoming *sweet*.

I hate this world—this dream—this horrible nightmare—with its churches and chicaneries, its books and blackguardisms, its fair faces and false hearts—its howling righteousness in front and utter hollowness at the back, and above all, its sanctified shopkeeping. What! Measure my soul according to what the bond-slaves of the world say!—Foh! Sister, you do not know the sannyāsin. "He stands on the head of the Vedas!" say the Vedas, because he is free from churches and sects and religions and prophets and books and all of that ilk. Missionary or no missionary, let them howl and attack me all they can. I take them as Bhartrihari says: "Go thou thy way, sannyāsin! Some will say, 'Who is this mad-man?' Others, 'Who is this chandāla?' Others will know thee to be a sage. Be glad at the prattle of the worldlings." But when they attack, know that the elephant passing through the market-place is always beset by curs, but he cares not. He goes straight *his own way*. So it is always when a great soul appears. There will be numbers to bark after him.

I am living with Landsberg at 54 W. 33rd Street. He is a brave and noble soul, Lord bless him! Sometimes I go to the Guernseys to sleep.

Lord bless you all, ever and ever, and may He lead you quickly out of this big humbug, the world. May you never be enchanted by this old witch, the world. May Śankara help you. May Umā open the door of Truth for you and take away all your delusions!

Yours etc.,
VIVEKANANDA

To Miss Mary Hale

228 WEST 39TH STREET, NEW YORK
10 February, 1895

DEAR SISTER,

I am astonished to learn that you have not received my letter yet. I wrote immediately after the receipt of yours and also sent you some booklets of three lectures I delivered in New York. These Sunday public lectures are now taken down by shorthand and printed. Three of them made two little pamphlets, several copies of which I have forwarded to you. I shall be in New York two weeks more and then I go to Detroit and come back to Boston for a week or two.

My health is very much broken down this year by constant work. I am very nervous. I have not slept a single night soundly this winter. I am sure I am working too much; yet a big work awaits me in England.

I shall have to go through it, and then I hope to reach India and have a rest all the rest of my life. I have tried, at least, to do my best for the world, leaving the result to the Lord. Now I am longing for rest. I hope I shall get some and the Indian people will give me up. How I should like to become dumb for some years and not talk at all!

I was not made for these struggles and fights of the world. I am naturally dreamy and restful. I am a born idealist and can only live in a world of dreams. The very touch of fact disturbs my visions and makes me unhappy. Thy will be done!

I am ever grateful to you four sisters. To you I owe everything I have in this country. May you be ever blessed and happy! Wherever I be, you will always be remembered with the deepest gratitude and sincerest love.

The whole of life is a succession of dreams. My ambition is to be a conscious dreamer—that is all. My love to all—to Sister Josephine.

Ever your affectionate brother,
VIVEKANANDA

To Mrs. Ole Bull

54 WEST 33RD STREET, NEW YORK
11 April, 1895

DEAR MRS. BULL,

. . . I am going away to the country tomorrow to Mr. Leggett for a few days.

A little fresh air will do me good, I hope. I have given up the project of removing from this house just now, as it will be too expensive, and moreover it is not advisable to change just now. I am working it up slowly. . . .

. . . Miss Hamlin has been helping me a good deal. I am very grateful to her. She is very kind and, I hope, sincere. She wants me to be introduced to the "right kind of people." This is the second edition of the "hold yourself steady" business, I am afraid. The only "right sort of people" are those whom the Lord sends—that is what I find from my life's experience. They alone can and will help me. As for the rest, Lord help them in a mass and save me from them!

Every one of my friends thought it would end in nothing, this living and preaching in poor quarters all by myself, and that *no ladies will ever come here.* Miss Hamlin especially thought that "she" and her "right sort of people" were *way up* from such things as to go and listen to a man who lives by himself in a poor lodging. But the "right kind" came for all that, day and night, and she too. Lord! How hard it is for man to believe in Thee and Thy mercies! Śiva! Śiva! Where is the right kind and where is the bad, Mother? It is all He! In the tiger and in the lamb, in the saint and sinner, all He! In Him I have taken refuge—body, soul, and Ātman. Will He leave me now, after carrying me in His arms all my life? Not a drop will be in the ocean, not a twig in the deepest forest, not a crumb in the house of the god of wealth, if the Lord is not merciful. Streams will be in the desert and the beggar will have plenty, if He wills it. He seeth the sparrow's fall. Are these but words, Mother, or literal, actual life?

Truce to this "right sort of presentation" and the like. Thou art my right, Thou my wrong, my Śiva. Lord, since I was a child I have taken refuge in Thee. Thou wilt be with me in the tropics or at the poles, on the tops of mountains or in the depths of the oceans. My Stay—my Guide in life—my Refuge—my Friend—my Teacher—my God—my real Self! Thou wilt never leave me, *never!* I know it as sure as anything. Sometimes I become weak, being alone and struggling against odds, my God, and I think of human help. Save Thou me for ever from these weaknesses, and may I never, never seek for help from any being but Thee! If a man puts his trust in another good man he is never betrayed, never forsaken. Wilt Thou forsake me, Father of all good, Thou who knowest that all my life I am Thy servant and Thine alone? Wilt Thou give me over to be played upon by others or dragged down by evil?

He will never leave me, I am sure, Mother.

Your son,
VIVEKANANDA

To Mr. E. T. Sturdy

NEW YORK, 24 April, 1895

DEAR FRIEND,

I am perfectly aware that although some truth underlies the mass of mystical thought which has burst upon the Western world of late, it is for the most part full of motives unworthy or insane. For this reason, I have never had anything to do with these phases of religion, either in India or elsewhere, and mystics as a class are not very favourable to me. . . .

I quite agree with you that only the Advaita philosophy can save mankind, whether in East or West, from "devil worship" and kindred superstitions, giving tone and strength to the very nature of man. India herself requires this quite as much as, or even more than, the West. Yet it is hard, uphill work, for we have first to create a taste, then teach, and lastly proceed to build up the whole fabric.

Perfect sincerity, holiness, gigantic intellect, and an all-conquering will—let only a handful of men work with these, and the whole world will be revolutionized. I did a good deal of platform work in this country last year, and received plenty of applause, but found that I was only working for myself. It is the patient upbuilding of character, the intense struggle to *realize* Truth, which alone will tell on the future of humanity. So this year I am hoping to work along this line —training up for practical Advaita realization a small band of men and women. I do not know how far I shall succeed. The West is the field for work, if a man wants to benefit humanity rather than his own particular sect or country. I agree perfectly as to your idea of a magazine. But I have no business capacity at all to do these things. I can teach and preach, and sometimes write. But I have intense faith in Truth. The Lord will send help and hands to work with me. Only let me be perfectly pure, perfectly sincere, and perfectly unselfish.

"Truth alone triumphs, not untruth; through Truth alone stretches the way to the Lord." (Yajur-Veda.) He who gives up the little self for the world will find the whole universe to be his. . . .

I am very uncertain about coming to England. I know no one there, and here I am doing some work. The Lord will guide, in His own time.

Yours etc.,
VIVEKANANDA

To Mr. E. T. Sturdy

19 WEST 38TH STREET, NEW YORK

DEAR FRIEND,

I received your last duly, and as I had a previous arrangement to come to Europe by the end of this August, I take your invitation as a divine call. . . .

Those who think that a little sugar-coating of untruth helps the spread of truth are mistaken, and will find in the long run that a single drop of poison poisons the whole mass. . . . The man who is pure and who dares, does all things. May the Lord ever protect you from illusion and delusion! I am ever ready to work with you, and the Lord will send us friends by the hundred, if only we be our own friends first. "The Ātman alone is the friend of the Ātman."

Europe has always been the source of social, and Asia, of spiritual, power; and the whole history of the world is the tale of the varying combinations of those two powers. Slowly a new leaf is being turned in the story of humanity. The signs of this are everywhere. Hundreds of new plans will be created and destroyed. Only the fit will survive, and what but the true and the good is the fit?

Yours etc.,
VIVEKANANDA

To Miss Mary Hale

54 WEST 33RD STREET, NEW YORK
22 June, 1895

DEAR SISTER,

The letters from India and the parcel of books reached me safe. . . .

This year I could hardly keep my head up and I did not go about lecturing. The three great commentaries on the Vedānta philosophy, belonging to the three great sects of Dualists, Qualified Monists, and Monists, are being sent to me from India. Hope they will arrive safe. Then I will have an intellectual feast indeed. I intend to write a book this summer on the Vedānta philosophy. This world will always be a mixture of good and evil, of happiness and misery. This wheel will ever go up and come down; dissolution and resolution are the inevitable law. Blessed are those who struggle to go beyond.

Well, I am glad all the "babies" are doing well, but sorry there was no "catch" even this winter, and every winter the chances are dwindling down. Here near my lodgings is the Waldorf Hotel, the rendezvous of lots of titled but penniless Europeans on show for "Yankee" heiresses to buy. You may have any selection here, the stock is so full and varied. There is the man who talks no English, there are others who lisp a few words which no one can understand, and others are there who talk nice English, but their chance is not so great as that of the dumb ones—the girls do not think them foreign enough who talk plain English fluently.

I read somewhere in a funny book that an American vessel was being foundered in the sea; the men were desperate and as a last solace wanted some religious service to be held. There was "Uncle Josh" on board who was an elder in the Presbyterian Church. They all began to entreat, "Do something religious, Uncle Josh! We are all going to die." Uncle Josh took his hat in his hand and took up a collection on the spot!!

That is all of religion he knew. And that is more or less characteristic of the majority of such people. Collections are about all the religion they know or will ever know. Lord bless them!

Good-bye for the present. I am going to eat something—I feel very hungry.

Yours affectionately,
VIVEKANANDA

To Miss Mary Hale

c/o MISS DUTCHER
THOUSAND ISLAND PARK, N. Y.
24 June, 1895

DEAR SISTER,

Many thanks for the Indian mail. I cannot express in words my gratitude to you. As you have already read in Max Müller's article on "Immortality" I sent Mother Church, he thinks that those we love in this life we must have loved in the past. So it seems I must have belonged to the Holy Family in some past life. . . .

My love to Mother Church and Father Pope and all the sisters. I am enjoying this place immensely—very little eating and a good deal of thinking and talking and study. A wonderful calmness is coming over my soul. Every day I feel I have no duty to do—I am always in eternal rest and peace. It is He that works. We are only the instruments. Blessed be His name! The threefold bondage of lust and gold and fame is as it were fallen from me for the time being, and once more, even here, I feel what sometimes I felt in India: "From me all difference has fallen, all right and wrong, all delusion and ignorance have vanished. I am walking in the path beyond the qualities. What law shall I obey, what disobey?" From that height the universe looks like a mud-puddle. Harih Om Tat Sat. He exists—nothing else does. I in Thee and Thou in me. Be Thou, Lord, my eternal refuge. Peace—peace—peace!

Ever with love and blessings,

Your brother,

VIVEKANANDA

To Miss Mary Hale

c/o MISS DUTCHER
THOUSAND ISLAND PARK, N. Y.
26 June, 1895

DEAR SISTER,

Many thanks for the Indian mail. It brought a good deal of good news. You are enjoying by this time the article by Prof. Max Müller on the "Immortality of the Soul," which I sent to Mother Church. The old man has taken in Vedānta bones and all and has boldly come out. I am so glad to know of the arrival of the rugs. Was there any duty to pay? If so I will pay that—I insist on it. There will come another big packet from the Rājā of Khetri containing some shawls and brocades and nick-nacks. I want to present them to different friends. But I am sure they are not going to arrive before some months.

I am asked again and again, as you will find from the letters from India, to come over. They are getting desperate. Now if I go to Europe I will go as the guest of Mr. Francis Leggett of New York. He will travel all over Germany, England, France, and Switzerland for six weeks. Thence I will go to India or I may return to America. I have a seed planted here and wish it to grow. This winter's work in New York was splendid and it may die if I suddenly go over to India—so I am not sure about going to India soon.

Nothing noticeable has happened during this visit to the Thousand Islands. The scenery is very beautiful and I have some of my friends here with me to talk God and soul to, ad libitum—eating fruits and drinking milk and so forth, and studying huge Sanskrit books on Vedānta which they have kindly sent me from India.

If I come to Chicago I cannot come at least within six weeks or more. Baby needn't alter any of her plans for me. I will see you all somehow or other before I go.

You fussed so much over my reply to Madras but it has produced a tremendous effect there. A recent speech by the President of the Madras Christian College embodies a large amount of my ideas and declares that the West is in need of Hindu ideas of God and man and calls upon the young men to go and preach to the West. This has created quite a furore, of course, amongst the Missions. What you allude to as being published in the *Arena*, I did not see a bit of it. The women did not make any fuss over me at all in New York. Your friend must have drawn on his imagination. They were not of the "bossing" type at all. I hope Father Pope will go to Europe, and Mother Church too. Travelling is the best thing in life. I am afraid I will die if made to stick to one place for a long time. Nothing like a nomadic life.

The more the shades around deepen—the more the end approaches—the more one understands the true meaning of life, that it is a dream; and we begin to understand the failure of everyone to grasp it, for they only attempted to get meaning out of the meaningless. To get reality out of a dream is boyish enthusiasm. "Everything is evanescent, everything is changeful"—knowing this, the sage gives up both pleasure and pain and becomes a witness of this panorama (the universe) without attaching himself to anything.

"They indeed have conquered birth and death even in this life whose minds have become fixed in *sameness*. God is pure and the same to all, therefore they are said to be *in* God." (Gitā.)

Desire, ignorance, and inequality, this is the trinity of bondage. Denial of the will to live, knowledge, and same-sightedness is the trinity of liberation. *Freedom* is the goal of the universe.

"Nor love nor hate, nor pleasure nor pain, nor death nor life, nor religion nor irreligion—not this, not this, not this."

Yours ever,
VIVEKANANDA

To Mr. E. T. Sturdy

19 WEST 38TH STREET, NEW YORK
2 August, 1895

DEAR FRIEND,

. . . Some Theosophists came to my classes in New York. But as soon as human beings perceive the glory of the Vedānta, all abracadabras fall off of themselves. This has been my uniform experience. Whenever mankind attains a higher vision, the lower vision disappears of itself. Multitude counts for nothing. A few heart-whole, sincere, and energetic men can do more in a year than a mob in a century. If there is heat in one body, then those others that come near it must catch it. This is the law. So success is ours so long as we keep up the heat, the spirit of truth, sincerity, and love. My own life has been a very chequered one, but I have always found the eternal words verified: "Truth alone triumphs, not untruth. Through truth alone lies the way to God."

May the Sat in you be always your infallible guide! May you speedily attain to freedom, and help others to attain it!

Ever yours in the Sat,
VIVEKANANDA

To Mr. E. T. Sturdy

19 West 38th Street, New York
9 August, 1895

Dear Friend,

. . . It is only just that I should try to give you a little of my views. I fully believe that there are periodic ferments of religion in human society, and that such a period is now sweeping over the educated world. While each ferment, moreover, appears broken into various little bubbles, these are all eventually similar, showing the cause or causes behind them to be the same. That religious ferment which at present is every day gaining a greater hold over thinking men has this characteristic, that all the little thought-whirlpools into which it has broken itself declare one single aim—a vision and a search after the Unity of Being. On planes physical, ethical, and spiritual, an ever broadening generalization— leading up to a concept of Unity Eternal—is in the air; and this being so, all the movements of the time may be taken to represent, knowingly or unknowingly, the noblest philosophy of unity man ever had—the Advaita Vedānta.

Again, it has always been observed that as a result of the struggles of the various fragments of thought in a given epoch, one bubble survives. The rest only arise to melt into it and form a single great wave, which sweeps over society with irresistible force.

In India, America, and England (the countries I happen to know about), hundreds of these are struggling at the present moment. In India, dualistic formulas are already on the wane; the Advaita alone holds the field in force. In America many movements are struggling for mastery. Now if anything was ever clear to me, it is that one of these must survive, swallowing up all the rest, to be the power of the future. Which one is it to be?

Referring to history, we see that only that fragment which is fit will survive, and what makes it fit to survive but character? Advaita will be the future religion of thinking humanity. No doubt of that. And of all the sects, they alone shall gain the day who are able to show most character in their lives—no matter how few they may be.

Let me tell you a little personal experience. When my Master left the body, we were a dozen penniless and unknown young men. Against us were a hundred powerful organizations, struggling hard to nip us in the bud. But Ramakrishna had given us one great gift—the desire, and the lifelong struggle, not to talk alone but to *live the life*. And today all India knows and reverences the Master, and the truths he taught are spreading like wildfire. Ten years ago I could not get a hundred persons together to celebrate his birthday anniversary. Last year there were fifty thousand.

Neither numbers, nor powers, nor wealth, nor learning, nor eloquence, nor anything else will prevail but purity, living the life, in one word, *anubhuti*, realization. Let there be but a dozen such lion-souls in each country, lions who have broken their own bonds, who have touched the Infinite, whose whole soul is gone to Brahman, who care neither for wealth, nor power, nor fame, and these will be enough to shake the world.

Here lies the secret. Says Patanjali, the father of Yoga: "When a man rejects all the superhuman powers, then he attains to the cloud of virtue." He sees God. He becomes God and helps others to become the same. This is all I have to preach. Doctrines have been expounded enough. There are books by the million. Oh, for an ounce of practice!

As to societies and organizations, these will come of themselves. Can there be jealousy where there is nothing to be jealous of? The number of those who will wish to injure us will be legion. But is not that the surest sign of our having the truth? The more I have been opposed, the more my energy has found expression. I have been honoured and worshipped by princes. I have been slandered by priests and laymen alike. But what of it? Bless them all! They are my very Self. And have they not helped me by acting as a spring-board from which my energy could take higher and higher flights?

. . . I have discovered one great secret—I have nothing to fear from *talkers* of religion. And the great ones who realize—they become enemies to none! Let talkers talk! They know no better! Let them have their fill of name and fame and money and woman. Let us hold on to realization, to being Brahman, to becoming Brahman. Let us hold on to truth unto death, and from life to life! Let us not pay the least attention to what others say, and if, after a lifetime's effort, one, only one, soul can break the fetters of the world and be free, we have done our work. Hari Om!

. . . One word more. Doubtless I do love India. But every day my sight grows clearer. What is India or England or America to us? We are the servants of that God who by the ignorant is called man. He who pours water at the root, does he not water the whole tree?

There is but one basis of well-being, social, political, or spiritual—to know that I and my brother are one. This is true for all countries and all people. And Westerners, let me say, will realize it more quickly than Orientals, who have almost exhausted themselves in formulating the idea and producing a few cases of individual realization.

Let us work without desire for name or fame or rule over others. Let us be free from the triple bonds of lust, greed of gain, and anger—and the truth will be with us!

VIVEKANANDA

To Mr. E. T. Sturdy

80 OAKLEY STREET, CHELSEA
31 October, 1895

DEAR FRIEND,

Just now two young gentlemen, Mr. Silverlock and his friend, left. . . . Both of them want to know the rituals of my creed! This opened my eyes. The world in general must have some form. In fact, in the ordinary sense, religion is philosophy concretized through rituals and symbols.

It is absolutely necessary to form some ritual and have a church. That is to say, we must fix on some ritual as fast as we can. If you can come Saturday morning or sooner, we shall go to the Asiatic Society Library; or you can procure

for me a book which is called *Hemādri Kośa*, from which we can get what we
want, and kindly bring the Upanishads. We shall fix something grand, from the
birth to the death of a man. A mere loose system of philosophy gets no hold on
mankind.

If we can get it through, before we have finished the classes, and publish it
by publicly holding a service or two under it, it will go on. They want to form
a congregation, and they want ritual; that is one of the reasons why ———— will
never have a hold on Western people.

The Ethical Society has sent me another letter thanking me for the acceptance
of their offer. Also a copy of their forms. They want me to bring with me a
book from which to read for ten minutes. Will you bring the Gitā (translation)
and the Buddhist *Jātaka* (translation) with you?

I will not do anything in this matter without seeing you first.

Yours with love and blessings,

VIVEKANANDA

To Mr. E. T. Sturdy

228 WEST 39TH STREET, NEW YORK
16 December, 1895

BLESSED AND BELOVED,

All your letters reached me by one mail today. Miss Muller also writes me one.
She has read in the *Indian Mirror* that Swami Krishnananda is coming over to
England. If that is so, he is the strongest man that I can get.

The classes I hold here are six in the week, besides a question class. The
general attendance varies between seventy and one hundred and twenty. Besides
every Sunday I have a public lecture. At first my lectures were in a small hall
holding about six hundred. But nine hundred would come as a rule, three hundred standing and about three hundred going off, not finding room. This week
therefore I have a bigger hall, with a capacity of twelve hundred people.

There is no admission charged in these lectures, but a collection covers the
rent. The newspapers have taken me up this week, and altogether I have stirred
up New York considerably this year. If I could have remained here this summer
and organized a summer place, the work would be going on sure foundations
here. But as I intend to come over in May to England, I shall have to leave it
unfinished. If, however, Krishnananda comes to England, and you find him
strong and able, and if you find the work in London will not be hurt by my
absence this summer, I would rather be here this summer.

Again, I am afraid my health is breaking down under constant work. I want
some rest. We are so unused to these Western methods, especially the keeping
to time. I will leave you to decide all these things. The *Brahmavādin* magazine is
going on here very satisfactorily. I have begun to write articles on bhakti, and also
send them a monthly account of the work. Miss Muller wants to come to America. I do not know whether she will or not. Some friends here are publishing
my Sunday lectures. I have sent you a few copies of the first one. I shall send
you, next mail, a few of the next two lectures, and if you like them I shall ask

them to send you more copies. Can you manage to get a few hundred copies sold in England? That will encourage them in publishing the subsequent ones.

Next month I go to Detroit, then to Boston and Harvard University. Then I shall have a rest, and then I come to England, unless you think that things will go on without me and with Krishnananda.

Ever yours with love and blessings,

VIVEKANANDA

To Miss S. Farmer

NEW YORK, 29 December, 1895

DEAR SISTER,

In this universe, where nothing is lost, where we live in the midst of death-in-life, every thought that is thought, in public or in private, in crowded thoroughfare or in the deep recesses of primeval forests, lives. They are continually trying to become self-embodied, and until they have fully embodied themselves they will struggle for expression, and no amount of repression can kill them. Nothing can be destroyed—those thoughts that caused evil in the past are also seeking embodiment, to be filtered through repeated expression and at last transfigured into perfect good.

This being so, there is a mass of thought which is at the present time struggling to get expression. This thought is telling us to give up our dreams of dualism, of good and evil, and the still wilder dream of suppressing evil. It teaches us that higher direction and not destruction is the law. It teaches us that it is not a world of bad and good, but good and better—and still better. It stops short of nothing but acceptance. It teaches that no situation is hopeless, and as such accepts every form of mental, moral, or spiritual thought where it already stands, and without a word of condemnation tells it that so far it has done good, now is the time to do better. What in old times was thought of as the elimination of bad, it teaches as the transfiguration of evil and the doing of better. It above all teaches that the kingdom of heaven is already in existence if we will have it, that perfection is already in man if he will see it.

The Greenacre meetings last summer were so wonderful simply because you opened yourself fully to that thought which has found in you so competent a medium of expression, and because you took your stand on the highest teaching of this thought that the kingdom of heaven already exists.

You have been consecrated and chosen by the Lord as a channel for converting this thought into life, and everyone that helps you in this wonderful work is serving the Lord.

Our Gītā teaches that he who serves the servants of the Lord is His highest worshipper. You are a servant of the Lord, and as a disciple of Krishna I will always consider it a privilege and worship to render you any service in the carrying out of your inspired mission, wherever I be.

Ever your affectionate brother,

VIVEKANANDA

To Miss Mary Hale

NEW YORK, 6 January, 1896

Many thanks, dear Sister, for your kind New Year's greetings. . . . The English people received me with open arms, and I have very much toned down my ideas about the English race. First of all, I found that those fellows—such as Lund, etc.—who came over from England to attack me were nowhere. Their existence is simply ignored by the English people. None but a person belonging to the English Church is thought to be *genteel*. Again, some of the best men of England belong to the English Church, and some of the highest in position and fame became my truest friends. This was quite another sort of experience from what I met in America, was it not?

The English people laughed and laughed when I told them about my experience with the Presbyterians and other fanatics here, and my reception in hotels, etc. I also found at once the difference in culture and breeding between the two countries, and came to understand why American girls go in shoals to be married to Europeans. Everyone was kind to me there, and I have left many noble friends of both sexes anxiously awaiting my return in the spring.

As to my work there, the Vedāntic thought has already permeated the higher classes of England. Many people of education and rank, and amongst them not a few clergymen, told me that the conquest of Rome by Greece was being re-enacted in England.

There are two sorts of Englishmen who have lived in India: one consisting of those who hate everything Indian—but they are uneducated; the other, to whom India is the holy land, its very air is holy—and they try to out-herod Herod in their Hinduism. They are awful vegetarians and they want to form a caste in England. Of course, the majority of the English people are firm believers in caste. I had eight classes a week apart from public lectures, and they were so crowded that a good many people, even ladies of high rank, sat on the floor and did not think anything of it. In England I found strong-minded men and women to take up the work and carry it forward with the peculiar English grip and energy. This year my work in New York is going on splendidly. Mr. Leggett is a very rich man of New York and very much interested in me. New Yorkers have more steadiness than any other people in this country, so I have determined to make my centre here. In this country my teachings are thought to be queer by the Methodist and Presbyterian aristocracy. In England it is the highest philosophy to the English Church aristocracy.

Moreover the talk and gossip so characteristic of the American woman are almost unknown in England. The English woman is slow, but when she works up to an idea she will have a hold on it sure, and they are regularly carrying on my work there and sending every week a report. Think of that. Here if I go away for a week everything falls to pieces.

My love to all—to Sam and to yourself. May the Lord bless you ever and ever!

Your affectionate brother,

VIVEKANANDA

To Śri Alasinga Perumal

17 February, 1896

Dear Alasinga,

. . . The work is terribly hard, and the more it is growing the harder it is becoming. I need a long rest very badly. Yet a great work is before me in England. . . . Have patience, my son—it will grow beyond all your expectations. . . . Every work has got to pass through hundreds of difficulties before succeeding. Those that persevere will see the light sooner or later. . . .

I have succeeded now in rousing the very heart of the American civilization, New York. But it has been a terrific struggle. . . . I have spent nearly all I had on this New York work and in England. Now things are in such a shape that they will go on.

To put the Hindu ideas into English and then make out of dry philosophy and intricate mythology and queer, startling psychology a religion which shall be easy, simple, popular, and at the same time meet the requirements of the highest minds—is a task that only those can understand who have attempted it. The abstract Advaita must become living—poetic—in everyday life; out of hopelessly intricate mythology must come concrete moral forms; and out of bewildering yogi-ism must come the most scientific and practical psychology— and all this must be put in such a form that a child may grasp it. That is my life's work. The Lord only knows how far I shall succeed. To work we have the right, not to the fruits thereof.

It is hard work, my boy, hard work! To keep oneself steady in the midst of this whirl of kāma-kānchana, and hold on to one's own ideals until disciples are moulded to conceive the ideas of realization and perfect renunciation, is indeed difficult work. Thank God, already there is great success. I cannot blame the missionaries and others for not understanding me—they hardly ever saw a man who did not care about women and money. At first they could not believe it—how could they? You must not think that the Western nations have the same ideas of chastity and purity as the Indians. Their equivalents are honesty and courage. . . . People are now flocking to me. Hundreds have become convinced that there are men who can really control their bodily desires, and reverence and respect for these principles are growing. All things come to him who waits.

May you be blessed for ever and ever!

Yours,

Vivekananda

To Miss Mary Hale

63 St. George's Road, London
May 1896

Dear Sister,

In London once more. The climate here in England is nice and cool. We have fire in the grate. We have a whole house to ourselves you know this time. It is small but convenient and in London things do not cost so much as in America, doncherknow—awe—What was I thinking?—awe—About your mother. I just wrote her a letter and will duly post it to her c/o Monroe & Co., 7 Rue Scribe, Paris. Some old friends are here—and Miss MacLeod came over from the Continent. She is good as gold and as kind as ever. We have a nice little family in the house. Another monk from India—poor man—a typical Hindu with nothing of that pluck and go which I have—he is always dreamy and gentle and sweet!! That won't do—I will try to put a little activity into him. I have had two classes already. They will go on for four or five months and after that to India I go. But—it is to Amérique—there where the heart is etc. etc. I love the Yankee land—I like to see new things. I do not care a fig to loaf about old ruins and mope a life out about old histories and keep sighing about the ancients. I have too much vigour in my blood for that. In America is the place, the people, the opportunity for everything new.

I have become horribly radical. I am just going to India to see what I can do in that awful mass of conservative jelly-fish—and then throw overboard all old associations and start a new thing, entirely new—simple, strong, new, and fresh as the first-born baby—throw all of the past overboard and begin anew.

The eternal, the infinite, the omnipresent, the omniscient is a principle— not a person. You, I, and everyone are but embodiments of that principle. The more of this infinite principle is embodied in a man, the greater is he—and all in the end will be the perfect embodiment of that principle, and thus all will be one, as they are now essentially. This is all that there is to religion— and the practice is through this feeling of oneness that is Love. Beyond this everything is mere superstition. All old fogy forms of gods are mere old superstitions. Now, why struggle to keep them alive? Why give thirsty people ditch-water to drink whilst the river of life and truth flows by? This is only human selfishness —nothing else. I am tired of defending old superstitions. I clearly see that I have spent my energy in vain in bolstering up rotten and falling notions.

Life is short—time is flying. That place and people where a man's ideas work best should be the country and the people for him. Oh, for a dozen bold hearts, large, noble, and sincere! I am very well indeed and enjoying life immensely.

Yours ever with love,
VIVEKANANDA

To Sister Nivedita

63 ST. GEORGE'S ROAD, LONDON
7 June, 1896

DEAR MISS NOBLE,

My ideal indeed can be put into a few words and that is: to preach unto mankind their divinity, and how to make it manifest in every movement of life.

This world is in chains of superstition. I pity the oppressed, whether man or woman, and I pity more the oppressors.

One idea that I see clear as daylight is that misery is caused by *ignorance* and nothing else. Who will give the world light? Sacrifice in the past has been

THE HOLY MOTHER AND SISTER NIVEDITA

13th Dec 96.

Dear Francisco

So Gopala has taken the female form!
It is fit that it should be so — the time
& the place considering. May all blessing
follow her through life. She was keenly
desired, prayed for and she comes as a blessing
to you and to your wife for life — I have not
the least doubt.

I wish she could have come to America
now, if only to fulfil the form "the Sages
of the east bringing presents to the western
baby". But the heart is there with all
prayers and blessings and the mind is more
powerful than the body.

I am starting on the 16th of this
month & take the steamer at Naples.
Will see Alberta etc in Rome surely.
With all love to the holy family
Yours ever in the Lord
Vivekananda

FACSIMILE OF A LETTER WRITTEN BY VIVEKANANDA TO MR.
FRANCIS H. LEGGETT CONGRATULATING HIM ON THE BIRTH
OF HIS DAUGHTER
(The word Gopala in the first sentence is an epithet of the
Baby Krishna, regarded as the Godhead by the Hindus, es-
pecially those of the Vaishnava tradition.)

the law—it will be, alas, for ages to come. The earth's bravest and best will have to sacrifice themselves for the good of many, for the welfare of all. Buddhas by the hundred are necessary with eternal love and pity.

The religions of the world have become lifeless mockeries. What the world wants is character. The world is in need of those whose life is one burning love— selfless. That love will make every word fall like a thunderbolt.

It is no superstition with you, I am sure. You have the making in you of a world-mover, and others will also come. Bold words and bolder deeds are what we want. Awake, awake, great one! The world is burning with misery. Can you sleep? Let us call and call till the sleeping gods awake, till the god within answers to the call. What more is in life? What greater work? The details come to me as I go. I never make plans. Plans grow and work themselves. I only say, awake, awake!

May all blessings attend you for ever!

Yours affectionately,

VIVEKANANDA

To Mr. Francis H. Leggett

63 St. George's Road, London, S. W.
6 July, 1896

DEAR FRANKINCENSE,

Your kind letter and the £40 for the publication duly reached me, and a beautiful letter from Mother.

Mrs. Bull writes to me to make out a power of attorney for you in regard to the books, which I send herewith.

Things are going on with me very well on this side of the Atlantic. The Sunday lectures were quite successful—so were the classes. The season has ended, and I too am thoroughly exhausted. I am going to take a tour in Switzerland with Miss Muller. The Galsworthys have been very, very kind. Joe brought them round splendidly. I simply admire Joe Joe for her tact and quiet ways. She is a feminine statesman. She could wield a kingdom. I have seldom seen such strong yet good common sense in a human being. I mean to return next autumn and take up the work in America.

Night before last I was at a party at Mrs. Martin's, about whom you must already know a good deal from Joe. Well, I found there how the work is growing silently yet surely in England. Almost every other man or woman came to me and talked about the work. This British Empire, with all its evils, is the greatest machine that ever existed for the dissemination of ideas. I mean to put my ideas in the centre of this machine, and it will spread them all over the world. Of course, all great work is slow, and the difficulties are too many, especially as we Hindus are a conquered race. Yet that is the very reason why it is bound to work, for spiritual ideals have always come from the downtrodden. The downtrodden Jews overwhelmed the Roman Empire with their spiritual ideals. You will be pleased to learn that I am also learning my lesson every day in patience and above all in sympathy. I think I am beginning to see the Divine even inside the bullying Anglo-Indians. I think I am slowly approaching to that state when I would be able to love the very "Devil" himself, if there were any.

At twenty I was a most unsympathetic, uncompromising fanatic. I would not walk on the foot-path on the theatre side of the street in Calcutta. At thirty-three I can live in the same house with prostitutes and never would think of saying a word of reproach to them. Is it degeneration? Or is it that I am broadening out into that universal love which is the Lord Himself? Again, I have heard that if one does not see the evil round him, he cannot do good work—he lapses into a sort of fatalism. I do not see that. On the contrary, my power of work is immensely increasing and becoming immensely effective. Some days I get into a sort of ecstasy. I feel that I must bless everyone, every being —love and embrace every being—and I literally see that evil is a delusion. I am in one of those moods now, dear Francis, and I am actually shedding tears of joy, as I am writing you now, at the thought of your and Mrs. Leggett's love and kindness to me. I bless the day I was born. I have had so much of kindness and love here, and that Love Infinite who brought me into being has guided every one of my actions, good or bad (don't be frightened); for what am I, what was I ever, but a tool in His hands for whose service I have given up everything—my beloved, my joy, my life, my soul? He is my playful darling. I am His playfellow. There is neither rhyme nor reason in the universe. What reason binds Him? He, the Playful One, is playing—these tears and laughter are all parts of the play. Great fun, great fun! as Joe says.

It is a funny world, and the funniest chap you ever saw is He, the Beloved. Infinite fun, is it not? Brotherhood or playmatehood? A shoal of romping children let out to play in this playground of the world, isn't it? Whom to praise? Whom to blame? It is all His play. They want an explanation, but how can you explain Him? He is brain-less, nor has He any reason. He is fooling us with little brains and reasons, but this time He won't find me napping—"you bet." I have learnt a thing or two. Beyond, beyond reason and learning and talking is the feeling, the "Love," the "Beloved." Ay, "Sakē,"[1] fill the cup and we will be mad.

Yours ever in madness,
VIVEKANANDA

To a Western Disciple

SWITZERLAND, August 1896

DEAR —,

Be you holy and above all sincere and do not for a moment give up your trust in the Lord, and you will see the light. Whatever is truth will remain for ever; whatever is not, none can preserve. We are helped in being born in a time when everything is quickly searched out. Whatever others think or do, lower not your standard of purity, morality, and love of God; above all beware of all secret organizations. No one who loves God need fear any jugglery. Holiness is the highest and divinest power on earth and in heaven. "Truth alone triumphs, not untruth. Through truth alone stretches the way to God." Do not

[1] Friend.

care for a moment who joins hands with you or not; be sure that you touch the hand of the Lord. That is enough. . . .

I went to the glacier of Monte Rosa yesterday and gathered a few hardy flowers growing almost in the midst of eternal snow. I send you one in this letter hoping that you will attain to a similar spiritual hardihood amidst all the snow and ice of this earthly life. . . .

Your dream was very, very beautiful. In dreams our souls read a layer of our mind which we do not read in our waking hours, and however unsubstantial imagination may be, it is behind the imagination that all unknown psychic truths lie. Take heart. We will try to do what we can for the good of humanity —the rest depends upon the Lord. . . .

Well, do not be anxious, do not be in a hurry. Slow, persistent, and silent work does everything. The Lord is great. We will succeed, my boy. We must. Blessed be His name! . . .

Here in America are no āśramas. Would there was one! How I would like it and what an amount of good it would do to this country!

VIVEKANANDA

To Miss Josephine MacLeod

c/o MISS MULLER
AIRLIE LODGE, RIDGEWAY GARDENS
WIMBLEDON, ENGLAND
7 October, 1896

Once more in London, dear Joe Joe, and the classes have begun already. Instinctively I looked about for one familiar face which never had a line of discouragement, never changed, but was always helpful, cheerful, and strengthening—and in my mind conjured up that face before me, in spite of a few thousand miles of space. For what is space in the realm of spirit? Well, you are gone to your home of rest and peace—for me, ever increasing mad work—yet I have your blessings with me always, have I not?

My natural tendency is to go into a cave and be quiet, but a fate behind pushes me forward and I go. Who could ever resist fate?

Why did not Christ say in the Sermon on the Mount, "Blessed are they that are always cheerful and always hopeful, for they have already the kingdom of heaven"? I am sure he must have said it, he with the sorrows of a whole world in his heart, he who likened the saintly soul to a child—but it was not noted down. Of a thousand things he said, they noted down only a few—I mean, remembered.

I now live mostly on fruits and nuts; they seem to agree with me well. If ever the old doctor with "land" up somewhere comes to see you, you may confide to him this secret. I have lost a good deal of my fat, but on days I lecture I have to go on solid food. How is Hollister?[1] I never saw a sweeter boy. May all blessings ever attend him through life!

[1] I.e. Hollister Sturges, the son of Mrs. Leggett by her first marriage.

I hear your friend Cola is lecturing on Zoroastrian philosophy. Surely the stars are not smiling on him. What about your Miss A—? And our Y—? What news about the brotherhood of the Z Z Z's? And our Miss (forgotten!)? I hear that half a ship-load of Hindus and Buddhists and Mohammedans and brotherhoods and what not have entered the U. S., and another cargo of Mahātmā-seekers, evangelists, etc. have entered India!! Good. India and the U. S. seem to be the two countries for religious enterprise. Have a care, Joe, this heathen corruption is dreadful. I met Madame S— in the street today. She does not come any more to my lectures. Good for her. Too much of philosophy is not good.

Do you remember that lady who used to come to every meeting too late to hear a word, but buttonholed me immediately after and kept me talking till a battle of Waterloo would be raging in my internal economy through hunger? She came, they are all coming and more. That is cheering.

Most of our friends came—one of the Galsworthys, too, the married daughter. Mrs. Galsworthy could not come today; it was very short notice. We have a hall now, a pretty big one holding about two hundred or more. There is a big corner which will be fitted up as a library. I have another man from India now to help me.

I enjoyed Switzerland immensely, also Germany. Prof. Deussen was very kind. We came together to London and had great fun here. Prof. Max Müller is very friendly too. In all, the English work is becoming solid and respected too, seeing that great scholars are sympathizing. Probably I shall go to India this winter with some English friends. So much about my own sweet self.

Now, what about the Holy Family? Everything is going on first rate, I am sure. You must have heard from Fox by this time. I am afraid I rather made him dejected the day before he sailed, by telling him that he could not marry Mabel[2] until he began to earn a good deal of money!! Is Mabel with you now? Give her my love. Also give me your present address.

How is Mother? Francis, same solid sterling gold as ever, I am sure.

Alberta working at her music and languages, and laughing a good deal, and eating a good many apples as usual, by the bye?

It is getting late in the night, so good night, Joe (Is strict etiquette to be followed in New York too?), and Lord bless you ever and ever! . . .

Ever yours with love and blessings,
VIVEKANANDA

P.S. Mr. and Mrs. Sevier, in whose house (flat) I am writing now, send their kindest regards.

V.

[2] I.e. Mabel MacLeod.

To Miss Mary Hale

14 GREYCOAT GARDENS
WESTMINSTER, LONDON
1 November, 1896

"Gold and silver," my dear Mary, "have I none, but such as I have I give to thee freely," and that is the knowledge that the goldness of gold, the silverness of silver, the manhood of man, the womanhood of woman, the reality of everything, is the Lord, and that this Lord we are all trying to realize from the beginningless past in the objective world, and in the attempt throwing up such "queer" creatures of our fancy as man, woman, child, body, mind, the earth, sun, moon, stars, the world, love, hate, property, wealth, etc., also ghosts, devils, angels, gods, God, etc.—the fact being that the Lord is in us; we are He, the eternal subject, the real ego, never to be objectified; and all this objectifying process is mere waste of time and talent.

When the soul becomes aware of this it gives up objectifying and falls back more and more upon the subjective. This is evolution—less and less in the body, more and more in the mind—man, meaning in Sanskrit manas, thought, being the highest form—the animal that thinks and not the animal that "senses" only. This is what in theology is called "renunciation." The formation of society, the institution of marriage, the love for children, our good works, morality and ethics, are all different forms of renunciation. Life in every society means the subjection of the will, of thirst, of desire.

This subjection of the will—the desire to jump out of ourselves, as it were —the struggle to objectify the subject—is the one phenomenon in the world of which all societies and social forms are various modes and stages.

Love is the easiest and smoothest way towards this self-surrender or subjection of the will; and hatred, the opposite. People have been cajoled through various stories or superstitions of heavens and hells and rulers above the sky, towards this one end of self-surrender. The philosopher does the same knowingly, without superstition, by giving up desires.

An objective heaven or millennium therefore has existence only in the fancy— but a subjective one is already in existence. The musk-deer, after vain search for the cause of the scent of the musk, at last will have to find it in himself.

Objective society will always be a mixture of good and evil—objective life will always be followed by its shadow, death, and the longer the life, the longer will also be the shadow. It is only when the sun is above our own head that there is no shadow. When God and good and everything else is in us, there is no evil.

In objective life every bullet has its billet—evil goes ever with good as its shadow. Every improvement is coupled with an equal degradation—the reason being that good and evil are not two things, but one, and the difference is only in manifestation—one of degree, not kind. Our very lives depend upon the death of others—plants or animals or bacilli!!

The other great mistake we often make is that good is taken as an ever increasing item, and evil as a diminishing one. From this it is argued that evil being diminished every day, there will come a time when good alone will remain. The fallacy lies in the assumption of a false premise. If good is increasing, so is evil. My desires have been much more keen than those of the masses among my race. My joys have been much greater than theirs—but my miseries a million times more intense. The same condition that makes you feel the least touch of good makes you feel the least touch of evil too. The same nerves that carry sensations of pleasure carry sensations of pain too, and the same mind feels both. The progress of the world means more enjoyment and more misery too. This mixture of life and death, good and evil, knowledge and ignorance, is what is called māyā—or the universal ignorance. You may go on for ever, inside māyā's net, seeking happiness—you will find much, and much evil too. To have good and no evil is childish nonsense. Two ways are left open—one, to give up all hope, take up the world as it is, and bear its pangs and pains in the hope of a crumb of happiness now and then. The other, to give up the search for pleasure, knowing it to be pain in another form, and seek truth; and those that dare to seek truth succeed in finding that truth is ever present—present in themselves. Then we also discover how that same truth is manifesting itself in both our relative error and knowledge. We find also that the same truth is bliss, which is manifesting itself as good and evil; and lastly we find that the same truth is real existence, manifesting itself as both life and death.

Thus we realize that all these phenomena are but the reflections, bifurcated or manifolded, of the one existence—Truth—Bliss—Unity, my real Self and the reality of everything else. Then and then only, perhaps, is it possible to do good without evil. For the knower of Truth has got control of the material of which both good and evil are manufactured, and he alone can manifest one or the other as he likes, and we know he manifests only good. This is jivanmukti —freedom while living—the goal of Vedānta as of all other philosophies.

Human society is in turn governed by the four castes—the priests, the soldiers, the traders, and the labourers. Each state has its glories as well as its defects. When the priest (brāhmin) rules, there is a tremendous exclusiveness on hereditary grounds. The persons of the priests and their descendants are hemmed in with all sorts of safeguards. None but they have any knowledge—none but they have the right to impart that knowledge. The glory of the priestly rule is that at this period is laid the foundation of the sciences. The priests cultivate the mind, for through the intellect they govern.

The military (kshattriya) rule is tyrannical and cruel, but not exclusive, and during that period the arts and social culture attain their height.

The commercial (vaiśya) rule comes next. It is awful in its silent, crushing, blood-sucking power. Its advantage is that as the trader himself goes everywhere, he is a great disseminator of ideas collected during the two previous states. It is still less exclusive than the military, but culture begins to decay.

Last will come the rule of the labourer (śudra). Its advantage will be the distribution of physical comforts; its disadvantage, (perhaps) the lowering of culture. There will be a great distribution of ordinary education, but extraordinary geniuses will be fewer and fewer.

If it is possible to form a state in which the knowledge of the priestly period, the culture of the military, the distributive spirit of the commercial, and the ideal of equality of the last can all be kept intact, minus their evils, it will be an ideal state. Is it possible?

Yet the first three have had their time. Now is the time for the last—the śudras must have it—none can resist. I do not know all the difficulties about the gold or silver standard (nobody seems to know much as to that), but this much I see, that the gold standard has been making the poor poorer and the rich richer. Bryan was right when he said, "We refuse to be crucified on a cross of gold." The silver standard will give the poor a little better chance in this unequal fight.

I am a socialist, not because I think it is a perfect system; but half a loaf is better than no bread. The other systems have been tried and found wanting. Let this one be tried—if for nothing else, for the novelty of the thing. A redistribution of pain and pleasure is better than always the same persons' having pain or pleasure. The sum total of good and evil in the world remains ever the same. The yoke will be lifted from shoulder to shoulder by new systems—that is all.

Let every dog have his day in this miserable world, so that after this experience of so-called happiness they may all come to the Lord and give up this vanity of a world and governments and all other botherations.

With love to all,

Your ever faithful brother,
VIVEKANANDA

To the Hale Sisters

39 VICTORIA STREET, LONDON, S.W.
28 November, 1896

DEAR SISTERS,

I think you are the four persons I love most in this world, somehow or other, and I am vain enough to believe that you four have the same love for me. Therefore I feel impelled to write a few lines to you before my departure for India. The work in London has been a roaring success. The English are not so bright as the Americans, but once you touch their heart it is yours for ever. Slowly I have gained, and it is surprising that in only six months of work I should have a steady class of one hundred and twenty persons, apart from public lectures. Here everyone means work—the practical Englishman. Captain and Mrs. Sevier and Mr. Goodwin are going with me to India to work and spend their own money on it!! There are scores here ready to do the same: men and women of position—beautiful young girls—ready to give up everything for an idea if they once feel convinced. And last, not the least, the help in the shape of money to start my work in India has come, and more will follow.

My ideas about the English have been revolutionized. I now understand why the Lord has blessed them above all other races—steady, sincere to the backbone, with great depths of feeling—only with a crust of stoicism on the surface. If that is broken you have your man.

Now I am going to start a centre in Calcutta and another in the Himālayas The Himālayan one will be an entire hill about seven thousand feet high—cool in summer, cold in winter. Captain and Mrs. Sevier will live there and it will be the centre for European workers, as I do not want to kill them by forcing on them the Indian mode of living and the fiery plains. My plan is to send out numbers of Hindu boys to every civilized country to preach, and get men and women from foreign countries to work in India. This would be a good exchange.

After having established the centres, I go about up and down like the gentleman in the Book of Job. Here I must end to catch the mail. Things are opening for me. I am glad and I know so are you.

Now all blessings be yours and all happiness.

With eternal love,
VIVEKANANDA

P.S. What about Dharmapala? What is he doing? Give him my love if you meet him.

V.

To Miss Mary Hale

DAMPFER "PRINZ-REGENT LUITPOLD"
3 January, 1897

DEAR MARY,

I received your letter forwarded from London in Rome. It was very, very kind of you to write such a beautiful letter and I enjoyed every bit of it. I do not know anything about the evolution of the orchestra in Europe. We are nearing Port Said after four days of frightfully bad sailing from Naples. The ship is rolling as hard as she can and you must pardon my scrawls under such circumstances.

From Suez begins Asia—once more Asia. What am I? Asiatic, European, or American? I feel a curious medley of personalities in me. You didn't write anything about Dharmapala—his goings and doings. I am much more interested in him than in Gandhi.

I land in a few days at Colombo and mean to "do" Ceylon a bit. There was a time when Ceylon had more than twenty million inhabitants and a huge capital, of which the ruins cover nearly a hundred square miles! The Ceylonese are not Dravidians but pure Āryans. It was colonized from Bengal about 800 B.C. and they have kept a very clear history of their country from that time. It was the greatest trade centre of the ancient world, and Anuruddhapura was the London of the ancients.

I enjoyed Rome more than anything in the West, and after seeing Pompeii I have lost all regard for the so-called "modern civilization." With the exception of steam and electricity, they had everything else, and infinitely more art conceptions and execution than the moderns.

Please tell Miss Locke that I was mistaken when I told her that the sculpturing of the human figure was not developed in India as among the Greeks. I am reading in Fergusson and other authorities that in Orissa or Juggernaut, which I did not visit, there are among the ruins human figures which, for beauty and anatomical skill, would compare with any production of the Greeks. There is a colossal figure of Death—a huge female skeleton covered with a shrivelled skin, in which the awful fidelity to anatomical details is frightening and disgusting, says my author. One of the female figures in a niche is exactly like the Venus de Medici, and so on. But you must remember that almost everything has been destroyed by the iconoclastic Mohammedans—yet the remnants are more than all the European debris put together! I have travelled eight years and not seen many of the masterpieces.

Tell Sister Locke also that there is a ruined temple in a forest in India which, along with the Parthenon of Greece, Fergusson considers as the climax of architectural art—each of its type—the one of conception, the other of conception and detail. The later Moghul buildings, etc.—the Indo-Saracenic architecture—do not compare a bit with the best types of the ancients.

I will be sure to come to see you married when you have fixed on your man, wherever I may be—or at least write a benedictory letter twice as long as Harriet's.

With all my love,

VIVEKANANDA

P.S. Just by chance saw Mother Church and Father Pope in Florence. You know of it already.

V.

To Miss Mary Hale

DARJEELING, 28 April, 1897

DEAR MARY,

A few days ago I received your beautiful letter. Yesterday came the card announcing Harriet's marriage. Lord bless the happy pair!—Is that the way?

The whole country here rose like one man to receive me. Hundreds of thousands of persons, shouting and cheering at every place, rājās drawing my carriage, arches all over the streets of the capitals, with blazing mottoes, etc.!!! The whole thing will soon come out in the form of a book, and you will have a copy soon.

But unfortunately I was already exhausted by hard work in England and this tremendous exertion in the heat of Southern India prostrated me completely. I had of course to give up the idea of visiting other parts of India and fly up to the nearest hill-station, Darjeeling. Now I feel much better and a month more in Almora will complete the cure. By the bye, I have just lost a chance of coming over to Europe. Rājā Ajit Singh and several other rājās start next Saturday for England. Of course, they tried hard to get me to go over with them. But unfortunately the doctors would not hear of my undertaking any physical or mental labour just now. So with the greatest chagrin I had to give it up, reserving it for the near future.

Dr. Barrows has reached America by this time, I hope. Poor man! He came here to preach the most bigoted Christianity, with the usual result that nobody listened to him. Of course, they received him very kindly, but it was my letter that did it. I could not put brains into him!! Moreover, he seems to be a queer man. I hear that he was mad at the national rejoicing over my coming home. You ought to have sent a brainier man anyway, for the Parliament of Religions has been made a farce in the Hindu mind by Barrows. On metaphysical lines no nation on earth can hold a candle to the Hindu—and curiously, all the fellows that come over here from Christian lands have that one antiquated foolishness of an argument that the Christians are powerful and rich and the Hindus are not, ergo Christianity is better than Hinduism. To which the Hindus very aptly retort that that is the very reason why Hinduism is a religion and Christianity is not, because in this beastly world it is blackguardism and that alone which prospers, and virtue always suffers. It seems, however advanced the Western nations are in scientific culture, they are mere babies in metaphysical and spiritual education.

Material science can only give worldly prosperity, whilst spiritual science is for eternal life. If there is no eternal life, still the enjoyment of spiritual thoughts as ideals is keener and makes a man happier, whilst the tomfoolery of materialism leads to competition and undue ambition and ultimate death, individual and national.

This Darjeeling is a beautiful spot, with a view of the glorious Kānchanjanghā (28,146 ft.) now and then, when the clouds permit it, and from a near hill-top one can catch a glimpse of the distant Gouriśanker (29,002 ft.) now and then. Then the people here are so picturesque—the Tibetans and Nepalese and above all the beautiful Lepcha women. Do you know one Colton Turnbull of Chicago? He was here a few weeks before I reached India. He seems to have had a great liking for me, with the result that the Hindu people all liked him very much.

What about Joe Joe, Mrs. Adams, Sister Josephine, and all the rest of our friends? Where are our beloved Mills? Grinding slow but sure? I wanted to send some nuptial presents to Harriet, but with your terrible duties I must reserve it for some time in the near future. Maybe I shall meet them in Europe very soon. I should have been very glad, of course, if you could have announced your engagement, and I could have fulfilled my promise by filling up half a dozen papers in one letter. Why do you not take Mr. Howe and finish up the business, and we may sing, All is well that ends well! What about Isabel? Has she got anybody? By the bye, I saw the Venus of What-do-you-call-it?—and you are right— Isabel's face is much like that statue. Of course, her hands are better, for the statue has only stumps—that is to say, to our uneducated taste. Anyhow, Isabel is beautiful because she is like that Venus, and that Venus is beautiful because she is like Isabel!! On the whole, I think she is much more beautiful than the statue, stumps notwithstanding.

My hair is turning grey in bundles and my face is getting wrinkled up all over—that losing of flesh has given me twenty years of age more. And now, no bread or rice or potatoes, not even a lump of sugar in my coffee!! I am living with a brāhmin family who all dress in knickerbockers, women excepted of course. I am also in knickers. It would have given you a surprise if you had seen me bounding from rock to rock like a chamois or galloping with might and main over up-and-down mountain roads.

I am very well here, for life in the plains has become a torture. I cannot put the tip of my nose out into the streets but there is a curious crowd!! Fame is not all milk and honey!! I am going to trim a big beard now it is grey. It gives a venerable appearance and saves one from American scandal-mongers. O thou white hair! how much thou canst conceal! All glory unto thee, hallelujah!

The mail time is nearly up, so I finish. Good dreams, good health, all blessings attend you.

With love to Father and Mother and you all,

Yours,
VIVEKANANDA

To Sister Nivedita

ALMORA, 20 June, 1897

MY DEAR MISS NOBLE,

. . . Let me tell you plainly. Every word you write I value, and every letter is welcome a hundred times. Write whenever you have a mind and opportunity, and whatever you like, knowing that nothing will be misinterpreted, nothing unappreciated. I have not had any news of the work for so long. Can you tell me anything? I do not expect any help from India, in spite of all the jubilating over me. They are so poor!

But I have started work in the fashion in which I myself was trained—that is to say, under the trees, and keeping body and soul together anyhow. The plan has also changed a little. I have sent some of my boys to work in the famine districts. It has acted like a miracle. I find, as I always thought, that it is through the *heart*, and that alone, that the world can be reached. The present plan is, therefore, to train up numbers of young men—from the highest classes, not the lowest; for the latter I shall have to wait a little—and the first attack will be made by sending a number of them over a district. When these sappers and miners of religion have cleared the way, there will then be time enough to put in theory and philosophy.

A number of boys are already in training, but the recent earthquake has destroyed the poor shelter we had to work in, which was only rented, anyway. Never mind. The work must be done without shelter, and under difficulties. . . . As yet it is shaven heads, rags, and casual meals. This must change, however, and will, for are we not working for it, head and heart? . . .

It is true in one way that the people here have so little to give up—yet renunciation is in our blood. One of my boys in training has been an executive engineer in charge of a district. That means a very big position here. He gave it up like straw! . . .

With all love,

Yours in the Truth,
VIVEKANANDA

To Miss Mary Hale

ALMORA, 9 July, 1897

DEAR SISTER,

I am very sorry to read between the lines the desponding tone of your letter, and I understand the cause. I must, to begin with, thank you for your warning. I understand your motive perfectly.

I had arranged to go with Ajit Singh to England, but the doctors not allowing, the plan fell through. I shall be so happy to learn that Harriet has met him. He will be only too glad to see any of you.

I had a lot of cuttings from different papers in America, fearfully criticizing my utterances about American women and furnishing me with the astounding news that I was outcasted! As if I had any caste to lose, being a sannyāsin!!

Not only no caste has been lost, but it has almost shattered the opposition to sea-voyage—my going to the West. If I am to be outcasted, it will have to be with half the ruling princes of India and all of educated India. On the other hand, a leading rājā of the caste to which I belonged before entering the order got up a public banquet in my honour, at which were most of the big bugs of that caste.

Sannyāsins, on the other hand, do not dine with anyone in India, as it would be beneath the dignity of gods to dine with mere mortals. We are Nārāyanas, and they are men. And dear Mary, these feet have been washed and wiped and worshipped by the descendants of a hundred kings, and there has been a progress through the country which none ever commanded in India.

It will suffice to say that the police are necessary to keep order if I venture out into the street!! That is outcasting indeed! Of course that took the starch out of the "missoos"—and who are they here? Nobodies. We are in blissful ignorance of their existence all the time. I had in a lecture said something about the missoos and the origin of that species, except the English Church gentlemen, and in that connexion had to refer to the very churchy women in America and their power of inventing scandals. This the missoos are parading as an attack on American women en masse, to undo my work there, as they well know that anything said against themselves will rather please the United States public. Now dear Mary, supposing I had said all sorts of fearful things against the "Yanks"— would that be paying off a millionth part of what they say of our mothers and sisters? "Neptune's waters" would be perfectly useless to wash off the hatred the Christian "Yanks" of both sexes bear to us "heathens of India"!! And what harm have we done them?

Let the "Yanks" learn to be patient under criticism and then criticize others. It is a well-known psychological fact that those who are ever ready to abuse others cannot bear the slightest touch of criticism from others. Then again, what do I owe them? Except your family, Mrs. Bull, the Leggetts, and a few other kind persons, who else has been kind to me? I had to work till I am at death's door and had to spend nearly the whole of that time in America, so that the Americans might learn to be broader and more spiritual. In England I worked only six months. There was not a breath of scandal save one, and that was through an American woman, which knowledge greatly relieved my English friends. Not only no attacks, but many of the best English Church clergymen became my firm friends, and without asking I got much help for my work and I am sure to get much more.

There is a society watching my work and getting help for it, and four respectable persons followed me to India to help my work, braving everything, and dozens were ready, and the next time I go, hundreds will be!!

Dear, dear Mary, do not be afraid for me. The Americans are big people only to European hotel-keepers and milliners and in their own imagination. The world is very, very big and there must be some place for me even if the "Yankees" rage. Anyhow, I am quite satisfied with my work. I never planned anything. I have taken things as they came. Only one idea was burning in my brain—to start the machine for elevating the Indian masses, and that I have succeeded in doing to a certain extent.

It would have made your heart glad to see how my boys are working in the midst of famine and disease and misery—nursing by the mat-bed of the cholera-stricken pariah and feeding the starving chandāla, and the Lord sends help to me, to them, to all. What are men? He is with me, the Beloved, as He was when I was in America, in England, when I was roaming about unknown from place to place in India. What do I care about what they say? The babies—they do not know any better. What? I, who have realized the Spirit, and the vanity of all earthly nonsense, to be swerved from my path by babies' prattle? Do I look like that?

I had to talk a lot about myself because I owed that to you. I feel my task is done—at most three or four years more of life are left. I have lost all wish for my salvation. I never wanted earthly enjoyments. I must see my machine in strong working order, and then, knowing for sure that I have put in a lever for the good of humanity, in India at least, which no power can drive back, I will sleep—without caring what will be next.

And may I be born again and again, and suffer thousands of miseries, so that I may worship the only God that exists, the only God I believe in, the sum total of all souls. And above all, my God the wicked, my God the miserable, my God the poor of all races, of all species, is the especial object of my worship.

"He who is in you and outside of you, who works through every hand, who walks through every foot—whose body you are—Him worship and break all other idols.

"He who is the high and the low, the saint and the sinner, the god and the worm—Him worship, the visible, the knowable, the real, the omnipresent. Break all other idols.

"In whom there is neither past life nor future birth, nor death, nor going nor coming, in whom we always have been and always will be one—Him worship. Break all other idols.

"Ay, fools, who are neglecting the living God and His infinite reflections, of which the world is full, and running after imaginary shadows leading to quarrels and fights—Him worship, the only visible One. Break all other idols."

My time is short. I have got to unbreast whatever I have to say, without caring if it smarts some or irritates a few. Therefore, my dear, dear Mary, do not be frightened at whatever drops from my lips, for the power behind me is not

Vivekananda, but He, the Lord, and He knows best. If I have to please the world, that will be injuring the world. The voice of the majority is wrong, seeing that they govern and seeing the sad state of the world.

Every new thought must create opposition—in the civilized, polite sneers, in the vulgar, savage howls and filthy scandals. Even these earthworms must stand erect, even children must see light.

The Americans are drunk with new wine. A hundred waves of prosperity have come and gone over my country. We have learnt the lesson which no child can yet understand: It is vanity—this hideous world is māyā. Renounce and be happy.

Give up the ideas of sex and possessions. There is no other road. Marriage and sex and money are the only living devils. All earthly love proceeds from the body, body, body. No sex, no possessions—as these fall off, the eyes open to spiritual visions—the soul regains its own infinite power.

How I wish I were in England to see Harriet! I have one wish left—to see you four sisters before I die, and that must happen.

Yours ever affectionately,

VIVEKANANDA

To Miss Josephine MacLeod

ALMORA, 10 July, 1897

MY DEAR JOE JOE,

I am glad to learn that you have at last found out that I have time to read your letters. . . .

Do come by all means. Only you must remember this: the Europeans and the Hindus (called "natives" by the Europeans) live as oil and water; mixing with natives is damning to the Europeans.

There are no good hotels to speak of even at the capitals. You will have to travel with a number of servants about you (cost cheaper than hotels). You will have to bear with people who wear only a loin-cloth; you will see me with only a loin-cloth about me. Dirt and filth everywhere, and brown people. But you will have plenty of men to talk philosophy to you. If you mix with the English much here, you will have more comforts but see nothing of the Hindus as they are. Possibly I will not be able to eat with you, but I promise that I will travel to a good many places with you and do everything in my power to make your journey pleasant. These things are what you are to expect; if anything good comes, so much the better. Perhaps Mary Hale may come over with you. There is a young lady, Miss Campbell, Orchard Lake, Orchard Island, Michigan, who is a great worshipper of Krishna and lives alone on that island, fasting and praying. She will give anything to be able to see India once, but she is awfully poor. If you bring her with you, I will anyhow manage to pay her expenses. If Mrs. Bull brings old Landsberg with her, that will be saving that fool's life, as it were. . . .

I had a great mind to go to Tibet this year; but they would not allow me, as the road is dreadfully fatiguing. However, I content myself with galloping hard over precipices on mountain ponies. (This is more exciting than your bicycle, even, although I had an experience of that at Wimbledon.) Miles and miles of uphill and miles and miles of downhill, the road a few feet broad hanging over sheer precipices several thousand feet deep below.

Ever yours in the Lord,

VIVEKANANDA

P.S.   The best time to arrive in India is October or the beginning of November. December, January, and February you see things all over, and then start by the end of February. From March it begins to get hot. Southern India is *always* *hot*.

V.

Goodwin has gone to work in Madras on a paper to be started there soon.

V.

To Miss Marie Halboister

ALMORA, 25 July, 1897

MY DEAR MARIE,

I have time, will, and opportunity now to clear my promise. So my letter begins. I have been very weak for some time, and with that and other things my visit to England this Jubilee season had to be postponed. I was very sorry, at first, not to be able to meet my nice and very dear friends once more, but karma cannot be avoided and I had to rest content with my Himālayas.

It is a sorry exchange, after all, for the beauty of the living spirit shining through the human face is far more pleasurable than any amount of material beauty. Is not the soul the Light of the world?

The work in London had to go slow for various reasons, and last though not least was *l'argent, mon amie!* When I am there *l'argent* comes in somehow, to keep the work going. Now everybody shrugs his shoulders. I must come again and try my best to revive the work.

I am having a good deal of riding and exercise, but I had to drink a lot of skimmed milk per prescription of the doctors, with the result that I am more to the front than back! I am always a forward man though—but I do not want to be too prominent just now, and I have given up drinking milk.

I am glad to learn that you are eating your meals with good appetite.

Do you know Miss Margaret Noble of Wimbledon? She is working hard for me. Do correspond with her if you can, and you can help me a good deal there. Her address is: Brantwood, Worple Road, Wimbledon.

So you saw my little friend Miss Orchard, and you liked her too—good. I have great hopes for her. And how I should like to be retired from life's activities entirely when I am very old, and hear the world ringing with the names of my dear, dear young friends like yourself and Miss Orchard, etc.!

By the bye, I am glad to find that I am aging fast; my hair is turning grey. "Silver threads among the gold"—I mean black—are coming in fast.

It is bad for a preacher to be young, don't you think so? I do, as I did all my life. People have more confidence in an old man and he looks more venerable. Yet old rogues are the worst rogues in the world, aren't they? The world has its code of judgement, which, alas, is very different from that of truth.

So your "Universal Religion" has been rejected by the *Revue des deux Mondes*. Never mind, try again with some other paper. Once the ice is broken, you get in at a quick rate, I am sure. And I am so glad that you love the work; it will make its way, I have no doubt of it. Our ideas have a future, ma chère Marie—and it will be realized soon.

I think this letter will meet you in Paris—your beautiful Paris—and I hope you will write me lots about French journalism and the coming "World's Fair" there.

I am so glad that you have been helped by Vedānta and Yoga. I am unfortunately sometimes like the circus clown who makes others laugh, himself miserable!!

You are naturally of a buoyant temperament. Nothing seems to touch you. And you are moreover a very prudent girl, inasmuch as you have scrupulously kept yourself away from "love" and all its nonsense. So you see you have made your good karma and planted the seed of your lifelong well-being. Our difficulty in life is that we are guided by the present and not by the future. What gives us a little pleasure now drags us on to follow it, with the result that we always buy a mass of pain in the future for a little pleasure in the present.

I wish that I had nobody to love and that I had been an orphan in my childhood. The greatest misery in my life has been my own people—my brothers and sisters and mother, etc. Relatives are like deadly clogs to one's progress, and is it not a wonder that people will still go on to find new ones by *marriage!!!*

He who is alone is happy. Do good to all, like everyone, but *do not love anyone*. It is a bondage, and bondage brings only misery. Live alone in your mind—that is happiness. To have nobody to care for and never to mind who cares for you is the way to be free.

I envy so much your frame of mind—quiet, gentle, light, yet deep and free. You are already free, Marie, free already. You are jivanmukta. I am more of a woman than a man; you are more of a man than a woman. I am always dragging others' pain into me, for nothing, without being able to do any good to anybody —just as women, if they have no children, bestow all their love upon a cat!!!

Do you think this has any spirituality in it? Nonsense! It is all material *nervous bondage*—that is what it is. Oh, to get rid of the thraldom of the flesh!!

Your friend Mrs. Martin very kindly sends me copies of her magazine every month—but Sturdy's thermometer is now below zero, it seems. He seems to be greatly disappointed with my non-arrival in England this summer. What could I do?

We have started two maths here, one in Calcutta, the other in Madras. The Calcutta math (a wretched rented house) was awfully shaken in the late earthquake.

We have got in a number of boys and they are in training; also we have opened famine relief in several places and the work is going on apace. We will try to start similar centres in different places in India.

In a few days I am going down to the plains and from there to the western part of the mountains. When it is cooler in the plains, I will make a lecture tour all over and see what work can be done.

Here I cannot find any more time to write—so many people are waiting. So here I stop, dear Marie, wishing you all joy and happiness.

May you never be lured by the flesh is the constant prayer of—

Ever yours in the Lord,
VIVEKANANDA

To Sister Nivedita

SRINAGAR, KASHMIR
1 October, 1897

DEAR MARGOT,

Some people do the best work when led. Not everyone is born to lead. The best leader, however, is one who "leads like the baby." The baby, though apparently depending on everyone, is the king of the household. At least, to my thinking, that is the secret. . . . Many feel, but only a few can express. It is the power of expressing one's love and appreciation and sympathy for others that enables one person to succeed better in spreading the idea than others. . . .

I shall not try to describe Kashmir to you. Suffice it to say, I never felt sorry to leave any country except this paradise on earth—and I am trying my best, if I can, to influence the Rājā in starting a centre. So much to do here, and the material so hopeful! . . .

The great difficulty is this: I see persons giving me almost the whole of their love. But I must not give anyone the whole of mine in return, for that day the work would be ruined. Yet there are some who will look for such a return, not having the breadth of the impersonal view. It is absolutely necessary for the work that I should have the enthusiastic love of as many as possible, while I myself remain entirely impersonal. Otherwise jealousy and quarrels will break up everything.

A leader must be impersonal. I am sure you understand this. I do not mean that one should be a brute, making use of the devotion of others for his own ends, and laughing in his sleeve meanwhile. What I mean is what I am—intensely personal in my love, but having the power to pluck out my own heart with my own hand, if it becomes necessary, "for the good of many, for the welfare of many," as Buddha said. Madness of love, and yet in it no bondage. Matter changes into spirit by the force of love. That is the very gist of our Vedānta. There is but One, seen by the ignorant as matter, by the wise as God. And the history of civilization is the progressive reading of spirit into matter. The ignorant see the person in the non-person. The sage sees the non-person in the person. Through pain and pleasure, joy and sorrow, this is the one lesson we are learning. . . .

Yours ever with love and truth,
VIVEKANANDA

To Sister Nivedita[1]

JAMMU, 3 November, 1897

MY DEAR MISS NOBLE,

. . . Too much sentiment hurts work. "Hard as steel and soft as a flower" is the motto.

I shall soon write to Sturdy. He is right to tell you that in case of trouble I will stand by you. You will have the whole of it, if I find a piece of bread in India—you may rest assured of that. I am going to write to Sturdy from Lahore, for which I start tomorrow. I have been here for fifteen days to get some land in Kashmir from the Mahārājā. I intend to go to Kashmir again next summer, if I am here, and start some work there.

With everlasting love,

Yours,
VIVEKANANDA

To Miss Mary Hale

SRINAGAR, KASHMIR
28 August, 1898

MY DEAR MARIE,

I could not find an earlier opportunity of writing you, and knowing that you were in no hurry for a letter, I will not make apologies. You are learning all about Kashmir and ourselves from Miss MacLeod's letters to Mrs. Leggett, I hear. Therefore it is needless to go into long rigmaroles about it.

The search for Heinsholdt's mahātmās in Kashmir will be entirely fruitless, and as the whole thing has first to be established as coming from a creditable source, the attempt will also be a little too early. How is Mother Church? Father Pope—and where? How are you laidies, young and old? Going on with the old game with more zest now that one has fallen from the ranks? How is the lady that looks like a certain statue in Florence? (I have forgotten the name.) I always bless her arms when I think of the comparison.

I have been away a few days. Now I am going to join the ladies. The party then goes to a nice quiet spot behind a hill, in a forest, through which a murmuring stream flows, to have meditation deep and long under the deodars (tree of God) cross-legged à la Buddha. This will be for a month or so, when by that time our good works will have spent their powers and we shall fall from this earthly paradise to earth again. Then we shall work out our karma a few months and shall have to go to hell in China for bad karma, and our evil deeds will make us sink in bad odour with the world in Canton and other cities. Then purgatory in Japan and regain paradise once more in the U. S. of America.

I wished to send you so many nice things—but alas! the thought of the tariff makes my desires vanish "like youth in women and beggars' dreams." By the bye, I am glad now that I am growing greyer every day. My head will be a full-blown white lotus by the time you see me next.

[1] This was the last letter received in England by Sister Nivedita.

Ah! Marie, if you could see Kashmir—only Kashmir—the marvellous lakes full of lotuses and swans (there are no swans, but geese—poetic licence) and the big black bee trying to settle on the wind-shaken lotus (I mean, the lotus nods him off, refusing a kiss—poetry), then you could have a good conscience on your death-bed. As this is the earthly paradise and as logic says one bird in the hand = two in the bush, a glimpse of this is wiser; but economically the other is better—no trouble—no labour—no expense—a little namby-pamby dolly life —and you enter, that is all.

My letter is becoming a bore (which is a lie, and I have come to like boar's flesh pickled, which the Mahārājā of Kashmir treated me with liberally several times), so I stop (it is sheer idleness). Good night—antipodese.

Ever yours in the Lord,
VIVEKANANDA

My address always is
The Math, Belur
Howrah District, Bengal
India

To Miss Mary Hale

THE MATH, BELUR, HOWRAH DISTRICT
16 March, 1899

MY DEAR MARY,

Thanks to Mrs. Adams; she roused you naughty girls to a letter at last— "out of sight, out of mind"—as true in India as in America. And the other young lady, who just left her love as she flitted by, deserves a ducking, I suppose.

Well, I have been in a sort of merry-go-round with my body, which has been trying to convince me for months that it too much exists. However, no fear, with four mental-healing sisters, as I have—no sinking just now. Give me a strong pull and a long pull, will you—all together—and then I am up!

Why do you talk so much about me in your one-letter-a-year, and so little about the four witches mumbling mantras over the boiling pot in a corner of Chicago?

Did you come across Max Müller's new book, "Ramakrishna, His Life and Sayings"? If you have not, do get it—and let Mother see it. How is Mother? Growing grey? And Father Pope? Who have been our last visitors from America, do you suppose? "Brother—Love is a drawing card" and "Meeses Meel." They have been doing splendidly in Australia and elsewhere—the same old fellers little changed if at all. I wish you could come to visit India—that will be some day in the future. By the bye, Mary, I heard a few months ago, when I was rather worrying over your long silence, that you were just hooking a milly,[1] and so busy with your dances and parties. That explained, of course, your inability to write. But milly or no milly, I must have my money—don't forget. Harriet is discreetly silent since she got her boy—but where is my money, please? Remind

[1] I.e. Millionaire.

her and her husband of it. If she is Woolley, I am a greasy Bengalee, as the English call us here. Lord, where is my money?

I have got a monastery on the Ganges now, after all, thanks to American and English friends. Tell Mother to look sharp—I am going to deluge your Yankee land with idolatrous missionaries.

Tell Mr. Woolley he got the sister but has not paid the brother yet. Moreover, it was the fat, black, queerly dressed apparition smoking in the parlour that frightened many a temptation away—and that was one of the causes which secured Harriet to Mr. Woolley. Therefore—I want to be paid for my great share in the work, etc. etc. etc. Plead strong, will you?

I do so wish I could come over to America with Joe Joe this summer. But man proposes and who disposes?—not God, surely, always. Well, let things slide as they will. Abhayananda is here—Marie Louise, you know—and she has been very well received in Bombay and Madras. She will be in Calcutta tomorrow, and we are going to give her a good reception too.

My love to Miss Howe, Mrs. Adams, to Mother Church and Father Pope, and all the rest of my friends across the seven oceans. We believe in seven oceans—one of milk, one of honey, one of curd, one of wine, one of sugar-cane juice, one of salt, one of—I forget what. To you four sisters I waft my love across the ocean of honey—and a little wine, just to make it palatable.

Ever sincerely, your brother

VIVEKANANDA

P.S.   Write when you find time between dances.

V.

To Miss Marie Halboister

c/o MISS NOBLE
21A HIGH STREET, WIMBLEDON
August 1899

MY DEAR MARIE,

I am in London again—this time not busy, not hustling about, but quietly settled down in a corner, waiting to start for the United States of America at the first opportunity. My friends are nearly all out of London in the country and elsewhere, and my health is not sufficiently strong.

So you are happy in the midst of your lakes and gardens and seclusion in Canada. I am glad, so glad to know that you are up again on top of the tide. May you remain there for ever!

You could not finish the Rāja-Yoga translation yet—all right, there is no hurry. Time and opportunity must come if it is to be done, you know; otherwise we vainly strive.

Canada must be beautiful now, with its short but vigorous summer, and very healthy.

I expect to be in New York in a few weeks, and don't know what next. I hope to come back to England next spring.

I fervently wish that no misery ever came near anyone; yet it is that alone that gives us an insight into the depths of our lives, is it not? In our moments of anguish gates barred for ever seem to open and let in many a flood of light.

We learn as we grow. Alas! we cannot use our knowledge here. The moment we seem to learn, we are hurried off the stage. And this is māyā.

This toy world would not be here, this play could not go on, if we were knowing players. We must play blindfolded. Some of us have taken the part of the rogue of the play; some, of the hero—never mind, it is all play. This is the only consolation. There are demons and lions and tigers and what not on the stage, but they are all muzzled. They snap but cannot bite. The world cannot touch our souls. If you want, even if the body be torn and bleeding, you may enjoy the greatest peace in your mind.

And the way to that is to attain hopelessness. Do you know that? Not the imbecile attitude of despair, but the contempt of the conqueror for the things he has attained, for the things he has struggled for and then throws aside as beneath his worth.

This hopelessness, desirelessness, aimlessness, is just harmony with nature. In nature there is no harmony, no reason, no sequence. It was chaos before; it is so still.

The lowest man is in consonance with nature in his earthy-headedness; the highest, the same in the fullness of knowledge. All three—the highest man, the lowest man, and nature—aimless, drifting, hopeless—all three happy.

You want a chatty letter, don't you? I have not much to chat about. Mr. Sturdy came for the last two days. He goes home to Wales tomorrow. I have to book my passage for N. Y. in a day or two.

None of my old friends have I seen yet except Miss Soutter and Max Gysic, who are in London. They have been very kind, as they always were.

I have no news to give you, as I know nothing of London yet. I don't know where Gertrude Orchard is, else would have written to her. Miss Kate Steel is also away. She is coming on Thursday or Saturday.

I had an invitation to stay in Paris with a friend, a very well educated Frenchman, but I could not go this time. I hope another time to live with him some days.

I expect to see some of our old friends and say good day to them.

I hope to see you in America sure. Either I may unexpectedly turn up in Ottawa in my peregrinations, or you come to New York.

Good-bye, all luck be yours.

Ever yours in the Lord,
VIVEKANANDA

To Mr. E. T. Sturdy

RIDGELY MANOR, 14 September, 1899

MY DEAR STURDY,

I have simply been taking rest at the Leggetts' and doing nothing. Abhedananda is here. He has been working hard. He goes in a day or two to resume his work in different places for a month. After that he comes to New York to work.

I am trying to do something in the line you suggested, but don't know how far an account of the Hindus will be appreciated by the Western public when it comes from a Hindu. . . .

Mrs. Johnson is of opinion that no spiritual person ought to be ill. It also seems to her now that my smoking is sinful, etc. etc. That was Miss Muller's reason for leaving me—my illness. They may be perfectly right, for aught I know—and you too—but I am what I am. In India the same defects, plus eating with Europeans, have been taken exception to by many. I was driven out of a private temple by the owners for eating with Europeans. I wish I were malleable enough to be moulded into whatever one desired, but unfortunately I never saw a man who could satisfy everyone. Nor can anyone who has to go to different places possibly satisfy all.

When I first came to America they ill-treated me if I had not trousers on. Next I was forced to wear cuffs and collars, else they would not touch me, etc. etc. They thought me awfully funny if I did not eat what they offered, etc. etc. . . .

In India the moment I landed they made me shave my head, and wear "kaupin" (loin-cloth), with the result that I got diabetes, etc. Saradananda never gave up his underwear; this saved his life, with just a touch of rheumatism and much comment from our people.

Of course, it is my karma, and I am glad that it is so. For though it smarts for the time, it is another great experience of life, which will be useful either in this one or in the next. . . .

As for me, I am always in the midst of ebbs and flows. I knew it always and preached always that every bit of pleasure will bring a large quota of pain, if not with compound interest. I have had a good deal of love given to me by the world; I deserve a good deal of hatred therefore. I am glad it is so, as it proves my theory of "every wave having its corresponding dip" on my own person.

As for me, I stick to my nature and principle: once a friend, always a friend—also to the true Indian principle of looking subjectively for the cause of the objective.

I am sure that the fault is mine, and mine only, for every wave of dislike and hatred that I get. It could not be otherwise. Thanking you and Mrs. Johnson for thus calling me once more to the internal, I remain

As ever, with love and blessings,

VIVEKANANDA

To Miss Mary Hale

RIDGELY MANOR, September 1899

MY DEAR MARY,

Yes, I have arrived. I had a letter from Isabel from Greenacre—I hope to see her soon and Harriet. Harriet W. has been uniformly silent. Never mind—I will bide my time, and as soon as Mr. Woolley becomes a millionaire, demand my money. You did not write any particulars about Mother Church and Father Pope—only the news of something about me in some newspaper. I have long ago ceased to take any interest in papers—only they keep me before the public and get a sale of my books "anyway," as you say. Do you know what I am trying to do now? Writing a book on India and her people—a short, chatty, simple something. Again, I am going to learn French. If I fail to do it this year I cannot "do" the Paris exposition next year properly. Well, I expect to learn much French here, where even the servants talk it.

You never saw Mrs. Leggett, did you? She is simply grand. I am going to Paris next year as her and Mr. Leggett's guest, as I did the first time.

I have now got a monastery on the Ganges for the teaching of philosophy and comparative religion, and as a centre of work.

What have you been doing all this time? Reading? Writing? You did not do anything. You could have written lots by this time. Even if you had taught me French, I would be quite a Froggy now—and you did not—only made me talk nonsense. You never went to Greenacre. I hope it is getting more strength every year.

Say, you twenty-four feet and six hundred pounds of Christian Science, you could not pull me up with your treatments. I am losing much faith in your healing powers. Where is Sam? "Bewaring" all this time, as he should? Bless his heart—such a noble boy!

I was growing grey fast but somehow it got checked. I am sorry—only a few grey hairs now; a research will unearth many, though. I like it and am going to cultivate a long white goatee. Mother Church and Father Pope were having a fine time on the Continent. I saw a bit on my way home. And you have been Cinderella-ing in Chicago—good for you. Persuade the old folks to go to Paris next year and take you along. There must be wonderful sights to see; the French are making a last great struggle, they say, before closing business.

Well—you did not write me for long—long. You do not deserve this letter—but I am so good, you know, especially as death is drawing near, I do not want to quarrel with anyone. I am dying to see Isabel and Harriet. I hope they have got a great supply of healing power at Greenacre Inn and will help me out of my present fall. In my days the Inn was well stored with spiritual food—and less of material stuffs. Do you know anything of osteopathy? There is an osteopath in New York working wonders, really. I am going to have my bones searched by him in a week.

Where is Miss Howe? She is such a noble soul, such a friend. By the bye, Mary, it is curious—your family—Mother Church and her clergy, both monastic and secular—have made more impression on me than any family I know of. Lord bless you ever and ever!

I am taking rest now, and the Leggetts are so kind. I feel perfectly at home. I intend to go to New York to see the Dewey procession.[1] I have not yet seen my friends there.

Write me all about yourselves—I so long to hear. You know Joe Joe, of course. I marred their visit to India with my constant breakdowns, and they were so good, so forgiving. For years Mrs. Bull and she have been my guardian angels. Mrs. Bull is expected here next week. She would have been here before

[1] A reference to the public celebration in honour of Admiral George Dewey after his return from Japan.

but her daughter had a spell of illness. She suffered much but is now out of danger. Mrs. Bull has taken one of the Leggetts' cottages here, and if the cold weather does not set in faster than usual, we are going to have a delightful month here even now. The place is so beautiful—well wooded and perfect lawns.

I tried to play golf the other day. I do not think it difficult at all—it only requires good practice. You never went to Philadelphia to visit your golfing friends? What are your plans? What do you intend to do the rest of your life? Have you thought out any work? Write me a long letter, will you? I saw a lady in a street in Naples, as I was passing, going along with three others—must have been Americans—so like you that I was almost going to speak to her. When I came near I saw my mistake.

Good-bye for the present. Write sharp.

Ever your affectionate brother,

VIVEKANANDA

To Miss Mary Hale

RIDGELY MANOR, 30 October, 1899

MY DEAR OPTIMIST,

I received your letter and am thankful that something has come to force optimistic *laissez faire* into action. Your questions have tapped the very source of pessimism, however. British rule in modern India has only one redeeming feature, though unconscious. It has brought India out once more on the stage of the world; it has forced upon it the contact of the outside world. If it had been done with an eye to the good of the people concerned, as circumstances favoured Japan, the results would have been more wonderful for India. No good can be done when the main idea is blood-sucking. On the whole the old regime was better for the people, as it did not take away everything they had, and there was some justice, some liberty.

A few hundred modernized, half educated, and denationalized men are all that modern English India has to show—*nothing else*. The Hindus were six hundred million in number, according to Ferishta, the Mohammedan historian, in the twelfth century. Now they are less than two hundred. In spite of the century of anarchy that reigned during the struggles of the English to conquer, the terrible massacre the English perpetrated in '57 and '58, and the still more terrible *famines* that have become the inevitable consequence of British rule (there never is a famine in a Native State) and that take off millions—yet there has been a good increase of population, but not yet what it was when India was entirely independent, that is, before the Mohammedan rule. Indian labour and produce can support five times as many people as there are now in India, with comfort, if the whole thing is not taken off from them.

This is the state of things (for the last four years)—even education will no more be permitted to spread, freedom of the press has been stopped already (of course, we have been disarmed long), the bit of self-government granted to us for some years is being quickly taken off. We are watching what next. For writing a few words of innocent criticism men are being hurried to *transportation for life*. Others are imprisoned *without any trial*, and nobody knows when his head will be off.

There has been a reign of terror in India for some years. English soldiers are killing our men and outraging our women—only to be sent home with passage and pension at our expense. We are in a *terrible* gloom. Where is the Lord? Mary, you can afford to be optimistic—can I? Suppose you simply publish this letter—the law just passed in India will allow the English Government in India to drag me from here to India and kill me without trial. And I know all your Christian Governments will only rejoice, because we are heathens. Shall I also go to sleep and become optimistic? Nero was the greatest optimistic person! They don't think it worth while to write these things even as news items!! If necessary, the news agent of Reuter gives exactly opposite news fabricated to order! Heathen-murdering is only a legitimate pastime for the Christian!! Your missionaries go to preach God and dare not speak a word of truth for fear of the English, who would kick them out the next day.

All the property and lands granted by the previous Governments for supporting education have been swallowed up—and the present Government spends even less than Russia in education. And what education?

The least show of originality is throttled. Mary, it is hopeless with us, unless there really is a God—who is the Father of all, who is not afraid of the strong—to protect the weak, and who is not bribed by wealth. Is there such a God? Time will show.

Well, I think I am coming to Chicago in a few weeks and talk of things fully. Don't quote your authority.

With all love,

Ever your brother,

VIVEKANANDA

P.S. As for religious sects, the Brāhmo-Samāj, Ārya-Samāj, and other sects have been useless mixtures. They were only voices of apology to our English masters to allow us to live!! We have started a *new India*—a *growth*—waiting to see what comes. We believe in new ideas only when the nation wants them, and what will be true for us. The test of truth for these Brāhmos is "what our masters approve"—with us, what the Indian reasoning and experience approve. The struggle has begun—not between the Brāhmos and us, for they are gone already—but a harder, deeper, and more terrible one.

V.

To Mr. E. T. Sturdy

c/o F. LEGGETT, ESQ.
RIDGELY MANOR, ULSTER COUNTY, N. Y.

MY DEAR STURDY,

Your last letter reached me after knocking about a little through insufficient address.

It is quite probable that very much of your criticism is just and correct. It is also possible that some day you may find that all this springs from your dislike of certain persons, and I was the scapegoat.

There need be no bitterness, however, on that account, as I don't think I ever posed for anything but what I am. Nor is it ever possible for me to do so, as an hour's contact is enough to make everybody notice my smoking, bad temper, etc. "Every meeting must have a separation"—this is the nature of things. I carry no feeling of disappointment even. I hope you will have no bitterness. It is karma that brings us together, and karma that separates.

I know how shy you are, and how loath to wound others' feelings. I perfectly understand months of torture in your mind, when you have been struggling to work with people who were so different from your ideal. I could not guess it before at all, else I could have saved you a good deal of unnecessary mental trouble. It is karma again.

The accounts were not submitted before, as the work is not yet finished, and I thought of submitting to my donor a complete account when the whole thing was finished. The work was begun only last year, as we had to wait for funds a long time, and my method is never to ask, but wait for voluntary help.

I follow the same idea in all my work, as I am so conscious of my nature's being positively displeasing to many, and wait till somebody wants me. I hold myself ready also to depart at a moment's notice. In this matter of departure I never feel bad, nor do I think much about it, as in the constant roving life I lead I am always doing it. Only so sorry I trouble others without wishing it. If there is any mail for me at your address, will you kindly send it over?

May all blessings attend you and yours for ever and ever, will be the constant prayer of

VIVEKANANDA

To Swami Brahmananda

U. S. A., 20 November, 1899

MY DEAR RAKHAL,

Got some news from Sarat's letter. . . . Get experience while still there is a chance; I am not concerned whether you win or lose. . . . I have no disease now. Again . . . I am going to tour from place to place. There is no reason for anxiety; be fearless. Everything will fly away before you; only don't be disobedient, and all success will be yours. . . . Victory to Kāli! Victory to the Mother! Victory to Kāli! Wah guru! Wah guru ki fateh![1]

. . . Really, there is no greater sin than cowardice; cowards are never saved—that is sure. I can stand everything else, but not that. Can I have any dealings with one who will not give that up? . . . If one gets one blow, one must return ten with redoubled fury. . . . Then only is one a man. . . . The coward is an object to be pitied.

I bless you all; today, on this day sacred to the Divine Mother, on this night, may the Mother dance in your hearts and bring infinite strength to your arms.

[1] "Victory unto the guru!"

VIVEKANANDA, THE WANDERING MONK

VIVEKANANDA TEMPLE AT THE BELUR MATH

THE BELUR MATH

Victory to Kāli! Victory to Kāli! Mother will certainly come down—and with great strength will bring all victory, world victory. Mother is coming, what fear? Whom to fear? Victory to Kāli! At the tread of each one of you the earth will tremble. . . . Victory to Kāli! Again onward, forward! *Wah guru!* Victory to the Mother! Kāli! Kāli! Kāli! Disease, sorrow, danger, weakness—all these have departed from you all. All victory, all good fortune, all prosperity is yours. Fear not! Fear not! The threat of calamity is vanishing, fear not! Victory to Kāli! Victory to Kāli!

VIVEKANANDA

P.S. I am the servant of the Mother; you are all servants of the Mother—what destruction, what fear is there for us? Don't allow egotism to enter your minds, and let love never depart from your hearts. What destruction can touch you? Fear not. Victory to Kāli! Victory to Kāli!

V.

To Sister Nivedita

LOS ANGELES, 6 December, 1899

DEAR MARGOT,

Your letter has arrived, but with it yet no change in my fortune. Would change be any good, do you think? Some people are made that way—to love being miserable. If I did not break my heart over the people I was born amongst, I would do it for somebody else. I am sure of that.

This is the way of some—I am coming to see it. We are all after happiness, true, but some are only happy in being unhappy—queer, is it not?

There is no harm in it, either, except that happiness and unhappiness are both infectious. Ingersoll said once that if he were God, he would make health catching, instead of disease—little dreaming that health is quite as catching as disease, if not more so!!

That is the only danger. No harm to the world in my being happy in being miserable, but others must not catch it. This is the great fact. No sooner does a prophet feel miserable for the state of man than he sours his face, beats his breast, and calls upon everyone to drink tartaric acid, munch charcoal, sit upon a dung-heap covered with ashes, and speak only in groans and tears!

I find they all have been wanting. Yes, they have. If you are really ready to take up the earth's burden, take it up by all means—but do not let us hear your groans and curses, do not frighten us with your sufferings, so that we come to feel we were better off with our own burdens.

The man who really takes up the burden blesses the world and goes his own way. He has not a word of condemnation, not a word of criticism—not because there was no evil, but because he has taken it on his own shoulders willingly, voluntarily. It is the Saviour who should go on his way rejoicing—not the saved.

This is the only light that I have caught this morning. This is enough, if it

has come to live with me and permeate my life. Come ye that are heavily
laden and lay all your burdens on me, and then do whatever you like and forget
that I ever existed.

Ever with love, your father,
VIVEKANANDA

To Mrs. Ole Bull

12 December, 1899

MY DEAR MRS. BULL,

You are perfectly right. I am brutal, very, indeed. But about the tenderness
etc., that is my fault. I wish I had less, much less, of that—that is my weakness—and alas! all my sufferings have come from that. Well, the municipality
is trying to tax us out—good, that is my fault as I did not make the Math
public property by a deed of trust. I am very sorry I use harsh language to my
boys, but they also know I love them more than anybody else on earth. I may
have had Divine help—true, but oh, the pound of flesh every bit of Divine
help has been to me!! I would be a gladder and better man without that. The
present looks very gloomy indeed, but I am a fighter and must die fighting—
not give way. That is why I get mad at the boys. I don't ask them to fight,
but ask them not to hinder my fight.

I don't grudge my fate. But oh, now I want a man, one of my boys, to stand
by me and fight against all odds! Don't you vex yourself; if anything is to be
done in India my presence is necessary, and I am much better in health.
Possibly the sea will make me better. Anyway I did not do anything this time
in America except bother my friends. Possibly Joe will help me out with the
passage, and I have some money with Mr. Leggett. I have hope of collecting
some money in India yet. I did not see any of my friends in different parts
of India. I have hope of collecting the fifteen thousand that will make up the
fifty thousand, and a deed of trust will bring down the municipal taxes. If I
cannot collect that, it is better to struggle and die for it than vegetate here
in America. My mistakes have been great, but every one of them was from
too much love. How I hate love! Would I had never had any bhakti! Indeed!
I wish I could be an Advaitist, calm and heartless. Well, this life is done. I will
try in the next. I am sorry, especially now, that I have done more injury to my
friends than I have given blessings to them. The peace, the quiet I am seeking,
I never found.

I went years ago to the Himālayas, never to come back—and my sister committed suicide, the news reached me there, and that weak heart flung me off
from the prospect of peace!! It is the weak heart that has driven me out of
India to seek some help for those I love, and here I am! Peace have I sought,
but the heart, that seat of bhakti, would not allow me to find it. Struggle and
torture, torture and struggle! Well, so be it then, since it is my fate; and the
quicker it is over, the better. They say I am impulsive, but look at the circumstances!!! I am sorry I have been the cause of pain to you, to you above all,

who love me so much, who have been so, so kind. But it is done—is a fact. I am now going to cut the knot or die in the attempt.

Ever your son,
VIVEKANANDA

P.S.   As Mother wants it, so let it be. I am going to beg of Joe a passage via San Francisco to India. If she gives it I start immediately via Japan. It would take a month. In India, I think, I can raise some money to keep things straight or on a better footing—at least to keep things from getting all muddled. The end is getting very dark and very much muddled; well, I expected it so. Don't think I give in for a moment. Lord bless you! If the Lord has made me His hack to work and die on the streets, let Him have it so. I am more cheerful just now after your letter than I have been for years—*Wah guru ki fateh!* Victory unto the guru!! Yes, let the world come, the hells come, the gods come, let Mother come. I fight and do not give in. Rāvana got his release in three births by fighting the Lord Himself! It is glorious to fight Mother.

All blessings on you and yours! You have done for me more, much more, than I ever deserved.

Love to Christine and Turiyananda.

VIVEKANANDA

To Miss Mary Hale

c/o MRS. BLODGETT
921 WEST 21ST STREET, LOS ANGELES
27 December, 1899

Mary Christmas and Happy New Year and many, many glorious returns of such for your birthday—all these wishes, prayers, greetings in one breath. I am cured, you will be glad to know. It was only indigestion and no heart or kidney affection—quoth the healers, nothing more. And I am walking three miles a day, after a heavy dinner.

Say—the person healing me insisted on my smoking! So I am having my pipe nicely and am all the better for it. In plain English, the nervousness etc. was all owing to dyspep and nothing more.

Well, six feet—I am strong enough to take you in my arms like a feather and pitch you a few hundred yards. That is what I feel. I am at work, too—working, working—not hard, but don't care—and want to make money this time. Tell this to Margot—especially the pipe business. You know who is healing me? No physician, no Christian Science healer, but a magnetic healing woman who skins me every time she treats me. Wonders—she performs operations by rubbing—internal operations, too, her patients tell me.

It is getting late in the night. I have to give up writing separate letters to Margot, Harriet, Isabel, and Mother Church. Wish is half the work. They all know how I love them dearly, *passionately*—so you become the medium for my spirit for the time, and carry them my New Year's messages.

It is exactly like Northern Indian winter here—only some days a little warmer. The roses are here and the beautiful palms. Barley is in the fields—the roses and many other flowers round about the cottage where I live. Mrs. Blodgett, my hostess, is a Chicago lady. Fat, old, and extremely witty. She heard me in Chicago and is very motherly.

I am so sorry the English have caught a Tartar in South Africa.—A soldier on duty outside a camp bawled out that he had caught a Tartar. "Bring him in," was the order from inside the tent. "He won't come," replied the sentry. "Then you come yourself," rang out the order again. "He won't let me either!" Hence the phrase "to catch a Tartar." Don't you catch any.

I am happy just now and hope to remain so for all the rest of my life. Just now I am a Christian Scientist—no evil, and "love is a drawing card."

I shall be very happy if I can make a lot of money. I am making some. Tell Margot I am going to make a lot of money and go home by way of Japan, Honolulu, China, and Java. This is a nice place to make money quick, and San Francisco is better, I hear.—Has she made any?

You could not get the millionaire. Why don't you start for a half or a quarter million? Something is better than nothing. We want the money—he may go into Lake Michigan, we have not the least objection.

We had a bit of an earthquake here the other day. I hope it has gone to Chicago and raised Isabel's mud-puddle up. It is getting late. I am yawning, so here I quit. Good-bye—all blessings, all love.

VIVEKANANDA

To Mrs. Ole Bull

17 January, 1900

MY DEAR DHIRĀMĀTĀ,

I received yours with the enclosures for Saradananda. . . .

Now it occurs to me that my mission from the platform is finished, and I need not break my health again by that sort of work.

It is becoming clearer to me that I should lay down all the concerns of the Math and for a time go back to my mother. She has suffered much through me. I must try to smooth her last days. Do you know, this was just exactly what the great Sankarāchārya himself had to do. He had to go back to his mother in the last few days of her life. I accept it, I am resigned. I am calmer than ever. The only difficulty is the financial part. Well, the Indian people owe me something. I will try Madras and a few other places in India. Anyhow, I must try, as I have forebodings that my mother has not very many years to live. Then again, this is coming to me as the greatest of all sacrifices to make, the sacrifice of ambition, of leadership, of fame. I am resigned and must do the penance. The one thousand dollars with Mr. Leggett, if a little more is collected, will be enough to fall back upon in case of need. Will you send me back to India? I am ready any time. Don't go to France without seeing me. I have become practical, at least compared to the visionary dreams of Joe and Margot. Let them work out their dreams for me—they are not more than

dreams. I want to make out a trust deed of the Math in the names of Saradananda, Brahmananda, and yourself. I will do it as soon as I get the papers from
Saradananda. Then I am quits.

I want rest, a meal, a few books, and I want to do some scholarly work.
Mother shows this light vividly now. Of course, you were the one to whom
She showed it first. I would not believe it then. But then, it is now shown that
though leaving my mother was a great renunciation in 1884, it is a greater
renunciation to go back to my mother now. Probably Mother wants me to
undergo the same that She made the great Āchārya undergo in olden days. Is it
so? I am surer of your guidance than of my own. Joe and Margot are great souls,
but to you Mother is now sending the light for my guidance. Do you see light?
What do you advise? At least do not go out of this country without sending
me home.

I am but a child; what work have I to do? My powers I passed over to you.
I see it. I cannot any more *tell* from the platform. Don't tell it to anyone—
not even to Joe. I am glad. I want rest; not that I am tired, but the next phase
will be the *miraculous touch and not the tongue*—like Ramakrishna's. The word
has gone to you, the boys, and to Margot. No more is it in me. I am glad. I am
resigned. Only get me out to India, won't you? Mother will make you do it,
I am sure.

Ever your son,
VIVEKANANDA

LOS ANGELES, CALIFORNIA
24 January, 1900

DEAR —,

I am afraid that the rest and peace I seek for will never come. But Mother
does good to others through me, at least some to my native land, and it is easier
to be reconciled to one's fate as a sacrifice. We are all sacrifices—each in his
own way. The great worship is going on—no one can see its meaning except
that it is a great sacrifice. Those that are willing escape a lot of pain. Those that
resist are broken into submission and suffer more. I am now determined to be
a willing one.

Yours etc.,
VIVEKANANDA

To Mrs. Ole Bull

LOS ANGELES, 15 February, 1900

DEAR DHIRĀMĀTĀ,

Before this reaches you, I am off to San Francisco. . . .

I can always work better alone, and am physically and mentally best when
entirely alone. I scarcely had a day's illness during my eight years of lone life
away from my brethren. Now I am again getting up, being alone. Strange, but
that is what Mother wants me to be—"wandering alone like the rhinoceros," as
Joe likes it. I think the conferences are ended. Poor Turiyananda suffered so
much and never let me know; he is so strong and good. Poor Niranjan, I learn

from Mrs. Sevier, is so seriously ill in Calcutta that I don't know whether he has passed away or not. Well, good and evil both love company; queer, they come in strings. I had a letter from my cousin telling me her daughter (the adopted little child) was dead. Suffering seems to be the lot of India! Good. I am getting rather callous of late. Good. Mother knows. I am so ashamed of myself—of this display of weakness for the last two years! Glad it is ended.

Ever your loving son,

VIVEKANANDA

To Miss Mary Hale

PASADENA, 20 February, 1900

MY DEAR MARY,

Your letter bearing the sad news of Mr. Hale's passing away reached me yesterday. I am sorry, because in spite of monastic training the heart lives on, and then Mr. Hale was one of the best souls I have met in life. Of course you are sorry—miserable—and so is Mother Church and Harriet and the rest, especially as this is the first grief of its kind you have met, is it not? I have lost many—suffered much—and the most curious cause of suffering when somebody goes off is the feeling that I was not good enough to that person. When my father died it was a pang for months, and I had been so disobedient.

You have been very, very dutiful. If you feel anything like that, it is only a form of sorrow.

Just now I am afraid life begins for you, Mary, in earnest. We may read books, hear lectures, and talk miles—but experience is the one teacher, the one eye-opener. It is best as it is. We learn—through smiles and tears we learn. We don't know why, but we see it is so, and that is enough. Of course, Mother Church has the solace of her religion. I wish we could all dream undisturbed good dreams.

You have had shelter all your life. I was in the glare—burning and panting all mine. Now for a moment you have caught a glimpse of the other side. My life is made up of continuous blows like that, and a hundred times worse, because of poverty, treachery, and my own foolishness! Pessimism! You will understand how it all comes. Well—well—what shall I say to you, Mary? You know all the talk. Only I say this, and it is true. If it were possible to exchange grief—and had I a cheerful mind—I would exchange mine for your grief ever and always. Mother knows best.

Your ever faithful brother,

VIVEKANANDA

To Mrs. Ole Bull

SAN FRANCISCO, 4 March, 1900

DEAR DHIRĀMĀTĀ,

I don't want to work. I want to be quiet and rest. I know the time and the place, but fate or karma, I think, drives me on—work, work. We are like cattle driven to the slaughter-house—hastily nibbling a bit of grass on the roadside as they are driven along under the whip. And all this is our work, our fear— fear, the beginning of misery, of disease, etc. By being so fearful to hurt, we hurt more. By trying so much to avoid evil, we fall into its jaws.

What a mass of namby-pamby nonsense we create round ourselves! It does us no good, it leads us on to the very thing we try to avoid—misery. . . .

Oh, to become fearless, to be daring, to be careless of everything! . . .

Yours etc.,

VIVEKANANDA

To Miss Mary Hale

1719 TURK STREET, SAN FRANCISCO
22 March, 1900

MY DEAR MARY,

Many thanks for your kind note. You are correct in saying that I have many other thoughts to think about besides the Indian people—but they all have to go to the background before the all-absorbing mission, my Master's work.

Would that this sacrifice were pleasant! It is not—and naturally makes one bitter at times; for know, Mary, I am yet a man and cannot wholly forget myself. Hope I shall some time—pray for me.

Of course I am not to be held responsible for Miss MacLeod's or Miss Noble's or anybody else's views regarding myself or anything else—am I? You never found me to smart under criticism?

I am glad you are going over to Europe for a long visit. Make a long tour— you have been long a house-dove.

As for me, I am tired, on the other hand, of eternal tramping. That is why I want to go back home and be quiet. I do not want to work any more. My nature is the retirement of the scholar. I never get it! I pray I shall get it now that I am all broken and worked out. Whenever I get a letter from Mrs. Sevier from her Himālayan home, I feel like flying off to the Himālayas. I am really sick of this platform work and eternal trudging and seeing new faces and lecturing.

You need not bother about getting up classes in Chicago. I am getting money in Frisco and shall soon make enough for my passage home.

How are you and the sisters? I expect to come to Chicago some time towards the first part of April.

VIVEKANANDA

SAN FRANCISCO, 25 March, 1900

DEAR —,

I am much better and am growing very strong. I feel sometimes that freedom is near at hand, and the tortures of the last two years have been great lessons in many ways. Disease and misfortune come to do us good in the long run, although at the time we feel that we are submerged for ever.

I am the infinite blue sky; the clouds may gather over me but I am the same infinite blue.

I am trying to get a taste of that peace which I know is my nature and everyone's nature. These tin-pots of bones and foolish dreams of happiness and misery—what are they?

My dreams are breaking. Om Tat Sat!

Yours,
VIVEKANANDA

To Miss Mary Hale

1719 TURK STREET, SAN FRANCISCO
28 March, 1900

WELL BLESSED MARY,

This is to let you know "I am very happy." Not that I am getting into a shadowy optimism, but my power of suffering is increasing. I am being lifted up above the pestilential miasma of this world's joys and sorrows. They are losing their meaning. It is a land of dreams. It does not matter whether one enjoys or weeps—they are but dreams, and as such must break sooner or later. How are things going on with you folks there? Harriet is going to have a good time in Paris. I am sure to meet her over there and *parler français!* I am getting by heart a French *dictionnaire!* I am making some money too—hard work morning and evening—yet better for all that. Good sleep—good digestion—perfect irregularity.

You are going to the East. I hope to come to Chicago before the end of April. If I can't I will surely meet you in the East before you go.

What are the McKindley girls doing? Eating grapefruit concoctions and getting plump? So on—life is but a dream. Are you not glad it is so? My! They want an eternal heaven! Thank God nothing is eternal except Himself. He alone can bear it, I am sure. Eternity of nonsense!!

Things are beginning to hum for me; they will presently roar. I will remain quiet, though, all the same. Things are not humming for you just now. I am so sorry—that is, I am trying to be, for I cannot be sorry for anything any more. I am attaining peace that passeth understanding—which is neither joy nor sorrow, but something above them both. Tell Mother that. My passing through the valley of death—physical, mental—these last two years, has helped me in this. Now I am nearing that *Peace*, the eternal *Silence*. Now I mean to see things as they are—everything in that Peace, perfect in its way. "He whose joy is only in himself, whose desires are only in himself"—he has learnt his lessons. This is the great lesson that we are here to learn, through myriads of births and heavens and hells: There is nothing to be sought for, asked for, desired, beyond one's self. The greatest thing I can obtain is myself. I am free—therefore I require none else for my happiness. Alone through eternity—because I was free, am free, and shall remain free for ever. This is Vedāntism. I preached the theory so long, but oh, joy! Mary, my dear sister, I am realizing it now every day. Yes, I am. I am free. Alone—Alone—I am the One without a second.

Ever yours in the Satchidānanda,

VIVEKANANDA

P.S.   Now I am going to be truly Vivekananda. Did you ever enjoy evil? Ha, ha—you silly girl—awl is gooood! Nonsense—some good, some evil. I enjoy the good and I enjoy the evil. I was Jesus and I was Judas Iscariot, both—my play, my fun. "So long as there are two, fear shall not leave thee." Ostrich method? Hide your heads in the sand?—and think there is nobody seeing you! Awl is gooood! Be brave and face everything. Come, good; come, evil—both welcome—both of you my play. I have no good to attain, no ideal to clinch up to, no ambition to fulfil. I, the diamond mine, am playing with pebbles, good and evil. Good for you, evil, come; good for you, good, you come too. If the universe tumbles round my ears, what is that to me? I am Peace that passeth understanding. Understanding only gives us good or evil. I am beyond—I am *Peace.*

V.

To Sister Nivedita

SAN FRANCISCO, 26 May, 1900

DEAR NIVEDITA,

All blessings on you. Don't despond in the least. *Śri wah guru! Śri wah guru!* You come of the blood of a kshattriya. Our yellow garb is the robe of death on the field of battle. Death for the cause is our goal, not success. *Śri wah guru!*

Black and thick are the folds of sinister fate. But I am the master. I raise my hand, and lo, they vanish! All this is nonsense and fear. I am the Fear of fear, the Terror of terror. I am the fearless, secondless One, I am the Ruler of destiny, the Wiper-out of fact. *Śri wah guru!* Steady, child, don't be bought by gold or anything else, and you win!

VIVEKANANDA

To Miss Mary Hale

VEDANTA SOCIETY
146 EAST 55TH STREET, NEW YORK
23 June, 1900

MY DEAR MARY,

Many, many thanks for your beautiful letter. I am very well and happy and the same as ever. A fall must come before a rise. So with me. I am very glad you are going to pray. Why don't you get up a Methodist camp-meeting? That will have a quicker effect, I am sure.

I am determined to get rid of all sentimentalism and emotionalism—and hang me if you ever find me emotional. I am the Advaitist. Our goal is *knowledge—*

no feelings, no love, as all that belongs to matter and superstition and bondage.
I am only Existence and Knowledge.

Greenacre surely will give you good rest, I am sure. I wish you all joy there.
Don't for a moment worry on my account. "Mother" looks after me. She is bringing me out fast from the hell of emotionalism, and bringing me into the light
of pure reason.

With everlasting wishes for your happiness,

Ever your brother,
VIVEKANANDA

P.S.   Margot starts on the twenty-eighth. I may follow in a week or two.
Nobody has any power over me, for I am the Spirit. I have no ambition. It is
all Mother's work; I have no part.

V.

I could not digest your letter as the dyspepsia was rather bad the last few days.

V.

Non-attachment has always been there. It has come in a minute. Very soon I
stand where no sentiment can touch me—no feeling.

V.

PARIS, 28 August, 1900

DEAR —,

Such is life—grind, grind! And yet what else are we to do? Grind, grind!
Something will come—some way will be opened. If it does not, as it probably
never will—then, then—what then? All our efforts are only to stave off—for a
season—the great climax, death. Oh, what would the world do without thee,
Death! Thou great healer!

The world as it is, is not real, is not eternal, thank the Lord! How can the
future be any better? That must be the effect of this one—at least like this, if not
worse!

Dreams, oh, dreams! Dream on! Dream, the magic of dream, is the cause of
this life; it is also the remedy. Dream, dream, only dream! Kill dream by dream!

I am trying to learn French, talking to ——— here. Some are very appreciative
already. Talk to all the world of the eternal riddle, the eternal spool of fate—
whose thread-end no one finds and everyone seems to find, at least to his own
satisfaction, at least for a time—to fool himself a moment, is it not?

Well, now great things are to be done—who cares for great things? Why not
do small things as well? One is as good as the other. The greatness of little things,
that is what the Gitā teaches, bless the old book! . . .

I had not much time to think of the body; so it must be well. Nothing is ever
well here. We forget the body at times, and that is being well and doing well.

We play our parts here—good or bad. When the dream is finished and we
have left the stage, we shall have a hearty laugh at all this—of this only I
am sure.

Yours etc.,
VIVEKANANDA

To Miss Josephine MacLeod

THE MATH, BELUR, HOWRAH
26 December, 1900

DEAR JOE,

This mail brought your letter including that of Mother and Alberta. What the learned friend of Alberta says about Russia is about the same as I think myself. Only there is one difficulty: Is it possible for the Hindu race to be Russianized?

Dear Mr. Sevier passed away before I could arrive. He was cremated on the bank of the river that flows by his āśrama, à la Hindu, covered with garlands, the brāhmins carrying the body and boys chanting the Vedas.

The cause has already two martyrs. It makes me love dear old England and its heroic breed. The Mother is watering the plant of future India with the best blood of England. Glory unto Her!

Dear Mrs. Sevier is calm. A letter she wrote me to Paris comes back this mail. I am going up tomorrow to pay her a visit. Lord bless her, dear brave soul!

I am calm and strong. Occasion never found me low yet; Mother will not make me now depressed.

It is very pleasant here, now the winter is on. The Himālayas will be still more beautiful with the uncovered snows.

The young man who started from New York, Mr. Johnston, has taken the vow of a brahmachārin and is at Mayavati.

Send the money to Saradananda in the Math, as I will be away in the hills.

They have worked all right as far as they could; I am glad, and feel myself quite a fool on account of my nervous chagrin.

They are as good and as faithful as ever, and they are in good health. Write all this to Mrs. Bull, and tell her she was always right and I was wrong, and I beg a hundred thousand pardons of her.

Oceans of love for her and for M—.

> I look behind and after
> And find that all is right;
> In my deepest sorrows
> There is a soul of light.

All love to Mother, Mrs. C—, to dear Jules Bois, and to you, dear Joe, pranams.

VIVEKANANDA

To Sister Christine

THE MATH, BELUR, 6 July, 1901

Things come to me by fits—today I am in a fit of writing. The first thing to do is, therefore, to pen a few lines to you. I am known to be nervous, I worry much; but it seems, dear Christine, you are not far behind in that trick. One of our poets says: "Even the mountains will fly, fire will be cold, yet the heart of the great will never change." I am small, very, but I know you are great, and my faith is always in your true heart. *I worry about everything except you.* I have dedicated you to the Mother. She is your shield, your guide. No harm can reach you—nothing can hold you down a minute, I know it.

Ever yours in the Lord,

VIVEKANANDA

To Mrs. Ole Bull

THE MATH, 14 June, 1902

DEAR DHIRĀMĀTĀ,

. . . In my opinion, a race must first cultivate a great respect for motherhood, through the sanctification and inviolability of marriage, before it can attain to the ideal of perfect chastity. The Roman Catholics and the Hindus, holding marriage sacred and inviolate, have produced great chaste men and women of immense power. To the Arab, marriage is a contract or a forceful possession, to be dissolved at will, and we do not find there the development of the idea of the virgin or the brahmachārin. Modern Buddhism—having fallen among races who have not yet come up to the evolution of marriage—has made a travesty of monasticism. So until there is developed in Japan a great and sacred ideal about marriage (apart from mutual attraction and love), I do not see how there can be great monks and nuns. As you have come to see that the glory of life is chastity, so my eyes also have been opened to the necessity of this great sanctification for the vast majority, in order that a few lifelong chaste powers may be produced. . . .

VIVEKANANDA

APPENDIX A

How HARD Swami Vivekananda had to work in the United States in order to inculcate the spiritual ideas of India on the Americans may be understood to some extent from the following schedule of class lectures he gave at 228 West 39th Street, New York, during the winter of 1895-96:

Mondays: Bhakti-Yoga . . . . . 11 a.m. and 8 p.m.
Wednesdays: Jnāna-Yoga . . . . 11 a.m. and 8 p.m.
Fridays: Question Class . . . .   8 p.m.
Saturdays: Rāja-Yoga . . . . . 11 a.m. and 8 p.m.

Besides this program, the Swami had to give public lectures and numerous interviews, and also carry on a heavy correspondence. All his letters had to be written in his own hand.

APPENDIX B

ON THE EVE of Swami Vivekananda's departure from England for India, a farewell meeting was organized on December 13, 1896, by his friends, students, and admirers, at the galleries of the Royal Institute of Painters in Water-Colours, in London. An illuminated address, the text of which is given below, was presented to the Swami:

"The students of the Vedānta philosophy in London under your remarkably able instruction feel that they would be lacking in their duty and privilege if they failed to record their warm and heartfelt appreciation of the noble and unselfish work you have set yourself to do, and the great help you have been to them in their study of religion.

"We feel the very deepest regret that you are so soon to leave England, but we should not be true students of the very beautiful philosophy you have taught us to regard so highly if we did not recognize that there are claims upon your work from our brothers and sisters in India. That you may prosper very greatly in that work is the united prayer of all who have come under the elevating influence of your teaching, and no less of your personal attributes, which, as a living example of Vedānta, we recognize as the most helpful encouragement to us one and all to become real lovers of God, in practice as well as in theory.

"We look forward with great interest and keen anticipation to your speedy return to this country, but, at the same time, we feel real pleasure that India, which you have taught us to regard in an altogether new light, and we should like to add, to love, is to share with us the generous service which you are giving to the world.

"In conclusion we would especially beg of you to convey our loving sympathy to the Indian people and to accept from us our assurance that we regard their cause as ours, realizing as we do from you that we are all One in God."

GLOSSARY

āchārya Religious teacher.

Ādityas Twelve deities (suns) constituting a group.

Advaita Non-duality; a school of Vedānta philosophy teaching the oneness of God, soul, and universe, whose chief exponent was Śankarāchārya (A. D. 788-820).

Advaitin Advaitist.

Advaitist A follower of Advaita, the philosophy of non-dualism.

agni Fire; the god of fire.

ahamkāra I-consciousness.

ahimsā Non-injury.

ākāśa The first of the five material elements that constitute the universe; often translated as "space" and "ether." The four other elements are vāyu (air), agni (fire), ap (water), and prithivi (earth).

akhanda Undivided.

Ānanda Bliss.

animā Minuteness; one of the supernatural powers, by which a yogi can make himself as small as an atom.

Annapurnā A name of the Divine Mother as the Giver of food.

antahkarana The inner organ; the mind.

Antaryāmin The Inner Controller.

apāna One of the modifications of the vital force in the body, by which unassimilated food and drink are eliminated.

āpani The same as the English pronoun "you," as used with reference to an elder.

āpta An illumined person, whose words are infallible.

āptavākya The words of an illumined person.

Āranyaka A part of the Brāhmana section of the Vedas, to be studied in the forest during the third stage of life; it deals mainly with the contemplation of deities.

Arjuna A hero of the epic Mahābhārata and a friend and disciple of Krishna.

Ārya Samāj A Hindu religious movement founded by Swami Dayananda (A. D. 1824-1883).

Āryāvarta The land of the Āryans.

āsana Posture.

āśrama Hermitage; also any one of the four stages of life: the celibate student stage (brahmacharya), the married householder stage (gārhasthya), the stage of retirement and contemplation (vānaprastha), and the stage of religious mendicancy (sannyāsa).

aśvattha tree The holy fig tree; sometimes used as a symbol of the universe.

Atharva-Veda   One of the four Vedas. See Vedas.

Ātman   The Self or Soul; denotes both the Supreme Soul and the individual soul, which, according to Non-dualistic Vedānta, are ultimately identical.

Avatāra   Incarnation of God.

avidyā   A term of Vedānta philosophy meaning ignorance, individual or cosmic.

Bhagavad Gitā   An important Hindu scripture, comprising eighteen chapters of the epic Mahābhārata and containing the teachings of Śri Krishna.

Bhagavān   The Lord; also used as a title of celebrated saints.

Bhāgavata (Purāna)   A well-known scripture dealing mainly with the life of Krishna.

bhakta   Devotee of God.

bhakti   Love of God.

bhakti-yoga   The path of devotion followed by dualistic worshippers.

bhakti-yogi   A follower of the path of devotion.

Bharata   A holy man who, according to the legend, cherished at the time of death the thought of his pet deer, and therefore was reincarnated as a deer.

Bhartrihari   A well-known Sanskrit poet and philosopher.

bhāshya   Commentary.

Bhishma   A hero of the Mahābhārata, celebrated for his devotion to truth.

bhoga   Enjoyment.

bodhisattva   A Buddhist saint on his way to the attainment of Nirvāna, or final illumination; this state is reached through a long series of unselfish deeds.

Bo-tree   The famous tree under which Buddha attained illumination.

Brahmā   The Creator God; the First Person of the Hindu Trinity, the other two being Vishnu and Śiva.

brahmachārin   A celibate student belonging to the first stage of life. See āśrama.

brahmachārini   A nun.

brahmacharya   The first of the four stages of life; the life of an unmarried student. See āśrama.

Brahmaloka   The plane of Brahmā, roughly corresponding to the highest heaven of the dualistic religions, where fortunate souls go after death and enjoy communion with the Personal God.

Brahman   The Absolute; the Supreme Reality of the Vedānta philosophy.

Brāhmana   That portion of the Vedas which gives the rules for the employment of the hymns at the various sacrifices, their origin and detailed explanation, etc. It is distinct from the Mantra portion of the Vedas.

Brahma Sutras   An authoritative treatise on Vedānta philosophy, ascribed to Vyāsa.

Brahmavidyā   The Knowledge of Brahman.

brāhmin   A member of the priestly caste, the highest caste in Hindu society.

Brāhmo   A member of the Brāhmo Samāj.

Brāhmo Samāj   A liberal Hindu religious movement founded by Rājā Rammohan Roy (A. D. 1774-1833).

Brihadāranyaka Upanishad   One of the major Upanishads. See Upanishads.

buddhi   The determinative faculty of the mind, which makes decisions; sometimes translated as "intellect."

Chaitanya A prophet born in A. D. 1485, who lived at Navadvip, Bengal, and emphasized the path of divine love for the realization of God.

chandāla Untouchable.

Chārvākas Followers of Chārvāka, an atheistic philosopher who denied the existence of God, soul, and hereafter and repudiated the authority of the Vedas.

Chhāndogya Upanishad One of the major Upanishads. See Upanishads.

Chit Consciousness.

chitta The mind-stuff; that part of the inner organ which is the storehouse of memory or which seeks for pleasurable objects.

Dakshineswar The village near Calcutta where Ramakrishna lived and communed with God.

darśanas The six systems of orthodox Hindu philosophy, namely, the Sāmkhya of Kapila, the Yoga of Patanjali, the Vaiśeshika of Kanāda, the Nyāya of Gautama, the Purva Mimāmsā of Jaimini, and the Vedānta or Uttara Mimāmsā of Vyāsa.

dayā Compassion.

deśa-kāla-nimitta Space, time, and causality.

devas (Lit., shining ones.) The gods of Hindu mythology.

devi Goddess.

Devi-Bhāgavata A Hindu scripture.

Dhammapāda A famous treatise of the Buddhists.

dhāranā Fixing the mind on a point; a stage in the process of meditation.

dharma Righteousness, duty; the inner constitution of a thing, which governs its growth.

dhoti The wearing-cloth of a Bengali Hindu.

dhyāna Concentration.

Diwan Prime Minister of the ruler of a Native State.

durātman Wicked soul.

Durgā A name of the Divine Mother.

Dyāvā-prithivi Sky and earth.

eight powers The supernatural powers manifested by the yogi, such as his ability to make himself subtle as an atom, light as cotton, all-pervasive, etc.

Ganapati Also known as Ganeśa, the Hindu deity with an elephant's head.

garden house A rich man's country house set in a garden.

Gārgi A woman seer mentioned in the Vedas.

Gāyatri A sacred verse of the Vedas recited daily by Hindus of the three upper castes after their investiture with the sacred thread.

Gitā Same as Bhagavad Gitā.

gopis The cowherd girls of Vrindāvan, playmates of Krishna.

gunas A term of the Sāmkhya philosophy, according to which prakriti (nature or matter), in contrast with Purusha (Soul), consists of three gunas—usually translated as "qualities"—known as sattva, rajas, and tamas. Tamas stands for inertia, rajas for activity or restlessness, and sattva for balance or wisdom.

guru   Spiritual preceptor.
gurudeva   The same as guru.

Hāldārpukur   A lake at Kāmārpukur, Śri Ramakrishna's birthplace.
Hanumān   The great monkey devotee of Rāma, mentioned in the Rāmāyana.
Hari   An epithet of the Godhead.
hatha-yogi   One who practices the disciplines of hatha-yoga.
Hiranyagarbha   (Lit., the Golden Germ or the Golden Womb.) The first mani-
    festation of Saguna Brahman, or Brahman with attributes, in the relative
    universe.
Holy Mother   The name by which Śri Ramakrishna's wife was known among
    his devotees.
Hum   A mystic word mentioned in the Tantra philosophy.

Idā   A nerve in the spinal column. See Sushumnā.
Indra   The king of the gods.
indriyas   The sense-organs, consisting of the five organs of perception, the five
    organs of action, and the mind.
Iśa Upanishad   One of the major Upanishads. See Upanishads.
Iśāna   A ruler; an epithet of Śiva and of Vishnu.
Ishta   The aspect of the Godhead which a devotee selects as his Chosen Ideal.
Ishta-nishthā   Single-minded devotion to the Chosen Ideal.
Iśvara   The Personal God.

Jagannāth   The Lord of the universe; a name of Vishnu.
Jains   The followers of Jainism, an important religious sect of India.
Janaka   A king in Hindu mythology who was endowed with the Knowledge of
    Brahman.
Jānaki   Sitā, the consort of Rāma.
japa   Repetition of the Lord's name or of a sacred formula taught to the dis-
    ciple by the spiritual teacher.
jiva   (Lit., living being.) The individual soul, which in essence is one with
    the Universal Soul.
jivanmukta   One who has attained liberation while living in the body.
jivanmukti   Liberation while dwelling in the body.
jivātman   The embodied soul.
jnāna   Knowledge of Reality arrived at through reasoning and discrimination;
    also the process of reasoning by means of which Ultimate Truth is attained.
Jnānakānda   The philosophical part of the Vedas, in contrast with the ritual-
    istic part.
jnāna-yoga   A form of spiritual discipline mainly based upon philosophical dis-
    crimination between the real and the unreal, and renunciation of the unreal.
jnāna-yogi   A follower of jnāna-yoga.
jnāni   One who follows the path of reasoning and discrimination to realize
    Ultimate Truth; generally used to denote a non-dualist.
Jumnā   A sacred river of India.
jyotish   Astronomy.

kaivalya   The term used in rāja-yoga for ultimate liberation, meaning independence of the soul from the body or matter.

Kāli   (Lit., the Black One.) An epithet of the Divine Mother; the Primal Energy.

Kālidāsa   The great Sanskrit poet and author of *Sakuntalā*.

Kaliyuga   The fourth of the cycles or world periods. According to Hindu mythology the duration of the world is divided into four yugas, namely, Satya, Tretā, Dwāpara, and Kali. In the first, also known as the Golden Age, there is a great preponderance of virtue among men, but with each succeeding yuga virtue diminishes and vice increases. In the Kaliyuga there is a minimum of virtue and a great excess of vice. The world is said to be now passing through the Kaliyuga.

kalpa   Cycle or world-period.

kāma-kānchana   Lust and greed.

Kamalākānta   A mystic poet of Bengal.

Kapila   The well-known founder of the Sāmkhya philosophy.

karma   Action in general; duty. The Vedas use the word chiefly to denote ritualistic worship and humanitarian action.

Karmakānda   The ritualistic part of the Vedas, in contrast with the philosophical part.

karma-yoga   A spiritual discipline, mainly discussed in the Bhagavad Gītā, based upon the unselfish performance of duty.

karma-yogi   A follower of karma-yoga.

karmis   Believers in the Vedic rituals.

Katha Upanishad   One of the major Upanishads. See Upanishads.

Keshab Chandra Sen   See Sen, Keshab Chandra.

Krishna   An Incarnation of God described in the *Mahābhārata* and the *Bhāgavata*.

Kshatra   A member of the warrior race.

kshattriya   A member of the second or warrior caste in Hindu society.

kumbhaka   Retention of breath; a process in prānāyāma, or breath-control, described in rāja-yoga and hatha-yoga.

Kundalini   (Lit., coiled-up serpent.) The word refers to the spiritual power dormant in all living beings. When awakened through the practice of spiritual disciplines, it rises through the spinal column, passes through various centres, and at last reaches the brain, whereupon the yogi experiences samādhi, or total absorption in the Godhead. See Sushumnā.

Kunti   The mother of the five Pāndava brothers.

Kurukshetra   A place near modern Delhi, where the great battle described in the Bhagavad Gītā was fought.

kutichaka   A monk who has a fixed abode.

Lakshmi   The Consort of Vishnu; the Goddess of Fortune.

lingam   The phallic symbol associated with Śiva.

Lotus   Each of the six centres along the Sushumnā is called a Lotus, since their form is like that of a lotus blossom. See Kundalini.

Madhva   Same as Madhvāchārya.

Madhvāchārya   The chief exponent of Dualistic Vedānta (A. D. 1199-1276).

Mahābhārata   A celebrated Hindu epic.

Mahānirvāna Tantra   One of the principal Tantras. The Tantras are systems of religious philosophy in which the Divine Mother, or Power, is regarded as Ultimate Reality.

mahāpurusha   Great soul.

mahāsamādhi   The highest state of God-consciousness; the word also signifies the death of an illumined person.

mahat   The cosmic mind.

mahātmā   Great soul.

mahātman   Great soul.

Maitreyi   A wife of the sage Yājnavalkya, mentioned in the Brihadāranyaka Upanishad.

Malabar   The southwestern part of India.

mamatā   My-ness.

manas   The faculty of doubt and volition; sometimes translated as "mind."

mantra   Sacred word by which a spiritual teacher initiates his disciple; Vedic hymn; sacred word in general.

Manu   The celebrated ancient lawgiver of India.

math   Monastery.

Mathurā   A city in Northern India, the birthplace of Krishna.

māyā   A term of Vedānta philosophy denoting ignorance obscuring the vision of Reality; the cosmic illusion on account of which the One appears as many, the Absolute as the relative.

māyāvādin   A believer in the doctrine of māyā.

Meru   A mythical mountain abounding in gold and precious stones. The abode of Brahmā, the Creator, and a meeting-place for the gods, demigods, rishis, and other supernatural beings, Meru is regarded as the axis around which the planets revolve.

Mimāmsakas   The followers of the Purva Mimāmsā school of philosophy, a system based upon the ritualistic part of the Vedas, whose chief exponent is Jaimini.

Mirābāi   A celebrated woman saint of India.

mlechcha   A non-Hindu, a barbarian. This is a term of reproach applied by orthodox Hindus to foreigners, who do not conform to the established usages of Hindu religion and society. The word corresponds to the "heathen" of the Christians and the "kafir" of the Mussulmans.

moksha   Liberation or emancipation, which is the final goal of life.

mrityu   Death.

mukti   Liberation from the bondage of the world, which is the goal of spiritual practice.

mumukshutvam   Yearning for liberation.

Mundaka Upanishad   One of the major Upanishads. See Upanishads.

Nachiketas   The spiritual seeker mentioned in the Katha Upanishad.

Nāda   The mystic word Om, the symbol of Brahman.

nāḍi   Nerve.

Naiyāikas   Followers of the Nyāya system of philosophy, founded by Gautama.

nāma   Name.

nāma-rupa   Name and form.

Nārada   A saint in Hindu mythology.

Nārāyana   An epithet of Vishnu, or the Godhead.

"Neti, neti"   (Lit., "Not this, not this.") The negative process of discrimination, advocated by the followers of Non-dualistic Vedānta.

Nimbārka   The name of a great Hindu philosopher.

Nirvāna   Final absorption in Brahman, or the All-pervading Reality, through the annihilation of the individual ego.

nirvikalpa samādhi   The highest state of samādhi, in which the aspirant realizes his total oneness with Brahman.

nishthā   Single-minded devotion.

nivritti   Renunciation or detachment.

niyama   Restraint of the mind; the second of the eight Yoga disciplines.

Nyāya   Indian Logic, one of the six systems of orthodox Hindu philosophy, founded by Gautama.

ojas   Virility.

Om   The most sacred word of the Vedas; also written Aum. It is a symbol both of the Personal God and of the Absolute.

Om Tat Sat   (Lit., Om That Reality.) The threefold designation of Brahman.

pāda   Section.

Panchavati   A group of five sacred trees planted by Śri Ramakrishna in the temple garden of Dakshineswar for his practice of spiritual discipline.

Pāndavas   The five sons of Pāndu: King Yudhishthira, Arjuna, Bhima, Nakula, and Sahadeva. They are some of the chief heroes of the Mahābhārata.

pandit   Scholar.

Pānini   The famous Sanskrit grammarian; also the grammar written by Pānini.

parā   Higher.

parā-bhakti   Supreme love of the Lord, characterized by complete selflessness.

paramahamsa   One belonging to the highest order of sannyāsins.

Parjanya   Rain-cloud; the god of rain.

Pārthasārathi   The charioteer of Arjuna; an epithet of Krishna.

Patanjali   The author of the Yoga system, one of the six systems of orthodox Hindu philosophy, dealing with concentration and its methods, control of the mind, and similar matters.

Pingalā   A nerve in the spinal column. See Sushumnā.

pitris   Forefathers.

Prahlāda   The young son of the wicked demon king Hiranyakaśipu, who nevertheless developed supreme devotion to God.

Prajāpati   The Creator God.

prakriti   Primordial nature; the material substratum of the creation, consisting of sattva, rajas, and tamas.

prāna   The vital breath, which sustains life in a physical body; the primal energy or force, of which other physical forces are manifestations. In the books of Yoga, prāna is described as having five modifications, according to its five different bodily functions: (1) prāna (which controls the breath), (2) apāna (which carries downward unassimilated food and drink), (3) vyāna (which pervades the entire body), (4) udāna (by which the contents of the stomach are ejected through the mouth, and by which the soul is conducted from the body at death), and (5) samāna (which carries nutrition throughout the body). Prāna is also a name of Saguna Brahman, or Brahman with attributes.

pranāyāma   Control of the breath; one of the disciplines of Yoga.

pratika   Substitute.

pratimā   Image.

pratyāhāra   Restraining the organs.

pravritti   Desire.

pujā   Ritualistic worship.

Purānas   Books of Hindu mythology.

Purusha   (Lit., person.) A term of Sāmkhya philosophy denoting the individual conscious principle. In Vedānta the term *Purusha* denotes the Self.

Qualified Monism   A school of Vedānta founded by Rāmānuja, according to which the soul and nature are modes of Brahman, and the individual soul is a part of Brahman.

Qualified Non-dualism   Same as Qualified Monism.

rajas   The principle of restlessness or activity in nature. See gunas.

rāja-yoga   A system of yoga ascribed to Patanjali, dealing with concentration and its methods, control of the mind, samādhi, and similar matters.

rāja-yogi   One who follows the disciplines of rāja-yoga.

Rāma   The hero of the *Rāmāyana*, regarded by the Hindus as a Divine Incarnation.

Ramakrishna   A great saint of Bengal, regarded as a Divine Incarnation (A. D. 1836-1886).

Rāmānuja   Same as Rāmānujāchārya.

Rāmānujāchārya   A great saint of Southern India, the foremost interpreter of the school of Qualified Non-dualistic Vedānta (A. D. 1017-1137).

Rāmāyana   A famous Hindu epic.

Rāmprasād   A Bengali mystic and writer of songs about the Divine Mother, who flourished in the late eighteenth and early nineteenth century.

Rāvana   The monster-king of Ceylon, who forcibly abducted Sitā, the wife of Rāma.

Rig-Veda   One of the four Vedas. See Vedas.

rishi   A seer of truth to whom the wisdom of the Vedas was revealed; a general name for saint or ascetic.

Rudra   An epithet of Śiva.

Rung   A mystic word mentioned in the Hindu scriptures.

rupa   Form.

Śaivas   The worshippers of Śiva.

Śāktas   Followers of the Śakti cult, in which Ultimate Reality is described as Power, or the Divine Mother.

Śakti   Power, generally the Creative Power of Brahman; a name of the Divine Mother.

Śākya Muni   A name of Buddha.

samādhi   Ecstasy, trance, communion with God.

samashti   Totality; the universal.

Sāma-Veda   One of the four Vedas. See Vedas.

Samhitā   A section of the Vedas containing a collection of hymns.

Sāmkhya   One of the six systems of orthodox Hindu philosophy, which teaches that the universe evolves as the result of the union of prakriti (nature) and Purusha (Spirit). It was founded by Kapila.

Sāmkhyas   Followers of the Sāmkhya philosophy.

samsāra   The relative world; the unceasing round of births and deaths.

samskāra   Mental impression or tendency created by an action.

samyama   A form of concentration described in rāja-yoga.

Śāndilya   A sage who wrote aphorisms on bhakti, or divine love.

Sankara   Same as Sankarāchārya.

Sankarāchārya   One of the greatest saints and philosophers of India, the foremost exponent of Advaita Vedānta (A. D. 788-820).

sannyāsa   The monastic life; the last of the four stages of life. See āśrama.

sannyāsin   A Hindu monk who has renounced the world in order to realize God.

sannyāsini   A woman who has embraced the monastic life.

śānta-bhakti   Bhakti, or love of God, characterized by a serene· attitude towards Him, as distinguished from such an attitude as that of a servant, friend, parent, or beloved.

śāntih   Peace.

Sarasvati   The Goddess of Learning.

sāri   The wearing-cloth of Hindu women, especially of those residing in Bengal.

śāstra   Scripture; sacred book; code of laws.

Sat   Reality; being.

Satchidānanda   (Lit., Existence-Knowledge-Bliss Absolute.) A name of Brahman, or Ultimate Reality.

sattva   The principle of balance or righteousness in nature. See gunas.

sāttvikas   Those in whom the quality of sattva is greatly developed.

Satyakāma   A sage mentioned in the Chhāndogya Upanishad.

śava   Corpse.

Self   The same as Brahman, or Pure Spirit. See footnote, p. 189.

self   The individual self. See footnote, p. 189.

Sen, Keshab Chandra   A leader of the Brāhmo Samāj (A. D. 1838-1884).

siddhis   The supernatural powers possessed by a yogi.

śishya   Disciple.

Sitā   The wife of Rāma.

Śiva   The Destroyer God; the Third Person of the Hindu Trinity, the other two being Brahmā and Vishnu.

Smritis   The sacred books of the Hindus, subsidiary to the Vedas, guiding their
   daily life and conduct; they include the epics, the Purānas, and the Manu-
   samhitā or Code of Manu.

"Soham"   (Lit., "I am He.") One of the sacred formulas of the Non-dualistic
   Vedāntist.

soma   A creeper whose juice was used in Vedic sacrifices.

Sonthāls   A primitive tribe of Central India.

Soul   The same as Brahman, or Pure Spirit. See footnote, p. 189.

soul   The individual soul. See footnote, p. 189.

Sphota   The idea that flashes in the mind when a sound is uttered.

śraddhā   Faith.

Śramana   Buddhist monk.

Śri   The word is often used as an honorific prefix to the names of deities and
   eminent persons, or of celebrated books generally of a sacred character; sometimes used as an auspicious sign at the commencement of letters, manuscripts,
   etc., also as an equivalent of the English term Mr.

Śruti   (Lit., hearing.) The Vedas, which in ancient India were transmitted
   orally from teacher to disciple.

śudra   A member of the fourth or labouring caste in Hindu society.

Sufis   A sect of liberal Moslems influenced by the teachings of Vedānta.

Śuka(deva)   The narrator of the Bhāgavata and son of Vyāsa, regarded as one
   of India's ideal monks.

Sushumnā   The Sushumnā, Iḍā, and Pingalā are the three most prominent
   nāḍis, or nerves, among the innumerable nerves in the nervous system. Of
   these, again, the Sushumnā is the most important, being the point of harmony of the other two, lying, as it does, between them. The Iḍā is on the
   left side, and the Pingalā on the right. The Sushumnā, through which the
   awakened spiritual energy rises, is described as the Brahmavartman, or Path-
   way to Brahman. It is situated within the spinal column and extends from
   the base of the spine to the brain. See Kundalini.

sutra   Aphorism.

svarga   Heaven.

Svāti   The star Arcturus, regarded as forming the fifteenth lunar asterism.

svayamvara   The choosing of a husband by a princess in ancient India.

Śvetaketu   A sage mentioned in the Chhāndogya Upanishad.

Śvetāśvatara Upanishad   One of the major Upanishads. See Upanishads.

Swami   (Lit., lord.) A title of the monks belonging to the Vedānta school.

Swamiji   A term of endearment and respect by which a Swami is addressed.

tamas   The principle of dullness or inertia in nature. See gunas.

tanmātras   The subtle elements of matter as originally evolved.

Tantra   A system of religious philosophy in which the Divine Mother, or
   Power, is regarded as Ultimate Reality; also the scriptures dealing with this
   philosophy.

tapas   Austerity.

tapasyā   Austerity.

Tat   That.

Tat tvam asi (Lit., "That thou art.") A sacred formula of the Vedas denoting the identity of the individual self and the Supreme Self.

Thugs A notorious band of robbers in India who used to waylay travellers and take away their possessions after killing them.

Tulsidās A celebrated Vaishnava poet and author of the version of the *Rāmāyana* associated with his name.

tumi A pronoun corresponding to the English *you* and used with reference to persons equal in rank or inferior.

tyāgi One who has renounced the world.

Umā The Consort of Śiva. She is an Incarnation of the Divine Mother.

upādhi A term of Vedānta philosophy denoting a limitation imposed upon the Self or upon Brahman through ignorance.

Upanishads The well-known Hindu scriptures containing the philosophy of the Vedas. They are one hundred and eight in number, of which eleven are called major Upanishads.

vaidhi bhakti Devotion to God characterized by formal rules regarding food, worship, etc.

vairāgya Renunciation.

Vaiśeshika One of the six systems of Hindu philosophy, founded by Kanāda.

Vaishnavas The followers of Vishnu; a dualistic sect which emphasizes the path of devotion as a spiritual discipline.

vaiśya A member of the third caste in Hindu society, which engages in agriculture, commerce, and cattle-rearing.

Vālmiki The author of the *Rāmāyana.*

Vāmadeva A sage in Hindu mythology.

vānaprasthin One who has entered the stage of retirement and contemplation. See *āśrama.*

Varuna A Vedic deity; the presiding deity of the ocean.

Vedānta (Lit., the essence or concluding part of the Vedas.) A system of philosophy mainly based upon the teachings of the Upanishads, the Bhagavad Gitā, and the *Brahma Sutras.*

Vedānta Sutras Same as *Brahma Sutras.*

Vedas The revealed scriptures of the Hindus, consisting of the Rig-Veda, Sāma-Veda, Yajur-Veda, and Atharva-Veda.

Vidyā Knowledge leading to liberation, i.e. to the realization of Ultimate Reality.

Virāt Consciousness limited or conditioned by the upādhi of the aggregate of gross bodies; an epithet of the Cosmic Soul.

Vishnu (Lit., the All-pervading Spirit.) The Preserver God; the Second Person of the Hindu Trinity, the other two being Brahmā and Śiva; also a name of the Supreme Lord.

Viśishtādvaita Qualified Non-dualistic Vedānta, as expounded by Rāmānujāchārya.

Viśishtādvaitist A follower of the philosophy of Qualified Non-dualism.

viśishtam Differentiation.

Viśwanāth   An epithet of Śiva.

viveka   Discrimination between the real and the unreal.

Vraja   The same as Vrindāvan, associated with the youthful exploits of Krishna.

Vrindāvan   A town on the banks of the Jumnā river, associated with Śri Krishna's childhood.

vritti   State; form.

vyādha   Hunter.

Vyāsa   The compiler of the Vedas, reputed author of the Mahābhārata and the Brahma Sutras, and father of Śukadeva.

Vyāsa Sutras   Same as Brahma Sutras.

Yājnavalkya   A sage described as a knower of Brahman in the Brihadāranyaka Upanishad.

Yajur-Veda   One of the four Vedas. See Vedas.

Yama   The king of death, a Vedic deity.

yama   Self-restraint, the first of the eight steps of rāja-yoga.

yoga   Union of the individual soul and the Supreme Soul. The discipline by which such union is effected. The Yoga system of philosophy, ascribed to Patanjali, is one of the six systems of orthodox Hindu philosophy, and deals with the realization of Truth through the control of the mind.

yogi   One who practises yoga.

Yudhishthira   The eldest of the five sons of Pāndu; one of the heroes of the Mahābhārata.

INDEX